VOYAGES
IN ENGLISH
GRAMMAR AND WRITING

Patricia Healey, I.H.M.
B.A., Immaculata University
M.A., Temple University
20 years teaching; 20 years in administration

Irene Kervick, I.H.M.
B.A., Immaculata University
M.A., Villanova University
46 years teaching

Anne B. McGuire, I.H.M.
B.A., Immaculata University
M.A., Villanova University
M.A., Immaculata University
16 years teaching; 14 years as elementary principal; 10 years staff development

Adrienne Saybolt, I.H.M.
B.A., Immaculata University
Pennsylvania State Board of Education, professional certification
M.A., St. John's University
40 years teaching

LOYOLAPRESS.

Loyola Press has made every effort to locate the copyright holders for the cited works used in this publication and to make full acknowledgment for their use. In the case of any omissions, the publisher will be pleased to make suitable acknowledgments in future editions. Continued on page 567.

Cover Design: Think Book Works   Cover Artist: Pablo Bernasconi
Interior Design: Joan Bledig/Loyola Press
Art Director: Judine O'Shea/Loyola Press
Editor: Ron Watson/Loyola Press

ISBN-13: 978-0-8294-2827-8
ISBN-10: 0-8294-2827-5

LOYOLA PRESS.
3441 N. Ashland Avenue
Chicago, Illinois 60657
(800) 621-1008
www.loyolapress.com

RRD / China / 10-09 / 1st Printing

Contents

PART 1 Grammar

PART 2 Written and Oral Communication

VOYAGES
IN ENGLISH
GRAMMAR AND WRITING

Welcome to *Voyages in English*, a core English language arts curriculum that has been an outstanding success in elementary and middle schools since 1942. From the time of first publication, *Voyages in English* (*Voyages*) has focused on providing students with the tools necessary to become articulate communicators of the English language. For over 65 years, those who wrote, published, and used *Voyages* for classroom instruction never abandoned the belief that communication skills are crucial for opportunities and success in education and eventually in employment.

With these expectations in mind, *Voyages* has advanced the best values of the past to meet the demands of communication in the twenty-first century. The curriculum meets the following goals:

- **Enable children to master grammar** through direct instruction, rigorous practice, written application, and ongoing assessment.

- **Guide children to experience, explore, and improve their writing** through the in-depth study of unique writing genres, writing skill lessons, and the implementation of the writing process.

- **Give children the speaking and writing practice and tools they need** to communicate with clarity, accuracy, and ease.

- **Provide children and teachers with opportunities to use technology** as a means to learn, assess, apply new skills, and communicate outside the school setting.

- **Provide master and novice teachers with support and straightforward, practical lesson plans** that can be presented with confidence.

When learning is presented as a positive opportunity and a challenging adventure, children respond. *Voyages in English* subscribes to this idea, just as previous editions have. Regular, consistent use of *Voyages* helps create successful communicators in school and—eventually—in society. So welcome to *Voyages in English: Grammar and Writing*—enjoy the journey!

COMPLETE AND COMPREHENSIVE

Voyages in English: Grammar and Writing for grades 3 through 8 fully prepares students to become literate masters of the written and spoken word. The components and lessons in this program are the result of decades of research and practice by experts in the field of grammar and writing. The result—better writers, readers, listeners, and speakers as well as happy teachers, principals, and parents!

Student Editions

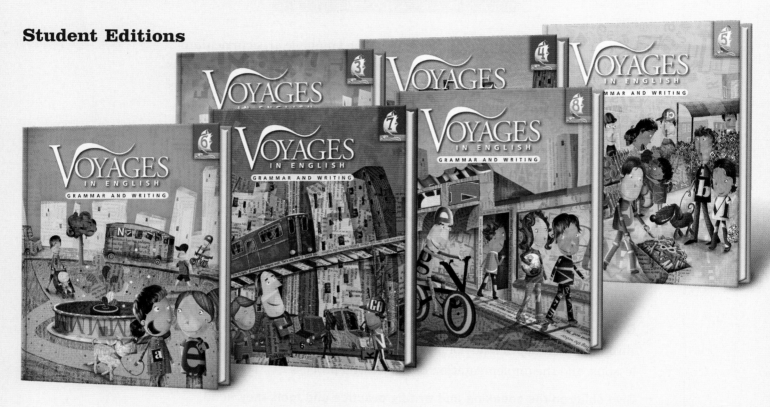

Teacher Editions

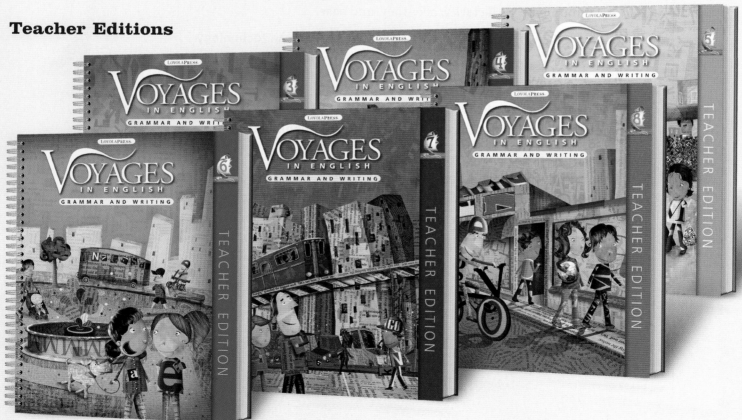

Practice Books
Grades 3–8

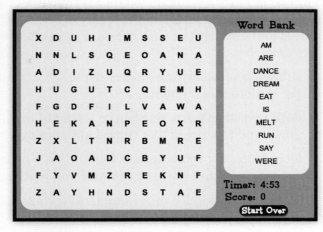

										Word Bank
X	D	U	H	I	M	S	S	E	U	AM
N	N	L	S	Q	E	O	A	N	A	ARE
A	D	I	Z	U	Q	R	Y	U	E	DANCE
H	U	G	U	T	C	Q	E	M	H	DREAM
F	G	D	F	I	L	V	A	W	A	EAT
H	E	K	A	N	P	E	O	X	R	IS
Z	X	L	T	N	R	B	M	R	E	MELT
J	A	O	A	D	C	B	Y	U	F	RUN
F	Y	V	M	Z	R	E	K	N	F	SAY
Z	A	Y	H	N	D	S	T	A	E	WERE

Timer: 4:53
Score: 0
Start Over

Additional Student Practice
www.voyagesinenglish.com

Assessment Books
Grades 3–8

Optional Customizable Assessment
Grades 3–8

ExamView® Assessment Suite Test Generator

Additional Teacher Support
www.voyagesinenglish.com

TWO CORE PARTS—ONE COHESIVE PROGRAM

Voyages in English is organized into two distinct parts: grammar and writing. The student books are divided in this way to help teachers tailor lesson plans to student needs and differentiate instruction. The benefits of this type of organization include the following:

- **Grammar lessons** have greater depth, giving students the tools needed to learn the structure of language.
- **Writing instruction** is relevant to students' lives, to the literature they read and enjoy, and to writing that they experience every day.
- **Integration opportunities** are built into the program, allowing teachers to show the relationship between grammar and writing.
- **Flexible planning** becomes simple, allowing for adaptations based on students' developmental levels.
- **Long-range and thematic planning** is effortless, allowing teachers to cover required standards.

PART I: GRAMMAR
The Structure of Language

- Parts of speech
- Usage
- Mechanics
- Agreement
- Punctuation/capitalization

PART II: WRITTEN AND ORAL COMMUNICATION
Written Expression

- Traits of effective writing
- Genre characteristics
- Sentence structure
- Word and study skills
- Seven-step writing process

INTEGRATION OPPORTUNITIES

Throughout the program, ample integration opportunities are built in to provide a systematic review of essential concepts.

Part I: Grammar
Writing Integration

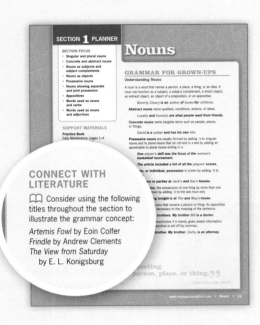

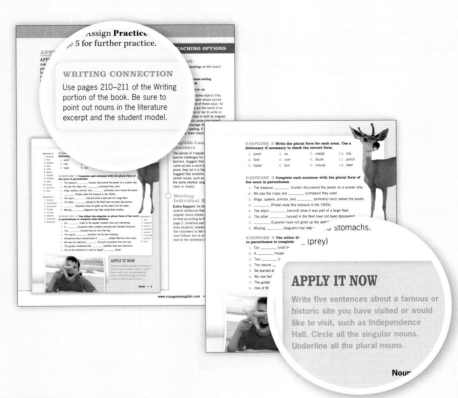

Part II: Written and Oral Communication
Grammar Integration

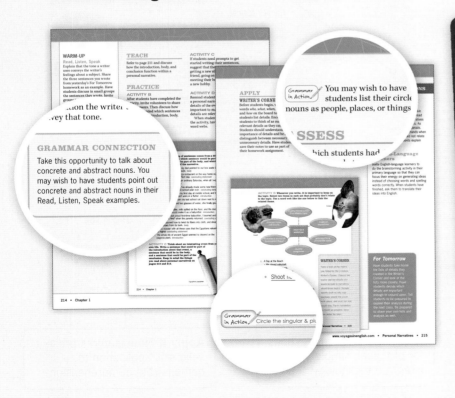

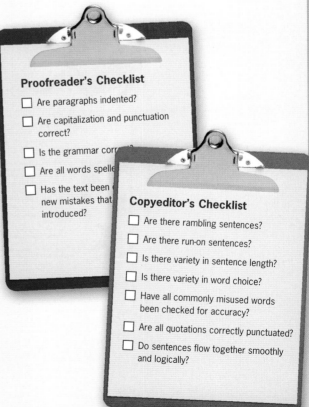

Proofreader's Checklist

- [ ] Are paragraphs indented?
- [ ] Are capitalization and punctuation correct?
- [ ] Is the grammar correct?
- [ ] Are all words spelled
- [ ] Has the text been
      new mistakes that
      introduced?

Copyeditor's Checklist

- [ ] Are there rambling sentences?
- [ ] Are there run-on sentences?
- [ ] Is there variety in sentence length?
- [ ] Is there variety in word choice?
- [ ] Have all commonly misused words been checked for accuracy?
- [ ] Are all quotations correctly punctuated?
- [ ] Do sentences flow together smoothly and logically?

Program Overview

STUDENT EDITION: GRAMMAR

An excellent education in the acquisition and application of language has never been exclusively about memorizing parts of speech in isolation or diagramming a sentence as an end in itself. Because of this, *Voyages in English* takes grammar further, helping students become polished, articulate, and intelligent communicators.

The grammar portion of the Student Edition focuses on the needs of the students and in building their confidence so that when they speak, others listen, and when they write, others understand their message and want to read more. In other words, *Voyages in English* has what it takes to help students succeed: more practice, more rigor, more application, more integration.

Thorough explanations and clear examples are provided for every grammar topic.

Ample practice ensures skill mastery.

Grammar in Action features challenge students to spot the importance of grammar in real-life writing.

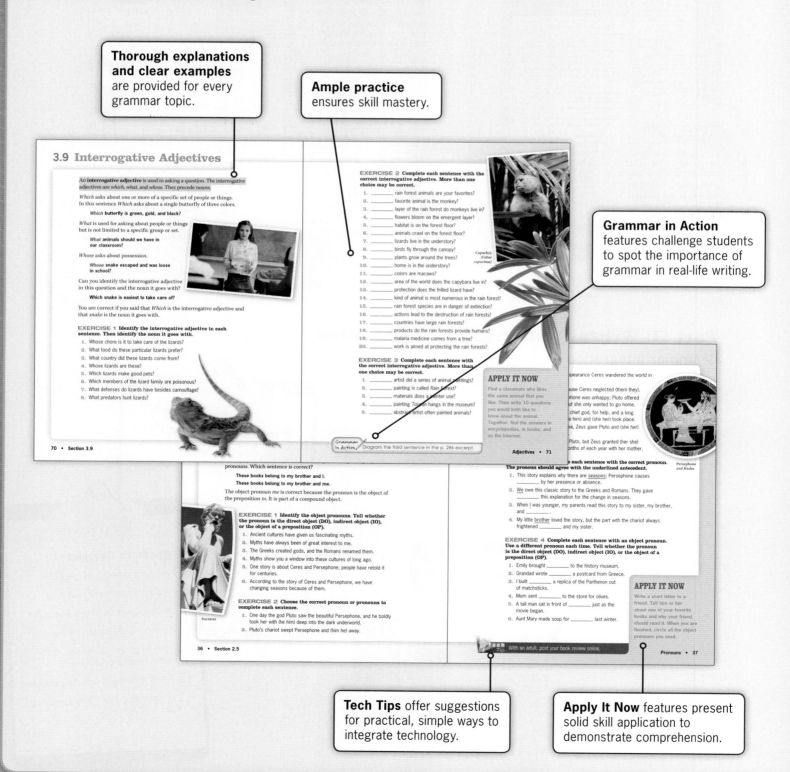

Tech Tips offer suggestions for practical, simple ways to integrate technology.

Apply It Now features present solid skill application to demonstrate comprehension.

A **Grammar Review** for every grammar section helps build student confidence and offers two full pages that can be used as review or informal assessment.

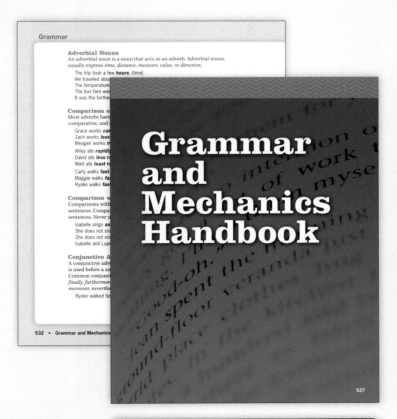

Adjective Review

3.1 Identify each descriptive adjective and the noun it describes.
1. Racing is a popular sport.
2. The sleek car was on the track.
3. The car made a quick stop.
4. A fiery crash scared the crowd.
5. The Brazilian driver won the race.

3.2 Identify each article and tell whether it is definite or indefinite.
6. Mom and Dad watched the swim meet.
7. The swimmer talked with an official.
8. Bruce swam the backstroke and the butterfly.

3.4 Identify each subject complement and the noun it describes.
15. According to some people, Frank Lloyd Wright was eccentric.
16. The architect became famous.
17. His designs looked odd to some people.
18. Most designs, however, were impressive.
19. Prairie-style homes are popular.

3.5 Identify each descriptive adjective. Tell whether it is positive, comparative, or superlative.
20. The classroom has a nice map.
21. What is the largest country in the world?
22. Vatican City is the smallest country.
23. Do you think more tourists will visit this year than last?

3.6 Rewrite the sentences to correct any errors in the use of comparative or superlative adjectives.
24. The cheetah is the faster land animal on earth.
25. Does a cheetah or a tiger have the softest fur?

26. Leopards are slowest than cheetahs.
27. The hunters saw most cougars in Canada than anywhere else.

3.7 Complete each sentence with the correct adjective: *little, less, least, few, fewer,* or *fewest.*
28. Sheila has ____ patience for polluters.
29. She has a ____ tips to save the environment.
30. Try to use ____ paper.
31. ____ cars on the road will reduce ozone gasses.
32. Which city has the ____ pollution?

3.8 Complete each sentence with the correct demonstrative adjective: *this, these, that,* or *those.* Use the directions in parentheses.
33. ____ (near) traffic is backed up for miles.
34. ____ (near) people are becoming frustrated.
35. ____ (far) lane of traffic is moving.
36. ____ (far) cars collided.
37. ____ (far) accident could have been prevented.

3.9 Complete each sentence with the correct interrogative adjective: *which, what,* or *whose.*
38. ____ game is this?

39. ____ team should we cheer for?
40. ____ seat is this?
41. ____ player hit the home run?
42. ____ snacks do they sell here?

3.10 Identify each indefinite adjective and the noun it goes with.
43. Some people travel to Egypt.
44. Anita and Juan saw several pyramids.
45. Both students learned interesting facts.
46. Pyramids were built with many stones.
47. All pyramids were built for the pharaohs.

3.11 Identify each adjective phrase and the noun it describes.
48. Elephants from Africa are the heaviest land animals.
49. Do you know the differences between African and Asian elephants?
50. A group of elephants is called a herd.
51. The trunks of these animals are useful body parts.
52. An elephant keeper is called mahout in India.

Tech Tip Go to www.voyagesinenglish.com for more activities.

Adjectives • 77

A **Grammar Challenge** follows each Grammar Review to extend the learning or offer another opportunity for informal assessment.

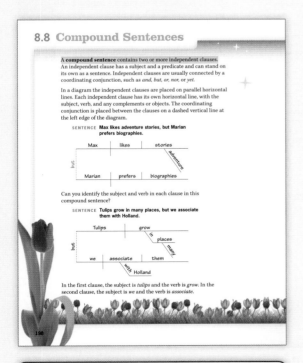

Adjective Challenge

Read the selection and then answer the questions.

1. The harbor is alive with ships from around the world. 2. Several freighters rock with the tide, graceful liners glide up to the piers, and tugs wander in and out of the harbor. 3. The tugs, which are smaller than the other vessels, look tiny when compared to the black hulls of the freighters. 4. Two pleasure boats cruise up the river. 5. Strains of cheerful music from their orchestras float toward both shores. 6. This port is a vivid glimpse of today's American coastal life.

1. Name an adjective used as a subject complement in sentence 1.
2. What word does the subject complement in sentence 1 describe?
3. Name the indefinite adjective in sentence 2.
4. Name the comparative adjective in sentence 3.
5. Name the two other degrees of the comparative adjective in sentence 3.
6. Name the three descriptive adjectives in sentence 3.
7. Name the numerical adjective in sentence 4.
8. What noun does the numerical adjective in sentence 4 describe?
9. Is the word pleasure used as a noun or an adjective in sentence 4?
10. Name the article in sentence 4.
11. Name the descriptive adjective in sentence 5.
12. Write the comparative and superlative forms for the descriptive adjective in sentence 5.
13. Name the indefinite adjective in sentence 5.
14. Name the indefinite article in sentence 6.
15. Name the demonstrative adjective in sentence 6.
16. Does the demonstrative adjective in sentence 6 describe a singular or plural noun?
17. Find an adjective that shows origin in the paragraph.
18. Does the paragraph contain any superlative adjectives?

78 • Adjective Challenge

8.8 Compound Sentences

A **compound sentence** contains two or more independent clauses. An independent clause has a subject and a predicate and can stand on its own as a sentence. Independent clauses are usually connected by a coordinating conjunction, such as *and, but, or, nor,* or *yet.*

In a diagram the independent clauses are placed on parallel horizontal lines. Each independent clause has its own horizontal line, with the subject, verb, and any complements or objects. The coordinating conjunction is placed between the clauses on a dashed vertical line at the left edge of the diagram.

SENTENCE **Max likes adventure stories, but Marian prefers biographies.**

Can you identify the subject and verb in each clause in this compound sentence?

SENTENCE **Tulips grow in many places, but we associate them with Holland.**

In the first clause, the subject is *tulips* and the verb is *grow.* In the second clause, the subject is *we* and the verb is *associate.*

198

Sentence Diagramming at every grade level helps students analyze, visualize, and unlock the English language.

Grammar

Adverbial Nouns
An adverbial noun is a noun that acts as an adverb. Adverbial nouns usually express *time, distance, measure, value,* or *direction.*

The trip took a few **hours**. (time)
We traveled about ____ miles.
The temperature was ____
The bus fare was ____
It was the farthest ____

Comparison o
Most adverbs have ____
comparative, and ____

Grace works **car**____
Zach works **less**____
Meagen works **m**____
Wiley ate **rapidly**____
David ate **less r**____
Matt ate **least ra**____
Carly walks **fast.**____
Maggie walks **fa**____
Ryoko walks **fast**____

Comparison w
Comparisons with ____
sentences. Compa ____
sentences. Never u ____
Isabelle sings **as**____
She does not sin ____
She does not sin ____
Isabelle and Lup ____

Conjunctive A
A conjunctive adve ____
is used before a c ____
Common conjunc ____
finally, furthermor ____
moreover, neverth ____
Ryoko walked fas ____

532 • Grammar and Mechanics

Grammar and Mechanics Handbook

527

The **Grammar and Mechanics Handbook** provides a quick reference tool for grammar, usage, and mechanics topics.

Program Overview

TEACHER EDITION: GRAMMAR

The core values and competencies that fortify *Voyages in English* have always been focused on high-level instruction that challenges the most able of students and supports those who struggle. Therefore, the Teacher Edition of *Voyages in English* is crafted with an easy-to-use, flexible format that includes support for teachers of all experience levels who serve children at all levels of development.

Background and Planning Support

An **at-a-glance skills list** provides focus for each grammar section.

Clear and straightforward grammar essentials provide all the background teachers need to teach the grammar topic.

Common Errors features alert teachers to errors students often make and advise how to correct them.

Detailed materials lists allow for easy planning.

Ideas for literature invite teachers to show grammar skills in context.

Diagramming basics review concepts so teaching is easier.

Grammar Expert questions and answers offer even more support to bring teachers up to speed on grammar.

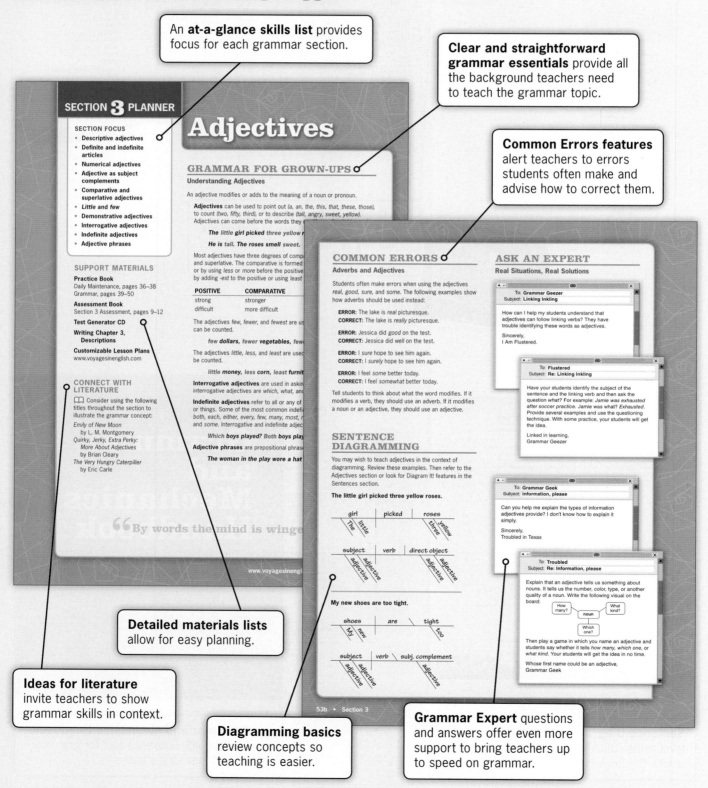

Instruction

An **easy four-step teaching approach** is implemented in every lesson: Teach, Practice, Apply, Assess.

Teaching Options allow teachers to tailor instruction to student needs through **Reteach, Multiple Intelligences, English-Language Learners,** and **Diagram It!**

Daily Maintenance features help maintain proficiency in grammatical concepts that have already been taught and assessed.

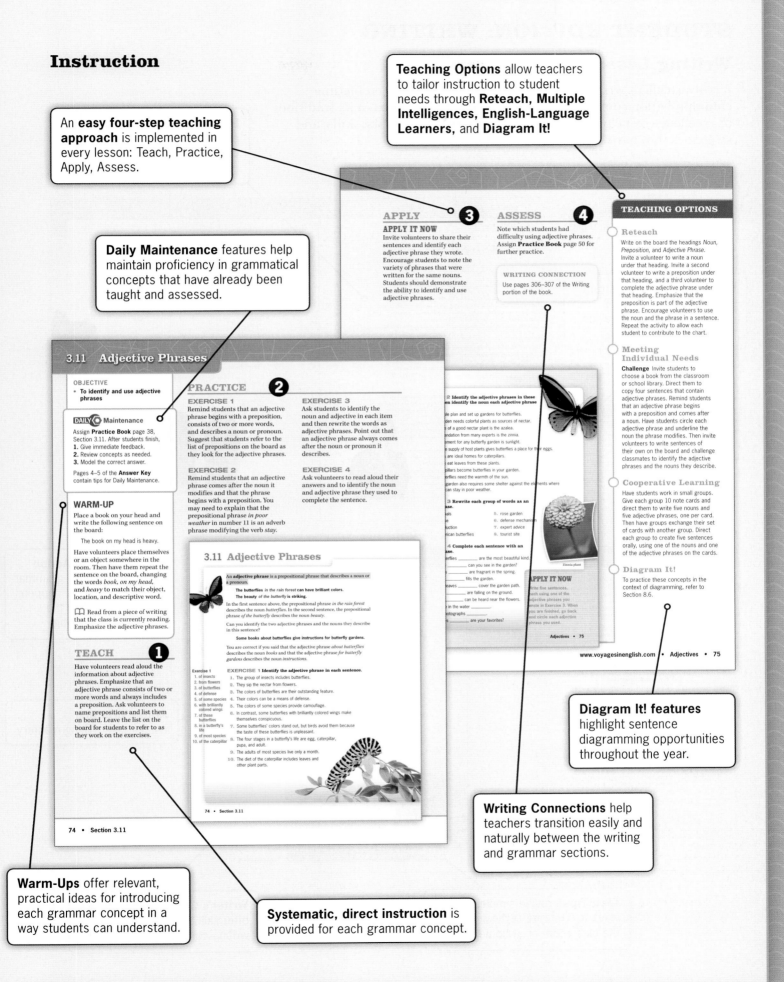

APPLY ③

APPLY IT NOW
Invite volunteers to share their sentences and identify each adjective phrase they wrote. Encourage students to note the variety of phrases that were written for the same nouns. Students should demonstrate the ability to identify and use adjective phrases.

ASSESS ④
Note which students had difficulty using adjective phrases. Assign **Practice Book** page 50 for further practice.

WRITING CONNECTION
Use pages 306–307 of the Writing portion of the book.

TEACHING OPTIONS

Reteach
Write on the board the headings *Noun, Preposition,* and *Adjective Phrase.* Invite a volunteer to write a noun under that heading. Invite a second volunteer to write a preposition under that heading, and a third volunteer to complete the adjective phrase under that heading. Emphasize that the preposition is part of the adjective phrase. Encourage volunteers to use the noun and the phrase in a sentence. Repeat the activity to allow each student to contribute to the chart.

Meeting Individual Needs
Challenge Invite students to choose a book from the classroom or school library. Direct them to copy four sentences that contain adjective phrases. Remind students that an adjective phrase begins with a preposition and comes after a noun. Have students circle each adjective phrase and underline the noun the phrase modifies. Then invite volunteers to write sentences of their own on the board and challenge classmates to identify the adjective phrases and the nouns they describe.

Cooperative Learning
Have students work in small groups. Give each group 10 note cards and direct them to write five nouns and five adjective phrases, one per card. Then have groups exchange their set of cards with another group. Direct each group to create five sentences orally, using one of the nouns and one of the adjective phrases on the cards.

Diagram It!
To practice these concepts in the context of diagramming, refer to Section 8.6.

3.11 Adjective Phrases

OBJECTIVE
- To identify and use adjective phrases

DAILY Maintenance
Assign **Practice Book** page 38, Section 3.11. After students finish,
1. Give immediate feedback.
2. Review concepts as needed.
3. Model the correct answer.
Pages 4–5 of the **Answer Key** contain tips for Daily Maintenance.

WARM-UP
Place a book on your head and write the following sentence on the board:

The book on my head is heavy.

Have volunteers place themselves or an object somewhere in the room. Then have them repeat the sentence on the board, changing the words *book, on my head,* and *heavy* to match their object, location, and descriptive word.

Read from a piece of writing that the class is currently reading. Emphasize the adjective phrases.

TEACH ①
Have volunteers read aloud the information about adjective phrases. Emphasize that an adjective phrase consists of two or more words and always includes a preposition. Ask volunteers to name prepositions and list them on board. Leave the list on the board for students to refer to as they work on the exercises.

PRACTICE ②

EXERCISE 1
Remind students that an adjective phrase begins with a preposition, consists of two or more words, and describes a noun or pronoun. Suggest that students refer to the list of prepositions on the board as they look for the adjective phrases.

EXERCISE 2
Remind students that an adjective phrase comes after the noun it modifies and that the phrase begins with a preposition. You may need to explain that the prepositional phrase *in poor weather* in number 11 is an adverb phrase modifying the verb *stay.*

EXERCISE 3
Ask students to identify the noun and adjective in each item and then rewrite the words as adjective phrases. Point out that an adjective phrase always comes after the noun or pronoun it describes.

EXERCISE 4
Ask volunteers to read aloud their answers and to identify the noun and adjective phrase they used to complete the sentence.

3.11 Adjective Phrases

An **adjective phrase** is a prepositional phrase that describes a noun or a pronoun.

The butterflies *in the rain forest* can have brilliant colors.
The beauty *of the butterfly* is striking.

In the first sentence above, the prepositional phrase *in the rain forest* describes the noun *butterflies.* In the second sentence, the prepositional phrase *of the butterfly* describes the noun *beauty.*

Can you identify the two adjective phrases and the nouns they describe in this sentence?

Some books about butterflies give instructions for butterfly gardens.

You are correct if you said that the adjective phrase *about butterflies* describes the noun *books* and that the adjective phrase *for butterfly gardens* describes the noun *instructions.*

Exercise 1
1. of insects
2. from flowers
3. of butterflies
4. of defense
5. of some species
6. with brilliantly colored wings
7. of these butterflies
8. in a butterfly's life
9. of most species
10. of the caterpillar

EXERCISE 1 Identify the adjective phrase in each sentence.
1. The group of insects includes butterflies.
2. They sip the nectar from flowers.
3. The colors of butterflies are their outstanding feature.
4. Their colors can be a means of defense.
5. The colors of some species provide camouflage.
6. In contrast, some butterflies with brilliantly colored wings make themselves conspicuous.
7. Some butterflies' colors stand out, but birds avoid them because the taste of these butterflies is unpleasant.
8. The four stages in a butterfly's life are egg, caterpillar, pupa, and adult.
9. The adults of most species live only a month.
10. The diet of the caterpillar includes leaves and other plant parts.

74 • Section 3.11

---

2 Identify the adjective phrases in these ... then identify the noun each adjective phrase ...

...le plan and set up gardens for butterflies.
...den needs colorful plants as sources of nectar.
...of a good nectar plant is the azalea.
...ndation from many experts is the zinnia.
...ment for any butterfly garden is sunlight.
...e supply of host plants gives butterflies a place for their eggs.
...s are ideal homes for caterpillars.
...eat leaves from these plants.
...pillars become butterflies in your garden.
...flies need the warmth of the sun.
...garden also requires some shelter against the elements where
...can stay in poor weather.

3 Rewrite each group of words as an ... ase.
...als
5. rose garden
...duction
6. defense mechanism
...rican butterflies
7. expert advice
8. tourist site

4 Complete each sentence with an ... ase.
...terflies _____ are the most beautiful kind.
... _____ can you see in the garden?
... _____ are fragrant in the spring.
...leaves _____ fills the garden.
... _____ cover the garden path.
... _____ are falling on the ground.
... _____ can be heard near the flowers.
...n in the water _____
...hotographs _____
... _____ are your favorites?

APPLY IT NOW
Write five sentences...
...each using one of the adjective phrases you...
...in Exercise 3. When you are finished, go back...
...d circle each adjective phrase you used.

Adjectives • 75

www.voyagesinenglish.com • Adjectives • 75

Diagram It! features highlight sentence diagramming opportunities throughout the year.

Writing Connections help teachers transition easily and naturally between the writing and grammar sections.

Warm-Ups offer relevant, practical ideas for introducing each grammar concept in a way students can understand.

Systematic, direct instruction is provided for each grammar concept.

74 • Section 3.11

STUDENT EDITION: WRITING

Writing Lessons

A truly excellent writing program always sets its sights on lifetime communication competence. *Voyages in English* is rooted in its tradition of excellence by helping students employ writing concepts, skills, and strategies that have stood the test of time.

Easy-to-follow, practical explanations and examples make writing relevant and engaging.

Link features demonstrate a writing concept or skill within the context of real-life writing or literary works.

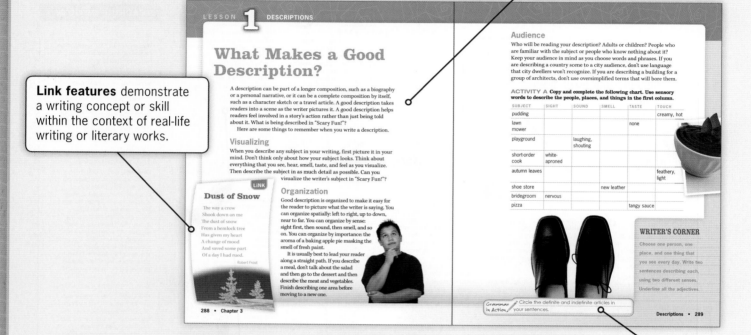

Grammar in Action features offer grammar application that happens naturally within the context of writing.

Ample practice encourages writing mastery.

Tech Tips provide simple, natural ways to integrate technology in the classroom or at home.

Writer's Corner experiences offer skill application for each writing concept.

Writer's Workshop

In the span of one year, students work through a seven-step writing process to develop and publish eight written pieces that span eight distinct writing genres, including research reports. The systematic and evolutionary development of each piece sets in motion the goal of producing reflective, creative, critical, and articulate communicators.

The seven-step writing process mirrors the process often used by professional writers:

- Prewriting
- Drafting
- Content editing
- Revising
- Copyediting
- Proofreading
- Publishing

> **Complete coverage of writing skills and the writing process** can increase standardized test-taking success.

> **Step-by-step practice** is led by a model student.

> **Traits of effective writing** are integrated in natural, relevant ways.

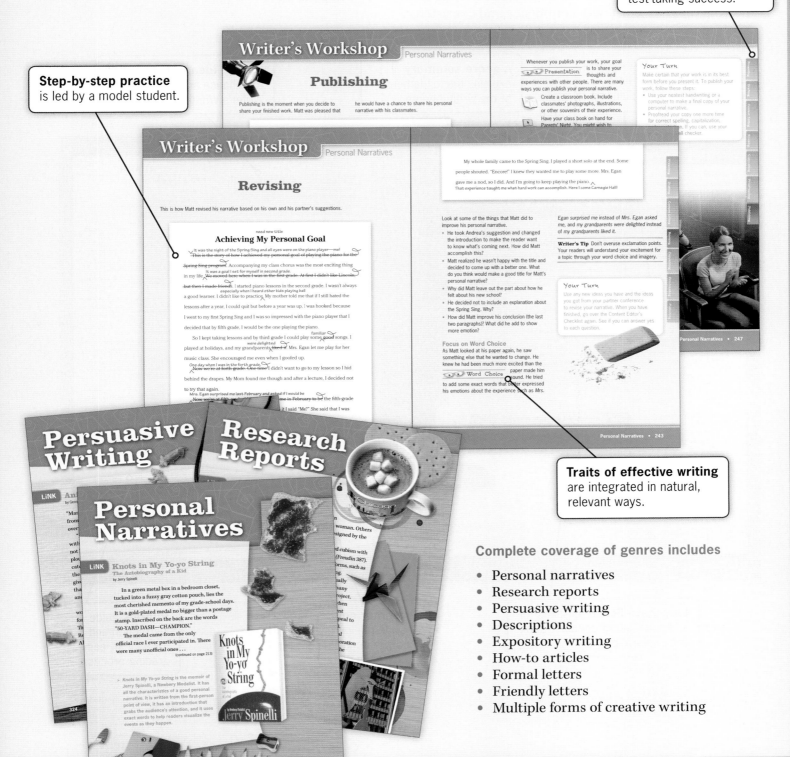

Complete coverage of genres includes

- Personal narratives
- Research reports
- Persuasive writing
- Descriptions
- Expository writing
- How-to articles
- Formal letters
- Friendly letters
- Multiple forms of creative writing

TEACHER EDITION: WRITING

Since all students deserve a strong, interesting, and challenging curriculum with high-level results, *Voyages in English* not only raises the bar for expected outcomes but also provides strong and consistent instructional steps and support for teachers. A clear, easy-to-follow format gives new teachers and seasoned professionals the tools and confidence they need to guide students.

Background and Planning Support

In the Genre Planner, teachers are provided with clear definitions of the elements and characteristics of the specific writing genres they will present, allowing them to teach with confidence and consistency.

Detailed materials lists allow for at-a-glance planning.

A **genre summary** explains the fundamentals of the writing genre.

Helpful ideas are presented to enhance and extend the Writer's Workshop.

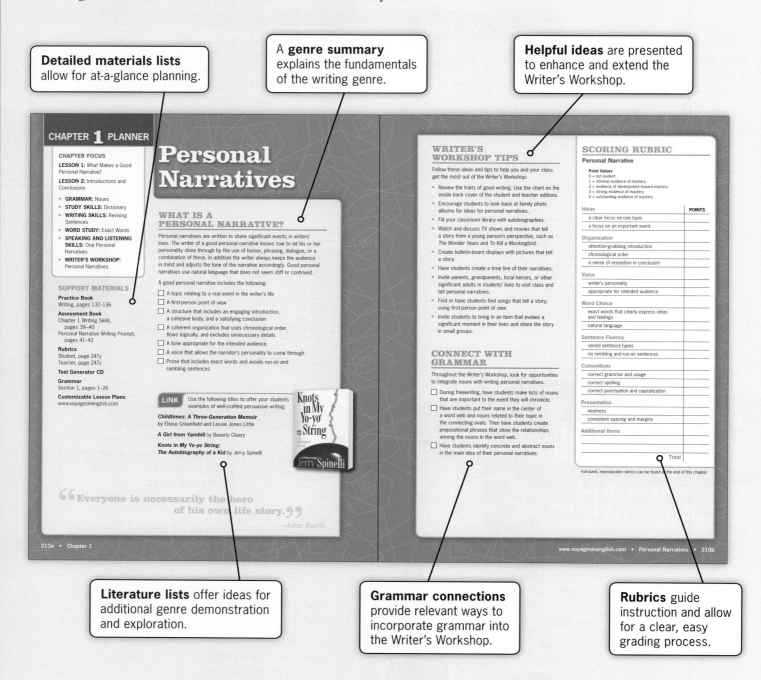

Literature lists offer ideas for additional genre demonstration and exploration.

Grammar connections provide relevant ways to incorporate grammar into the Writer's Workshop.

Rubrics guide instruction and allow for a clear, easy grading process.

Instruction

Read, Listen, Speak features offer small-group discussion of the writing assignment.

Systematic, direct instruction is provided for each topic.

A **simple four-step teaching approach:** Teach, Practice, Apply, Assess

Activities in a variety of learning styles: **Reteach, Multiple Intelligences,** and **English-Language Learners**

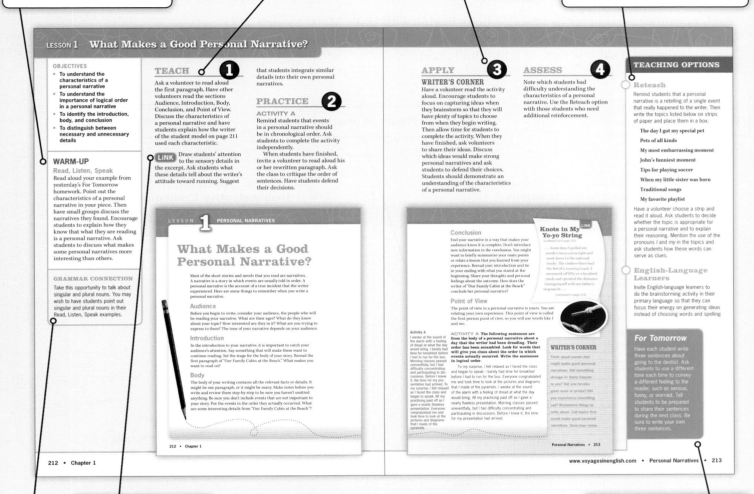

Link offers ways that popular writing can be used as a model.

Grammar Connections allow seamless integration between writing and grammar.

For Tomorrow features provide practical writing assignments and additional practice for homework or in-class study.

Rubrics

The Teacher Editions provide reproducible rubrics for students and teachers.

Program Overview

PRACTICE BOOK: PRACTICE MAKES PERFECT

Research shows that the more exposure and practice children have using newly introduced skills, the more likely they are to internalize and master them. That's why *Voyages in English* provides ample opportunity for additional practice.

Grammar Section Practice

Each grammar section of the Practice Book begins with Daily Maintenance opportunities that are described in each Teacher Edition lesson. Every grammar topic receives at least one page of additional practice.

Easy-to-understand directions

Plenty of practice

A **clear explanation** of the grammar skill

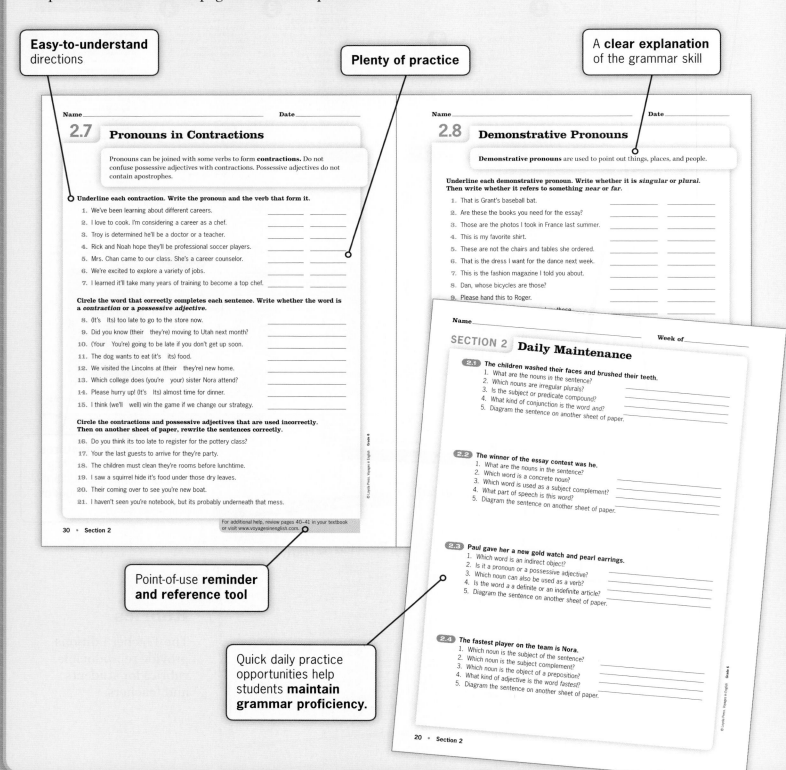

2.7 Pronouns in Contractions

Pronouns can be joined with some verbs to form **contractions.** Do not confuse possessive adjectives with contractions. Possessive adjectives do not contain apostrophes.

Underline each contraction. Write the pronoun and the verb that form it.

1. We've been learning about different careers.
2. I love to cook. I'm considering a career as a chef.
3. Troy is determined he'll be a doctor or a teacher.
4. Rick and Noah hope they'll be professional soccer players.
5. Mrs. Chan came to our class. She's a career counselor.
6. We're excited to explore a variety of jobs.
7. I learned it'll take many years of training to become a top chef.

Circle the word that correctly completes each sentence. Write whether the word is a *contraction* or a *possessive adjective.*

8. (It's Its) too late to go to the store now.
9. Did you know (their they're) moving to Utah next month?
10. (Your You're) going to be late if you don't get up soon.
11. The dog wants to eat (it's its) food.
12. We visited the Lincolns at (their they're) new home.
13. Which college does (you're your) sister Nora attend?
14. Please hurry up! (It's Its) almost time for dinner.
15. I think (we'll well) win the game if we change our strategy.

Circle the contractions and possessive adjectives that are used incorrectly. Then on another sheet of paper, rewrite the sentences correctly.

16. Do you think its too late to register for the pottery class?
17. Your the last guests to arrive for they're party.
18. The children must clean they're rooms before lunchtime.
19. I saw a squirrel hide it's food under those dry leaves.
20. Their coming over to see you're new boat.
21. I haven't seen you're notebook, but its probably underneath that mess.

For additional help, review pages 40–41 in your textbook or visit www.voyagesinenglish.com.

30 • Section 2

2.8 Demonstrative Pronouns

Demonstrative pronouns are used to point out things, places, and people.

Underline each demonstrative pronoun. Write whether it is *singular* or *plural*. Then write whether it refers to something *near* or *far*.

1. That is Grant's baseball bat.
2. Are these the books you need for the essay?
3. Those are the photos I took in France last summer.
4. This is my favorite shirt.
5. These are not the chairs and tables she ordered.
6. That is the dress I want for the dance next week.
7. This is the fashion magazine I told you about.
8. Dan, whose bicycles are those?
9. Please hand this to Roger.

SECTION 2 Daily Maintenance

Week of _____

2.1 The children washed their faces and brushed their teeth.
1. What are the nouns in the sentence?
2. Which nouns are irregular plurals?
3. Is the subject or predicate compound?
4. What kind of conjunction is the word and?
5. Diagram the sentence on another sheet of paper.

2.2 The winner of the essay contest was he.
1. What are the nouns in the sentence?
2. Which word is a concrete noun?
3. Which word is used as a subject complement?
4. What part of speech is this word?
5. Diagram the sentence on another sheet of paper.

2.3 Paul gave her a new gold watch and pearl earrings.
1. Which word is an indirect object?
2. Is it a pronoun or a possessive adjective?
3. Which noun can also be used as a verb?
4. Is the word a a definite or an indefinite article?
5. Diagram the sentence on another sheet of paper.

2.4 The fastest player on the team is Nora.
1. Which noun is the subject of the sentence?
2. Which noun is the subject complement?
3. Which noun is the object of a preposition?
4. What kind of adjective is the word fastest?
5. Diagram the sentence on another sheet of paper.

20 • Section 2

Point-of-use **reminder and reference tool**

Quick daily practice opportunities help students **maintain grammar proficiency.**

Writing Chapter Practice

The writing portion of the Practice Book is in one-to-one correspondence with the Student Edition and the Teacher Edition.

Clear directions

A concise definition of the lesson topic

Targeted practice

Handy reference for review

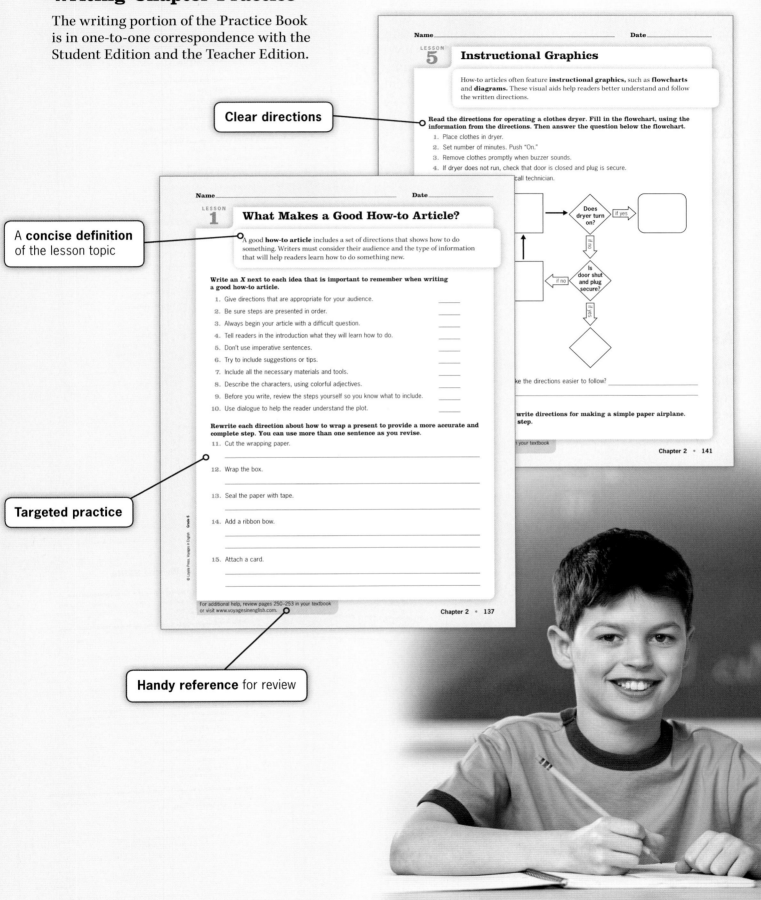

LESSON 5

Instructional Graphics

How-to articles often feature **instructional graphics,** such as **flowcharts** and **diagrams.** These visual aids help readers better understand and follow the written directions.

Read the directions for operating a clothes dryer. Fill in the flowchart, using the information from the directions. Then answer the question below the flowchart.

1. Place clothes in dryer.
2. Set number of minutes. Push "On."
3. Remove clothes promptly when buzzer sounds.
4. If dryer does not run, check that door is closed and plug is secure.
5. ...call technician.

Does dryer turn on?

if yes

if no

Is door shut and plug secure?

if no

if yes

...ke the directions easier to follow? _____

...write directions for making a simple paper airplane.
...step.

...n your textbook

Chapter 2 • 141

LESSON 1

What Makes a Good How-to Article?

A good **how-to article** includes a set of directions that shows how to do something. Writers must consider their audience and the type of information that will help readers learn how to do something new.

Write an X next to each idea that is important to remember when writing a good how-to article.

1. Give directions that are appropriate for your audience. _____
2. Be sure steps are presented in order. _____
3. Always begin your article with a difficult question. _____
4. Tell readers in the introduction what they will learn how to do. _____
5. Don't use imperative sentences. _____
6. Try to include suggestions or tips. _____
7. Include all the necessary materials and tools. _____
8. Describe the characters, using colorful adjectives. _____
9. Before you write, review the steps yourself so you know what to include. _____
10. Use dialogue to help the reader understand the plot. _____

Rewrite each direction about how to wrap a present to provide a more accurate and complete step. You can use more than one sentence as you revise.

11. Cut the wrapping paper.
    _____

12. Wrap the box.
    _____

13. Seal the paper with tape.
    _____

14. Add a ribbon bow.
    _____
    _____

15. Attach a card.
    _____
    _____

For additional help, review pages 250–253 in your textbook or visit www.voyagesinenglish.com.

© Loyola Press. Voyages in English. Grade 6

Chapter 2 • 137

ASSESSMENT BOOK: THE KEY TO INFORMED INSTRUCTION

Effective assessment helps teachers note progress, guide instruction, and reveal opportunities for differentiation. Each day, in various ways, *Voyages in English* offers a variety of assessment opportunities that help teachers obtain targeted information about their students' development.

Assess Grammar

Each grammar assessment challenges students to display their knowledge of previously taught content.

Assess Over Time

Summative assessments offer teachers the ability to assess over time—combining two or more grammar sections into one test.

Assess Writing

The writing assessments ask students to show their knowledge of specifically taught skills as well as use the writing process to craft a written piece. Writing-process assessments help prepare students for standardized tests.

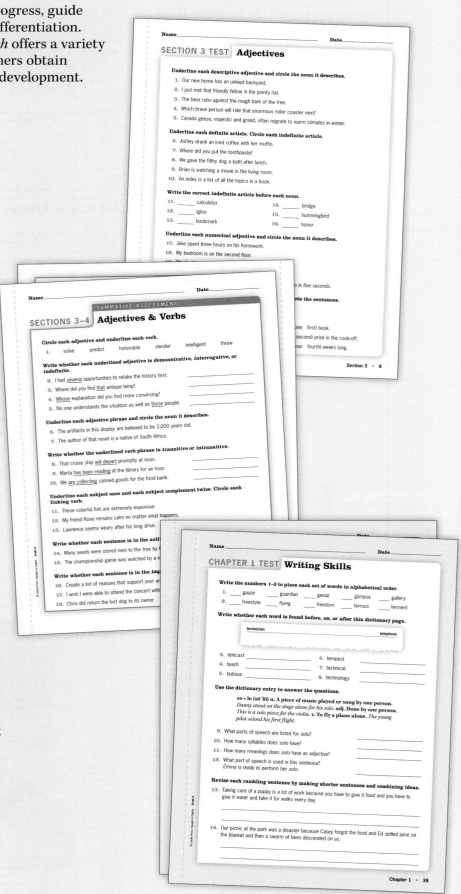

Assess According to Class Needs
ExamView® Assessment Suite Test Generator

Today's teachers need flexibility to customize assessment to meet the needs of all students, offer assessment in a variety of formats, and analyze results quickly and easily. Therefore, *Voyages in English* is proud to offer the ExamView® Assessment Suite Test Generator, "a complete toolset in three seamless applications."

Voyages in English Test Generator is available for separate purchase. With this CD, teachers can build comprehensive tests with the Test Generator, administer customized tests with the Test Player, and analyze results with the Test Manager.

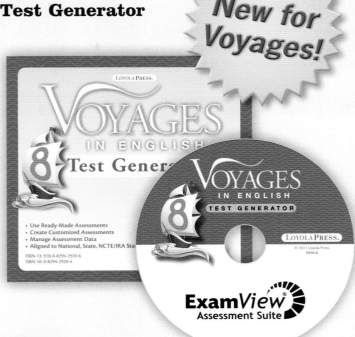

Each grade-level CD provides teachers with the following:

- Preformatted yet customizable assessments that correspond with the Assessment Book while offering 25% new test items for each test

- Alignment to key national and state standards

- The ability to save questions in Question Banks for compilation into multiple study guides and assessments

- Wide variety of question selection methods and question types

- Question-scrambling capability for multiple test versions and secure test conditions

- Multiple test-delivery methods: printed, LAN, or export the test as an HTML file to be manually posted to a Web site

- Grade assessments through a variety of scanning methods, track progress, and generate reports

- On-screen help

Contact your sales representative at **800-621-1008** for more information or visit us online at **www.voyagesinenglish.com**.

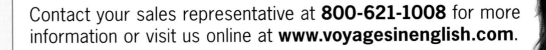

STUDENTS: TECHNOLOGY INTEGRATION

In the Book

Students are invited to communicate, collaborate, research, and problem-solve using technology. Online resources and digital tools are suggested to enhance writing and reinforce grammar topic application.

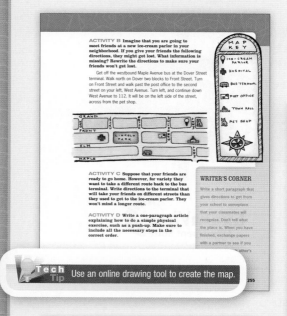

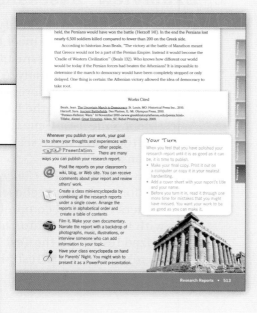

Students explore ways to publish their work using technology.

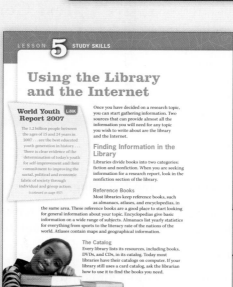

Direct technology instruction embedded into student lessons

Tech Tips invite students to creatively apply their grammar skills, using a variety of technologies.

On the Web

Find additional opportunities for students to strengthen and polish their grammar and writing skills at www.voyagesinenglish.com.

Interactive games for more practice

Grammar and Mechanics Handbook for at-home use

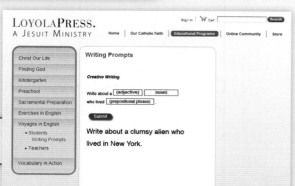

Additional writing activities expand learning.

TEACHERS: TECHNOLOGY INTEGRATION

In the Book

Easy, practical tips allow teachers to make technology a natural part of the language-arts classroom.

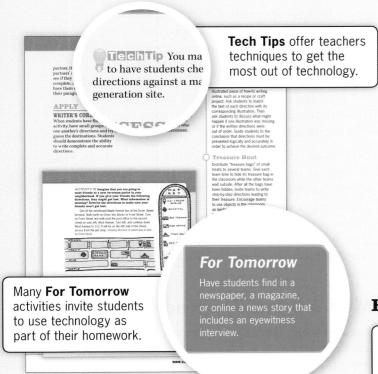

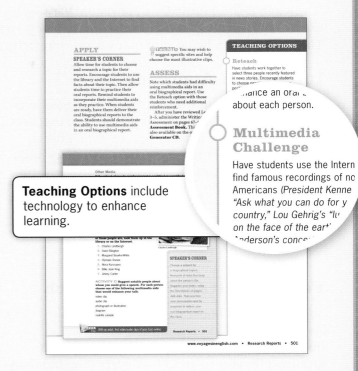

Tech Tips offer teachers techniques to get the most out of technology.

Teaching Options include technology to enhance learning.

For Tomorrow

Have students find in a newspaper, a magazine, or online a news story that includes an eyewitness interview.

Many **For Tomorrow** activities invite students to use technology as part of their homework.

For the Computer

Optional ExamView® Assessment Suite Test Generator (see page OV-17)

On the Web

Plenty of online support, including professional development and planning.

Ask An Expert provides additional teacher background to common questions.

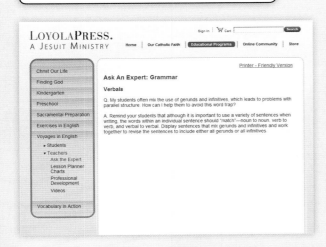

Research document explains how *Voyages* is based and anchored in research.

Lesson Plan Charts show how to integrate the grammar and writing sections.

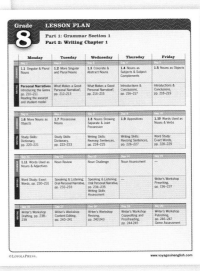

CREATING A PLAN THAT WORKS FOR YOU

Voyages in English provides a consistent, systematic teaching plan for student success and excellence in writing and grammar proficiency—with room for individual adaptation. The program can be used in many ways, supporting each teacher's personal style.

Integrated Approach

Many teachers follow the integration suggestions that are provided in the book. To do this, teachers follow the Teacher Edition step by step. This is especially helpful to new teachers. Teachers build their plans based on the suggestions in the wrap-around text, leading them to toggle between the grammar and writing portions of the textbook. They cover the grammar lessons, writing skills, and the Writer's Workshops.

Focus on Grammar Approach

Some teachers choose to separate the book sections and focus on grammar for direct instruction. They teach grammar as part of a grammar/language arts block every day, and then have students work through the writing portion of the book at a different time, such as during reading time as seatwork. They may also choose to teach writing less often than grammar.

Focus on Writing Approaches

Some teachers provide direct instruction throughout the writing chapters and have students work through the grammar portion of the book during their reading time. Or they assess students' grammar skills and teach only the sections in which students need further development, freeing up time to focus on the writing chapters.

Other teachers follow the writing lesson plans, but as soon as the students have a grasp of the genre characteristics, they begin the Writer's Workshop. The teacher continues teaching the writing skills lessons as needed only. This allows students more time to work on their final piece while they learn how to improve their writing and grammar skills.

Mixed-Order Approach

Teachers who integrate grammar and writing instruction into their set reading curriculum schedule often teach the grammar sections and writing chapters in an order that suits the stories that students are experiencing. For example, if students are reading an autobiography in reading class, teachers may choose to have students experience the personal narrative writing chapter and the pronouns grammar section.

LESSON PLANS FOR THE INTEGRATED APPROACH

If you choose to implement the integrated approach, then use the following as a guide for how each grammar section and writing chapter work together.

Grade 3

Grammar	Writing
Sentences	Personal Narratives
Nouns	How-to Articles
Pronouns	Descriptions
Verbs	Personal Letters
Adjectives	Book Reports
Adverbs and Conjunctions	Persuasive Writing
Punctuation and Capitalization	Creative Writing
Diagramming	Research Reports

Grade 4

Grammar	Writing
Sentences	Personal Narratives
Nouns	Formal Letters
Pronouns	Descriptions
Adjectives	How-to Articles
Verbs	Persuasive Writing
Adverbs and Conjunctions	Creative Writing
Punctuation and Capitalization	Expository Writing
Diagramming	Research Reports

Grade 5

Grammar	Writing
Nouns	Personal Narratives
Pronouns	How-to Articles
Adjectives	Business Letters
Verbs	Descriptions
Adverbs	Book Reports
Prepositions, Conjunctions, and Interjections	Creative Writing
Sentences	Persuasive Writing
Punctuation and Capitalization Diagramming	Research Reports

Grade 6

Grammar	Writing
Nouns	Personal Narratives
Pronouns	How-to Articles
Adjectives	Descriptions
Verbs	Persuasive Writing
Adverbs	Expository Writing
Sentences	Business Letters
Conjunctions, Interjections, Punctuation, and Capitalization	Creative Writing
Diagramming	Research Reports

Grade 7

Grammar	Writing
Nouns Adjectives	Personal Narratives
Pronouns	Business Letters
Verbs	How-to Articles
Verbals	Descriptions
Adverbs Prepositions	Book Reviews
Sentences	Creative Writing
Conjunctions and Interjections Punctuation and Capitalization	Expository Writing
Diagramming	Research Reports

Grade 8

Grammar	Writing
Nouns Adjectives	Personal Narratives
Pronouns	How-to Articles
Verbs	Business Letters
Verbals	Descriptions
Adverbs Prepositions	Expository Writing
Sentences	Persuasive Writing
Conjunctions and Interjections Punctuation and Capitalization	Creative Writing
Diagramming	Research Reports

How to Use This Program

LESSON PLANNING MADE EASY

Each grammar section provides a developmentally appropriate study of a part of speech that includes grammar lessons with ample practice, a review lesson, and a challenge lesson. The Writing Connection that culminates each grammar lesson leads to the writing portion of the book to create an opportunity for integration between the two main parts. Each writing chapter in *Voyages in English* is a study of a single genre—a chapter opener, six lessons, and the genre's Writer's Workshop. Here are the main instructional elements for each grammar section and writing chapter.

PART I: GRAMMAR

- Daily Maintenance
- Warm-Up
- Practice
- Review
- Challenge

PART II: WRITTEN AND ORAL COMMUNICATION

- Literature excerpt
- Student model
- Genre lessons
- Writing skills lessons
- Writer's Workshops

If You Teach Grammar and Writing Three Days a Week,

- condense *Voyages* into a three-day-a-week plan.
- complete two of the activities and exercises shown in each grammar section and writing page span.

	Monday	Wednesday	Friday
GRAMMAR	**1.1** Singular and Plural Nouns **1.2** More Singular and Plural Nouns	**1.3** Concrete and Abstract Nouns	**1.4** Nouns as Subjects and Subject Complements
WRITING	**Personal Narratives** Introducing the Genre, pp. 210–211	What Makes a Good Personal Narrative?, pp. 212–215	Introductions and Conclusions, pp. 216–219

If You Teach Grammar and Writing Every Day,

- apply this five-day-a-week plan throughout the program.
- complete all the activities and exercises shown in each grammar section and writing page span.

	Monday	Tuesday	Wednesday	Thursday	Friday
	Day 1	**Day 2**	**Day 3**	**Day 4**	**Day 5**
GRAMMAR	**1.1** Singular and Plural Nouns	**1.2** More Singular and Plural Nouns	**1.3** Concrete and Abstract Nouns	**1.4** Nouns as Subjects and Subject Complements	**1.5** Nouns as Objects
WRITING	**Personal Narratives** Introducing the Genre pp. 210–211 Reading the Excerpt and Student Model	What Makes a Good Personal Narrative?, pp. 212–213	What Makes a Good Personal Narrative?, pp. 214–215	Introductions and Conclusions, pp. 216–217	Introductions and Conclusions, pp. 218–219
	Day 6	**Day 7**	**Day 8**	**Day 9**	**Day 10**
GRAMMAR	**1.6** More Nouns as Objects	**1.7** Possessive Nouns	**1.8** Nouns Showing Separate and Joint Possession	**1.9** Appositives	**1.10** Words Used as Nouns and Verbs
WRITING	Study Skills: Dictionary, pp. 220–221	Study Skills: Dictionary, pp. 222–223	Writing Skills: Revising Sentences, pp. 224–225	Writing Skills: Revising Sentences, pp. 226–227	Word Study: Exact Words, pp. 228–229
	Day 11	**Day 12**	**Day 13**	**Day 14**	**Day 15**
GRAMMAR	**1.11** Words Used as Nouns and Adjectives	Noun Review	Noun Challenge	Noun Assessment	—
WRITING	Word Study: Exact Words, pp. 230–231	Speaking & Listening Skills: Oral Personal Narratives, pp. 232–233	Speaking & Listening Skills: Oral Personal Narratives, pp. 234–235 Writing Skills Assessment	—	Writer's Workshop Prewriting, pp. 236–237
	Day 16	**Day 17**	**Day 18**	**Day 19**	**Day 20**
WRITING	Writer's Workshop Drafting, pp. 238–239	Writer's Workshop Content Editing, pp. 240–241	Writer's Workshop Revising, pp. 242–243	Writer's Workshop Copyediting and Proofreading, pp. 244–245	Writer's Workshop Publishing, pp. 246–247 Genre Assessment

Go to www.voyagesinenglish.com to find sample lesson plans for the whole year—one for each grammar section and writing chapter in the program.

INTRODUCING THE PROGRAM ON DAY ONE

Warm-Up

As a class, work together to write a three-sentence "text message" about a favorite book. Challenge students to use common text abbreviations, such as *LOL*, and convey the message in as few words and letters as possible. Write student ideas on the chalkboard. Read aloud the message two ways: literally and as it is intended. Together, note the differences in how the message sounds.

Explain to students that as technology moves us away from using standard English grammar and writing, it is even more important to learn, master, and use them correctly. Tell students that using grammar and writing correctly will help them be better readers, writers, listeners, and speakers as well as better students and workers when they are adults.

Teach

Guide students on a book walk through the textbook. Review the Table of Contents and the book's organization and contents. Explain that students will be using *Voyages in English* in their journey to master English grammar and writing.

Practice

Provide students with a minute or two to review the book's contents. Tour the room, pointing out interesting book features to individual students.

Apply

Have students go on their first *Voyages in English* scavenger hunt. Ask students to find features such as a grammar lesson, writing lesson, Writer's Workshop, Link, Grammar in Action, and Tech Tip. Award points or prizes to the students who are first to find the features.

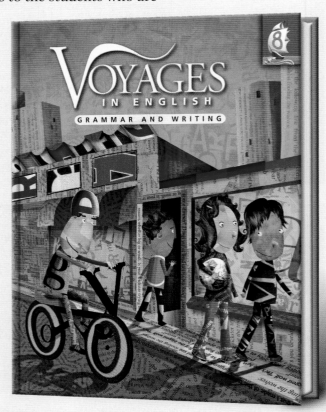

Assess

Ask students the following questions: *Why is it important to study grammar and writing? What is one thing we will be learning this year? Which skill or topic might be most challenging for you? What do you think will be easiest to learn?*

Extend

Have students study their book covers. Say: *We know that words are powerful. When words are used carefully and correctly, they can take us where we want to go in life. Look at your cover. Choose a person in it. Where do you think he or she is going in life? Take a few minutes to jot some ideas.*

Invite student volunteers to share their ideas. Close by saying: *Now we're going to go on a voyage together— to learn about words and writing so that we can go where we want to go. Let's get started!*

SECTION FOCUS
- **Singular and plural nouns**
- **Nouns as subjects and subject complements**
- **Nouns as objects and object complements**
- **Appositives**
- **Possessive nouns**

SUPPORT MATERIALS

Practice Book
Daily Maintenance, pages 1–2
Grammar, pages 3–10

Assessment Book
Section 1 Assessment, pages 1–2

Test Generator CD

Writing Chapter 1,
**   Personal Narratives**

Customizable Lesson Plans
www.voyagesinenglish.com

CONNECT WITH LITERATURE

📖 Consider using the following titles throughout the section to illustrate the grammar concept:

Grape Thief by Kristine L. Franklin
Just Ella by Margaret Peterson
    Haddix
Mud City by Deborah Ellis

Nouns

GRAMMAR FOR GROWN-UPS

Understanding Nouns

A **noun** is a word that names a person, a place, a thing, or an idea. A noun has many different functions within a sentence. A noun can function as a subject, a subject complement, a direct object, an indirect object, an object complement, an object of a preposition, or an appositive.

The **subject** tells what the sentence is about.

> *Dogs make great pets.*

A **subject complement** follows a linking verb and renames the subject. Common linking verbs are *be* and its various forms (*am, is, are, was, were*), *become, feel, taste, remain, appear, grow,* and *seem.*

> *George Washington was the first president.*

A **direct object** answers the question *whom* or *what* after the verb.

> *Marcus ate the entire salad.*

An **indirect object** tells *to whom* or *for whom*, or *to what* or *for what*, an action is done.

> *Maria gave her friend a beautiful gift.*

Just as a subject complement renames the subject, an **object complement** renames the direct object.

> *The school newspaper called the play a great success.*

A noun can also be the **object of a preposition.** Some common prepositions are *in, into, on, to, by, for, from, with,* and *without.*

> *I threw the ball to my friend.*

An **appositive** is a word that follows a noun and renames it. An appositive is restrictive if it is necessary to the meaning of the sentence.

> *I have three sisters. My sister Laurel is a photographer.*

An appositive is nonrestrictive if it merely gives added information. A nonrestrictive appositive is set off by commas.

> *My only sister, Laurel, is a photographer.*

"Grammar is a piano I play by ear. All I know about grammar is its power."

—Joan Didion

COMMON ERRORS

Understanding Subject-Verb Agreement

Writers sometimes mistake a noun contained in a prepositional phrase for the subject of the sentence and subsequently use an incorrect form of the verb.

ERROR: The set of glasses are not clean.
CORRECT: The set of glasses is not clean.

ERROR: The placement of nouns are important
CORRECT: The placement of nouns is important.

The subjects *set* and *placement* are singular. The plural words *glasses* and *nouns* are part of prepositional phrases that modify the subjects.

Remind students that the proximity of a noun to a verb is not always an indicator of subject. Guide your students to read their writing carefully to avoid this kind of error and to include an extra read during revision time to find and fix this kind of error.

SENTENCE DIAGRAMMING

You may wish to teach nouns in the context of diagramming. Review these examples. Then refer to the Diagramming section or look for Diagram It! features in the Nouns section.

Mrs. Leder is my favorite teacher.

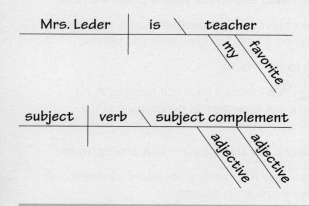

He offered Steven a job.

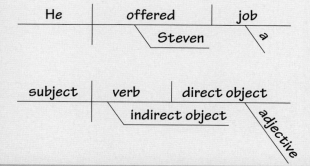

ASK AN EXPERT

Real Situations, Real Solutions

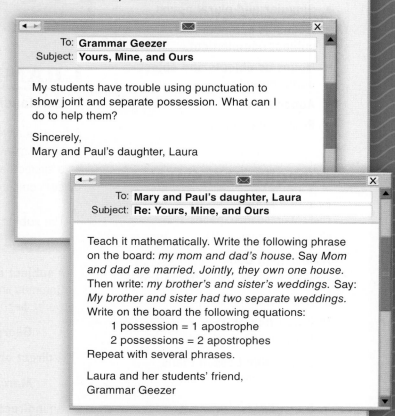

To: **Grammar Geezer**
Subject: **Yours, Mine, and Ours**

My students have trouble using punctuation to show joint and separate possession. What can I do to help them?

Sincerely,
Mary and Paul's daughter, Laura

To: **Mary and Paul's daughter, Laura**
Subject: **Re: Yours, Mine, and Ours**

Teach it mathematically. Write the following phrase on the board: *my mom and dad's house*. Say *Mom and dad are married. Jointly, they own one house.* Then write: *my brother's and sister's weddings*. Say: *My brother and sister had two separate weddings.* Write on the board the following equations:
1 possession = 1 apostrophe
2 possessions = 2 apostrophes
Repeat with several phrases.

Laura and her students' friend,
Grammar Geezer

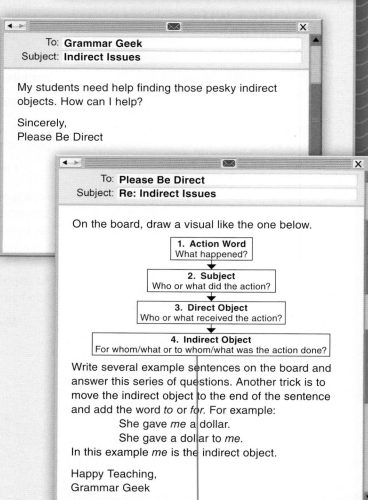

To: **Grammar Geek**
Subject: **Indirect Issues**

My students need help finding those pesky indirect objects. How can I help?

Sincerely,
Please Be Direct

To: **Please Be Direct**
Subject: **Re: Indirect Issues**

On the board, draw a visual like the one below.

> **1. Action Word**
> What happened?
>
> **2. Subject**
> Who or what did the action?
>
> **3. Direct Object**
> Who or what received the action?
>
> **4. Indirect Object**
> For whom/what or to whom/what was the action done?

Write several example sentences on the board and answer this series of questions. Another trick is to move the indirect object to the end of the sentence and add the word *to* or *for*. For example:
She gave *me* a dollar.
She gave a dollar to *me*.
In this example *me* is the indirect object.

Happy Teaching,
Grammar Geek

SECTION ONE
Nouns

1.1 Singular and Plural Nouns

OBJECTIVES

- **To identify and use singular and plural nouns**
- **To form the plurals of nouns ending in *s*, *x*, *z*, *ch*, and *sh***
- **To form the plurals of nouns that end in *y* preceded by a vowel and those that end in *y* preceded by a consonant**
- **To recognize the plural forms of irregular nouns and the plural forms of nouns that do not change in the plural form**

DAILY Maintenance

Assign **Practice Book** page 1, Section 1.1. After students finish,
1. Give immediate feedback.
2. Review concepts as needed.
3. Model the correct answer.

Pages 4–5 of the **Answer Key** contain tips for Daily Maintenance.

WARM-UP

Write the headings *One* and *More Than One* on the board. Have small groups list people, places, and things. Then have a student from each group write the words on the board under the appropriate heading. Erase and switch the headings. Ask students to change the singular words to make them fit under the new heading and to do the same for the plurals.

📖 Read from a piece of writing that the class is currently reading. Emphasize the singular and plural nouns.

TEACH

Invite a student to read aloud the definitions for singular and plural nouns at the top of the page. Ask students to share nouns they know. Write these words on the board. Help students distinguish between nouns that are singular and nouns that are plural.

Ask volunteers to take turns reading the rules that explain how to make nouns plural. Review the list of nouns on the board and help students determine which rule applies to each word.

PRACTICE

EXERCISE 1

After students have identified which nouns are singular and which nouns are plural, have volunteers write on the board the singular and plural forms for all the nouns. Encourage students to state the rule that applies to making each noun plural.

EXERCISE 2

Review students' answers for accuracy. You may wish to have students go back to their dictionaries to check incorrect responses. Encourage students to state the rule that applies to making each noun plural.

1.1 Singular and Plural Nouns

A **noun** is a name word. A **singular noun** names one person, place, thing, or idea. A **plural noun** names more than one person, place, thing, or idea.

Add *-s* to most nouns to form the plurals.

SINGULAR	PLURAL	SINGULAR	PLURAL
artifact	artifacts	minute	minutes

Add *-es* to form the plural of a noun ending in *s*, *x*, *z*, *ch*, or *sh*.

SINGULAR	PLURAL	SINGULAR	PLURAL
guess	guesses	crash	crashes

Form the plural of a noun ending in *y* preceded by a vowel by adding *-s*.

SINGULAR	PLURAL	SINGULAR	PLURAL
monkey	monkeys	birthday	birthdays

Form the plural of a noun ending in *y* preceded by a consonant by changing the *y* to *i* and adding *-es*.

SINGULAR	PLURAL	SINGULAR	PLURAL
baby	babies	victory	victories

Some plural nouns are not formed by adding *-s* or *-es*. Check a dictionary for the correct plural form.

SINGULAR	PLURAL	SINGULAR	PLURAL
ox	oxen	goose	geese
oasis	oases	medium	media

The plural forms of some nouns are the same as the singular forms.

SINGULAR	PLURAL	SINGULAR	PLURAL
series	series	corps	corps
sheep	sheep	Portuguese	Portuguese

APPLY

APPLY IT NOW

As students work, remind them to check a dictionary if they are uncertain about a word's plural form. Ask volunteers to read their sentences aloud and identify which form of the noun is used. Students should demonstrate an understanding of singular and plural nouns and forming the plurals of regular and irregular nouns.

ASSESS

Note which students had difficulty with singular and plural nouns. Assign **Practice Book** page 3 for further practice.

WRITING CONNECTION

Use pages 222–223 of the Writing portion of the book. Be sure to point out nouns in the literature excerpt and the student model.

Exercise 1
1. ranches
2. barrels
3. buses
4. taxi
5. berry
6. journey
7. colonies
8. fishermen
9. parties
10. lily
11. crisis
12. buzzes
13. data
14. theses
15. larvae
16. woman

Exercise 2
1. children
2. dishes
3. discoveries
4. genes
5. species
6. displays
7. peaches
8. potatoes
9. berries, peas, tomatoes
10. farmer's markets

Apply It Now
1. princesses
2. inquiries
3. species
4. buffalos or buffaloes
5. churches
6. chimneys
7. processes
8. appendixes or appendices
9. flurries

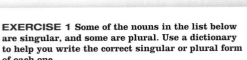

EXERCISE 1 Some of the nouns in the list below are singular, and some are plural. Use a dictionary to help you write the correct singular or plural form of each one.

1. ranch	5. berries	9. party	13. datum
2. barrel	6. journeys	10. lilies	14. thesis
3. bus	7. colony	11. crises	15. larva
4. taxis	8. fisherman	12. buzz	16. women

EXERCISE 2 Complete each sentence with the plural form of the noun or nouns in parentheses.

1. Adults always tell _____ (child) to eat their fruits and vegetables.
2. A lot of the food we buy and put on our _____ (dish) is changing.
3. Every day there are new _____ (discovery) in genetic engineering.
4. Genetic engineering is the science of changing organisms by making changes in their _____ (gene).
5. It can produce changes in _____ (species).
6. For example, it can make tomatoes that are redder and look more attractive in supermarket _____ (display).
7. In the future there may be _____ (peach) that are resistant to frost.
8. Scientists also hope to produce _____ (potato) that are resistant to disease.
9. But nothing tastes as good as the _____ (berry, pea, and tomato) that you can grow yourself.
10. We grow more vegetables than we can eat, so we sell the rest at _____ (farmer's market) around the state.

APPLY IT NOW

Look up each singular noun in a dictionary and write the plural form. Then use either the singular or plural form in a sentence.

1. princess	6. chimney
2. inquiry	7. process
3. species	8. appendix
4. buffalo	9. flurry
5. church	

Nouns • 3

1.2 More Singular and Plural Nouns

OBJECTIVES

- **To form the plural of nouns ending in *o* and *f* or *fe***
- **To form the plural of compound nouns and words ending in *ful***
- **To recognize nouns that always appear in the plural form and nouns that appear in the plural form but are singular**

 **Maintenance**

Assign **Practice Book** page 1, Section 1.2. After students finish,
1. Give immediate feedback.
2. Review concepts as needed.
3. Model the correct answer.

Pages 4–5 of the **Answer Key** contain tips for Daily Maintenance.

WARM-UP

Have students look around the room. In the space of one minute, have them write down the names of as many objects as they can. Challenge students to say the plural form of each object. Have students write on the board a list of plural nouns. Make sure to include some plural nouns that do not end in *s*.

📖 Read from a piece of writing that the class is currently reading. Emphasize the singular and plural nouns.

TEACH

Review the definitions of singular and plural nouns. Invite volunteers to read aloud the rules for forming plurals. After students read each rule, point out examples from the Warm-Up activity. Challenge students to find additional examples of each rule.

PRACTICE

EXERCISE 1

Review students' work for accuracy. After confirming the plural of each noun, ask students to identify which rule applies to each plural form.

EXERCISE 2

Remind students that not all words that end in *s* are plural and that some plurals do not end in *s*. Point out that words such as *deer* and *fish* can be both singular and plural. Have students work in pairs to decide whether or not the words in the list are singular or plural. Remind students to use a dictionary to find the plurals of unfamiliar nouns.

1.2 More Singular and Plural Nouns

If a noun ends in *o* preceded by a vowel, form the plural by adding -*s*.

SINGULAR	PLURAL	SINGULAR	PLURAL
studio	studios	stereo	stereos

If a noun ends in *o* preceded by a consonant, form the plural by adding -*es*. There are exceptions to this rule. Always check a dictionary.

SINGULAR	PLURAL	SINGULAR	PLURAL
tomato	tomatoes	hero	heroes
EXCEPTIONS		EXCEPTIONS	
piano	pianos	kimono	kimonos
zero	zeros or zeroes	cello	cellos

For most nouns ending in *f* or *fe*, form the plurals by adding -*s*. For some nouns, however, you must change the *f* or *fe* to *ves*. Always check a dictionary.

SINGULAR	PLURAL	SINGULAR	PLURAL
roof	roofs	loaf	loaves

Form the plurals of most compound nouns by adding -*s*.

SINGULAR	PLURAL	SINGULAR	PLURAL
disc drive	disc drives	fireplace	fireplaces
cover-up	cover-ups	drive-in	drive-ins

Form the plurals of some compound nouns by adding -*s* to the principal words or by making the principal word plural. Always check a dictionary.

SINGULAR	PLURAL	SINGULAR	PLURAL
brother-in-law	brothers-in-law	man-of-war	men-of-war

Form the plurals of compounds ending in *ful* by adding -*s*.

SINGULAR	PLURAL	SINGULAR	PLURAL
handful	handfuls	spoonful	spoonfuls

Exercise 1
1. ladies
2. suffixes
3. trespassers
4. radios
5. dispatches
6. sisters-in-law
7. jockeys
8. eyeteeth
9. chimneys
10. burros
11. mumps
12. shelves
13. alumni
14. foxes
15. cargos
16. sketches
17. fish or fishes
18. hooves
19. mice
20. cacti, cactuses, or cactus

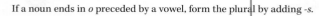

APPLY

APPLY IT NOW

After students have finished, challenge partners to compare their lists and to identify which nouns are plural and which nouns are singular. Students should demonstrate an understanding of forming irregular plurals and of nouns that have the same singular and plural form.

💡 **TechTip** Suggest that students look online for a graphic organizer such as a word web. Students can enter the location of the campsite in the center space, and plural and singular nouns describing items needed for camping in the rest of the web.

ASSESS

Note which students had difficulty with singular nouns and plural nouns. Assign **Practice Book** page 4 for further practice.

WRITING CONNECTION

Use pages 224–225 of the Writing portion of the book.

TEACHING OPTIONS

Reteach

Write on the board a plural noun that corresponds to each rule. Challenge students to identify whether the word is plural. Then ask students to read the rule to which the plural form applies.

Observe and Apply

While students are exploring literary forms or reading literature texts in class, call attention to plural nouns that follow the rules on this page. Encourage students to look for similar plurals as they read on their own. Have students write these plural nouns in their notebooks to share with the class.

Cooperative Learning

Have students generate a list of five singular nouns for which they feel that forming the plural is tricky. Then have groups review the rules for forming plurals on pages 2–3 and discuss the proper plural form for all the tricky nouns. Have each group share a few examples with the class.

Meeting Individual Needs

Auditory You might find that some students have an easier time learning these rules by listening rather than by reading. Suggest that students chant the rules, along with examples, infusing the chants with a predictable rhythm. Point out that this procedure may help impress the rules upon students memories.

Exercise 2
Singular Nouns
corps
salmon
deer
Balinese
cod
crisis
Inuit
trout
woman
goose
species
larva
swine
series
radius
treasure

Plural Nouns
zoos
potatoes
corps
salmon
children
taxes
deer
Balinese
cod
miracles
victories
vertebrae
Inuit
oases
data
trout
men
grouse
species
swine
series
strata

Some nouns are used only in the plural form.

clothes   **pliers**   **jeans**

Some nouns are plural in form but singular in meaning and use.

politics   **measles**   **news**

EXERCISE 1 Write the plural of each noun. Check a dictionary if you are not sure of a plural form.

1. lady
2. suffix
3. trespasser
4. radio
5. dispatch
6. sister-in-law
7. jockey
8. eyetooth
9. chimney
10. burro
11. mumps
12. shelf
13. alumnus
14. fox
15. cargo
16. sketch
17. fish
18. hoof
19. mouse
20. cactus

EXERCISE 2 Write these words in two columns, one column with singular forms and the other with plural forms. Some words will go into both columns. Check a dictionary if necessary.

zoos	Balinese	oases	species
potatoes	cod	data	larva
corps	crisis	trout	swine
salmon	miracles	men	series
children	victories	woman	strata
taxes	vertebrae	goose	radius
deer	Inuit	grouse	treasure

APPLY IT NOW

You and your friends are planning a camping trip. Create a list of supplies that you will need for the whole group. Use both singular and plural nouns.

🔧 **TechTip** With an adult, search online for camping necessities.

Nouns • 5

1.3 Nouns as Subjects and Subject Complements

OBJECTIVES
- To identify the subject of a sentence
- To identify the subject complement of a sentence

 **Maintenance**

Assign **Practice Book** page 1, Section 1.3. After students finish,
1. Give immediate feedback.
2. Review concepts as needed.
3. Model the correct answer.

Pages 4–5 of the **Answer Key** contain tips for Daily Maintenance.

WARM-UP

Distribute three sets of note cards, each with a noun and phrase as shown below. Ask pairs of students to construct sentences using all the words on the cards.

Football	his favorite sport
Steve	the star
Fans	the cheerleaders

Ask students to think about what function each phrase plays in the sentence.

📖 Read from a piece of writing that the class is currently reading. Emphasize the nouns used as subjects and subject complements.

TEACH

Invite a volunteer to read the definition of subject and another volunteer to read the definition of subject complement. Discuss how the terms differ and encourage students to give examples of a subject and a subject complement within a sentence.

Tell students that adjectives preceded by linking verbs can also be subject complements. See page 18 for adjectival subject

complements and their linking verbs. Tell students that an adjectival complement describes the subject, unlike a noun complement which renames the subject. Discuss these differences.

After students read their sentences aloud, have volunteers identify the linking verbs. Then ask students to name the subject and the subject complement in each sentence.

PRACTICE

EXERCISE 1
Remind students that a subject is what or who the sentence is about. Point out that in many cases the subject is a noun. Have students identify the subject as a person, a place, or a thing to confirm their answers. As a class, identify the subject complements.

EXERCISE 2
Stress that the subject complement renames or identifies the subject and reveals more information about it. Have students identify the subject complements and tell what extra information is given about the subjects.

EXERCISE 3
Point out that in Exercise 2, the subject was usually at the beginning of the sentence and

---

1.3 Nouns as Subjects and Subject Complements

A noun can be used as the subject of a sentence. The **subject** tells what or who the sentence is about.

In this sentence the noun *wars* is the subject.

> **Wars** have occurred throughout human history.

A noun or pronoun that renames or identifies the subject is a **subject complement.** A subject complement follows a linking verb such as *be* and its various forms *(am, is, are, was, were),* *become,* and *remain.*

In this sentence *World War II* is the subject and *conflict* is the subject complement.

> *World War II* **was a major** *conflict* **of the 20th century.**

What are the subject and the subject complement in this sentence?

> **Winston Churchill became the prime minister of England for the first time in 1940.**

To find the subject, ask yourself *who* or *what* the sentence is about *(Winston Churchill).* Then see if there is a linking verb. If so, ask *Is the linking verb followed by a noun that renames the subject?* That noun is the subject complement *(prime minister).*

EXERCISE 1 Name the subject of each sentence. Name the subject complements if there are any.

1. Winston Churchill's role in World War II was crucial.
2. His most important contribution was to give the British people hope.
3. German planes were bombing London primarily by night.
4. Great Britain needed aid during the war.
5. President Franklin D. Roosevelt convinced the United States to help Britain.
6. Churchill was a brilliant orator and a source of strength.
7. His six-volume publication *The Second World War* earned Churchill the Nobel Prize for literature.
8. Churchill was also an officer in the British army, a historian, and an artist.
9. London is a city that has seen its share of wars.

Exercise 1
1. role
2. contribution
3. planes
4. Great Britain
5. President Franklin D. Roosevelt
6. Churchill, orator
7. publication
8. Churchill, officer, historian, artist
9. London, city

followed by the linking verb and the subject complement. Explain that recognizing the location of the subject and subject complement in a sentence may help students decide which they have added to the sentences in this exercise.

APPLY

APPLY IT NOW

To help students begin writing, review that the subject complement renames the subject and provides extra information about it. Have students exchange papers to identify the subject of each sentence. Have students discuss what each sentence is about.

Students should demonstrate an understanding of subjects and subject complements.

ASSESS

Note which students had difficulty with subjects and subject complements. Assign **Practice Book** pages 5–6 for further practice.

WRITING CONNECTION

Use pages 226–227 of the Writing portion of the book.

TEACHING OPTIONS

Reteach

Point to objects in the room and encourage volunteers to suggest sentences about the objects, including a subject and a subject complement in each sentence. For example, point to a flag and elicit from students a sentence such as *The flag is a symbol of the United States.* Write students' sentences on the board. Have volunteers circle the subjects and underline the subject complements.

Meeting Individual Needs

Interpersonal Have students write sentences that tell about people, places, and things in their lives. Tell students to use the sentence structure that includes a subject and a subject complement. You might use the following as sentence starters to prompt ideas:

_____ **is the city where I was born.**

_____ **is my (brother, sister, aunt, uncle, and so on).**

My dog is a _____.

Have students circle the subject of each sentence and then underline the subject complement.

Meeting Individual Needs

Extra Support For students who have difficulty identifying the subject complement, suggest that they ask questions as they read each sentence. Use the example given on page 6: *Winston Churchill became the prime minister of England for the first time in 1940.* Have students locate the subject—*Winston Churchill.* Then ask a question about the subject: *Who was Winston Churchill?* The answer—*the prime minister*—will be the subject complement. Encourage students to try this strategy with other sentences.

Exercise 2
Subjects are underlined once. Subject complements are underlined twice.

EXERCISE 2 Identify the subject of each sentence. Then name the subject complement if there is one.

1. The United Kingdom includes England, Scotland, Wales, and Northern Ireland.
2. Great Britain is only England, Wales, and Scotland.
3. The British monarch remains a symbol of the nation.
4. The reigning monarch has little real power.
5. The real ruler of Britain is Parliament.
6. Parliament is the legislature, similar to the U.S. Congress.
7. Cricket has been a popular British sport.
8. Baseball had its origins in cricket.
9. Shepherd's pie is a popular British food.
10. Its main ingredients are beef and potatoes.
11. Tea with milk and sugar is a popular hot beverage with most Britons.
12. The favorite British sport football is called soccer in America.
13. The Welsh prefer rugby.

Exercise 3
Answers will vary.
1. subject complement
2. subject
3. subject complement
4. subject complement
5. subject
6. subject
7. subject complement
8. subject complement

EXERCISE 3 Complete each sentence. Then tell whether you added a subject or a subject complement.

1. My favorite place around here is _____.
2. _____ is a spot that is just beautiful.
3. My favorite food has always been _____.
4. A food I liked when I was younger was _____.
5. _____ remains a popular sport with people my age.
6. _____ became my favorite kind of music.
7. London is a _____ that history buffs love to visit.
8. Old English sheepdogs are _____ that are considered highly intelligent.

APPLY IT NOW

Write five sentences, each one using a subject complement and telling about something you either enjoy or do not enjoy. Use the verbs *become* and *remain* in two of the sentences.

Nouns • 7

1.4 Nouns as Objects and Object Complements

OBJECTIVES

- **To recognize and identify the direct object of a sentence**
- **To recognize and identify the indirect object of a sentence**
- **To understand that a noun can be the object of a preposition**
- **To understand that a noun can be an object complement**

DAILY Maintenance

Assign **Practice Book** page 1, Section 1.4. After students finish,
1. Give immediate feedback.
2. Review concepts as needed.
3. Model the correct answer.

Pages 4–5 of the **Answer Key** contain tips for Daily Maintenance.

WARM-UP

Write the following sentences on the board. Ask students how these sentences are different.

Maureen threw.

Maureen threw a ball.

Remind students that asking *what* or *whom* when reading a sentence can provide important information and help identify the parts of a sentence.

📖 Read from a piece of writing that the class is currently reading. Emphasize the nouns used as objects and as object complements.

TEACH

Write the following sentence on the board. Ask a volunteer to read aloud the definitions of a direct object and an indirect object at the top of the page.

My friend baked me an apple pie.

Ask students what is being baked. Then erase *an apple pie* from the sentence. Ask students how the meaning of the sentence changed

and what the function of each noun is.

Ask students to write a sentence that has an object complement. Have volunteers read their sentences aloud. As a class, identify the object complements.

PRACTICE

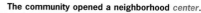

EXERCISE 1
Remind students that in most cases the direct object will appear after the verb. Point out that the direct object will also answer the question *what* or *whom*. Read the first sentence aloud. Then ask, *What do some high school students*

take? (classes) Be sure students understand that *classes* is the direct object. When students have completed the exercise, review their answers. Continue in this way for indirect objects, objects of prepositions, and object complements. Encourage students to ask questions that can be answered by these nouns.

EXERCISE 2
Have students complete the exercise independently and then share their answers with a partner. Encourage students to discuss any difficulty they had.

1.4 Nouns as Objects and Object Complements

A noun can be used as a direct object. The **direct object** answers the question *whom* or *what* after the verb. In this sentence the direct object is *center*. It answers the question *What did the community open?*

The community opened a neighborhood *center.*

A noun can be used as an indirect object. An **indirect object** tells *to whom* or *for whom*, or *to what* or *for what*, an action is done. In this sentence the indirect object is *children*. It answers the question *To whom does the center offer classes?*

The center offers *children* **classes.**

A noun can be the **object of a preposition** when it follows a preposition such as *in, into, on, to, by, for, from, with,* or *without*. In this sentence *ceramics* is the object of the preposition *in*. It answers the question *What did I take a class in?*

I took a class in *ceramics* **there.**

A noun can be an object complement. Just as a subject complement renames the subject, an **object complement** renames the direct object. In this sentence *pot* is the direct object. The noun *masterpiece* is an object complement that renames *pot*.

I called my first ceramic pot a *masterpiece.*

Some common verbs that take object complements are *appoint, call, consider, choose, elect, make,* and *name*.

Exercise 1
1. classes
2. computer
3. pictures
4. art show
5. parents
6. money
7. donations

EXERCISE 1 Name the direct object in each sentence.
1. Some high school students take art classes every Saturday.
2. Some students use the computer in art class.
3. Students draw pictures on the computer.
4. The students are planning an art show.
5. They will invite their parents.
6. Hopefully, the show will raise money for supplies.
7. Professional artists in our community often make donations too.

8 • Section 1.4

APPLY

APPLY IT NOW

Explain that students use direct objects, indirect objects, object complements, and objects of prepositions frequently, but they may have never considered the words in terms of sentence structure. Students should be able to demonstrate an understanding of direct and indirect objects and objects of prepositions.

TechTip Create a class blog that contains sample sentences written by students. Then have the class review each sentence for direct objects, indirect objects, objects of prepositions, and object complements.

ASSESS

Note which students had difficulty with nouns used as objects and object complements. Assign **Practice Book** pages 7–8 for further practice.

WRITING CONNECTION

Use pages 228–229 of the Writing portion of the book.

Reteach

Choose something that the class is currently reading, such as a textbook, a magazine, or a literary work. Invite students to read aloud sentences from the text for you to write on the board. Work with the class to analyze the sentences to identify direct objects, indirect objects, objects of prepositions, and object complements. You might also challenge students to find sentences with examples of each, then confirm their choices as the entire class analyzes the sentences.

Cooperative Learning

Invite students to help one another identify and understand nouns as objects and object complements in their own writing. Encourage students to work as a group to write a brief review of a movie, a CD, a TV show, a book, a video game, or another form of entertainment. Have all students contribute sentences to the piece. Then have students read their review as a group, underlining the nouns in each sentence. Instruct students to identify how the nouns are used. Encourage students to offer suggestions to their classmates on how to identify noun usage in the future.

Meeting Individual Needs

Kinesthetic Invite students to identify nouns by acting out these sentences:

> **I am giving a boy my book.**
>
> **I am jumping on the floor.**
>
> **I dropped my pencil on the floor.**
>
> **I am writing a letter to my friend.**

As students act out these and other sentences you generate, have volunteers identify the function of each noun in the sentence—as a direct object, indirect object, object of a preposition, or object complement.

---

8. schools
9. students
10. center
11. students
12. students
13. photographers
14. lake
15. sunlight
16. experience
17. spokesperson
18. teacher
19. topic

Name the indirect object in each sentence.

8. Mrs. Simpson, the coordinator of the center, sends schools fliers with information on the center's courses.
9. The center offers students classes on Saturdays.
10. Many teachers give the center their time voluntarily.
11. Local artists give students special instruction once in a while.

Name the object of a preposition in each sentence.

12. Mr. Susick organized a field trip for the art students.
13. The exhibition including works by famous photographers was fascinating.
14. An image of a quiet lake was my favorite photo.
15. The picture showed water evaporating in the sunlight.

Name the object complement in each sentence.

16. Everyone declared the field trip an enjoyable experience.
17. To express our thanks, we appointed Ed spokesperson.
18. The class considers Mr. Susick a good teacher.
19. He makes history an exciting topic.

Exercise 2

1. direct object, object of a preposition
2. indirect object, direct object
3. object of a preposition
4. direct object, object of a preposition
5. direct object
6. direct object, object complement

EXERCISE 2 Tell whether each underlined noun is a direct object, an indirect object, an object of a preposition, or an object complement.

1. My family attended an <u>exhibit</u> on <u>life</u> in the 1600s.
2. I gave my <u>parents</u> the <u>trip</u> to the exhibit as a present.
3. We were first to arrive at the <u>exhibit</u> that day.
4. We saw life-sized <u>mannequins</u> in period <u>costumes</u>.
5. Mannequins of the 1920s wore shiny dance <u>outfits</u>.
6. We considered the <u>exhibit</u> a real learning <u>experience</u>.

APPLY IT NOW

Write five sentences about an extracurricular activity that you have enjoyed. Use at least one direct object, one indirect object, and one object of a preposition in your sentences. Label the direct objects, indirect objects, and objects of prepositions.

 Post sentences on your class blog for peer review.

OBJECTIVES

- **To identify appositives and appositive phrases in sentences**
- **To distinguish between restrictive and nonrestrictive appositives**

Maintenance

Assign **Practice Book** page 2, Section 1.5. After students finish,
1. Give immediate feedback.
2. Review concepts as needed.
3. Model the correct answer.

Pages 4–5 of the **Answer Key** contain tips for Daily Maintenance.

WARM-UP

Write the following sentences on the board:

> The skater won a medal.

> The skater was a teenager.

Show students how they can combine the two sentences.

> The skater, a teenager, won a medal.

Ask students how combining sentences might help make their writing concise and more interesting.

📖 Read from a piece of writing that the class is currently reading. Emphasize the appositives.

TEACH

Invite volunteers to take turns reading the page. Pause after each example and discuss it before moving on to the next example. Reiterate that an appositive follows and explains or identifies a noun. Have students suggest sentences with appositives for objects in the classroom and for people in the school. (*Our art teacher, Mrs. Fleming, is teaching us how to use a pottery wheel.*)

PRACTICE

EXERCISE 1
Remind students that an appositive provides information that helps identify a noun. After students identify the appositives in each sentence, invite them to compose their own sentences, using the structure of the sentences in the exercise. Have students underline the appositives in their sentences. Use sentence 2 as an example: *She spent most of her youth in Concord, a town near Boston. (My brother spent last year in Casper, a town in Wyoming.)*

EXERCISE 2
To guide students through this exercise, remind them that commas are used to set off an appositive word or phrase that is not critical to understanding the sentence. Take time to analyze each sentence and its appositive, encouraging students to explain their decision making, confirming the sentences that are correct, and revising the sentences that are not. Call on volunteers to identify the appositive phrases and to tell whether each is restrictive or nonrestrictive.

1.5 Appositives

Louisa May Alcott

An **appositive** is a word that follows a noun and helps identify it. An appositive names the same person, place, thing, or idea as the noun it explains. An **appositive phrase** is an appositive and its modifiers.

In the first sentence below, *writer* is the appositive in the appositive phrase *a 19th-century writer* that explains the noun *Louisa May Alcott*. The appositive is set off by commas because it is **nonrestrictive**, which means the appositive is not crucial to understanding the sentence. In the second sentence below, the noun *Little Women* is an appositive that explains the noun *novel*. Here the appositive is not set off by commas because it is **restrictive**. The appositive is necessary in order to know which novel is meant.

Louisa May Alcott, a 19th-century writer, produced many novels.
Her most popular work is the novel *Little Women*.

In the first example below, the appositive is not set off by commas because the writer's name is necessary in order to know which 19th-century writer is meant. The appositive in the second sentence is set off by commas because it is nonrestrictive. It is not necessary for the meaning of the sentence.

The 19th-century writer Louisa May Alcott produced many novels.
Little Women, **a novel by Louisa May Alcott, is her most popular work.**

In the first example below, the appositive *Abigail* is nonrestrictive—Alcott had only one mother. In the second example, the appositive *Elizabeth* is restrictive because it is necessary in order to know which of Alcott's three sisters is meant.

Alcott's mother, *Abigail*, **encouraged Louisa in her writing.**
Alcott's sister *Elizabeth* **was probably the model for Beth.**

EXERCISE 1 Identify the appositive in each sentence. Then tell which noun the appositive explains.

1. Louisa May Alcott, a famous American writer, was born in Germantown, Pennsylvania, in 1832.

APPLY

APPLY IT NOW

Encourage students to include information about their novels or movies in the form of appositives. Have students exchange their papers with partners to identify each other's appositives. Students should be able to compose sentences that contain restrictive and nonrestrictive appositives, and to identify each kind of appositive.

TechTip Suggest that students search for a movie or CD review online with an adult. Ask students to look for examples of appositives within the review.

ASSESS

Note which students had difficulty with appositives. Assign **Practice Book** page 9 for further practice.

> ### WRITING CONNECTION
> Use pages 230–231 of the Writing portion of the book.

TEACHING OPTIONS

Reteach

Assign partners a topic, such as a sport or a location. Have each student write two closely related simple sentences without appositives. Then have partners exchange sentences and combine the sentences into one sentence using an appositive. Ask volunteers to read their sentences aloud. Have the class identify the appositive and whether it is restrictive or nonrestrictive.

Meeting Individual Needs

Auditory Suggest that students talk to you and one another, using appositives in their speech. Give the following examples:

> **Hand me that pencil with the big eraser.**

> **I spoke to the board member Ms. Goggin today.**

Ask volunteers to share their sentences. Write these sentences on the board and have students identify the appositives.

Meeting Individual Needs

Extra Support Invite students who have difficulty with appositives to write about a well-known person, such as someone in sports, entertainment, or literature. Insert appositives in each student's work. Then ask students to analyze the sentences. Use these examples:

> **I think Alex Rodriguez, the baseball player, is the best athlete.**

> **I think the baseball player Alex Rodriguez is the best athlete.**

Diagram It!

To practice appositives in the context of diagramming, turn to Section 11.2.

Exercise 1
Appositives are underlined once. Nouns to which they refer are underlined twice.

Exercise 2
1. characters, nonrestrictive
2. Jo, restrictive
3. tale, nonrestrictive
4. conflict, nonrestrictive
5. example, nonrestrictive
6. Kendall, restrictive; Bette, nonrestrictive
7. Kendall, Bette, Margaret, Alden, nonrestrictive
8. Connecticut, restrictive
9. part, nonrestrictive

2. She spent most of her youth in Concord, a town near Boston.
3. She was the daughter of the teacher Bronson Alcott.
4. Louisa, a good student, was educated at home.
5. Her family was poor but had contact with the famous American intellectuals Ralph Waldo Emerson, Nathaniel Hawthorne, and Henry David Thoreau.
6. She eventually became editor of the children's magazine, Merry Museum.
7. My home state, Pennsylvania, was home to many famous people.

Henry David Thoreau

EXERCISE 2 Identify the appositive in each sentence and decide whether it is restrictive or nonrestrictive. Correct the sentences with nonrestrictive appositives by adding commas where necessary.

1. The Marches, the characters in *Little Women*, are based on Louisa May Alcott's family.
2. The character Jo was based on Louisa herself.
3. The novel, a tale of the trials and hardships of four sisters, follows them as they grow up.
4. The novel takes place during the Civil War, the conflict between the North and South.
5. The book, an early example of realistic fiction for children, supports family values.
6. My sister Kendall wants to write books like Alcott's, and my baby sister, Bette, will illustrate them.
7. I also have four sisters, Kendall, Bette, Margaret, and Alden, just like Alcott's character.
8. We grew up in Connecticut, a northern state.
9. Connecticut, part of New England, was also involved in the Civil War.

APPLY IT NOW

Write a paragraph about a novel or movie with which you are familiar. Summarize it, using both types of appositives to explain any nouns in your paragraph. Label each appositive as restrictive or nonrestrictive. Be sure to use appropriate punctuation.

TechTip With an adult, search for reviews online.

Nouns • 11

OBJECTIVES

- **To understand the concept of a possessive noun**
- **To use apostrophes correctly in singular and plural possessive nouns**
- **To write separate and joint possessive forms with two or more nouns**

 **DAILY** **Maintenance**

Assign **Practice Book** page 2, Section 1.6. After students finish,
1. Give immediate feedback.
2. Review concepts as needed.
3. Model the correct answer.

Pages 4–5 of the **Answer Key** contain tips for Daily Maintenance.

WARM-UP

Write the following on the board:

> 2 taco's today for 99¢

Ask students if this sentence is correct. Point out that people sometimes confuse the possessive noun form *'s* with the *s* that follows a plural noun. Ask students to name other examples they have seen on billboards or signs or in advertisements.

📖 Read from a piece of writing that the class is currently reading. Emphasize the possessive nouns.

TEACH

Tell students that *possession* suggests ownership. Pick up a pencil and say, *This pencil is mine. This pencil is my possession.*

Ask students to say a sentence that identifies the owner of the pencil and lead them to the phrase *the teacher's pencil*. Ask a student to write this phrase on the board Make sure the phrase is written correctly *(the teacher's pencil)*. Be sure to note whether they have included the apostrophe in the correct position. Refer back to the

Warm-Up sentence. Point out that *taco's* implies ownership and is incorrect.

Ask volunteers to read the definition and examples of possessive nouns. Encourage students to suggest additional possessives for each rule and to write these examples in their notebook.

Have students read aloud the definitions of separate and joint possession. Ask volunteers to write sentences on the board, leaving blanks for the possessive nouns. Have volunteers fill in the blanks with the correct possessive forms.

PRACTICE

EXERCISE 1

After students have completed the exercise, start a chart on the board with the column headings *Singular Possessive* and *Plural Possessive*. For each sentence in the exercise, invite a volunteer to write the possessive form of the noun in the correct column of the chart. Ask students how they chose the singular or plural possessive form.

EXERCISE 2

Ask volunteers to write one of their sentences on the board and to underline the possessive nouns. Discuss whether the possessive

---

1.6 Possessive Nouns

A **possessive noun** expresses possession, or ownership. The sign of the possessive is usually *'s*.

To form the singular possessive, add *-'s* to the singular form of the noun.

| boy | boy's | Tommy | Tommy's |

To form the possessive of plural nouns ending in *s*, add the apostrophe only. If the plural form of a noun does not end in *s*, add *-'s*.

| students | students' | women | women's |
| teachers | teachers' | children | children's |

The singular possessive of a proper name ending in *s* is usually formed by adding *-'s*.

| Alexis | Alexis's | Mrs. Hess | Mrs. Hess's |

To form the plural possessive of a proper noun, first form the plural of the noun and then add an apostrophe.

| Jones | Joneses' | Adams | Adamses' |

The possessive of compound nouns is formed by adding *-'s* to the end of the term.

| editor in chief | editor in chief's |
| mothers-in-law | mothers-in-law's |

If two or more nouns are used together to indicate separate possession—that is, each person owns something independently— *-'s* is used after each noun.

> J. K. *Rowling's* and Shel *Silverstein's* writings provide wonderful entertainment.

If two or more nouns are used together to indicate joint possession—that is, to show that one thing is owned together— *-'s* is used after the last noun only.

> *Terri and Shari's* garden is beautiful.

form was written correctly. Encourage students to tell the rule they applied for making the possessive form of each noun.

APPLY

APPLY IT NOW

Ask students to share their sentences with the class. Discuss the possessive forms that were used and whether they were formed correctly. You may wish to list these on the board. Ask volunteers to give the singular forms for the plural possessive nouns and the plural forms for the singular possessive nouns. Challenge students to find

examples of separate and joint possession. Students should demonstrate an understanding of possessive nouns.

ASSESS

Note which students had difficulty with possessive nouns. Assign **Practice Book** page 10 for further practice.

WRITING CONNECTION

Use pages 232–233 of the Writing portion of the book.

Exercise 1
1. city's
2. farmers'
3. sellers'
4. customers'
5. family's
6. woman's
7. Mrs. Prentiss's
8. bush's
9. Prentisses'

Exercise 2
Sentences will vary. The possessive forms, however, should be as shown below.
1. Finn and Meg's
2. Mary's and Anna's
3. Michael and Fiona's
4. Lilly's and Fran's
5. Richard's and Les's
6. Claude and Pilar's
7. Pip's and Eli's

EXERCISE 1 Complete each sentence, using the singular possessive or plural possessive form of the noun in parentheses.

1. On Sunday mornings our _____ (city) park department holds "green markets."

2. At a local park, space is cleared, and many _____ (farmer) products are displayed in booths.

3. The _____ (seller) products are all fresh from their farms and look very tempting.

4. Many _____ (customer) arms are soon filled with packages and bags containing vegetables and fruits.

5. My _____ (family) visit to the green market last week was a great success.

6. One _____ (woman) stand displayed homemade jam.

7. We couldn't resist, and we bought several jars of _____ (Mrs. Prentiss) blackberry jam.

8. Her prize blackberry _____ (bush) fruit is so sweet, it needs no sugar.

9. Her whole family helps her each year; it is all of the _____ (Prentiss) hard work that makes their jam the best.

EXERCISE 2 Based on the information given for each item, write your own sentence that indicates either separate or joint ownership.

1. Finn and Meg have a roadside stand. It features vegetables.

2. Mary has a garden plot. Anna has her own garden plot. These garden plots produce herbs.

3. Michael and Fiona grow sunflowers together. Their sunflowers have won prizes.

4. Lilly sells flowers. Fran also sells flowers. Their stands are at the mall.

5. Richard and Les each have farm stands. The farm stands are very profitable.

6. Claude planted a strawberry patch. His little sister Pilar helps him water it. Their strawberries are juicy and sweet.

7. Pip grows wonderful tomatoes. Eli grows tasty mangos. They make good salsa with their harvests.

APPLY IT NOW

Write five sentences about achievements of family, friends, or others that you admire. Use both single and plural possessive nouns in your sentences. Include at least one sentence that indicates separate or joint possession accurately.

Nouns • 13

ASSESS

Use the Noun Review as homework, as a practice test, or as an informal assessment. Following are some options for use.

Homework

You may wish to assign one group the odd items and another group the even items. When you next meet, review the correct answers as a group. Be sure to model how to arrive at the correct answer.

Practice Test

Use the Noun Review as a diagnostic tool. Assign the entire review or just specific sections. After students have finished, identify which concepts require more attention. Reteach concepts as necessary.

Noun Review

1.1
1. People, families, hobbies
2. cousins, members, corps
3. queries
4. mice
5. media
6. tomatoes
7. geese
8. loaves
9. oxen
10. crises
11. halves
12. inquiries
13. colonies
14. matrices
15. lives

1.2
16. boats
17. foxes
18. radios
19. potatoes
20. zeros or zeroes
21. maids of honor
22. spoonfuls
23. deer
24. drive-ins

1.3
25. Newfoundland: subject; province: subject complement
26. province: subject; island: subject complement

1.1 Complete the sentences with the plural form of the nouns in parentheses.

1. ___ (People) in both our ___ (family) have unique ___ (hobby).
2. My twin ___ (cousin) are ___ (member) of the youth and adult ballet ___ (corps).
3. Monique answers e-mail ___ (query) about homework.
4. My little sister raises ___ (mouse) for the pet store.
5. David is an artist who works in several (medium).
6. My mother raises ___ (tomato) in the garden.
7. Every autumn, flocks of Canadian ___ (goose) fly south.
8. Every morning the bakery bakes hundreds of ___ (loaf) of bread.

Write the plural of each noun.

9. ox
10. crisis
11. half
12. inquiry
13. colony
14. matrix
15. life

1.2 Write the plural of each noun.

16. boat
17. fox
18. radio
19. potato
20. zero
21. maid of honor

22. spoonful
23. deer
24. drive-in

1.3 Identify the subject of each sentence. Then name the subject and the subject complement if there is one.

25. Newfoundland is a province in Canada.
26. This province is an island off the east coast of Canada.
27. The island has miles of jagged coastline.
28. Newfoundlands, huge black dogs, originated there.
29. Brave animals such as Newfoundlands are the subjects of some fables and dramatic novels.
30. The Newfoundland is courageous yet gentle.
31. These dogs are both amazing water-rescuers and wonderful companions.

1.4 Tell whether each underlined word is a direct object, an indirect object, an object of a preposition, or an object complement.

32. Many experts recommend music lessons for children.
33. Our local arts center sends parents the information about music instruction in September.
34. I have studied the flute for 10 years.
35. I called my first lesson a disaster.

27. island: subject
28. Newfoundlands: subject
29. animals: subject; subjects: subject complement
30. Newfoundland, subject
31. dogs: subject; water-rescuers, companions: subject complements

1.4
32. lessons: direct object; children: object of a preposition
33. parents: indirect object; information: direct object; instruction: object of a preposition; September: object of a preposition
34. flute: direct object; years: object of a preposition
35. lesson: direct object; disaster: object complement
36. Mr. Ramos: direct object; teacher: object complement
37. students: indirect object; chance: direct object
38. jazz: direct object
39. Kind of Blue: object complement
40. Answers will vary.
41. Answers will vary.
42. Answers will vary.
43. Answers will vary.

Informal Assessment

Use the review as preparation for the formal assessment. Count the review as a portion of the grade. Have students work to find the correct answers and use their corrected review as a study guide for the formal assessment.

WRITING CONNECTION

Use pages 234–235 of the Writing portion of the book.

Putting It All Together

Ask students to choose a passage from a favorite book or from an interesting newspaper, magazine, or online article and to copy it. Suggest that they use triple spacing if they are typing on a computer or to write on every third line if they are writing on paper. Write these directions on the board:

- **Circle all nouns.**
- **Underline with one line all nouns used as subjects.**
- **Underline with two lines all nouns used as subject complements.**
- **Write *DO* above all direct objects.**
- **Write *IO* above all indirect objects.**

Suggest that students work in pairs and check each other's work.

English–Language Learners

Remind students to refer to their word bank files of vocabulary and grammar rules as they complete the review items. Encourage students to add any new vocabulary or grammar rules and concepts. Students may wish to print out these files and put them in a grammar-and-vocabulary binder to use at home.

1.5

44. Harriet Tubman, a slave born on a plantation in Maryland, led other slaves to freedom on the Underground Railroad.
45. The slave and preacher Nat Turner led a revolt and became a hero to Tubman.
46. Tubman's mother, Harriet Greene, worked as a slave for the Brodas family.
47. Over many years Harriet traveled the Underground Railroad, a series of safe houses for slaves.
48. The Underground Railroad involved the efforts of many "conductors," individuals responsible for moving fugitives from one safe house to the next.
49. nonrestrictive
50. restrictive
51. restrictive
52. nonrestrictive
53. nonrestrictive

36. I consider Mr. Ramos a good teacher.
37. He offers students the chance to learn different kinds of music.
38. I love jazz more than any other type of music.
39. I especially love Miles Davis's masterpiece called "Kind of Blue."

Use the following words in sentences as the part of speech indicated in parentheses.

40. leaves (direct object)
41. friends (indirect object)
42. jacket (object of a preposition)
43. experience (object complement)

1.5 Identify the appositive in each sentence. Correct the sentences with nonrestrictive appositives by adding commas where necessary.

44. Harriet Tubman a slave born on a plantation in Maryland led other slaves to freedom on the Underground Railroad.
45. The slave and preacher Nat Turner led a revolt and became a hero to Tubman.
46. Tubman's mother Harriet Greene worked as a slave for the Brodas family.
47. Over many years Harriet traveled the Underground Railroad a series of safe houses for slaves.
48. The Underground Railroad involved the efforts of many "conductors" individuals responsible for moving fugitives from one safe house to the next.

Identify the appositive in each sentence as restrictive or nonrestrictive.

49. Nellie, the horse with the black mane, is very difficult to ride.
50. Louise is a descendant of the writer Oscar Wilde.
51. Steven King's book *It* is about a scary clown.
52. J.K. Rowling, the author of the Harry Potter series, hails from England.
53. George Washington, a great army general during the Revolution, led his troops across the Delaware in the dead of winter.

1.6 Write the possessive form of each noun.

54. neighbors
55. teens
56. mothers-to-be
57. principals
58. Father Jess
59. woman
60. boys
61. the Davises
62. separate possession: music of Bach and of Mozart
63. joint possession: cars of Mom and Dad
64. separate possession: reports of Darnell and Melissa

1.6

54. neighbors'
55. teens'
56. mothers-to-be's
57. principals'
58. Father Jess's
59. woman's
60. boys'
61. The Davises'
62. Bach's and Mozart's music
63. Mom and Dad's cars
64. Darnell's and Melissa's

Tech Tip Go to www.voyagesinenglish.com for more activities.

TechTip Encourage students to further review nouns, using the additional practice and games at www.voyagesinenglish.com.

ASSESS

EXERCISE 1

Have volunteers read the directions and the paragraph aloud. If students have difficulty with any of the questions, remind them that they should refer to the section that teaches that skill. This activity can be done individually, in small groups, or with the class as a whole.

EXERCISE 2

Have students complete the second exercise. Be sure to check that their paragraphs contain all the items listed.

After you have reviewed nouns, administer the Section 1 Assessment on pages 1–2 in the **Assessment Book,** or create a customized test with the optional **Test Generator CD.**

Noun Challenge

EXERCISE 1 Read the selection and then answer the questions.

1. A painting by the celebrated American artist James McNeill Whistler hangs in the Louvre. 2. *An Arrangement in Gray and Black* is the imposing title of this portrait, but to the millions who know and love it, the likeness is best known as *Whistler's Mother.* 3. At first the picture brought the artist little recognition. 4. Many years later, however, it was the opinion of more than one committee of critics that this picture alone would have made Whistler a true master. 5. For connoisseurs of art, the beauty of this painting lies in the perfect placement of objects and the harmony achieved through its many tones of gray. 6. Its appeal to the heart of the ordinary person rests in the noble traits of motherhood that Whistler has captured and enshrined forever on canvas.

1. What is the subject of sentence 1?
2. Name an appositive in sentence 1 and identify it as either restrictive or nonrestrictive.
3. Name a possessive noun in sentence 2.
4. What is the subject complement in sentence 2?
5. Identify the object of a preposition in sentence 2.
6. What are the direct object and the indirect object in sentence 3?
7. Name the object complement in sentence 4.
8. Identify the objects of the prepositions in sentence 4.
9. What is the singular form of the word *connoisseurs,* used in sentence 5?
10. Which nouns in sentence 6 are objects of prepositions?

Exercise 1
1. painting
2. James McNeill Whistler, restrictive
3. Whistler's
4. title
5. millions
6. direct object: recognition; indirect object: artist
7. master
8. committee, critics
9. connoisseur
10. heart, person, traits, motherhood, canvas

EXERCISE 2 Read the following and respond.

Musicians, like painters, have unique artistic styles. Their music is often categorized in a genre such as rock, jazz, classical, or hip-hop. Write a paragraph identifying one of your favorite musicians or bands and why. Do you like the vocals or the instruments? Do you enjoy the lyrics? Explain, using at least one each of the following:

1. a direct object or an indirect object
2. a subject complement or an object complement
3. an object of a preposition
4. a possessive noun
5. and an appositive

Exercise 2
Answers will vary.

SECTION FOCUS

- **Descriptive adjectives, position of adjectives**
- **Demonstrative, interrogative, and indefinite adjectives**
- **Comparative and superlative adjectives**
- *Few* and *little*
- **Adjective phrases and clauses**

SUPPORT MATERIALS

Practice Book
Daily Maintenance, pages 11–12
Grammar, pages 13–19

Assessment Book
Section 2 Assessment, pages 3–4

Test Generator CD

**Writing Chapter 1,
    Personal Narratives**

Customizable Lesson Plans
www.voyagesinenglish.com

CONNECT WITH LITERATURE

📖 Consider using the following titles throughout the section to illustrate the grammar concept:

Double Dutch by Sharon M. Draper
If You Were an Adjective by Michael Dahl
Swimming Upstream: Middle School Poems by Kristine O'Connell George

Adjectives

GRAMMAR FOR GROWN-UPS

Understanding Adjectives

The word *adjective* comes from the Latin word *adjectivum*, meaning "something that is added." An **adjective** modifies or adds to the meaning of a noun or pronoun.

A **descriptive adjective** describes a noun's or pronoun's number, color, size, type, or other qualities. Most adjectives appear before the noun they describe, but adjectives may also directly follow nouns.

> *Fragrant **flowers will bloom in the spring.***
>
> *Flowers, colorful **and** fragrant, **will bloom in the spring.***

An adjective can act as a subject complement or an object complement.

> ***The vase is** green. **(subject complement)**
>
> ***The artist painted the vase** green. **(object complement)**

Demonstrative adjectives point out definite people, places, things, or ideas. The demonstrative adjectives are *this, that, these,* and *those.*

> *These **dishes are dirty.***

Interrogative adjectives, such as *what, which,* and *whose,* are used to ask questions.

> *What **will be served for dinner?***

Indefinite adjectives refer to any or all of a group. Indefinite adjectives include a*ll, another, any, both, each, either, few, many, more, most, much, neither, other, several,* and *some.*

> *Both **animals have similar characteristics.***
>
> *Another **student has my book.***

Most adjectives have three degrees of comparison. The **positive** degree shows a quality of a noun. The **comparative** degree compares two items. The **superlative** degree compares three or more items.

> ***The kitchen is** warm.*
>
> ***The kitchen is** warmer **than the dining room.***
>
> ***The kitchen is the** warmest **room in the house.***

" The adjective is the banana peel
of the parts of speech. "

—Clifton Fadiman

COMMON ERRORS

Understanding *Few* and *Less*

Few, fewer, and *fewest* refer to number and are used with plural nouns. *Little, less,* and *least* refer to degree or amount and are used with singular nouns.

ERROR: I need less hours of sleep than you do.
CORRECT: I need fewer hours of sleep than you do.
I need less sleep than you do.

ERROR: That candidate proposed the least taxes.
CORRECT: That candidate proposed the fewest taxes.
That candidate proposed the least money in taxes.

As students write, remind them to check for this error. You might ask students to find this common error in newspaper, magazine, or online articles or in television commercials.

SENTENCE DIAGRAMMING

You may wish to teach adjectives in the context of diagramming. Review these examples. Then refer to the Diagramming section or look for Diagram It! features in the Adjectives section.

The boy in the blue hat threw the rock.

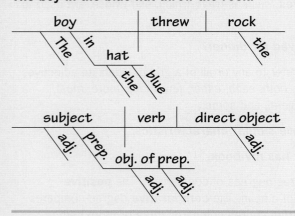

A figure that has five sides is a pentagon.

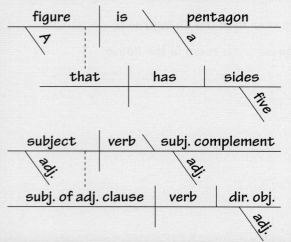

ASK AN EXPERT

Real Situations, Real Solutions

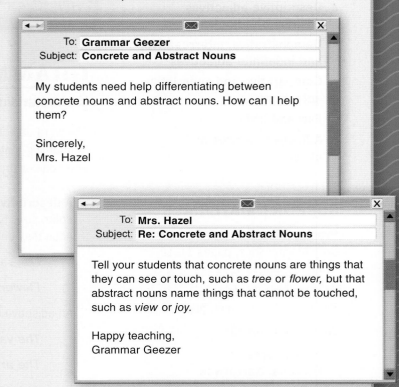

To: **Grammar Geezer**
Subject: **Concrete and Abstract Nouns**

My students need help differentiating between concrete nouns and abstract nouns. How can I help them?

Sincerely,
Mrs. Hazel

To: **Mrs. Hazel**
Subject: **Re: Concrete and Abstract Nouns**

Tell your students that concrete nouns are things that they can see or touch, such as *tree* or *flower,* but that abstract nouns name things that cannot be touched, such as *view* or *joy*.

Happy teaching,
Grammar Geezer

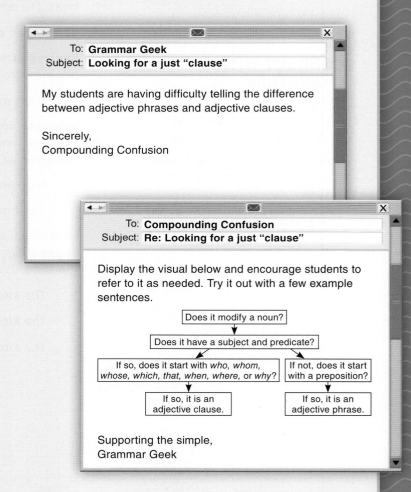

To: **Grammar Geek**
Subject: **Looking for a just "clause"**

My students are having difficulty telling the difference between adjective phrases and adjective clauses.

Sincerely,
Compounding Confusion

To: **Compounding Confusion**
Subject: **Re: Looking for a just "clause"**

Display the visual below and encourage students to refer to it as needed. Try it out with a few example sentences.

Does it modify a noun?
Does it have a subject and predicate?
If so, does it start with *who, whom, whose, which, that, when, where,* or *why*?
If not, does it start with a preposition?
If so, it is an adjective clause.
If so, it is an adjective phrase.

Supporting the simple,
Grammar Geek

OBJECTIVES

- **To recognize that the purpose of an adjective is to modify a noun**
- **To recognize adjectives as words that tell number, color, type, and other qualities**
- **To distinguish between adjectives used as subject complements and as object complements**

 **Maintenance**

Assign **Practice Book** page 11, Section 2.1. After students finish,
1. Give immediate feedback.
2. Review concepts as needed.
3. Model the correct answer.

Pages 4–5 of the **Answer Key** contain tips for Daily Maintenance.

WARM-UP

Show the front page of a newspaper to the class. Have students name words in the headlines that describe nouns or pronouns. Then read the headlines without the adjectives. Discuss how these words change students' impressions of the headlines.

📖 Read from a piece of writing that the class is currently reading. Emphasize the descriptive adjectives and their positions.

TEACH

Ask a volunteer to read aloud the paragraph that defines descriptive adjectives and their placement. Write the example sentence on the board. Then write it again with the words *thick and hot* before *ashes*. Encourage students to point out the difference between the two sentences. Discuss that writers sometimes place adjectives after the noun they describe for added emphasis.

Ask volunteers to read the definitions of subject and object complements. Have students write on the board sentences containing subject or object complements. As a class, identify the complement and determine if each is a subject or an object complement. Remind students to ask themselves: *What noun does the complement describe?*

PRACTICE

EXERCISES 1 & 2

Have students complete the exercises independently. Before students begin Exercise 2, review the difference between a subject

complement and an object complement. Encourage students to identify strategies that might help them make this distinction. When students have finished, ask them to discuss both the position of the adjectives and their function in the sentence.

EXERCISE 3

Ask volunteers to read their sentences aloud and to tell whether the adjective appears before or after the noun, and whether it is a subject complement or an object complement. For the second part, write the first noun, *ocean,* on the board. Challenge students to brainstorm

2.1 Descriptive Adjectives, Position of Adjectives

A descriptive adjective describes a noun's or pronoun's number, color, size, type, or other qualities. An adjective usually goes before the word it describes. However, adjectives may also directly follow nouns. In this sentence the adjectives *thick* and *hot* describe the noun *ashes*.

Ashes, **thick** and **hot**, rained down on Pompeii.

In this sentence the adjectives *eminent* and *Roman* describe the noun *writer*.

An *eminent Roman* writer described the disaster.

An adjective acts as a **subject complement** when it follows a linking verb and describes the subject. Linking verbs include the different tenses of the verbs *be, become, taste, sound, feel, look, remain, appear,* and *seem*. In this sentence *fearful* describes the subject *people*.

People were *fearful* because of the disaster.

An adjective can also act as an **object complement** when it follows a direct object and describes it. In these sentences *fearful* describes the direct object *people*, and *happy* describes *brother*.

The disaster left people *fearful*.
Our new puppy made my brother very *happy*.

EXERCISE 1 Name the descriptive adjectives in each sentence.

1. Pompeii was an Italian city that was destroyed by a volcanic eruption in AD 79.
2. The sudden eruption of Mount Vesuvius was a surprise to the residents of ancient Pompeii.
3. Wealthy Romans built palatial villas in the bustling town.
4. Before the huge eruption, trees and gardens covered the mountain's gentle slopes.
5. Powerful forces, however, were building within the peaceful mountain, causing extreme pressure.
6. Archaeological digs unearthed startling evidence that the unfortunate people were stopped in their tracks.
7. The excavated town reveals a moment of daily Roman life frozen in time.

Exercise 1
1. Italian, volcanic
2. sudden, ancient
3. Wealthy, palatial, bustling
4. huge, gentle
5. Powerful, peaceful, extreme
6. Archaeological, startling, unfortunate
7. excavated, daily Roman

18 • Section 2.1

as many appropriate descriptive adjectives as possible. Have students complete the exercise independently.

APPLY

APPLY IT NOW

Encourage students to use adjectives that appeal to a variety of senses, not just what can be seen. Students should demonstrate an understanding of descriptive adjectives and their positions within a sentence.

 The subject complements on page 223 are *still,*

peculiar, heavy, and *difficult.* You may wish to ask volunteers to name the linking verbs, which are *became, smelled, was,* and *was.*

ASSESS

Note which students had difficulty with descriptive adjectives. Assign **Practice Book** page 13 for further practice.

WRITING CONNECTION

Use pages 236–237 of the Writing portion of the book.

Reteach

Encourage students to choose a passage from a literary text that they particularly enjoy. Have students write their passages on poster board large enough for everyone to see. Each day review several passages. Challenge students to identify the adjectives and to explain how each is used in the sentence: as a descriptive adjective before or after a noun, as a subject complement, or as an object complement.

Meeting Individual Needs

Visual Have students create a drawing, emphasizing the details. Tell students to color the picture using markers, crayons, or colored pencils. Once students have completed their drawings, have them trade with a partner. Have students write a paragraph about the picture. Encourage students to use as many descriptive adjectives as possible. Also, challenge students to vary the position of their adjectives.

Cooperative Learning

On sentence strips write incomplete sentences that lack either subject or object complements, such as those below. Provide small groups with several sentence strips. Have students work together to complete the sentences with descriptive adjectives. Then direct groups to exchange sentence strips and to label the subject complements as *SC* and the object complements as *OC*. Have a volunteer from each group explain the use of the subject and object complements.

> **Marta painted the house ____.**
> (green; object complement)
>
> **The building is ____ and ____.**
> (tall, modern; subject complement)

Exercise 2
1. top, before
2. cloud, after, after
3. day, after, subject complement
4. rock, after, after, gas, before
5. blanket, before, pumice stone, before
6. scene, after, object complement
7. city, after, subject complement
8. volcano, after, subject complement
9. rescuers, after, object complement

Exercise 3
Answers will vary.

EXERCISE 2 In each sentence identify the nouns modified by the italicized adjectives. Then tell whether each adjective comes before the noun or after the noun, and identify if it is used as a subject complement or as an object complement.

1. In AD 79, on August 24, the *entire* top of Mount Vesuvius blew off.
2. A cloud, *huge* and *threatening,* formed over the mountain.
3. The day became *dark* as night.
4. The volcano spewed out rock, *black* but *hot,* and *poisonous* gas.
5. A *thick* blanket of ash, *fine* pumice stone, and other debris covered Pompeii to a depth of 20 feet.
6. Survivors called the scene *infernal.*
7. The city remained *buried* for centuries.
8. The volcano proved *deadly* again in 1631, when it buried a new city.
9. Discovery of old Pompeii beneath the new city's ruins left rescuers *speechless.*

EXERCISE 3 Use the following descriptive adjectives in sentences of your own.

1. historic
2. noisy
3. energetic
4. magnificent
5. mysterious
6. sparkling
7. crowded
8. Japanese
9. sincere
10. excited
11. thoughtful
12. colorful

Use an appropriate descriptive adjective with each noun.

13. ocean
14. skyline
15. painting
16. movie
17. idea
18. shirt
19. shoes
20. music
21. mail
22. hawk
23. beach
24. statue

APPLY IT NOW

Think of an amazing event that you've experienced. Brainstorm a list of adjectives to describe what you saw, heard, and felt. Then write a paragraph describing it. Include adjectives before and after the words they modify, two subject complements, and two object complements.

Grammar in Action. Identify the subject complements in the first paragraph of the p. 223 excerpt.

Adjectives • 19

OBJECTIVES

- To recognize *this, that, these,* and *those* as demonstrative adjectives
- To recognize *what, which,* and *whose* as interrogative adjectives
- To recognize singular and plural indefinite adjectives

DAILY Maintenance

Assign **Practice Book** page 11, Section 2.2. After students finish,
1. Give immediate feedback.
2. Review concepts as needed.
3. Model the correct answer.

Pages 4–5 of the **Answer Key** contain tips for Daily Maintenance.

WARM-UP

Point to objects in the classroom and encourage students to write questions about each object. Offer an example such as *Which pen is mine?* Have students work in pairs to answer the questions, such as *Both pens are yours.*

📖 Read from a piece of writing that the class is currently reading. Emphasize the demonstrative, interrogative, and indefinite adjectives.

TEACH

Have three volunteers read aloud the demonstrative adjectives, interrogative adjectives, and indefinite adjectives sections. Discuss how these adjectives are different. Lead students to understand the following: A demonstrative adjective identifies a specific noun, such as *this book,* an interrogative adjective poses a question, such as *whose book?* and an indefinite adjective suggests a vague number, such as *several books.* Challenge students to create more examples using the adjectives on the page.

PRACTICE

EXERCISE 1

Ask volunteers to suggest alternative words to help recall the meanings of *demonstrative, interrogative,* and *indefinite. (For* demonstrative *you might suggest* demonstrate; *for* interrogative *use* questioning; *and for* indefinite *offer* vague *or* unsure.*)* Tell students to consider these "translations" as they identify the adjectives in the exercise. Review students' answers, guiding them through any misconceptions.

EXERCISE 2

Before students begin this exercise, you might have them create a chart with the three headings *Demonstrative, Interrogative,* and *Indefinite.* Have students write the adjectives from this page in the chart. Encourage students to refer to this chart as they complete the exercise. Invite volunteers to read their completed sentences aloud and to explain how they determined which adjective to use in each sentence.

2.2 Demonstrative, Interrogative, and Indefinite Adjectives

Demonstrative adjectives point out definite people, places, things, or ideas. The demonstrative adjectives are *this, that, these,* and *those.*

DEMONSTRATIVE ADJECTIVES

This glass is half full.
Those glasses need to be washed.

Interrogative adjectives are used in questions. The interrogative adjectives are *what, which,* and *whose. Which* is usually used to ask about one or more of a specific set of items.

INTERROGATIVE ADJECTIVES

What equipment do you need?
Which bat is mine?
Whose uniform is this?

Indefinite adjectives refer to any or all of a group. Indefinite adjectives include *all, another, any, both, each, either, few, many, more, most, much, neither, other, several,* and *some.* Note that *another, each, every, either,* and *neither* are always singular.

INDEFINITE ADJECTIVES

Each student receives a progress report once a week. (singular)
Every student should write a thank-you note. (singular)
Neither friend was at home when I called. (singular)
Few students are chosen for this honor. (plural)
I am thankful for the *many* gifts I have received. (plural)

Exercise 1
1. demonstrative
2. interrogative
3. interrogative
4. indefinite
5. indefinite

EXERCISE 1 Tell whether each italicized adjective is demonstrative, interrogative, or indefinite.

1. *This* vase holds a beautiful arrangement of summer flowers.
2. *What* flowers are these?
3. *Whose* flower arrangement is this?
4. The placement of *each* blossom is perfect.
5. *Both* arrangements in this room have a variety of colorful flowers.

APPLY

APPLY IT NOW

Provide sample questions for students. For example, if they wanted to learn about national parks, students might ask the following:

<u>Whose</u> responsibility is it to oversee the park's <u>many</u> aspects?

How is <u>this</u> park different?

Is <u>every</u> park open all year, or are only a <u>few</u> parks open all year?

Students should show an understanding of demonstrative, interrogative, and indefinite adjectives.

TechTip Build a classroom blog or wiki. Many free tools to build blogs and wikis can be found by searching the Internet.

ASSESS

Note which students had difficulty with demonstrative, interrogative, and indefinite adjectives. Assign **Practice Book** pages 14–15 for further practice.

WRITING CONNECTION

Use pages 238–239 of the Writing portion of the book.

6. demonstrative
7. indefinite
8. demonstrative
9. indefinite
10. indefinite
11. indefinite
12. indefinite
13. demonstrative

6. *That* vase holds a bouquet of herbs.

7. *Some* herbs are said to have healing powers.

8. With its tiny blue blossoms, *this* rosemary is decorative as well.

9. Adding *several* large sprigs of rosemary to bathwater is thought to help sprains and pulled muscles.

10. Lavender also has *many* uses in healing.

11. Aloe is *another* plant used for healing.

12. *Each* fleshy leaf contains fluid that takes the sting out of sunburn.

13. *This* plant can also be used to treat acne.

Exercise 2
Answers may vary.
1. some
2. Which
3. Those
4. Whose
5. that
6. few, many
7. all, any
8. This, any
9. What
10. Each
11. These, many
12. Some, other

EXERCISE 2 Complete each sentence with an adjective of the type indicated in parentheses.

1. Long before there were pills, _____ people used herbs and other plants to treat illnesses. (indefinite)

2. _____ herbs did they use? (interrogative)

3. _____ herbs included rosemary, sage, and lavender. (demonstrative)

4. _____ advice do you seek when you are sick? (interrogative)

5. Why do you value _____ advice? (demonstrative)

6. Although _____ doctors prescribe herbs to treat illnesses today, a great _____ have proven to be effective treatments. (indefinite)

7. It is important to be careful with _____ treatments, because the improper application of _____ treatment can be dangerous. (indefinite)

8. _____ rule is very important to follow: never mix _____ pills or medicinal herbs without a doctor's approval. (demonstrative, indefinite)

9. _____ consequences are there for mixing treatments? (interrogative)

10. _____ different herb and pill contains different chemicals. (indefinite)

11. _____ chemicals, when combined, can have _____ unexpected effects. (demonstrative, indefinite)

12. _____ cold medications, when mixed with _____ cold medications or herbs, can have life-threatening side-effects. (indefinite, indefinite)

APPLY IT NOW

Think of a health-related topic you'd like to survey people about, such as eating habits or exercise. Write five questions about the topic, using interrogative adjectives in the questions. Have classmates answer your questions. Report group results, using indefinite and demonstrative adjectives.

 Tech Tip Post your results on your class blog or wiki.

Adjectives • 21

OBJECTIVES

- **To identify and use comparative and superlative adjectives**
- **To form comparative and superlative adjectives using the suffixes -er and -est and the words more, most, less, and least**
- **To recognize irregular comparative and superlative adjectives**

DAILY Maintenance

Assign **Practice Book** page 11, Section 2.3. After students finish,
1. Give immediate feedback.
2. Review concepts as needed.
3. Model the correct answer.

Pages 4–5 of the **Answer Key** contain tips for Daily Maintenance.

WARM-UP

Write these slogans on the board:

Travel to the warmest beach around!

Better than the bargain brand!

Tell students that in advertisements, slogans, and many kinds of writing, we compare things. Ask students what is being compared in each sentence (*one beach to all the other beaches in the area; one product that is better than another product*). Then ask what words show that something is being compared.

📖 Read from a piece of writing that the class is currently reading. Emphasize the comparative and superlative adjectives.

TEACH

Have a volunteer read aloud the definitions of positive, comparative, and superlative adjectives. Emphasize that the positive degree of an adjective

only expresses a quality, and that it does not compare a quality as the comparative and superlative degrees do.

Invite a volunteer to read aloud how comparative and superlative adjectives are used and how they are formed.

Write these words on the board: *warm, worthy, young, short, easy, complicated, durable, studious, responsible, bothersome.* Call on volunteers to give the comparative and superlative degrees of these adjectives. Remind students that some adjectives might require the use of the words *more* or *most,* or *less* or *least.*

PRACTICE

EXERCISE 1

Tell students the words *most* and *least* and adjectives that end in *est* are usually preceded by the word *the.* Explain that if students see the word *than,* they should use the word *more* or *less,* or an adjective that ends in *er.* When students have completed the exercise, review students' answers and encourage them to explain their adjective choices.

2.3 Comparative and Superlative Adjectives

Most adjectives have three degrees of comparison: positive, comparative, and superlative. The **positive** degree of an adjective shows a quality of a noun. The **comparative** degree is used to compare two items or two sets of items. This form is often followed by *than.* The **superlative** degree is used to compare three or more items.

For adjectives of one syllable and some adjectives of two syllables (including those ending in *y*), the comparative degree is formed by adding *-er* to the positive form, and the superlative degree is formed by adding *-est* to the positive form.

POSITIVE	COMPARATIVE	SUPERLATIVE
warm	warmer	warmest
sunny	sunnier	sunniest
fine	finer	finest
hot	hotter	hottest

For adjectives of three or more syllables and many adjectives of two syllables, the comparative degree is formed by using *more* or *less* with the positive form, and the superlative degree is formed by using *most* or *least* with the positive form.

POSITIVE	COMPARATIVE	SUPERLATIVE
important	more important	most important
extreme	more extreme	most extreme
thoughtful	less thoughtful	least thoughtful
resistant	less resistant	least resistant

Certain adjectives have irregular comparisons.

POSITIVE	COMPARATIVE	SUPERLATIVE
good	better	best
bad	worse	worst
many	more	most
little	less	least

Some adjectives, such as *dead, perfect,* and *eternal* cannot be compared. If you are uncertain about comparatives and superlatives, always check a dictionary.

EXERCISE 2

Invite volunteers to read their sentences aloud. Encourage students to review the three degrees of comparison to decide which sentences to rewrite.

APPLY

APPLY IT NOW

Before students start writing their sentences, briefly discuss the proper use of the words *bad, worse, worst, good, better,* and *best.* Students should demonstrate an understanding of comparative and superlative adjectives.

TechTip Encourage students to search for these images on Web sites that feature travel articles.

ASSESS

Note which students had difficulty with comparative and superlative adjectives. Assign **Practice Book** page 16 for further practice.

WRITING CONNECTION

Use pages 240–241 of the Writing portion of the book.

TEACHING OPTIONS

Reteach

Distribute old magazines. Instruct students to cut out pictures that can be used to illustrate the positive, comparative, and superlative forms of adjectives. Have students write sentences on note cards describing the pictures, using one of the three degrees of comparison in each sentence. Display students' pictures and sentences in the classroom and refer to them when students practice this skill.

English-Language Learners

The rules for comparing adjectives vary from one language to another. In Spanish, for example, the word for *more* is placed in front of an adjective to make it comparative. Many adjectives that are irregular in English are also irregular in other languages, such as *good, better,* and *best.* If possible, make a chart to show how adjectives are compared in the various languages spoken by students. Write the same sentence in several languages as examples.

Meeting Individual Needs

Interpersonal Play 20 Questions with the class. Have one student think of an object in the classroom without naming the object. Direct the other students to ask up to 20 questions that use the positive, comparative, and superlative forms of adjectives, for example, *Is the object bigger than this book?* Have students reverse roles after the object has been correctly named.

Exercise 1
1. longer
2. oldest
3. better
4. most beautiful
5. more extensive
6. smallest, most

Exercise 2
1. In my opinion Maryland is the most pleasant state.
2. No change
3. Summer heat and humidity are no worse than they are in many other places I could name.
4. Night skies over Chesapeake Bay are at their most brilliant in winter, when the air is cold and clear.
5. The seafood in Maryland is better and fresher than in other places, and crab cakes are the most delicious seafood dish.
6. The southern states make the best southern fried chicken.
7. I think Alabama has the tastiest cooking of them all.

EXERCISE 1 Complete each sentence with the comparative or superlative form of the adjective in parentheses.

1. Alaska's coastline is _____ (long) than that of all the other states combined.
2. The _____ (old) rock in the world, 3.8 billion years old, was found in Minnesota.
3. The pueblos at Taos, New Mexico, are in _____ (good) condition than any other pueblos in the United States.
4. Some people consider the stalagmites and stalactites in Lechuguilla Cave in the Carlsbad Caverns of Kentucky the _____ (beautiful) in the world.
5. Mammoth Cave, also in Kentucky, has a _____ (extensive) cave system than the Carlsbad Caverns do.
6. Although Rhode Island is the _____ (small) U.S. state, it has some of the _____ (many) beautiful beaches in New England.

EXERCISE 2 Rewrite each sentence to correct errors in comparison. Not every sentence requires rewriting.

1. In my opinion Maryland is the pleasantest state.
2. I think that the weather there is more temperate than it is in any other Middle Atlantic state.
3. Summer heat and humidity are no worser than they are in many other places I could name.
4. Night skies over Chesapeake Bay are at their brilliantest in winter, when the air is cold and clear.
5. The seafood in Maryland is more better and fresher than in other places, and crab cakes are the deliciousest seafood dish.
6. The southern states make the bestest southern fried chicken.
7. I think Alabama has the tastest cooking of them all.

APPLY IT NOW

What do you think are the best aspects of a place where you would like to visit? Write six sentences to convince someone else that your choice is a great place. Use positive, comparative, and superlative forms of adjectives in your writing. Consult a dictionary as needed.

Tech Tip With an adult, search online for images of these places.

Adjectives • 23

OBJECTIVES

- **To distinguish between concrete nouns and abstract nouns**
- **To use the adjectives *few, fewer, fewest* and *little, less, least* correctly in comparisons**

 **DAILY** ⚙ **Maintenance**

Assign **Practice Book** page 11, Section 2.4. After students finish,
1. Give immediate feedback.
2. Review concepts as needed.
3. Model the correct answer.

Pages 4–5 of the **Answer Key** contain tips for Daily Maintenance.

WARM-UP

Write the words *error* and *knowledge* on the board. Ask students if they can count the number of errors made on a math test. Confirm that they can. Then ask students whether they can count how much knowledge of mathematics someone has. Confirm that they cannot.

📖 Read from a piece of writing that the class is currently reading. Emphasize the uses of *few* and *little*.

TEACH

Invite a volunteer to read the concrete nouns and abstract nouns section. Ask another volunteer to read how the words *few, fewer, fewest* and *little, less, least* are used to modify these nouns.

Explain that *fewer* tells how many and modifies a plural noun, while the word *less* describes how much. Refer to the Warm-Up activity to show the connection between concrete and abstract nouns and the words *few, fewer, fewest,* and *little, less, least.*

PRACTICE

EXERCISE 1

To guide students through this activity, suggest that they consider if the thing referred to by the noun can be touched or seen. Explain that if students cannot touch or see it, then the noun is abstract. Remind students that only things that can be seen and touched are concrete. Review students' charts and discuss any word that students find challenging.

EXERCISE 2

Before students begin, you might give this helpful hint: If the noun can be made plural, use the words *few, fewer,* and *fewest.* If the noun cannot be made plural, use the words *little, less,* and *least.* After students have finished, discuss strategies that students used to make the right word choices.

EXERCISE 3

Tell students to first locate the noun to be modified in each sentence. Then have students complete the sentences. Ask students to exchange papers with partners to check each other's work.

2.4 *Few and Little*

Concrete nouns name things that you can see, touch, or count. They can be made plural because they can be counted: *chair, screwdriver, hat, river.* **Abstract nouns** name things that generally cannot be seen, touched, or counted. They express qualities or conditions: *life, patience, happiness, disgust.* They generally cannot be made plural. For some nouns you can use either *less* or *fewer* depending on the noun's usage in the sentence.

Use the adjectives *few, fewer,* and *fewest* to compare concrete nouns that can be counted. Note that the noun *errors* is in the plural form.

USING: *FEW, FEWER, FEWEST*

Anthony's report contained *few* errors.
Cynthia's report contained *fewer* errors than Anthony's did.
Jackie's report contained the *fewest* errors of all.

Use the adjectives *little, less,* and *least* to compare abstract nouns by quantity. They are used for nouns that cannot be counted, such as *love, maturity,* or *sleep.* Note that the nouns *motivation* and *effort* are singular.

USING: *LITTLE, LESS, LEAST*

Anthony showed only a *little* motivation for writing his report.
Lydia put even *less* effort into her report than Anthony did.
Of all the students, Debbie showed the *least* motivation or effort.

EXERCISE 1 Place these words in two columns, one with concrete nouns and the other with abstract nouns.

penny	strength	oxygen	sadness
jewelry	newspaper	justice	chemistry
patriotism	gold	quality	bottle
scenery	weather	hammer	milk
mountain	thunder	belief	necklace
sandwich	tennis	apple	confidence
knowledge	safety	leadership	work

Exercise 1

Concrete: penny, jewelry, mountain, sandwich, newspaper, gold, hammer, apple, bottle, milk, necklace

Abstract: patriotism, scenery, knowledge, strength, weather, thunder, tennis, safety, oxygen, justice, quality, belief, leadership, sadness, chemistry, confidence, work

APPLY

APPLY IT NOW

Ask volunteers to read aloud one or more sentences as you write them on the board. Have students make note of the adjective—*less* or *fewer*—and the word it describes. Students should demonstrate an understanding of when and how to use the words *few* and *little* and their various forms.

TechTip After students post their work, have them check one another's work to see whether the words *few* and *less* were used correctly.

ASSESS

Note which students had difficulty with the words *few* and *little*. Assign **Practice Book** page 17 for further practice.

WRITING CONNECTION

Use pages 242–243 of the Writing portion of the book.

TEACHING OPTIONS

Reteach

Review the correct use of adjectives in the comparative and superlative degrees, including *fewer* and *less*. Then distribute note cards to pairs of students on which a variety of adjectives (including *few* and *little*) are written, one per card. Invite one student to hold up a note card and read the adjective aloud. Have the other student provide a sentence using the adjective in the comparative degree. The first student can then provide a similar sentence, this time using the adjective in the superlative degree. Have students repeat the activity with all the cards.

Meeting Individual Needs

Intrapersonal Invite students to note everyday observations in their journals, using a variety of adjectives to describe and compare the things they see and hear. Encourage students to use comparative and superlative adjectives in their writing, such as *more, most, less,* and *least, few, little*. Suggest that students refer to these observations later for ideas for poems and essays.

Cooperative Learning

Have partners take turns comparing two or more games, sports, or hobbies, using adjectives in the comparative and superlative degrees. Encourage students to be aware of the correct use of these forms in everyday conversation. Tell students to pay attention to their partners' sentences and to offer corrections if needed.

Exercise 2

The correct word is underlined.

1. concrete
2. abstract
3. concrete
4. abstract
5. concrete
6. concrete
7. abstract
8. abstract
9. concrete
10. abstract

EXERCISE 2 Tell whether the noun being compared in each sentence is abstract or concrete. Then choose the correct word to complete the sentence.

1. Our school's "garage sale" attracted (fewer less) people this year than it did last year.
2. I think there was (fewer less) publicity for the auction this year.
3. I saw (fewer less) bands in the parade this July 4th.
4. People had (fewer less) enthusiasm for the rodeo this year.
5. We definitely collected (fewer less) vegetables to sell at the market.
6. I have (fewer less) jewelry than my older sister.
7. My father has (fewer less) talent in the kitchen than my grandmother.
8. An athlete has to master (fewer less) skills in diving than in gymnastics, but both are very difficult sports.
9. After riding the carousel, Molly had the (fewest littlest) tickets left for the carnival.
10. Fish cannot live in some parts of the ocean because pollution has left too (few little) oxygen in the water.

Exercise 3

1. less
2. less
3. fewer
4. fewer
5. less
6. fewer
7. fewer
8. less, fewer
9. less, few
10. less, fewer

EXERCISE 3 Complete each sentence with *fewer* or *less.*

1. All of us had _____ time to work on the class yearbook this year than we had last year.
2. All of us had _____ homework last year.
3. Some of us had _____ after-school activities last year too.
4. Generally, we had many _____ hours to work on the yearbook this year.
5. We also got _____ help from faculty advisors.
6. As a result, there were _____ errors in last year's yearbook.
7. Also, there are _____ pages in this year's book.
8. There is _____ material on school activities and _____ photos.
9. There is also _____ space for seniors' comments and quotes, although _____ seniors are likely to complain.
10. Everyone is _____ enthusiastic about this year's yearbook, and we will print _____.

APPLY IT NOW

Write five sentences about a change in your life over the past year—something you now spend less time doing. Use any forms of *few* or *less* in your sentences at least three times each.

TechTip Post your work on the class blog or wiki for peer review.

Adjectives • 25

OBJECTIVES

- **To understand that a prepositional phrase can be used as an adjective**
- **To recognize adjective clauses**
- **To distinguish between restrictive adjective clauses and nonrestrictive adjective clauses**

Maintenance

Assign **Practice Book** page 12, Section 2.5. After students finish,
1. Give immediate feedback.
2. Review concepts as needed.
3. Model the correct answer.

Pages 4–5 of the **Answer Key** contain tips for Daily Maintenance.

WARM-UP

Write the following sentence starters on the board. Have students complete them. Then encourage students to create five more sentences following these sentence starters.

The freckled young boy in _____.

The bashful girl who _____.

The fat black cat that _____.

📖 Read from a piece of writing that the class is currently reading. Emphasize the adjective phrases and clauses.

TEACH

Have several students write their Warm-Up sentences on the board. Point out their use of adjective phrases and clauses. Then invite a volunteer to read the adjective phrase paragraph and example. Underline the adjective phrases in students' examples while the student is reading. Then ask a student to read aloud the clauses paragraph. Underline the adjective clauses in the students' examples.

Discuss how adjective phrases and adjective clauses differ.

Ask a student to read the restrictive and nonrestrictive adjective clauses paragraph. Encourage questions and offer clarification as needed. Discuss how the two examples differ and why one clause is restrictive and the other is not.

PRACTICE

EXERCISE 1

For this exercise, suggest that students read each sentence completely. Then ask them to locate the prepositional phrase. Have volunteers write the sentences on the board, underlining the nouns and circling the adjective phrases.

EXERCISE 2

To help students complete this exercise, review the difference between restrictive and nonrestrictive clauses. Encourage students to explain the difference to help identify these clauses. Invite volunteers to read the adjective clauses and give the nouns they modify. Ask other volunteers to decide whether the clauses are restrictive or nonrestrictive.

2.5 Adjective Phrases and Clauses

A **prepositional phrase** is made up of a preposition, the object of the preposition, and any modifiers. A prepositional phrase can be used as an adjective. Prepositions that begin adjective phrases include *with, to, in, at, of, under,* and *over.* In this sentence the prepositional phrase *in bright colors* modifies the noun *shirts.* It is an **adjective phrase.**

> **Shirts** *in bright colors* **are often worn by people in warm climates.**

A **clause** is a group of words that has a subject and a predicate. A dependent clause does not express a complete thought. Some dependent clauses are **adjective clauses.** They describe nouns. In this sentence *which has many rich cultural traditions* is a dependent clause. The dependent adjective clause modifies *Hawaii.*

> **Hawaii,** *which has many rich cultural traditions,* **is both a beautiful and an interesting place to visit.**

A **restrictive adjective clause** is necessary to the meaning of a sentence. A **nonrestrictive clause** is not necessary to the meaning. Nonrestrictive clauses are set off with commas. Adjective clauses are introduced by *who, whom, whose, that, which, where,* and *when.* As a general rule, the relative pronoun *that* is used in restrictive clauses and *which* in nonrestrictive ones. Note that proper nouns are usually followed by nonrestrictive clauses.

> **The shirt** *that I bought* **has red flowers on a white background.**
> (restrictive—necessary in order to know which shirt)
> **Maui,** *which is one of the Hawaiian Islands,* **is a popular tourist destination.** (nonrestrictive—not necessary in order to identify the specific island)

EXERCISE 1 Identify the adjective phrases and name the words they modify.

1. Our trip to Hawaii was a great success.
2. When we left Boston, the temperature at Logan Airport was freezing.
3. When we landed, we felt the warmth of the Hawaiian sunshine.
4. Dad quickly shed his coat with the heavy lining.
5. We saw people in short-sleeved shirts.

Exercise 1
Adjective phrases are underlined once. Nouns they modify are underlined twice.

APPLY

APPLY IT NOW

Tell partners to take turns reading their sentences to each other. Encourage one student to listen for the clause and the noun it modifies. Have that student tell the clause and noun for the partner to confirm. Students should demonstrate an understanding of adjective phrases and clauses.

 Grammar in Action. The adjective phrases on page 222 are *to all language, of things, of inquiry,* and *of the word.* To assist students, you may want to point out the prepositions in each phrase. Challenge students to identify the nouns modified by each phrase *(key, knowledge, field, meaning).*

ASSESS

Note which students had difficulty with adjective phrases and clauses. Assign **Practice Book** pages 18–19 for further practice.

WRITING CONNECTION

Use pages 244–245 of the Writing portion of the book.

Use pages 244–245 of the Writing portion of the book.

Exercise 2

Adjective clauses are underlined once. Nouns they modify are underlined twice.

1. nonrestrictive
2. nonrestrictive
3. nonrestrictive
4. nonrestrictive
5. nonrestrictive
6. restrictive
7. restrictive
8. restrictive
9. restrictive
10. restrictive
11. restrictive
12. nonrestrictive

EXERCISE 2 In each sentence identify the adjective clause and name the noun it modifies. Then tell whether the clause is restrictive or nonrestrictive.

1. Hawaiian shirts, which are colorful shirts with short sleeves, are a popular clothing item in many places today.
2. The shirts were first manufactured commercially in Hawaii in 1936 by Ellery J. Chun, who named them Aloha shirts.
3. An ancestor of the Aloha shirt was the "thousand-mile shirt," which was a sturdy garment worn by missionaries.
4. The Hawaiians, who up to that time had not worn Western-style garments, supposedly added patterns and color to the shirts.
5. Early shirts were of tapa cloth, which Hawaiians produced from the bark of the paper mulberry plant.
6. Patterns were taken from native flowers and other vegetation that grew on the islands.
7. The fabric that became popular for the shirts was rayon because it was easier to dye than natural fibers.
8. The 1950s was the period that Hawaiian shirts became popular throughout the United States.
9. At the time, celebrities such as Frank Sinatra and Elvis Presley wore them in movies, and then fans who wanted to imitate these stars began to wear them also.
10. Hawaiians say that Hawaii is the only place that authentic Aloha shirts can ever be produced.
11. I have a Hawaiian shirt that I got when I visited Maui.
12. Maui, which is a Hawaiian island with a fertile valley between two volcanoes, is also called the "Valley Island."

APPLY IT NOW

For each word below, write a sentence containing an adjective clause modifying it.

homework	park
gift	mouse
holiday	toys
television	Ohio
man	

Grammar in Action. Find the adjective phrases in the p. 222 excerpt.

Adjectives • 27

TEACHING OPTIONS

Reteach

Choose sentences from a classroom text that include adjective phrases and adjective clauses. Write the sentences on chart paper. Then display the paper and discuss the sentences with the class. Challenge students to identify the phrases and clauses in the sentences and to tell which nouns the phrases or clauses modify. Have students work with partners to find an example from the same text of each type of phrase or clause: an adjective phrase, a restrictive adjective clause, a nonrestrictive adjective clause. Invite students to share their sentences with the class.

Meeting Individual Needs

Extra Support For students who have difficulty distinguishing the difference between adjective phrases, nonrestrictive adjective clauses, and restrictive adjective clauses, review the sentences in the exercises. Set up a three-column chart, for phrases and each type of clause, and ask students to write each sentence in the appropriate column. Then have students compare the sentences in each column, noticing the things they have in common. Tell students to think about these common structures and features when they review sentences in the future.

Curriculum Connection

Bring an art book to class from your school or local library. Choose a piece of art, such as a painting, and invite students to describe images they see. Challenge students to include adjective phrases and adjective clauses in their descriptions.

Diagram It!

To practice these concepts in the context of diagramming, turn to Section 11.8.

To practice these concepts in the context of diagramming, turn to Section 11.8.

Adjective Review

ASSESS

Use the Adjective Review as homework, as a practice test, or as an informal assessment. Following are some options for use.

Homework

You may wish to assign one group the odd items and another group the even items. When you next meet, review the correct answers as a group. Be sure to model how to arrive at the correct answer.

Practice Test

Use the Adjective Review as a diagnostic tool. Assign the entire review or only specific sections. After students have finished, identify which concepts require more attention. Reteach concepts as necessary.

Adjective Review

2.1
1. Seven, different, ancient, Chinese
2. seven, difficult, subject complement
3. simple, frustrated, object complement
4. finite, complicated, subject complement
5. addictive, object complement
6. logical, American
7. popular, subject complement, Japanese
8. symbol-based, subway
9. occupied, object complement

2.2
10. indefinite
11. interrogative
12. indefinite
13. demonstrative
14. indefinite
15. interrogative
16. indefinite
17. interrogative
18. demonstrative, indefinite
19. indefinite, indefinite
20. indefinite

2.1 Name the descriptive adjectives in each sentence. Identify adjectives used as subject complements or object complements.

1. Seven different shapes make up an ancient Chinese puzzle called a tangram.
2. Rearranging the seven pieces is difficult for some people.
3. The seemingly simple puzzle leaves many frustrated.
4. A description of a finite set of patterns called a convex is highly complicated.
5. Some players find the puzzle addictive.
6. Sudoku is a logical puzzle invented by an American architect.
7. It became popular in Japan first, however, which is why it has a Japanese name.
8. Suduko is a symbol-based puzzle that entertains subway commuters everywhere.
9. Sudoko keeps my sister occupied whenever we travel long distances.

2.2 Identify each underlined adjective as demonstrative, interrogative, or indefinite.

10. Every ninth grader has to write a research paper.
11. Which topic have you chosen?
12. I've read several sample papers in the library.
13. Those students certainly did extensive research.

14. Each paper receives a grade for content and a grade for writing.
15. Whose computer will you be using?
16. Neither machine was working last week.
17. What department do we need to contact to have them fixed?.
18. Those computers crash several times a week.
19. I worry that I will lose my work each time I use them, so I save my files every half hour.
20. Neither Jesse nor Suzanne are in the habit of saving their work.

2.3 Identify the following words as positive, comparative, or superlative.

21. brighter
22. most generous
23. extensive
24. shady
25. most difficult
26. less extreme
27. least tolerant
28. hyper

Write the positive, comparative, and superlative forms of each word.

29. delicate
30. healthy
31. extreme
32. eternal
33. red
34. little

2.3
21. comparative
22. superlative
23. positive
24. positive
25. superlative
26. comparative
27. superlative
28. positive
29. delicate, more delicate, most delicate
30. healthy, healthier, healthiest
31. extreme, more extreme, most extreme
32. cannot be compared
33. red, redder, reddest
34. little, less, least
35. wise, wiser, wisest
36. fanciful, more fanciful, most fanciful
37. hot, hotter, hottest
38. common, more common or commoner, most common or commonest
39. much, more, most
40. far, farther or further, farthest or furthest

Informal Assessment

Use the review as preparation for the formal assessment. Count the review as a portion of the grade. Have students work to find the correct answers and use their corrected review as a study guide for the formal assessment.

WRITING CONNECTION

Use pages 246–247 of the Writing portion of the book.

Putting It All Together

To help students review the many ways adjectives are used, ask them to gather all their Apply It Now activities. Have students review all five assignments. Then ask them to complete the following activities:

- Write an advertisement for your favorite game, such as a video game or a board game. In your advertisement, circle all the adjectives and note their position within each sentence.

- Write a short paragraph comparing two athletes, actors, or musicians. Incorporate demonstrative, interrogative, and indefinite adjectives whenever possible. Underline these adjectives, and circle all the comparative and superlative adjectives.

- Take a survey among classmates to see how many use the adjectives *few, fewer, fewest* and *little, less, least* correctly. Use examples gathered in the 2.4 Apply It Now and quiz your classmates.

- Write a detailed sentence about your favorite type of food. Include at least one adjective clause. Then diagram the sentence.

2.4

41. people: concrete; aroma: abstract; bakery: concrete; Few
42. resolve: abstract; treats: concrete; less
43. trips: abstract; Main Street: concrete; temptation: abstract; fewer
44. time: abstract; route: concrete; little
45. diligence: abstract; mistakes: abstract; fewer
46. homework: abstract; quizzes, concrete; least
47. subjects: concrete; amount: abstract; fewest

2.5

48. Our research trip to the Field Museum was a huge success. (adjective phrase that modifies *trip*)
49. We wanted to get firsthand information about the *T. rex* Sue, whose skeleton is the largest and most complete ever discovered. (adjective clause that modifies *Sue*)

35. wise
36. fanciful
37. hot
38. common
39. much
40. far

2.4 Identify each noun as concrete or abstract. Then complete each sentence with the correct form of *few* or *little.*

41. _____ people can resist the aroma that comes from a bakery.
42. I have _____ resolve than Ali when we see the sweet treats.
43. I try to make _____ trips down Main Street so I can avoid temptation.
44. It only takes a _____ time to take an alternate route.
45. Greater diligence results in _____ mistakes.
46. Of all my teachers, she gives the _____ homework but the most quizzes.
47. Isabella had the _____ subjects to study, but the most amount of work.

2.5 Identify each adjective phrase and adjective clause and tell the words they modify. Then add commas where necessary.

48. Our research trip to the Field Museum was a huge success.
49. We wanted to get firsthand information about the *T. rex* Sue whose skeleton is the largest and most complete ever discovered.

50. *T. rex* which is a species of dinosaur weighed five to seven tons.
51. The museum storyteller told us a story that was fascinating.
52. It was about a dinosaur in the water, and it was much bigger than the ones on land.

Identify the following groups of words as either adjective phrases or adjective clauses, then use them in sentences.

53. on the floor
54. which is blue
55. on your left
56. by the river
57. who is a student
58. which sits by the door
59. beside Miguel
60. that we built
61. under the bridge
62. whom are ill
63. who got the job

For the sentences that you wrote in the preceding exercise, change three nonrestrictive clauses to restrictive clauses, OR three restrictive clauses to nonrestrictive clauses. Rewrite the sentences as necessary.

50. *T. rex, which is a species of dinosaur, weighed five to seven tons.* (adjective clause that modifies *T. rex*)
51. The museum storyteller told us a story that was fascinating. (adjective clause that modifies *story*)
52. It was about a dinosaur in the water; and it was much bigger than the ones on land (adjective phrases that modify dinosaur, ones)
53. adjective phrase
54. adjective clause
55. adjective phrase
56. adjective phrase
57. adjective clause
58. adjective clause
59. adjective phrase
60. adjective clause
61. adjective phrase
62. adjective clause
63. adjective clause

Sentences will vary.

Tech Tip Go to www.voyagesinenglish.com for more activities.

Adjectives • 29

TechTip Encourage students to further review adjectives, using the additional practice and games at www.voyagesinenglish.com.

Adjective Challenge

ASSESS

EXERCISE 1
Encourage students to read the paragraph twice before answering the questions. If students have difficulty with any question, suggest that they refer to the section that teaches that skill. This activity can be done individually, in small groups, or as a whole class.

EXERCISE 2
Then have students complete the second exercise. Be sure to check that their poems contain the items listed.

After you have reviewed adjectives, administer the Section 2 Assessment on pages 3–4 in the **Assessment Book,** or create a customized test with the optional **Test Generator CD.**

You may also wish to administer the Sections 1–2 Summative Assessment on pages 33–34 of the **Assessment Book.** This test is also available on the optional **Test Generator CD.**

WRITING CONNECTION
Students can complete a formal personal narrative using the Writer's Workshop on pages 248–259.

Adjective Challenge

EXERCISE 1 Read the selection and then answer the questions.

1. Suppose birds became extinct. 2. We can appreciate the negative consequences of such an event when we consider the many ways that birds help us. 3. The destruction of harmful insects, which is perhaps birds' most important function, makes farmers' tasks easier. 4. Further, some birds help keep weeds under control by eating their seeds, while many larger birds prevent mice and rats from becoming really bad pests. 5. You can see why we consider birds essential in our ecosystem. 6. They are among our greatest benefactors. 7. Every action that we can take now to save our bird population will pay off in the future.

1. What is the subject complement in sentence 1?
2. Find an adjective clause in sentence 2. What noun does it modify? Is it restrictive or nonrestrictive? What is the relative pronoun?
3. Name the superlative form of an adjective in sentence 3. What are its positive and comparative forms?
4. What is the object complement in sentence 3? What is its degree of comparison?
5. Find an adjective clause in sentence 3. What noun does it modify? Is it restrictive or nonrestrictive? What is the relative pronoun?
6. Name two indefinite adjectives in sentence 4. What noun does each one modify?
7. Give the degrees of comparison for the adjective *bad* in sentence 4.
8. What is the object complement in sentence 5?
9. Name the superlative form of an adjective used in sentence 6. What are its positive and comparative forms?
10. Name the indefinite adjective in sentence 7.

EXERCISE 2 Descriptive imagery in poems require adjectives. Write a descriptive poem in which you use the following:

1. a demonstrative, an interrogative, or an indefinite adjective
2. an adjective clause
3. a comparative or a superlative adjective

Exercise 1
1. extinct
2. that birds help us; ways; restrictive; that
3. most important; important; more important
4. easier; comparative
5. which is perhaps birds' most important function; destruction, nonrestrictive; which
6. some, many; birds, birds
7. bad, worse, worst
8. essential
9. greatest; great, greater
10. Every

Exercise 2
Answers will vary.

30 • Adjective Challenge

SUPPORT MATERIALS

Practice Book
Daily Maintenance, pages 20–22
Grammar, pages 23–37

Assessment Book
Section 3 Assessment, pages 5–8

Test Generator CD

Writing Chapter 2,
   How-to Articles

Customizable Lesson Plans
www.voyagesinenglish.com

CONNECT WITH LITERATURE

📖 Consider using the following titles throughout the section to illustrate the grammar concept:

I And You And Don't Forget Who: What Is a Pronoun? by Brian P. Cleary
Monster by Walter Dean Myers

Pronouns

GRAMMAR FOR GROWN-UPS

Understanding Pronouns

Pronouns are words used in place of nouns. The word, phrase, or clause to which a pronoun refers is its **antecedent.** Pronouns have the qualities of person, gender, number, and case, and they add variety to sentences, making them less repetitive.

Pronouns must match their antecedent in person (who is speaking), number (whether they refer to one or more), and gender (whether the antecedent is masculine, feminine, or neuter).

PERSONAL PRONOUNS	SINGULAR	PLURAL
First Person (speaker)	I, me	we, us
Second Person (spoken to)	you	you
Third Person (spoken of)	he, she, it	they
	him, her, it	them

There are three **cases** of personal pronouns. The cases are **subject** (*I, you, he, she, it, we, they*), **object** (*me, you, him, her, it, us, them*), and **possessive** (*mine, yours, his, hers, its, ours, theirs*).

Possessive pronouns stand alone.

> *This book is* **mine.**

Possessive adjectives, such as *my, your,* and *his,* modify nouns.

> **Your** *book is on the table.*

An **intensive pronoun** is used to emphasize a preceding noun or pronoun.

> *She* **herself** *made dinner.*

A **reflexive pronoun** is used as an object and refers to or renames the subject.

> *I hurt* **myself.**

A **demonstrative pronoun** points out a definite person, place, or thing.

> **This** *is the spot I left my keys.*

An i**ndefinite pronoun** identifies no particular person, place, or thing.

> **Somebody** *ate the last piece of watermelon.*

> ❝ The frank yet graceful use of 'I'
> distinguishes a good writer from a bad. ❞
>
> —Ambrose Bierce

COMMON ERRORS

Contractions and Possessives

Students sometimes confuse the words *who's* and *whose* to show possession. *Whose* is the possessive form, while *who's* is simply a contraction.

ERROR: Who's cat is in the tree?
CORRECT: Whose cat is in the tree?

Guide students to be careful with spelling when showing possession. Also point out that pronouns never use apostrophes to show possession; only nouns do (*Corey's, his; Elena's, hers; the cat's, its*).

SENTENCE DIAGRAMMING

You may wish to teach adjectives in the context of diagramming. Review these examples. Then refer to the Diagramming section or look for Diagram It! features in the Adjectives section.

I myself prefer oatmeal cookies.

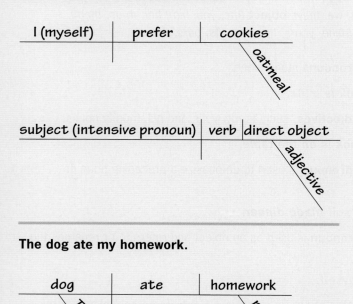

The dog ate my homework.

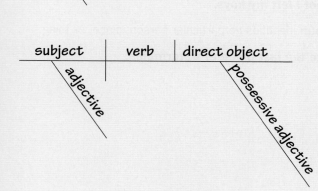

ASK AN EXPERT

Real Situations, Real Solutions

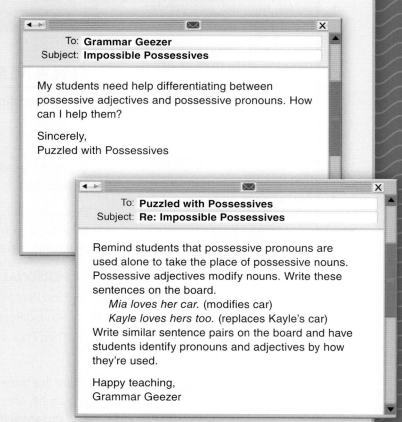

To: **Grammar Geezer**
Subject: **Impossible Possessives**

My students need help differentiating between possessive adjectives and possessive pronouns. How can I help them?

Sincerely,
Puzzled with Possessives

To: **Puzzled with Possessives**
Subject: **Re: Impossible Possessives**

Remind students that possessive pronouns are used alone to take the place of possessive nouns. Possessive adjectives modify nouns. Write these sentences on the board.
  Mia loves her car. (modifies car)
  Kayle loves hers too. (replaces Kayle's car)
Write similar sentence pairs on the board and have students identify pronouns and adjectives by how they're used.

Happy teaching,
Grammar Geezer

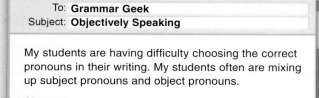

To: **Grammar Geek**
Subject: **Objectively Speaking**

My students are having difficulty choosing the correct pronouns in their writing. My students often are mixing up subject pronouns and object pronouns.

Sincerely,
Pronoun Perplexion

To: **Pronoun Perplexion**
Subject: **Re: Objectively Speaking**

Try using this visual to help your students grasp the difference between subject and object pronouns. You may wish to have students write it in their notebooks for quick reference.

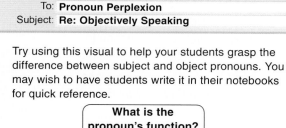

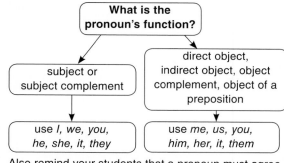

Also remind your students that a pronoun must agree with its antecedent in person, number, and gender.

Supporting the simple,
Grammar Geek

OBJECTIVES

- **To identify personal pronouns**
- **To name the person, number, and gender of personal pronouns**
- **To use personal pronouns correctly**

Assign **Practice Book** page 20, Section 3.1. After students finish,
1. Give immediate feedback.
2. Review concepts as needed.
3. Model the correct answer.

Pages 4–5 of the **Answer Key** contain tips for Daily Maintenance.

WARM-UP

Read the following paragraph aloud:

> Sarah learned to read when Sarah was two years old. Sarah had a favorite book. Sarah's favorite book was *The Wind in the Willows*. Immediately, Sarah wanted to share the book with someone. Sarah has a sister who wants to read the book too.

Suggest that there is a word students might use in place of *Sarah* that would avoid repeating the name. Ask students to name this word.

📖 Read from a piece of writing that the class is currently reading. Emphasize the use of pronouns.

TEACH

Write several pairs of sentences on the board such as *James is standing. He is wearing a red shirt.* Ask which word in the second sentence identifies the person *(he)*. Explain that *he* is a pronoun—a word that replaces a noun, in this case the person's name. Point out that the noun the pronoun refers to, *James,* is called the antecedent.

Continue, using a variety of pronouns.

Invite a volunteer to read aloud the definition of a pronoun and the words listed as pronouns in the chart. Have students read the rest of the page silently. Review the terms *person, number,* and *gender* and how these are used to identify pronouns.

PRACTICE

EXERCISE 1

Have partners locate the pronouns in each sentence. Encourage students to discuss their choices and to explain to one another if the pronouns are first person,

second person, or third person; plural or singular; and, if appropriate, masculine, feminine, or neuter.

EXERCISE 2

Have students write their answers independently. Ask volunteers to take turns reading aloud their sentences. Have the rest of the class determine if the answer is correct.

EXERCISE 3

Have students complete this exercise independently. Discuss answers as a class when students have finished.

3.1 Person, Number, and Gender of Pronouns

A **pronoun** is a word used in place of a noun. **Personal pronouns** are one kind of pronoun. Look at this chart.

PERSONAL PRONOUNS	SINGULAR	PLURAL
FIRST PERSON (SPEAKER)	I me	we us
SECOND PERSON (SPOKEN TO)	you you	you you
THIRD PERSON (SPOKEN OF)	he, she, it him, her, it	they them

Personal pronouns change form depending on **person**—whether they refer to the one who is speaking, is spoken to, or is spoken of.

Personal pronouns also may have different forms depending on **number**—whether they refer to one person or thing (singular) or to more than one person or thing (plural).

Third person singular personal pronouns also change form depending on the **gender** (feminine, masculine, or neuter) of the **antecedent,** the word the pronoun refers to.

Can you identify the type (person, number, and gender) of the pronouns in these sentences?

> *I* am taking computer science as an elective.
> Frank hasn't decided on an elective yet, but *he* is thinking of taking band.

In the first sentence, *I* is a first person singular pronoun. In the second sentence, *he* is third person singular and masculine. It agrees with its antecedent *Frank.*

Pronouns allow writers to avoid the constant repetition of nouns and make their writing sound more natural.

APPLY

APPLY IT NOW

Read aloud these sentences: "I enjoyed reading *Great Expectations. Great Expectations* was a great book. *Great Expectations* has many interesting characters. I would recommend *Great Expectations* to other people." Ask students how they might improve these sentences. Confirm that continual use of the book's title becomes redundant and that using pronouns makes writing smoother. Review students' work to make sure they have identified the personal pronouns and antecedents correctly.

Students should demonstrate an understanding of pronoun usage.

ASSESS

Note which students had difficulty identifying person, number, and gender of pronouns. Assign **Practice Book** pages 23–24 for further practice.

WRITING CONNECTION

Use pages 260–261 of the Writing portion of the book. Be sure to point out pronouns in the literature excerpt and student model.

TEACHING OPTIONS

Reteach

Remind students that pronouns are used in place of nouns. Write the pronouns *I, we, he, she, they, you,* and *it* on note cards. Have students take a card and suggest a noun that could have been replaced by that pronoun. Then have students use the pronoun in a sentence.

Cooperative Learning

Encourage partners to take turns describing the plot of a movie or the ongoing action of a sporting event. Instruct the partner who is listening to raise a hand every time he or she hears a pronoun. Point out the frequency with which students use pronouns.

English-Language Learners

Write female names, male names, plural nouns, and singular nouns on note cards. On separate cards, write the pronouns *he, she, him, her, they,* and *it*. Encourage students to match the pronoun cards with the correct name or noun cards. Then ask students to write the same nouns and pronouns from their primary language on the backs of the cards to help use for review at home.

Exercise 1
1. first person singular
2. third person singular masculine; third person singular masculine
3. first person singular; second person plural or singular
4. third person singular neuter
5. third person singular masculine
6. third person singular masculine
7. third person plural
8. first person singular; first person singular; third person singular masculine
9. third person singular feminine; first person singular
10. first person singular
11. first person singular
12. third person plural

EXERCISE 1 Identify the pronouns in each sentence. For each pronoun, tell the person, number, and, if appropriate, gender.

1. Recently I discovered short stories by Jack London.
2. People know him from the novels he wrote about Alaska.
3. One of those stories, "To Build a Fire," is the first story that I will recommend to you.
4. It is about a man traveling through Alaska.
5. He does not understand what cold can do.
6. He hikes through the snow with a dog.
7. As they traveled through the terrible cold, the dog began to mistrust the man.
8. I felt I was with that man, watching him.
9. Beverly says she felt the same way I did.
10. I read that *White Fang* is also set in Alaska.
11. Those novels sound interesting to me.
12. The librarians say they will put the books on reserve.

Jack London

EXERCISE 2 Complete each sentence with a pronoun. Use the directions in parentheses.

1. This year ___we___ will have a chance to choose some classes ourselves. (first person, plural)
2. Our teachers created the courses, and ___they___ call these *electives*. (third person, plural)
3. ___I___ am trying to decide between art and keyboarding. (first person, singular)
4. My mom wants me to take keyboarding, so I'll probably take ___it___. (third person, singular, neuter)
5. What will ___you___ take? (second person, singular)
6. Maybe ___we___ will be in the same class. (first person, plural)

Exercise 3
1. they or them
2. you
3. us or we
4. he or she; him or her

EXERCISE 3 Change the following nouns to appropriate pronouns.

1. Jorge and Jack
2. you and your family
3. me and the dog
4. our teacher

APPLY IT NOW

Write a paragraph about a short story that you have read. Your purpose is to convince a friend either to read or not to read it. In your finished paragraph, underline all the personal pronouns and circle their antecedents.

Pronouns • 33

3.2 Subject Pronouns

OBJECTIVE

- To recognize and know when to use the subject pronouns *I, we, you, he, she, it,* and *they*

 **Maintenance**

Assign **Practice Book** page 20, Section 3.2. After students finish,
1. Give immediate feedback.
2. Review concepts as needed.
3. Model the correct answer.

Pages 4–5 of the **Answer Key** contain tips for Daily Maintenance.

WARM-UP

Write on the board the following sentence:

Billy and me were friends.

Ask whether the sentence sounds correct. Then invite volunteers to discuss their answers with the class. Suggest that there are times when what may sound correct is not actually correct.

📖 Read from a piece of writing that the class is currently reading. Emphasize the subject pronouns.

TEACH

Write the following sentence on the board:

_____ did the job.

Discuss the different pronouns that could be used to complete this sentence based on person, number, and gender *(I, we, you, he, she, it,* and *they*). Tell students that these are the subject pronouns.

Remind students that in addition to being subjects, these pronouns can also be used as subject complements. Model this by acting as if you are making a phone call to a student. Say: *May I speak to [student's name]?* Encourage the student to answer using a pronoun *(This is him/her*

or *This is he/she).* If the student answers with *him* or *her,* model the correct answer. *(This is he/she.)* Remind students that what sounds correct might not always be so. Then have students read the definition and example sentence for subject pronouns. You may also wish to take this opportunity to review subject complements on pages 6–7.

PRACTICE

EXERCISE 1

When students have finished, invite volunteers to read aloud the sentences and to state reasons for their pronoun choices.

EXERCISE 2

Ask students to define *subject* and *subject complement.* Encourage volunteers to take turns reading their sentences aloud. Ask students if they agree with the pronoun choices and to explain their reasoning.

EXERCISE 3

Have partners rewrite the incorrect sentences. Then have students read their corrected sentences aloud. Point out that the incorrect pronouns are not subject pronouns and that the correct replacements are all subject pronouns.

3.2 Subject Pronouns

A **subject pronoun** can be the subject or subject complement in a sentence. The subject pronouns are *I, we, you, he, she, it,* and *they.*

> **I watched the movie twice.** (subject)
> **The actor who won the award was he.** (subject complement)

One common error is not using a subject pronoun when it is part of a compound subject or complement. How would you edit these sentences?

> **Cynthia and me went to the movies.**
> **The students attending the play were her and Gregory.**

You are correct if you changed *me* to *I* in the first sentence. The pronoun is part of a compound subject, so the subject form of the pronoun is needed.

You are also correct if you changed *her* to *she* in the second sentence. It is part of a compound subject complement: *she and Gregory* rename the subject—*students.*

EXERCISE 1 Choose the correct pronoun to complete each sentence.

1. My friends and (me <u>I</u>) watch old movies together.
2. (Us <u>We</u>) usually meet at Elisa's house.
3. (<u>She</u> Her) and Peter provide refreshments.
4. (<u>They</u> Them) often have juice and soda.
5. Jane and (<u>I</u> me) usually bring popcorn to pop.
6. David knows a lot about old films, and the ones who usually choose the films are Elisa and (<u>he</u> him).
7. Sometimes (<u>we</u> us) vote on the film to see the next time.
8. David and (<u>she</u> her) suggested *The Sound of Music.*
9. Kevin and (<u>he</u> him) had never seen the film.
10. It was (<u>they</u> them) who really wanted to see the film.
11. But (us <u>we</u>) all enjoyed it.
12. Next week, (<u>she</u> her) will choose the movie with us.
13. (Us <u>We</u>) decided to pick another musical that we all enjoy.
14. (<u>He</u> Him) is a terrible singer, so we are hoping that he won't sing along!

APPLY

APPLY IT NOW

Before students begin to write, have them recite the subject pronouns *I, we, you, he, she, it*, and *they*. When reviewing students' work, help them identify the subject of each sentence, especially if they have used an incorrect pronoun. Students should demonstrate an understanding of subject pronouns.

💡 **TechTip** Make sure you examine students' reviews for clarity and appropriate content before you allow them to post online.

ASSESS

Note which students had difficulty identifying subject pronouns. Assign **Practice Book** page 25 for further practice.

WRITING CONNECTION

Use pages 262–263 of the Writing portion of the book.

TEACHING OPTIONS

Reteach

Say sentences to the class that use subject pronouns incorrectly. After each sentence, ask students to suggest corrections. Encourage students to explain their ideas. Then have students say the sentence with the correct subject pronoun. Challenge students to find 10 examples of correctly used subject pronouns in print sources other than an English or language arts textbook.

Meeting Individual Needs

Auditory Some students may find it helpful to rely on the sound of a pronoun in context to decide the correct pronoun to use, especially with compound subjects. For the sentences in Exercise 1, have students ignore the subjects. Then have students try each pronoun choice with the verb (adjusting the verb if needed). For sentence 1, for example, students compare *I watch* and *Me watch*.

Cooperative Learning

Encourage volunteers to tell about humorous experiences that involved a number of friends or family members. Challenge students to listen for pronouns used as subjects and subject complements and to call attention to these words by raising a pencil in the air.

Exercise 2
1. subject
2. subject
3. subject
4. subject
5. subject
6. subject
7. subject complement
8. subject complement
9. subject complement
10. subject
11. subject complement
12. subject

EXERCISE 2 In each sentence use the correct pronoun for the underlined words. Tell whether the pronoun is a subject or a subject complement.

1. My friends and I planned to see *The Sound of Music*, and ___we___ saw it together yesterday.

2. The movie won an Oscar, and ___it___ is considered a classic.

3. The main character in the film is Maria. ___She___ is in a convent at the beginning of the movie.

4. Maria gets a job taking care of children. ___They___ seem well behaved, but they are quite mischievous with Maria.

Scene from *The Sound of Music*

5. ___They___ are called the von Trapp family.

6. Their father is a widower, and ___he___ was strict with them.

7. Captain von Trapp was a military officer, and it was ___he___ that the Germans wanted for their own military.

8. Nancy likes sentimental movies, and the person who was crying at the end was ___she___.

9. Elaine and I knew the words of the songs, and it was ___we___ who sang along during the film.

10. The von Trapp family now live in Stowe, Vermont, where ___they___ settled after their daring escape.

11. At the lodge, guests can join the family in sing-alongs, and ___they___ can enjoy its beautiful mountain views.

12. Guests can also learn maple sugaring, or ___they___ can ski all day and night.

Exercise 3
1. Correct
2. It was she who wrote the book on which the musical was based.
3. She and her family were well-known singers.
4. Her husband and she were from Austria.
5. He and she met when she was caring for one of his children.
6. Correct
7. Their children and they traveled around the world.

EXERCISE 3 Rewrite the sentences so that the use of subject pronouns is correct. Not all the sentences have errors.

1. *The Sound of Music* was based on a real-life story of a woman. She was Maria von Trapp.

2. It was her who wrote the book on which the musical was based.

3. Her and her family were well-known singers.

4. Her husband and her were from Austria.

5. Him and her met when she was caring for one of his children.

6. They escaped from Austria by hiking over the Alps.

7. Their children and them traveled around the world.

APPLY IT NOW

Write the plot of a movie you like and give your reaction to the film. After you have finished, check that you have used subject pronouns correctly, especially in compound subjects.

Tech Tip Post your review online.

Pronouns • 35

3.3 Object Pronouns

OBJECTIVE
- **To recognize and know when to use the object pronouns**

 **Maintenance**

Assign **Practice Book** page 20, Section 3.3. After students finish,
1. Give immediate feedback.
2. Review concepts as needed.
3. Model the correct answer.

Pages 4–5 of the **Answer Key** contain tips for Daily Maintenance.

WARM-UP

Have a male student and a female student stand at the front of the room. Place a ruler and a sheet of paper on your desk. Then say *Please give the ruler to [male student's name].* Ask students to write a sentence about this action without using the word *ruler* or the male student's name. *(Please give it to him.)* Have students share their sentences with the class. Then do the same with the paper and the female student. Ask students what function the replacement words play and how these can be beneficial to students' writing.

Read from a piece of writing that the class is currently reading. Emphasize the object pronouns.

TEACH

Encourage students to explain their understanding of the object of a sentence. If necessary, you may wish to review object complements on pages 8–9. Then invite volunteers to take turns reading about object pronouns. Have students recite sentences they might say every day, using object pronouns. *(I saw him. I did it. She thanked me.)*

Point out that the object in the pair of example sentences is a compound object, *Kristi and*

me. To help students choose the correct pronoun, suggest that they read the sentences again, this time using a simple object.

> The Gettysburg Address was memorized by me.

> The Gettysburg Address was memorized by I.

Tell students that by eliminating one part of the compound object, they can more easily recognize that the pronoun should be an object pronoun *(me)* rather than a subject pronoun *(I).*

PRACTICE

EXERCISES 1 & 2
Review the difference between direct objects and indirect objects. Then discuss objects of prepositions. Have students complete the exercises independently. Ask partners to compare answers. Suggest that students share any discrepancies with the class to determine the correct answers.

EXERCISE 3
Tell students that they should identify every pronoun in each sentence. Then have students determine how each pronoun is

---

3.3 Object Pronouns

An **object pronoun** can be used as the object of a verb or a preposition. The object pronouns are *me, us, you, him, her, it,* and *them.*

> **Abraham Lincoln was the president during the Civil War. The nation elected *him* in 1860.** (direct object, answers *who? what?*)
> **Lincoln liked to entertain people, and he often told *them* amusing stories.** (indirect object, answers *to whom? to what?*)
> **"With malice toward none, with charity for all" was written by *him*.** (object of a preposition)

One of the sentences below shows a common error in object pronoun usage. Which sentence is correct?

> **The Gettysburg Address was memorized by Kristi and I.**
> **The Gettysburg Address was memorized by Kristi and me.**

If you chose the second sentence, you are correct. The object pronoun *me* should be used as the object of the preposition. It is part of the compound object *Kristi and me.*

EXERCISE 1 Identify the object pronouns. Tell whether each is a direct object, an indirect object, or an object of a preposition.

1. Mrs. Urbanski read <u>us</u> the Gettysburg Address.
2. She gave a fine dramatic reading of <u>it</u>.
3. She explained the speech's importance to <u>us</u>.
4. A cemetery was being established at Gettysburg, and Lincoln and others were dedicating <u>it</u>.
5. The Civil War ended two years after he delivered <u>it</u>.
6. Many soldiers had died at the site, and the cemetery honored <u>them</u>.
7. Lincoln was asked to speak, and the event became an occasion for <u>him</u> to explain the reasons for the war.
8. Historians say that the address was important; to <u>them</u> the words defined the nation as one people dedicated to one principle—equality.
9. The address was important to Americans; the speech gave <u>them</u> a reaffirmation of the basic beliefs of liberty and equality.
10. Some people call <u>it</u> one of the greatest speeches in American history.

Exercise 1
1. indirect object
2. object of a preposition
3. object of a preposition
4. direct object
5. indirect object
6. direct object
7. object of a preposition
8. object of a preposition
9. indirect object
10. direct object

Lincoln delivering the Gettysburg Address

36 • Section 3.3

used and whether the correct form of the pronoun is used. Review students' sentences and help them make corrections as necessary.

EXERCISE 4

Ask volunteers to share their answers. Encourage students to provide their reasoning for each answer.

APPLY

APPLY IT NOW

If students have trouble identifying an object pronoun, suggest that they circle all the pronouns in their writing and determine which pronouns are subject pronouns. Explain that the remaining pronouns will mainly be object pronouns. If needed, help students understand any errors. Students should demonstrate an understanding of object pronouns.

ASSESS

Note which students had difficulty identifying object pronouns. Assign **Practice Book** page 26 for further practice.

WRITING CONNECTION

Use pages 264–265 of the Writing portion of the book.

Reteach

Say the beginning of a sentence for students to complete with an object pronoun. You might use classroom props as needed. For example:

I asked _____ for the answer.
(you her him)

I gave my pencil to _____.
(you her him)

I saw _____ at lunch.
(them)

For each sentence, have students identify the pronoun as the direct object, the indirect object, or the object of a preposition.

Meeting Individual Needs

Intrapersonal Have students write about a group activity in which they recently participated. Encourage them to substitute object pronouns for the names of people and things. Review students' work to make sure they are using object pronouns correctly.

Meeting Individual Needs

Kinesthetic To help students understand the relationship between a verb, a direct object, and an indirect object, write on the board the following sentences:

He gives her a sheet of paper.

She hands me the eraser.

I lend her the ruler.

Read the sentences aloud and invite students to act out the action of each sentence, using classroom objects. Review each sentence, inserting the preposition *to* before each indirect object: *He gives a sheet of paper to her.* Tell students that this will help demonstrate that an indirect object tells *to whom* or *to what* or *for whom* or *for what* that verb's action is performed.

Exercise 2
1. object of a preposition
2. indirect object
3. object of a preposition
4. indirect object
5. direct object
6. indirect object

Exercise 3
1. Lincoln is one of the most honored presidents; perhaps Americans admire George Washington and him the most.
2. Correct
3. We learned that speeches were given at Gettysburg by both Edward Everett and him.
4. Mrs. Urbanski called on Susan and me for a dramatic reading of the speech.
5. Our reading was listened to attentively by her and the class.

Exercise 4
1. her, me
2. him
3. them
4. you

EXERCISE 2 Complete each sentence with a pronoun. Then tell whether the word you added is a direct object, an indirect object, or an object of a preposition.

1. Lincoln was not the first speaker. Edward Everett, the orator who spoke before ___him___, addressed the crowd for two hours.
2. As Everett spoke, people gave ___him___ polite attention.
3. Lincoln's speech was completed in a few minutes, but even today we are moved by ___it___.
4. Lincoln believed that those who died in battle had consecrated the ground, and he gave ___them___ credit for their sacrifice.
5. Many people present were expecting a long speech from Lincoln; he must have disappointed ___them___.
6. A few people in the crowd must have realized that Lincoln had given ___them___ something memorable.

Abraham Lincoln

EXERCISE 3 Rewrite the sentences so that the use of object pronouns is correct. Not all sentences have errors.

1. Lincoln is one of the most honored presidents; perhaps Americans admire George Washington and he the most.
2. Perhaps the most famous speech in the history of the country was given by him.
3. We learned that speeches were given at Gettysburg by both Edward Everett and he.
4. Mrs. Urbanski called on Susan and I for a dramatic reading of the speech.
5. Our reading was listened to attentively by she and the class.

EXERCISE 4 Write the correct form of the personal pronoun indicated in parentheses.

1. Lincoln's speech was presented to the class by both (third person singular feminine) and (first person singular).
2. For the original speech in 1863, it is estimated that over 15,000 people came to listen to (third person singular masculine).
3. After the students listened to the speech, we helped (third person plural) repeat it.
4. We agreed that Lincoln made the nation a better place for both (second person singular) and me.

APPLY IT NOW

Write a brief paragraph about an imaginary encounter with someone you admire. After you have finished, find and underline all the object pronouns in your writing. Remember that you should use pronouns in your writing to avoid repetition and make your writing sound more natural.

Pronouns • 37

3.4   Pronouns after *Than* or *As*

OBJECTIVES
- To understand how to use the conjunctions *than* or *as* to connect two clauses
- To recognize when to use a subject pronoun or an object pronoun in the second clause of a sentence using *than* or *as*

 **Maintenance**

Assign **Practice Book** page 20, Section 3.4. After students finish,
1. Give immediate feedback.
2. Review concepts as needed.
3. Model the correct answer.

Pages 4–5 of the **Answer Key** contain tips for Daily Maintenance.

WARM-UP

Have a male and a female student of different heights stand in front of the room. Have one student stand a few steps closer to the board and tell one student to smile. Then have the rest of the class write sentences comparing the students' heights, facial expressions, and distance from the board. Tell students their sentences must contain either the word *than* or *as*, and cannot contain the students' names. Have volunteers share and discuss their sentences with the class.

Read from a piece of writing that the class is currently reading. Emphasize the pronouns after *than* or *as*.

TEACH

Write the following sentence on the board:

He is taller than her.

Ask volunteers to read aloud the explanation of how to use pronouns that follow *than* or *as*. Survey the class by asking how many students think the sentence

on the board is correct. Then explain that part of the clause after *than her* has been omitted. Demonstrate this by adding *is tall* at the end of the sentence. Students can confirm that the pronoun *her* is incorrect. Remind students that they should use subject pronouns after *than* or *as*.

PRACTICE

EXERCISE 1
Point out that each pronoun has already been identified in the sentences. Have students determine to what each pronoun is being compared. Read each sentence aloud for students to hear

the language. Have them write their answers. Invite volunteers to share their answers and to discuss the comparison in each sentence.

EXERCISE 2
Tell students to be aware of the purpose of each pronoun in the sentence. Ask them to consider the following: *Is the pronoun being used as the subject of a clause? Is it being used as a direct object or an indirect object of a clause?* Ask partners to determine the correct pronouns. Then have small groups compare and explain their answers. Monitor the groups to make sure students are using pronouns correctly.

3.4 Pronouns After *Than* or *As*

The words *than* or *as* are used in comparisons. Often these conjunctions join two clauses.

> Jacob is as good a singer *as* she is.
> Teachers choose him for solos more often *than* they choose her.

Sometimes, however, part of the second clause is omitted. You may need to add the missing parts mentally to determine whether to use a subject pronoun or an object pronoun after *than* and *as*.

Study these examples. The words that can be omitted from the clauses are in brackets.

> Emily is a better dancer than *she* [is a good dancer].
> Emily's dancing impressed me more than [it impressed] *them*.

In the first sentence, the pronoun after *than* is the subject of the clause. So the correct pronoun is *she*—a subject pronoun. In the second sentence, the pronoun after *than* is the direct object of the verb *impressed*. So the correct pronoun is *them*—an object pronoun.

In sentences where either a subject or an object pronoun could be correct, it is important to express the comparison completely to avoid confusion.

> I've known Jacob longer than she [has known Jacob].
> I've known Jacob longer than [I've known] her.

As you come across sentences with *than* and *as*, remember to supply missing words mentally to check for correct pronoun usage.

EXERCISE 1 Identify the word to which the underlined pronoun is compared in each sentence.

1. The theater interests Rosa more than <u>me</u>.
2. Gordon has taken more dancing lessons than <u>she</u>.
3. Janice is a more experienced actress than <u>she</u>.
4. Ian has been in more plays than <u>I</u>.
5. Our drama teacher has chosen Diana for bigger parts than <u>her</u>.
6. Being onstage scares me more than <u>him</u>.
7. Will is as good a dancer as <u>he</u>.
8. The drama teacher has helped Lewis more than <u>him</u>.
9. Alicia memorizes lines faster than <u>they</u>.
10. Brian has tutored Lydia more than <u>her</u>.

Exercise 1
1. Rosa
2. Gordon
3. Janice
4. Ian
5. Diana
6. me
7. Will
8. Lewis
9. Alicia
10. Lydia

38 • Section 3.4

EXERCISE 3

Have students complete this activity independently. If students encounter any difficult sentences, have them add the missing part of the clause to the end of the sentence. Discuss any discrepancies as a class.

APPLY

APPLY IT NOW

Review students' sentences for correct pronoun usage. Direct students who appear to be having problems to complete the missing part of the clause first to determine the purpose of the pronoun in the sentence. You might choose to read selected sentences to the class as examples of proper usage. Students should demonstrate an understanding of pronouns after *than* or *as*.

ASSESS

Note which students had difficulty identifying how to use pronouns after *than* or *as*. Assign **Practice Book** page 27 for further practice.

> **WRITING CONNECTION**
>
> Use pages 266–267 of the Writing portion of the book.

TEACHING OPTIONS

Reteach

Invite the class to write a group critique comparing two stories or books the class has recently read. Encourage students to suggest sentences for the critique as you write them on poster board. Write some of the sentences correctly but write others with incorrect pronouns. Challenge students to watch as you write the sentences and to correct you as necessary.

Curriculum Connection

Invite students to make comparisons, using topics they are learning in other subjects. For example, in geography students might compare the size of countries or other landforms; in math students might compare measurements; in science students might compare animals. Have students write several sentences comparing ideas from other subjects. Review the sentences with the class to determine if the pronouns have been used properly.

EXERCISE 2 Choose the correct pronoun to complete each sentence.

1. Everyone is as excited about the drama club's new musical as (I me).
2. Elena has sold more tickets than (she her).
3. Elena's a good salesperson, so the drama teacher has given her more tickets to sell than (they them).
4. I have passed out more fliers to friends than (they them).
5. Carol knew her lines. During rehearsal, the teacher had to give Edward more help with lines than (she her).
6. Edward's singing impressed me as much as (she her). We had never heard him sing as well.
7. No one is as talented at singing and dancing as (she her).
8. The ending of the play surprised me as much as (they them)—there was a big gasp from the audience.
9. The play was as entertaining to me as it was to (she her).
10. No one worked harder than the drama coach, and no one was more pleased about the success of the play than (he him).

Exercise 3
1. walks
2. sing
3. swims
4. are good
5. am old
6. is proficient
7. finished
8. prepare
9. is witty
10. climbs
11. drove
12. skied
13. arrived
14. recognized the star
15. are fast

EXERCISE 3 Choose the correct pronoun to complete each sentence. Then tell the word or words that have been omitted from each sentence.

1. Evelyn walks more quickly than (she her).
2. Dustin sings better than (I me).
3. Sasha swims as fast as (he him).
4. That band is as good as (we us).
5. Juan is older than (I me).
6. I hope to be as proficient as (she her).
7. Ben finished his homework before (I me).
8. She prepares her work better than (I me)
9. Darnell is not so witty as (he him).
10. Antonio climbs as well as (she her).
11. He drove no faster than (we us).
12. Sarita skied down a steeper trail than (she her).
13. I arrived at the movies before (he him).
14. Ed recognized the star sooner than (she her).
15. Our sprinters are faster than (they them).

APPLY IT NOW

Write seven sentences in which you compare skills of famous athletes and entertainers. Use *than* and *as* followed by personal pronouns.

Pronouns • 39

3.5 Possessive Pronouns and Adjectives

OBJECTIVES

- **To identify and understand how to use possessive pronouns**
- **To recognize the difference between possessive pronouns and possessive adjectives**

 **Maintenance**

Assign **Practice Book** page 21, Section 3.5. After students finish,
1. Give immediate feedback.
2. Review concepts as needed.
3. Model the correct answer.

Pages 4–5 of the **Answer Key** contain tips for Daily Maintenance.

WARM-UP

Walk around the room, asking students specific questions such as these:

Is your name Joe?

Whose pencil is this?

Have students answer these questions with complete sentences. *(No, my name is Brad.)* Ask these questions to several students. Then discuss the word *possession* and what it means to each student.

📖 Read from a piece of writing that the class is currently reading. Emphasize the possessive pronouns and adjectives.

TEACH

Ask several students to hold up objects that are at or near their desks. Make statements about the objects, using possessive pronouns. For example:

This pen is yours.

This classroom is ours.

Challenge students to identify which words are pronouns. Then have volunteers read aloud the explanations about possessive pronouns. Pause before the

paragraph about possessive adjectives to review the previous information.

Have a volunteer read aloud the sentences that have examples of possessive pronouns. Have another volunteer read aloud the examples of possessive adjectives. Encourage students to explain how these possessives differ.

PRACTICE

EXERCISE 1

Have students complete the exercise independently. Then let them work with a partner to compare answers. Encourage students to discuss their answers

if they differ. Help students reach conclusions about the correct answers.

EXERCISE 2

Remind students that an antecedent is the noun to which a pronoun refers. Have students work on the exercise independently. Discuss students' answers.

EXERCISE 3

Invite a volunteer to read aloud the paragraph above the chart on page 40, which defines possessive pronouns. After students rewrite the sentences, invite volunteers to write on the board the corrected sentences. Review the sentences

---

3.5 Possessive Pronouns and Adjectives

Possessive pronouns show possession, or ownership. They take the place of possessive nouns.

> The paints are *Jerome's*. (possessive noun)
> The paints are *his*. (possessive pronoun)

Possessive pronouns change in form to indicate person, number, and gender. Make sure possessive pronouns agree with their antecedents. Be careful of the spelling. Unlike possessive nouns, possessive pronouns do not contain apostrophes. Study the chart.

POSSESSIVE PRONOUNS	SINGULAR	PLURAL
FIRST PERSON	mine	ours
SECOND PERSON	yours	yours
THIRD PERSON	his, hers, its	theirs

Possessive pronouns have the same roles in sentences as nouns do.

> **Hers** is the large painting. (subject)
> That sculpture is *his*. (subject complement)
> Have you seen *mine*? (direct object)

Words similar to possessive pronouns are possessive adjectives. The possessive adjectives are *my, our, your, his, her, its,* and *their*. Possessive pronouns stand alone. **Possessive adjectives** always precede the nouns they modify.

POSSESSIVE PRONOUNS	POSSESSIVE ADJECTIVES
Mine is on that wall.	*My* painting is on that wall.
Hers is beautiful.	*Her* ceramic pot is beautiful.

EXERCISE 1 Identify the possessive pronoun or possessive adjective in each sentence. Identify the noun each possessive adjective modifies.

1. The art department was organizing <u>its</u> annual art show. (art show)
2. Entrants could submit watercolors, ceramics, sculptures, and so on; the choice of medium was <u>theirs</u>.
3. Even <u>our</u> teachers could enter the show. (teachers)

Exercise 1
Possessive pronouns are underlined once. Possessive adjectives are underlined twice.

40 • Section 3.5

to make sure they are correct and ask students to explain their corrections.

EXERCISE 4

Read the sentences to the class. Ask volunteers for possible answers. Discuss any discrepancies.

APPLY

APPLY IT NOW

Encourage students who do not have siblings to imagine that they have taken a classmate's book by mistake. Have students circle each possessive pronoun and possessive adjective they used.

Students should demonstrate an understanding of possessive pronouns and possessive adjectives.

ASSESS

Note which students had difficulty identifying possessive pronouns and possessive adjectives. Assign **Practice Book** pages 28–29 for further practice.

WRITING CONNECTION

Use pages 268–269 of the Writing portion of the book.

Use pages 268–269 of the Writing portion of the book.

Assign **Practice Book** pages 28–29 for further practice.

EXERCISE 2 Complete the sentences with possessive pronouns. The pronoun should refer to the underlined antecedent.

1. <u>Raphael</u> likes to work with clay. That clay sculpture of a basketball player shooting a basket must be ___his___.
2. I know <u>Jill</u> submitted an acrylic piece. Do you think that the picture with the big colorful fruit is ___hers___?
3. Did <u>you</u> decide to do a collage? Is the collage with pictures from magazines ___yours___?
4. <u>Yolanda and Michael</u> decided to work together. I think the sculpture made from old bicycle wheels is ___theirs___.
5. <u>Lila</u> does wonderfully detailed pencil drawings. I'm sure that drawing of a cactus is ___hers___.

Exercise 3
1. A panel of students and teachers is judging the prizewinners. That difficult decision is theirs.
2. Everyone was impressed by Jill's painting, so no one was surprised when the top prize became hers.
3. The eighth-grade teacher's pencil portrait of her mother earned her a special prize.
4. The pieces of artwork from the show now hang throughout the school. Ours are in the library.

Exercise 4
Answers will vary.

EXERCISE 3 Rewrite the sentences so that the use of possessive pronouns and possessive adjectives is correct.

1. A panel of students and teachers is judging the prizewinners. That difficult decision is their's.
2. Everyone was impressed by Jill's painting. So no one was surprised when the top prize became hers'.
3. The eighth-grade teacher's pencil portrait of hers mother earned her a special prize.
4. The pieces of artwork from the show now hang throughout the school. Ours' are in the library.

EXERCISE 4 Complete the sentences with appropriate possessive pronouns.

1. That blue sweater is not _____.
2. Take _____ but leave _____.
3. _____ is not as warm as _____.
4. The book is _____ but that is _____.
5. Mr. Rodriguez sold _____.
6. _____ ran away.
7. The umbrella with the purple stripes is _____.
8. Someone stole _____.
9. _____ was left on the beach.

APPLY IT NOW

Imagine that you took your brother's or sister's books to school and your brother or sister took yours. In 10 sentences, explain how this happened. Use at least three possessive pronouns to keep your writing from becoming repetitive.

Pronouns • 41

TEACHING OPTIONS

Reteach

Gather magazine articles on which students can write. Distribute the articles and ask students to circle the possessive pronouns and possessive adjectives. As you check students' work, encourage them to explain the difference between possessive nouns and possessive adjectives.

Meeting Individual Needs

Auditory Help students come up with sentences to practice using possessive pronouns and possessive adjectives. Invite each student to choose an object in the classroom to speak about. Have students say sentences about the object, first using a possessive adjective and then using a possessive pronoun. For example:

This is my book. It is mine.

This is her book. It is hers.

This is our book. It is ours.

This is your book. It is yours.

This is their book. It is theirs.

This is his book. It is his.

Meeting Individual Needs

Extra Support Write the possessive pronouns and the possessive adjectives on individual note cards. Place the cards in a stack and have partners choose a card. Tell students to write several sentences using their pronoun or adjective. Review partners' sentences with the class to confirm that they are correct.

OBJECTIVE

- To identify and distinguish between intensive and reflexive pronouns

 **Maintenance**

Assign **Practice Book** page 21, Section 3.6. After students finish,
1. Give immediate feedback.
2. Review concepts as needed.
3. Model the correct answer.

Pages 4–5 of the **Answer Key** contain tips for Daily Maintenance.

WARM-UP

Write on the board the word *self*. Then perform an action such as tossing a pencil up in the air and catching it. Have half the class write a sentence about the action you performed that contains *self*. *(The teacher threw the pencil to himself.)* Have the other half write a sentence that does not contain *self*. Ask students to share their sentences. Briefly discuss the examples. Then ask the class how *self* functions in a sentence.

Read from a piece of writing that the class is currently reading. Emphasize the intensive and reflexive pronouns.

TEACH

Ask students to name words that end in *self* or *selves*. List their responses on the board *(myself, himself, herself, yourself, itself, themselves, yourselves, ourselves)*. Tell students that these words are pronouns. Encourage volunteers to take turns reading the intensive and reflexive pronouns sections. Discuss how the two types of pronouns differ. Challenge students to use the pronouns in sentences.

PRACTICE

EXERCISE 1

Review that an antecedent is a noun that a pronoun replaces to avoid repetition. Have partners identify the intensive or reflexive pronoun in each sentence. Encourage students to determine the antecedent to which the pronoun refers. Then review students' answers with the class.

EXERCISE 2

Allow students to refer to the chart of intensive and reflexive pronouns to confirm their answers. Then have volunteers share their pronouns. Discuss any discrepancies with the class.

EXERCISE 3

Challenge students to complete this exercise independently. Invite volunteers to write on the board their completed sentences. Discuss the answers as a class. Have students identify the antecedent in each sentence.

3.6 Intensive and Reflexive Pronouns

Intensive pronouns and reflexive pronouns end in *self* or *selves*.

An **intensive pronoun** is used to emphasize a preceding noun or pronoun.

> I *myself* researched family vacation spots on the Internet.
> My mother *herself* was surprised at all the information I found.

A **reflexive pronoun** is usually the object of a verb or a preposition. The reflexive pronoun refers back to the subject of the clause or sentence.

> I enjoyed *myself* at the cabin. (direct object)
> They cooked *themselves* meals over an outdoor grill. (indirect object)
> My mother packed the car by *herself*. (object of a preposition)

The chart shows forms of intensive and reflexive pronouns. These pronouns should agree with their antecedents in person, number, and gender.

INTENSIVE AND REFLEXIVE PRONOUNS	SINGULAR	PLURAL
FIRST PERSON	myself	ourselves
SECOND PERSON	yourself	yourselves
THIRD PERSON	himself herself itself	themselves

Note that *hisself* and *theirselves* are not good usage. What words from the chart would you use instead of those words? You are correct if you said *himself* and *themselves*.

It is also incorrect to use forms with *self* instead of subject and object pronouns.

> Edward and I (*not* myself) don't know how to swim.
> The meal was made by Hans and me. (*not* myself)

> Grandpa and you (*not* yourself) are great pals.
> Grandpa relies on Maya and you. (*not* yourself)

APPLY

APPLY IT NOW

Remind students that when they write about their experiences, they are writing in the first person or from the first person point of view. Tell students they will probably use the pronoun *myself* often. Challenge students to include other people in their descriptions to practice using other intensive and reflexive pronouns. Students should demonstrate an understanding of intensive and reflexive pronouns.

TechTip Have students review and critique one another's work. You may wish to post the reviews on a class blog for the authors to see and use for revisions.

ASSESS

Note which students had difficulty identifying intensive and reflexive pronouns. Assign **Practice Book** page 30 for further practice.

WRITING CONNECTION

Use pages 270–271 of the Writing portion of the book.

Reteach

Write the intensive and reflexive pronouns on note cards, one per card. You will need enough cards for the whole class, so write each pronoun on several different cards. Give one card to each student. Tell students to listen closely as you say sentences, pausing where a pronoun needs to be included. Ask students whose cards have the pronoun that fits the sentence to hold up their cards. Check the cards to make sure that all the words on the cards are correct. Discuss any differences of opinion about the correct pronoun for each sentence. After completing several sentences, have students trade cards. Then continue with additional sentences.

Meeting Individual Needs

Auditory Encourage students to include intensive and reflexive pronouns in a class discussion. For example, if the class is discussing a novel that students are reading, students might say "I myself found this part exciting. The characters themselves were very resourceful." You might make the activity a game, keeping score by noting the times each student includes an intensive or a reflexive pronoun in a sentence.

Meeting Individual Needs

Intrapersonal Encourage students to reflect on the day, infusing their writing with intensive and reflexive pronouns. Explain that students do not need to include these words every time they write but that for this journal entry, you would like them to practice using intensive and reflexive pronouns.

Exercise 1
1. themselves, parents
2. ourselves, we
3. myself, I
4. himself, father
5. itself, lake

EXERCISE 1 Identify the intensive or reflexive pronoun in each sentence. Then identify its antecedent.

1. My parents decided on our vacation plans for this year themselves—with the help of my cousins' family.
2. As we prepared ourselves for the vacation, we wondered how we would get along with our cousins for a month.
3. I packed my suitcase myself, but I knew I had forgotten something.
4. My father drove most of the way to the lake himself.
5. The lake itself was beautiful, though the mountains were rather barren.

EXERCISE 2 Complete each sentence with an intensive or a reflexive pronoun. The pronoun should refer to the underlined antecedent.

1. We treated ourselves to the rental of a sailboat.
2. My older sister proved herself to be a good skipper.
3. I myself learned a little about handling the boat.
4. Our parents themselves informed us about safety rules.

Exercise 3
Antecedents are underlined.

EXERCISE 3 Complete each sentence with an intensive or a reflexive pronoun. Then identify its antecedent.

1. Maya blamed herself for the misunderstanding.
2. Josh cut himself on a piece of the broken ketchup bottle.
3. Every woman must answer for herself.
4. The firefighters themselves could not find the source of the smoke.
5. Levi himself had been hiking in the forest that afternoon.
6. You yourself heard the judge's verdict.
7. The fugitives hid themselves from the sheriff.
8. We ourselves were responsible for the broken window.
9. Kim's turtle hid itself behind a pile of stuffed animals.
10. You and your classmates disagreed among yourselves.
11. I myself made the birdhouse.
12. Louis XIV called himself the Sun King.

APPLY IT NOW

Describe a project you have undertaken that proved to be more than you had expected. Use two intensive and reflexive pronouns in your description.

TechTip Post your description on a class blog or wiki.

Pronouns • 43

3.7 Agreement of Pronouns and Antecedents

OBJECTIVE

- To recognize that a pronoun must agree with its antecedent in person, number, and gender

 **Maintenance**

Assign **Practice Book** page 21, Section 3.7. After students finish,

1. Give immediate feedback.
2. Review concepts as needed.
3. Model the correct answer.

Pages 4–5 of the **Answer Key** contain tips for Daily Maintenance.

WARM-UP

Give each student a note card. Have half the class write a noun on their card. Encourage some students to write plural nouns and some to write proper nouns to be sure that a variety of nouns are written. Have the other half write object pronouns on their cards. Then have each noun student find the pronoun that matches his or her noun and stand next to that student. Discuss any incorrect pairings.

Read from a piece of writing that the class is currently reading. Emphasize the agreement of pronouns and antecedents.

TEACH

Say these sentences to the class: *Maya Angelou is a well-loved poet. He has written many wonderful poems.* Ask students to explain what is wrong with the sentences and confirm that the pronoun *he* does not match, or agree with, the noun that it refers to, *Maya Angelou.* Remind students that a correctly chosen pronoun agrees with its antecedent in person, number, and gender.

Invite students to take turns reading aloud the explanation of agreement of pronouns and antecedents. Ask students to offer sentences using correct agreement between pronouns and antecedents.

PRACTICE

EXERCISE 1

Tell students that they should identify only those pronouns that refer to the underlined words. When students have finished, read each sentence aloud and invite a volunteer to explain the pronoun or pronouns he or she identified. Encourage the rest of the class to discuss the answer.

EXERCISE 2

Have partners identify the underlined pronouns and their antecedents. Invite partners to share their answers with the class.

EXERCISE 3

Challenge students to complete this exercise independently. Encourage students to question whether the pronoun fits the rules for its place in the sentence. Suggest questions such as these: *Is it the subject of the sentence? Is it a direct object? Does it agree with its antecedent?* Invite volunteers to share their answers and discuss why each pronoun is correct.

3.7 Agreement of Pronouns and Antecedents

The word to which a pronoun refers is called its **antecedent.** Pronouns agree with their antecedents in person, number, and gender. You need to make sure you use the correct person, number, and gender when you replace a noun or a pronoun with another pronoun.

> *Lloyd Alexander* wrote *Time Cat*, and *he* has written several other fantasy books.

The antecedent of the subject pronoun *he* is *Lloyd Alexander,* so the third person singular masculine form is used.

In the following, what is the antecedent of *he*? of *her*?

> *Lloyd Alexander* wrote about *Vesper Holly.* He places her in exciting and dangerous situations.

You are correct if you answered *Lloyd Alexander* for the antecedent of *he*. The subject pronoun *he* is third person singular masculine. The antecedent of *her* is *Vesper Holly.* The object pronoun *her* is third person singular feminine to agree with its antecedent.

Mark Twain

EXERCISE 1 Identify the pronoun or pronouns that refer to each underlined antecedent.

1. <u>Readers</u> are interested in time travel, and many books on this topic will appeal to <u>them</u>.
2. Mark Twain is probably best known for his books set near the <u>Mississippi</u>, but he also wrote books set far from <u>it</u>—in other times and places.
3. Twain's <u>novel</u> *A Connecticut Yankee in King Arthur's Court* is set in the year AD 528, and <u>it</u> is, in fact, a time-travel book.
4. <u>Hank Morgan</u>, the main character, travels to the past, where <u>he</u> uses his knowledge of 19th-century technology to get <u>himself</u> a good life and even a place at the Round Table itself.
5. <u>Twain</u> uses the book to critique the society of <u>his</u> time, and yet <u>he</u> makes readers laugh at the humorous situations that befall the main character.

EXERCISE 4
Read each sentence aloud. Discuss possible answers as a class.

APPLY

APPLY IT NOW
Encourage students to be creative as they write. Suggest that they choose an era that interests or inspires them. Challenge students to let their imaginations take over. When their stories are completed, remind students to identify the pronouns and their antecedents. Students should demonstrate an understanding of agreement of pronouns and antecedents.

Grammar in Action. The pronoun antecedents are *sap* and *scum*. Ask students to identify which pronoun replaces each antecedent. (*It* replaces *sap, and* that *replaces* scum.)

ASSESS

Note which students had difficulty with agreement of pronouns and antecedents. Assign **Practice Book** page 31 for further practice.

WRITING CONNECTION
Use pages 272–273 of the Writing portion of the book.

Exercise 2
1. first person singular
2. third person singular neuter
3. third person singular neuter
4. third person singular masculine
5. third person singular masculine
6. first person plural
7. third person plural

EXERCISE 2 Identify the antecedent for each underlined pronoun. Then tell the person, number, and, as appropriate, gender of that antecedent.

1. I have a book to recommend, a favorite of <u>mine</u>.
2. The <u>book</u> is about time travel, and <u>it</u> entertains from start to finish.
3. The <u>title</u> is *Time Cat,* and the title <u>itself</u> describes the content.
4. <u>Gareth</u>, a cat who lives in the present, has the ability to travel into the past, where <u>he</u> has adventures at different times in history.
5. <u>Gareth</u> takes his master, Jason, with <u>him</u>.
6. <u>Gareth</u> and <u>Jason</u> travel to nine different times and places, and <u>they</u> experience everyday life in each.
7. The <u>adventures</u> they have are so much fun that I forgot I was actually learning from <u>them</u>.

EXERCISE 3 Complete each sentence with the appropriate pronoun. Make sure your choice agrees with its antecedent in person, number, and, where appropriate, gender.

1. Ms. Chaplin, our social studies teacher, has made an assignment that, ___she___ said, is completely different from her usual ones.
2. We are to write a story, and ___it___ is to be set in a time and place we've learned about in class.
3. She ___herself___ will do the assignment along with us.
4. I've spoken to some students, and ___they___ told me that they plan to do a lot of research.
5. Some students have chosen their periods, and I've chosen ___mine___—the colonial period in America.

EXERCISE 4 Complete each sentence with a possessive pronoun that agrees with its antecedent.

1. Brian has finished ___his___ dinner and is now clearing the table.
2. Janet is going to the movies, and Phillip is going with ___her___.
3. The clean-up crew finished early because one of the teams helped ___them___.
4. We could not take any of the kittens into ___our___ home until the vet had checked them.

APPLY IT NOW
Imagine you have received the assignment described in Exercise 3. Describe the period in history that you would use as your setting and tell why you chose it. Underline all the pronouns and circle their antecedents.

Grammar in Action. Identify pronoun antecedents in the last paragraph of the p. 261 excerpt.

Pronouns • 45

3.8 Interrogative and Demonstrative Pronouns

 **Maintenance**

Assign **Practice Book** page 21, Section 3.8. After students finish,
1. Give immediate feedback.
2. Review concepts as needed.
3. Model the correct answer.

Pages 4–5 of the **Answer Key** contain tips for Daily Maintenance.

WARM-UP

Tell students to place an object on their desk. Have partners ask each other questions about the object. *(Who bought that pen?)* Tell students to answer the questions. List the words that begin each sentence on the board *(who, whom, whose, which, what, this, that, those, these)*.

📖 Read from a piece of writing that the class is currently reading. Emphasize interrogative and demonstrative pronouns.

TEACH

Write on the board the following sentences:

Who wrote this book?

What is this book about?

Which is your favorite character?

Ask students what these sentences have in common. Confirm that they are all questions. Then ask students if they see any pronouns in the sentences. Circle the pronouns *Who, What,* and *Which*. Explain that these pronouns ask a question. Ask students if they can think of any other words that ask questions *(whom, whose).*

Then invite volunteers to take turns reading about interrogative pronouns.

After discussing interrogative pronouns, invite volunteers to read the demonstrative pronouns section. Encourage students to explain the difference between *this* and *these* and between *that* and *those*. Challenge students to use these words in sentences, referring to a book they have read in class. *(This book is my favorite. I didn't like that book as much. Those characters were boring. These characters came alive for me.)*

PRACTICE

EXERCISES 1 & 2
Tell students that the sentences in these exercises ask questions. Review the interrogative pronouns. Then have students complete the sentences independently. Discuss the answers with the class, clarifying any confusion students may have.

EXERCISE 3
Ask students what the directions mean by "Be sure to use the correct number." After students offer ideas, remind students that pronouns can be singular or plural. Point out that in the

---

3.8 Interrogative and Demonstrative Pronouns

Interrogative pronouns are used to ask questions. The interrogative pronouns are *who, whom, whose, which,* and *what.*

Who refers to persons. It is often the subject of a question.

> **Who visited New York?** (subject)

Whom refers to persons. It is the object of a verb or a preposition.

> **Whom did you visit there?** (direct object)
> **With whom did you go on the trip?** (object of a preposition)

Whose is used when asking about possession. *Which* is used when asking about a group or class. *What* is used for asking about things and seeking information.

> **Whose are those photos of New York?**
> **Which of the other states would you like to visit?**
> **What did you take with you on your trip?**

What is the error in the sentence below?

> **Who did you show your photos to?**

The interrogative pronoun must be in the object form because it is the object of the preposition *to.* Therefore, *whom* is the correct choice.

Exercise 1
1. Who
2. What
3. Which
4. Which
5. What
6. Who
7. whom
8. whom
9. Who
10. What

The **demonstrative pronouns** point out a particular person, place, or thing. They are *this, that, these,* and *those.*

> **This is a picture of a historic skyscraper.** (near)
> **That is a picture of my grandmother with whom I stayed.** (far)
> **These are some souvenirs I bought.** (near)
> **Those are presents for you.** (far)

EXERCISE 1 Complete each question with an interrogative pronoun.

1. _____ has ever visited Arizona?
2. _____ are some of the sights you can see there?
3. _____ of the cities did you visit?
4. _____ of the Native American nations have lived in Arizona?
5. _____ were the various types of Native American dwellings?

sentences, antecedents, as well as the verb, help determine the correct pronoun. Explain that the singular pronoun *this* will have a singular verb, such as *is* and that the plural pronoun *these* will have a plural verb, such as *are*. Have students work with partners to choose the correct pronouns. Then discuss students' answers.

APPLY

APPLY IT NOW

Encourage students to think about a state they would like to visit. As they write, remind students to consider which pronoun best fits each question.

TechTip Most states have .gov sites with rich resources for further reading about state histories and indigenous cultures.

ASSESS

Note which students had difficulty with interrogative and demonstrative pronouns. Assign **Practice Book** pages 32–33 for further practice.

WRITING CONNECTION

Use pages 274–275 of the Writing portion of the book.

Reteach

Review the uses of interrogative and demonstrative pronouns. Then provide groups with short stories or novels and have students find sentences that use each interrogative pronoun and each demonstrative pronoun. Instruct students to copy the sentences onto note cards, one sentence per card. As students work, prepare a bulletin-board display with a heading for each pronoun: *Who, Whom, Whose, Which, What, This, That, These,* and *Those.* Direct each group to place their cards under the applicable headings. Discuss the sentences, pointing out the agreement in number.

Meeting Individual Needs

Logical Make statements and challenge students to form questions with interrogative pronouns. For example:

> **Geography is my favorite subject. Which is your favorite subject?**

> **Ernest Hemingway wrote many short stories.**
> **Who wrote many short stories?**
> **What did Ernest Hemingway write?**

Invite students to write their questions as a way to reinforce interrogative pronoun use. For demonstrative pronouns, point to objects (plural and singular, near and far) for students to identify: this book, those encyclopedias; this globe, that map.

---

6. _____ was instrumental in preserving the ancient ruins?

7. By _____ was the area ruled in the 1600s?

8. From _____ was the area of Arizona purchased for the United States?

9. _____ are some famous Arizonians?

10. _____ is the best time of the year to visit Arizona?

Exercise 2
1. Who
2. whom
3. Who
4. whom
5. Who
6. whom
7. Whom
8. Who

EXERCISE 2 Complete each sentence with *who* or *whom*.

1. _____ is the first settler to explore Arizona?

2. By _____ were you told?

3. _____ do you think built ruins?

4. With _____ did you come to the presentation?

5. _____ brought the tortillas?

6. For _____ are these remarks intended?

7. _____ should we invite on our canyon hike?

8. _____ can it be?

Exercise 3
1. These
2. that
3. This, that
4. those
5. these
6. those
7. These
8. that
9. That
10. These

EXERCISE 3 Complete each sentence by adding the correct demonstrative pronoun. Use the directions in parentheses. Be sure to use the correct number.

1. _____ (near) are some examples of Native American art from Arizona.

2. What kind of doll is _____ (far)?

3. _____ (near) is a kachina doll. And so is _____ (far).

4. Are _____ (far) special kinds of dolls?

5. Yes, in Hopi culture, _____ (near) represent spirits that visit a village to help people live in harmony with nature.

6. What are _____ (far)—the round objects with feathers?

7. _____ (near) are dream catchers. According to Navajo legend, they capture bad dreams and let good dreams pass.

8. What is _____ (far) on the silver bracelet?

9. _____ (far) is a piece of turquoise. It's a traditional gemstone in jewelry of the Southwest.

10. _____ (near) are all fascinating objects with interesting stories.

APPLY IT NOW

Write seven questions about a state that interests you, using at least three different interrogative pronouns. Then find the answers to your own questions.

Tech Tip With an adult, research your state online.

Pronouns • 47

3.9 Relative Pronouns

OBJECTIVE

- To identify and use the relative pronouns *who, whom, that, whose,* and *which*

 **Maintenance**

Assign **Practice Book** page 22, Section 3.9. After students finish,
1. Give immediate feedback.
2. Review concepts as needed.
3. Model the correct answer.

Pages 4–5 of the **Answer Key** contain tips for Daily Maintenance.

WARM-UP

Write on the board the following sentence:

> The teacher uses books are big and heavy.

Ask students what is missing from this sentence. Encourage students to tell what function the missing word plays in the sentence.

📖 Read from a piece of writing that the class is currently reading. Emphasize the relative pronouns.

TEACH

Write the following sentences on the board for students to analyze:

> I sent a letter to my friend who lives in Colorado.

> The grass that was recently mowed smells wonderful.

Challenge students to tell you which part of the sentence is the independent clause and which part is the dependent clause. As students offer ideas, edit the sentences until only the main subject and verb of each remain.

> I sent a letter to my friend.

> The grass smells wonderful.

Point out that the remaining words form the independent clause of each sentence. Explain that the removed words form the dependent clause. Then ask students which words connect the independent and dependent clauses *(who, that).* Explain that these connecting words are relative pronouns. Then invite students to take turns reading about relative pronouns. Pause after each example to discuss the sentence.

PRACTICE

EXERCISE 1

Encourage partners to identify the relative pronoun and antecedent in each sentence. Then ask volunteers to write the sentences on the board. Have students circle the relative pronoun and underline its antecedent. Check students' work for accuracy.

EXERCISE 2

Challenge students to determine the function of the pronoun in each dependent clause *(subject, direct object, indirect object, object of a preposition).* Have students complete the exercise independently. Then discuss students' answers.

EXERCISE 3

Have students complete the exercise independently. Discuss the correct answers as a class.

3.9 Relative Pronouns

A **relative pronoun** is used to join a dependent clause to its antecedent in the independent clause. The relative pronouns are *who, whom, that, whose,* and *which.*

> The Chinese use certain medical treatments *that* are not common practices in the West.

The relative pronoun *that* joins the dependent clause—*that are not common practices in the West*—to the independent clause—*The Chinese use certain medical treatments.* The antecedent of *that* is *treatments.*

The relative pronouns *who* and *whom* refer to persons.

> The Chinese, *who* have one of the world's oldest civilizations, have a written history going back more than 3,500 years.

The relative pronoun *that* refers to people, animals, places, or things. The relative pronoun *whose* often refers to people but also can refer to animals, places, or things. The relative pronoun *which* refers to animals, places, or things.

> People *that* the Chinese influenced included the Koreans.
> The Chinese, *whose* civilization is ancient, developed paper first.
> Chinese culture, *which* was respected, influenced many other cultures throughout Asia.

Which of the following is correct?

> People *who* the Chinese influenced included the Japanese.
> People *whom* the Chinese influenced included the Japanese.

The second sentence is correct. The relative pronoun is the direct object in the dependent clause, so the object form *whom* is correct. Use *who* when the relative pronoun is the subject in a dependent clause. Use *whom* when the relative pronoun is an object in a dependent clause—a direct object, an indirect object, or an object of a preposition.

> Other Asians, *who* admired the Chinese, adopted aspects of Chinese language and culture. (subject)
> The Chinese, for *whom* acupuncture is a common practice, use medical treatments different from those in the West. (object of a preposition)

48 • Section 3.9

APPLY

APPLY IT NOW

Write on a sheet of poster board the heading *Relative Pronouns in Action*. Invite students to share their annotated sentences with the class. Then invite students to arrange their sentences on the poster board to create a relative-pronouns collage. Students should demonstrate an understanding of relative pronouns.

Grammar in Action. The relative pronoun on page 260 is *which*. Point out that although *which* is preceded by a semi-colon, it is still a relative pronoun. Ask students to identify the dependent clause that begins with *which (which being properly accommodated with a tail, loop, and string)*. Then ask students to identify what the dependent clause modifies *(kite)*.

ASSESS

Note which students had difficulty identifying relative pronouns. Assign **Practice Book** pages 34–35 for further practice.

WRITING CONNECTION

Use pages 276–277 of the Writing portion of the book.

TEACHING OPTIONS

Reteach

Encourage students to talk about other subjects they are studying, using sentences that include dependent clauses and relative pronouns. Write students' sentences on the board and help students analyze the sentences to determine whether the relative pronouns have been used correctly. Suggest additional sentences to analyze for their clauses, relative pronouns, and antecedents.

Meeting Individual Needs

Extra Support Write on the board the sentence pairs that follow. Help students combine the sentences, using the relative pronouns in parentheses. Discuss the relationship between the relative pronouns and their antecedents.

I met the author. The author wrote the best seller. (who)
(I met the author who wrote the best seller.)

This is the bicycle. The bicycle was on sale last week. (that)
(This is the bicycle that was on sale last week.)

This is the neighbor. I bought the puppy from the neighbor. (whom)
(This is the neighbor from whom I bought the puppy.)

Exercise 1
Relative pronouns are underlined twice. Antecedents are underlined once.

EXERCISE 1 Identify each relative pronoun. Then find its antecedent.

1. The Chinese use medical procedures that rely on the body's natural ability to heal itself.
2. Many Westerners also believe in this approach, which is thousands of years old.
3. In the 12th century, Chinese medical information was written down in a huge volume that Chinese practitioners still use today.
4. Anyone who is treated by a Chinese practitioner has probably received acupuncture.
5. The patient is treated with fine needles that are used for pain relief and other therapeutic purposes.
6. They are inserted in areas of the body called meridians, which are considered channels of energy in the body.

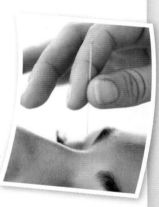

Exercise 2
1. who, subject
2. whom, object of a preposition
3. who, subject
4. who, subject
5. whom, direct object

EXERCISE 2 Complete each sentence with *who* or *whom*. Then tell how that pronoun functions in the dependent clause.

1. Herbal medicine is popular with people _____ live in the West.
2. Usually, herbal treatments are specially selected for the patient to _____ they are prescribed.
3. Patients typically give detailed case histories to practitioners _____ specialize in herbal medicine.
4. Many of the people _____ practice herbal medicine follow ancient Chinese traditions.
5. A naturopathic doctor is someone _____ you might consult about herbal remedies.

Exercise 3
Answers will vary.

EXERCISE 3 Add dependent clauses that begin with relative pronouns where indicated in the following sentences.

1. Mr. Li, (dependent clause), studies the art of combining medicinal herbs.
2. Special herbs, (dependent clause), help ease his patients of their pain.
3. The Chinese, (dependent clause), commonly use herbs such as ginseng and licorice.

APPLY IT NOW

Look in magazines and newspapers for five sentences containing relative pronouns. For each, underline the dependent clause, circle the relative pronoun, and draw an arrow from that pronoun to its antecedent.

Grammar in Action. Identify the relative pronoun in the p. 260 excerpt.

Pronouns • 49

3.10 Indefinite Pronouns

OBJECTIVE
- **To identify indefinite pronouns**

 **Maintenance**

Assign **Practice Book** page 22, Section 3.10. After students finish,
1. Give immediate feedback.
2. Review concepts as needed.
3. Model the correct answer.

Pages 4–5 of the **Answer Key** contain tips for Daily Maintenance.

WARM-UP

Write the following words on large sheets of paper: *any, every, some, body, one, thing*. Give these seven sheets to different students. Have students holding *body, one,* and *thing* stand in the front of the room. Have the student holding *any* stand next to the student holding *body*. Have both students hold up their sheets. Ask students to write the word that is formed. Have the student holding *any* repeat with *one* and *thing*. Repeat the entire process for *every* and *some*. List on the board the words formed. Ask students how these words are used in writing.

📖 Read from a piece of writing that the class is currently reading. Emphasize the indefinite pronouns.

TEACH

Invite volunteers to read aloud the indefinite pronouns section. Ask students if they are familiar with these words. Read the list of indefinite pronouns. Assign a word to each student, and challenge the student to provide a sentence for that word, using it as a pronoun.

Have a volunteer look up the meaning of the word *indefinite* (*not precise, vague*). Then discuss why these pronouns are called indefinite pronouns. Remind students that some of these words

can also be used as adjectives. Ask a volunteer to explain how to tell the difference. *(A pronoun replaces a noun; an adjective modifies a noun.)*

PRACTICE

EXERCISE 1
Suggest that students complete this exercise, using the chart on top of the page. Point out that the words appear in alphabetical order and that if students question whether a word is an indefinite pronoun, they can look for the word in the list. Let students work independently. Then discuss students' answers as a class.

EXERCISE 2
Tell students that as they search for indefinite pronouns, they will come across other pronouns. Have students create a two-column chart—one column for indefinite pronouns, another for other pronouns. Have students use the chart to list the pronouns they find. Read aloud the sentences and have volunteers name the pronouns and identify the function of each.

EXERCISE 3
Ask volunteers to read aloud their sentences for each indefinite pronoun. Discuss these sentences as a class.

3.10 Indefinite Pronouns

An **indefinite pronoun** refers to any or all of a group of people, places, or things.

SINGULAR		PLURAL	SINGULAR AND PLURAL
another	neither	both	all
anybody	nobody	few	any
anyone	no one	many	more
anything	nothing	others	most
each	one	several	none
either	other		some
everybody	somebody		
everyone	someone		
everything	something		
much			

Like nouns, indefinite pronouns act as subjects and objects.

Many **have visited the Rock and Roll Hall of Fame and Museum.** (subject)

I read *something* **about the museum online.** (direct object)

I hadn't heard of *either* **of those musicians.** (object of a preposition)

She was the *one* **who sang the anthem.** (subject complement)

Some of these words can also be used as adjectives.

Many **musicians are in the Rock and Roll Hall of Fame.**

Many is an adjective that modifies the noun *musicians*.

Rock and Roll Hall of Fame and Museum

EXERCISE 1 Identify the indefinite pronouns in these sentences. Not every sentence contains an indefinite pronoun.

1. Few may know that the Rock and Roll Hall of Fame and Museum is fairly new; it was opened in Cleveland in 1995.
2. Someone had the idea for a Rock and Roll Hall of Fame in the 1980s.
3. Its purpose was to honor musicians and others who had contributed to rock-and-roll history.
4. All of those in the hall are acknowledged "greats."
5. Several are elected to the Rock Hall annually as new members.
6. A panel of 1,000 rock-and-roll experts choose them.
7. A big contribution to rock and roll was made by each.
8. The Hall of Fame building impresses everyone.

Exercise 1
1. Few
2. Someone
3. others
4. All
5. Several
6. no indefinite pronoun
7. each
8. everyone
9. no indefinite pronoun
10. Many
11. Each
12. no indefinite pronoun
13. few
14. someone

APPLY

APPLY IT NOW

After surveying fellow classmates, encourage students to write a summary of their findings. Have students circle the indefinite pronouns in their writing. You might display students' work on a bulletin board titled *Our Class Music Hall of Fame.* Students should demonstrate an understanding of indefinite pronouns.

💡 **TechTip** Many computers have PowerPoint already installed, but your local library can also help.

ASSESS

Note which students had difficulty identifying indefinite pronouns. Assign **Practice Book** page 36 for further practice.

WRITING CONNECTION

Use pages 278–279 of the Writing portion of the book.

TEACHING OPTIONS

Reteach

Have students vote on a topic to write about, such as music, sports, the community, or a school event. Write each indefinite pronoun on a separate note card and give one to each student. Make sure you have enough cards so that each student gets one. Then ask each student to write one sentence with the indefinite pronoun on his or her card. Instruct students to write their sentences on strips of paper that you provide. Have students share their sentences with the class. Collect the strips and, working with the class, arrange the sentences into a cohesive paragraph that tells about the topic the class has chosen.

Meeting Individual Needs

Auditory Invite pairs to create their own set of indefinite pronoun cards. Tell partners to shuffle the cards and put them facedown. Instruct one partner to pick the first card, think of a sentence for the word, and say the sentence. Encourage the other partner to listen closely and to identify the indefinite pronoun. Encourage students to continue until all the cards have been used or until the end of the lesson.

9. It features bold geometric shapes and a 162-foot tower.
10. Many have performed at the Rock Hall.
11. Each have found the experience to be thrilling.
12. Someday I plan to visit it too.
13. I don't know the names of every rock star elected to the Rock Hall, but I know quite a few.
14. Maybe I will be someone elected to the Hall of Fame.

Chuck Berry

Exercise 2

Indefinite pronouns are underlined.

1. direct object
2. subject
3. subject
4. subject complement
5. subject
6. subject complement
7. subject
8. subject
9. subject; subject
10. subject complement; object of a preposition

EXERCISE 2 Identify the indefinite pronoun or pronouns in each sentence. Then tell what its function is in the sentence.

1. It should surprise nobody that Elvis Presley was among the original inductees to the Rock and Roll Hall of Fame and Museum.
2. Everybody called him the King for his role in popularizing rock and roll.
3. Actually, some credit Chuck Berry, also an original inductee, with inventing the new musical style.
4. He did something that no one had done before—combine country and western with rhythm and blues.
5. Both of these styles merged to develop into rock and roll in the 1950s.
6. Aretha Franklin was one of the first women members.
7. Most know her as the Queen of Soul.
8. Several of her songs sold more than a million copies.
9. Not all the inductees are actually rock-and-roll musicians; some are placed in a special category.
10. Bessie Smith, a blues singer of the early 1900s, for example, is one of several in the category "Early Influences."

Exercise 3

Answers will vary.

EXERCISE 3 Write sentences using the following indefinite pronouns.

1. everybody
2. somebody
3. all
4. some
5. much
6. each
7. several
8. either

APPLY IT NOW

Talk to seven people about what they know about rock and roll and its musicians and what they think of this type of music. Write a paragraph with your results. Include at least four indefinite pronouns.

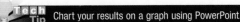

Tech Tip Chart your results on a graph using PowerPoint.

Pronouns • 51

OBJECTIVE
- **To use singular and plural indefinite pronouns**

 **Maintenance**

Assign **Practice Book** page 22, Section 3.11. After students finish,
1. Give immediate feedback.
2. Review concepts as needed.
3. Model the correct answer.

Pages 4–5 of the **Answer Key** contain tips for Daily Maintenance.

WARM-UP

Say the following sentence aloud:

Both is good places to eat.

Have students identify the word that makes the sentence incorrect. Ask students to change the word and explain why they changed it.

📖 Read from a piece of writing that the class is currently reading. Emphasize the agreement with indefinite pronouns.

TEACH

Choose several sentences from the exercises on pages 50–51 where the indefinite pronoun is the subject of the sentence. You might use Exercise 1, sentences 4, 5, 10; or Exercise 2, sentences 3, 7, 9. Write the sentences on the board. Challenge students to identify the subject and the verb in each sentence. Make a chart for students to compare.

EXERCISE 1	SUBJECT	VERB
ITEM 4	All	are
ITEM 5	Several	are
ITEM 10	Many	have

EXERCISE 2	SUBJECT	VERB
ITEM 3	some	credit
ITEM 7	Most	know
ITEM 9	all	are

Point out that the indefinite pronouns and the verbs agree in number.

Invite volunteers to take turns reading aloud the explanation of agreement with indefinite pronouns. To help students remember which indefinite pronouns are singular, which are plural, and which can be both, refer them to page 50.

PRACTICE

EXERCISE 1
Suggest that students complete their own three-column chart of indefinite pronouns for reference. As students complete the exercise, encourage them to refer to their charts to determine the correct verb form. Then have partners compare and discuss their answers.

EXERCISE 2
You may wish to review which indefinite pronouns are plural. Have students complete the exercise independently. Then discuss the answers as a class.

EXERCISE 3
Have partners read each sentence quietly and decide if the sentence is correct or incorrect. Tell students that if it is incorrect, they should rewrite the sentence.

3.11 Agreement with Indefinite Pronouns

Most indefinite pronouns are singular, but some are plural. When an indefinite pronoun acts as the subject of a sentence, the verb needs to agree with it in number.

Singular indefinite pronouns include *another, anybody, anyone, anything, each, either, everybody, everyone, everything, much, neither, nobody, no one, nothing, one, other, somebody, someone,* and *something.* They take singular verbs.

No one is able to predict earthquakes.

In the above sentence, *no one* is followed by *is,* the third person singular form of the verb *be.*

Which verb correctly completes the following sentence?

Everyone (want wants) us to be able to predict them.

The correct answer is *wants.* It is a third person singular verb, to agree with the singular indefinite pronoun. Remember that third person singular verbs end in *s.*

Plural indefinite pronouns include *both, few, many, others,* and *several.* They take plural verbs.

Many are working to try to predict earthquakes.

Some indefinite pronouns can be either singular or plural, depending on how they are used in a sentence. These include *all, any, more, most, none,* and *some.* These pronouns are singular and take a singular verb when they are followed by a phrase with a singular noun or an abstract noun. They are plural and take a plural verb when they are followed by a phrase with a plural noun.

SINGULAR	PLURAL
All of the building was destroyed.	*All* of the buildings were destroyed.

When all have finished, invite students to share their sentences with the class.

APPLY

APPLY IT NOW

Before students begin to write, encourage them to recall groups of objects they have seen and to think how indefinite pronouns can be used to describe these things. When students feel they have some ideas for sentences, let them begin to write. Ask students to circle the indefinite pronouns and to analyze their sentences to make sure the pronouns and the verbs agree. Students should demonstrate an understanding of agreement with indefinite pronouns.

ASSESS

Note which students had difficulty with agreement with indefinite pronouns. Assign **Practice Book** page 37 for further practice.

WRITING CONNECTION

Use pages 280–281 of the Writing portion of the book.

TEACHING OPTIONS

Reteach

Write each indefinite pronoun on a separate note card and shuffle the cards. Pick a card from the deck, hold it up for the class to read, and ask the class to say whether the pronoun goes with a single verb, a plural verb, or either type of verb. Then use the word in a sentence that is either correct or incorrect. Ask the class to listen closely and to correct your sentence if needed. Encourage students to explain their thinking as they respond.

Cooperative Learning

Ask small groups to discuss something about the school that they would like to change or add. For example, they might like a new library or more after-school activities. Encourage students to work together to write an essay about the change, using indefinite pronouns to state their case.

Meeting Individual Needs

Extra Support Some students might have difficulty with verb agreement using indefinite pronouns such as *everybody, everything,* and *everyone* because the word *every* seems to imply *more than one.* Suggest that when students see these words, they should think in singular terms by inserting the word *single: every single thing, every single one, every single body.* Work with students as they compose sentences with these indefinite pronouns to help them become more familiar with singular verb agreement.

EXERCISE 1 Choose the correct verb to complete each sentence. Make sure the verb agrees with its subject.

1. (Has Have) anybody been able to predict earthquakes?
2. Some (says say) that we don't know much in this area of science.
3. Scientists can tell us where quakes might occur in the future, but no one (is are) really more definite than that.
4. All of the efforts so far (has have) not created anything to predict a quake reliably.
5. Among cultures in earthquake regions, several (has have) tried for centuries to predict quakes.
6. One of those attempts (was were) an ancient Chinese device that actually picked up the earth's vibrations and pointed out the direction of the quake.
7. None of the proposed methods for predicting earthquakes, however, (has have) proved successful.

Exercise 2

Indefinite pronouns are underlined once. Verbs are underlined twice.

Exercise 3

1. Correct
2. Correct
3. Many say that the air smells different after an earthquake.
4. Everyone agrees that the experience is indescribable.
5. Correct
6. Of my two friends in California, both have firsthand knowledge of this phenomenon.
7. Neither, however, has been hurt by the earthquakes.
8. Everybody in earthquake zones needs to learn about emergency procedures.

EXERCISE 2 Identify the indefinite pronoun in each sentence. Then choose the verb that agrees with it.

1. Several of the students (wear wears) parkas in the winter.
2. Neither of the girls (play plays) in the band.
3. Both of the boys usually (forget forgets) their homework.
4. One of the answers (is are) wrong.
5. Many of the employees (eat eats) their lunches in the diner.

EXERCISE 3 Rewrite the sentences to correct errors in agreement between subject and verb. Not all sentences have errors.

1. Nobody is likely to forget being in an earthquake.
2. Nothing feels scarier than having the whole world shaking around you.
3. Many says that the air smells different after an earthquake.
4. Everyone agree that the experience is indescribable.
5. Some experience several quakes in a lifetime.
6. Of my two friends in California, both has firsthand knowledge of this phenomenon.
7. Neither, however, have been hurt by the earthquakes.
8. Everybody in earthquake zones need to learn about emergency procedures.

APPLY IT NOW

Write eight sentences describing a collection of things, such as the contents of your backpack. Use four indefinite pronouns in your paragraph. Underline the verbs with which the indefinite pronouns agree.

Pronouns • 53

Pronoun Review

ASSESS

Use the Pronoun Review as homework, as a practice test, or as an informal assessment. Following are some options for use.

Homework

You may wish to assign one group the odd items and another group the even items. When you next meet, review the correct answers as a group. Be sure to model how to arrive at the correct answer.

Practice Test

Use the Pronoun Review as a diagnostic tool. Assign the entire review or just specific sections. After students have finished, identify which concepts require more attention. Reteach concepts as necessary.

Pronoun Review

3.1 Identify each pronoun, and tell its person, number, and gender.

1. I am trying to decide whether to take French or Spanish as an elective.
2. Julia decided to take German because she is going to visit a friend in Hamburg next summer.
3. You should take a foreign-language course.
4. Jack and Ryan think they might take Japanese.

3.2 Choose the correct subject pronoun to complete each sentence.

5. (I Me) am reading *The Hobbit* for my book club.
6. My friends really liked the *Lord of the Rings* movies, and it was (they them) who picked the book.
7. (They Them) will make the discussion exciting.
8. My brother and (I me) really like the book, especially the part about the dragon.

3.3 Identify the underlined pronoun in each sentence as a direct object, an indirect object, or an object of a preposition.

9. Lewis and Clark took a dog with <u>them</u> out West.
10. The Native Americans wanted to trade skins for <u>it</u>.
11. Lewis was the first to observe coyotes, which always saluted <u>him</u> by barking.

12. The grizzly bears gave <u>them</u> a real fright.
13. Once, when a bear came close to camp, Lewis and Clark and several men with rifles killed <u>it</u>.

3.4 Choose the correct pronoun to complete each sentence. Then identify the word to which the pronoun is compared.

14. Jim and Sarah are learning sign language, but Jim is becoming a better signer than (her she).
15. Sarah also takes a Spanish class but thinks the signing class is more exciting than (them it).
16. Ms. Ramos is an excellent teacher, and Sarah wants to be as good as (she her).

3.5 Rewrite the sentences and replace each possessive adjective and noun with the correct possessive pronoun.

17. My Chumbawumba CD is in the car.
18. We switched, and he gave me his Joni Mitchell CD.
19. Our CD collection has more than a thousand titles.
20. We went to our friends' house to see their collections.

3.1
1. I, first person singular
2. she, third person singular feminine
3. You, second person singular or plural
4. they, third person plural

3.2
5. I
6. they
7. They
8. I

3.3
9. object of a preposition
10. object of a preposition
11. direct object
12. indirect object
13. direct object

3.4
14. she, Jim
15. it, class
16. she, Ms. Ramos

3.5
17. Mine is in the car.
18. We switched, and he gave me his.
19. Ours has more than a thousand titles.
20. We went to our friends' house to see theirs.

Informal Assessment

Use the review as preparation for the formal assessment. Count the review as a portion of the grade. Have students work to find the correct answers and use their corrected review as a study guide for the formal assessment.

WRITING CONNECTION

Use pages 282–283 of the Writing portion of the book.

TEACHING OPTIONS

Putting It All Together

Ask students to copy a passage in a textbook from another subject. Suggest that they use double-spacing. Write these directions on the board:

- **Circle the personal pronouns**
- **Underline the pronouns used as subjects.**
- **Underline with two lines the pronouns used as subject complements.**
- **Underline with three lines the pronouns used as direct objects**

3.6
21. reflexive, We
22. intensive, mother
23. reflexive, I
24. intensive, You

3.7
25. they
26. She
27. him
28. he

3.8
29. Whose
30. which
31. whom
32. This or That

3.9
33. that, tunnel
34. who, People
35. whom, Commuters

3.10
36. each
37. something, everybody
38. anybody, several
39. some

3.11
40. Has anybody ever walked the 3,750 miles atop the Great Wall of China?
41. Nobody knows how many people were needed to complete the wall.
42. Some think the wall stands as a reminder of the strength of the Chinese people.

3.6 Identify the underlined pronouns as intensive or reflexive. Then tell their antecedents.

21. We prepared ourselves for writing a research paper on American history.
22. My mother herself was amazed that we had to write 10 pages each.
23. I amazed myself when I thought of a good topic and started the paper early.
24. You yourself should start any project at least a month before it is due.

3.7 Complete each sentence with the pronoun that agrees with the antecedent.

25. Josh and Cara wanted a new pet, so _____ went to the animal shelter.
26. _____ wanted a kitten, but he wanted a dog.
27. Josh couldn't decide until a gray cat jumped onto _____.
28. Josh loved the cat, and _____ named it Cannonball.

3.8 Complete each sentence with an appropriate interrogative or demonstrative pronoun.

29. _____ is the book on astronomy?
30. Do you know _____ of the planets are visible tonight?
31. From _____ did you get the book?
32. _____ is a fascinating book.

3.9 Identify the relative pronoun and its antecedent in each sentence.

33. The Chunnel is a train tunnel that connects France and England.
34. People who travel by Chunnel can make the journey in about one hour.
35. Commuters, for whom crossing quickly is important, use this option.

3.10 Identify the indefinite pronoun or pronouns in each sentence.

36. The speaker told the eighth graders that each person should visit a farm at least once.
37. A farm has something to offer everybody.
38. Not just anybody can learn to work on a farm; several skills require a lot of practice.
39. Even among farmers, some say that they have never mastered farming.

3.11 Rewrite the sentences to correct errors between subject and verb.

40. Have anybody ever walked the 3,750 miles atop the Great Wall of China?
41. Nobody know how many people were needed to complete the wall.
42. Some thinks the wall stand as a reminder of the strength of the Chinese people.

 Go to www.voyagesinenglish.com for more activities.

Pronouns • 55

TechTip Encourage students to further review pronouns, using the additional practice and games at www.voyagesinenglish.com.

ASSESS

EXERCISE 1
Encourage students to read the paragraph twice before answering the questions. If students have difficulty with any question, suggest that they refer to the section that teaches that skill. This activity can be done individually, in small groups, or as a whole class.

EXERCISE 2
Have students complete the second exercise. Be sure to check that their paragraphs contain all the items listed.

After you have reviewed pronouns, administer the Section 3 Assessment on pages 5–8 in the **Assessment Book,** or create a customized test with the optional **Test Generator CD.**

WRITING CONNECTION
Use pages 284–285 of the Writing portion of the book.

Students can complete a formal how-to article using the Writer's Workshop on pages 286–297.

Pronoun Challenge

EXERCISE 1 Read the selection and then answer the questions.

1. Each of you, boys and girls, belongs to two important societies: the family and the state. 2. "What," you may ask, "is the obligation that is imposed by membership in these societies?" 3. The answer is this. 4. You must give a respectful obedience to those in authority, perform your duties conscientiously, and strive to live in harmony with other members. 5. In other words, you must develop in yourself whatever will make you a valued member of each group. 6. Such is the attitude of every worthwhile person. 7. It should also be yours.

1. What kind of pronoun is the first word in the selection?
2. Name the personal pronoun in sentence 1. Is it singular or plural?
3. What is the person and number of the pronoun *you* in sentence 2? How is it used in the sentence?
4. What is the interrogative pronoun in sentence 2? How is it used?
5. What is the relative pronoun in sentence 2? What is its antecedent?
6. What is the demonstrative pronoun in sentence 3?
7. In sentence 4, what personal pronoun is used as a subject?
8. What is the pronoun in sentence 6? What kind of pronoun is it?
9. What is the gender of the pronoun *it* in sentence 7?
10. Find the reflexive pronoun in the selection. What sentence is it in? How is it used in the sentence?
11. Find the possessive pronoun in the paragraph. What sentence is it in?

EXERCISE 2 Do you agree with the paragraph above? Would you add anything else? Follow the instructions below.

Write a short response to this paragraph explaining how you would change it, what you might add or remove, and why. You can also give examples from your own experience. Be sure to include an interrogative pronoun, a subject pronoun, and an object pronoun. Then identify the subject pronoun as either a subject or a subject complement. Identify the object pronoun as a direct object, an indirect object, or an object of a preposition. Finally, correctly use either *who* or *whom* at least once in your response.

Exercise 1
1. indefinite pronoun
2. you; plural
3. second person, singular or plural; subject
4. What; subject
5. that; obligation
6. this
7. You
8. such; indefinite
9. neuter
10. yourself; #5; object of a preposition
11. yours; #7

Exercise 2
Answers will vary.

Verbs

SUPPORT MATERIALS

Practice Book
Daily Maintenance, pages 38–40
Grammar, pages 41–53

Assessment Book
Section 4 Assessment, pages 9–12

Test Generator CD

**Writing Chapter 3,
    Business Letters**

Customizable Lesson Plans
www.voyagesinenglish.com

CONNECT WITH LITERATURE

📖 Consider using the following titles throughout the section to illustrate the grammar concept:

The Call of the Wild by Jack London
The Misfits by James Howe
Nouns and Verbs Have a Field Day by Robin Pulver and Lynn Rowe Reed

GRAMMAR FOR GROWN-UPS

Understanding Verbs

A verb shows action or state of being. Every sentence must have a verb.

Verbs can be transitive or intransitive. A **transitive verb** expresses an action that passes from a doer to a receiver. It has a direct object.

> *Ron read the book.*

An **intransitive verb** does not have a receiver for its action. Therefore, it does not have a direct object.

> *The cat slept.*

A **linking verb** expresses state of being. It links the subject of a sentence with a subject complement.

> *She is a doctor.*

The verb *be* in its various forms is the most common linking verb. Other verbs used as linking verbs include *seem, appear, remain, stay, feel, become,* and *continue.*

Verb forms indicate **tense**—whether the action takes place in the past, the present, or the future. The **simple present** tense (*run/runs*) describes habitual action or things that are always true. The **simple past** (*ran*) describes something that happened in the past. The **future** with *will* and the future with *going* to indicate action that will take place in the future.

Progressive tenses (*is running, was running, will be running*) show continuing action. **Perfect tenses** (*have run, had run, will have run*) show a relationship between the present time and the time of the action.

Verb forms also show **mood**. The **indicative mood** is used to state or deny a fact or to ask a question: *The boy is running.* The **imperative mood** expresses a command: *Please stop. Don't run!* The **subjunctive mood** expresses a wish or desire; a condition that is contrary to fact; or a demand, recommendation, or necessity after that: *I insist that he stop running.*

> ❝One of the glories of English simplicity is the possibility of using the same word as noun and verb.❞
>
> —Edward Sapir

COMMON ERRORS

Eternal Truths and Tense

There are some statements that are always understood to be true, such as *two plus two equals four*. For statements such as these, you must always write in the present tense. But, alas, this doesn't always happen. Sometimes folks who are writing in the past tense write an "eternal truth" in past tense as well. This shouldn't happen.

ERROR: Jake said that Mars was the fourth planet from the sun.
CORRECT: Jake said that Mars is the fourth planet from the sun.

ERROR: Lori knew that two times four was eight.
CORRECT: Lori knew that two times four is eight.

ERROR: Barry told me that the United States had 50 states.
CORRECT: Barry told me that the United States has 50 states.

When working on subject-verb agreement with students, be sure to spend some time on eternal truths. Challenge students to watch for these in their own speaking and writing, and to make corrections whenever they catch errors.

SENTENCE DIAGRAMMING

You may wish to teach verbs in the context of diagramming. Review these examples. Then refer to the Diagramming section or look for Diagram It! features in the Verbs section.

Kathryn has been playing piano for two years.

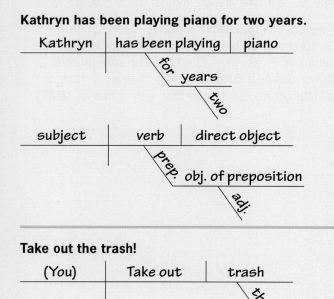

Take out the trash!

ASK AN EXPERT

Real Situations, Real Solutions

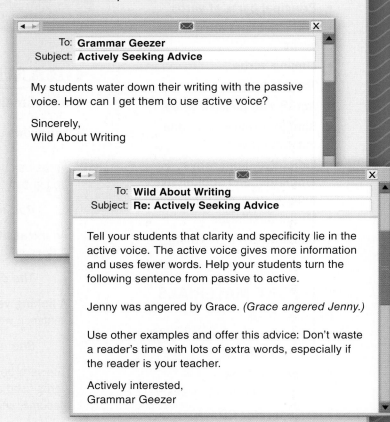

To: **Grammar Geezer**
Subject: **Actively Seeking Advice**

My students water down their writing with the passive voice. How can I get them to use active voice?

Sincerely,
Wild About Writing

To: **Wild About Writing**
Subject: **Re: Actively Seeking Advice**

Tell your students that clarity and specificity lie in the active voice. The active voice gives more information and uses fewer words. Help your students turn the following sentence from passive to active.

Jenny was angered by Grace. *(Grace angered Jenny.)*

Use other examples and offer this advice: Don't waste a reader's time with lots of extra words, especially if the reader is your teacher.

Actively interested,
Grammar Geezer

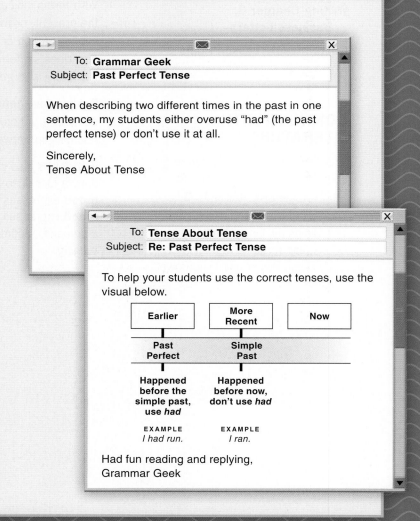

To: **Grammar Geek**
Subject: **Past Perfect Tense**

When describing two different times in the past in one sentence, my students either overuse "had" (the past perfect tense) or don't use it at all.

Sincerely,
Tense About Tense

To: **Tense About Tense**
Subject: **Re: Past Perfect Tense**

To help your students use the correct tenses, use the visual below.

Earlier	More Recent	Now
Past Perfect	Simple Past	
Happened before the simple past, use *had*	Happened before now, don't use *had*	
EXAMPLE *I had run.*	EXAMPLE *I ran.*	

Had fun reading and replying,
Grammar Geek

OBJECTIVES

- **To recognize that verbs are words that show action or state of being**
- **To recognize the base, past, present participle, and past participle forms of a verb**
- **To recognize how to use the auxiliary verbs** *be, have, do, can, may, might, should, could,* **and** *will*

DAILY Maintenance

Assign **Practice Book** page 38, Section 4.1. After students finish,
1. Give immediate feedback.
2. Review concepts as needed.
3. Model the correct answer.

Pages 4–5 of the **Answer Key** contain tips for Daily Maintenance.

WARM-UP

Toss a beanbag to a student and ask that student to name his or her favorite activity *(play baseball)*. Then have that student toss the beanbag to another student. Tell students that whoever catches the beanbag must say an action that would occur in the activity named by the first student *(run, throw, swing)* and then toss the beanbag to another student. List students' responses on the board.

📖 Read from a piece of writing that the class is currently reading. Emphasize the principal parts of verbs.

TEACH

Ask a volunteer to read aloud the information about principal parts of verbs. Point out that the past participle and present participle of a verb are always used with an auxiliary verb. Tell students that irregular verbs require more than simply adding *-ed* to form the past and past participle principal parts.

Invite a volunteer to read aloud the remainder of the page. Then write on the board the following sentences:

They <u>talk</u> to each other.

I <u>write</u> stories.

Tell students that the underlined words are the present, or base, form of the verb. Have students rewrite each sentence using the past, past participle, and present participle forms of the verb. Ask volunteers to share their sentences. Point out again that the past participle and present participle are used in verb phrases with auxiliary verbs.

PRACTICE

EXERCISE 1
Have students discuss with partners which verbs are verb phrases and which parts of the phrases are auxiliary verbs.

EXERCISE 2
Remind students that past participles and present participles are combined with auxiliary verbs to form a verb phrase. Have students complete the exercise independently. Then have partners compare answers. Encourage students to identify the verbs that are irregular.

4.1 Principal Parts of Verbs

Aztec calendar

Verbs show action or state of being.

We *read* several Mexican folktales. (action)
Folktales *are* traditional stories of a people. (state of being)

The principal parts of a verb are the **base form,** the **past,** and the **past participle.** A fourth part, the **present participle,** is formed by adding *-ing* to the base form of the verb. Participles have three functions in sentences. They can be part of a verb phrase, or they can function as an adjective or a noun.

BASE	PAST	PAST PARTICIPLE	PRESENT PARTICIPLE
talk	talked	talked	talking

Regular verbs, such as *talk,* form the past and past participle by adding *-d* or *-ed* to the base form. Irregular verbs, such as the ones below, do not form the past and past participle in this way. If you are unsure of the principal parts of a verb, check a dictionary.

BASE	PAST	PAST PARTICIPLE	PRESENT PARTICIPLE
hide	hid	hid	hiding
freeze	froze	frozen	freezing

A **verb phrase** is two or more verbs that work together as a unit. A verb phrase may have one or more **auxiliary verbs** and a **main verb.**

One folktale *is called* "The Legend of the Volcanoes."

In the sentence above, the main verb is the past participle *called,* and the auxiliary verb *is* is a form of the verb *be.* Note that the past participle is often used with auxiliary verbs, but the past stands alone.

Can you find the main verb and the auxiliary verb in this sentence?

The volcano *has emitted* smoke for years.

You are correct if you said that *has* is the auxiliary verb and that *emitted,* a past participle, is the main verb.

Common auxiliary verbs are *be* and *have* and their various forms, as well as *do* and *did.* Other auxiliary verbs include *can, may, might, should, could,* and *will.*

APPLY

APPLY IT NOW

As students summarize their folktales or legends, remind students that most folktales are told in the past tense. Challenge students to use all four principal parts correctly. Invite students to read their stories aloud and have classmates consider whether the principal parts were used correctly. Students should demonstrate an understanding of the principal parts of verbs.

Grammar in Action. The three past principal parts are *fit, impressed,* and *enclosed.* Follow up by asking students if each verb is regular or irregular.

ASSESS

Note which students had difficulty using verbs and choosing the proper verb form. Assign **Practice Book** page 41 for further practice.

WRITING CONNECTION

Use pages 298–299 of the Writing portion of the book. Be sure to point out verbs in the literature excerpt and the student model.

Exercise 1
Main verbs are underlined once. Auxiliary verbs are underlined twice.

EXERCISE 1 Underline the verbs and verb phrases in the sentences. Then identify the auxiliary verb and the main verb in each verb phrase.

1. The most famous volcano in Mexico <u>is called</u> Popocatépetl.
2. Its name <u>means</u> "smoking mountain."
3. The volcano <u>has been</u> an active one for hundreds of years.
4. It <u>lies</u> close to Mexico City.
5. According to Aztec legends, this volcano <u>was</u> once a warrior that <u>had been transformed</u> into a volcano.
6. Kilauea, the earth's most active volcano, <u>is located</u> in Hawaii.
7. It <u>is</u> the youngest volcano on the big island of Hawaii.
8. This volcano <u>has erupted</u> continuously since 1983!
9. It <u>was believed</u> to be the home of Pele, the Hawaiian volcano goddess, by ancient Hawaiians.

Exercise 2
1. past
2. past participle
3. past; past
4. past participle
5. past participle
6. past; past participle; past participle
7. past; past
8. past; past
9. past
10. past participle
11. past participle

EXERCISE 2 Identify each verb or verb phrase. Tell whether each main verb is the past form or the past participle form.

1. An ancient ruler and his wife <u>had</u> a beautiful baby.
2. The daughter <u>was named</u> Iztaccíhuatl.
3. When she <u>grew</u> up, she <u>fell</u> in love with a warrior, Popoca.
4. Popoca <u>was called</u> to battle.
5. The king <u>had promised</u> Popoca his daughter's hand for a victory.
6. A false message <u>came</u> to the king that Popoca <u>had won</u> but that he <u>had been killed</u> in battle.
7. When Iztaccíhuatl <u>heard</u> the news, she <u>died</u> of sadness.
8. When Popoca <u>arrived</u> back home, he <u>learned</u> of Iztaccíhuatl's death.
9. He <u>died</u> of grief.
10. According to myth, the lovers <u>were transformed</u> into volcanos.
11. <u>Have</u> you <u>noticed</u> his name within the name of the volcano Popocatépetl?

Popocatépetl volcano

APPLY IT NOW

Write a brief summary of a folktale or a legend you know. Use each of the four verb forms at least once, and label them accordingly.

Grammar in Action. Identify three past principal parts in the p. 298 letter.

Verbs • 59

Reteach

Begin a chart like the one below. Have students suggest verbs to complete the chart, identifying the verbs as regular or irregular. Invite students to use the principal parts of each verb in a sentence.

Base	Past	Past Participle	Regular or Irregular
jump	jumped	jumped	regular
mark	marked	marked	regular
throw	threw	thrown	irregular

Cooperative Learning

Invite small groups to select a folktale, a fairy tale, or a passage from a grade-appropriate novel that they enjoy. As students read the story, have them list and discuss the verbs, identifying the verb forms and auxiliary verbs. Make sure students note whether the verbs are regular or irregular.

English-Language Learners

Pair English-language learners with students who have a firm grasp on verb usage. Invite students to say simple sentences with base-form verbs such as *We study in school.* Then encourage students to work with the English-language learners to repeat the sentences in the past form: *We studied in school.*

OBJECTIVES

- **To recognize that a transitive verb expresses an action that passes to a receiver**
- **To recognize and use phrasal verbs**
- **To recognize that an intransitive verb does not have a receiver for its action**
- **To distinguish between transitive and intransitive usage**

DAILY Maintenance

Assign **Practice Book** page 38, Section 4.2. After students finish,
1. Give immediate feedback.
2. Review concepts as needed.
3. Model the correct answer.

Pages 4–5 of the **Answer Key** contain tips for Daily Maintenance.

WARM-UP

Tell one side of the class that they are the doers and tell the other side that they are the receivers. Have the doers say several verbs. Write each on the board. Then have each receiver use the verbs to make sentences that have receivers. Tell students that some verbs will not have a receiver.

Read from a piece of writing that the class is currently reading. Emphasize the transitive and intransitive verbs.

TEACH

Have a volunteer read aloud the transitive verb and phrasal verb paragraphs. Tell students that transitive verbs express action passed from a doer to a receiver. Emphasize that this receiver is a noun or pronoun. Invite volunteers to suggest sentences that use transitive verbs. Have students point out the direct objects in these sentences.

Ask students to list on the board as many phrasal verbs as they can. Challenge students to create sentences using the phrasal verbs.

Have a volunteer read about intransitive verbs. Say this sentence: *The children slept peacefully.* Have students identify the verb *(slept)*, then ask them whether the verb has a receiver *(no)*. Explain that a verb that does not have a receiver is an intransitive verb. Encourage students to suggest other examples of sentences with intransitive verbs.

PRACTICE

EXERCISE 1

Have partners read each sentence and identify the verb, verb phrase, or phrasal verb. Encourage partners to determine whether the verbs are transitive or intransitive. You may wish to combine student pairs to form larger groups and have the groups compare their answers.

EXERCISE 2

Invite a volunteer to explain the difference between a transitive verb and an intransitive verb. Suggest that students create a

---

4.2 Transitive and Intransitive Verbs

A **transitive verb** expresses an action that passes from a doer to a receiver. The receiver of the action is the direct object. To determine whether there is a direct object, ask *whom* or *what* after the verb.

The ancient Greeks *created* myths.

The verb *created* is transitive. Its direct object is *myths*.

Some transitive verbs are phrasal verbs. A **phrasal verb** is a combination of a main verb and a preposition or an adverb, such as *clear out, nail down, nose out, root out, saddle up,* and *win over*. Although it may appear to be the object in a prepositional phrase, the noun or pronoun that follows a phrasal verb is a direct object. In the following sentence, *up this horse* is not a prepositional phrase.

Saddle up this horse. (*Saddle up* is the phrasal verb; *horse* is the direct object.)

An **intransitive verb** does not have a receiver for its action. It does not have a direct object.

A family of gods *sat* on Mount Olympus.

Can you tell whether the verb in this sentence is transitive or intransitive? How can you tell?

The myths *provided* explanations of things in the world.

The verb *provided* is transitive. Its direct object is *explanations*. Some verbs may be transitive or intransitive, depending on their use in the sentence.

Hercules *fought* a huge lion. (transitive)
The gods *fought* among themselves. (intransitive)

EXERCISE 1 Identify the verb, verb phrase, or phrasal verb in each sentence. Then tell whether the verb is transitive or intransitive.

1. The Greek gods <u>watched over</u> human affairs.
2. From high on Mount Olympus, they <u>watched</u>.
3. People still <u>tell</u> the Greek myths.

Exercise 1
1. transitive
2. intransitive
3. transitive

chart with two columns to sort the verbs: *Transitive Verb and Receiver* and *Intransitive Verb*.

EXERCISE 3

Invite a volunteer to define a *phrasal verb*. Then have partners complete the exercise. Suggest students use the chart that they created in Exercise 2 for help.

APPLY

APPLY IT NOW

Make sure students have used the verbs correctly. For the sentences in which transitive verbs are used, ask students to identify the receiver of the action. Students should demonstrate an understanding of transitive and intransitive verbs.

ASSESS

Note which students had difficulty using and distinguishing between transitive and intransitive verbs. Assign **Practice Book** page 42 for further practice.

WRITING CONNECTION

Use pages 300–301 of the Writing portion of the book.

Reteach

Provide groups with discarded magazines. Invite students to cut out large, interesting photographs, one that might depict a transitive verb (*The girl is brushing her hair*) and one that might depict an intransitive verb (*The car sped away*). Instruct students to glue their pictures to poster board. Then challenge students to write a sentence caption for each picture. Have the students underline the verbs and identify them as either transitive or intransitive.

Meeting Individual Needs

Challenge Invite students to copy on a sheet of paper four or five sentences from a magazine, newspaper, or online article. Then ask students to underline the verbs or verb phrases. Challenge students to identify the transitive verbs. Invite volunteers to read aloud one example and to explain how they arrived at their choices. (*The action has a receiver.*)

Meeting Individual Needs

Extra Support Begin a chart on the board with the following column headings: *Sentence, Verb, Type,* and *Receiver*. Enter the following information as an example:

Sentence:	**He caught the ball.**
Verb:	**caught**
Type:	**transitive**
Receiver:	**ball**

Ask a volunteer to write in the first column a sentence with an action verb and the verb or verb phrase in the second column. Discuss the sentence further, having the student enter the information in the appropriate columns. Have other volunteers write sentences and fill in the columns. Discuss each sentence with the class.

---

4. transitive
5. intransitive
6. transitive
7. intransitive
8. transitive

4. Some of the myths <u>describe</u> such heroes as Hercules and Perseus.
5. People sometimes <u>prayed</u> to the gods for help.
6. The Greeks <u>called</u> the messenger of the gods Hermes.
7. I <u>have read</u> about Greek heroes in class.
8. The lives of Greek gods and heroes <u>make</u> fascinating stories.

Exercise 2
Verbs are underlined once. Direct objects are underlined twice.

1. intransitive
2. transitive
3. intransitive
4. transitive
5. intransitive
6. transitive
7. transitive
8. transitive
9. transitive
10. intransitive
11. transitive
12. transitive
13. transitive
14. intransitive
15. intransitive
16. transitive

EXERCISE 2 Identify the verb, verb phrase, or phrasal verb in each sentence. Tell whether it is transitive or intransitive. For each transitive verb, identify the direct object.

1. The young hero Perseus <u>lived</u> with his mother, Danae.
2. A king <u>wanted</u> Perseus's <u>mother</u> for his wife.
3. The king <u>did</u> not <u>get along</u> with Perseus.
4. He <u>challenged</u> <u>Perseus</u> to an impossible feat.
5. The king <u>was wishing</u> for Perseus's death.
6. The brave Perseus <u>accepted</u> the <u>challenge</u>.
7. The king <u>requested</u> the <u>head</u> of a monster.
8. Medusa, the monster, <u>had</u> <u>snakes</u> for hair.
9. One sight of the monster <u>turned</u> <u>people</u> into stone.
10. Medusa once <u>had boasted</u> of her beauty.
11. The gods <u>had punished</u> <u>her</u> for that boast.
12. The gods now <u>were looking</u> after <u>Perseus</u>.
13. One goddess <u>lent</u> Perseus a bright <u>shield</u>.
14. Perseus <u>was walking</u> along in search of Medusa.
15. Eventually, he <u>came</u> to Medusa's island home.
16. How could he <u>bring about</u> the monster's <u>death</u>?

Exercise 3
Verbs are underlined once. Direct objects are underlined twice.

1. intransitive
2. transitive
3. intransitive
4. intransitive, phrasal verb

EXERCISE 3 Identify the verbs. Tell whether they are transitive or intransitive. For each transitive verb, identify the direct object. Identify any transitive verbs that are phrasal verbs.

1. What movies <u>are shown</u> at that theater?
2. Brad Pitt <u>played</u> the Greek <u>hero</u> Achilles in one movie.
3. Achilles and Hector <u>fought</u> against each other in one battle scene.
4. We all <u>cleared out</u> of the theater afterward.

APPLY IT NOW

Write two sentences for each of the verbs *read, fight,* and *practice.* In one sentence use the verb as a transitive verb and in the other as an intransitive verb.

Verbs • 61

OBJECTIVE

- To recognize how to use and how to avoid mistakes with troublesome verbs: teach/ learn, take/bring, lend/borrow, lie/lay, rise/raise, and sit/set

DAILY Maintenance

Assign **Practice Book** page 38, Section 4.3. After students finish,
1. Give immediate feedback.
2. Review concepts as needed.
3. Model the correct answer.

Pages 4–5 of the **Answer Key** contain tips for Daily Maintenance.

WARM-UP

Write the following sentences on the board. Ask students to choose the correct verb in each sentence.

Dr. Bell (sit set) his glasses down.

The student (rose raised) his hand.

Challenge students to point out two things that the correct verbs have in common. *(Both verbs are transitive, and both verbs are irregular.)*

📖 Read from a piece of writing that the class is currently reading. Emphasize the troublesome verbs.

TEACH

Have volunteers read aloud the information about troublesome verbs. Ask students to explain why these verbs can be troublesome and why people sometimes use the verbs incorrectly. Point out that the past principal part of *lie* is *lay* and remind students to be careful when they come across this word in writing. Challenge students to say a sentence using each verb. Discuss if the verb has been used properly.

Emphasize that *lay, raise,* and *set* take direct objects and are therefore transitive verbs. Also

point out that *lie, rise,* and *sit* are intransitive, therefore they do not have direct objects. Point out that *lie, rise,* and *sit* are often followed by prepositional phrases that tell how or why. Tell students that finding a direct object can help them determine if *lay* is the past principal part (of *lie*) or the present principal part.

PRACTICE

EXERCISE 1

Encourage students to complete the activity independently. Then have partners exchange papers to check and compare answers. Have

students confer about any answers that differ. Discuss each sentence with the class, inviting students to explain their verb choices.

EXERCISE 2

Remind students that *lay* can be the past principal part of *lie*. Have partners complete this exercise. Suggest that one partner read a sentence aloud and then have the partners discuss whether the sentence is correct. Challenge students to discuss the verb and decide whether it is being used properly. Then have the partners work together to rewrite the incorrect sentences.

4.3 Troublesome Verbs

The following pairs of verbs often cause usage problems. Study the differences to avoid mistakes.

Teach (taught, taught) means "to give knowledge."
Learn (learned, learned) means "to receive knowledge."

> He *taught* history.
> I *learned* a lot in his class.

Take (took, taken) means "to carry from a near place to a more distant place."
Bring (brought, brought) means "to carry from a distant place to a near place."

> Don't *take* that book to Jim's house.
> Please *bring* several sharp pencils for the test.

Lend (lent, lent) means "to let someone use something of yours."
Borrow (borrowed, borrowed) means "to take something and use it as one's own with the idea of returning it."

> Please *lend* me your coat.
> He *borrowed* a warm coat.

Lie (lay, lain, lying) means "to recline." It does not take a direct object.
Lay (laid, laid, laying) means "to place." It takes a direct object. Notice the differences in the principal parts of *lie* and *lay*.

> *Lie* down here.
> *Lay* the blanket on the bed.

Rise (rose, risen) means "to get up." It does not take a direct object.
Raise (raised, raised) means "to lift up" or "to bring to maturity." It takes a direct object.

> Please *rise* now.
> They *raise* the flag each morning.

Sit (sat, sat) means "to take a seat." It does not take a direct object.
Set (set, set) means "to put down." It takes a direct object.

> *Sit* down in the kitchen.
> *Set* the groceries on the table.

EXERCISE 3

Have students recall that *lay* and *raise* are transitive verbs and therefore have direct objects. Invite a volunteer to read each sentence aloud. Ask another volunteer to provide the correct answer.

APPLY

APPLY IT NOW

Make sure students understand that they should write one sentence for each troublesome verb (or two sentences for each troublesome verb pair). You may wish to write the verb pairs on the board before students begin this activity. Students should demonstrate an understanding of troublesome verbs.

ASSESS

Note which students had difficulty using troublesome verbs. Assign **Practice Book** pages 43–44 for further practice.

WRITING CONNECTION

Use pages 302–303 of the Writing portion of the book.

TEACHING OPTIONS

Reteach

Assign a pair of troublesome verbs to partners. Tell them to work together to write two sentences for each verb. Then ask one partner to read the sentences aloud. Ask the class to listen carefully for proper usage. Discuss any usage discrepancies.

English-Language Learners

The slight differences in these verbs might be particularly confusing to English-language learners. Review the sentences in the lesson that provide examples of proper usage. As you say each sentence, act out the verb. Then invite students to say the sentence with you and to act it out as well. Encourage students to suggest another sentence for the verb and to act out the verb in the new sentence.

Meeting Individual Needs

Visual Have students list three troublesome verbs that they have had problems with in the past. Encourage students to write the meaning of each verb, to write a sentence using the verb, and to create a drawing illustrating its meaning. Also challenge students to write the past, past participle, and present participle forms of each verb.

EXERCISE 1 Choose the correct verb to complete each sentence.

1. He (learned <u>taught</u>) us how to project our voices onstage and gave lots of other tips about acting.
2. Don't (<u>set</u> sit) the paint can there while you're working.
3. Don't (<u>take</u> bring) that brush; I still need it.
4. Come and (set <u>sit</u>) down; you look exhausted.
5. After painting all afternoon, I had to (<u>lie</u> lay) down and rest.
6. Whose job is it to (rise <u>raise</u>) the curtain?
7. Do you know where I've (lain <u>laid</u>) my script?
8. My sister (borrowed <u>lent</u>) me her silk blouse for the performance.
9. I even (lent <u>borrowed</u>) her best scarf.
10. At the last minute, my mother didn't remember where she (lay <u>laid</u>) the tickets.
11. She had (<u>set</u> sit) them on the hall table.
12. They were (<u>lying</u> laying) there when we looked for them.

Exercise 2

1. Correct
2. The community center lent us extra chairs for the performance.
3. The members of the audience rose to their feet and applauded.
4. The entire experience taught us a lot about the theater and acting.
5. The experience was so exhausting that I lay in bed resting until 10 o'clock the next morning.
6. Correct

EXERCISE 2 Rewrite any incorrect sentence to correct the use of a troublesome verb. Not all the sentences have errors.

1. We're selling T-shirts for the play at the door; we hope to raise money for next term's play.
2. The community center borrowed us extra chairs for the performance.
3. All the members of the audience raised to their feet and applauded.
4. The entire experience learned us a lot about the theater and acting.
5. The experience was so exhausting that I laid in bed resting until 10 o'clock the next morning.
6. The babysitter laid the sleeping infant in the crib.

EXERCISE 3 Choose the correct verb to complete each sentence.

1. Don't forget to _____ your fishing rod with you on your camping trip. (<u>take</u> bring)
2. The audience _____ from their seats and applauded the musician. (raise <u>rose</u>)
3. _____ your boots and socks by the woodstove so they will dry out by morning. (Lie <u>Lay</u>)

APPLY IT NOW

Use each troublesome verb on the preceding page in a sentence to illustrate its correct use.

Verbs • 63

OBJECTIVES

- **To recognize the function of linking verbs**
- **To identify linking verbs in a sentence**

DAILY Maintenance

Assign **Practice Book** page 38, Section 4.4. After students finish,
1. Give immediate feedback.
2. Review concepts as needed.
3. Model the correct answer.

Pages 4–5 of the **Answer Key** contain tips for Daily Maintenance.

WARM-UP

Write *is, was, remain, sound, feel,* and *seem* on the board. Arrange the class into teams of three. Tell students they are going to compete in sentence relays. Hand a "baton" (a paper towel roll) to a student. Have that student say a noun and hand the baton to the next person, who chooses a verb from the list on the board. Have that student hand the baton to the third person, who completes the sentence. Repeat the activity with each team. You may wish to use a stopwatch to time each team.

📖 Read from a piece of writing that the class is currently reading. Emphasize the linking verbs.

TEACH

Tell students that not all verbs express action. Then invite a volunteer to begin reading about linking verbs. Discuss the chart with students. Challenge students to generate similar sentences. On the board write the verbs used in the sentences that students suggest. Have a student read aloud these verbs. Ask volunteers to read aloud the rest of the page. Refer to your list as you point out that several verbs mentioned are the verbs students have been using.

Point out that sometimes a linking verb might appear to be an action verb. Tell students that there is a test to determine if a verb is a linking verb or an action verb. Explain that if students can replace a verb with a form of the verb *be*, it is a linking verb. Let students try replacing each linking verb on the page to practice this test.

PRACTICE

EXERCISE 1

Review subject complements on page 6. Have partners guide each other through the sentences— identifying verbs, categorizing them as action or linking verbs, and finding the subject complements.

EXERCISE 2

Review transitive and intransitive verbs on page 60. Challenge students to work independently. Have volunteers share their answers with the class. You might record the verb for each sentence in a three-column chart, with the headings *Transitive, Intransitive,* and *Linking.*

4.4 Linking Verbs

Not all verbs express action. **A linking verb** joins the subject with a **subject complement.** The subject complement is a noun or pronoun that renames the subject, or an adjective that describes the subject.

SUBJECT	LINKING VERB	SUBJECT COMPLEMENT
Woody Guthrie	**was**	**a folk singer.** (noun)
It	**was**	**he who popularized folk music.** (pronoun)
His songs	**remain**	**popular.** (adjective)

The verb *be* in its various forms (*am, is, are, was, were, will be, has been, had been,* and so on) is the most common linking verb. Other common linking verbs are *appear, become, feel, grow, look, remain, seem, smell, sound, stay, taste,* and *turn.*

Some of these verbs can function as either action verbs or linking verbs.

Miriam Makeba's name *remains* **famous in the music world.** (linking verb)
She *remained* **in the United States for many years.** (action verb—an intransitive verb)
Makeba's voice *sounded* **powerful.** (linking verb)
Makeba courageously *sounded* **her protest against apartheid to the world.** (action verb—a transitive verb with the direct object *protest*)

When words such as *remain* and *sound* are used as linking verbs, a form of the verb *be* can be substituted for the original verb.

Miriam Makeba's name *is* **famous in the music world.**
Makeba's voice *is* **powerful.**

EXERCISE 1 Identify the linking verbs and the subject complements in these sentences. Not every sentence has a linking verb.

1. Woody Guthrie <u>was</u> a <u>songwriter</u>.
2. He <u>became</u> <u>famous</u> for his songs about the United States and its people.
3. Many of his songs <u>are</u> <u>accounts</u> of working people during the Great Depression of the 1930s.
4. His <u>was</u> a <u>voice</u> of protest against injustice.

Exercise 1
Linking verbs are underlined once. Subject complements are underlined twice. Item #8 does not have a linking verb.

Woody Guthrie

64 • Section 4.4

EXERCISE 3

Invite volunteers to list on the board the linking verbs. Then have students identify the word to which the verb is linked. Discuss answers as a class.

APPLY

APPLY IT NOW

Suggest that students write their sentences about one subject. Have volunteers share their work with the class. Students should demonstrate an understanding of linking verbs.

TechTip Suggest that students post their sentences on a class blog. Then have students review classmates' use of linking verbs and offer feedback.

ASSESS

Note which students had difficulty recognizing linking verbs. Assign **Practice Book** page 45 for further practice.

WRITING CONNECTION

Use pages 304–305 of the Writing portion of the book.

WRITING CONNECTION

Use pages 304–305 of the Writing portion of the book.

---

5. "This Land Is Your Land" remains his most famous song.
6. It is a celebration of the country from one coast to the other.
7. In certain verses the song becomes bitter, lamenting the gap between rich and poor.
8. The song ends on a hopeful note, however.
9. Many people feel proud of their heritage because of the song.
10. To some, the song is our informal national anthem.

Exercise 2
1. linking
2. intransitive
3. transitive
4. transitive
5. transitive
6. transitive
7. transitive
8. linking
9. transitive
10. intransitive

EXERCISE 2 Identify the verb or verb phrase in each sentence. Then tell whether that verb is transitive, intransitive, or linking.

1. Miriam Makeba was a famous singer with an incredible voice.
2. She had lived in Johannesburg, South Africa.
3. At that time in South Africa, the system of apartheid separated black people from white people.
4. Makeba voiced her opposition to apartheid.
5. Because of this, she gained enemies.
6. She began a musical career in the United States in the 1950s.
7. She introduced African music to the West.
8. She became popular around the world for her music.
9. Her music blended different styles, including jazz and African strains.
10. Miriam Makeba returned to South Africa after the fall of apartheid.

Miriam Makeba

Exercise 3
Linking verbs are underlined once. The word it is linked with is underlined twice.
1. adjective
2. noun
3. adjective
4. pronoun
5. noun
6. adjective

EXERCISE 3 Identify the linking verb in each sentence. Identify the word to which the verb is linked. Tell whether the verb links the subject with a noun, a pronoun, or an adjective.

1. Noah's guitar is beautiful.
2. We are a popular band.
3. The audience's mood grew enthusiastic during our first set.
4. It was she who chose the songs.
5. A banjo is a string instrument that Noah also plays.
6. Samantha always remains calm onstage.

APPLY IT NOW

Use the linking verbs *was, appear, become, feel, look, seem, sound, smell,* and *taste* in nine sentences. Label each subject complement as a noun, a pronoun, or an adjective.

 Tech Tip Post sentences on your class blog for peer review.

Verbs • 65

TEACHING OPTIONS

Reteach

Choose a person who is well known to students, such as someone in the community, a celebrity, a historical figure, or a character in a novel. Encourage students to suggest sentences that tell about this person. Write their sentences on chart paper. As you review the sentences, ask students to identify the verbs as action verbs or linking verbs.

Mia Hamm is a soccer player.

She plays professional soccer.

Her play seems effortless.

She knows the necessary moves to get the ball down the field.

Curriculum Connection

Invite each student to choose a topic that he or she is learning about in science or social studies. Encourage students to write about the topic, explaining and describing it. When the writing is complete, have students underline the verbs in their pieces and identify each as either an action verb or a linking verb.

We are learning about crustaceans.

Crustaceans live in the ocean.

Their hard outsides are actually shells.

Inside you can find their soft bodies.

Meeting Individual Needs

Auditory Have volunteers read aloud three sentences from a novel. As students read, encourage the other class to identify the verbs. Discuss whether the verbs express action or are linking verbs. Challenge students to explain their choices.

 **Maintenance**

Assign **Practice Book** page 39, Section 4.5. After students finish,
1. Give immediate feedback.
2. Review concepts as needed.
3. Model the correct answer.

Pages 4–5 of the **Answer Key** contain tips for Daily Maintenance.

WARM-UP

Take a small, soft object such as a beanbag and toss it to a student. Tell half of the class to write a sentence that begins with *The teacher,* describing what happened. *(The teacher tossed a beanbag.)* Instruct the other half of the class to write a sentence that begins with *The beanbag.* *(The beanbag was thrown by the teacher.)* Have volunteers from each half of the class write their sentences on the board.

📖 Read from a piece of writing that the class is currently reading. Emphasize the active and passive voices.

TEACH

Read the sentences students wrote on the board from the Warm-Up. Challenge students to tell how the sentences differ. Point out that the verb in the sentence beginning with *The teacher* is more immediate, or active, and that the verb in the sentence beginning with *The beanbag* contains *was,* which is not as immediate, or passive.

Invite students to take turns reading aloud about active and passive voice. Lead students to see that if the subject of a verb is the doer of the action, the verb is in the active voice. Tell students that when the subject of a verb is the receiver of the action, the verb is in the passive voice. Discuss how the passive voice is often formed by combining a form of *be* plus the past participle of the main verb.

PRACTICE

EXERCISE 1

Read the sentences aloud, asking students to follow along in their books. Have students write each verb or verb phrase and identify it as active or passive. After reading the last sentence, review the students' answers and discuss both active and passive voices.

EXERCISE 2

Invite a volunteer to explain the difference between active and passive voices. Encourage students to remember this description as they rewrite the sentences in the exercise.

EXERCISE 3

Remind students that passive voice is often formed by combining a form of *be* with the past participle of the main verb. Have partners

---

4.5 Active and Passive Voices

A transitive verb has voice. When a transitive verb is in the **active voice,** the subject is the doer of the action.

> Congress *passed* the bill.

In the **passive voice,** the subject is the receiver of the action.

> The bill *was passed* by Congress.
> The bill *was being studied* in committee.

In the first sentence, *Congress,* the subject, is the doer of the action *passed.* The verb, therefore, is in the active voice. In the second sentence, the subject *bill* is the receiver of the action *was passed.* The verb, therefore, is in the passive voice.

A verb in the passive voice is formed by combining some form of *be* with the past participle of the main verb. Only transitive verbs can be used in the passive voice. Which of the following sentences is in the passive voice?

> Nicole writes articles for the magazine.
> The articles for the magazine are written by Nicole.

You are correct if you said the second sentence is in the passive voice. The subject *articles* is the receiver of the action, and the verb consists of a form of *be (are)* plus the past participle of the verb *write (written).*

Sentences in the active voice are generally more alive and direct.

> I gave the speech. (active voice)
> The speech was given by me. (passive voice)

Sometimes, though, passive voice can be the better choice; for example, when the doer of the action is unknown or unimportant.

> Every house on the street was painted a different color.

EXERCISE 1 Identify the verb or verb phrase in each sentence and tell whether it is in the active voice or the passive voice.

1. The Constitution of the United States <u>was ratified</u> in 1788.
2. The original Constitution <u>did</u> not <u>include</u> a bill of rights.
3. Many people <u>wanted</u> a statement of the limitation of the government's power over individuals.

Exercise 1
1. passive
2. active
3. active
4. passive
5. active
6. passive
7. passive
8. active
9. passive
10. passive

complete this exercise. Discuss possible revisions for each sentence.

APPLY

APPLY IT NOW

Tell students that sometimes the passive voice is more effective in nonfiction texts because readers do not always need to know the doer of the action. After students have finished, have them rewrite the sentences so they are in the opposite voice. Students should demonstrate an understanding of active and passive voices.

💡 **TechTip** Suggest that students find their science article through a well-known organization such as NASA or NOAA.

ASSESS

Note which students had difficulty recognizing active and passive voice. Assign **Practice Book** page 46 for further practice.

> **WRITING CONNECTION**
> Use pages 306–307 of the Writing portion of the book.

WRITING CONNECTION
Use pages 306–307 of the Writing portion of the book.

TEACHING OPTIONS

TEACHING OPTIONS

Reteach

Invite the class to brainstorm a list of 20 action verbs. Record their list on the board. Then ask partners to select five verbs from the list and to take turns using them in sentences in both the passive and active voices. Encourage students to work together to write their sentences, circling the verbs and verb phrases and indicating whether each is in the active or passive voice.

Meeting Individual Needs

Interpersonal Have students work with partners. Encourage one partner to describe an event that he or she observed, such as a soccer match, a concert, or a festival. Challenge the other partner to listen closely for the use of active or passive voice and to write down the verbs he or she hears. Afterward, have partners discuss the use of the verbs and how it affected the description. Then have partners switch roles.

Cooperative Learning

Have partners create a story about two characters. Encourage students to write about a funny or mysterious situation. Instruct one student to write the story in the active voice and the other student to write the story in the passive voice. Encourage students to discuss how they create each voice while they write. Remind students to include plot twists and interesting details in their stories. Ask volunteers to share their stories with the class.

Exercise 2

1. A strong central government was established by the Constitution.
2. Revolutionary leaders Patrick Henry and Samuel Adams opposed the Constitution.
3. The Constitution was approved by the states only after a long debate.
4. The power of the larger states was feared by the small states.
5. The writers of the Constitution proposed two houses of the legislature.
6. Strong representation for small states was ensured by the upper house—the Senate with two senators from each state.

Exercise 3
Answers will vary.

---

4. For them the American Revolution <u>was fought</u> precisely for these rights.
5. Leaders in favor of ratification <u>promised</u> a bill of rights.
6. Personal rights <u>were outlined</u> in the proposed bill.
7. These rights <u>were incorporated</u> into amendments to the Constitution.
8. The first 10 amendments to the Constitution <u>form</u> the Bill of Rights.
9. Basic freedoms, such as freedom of speech, freedom of religion, freedom of the press, and a right to trial by jury <u>are guaranteed</u> by the Bill of Rights.
10. The rights <u>are recognized</u> as essential to the foundations of American democracy.

EXERCISE 2 Rewrite each sentence in the voice indicated.

1. The Constitution established a strong central government. (passive)
2. The Constitution was opposed by revolutionary leaders Patrick Henry and Samuel Adams. (active)
3. The states approved the Constitution only after a long debate. (passive)
4. The small states feared the power of the larger states. (passive)
5. Two houses of the legislature were proposed by the writers of the Constitution. (active)
6. The upper house—the Senate with two senators from each state—ensured strong representation for small states. (passive)

EXERCISE 3 Rewrite the following sentences. Change the verbs in the active voice to the passive voice or the verbs in the passive voice to the active voice.

1. The Iroquois nation wrote a constitution that inspired our own.
2. Other ideals were imported from Europe.
3. The two houses of the legislature are similar to England's government.
4. Healthy debate strengthens our civilization.
5. Our respect for one another must not be lost despite our differences.
6. The Constitution protects minorities from the tyranny of the majority.

APPLY IT NOW

Find a science article in a magazine or newspaper and identify four transitive verbs—two active and two passive. Label each one accordingly.

💡 **Tech Tip** With an adult, find a science article online.

Verbs • 67

OBJECTIVES

- To identify verbs in the simple, progressive, and perfect tenses
- To form verbs in the simple, progressive, and perfect tenses

 **Maintenance**

Assign **Practice Book** page 39, Section 4.6. After students finish,
1. Give immediate feedback.
2. Review concepts as needed.
3. Model the correct answer.

Pages 4–5 of the **Answer Key** contain tips for Daily Maintenance.

WARM-UP

Place a chair at the front of the classroom and have a volunteer sit in the chair, facing the class. Write an occupation on the board, such as chef or nurse. Tell students to call out clues to help the volunteer guess what job he or she had in the past. Ask students to begin their clues with *You used to be _____.* When the volunteer guesses his or her past occupation, write a future career for the same volunteer. Have students begin each clue with *You will be _____.* Repeat with several students.

📖 Read from a piece of writing that the class is currently reading. Emphasize the simple, progressive, and perfect tenses.

TEACH

Say the following sentences as you write them on the board.

Marcus eats lunch at noon.

Janie ate lunch earlier.

Andre will eat lunch soon.

Latrell is going to eat lunch too.

Ask volunteers to explain how the sentences are the same. *(All mention eating lunch.)* Then

challenge students to explain how the sentences are different. *(The verbs have different tenses.)* Prompt students to identify the tense of each verb.

Ask a volunteer to read the first two paragraphs and the example sentences. Discuss how progressive tenses differ from simple tenses; make sure students indicate the use of the auxiliary verb *be*. Encourage students to suggest sentences for each progressive verb tense.

Continue in this way with the perfect tenses. Ask students to explain how perfect tenses differ from progressive tenses. Stress that the perfect tense includes the

auxiliary verb *have*. Discuss the use of *been* to form the passive voice. Then challenge students to suggest sentences for both perfect and progressive verb tenses.

PRACTICE

EXERCISE 1
Read the first sentence to the class. Ask a volunteer to provide the correct answer. Then have students complete the exercise independently. When students are finished, review their answers.

EXERCISE 2
Make sure students understand that for each sentence they must

---

4.6 Simple, Progressive, and Perfect Tenses

Verb forms indicate **tense,** or the time of the action. **Simple tenses** are the **present tense,** the **past tense,** and the **future tense.**

Progressive tenses consist of a form of the auxiliary verb *be* and the present participle of the main verb. Verbs in the progressive tense indicate continuing, or ongoing, action.

Present progressive:	Alyssa *is studying* Italian.
Past progressive:	Alyssa *was studying* Italian last term.
Future progressive:	Alyssa *will be studying* Italian for many years.

Perfect tenses consist of a form of the auxiliary verb *have* and the past participle of the main verb. The **present perfect** tells about an action that took place at an indefinite time in the past or that started in the past and continues into the present. The **past perfect** tells about an action that was completed before another past action. The **future perfect** tells about an action that will be completed before a specific time in the future.

Present perfect active:	I *have read* the book on Venice.
Past perfect active:	I *had read* the book before my trip.
Future perfect active:	I *will have read* the book by the time I leave.

In the perfect tenses, the passive voice is formed by inserting *been* between the auxiliary verb *have* and the main verb.

Present perfect passive:	A plan to save Venice *has been undertaken* recently.
Past perfect passive:	The solution *had been proposed* a while ago.
Future perfect passive:	Perhaps the plan *will have been implemented* by the time I visit.

Progressive forms of the perfect tenses indicate ongoing actions.

Present perfect progressive:	I *have been planning* for months.
Past perfect progressive:	I *had been studying* Italian for a while before I understood it.
Future perfect progressive:	I *will have been studying* Italian for a long time before I am fluent.

68 • Section 4.6

choose the correct tense of the verb and write it in the correct voice. Encourage partners to discuss their answers and to make sure their verb choices fit both criteria—tense and voice. Invite volunteers to share their verbs with the class.

APPLY

APPLY IT NOW

Encourage students to write freely, expressing their ideas in sentences that seem appropriate to the piece. Then have students reread their work, circling the verbs and identifying their tense.

Students should demonstrate an understanding of simple, progressive, and perfect tenses.

ASSESS

Note which students had difficulty identifying simple, progressive, and perfect verb tenses. Assign **Practice Book** page 47 for further practice.

> **WRITING CONNECTION**
> Use pages 308–309 of the Writing portion of the book.

Use pages 308–309 of the Writing portion of the book.

Exercise 1

The verbs are underlined.

1. present perfect, active
2. future perfect passive
3. past perfect active
4. future perfect passive

Exercise 2

1. was built
2. has driven
3. have used
4. has contributed
5. is causing
6. was decided; had been proposed
7. are constructing
8. will block
9. oppose
10. will be working
11. hope; will have solved
12. has been adding

EXERCISE 1 Identify the verbs in these sentences. Tell the tense and voice of each verb.

1. Carlos has purchased a new digital camera.
2. The check will have been mailed before the payment is due.
3. Louise had trained hard before the race.
4. The act will have been performed by the time you get there.

EXERCISE 2 Complete the sentences with the verbs in parentheses. Use the tense and voice indicated.

1. Venice _____ (build—simple past, passive) on pilings in the marshy ground.
2. The weight of the city buildings _____ (drive—present perfect, active) the pilings down into the muddy land.
3. The city's residents and visitors _____ (use—present perfect, active) well water from beneath the city.
4. This also _____ (contribute—present perfect, active) to the gradual sinking of the city.
5. Global warming now _____ (cause—present progressive, active) a rise in the water level in the sea and the lagoon.
6. A plan finally _____ (decide—simple past, passive) on in 2001 after many plans _____ (propose—past perfect, passive).
7. Workers _____ (construct—present progressive, active) gates at entrances to the lagoon.
8. These _____ (block—simple future, active) high waters.
9. Some _____ (oppose—simple present, active) this plan for environmental reasons.
10. The city _____ (work—future progressive, active) on the gates for many years.
11. I _____ (hope—simple present, active) the city _____ (solve—future perfect, active) the flooding problem with this plan.
12. The beauty of Venice's waterways _____ (add—present perfect progressive) romance to this city for centuries.

APPLY IT NOW

Write a paragraph about a place that you plan to visit, using at least six verbs and three different tenses. Include information about the place's history, why you want to visit it, what you plan to do there, and how you are preparing for the trip. Circle the verbs you use and label their tenses.

Verbs • 69

TEACHING OPTIONS

Reteach

Help students identify verb tenses by creating a chart of simple tenses and the active and passive voices.

SIMPLE TENSES
Active Voice

Present	Past	Future
check	checked	will check

Passive Voice

Present	Past	Future
is checked	was checked	will be checked

Have students complete similar charts for progressive-tense verbs and perfect-tense verbs. Display the charts. Encourage students to refer to the charts while completing the exercises and activities about verb tenses.

Cooperative Learning

Have students work in groups of three or four. Assign a verb to each group and challenge members to come up with sentences that demonstrate an understanding of the present, past, and future of simple, progressive, and perfect tenses. Provide students with poster paper and markers. Tell students to write their sentences on the paper in large letters. When students have finished, have them share and discuss their sentences with the class.

Meeting Individual Needs

Challenge Encourage students to choose a nonfiction book about a topic that is of special interest to them. Tell students to choose a chapter or a few pages from the book that particularly captured their interest and to copy a paragraph from that passage, circling the verbs and verb phrases. Work with each student to identify the tenses and voice of those verbs.

4.7 Indicative, Imperative, and Emphatic Moods

OBJECTIVES

- **To recognize how verbs express the indicative mood, imperative mood, and emphatic mood**
- **To identify the indicative mood, imperative mood, and emphatic mood**

 **Maintenance**

Assign **Practice Book** page 39, Section 4.7. After students finish,
1. Give immediate feedback.
2. Review concepts as needed.
3. Model the correct answer.

Pages 4–5 of the **Answer Key** contain tips for Daily Maintenance.

WARM-UP

Play a game of Simon Says with the class. After completing the game, encourage students to discuss the ways in which the sentences you stated are similar. Ask volunteers to point out how some sentences were different.

📖 Read from a piece of writing that the class is currently reading. Emphasize the indicative, imperative, and emphatic moods.

TEACH

Write the word *mood* on the board and invite students to explain what the word *mood* means to them. List students' ideas on the board. Then ask a volunteer to read aloud about mood and indicative mood, including the example sentences. You may wish to have a volunteer look up the meaning of the word *indicative* to reinforce the meaning of the indicative mood.

Invite a volunteer to read about the imperative mood. Point out that the sentences used when playing Simon Says were all examples of the imperative mood. Then compare the two types of moods. On the board, start a two-column chart, one column for indicative mood and the other for imperative mood. Have students suggest sentences for each and write their sentences on the chart.

Have a volunteer read about the emphatic mood. Add a column to the chart on the board. Have students provide sentences in the emphatic mood. Leave the chart displayed so students have examples to reference as they complete the exercises.

PRACTICE

EXERCISE 1

Let students work with partners to complete this exercise. Encourage partners to confer about their verb choices and to discuss whether the verbs express the indicative, imperative, or emphatic mood. You might combine student pairs to form larger groups, encouraging the groups to discuss their answers.

EXERCISE 2

Challenge students to rewrite these sentences independently. Then invite volunteers to write their sentences on the board. Discuss students' revisions with the class, working through both the indicative and imperative sentences.

4.7 Indicative, Imperative, and Emphatic Moods

Verb forms also indicate mood. There are four **moods** in English: indicative, imperative, emphatic, and subjunctive. You will examine the first three in this section and the fourth in the next section.

The **indicative mood** is the form of a verb that is used to state a fact or ask a question.

> We *are working* on the project together.
> *Have* you ever *painted* a T-shirt?

Note that all the tenses studied in Section 4.6—simple, progressive, and perfect—are forms of the indicative mood.

The **imperative mood** is the form of a verb that is used to give commands. The subject of a verb in the imperative mood is almost always in the second person, either singular or plural. The subject *you* usually is not expressed. To form the imperative mood, use the base form of the verb. For negative sentences, use *do not* or *don't*.

> *Plan* your design carefully.
> *Do not start* without a definite design.

In both the above sentences, the subject *you* is understood.

To form a command using the first person, use *let's (let us)* before the base form of the verb.

> *Let's get* the materials for our project.

The **emphatic mood** is the form of a verb that gives special force to a simple present or past tense verb. For the present tense, use *do* or *does* before the base form of the verb. For the past tense, use *did* before the base form of the word. Do not confuse this with *do, does,* and *did* used as auxiliary verbs in questions or negative sentences.

> I *do like* your idea.

EXERCISE 1 Identify the verb or verb phrase in each sentence. Then tell whether the sentence is in the indicative, imperative, or emphatic mood.

1. I <u>do hope</u> to paint a T-shirt for the school logo contest.
2. We <u>can work</u> together.
3. What <u>do</u> we <u>need</u> for the project?

Exercise 1
1. emphatic
2. indicative
3. indicative

EXERCISE 3

Have students complete this exercise independently. Encourage students to answer using a three-column chart with columns for verb, mood, and tense. Remind students that they will only identify the tense if the verb is in the emphatic mood.

APPLY

APPLY IT NOW

Point out that students often find the imperative mood when they read instructions. Then have students write instructions for a fire drill, changing some sentences into the indicative and emphatic moods. Students should demonstrate an understanding of the indicative, imperative, and emphatic moods.

ASSESS

Note which students had difficulty identifying indicative, imperative, and emphatic moods. Assign **Practice Book** page 48 for further practice.

WRITING CONNECTION

Use pages 310–311 of the Writing portion of the book.

TEACHING OPTIONS

Reteach

Prepare a note card for each student. On each card write a sentence in either the imperative, indicative, or emphatic mood. Then pass out the cards at random. Tell students to decide whether their sentences are indicative, imperative, or emphatic. Have students compare their cards to those of other students. Have volunteers read their sentences aloud and identify the mood of their sentences.

Meeting Individual Needs

Kinesthetic Have small groups create and act out a scene, using the indicative, imperative, and emphatic moods. Have students place their scene in a retail shop, such as a grocery store. Ask students to identify jobs for themselves within this store, such as manager, clerk, or stocker. Have one student play the role of a customer. Ask students to improvise a scene in which they give one another orders or make requests that would be natural for their characters. For example, a manager might say *Please help this customer.* Encourage students to be creative. Then discuss each scene with the class, focusing on the use of each mood.

English-Language Learners

Say simple directions and ask students to follow those directions. After students have completed the assigned activity, have them explain what they just did using an indicative or emphatic sentence.

Teacher: Write your name.
(Student writes his or her name.)

Student: I wrote my name.
Or   I did write my name.

Continue until you feel the students understand these moods of the verbs.

---

4. imperative
5. indicative
6. imperative
7. indicative
8. imperative
9. imperative
10. indicative

4. <u>Get</u> a couple of T-shirts, some fabric paints, and a piece of cardboard.
5. Why <u>do</u> we <u>need</u> the cardboard?
6. <u>Put</u> the cardboard inside the T-shirt.
7. The cardboard <u>stops</u> paint from soaking onto the back of the T-shirt.
8. <u>Do</u> not <u>paint</u> the shirt without the cardboard inside!
9. Please <u>choose</u> a design.
10. I <u>am thinking</u> of a slogan about learning and cooperation.

Exercise 2
1. Apply the fabric paint with a brush or a sponge.
2. Squeeze paint from the tube right onto the shirt to draw lines.
3. Do not put the painted shirt on immediately.
4. Let the paint dry first.
5. Use different colored T-shirts to get different background effects.
6. Hand me the fabric paint.
7. Tell me which colors you like.
8. Pick from the rack of paints on the wall.

EXERCISE 2 **Rewrite the following sentences in the imperative mood.**
1. You can apply the fabric paint with a brush or a sponge.
2. It is a good idea to squeeze paint from the tube right onto the shirt to draw lines.
3. You should not put the painted shirt on immediately.
4. It is necessary to let the paint dry first.
5. You can use different colored T-shirts to get different background effects.
6. Would you hand me the fabric paint?
7. Can you tell me which colors you like?
8. You can pick from the rack of paints on the wall.

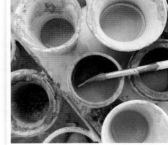

Exercise 3
1. indicative
2. indicative
3. indicative
4. imperative
5. emphatic, present
6. indicative
7. imperative
8. imperative
9. imperative
10. indicative
11. emphatic, past

EXERCISE 3 **Identify the verb or verb phrase in each sentence. Then tell whether the verb is in the indicative or the imperative mood. If the verb is in the emphatic mood, tell its tense.**
1. The soccer team's annual car wash <u>is</u> this afternoon.
2. We <u>need</u> money for new uniforms.
3. The Art Club <u>made</u> signs for us.
4. <u>Hang</u> one sign at each end of the block.
5. Good advertising really <u>does work</u>!
6. <u>Do</u> we <u>have</u> enough buckets and sponges?
7. <u>Put</u> soapy water in the buckets.
8. <u>Rinse</u> the soap off the cars with the hoses.
9. <u>Use</u> these rags to dry the cars.
10. Drivers <u>will be</u> happy about their clean cars!
11. We <u>did have</u> fun last year too.

APPLY IT NOW

Write your school's fire drill instructions, using two of each type of verb: imperative, indicative, and emphatic.

Verbs • 71

OBJECTIVES

- **To recognize how verbs are used to express the subjunctive mood**
- **To identify and use the subjunctive mood**

DAILY Maintenance

Assign **Practice Book** page 39, Section 4.8. After students finish,
1. Give immediate feedback.
2. Review concepts as needed.
3. Model the correct answer.

Pages 4–5 of the **Answer Key** contain tips for Daily Maintenance.

WARM-UP

Arrange the class into four groups. Give a note card to each group with one of the following sentence starters on it:

If I were _____.

My brother wishes that _____.

My boss recommends that _____.

Whether it rains or not, I _____.

Have groups write as many endings as they can that complete the sentence starters. Then ask a volunteer from each group to write one sentence on the board and say what the sentence expresses *(a wish, a desire, a recommendation, an uncertainty)*.

📖 Read from a piece of writing that the class is currently reading. Emphasize the subjunctive mood.

TEACH

Use the sentences on the board from the Warm-Up. Explain that each sentence is in the subjunctive mood. Ask a volunteer to read the information about the subjunctive mood. Then have students create new sentences to fit each category.

Emphasize that subjunctive constructions after words such as *insist, recommend,* or *suggest* should not include *should* or *would.*

PRACTICE

EXERCISE 1

Before engaging students in this exercise, elicit from them their own strategies for understanding the subjunctive mood. Read aloud each sentence in the exercise as students follow along and write their answers. Ask a few volunteers to share their answers with the class. Work with students on each sentence to help them learn how to identify the mood.

EXERCISE 2

Suggest that students use the example sentences to identify what each sentence in the exercise expresses. When students have finished, let them exchange papers with partners. Have partners explain their answers when they come upon different verb choices. Challenge students to work through those sentences to arrive at the correct answer.

EXERCISE 3

Review the different expressions that the subjunctive mood creates *(wish or desire, contrary to the fact, demand, recommendation, uncertainty)*. Have students

---

4.8 Subjunctive Mood

The **subjunctive mood** of a verb can express a wish or desire or a condition that is contrary to fact. The past tense is used to state present wishes or desires or contrary-to-fact conditions. The past perfect tense is used to state past wishes, desires, or contrary-to-fact conditions. Note the use of *could* and *would have* in the contrary-to-fact sentences.

Wish or desire:	I wish my new bike *were* here already.
	I wished I *had bought* a computer.
Contrary-to-fact condition:	If I *were* in the market for a bike, I *could research* prices on the Internet.
	If you *had worked* more hours, you *would have earned* enough to buy a computer.

The subjunctive mood is also used to express a demand or recommendation after *that* or to express an uncertainty after *if* or *whether*. The base form of the verb is used in the clause after *that, if,* or *whether.*

Demand after *that*:	I must insist that your mother *be* with you when you buy it.
Recommendation after *that*:	I recommended that James *compare* prices before buying a new bike.
Uncertainty:	Whether Joe's suggestion *be* good or bad, I'm sticking with my decision.
	Whether he *buy* a bike or a computer, James will be happy.

EXERCISE 1 Tell whether each of the following sentences is in the subjunctive, indicative, emphatic, or imperative mood.

1. You could choose from games, clothing, and lots of other things if you were to shop online.
2. I do believe you could order everything you need online.
3. I recommend that he follow simple tips for shopping online.
4. Consumer experts urge that every buyer check out the reliability of online merchants.
5. Experts also suggest that every consumer keep copies of online transactions and purchases.
6. Buy only from well-known companies.
7. Check out the special sales.
8. If he were buying a computer, he says that he would shop online.

Exercise 1
1. subjunctive
2. emphatic
3. subjunctive
4. subjunctive
5. subjunctive
6. imperative
7. imperative
8. subjunctive
9. emphatic
10. indicative

complete this exercise independently. When students have finished, have volunteers share their answers. Discuss each sentence and how students arrived at their answers.

APPLY
APPLY IT NOW

Make sure the verbs in the subjunctive mood have been used correctly. Invite volunteers to share their sentences with the class. Students should demonstrate an understanding of the subjunctive mood.

 Grammar in Action. Students should identify the following sentence as subjunctive mood: *If we had a skate park, kids would no longer bother adults downtown.*

ASSESS

Note which students had difficulty identifying the subjunctive mood. Assign **Practice Book** page 49 for further practice.

WRITING CONNECTION

Use pages 312–313 of the Writing portion of the book.

TEACHING OPTIONS

Reteach

Have the class choose something they would like to change at their school or something they would like to add to it, for example, a new playing field. Direct students to suggest sentences in the subjunctive mood as you write them on chart paper. Write the sentences exactly as students say them. Then review the sentences, asking the class if the verbs have been used correctly.

Meeting Individual Needs

Intrapersonal Encourage students to spend a few minutes writing sentences in the subjunctive mood in their journals. Suggest that the sentences reflect something students think or feel about school, for example: *I wish the lunches in the school cafeteria were better. I recommend that the teachers be more lenient when it comes to homework.*

Curriculum Connection

Encourage students to think about a topic they are studying in science or social studies that they would like to tell others about. Suggest, for example, that perhaps they are learning about the importance of voting or why we should not pollute the world's oceans. Challenge students to write an essay about the topic, paying attention to the use of the subjunctive mood. For example:

> **I recommend that everyone pay attention to what he or she puts in the world's oceans. It does make a difference.**

---

9. Many of my friends do shop online.

10. Some things you buy don't fit or are not what you expected.

Exercise 2

Verbs are underlined.

1. wish or desire
2. contrary-to-fact condition
3. recommendation
4. wish or desire
5. uncertainty
6. demand
7. contrary-to-fact condition
8. contrary-to-fact condition
9. wish or desire
10. recommendation

EXERCISE 2 Identify each verb in the subjunctive mood. Tell what each verb expresses: a wish or desire, a contrary-to-fact condition, a demand, recommendation after *that*, or an uncertainty.

1. Long live the King!
2. My sister would play the piano if she were here.
3. The store clerk recommended that you wash the new jeans before wearing them.
4. May she be happy in her new job!
5. Whether he be honest or not, we have to trust him.
6. Akira insisted that her little sister go to bed after the movie.
7. He looks as if he just swallowed a lemon.
8. If I were you, I would read the assignment.
9. May all your dreams come true.
10. I suggest that she report her missing wallet to the police immediately.

Exercise 3

1. contrary-to-fact condition
2. contrary-to-fact condition
3. demand after *that*
4. demand after *that*
5. recommendation after *that*
6. uncertainty
7. contrary-to-fact condition
8. wish or desire

EXERCISE 3 Choose the correct forms to complete the sentences. Tell what each verb expresses.

1. If I (was were) you, I would send those boots back.
2. You wouldn't have to ship them if you (live lived) in the city.
3. You must insist that the company (takes take) them back.
4. You must demand that the company (gives give) you your money back or (sends send) you a pair in a bigger size.
5. I recommend that you (be are) firm with them.
6. Whether the pair of boots (be are) sturdy enough is another question.
7. If the company (was were) in town, I'd talk to the president.
8. I wish that I (own owned) boots like that—but in the right size.

APPLY IT NOW

Write three sentences using the following phrases about consumer issues, such as online shopping. When you have finished, circle all the verbs in the subjunctive mood.

Experts suggest that . . .

If I were . . .

I recommend that . . .

Grammar in Action. Identify the subjunctive mood in the letter on p. 299.

Verbs • 73

4.9 Modal Auxiliaries

OBJECTIVES

- **To recognize that the purpose of modal auxiliaries is to express permission, possibility, ability, necessity, obligation, or intention**
- **To recognize and use the common modal auxiliaries** *may, might, can, could, must, should, will,* **and** *would*

Maintenance

Assign **Practice Book** page 40, Section 4.9. After students finish,
1. Give immediate feedback.
2. Review concepts as needed.
3. Model the correct answer.

Pages 4–5 of the **Answer Key** contain tips for Daily Maintenance.

WARM-UP

Write on the board the following words: *may, might, can, could, must, should, will, would.* Tell students to imagine that they are stranded in the wilderness. Have each student generate an idea for survival, using one of the verbs on the board. (*I would create a shelter immediately.*) Have volunteers share their ideas with the class.

📖 Read from a piece of writing that the class is currently reading. Emphasize the modal auxiliaries.

TEACH

Start a chart on the board with the following headings: *Permission, Possibility, Ability, Necessity, Obligation, Intention.* Invite a volunteer to read aloud the information about modal auxiliaries. Have students write the modal auxiliaries under the correct headings in the chart. Point out that some headings will have more than one modal auxiliary and that some modal

auxiliaries will fit under more than one heading.

Review the example sentences and encourage students to suggest sentences of their own for each modal auxiliary. You may wish to leave the chart on the board for students to reference as they complete the exercises.

PRACTICE

EXERCISE 1

Challenge students to complete this exercise independently. Then assign a sentence to each of 10 volunteers and ask them

to write the sentences on the board, underline the verb phrase, and write which type of modal auxiliary the sentence includes. Invite the rest of the class to check their own work against their classmates' sentences on the board. Discuss any problematic sentences.

EXERCISE 2

Let students work with partners to complete this exercise. Encourage them to help each other come up with appropriate verb phrases that include the modal auxiliary. Ask volunteers to read their completed sentences to the class.

4.9 Modal Auxiliaries

Modal auxiliaries are used to express permission, possibility, ability, necessity, obligation, and intention. They are used with main verbs that are in the base form.

The common modal auxiliaries are *may, might, can, could, must, should, will,* and *would.* Study the verb phrases in each of these sentences.

Permission: Anyone who needs help *may request* a tutor.
Possibility: I *might need* some help with my math.
Ability: Laurel *can solve* equations easily.
Necessity: You *must complete* your homework on time.
Obligation: I *should study* more.
Intention: Andy *will help* you with that paper.

For verb phrases with auxiliaries, the passive voice is formed by inserting *be, have been,* or *had been* between the modal auxiliary and the past participle.

The homework *could be done* in an hour.
The project *must have been completed* yesterday.

Some auxiliaries that include forms of *have* indicate contrary-to-fact conditions.

I *could have completed* my homework on Friday [but I didn't].
I *should have started* my homework earlier [but I didn't].

EXERCISE 1 Identify the verb phrase with a modal auxiliary in each sentence. Tell whether the verb phrase expresses permission, possibility, ability, necessity, obligation, or intention.

1. My parents say that I <u>should get</u> better grades.
2. In fact, they say that I <u>must get</u> better grades.
3. I agree that I <u>could have studied</u> more last term.
4. I <u>should have started</u> on my projects before the deadlines.
5. I <u>will</u> also <u>try</u> to get help if I need it.
6. My teacher said I <u>may ask</u> for help if I need it.
7. Helpful tips like these <u>can be used</u> by any student.
8. Especially for students who <u>may have lost</u> their discipline.
9. My sister <u>can study</u> for hours on end.
10. My grades <u>must be raised</u> by the end of this semester.

Exercise 1
Verb phrases are underlined.
1. obligation
2. necessity
3. possibility
4. obligation
5. intention
6. permission
7. ability
8. possibility
9. ability
10. necessity

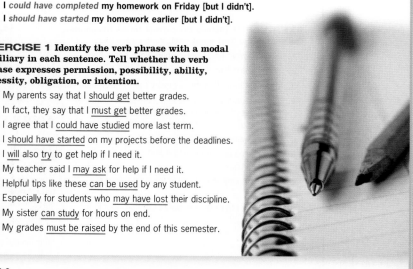

APPLY

APPLY IT NOW

When checking the tips, make sure students not only use modal auxiliaries correctly but also know the purpose of each. You may wish to have students write the purpose of the modal auxiliary after each sentence. For students who appear to struggle, suggest they use the chart they created during the lesson. Students should demonstrate an understanding of modal auxiliaries.

ASSESS

Note which students had difficulty recognizing modal auxiliaries and their purposes. Assign **Practice Book** page 50 for further practice.

WRITING CONNECTION

Use pages 314–315 of the Writing portion of the book.

TEACHING OPTIONS

Reteach

Write each modal auxiliary on a separate note card and put the note cards facedown in a pile on a table at the front of the room. Invite a volunteer to pick a card, read the word, and return the card to the pile. Challenge the student to say a sentence that uses that word. Then invite the rest of the class to identify its purpose, such as whether it expresses permission, possibility, ability, necessity, obligation, or intention. Continue as time permits.

Meeting Individual Needs

Challenge Have students complete the sentences in Exercise 2, but have students use a modal auxiliary that has a meaning other than the one indicated. Challenge students to identify what is expressed in each new sentence. Encourage students to discuss how the meaning of each sentence changes according to the modal auxiliary used.

Observe and Apply

Display a photo or an illustration that shows people. Have students describe the picture, expressing the thoughts, actions, and ideas of the people in the picture. Challenge students to use modal auxiliaries in their sentences.

> **He should have brought an umbrella.**
>
> **She must be feeling sad.**
>
> **She might be missing a friend.**
>
> **He can jump far.**

Exercise 2

1. should have
2. should write
3. could write or might write
4. must do
5. should have
6. could start or might start
7. can have
8. may sit
9. can hear
10. should ask
11. might make or could make
12. could study or might study
13. must do
14. can do
15. could help or might help
16. could review or might review

EXERCISE 2 Complete each sentence with a verb phrase containing a modal auxiliary. Use the verb in parentheses with the meaning indicated. More than one modal auxiliary may be correct for some sentences.

1. Every student _____ (have—obligation) an assignment book.
2. You _____ (write—obligation) your assignments down.
3. You even _____ (write—possibility) a schedule for completing long-term assignments.
4. That way you know at a glance what you _____ (do—necessity) every day to complete projects.
5. You _____ (have—obligation) a regular time to do homework.
6. For example, you _____ (start—possibility) your assignments right after school.
7. Then you _____ (have—ability) the evenings free.
8. My teachers said that I _____ (sit—permission) nearer the front in class.
9. This way I _____ (hear—ability) them better.
10. You _____ (ask—obligation) questions about what you don't understand.
11. You _____ (make—possibility) a list of questions as you do your homework.
12. You _____ (study—possibility) with someone else.
13. You _____ (do—necessity) your tasks; otherwise, you are letting someone else down.
14. I _____ (do—ability) math better than my brother, so I help him with math and he helps me with English.
15. Here's another tip that _____ (help—possibility) you.
16. You _____ (review—possibility) material regularly—not just before tests.

APPLY IT NOW

Write six study tips for a younger student. Use at least four modal auxiliaries in your writing.

Verbs • 75

OBJECTIVES

- **To use verbs that agree with subjects in person and number**
- **To recognize when to use *doesn't* and *don't***
- **To recognize which verbs to use with *you* as the subject**
- **To understand that *there is* and *there are* agree with the subject**
- **To identify intervening phrases in order to achieve correct subject-verb agreement**

 **Maintenance**

Assign **Practice Book** page 40, Section 4.10. After students finish,
1. Give immediate feedback.
2. Review concepts as needed.
3. Model the correct answer.

Pages 4–5 of the **Answer Key** contain tips for Daily Maintenance.

WARM-UP

Write on the board four sets of lists, one for each of four teams. For each team, list subjects varying in person and number and list verbs so that each subject has a matching verb. Have students conduct a relay race in which one student from each team draws a line from a subject to a verb that correctly matches in person and number. That student then hands the chalk to the next student in line and so on until all the subjects and verbs are correctly matched.

📖 Read from a piece of writing that the class is currently reading. Emphasize the agreement of subjects and verbs.

TEACH

Read aloud the information about subject and verb agreement. Pause after each heading and ask volunteers to add examples of sentences in which the subjects and verbs agree. Point out that before students can decide if a subject and verb agree, they must identify the subject and determine its person and number. Say random sentences for the class and ask students if the subjects and the verbs agree. Include sentences with subjects and verbs that do not agree.

PRACTICE

EXERCISE 1
Let students work with partners to complete this exercise. Suggest that partners discuss the verbs, saying the sentences aloud. Then discuss the answers with the class.

EXERCISE 2
Encourage students to complete the sentences independently. Suggest that students first locate the subject to help them choose the correct verb form.

EXERCISE 3
Have students complete this exercise independently. Review students' work as a group to reinforce correct answers and to work through incorrect answers.

EXERCISE 4
Review subject-verb agreement when *you* is the subject. Ask volunteers to write on the board their revised sentences. Discuss

4.10 Agreement of Subject and Verb—Part I

A **verb** agrees with its subject in person and number. Remember that a third person singular subject requires the verb form ending *-s* or *-es* for a present tense verb.

> Several <u>towns</u> *re-create* life at different times in the past. (base form of the verb with a plural subject)
> <u>Williamsburg</u> *re-creates* colonial life. (base form plus -s with a singular subject)

Doesn't* and *Don't
Use *doesn't* when the subject is third person singular.

> <u>Williamsburg</u> *doesn't* have automobiles.

Use *don't* in other cases.

> I *don't* know where Williamsburg is located.

***You* as the Subject**
Use *are* and *were* with *you* whether the subject is singular or plural. Do not use *is* or *was* with the subject *you*.

> *Were* <u>you</u> at the historic reenactment of our town's founding?

There Is* and *There Are
When *there is* or *there are* introduces a sentence, the subject follows the verb. Use *there is (was, has been)* with singular subjects. Use *there are (were, have been)* with plural subjects.

> *There is* a historic <u>village</u> in Massachusetts. (singular subject)
> *There are* several reconstructed colonial <u>towns</u> on the East Coast. (plural subject)

Be careful when using the contraction *there's;* it must be followed by a singular subject.

Phrases Between the Subject and the Verb
When there is an intervening phrase between the subject and the verb, the verb must agree with the subject, not with the noun or pronoun in the intervening phrase.

> A <u>place</u> with historic sites *is* Williamsburg, Virginia.
> Several other <u>towns</u>, including Old Sturbridge Village, *are* historic sites.

each sentence and encourage students to provide alternative revisions.

APPLY

APPLY IT NOW

To get students started, suggest that they list interesting features about their chosen places. Then have students include each feature in a sentence. Help students work out any problems that arise. Students should demonstrate an understanding of subject-verb agreement.

ASSESS

Note which students had difficulty writing sentences with subjects and verbs that agree. Assign **Practice Book** page 51 for further practice.

WRITING CONNECTION

Use pages 316–317 of the Writing portion of the book.

TEACHING OPTIONS

Reteach

On the board, write sentences in which the subject and the verb do not agree. Use the words *doesn't/don't*, *you*, and *there's/there is/there are* in the sentences. Also write sentences with phrases that intervene between the subject and the verb. Challenge students to come to the board to correct the incorrect sentences. Read the corrected sentences aloud and have students explain why the subjects and verbs now agree.

Meeting Individual Needs

Extra Support To make it easier to see if the subject and verb in a sentence agree, tell students to put prepositional phrases and adjective clauses in parentheses. Explain that if the words in parentheses are omitted from a sentence, it should still make grammatical sense. Provide several examples and have students use this technique to identify the subjects and choose the correct verbs.

Meeting Individual Needs

Auditory Tell students that maintaining correct subject-verb agreement is important not only when writing but also when speaking. Ask each student to write two sentences, one with correct and one with incorrect subject-verb agreement. Call on volunteers to read their sentences aloud. Ask students to listen closely to identify which sentences are correct and which are incorrect. Ask students to correct the incorrect sentences.

EXERCISE 1 Choose the correct form of the verb in each sentence.

1. One of the most famous tourist attractions in the United States (is are) Williamsburg, Virginia.
2. You (was were) at Williamsburg once, (wasn't weren't) you?
3. Williamsburg (takes take) visitors back to life in the 1700s.
4. There (is are) houses there built in the 1700s.
5. The town (doesn't don't) have all original houses; there (is are) also buildings reconstructed in the colonial style.
6. Some interesting sites in the town (includes include) shops of a wig maker, a saddle maker, and a silversmith.

Antique map of Virginia

EXERCISE 2 Complete each sentence with *doesn't* or *don't*.

1. __Don't__ you want to visit a historic town?
2. __Doesn't__ Sturbridge Village have a covered bridge?
3. The village __doesn't__ re-create life in the 1700s, but the 1800s.
4. Nat __doesn't__ know what a blacksmith does.
5. __Doesn't__ the town have a Web site?
6. We __don't__ have to pay to get in because we are students.

EXERCISE 3 Name the subject of each sentence. Then choose the correct form of the verb to complete each sentence.

1. Several members of the staff (practice practices) here on Saturday mornings.
2. The delightful re-creation of the village (account accounts) for the extensive tourist trade.
3. A stack of hot pancakes (was were) placed on the table.
4. Jacqueline's tales of her trip (was were) great.

Exercise 4

1. Correct
2. Activities include a horse-and-buggy ride.
3. Were you ever on a horse and buggy?
4. There are places for visitors to see traditional crafts.
5. A task of blacksmiths was to make wheels for buggies.

EXERCISE 4 Rewrite the sentences to achieve correct subject-verb agreement. Not every sentence requires rewriting.

1. Are you interested in visiting Sturbridge Village?
2. Activities includes a horse-and-buggy ride.
3. Was you ever on a horse and buggy?
4. There is places for visitors to see traditional crafts.
5. A task of blacksmiths were to make wheels for buggies.

APPLY IT NOW

Write ten sentences about an interesting place you have visited. Incorporate the phrase below. Make sure that the subjects and verbs agree.
One of the most interesting places . . .

Verbs • 77

OBJECTIVES
- **To use the correct verbs to agree with compound subjects**
- **To identify and use the verbs that agree with collective nouns, indefinite pronouns, and special nouns used as the subjects of sentences**

 **DAILY Maintenance**

Assign **Practice Book** page 40, Section 4.11. After students finish,
1. Give immediate feedback.
2. Review concepts as needed.
3. Model the correct answer.

Pages 4–5 of the **Answer Key** contain tips for Daily Maintenance.

WARM-UP

Write the following on the board: *macaroni and cheese, peanut butter and jelly, the dog and I, pants, team.* Have volunteers use an item from the list as a subject in a sentence. Discuss if the subject and verb agree for each sentence.

📖 Read from a piece of writing that the class is currently reading. Emphasize the agreement of subjects and verbs.

TEACH

Write the following on the board and ask students to guess definitions of each:

Compound subjects

Collective nouns

Indefinite pronouns

Unusual plurals

Tell students that these types of subjects require special attention. Assign a volunteer to each term and invite that volunteer to read the information in the text. After each example, challenge students to come up with a similar sentence that reflects the rule.

Ask students to explain why the subject-verb agreement for each type of subject is tricky. Explain that, when these nouns or pronouns are used as subjects, writers (and speakers) must be careful to choose the correct verbs.

PRACTICE

EXERCISE 1
Tell students to first identify the subject and then to determine whether it is singular or plural. Challenge students to complete the exercise independently. Then have partners check each other's answers. Encourage students to discuss answers that differ

and to agree on the correct answer. Remind students that their answers should be based on whether a subject is plural or singular.

EXERCISE 2
Have students complete this activity independently. Ask volunteers to share their answers. Discuss each sentence with the class.

EXERCISE 3
Have small groups work together to rewrite the incorrect sentences. Give each group a large sheet of poster board and a marker. Ask the groups to write their

---

4.11 Agreement of Subject and Verb—Part II

Compound subjects with *and* usually take a plural verb. If the subjects connected by *and* refer to the same person or thing or express a single idea, the verb is singular.

> Lumber and medicine *are* just two products of forests.
> Fire safety and prevention *is* the subject of the talk.

When *each, every, many a,* or *no* precedes a compound subject connected by *and* or *or,* use a singular verb.

> Every adult and child *is* contributing to the cleanup.

When a compound subject is connected by *or* or *nor,* the verb agrees with the subject closer to it.

> Neither the exhausting work nor the harsh living conditions *deter* wildland firefighters from their job.
> Neither the harsh living conditions nor the exhausting work *deters* wildland firefighters from their job.

A **collective noun** names a group of people or things considered as a unit. Examples include *audience, band, herd,* and *public.* A collective noun usually requires a singular verb. However, when the meaning suggests that the members are being considered as separate individuals, use a plural verb.

> The firefighting team *uses* tools such as helicopters.
> The team *don't take* any vacations during fire season.

Indefinite pronouns such as *another, anyone, anybody, anything, each, everyone, everybody, everything, either, neither, no one, nobody, nothing, one, other, somebody, someone,* and *something* are singular and take singular verbs.

> Everyone *is* responsible for forest fire prevention.

Some nouns that are **plural in form are singular in meaning** and require singular verbs. These include *aeronautics, civics, economics, mathematics, measles, news,* and *physics.*

Other nouns that are **plural in form refer to one thing** and require plural verbs. These nouns include *ashes, clothes, goods, pliers, pants, proceeds, thanks, trousers,* and *scissors.*

78 • Section 4.11

correct sentences on the poster board. Display all the groups' posters. Working with the class, compare the sentences and note any discrepancies. Review how to arrive at the correct subject-verb agreement.

APPLY

APPLY IT NOW

Students' sentences should contain correct subject-verb agreement. If necessary, give examples for each. Students should demonstrate an understanding of subject and verb agreement.

ASSESS

Note which students had difficulty identifying singular and plural subjects and their correct verbs. Assign **Practice Book** pages 52–53 for further practice.

WRITING CONNECTION

Use pages 318–319 of the Writing portion of the book.

EXERCISE 1 Choose the correct form of the verb to complete each sentence.

1. The news of a large nearby forest fire (was were) on the radio.
2. My family and I (was were) among those who evacuated the area.
3. When we left, ashes (was were) floating around us.
4. Everyone (was were) worried about what we would find.
5. Neither my brother nor I (was were) really prepared for the devastation we saw as we drove through the forest.
6. After a big fire, nothing in the forest (seems seem) to be alive.
7. Fortunately, everything at our house (was were) OK—just the outside was dirty from smoke.

Exercise 2

Subjects are underlined.

1. calls
2. wants
3. Has
4. comes
5. wants
6. rides
7. is
8. keeps

EXERCISE 2 Identify the subject of each sentence. Then choose the correct form of the verb to complete the sentence.

1. Somebody always (call) when I am asleep.
2. Nobody (want) to drive anywhere in this snowstorm.
3. (Have) anyone taken my ticket?
4. One of her favorite beverages (come) from Brazil.
5. Neither of the children (want) to leave the beach.
6. Each of the clowns (ride) a unicycle.
7. (Be) either of your brothers going on the hike?
8. Someone (keep) asking me your name.

Exercise 3

1. Damage from the fire was in the millions, but mathematics alone does not tell the human story.
2. No one living along that road still has a house.
3. Correct
4. Thanks are due to all who helped.
5. Every firefighter and police officer has put in heroic and tireless work in protecting the community.

EXERCISE 3 Rewrite the following sentences to correct errors in subject-verb agreement. Not every sentence requires rewriting.

1. Damage from the fire was in the millions, but mathematics alone do not tell the human story.
2. No one living along that road still have a house.
3. From all over the country, goods are arriving to help those who have been left homeless.
4. Thanks is due to all who helped.
5. Every firefighter and police officer have put in heroic and tireless work in protecting the community.

APPLY IT NOW

Write five sentences using one of the following subjects: *each neither, either, somebody, everyone.* Make sure the subjects and verbs agree.

Verbs • 79

Verb Review

ASSESS

Use the Verb Review as homework, as a practice test, or as an informal assessment. Following are some options for use.

Homework

You may wish to assign one group the odd items and another group the even items. When you next meet, review the correct answers as a group. Be sure to model how to arrive at the correct answer.

Practice Test

Use the Verb Review as a diagnostic tool. Assign the entire review or just specific sections. After students have finished, identify which concepts require more attention. Reteach concepts as necessary.

Verb Review

4.1 Identify the principal part of each main verb and the auxiliary verb.

1. I am learning about volcanoes around the world.
2. More volcanoes are located under the sea than on land.
3. Most undersea volcanoes are naturally hidden from view.
4. Undersea volcanoes eventually may grow high enough to break the ocean surface.
5. The Hawaiian Islands formed from volcanic mountains.

4.2 Identify the verbs or verb phrases in each sentence. Then tell whether the verb is transitive or intransitive.

6. In the Middle Ages, nobles controlled vast areas of land.
7. The nobles lived in castles, some of which are still standing today.
8. I have read many stories about knights in the Middle Ages.
9. We read about King Arthur last year in literature class.

4.3 Replace the troublesome verbs in each sentence.

10. My mom borrowed me her Bob Dylan CDs.
11. I set down in the living room and listened to one of his first recordings.
12. My eighth-grade music teacher learned us "Blowin' in the Wind."
13. Just lie that sheet music over on the table.

4.4 Identify the linking verbs and the subject complements. Tell whether the subject complement is an adjective, a noun, or a pronoun.

14. Maria Tallchief was America's first great prima ballerina.
15. It was she who popularized many of the characters in the world's most famous ballets.
16. Her performances remain memorable.
17. Tallchief became enthusiastic about dance after attending a pow-wow of the Osage people.

4.5 Identify each verb or verb phrase, and tell whether it is in the active voice or the passive voice.

18. Last spring a primary election was held to select nominees for the U.S. Senate.
19. Several candidates were slated from each party.
20. My candidate had legislative experience in the state senate.
21. His speeches were delivered to groups all over the state.
22. He won the primary election by a wide margin.

4.6 Complete each sentence with the verb indicated in parentheses. Use the tense and voice indicated.

23. My brother Frank _____ (travel—simple present, active) frequently for business.
24. Over the last 10 years, he _____ (accumulate—present perfect, active) millions of frequent-flier miles.

4.1
Auxiliary verbs are underlined.
1. present participle
2. past participle
3. past participle
4. base
5. past

4.2
Verbs or verb phrases are underlined
6. transitive
7. intransitive; intransitive
8. transitive
9. intransitive

4.3
10. lent
11. sat
12. taught
13. lay

4.4
Linking verbs are underlined once. Subject compliments are underlined twice.
14. noun
15. pronoun
16. adjective
17. adjective

4.5
Verbs or verb phrases are underlined.
18. passive
19. passive
20. active
21. passive
22. active

Informal Assessment

Use the review as preparation for the formal assessment. Count the review as a portion of the grade. Have students work to find the correct answers and use their corrected review as a study guide for the formal assessment.

WRITING CONNECTION

Use pages 320–321 of the Writing portion of the book.

TEACHING OPTIONS

Putting It All Together

Have students copy a section from their favorite book. Ask students to use double-spacing if they are typing on a computer or to write on every other line if using pen and paper. Write the following directions on the board:

- **Underline all the verbs.**
- **Write either _T_ for transitive or _I_ for intransitive above the verbs.**
- **Determine if a verb is active or passive. Write either _A_ or _P_ in the left-hand margin.**
- **Circle all the verbs that are in the subjunctive mood.**
- **Draw a box around any modal auxiliaries.**

Have students exchange papers with a partner and discuss the choices each made and why.

4.6
23. travels
24. has accumulated
25. will be redeeming

4.7
26. have paddled, indicative; (have) portaged, indicative
27. Get, imperative
28. can be, indicative

4.8
The correct verb is underlined. Item #32 is not in the subjunctive mood.

4.9
33. might visit
34. must raise
35. can accomplish

4.10
36. Were
37. include
38. is
39. is
40. Correct

4.11
41. are
42. deter
43. was
44. Correct

---

25. Frank and his fiancée _____ (redeem—future progressive, active) those miles for their upcoming honeymoon trip.

4.7 Identify each verb or verb phrase, and tell whether the sentence is in the indicative or imperative mood.

26. When have you last paddled and portaged in the Boundary Waters Canoe Area Wilderness?
27. Get fit for this kind of trip.
28. Carrying unnecessary items can be maddening.

4.8 Identify the correct form of the verb to complete each sentence. Identify which sentences are not in the subjunctive mood.

29. The counselor recommends that Eric (receive receives) training as a chef.
30. He wishes the institute (was were) closer to home.
31. I insist that someone (be is) with you when you walk home tonight.
32. That kind of training (helps help) a person get a job.

4.9 Complete each sentence with a verb phrase containing a modal auxiliary verb. Use the meaning indicated in parentheses after the sentence.

33. Our class _____ (visit) Washington, D.C. (possibility)

---

34. We _____ (raise) enough money to finance half of the cost. (necessity)
35. The eighth graders I know _____ (accomplish) this goal easily. (ability)

4.10 Correct the following sentences for subject-verb agreement. Not all the sentences have errors.

36. Was you the one who asked about Mackinac Island?
37. Activities on the island includes biking and sailing.
38. A popular stop for tourists are the Grand Hotel.
39. A race with hundreds of sailboats are held every year.
40. The race across Lake Michigan begins in Chicago.

4.11 Correct the following sentences for subject-verb agreement. Not all the sentences have errors.

41. The sandhill crane and the arctic tern is just two kinds of birds that migrate.
42. Neither the cold nor the wet conditions deters avid birdwatchers.
43. A flock of migrating swans were sighted last week.
44. Everyone here is excited when the birds start arriving.

 Tech Tip Go to www.voyagesinenglish.com for more activities.

Verbs • 81

Tech Tip Encourage students to further review verbs, using the additional practice and games at www.voyagesinenglish.com.

ASSESS

Encourage students to read the paragraph twice before answering the questions independently. If students have difficulty with any question, suggest that they refer to the section that teaches the skill. This activity can be done individually, in small groups, or as a whole class.

After you have reviewed verbs, Administer the Section 4 Assessment on pages 9–12 in the **Assessment Book,** or create a customized test with the optional **Test Generator CD.**

You may also wish to administer the Sections 3–4 Summative Assessment on pages 35–36 of the **Assessment Book.** This test is also available on the optional **Test Generator CD.**

WRITING CONNECTION

Use pages 322–323 of the Writing portion of the book.

Students can complete a formal business letter using the Writer's Workshop on pages 324–335.

Verb Challenge

Read the selection and then answer the questions.

1. You probably have heard the name UNESCO. 2. Do you know the meaning of its letters? 3. They stand for United Nations Educational, Scientific, and Cultural Organization. 4. This organization was founded in 1945, after World War II, at the same time as the United Nations itself. 5. As the many letters in UNESCO's name suggest, the organization's mission is broad. 6. It builds schools in countries devastated by war or poverty. 7. It has helped in the preservation of historic places through the World Heritage program. 8. By 2003 there were more than 700 such sites around the world, including the Grand Canyon and the historic pueblos of the United States. 9. Currently, UNESCO is actively working toward a number of concrete goals. 10. One goal is that by 2015 everyone will have access to free public education. 11. By 2015 UNESCO also hopes that it will have cut in half the number of people in extreme poverty. 12. Its overall goal is even loftier—to help build peace. 13. Let's all work to help it succeed. 14. You can learn more about UNESCO at its Internet site, www.unesco.org. 15. I recommend that everyone read the information at that site.

Verb Challenge
1. past participle
2. Do know
3. was founded; simple past, passive
4. is; adjective
5. builds; transitive
6. has helped; present perfect, active
7. is working; present progressive, active
8. will have cut; future perfect, active
9. Let's work; sentence 13
10. can learn; sentence 14
11. read; sentence 15

1. Which principal part of the verb *hear* is used in sentence 1?
2. What is the verb phrase in sentence 2?
3. What is the verb phrase in sentence 4? What are its tense and voice?
4. What is the linking verb in sentence 5? What part of speech is its subject complement?
5. What is the verb in sentence 6? Is it transitive or intransitive?
6. What is the verb phrase in sentence 7? What are its tense and voice?
7. What is the verb phrase in sentence 9? What are its tense and voice?
8. What is the verb phrase in sentence 11? What are its tense and voice?
9. Find the verb in the imperative mood in the selection. What sentence is it in?
10. Find the verb phrase with a modal auxiliary in the selection. What sentence is it in?
11. Find the verb in the subjunctive mood in the selection. What sentence is it in?

SUPPORT MATERIALS

Practice Book
Daily Maintenance, pages 54–56
Grammar, pages 57–70

Assessment Book
Section 5 Assessment,
     pages 13–16

Test Generator CD

**Writing Chapter 4,
   Descriptions**

Customizable Lesson Plans
www.voyagesinenglish.com

CONNECT WITH LITERATURE

📖 Consider using the following titles throughout the section to illustrate the grammar concept:

*Only Passing Through: The Story
   of Sojourner Truth* by Anne
   Rockwell
Surviving the Applewhites by
   Stephanie S. Tolan

Verbals

GRAMMAR FOR GROWN-UPS

Understanding Verbals

Verbals are verb forms that are used as other parts of speech. The three verbal forms are the participle, the gerund, and the infinitive.

A **participle** is a verb form that is used as an adjective. A participle often ends in *ing* (present participle) or in *ed* (past participle).

> *The barking **dog chased the ball.***

> *The caged **bird would not stop singing.***

A participle can be a single word, as in the examples above, or as part of a participial phrase. A **participial phrase** consists of the participle, an object or a complement, and any modifiers. Participles can have complements, objects, and adverb modifiers.

> *Munching a carrot, **Kevin walked across the lunchroom.***

A **gerund** is the *-ing* form of a verb that is used as a noun. A gerund can be used as a subject, a complement, an object of a preposition, an indirect object, a direct object, or an appositive.

> *Running **is my main form of exercise.*** (subject)

> *Jorge's favorite pastime is swimming.* (direct object)

> *The family business, catering parties, **is a lot of work.***
> (appositive)

An **infinitive** can be used as a noun, an adjective, or an adverb. An infinitive consists of the base form of the verb generally preceded by *to*.

> *To finish **my homework is my goal.*** (noun)

> *I had a chance to ride **in a helicopter.*** (adjective)

> *Nicole went to watch **a movie.*** (adverb)

> ❝ To boldly go
> where no man has gone before. ❞
>
> —James Tiberius Kirk, *Star Trek*

COMMON ERRORS

Using the Possessive with Gerunds

Remember that a gerund is a noun. When you use a noun or a pronoun before a gerund, it should be in the possessive form. This rule is broken so often that incorrect sentences begin to sound correct—unless you pay close attention

ERROR: My teacher objects to me going on the trip.
CORRECT: My teacher objects to my going on the trip.

A good way to check is this: if the meaning of a sentence changes drastically when you drop the gerund or gerund phrase, you need a possessive.

SENTENCE: Natalie loves him cooking pasta.
DROP THE GERUND: Natalie loves him. (The meaning of the sentence has changed!)
CORRECT: Natalie loves his cooking pasta.

SENTENCE DIAGRAMMING

You may wish to teach verbs in the context of diagramming. Review these examples. Then refer to the Diagramming section or look for Diagram It! features in the Verbals section.

Fishing is my favorite activity.

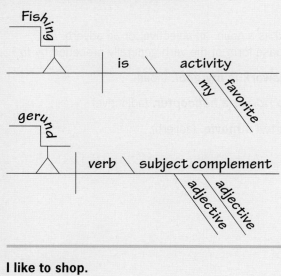

I like to shop.

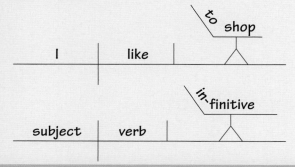

ASK AN EXPERT

Real Situations, Real Solutions

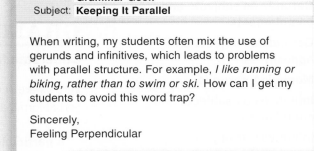

To: **Grammar Geek**
Subject: **Keeping It Parallel**

When writing, my students often mix the use of gerunds and infinitives, which leads to problems with parallel structure. For example, *I like running or biking, rather than to swim or ski.* How can I get my students to avoid this word trap?

Sincerely,
Feeling Perpendicular

To: **Feeling Perpendicular**
Subject: **Re: Keeping It Parallel**

Remind your students that although it is important to use a variety of sentences when writing, the words within an individual sentence should "match"—noun to noun, verb to verb, and verbal to verbal. Display a variety of sentences that mix gerunds and infinitives and work together to revise the sentences to include either all gerunds or all infinitives. Have students explain the changes they make.

They'll be parallel in no time,
Grammar Geek

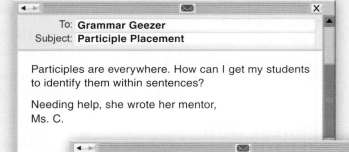

To: **Grammar Geezer**
Subject: **Participle Placement**

Participles are everywhere. How can I get my students to identify them within sentences?

Needing help, she wrote her mentor,
Ms. C.

To: **Ms. C**
Subject: **Re: Participle Placement**

You're right. Participles can occur almost anywhere in a sentence. To help your students identify participles, display the visual below.

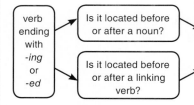

Use the visual to analyze several sentences with the class.

Loving her job, she happily replied,
Grammar Geezer

5.1 Participles

OBJECTIVES

- **To identify participles and the words they modify**
- **To use the correct tense of participles in sentences**

 **DAILY Maintenance**

Assign **Practice Book** page 54, Section 5.1. After students finish,
1. Give immediate feedback.
2. Review concepts as needed.
3. Model the correct answer.

Pages 4–5 of the **Answer Key** contain tips for Daily Maintenance.

WARM-UP

Write the following on the board:

I _____ across the room.

I am a _____ monkey.

Have groups sit in chairs across from each other. Ask one student from each group to stand. Explain that you will call out an action such as skip or dance. Have the standing students perform the action. Ask students to complete the sentences on the board, using the performed actions. *(I danced across the room. I am a dancing monkey.)* Then discuss how the verb is different and how it functions differently in each sentence.

📖 Read from a piece of writing that the class is currently reading. Emphasize the participles.

TEACH

Write these sentences on the board:

The cat purred softly.

The cat rested in my lap.

Challenge students to combine the sentences. *(Resting in my lap, the cat purred softly. Purring softly, the cat rested in my lap.)*

Read aloud the definitions for *verbals, participle,* and *participial phrase.* Challenge students to identify the participle in the sentence they wrote *(resting* or *purring).* Explain that, although *resting* and *purring* have some properties of verbs, they are used in these sentences as adjectives to modify the noun *cat.*

Explain that participles, like verbs, have tenses. Write on the board these sentences:

Satisfied with its meal, the cat rested in my lap.

Having eaten its meal, the cat rested in my lap.

Purring contentedly, the cat rested in my lap.

Ask volunteers to circle each participial phrase and underline the participle. Help students identify the tense of the participles. *(Satisfied is past participle,* having eaten *is present participle,* purring *is present participle.)*

PRACTICE

EXERCISE 1
Remind students that participles end in *-ing* or *-ed* and function as adjectives. Have volunteers read each sentence aloud and identify the participle.

5.1 Participles

Verbals are words made from verbs to function as another part of speech. There are three kinds of verbals: participles, gerunds, and infinitives.

A **participle** is a verb form that is used as an adjective; it describes a noun or pronoun. Participles often end in *-ing* or *-ed.*

> After graduation from high school, Jason spent some time *assisting* his mother in her classroom.

In this sentence *assisting* is a participle. It resembles an adjective because it modifies the noun *time.*

Just like other verb forms, participles show time through tense. Present participles end in *-ing,* and past participles often end in *-ed.* Participles can also be active or passive.

Present Participle:	*Reading* Marjorie Kinnan Rawlings's novels and stories, I learned about life in rural Florida. (active)
	Being treated as an outsider, Rawlings did not gain her new neighbors' acceptance at first. (passive)
Past Participle:	*Worried* by their views, she tried to make friends. (active)
	Accepted by her new neighbors, Rawlings started to learn more about their lives. (passive)
Perfect Participle:	*Having won* a Pulitzer Prize, Rawlings started to earn a living from her writing. (active)
	Having been awarded a Pulitzer Prize, Rawlings gained prestige as a writer. (passive)

Like appositives, a participle that is **nonrestrictive**—not essential to a sentence—is set off by commas. A participle that is **restrictive**—essential to the meaning of a sentence—is not set off by commas.

A **participial phrase** is made up of the participle, its object or complement, and any modifiers.

> *Left out in the rain,* the library book is now ruined.

In this sentence the participial phrase *Left out in the rain* describes the noun *book* and includes the prepositional phrase *in the rain,* which acts as an adverb telling where. A participial phrase can come before or after the word it describes.

84 • Section 5.1

EXERCISES 2

Have students work independently. Then invite volunteers to identify each participial phrase and its participle. Ask other volunteers to identify the nouns or pronouns being modified.

EXERCISE 3

Review tenses of participles. Suggest students exchange papers with partners to check answers.

APPLY

APPLY IT NOW

If needed, provide students with example sentences that model correct participial phrase usage. Students should demonstrate an understanding of participles.

ASSESS

Note which students had difficulty identifying participles. Assign **Practice Book** pages 57–58 for further practice.

WRITING CONNECTION

Use pages 336–337 of the Writing portion of the book. Be sure to point out verbals in the literature excerpt and student model.

Reteach

Ask volunteers to identify sentences from magazine and newspaper articles that contain examples of participial phrases. Review the function, form, and position of participles. Then have students copy five such sentences and use highlighters to identify the participial phrases. Direct students to use a pen to underline the participle and circle the noun or pronoun that is modified. Have students exchange papers with partners and review each other's work.

Meeting Individual Needs

Extra Support Write on the board a sentence and create a chart such as the following:

Stretching gracefully, the dancer warms up.

Phrase	Participle	Modifies
Stretching gracefully	stretching	dancer

Invite students to contribute to the chart as they find participial phrases in their own reading. Tell students to write the phrase, the participle, and the word it modifies. Review students' findings for further discussion.

Meeting Individual Needs

Auditory Read aloud the following sentences: *The quarterback threw a touchdown pass. The quarterback scrambled to avoid a tackle.* Have a volunteer combine the sentences, using a participial phrase. (*Scrambling to avoid a tackle, the quarterback threw a touchdown pass.*) Direct each student to write a pair of related sentences. Then have students read their sentences aloud. Challenge the class to listen closely and suggest a way to combine the sentences, using a participial phrase.

Exercise 1
Participles are underlined.

EXERCISE 1 Identify the participle in each sentence.

1. Raised around Washington, D.C., Rawlings loved to write stories and submit them to local newspapers.
2. Beginning her career as a journalist, she wrote for newspapers and created a syndicated column.
3. Devoting herself to fiction, Rawlings wrote many notes about her new life in Florida.

Exercise 2
Participial phrases are underlined.

1. becoming, Marjorie Kinnan Rawlings
2. Fascinated, Rawlings
3. Having bought, she
4. inhabited, grove
5. Having hoped, she
6. having sold, Rawlings
7. Pursuing, Rawlings
8. found, subjects
9. based, movie

EXERCISE 2 Identify the participial phrase in each sentence. Name each participle and tell the noun or pronoun it describes.

1. Writer Marjorie Kinnan Rawlings, becoming tired of city life, went to live in Florida in 1928.
2. Fascinated by the simple way of life on a visit to Florida, Rawlings decided to move there.
3. Having bought an orange grove, she planned to farm.
4. Already inhabited by a couple of cows and some chickens, the orange grove became her home.
5. Having hoped for a quiet life, she soon realized the difficulties.
6. Rawlings, having sold everything for the grove, could only stay and try to solve her problems.
7. Pursuing her ambition as a writer, Rawlings continued to work.
8. The subjects found in her own life and surroundings became the topics in her book *Cross Creek*.
9. A movie based on the book was made in 1983.

Exercise 3
Participial phrases are underlined.

1. *The Yearling*, set, present
2. fawn, Having lost, perfect
3. boy, living, present
4. boy, Facing, present
5. *The Yearling*, Having been recommend, perfect

EXERCISE 3 Identify the participial phrase in each sentence and tell the noun it describes. Then identify the participle and tell whether it is present, past, or perfect.

1. Rawlings's novel *The Yearling*, set in rural Florida in the 1800s, is perhaps her most famous book.
2. Having lost its mother, a fawn is adopted by a boy.
3. For the boy, living on an isolated farm with his parents, the fawn becomes the center of his life.
4. Facing problems with the deer, the boy has to make a decision.
5. Having been recommended by a librarian, *The Yearling* became the first book I read this year.

APPLY IT NOW

Write six sentences, each using one of the following participles in a participial phrase: arriving, crying, having lost, written, having finished, starring.

Verbals • 85

OBJECTIVES
- To identify participial adjectives and the nouns they modify
- To identify and correct dangling and misplaced participles

DAILY Maintenance

Assign **Practice Book** page 54, Section 5.2. After students finish,
1. Give immediate feedback.
2. Review concepts as needed.
3. Model the correct answer.

Pages 4–5 of the **Answer Key** contain tips for Daily Maintenance.

WARM-UP

Have a student from each of two teams stand in the front of the room. Read aloud a sentence with a dangling participle, such as the following:

Joe found a dollar walking his dog.

Explain that the first student to identify the error and to correct it earns a point. Repeat as time allows. Tell students that the team with the most points wins.

Read from a piece of writing that the class is currently reading. Emphasize the placement of participles.

TEACH

Ask a volunteer to read aloud the introductory sentence about participles used as adjectives and the example sentences. Discuss the sentences in detail, asking students how each participial adjective is used. Elicit from them that *spinning* appears before the noun that it modifies *(wheel)*, that *desired* appears after the noun it modifies *(results)*, and that *delighted* follows the linking verb *is*.

Challenge students to suggest other examples of participial adjectives. Write their responses on the board. To get students started, offer these examples: *a soaking rainstorm, a closed door, a surprising answer,* and *a startled scream.*

Have a student read aloud about dangling and misplaced participles. Discuss how these errors can lead to confusion and lack of clarity.

PRACTICE

EXERCISE 1
Remind students that adjectives describes nouns. Tell students

that when they find a participial adjective, they should identify the word it describes. Let students exchange papers to check and discuss their answers.

EXERCISE 2
Direct partners to identify the dangling participle and the noun or pronoun that the participial phrase should modify. Stress that the participial phrase should be close to the word it describes. Encourage students to work together to rewrite the sentences.

EXERCISE 3
Have students work independently to revise the paragraph. Remind

---

5.2 Placement of Participles

If a participle is used alone as an adjective before or after the word it modifies, or after a linking verb, the participle is a **participial adjective.**

> I made my ceramic pot on a *spinning* wheel.
> My ceramic project did not produce the results *desired.*
> Miriam, on the other hand, is *delighted* with her pot.

A participial adjective after a linking verb should not be confused with a participle that is part of a verb phrase.

> This exercise is *relaxing* to me. (participial adjective modifying *exercise*)
> This exercise is *relaxing* my tense muscles. (part of the verb phrase *is relaxing*)

Asking these questions can help determine whether a participle is a participial adjective or as part of a verb phrase:

- Can the participle be used in front of the noun *(relaxing exercise)*?
- Does it makes sense when used after *seems (seems relaxing)*?
- Can it be compared *(most relaxing)* or modified *(very relaxing)*?

If the answer to these questions is yes, the participle is a participial adjective.

A participial phrase acts as an adjective and therefore must describe a noun or pronoun. A participial phrase that does not appear to modify any word in the sentence is called a **dangling participle**—something to avoid in your writing.

> Dangling participle: *Having worked hard on the ceramic project,* **the finished pot was disappointing.**
> Correction: *Having worked hard on the ceramic project,* **I was disappointed in the finished pot.** (The participial phrase modifies *I.*)

A **misplaced participle** is a participial phrase that seems to modify the wrong word or more than one word in a sentence.

> Misplaced participle: *Covered with a glaze,* **the instructor put the pot into the kiln.**
> Correction: *Covered with a glaze,* **the pot was placed into the kiln. OR**
> **The instructor put the pot,** *covered with a glaze,* **into the kiln.**

Notice that in both sentences, some words had to be added or changed.

students that participial phrases act as adjectives and must modify nouns or pronouns.

APPLY

APPLY IT NOW

Have students circle the participial adjectives in their review. Then have students share their work with a partner. Students should demonstrate an understanding of the placement of participles.

 Grammar in Action. The two participial adjectives are *contrasting* and *steaming*. Ask students which nouns these

participial adjectives describe (*odors* and *peanuts*).

ASSESS

Note which students had difficulty identifying the correct placement of participles. Assign **Practice Book** pages 59–60 for further practice.

WRITING CONNECTION

Use pages 338–339 of the Writing portion of the book.

TEACHING OPTIONS

Reteach

Have small groups create posters that illustrate dangling and misplaced participles and ways to correct them. Suggest that students first write two or three sentences that have dangling participles. Direct students to illustrate the sentences in a humorous, literal way, for example, *Shining brightly, I saw the moon in the night sky.* Discuss how students might draw a person "shining brightly." Then instruct students to rewrite the sentences so they are correct. Proceed in the same way with misplaced modifiers. Display the posters in the classroom.

Curriculum Connection

Invite students to look through a science or social studies textbook for five examples of participial adjectives or participial phrases. Have students write their examples on chart paper to share with the class. Discuss the sentences and challenge the class to identify the participial adjectives and phrases. Encourage students to identify possible dangling participles and help them determine whether those sentences need correcting.

Diagram It!

To practice these concepts in the context of diagramming, turn to Section 11.5.

Exercise 1
Participial adjectives are underlined.

Exercise 2
Possible answers:
1. Having seen van Gogh's painting *Sunflowers*, I hung a copy of it in my room.
2. Being a lover of art, I am not bored by visiting a museum.
3. Correct
4. Correct
5. Desiring vivid colors, I chose acrylic paints for the work.
6. Having been assigned an art project at school, I felt that a collage was a good idea.
7. Making my collage, I used lots of colorful magazines.
8. Looking at magazines, I spent hours deciding on the right subjects.

Exercise 3
The students studied the works of art hanging on the walls. Then, carrying a clipboard, a judge looked at my collage. Smiling, he looked at it for a long time. Waving a blue ribbon, he pointed to my collage. Wearing a big grin, I shook the judge's hand.

EXERCISE 1 Identify the participial adjective in each sentence.
1. Vincent van Gogh was not a <u>known</u> painter during his lifetime.
2. Today he is an <u>admired</u> artist.
3. The <u>striking</u> colors of his paintings draw many to them.
4. Their <u>vibrating</u> surfaces, often with thick brush strokes visible, seem to have a life of their own.
5. The <u>tortured</u> artist of these works had a difficult life.
6. A <u>caring</u> brother helped support him.
7. Van Gogh felt increasingly <u>isolated</u>.
8. The <u>rejected</u> artist experienced a mental breakdown.
9. One of his famous paintings is the <u>moving</u> *Starry Night*.
10. It is full of life with its <u>swirling</u> forms.

Vincent van Gogh, a self-portrait

EXERCISE 2 Rewrite the sentences to correct dangling participles. Not all the sentences need correcting.
1. Having seen van Gogh's painting *Sunflowers*, a copy is now hanging in my room.
2. Being a lover of art, museum visits aren't boring to me.
3. I know many techniques, having taken art classes at the museum.
4. Inspired by the works in the museum, I began one myself.
5. Desiring vivid colors, acrylic paints were chosen for the work.
6. Having been assigned an art project at school, a collage seemed a good idea to me.
7. Making my collage, lots of colorful magazines were needed.
8. I spent hours deciding on the right subjects looking at magazines.

EXERCISE 3 Rewrite the following paragraph. Revise any sentences that contain a misplaced participle.

Hanging on the walls, the students studied the works of art. Then a judge looked at my collage carrying his clipboard. Smiling, he looked at it for a long time. He pointed to my collage waving a blue ribbon. I shook the judge's hand wearing a big grin.

APPLY IT NOW

Write a short review of a movie, a book, or a TV program. Use at least two of the following words as participial adjectives: *bored, surprising, exhilarating, confused,* and *breathtaking*.

Grammar in Action. Find two participial adjectives in the p. 337 model.

Verbals • 87

OBJECTIVE
- **To identify gerunds and gerund phrases as subjects and subject complements**

DAILY Maintenance

Assign **Practice Book** page 54, Section 5.3. After students finish,
1. Give immediate feedback.
2. Review concepts as needed.
3. Model the correct answer.

Pages 4–5 of the **Answer Key** contain tips for Daily Maintenance.

WARM-UP

Have volunteers stand up. Then have them take turns saying as many of their favorite activities as they can, using only the present participle *(swimming, running, sleeping, and so on)*. List the activities on the board. Have students choose one activity and write a brief paragraph about it.

📖 Read from a piece of writing that the class is currently reading. Emphasize the gerunds used as subjects and subject complements.

TEACH

Ask volunteers to read aloud their paragraphs from the Warm-Up. When you hear students use a gerund as a subject or a subject complement, write the sentence on the board. Have several volunteers read their paragraphs so that you can list at least two examples of a gerund as a subject and two examples of a gerund as a subject complement.

Point out the gerunds in students' sentences. Challenge students to identify the functions of the gerunds in each sentence. Elicit that they are used as subjects or subject complements.

Write the word *gerund* on the board and invite a volunteer to read aloud the definition of a

gerund. Have volunteers read aloud the paragraphs and the examples in the text. Encourage students to suggest their own sentences with gerunds.

PRACTICE

EXERCISE 1
Have partners identify the gerunds or gerund phrases in each sentence. Then discuss the answers with the entire class. Make sure that students recognize that gerunds are verbs with the *-ing* ending that are used as nouns in sentences.

EXERCISE 2
When students have finished, have volunteers read aloud their sentences. Discuss any troublesome sentences with the class.

EXERCISE 3
Have students complete this exercise independently. Explain that after identifying the gerund phrase and its function, students should identify the direct object of the gerund phrase—not the direct object of the sentence.

EXERCISE 4
Tell students to complete each sentence with a gerund or a

5.3 Gerunds as Subjects and Subject Complements

A **gerund** is a verb form ending in *-ing* that is used as a noun. Because it acts as a noun, a gerund can be used in a sentence as a subject, a subject complement, a direct object, an object of a preposition, or an appositive. You will study the first two functions in this section and the remaining three in the next section.

> **Running** is his main form of exercise. (subject)
> **Currently my favorite exercise is** *swimming*. (subject complement)

A **gerund phrase** may have objects and complements, and it may contain modifiers. The entire gerund phrase acts as a noun. In the first sentence below, *Reading books* is the gerund phrase; *Reading* is the gerund and *books* is its direct object. In the second sentence below, *skateboarding in the park* is the gerund phrase, and *skateboarding* is the gerund.

> **Reading books** is Mom's favorite form of recreation.
> **Lynne's favorite activity is** *skateboarding in the park*.

How do the gerunds function in the above sentences? You are right if you said the gerund acts as the subject of the first sentence and as the subject complement in the second.

Gerunds can be active or passive.

> *Making the team* **is Kevin's goal.** (active)
> *Being chosen for the team* **is Kevin's goal.** (passive)

EXERCISE 1 Identify the gerund or gerund phrase in each sentence. Tell whether each is a subject or subject complement.

1. Getting some exercise every day is important.
2. Exercising every day will keep the heart healthy.
3. A common exercise for people of all ages is biking.
4. Participating in a sport is a good exercise also.
5. Being inactive much of the time can make you feel tired.
6. Remaining active can restore energy.
7. A good way to exercise may be walking to school.
8. According to Mom, the best exercise for me is cleaning my room.

Exercise 1
Gerunds and gerund phrases are underlined.
1. subject
2. subject
3. subject complement
4. subject
5. subject
6. subject
7. subject complement
8. subject complement

88 • Section 5.3

gerund phrase that tells about themselves. Review students' work individually.

APPLY

APPLY IT NOW

Write on the board an example such as the following:

> Washing your hands before eating is a healthful idea.

Have partners review each other's sentences. Students should demonstrate an understanding of gerunds as subjects and subject complements.

TechTip Provide students time to review their classmates' work on the class blog. Suggest students write the tips they find most useful in their notebooks.

ASSESS

Note which students had difficulty identifying and using gerunds and gerund phrases. Assign **Practice Book** page 61 for further practice.

WRITING CONNECTION
Use pages 340–341 of the Writing portion of the book.

Reteach

Have students list on a sheet of paper five verbs in the present tense, for example, *joke, tell, walk, catch,* and *fly.* Direct students to exchange papers with partners and to write sentences using the verbs as gerunds. Instruct students to use the gerunds as subjects and then as subject complements for a total of 10 sentences. Have partners review each other's work.

Meeting Individual Needs

Interpersonal Create a two-column chart as shown. Invite students to write actions that can be hurtful and actions that can be caring in the appropriate columns.

Hurtful	Caring
calling someone names	giving a compliment
picking on someone	inviting someone to join you

Challenge students to include the phrases in sentences that might be put on a poster to display in the classroom.

English-Language Learners

Write the following sentence on the board:

> _____ is an activity I can do.

Challenge students to name gerunds depicting actions. Have students first pantomime the action and then write the verb in the sentence.

> **Reading is an activity I can do.**
>
> **Painting is an activity I can do.**
>
> **Singing is an activity I can do.**
>
> **Running is an activity I can do.**

Exercise 2

Gerund phrases are underlined.

1. Stretching all the muscles is an important warm-up routine.
2. Finishing the course was the best part of the workout.
3. Jogging quickly around the block has been my evening routine.
4. Refusing to quit is a characteristic of good runners.

Exercise 3

Gerunds and gerund phrases are underlined.

1. subject
2. subject
3. subject, fruits and vegetables
4. subject complement
5. subject, breakfast
6. subject complement, teeth
7. subject complement, sleep
8. subject complement, energy
9. subject
10. subject, time

Exercise 4

Answers will vary.

1. subject complement
2. subject
3. subject complement
4. subject
5. subject
6. subject
7. subject complement
8. subject

EXERCISE 2 Identify the gerund phrase in each sentence. Rewrite the sentence by substituting the gerund phrase for the subject.

EXAMPLE **My favorite activity is running long distances.**
Running long distances is my favorite activity.

1. An important warm-up routine is stretching all the muscles.
2. The best part of the workout was finishing the course.
3. My evening routine has been jogging quickly around the block.
4. A characteristic of good runners is refusing to quit.

EXERCISE 3 Identify the gerund or gerund phrase in each sentence. Tell whether each is a subject or a subject complement. Identify any direct objects in the gerund phrase.

1. Eating properly is essential to good health.
2. Staying away from fats and sweets is a good idea.
3. Choosing fruits and vegetables for snacks can be a healthful alternative to junk food.
4. Another good idea is snacking on low-fat popcorn.
5. Eating a good breakfast gives you energy in the morning.
6. A basic health habit is brushing your teeth after every meal.
7. Another good health habit is getting enough sleep.
8. One function of sleep is restoring energy to your body.
9. Relaxing is important too.
10. Taking time for some favorite activity every day is good for you.

EXERCISE 4 Complete each sentence with a gerund or a gerund phrase. Tell how it functions in the sentence.

1. My favorite free-time activity is _____.
2. _____ is my least favorite activity.
3. The best way to spend an afternoon is _____.
4. _____ is a boring way to exercise.
5. _____ is my favorite way to exercise.
6. _____ is one food habit I should change.
7. One health habit I need to change is _____.
8. _____ is a good way to stay active.

APPLY IT NOW

What do you think are important health tips for students your age to follow? Make a list of five tips. Use gerunds in your tips. Compare your tips with those of your classmates.

TechTip Post your tips on the class blog for comparison.

Verbals • 89

5.4 Gerunds as Objects and Appositives

OBJECTIVE

- **To recognize gerunds used as direct objects, as objects of prepositions, and as appositives**

 **Maintenance**

Assign **Practice Book** page 54, Section 5.4. After students finish,
1. Give immediate feedback.
2. Review concepts as needed.
3. Model the correct answer.

Pages 4–5 of the **Answer Key** contain tips for Daily Maintenance.

WARM-UP

Have students write all the functions of a noun *(subject, subject complement, direct object, indirect object, object of a preposition, object complement* and *appositive)*. Have the first student to complete this list write his or her three favorite activities on the board. Then write on the board the sentence starters below. Instruct students to use the activities on the board to complete the sentences.

People enjoy _____.

I stay fit by _____.

My favorite activity, _____, takes up a lot of my time.

📖 Read from a piece of writing that the class is currently reading. Emphasize the gerunds used as objects and appositives.

TEACH

Ask volunteers to read aloud their Warm-Up sentences. Point out that students had to turn the activities into gerunds to complete each sentence. Then ask volunteers to identify the function of the gerunds in each sentence *(direct object, object of a preposition, appositive)*. Challenge students to explain direct objects, objects of prepositions, and appositives. Review as needed.

Invite volunteers to take turns reading aloud the text about gerunds used as objects and as appositives. Encourage students to offer more examples for each type of gerund.

PRACTICE

EXERCISE 1

Have students work in pairs. Suggest that they take turns identifying the gerund phrase and the function of the phrase in each sentence. Then make larger groups by combining two student pairs. Have these students compare their work and discuss any discrepancies. Encourage students to record discrepancies on a separate sheet and to discuss these sentences with the class.

EXERCISES 2 & 3

Have students complete these exercises independently. Remind students that gerunds always take the *-ing* form of a verb. Also point out that when a gerund phrase functions as an appositive, there must be a comma before and after the gerund phrase.

5.4 Gerunds as Objects and Appositives

A gerund can be used as a direct object.

> **Many parents consider** *naming their children after family members.*

The gerund phrase *naming their children after family members* is the object of the verb *consider.*

A gerund can be used as the object of a preposition.

> **Many parents decide on a name by** *looking through books.*

The gerund phrase *looking through books* is the object of the preposition *by.*

A gerund can be used as an appositive, a word or group of words that renames a noun and gives more information about it.

> **Genealogy,** *exploring one's family roots,* **often involves research into last names.**

The gerund phrase *exploring one's family roots* explains the noun *genealogy.*

What are the gerund phrases in these sentences? Can you identify their functions in the sentences?

> **Abernathy's wish, being called Abe, seems understandable.**
> **He prefers being called by his nickname rather than by his given name.**

You are correct if you said that in the first sentence, the gerund phrase *being called Abe* is used as an appositive. It explains the noun *wish.* You are also correct if you said that in the second sentence, the gerund phrase *being called by his nickname* is the direct object of the verb *prefers.*

EXERCISE 1 Identify the gerund phrase in each sentence. Tell whether the gerund phrase is used as a direct object, an object of a preposition, or an appositive.

1. People began <u>using nicknames</u> a long time ago.
2. The idea behind a nickname, <u>using a name other than a person's given one</u>, suggests a desire for informality.
3. Some parents like <u>naming their children after relatives and friends</u>.
4. Parents, however, may get tired of <u>repeating a child's given name</u>.

Exercise 1
Gerund phrases are underlined.
1. direct object
2. appositive
3. direct object
4. object of a preposition
5. direct object
6. object of a preposition
7. appositive
8. object of a preposition
9. object of a preposition
10. object of a preposition
11. direct object
12. direct object

APPLY

APPLY IT NOW

Encourage students to use gerunds in as many different ways as possible. When students have finished, invite volunteers to read their sentences aloud. Ask students to identify the gerunds and their functions. Students should demonstrate an understanding of gerunds.

ASSESS

Note which students had difficulty recognizing gerunds used as direct objects, objects of prepositions, and appositives. Assign **Practice Book** page 62 for further practice.

WRITING CONNECTION

Use pages 342–343 of the Writing portion of the book.

TEACHING OPTIONS

Reteach

Write the following on the board:

    1—direct object

    2—object of a preposition

    3—appositive

    4—subject

    5—subject complement

    6—your choice

Give students a list of 20 action verbs in the present tense and one die. Tell students to take turns tossing the die and using the verbs from the list as gerunds in sentences, according to the number key on the board. For example, if a student chooses the verb *listen* and rolls the number 2, he or she must use the gerund *listening* as an object of a preposition. Instruct students to take turns until all the verbs have been used.

English-Language Learners

Students may benefit from extra support in identifying and recognizing gerunds. Pair English-language learners with students who are fluent in English. Provide partners with three note cards labeled *direct object*, *object of a preposition*, and *appositive*. Place the cards faceup on a table. Then direct students to review sentences in the exercises and work together to select the card that identifies each gerund use.

5. They may consider <u>finding a short, informal name,</u> or one may present itself as a term of endearment.

6. The practice of <u>shortening a name</u> is common; for example, Samantha to Sam.

7. One common practice, <u>calling people by a physical trait,</u> produces names such as Red (a person with red hair).

8. With the use of irony, Shorty may become the way of <u>designating an extremely tall person.</u>

9. Sometimes a particular action leads to <u>obtaining a specific nickname.</u>

10. For <u>winning a battle at a place named Tippecanoe,</u> President William Henry Harrison was given that as a nickname.

11. The famous Beatle Ringo Starr loved <u>wearing lots of rings</u>—and so came his nickname.

12. Usually one person starts <u>calling a person by a nickname,</u> which is then picked up by others.

Exercise 2
Answers will vary.

EXERCISE 2 Complete each sentence with an appropriate gerund phrase used as a direct object.

  1. Do you enjoy _____?

  2. We should avoid _____.

  3. Have they begun _____?

Exercise 3
Answers will vary.
1. object of a preposition
2. direct object
3. direct object
4. appositive
5. object of a preposition
6. direct object

EXERCISE 3 Complete each sentence with a gerund. Then tell whether it is used as a direct object, an object of a preposition, or an appositive.

  1. I am really good at _____.

  2. I really dislike _____.

  3. My favorite pastimes include _____.

  4. The latest style, _____, is something I might try.

  5. I am thinking of _____ next year.

  6. I spent my entire day _____.

Ringo Starr

APPLY IT NOW

Write five sentences about your morning routine. Use four gerunds and identify how they are used.

Verbals • 91

OBJECTIVES

- **To use possessive forms with gerunds**
- **To distinguish between *-ing* verb forms**

DAILY Maintenance

Assign **Practice Book** page 55, Section 5.5. After students finish,
1. Give immediate feedback.
2. Review concepts as needed.
3. Model the correct answer.

Pages 4–5 of the **Answer Key** contain tips for Daily Maintenance.

WARM-UP

Write on the board the following parts of speech and their respective sounds:

GERUND	PARTICIPLE	VERB
cough	bark	buzz

Explain that you will write a sentence on the board and point to a word in the sentence. Challenge students to identify the part of speech by making the sound listed on the board. Explain that students who make the incorrect sound are out of the game.

📖 Read from a piece of writing that the class is currently reading. Emphasize the possessives with gerunds and the use of *-ing* verb forms.

TEACH

Write the following sentence on the board:

Our electing Jenna as class president demonstrates the democratic process.

Have a student circle the gerund in the sentence *(electing)*. Then ask the class to explain the function of the word that comes before

electing and to confirm that the word *Our* shows possession. Invite volunteers to read aloud about possessives with gerunds. Encourage students to suggest additional sentences and to write their responses on the board below the example sentence.

Point out that students have discovered several ways that a verb ending in *-ing* can be used. Elicit from students what they recall about the functions of gerunds, participial adjectives, and participles in verb phrases. Encourage students to review these uses. Challenge students to suggest several sentences demonstrating each usage.

PRACTICE

EXERCISE 1

Review words that show possession, such as the adjectives *my, your, our*, and nouns created with an apostrophe or an apostrophe and *s*. Have students complete this exercise independently, choosing the correct word for each sentence. When students have finished, have them exchange papers with partners to compare answers.

EXERCISE 2

Review how to distinguish between gerunds, participial adjectives, and participles in verb

5.5 Possessives with Gerunds, Using *-ing* Verb Forms

Gerunds may be preceded by a possessive form—either a possessive noun or a possessive adjective. These possessives describe the doer of the action of the gerund.

> *Our* choosing Florida as a vacation spot **was a good idea.** (not *Us choosing Florida*)
>
> **The worst moment was** *Kendra's* getting lost at the park. (not *Kendra getting lost*)

What is the correct choice of word in these sentences?

(You Your) offering to feed the cat is much appreciated.

I was surprised by (Ian Ian's) calling to wish me a good trip.

If you chose *Your* and *Ian's*, you are correct. These are the possessive forms, the form to use before a gerund.

Whether an *-ing* form of a verb is a participle or a gerund depends upon the emphasis in the sentence. When the emphasis is on the doer, the word is a participle; when it is on the action, the word is a gerund.

> **The coach watched the girls** *swimming*. (The girls—the doers—are the center of the coach's attention; therefore, *swimming* is a participle modifying *girls*.)
>
> **The coach watched the girls'** *swimming*. (The swimming of the girls—the action and not the girls themselves—is what the coach is watching; therefore, *swimming* is a gerund and *girls'* must be possessive.)

EXERCISE 1 Choose the correct word to complete each sentence.

1. My (family family's) getting ready to go on a trip was a huge task.
2. First, (us our) deciding on Florida as a destination required a lot of negotiation.
3. My (brother brother's) finally agreeing to a Florida vacation which made it possible for us to start making plans.
4. (Dad Dad's) making reservations at a beach resort sounded great to me.
5. (Us Our) packing for the trip also was a major task.

phrases. Have students complete the exercise independently. Discuss the answers with the class.

EXERCISE 3
Read aloud each sentence and ask a volunteer to provide the correct answer. Encourage students to share their reasons for selecting each answer.

APPLY

APPLY IT NOW
Invite volunteers to write their sentences on the board. Then ask students to identify how *driving* functions in each sentence.

Students should demonstrate an understanding of *-ing* verb forms.

ASSESS

Note which students had difficulty using possessive forms with gerunds, as well as distinguishing between *-ing* verb forms. Assign **Practice Book** page 63 for further practice.

WRITING CONNECTION
Use pages 344–345 of the Writing portion of the book.

TEACHING OPTIONS

Reteach
Review the uses of *-ing* words as gerunds, participial adjectives, and verbs in verb phrases. Assign small groups one of the *-ing* uses. Provide each group with magazines, textbooks, and other reading materials. Have students find examples of *-ing* words according to the usage assigned to them. Direct students to copy the examples onto poster paper to share with the class.

Meeting Individual Needs

Extra Support Create a chart like the one below. Have students suggest verbs for the chart. Guide students as they construct sentences for each usage.

dancing

Gerund:
Dancing is a good way to stay in shape.

Participial Adjective:
Have you ever seen a dancing bear?

The woman dancing in the movie is famous.

Part of a Verb Phrase:
Jerome is dancing in the school musical.

Diagram It!
To practice these concepts in the context of diagramming, turn to Section 11.6.

6. (Gina **Gina's**) taking so many clothes is silly, and it just means more stuff to carry.

7. I said, "(You **Your**) worrying so much about clothes is not necessary, Gina."

8. (Me **My**) calling the hotel to ask what one wears in Florida in April is probably not the best plan.

9. I think that (Mom **Mom's**) suggesting that we watch the weather forecast is a good one.

10. (Milly **Milly's**) offering to check the newspaper is another helpful idea.

Exercise 2
1. gerund
2. part of a verb phrase
3. participial adjective
4. part of a verb phrase
5. gerund
6. participial adjective
7. part of a verb phrase

EXERCISE 2 Tell whether the italicized word in each sentence is a gerund, a participial adjective, or part of a verb phrase.

1. *Running* around all day has left me exhausted.

2. Thoughts about Florida's beaches have been *running* through my head.

3. I would prefer to be relaxing near the *running* water of a river.

4. Many flights are now *running* between Chicago and Miami.

5. *Sitting* in the plane was not an exciting experience for me.

6. Then *sitting* on the beach, I realized how tranquil the sun, sand, and water felt.

7. After my family had been *sitting* for dinner, we all took a walk on the beach path.

EXERCISE 3 Read the directions after each sentence. Then tell which word correctly completes each sentence.

1. On the plane we listened to the (babies **babies'**) crying. (Emphasis is on the doer.)

2. We also listened intently to the (pilots **pilot's**) speaking. (Emphasis is on the action.)

3. At the beach my family enjoyed watching the (teens **teens'**) surfing. (Emphasis is on the doer.)

4. Above us we could hear the (birds **birds'**) calling. (Emphasis is on the action.)

5. I could hear my (siblings **siblings'**) laughing as they splashed in the surf. (Emphasis is on the doer.)

APPLY IT NOW
Use the word *driving* in three sentences—as a gerund, a participial adjective, and part of a verb phrase. Have a partner identify how the word is used in each sentence.

Verbals • 93

5.6 Infinitives as Subjects and Subject Complements

OBJECTIVE

- **To identify infinitives and infinitive phrases used as subjects and subject complements**

Maintenance

Assign **Practice Book** page 55, Section 5.6. After students finish,

1. Give immediate feedback.
2. Review concepts as needed.
3. Model the correct answer.

Pages 4–5 of the **Answer Key** contain tips for Daily Maintenance.

WARM-UP

Write the following sentence starters on the board:

> To _____ is part of a(n) _____'s job.

> A basic part of being a(n) _____ is to _____.

Have students form teams of four. Ask each team to choose a profession *(astronaut, chef, nurse)*. Have students complete each starter sentence. Then invite volunteers from each group to write their sentences on the board.

📖 Read from a piece of writing that the class is currently reading. Emphasize the infinitives used as subjects and subject complements.

TEACH

Read aloud the definition of an infinitive and the example sentences. Invite volunteers to underline the infinitives in the sentences on the board. Then write the following sentence on the board:

> I will write a letter to my cousin.

Have students say the phrase that begins with the word *to* (*to my cousin*).

Ask students to explain how this phrase differs from the infinitives in the Warm-Up sentences. *(The phrase* to my cousin *does not contain a verb, so it is not an infinitive. The phrase is a prepositional phrase.)*

Invite volunteers to take turns reading aloud about infinitives. Point out the infinitives in the examples that are used as subjects and subject complements. Encourage students to provide other examples of infinitives as subjects and subject complements. Write their suggestions on chart paper to post in the room.

PRACTICE

EXERCISE 1

Have students work with partners. Encourage students to identify the infinitives and infinitive phrases in each sentence. Remind students that they need to look for the word *to* followed by a verb.

EXERCISE 2

Point out that although the infinitives in this exercise always function as subjects, infinitives and infinitive phrases can also be nouns, adjectives, or adverbs. Have volunteers read aloud their completed sentences. Discuss each answer.

5.6 Infinitives as Subjects and Subject Complements

An **infinitive** is a verb form, usually preceded by *to*, that is used as a noun, an adjective, or an adverb.

To cook is a necessary skill. (infinitive used as noun)
I have a meal to prepare. (infinitive used as adjective)
I went to get a cookbook from the library. (infinitive used as adverb)

Like participles and gerunds, infinitives can appear alone or in phrases. An **infinitive phrase** consists of the infinitive, its object, and any modifiers. In the examples above, *to cook* and *to prepare* are examples of infinitives used alone. *To get a cookbook from the library* is an infinitive phrase.

When infinitives are used as nouns, they function as subjects, complements, objects, or appositives.

To make an appetizing meal was my goal. (subject)
My task was to learn a few recipes. (subject complement)
I want to surprise my family. (direct object)
My goal, to prepare a whole meal, **was ambitious.** (appositive)

Are the infinitives in the following sentences subjects or subject complements?

My hope is to learn some easy recipes.
To make a pie seems too difficult right now.

You are right if you said that the infinitive in the first sentence, *to learn some easy recipes,* is a subject complement and that the one in the second sentence, *to make a pie,* is a subject.

Infinitives can be active or passive, and they can also have perfect forms.

Simple active:	**My job is** to peel **the potatoes.**
Simple passive:	**These potatoes are** to be peeled **for the stew.**
Perfect active:	**My goal is** to have peeled **the potatoes by six o'clock.**
Perfect passive:	**Those potatoes were** to have been peeled **by my sister.**

94 • Section 5.6

EXERCISE 3

Encourage students to complete this exercise independently. Remind them that the sentences must be completed with an infinitive—a verb preceded by the word *to*. Invite volunteers to write their sentences on the board. As a class, identify each infinitive as a subject or a subject complement.

APPLY

APPLY IT NOW

Tell students that their poems can be about any emotion they choose. When students have finished, invite volunteers to read their poems aloud. Students should demonstrate an understanding of infinitives used as subjects and subject complements.

ASSESS

Note which students had difficulty identifying infinitives and infinitive phrases used as subjects and subject complements. Assign **Practice Book** page 64 for further practice.

WRITING CONNECTION

Use pages 346–347 of the Writing portion of the book.

Reteach

Write sentences with infinitive phrases as the subject and as the subject complement on separate note cards, one sentence per card, one card for each student. Pass out the cards. Invite each student to read the sentence on his or her card, to name the infinitive phrase, and then to identify it as the subject or the subject complement. Tape the cards to a two-column chart, sorting them according to the usage of the infinitive phrase.

Observe and Apply

Tell students that one of the most famous uses of infinitives as nouns in the English language is the "To Be or Not to Be" monologue from William Shakespeare's *Hamlet*. Distribute copies of the monologue and have students highlight the infinitive phrases. Encourage students to use a dictionary to look up any unfamiliar words. Challenge students to identify any gerunds in the monologue.

Cooperative Learning

Challenge each pair of students to create a silly fill-in-the-blank story. Explain that each story should include sentences that are missing infinitive phrases for the subject or the subject complement. Tell students that the stories should be brief. Later have each pair exchange its story with another pair. Encourage students to complete each other's story with infinitive phrases.

Exercise 1
Infinitive phrases are underlined.

1. subject
2. subject complement
3. subject complement
4. subject
5. subject
6. subject
7. subject
8. subject complement
9. subject
10. subject complement
11. subject complement, subject complement

EXERCISE 1 Identify the infinitive phrase in each sentence. Tell whether it is used as a subject or a subject complement.

1. To read about the history of spices can be fascinating.
2. One basic use of spices such as cinnamon, ginger, cloves, and pepper has been, of course, to flavor food.
3. Another use was to be put into medicines.
4. For centuries, to own spices was like owning gold.
5. To possess a few peppercorns gave one significant wealth.
6. During the Middle Ages, to control the spice trade to the West was the prerogative of the Arabs.
7. To find a sea route to the riches—and spices—of the East was a race.
8. The Portuguese plan was to travel east around Africa.
9. To find a shorter route west was Columbus's goal.
10. Queen Isabella was displeased with Columbus's attempt to enslave the natives of the New World, however.
11. She ordered officers to arrest him and to bring him back to Europe.

Christopher Columbus

Exercise 2
Answers will vary.

EXERCISE 2 Complete each sentence with an appropriate infinitive or infinitive phrase.

1. _____ is an accomplishment.
2. _____ is a good feeling.
3. _____ can be dangerous.
4. _____ requires a lot of studying.
5. _____ makes me happy.

Exercise 3
Answers will vary.

1. subject complement
2. subject
3. subject
4. subject
5. subject complement

EXERCISE 3 Complete the sentences with infinitives. Tell if they are used as subjects or subject complements.

1. Something I would like to learn is _____.
2. _____ is a dream of mine.
3. _____ would be very fascinating.
4. _____ is an important skill.
5. One way to study for a test is _____.

APPLY IT NOW

Imagine describing emotions to a robot that does not understand them. Write a poem to the robot that explains an emotion. Follow this model, using three infinitives in the description.

Sadness is
  to lose a friend,
  to see the dying leaves in fall,
  to feel alone.

Verbals • 95

5.7 Infinitives as Objects

OBJECTIVE
- To identify infinitives, infinitive phrases, and infinitive clauses used as direct objects

DAILY Maintenance

Assign **Practice Book** page 55, Section 5.7. After students finish,
1. Give immediate feedback.
2. Review concepts as needed.
3. Model the correct answer.

Pages 4–5 of the **Answer Key** contain tips for Daily Maintenance.

WARM-UP

Write on note cards sentences that use infinitive phrases as direct objects. Then play musical chairs with the class. Give the student who is left standing one of the note cards. Have the student read the sentence aloud and identify the infinitive and infinitive phrase in the sentence. Repeat this game as time allows.

📖 Read from a piece of writing that the class is currently reading. Emphasize the infinitives used as direct objects.

TEACH

Review direct objects with these simple sentences:

I walked the dog.

The band played music.

Invite volunteers to identify the direct object in each sentence *(dog, music)*. Then have students explain what a direct object is, for example, the direct object receives the action or answers the questions *whom* or *what* after the verb.

Discuss several Warm-Up sentences. Point out that the infinitive phrases are direct objects in each sentence. Then invite volunteers to read aloud

about infinitive phrases as direct objects. You might pose questions for the first three example sentences. For example:

What did Gandhi try? He tried *to obtain freedom for India.*

Read aloud the two example sentences. Be sure students understand that *people* and *them* are each the subject of an infinitive clause and that the entire clause is the direct object.

PRACTICE

EXERCISE 1
Encourage students to complete this exercise independently. If

students have trouble finding the infinitive phrase, suggest they look for the word *to*, followed by a verb, or ask the question *whom* or *what* after the verb. Have students exchange papers with partners to compare and discuss their answers.

EXERCISE 2
Suggest that students write example sentences with infinitive phrases as the subject, the subject complement, and the direct object. Remind students that infinitives used as direct objects can have subjects. Have students refer to their examples as they complete the exercise.

5.7 Infinitives as Objects

When an infinitive functions as a noun, it can be used as a direct object.

In the 1900s Mahatma Gandhi tried *to obtain freedom for India.*
He also hoped *to gain rights for all Indians.*
He wanted *to make the world aware of the issues.*

An infinitive used as a direct object may be preceded by a noun or a pronoun. This noun or pronoun, the subject of the infinitive, tells the doer of the action of the infinitive. The infinitive and its subject form an **infinitive clause**. This construction always follows the main verb of the sentence, and a pronoun used as its subject is always in the object form.

Gandhi encouraged _people_ *to engage in protest.*
He urged _them_ *to act in nonviolent protest of unjust laws.*

In the second sentence, *them to act in nonviolent protest of unjust laws* is an infinitive clause, and *them*, the object form of *they*, is the subject.

Mahatma Gandhi

EXERCISE 1 Identify the infinitive phrase and the main verb in each sentence.

1. Mahatma Gandhi hoped to secure India's independence from British rule.
2. The British had begun to rule in India in the 1700s.
3. As a young man, Gandhi failed to do well in college.
4. Gandhi eventually managed to get a law degree in England.
5. Back in India, he failed to become a successful lawyer because of his shyness.
6. Taking a job in South Africa, he learned to talk effectively in public.
7. He wanted to gain rights for Indians in South Africa.
8. He tried to make service to others his primary goal.
9. In 1914 Gandhi decided to give up his now successful law practice in South Africa.
10. He wanted to go back to his homeland, India.
11. He was determined to bring freedom to his country.

Exercise 1
Infinitive phrases are underlined once. Verbs are underlined twice.

96 • Section 5.7

EXERCISE 3

Have volunteers read aloud their completed sentences. Ask students whether an infinitive or an infinitive phrase was added.

APPLY

APPLY IT NOW

If students have trouble thinking of people, suggest names such as Sojourner Truth, Eleanor Roosevelt, César Chávez, and Jackie Robinson. Invite volunteers to read their sentences aloud. Students should demonstrate an understanding of infinitives used as direct objects.

ASSESS

Note which students had difficulty identifying infinitives, infinitive phrases, and infinitive clauses used as direct objects. Assign **Practice Book** page 65 for further practice.

WRITING CONNECTION

Use pages 348–349 of the Writing portion of the book.

Reteach

Invite each student to write a sentence that includes an infinitive phrase as the direct object. Explain that the sentences should be about something adventurous, for example, *Reisha wants to hike the Grand Canyon. Matthew wants to visit London. Carrie wants to dig for dinosaur bones in the desert.* Have students write their sentences on strips of paper. Tell students to cut the subject and verb apart from the direct object. Collect the parts. Display the strips with the subjects and verbs and read aloud the strips with the infinitive phrases used as direct objects. Let students have fun matching the adventures to their classmates who chose them.

Curriculum Connection

Remind students that they learned some things about Gandhi and the country of India while completing the exercises. Invite students to research what India is like today. Challenge them to write a brief report about India that explains its government, its culture, or its geography. Encourage students to include infinitive phrases in their writing.

Meeting Individual Needs

Challenge Have partners work together to write 10 sentences on a single topic, using infinitive phrases as direct objects. Have students write their sentences on the board, one pair at a time. Encourage the partners to read aloud the sentences and to underline on the board the infinitive phrases used as direct objects for the rest of the class to see and discuss.

Exercise 2
Infinitive phrases and clauses are underlined.
1. subject
2. direct object
3. direct object
4. subject
5. direct object
6. direct object
7. direct object
8. subject complement
9. direct object
10. direct object
11. subject complement
12. direct object
13. direct object
14. subject
15. direct object
16. direct object
17. direct object

EXERCISE 2 Identify the infinitive phrase or clause used as a noun in each sentence. Note whether it is a subject, a subject complement, or a direct object.

1. <u>To end the inequities of the Indian caste system</u> became one of Gandhi's goals, along with independence.
2. Gandhi started <u>to study famous religious works</u>.
3. He refused <u>to accept material items as essential</u>.
4. <u>To reject violence</u> was a goal that Gandhi adopted after an incident in South Africa.
5. He had refused <u>to move from a first-class car to a third-class car on a train</u>.
6. Officials had forced <u>him to leave the train</u>.
7. As a result of that incident, Gandhi had resolved never <u>to use violence as a way of action</u>.
8. His plan was <u>to change society without violence</u>.
9. Gandhi convinced <u>others to join his struggle for rights</u>.
10. He urged <u>Indians to participate in a program of civil disobedience</u>.
11. The British leaders' response was <u>to put him into prison because of his acts of civil disobedience</u>.
12. Gandhi managed <u>to gain world attention for his cause</u>.
13. He decided <u>to lead a 24-day march to the sea against the British monopoly on salt</u>.
14. <u>To pick up some salt from the shore</u> was a symbol of protest.
15. People began <u>to ignore the law against homemade salt</u>.
16. Eventually the British invited <u>Gandhi to participate in a conference on India's fate</u>.
17. After World War II, the British promised <u>to grant independence to India</u>.

Mahatma Gandhi breaking the salt law by picking up a lump of natural salt at Dandi, Gujarat

Exercise 3
Answers will vary.

EXERCISE 3 Complete each sentence with an appropriate infinitive or infinitive phrase used as a direct object.

1. Gandhi intended _____.
2. Officials vowed _____.
3. The British managed _____.
4. The Indians continued _____.
5. From Gandhi, people should try _____.

APPLY IT NOW

Write six sentences about a person you admire for helping others. Include three infinitives as direct objects in your writing.

Verbals • 97

OBJECTIVE
- **To identify infinitives and infinitive phrases used as appositives**

 **DAILY** Maintenance

Assign **Practice Book** page 55, Section 5.8. After students finish,
1. Give immediate feedback.
2. Review concepts as needed.
3. Model the correct answer.

Pages 4–5 of the **Answer Key** contain tips for Daily Maintenance.

WARM-UP

Write *My Goals* on the board. Then throw a beanbag to a student. Instruct the student to tell one of his or her goals, using an infinitive phrase *(to make the baseball team)*. Then tell the student to throw the beanbag to another student who will do the same. Continue this activity with several students.

📖 Read from a piece of writing that the class is currently reading. Emphasize the infinitives used as appositives.

TEACH

Review the definition of an appositive. Then tell students to turn an infinitive phrase from the Warm-Up into an appositive within a sentence. *(My goal, to make the baseball team, will require hard work.)* Have several volunteers write their sentences on the board and underline the appositives.

Invite volunteers to take turns reading about infinitives as appositives in the text. Encourage students to query any points they would like clarified.

PRACTICE

EXERCISE 1
Allow students to work with partners to complete this exercise. Encourage students to take turns reading the sentences aloud and repeating the infinitive phrases. Suggest that students identify the word that each appositive renames so that they gain a firm grasp of its function in the sentence. Have students share their answers with the class.

EXERCISE 2
Challenge students to complete this exercise independently. Explain that their prior knowledge of subjects, subject complements, direct objects, and appositives will be called upon as they complete this exercise. Have volunteers write their sentences on the board, underlining the infinitive phrases and explaining their uses in the sentences.

EXERCISE 3
Have students complete this activity independently. Tell student that the infinitives can be used as subjects, subject complements, direct objects, objects of prepositions, or appositives

---

5.8 Infinitives as Appositives

Washington, D.C., as originally laid out, from a 1793 engraving

An infinitive that functions as a noun can be used as an **appositive.** An appositive is a word or group of words put after a noun or pronoun to rename it or to give more information about it.

> My suggestion, *to do a project on Washington, D.C.,* was accepted by the group.

The infinitive phrase in red acts as an appositive, renaming and telling something about the noun *suggestion.*

Infinitive appositives appear in various positions.

> **Subject:** The team's goal, *to win first place in the conference,* meant practicing every day.
> **Subject complement:** Improvement was our aim, *to do better at each meet.*
> **Direct object:** The team set its own rules, *to practice daily and to work hard.*
> **Indirect object:** We gave the objective, *to bring home a trophy,* our best efforts.

EXERCISE 1 Identify the infinitive phrase used as an appositive in each sentence. Tell what word the appositive renames.

1. The government leaders expressed their <u>desire</u>, <u>to build a magnificent capital for the new country</u>.
2. The final <u>choice</u>, <u>to build a city between Virginia and Maryland</u>, was made in the 1790s.
3. Pierre L'Enfant's <u>task</u>, <u>to design the capital of the United States</u>, was given to him by George Washington.
4. L'Enfant had a <u>vision</u>, <u>to create a city of wide avenues and vistas</u>.
5. His original <u>plan</u>, <u>to have three separate areas for the three branches of government</u>, was not implemented.
6. Pennsylvania Avenue, a wide boulevard connecting the Capitol Building to the White House, had a special <u>purpose</u>, <u>to serve as a place for ceremonial processions</u>.

Exercise 1

Infinitive phrases used as appositives are underlined once. Words the appositive renames are underlined twice.

The Capitol when first occupied by Congress in 1800

APPLY

APPLY IT NOW

Have students brainstorm historical places, events, and objects, such as Williamsburg, Boston, the Revolutionary War, the White House, and the presidential seal. Invite volunteers to read their sentences aloud. Students should demonstrate an understanding of infinitives used as nouns.

TechTip Remind students that they should only use reliable Web sites for online research. If you have a computer in the classroom, show students several examples of reliable sites.

ASSESS

Note which students had difficulty identifying infinitives and infinitive phrases used as appositives. Assign **Practice Book** page 66 for further practice.

WRITING CONNECTION

Use pages 350–351 of the Writing portion of the book.

Exercise 2

Infinitive phrases or clauses used as nouns are underlined.

1. appositive
2. direct object
3. direct object
4. subject complement
5. direct object
6. subject
7. direct object
8. subject complement
9. subject
10. appositive
11. direct object
12. direct object
13. direct object
14. subject
15. direct object

Exercise 3

Infinitives are underlined.

1. subject
2. direct object
3. subject complement
4. subject complement
5. appositive

EXERCISE 2 Identify the infinitive phrase or clause used as a noun in each sentence. Tell whether it is used as a subject, a subject complement, a direct object, or an appositive.

1. The purpose of the Liberty Bell, to mark the 50th anniversary of Pennsylvania's charter, showed the importance of the charter's freedoms to the colony.

2. In 1751 the colony's assembly ordered the bell to be made.

3. The assembly planned to place the bell in the State House, now Independence Hall, in Philadelphia.

4. Their decision was to order the bell from England.

5. A flaw in the bell caused it to crack during its hanging.

6. To recast the bell was the task given to two Philadelphia foundry workers.

7. The tone of the recast bell failed to please people.

8. Despite the arrival of a new bell from England, the final decision was to keep the recast bell in place.

9. To ring for these major events became the fabled task of the bell: the Battles of Lexington and Concord and the Declaration of Independence on July 8, 1776.

10. The fate of the bell, to ring for all important occasions, made it a national relic.

11. People began to call it the Liberty Bell in the 1830s.

12. No one knows for sure when the bell began to crack.

13. People continued to use it until 1846.

14. To give the bell a symbolic tap is a tradition on July 4.

15. Now visitors from all over the country want to view it on visits to Philadelphia.

EXERCISE 3 Identify the infinitive used as a noun in each sentence and tell its function.

1. To reach the finish line of the Philadelphia marathon was reward enough for Ty.

2. He tried to run at an even pace.

3. He seemed to collapse at the halfway point.

4. Yao's job was to pace him though the last two miles.

5. Karl's task, to bring water along, was crucial.

APPLY IT NOW

Write five sentences about a specific historical topic. Use four infinitives as nouns in your writing.

Tech Tip With an adult, research your historical topic online.

Verbals • 99

5.9 Infinitives as Adjectives

OBJECTIVE

• To identify infinitives and infinitive phrases used as adjectives

 **Maintenance**

Assign **Practice Book** page 56, Section 5.9. After students finish,
1. Give immediate feedback.
2. Review concepts as needed.
3. Model the correct answer.

Pages 4–5 of the **Answer Key** contain tips for Daily Maintenance.

WARM-UP

Reinforce that adjectives are words that describe. Put several small objects in a bag. Have a student pick an object from the bag. Ask the rest of the class to close their eyes. Then have the student describe the object. Encourage the student to make the description as vivid as possible. Have the rest of the class guess what the object is. Repeat this activity as time allows.

📖 Read from a piece of writing that the class is currently reading. Emphasize the infinitives used as adjectives.

TEACH

Review the various ways that infinitive phrases can be used—as subjects, subject complements, objects, and appositives. Point out that infinitive phrases used in these ways all function as nouns.

Explain that infinitive phrases also can function as adjectives. Then have volunteers take turns reading aloud about infinitives used as adjectives. Pause after the example sentences and discuss each.

Challenge students to create sentences that include infinitive phrases used as adjectives. Write the sentences on the board to

discuss in more detail. Point out any sentences that use infinitive phrases in other ways, such as direct objects or as subjects. Lead students to see that to be an adjective, a phrase must describe a noun or pronoun—not function as a noun itself. Help students restructure sentences as necessary so that the infinitive phrases are used as adjectives.

PRACTICE

EXERCISE 1

Explain that an infinitive or infinitive phrase, when functioning as an adjective, always follows the word it modifies. Have

students complete the exercise independently. Then have students exchange papers with partners to check and compare answers.

EXERCISE 2

Allow students to work with partners as they consider the placement and function of each phrase. Suggest that students ask themselves *How does this phrase function? Is it a noun? Does it describe a noun?* Have partners take turns sharing answers with the class. Confirm, revise, and discuss students' work as necessary.

5.9 Infinitives as Adjectives

Infinitives can be used as adjectives to describe nouns and pronouns. These infinitives follow the words they describe.

I got a <u>chance</u> **to read** a book by Dorothy M. Johnson.
The book was a great <u>way</u> *to learn* about the West.
The book, *Buffalo Woman*, was definitely <u>one</u> to recommend to others.

Native American buffalo skin tepees on the Great Plains in the 1800s

In the first two sentences, the infinitives modify the nouns *chance* and *way*. In the third sentence, the infinitive modifies the indefinite pronoun *one*.

Can you find the infinitives or infinitive phrases used as adjectives and the nouns they describe in the sentences below?

Johnson had the ability to take readers into the past.
Lists of Western novels to read always include her books.

The infinitive phrase *to take readers into the past* acts as an adjective describing *ability* in the first sentence. *To read* acts as an adjective describing the noun *novels* in the second sentence.

A pronoun used as the subject, subject complement, or direct object of an infinitive is always in the object form.

Juanita's parents expected the winner to be *her*.
Our team cheered for the winner to be *her* or *me*.

EXERCISE 1 Identify the infinitive phrase used as an adjective in each sentence. Then tell the noun it describes.

1. A <u>decision</u> <u>to go to Montana</u> influenced Dorothy M. Johnson's life.
2. Her family's move led to her <u>desire</u> <u>to study the West</u>.
3. Writing gave her a <u>way</u> <u>to share her fascination with the American West</u>.
4. Johnson wrote <u>stories</u> <u>to entertain both lovers of Western novels and general readers alike</u>.
5. One of her <u>books</u> <u>to be made into a film</u> was *The Man Who Shot Liberty Valance*.
6. She was praised for her <u>efforts</u> <u>to portray Native Americans correctly</u>.

Exercise 1
Infinitive phrases used as adjectives are underlined once. Described nouns are underlined twice.

EXERCISE 3

Complete this exercise as a class. Challenge students to identify what words are described by the infinitive phrases.

APPLY

APPLY IT NOW

Ask volunteers to write example sentences on the board. When students have finished, have them exchange papers with a partner and discuss the infinitives used. Students should demonstrate an understanding of infinitives.

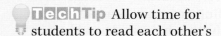 **TechTip** Allow time for students to read each other's

work on the class blog. Encourage students to make note of interesting or confusing uses of infinitives. Discuss these as a class.

ASSESS

Note which students had difficulty identifying infinitives and infinitive phrases used as adjectives. Assign **Practice Book** page 67 for further practice.

WRITING CONNECTION

Use pages 352–353 of the Writing portion of the book.

TEACHING OPTIONS

Reteach

Write the following items on separate note cards:

a building	to construct
a puppy	to love
a movie	to see
a book	to read
a journal	to write in
a place	to visit

Display the cards in two columns, as shown above, but in random order. Let students match each noun with an appropriate infinitive. Then have students write sentences for each pair of cards, for example:

The town council is determining which building to construct in place of the old warehouse.

Our family would really like a puppy to love.

The movie to see this year is based on a best-selling novel.

I am looking for a book to read.

For English class I need a journal to write in.

Egypt is a fascinating place to visit.

Observe and Apply

Display a poster that you think students would like to describe. Find a poster that is illustrated with photographs or drawings. Challenge students to suggest sentences that describe the poster and the images in the poster, for example:

This poster presents an opportunity to talk about the wildlife in a rain forest.

The monkey looks as if it is choosing which tree to climb.

Have students write sentences on strips of paper to display around the poster and to serve as captions.

Exercise 2
Infinitive phrases and clauses are underlined.
1. adjective, monument
2. adjective, project
3. noun
4. adjective, invitation
5. noun
6. noun
7. adjective, efforts
8. noun
9. noun
10. adjective, work
11. noun
12. adjective, ceremony
13. noun
14. adjective, Work
15. adjective, money
16. adjective, Blasts
17. adjective, date

EXERCISE 2 Identify the infinitive phrase or clause in each sentence. Tell whether each is used as an adjective or a noun. For those used as adjectives, tell the word that the infinitive phrase describes.

1. A huge monument to honor Native Americans is being built in South Dakota.
2. The project to build the memorial began in 1948.
3. Sioux chief Henry Standing Bear asked a sculptor to make it.
4. Korczak Ziolkowski accepted the invitation to carve the sculpture.
5. The chief wanted to portray Crazy Horse.
6. The Sioux consider him to be a great leader.
7. Crazy Horse's efforts to serve his people and protect their culture earned him the honor.
8. The final design was to show the chief on horseback.
9. Korczak Ziolkowski's task, to carve a gigantic statue out of a mountain, was an immense one.
10. Work to make the face of the chief began in 1988.
11. To carve out just the face took 10 years.
12. The ceremony to dedicate the face took place in 1998.
13. Ziolkowski, having died in 1982, failed to see this stage of work.
14. Work to carve the sculpture continues.
15. The money to build the statue comes from private contributions.
16. Blasts to remove stone take place several times a week.
17. The date to see the finished statue is still far in the future.

Crazy Horse Memorial in Black Hills, South Dakota

Korczak Ziolkowski

Exercise 3
Infinitive phrases are underlined.

EXERCISE 3 Identify the infinitive phrase in each sentence.

1. The Crazy Horse sculpture is a great monument to visit in South Dakota.
2. The Sioux want to share his history with the public.
3. Preserving his culture is an important issue to the Sioux.

APPLY IT NOW

In a paragraph describe a community service project in which you would like to participate. Pick three of the sentence starters below to explain why, using infinitive phrases.

With this project, I want . . .
This is a chance . . .
It is important . . .
Our community deserves . . .
My idea is . . .
I volunteer . . .

Tech Tip Post your paragraph on the class blog.

Verbals • 101

OBJECTIVE

- **To identify infinitives and infinitive phrases used as adverbs**

 **DAILY Maintenance**

Assign **Practice Book** page 56, Section 5.10. After students finish,
1. Give immediate feedback.
2. Review concepts as needed.
3. Model the correct answer.

Pages 4–5 of the **Answer Key** contain tips for Daily Maintenance.

WARM-UP

On a set of colored note cards, list verbs, one per card. Then on a set of a different color, list adverbs. Have a student draw a card from the verb stack and pantomime the word on the card. Then have three students select cards from the adverb stack. Have one student read aloud the adverb on the card. Have the student pantomiming the verb incorporate the adverb into his or her performance. Then have another student read an adverb card and have the performing student pantomime the verb. Continue as long as time permits.

📖 Read from a piece of writing that the class is currently reading. Emphasize the infinitives used as adverbs.

TEACH

Write the following sentence on the board and read it aloud:

Sometimes this class is too unruly to handle.

Invite volunteers to underline the infinitive phrase. Ask students to determine the function of the phrase *(adverb)*. Challenge students to figure out which word the phrase describes *(unruly—an adjective)*.

Invite volunteers to read aloud the text about infinitives used as adverbs. Because this concept might be difficult for students to grasp, spend adequate time providing examples and responding to students' queries.

PRACTICE

EXERCISE 1

Have students work with partners to complete this exercise. Encourage students to discuss their ideas and to come up with conclusive answers. Discuss the sentences as a class.

EXERCISE 2

Remind students that an infinitive phrase used as an adverb can modify another adverb, an adjective, or a verb. Have them to complete the exercise with partners. Review students' work as a class.

EXERCISES 3 & 4

Have students work on the exercises independently. Invite volunteers to write the sentences on the board. Have students underline each infinitive phrase and write *noun, adjective,* or *adverb* to identify its usage. If the infinitive phrase is an adverb or adjective, have students identify

---

5.10 Infinitives as Adverbs

An infinitive can be used as an adverb to describe a verb, an adjective, or another adverb. These infinitives follow the words they modify.

Butch went to Montana *to take a special vacation on a dude ranch.* (describing the verb *went*)

He was excited *to ride a horse for the first time.* (describing the adjective *excited*)

He wasn't experienced enough *to stay on the horse at first.* (describing the adverb *enough*)

Identify the infinitives used as adverbs in these sentences. What does each infinitive phrase describe?

I didn't know enough to write about the Oregon Trail.
I was determined to learn more about it.
I visited the library to get a book on traveling west.

In the first sentence, the infinitive phrase *to write about the Oregon Trail* describes the adverb *enough.* In the second sentence, the infinitive phrase *to learn more about it* describes the adjective *determined.* In the third sentence, *to get a book on traveling west* explains the verb *visited.* An infinitive that describes a verb often answers the questions *why* or *how* about the verb.

EXERCISE 1 Identify the infinitive phrase used as an adverb in each sentence. The word it describes is italicized. Give its part of speech: adjective, adverb, or verb.

1. Susan *traveled* to the West last summer to participate in a historic adventure tour.
2. She *went* to take a trip in a covered wagon.
3. Susan was *eager* to try the pioneer experience.
4. She was *happy,* however, to learn about the wagons.
5. Rubber wheels *were used* to make the ride less bumpy.
6. A farmhand *was provided* to drive each wagon.
7. Each participant *could sit* in the front to drive the horses.
8. On her turn Susan was strong *enough* to control the horses on her own.

Exercise 1
Infinitive phrases used as adverbs are underlined.
1. verb
2. verb
3. adjective
4. adjective
5. verb
6. verb
7. verb
8. adverb

the word it describes. Discuss the sentences with the class.

APPLY

APPLY IT NOW

Review examples of infinitives used as nouns, adjectives, and adverbs. Invite volunteers to write their sentences on the board and to identify the infinitive phrases. Students should demonstrate an understanding of infinitive phrases.

 Remind students that adverbs can modify verbs, adjectives, and other adverbs. In this model the

infinitive *to find* functions as an adverb.

ASSESS

Note which students had difficulty identifying infinitives and infinitive phrases used as adverbs. Assign **Practice Book** page 68 for further practice.

WRITING CONNECTION

Use pages 354–355 of the Writing portion of the book.

TEACHING OPTIONS

Reteach

Review that one way to determine if an infinitive phrase is used as an adverb is to use the question words *how* or *why*. Have students pose these questions for each sentence in Exercise 1, for example:

Why did Susan travel?
(to participate in a historic adventure tour)

Make sure students realize that the answers to the *why* and *how* questions are the adverb infinitive phrases from the sentences.

Cooperative Learning

Challenge small groups to write instructions for a task such as making a paper airplane, operating the class computer, or cooking a recipe. Encourage students to use infinitive phrases as adverbs while writing the steps in the instructions. Then have volunteers read aloud their instructions. Ask other students to listen for the infinitive phrases used as adverbs. Discuss the phrases and the words they modify.

Meeting Individual Needs

Auditory Invite students to work with partners, asking each other *how* and *why* questions about the school or about things they are doing in school. Challenge students to answer their classmates with sentences that include infinitive phrases used as adverbs. Offer this example.

> **Question: Why are you studying plants in science?**
>
> **Answer: We are studying to learn how they reproduce.**

If possible, let students record their question-and-answer sessions. Have students play back the recordings and write the sentences with infinitive phrases used as adverbs.

Exercise 2
Infinitive phrases used as adverbs are underlined.
1. sat, verb
2. were provided, verb
3. stopped, verb
4. easy, adjective
5. slowly, adverb

EXERCISE 2 Identify the infinitive phrase used as an adverb in each sentence. Then tell the word the infinitive phrase describes and the word's part of speech.

1. At night everyone sat around the campfire to tell stories.
2. Mattresses were provided to sleep on in the wagons.
3. The wagon train stopped regularly to give participants chances for hiking and exploring.
4. The pace of the wagon train was easy to manage.
5. It traveled slowly to allow time for enjoying nature—10 miles a day instead of the 15 miles a day of the pioneers.

Exercise 3
Infinitive phrases are underlined.
1. adjective
2. noun
3. adjective
4. adverb
5. noun
6. adverb
7. noun
8. adverb
9. adjective
10. noun, adverb

EXERCISE 3 Identify the infinitive phrase in each sentence. Tell whether each is used as a noun, an adjective, or an adverb.

1. The original pioneers faced hardships to get to the West.
2. People hoped to have a better life in the West.
3. The dangers to be faced on the trip included harsh weather, accidents, disease, and sometimes starvation.
4. The wagons, with springs only under the driver's seat, were bumpy to ride in.
5. Usually people chose to walk alongside the wagons with their cattle and sheep.
6. The pace was sometimes difficult to maintain.
7. A train usually began to move at seven in the morning.
8. At five the train stopped to rest for the night.
9. At longer stopovers women had the chance to do chores.
10. To arrive at a watering hole was excuse enough to stop.

Exercise 4
Infinitive phrases used as adverbs are underlined.
1. struggled, verb
2. was needed, verb
3. difficult, adjective
4. shared, verb
5. anxious, adjective

EXERCISE 4 Identify the infinitive phrase used as an adverb in each sentence. Then tell the word the infinitive phrase describes and the word's part of speech.

1. Some pioneers struggled to establish new lives.
2. Grass was needed to feed the horses and cattle.
3. Some areas were too difficult to pass through.
4. Travelers shared goods to lighten their loads.
5. Many pioneers were anxious to return to the East.

APPLY IT NOW

Choose two of the following infinitive phrases. Write three sentences for each, using it as a noun, an adjective, and an adverb.
to study a foreign language
to see the new museum
to play the guitar
to go to a rock concert

Grammar in Action. Find an infinitive phrase functioning as an adverb in the p. 337 excerpt.

Verbals • 103

OBJECTIVES

- To identify infinitives used without *to*
- To arrange words in sentences to avoid split infinitives

 **Maintenance**

Assign **Practice Book** page 56, Section 5.11. After students finish,
1. Give immediate feedback.
2. Review concepts as needed.
3. Model the correct answer.

Pages 4–5 of the **Answer Key** contain tips for Daily Maintenance.

WARM-UP

Place a wastepaper basket at the front of the room. Put several balled-up pieces of paper on your desk. Then have two teams compete by identifying the infinitives in sentences you write on the board. Be sure that each sentence contains a hidden or a split infinitive. Explain that the first student to identify the infinitive gets to throw a paper ball into the basket. Tell students that each basket is worth one point and that the team with the most points wins.

📖 Read from a piece of writing that the class is currently reading. Emphasize the hidden and split infinitives.

TEACH

Explain that the Warm-Up sentences have infinitives but that the infinitives are not readily noticeable. Point out that sometimes infinitive phrases can appear without the word *to*. Tell students that this type of infinitive is called a hidden infinitive. Invite a volunteer to read aloud about hidden infinitives. Challenge students to suggest sentences with hidden infinitives for the verbs

hear, see, feel, let, make, dare, need, and *help.*

Tell students that sometimes people "split" an infinitive, which means that they place a word between *to* and the verb. Point out several examples from the Warm-Up sentences. Have a volunteer read aloud about split infinitives. Encourage students to offer examples of split infinitives, while other students "repair" the splits by rewording the sentences.

PRACTICE

EXERCISE 1

Review the words that can help students locate hidden infinitives,

such as *hear, see, feel, let, make, dare, need,* and *help.* Allow students to work with partners to complete this activity. Ask students to share their answers with the class. Discuss in more detail the sentences that seemed to be most troublesome.

EXERCISE 2

Remind students that good writers try to avoid split infinitives. Mention that the word that is splitting the infinitive can usually be placed in more than one place in the sentence. Invite volunteers to write their corrected sentences on the board. Discuss how

---

5.11 Hidden and Split Infinitives

The word *to* is called the sign of the infinitive, but sometimes infinitives appear in sentences without the *to.* Such infinitives are called **hidden infinitives.**

After verbs of perception such as *hear, see,* and *feel,* the infinitive is used without a *to.* This is also the case for the verbs *let, make, dare, need,* and *help.*

> We <u>heard</u> the astronomer *talk* about the comet.
> We would not <u>dare</u> *use* Marshall's telescope without his permission.

The *to* is also omitted after the prepositions *but* and *except* and the conjunction *than.*

> Marshall does little but *talk* about the comet these days.
> I'd rather do an experiment than *read* about science.

An adverb placed between *to* and the verb results in a **split infinitive.** Good writers try to avoid split infinitives. To avoid a split infinitive, put the adverb where it sounds best.

> Split infinitive: We were told to carefully view each star.
> Improved: We were told to view each star carefully.
>
> Split infinitive: Marshall told us to not damage his telescope.
> Improved: Marshall told us not to damage his telescope.

Where to place the adverb you remove from the middle of the infinitive depends on the meaning of the sentence.

> Split infinitive: We started to optimistically watch the sky for the comet.
> Improved: Optimistically we started to watch the sky for the comet. OR
>   We started to watch the sky for the comet optimistically.

Exercise 1
Hidden infinitives are underlined.

EXERCISE 1 Identify the hidden infinitive in each sentence.

1. Many people saw the comet <u>appear</u> in the sky.
2. Watching the comet streak across the sky made us <u>feel</u> small.
3. Marshall let us <u>borrow</u> his telescope for one night to see Halley's comet.

students revised the sentences to remove the split infinitives.

EXERCISE 3

Complete this exercise as a class. Discuss the differences in the placement of each adverb.

APPLY

APPLY IT NOW

Encourage students to show you where they included hidden infinitives. Question students to make sure they know why the infinitives are considered hidden. *(They do not have the word* to.*)* Students should demonstrate an understanding of hidden infinitives.

ASSESS

Note which students had difficulty identifying infinitives used without *to* and with arranging words in sentences to avoid split infinitives. Assign **Practice Book** pages 69–70 for further practice.

> ### WRITING CONNECTION
>
> Use pages 356–357 of the Writing portion of the book.

TEACHING OPTIONS

Reteach

Write the following words at the top of separate sheets of paper: *help, need, dare, let, make, but, except, than, hear, see, feel, watch.* Assign one of these words to each student and have the student use the word in a sentence with a hidden infinitive. Direct students to write their sentences on the appropriate paper for that word. Review the sentences. Have students find the hidden infinitives.

English-Language Learners

Provide students with additional practice in recognizing and avoiding split infinitives. Ask students fluent in English to write several example sentences with split infinitives. Have English-language learners identify the split infinitives. Encourage students to suggest revisions for the split infinitives.

Curriculum Connection

Remind students that comets are objects in space. Encourage students to research other objects in space, such as planets, the moon, distant stars, a galaxy, or the asteroid belt. Ask students to write a description of a real or an imagined feature of space, using hidden infinitives. Combine students' work into an Out in Space anthology. Let students read their classmates' work, noting any hidden infinitives they find.

Diagram It!

To practice these concepts in the context of diagramming, turn to Section 11.7.

Exercise 2
Possible answers:

1. I was determined to view the next solar eclipse safely.

2. I knew enough not to look directly at the sun.

3. I went to the library to research the topic thoroughly so that I could do so safely.

4. I was warned to keep my back to the sun constantly throughout the eclipse.

5. Easily I managed to make a pinhole projector.

6. I was able to obtain readily the two necessary pieces of cardboard needed to make it.

7. I needed simply to cut a small hole in one piece.

8. I needed to place the two pieces properly in alignment during the eclipse.

9. I would look through the hole to see the sun's reflection clearly on the other piece of cardboard.

10. Immediately I wanted to test out the device—but I had to wait for the eclipse, of course.

Exercise 3
Accept any answers that do not contain split infinitives.

4. I prefer to see the comet in the sky firsthand rather than <u>view</u> a video of it.

5. We knew that we would see the comet <u>shine</u> more clearly with a telescope.

6. We dared not <u>damage</u> it.

7. He need not <u>worry</u> about us—we are always careful with things we borrow.

8. My father helped us <u>place</u> the telescope in our window.

9. I did nothing all day but <u>think</u> about viewing the comet.

10. When will people watch the comet <u>blaze</u> across the sky again?

EXERCISE 2 Rewrite the sentences so that they do not contain split infinitives.

1. I was determined to safely view the next solar eclipse.

2. I knew enough to not look directly at the sun.

3. I went to the library to thoroughly research the topic so that I could do so safely.

4. I was warned to constantly keep my back to the sun throughout the eclipse.

5. I managed to easily make a pinhole projector.

6. I was able to readily obtain the two necessary pieces of cardboard needed to make it.

7. I needed to simply cut a small hole in one piece.

8. I needed to properly place the two pieces in alignment during the eclipse.

9. I would look through the hole to clearly see the sun's reflection on the other piece of cardboard.

10. I wanted to immediately test out the device—but I had to wait for the eclipse, of course.

EXERCISE 3 Rewrite each sentence to include the adverb in parentheses. Avoid creating a split infinitive.

1. Gail hopes to become a professional astronomer. (eventually)

2. She plans to identify all the constellations. (correctly)

3. She appears to have most of them identified. (already)

4. Her uncle, Captain Matthews, learned how to land planes. (skillfully)

5. He has landed planes in bad weather. (carefully)

APPLY IT NOW

Write a short description of what you see, hear, and feel while outside at night. Use two hidden infinitives in your writing and identify them.

Verbals • 105

Verbal Review

ASSESS

Use the Verbal Review as homework, as a practice test, or as an informal assessment. Following are some options for use.

Homework

You may wish to assign one group the odd items and another group the even items. When you next meet, review the correct answers as a group. Be sure to model how to arrive at the correct answer.

Practice Test

Use the Verbal Review as a diagnostic tool. Assign the entire review or only specific sections. After students have finished, identify which concepts require more attention. Reteach concepts as necessary.

Verbal Review

5.1 Identify each participial phrase, each participle, and the noun or pronoun each participle describes. Then identify the participle as present, past, or perfect.

1. Walking through the open-air market, Jin stopped at each stall.
2. Having decided to make empanadas, she needed fresh ingredients.
3. Filled with meat, cheese, or fruit, empanadas are popular Latin American pastries.
4. Having purchased the ingredients, Jin went home.

5.2 Identify the participial adjective or participial phrase in each sentence. Correct any sentences that have a dangling participle.

5. The conductor quieted the waiting audience.
6. Tapping his baton, the orchestra began to play.
7. Being a fan of classical music, the concert was enjoyable.

5.3 Identify each gerund phrase. Tell whether each gerund is a subject or a subject complement.

8. Training for a 26.2-mile race is a serious commitment.
9. Stretching before a race can help prevent injuries.
10. A recommendation is drinking enough water to stay hydrated.

5.4 Identify the gerund phrase in each sentence and tell whether it is used as a direct object, an object of a preposition, or an appositive.

11. In many countries people enjoy drinking tea.
12. According to folklore, the Chinese accidentally discovered the drink by dropping some leaves of the plant into hot water.
13. The practice, drinking tea, was at first only for the wealthy.
14. Some Americans began serving tea over ice cubes.

5.5 Choose the correct word to complete each sentence.

15. (Me My) writing the winning story would be great.
16. I was happy with (Carl's Carl) editing of my story.
17. (Her She) entering the contest took courage.
18. We applauded (his him) winning the award.

5.6 Identify each infinitive phrase and tell whether it is used as a subject or a subject complement.

19. To explore west of the Mississippi was one of President Thomas Jefferson's goals.
20. As Jefferson's personal secretary, Meriwether Lewis's main duty was to help plan for westward expansion.

5.1

1. walking through the open-air market, walking, Jin, present
2. having decided to make empanadas, having decided, she, perfect
3. Filled with meat, seafood, cheese, or fruit; filled, empanadas; past
4. Having purchased the ingredients, Having purchased, Jin, perfect

5.2

5. waiting, participial adjective
6. tapping his baton, dangling participle; possible answer: Tapping his baton, the conductor instructed the orchestra to begin to play.
7. Being a fan of classical music, dangling participle; possible answer: Being a fan of classical music, I enjoyed the concert.

5.3

8. Training, subject
9. Stretching, subject
10. drinking, subject complement

5.4

11. direct object
12. object of a preposition
13. appositive
14. direct object

Informal Assessment

Use the review as preparation for the formal assessment. Count the review as a portion of the grade. Have students work to find the correct answers and use their corrected review as a study guide for the formal assessment.

WRITING CONNECTION

Use pages 358–359 of the Writing portion of the book.

5.6
19. subject
20. subject complement
21. subject
22. subject complement
23. subject complement

5.7
24. attempted
25. hoped
26. wanted
27. managed

5.8
28. idea
29. plan
30. decision
31. purpose

5.9
32. chance
33. way
34. items
35. technique

5.10
36. adjective
37. adverb
38. adjective
39. verb

5.11
40. organize
41. The volunteers were told to consider their duties seriously.
42. sell
43. I decided definitely to donate an item.

21. To serve as a commander for the expedition was an honor for Lewis.
22. The purpose of the expedition was to gather information about the West.
23. William Clark's responsibility as chief cartographer was to map the expedition.

5.7 Identify each infinitive phrase and the verb of which it is a direct object.

24. Henry Ford first attempted to establish an auto manufacturing company in 1899.
25. He hoped to revolutionize the manufacturing industry.
26. He wanted to use standardized parts and division of labor.
27. In 1903 he founded Ford and managed to start the world's first moving assembly line.

5.8 Identify each infinitive phrase and tell the word each appositive explains.

28. My idea, to write a report on the Normandy Invasion, required a great deal of research.
29. The plan, to turn the tide in favor of the Allies, succeeded.
30. The decision to postpone the invasion because of the weather was a good one.
31. The purpose of Memorial Day, to honor soldiers killed in battle, seemed especially important on the 60th anniversary of D-Day.

5.9 Identify the infinitive phrases used as adjectives. Tell the noun each infinitive phrase describes.

32. Felicity got the chance to browse London's famous flea markets.
33. Rummaging through the stalls is a great way to find hidden treasures.
34. She bought items to fix and resell at her store.
35. Bargaining is one technique to get a good deal.

5.10 Identify the infinitive phrases used as adverbs. Tell whether the phrase modifies a verb, an adjective, or an adverb.

36. Pedro was anxious to work toward his goal.
37. He practiced enough to become proficient.
38. The surfers thought some waves were too big to ride.
39. The surfers met on the shore to pack up their gear.

5.11 Identify any hidden infinitives. Rewrite any sentence to correct a split infinitive.

40. Magdalena helped the club organize a fund-raiser for charity.
41. The volunteers were told to seriously consider their duties.
42. Do you think they'll let me sell tickets?
43. I decided to definitely donate an item.

Go to www.voyagesinenglish.com for more activities.

Verbals • 107

Meeting Individual Needs

Challenge Help students review verbals by having them complete three of the following exercises:

- Look through a magazine or newspaper article and find three examples of participial phrases. Underline each phrase and circle the noun or pronoun the participial phrase modifies.

- Write six sentences about someone you know. Use a gerund as a subject in two sentences, a gerund as a subject complement in two sentences, and a gerund as an appositive in two sentences.

- Write a paragraph about a sibling or a good friend. Include infinitives used as direct objects. Share your work with a partner and point out the infinitives used as direct objects.

- Watch a local news program and note how many times infinitives are used in the reporting. Choose five infinitives and use each in a sentence.

- Write a paragraph about your favorite season. Include at least one split infinitive and one hidden infinitive. Work with a partner and see if he or she can find the hidden and split infinitives.

TechTip Encourage students to further review verbals, using the additional practice and games at www.voyagesinenglish.com.

Verbal Challenge

ASSESS

Encourage students to read the paragraph twice before answering the questions independently. If students have difficulty with any question, suggest that they refer to the section that teaches the skill. This activity can be completed by individuals, by small groups, or by the class working as a whole.

After you have reviewed verbals, administer the Section 5 Assessment on pages 13–16 in the **Assessment Book,** or create a customized test with the optional **Test Generator CD.**

WRITING CONNECTION

Use pages 360–361 of the Writing portion of the book.

Students can complete a formal description using the Writer's Workshop on pages 362–373.

Verbal Challenge

Read the selection and then answer the questions.

1. Ever since fourth grade, I have been wanting to visit the battle monument in Concord, Massachusetts. 2. We were expected to memorize the "Concord Hymn" by Ralph Waldo Emerson. 3. I enjoyed reciting it, and I still know it by heart. 4. Emerson wrote the poem in 1837 for the dedication to be put on the battle monument. 5. The monument was raised to honor the Minutemen, soldiers who fought for America's independence from England, at the battles of Lexington and Concord in 1775. 6. Traveling through New England last year, my family was passing near Concord. 7. This made it possible for me to realize my dream to see the monument. 8. It was the dead of winter, and the setting sun cast a reddish-orange glow over everything. 9. Wearing only our thin jackets, Dad, my little sister, and I were freezing, but nobody complained. 10. I cannot think of a better way to see this historic site. 11. I recited a verse of the poem in honor of visiting this piece of American history.

1. In sentence 1, what is the infinitive phrase? How is it used in the sentence?
2. In sentence 3, what is the gerund phrase? How is it used in the sentence?
3. In sentence 4, what is the infinitive phrase? How is it used in the sentence?
4. In sentence 5, what is the infinitive phrase? How is it used in the sentence?
5. How does the phrase *Traveling through New England last year* function in sentence 6?
6. How is the word *passing* used in sentence 6?
7. How is the word *setting* used in sentence 8?
8. What is the participial phrase in sentence 9? What words does it describe?
9. In sentence 10, what is the infinitive phrase? How is it used in the sentence?
10. How is the phrase *visiting this piece of American history* used in sentence 11?

Minute Man National Historical Park in Concord, Massachusetts

Verbal Challenge

1. to visit the battle monument in Concord, Massachusetts; direct object
2. reciting it; direct object
3. to be put on the battle monument; adjective
4. to honor the Minutemen; adverb
5. present participle modifying *family*
6. as a verb in a verb phrase
7. adjective
8. Wearing only our thin jackets; Dad, sister, I
9. to see this historic site; adjective
10. object of a preposition

Adverbs

SECTION FOCUS
- Types of adverbs
- Interrogative adverbs, adverbial nouns
- Comparative and superlative adverbs
- Adjectives and adverbs with *as . . . as, so . . . as*, and *equally*
- Adverb phrases and clauses

SUPPORT MATERIALS

Practice Book
Daily Maintenance, pages 71–72
Grammar, pages 73–80

Assessment Book
Section 6 Assessment, pages 17–18

Test Generator CD

Writing Chapter 5, Expository Writing

Customizable Lesson Plans
www.voyagesinenglish.com

CONNECT WITH LITERATURE

Consider using the following titles throughout the section to illustrate the grammar concept:

Cuba 15 by Nancy Osa
Dearly, Nearly, Insincerely: What Is an Adverb by Brian P. Cleary
Hush by Jacqueline Woodson

GRAMMAR FOR GROWN-UPS

Understanding Adverbs

Adverbs modify verbs, adjectives, or other adverbs. Although adverbs commonly end in *ly* (*quickly, early, fairly*), some do not (*fast, ever, very*).

Adverbs of time tell *when* or *how often*.

> **George does his homework daily.**

Adverbs of place tell *where*.

> **Brooke put the dog outside.**

Adverbs of manner tell *how* or *in what manner*.

> **The teacher briskly wrote the notes on the board.**

Adverbs of degree tell *how much* or *how little*.

> **I was extremely unhappy with my meal.**

Adverbs of affirmation confirm the truth of a statement.

> **Maria definitely enjoys going to the movies.**

Adverbs of negation express a negative statement or refusal.

> **I have never rode my bike without a helmet.**

Just as with adjectives, adverbs can be compared. These adverbs have **positive, comparative,** and **superlative** forms. With most adverbs that end in *-ly*, the comparative is formed by adding *more* and the superlative is formed by adding *most*.

> **My brother writes smoothly.** (positive)

> **My sister writes more smoothly than he** (comparative)

> **I write most smoothly of all my siblings.**

However, comparative and superlative forms of adverbs that do not end in *ly* are formed by adding *-er* or *-est* (*fast, faster, fastest*).

> **❝I adore adverbs; they are the only qualifications I really much respect.❞**
>
> —Henry James

COMMON ERRORS

Using Adjectives and Adverbs

Sometimes students use an adjective in place of an adverb. Some students will drop the *ly* of the adverb and incorrectly use an adjective.

> **ERROR:** David threw the ball weak.
> **CORRECT:** David threw the ball weakly.
>
> **ERROR:** The dog barks loud.
> **CORRECT:** The dog barks loudly.

Often, if a word answer the question *how,* it is an adverb and will end in *ly. He throws how? He throws weakly.*

SENTENCE DIAGRAMMING

You may wish to teach verbals in the context of diagramming. Review these examples. Then refer to the Diagramming section or look for Diagram It! features in the Verbals section.

The spy quietly and carefully climbed the fence.

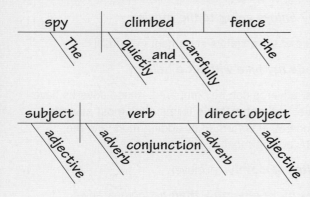

Betsy threw the towel in the hamper.

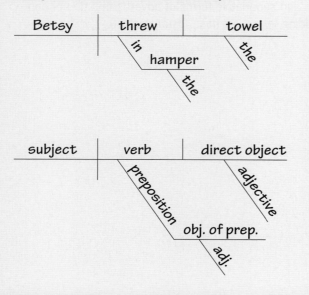

ASK AN EXPERT

Real Situations, Real Solutions

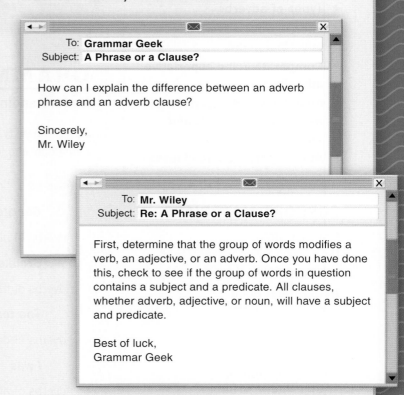

To: **Grammar Geek**
Subject: **A Phrase or a Clause?**

How can I explain the difference between an adverb phrase and an adverb clause?

Sincerely,
Mr. Wiley

To: **Mr. Wiley**
Subject: **Re: A Phrase or a Clause?**

First, determine that the group of words modifies a verb, an adjective, or an adverb. Once you have done this, check to see if the group of words in question contains a subject and a predicate. All clauses, whether adverb, adjective, or noun, will have a subject and predicate.

Best of luck,
Grammar Geek

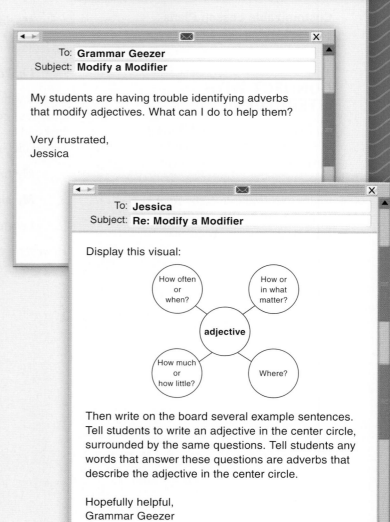

To: **Grammar Geezer**
Subject: **Modify a Modifier**

My students are having trouble identifying adverbs that modify adjectives. What can I do to help them?

Very frustrated,
Jessica

To: **Jessica**
Subject: **Re: Modify a Modifier**

Display this visual:

Then write on the board several example sentences. Tell students to write an adjective in the center circle, surrounded by the same questions. Tell students any words that answer these questions are adverbs that describe the adjective in the center circle.

Hopefully helpful,
Grammar Geezer

Adverbs

OBJECTIVE

- **To identify adverbs of time, place, manner, degree, affirmation, and negation**

DAILY Maintenance

Assign **Practice Book** page 71, Section 6.1. After students finish,
1. Give immediate feedback.
2. Review concepts as needed.
3. Model the correct answer.

Pages 4–5 of the **Answer Key** contain tips for Daily Maintenance.

WARM-UP

Write on the board a list of adverbs and a list of verbs. Toss a beanbag to a student. Have that student choose one adverb and one verb from each list, say the words aloud, and toss the beanbag to another student. Instruct this student to act out the word combination *(softly speak, briskly write)*. Continue the activity by rotating students who choose word combinations with students performing the actions.

📖 Read from a piece of writing that the class is currently reading. Emphasize the types of adverbs.

TEACH

Read aloud the definition of an adverb and the example sentences. Have students close their eyes. Then read aloud the following sentences:

The boy walked through the hall.

The boy walked quickly through the hall.

Ask a volunteer to identify the adverb in the second sentence *(quickly)*. Discuss how the adverb created a clearer image.

Point out that *quickly* tells the manner in which the boy walked and is an adverb of manner. Have

volunteers read aloud about each type of adverb. Discuss the example sentences and encourage students to suggest additional sentences.

PRACTICE

EXERCISE 1

Write on the board a chart with the following headings: *Time, Place, Degree, Manner, Affirmation,* and *Negation.* Have volunteers write the adverbs from the sentences under the correct headings.

EXERCISE 2

Use the chart from Exercise 1 to review the ways adverbs can be used—to express time, place, manner, degree, affirmation, or negation. Have students complete this exercise independently. Then have partners exchange papers to compare their answers.

EXERCISE 3

Remind students that adverbs can describe verbs, adjectives, or other adverbs. Have students work with partners to complete this exercise. Combine two sets of partners and have the larger groups discuss their answers.

6.1 Types of Adverbs

An **adverb** is a word used to describe a verb, an adjective, or another adverb. It is also called a simple adverb. There are several types of adverbs.

> **Many stories are told** *orally*. (The adverb *orally* describes the verb phrase *are told*.)
> **Oral storytelling has an** *extremely* **long history.** (The adverb *extremely* describes the adjective *long*.)
> **Jackson tells stories** *very* **dramatically.** (The adverb *very* describes the adverb *dramatically*.)

An **adverb of time** tells when or how often. Some adverbs of time are *again, early, frequently, now, then,* and *weekly*.

> **I** *recently* **heard a strange story.**

An **adverb of place** tells where. Some adverbs of place are *above, away, up, forward, here, nearby,* and *there*.

> **Sit** *down*, **and listen to the story.**

An **adverb of manner** tells how or in what manner. These adverbs include *carefully, slowly,* and *enthusiastically*.

> **Everyone listens** *attentively* **to Jackson's stories.**

An **adverb of degree** tells how much or how little. Some adverbs of degree are *almost, hardly, many, quite, seldom,* and *very*.

> **Some of his stories are** *quite* **scary.**

An **adverb of affirmation** tells whether a statement is positive or expresses consent or approval. The adverbs of affirmation include *allegedly, indeed, positively, undoubtedly,* and *yes*.

> **This author** *undoubtedly* **has traveled widely.**
> *Indeed*, **his biography refers to him as a world traveler.**

An **adverb of negation** expresses a negative condition or refusal. Among the adverbs of negation are *no, not,* and *never*.

> **I** *never* **expect to see any science fiction books by him.**
> **That is** *not* **where his interests lie.**

APPLY

APPLY IT NOW

Have volunteers read aloud their stories, first with the adverbs and then without. Ask students to compare the two versions. Students should demonstrate an understanding of adverbs.

💡 **TechTip** Have students highlight each adverb before posting their stories on the class Web site. Then have students review their classmates' stories and create a list of effective adverbs.

ASSESS

Note which students had difficulty identifying adverbs. Assign **Practice Book** page 73 for further practice.

WRITING CONNECTION

Use pages 374–375 of the Writing portion of the book. Be sure to point out adverbs in the literature excerpt and the student model.

TEACHING OPTIONS

Reteach

Have students search through magazines and choose six pictures showing a variety of situations. Instruct students to cut out the pictures, glue them to poster board, and write a corresponding sentence below each picture. Tell students that they should describe each picture with a different type of adverb (*time, place, manner, degree, affirmation, negation*). Encourage students to give their posters catchy titles. Invite volunteers to share their work with the class.

English-Language Learners

Discuss how to identify adverbs that do not end in the suffix *ly*. Write these adverbs on the board:

again	**now**	**somewhere**
always	**often**	**soon**
ever	**perhaps**	**then**
just	**rather**	**there**
later	**so**	**too**
never	**sometimes**	**yet**
not		

Suggest that students record these words in their notebooks. Have small groups take turns using the words in sentences. Suggest that as one student provides a sentence, the other students identify the adverb and the word the adverb describes.

Cooperative Learning

Direct each student to write 10 sentences that contain adverbs. Tell students to exchange papers and to identify the adverbs in their partners' sentences. Then encourage students to work together to revise their sentences by changing the adverbs so that the sentences express ideas that are opposites of the original sentences.

Exercise 1
1. negation, time
2. degree, manner
3. affirmation, negation, place
4. manner, manner
5. affirmation, manner, place

EXERCISE 1 Identify the italicized words in each sentence as adverbs of time, place, degree, manner, affirmation, or negation.

1. Bill was *not* able to recall the story *recently*.
2. He started *quite calmly*.
3. *Allegedly*, the lion had *never* been seen running *away*.
4. Walking *confidently* toward the lion, she talked *steadily* to it.
5. The lion *undoubtedly* was curious and *slowly* stood *up*.

Exercise 2
Adverbs are underlined.
1. degree
2. affirmation
3. time
4. time
5. manner
6. time
7. manner
8. degree
9. degree
10. time

EXERCISE 2 Identify the adverb in each sentence and tell whether it is an adverb of time, place, manner, degree, affirmation, or negation.

1. The <u>highly</u> unusual stories that make the rounds throughout the country are called urban legends.
2. You <u>certainly</u> have heard some of these.
3. People <u>sometimes</u> hear stories about alligators living in sewers.
4. According to legend, baby alligators <u>once</u> were given as pets.
5. When families got tired of tending to the alligators, they <u>irresponsibly</u> abandoned them.
6. The alligators <u>eventually</u> got into the sewer system.
7. Alligators <u>quickly</u> multiplied.
8. They grew <u>terribly</u> large.
9. Rumors spread of the <u>extremely</u> dangerous threat.
10. Some people claimed that the alligators <u>occasionally</u> entered houses through the plumbing system.

Exercise 3
Adverbs are underlined.
1. untrue, adjective
2. persist, verb; strong, adjective
3. are told, verb
4. have heard, verb
5. may appeal, verb

EXERCISE 3 Identify the adverb or adverbs in each sentence. Tell the word that each adverb describes and give the word's part of speech.

1. People frighten one another with <u>totally</u> untrue stories.
2. The legends <u>still</u> persist despite <u>emphatically</u> strong denials by police.
3. Such tales are told <u>confidently</u> by the storytellers.
4. Tellers <u>usually</u> have heard them from a "friend of a friend."
5. The accounts <u>simply</u> may appeal because they are scary.

APPLY IT NOW

Write a brief paragraph about a story you like to tell. Use adverbs of manner such as *calmly, happily, hesitantly, determinedly,* and *rapidly* to add detail to your writing.

 Tech Tip Post your story on the class Web site.

Adverbs • 111

OBJECTIVES

- **To identify and use interrogative adverbs**
- **To identify adverbial nouns and to tell what they express**

 **Maintenance**

Assign **Practice Book** page 71, Section 6.2. After students finish,
1. Give immediate feedback.
2. Review concepts as needed.
3. Model the correct answer.

Pages 4–5 of the **Answer Key** contain tips for Daily Maintenance.

WARM-UP

Prepare note cards with adverbial nouns such as *years, inches,* and *south.* Have students choose a card and say a sentence using the word. *(High school lasts only a few years.)* Write on the board students' sentences. Then have students turn the written sentences into questions. *(How long does high school last?)*

📖 Read from a piece of writing that the class is currently reading. Emphasize the interrogative adverbs and adverbial nouns.

TEACH

Write the following words on the board: *why, where, when,* and *how.* Ask students what these words have in common. *(All these words ask questions.)* Read aloud about interrogative adverbs. Tell students that each interrogative adverb expresses a specific type of question.

Read from the board several Warm-Up sentences. Point out that sometimes a noun functions as an adverb and is called an adverbial noun. Guide students to understand the difference between adverbial nouns and direct objects. Explain that a direct object answers the question *what* after

a transitive verb. Ask a student to read aloud about adverbial nouns. Challenge students to think of other adverbial nouns *(pints, inches, feet).*

PRACTICE

EXERCISE 1

Have small groups complete this exercise. Challenge students to identify each adverb as an adverb of time, place, manner, degree, affirmation, or negation.

EXERCISE 2

Point out that interrogative adverbs are easy to identify, but adverbial nouns are more challenging. Have students complete the exercise independently. Then have small groups discuss their answers.

EXERCISE 3

Invite volunteers to write their completed sentences on the board. Have students check their own sentences against the sentences on the board. Point out that adverbial nouns may appear to be direct objects, but adverbial nouns tell *how far, how long,* and *how costly*— all questions typically answered by adverbs.

6.2 Interrogative Adverbs and Adverbial Nouns

An **interrogative adverb** is used to ask a question. The interrogative adverbs are *how, when, where,* and *why.* Interrogative adverbs are used to express or to query reason, place, time, or method.

Reason: *Why* did the railroads lose some of their importance?
Place: *Where* did first public railroads run?
Time: *When* did your train arrive?
Method: *How* do you usually travel long distances?

An **adverbial noun** is a noun that acts as an adverb by describing a verb. Adverbial nouns are used to express time, distance, measure, value, or direction.

Time: I spent 21 *hours* on the train.
Distance: We traveled nearly 1,000 *miles* on the trip.
Measure: The container held two *quarts* of water.
Value: The meal cost several *dollars* more than we expected.
Direction: The train traveled *west* throughout the night.

An adverbial noun should not be mistaken for a direct object. A direct object follows a transitive verb and answers the question *what.*

He crossed out three *weeks* on the calendar.

Her cold lasted three *weeks.*

In the first sentence, *three weeks* is an adverb telling how long the cold lasted. In the second sentence, *three weeks* is a direct object telling what was crossed out.

EXERCISE 1 Identify the adverb or adverbs in each sentence. Point out which ones are interrogative adverbs.

1. The rusty car rolled forward slowly.
2. When did the car start to approach the corner?
3. It barely scraped Tom's car.
4. Tom quickly jumped out and started sadly, shaking his head.
5. How long did he chase the empty car?
6. The car just kept rolling away from him.

Exercise 1
1. forward, slowly
2. When, interrogative
3. barely
4. quickly, out, sadly
5. How, interrogative
6. just, away

APPLY

APPLY IT NOW

Encourage students to express such ideas as how far they traveled and how long they stayed, which will provide opportunities for the use of adverbial nouns. Students should demonstrate an understanding of interrogative adverbs and adverbial nouns.

TechTip Have students review their classmates' interviews. Challenge students to identify adverbial nouns that express time, distance, measure, value, and direction.

ASSESS

Note which students had difficulty identifying interrogative adverbs and adverbial nouns. Assign **Practice Book** pages 74–75 for further practice.

WRITING CONNECTION

Use pages 376–377 of the Writing portion of the book.

Exercise 2
1. When, interrogative adverb, time
2. years, adverbial noun, time
3. Where, interrogative adverb, place
4. thousands, adverbial noun, measure
5. miles, adverbial noun, distance
6. miles, adverbial noun, distance
7. Where, interrogative adverb, place
8. west, adverbial noun, direction
9. north, adverbial noun, direction; south, adverbial noun, direction
10. miles, adverbial noun, distance
11. Why, interrogative adverb, reason
12. millions, adverbial noun, value

EXERCISE 2 Identify the interrogative adverbs and adverbial nouns in these sentences. Tell what each interrogative adverb expresses—reason, place, time, or method. Tell what each adverbial noun expresses—time, distance, measure, value, or direction.

1. When was the great era of railroads?
2. It started approximately 200 years ago.
3. Where did the first successful railroad trip by steam engine take place?
4. A load might weigh thousands of pounds—including ten tons of iron and five wagons—and be pulled by a single engine.
5. The first trip covered nearly 10 miles of track.
6. The tracks went many miles across the United States.
7. Where did the two ends of the transcontinental railroad finally meet?
8. The railroads took settlers west across the United States.
9. In the United States today the largest number of train passengers moves north and south along the East Coast.
10. Some passenger trains travel 267 miles an hour; however, airplanes are often more convenient for long distances.
11. Why are railroads still important?
12. Although they cost millions of dollars to maintain, trains still carry many tons of freight from place to place.

Exercise 3
Answers will vary.
Possible answers:
1. How
2. Where
3. 1,000 miles
4. four hours
5. Why
6. 10 dollars
7. two days
8. When
9. How

EXERCISE 3 Complete the sentences with interrogative adverbs or adverbial nouns. Use the clues in parentheses.

1. _____ did you travel on your last vacation? (method)
2. _____ did you go? (place)
3. We traveled approximately _____. (distance)
4. The trip took _____. (time)
5. _____ did you choose to visit a theme park? (reason)
6. We paid _____ to rent a campsite. (value)
7. I researched the location for _____. (time)
8. _____ did you finally decide? (time)
9. _____ did you make your decision? (method)

APPLY IT NOW

With a partner, interview each other about trips you have taken. Write five interview questions using interrogative adverbs. Use at least one adverbial noun in each of your answers.

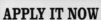 Post your interview on the class blog or wiki.

Adverbs • 113

OBJECTIVE
- **To identify adverbs and name their form of comparison**

 **Maintenance**

Assign **Practice Book** page 71, Section 6.3. After students finish,
1. Give immediate feedback.
2. Review concepts as needed.
3. Model the correct answer.

Pages 4–5 of the **Answer Key** contain tips for Daily Maintenance.

WARM-UP

Have three students stand in front of the classroom. Tell one student to clap. Ask the class how the student clapped *(loud, fast)*. Then have the other student outdo the first student's clapping. Ask the class again how that student clapped *(louder, faster)*. Then ask the last student to outdo the second student's clapping. Ask the class how this student's clapping compared to the previous two *(loudest, fastest)*. Repeat with additional actions such as jumping, running, and talking.

📖 Read from a piece of writing that the class is currently reading. Emphasize the comparative and superlative adverbs.

TEACH

Write on the board the following sentences:

The first student clapped fast.

The second student clapped faster than the first.

The third student clapped fastest of all.

Invite a volunteer to identify the adverb in the first sentence *(fast)*. Explain that the two students are being compared in the second sentence and point out the use of

than. Emphasize that more than two students are being compared in the third sentence.

Have students compare the example sentences in the book with the sentences on the board. Have volunteers read about comparative and superlative adverbs and the charts of example adverbs.

PRACTICE

EXERCISE 1
Review the adverb charts and suggest that students refer to them as needed. Invite volunteers to write on the board their comparative and superlative

adverbs. Discuss student's responses, especially the irregular forms.

EXERCISE 2
Remind students that the comparative form of an adverb is used to compare two thing and that the superlative form is used to compare more than two things. Point out that the positive form is used when nothing is being compared.

EXERCISE 3
Tell students to check the number of things being compared in the sentence. Remind students that if more than two things are being

6.3 Comparative and Superlative Adverbs

Some adverbs can be compared. Like adjectives, they have **comparative** and **superlative** forms.

Positive:	My sister packs *quickly*.
Comparative:	My mom packs *more quickly* than my sister.
Superlative:	I pack *most quickly* of all in the family.

The comparative and superlative forms of most adverbs that end in *ly* are formed by adding *more* or *most* (or *less* or *least*) before the positive form of the adverb. The comparative and superlative forms of many adverbs that do not end in *ly* are formed by adding *-er* or *-est*. Using *more* or *most* (or *less* or *least*) with adverbs that end in *er* or *est* is incorrect. Avoid constructions such as *more faster* and *more better*.

POSITIVE	COMPARATIVE	SUPERLATIVE
carefully	more (or less) carefully	most (or least) carefully
hastily	more (or less) hastily	most (or least) hastily
fast	faster	fastest
late	later	latest

Some adverbs have irregular comparisons.

ADVERB	COMPARATIVE	SUPERLATIVE
well	better	best
badly	worse	worst
far	farther	farthest
little	less	least
much	more	most

EXERCISE 1 Write the comparative and superlative forms of the following adverbs.

1. easily
2. noisily
3. hurriedly
4. early
5. beautifully
6. soon
7. cautiously
8. well
9. effectively
10. desperately
11. simply
12. nervously
13. high
14. powerfully
15. sloppily

Exercise 1
More/less or *most/least* are used with all the words except the following:
4. earlier, earliest
6. sooner, soonest
8. better, best
13. higher, highest

compared, students should use the superlative form.

EXERCISE 4
Point out that the comparative and superlative forms of most adverbs that end in *ly* are formed by adding *more* or *most* before the positive form of the adverb. Invite volunteers to read their sentences aloud.

APPLY
APPLY IT NOW
Invite volunteers to read their sentences aloud. Point out proper usage of comparative and superlative adverbs.

Students should demonstrate an understanding of comparative and superlative adverbs.

ASSESS
Note which students had difficulty identifying comparative and superlative adverbs. Assign **Practice Book** page 76 for further practice.

> ### WRITING CONNECTION
> Use pages 378–379 of the Writing portion of the book.

Exercise 2
Adverbs are underlined.
1. positive
2. comparative
3. positive
4. superlative

Exercise 3
1. more frequently
2. hardest
3. more carefully
4. most highly
5. better
6. least
7. most
8. more/less readily

Exercise 4
1. Of all publications *The Guinness Book of World Records* probably covers world records most comprehensively.
2. For example, it tells about people who have traveled farthest.
3. Correct
4. In addition to traveling farthest, he probably also has traveled the longest time—more than 30 years.
5. Of all the books I own, I read the record books most eagerly.

EXERCISE 2 Identify the adverb in each sentence. Tell whether the adverb is positive, comparative, or superlative.

1. The editor examined the manuscript <u>closely</u>.
2. The wind blew <u>more strongly</u> as we reached the open water.
3. Are you <u>adequately</u> prepared for this test?
4. The judge listened <u>most attentively</u>.

EXERCISE 3 Complete each sentence with the correct comparative or superlative form of the adverb in parentheses.

1. With Mom in the Army, we move much _____ (frequently) than most other families.
2. My mom always works _____ (hard) of all of us.
3. No one plans a move _____ (carefully) than she does.
4. She is the _____ (highly) organized person I know.
5. She works _____ (good) than any moving company.
6. Of cleaning, doing laundry, and packing, I don't know which is my _____ (little) favorite task.
7. What I find _____ (much) distressful is saying good-bye.
8. I can make friends _____ (readily) now that I'm getting older.

EXERCISE 4 Rewrite the sentences to correct the use of adverbs in comparisons. Not all the sentences have errors.

1. Of all publications *The Guinness Book of World Records* probably covers world records most comprehensive.
2. For example, it tells about people who have traveled most farthest.
3. Arthur Blessitt has walked farther than anyone else—about 37,502 miles in 310 countries.
4. In addition to traveling most farthest, he probably also has traveled the longest time—about 30 years.
5. Of all the books I own, I read the record books more eagerly.

APPLY IT NOW
Write six sentences using the following adverbs. Use the degree of comparison indicated in parentheses.
carefully (comparative)
well (superlative)
little (superlative)
sloppily (superlative)
confidently (comparative)
effectively (superlative)

Adverbs • 115

6.4 As . . . As, So . . . As, and *Equally*

OBJECTIVES

- **To distinguish between** *as . . . as* **and** *so . . . as*
- **To recognize the correct use of the adverb** *equally*

 **Maintenance**

Assign **Practice Book** page 71, Section 6.4. After students finish,
1. Give immediate feedback.
2. Review concepts as needed.
3. Model the correct answer.

Pages 4–5 of the **Answer Key** contain tips for Daily Maintenance.

WARM-UP

Write on the board a list of nouns and a list of verbs, using students' suggestions. Then have students write comparisons using two nouns and a verb from the board, and the word *as* or *equally*. Ask volunteers to read their sentences aloud. Discuss the use of adverbs in each sentence.

📖 Read from a piece of writing that the class is currently reading. Emphasize the comparisons with *as . . . as, so . . . as,* and *equally*.

TEACH

Display two items that are the same size, such as two pens. Challenge students to create a sentence that compares the items. Write several of the students' sentences on the board. *(This pen is as long as that pen.)*

Ask students to explain the function of *as . . . as* in the sentences. Elicit that these words are used to compare the two items in a positive way.

Have students create a sentence that compares the items in a negative way. *(This pen doesn't write so smoothly as that pen.)* Point out that *so . . . as* is used in the negative comparison. Invite volunteers to take turns reading

aloud about *as . . . as* and *so . . . as*. Challenge students to create sentences that use *so . . . as* in a comparison.

Invite a student to read aloud about the word *equally*. Challenge students to suggest sentences that include *equally*.

PRACTICE

EXERCISE 1

Ask students to explain when they should use the comparison *so . . . as*. Discuss its use in negative comparisons and tell students to look for signal words such as *not* or *no*. Have students complete the

exercise independently and then compare answers with a partner.

EXERCISE 2

Have students complete this exercise independently. Invite volunteers to read aloud their answers. Discuss each sentence with the class, telling students to compare their choices with those that were read aloud.

EXERCISE 3

Remind students that *as* should not be used between *equally* and the adverb or adjective in comparisons. Have students complete this activity independently. Ask volunteers

---

6.4 As . . . As, So . . . As, and *Equally*

The Nile River in Egypt

Both adjectives and adverbs can be used in comparisons.

A particular usage problem may come up in comparisons with *as . . . as* or *so . . . as*. Study the following examples of adverb comparisons.

> The Yukon River flows **as** far in North America **as** the Orinoco River does in South America.
> The Nile River doesn't flow quite **so** forcefully **as** the Amazon River does.
> The Nile River doesn't flow quite **as** forcefully **as** the Amazon River.

In the first sentence, the comparison is positive. In that sentence only *as . . . as* may be used. In the second and third sentences, the comparison is negative; the sentences contain *not*. In a sentence with a negative comparison, either *as . . . as* or *so . . . as* may be used.

The same rules for using *as . . . as* and *so . . . as* apply to adjectives used in comparisons. A positive comparison may use only *as . . . as*. A negative comparison may use *as . . . as* or *so . . . as*.

> The Chang Jiang River is nearly **as** long **as** the Amazon.
> The Mississippi River isn't **so** long **as** the Amazon.

Equally is also used in comparisons. Never use *as* between *equally* and the adverb or adjective.

> The two rivers are **equally** impressive.
> Both rivers are **equally** dangerous.

EXERCISE 1 Complete each sentence with *so* or *as*.

1. The Monongahela River is not ___so / as___ long as the Allegheny River.
2. The Allegheny River, however, doesn't flow ___so / as___ powerfully as the Monongahela River.
3. The use of the rivers for transportation is ___as___ old as the history of the country.
4. Pittsburgh, where the Monongahela and the Allegheny meet, is ___as___ historic as any city west of the Appalachians.
5. The ocean is not ___as___ accessible as a river.

---

to read their sentences aloud. Encourage students to explain each answer.

APPLY

APPLY IT NOW

Before students begin writing, ask them which words are used in a positive comparison (*as . . . as*). Then ask which words are used in a negative comparison (*as . . .as* or *so . . . as*). Invite volunteers to share their sentences. Students should demonstrate an understanding of using *as . . . as, so . . . as,* and *equally* when making comparisons.

 Students should identify the following comparison in the excerpt:

> Greece is only half as large as the state of New York . . .

ASSESS

Note which students had difficulty using *as . . . as, so . . . as,* and *equally* in comparisons. Assign **Practice Book** pages 77–78 for further practice.

WRITING CONNECTION

Use pages 380–381 of the Writing portion of the book.

Exercise 2
Items #4, 6, 7, 8, 11
can be either *so* or *as*

EXERCISE 2 Choose the word or words that correctly complete each sentence.

1. The two rivers that meet at Pittsburgh, the Allegheny and the Monongahela, are (equally impressive   equally as impressive).

2. In the 1700s the area where the two rivers meet to form the Ohio River was (as so) strategic as any in the West.

3. During the French and Indian War, the French and the British were (equally desirous   equally as desirous) to control it.

4. In fact, there wasn't any outpost (as so) important to the French as it was, because it allowed passage from their northern to their southern colonies.

5. Few attacks ended (as so) disastrously as that of British General Edward Braddock on French-held Fort Duquesne in 1754.

6. His army, however, was not (as so) large as the British army that successfully captured the fort in 1758.

7. Pittsburgh did not figure (so as) importantly as did cities farther east during the Revolutionary War.

8. More recent periods in history are not (as so) fascinating to me as the colonial period.

9. I say that is because I'm (as so) much of a history buff as my father.

10. My father and mother tell me that the 1700s suit me (as so) well as my own time.

11. People today do not work (as so) rigorously to survive as they did in the 1700s, so I'm not sure I agree.

EXERCISE 3 Choose the word or words that correctly complete each sentence.

1. Cedric's bicycle is (as equally as) good as mine.

2. That end of the pool is not (equally so) deep as this end.

3. Tia and Max play the drums (equally equally as) well.

4. San Francisco has (as so) much fog as London.

The Allegheny River in Pittsburgh, Pennsylvania

APPLY IT NOW

Use *as . . . as* or *so . . . as* in sentences to compare one of the following sets of items. Choose items that you have opinions about.

two songs	two sports
two books	two school subjects
two movies	two music groups

Adverbs • 117

Grammar in Action. Find the adverb comparison in the p. 374 excerpt.

Reteach

Invite students to look through textbooks and magazines for pictures with interesting images. Then display two of the chosen pictures side by side. Encourage students to describe the pictures in sentences, using the words *as . . . as, so . . . as,* and *equally* similarly to the examples below. Display students' sentences to reinforce correct sentence construction.

> **These people are smiling as happily as those people are.**
>
> **The colors in this picture do not glow so vibrantly as the colors in that picture.**
>
> **The rafting and the hiking in these pictures seem to be equally enjoyable.**

Meeting Individual Needs

Auditory Assign small groups a topic, such as sports, cities, or video games. Invite students to talk about their topics, using the comparisons *as . . . as, so . . . as,* and *equally*. Have one group member record at least five of the group's sentences. Ask volunteers to share these sentences with the class.

Meeting Individual Needs

Interpersonal Have groups discuss the plots of their favorite movies. Encourage students to create comparisons between the movies, using *as . . . as, so . . . as,* and *equally*. Encourage students to raise their hands every time they hear a comparison correctly. Challenge students to correct any incorrect comparisons (such as using *so . . . as* for a positive comparison).

6.5 Adverb Phrases and Clauses

OBJECTIVES

- **To identify prepositional phrases as adverb phrases**
- **To identify dependent clauses as adverb clauses**

 **Maintenance**

Assign **Practice Book** page 72, Section 6.5. After students finish,
1. Give immediate feedback.
2. Review concepts as needed.
3. Model the correct answer.

Pages 4–5 of the **Answer Key** contain tips for Daily Maintenance.

WARM-UP

Write on the board the following sentence:

> In the morning I quickly ate my toast in the car.

Ask a volunteer to circle the part of the sentence that shows the action *(ate)* and who performed the action *(I)*. Ask another volunteer to underline the parts of the sentence that show how the action was done *(quickly)*, when the action was done *(in the morning)*, and where the action was done *(in the car)*.

📖 Read from a piece of writing that the class is currently reading. Emphasize the adverb phrases and clauses.

TEACH

Remind students that adverbs describe verbs, adjectives, or other adverbs. Then have a volunteer read aloud about adverb phrases. Discuss the example sentences. Have students say sentences containing prepositional phrases that answer one of these questions: *when, where, why, how, to what extent,* and *under what condition.*

Ask a volunteer to read aloud about adverb clauses. Challenge students to explain how adverb

phrases and adverb clauses differ. Remind students that a predicate is a verb or verb phrase that tells what the subject does or is. Then have students create sentences that include adverb clauses, using the conjunctions listed at the bottom of the page.

PRACTICE

EXERCISE 1

Remind students that an adverb phrase is a prepositional phrase that answers one of the following questions: *when, where, why, how, to what extent,* and *under what condition.* Allow students to work

together to locate each adverb phrase and the word it describes. Challenge students to identify the modified word as a verb, an adjective, or an adverb.

EXERCISE 2

Have a volunteer read aloud the common conjunctions that introduce adverb clauses. Have partners complete this activity. Discuss the answers as a class.

EXERCISE 3

Review the difference between an adverb phrase and an adverb clause. Remind students that adverb clauses contain

---

6.5 Adverb Phrases and Clauses

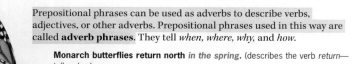

Prepositional phrases can be used as adverbs to describe verbs, adjectives, or other adverbs. Prepositional phrases used in this way are called **adverb phrases**. They tell *when, where, why,* and *how.*

Monarch butterflies return north *in the spring.* (describes the verb *return*— tells *when*)
Some monarch butterflies migrate *from Canada.* (describes the verb *migrate*—tells *where*)

What are the adverb phrases in these sentences? What does each describe?

Many butterflies travel to Mexico.
They are vulnerable to habitat loss.
They begin their migration early in the autumn.

You are correct if you answered as follows: In the first sentence, the adverb phrase *to Mexico* describes the verb *travel.* In the second sentence, the adverb phrase *to habitat loss* describes the adjective *vulnerable.* In the third sentence, the adverb phrase *in the autumn* describes the adverb *early.*

A **clause** is a group of words containing a subject and a predicate. A **dependent clause** is one that does not express a complete thought and that cannot stand alone. A dependent clause that acts as an adverb is called an **adverb clause**. Like adverbs and adverb phrases, adverb clauses tell *how, when, where, why, to what extent,* or *under what condition.*

Unlike most other insects, monarch butterflies migrate *because they cannot survive the cold.* (The adverb clause tells *why* and describes the verb *migrate* in the main clause.)
When it gets cold, **the butterflies begin migration.** (The adverb clause tells *when* and describes the verb *begin.*)

Some common conjunctions used to introduce adverb clauses are *after, although, as, because, before, if, in order that, provided that, since, so that, unless, until, when, whenever, where, wherever, whether,* and *while.*

Exercise 1
1. in North America, spend
2. During the summer, are spread; over a wide area, are spread
3. In the fall, migrate; to their winter homes, migrate
4. to the same winter homes, fly; by the previous generation of butterflies, used
5. During the flight, are vulnerable; to predators, are vulnerable
6. to Mexico, fly; in large groups, fly
7. in a Mexican forest, winter
8. in the same place, congregate

118 • **Section 6.5**

subjects and predicates. Have students complete this activity independently. Then have volunteers share their answers.

APPLY

APPLY IT NOW

Tell students to copy each sentence that contains an adverb phrase or adverb clause. Have students underline the phrase or clause and identify the word that it describes. Students should demonstrate an understanding of adverb phrases and clauses.

ASSESS

Note which students had difficulty identifying prepositional phrases as adverb phrases and dependent clauses as adverb clauses. Assign **Practice Book** pages 79–80 for further practice.

WRITING CONNECTION

Use pages 382–383 of the Writing portion of the book.

Use pages 382–383 of the Writing portion of the book.

TEACHING OPTIONS

Reteach

Start a chart on the board with the headings *Adverb Phrases* and *Adverb Clauses*. Brainstorm phrases and clauses for each column. Write students' responses in the chart. Review the phrases and clauses on the chart and ask whether they have been listed correctly. Then direct students to use the phrases and clauses in sentences.

Meeting Individual Needs

Challenge Invite a student to write on the board a simple subject-and-verb sentence.

My dog plays.

Challenge the student to add other clauses and phrases to that sentence.

My dog plays in the yard.

When snow covers the ground, my dog plays in it.

Emphasize how the added clauses and phrases make the simple sentence more informative. Then encourage students to come up with additional sentences.

Cooperative Learning

Extra Support Tell students that adverb phrases and adverb clauses can be located at the beginning, in the middle, or at the end of a sentence. Invite volunteers to read aloud the sentences in Exercises 1 and 2. Then have students read each sentence again, changing the position of the adverb phrase or adverb clause. Encourage students to discuss how each change affects the sentence.

EXERCISE 1 Identify the adverb phrase in each sentence. Name the word the adverb phrase describes.

1. Monarch butterflies spend summer in North America.
2. During the summer they are spread over a wide area.
3. In the fall they migrate to their winter homes.
4. Some monarch butterflies fly to the same winter homes used by the previous generation of butterflies.
5. During the flight they are, of course, vulnerable to predators.
6. Many monarch butterflies fly to Mexico in large groups.
7. Most monarch butterflies winter in a Mexican forest.
8. Millions congregate in the same place.

Monarch butterflies in the Sierra Chincua Butterfly Sanctuary in Angangueo, Michoacan, Mexico

EXERCISE 2 Identify the adverb clause in each sentence. Name the word or words the adverb clause describes.

1. Because they make a long migratory flight rather quickly, monarch butterflies born at the end of summer have special features.
2. Although they look like their parents, they differ in some ways.
3. Because their bodies store a lot of fat in the abdomen, they have enough fuel for their long flight.
4. They leave for the south before the weather gets cold.
5. If they stay too long, they cannot make the trip.
6. Butterflies cannot fly in cold weather because they are cold-blooded animals.
7. As they migrate southward, they stop to get nectar and actually gain weight on the trip.

EXERCISE 3 Identify the underlined words in each sentence as an adverb phrase or adverb clause. Name the word it describes.

1. Strike <u>while the iron is hot</u>.
2. The greyhound ran faster <u>than the rabbit could</u>.
3. The ants climbed <u>over my sandwich</u>.
4. An honest woman speaks <u>as she thinks</u>.
5. Raphael acted <u>with courage</u>.

APPLY IT NOW

Find an article about an animal that interests you. Try to identify all the adverb phrases and clauses in it. Write a five-sentence summary of the article without looking back at it. Use at least one adverb phrase and one adverb clause in your summary.

Adverbs • 119

Exercise 2

1. Because they make a long migratory flight rather quickly, have
2. Although they look like their parents, differ
3. Because their bodies store a lot of fat in the abdomen, have
4. before the weather gets cold, leave
5. If they stay too long, can make
6. because they are cold-blooded animals, can fly
7. As they migrate southward, stop

Exercise 3

Modified words are underlined.

1. adverb clause
2. adverb clause
3. adverb phrase
4. adverb clause
5. adverb phrase

Adverb Review

ASSESS

Use the Adverb Review as homework, as a practice test, or as an informal assessment. Following are some examples for use.

Homework

You may wish to assign one group the odd items and another group the even items. When you next meet, review the correct answers as a group. Be sure to model how to arrive at the correct answer.

Practice Test

Use the Adverb Review as a diagnostic tool. Assign the entire review or only specific sections. After students have finished, identify which concepts require more attention. Reteach concepts as necessary.

Adverb Review

6.1
1. frequently, time, walks
2. enthusiastically, manner, waits
3. hardly, degree, up
4. away, place, scampered
5. certainly, affirmation, happy
6. never, negation, are
7. far, place, walk
8. playfully, manner, tugs
9. quite, degree, tired
10. everywhere, place, travel
11. usually, time, run

6.2
12. interrogative adverb
13. interrogative adverb
14. adverbial noun
15. interrogative adverb
16. adverbial noun
17. adverbial noun
18. interrogative adverb
19. adverbial noun
20. adverbial noun
21. interrogative adverb
22. adverbial noun
23. adverbial noun

6.1 Identify the simple adverb in each sentence. Tell its type and the word the adverb describes.

1. Erin frequently walks her dog on the trail.
2. Her dog, Rufus, waits enthusiastically at the door in the morning.
3. The sun is hardly up when they begin their walk.
4. Rufus scampered away from Erin.
5. Rufus is certainly happy on those morning walks.
6. Their morning walks are never short.
7. They walk far from home.
8. Rufus tugs playfully on his leash.
9. They are quite tired at the end of their walk.
10. Erin and Rufus travel everywhere together.
11. They usually run around the park.

6.2 Identify the underlined word in each sentence as an interrogative adverb or an adverbial noun.

12. When will Donna arrive home from school?
13. Why was her bus so late?
14. It had to stop many times.
15. Why did the traffic jam occur?
16. Donna spent two hours on the bus.

17. In that time the bus traveled three miles.
18. Where was the bus stuck?
19. The bus moved only inches at a time.
20. Donna's trip usually takes 30 minutes.
21. How did Donna feel when she finally arrived home?
22. It seemed like she was riding the bus all night.
23. Donna only lives 12 blocks from school.

6.3 Write the comparative and superlative forms of the following adverbs. If the comparative form is given, write the superlative form.

24. skillfully
25. less carefully
26. fast
27. far
28. well
29. much
30. little
31. badly
32. simply
33. less readily
34. soon
35. actively
36. less effectively
37. early
38. slow

6.3
24. more/less skillfully, most/least skillfully
25. least carefully
26. faster, fastest
27. farther, farthest
28. better, best
29. more, most
30. less, least
31. worse, worst
32. more/less simply, most/least simply
33. least readily
34. sooner, soonest
35. more/less actively, most/least actively
36. least effectively
37. earlier, earliest
38. slower, slowest

6.4
39. so/as
40. as
41. equally
42. so/as
43. as
44. so/as
45. equally
46. as
47. equally
48. so/as
49. so/as
50. as
51. equally

Informal Assessment

Use the review as preparation for the formal assessment. Count the review as a portion of the grade. Have students work to find the correct answers and use their corrected review as a study guide for the formal assessment.

WRITING CONNECTION

Use pages 384–385 of the Writing portion of the book.

6.5

52. at her grandparents' house, phrase, vacation
53. When Julia arrived, clause, hugged
54. in San Francisco, phrase, live
55. over the bay, phrase, looks
56. Although Julia enjoys the hot weather of southern California, clause, appreciates
57. whenever she visits San Francisco, clause, goes
58. to Chinatown, phrase, goes; with her grandparents, phrase, goes
59. to Angel Island Park, phrase, take
60. when they immigrated to America, clause, arrived
61. After they go to Chinatown, clause, walk; along the wharf, phrase, walk
62. where they catch the ferry, clause, is
63. Because Julia likes animals, clause, go
64. Before Julia goes home, clause, go
65. In the shopping bags, phrase, are

6.4 Complete each sentence with *so, as,* or *equally.*

39. This year's art fair wasn't _____ crowded as last year's.
40. The painting was _____ realistic as a photograph.
41. The artists are _____ talented, judging from the exhibits.
42. This mosaic isn't _____ colorful as the other one.
43. She sculpts _____ well as she paints.
44. Larry doesn't like art _____ much as he likes music.
45. Pottery and quilts are _____ remarkable.
46. This painting is _____ striking as that one.
47. The judges thought the two paintings were _____ impressive.
48. Sarah's paintings aren't _____ interesting as her sculptures.
49. Sarah doesn't work on her paintings _____ often as she works on her sculpture.
50. Kim's collage was _____ colorful as her photograph.
51. The crowd believed her two pieces were _____ striking.

6.5 Identify the adverb phrase or adverb clause in each sentence. Tell whether each is a phrase or a clause, and identify the word it describes.

52. Julia spent her vacation at her grandparents' house.
53. When Julia arrived, her grandparents hugged her.
54. Her grandparents live in San Francisco.
55. Their house looks over the bay.
56. Although Julia enjoys the hot weather of southern California, she appreciates San Francisco's cooler air temperature even more.
57. Julia goes sightseeing whenever she visits San Francisco.
58. She usually goes to Chinatown with her grandparents.
59. They also take a ferry to Angel Island Park.
60. Angel Island Park is where her grandparents first arrived when they immigrated to America.
61. After they go to Chinatown, they often walk along the wharf.
62. That is where they catch the ferry to Angel Island State Park.
63. Because Julia likes animals, they also go to the San Francisco Zoo.
64. Before Julia goes home, they all go shopping.
65. In the shopping bags are many souvenirs.

 Tech Tip Go to www.voyagesinenglish.com for more activities.

Adverbs • 121

TEACHING OPTIONS

Putting It All Together

Review that adverbs are words, phrases, or clauses that describe a verb, an adjective, or another adverb. Remind students that adverbs answer the questions *how, how often, where, how much, how little, when, why, to what extent,* or *under what condition.* Write on the board the following headings:

Time

Manner

Degree

Affirmation

Negation

Interrogative

Adverbial Noun

Comparative and Superlative

Adverb Phrase

Adverb Clause

Have each student write on a note card a sentence containing an adverb, an adverb phrase, or an adverb clause. Collect the cards. Ask volunteers to choose cards and read the sentences aloud. Challenge students to identify the adverb, adverb phrase, or adverb clause and to write it below the proper heading on the board.

Tech Tip Encourage students to further review adverbs, using the additional practice and games at www.voyagesinenglish.com.

Adverb Challenge

ASSESS

EXERCISE 1
Encourage students to read the paragraph twice before answering the questions independently. If students have difficulty with any question, suggest that they refer to the section that teaches the skill. This activity can be completed by individuals, by small groups, or by the class working as a whole.

EXERCISE 2
Read aloud the directions for Exercise 2. Have students complete this activity independently. When students have finished, invite volunteers to read their paragraphs aloud. Challenge students to raise their hands every time they hear an adverb.

After you have reviewed adverbs, administer the Section 6 Assessment on pages 17–18 in the **Assessment Book,** or create a customized test with the optional **Test Generator CD.**

You may also wish to administer the Sections 5–6 Summative Assessment on pages 37–38 of the **Assessment Book.** This test is also available on the optional **Test Generator CD.**

WRITING CONNECTION
Use pages 386–387 of the Writing portion of the book.

Adverb Challenge

EXERCISE 1 Read the selection and answer the questions.

1. The first astronauts had to be very brave. 2. They ventured to places where no one had ever been. 3. Carefully trained physically and scientifically, they began to explore parts of the universe that previously were seen only from a distance. 4. They were indeed modern pioneers. 5. They were probably more thoroughly trained than the recent astronauts who have left Earth's atmosphere on space shuttles.

6. As space exploration has advanced, inhabited Earth-orbiting stations that were once idly dreamed about have become a reality. 7. The possibility of space travel is not so much a question anymore as that of how long human bodies can stay in space without damage.

American astronaut Edwin "Buzz" Aldrin walking near the lunar module on the moon

1. What is the adverb in the first sentence? What part of speech is the word it describes?
2. In sentence 2 is *where* an interrogative adverb, a conjunction, or an adverbial noun? What word does it describe?
3. In sentence 2 which adverb shows time? What does it describe?
4. In sentence 4 find an adverb. What type of adverb is it?
5. In sentence 5 find the adverb in the comparative form. Give its positive and superlative forms.
6. In sentence 5 find the adverb phrase. What does it describe?
7. In sentence 6 find the adverb clause.
8. In sentence 6 find the adverb of manner.
9. In sentence 7 is *without damage* an adverb phrase or adjective phrase? What does it describe?

EXERCISE 2 Write a paragraph, following these instructions.

Describe an extracurricular activity you enjoy. In your description, use at least two simple adverbs, a comparative adverb, a superlative adverb, an adverb phrase, and an adverb clause. Explain how, when, and where you participate in the activity, as well as why you participate.

Exercise 1
1. very; adjective
2. conjunction; places
3. ever; had been
4. indeed; adverb of affirmation
5. more thoroughly; thoroughly, most thoroughly
6. on space shuttles; have left
7. As space exploration has advanced
8. idly
9. adverb phrase; can stay

Exercise 2
Answers will vary.

SECTION FOCUS
- **Single and multiword prepositions**
- **Troublesome prepositions**
- **Words used as adverbs and prepositions**
- **Prepositional phrases as adjectives**
- **Prepositional phrases as adverbs**
- **Prepositional phrases as nouns**

SUPPORT MATERIALS

Practice Book
Daily Maintenance, pages 81–82
Grammar, pages 83–89

Assessment Book
Section 7 Assessment,
  pages 19–20

Test Generator CD

Writing Chapter 5,
  Expository Writing

Customizable Lesson Plans
www.voyagesinenglish.com

CONNECT WITH LITERATURE

📖 Consider using the following titles throughout the section to illustrate the grammar concept:

Casey at the Bat: A Ballad of the Republic Sung in the Year 1888 by Ernest L. Thayer
Fly with Poetry: An ABC of Poetry by Avis Harley
Under, Over, by the Clover: What Is a Preposition? by Brian P. Cleary

Prepositions

GRAMMAR FOR GROWN-UPS

Understanding Prepositions

A **preposition** is a word that shows a relationship between a noun or pronoun and other words within the sentence.

Here are some common prepositions.

about	*before*	*down*	*of*
above	*behind*	*for*	*on*
after	*below*	*from*	*to*
at	*by*	*into*	*with*

A **prepositional phrase** is a group of words containing a preposition, the **object of the preposition** (a noun or pronoun that follows the preposition), and any modifiers of the object of the preposition. Prepositional phrases usually serve as adjectives or adverbs.

> **The boy** *in the green shirt* **raised his hand.** (adjective)

> **The chef dropped the ingredients** *into the pot*. (adverb)

In addition to being adjectives or adverbs, prepositional phrases can also be nouns.

> *In my bedroom* **is where I usually hang out.** (subject)

> **My time for doing homework is** *after dinner*. (subject complement)

Some words can be either prepositions or adverbs. A word being used as a preposition is always part of a phrase. A word being used as an adverb will describe the verb.

> **As I climbed the ladder, a cat walked** *below me*. (preposition)

> **As I climbed the ladder, a cat walked** *below*. (adverb)

> ❝With enough verbs and prepositions, anything can happen.❞
>
> —Michael Wakcher

COMMON ERRORS

Misused Prepositions

Can you use the prepositions *between* and *among* interchangeably? In most cases, the answer is no. As a general rule, *between* is used to express one-to-one relationships, and *among* is used to describe collective or undefined relationships.

> **ERROR:** The squirrel scampered between the flowers.
> **CORRECT:** The squirrel scampered among the flowers.

> **ERROR:** I had to choose among the red and the blue.
> **CORRECT:** I had to choose between the red and the blue.

When students check their writing, have them read for the use of these prepositions. Work with students to choose the correct word based on its context.

SENTENCE DIAGRAMMING

You may wish to teach conjunctions and interjections in the context of diagramming. Review these examples. Then refer to the Diagramming Section or look for Diagram It! features in the Conjunctions and Interjections section.

The car with red paint is ours.

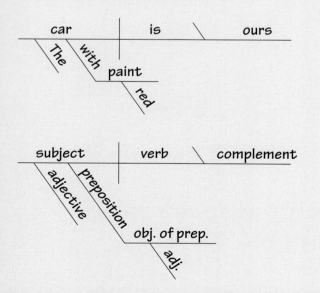

ASK AN EXPERT

Real Situations, Real Solutions

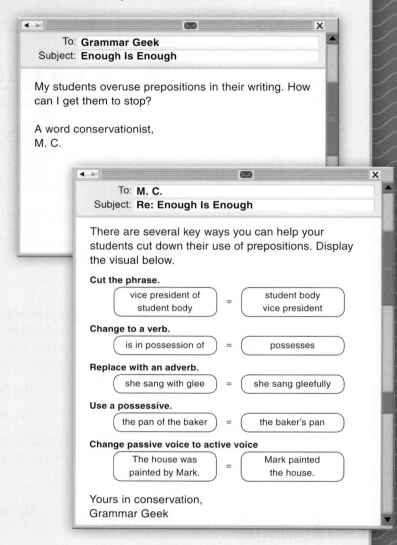

To: Grammar Geek
Subject: Enough Is Enough

My students overuse prepositions in their writing. How can I get them to stop?

A word conservationist,
M. C.

To: M. C.
Subject: Re: Enough Is Enough

There are several key ways you can help your students cut down their use of prepositions. Display the visual below.

Cut the phrase.

| vice president of student body | = | student body vice president |

Change to a verb.

| is in possession of | = | possesses |

Replace with an adverb.

| she sang with glee | = | she sang gleefully |

Use a possessive.

| the pan of the baker | = | the baker's pan |

Change passive voice to active voice

| The house was painted by Mark. | = | Mark painted the house. |

Yours in conservation,
Grammar Geek

After school is my practice time.

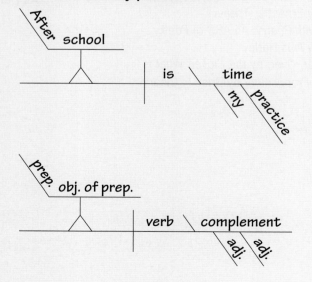

OBJECTIVE

- **To identify single-word and multiword prepositions and the objects of prepositions**

DAILY Maintenance

Assign **Practice Book** page 81, Section 7.1. After students finish,
1. Give immediate feedback.
2. Review concepts as needed.
3. Model the correct answer.

Pages 4–5 of the **Answer Key** contain tips for Daily Maintenance.

WARM-UP

Place markers throughout the classroom. Have students locate as many markers as they can. Then ask students who have markers where they were found *(under the desk, by the door, and so on)*. List student's responses on the board.

Read from a piece of writing that the class is currently reading. Emphasize the single and multiword prepositions.

TEACH

Invite students to share what they know about prepositions. Then ask volunteers to write on the board sentences using the prepositional phrases from the Warm-Up. Have a volunteer read aloud about prepositions and prepositional phrases. Challenge students to read the sentences on the board and to identify the prepositions and the prepositional phrases.

Have each student choose a common preposition from the list and say a prepositional phrase using that preposition. Then read aloud about multiword prepositions, including the examples. Discuss how multiword prepositions are similar to and different from single-word prepositions. Challenge students

to suggest sentences for each multiword preposition.

PRACTICE

EXERCISE 1
Review nouns as objects of prepositions on page 8. Tell students that each sentence has at least two prepositions. Point out that some prepositions are multiword prepositions.

EXERCISE 2
Review that a prepositional phrase includes the preposition, the object of the preposition, and any words that describe the object. Suggest that students

review the prepositions in both lists on page 124. Point out that *to* can be a preposition or the beginning of an infinitive, as it is in the introductory phrase in item 12. Have students complete this activity with partners. Then discuss the answers. Challenge students to identify the objects of the prepositions.

EXERCISE 3
Remind students that a preposition shows the relationship between a noun or pronoun and another word in a sentence. Encourage students to identify the words that have a relationship before determining which

---

7.1 Single and Multiword Prepositions

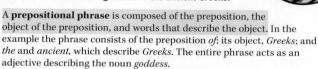

A **preposition** shows the relationship between a noun or pronoun and some other word in the sentence. In this sentence the preposition *of* shows the relationship between *goddess* and *Greeks*.

Gaia was the earth goddess *of* the ancient Greeks.

A **prepositional phrase** is composed of the preposition, the object of the preposition, and words that describe the object. In the example the phrase consists of the preposition *of*; its object, *Greeks*; and *the* and *ancient*, which describe *Greeks*. The entire phrase acts as an adjective describing the noun *goddess*.

Here are some common prepositions.

about	behind	from	since
above	beside	in	through
across	between	into	throughout
after	beyond	near	to
against	by	of	toward
among	down	off	under
around	during	on	up
at	except	over	with
before	for	past	without

Multiword prepositions are made up of more than one word but are treated as single words. In each of the following sentences, the prepositional phrase is in red italics and the preposition is underlined.

> *In addition to Gaia*, another early deity was her consort, Uranus.
> *According to Greek mythology*, the Titans were their children.

Here are some common multiword prepositions.

according to	in addition to	in spite of	out of
because of	in front of	instead of	outside of
by means of	in regard to	on account of	prior to

EXERCISE 1 Identify the preposition or prepositions in each sentence. Name the object of each preposition.

1. Because of the princess's beauty, many men fell in love with her at first sight.
2. A shepherd living near the king's palace sang to the princess.

Exercise 1
1. Because of, beauty; in, love; with, her; at, sight
2. near, palace; to, princess
3. to, singing; with, smiles
4. On account of, need; for, happiness; because of, cleverness

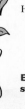

preposition to use. Complete the first sentence as a class. Then have students complete the activity independently.

APPLY

APPLY IT NOW

Discuss possible settings for students' humorous stories, such as a ball game, a concert, a mall, or a family vacation. Tell students that they should keep their settings in mind as they think of prepositional phrases. Students should demonstrate an understanding of prepositional phrases.

ASSESS

Note which students had difficulty identifying prepositions. Assign **Practice Book** page 83 for further practice.

WRITING CONNECTION

Use pages 388–389 of the Writing portion of the book.

Reteach

Write on the board a chart with the three columns shown below. Then write on the board a sentence with a prepositional phrase. Challenge students to identify the phrase and to write it in the first column. Invite a volunteer to write the preposition in the second column and the object of the preposition in the third column. Continue with other sentences and additions to the chart. You may wish to use the following sentence to get the chart started:

The goalie kicked the soccer ball across the field.

Prepositional Phrase	Preposition	Object of the Preposition
across the field	across	field

English-Language Learners

Students who are learning English may benefit from a kinesthetic and visual approach to identifying prepositions. Place a pencil in different places around the room. Work with students to generate sentences with prepositional phrases that identify the pencil's location.

The pencil is <u>behind</u> the book.

The pencil is <u>in front of</u> you.

The pencil is <u>across</u> the room.

The pencil is <u>on</u> the desk.

The pencil is <u>inside</u> the drawer.

The pencil is <u>under</u> the table.

Write each phrase on a note card. Place the note card at the location mentioned in the phrase. Use hand motions to indicate the location as well as the meaning of the preposition. Invite the student who created that sentence to repeat the gestures with you as the student reads aloud the preposition.

Exercise 2

1. before the gods, before; of Mount Olympus, of
2. of the Titan Cronos, of
3. by a son, by
4. Because of the warning, because of
5. through the aid, through; of his mother, of
6. against his father, against
7. to Zeus, to
8. with thunderbolts, with; for weapons, for
9. During a battle, During; from cliffs, from; onto the Titans, onto
10. on them, on; out of fear, out of
11. By means of this victory, By means of
12. to the lowest level, to; of the universe, of

Exercise 3

1. On account of
2. from
3. up
4. throughout
5. in
6. on

3. The princess responded to his singing with smiles.
4. On account of the princess's need for happiness and because of the shepherd's cleverness, the king allowed the marriage.

EXERCISE 2 Identify the prepositional phrase or phrases in each sentence. Name the preposition.

1. The Titans ruled the universe before the gods of Mount Olympus.
2. Zeus was a son of the Titan Cronos.
3. It was prophesied that Cronos would be overthrown by a son.
4. Because of the warning, Cronos swallowed his children.
5. Zeus escaped this fate through the aid of his mother.
6. Eventually, Zeus did revolt against his father.
7. The three one-eyed Cyclopes and the three hundred-armed Hecatoncheires gave aid to Zeus.
8. The Cyclopes provided Zeus with thunderbolts for weapons.
9. During a battle Hecatoncheires hurled rocks from cliffs onto the Titans.
10. The Titans thought the mountains were falling on them and fled out of fear.
11. By means of this victory, Zeus became ruler.
12. To punish the Titans, he sent them underground, to the lowest level of the universe.

EXERCISE 3 Choose the best preposition to complete each sentence. Use each preposition once.

from	on	throughout
in	up	on account of

1. _____ his part in the revolt, the Titan Atlas was punished.
2. His punishment was different _____ that of the other Titans.
3. He was given the task of holding _____ the sky.
4. The weight of the world is on his shoulders _____ all eternity.
5. Some say that earthquakes and tidal waves are signs of Atlas's faltering _____ his duty.
6. Because Atlas's image was _____ the cover of many medieval collections of maps, such books are now called atlases.

APPLY IT NOW

Brainstorm with a partner at least 10 prepositional phrases. Then write a humorous story, using as many of those phrases as possible.

Prepositions • 125

7.2 Troublesome Prepositions

OBJECTIVE

- **To use troublesome prepositions correctly**

 **Maintenance**

Assign **Practice Book** page 81, Section 7.2. After students finish,
1. Give immediate feedback.
2. Review concepts as needed.
3. Model the correct answer.

Pages 4–5 of the **Answer Key** contain tips for Daily Maintenance.

WARM-UP

Write the following prepositions on note cards, one per card: *beside, besides, in, into, between, among.* Have a volunteer select a card and draw on the board a picture depicting the preposition. Tell students to guess the preposition. Have volunteers take turns drawing prepositions as time permits.

📖 Read from a piece of writing that the class is currently reading. Emphasize the troublesome prepositions.

TEACH

Have students listen closely as you say the following sentences:

I wanted to sit <u>besides</u> my best friend at the assembly.

Instead, I sat <u>among</u> two teachers.

I was angry <u>at</u> the teachers for splitting us up because we don't talk that much.

Ask students if the prepositions have been used correctly and confirm that they have not. Invite volunteers to read aloud about troublesome prepositions.
   Review the correct usage of *like, as if,* and *as though.* Tell students that *similar to* or *such as* can be

substituted for *like* when checking whether it is the correct word choice.

   He looks like Brad Pitt.

   He looks similar to Brad Pitt.

Tell students to create sentences with *as if, as though, in,* and *into.*

PRACTICE

EXERCISE 1

Have students work with partners to select the correct prepositions. Encourage students to refer to the information in the lesson to guide

their choices. Combine two sets of partners and have the larger group compare and discuss their answers.

EXERCISE 2

Challenge students to complete this exercise independently. After students have finished, read aloud each sentence and ask students if it is correct. Then choose a student to identify the incorrect preposition, to supply the correct one, and to read the revised sentence. Ask the rest of the class if they agree. Discuss any discrepancies students may have.

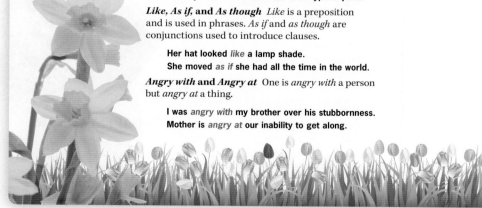

7.2 Troublesome Prepositions

Beside and ***Besides*** *Beside* means "next to." *Besides* means "in addition to."

   Plant the hyacinths *beside* the daffodils.
   Besides my mother, my brother likes to garden.

In and ***Into*** *In* means "within" or "inside." *Into* means "movement from the outside to the inside."

   The dog was *in* its cage.
   We didn't dare put the puppy *into* the same cage.

Between and ***Among*** *Between* is used to speak of two people, places, or things. *Among* is used to speak of more than two.

   What is the difference *between* daffodils and jonquils?
   Choosing *among* the many colors of crocuses was not easy.

Between *Between* implies a connection between at least two things and should never be used with the singular *each* or *every.*

   Leave a space *between* the boards. (not between each board)
   We rested *between* laps. (not between every lap)

Differ with, Differ on, and ***Differ from*** You *differ with* someone when you disagree. You usually *differ on* things. *Differ from* describes differences between people or things.

   I *differed with* mother over the prettiest tulip.
   We *differ on* the kinds of herbs to plant.
   This lily *differs from* that one in its type of petal.

Like, As if, and ***As though*** *Like* is a preposition and is used in phrases. *As if* and *as though* are conjunctions used to introduce clauses.

   Her hat looked *like* a lamp shade.
   She moved *as if* she had all the time in the world.

Angry with and ***Angry at*** One is *angry with* a person but *angry at* a thing.

   I was *angry with* my brother over his stubbornness.
   Mother is *angry at* our inability to get along.

APPLY

APPLY IT NOW

You might suggest that students write sentences with a connected theme, for example, planting flowers. Brainstorm some possible topics with the class. Invite volunteers to read their sentences aloud. Students should demonstrate an understanding of troublesome prepositions.

Grammar in Action. Students should identify the prepositions *by, by,* and *of* in the excerpt. Challenge students to identify the objects of the prepositions *(sea and mountains, itself,* and *people).*

ASSESS

Note which students had difficulty using troublesome prepositions correctly. Assign **Practice Book** page 84 for further practice.

WRITING CONNECTION

Use pages 390–391 of the Writing portion of the book.

TEACHING OPTIONS

Reteach

Start a two-column chart with the headings shown below. List in the first column a preposition from page 126. Invite students to suggest sentences that use the preposition correctly and write these in the second column. Have students compare sentences for preposition pairs (such as *between, among* or *beside, besides*). You may wish to get the chart started with these examples:

Preposition	Sentences
between	The argument was between Lee and Susan.
among	I am a science whiz among my classmates.

Cooperative Learning

Ask small groups to select a poster, an illustration, or a photograph that would be fun to describe. Tell students to work together to write sentences that tell about the image, using prepositional phrases to enhance their writing.

> **The dog is napping beside the cat.**
>
> **Besides the napping dog, a cat and a mouse are also in the picture.**
>
> **Do you see the mouse among the flowers?**

Have groups present the images they have chosen and take turns reading aloud their sentences. Encourage students to listen closely for the proper usage of each preposition.

Meeting Individual Needs

Extra Support Provide students with magazines, newspapers, and advertisements. Have small groups find examples of the troublesome prepositions from this lesson. Ask students to write examples on the board and determine whether the prepositions were used correctly.

EXERCISE 1 Choose the correct preposition to complete each sentence.

1. My mother, brother, and I order bulbs and seeds; (between <u>among</u>) the three of us, we receive many gardening catalogs.

2. We have a large pile of them (<u>beside</u> besides) the phone.

3. We each draw a diagram of our backyard, planning what new plants to grow (<u>beside</u> besides) those that are already there.

4. (Beside <u>Besides</u>) flowers, we also grow herbs and vegetables.

5. Our plans usually differ (on <u>from</u>) one another somewhat.

6. We talked about planting shrubs (between each walkway <u>between walkways</u>).

7. I differed (<u>with</u> from) my brother on what bulbs to plant.

8. A heated argument broke out (among <u>between</u>) us.

9. Mother looked (like <u>as if</u>) she was going to yell at us.

10. Since we differed (<u>on</u> from) the plan, she made the final decision.

11. Mother chided us for getting so easily (<u>angry with</u> angry at) each other.

12. At first I was (angry with <u>angry at</u>) her decision.

13. The garden will look (<u>like</u> as if) a rainbow.

14. Our yard will look (like <u>as though</u>) it was professionally landscaped.

Tulip bulbs

EXERCISE 2 Rewrite the sentences to correct errors in preposition usage. Not all the sentences have errors.

1. I read my mother's book about tulips like it were a novel.

2. I learned about the differences between "broken," "parrot," and "regular" tulips.

3. Beside information on types of tulips, the book explained how in the 1600s in the Netherlands, tulips were more valuable than gold.

4. My mother is now angry at me because I left the book in the garden, and it got damp with dew.

5. I, of course, differ with my mother on whether my admittedly careless action merits punishment.

Exercise 2

1. I read my mother's book about tulips as if it were a novel.

2. I learned about the differences among "broken," "parrot," and regular tulips.

3. Besides information on types of tulips, the book explained how in the 1600s in the Netherlands, tulips were more valuable than gold.

4. My mother is now angry with me because I left the book in the garden, and it got damp with dew.

5. Correct

APPLY IT NOW

Choose four sets of troublesome prepositions. Write eight sentences showing the correct use of the prepositions in each set.

Grammar in Action. Identify the prepositions in the last sentence of the excerpt on p. 374.

Prepositions • 127

OBJECTIVE
- **To distinguish between prepositions and adverbs**

DAILY Maintenance

Assign **Practice Book** page 81, Section 7.3. After students finish,
1. Give immediate feedback.
2. Review concepts as needed.
3. Model the correct answer.

Pages 4–5 of the **Answer Key** contain tips for Daily Maintenance.

WARM-UP

List on the board different areas of the school, such as the classroom, cafeteria, and gym. Tell students to choose two locations from the board and write directions for going from one place to the other. Invite volunteers to read aloud their directions. Ask students to identify words used as adverbs and words used as prepositions.

📖 Read from a piece of writing that the class is currently reading. Emphasize the words used as adverbs and prepositions.

TEACH

Write on the board this short poem:

> Worms crawl above the ground.
> Worms crawl below.
> Worms can help your garden grow.

In the first line, have students identify the preposition *(above)* and the prepositional phrase *(above the ground)*. Then ask students how the word *below* is used in the second line. Ask a volunteer to tell what its function is *(adverb)* and what it describes *(crawl)*.

Ask volunteers to read aloud about words used as adverbs and prepositions. Have students compare the example sentences with the sentences in the poem.

Ask which sentences are similar to line 1 *(the first sentence of each pair)* and which sentences are similar to line 2 *(the second sentence of each pair)*.

Have students suggest two sentences, using the same word as an adverb and as a preposition.

PRACTICE

EXERCISE 1

Complete the first two items as a class. Encourage several students to suggest possible words that complete each prepositional phrase. Then have students complete the remaining sentences independently. Start a simple chart on the board with one column for each sentence. Enter students' different answers in the appropriate columns to show the variety of correct answers.

EXERCISES 2 & 3

Remind students that a preposition is always part of a phrase that ends with a noun or pronoun. Guide students in completing the first two sentences in Exercise 2. Then have students complete the exercises independently. Tell students to exchange their completed papers with partners to check the answers.

7.3 Words Used as Adverbs and Prepositions

Some words can be either adverbs or prepositions.

> **As we sat on the mountaintop, an eagle flew** *below* **us.**
> **As we sat on the mountaintop, an eagle flew** *below***.**

In the first sentence, the adverb phrase *below us* contains the preposition *before* and the object *us*. The phrase describes the verb *flew*. In the second sentence, the word *below* functions as an adverb describing *flew*.

What part of speech is the word *beneath* in each of these sentences?

> **We dug** *beneath* **the porch in search of treasure.**
> **We really had no idea what lay** *beneath***.**

You are correct if you said that in the first sentence, the word *beneath* is a preposition, part of the phrase *beneath the porch*. In the second sentence, *beneath* is not part of a phrase. You are correct if you said that it is an adverb describing the verb *lay*.

To distinguish between a preposition and an adverb, remember that a preposition is always part of a phrase that ends with a noun or pronoun as its object.

EXERCISE 1 In the following sets of sentences, the word italicized in the first sentence is used as an adverb. Use the word as a preposition in the second sentence by adding an object.

1. Let's climb *up*.
   Let's climb up _____.
2. Let's rest *after*.
   Let's rest after _____.
3. We can look *around*.
   We can look around _____.
4. The cabin is *near*.
   The cabin is near _____.
5. I would rather stay *inside*.
   I would rather stay inside _____.

Exercise 1
Answers will vary.

EXERCISE 4

Encourage students to complete the exercise independently. Then assign the sentences to five volunteers and have them write on the board the completed sentences. Review each sentence with the class.

APPLY

APPLY IT NOW

Have students write *ADV* above the adverbs and *PREP* above the prepositions. Then have partners check each other's sentences. Students should demonstrate an understanding of words used as adverbs and prepositions.

ASSESS

Note which students had difficulty distinguishing between prepositions and adverbs. Assign **Practice Book** page 85 for further practice.

WRITING CONNECTION

Use pages 392–393 of the Writing portion of the book.

TEACHING OPTIONS

Reteach

Write the following words on note cards: *above, across, after, around, before, behind, below, beside, between, down, near, over, past, through, under,* and *up.* Place the note cards facedown in a pile. Invite a volunteer to pick a card, read the word aloud, and create a sentence using the word as a preposition. Have another volunteer suggest a sentence that uses the word as an adverb. Write both sentences on the board for students to compare. Call on volunteers until all the cards have been used.

Curriculum Connection

Challenge students to find words in materials from another subject area that can be used as prepositions or as adverbs. Tell students to begin a chart with two columns: *Adverbs* and *Prepositions.* Suggest that students write sentences on their charts as they locate these words in their reading. Have students compare their findings.

Meeting Individual Needs

Challenge Encourage students to have fun writing simple poems similar to the worm poem discusses at the beginning of the lesson. Explain that each poem should have a preposition and an adverb.

> **The rain fell outside the house.**
> **It also fell inside.**
> **From so much rain we could not**
>   **hide.**

Invite students to write and illustrate their poems on poster paper. Display the poems around the room. Encourage students to read one another's work and identify the prepositions and adverbs.

Exercise 2
1. preposition
2. adverb
3. adverb
4. preposition
5. preposition
6. preposition
7. adverb
8. preposition

EXERCISE 2 Tell whether each italicized word is an adverb or a preposition.

1. Have you ever wanted to climb *up* a mountain?
2. You get to the top, look *down,* and feel that you have achieved something special.
3. Some beginners start climbing *indoors.*
4. There are special places for climbing *in* some gyms.
5. Perhaps there is such a gym *near* your home.
6. Many kids start climbing *with* special harnesses.
7. It can be a bit scary at first when you look *below.*
8. Many gyms have lower walls *with* bigger grips for kids.

Exercise 3
1. down, adverb
2. on, preposition
3. outside, preposition
4. in, adverb
5. outside, adverb
6. in, preposition
7. away, adverb

EXERCISE 3 Identify the adverb or preposition in each sentence.

1. The rain splashed down while we were running toward shelter.
2. Inez piled the reports on my desk.
3. Sheila left the note outside your door.
4. Suddenly, the door opened, and in rushed Michelle.
5. The gorilla and his band stood outside.
6. Is that your snake slithering in the sand under the porch?
7. Her father got a new job so Jane is moving away.

Exercise 4
1. down, adverb
2. from, preposition
3. toward, preposition
4. within, preposition
5. before, adverb

EXERCISE 4 Choose the best word to complete each sentence. Use each word once. Tell whether each word is used as an adverb or a preposition.

before   down   from   toward   within

1. Have you ever sat _____ at a local beach or park and unexpectedly heard the sound of music?
2. It might be coming _____ a bandstand, a café, or a street corner.
3. The sound may be carried _____ you on a breeze.
4. As the sound continues, it may appeal to something _____ you.
5. It may remind you of something that happened _____ .

APPLY IT NOW

Imagine that you are a world-class mountain climber. Write 10 sentences about your adventures and accomplishments. Use some of the following words as prepositions or adverbs in your description: *above, after, before, below, down, in, off, through, under, up.* Identify the use of each of these words.

Prepositions • 129

OBJECTIVE

- To identify prepositional phrases used as adjectives

 **Maintenance**

Assign **Practice Book** page 81, Section 7.4. After students finish,
1. Give immediate feedback.
2. Review concepts as needed.
3. Model the correct answer.

Pages 4–5 of the **Answer Key** contain tips for Daily Maintenance.

WARM-UP

Write on the board the following sentences:

We bought tickets for the game.

Dr. Watson is the doctor for my entire family.

The store on the corner is always open.

Ask volunteers to underline the prepositional phrases *(for the game, for my entire family, on the corner)*. Then discuss what questions are answered by the prepositional phrases. *(What tickets were bought? For whom is he the doctor? Which store is open?)*

📖 Read from a piece of writing that the class is currently reading. Emphasize the prepositional phrases used as adjectives.

TEACH

Have volunteers read aloud about adjective phrases, pausing after each example sentence. Review that adjectives describe nouns. Have students identify each adjective phrase and the word it describes. Point out that the prepositional phrases in the Warm-Up sentences are all examples of adjective phrases. Challenge students to suggest sentences that include adjective phrases.

PRACTICE

EXERCISE 1

Ask students to define *adjective phrase*. Then have partners complete this exercise. Suggest that students identify each prepositional phrase first, then determine if it is an adjective phrase and what word it describes.

EXERCISE 2

Remind students that adjective phrases modify pronouns as well as nouns. Then have students complete the exercise independently. Invite volunteers to share their answers.

EXERCISE 3

Have students complete this exercise in small groups. Ask volunteers to read aloud their phrases. List on the board some of the phrases to demonstrate the different prepositions that can be used. Discuss answers for items 9 through 16. Point out that a variety of correct phrases can be produced for each noun.

EXERCISE 4

Review troublesome prepositions on page 126. Have students complete this exercise independently. Invite volunteers to write their sentences on the board. Challenge students

---

7.4 Prepositional Phrases as Adjectives

A prepositional phrase that describes a noun or pronoun is an **adjective phrase**.

Flowers are the large, showy blossoms *on a plant*.
The function *of the flowers* **is to produce seeds.**

Both of the italicized prepositional phrases are adjective phrases. In the first sentence, the prepositional phrase *on a plant* tells something about *blossoms*, a noun. In the second sentence, the prepositional phrase *of the flowers* describes the noun *function*.

In the following sentences, what are the adjective phrases, and what do they describe?

The meaning of flowers can vary.
The lotus, a water lily, is the national flower of India.

You are correct if you said that *of flowers* describes the noun *meaning*. In the next sentence, *of India* describes *flower*.

EXERCISE 1 Identify the adjective phrase or phrases in each sentence.

1. The international customs for flowers vary.
2. Suppose friends in Japan invite you home.
3. A small gift from the guest is expected.
4. It is best not to take a gift of cut flowers, however.
5. Cut flowers are usually considered gifts for sick people or for courting couples.
6. A popular custom in France takes place on May 1.
7. People exchange bunches of lilies of the valley.
8. The flowers are a sign of friendship.
9. Carnations are not a good gift for Europeans because many think the flowers are a sign of bad luck.
10. Purple has associations with mourning, so don't give flowers of that color unless it is appropriate.
11. People in the United States often give gifts of flowers or candy on special occasions.

130 • Section 7.4

---

to identify the adjective phrases in the sentences.

APPLY

APPLY IT NOW

Suggest that students review their work to see where they might insert additional adjective phrases. Have students revise their writing, inserting the additional adjective phrases. Then ask students to underline the adjective phrases and to circle the nouns that the phrases describe. Students should demonstrate an understanding of prepositional phrases used as adjectives.

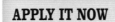 **TechTip** Suggest students use an online encyclopedia to conduct their research.

ASSESS

Note which students had difficulty identifying prepositional phrases used as adjectives. Assign **Practice Book** page 86 for further practice.

WRITING CONNECTION

Use pages 394–395 of the Writing portion of the book.

Use pages 394–395 of the Writing portion of the book.

Exercise 2
1. appearance
2. taste
3. plants
4. One
5. blossom
6. cavity; quarts
7. feature
8. that
9. scent
10. attraction
11. pollination

Exercise 3
Answers may vary.
Possible answers:
1. the gate of a garden
2. a garden of roses
3. the bark of a tree
4. food for a plant
5. a bed of flowers
6. a box in which to grow flowers
7. a bottle of water
8. a catalog for gardening
9. a tree in the forest
10. a flower from my garden
11. the house around the corner
12. my garden in the backyard
13. a path through the woods
14. a row of daisies
15. a bed of petunias
16. a bag of potting soil

EXERCISE 2 Identify the adjective phrase or phrases in each sentence. Name the noun or pronoun the adjective phrase describes.

1. The appearance of some flowers is truly weird.
2. Yet some gardeners have a taste for the exotic.
3. The plants in their gardens might include unusual flowers.
4. One from Borneo is called *Rafflesia arnoldii*.
5. The blossom on this Malaysian parasitic plant can be three feet across.
6. A cavity at its center holds several quarts of water.
7. That's not the most unusual feature of the flower, however.
8. The flower's foul odor resembles that of rotting flesh.
9. Why would a flower give off a scent like that?
10. The repugnant smell is actually an attraction for flies.
11. The plant requires pollination by flies.

Rafflesia arnoldii

EXERCISE 3 Rewrite each group of words as an adjective phrase.

1. garden gate
2. rose garden
3. tree bark
4. plant food

5. flower bed
6. flower box
7. water bottle
8. gardening catalog

Write an adjective phrase to describe each noun.

9. tree
10. flower
11. house
12. garden

13. path
14. row
15. bed
16. bag

EXERCISE 4 Write an adjective phrase using each preposition. Use the adjective phrase in a sentence. Answers will vary.

1. beside
2. between
3. among
4. into

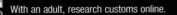 **Tech Tip** With an adult, research customs online.

APPLY IT NOW

Write a brief paragraph about a custom related to flowers for holidays or gift giving. Use at least five adjective phrases in your writing.

Prepositions • 131

OBJECTIVE

• **To identify prepositional phrases used as adverbs**

 **DAILY Maintenance**

Assign **Practice Book** page 82, Section 7.5. After students finish,
1. Give immediate feedback.
2. Review concepts as needed.
3. Model the correct answer.

Pages 4–5 of the **Answer Key** contain tips for Daily Maintenance.

WARM-UP

Write on the board the following paragraph:

My best friend Seth was born in Michigan. He moved to my town when he was seven. We hang out every weekend and play for hours. Every summer we go camping in the woods. We were there for three days. Seth and I are like brothers.

Invite volunteers to underline the parts of sentences that answer *how, when, where, why, to what extent,* and *under what condition.*

📖 Read from a piece of writing that the class is currently reading. Emphasize the prepositional phrases used as adverbs.

TEACH

Remind students that an adverb describes a verb, an adjective, or another adverb. Ask students which questions an adverb helps answer, and write on the board the question words *how, when, where, why, to what extent,* and *under what condition.* Then write a simple sentence for students to practice inserting adverbs.

I went to school.

How? I went to school <u>in a rush</u>.

When? I went to school <u>in the morning</u>.

Challenge students to provide additional sentences with prepositional phrases answering the other adverb questions. Then invite volunteers to read aloud about adverb phrases.

PRACTICE

EXERCISE 1

Remind students that adverbs can modify verbs, adjectives, and other adverbs. Then point out that the adverb phrase in each sentence has already been identified. Complete the first sentence as a class. Then have partners complete the exercise. Invite volunteers to share their answers.

EXERCISE 2

Have partners discuss each sentence and identify the adverb phrase and the word it describes. Then ask volunteers to explain whether each adverb phrase answers the question *how, when, where, why, to what extent,* or *under what condition.*

EXERCISE 3

Suggest that students write phrases that tell about Charlotte Forten, the woman featured in Exercises 1 and 2, or that they apply the phrases to their own experiences. You may wish to have students write these sentences in their notebooks.

7.5 Prepositional Phrases as Adverbs

Adverb phrases are prepositional phrases that are also used as adverbs—to describe verbs, adjectives, or other adverbs.

Like single-word adverbs, adverb phrases answer the questions *how, when, where, why, to what extent,* and *under what condition.*

> **Adverb:** The abolitionists worked *dedicatedly* to free slaves.
> **Adverb phrase:** The abolitionists worked *with dedication* to free slaves.

What are the adverb phrases in the sentences below? What does each describe?

> **Antislavery action began in colonial times.**
> **Many people were angry at slavery's existence.**
> **The movement gained momentum early in the 19th century.**

In the first sentence, the adverb phrase *in colonial times* describes the verb *began.* In the second sentence, the adverb phrase *at slavery's existence* describes the adjective *angry.* In the third sentence, the phrase *in the 19th century* modifies the adverb *early.*

EXERCISE 1 Tell what each italicized adverb phrase describes.

1. Charlotte Forten <u>went</u> *to the South* during the Civil War.
2. As an African American, she <u>was committed</u> *to the abolitionist cause.*
3. She was very <u>sensitive</u> *to the needs* of others.
4. She <u>brought</u> her ideals *to her work.*
5. Forten <u>came</u> *from an influential and affluent family.*
6. <u>Early</u> *in her life* she lived in Philadelphia.
7. She <u>went</u> *to Massachusetts* and attended a school for teachers.
8. She <u>began</u> her teaching career *in the Salem schools.*
9. There she taught grammar school until the onset of tuberculosis forced her to <u>return</u> *to Philadelphia.*
10. Forten <u>taught</u> successfully *during many phases* of her life.

Exercise 2

1. In 1862, went; to South Carolina, went
2. on her deepest beliefs, was acting
3. by means of her teaching skills, helped
4. In spite of her commitment, faced
5. in a special local dialect, spoke

A U.S. Army officer explains the duties of freedom to former slaves after the Emancipation Proclamation in 1863.

132 • Section 7.5

EXERCISE 4

Review adjective phrases on page 130. Have students complete this exercise independently. Discuss students' answers. Then challenge students to write the questions that the phrases answer. *(What was the raft made of?)*

APPLY

APPLY IT NOW

Instruct students to copy a page or passage from their research, underline the adverb phrases, and circle the words that the phrases describe. Students should demonstrate an understanding of prepositional phrases used as adverbs.

ASSESS

Note which students had difficulty identifying prepositional phrases used as adverbs. Assign **Practice Book** page 87 for further practice.

WRITING CONNECTION

Use pages 396–397 of the Writing portion of the book.

Reteach

Write on strips of paper a variety of prepositional phrases. Place the strips in a box. Ask a student to choose a strip and to read aloud the prepositional phrase. Then challenge students to provide sentences that use the phrase as an adverb phrase.

Meeting Individual Needs

Challenge Write prepositions on the board. Invite students to use the prepositions in adverb phrases related to travel, such as *on the road, through the town,* and *to the landmark.* Then have students write paragraphs about traveling, incorporating the adverb phrases on the board. Discuss the paragraphs, focusing on the effective use of adverb phrases.

Meeting Individual Needs

Extra Support Write simple noun-verb sentences on the board, such as these: *We play. I sang. Our class voted. My family traveled. The fish swam.* Point out that these sentences do not provide much information or detail about the action. Ask students to think of adverb phrases that expand these simple sentences. Encourage students to write their sentences on the board. Provide these examples:

We play <u>on the school field</u>.

I sang <u>in the school musical</u>.

Our class voted <u>for a class president</u>.

My family traveled <u>to Florida</u>.

The fish swam <u>in the ocean</u>.

---

6. with the language, unfamiliar
7. to her students, strange
8. with the islanders, did bond
9. Under physical and emotional stress, grew
10. after two years, left
11. in disappointment, departed
12. for equality, spoke; in many forums, spoke; for many years, spoke
13. for her diaries, famous
14. in her life; Later

Exercise 3

Possible answers:
1. She acted with courage during difficult times.
2. She studied with diligence to become a teacher.
3. She worked with determination to help others.
4. She wrote with clarity in her diary.
5. She wrote with honesty about her experiences.
6. She wrote with regularity in her diary.

Exercise 4

Prepositional phrases are underlined.
1. adverb, adverb, adverb, adverb
2. adjective, adjective
3. adjective, adjective, adverb
4. adverb

EXERCISE 2 Identify the adverb phrase or phrases in each sentence. Name the word or words the adjective phrase describes.

1. In 1862 Charlotte Forten went to South Carolina.
2. She was acting on her deepest beliefs.
3. She helped other African Americans by means of her teaching skills.
4. In spite of her commitment, she faced many difficulties.
5. Her pupils spoke in a special local dialect.
6. Forten was unfamiliar with the language.
7. Normal school routines were strange to her students.
8. Forten did not bond closely with the islanders.
9. Under physical and emotional stress, she grew ill.
10. She left the island of Saint Helena after two years.
11. She departed in disappointment.
12. Forten spoke for equality in many forums for many years.
13. Forten is now famous for her diaries.
14. Later in her life she married Presbyterian minister Francis J. Grimké.

Charlotte Forten Grimké

EXERCISE 3 Rewrite each italicized adverb as an adverb phrase. Use the phrase in a sentence.

1. acted *courageously*
2. studied *diligently*
3. worked *determinedly*
4. wrote *clearly*
5. wrote *honestly*
6. wrote *regularly*

EXERCISE 4 Identify the prepositional phrase or phrases in each sentence. Tell whether the prepositional phrase is being used as an adjective or an adverb.

1. Thor Heyerdahl led the *Kon-Tiki* expedition <u>from Peru</u> <u>to Polynesia</u> <u>on a raft</u> made <u>of balsa logs</u>.
2. The purpose <u>of the expedition</u> was to prove that the Inca Peruvians were the settlers <u>of Polynesia</u>.
3. Worshipping the Sun god Kon was a practice <u>of the early South American Indians</u>, <u>according to legend</u>.
4. The *Kon-Tiki* was damaged <u>on a reef</u>, but the men survived and completed their voyage.

APPLY IT NOW

Use an encyclopedia, a textbook, or the Internet to get more information on the abolitionists or on Charlotte Forten. Write seven sentences about what interests you. Use at least five adverb phrases and underline them.

Prepositions • 133

7.6 Prepositional Phrases as Nouns

OBJECTIVE
- **To identify prepositional phrases used as nouns**

 **Maintenance**

Assign **Practice Book** page 82, Section 7.6. After students finish,
1. Give immediate feedback.
2. Review concepts as needed.
3. Model the correct answer.

Pages 4–5 of the **Answer Key** contain tips for Daily Maintenance.

WARM-UP

Have students form two lines and stand facing each other. Ask a student in the first line to say a prepositional phrase *(by plane)*. Then have a student from the second line complete the phrase, making it the subject of a sentence. *(By plane is the best way to travel.)* Continue as time permits.

📖 Read from a piece of writing that the class is currently reading. Emphasize the prepositional phrases used as nouns.

TEACH

Write on the board several Warm-Up sentences. Challenge students to tell how the phrases are used in the sentences. *(The phrases function as subjects.)* Ask a student to transpose the subject and subject complement from a Warm-Up sentence. *(The best way to travel is by plane.)* Challenge students to identify the function of the prepositional phrase *(subject complement).*

Ask volunteers to read aloud about prepositional phrases used as nouns. Have students compare the example sentences with the Warm-Up sentences. Encourage students to provide other examples of prepositional phrases used as nouns.

PRACTICE

EXERCISE 1
Review prepositional phrases used as subjects and as subject complements. Then have partners complete this exercise. Ask partners to share their answers with the class. Discuss any discrepancies students may have.

EXERCISE 2
Review how prepositional phrases are used as adjectives, adverbs, and nouns. Discuss signals that can help students identify how each phrase is used. Point out that an adjective phrase describes a noun or pronoun, so it is usually preceded by a noun or pronoun. Tell students that an adverb phrase usually describes a verb, so it is preceded by a verb. Explain that a noun phrase can be the subject or subject complement in a sentence. Have partners complete this activity.

EXERCISE 3
Have students complete this exercise independently. Invite volunteers to read aloud their sentences. After students have read their sentences, challenge students to use each prepositional phrase in a different way.

7.6 Prepositional Phrases as Nouns

A prepositional phrase can be used as a noun.

> **Before dinner is my usual time to do homework.**

Before dinner is a prepositional phrase used as the subject of the verb *is*.

A prepositional phrase may appear in any position where a noun can be used in a sentence.

> **My time for playing the guitar is *after dinner*.**

In the above sentence, the prepositional phrase acts as a subject complement.

Which of these sentences uses a prepositional phrase as a noun?

> **Inside the display case lay a beautiful antique quilt.**
> **On the lawn was the best place to take the class photos.**

You are correct if you chose the second sentence. The prepositional phrase *on the lawn* is the subject of the verb *was*.

EXERCISE 1 Identify the prepositional phrase used as a noun in each sentence. Tell how the prepositional phrase functions in the sentence.

1. In front of the camera sometimes seems an uncomfortable place.
2. Behind the camera can also be a difficult place to be.
3. During bad weather is usually not a good time to take pictures.
4. Because of the light, a good time to take landscapes is in the early morning or the early evening.
5. A bad place to pose a subject is in front of a cluttered background.
6. In front of a strong sun is usually a bad place to take a picture.

EXERCISE 2 Identify the prepositional phrases in these sentences. Then tell whether each prepositional phrase is an adjective phrase, an adverb phrase, or a noun phrase.

1. A surprising time to receive a gift that changes one's life is at age 48.
2. However, that is exactly what happened to Julia Cameron.
3. Cameron's life changed with the gift of a camera.
4. Cameras of the 1860s were quite different from those of today.

Exercise 1
1. subject of *seems*
2. subject of *can be*
3. subject of *is*
4. subject complement of *time*
5. subject complement of *place*
6. subject of *is*

Exercise 2
1. at age 48, noun
2. to Julia Cameron, adverb
3. with the gift, adverb; of a camera, adjective
4. of the 1860s, adjective; from those, adverb; of today, adjective

APPLY

APPLY IT NOW

Encourage students to include at least five prepositional phrases used as nouns in their writing. Tell students to underline the phrases and to share them with the class. Students should demonstrate an understanding of prepositional phrases used as nouns.

TechTip Have students identify their favorite picture and description on the class blog. Discuss what students liked about their favorite picture.

ASSESS

Note which students had difficulty identifying prepositional phrases used as nouns. Assign **Practice Book** pages 88–89 for further practice.

WRITING CONNECTION

Use pages 398–399 of the Writing portion of the book.

TEACHING OPTIONS

Reteach

Write these sentence starters on the board:

_____ is the time for skiing.

_____ is the best place for the new shopping mall.

Ask students to complete each sentence with a prepositional phrase used as a noun. Point out that in each sentence the prepositional phrase is the subject.

Write the following sentence starters for students to complete:

My homework time is _____.

Our science lab is _____.

Explain that in these sentences the prepositional phrases are subject complements.

Cooperative Learning

Have partners name an event or a place. Encourage each student to expand upon that idea by writing a sentence that includes a prepositional phrase used as a noun.

Noun: movie

Sentence: During the movie is not a good time to talk.

Encourage partners to listen closely to each other's sentences to determine whether the sentence structure is correct and whether the prepositional phrase has been used as a noun.

Observe and Apply

Display a series of photographs or illustrations from specific time periods, events, or places. Encourage students to write sentences that describes each image. Tell students to use prepositional phrases as nouns in their sentences.

5. of their use, adjective; with photography, adverb
6. On Cameron's estate's lawn, noun
7. of her family and friends, adjective
8. for these photographs, adverb
9. of literature, adjective; as the characters, adverb; in it, adjective
10. of her efforts, adjective
11. of famous people, adjective
12. by her, adjective; of the naturalist Charles Darwin and the philosopher Thomas Carlyle, adjective
13. of the poet Alfred, Lord Tennyson, adjective; among her greatest work, adverb
14. for her work, adjective
15. of the sitter, adjective
16. for the out-of-focus technique, adverb; of certain pictures, adjective
17. because of this, adverb; for long periods, adverb; of time, adjective
18. According to her, adverb; behind the camera, noun

Exercise 3
Answers will vary.

5. Cameron gained mastery of their use, however, and became fascinated with photography.
6. On Cameron's estate's lawn was a wonderful place to take photos.
7. She took pictures of her family and friends.
8. Often her friends and relatives dressed up for these photographs.
9. Sometimes they would choose a work of literature and dress as the characters in it.
10. The results of her efforts are dreamy and romantic photographs that spark the imagination.
11. She also began to take photographs of famous people.
12. There are photos by her of the naturalist Charles Darwin and the philosopher Thomas Carlyle.
13. Her portrait of the poet Alfred, Lord Tennyson is her most famous and is counted among her greatest work.
14. She received praise and awards for her work.
15. Some people have remarked that Cameron's portraits capture the vitality of the sitter.
16. Some people, however, criticize her work for the out-of-focus technique of certain pictures.
17. She used long exposures, and because of this, her sitters had to remain still for long periods of time.
18. According to her, however, behind the camera was the most difficult place to be.

Alfred, Lord Tennyson portrait by Julia Cameron

EXERCISE 3 Write sentences using the following prepositional phrases as indicated in parentheses.

1. in the box (adjective phrase)
2. over the hill (adverb phrase)
3. inside the house (noun phrase)
4. after school (adverb phrase)
5. next to the fire (adjective phrase)
6. on the road (noun phrase)

APPLY IT NOW

Write seven sentences about a photo that is important to you. It may be one you took, one given to you, one with you in it, or one of an important event. Identify the prepositional phrases in your writing and tell how they function in the sentence.

Post your writing and photo on the class blog.

Preposition Review

ASSESS

Use the Preposition Review as homework, as a practice test, or as an informal assessment. Following are some examples for use.

Homework

You may wish to assign one group the odd items and another group the even items. When you next meet, review the correct answers as a group. Be sure to model how to arrive at the correct answer.

Practice Test

Use the Preposition Review as a diagnostic tool. Assign the entire review or only specific sections. After students have finished, identify which concepts require more attention. Reteach concepts as necessary.

Preposition Review

7.1
Prepositional phrases are underlined.
1. According to, on
2. From, to
3. Through, about
4. In spite of, in
5. in
6. On account of, by
7. in, for
8. by
9. throughout, in

7.2
10. from
11. Besides
12. from
13. with
14. beside
15. Among
16. on
17. Between
18. Besides
19. into
20. with

7.1 Identify the prepositional phrase or phrases in each sentence. Name the preposition.

1. According to experts, the giant squid is the largest invertebrate on earth.

2. From end to end, the giant squid can measure 75 feet long.

3. Through research, scientists have tried to learn more about the mysterious creature.

4. In spite of scientists' efforts, no one has seen a giant squid alive in its natural habitat.

5. It is believed that giant squid live in much deeper waters.

6. On account of its unusual appearance, humans have long been fascinated by the creature.

7. Recently, scientists have filmed a giant squid alive in its habitat for the first time.

8. They were rarely seen but had been occasionally caught by fishers.

9. Giant squid are found throughout the world but are rare in polar and tropical regions.

7.2 Choose the correct preposition to complete each sentence.

10. How does crocheting differ (with from) knitting?

11. (Beside Besides) a different number of needles, the two crafts require different skills.

12. Take the ball of yarn (from off) the pile and bring it to your grandmother.

13. I was angry (with at) my mother for making me wear the ugly, handmade sweater.

14. While learning how to knit, I sat (beside besides) my grandmother.

15. (Between Among) the three of us, there was enough knitting skill to produce one scarf.

16. My mother and grandmother differ (with on) which craft they like better.

17. (Between Among) you and me, I am a better knitter than my mother.

18. (Besides Beside) scarves, it is better to buy professionally made knit items.

19. Put the leftover yarn (in into) the sewing box.

20. I differ (on with) my mother about the best kinds of items to knit.

7.3 Tell whether each underlined word is an adverb or a preposition.

21. The horses galloped around the pasture.

22. Excited about riding the horses, we saddled up.

23. Because it was our first time horseback riding, we stayed near the barn.

24. We rode along a path.

25. We rode around for a half hour or so.

26. Let's brush down the horses.

7.3
21. preposition
22. adverb
23. preposition
24. preposition
25. adverb
26. adverb
27. preposition
28. adverb
29. adverb

7.4
30. from the United States, People
31. in Europe, country
32. for art lovers, museums
33. from Belgium, Chocolate
34. for a vacation, spot
35. along the Mediterranean Sea, beaches
36. of Switzerland, mountains
37. on European trains, Travel

Informal Assessment

Use the review as preparation for the formal assessment. Count the review as a portion of the grade. Have students work to find the correct answers and use their corrected review as a study guide for the formal assessment.

After students have reviewed the section, assign the Preposition Challenge on page 138.

Putting It All Together

Review prepositions by having students complete the following exercises:

- Make a list of three single prepositions and three multiword prepositions. Use each preposition in a sentence.

- Review the list of troublesome prepositions on page 126. Find examples in magazines of each preposition used correctly.

- Write definitions of an adverb and a preposition. Then choose two words that can be used as both a preposition and an adverb. Write sentences using the words as both prepositions and adverbs.

- Create a list of 10 nouns. Exchange lists with a partner and for each noun write a sentence that contains a prepositional phrase used as an adjective.

- Find examples of prepositional phrases used as nouns in online articles. Underline the prepositional phrase and label it as *SUB* if it is a subject or *COMP* if it is a subject complement.

7.5

38. for her cooking, is known
39. to the grocery store, went
40. with attention, shopped
41. to the produce section, went
42. with confidence, cooked
43. with fanfare, was served
44. with gusto, ate
45. by all the guests, was praised
46. at the outcome, happy
47. to her next party, invited

7.6

48. After school, noun phrase
49. in her notebook, adverb phrase
50. with a dictionary, adverb phrase
51. for two hours, adverb phrase
52. in his backpack, adverb phrase
53. for English homework, adjective phrase
54. to the last question, adjective phrase
55. on the teacher's desk, adverb phrase

---

27. They rode <u>beneath</u> the hot sun.
28. After the long ride, the horses rested <u>inside</u>.
29. We went <u>in</u> and had a cool drink.

7.4 Identify the adjective phrase in each sentence. Name the noun the adjective phrase describes.

30. People from the United States often visit European countries.
31. France is a country in Europe.
32. Paris has many museums for art lovers.
33. Chocolate from Belgium is delicious.
34. Rome is an ideal spot for a vacation.
35. The beaches along the Mediterranean Sea attract many tourists.
36. Hikers enjoy the mountains of Switzerland.
37. Travel on European trains is inexpensive and convenient.

7.5 Identify the adverb phrase in each sentence. Name the word or words each phrase describes.

38. Marcy is known for her cooking.
39. She went to the grocery store.
40. She shopped with attention to freshness and quality.
41. Marcy went to the produce section.
42. She cooked with confidence.
43. The meal was served with fanfare.

---

44. The guests ate the food with gusto.
45. The food was praised by all the guests.
46. Marcy was happy at the outcome.
47. Marcy invited us to her next party.

7.6 Identify the prepositional phrase in each sentence. Tell whether each phrase is an adjective phrase, an adverb phrase, or a noun phrase.

48. After school is the best time to do homework.
49. Kara wrote the answers in her notebook.
50. She always reads with a dictionary nearby.
51. The students studied for two hours.
52. To stay organized, Louis puts his books and pencils in his backpack.
53. The assignment for English homework is page 230.
54. Do you know the answer to the last question?
55. Put your homework on the teacher's desk.

Tech Tip Go to www.voyagesinenglish.com for more activities.

Tech Tip Encourage students to further review prepositions, using the additional practice and games at www.voyagesinenglish.com.

Preposition Challenge

EXERCISE 1
Encourage students to read the paragraph twice before answering the questions. If students have difficulty with any of the questions, remind them that they should refer to the section that teaches the skill. This activity can be completed by individuals, small groups, or the class working as a whole.

EXERCISE 2
Have volunteers read their passages aloud for Exercise 2. Instruct the rest of the class to raise their hands when they hear a prepositional phrase as a subject, to raise a pencil when they hear a prepositional phrase as an adjective, and to clap once when they hear a prepositional phrase as an adverb.

After you have reviewed prepositions, administer the Section 7 Assessment on pages 19–20 in the **Assessment Book,** or create a customized test with the optional **Test Generator CD.**

WRITING CONNECTION
Students can complete a formal expository essay using the Writer's Workshop on pages 400–411.

Preposition Challenge

EXERCISE 1 Read the selection and then answer the questions.

1. Less than a minute remained in the final Northern League basketball game of the season. 2. The contest had been an exciting, hard-fought battle between our Mayfair team and the Lincoln players. 3. At that game was definitely the place to be that January night. 4. Everything depended on what we did in the next few seconds, because Lincoln held a one-point lead. 5. In spite of close guarding, one of our players made a deft hook shot into the basket. 6. Spectators stood up and cheered loudly as those two precious points put us in the lead by one point. 7. Lincoln, now in possession of the ball, certainly was desperate to score. 8. The ball sailed harmlessly through the air and over the basket, however. 9. It fell into eager hands from our team as a loud blast from a horn announced not only the end of the game but also a victory for Mayfair. 10. Our team had come through.

1. Name the prepositions in sentence 1.
2. What is the prepositional phrase in sentence 2? Is it used as an adverb, an adjective, or a noun?
3. How is the prepositional phrase *at that game* used in sentence 3?
4. How is the prepositional phrase *into the basket* used in sentence 5?
5. Name the multiword preposition in sentence 5.
6. In sentence 6 is the word *up* used as an adverb or a preposition? How do you know?
7. Find two adverb phrases in sentence 8. What does each describe?
8. How many adjective phrases can you find in sentence 9? Name them and the words they describe.

EXERCISE 2 Prepositional phrases add important details to sentences in a narrative or an expository essay. Follow these instructions.

Think of an important or eventful story about your family that was told to you by a relative. In one to three paragraphs, record the story and its importance to you and your family. Use prepositional phrases as nouns, adjectives, and adverbs. Label each.

Exercise 1
1. in, of
2. between our Mayfair team and the Lincoln players; adjective
3. noun
4. adverb
5. In spite of
6. adverb; It is not followed by an object.
7. through the air, sailed; over the basket, sailed
8. five: into eager hands, fell; from our team, hands; from a horn, blast; of the game, end; for Mayfair, victory

Exercise 2
Answers will vary.

Sentences

SUPPORT MATERIALS

Practice Book
Daily Maintenance, pages 90–92
Grammar, pages 93–106

Assessment Book
Section 8 Assessment,
  pages 21–24

Test Generator CD

**Writing Chapter 6,
  Persuasive Writing**

Customizable Lesson Plans
www.voyagesinenglish.com

CONNECT WITH LITERATURE

📖 Consider using the following titles throughout the section to illustrate the grammar concept:

All Creatures Great and Small by
  James Herriot
Flowers for Algernon by Daniel
  Keyes
Hoot by Carl Hiaasen

GRAMMAR FOR GROWN-UPS

Understanding Sentences

A sentence is a group of words that contains a subject and a predicate and expresses a complete thought. A **declarative sentence** makes a statement. An **interrogative sentence** asks a question. An **imperative sentence** gives a command. An **exclamatory sentence** expresses strong emotion.

A sentence consists of one or more clauses. A **clause** is a group of words that contains a subject and a predicate. An **independent clause** expresses a complete thought.

A **dependent clause** does not express a complete thought. A dependent clause may function as a noun, an adjective, or an adverb.

A **noun clause** is a dependent clause that functions as a subject, a subject complement, an object of a preposition, or an appositive.

> *Whoever is interested* **can go to the store.**

> *I can see* **that you are a Red Sox fan.**

An **adjective clause** describes a noun or pronoun.

> *France is the place* **where my grandfather was born.**

An **adverb clause** describes a verb, an adjective, or an adverb.

> *After the game was complete,* **my mother surprised us with dessert.**

Sentences can be **simple,** having one independent clause *(The baby cries.);* **compound,** having two or more independent clauses *(Jeri plays drums, and Marco plays guitar.);* or **complex,** having an independent clause and at least one dependent clause. *(Because it was late, we had to go home.)*

> **"Words are the coins making up the currency of sentences, and there are always too many small coins."**
>
> —Jules Renard

COMMON ERRORS

Overusing Commas

The overuse of commas is one of the most common errors made by developing writers. One general rule is the following: don't split two parts of a single predicate.

ERROR: The weather was hot, and extremely humid.
CORRECT: The weather was hot and extremely humid.

ERROR: Jamaal is smart, and hard working.
CORRECT: Jamaal is smart and hard working.

When students check their writing, have them read for comma usage. Remind students to remove commas if they were used to separate two parts of a single predicate.

SENTENCE DIAGRAMMING

You may wish to teach sentences in the context of diagramming. Review these examples. Then refer to the Diagramming section or look for Diagram It! features in the Sentences section.

The turtle walked and the hare sprinted.

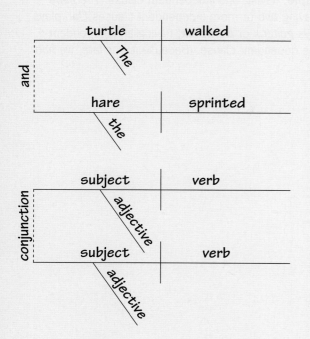

ASK AN EXPERT

Real Situations, Real Solutions

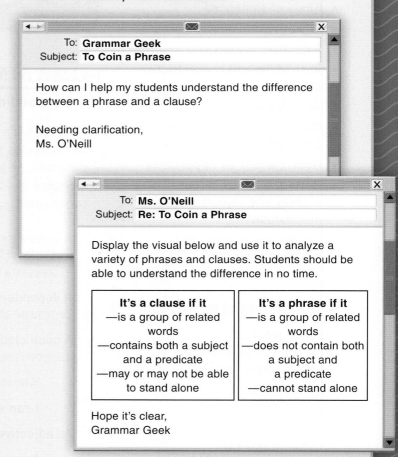

To: **Grammar Geek**
Subject: **To Coin a Phrase**

How can I help my students understand the difference between a phrase and a clause?

Needing clarification,
Ms. O'Neill

To: **Ms. O'Neill**
Subject: **Re: To Coin a Phrase**

Display the visual below and use it to analyze a variety of phrases and clauses. Students should be able to understand the difference in no time.

It's a clause if it	**It's a phrase if it**
—is a group of related words	—is a group of related words
—contains both a subject and a predicate	—does not contain both a subject and a predicate
—may or may not be able to stand alone	—cannot stand alone

Hope it's clear,
Grammar Geek

The turtle walked while the hare sprinted.

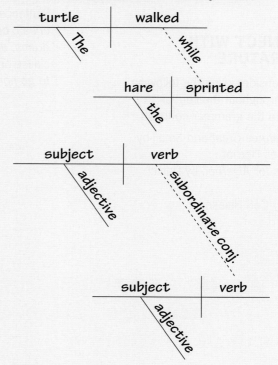

Sentences

8.1 Kinds of Sentences

OBJECTIVES

- **To classify sentences according to use**
- **To identify the subject and the predicate as the essential parts of a sentence**
- **To identify the complete and simple subject and complete and the simple predicate in a sentence**

 **DAILY Maintenance**

Assign **Practice Book** page 90, Section 8.1. After students finish,
1. Give immediate feedback.
2. Review concepts as needed.
3. Model the correct answer.

Pages 4–5 of the **Answer Key** contain tips for Daily Maintenance.

WARM-UP

Write on the board the following sentences:

Can you stop singing?

It would be nice if you stopped singing.

Stop singing.

Good grief, stop singing!

Have four groups each choose a sentence. Instruct them to act out a short scene for that sentence. Encourage students to create a story to accompany the sentence.

📖 Read from a piece of writing that the class is currently reading. Emphasize the kinds of sentences.

TEACH

Ask volunteers to read aloud the first paragraph. Have students suggest additional example sentences. Write the suggestions on the board and have students identify the simple subjects and the simple predicates.

Read aloud the second paragraph. Have volunteers

identify the complete subjects and the complete predicates in the sentences on the board.

Invite volunteers read aloud about the four kinds of sentences. Point out that the scenes from the Warm-Up were based on each of the four kinds of sentences. Discuss when students might use each kind of sentence.

PRACTICE

EXERCISE 1

Suggest that students refer to the Warm-Up sentences to help classify the sentences in this exercise. Have partners compare their answers. Tell students to

discuss reasons for any answers that differ.

EXERCISE 2

Suggest that students create charts to record their answers. Explain that the first and second columns are for the complete subject and the complete predicate, and that the third and fourth columns are for the simple subject and the simple predicate.

EXERCISE 3

Write on the board a chart similar to the one used in Exercise 2. Invite volunteers to complete the chart for each sentence. Discuss each sentence with the class.

8.1 Kinds of Sentences

A sentence is a group of words that expresses a complete thought. The essential parts of a sentence are the subject and the predicate. The **subject** tells who or what the sentence is about. The **predicate** names an action or a state of being. In this sentence the simple subject is the noun *Web site*. The simple predicate is the verb *lists*.

A special *Web site* | *lists* the times in major world cities.

The **complete subject** is the simple subject plus all the words and phrases that go with it. The **complete predicate** is the verb and all the words and phrases that go with it. In the sentence above, a vertical line separates the complete subject and complete predicate.

A **declarative sentence** makes a statement. It ends with a period.

I have a new watch.

An **interrogative sentence** asks a question. It ends with a question mark.

Are you late for school?

An **imperative sentence** gives a command. It usually ends with a period but may end with an exclamation point. In imperative sentences the subject *you* is understood.

(You) Tell me the time of the game.

An **exclamatory sentence** expresses a strong emotion. It ends with an exclamation point.

We are so late!

EXERCISE 1 Tell whether each sentence is declarative, interrogative, imperative, or exclamatory.

1. For most of the 19th century, each community in the country determined its own time.
2. What unbelievable confusion there was!
3. Two neighboring towns might have different times.
4. Why did the situation change?
5. Guess the answer.

Exercise 1
1. declarative
2. exclamatory
3. declarative
4. interrogative
5. imperative
6. declarative
7. interrogative
8. declarative
9. declarative
10. exclamatory

140 • Section 8.1

140 • Section 8.1

APPLY

APPLY IT NOW

Ask students to identify each kind of sentence and to circle the simple subject and underline the simple predicate. Students should demonstrate an understanding of the different kinds of sentences.

ASSESS

Note which students had difficulty identifying the different kinds of sentences. Assign **Practice Book** page 93 for further practice.

TechTip Have students review their classmates' paragraphs. Challenge students to identify the complete subjects and complete predicates.

WRITING CONNECTION

Use pages 412–413 of the Writing portion of the book. Be sure to point out the kinds of sentences in the literature excerpt and the student model.

Exercise 2

Complete subjects are underlined once. Complete predicates are underlined twice.

1. lines, separate
2. Prime Meridian, runs
3. longitude, marks
4. United States, has
5. hour, is lost
6. You, can determine
7. New York City, is
8. Denver, is
9. Variations, exist
10. places, do change

Exercise 3

Complete subjects are underlined once. Complete predicates are underlined twice.

1. declarative
2. exclamatory
3. declarative
4. interrogative
5. (You), imperative
6. declarative

6. In the 1880s, the railroads demanded standardized time.
7. How were the changes decided?
8. In 1884, delegates from more than 27 countries met in Washington, D.C.
9. They divided the earth into 24 time zones.
10. What a historical event it was!

EXERCISE 2 Identify the complete subject and the complete predicate in each sentence. Then name the simple subject and the simple predicate.

1. Imaginary lines on the globe separate the 24 time zones.
2. The prime meridian runs through Greenwich, England.
3. Zero degree longitude marks the start of time zones.
4. The continental United States has four time zones: eastern, central, mountain, and Pacific.
5. One hour is lost for every time zone to the west.
6. You can determine the different times fairly easily.
7. New York City is three hours later than Los Angeles.
8. At the same moment, Denver is one hour earlier than Chicago.
9. Variations still exist in the United States, however.
10. Some places don't change to daylight saving time in the spring.

EXERCISE 3 Identify the complete subject and complete predicate in each sentence. Then tell whether each sentence is declarative, interrogative, imperative, or exclamatory.

1. My family and I drove from Florida to New Mexico.
2. The scenery was amazing!
3. My father asked us a hard question.
4. Who knows how many time zones we will cross?
5. Look at a map and guess again.
6. The correct answer was two time zones.

APPLY IT NOW

Write six sentences about a time when you were either too late or too early. Use at least one of each of the four sentence types: declarative, interrogative, imperative, and exclamatory. Identify the simple subjects and the simple predicates in your writing.

Tech Tip Post your paragraph on the class blog for peer review.

Sentences • 141

8.2 Adjective and Adverb Phrases

OBJECTIVES
- **To identify prepositional, participial, and infinitive phrases**
- **To classify phrases used as adjectives or adverbs in a sentence**

 **Maintenance**

Assign **Practice Book** page 90, Section 8.2. After students finish,
1. Give immediate feedback.
2. Review concepts as needed.
3. Model the correct answer.

Pages 4–5 of the **Answer Key** contain tips for Daily Maintenance.

WARM-UP

Ask five volunteers to stand in a different part of the classroom and to hold an object. Then have students ask questions about themselves or about their object. *(Where am I standing?)* Tell students to answer, using a prepositional phrase *(by the door)* or a participial phrase *(guarding the door).*

📖 Read from a piece of writing that the class is currently reading. Emphasize the adjective and adverb phrases.

TEACH

Invite volunteers to take turns reading aloud about phrases. Pause after each example and discuss the example sentence. Encourage students to explain what features in the phrase help identify it as a prepositional, a participial, or an infinitive phrase. Challenge students to name the word each phrase describes or provides more information about. To help them locate that word, suggest that they ask themselves, *What questions does this phrase answer?*

Create a chart on the board similar to the one below. Instruct students to write this in their notebooks and to use for reference with later exercises.

TYPE	FORM	FUNCTION
Prepositional phrase	Begins with preposition, ends with noun	adjective or adverb
Participial phrase	Begins with *-ing* or *-ed* form of a verb	adjective
Infinitive phrase	Begins with *to* and base form of verb	adjective, adverb, or noun

PRACTICE

EXERCISE 1
Remind students to use the chart for help if needed. Have partners complete this activity. Invite volunteers to share their answers. Discuss the sentences to help students understand the correct answers.

EXERCISE 2
Review the clues students can use to help identify phrases. Have partners help each other find phrases, identify their type, and classify their function as adverbs or adjectives. Discuss the sentences with the class.

8.2 Adjective and Adverb Phrases

A **phrase** is a group of words that is used as a single part of speech. Unlike a sentence or a clause, a phrase does not contain a subject or a predicate. Several types of phrases function as adjectives and as adverbs.

A **prepositional phrase** is made up of a preposition, the object of the preposition, and modifiers of the object.

> **The Marine Corps was established** *in 1798.*
> (adverb phrase describing the verb *was established*)
> **The initial corps was a group** *within the United States Navy.* (adjective phrase describing the noun *group*)

A **participial phrase** is made up of a present or past participle and any words that go with it. Participial phrases always act as adjectives.

> *Participating in every major war,* **the Marine Corps has a long history.**
> (participial phrase describing the proper noun *Marine Corps*)

An **infinitive phrase** is made up of an infinitive—*to* and the base form of a verb—and any words that go with it. An infinitive phrase acts as an adjective, an adverb, or a noun.

> **A good place** *to find information about songs* **is the Internet.**
> (infinitive phrase acting as an adjective describing the noun *place*)
> **There wasn't time enough** *to find all the information this afternoon.*
> (infinitive phrase acting as an adverb describing the adjective *enough*)
> *To earn a dog biscuit* **is the reason my dog performs tricks for me.**
> (infinitive phrase acting as a noun)

EXERCISE 1 Tell whether each italicized phrase is prepositional, participial, or infinitive. Then tell whether the phrase is used as an adjective or an adverb.

1. The Barbary Coast is part *of North Africa.*
2. Tripoli, Morocco, Algiers, and Tunis, *bordering the Mediterranean Sea,* made up the Barbary States.
3. *In the 1700s and early 1800s,* pirates from the Barbary States robbed and terrorized the ships of other countries.
4. Countless efforts *to stop these raids* failed.
5. The North Africans, *dubbed "the Barbary pirates,"* ruled the sea.
6. The pirates' offers *to spare U.S. ships* were rejected.

Exercise 1
1. prepositional, adjective
2. participial, adjective
3. prepositional, adverb
4. infinitive adjective
5. participial, adjective
6. infinitive, adjective
7. infinitive, adverb
8. prepositional, adverb
9. infinitive, adverb
10. prepositional, adverb
11. participial, adjective
12. prepositional, adjective

EXERCISE 3

Review the information in the chart from the Teach section. Have students complete this activity independently. Invite volunteers to read aloud their sentences. Challenge students to identify the phrase in each sentence and tell whether it is acting as an adjective or an adverb phrase.

APPLY

APPLY IT NOW

Brainstorm possible topics such as eating a snack or walking the dog. Invite volunteers to write on the board sentences from their paragraphs containing different types of phrases. Students should demonstrate an understanding of adjective and adverb phrases.

ASSESS

Note which students had difficulty identifying adjective and adverb phrases. Assign **Practice Book** page 94 for further practice.

WRITING CONNECTION

Use pages 414–415 of the Writing portion of the book.

TEACHING OPTIONS

Reteach

Write on strips of paper a variety of prepositional, participial, and infinitive phrases. Place the strips in a box and mix them up. Ask students to take turns selecting a strip and reading aloud the phrase. Have students classify the phrase and explain the reasons for their choices. Help students write sentences that include the phrases. Invite volunteers to decide whether each phrase is used as an adverb or as an adjective.

Meeting Individual Needs

Extra Support Ask students to copy a paragraph from a favorite book, writing each sentence on a separate line. Have students locate the phrases and name the type of phrase. Then have students tell whether the phrases are used as adjectives or adverbs. Reinforce concepts by encouraging students to explain the reasons for their answers.

Meeting Individual Needs

Auditory Have partners play a guessing game in which one student describes aspects of a game, sport, or task while the other student tries to guess the subject of the description. Instruct the student giving the clues to use prepositional, participial, or infinitive phrases. Have students reverse roles after each subject is guessed or revealed.

7. *To let the ships pass,* the pirates demanded payment.

8. The offers were greeted *with the slogan* "Millions for defense but not a cent for tribute."

9. Several countries finally banded together *to stop the pirates.*

10. A fleet of U.S. warships commanded *by Stephen Decatur* set out for the Barbary Coast.

11. *Joining European warships,* the U.S. fleet helped drive the pirates from the sea.

12. When you hear the words *to the "Marine Hymn,"* you will now understand "to the shores of Tripoli."

Burning of the American ship *Philadelphia* held by Barbary pirates in Tripoli Harbor in 1804

Stephen Decatur

Exercise 2

Phrases are underlined.

1. prepositional, adjective
2. infinitive, adverb
3. participial, adjective; prepositional, adjective
4. infinitive, adjective
5. prepositional, adverb; prepositional, adverb

Exercise 3

Answers will vary.

1. infinitive
2. participial
3. prepositional
4. prepositional
5. infinitive
6. participial
7. infinitive
8. prepositional
9. prepositional
10. participial

EXERCISE 2 Identify the phrases in these sentences. Tell whether each is prepositional, participial, or infinitive and whether it acts as an adjective or as an adverb.

1. I am studying the songs of the military services.
2. I searched the Internet to find the lyrics.
3. Reading the lyrics, I had some questions about their meaning.
4. My desire to understand the lyrics sparked new research.
5. I even studied about the Barbary pirates for hours.

EXERCISE 3 Use these phrases in sentences of your own. Tell whether each phrase is prepositional, participial, or infinitive. Then tell whether the phrase is used as an adjective or an adverb.

1. to rescue captives
2. guarding our shores
3. at sea
4. with secret maps
5. to find buried treasure
6. sailing the seas
7. to explore new lands
8. throughout the world
9. in a day
10. changing the course of history

APPLY IT NOW

Write six sentences explaining your after-school routine. Use at least one prepositional phrase, one participial phrase, and one infinitive phrase. Identify each phrase and tell whether it acts as an adjective or as an adverb.

8.3 Adjective Clauses

OBJECTIVE

- **To identify adjective clauses and the words they describe**

 **Maintenance**

Assign **Practice Book** page 90, Section 8.3. After students finish,
1. Give immediate feedback.
2. Review concepts as needed.
3. Model the correct answer.

Pages 4–5 of the **Answer Key** contain tips for Daily Maintenance.

WARM-UP

Write on the board several clauses such as the following:

> that I was given
>
> who lived in France
>
> where my friend was born

Tell students to write a sentence for each clause.

📖 Read from a piece of writing that the class is currently reading. Emphasize the adjective clauses.

TEACH

Write the following lines on the board. Discuss what the two lines have in common and how they differ.

> We love scary movies.
>
> the movies that we saw

Elicit that the two lines are similar in that they both have subjects and verbs *(We love, we saw)* but differ because only one is a complete sentence. Point out that *that we saw* is an incomplete thought and therefore is a dependent clause, not a sentence.

Invite volunteers to write on the board their Warm-Up sentences. Point out that these sentences contain dependent clauses. Have volunteers read aloud about clauses and adjective clauses.

Then have volunteers identify the adjective clauses in the sentences on the board. Challenge students to identify what word is being described by each clause. Ask volunteers to suggest additional sentences that contain adjective clauses.

PRACTICE

EXERCISE 1

Have students complete this exercise independently. Explain that they must identify each adjective clause and the noun or pronoun it modifies. Have partners exchange their completed papers to check and compare answers.

EXERCISE 2

Review relative pronouns and subordinate conjunctions. Then have students complete the exercise independently. Invite volunteers to share their answers with the class.

EXERCISE 3

Make clear that the noun that should be modified in each sentence appears in italics. Assign a number from one through eight to each student. Have students with number one write their new versions of sentence 1 on the board. Point out how the sentences differ in their content, yet they are similar in their use of an adjective

---

8.3 Adjective Clauses

A **clause** is a group of words that contains a subject and a predicate. An **independent clause** is one that expresses a complete thought and so can stand on its own.

> **Boston has many historic sites.**

A **dependent clause** cannot stand alone.

> **One site** *that tourists visit* **is south of town.**
> **Some events** *about which I studied* **occurred in Boston.**

Notice that neither of the groups of words in red expresses a complete thought, even though each has a subject and a verb.

An **adjective clause,** one type of dependent clause, describes a noun or a pronoun. Most adjective clauses begin with one of the **relative pronouns** *who, whom, whose, which,* or *that.* The word in the independent clause to which the relative pronoun relates is its **antecedent.** In this sentence the adjective clause modifies *Madison. Madison* is the antecedent of the relative pronoun *which.*

> **Madison,** *which is in Wisconsin,* **has several lakes.**

Can you identify the adjective clause, the relative pronoun, and the antecedent of the pronoun in this sentence?

> **I visited the school that my mother attended.**

The adjective clause is *that my mother attended.* The relative pronoun is *that,* and *school* is its antecedent.

Some adjective clauses begin with a subordinate conjunction such as *when, where,* or *why.*

> **Madison is the place** *where my mother went to school.*

EXERCISE 1 Identify the adjective clause in each sentence. Name the noun or pronoun that the adjective clause describes.

1. I traveled to Newfoundland with my uncle Joel, <u>who had invited me on the trip.</u>
2. Joel is a person <u>whose ideas for adventures always turn out well.</u>
3. His plan, <u>which he presented as a trip to Newfoundland during the winter,</u> was unusual.

Exercise 1
Adjective clauses are underlined.
1. Joel
2. person
3. plan

clause. Continue until numbers two through eight have presented their sentences.

APPLY

APPLY IT NOW

Tell students that they can choose other sightseeing attractions beside those in the list. When students have finished, invite volunteers to read their sentences aloud. Discuss sentences that present any problems. Students should demonstrate an understanding of adjective clauses.

TechTip Review how to evaluate a Web site to be sure that it is credible. Then ask students to create a multimedia presentation, using PowerPoint or other similar software.

ASSESS

Note which students had difficulty identifying adjective clauses. Assign **Practice Book** page 95 for further practice.

WRITING CONNECTION

Use pages 416–417 of the Writing portion of the book.

4. people
5. person
6. New England
7. blizzard
8. place
9. ferry
10. ferry
11. plan
12. adventure

4. It seemed suited to people who love cold weather.
5. I, however, am not a person who likes cold weather.
6. We headed to New England, which was blanketed in snow.
7. A blizzard, which hadn't been forecast, forced us to stop.
8. So New Brunswick was the place where we stayed for several days—indoors.
9. We eventually made it to the ferry that would take us across the Gulf of St. Lawrence to Newfoundland.
10. The ferry, which had an icebreaker on its bow, chopped through the ice floes.
11. Our plan, which was to see the winter landscape, was hindered by another few days of bad weather.
12. This was the one adventure of Uncle Joel's that didn't please me.

Exercise 2
Adjective clauses are underlined.
1. relative pronoun
2. subordinate conjunction
3. relative pronoun
4. subordinate conjunction

EXERCISE 2 Identify the adjective clause in each sentence. Tell whether it begins with a relative pronoun or a subordinate conjunction.

1. Quebec, which is located in Canada, sits on the banks of the St. Lawrence River.
2. It is a city where people enjoy dogsled races and other winter activities.
3. It is in a region that is very cold.
4. Quebec is the Canadian city where many Americans travel for Winter Carnival.

Exercise 3
Answers will vary.

EXERCISE 3 Rewrite the following sentences, inserting an adjective clause after the italicized words.

1. The *trip* was my favorite one.
2. I remember the *day*.
3. I'll never forget the *place*.
4. The *hotel* was a lovely one.
5. Every day we went to the *park*.
6. The *pool* was a welcome sight.
7. I watched the *game* in the lobby.
8. She wrote the *guidebook*.

Tech Tip With an adult, research one of the places online.

APPLY IT NOW

Choose one of the following sightseeing attractions. Write five sentences about it, each containing an adjective clause.

Mount Rushmore
Golden Gate Bridge
Niagara Falls
Lake Placid
Gateway Arch
Mississippi River
Manhattan
Great Plains

Sentences • 145

TEACHING OPTIONS

Reteach

Reinforce the concept of adjective clauses by charting sentences that students suggest. In the first row of the chart write the sentence. Invite a volunteer to write the adjective clause in the second row. Have another volunteer write the noun that the clause modifies in the third row. Encourage students to decide on a topic that most have knowledge about, such as a local park or shopping mall.

Sentence:
The mall is a place that appeals to teens.

Adjective Clause:
that appeals to teens

Noun Being Modified:
place

Curriculum Connection

Invite students to write about a topic from another subject, such as science, social studies, art, music, or geography. Encourage students to include adjective clauses. Have students underline the adjective clauses and circle the nouns or pronouns that are described by the clauses. Have students write their sentences on the board. Discuss the sentences with the class.

Cooperative Learning

Have small groups copy the sentences from Exercise 1 onto a sheet of paper. Direct students to cut each sentence apart, separating the adjective clause from the rest of the sentence. Have students place the parts in two piles and shuffle each pile. Challenge students to put the sentences back together, identifying the adjective clauses and the nouns the clauses describe. Suggest that students check their sentences against the sentences in Exercise 1.

OBJECTIVE

- To distinguish between restrictive and nonrestrictive adjective clauses

Assign **Practice Book** page 90, Section 8.4. After students finish,
1. Give immediate feedback.
2. Review concepts as needed.
3. Model the correct answer.

Pages 4–5 of the **Answer Key** contain tips for Daily Maintenance.

WARM-UP

Write on the board the following sentences:

The boy in the green shirt ate the last piece of cake.

Patrick, the boy in the green shirt, did the dishes.

Have volunteers point out differences between the two sentences. Then give students several minutes to write as many similar sentence pairs as possible.

📖 Read from a piece of writing that the class is currently reading. Emphasize the restrictive and nonrestrictive clauses.

TEACH

Write on the board the word *restrictive*. Lead students to a definition of the term by discussing what *restrict* means *(to keep something within limits).* Ask volunteers to explain how restriction might apply to a clause. *(It limits the word that is being described.)* Explain that sometimes an adjective clause is necessary to make the meaning of a sentence clear. Tell students that this type of clause is restrictive.

Point out that other adjective clauses can be taken out of a sentence and the meaning remains

the same. Explain that these clauses, called nonrestrictive clauses, are not necessary to the sentence.

Invite students to read aloud about restrictive and nonrestrictive clauses. Have students pause after each example sentence and then say the sentence again without the adjective clause. Explain that the sentences with restrictive clauses seem incomplete without the adjective clauses. Elicit from students the observation that without the restrictive clauses, the reader does not know which arena, which empire, or which structures.

Have students write on the board their sentences from the Warm-Up. Challenge students to find the clauses and label each as restrictive or nonrestrictive.

PRACTICE

EXERCISE 1

Invite volunteers to explain how they can distinguish between restrictive and nonrestrictive clauses. Have students complete this exercise independently. Then ask small groups to discuss their answers.

8.4 Restrictive and Nonrestrictive Clauses

Some adjective clauses, called **restrictive clauses,** are essential to the meaning of the sentences in which they appear. Without them, the sentences no longer make sense. An adjective clause that is not essential to the meaning of the independent clause and that can be removed without affecting the sense of the sentence is a **nonrestrictive clause.**

A large arena *that stands in modern Rome* has survived through centuries. (restrictive clause)
The Coliseum, *which is a major tourist attraction,* was built by the ancient Romans. (nonrestrictive clause)

Can you tell which clauses are restrictive and which are nonrestrictive in the following sentences?

The ancient Romans, *who created a large empire,* left buildings throughout much of the Mediterranean.
The empire *that they created* lasted for centuries.
The structures *that the Romans built* included aqueducts and arenas.

The adjective clause in the first sentence is nonrestrictive, and those in the second and third sentences are restrictive. In the first sentence, the adjective clause can be removed without changing the basic meaning of the sentence. Removing the adjective clauses from the other sentences would make the sentences unclear.

Note the following characteristics of adjective clauses:

- A nonrestrictive clause is set off by commas.
- A restrictive clause does not have commas.
- A proper noun is usually followed by a nonrestrictive clause.
- The relative pronoun *that* is generally used for restrictive clauses, and *which* is used for nonrestrictive clauses.

EXERCISE 1 Identify the adjective clause in each sentence. Tell whether the adjective clause is restrictive or nonrestrictive.

1. The Coliseum, which is one of the most famous buildings in the world, stands in central Rome.
2. It is a magnificent monument that was left by the ancient Romans.
3. The Romans, whose skill at building was famous, created a great empire.

Exercise 1
Adjective clauses are underlined.

1. nonrestrictive
2. restrictive
3. nonrestrictive
4. restrictive
5. nonrestrictive
6. restrictive
7. nonrestrictive
8. nonrestrictive
9. nonrestrictive
10. restrictive

The Coliseum

EXERCISE 2

Have partners complete this exercise. When students have finished, ask volunteers to write each sentence on the board. Have students underline the adjective clause and add commas where necessary.

APPLY

APPLY IT NOW

Encourage students to explain why they labeled clauses restrictive or nonrestrictive. Have students share their findings in small groups to further reinforce the concept. Students should demonstrate an understanding of restrictive and nonrestrictive adjective clauses.

ASSESS

Note which students had difficulty distinguishing between restrictive and nonrestrictive adjective clauses. Assign **Practice Book** pages 96–97 for further practice.

WRITING CONNECTION

Use pages 418–419 of the Writing portion of the book.

TEACHING OPTIONS

Reteach

Ask students to suggest sentences that tell about a book the class is currently reading. Encourage students to include adjective clauses in their sentences. Write the sentences on the board. Discuss each sentence, asking students to identify the adjective clause and the noun or pronoun that the clause describes. Then have students classify the clause as restrictive or nonrestrictive.

Meeting Individual Needs

Extra Support Invite students to rewrite the sentences from Exercise 1 without the adjective clauses. Direct students to read the sentences silently, asking if the sentences are complete. Have students draw stars beside those sentences that seem to be lacking information and then check those sentences against the complete sentences in the exercise. Point out that the sentences with restrictive clauses are the sentences that students should have drawn stars beside.

Meeting Individual Needs

Intrapersonal Invite students to write about a hobby or an activity that they enjoy. Encourage students to include adjective clauses. Then have students underline each adjective clause and write *R* to identify a restrictive clause or *N* to identify a nonrestrictive clause.

---

4. Roman structures that are still standing include amphitheaters, aqueducts, arches, and roadways.

5. The Coliseum, which was built in only 10 years, has been standing since the first century AD.

6. The emperor who started the building was Vespasian.

7. The huge structure, which rises more than 187 feet in the air, is about 600 feet long and about 500 feet wide.

8. It had more than 80 entrances, which were numbered for easy access.

9. The structure could hold more than 45,000 people, who came for public entertainments provided by the emperor.

10. The entertainment that it provided for audiences included combats between gladiators and frequently with wild animals.

Exercise 2
Adjective clauses are underlined.

1. nonrestrictive, Gladiators, whose name comes from the Latin word for sword, were a class of professional fighters.

2. restrictive

3. nonrestrictive, The pairs, which could sometimes number up to 5,000 couples in one amphitheater, were trained in fighting.

4. restrictive

5. restrictive

6. nonrestrictive, Spartacus, who was forced to fight as a gladiator, escaped with 70 other gladiators.

7. restrictive

8. nonrestrictive, The bloody gladiator games, which continued until 404 AD, were finally banned by the emperor Honorius.

EXERCISE 2 Identify the adjective clause in each sentence and tell whether the clause is restrictive or nonrestrictive. Rewrite the sentences with nonrestrictive clauses, adding commas where necessary.

1. Gladiators whose name comes from the Latin word for *sword* were a class of professional fighters.

2. Pairs of gladiators would fight each other in games that were part of the public entertainment of Rome.

3. The pairs which could sometimes number up to 5,000 couples in one amphitheater were trained in fighting.

4. A gladiator who was defeated was killed by the victor.

5. Some gladiators were slaves that had been sold to gladiator schools.

6. Spartacus who was forced to fight as a gladiator escaped with 70 other gladiators.

7. It was Spartacus and his followers who eventually freed 100,000 slaves before being captured by the Roman army.

8. The bloody gladiator games which continued until 404 AD were finally banned by the emperor Honorius.

APPLY IT NOW

Copy five sentences with adjective clauses that you locate in books. Underline the adjective clauses and indicate whether each is restrictive or nonrestrictive.

Sentences • 147

OBJECTIVE
- **To identify adverb clauses and subordinate conjunctions**

 **DAILY ⚙ Maintenance**

Assign **Practice Book** page 91, Section 8.5. After students finish,
1. Give immediate feedback.
2. Review concepts as needed.
3. Model the correct answer.

Pages 4–5 of the **Answer Key** contain tips for Daily Maintenance.

WARM-UP

Have partners conduct short interviews about their hobbies and interests, modeled on the following:

Q: When did you start playing soccer?

A: I started playing soccer when I was seven.

Have the interviewer ask questions beginning with the following words: *how, when, where, why, in what way*. Make sure students answer in complete sentences.

📖 Read from a piece of writing that the class is currently reading. Emphasize the adverb clauses.

TEACH

Ask students the definition of an adverb. *(An adverb describes a verb, an adjective, or another adverb.)* Write the following on the board:

Alex finished.

Add words to the sentence and discuss each addition with the class.

Alex finished early.

Alex finished before the due date.

Alex finished after the report was due.

Point out that in the first sentence, the adverb *early* is added; in the second sentence, a phrase *(before the due date)* is added; and in the last sentence, a clause *(after the report was due)* is added. Lead students to note that the three additions all function as adverbs modifying *finished*, but only the modifier in the last sentence contains a subject and a predicate. Explain that it is an adverb clause.

Ask volunteers to read aloud about adverb clauses. Have students pause after the example sentences to identify the verbs that the adverb clauses describe.

PRACTICE

EXERCISE 1
Challenge students to complete the exercise independently. Suggest that they refer to the list of subordinate conjunctions if they need help. When students have finished, have small groups discuss their answers.

EXERCISE 2
Review the subordinate conjunctions that introduce adverb clauses. Let students remain in their groups from Exercise 1 to discuss the sentences, the clauses, and the words being described. Then discuss the

---

8.5 Adverb Clauses

Dependent clauses may act as adverbs, describing or giving information about verbs, adjectives, or other adverbs. These clauses, called **adverb clauses,** tell *where, when, why, in what way, to what extent (degree),* or *under what condition.*

> **Wherever they went,** King Arthur's knights helped the weak and the poor.

The adverb clause tells *where* and describes the verb *helped* in the independent clause.

Adverb clauses are introduced by subordinate conjunctions, some of which are listed below.

after	because	since	until
although	before	so long as	when
as if	even though	so that	whenever
as long as	if	than	where
as soon as	inasmuch as	though	wherever
as though	in order that	unless	while

A **subordinate conjunction** joins an adverb clause to an independent clause. Find the subordinate conjunctions in these sentences. What does each adverb clause tell about?

> **Even though there may have been a real King Arthur, the stories we read about him are legends.**
> **People have loved the tales of King Arthur since they were written down during the Middle Ages.**

In the first sentence, the subordinate conjunction *even though* introduces an adverb clause that tells a condition—*even though there may have been a real King Arthur.* In the second sentence, the subordinate conjunction *since* introduces an adverb clause that shows time—*since they were written down during the Middle Ages.*

An adverb clause can come before or after the independent clause. When an adverb clause begins a sentence, it is usually followed by a comma.

> *Since they were written down during the Middle Ages,* **the tales of King Arthur have been popular.**

148 • Section 8.5

answers as a class. Encourage students to determine what question the clause answers. Tell students that if the clause answers the question *where, when, why, in what way, to what extent (degree),* or *under what condition,* the clause is an adverb clause.

APPLY

APPLY IT NOW

Suggest that students set up a chart with two columns: one for adverb clauses and one for adjective clauses. Encourage students to write each sentence with an adjective or adverb clause that they locate in their passages.

Suggest that students underline each clause and circle the word it describes. Students should demonstrate an understanding of adverb clauses.

ASSESS

Note which students had difficulty identifying adverb clauses and subordinate conjunctions. Assign **Practice Book** page 98 for further practice.

WRITING CONNECTION

Use pages 420–421 of the Writing portion of the book.

Reteach

Write each subordinate conjunction on page 148 on a separate note card and place the cards in a box. Invite a volunteer to choose a card and to suggest a sentence that uses that conjunction to form an adverb clause in a sentence. Write the sentence on the board and ask volunteers if the sentence and the adverb clause are correct. Continue the activity until all the cards have been used.

Meeting Individual Needs

Interpersonal Have partners take turns role-playing being a "new kid" in school. Have the "old" student tell the new kid things about the school. Encourage the new kid to listen closely for sentences that include adverb clauses. Tell the new kid that after each sentence, he or she should repeat the adverb clause.

> **So that you don't get lost, you should carry a map of the school.**
>
> **If you get confused, ask a teacher for help.**
>
> **Although the school might seem confusing, you'll get the hang of it.**

Instruct each student to say five sentences as he or she assumes the role of the old student.

Diagram It!

To practice adverb clauses in the context of diagramming, turn to Section 11.9.

Exercise 1
Adverb clauses are underlined.

1. If
2. although
3. As
4. so that
5. Because
6. After
7. When
8. As
9. While
10. After

EXERCISE 1 Identify the adverb clause in each sentence. Name the subordinate conjunction.

1. If you want to read some good stories, read the tales about King Arthur and the Knights of the Round Table.

2. Here is one version of the ending, although there are other versions.

3. As the years passed, Arthur's knights died or went away.

4. An evil knight, Mordred, plotted so that he could have power.

5. Because Mordred wanted to take the throne from Arthur, a great battle occurred.

6. After the day-long battle ended, only Arthur, two of his knights, and Mordred were left standing.

7. When Arthur saw Mordred on the battlefield, he was able to strike a fatal blow to the evil knight's heart.

8. As Mordred was falling, however, he swung one last blow with his sword and wounded Arthur.

9. While he lay wounded, Arthur told his loyal knight Sir Bedivere to throw Excalibur, Arthur's magic sword, into the nearby lake.

10. After Bedivere dragged Arthur to the shore, a boat appeared with three women who carried Arthur away.

Tintagel Castle in Cornwall, England, which is associated with the legend of King Arthur

Exercise 2
Dependent clauses are underlined.

1. adverb clause
2. adverb clause
3. adjective clause
4. adjective clause
5. adverb clause
6. adjective clause
7. adjective clause

EXERCISE 2 Identify the dependent clause in each sentence. Tell whether it is an adjective clause or an adverb clause.

1. No one knows Arthur's fate after he disappeared into the mists.

2. Perhaps the women healed his wounds unless it was too late.

3. In some versions Arthur lives on Avalon, which is an island of mists and mystery.

4. The version of the legend that I read ends with no clear answer.

5. Even though the ending is unclear, Arthur's values of honor, fairness, and bravery live on.

6. Another version of the King Arthur myth, from the viewpoint of his sister, was written in 1982.

7. The book, which is called The Mists of Avalon, was a best seller.

APPLY IT NOW

Choose a passage from another textbook and list the adjective and adverb clauses in it.

8.6 Noun Clauses as Subjects

OBJECTIVE

- To identify and use noun clauses as subjects

 **Maintenance**

Assign **Practice Book** page 91, Section 8.6. After students finish,

1. Give immediate feedback.
2. Review concepts as needed.
3. Model the correct answer.

Pages 4–5 of the **Answer Key** contain tips for Daily Maintenance.

WARM-UP

Write on the board the following sentence starters:

> What _____ is against the rules.
>
> Whether _____ is not important.
>
> That _____ had been obvious to everyone.

Have students write two sentences for each starter. Invite volunteers to write their sentences on the board.

📖 Read from a piece of writing that the class is currently reading. Emphasize the noun clauses used as subjects.

TEACH

Ask students to separate their Warm-Up sentences into complete subjects and complete predicates. Lead students to see that each subject is a clause and therefore a noun clause.

Invite volunteers to read aloud about noun clauses as subjects. Have students pause after each set of example sentences. Discuss the information, making sure students understand why these words form a clause and how the clause functions as the subject of the sentence. Challenge students to offer example sentences, using the introductory words listed on this page.

PRACTICE

EXERCISE 1

Remind students that the noun clauses in these sentences will probably appear before the verb. Suggest that students identify the complete predicate and then determine whether the words that precede it form a noun clause used as a subject. Instruct students to work independently. Have partners exchange papers and compare answers.

EXERCISE 2

Emphasize that although no single noun clause is correct for a sentence, each noun clause must be formed correctly. Invite several volunteers to write their sentences on the board. Discuss each sentence with the class. Point out how the noun clause has been formed and how it functions as the subject of the sentence.

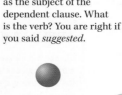

8.6 Noun Clauses as Subjects

Dependent clauses can be used as nouns. These clauses, called **noun clauses,** function as subjects, complements, appositives, direct objects, indirect objects, and objects of prepositions. Although a noun clause is a basic part of the independent clause and cannot be eliminated, it is still a dependent clause. A noun clause used as a subject generally takes the singular form of the verb.

Compare these sentences.

> My *worry* must have been evident from my facial expression.
> *That I was worried* must have been evident from my facial expression.

In the first sentence, the noun *worry* is the subject. In the second sentence, the clause *that I was worried* is the subject. The clause does the work of a noun, and so it is a noun clause.

Most noun clauses begin with one of the following introductory words: *that, who, whom, whoever, whomever, how, why, when, whether, what, where,* and *whatever.*

Compare the noun clauses in these sentences. How do the noun clauses, which are in red, function?

> *That* we needed entertainment for my little brother's birthday party **was never in doubt.**
> *Whoever* suggested a clown **had a good idea.**

Both noun clauses are subjects: in the first sentence, the subject of the verb *was,* and in the second sentence, the subject of *had.*

In the first sentence, *That* introduces the clause but serves no specific function within the dependent clause. In the second sentence, however, *Whoever* acts as the subject of the dependent clause. What is the verb? You are right if you said *suggested.*

150 • Section 8.6

APPLY

APPLY IT NOW

Write on the board several example sentences. Point out that each sentence begins with the noun clause. Invite volunteers to share their sentences with the class. Students should demonstrate an understanding of noun clauses used as subjects.

ASSESS

Note which students had difficulty identifying and using noun clauses as subjects. Assign **Practice Book** pages 99–100 for further practice.

WRITING CONNECTION

Use pages 422–423 of the Writing portion of the book.

Write on the board the complete predicates from Exercise 1.

TEACHING OPTIONS

Reteach

Write on the board the complete predicates from Exercise 1. Ask volunteers to read aloud the predicates. Have the class brainstorm themes that could include sentences containing these predicates. Choose one theme and encourage students to write noun clauses as subjects to complete the sentences in a way that develops the theme. Help students write their clauses as necessary.

Meeting Individual Needs

Extra Support Remind students that although some of the same words, such as *that, who, whoever,* and *which,* introduce noun and adjective clauses, the clauses have different functions. Write these and similar sentences on the board. Discuss the function of each clause.

> **The route that they took was long and dangerous.**

> **That they made the journey so quickly is a tremendous feat.**

Explain that the clause *that they took* appears before the verb *was* and could be mistaken for a noun clause. However, explain that the clause modifies the word *route* and therefore is an adjective clause. Point out the clause *That they made the journey so quickly* is the subject of the sentence, so the clause is a noun clause.

Encourage students to compose sentences that use the same introductory words for adjective clauses and noun clauses. Have partners exchange papers, circle the adjective clauses, and underline the noun clauses.

Exercise 1
Noun clauses are underlined.

EXERCISE 1 Identify the noun clause used as the subject in each sentence.

1. That the magician was late for Angelica's party surprised us all.
2. What we should do next was the question.
3. How we could keep the children quiet was our greatest concern.
4. That they were happy playing games soon became clear.
5. Whether they would pay attention to the magician was uncertain.
6. Why he did not call to explain his lateness disturbed me, especially since we had talked the day before.
7. That he had lost the address and phone number did not occur to us.
8. How he finally found the house was in itself a mystery.
9. That the children enjoyed the performance was obvious in their laughter.
10. That our food arrived cold was disappointing.
11. Whoever chose the movie deserves the credit too.
12. Whether I'll ever help out at another birthday party is a big question.

Exercise 2
Answers will vary.

EXERCISE 2 Complete each sentence with an appropriate noun clause used as the subject.

1. _____ was my favorite slogan.
2. _____ continues to be important to me.
3. _____ has always interested me.
4. _____ disturbs me.
5. _____ is puzzling.
6. _____ seems to be what I enjoy about school.
7. _____ is what I am most proud of.
8. _____ was thinking ahead.
9. _____ is what I was trying to achieve.
10. _____ will involve everybody.

APPLY IT NOW

Use each noun clause as the subject of a sentence.

- that we would win the game
- how I mastered that skill
- whether I'll ever learn French
- what pleases me the most
- why I like my best friend

Sentences • 151

OBJECTIVE
- **To identify and use noun clauses as subject complements**

 **Maintenance**

Assign **Practice Book** page 91, Section 8.7. After students finish,
1. Give immediate feedback.
2. Review concepts as needed.
3. Model the correct answer.

Pages 4–5 of the **Answer Key** contain tips for Daily Maintenance.

WARM-UP

Give students note cards that contain nouns and noun clauses similar to the following:

family	what is important to him
lunch	when I hang out with my friends

Have students write a sentence containing both the noun and the noun clause. Instruct students to use the noun as the subject and to use a form of *be* as the predicate in their sentences.

📖 Read from a piece of writing that the class is currently reading. Emphasize the noun clauses used as subject complements.

TEACH

Write on the board the term *subject complement* and elicit from students the characteristics of a subject complement. Confirm that a subject complement follows a linking verb and provides more information about the subject of a sentence. Invite volunteers to write on the board their Warm-Up sentences and to underline the subject. Point out that the subject complements in the Warm-Up sentences are the noun clauses from the note cards.

Have volunteers read aloud about noun clauses as subject complements. Help students understand why some subject complements are not noun clauses. *(They do not have subjects and verbs.)*

Tell students that every clause has a subject and a predicate. Then help students compose noun clauses as subject complements for the subject *One decision*.

PRACTICE

EXERCISE 1
Review the clue words that can help students locate noun clauses, such as *that*, *who*, *how*, and *why*.

Have students complete the exercise independently. Then ask partners to compare answers.

EXERCISE 2
Point out that because these clauses function as subject complements, they will follow the verbs. Have partners complete this exercise.

EXERCISE 3
Review the example sentences that contain noun clauses as subject complements. Have students complete this activity independently. Invite volunteers to write their sentences on the board. Analyze the sentences

---

8.7 Noun Clauses as Subject Complements

Noun clauses can be used as subject complements.

> **The issue in the balance was** *the control of the Roman world.*
> **The issue in the balance was** *who would control the Roman world.*

In the first sentence, the subject is *issue*. The verb *was* links the subject to the subject complement, the noun *control*. In the second sentence, *issue* is again the subject. The linking verb *was* joins the subject to the subject complement, the entire noun clause *who would control the Roman world*.

What are the subject complements in the following sentences? Which one is a noun clause?

> **The ruler would be the winner of the battle of Actium.**
> **The ruler would be whoever won the battle of Actium.**

In the first sentence, the noun *winner* is the subject complement. In the second sentence, the noun clause *whoever won the battle of Actium* is the subject complement. Its subject is *whoever*, and its verb is *won*.

EXERCISE 1 Identify the noun clause in each sentence. Tell if it is a subject or a subject complement.

1. My teacher's belief is <u>that American history is the most exciting subject to share with students</u>.
2. <u>Why the study of ancient civilization is more interesting to me</u> is a puzzle.
3. My suspicion is <u>that where an American grows up makes a real difference</u>.
4. <u>That they are somehow participants in Revolutionary history</u> might be the feeling of people from Boston.
5. My guess is <u>that my interest in science fiction has something to do with my interest in ancient civilizations</u>.
6. <u>How such things influence each other</u> is something to explore.
7. The fact is, I suppose, <u>that you can't really account for taste</u>.
8. The lucky thing is <u>that my preferences enable me to learn about both topics</u>.

Boston antique engraving. 1854

Exercise 1
Noun clause are underlined.
1. subject complement
2. subject
3. subject complement
4. subject
5. subject complement
6. subject
7. subject complement
8. subject complement

152 • Section 8.7

with the class to determine if the completions include noun clauses used as subject complements.

APPLY

APPLY IT NOW

Mention to students that it may be difficult to include a noun clause as a subject complement in every sentence. Recommend that students include such noun clauses only as warranted. Have students highlight the sentences that have noun clauses as complements and underline each of those noun clauses. Review students' work to confirm that they understand the concept. Students should

demonstrate an understanding of noun clauses used as subject complements.

ASSESS

Note which students had difficulty identifying and using noun clauses as subject complements. Assign **Practice Book** pages 101–102 for further practice.

WRITING CONNECTION

Use pages 424–425 of the Writing portion of the book.

Use pages 424–425 of the Writing portion of the book.

Reteach

Invite students to talk about a recent news event. Encourage them to present their ideas, using subject complements. Write students' sentences on the board. Ask volunteers to label parts of the sentences: *subject, verb,* and *subject complement.* Have students circle each word that signals a noun clause used as a subject complement. Discuss the sentences to make sure students understand the concept of a noun clause used as a subject complement.

Cooperative Learning

Organize the class into groups of four or five students. Tell each student to write on a sheet of paper the beginning of a sentence that needs a subject complement. For example:

> **My point is _____.**
>
> **The fact of the matter is _____.**
>
> **The question remains _____.**
>
> **My feelings about the test are _____.**

When students have written their sentence starters, tell group members to pass their papers to the students on the right. Instruct each student to write a noun clause as a subject complement to complete the sentence starter. When students have finished their first round, ask them to pass their papers to the right once again. Advise students to continue adding subject complements and passing the sentence starters to their right until students receive their original sentence starters. Students can then complete their own sentence starters. Invite students to take turns reading aloud the completed sentences.

Cleopatra VII Thea Philopator

Exercise 2
Noun clause are underlined.

1. fact
2. question
3. hope
4. situation
5. advice
6. belief
7. hope
8. concern
9. truth
10. event
11. question
12. outcome

EXERCISE 2 Identify the noun clause used as the complement in each sentence. Name the subject about which the noun clause gives information.

1. The fact is that the battle of Actium changed the world.
2. The question was who would rule Rome.
3. Mark Antony's hope was that he would defeat Octavius.
4. The situation was that he had been living in Egypt with Cleopatra.
5. Cleopatra's advice was that they fight a battle at sea.
6. Her belief was that Antony's forces would win.
7. Cleopatra's hope was that she would be queen of Rome.
8. The generals' concern was that Cleopatra couldn't be trusted.
9. The truth is that Antony might have won.
10. The surprising event was that Cleopatra sailed away.
11. The big question was why Antony and his ships followed her.
12. The outcome was that Octavius and his navy won the battle.

Sea battle of Actium in 31 BC, in which Octavius defeated Antony and Cleopatra

Exercise 3
Answers will vary.

EXERCISE 3 Complete each sentence with an appropriate noun clause used as the subject complement.

1. My teacher's greatest characteristic is _____.
2. The best attribute of our school is _____.
3. My favorite saying used to be _____.
4. What I've always wondered is _____.
5. The best lesson I've learned is _____.
6. The fact remains _____.
7. Still, it seems _____.
8. My hope is _____.
9. The question remains _____.
10. An answer might be _____.
11. The outcome might be _____.
12. My biggest wish is _____.

APPLY IT NOW

Write five sentences using noun clauses as complements to describe a friend, a teacher, or a family member.

Sentences • 153

OBJECTIVE
- To identify and use noun clauses as appositives

 **DAILY Maintenance**

Assign **Practice Book** page 91, Section 8.8. After students finish,
1. Give immediate feedback.
2. Review concepts as needed.
3. Model the correct answer.

Pages 4–5 of the **Answer Key** contain tips for Daily Maintenance.

WARM-UP

Write on the board the following sentences:

My dog hurt his paw.

I've had my dog for six years.

Tell students to combine the two sentences to make one sentence.

📖 Read from a piece of writing that the class is currently reading. Emphasize the noun clauses used as appositives.

TEACH

Have a volunteer explain how an appositive differs from a subject complement. Then invite volunteers to read aloud about noun clauses used as appositives. Have several students write on the board their Warm-Up sentences. Challenge students to identify the appositives.

Point out that noun clauses used as appositives are sometimes mistaken for adjective clauses. Share with students a technique for distinguishing between a noun clause used as an appositive and an adjective clause that modifies the preceding noun or pronoun. Lead students to see that because an appositive is a restatement of

the preceding noun or pronoun, the two can be connected by the linking verb *is* and make sense. Write on the board the following sentences:

The story <u>that he lost his keys again</u> amused us.

The story <u>that he told</u> amused us.

Tell students that *The story is that he lost his keys* makes sense, but that *The story is that he told* does not make sense.

Encourage students to supply other examples of noun clauses used as appositives and adjective clauses that modify a preceding noun or pronoun.

PRACTICE

EXERCISE 1
Review the technique for distinguishing between noun clauses and adjective clauses. Model the first sentence for the class. Then have students complete this exercise independently. When students have finished, discuss each sentence and guide them to recognize which clauses are noun clauses used as appositives and which clauses are adjective clauses.

EXERCISE 2
Discuss how students can distinguish between a noun clause

8.8 Noun Clauses as Appositives

Noun clauses can be used as appositives. An **appositive** is a word or group of words that follows a noun and renames it, or gives more information about it.

> The theme of many folktales is *that people have moral and social responsibilities.* (subject complement)
> The theme *that people have moral and social responsibilities* is important in folktales. (appositive)

In the first sentence, the italicized noun clause is a subject complement. It describes the subject *theme* and follows the linking verb *is.* In the second sentence, the italicized noun clause is an appositive. It explains the noun that precedes it, *theme.*

Can you identify the noun clause used as an appositive in the following sentence and what it explains?

> The principle that friendship is essential is in many folktales.

You are correct if you said the noun clause is *that friendship is essential* and that it follows and renames the noun *principle.*

Adjective clauses are sometimes confused with noun clauses used as appositives. An appositive renames the noun or pronoun it follows. An adjective clause describes a noun or pronoun.

> The folktale *that I read* was about the trickster Spider Ananse. (adjective clause)
> The theme *that weakness can overcome strength* is developed in some of the Ananse tales. (noun clause)

In the first sentence, *that* acts as a relative pronoun. Its antecedent is *folktale,* and it is the object of the verb *read* in the adjective clause. In the second sentence, *that* introduces the noun clause but has no other function in the clause; it is strictly an introductory word.

EXERCISE 1 Identify the noun clauses used as appositives in these sentences. Not all sentences have noun clauses.

1. It is a fact <u>that folktales are popular</u>.
2. Many folktales from around the world have themes and plots that are similar to one another.
3. It is a fact <u>that African folktales have universal themes</u>.
4. The people's hope <u>that they could communicate with the sky god</u> led them to build a high tower in an old Nigerian tale called "Why the Sky Is Far Away."

Exercise 1
Noun clauses are underlined.

used as an appositive and an adjective clause. Invite volunteers to write their sentences on the board. Discuss the sentences and have students determine whether each clause is a noun clause used as an appositive. Have volunteers make suggestions for the revision of incorrect sentences.

APPLY

APPLY IT NOW

Ask students to review their work and to highlight the sentences that include noun clauses used as appositives. Encourage students to explain why a specific clause

is a noun clause and not an adjective clause. Students should demonstrate an understanding of noun clauses used as appositives.

ASSESS

Note which students had difficulty identifying and using noun clauses as appositives. Assign **Practice Book** page 103 for further practice.

WRITING CONNECTION

Use pages 426–427 of the Writing portion of the book.

5. The punishment that people have to plow fields and that the sky is far away was the result of their action.
6. The tale's theme that people will be punished for wasting resources has a lesson for all of us today.
7. The message that people accepting society's values are rewarded is another common theme in African folktales.
8. Qualities that are valued in African tales include wisdom, friendship, love, and heroism.
9. Qualities that are not valued include foolishness and disloyalty.
10. It is a fact that wit and trickery are sometimes rewarded in African tales.
11. Characters that try to trick others are also sometimes fooled or punished, however, as in the Ananse tales.
12. The moral that caution is needed along with good sense is found in West African tales of Zomo the Rabbit trickster.

Exercise 2
Answers will vary.

EXERCISE 2 Complete each sentence with a noun clause used as an appositive.

1. The theme _____ is important in folktales.
2. The saying _____ is important to me.
3. I read a folktale, and I appreciated its message _____.
4. The fact _____ is surprising to me.
5. Did you hear the legend _____?
6. Claudia's story _____ was a big hit around the campfire.
7. Do you believe the story _____.
8. The moral _____ is sometimes forgotten among friends.
9. It was my grandfather's hope _____.
10. The rumor was _____.

APPLY IT NOW

Choose a folktale that you have enjoyed. Write an e-mail recommending the story to a friend. Use at least two noun clauses as appositives.

Sentences • 155

TEACHING OPTIONS

Reteach

On strips of paper, write pairs of sentences, one with a noun clause used as an appositive and the other with an adjective clause. Display the pairs of strips. Invite students to read the strips aloud. Ask students to select the sentence in each pair that contains a noun clause used as an appositive and to put those sentences in a pile. Have students read all the appositive sentences to reinforce the feel and language of noun clauses used as appositives. Sentences for the strips might include the following:

The message that was in the book could be followed by everyone.
(adjective clause)
The message that we all get along is a universal one.
(noun clause as an appositive)

The news that we heard from the principal was surprising.
(adjective clause)
The news that the school would close early was a welcome surprise.
(noun clause as an appositive)

The hope that we all cherished is an optimistic one.
(adjective clause)
The hope that we can have a fresh start is an optimistic one.
(noun clause as an appositive)

Meeting Individual Needs

Intrapersonal Invite students to explain in their journals what students know about adjective clauses and noun clauses used as appositives. Suggest that students conclude their writing with a sentence that includes an appositive. You might supply these sentence starters:

The lesson that _____.

The idea that _____.

OBJECTIVE
- **To identify and use noun clauses as direct objects**

DAILY Maintenance

Assign **Practice Book** page 92, Section 8.9. After students finish,
1. Give immediate feedback.
2. Review concepts as needed.
3. Model the correct answer.

Pages 4–5 of the **Answer Key** contain tips for Daily Maintenance.

WARM-UP

Write on the board the following sentence starters:

I asked how _____.

The girl thought that _____.

She does not know what _____.

Have students in small groups write as many sentences as they can within four minutes. The group with the most sentences wins.

📖 Read from a piece of writing that the class is currently reading. Emphasize the noun clauses as direct objects.

TEACH

Review that a direct object receives the action of the verb. Have volunteers read aloud about noun clauses used as direct objects. Pause after the first two example sentences and discuss the direct objects and the questions they answer. Then have students write on the board their Warm-Up sentences. Challenge students to identify the direct objects.

Discuss the importance of retaining *that* in some sentences. Point out that the fourth example sentence implies that from where I am situated, I can see you studying in the library, but the fifth example sentence implies

that you have made a decision to study in the library.

Remind students that only transitive verbs take direct objects and that this remains true even when the direct object is a clause.

PRACTICE

EXERCISE 1
Remind students that the direct object often appears directly after the verb of the independent clause. Tell students to identify the entire noun clause used as a direct object. When students have finished, have partners exchange papers and compare answers.

EXERCISE 2
Have students remain with their partners from Exercise 1. Encourage partners to decide whether each direct object is a noun or a noun clause. Discuss each sentence, inviting students to explain the reasons for their answers.

EXERCISE 3
Review examples of noun clauses used as subjects, subject complements, appositives, and direct objects. Then point out some common introductory words for noun clauses, such as *that* and *how*. Have students complete this

---

8.9 Noun Clauses as Direct Objects

A noun clause can act as a direct object. Recall that a direct object receives the action of the verb and answers the question *who* or *what* after a verb.

We wondered *how we would raise money for new computers.*
We decided *that we would hold a car wash.*

The introductory word *that* is frequently dropped from a noun clause used as a direct object.

I think *our fund-raising activity was a success.*

When verbs such as *feel, learn, say, see,* and *think* are followed by a noun clause, be careful to retain *that* if omitting it changes the meaning.

I see *you study in the library.*
I see *that you study in the library.*

The words in red in each sentence are noun clauses that serve as the direct object of the verb. How do the meanings of the sentences differ?

Which of these sentences contains a noun clause used as a direct object?

Each student will do *whatever he or she has the time or talent for.*
Each student will do the task *that he or she has the time or talent for.*

In the first sentence, the action of the verb is received by the noun clause *whatever he or she has the time or talent for.* In the second sentence, the noun *task* is the object, and it is followed by the adjective clause *that he or she has the time or talent for.*

EXERCISE 1 Identify the noun clause used as a direct object in each sentence.

1. Our class decided <u>that it wanted to organize a fund-raising project for new computers for classrooms</u>.

2. The class decided <u>whether it would hold a car wash or do some other fund-raising activity</u>.
3. Jo suggested <u>that we make and sell a cookbook</u>.
4. Although the idea wasn't popular at first, the class eventually decided <u>that it was a good idea</u>.
5. Then we discussed <u>how we would make and sell the book</u>.

Exercise 1
Noun clauses are underlined.

156 • Section 8.9

exercise independently. When students have finished, discuss their answers.

APPLY

APPLY IT NOW

Encourage students to write their sentences as an informational poster, telling others about the class activity. Display the posters. Discuss the sentences, encouraging students to identify the noun clauses used as direct objects. Students should demonstrate an understanding of noun clauses used as direct objects.

Grammar in Action. Students should identify the noun clause *what we can do to protect them.* Remind students that the direct object answers the question *who* or *what.*

ASSESS

Note which students had difficulty identifying and using noun clauses as direct objects. Assign **Practice Book** page 104 for further practice.

WRITING CONNECTION

Use pages 428–429 of the Writing portion of the book.

TEACHING OPTIONS

Reteach

Invite students to look through books in the classroom for sentences that have direct objects. Tell students to copy the sentences onto sentence strips. Display the sentence strips and review each sentence. Ask students to sort the sentences into two groups: nouns or pronouns as direct objects and noun clauses as direct objects. Help students distinguish between a noun as a direct object and a noun clause as a direct object. *(A noun may be a single word or a phrase. A noun clause will have an introductory word and a subject and a predicate.)*

Cooperative Learning

Ask small groups to brainstorm a fund-raising idea similar to that discussed in the exercises. Tell students to write sentences explaining their ideas and to include in their sentences noun clauses as direct objects. Suggest that students design posters to help advertise their fund-raising campaigns.

Meeting Individual Needs

Auditory Invite representatives from the groups organized for the Cooperative Learning activity to speak to the class. Have group members read aloud their plans for raising money. Ask the rest of the class to listen closely to each set of plans, focusing on sentences that include noun clauses as direct objects. Have students raise their hands when they hear such a clause. Invite the speaker to repeat the sentence for reinforcement.

Exercise 2
Direct objects are underlined.

1. noun clause
2. noun clause
3. noun clause
4. noun clause
5. noun clause
6. noun
7. noun
8. noun clause
9. noun
10. noun clause
11. noun
12. noun
13. noun clause
14. noun
15. noun clause

Exercise 3
Noun clauses are underlined.

1. appositive
2. subject
3. subject complement
4. subject
5. direct object
6. direct object

EXERCISE 2 Identify the direct object in each sentence. Tell whether the direct object is a noun or a noun clause.

1. We knew that we wanted to collect favorite recipes from as many people as possible.
2. We asked whoever was involved with the school for recipes— parents, teachers, and others in the community.
3. We of course asked that the cafeteria workers submit recipes.
4. We requested whatever were people's very best recipes.
5. We wondered how we should organize the recipes.
6. We received multiple recipes from many people.
7. We got many recipes that were repeats, for example, 10 recipes for zucchini bread.
8. One teacher suggested that we divide our cookbook into sections.
9. So we put the recipes into categories that we labeled Appetizers, Soups, Main Courses, and Desserts.
10. Now we hope that people will buy the printed books for themselves and as gifts.
11. We will use all the money that we collect for computers.
12. Our bills include only the cost of printing the book.
13. Everyone agrees that the project was a lot of hard work.
14. My family has tried out several dishes that were in the book.
15. Now someone has proposed that we have a fund-raising dinner with foods from the recipes.

EXERCISE 3 Identify the noun clause in each sentence. Tell whether the noun clause is used as a direct object, a subject, a subject complement, or an appositive.

1. Keisha's fear that the frame would fall off the wall seemed unreasonable.
2. How such a thing might happen was not clear to us.
3. The fact was that the frame was too heavy.
4. That it wobbled and fell to the floor surprised us.
5. Keisha showed us that the frame was heavier than the nails we used to hold it in place.
6. She suggested that we find anchors to hold up the frame.

APPLY IT NOW

Write a paragraph about a class project in which you participated. Include five noun clauses as direct objects in your writing.

Grammar in Action. Identify the noun clause used as a direct object in the first paragraph in the p. 413 excerpt.

Sentences • 157

OBJECTIVE
- **To identify and use noun clauses as objects of prepositions**

Assign **Practice Book** page 92, Section 8.10. After students finish,
1. Give immediate feedback.
2. Review concepts as needed.
3. Model the correct answer.

Pages 4–5 of the **Answer Key** contain tips for Daily Maintenance.

WARM-UP

Hide pencils throughout the classroom (under a desk, by the trash can, in a box). Instruct students to search for the pencils. When students find a pencil, tell them to write on the board a sentence stating where they found the pencil. (*I found the pencil in a box.*)

📖 Read from a piece of writing that the class is currently reading. Emphasize noun clauses used as objects of prepositions.

TEACH

Ask students what the sentences on the board have in common. Lead students to say that each contains a prepositional phrase. Have volunteers underline the preposition in each phrase and circle the object of each preposition. Point out that in these phrases the object is a noun.

Invite volunteers to read the text aloud. Have students pause every few paragraphs so you can discuss the information. Help students understand that the objects of the prepositions in the example sentences are clauses because they have subjects and predicates. Ask students to identify the subjects and predicates of the clauses. Then have students

write example sentences that contain noun clauses as objects of prepositions.

PRACTICE

EXERCISE 1
Have students reread the example sentences from the text. Emphasize that the adjective clause in the first sentence describes the desert and that the noun clause in the second sentence is the object of a preposition. Challenge students to determine whether each clause in the exercise acts as a noun. Have partners complete this exercise.

EXERCISE 2
Review prepositional phrases and objects of prepositions. Then read aloud example sentences that contain noun clauses as objects of prepositions. Have students complete this exercise independently. Invite volunteers to share their answers.

EXERCISE 3
Review example sentences that contain noun clauses used as subjects, direct objects, appositives, and objects of prepositions. Then have students complete this activity with partners.

8.10 Noun Clauses as Objects of Prepositions

Noun clauses can function as objects of prepositions.

> **We learned** *about desert biomes.*
> **We learned** *about what the characteristics of desert biomes are.*

What is the noun clause in this sentence? How is it used?

> **I am interested in how animals adapt to dry environments.**

The noun clause is *how animals adapt to dry environments.* The entire noun clause is the object of the preposition *in.*

An adjective clause can be confused with a noun clause used as the object of a preposition. An adjective clause describes a noun or pronoun in the independent clause. The introductory word of the adjective clause, usually a relative pronoun, has an antecedent in the independent clause.

> **A desert** *in which temperatures are low* **is called a cold desert.**
> (adjective clause)
> **We studied about** *which animals can survive in the Red Desert.* (noun clause)

In the first sentence, *which* is a relative pronoun. Its antecedent is *desert,* and it acts as the object of the preposition *in.* In the second sentence, *which* introduces the noun clause but has no antecedent in the independent clause.

What is the correct choice of pronoun in this sentence?

> **The vaccine was taken by (whoever whomever) had a chance of contracting the disease.**

You are correct if you said *whoever.* In the noun clause, *whoever* acts as the subject of the verb *had.* The form of the pronoun is determined by its role in the subordinate clause.

EXERCISE 1 Identify each noun clause used as the object of a preposition. Not all sentences have such a clause.

1. Many species of animals make their homes in <u>what is sometimes referred to as the American Serengeti</u>.
2. Wyoming's Red Desert covers more than five million acres.
3. It is a basin with <u>what are considered bad winters</u>.
4. Surrounding the basin are mountains with rugged gaps where the wind whistles.

Exercise 1
Noun clauses are underlined.

APPLY

APPLY IT NOW

Have students consider a job they might like to have that could make a positive contribution to society. Encourage students write their ideas in their notebooks. Suggest that students underline the noun clauses. As you review students' work, help them describe the function of each noun clause they've included: subject, direct object, object of a preposition, or appositive. Students should demonstrate an understanding of noun clauses used as objects of prepositions.

ASSESS

Note which students had difficulty identifying and using noun clauses as objects of prepositions. Assign **Practice Book** page 105 for further practice.

WRITING CONNECTION

Use pages 430–431 of the Writing portion of the book.

TEACHING OPTIONS

Reteach

Display a poster, an illustration, or a photograph. Ask students to describe the image, using sentences that include noun clauses as objects of prepositions. Write students' sentences on the board to analyze as a class. For example:

> **I see a tall building with what seem to be gargoyles at the top.**

> **The gargoyles are peering over what looks like the city of Paris.**

Have students copy the sentences into their notebooks as examples of the correct use of noun clauses as objects of prepositions.

English-Language Learners

To help students recognize how noun clauses are used as objects of prepositions, write the following on the board:

> **I throw the ball to you.**

Explain that *to you* is a prepositional phrase, *to* is the preposition, and *you* is the object of the preposition. Rewrite the sentence so that the object of the preposition is a noun clause:

> **I throw the ball with <u>what many consider perfect precision</u>.**

> **I throw the ball near <u>whichever of the bases is covered</u>.**

Underline each noun clause and point out how it differs from a simple noun or pronoun. Invite students to circle the simple subject and simple predicate of each clause (*many consider, whichever is*).

Diagram It!

To practice noun clauses in the context of diagramming, turn to Section 11.10.

---

5. There are steppes that antelope graze on.
6. Scientists explain about <u>how the antelope migrate hundreds of miles each spring</u>.
7. The animals move to <u>where they can find food</u>.
8. Horned toads and rattlesnakes make their homes in <u>what is an unusual environment for reptiles</u>.
9. Reptiles are usually found where climates are warmer.
10. Nevertheless, the Red Desert is an area that needs protection.

Exercise 2
Answers will vary.

EXERCISE 2 Complete each sentence with an appropriate noun clause used as the object of a preposition.

1. Jesse will give her tickets to _____.
2. We could not see the stage from _____.
3. There was a disagreement about _____.
4. We should make use of _____.

Exercise 3
Noun clauses are underlined.
1. object of a preposition
2. subject
3. direct object
4. subject
5. subject
6. direct object
7. subject
8. direct object
9. subject
10. appositive

EXERCISE 3 Identify the noun clause in each sentence. Tell if the noun clause is the subject, an appositive, the direct object, or the object of a preposition.

1. Jonas Salk was interested in <u>how polio could be prevented</u>.
2. <u>That the disease had been around since ancient times</u> was well documented.
3. Salk believed <u>that his vaccine could prevent it</u>.
4. <u>Whoever volunteered to do so</u> took part in the tests.
5. <u>That he tried it on his own family early on</u> is remarkable.
6. He found <u>that none of them got sick</u>.
7. <u>That his vaccine was a success</u> became known rather quickly.
8. In 1954 the U.S. government decided <u>that all school children should be inoculated</u>.
9. <u>That the disease is incurable</u> is still true.
10. The fact <u>that polio is now rare</u> is due primarily to Jonas Salk.

Jonas Salk standing in front of the Salk Institute in La Jolla, California

Microscopic view of the polio virus

APPLY IT NOW

Write five sentences about a job that interests you. Use a noun clause as a subject, a direct object, and the object of a preposition at least once each.

Sentences • 159

OBJECTIVE

- **To identify and write simple, compound, and complex sentences**

 **Maintenance**

Assign **Practice Book** page 92, Section 8.11. After students finish,
1. Give immediate feedback.
2. Review concepts as needed.
3. Model the correct answer.

Pages 4–5 of the **Answer Key** contain tips for Daily Maintenance.

WARM-UP

Place a line of tape down the middle of the classroom. Designate one side as Independent and the other as Dependent. Read a variety of simple, compound, and complex sentences. Tell students that if they think the sentence contains a dependent clause, they should stand on the dependent side of the line. Have students who stand on the wrong side sit down. Repeat as time permits.

Read from a piece of writing that the class is currently reading. Emphasize the simple, compound, and complex sentences.

TEACH

Write the following sentence on the board:

A new diner is opening at the mall.

Ask students to identify the complete subject (*A new diner*) and the complete predicate (*is opening at the mall*). Explain that because this sentence has only one independent clause, it is a simple sentence. Invite students to add another independent or another dependent clause to the sentence. Write on the board students' sentences. Help them recognize which sentences have two independent clauses and which have an independent clause and a dependent clause.

Invite volunteers to read aloud about simple, compound, and complex sentences. Direct students to match these names to the sentences on the board. Ask students to explain the differences between compound and complex sentences.

Tell students that sentences which have two independent clauses and a dependent clause are called compound-complex. Encourage volunteers to write examples on the board.

PRACTICE

EXERCISE 1

Remind students that if a sentence has two sets of subjects and predicates, students must determine whether the clauses are independent or dependent. Have partners complete this exercise.

EXERCISE 2

Tell students that the most important of the two sentences should remain an independent clause. If students determine that the sentences are of equal importance, tell students they should write a compound sentence.

8.11 Simple, Compound, and Complex Sentences

Sentences can be classified according to their structure. In the examples below, subjects are in red and verbs are underlined.

A **simple sentence** is a single independent clause. It has a subject and a predicate, either or both of which can be compound.

> *Chicago* <u>borders</u> Lake Michigan.
> *Willis Tower* and the *John Hancock Center* <u>are</u> among the city's tall buildings.
> Many *Chicagoans* <u>swim</u> and <u>sunbathe</u> along Lake Michigan.

A **compound sentence** contains two or more independent clauses. The independent clauses in compound sentences are commonly connected in one of three ways: (1) by a comma and one of the coordinating conjunctions *and, or, but, nor, so,* or *yet;* (2) by a semicolon; or (3) by a semicolon followed by an adverb such as *therefore, however,* or *nevertheless* and a comma.

> *Chicago* <u>boasts</u> many old skyscrapers, but *it* also <u>has</u> many modern ones.
> *Chicago* <u>was</u> on the main railroad lines; consequently, *its industries* <u>grew</u> rapidly in the mid-1800s.

A **complex sentence** has one independent clause and at least one dependent clause, which may function as an adjective, an adverb, or a noun.

> Because *Chicago* <u>welcomes</u> immigrants from all over the world, *it* boasts many ethnic restaurants. (adverb clause *Because Chicago welcomes immigrants from all over the world*)
> The *city,* which <u>burned</u> in a fire in 1871, <u>was</u> quickly rebuilt. (adjective clause *which burned in a fire in 1871*)
> Originally, many *people* <u>claimed</u> that the *fire* <u>was caused</u> by a cow. (noun clause *that the fire was caused by a cow*)

The Chicago Water Tower, built in 1869 by architect William W. Boyington

EXERCISE 1 Tell whether each sentence is simple, compound, or complex.

1. The Chicago River system is 156 miles long.
2. The river was originally only 2 feet deep, but now it has been dug to a depth of 26 feet.

Exercise 1
1. simple
2. compound
3. complex
4. compound
5. compound
6. complex
7. simple
8. compound
9. complex
10. simple

EXERCISE 3

Have partners create a two-column chart in which they can record their answers, one column for independent clauses and the other for dependent clauses. Have partners circle the subjects and underline the verbs in the clauses. Ask volunteers to record their answers on a class chart, to which the rest of the class can compare their answers.

APPLY

APPLY IT NOW

Review how to differentiate among simple, compound, and complex sentences. Have volunteers read aloud their sentences. Students should demonstrate an understanding of simple, compound, and complex sentences.

ASSESS

Note which students had difficulty identifying simple, compound, and complex sentences. Assign **Practice Book** page 106 for further practice.

WRITING CONNECTION

Use pages 432–433 of the Writing portion of the book.

Reteach

Tell students that they are going to have a scavenger hunt. Choose a book that the class is reading. Have students go to the same page. Present them with a clue to a specific sentence on the page. For example:

> **I am looking at paragraph 3.**
> **I see a complex sentence.**
> **It has a noun clause used as the object of a preposition. Find the sentence.**

Encourage a volunteer to read the sentence aloud. Ask him or her to tell how the sentence matches your description. Continue with other pages and other types of sentences. You might invite students to choose sentences for you and their classmates to find.

Meeting Individual Needs

Auditory Encourage small groups to record conversations. Have students replay the conversation, stopping it after each sentence to indicate whether it is a simple, compound, or complex sentence. Ask students to identify the independent and dependent clauses in the compound and complex sentences and to note any compound subjects or compound predicates.

Diagram It!

To practice compound sentences in the context of diagramming, turn to Section 11.3.

---

3. In the 19th century, the river was a source of disease because it was so polluted.
4. The river flowed into Lake Michigan, and the lake was the source of water for the city of Chicago.
5. In 1900 sanitary engineers reversed the flow of the river; therefore, it now runs backward, out of Lake Michigan.
6. Although cities downriver complained, this feat reduced the number of epidemics in the Chicago metropolitan area.
7. At one time Chicago had 52 movable bridges across the river.
8. There are only 45 of those bridges left, but that is still the highest number of any city in the world.
9. Chicago is like a museum of movable bridges because it has so many different styles, including swing bridges and lift bridges.
10. On St. Patrick's Day the river is dyed green in celebration.

Heron

Exercise 2
Answers will vary.

EXERCISE 2 Combine each pair of simple sentences into one compound sentence.

1. A lake, like Lake Michigan, is a large body of standing water. A pond is a small body of standing water.
2. In Chicago, summer days are warm. Winters are very cold.
3. The Chicago Cubs play baseball in the National League. The Chicago White Sox play in the American League.
4. Chicago has warm, beautiful summers. Chicago has very cold, windy winters.

Exercise 3
Independent clauses are underlined. Dependent clauses are listed below.

1. Dependent: although other kinds also live there
2. Dependent: that have been seen along the banks
3. Both are independent clauses.
4. Dependent: that new walkways and riverside restaurants will attract visitors to the riverbanks
5. Both are independent clauses.

EXERCISE 3 Identify the clauses in each sentence and tell whether they are dependent or independent.

1. Carp, goldfish, catfish, and sunfish are the main fish species in the Chicago River, although other kinds also live there.
2. Birds that have been seen along the banks include herons, kingfishers, warblers, and ducks.
3. The river had been too polluted for recreational use, but now boaters paddle throughout its length.
4. The city hopes that new walkways and riverside restaurants will attract visitors to the riverbanks.
5. Beaver and muskrat live in the river, and even mink have been seen there.

APPLY IT NOW

Write two examples each of simple, compound, and complex sentences. Identify each type of sentence, circle the subjects, and underline the verbs, including those within dependent clauses.

Sentences • 161

Sentence Review

ASSESS

Use the Sentence Review as homework, as a practice test, or as an informal assessment. Following are some options for use.

Homework

You may wish to assign one group the odd items and another group the even items. When you next meet, review the correct answers as a group. Be sure to model how to arrive at the correct answer.

Practice Test

Use the Sentence Review as a diagnostic tool. Assign the entire review or only specific sections. After students have finished, identify which concepts require more attention. Reteach concepts as necessary.

Sentence Review

8.1
Complete subjects are underlined once. Complete predicates are underlined twice.

1. question mark
2. (You), period
3. question mark
4. period
5. period

8.2
6. before daybreak, prepositional, adverb
7. Watching through binoculars, participial, adjective
8. to call for assistance, infinitive, adjective
9. into the water, prepositional, adverb
10. Reaching safety, participial, adjective

8.1 Add the correct end punctuation to each sentence. Then identify the complete subject and complete predicate.

1. Do you know what to do in case of severe weather
2. Go to the basement, please
3. What are the warning signs of severe weather
4. Funnel clouds develop from the colliding of hot and cold air
5. Destructive tornados occur frequently in spring

8.2 Identify the adjective phrase or adverb phrases in these sentences. Tell whether each is prepositional, participial, or infinitive.

6. They sailed before daybreak.
7. Watching through binoculars, the Coast Guard captain spotted a boat.
8. The captain's efforts to call for assistance were successful.
9. The crew lowered lifeboats into the water.
10. Reaching safety, the crew was relieved.

8.3 Identify the adjective clause in each sentence and the noun or pronoun that the adjective clause describes.

11. Willis Tower, which is in Chicago, is a world-famous skyscraper.
12. Wacker Drive is the street where it is located.
13. The views from the buildings that overlook Lake Michigan are spectacular.

14. A tourist, who was from China, viewed the distant skyline through a high-powered telescope.
15. The floor where visitors can see the entire city is called the Skydeck.

8.4 Identify the adjective clause in each sentence. Tell whether the adjective clause is restrictive or nonrestrictive. Add commas where necessary.

16. His garden which was at the back of the lot contained a wide variety of vegetables.
17. The beans that did so well last year are not available.
18. Tomatoes, strawberries, and rhubarb are plants that grow hardily.
19. Mulch is organic material that has decomposed.
20. Weeding which is my least favorite gardening task must be done frequently.

8.5 Identify the adverb clause in each sentence and each subordinate conjunction.

21. Whenever you want to leave, I will be ready.
22. As soon as she puts on her coat, we can leave.
23. Make certain that you have your keys before we lock the door.
24. Dad did the grocery shopping while Mom ran errands.
25. We'll buy peaches if they look ripe.

8.3
11. which is in Chicago, Willis Tower
12. where it is located, street
13. that overlook Lake Michigan, buildings
14. who was from China, tourist
15. where visitors can see the entire city, floor

8.4
16. nonrestrictive—His garden, which was at the back of the lot, contained a wide variety of vegetables.
17. restrictive
18. restrictive
19. restrictive
20. nonrestrictive—Weeding, which is my least favorite gardening task, must be done frequently.

8.5
Adverb clauses are underlined.
21. Whenever
22. As soon as
23. before
24. while
25. if

Informal Assessment

Use the review as preparation for the formal assessment. Count the review as a portion of the grade. Have students work to find the correct answers and use their corrected review as a study guide for the formal assessment.

WRITING CONNECTION

Use pages 434–435 of the Writing portion of the book.

Putting It All Together

Ask students to complete the following exercises:

- Choose an article from a newspaper or a magazine. Underline the complete subjects and circle the complete predicates.

- Choose a topic such as your favorite movie, book, or musician and write three paragraphs about it. Make sure you use at least 10 clauses (adjective, adverb, or noun). Underline each clause and label what type of clause it is. If the clause is a noun clause, identify its function (subject, subject complement, appositive, direct object, or object of a preposition).

- Think about the last sporting event or school function you watched. Write two paragraphs describing it. Make sure your writing includes at least two simple, two compound, and two complex sentences. Label each sentence as simple, compound, or complex.

8.7
Noun clauses used as complements are underlined.
31. advice
32. belief
33. thought
34. what
35. fact

8.9
Direct objects are underlined.
40. noun clause
41. noun clause
42. noun
43. noun clause

8.11
48. simple
49. compound
50. complex
51. complex

8.6 Identify the noun clause used as the subject in each sentence.

26. Whoever alerted the fire-fighters will receive a commendation.

27. That they were able to extinguish the fire relieved us.

28. That residents were still inside the building was our worry.

29. How everyone escaped was a miracle.

30. Whether they will be able to go back inside is yet to be decided.

8.7 Identify the noun clause used as a complement in each sentence. Name the subject it describes.

31. The doctor's advice was that he exercise and watch his diet.

32. The doctor's belief is that walking is the best exercise.

33. The thought is that walking at least 10,000 steps a day is beneficial.

34. What I wonder is how people count their steps.

35. The fact is that a pedometer makes it easy to count them.

8.8 Identify the noun clause used as an appositive in each sentence.

36. It is a fact that kindness is contagious.

37. The theme that good defeats evil is common in literature and movies.

38. The advice, how to avoid insect bites, was quite timely.

39. The saying that old friends and new friends are special in different ways is probably true.

8.9 Identify the direct object in each sentence. Tell whether it is a noun or a noun clause.

40. Jasmine wondered how she would get to school on time.

41. She knew that she was late.

42. She gave excuses to explain her lateness.

43. Jasmine promised that she would not dawdle anymore.

8.10 Identify the noun clause used as the object of a preposition in each sentence.

44. We learned about how long the life of a fruit fly is.

45. There are stages through which a fruit fly must go.

46. Our group reported on how the various changes take place.

47. I am interested in what are the possible benefits from fruit flies.

8.11 Tell whether each sentence is simple, compound, or complex.

48. Most tulips bloom in the spring.

49. The flower originated in Holland, but it is extremely popular in the United States.

50. Because tulips must be exposed to cold in order to blossom, gardeners plant their bulbs in the fall.

51. Tulips, which are available in many colors, make wonderful flower arrangements.

Tech Tip Go to www.voyagesinenglish.com for more activities.

Sentences • 163

TechTip Encourage students to further review sentences, using the additional practice and games at www.voyagesinenglish.com.

www.voyagesinenglish.com • Sentences • 163

Sentence Challenge

ASSESS

Encourage students to read the selection twice before answering the questions independently. If students have difficulty with any questions, remind them that they should refer to the section that teaches the skill. This activity can be completed by individuals, by small groups, or by the class as a whole.

After you have reviewed sentences, administer the Section 8 Assessment on pages 21–24 in the **Assessment Book,** or create a customized test with the optional **Test Generator CD.**

You may also wish to administer the Sections 7–8 Summative Assessment on pages 39–40 of the **Assessment Book.** This test is also available on the optional **Test Generator CD.**

WRITING CONNECTION

Use pages 436–437 of the Writing portion of the book.

Students can complete a formal persuasive essay using the Writer's Workshop on pages 438–449.

Sentence Challenge

Read the selection and then answer the questions.

1. New Year's celebrations vary around the world, and they even occur at different times. 2. Still, there are some similarities among the many customs.

3. One way to celebrate the new year is with fireworks. 4. In the past the belief that the noise of fireworks scared off evil spirits was a reason for their use. 5. Now although the fireworks are still part of the celebrations, people seem to use them more for their visual entertainment aspects.

6. What people eat on New Year's is also important. 7. In many places people eat foods that are sweet. 8. Why do they do this? 9. The reason is that they want a "sweet," or good, new year. 10. People in Israel, for example, dip apples into honey. 11. Sometimes foods that are eaten symbolize hoped-for wealth. 12. People in many places eat lentils, which look like tiny coins. 13. In other places people eat cabbage because it looks like paper money. 14. Others eat round foods, such as doughnuts, that symbolize the cycle of life.

15. Think about how and when your family and culture celebrate the new year. 16. Whatever you do, have a happy new year!

1. Is sentence 1 a simple, compound, or complex sentence?
2. Identify the infinitive phrase in sentence 3. Is it used as an adjective or as an adverb?
3. What is the noun clause in sentence 4? How is it used?
4. Is sentence 5 a simple, compound, or complex sentence?
5. Find the dependent clause in sentence 7. How is it used?
6. What is the noun clause in sentence 9? How is it used?
7. Identify the simple and complete subjects and simple and complete predicates in sentence 10.
8. Is sentence 11 a simple, compound, or complex sentence?
9. Find the adjective clause in sentence 12. Is it restrictive or nonrestrictive?
10. What is the dependent clause in sentence 13? How is it used?
11. Is sentence 15 a simple, compound, or complex sentence?
12. Find any sentences that are interrogative, imperative, or exclamatory in the selection.

Sentence Challenge
1. compound
2. to celebrate the new year; adjective
3. that the noise of fireworks scared off evil spirits; as an appositive
4. complex
5. that are sweet; as an adjective clause
6. that they want a "sweet," or good, new year; as a subject complement
7. People, People in Israel; dip, dip apples into honey
8. complex
9. which look like tiny coins; nonrestrictive
10. because it looks like paper money; as an adverb clause
11. simple
12. interrogative: sentence 8, imperative: sentence 15, exclamatory: sentence 16

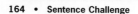

164 • Sentence Challenge

SECTION FOCUS
- **Coordinating conjunctions**
- **Correlative conjunctions**
- **Conjunctive adverbs**
- **Subordinate conjunctions**
- **Troublesome conjunctions**
- **Interjections**

Conjunctions and Interjections

SUPPORT MATERIALS

Practice Book
Daily Maintenance, pages 107–108
Grammar, pages 109–116

Assessment Book
Section 9 Assessment,
    pages 25–26

Test Generator CD

Writing Chapter 7,
    Creative Writing

Customizable Lesson Plans
www.voyagesinenglish.com

CONNECT WITH LITERATURE

📖 Consider using the following titles throughout the section to illustrate the grammar concept:

*Find Your Function at Conjunction
    Junction* by Pamela Hall
If You Were a Conjunction
    by Nancy Loween
*Just Me and 6,000 Rats: A Tale of
    Conjunctions* by Rick Walton

GRAMMAR FOR GROWN-UPS

Understanding Conjunctions and Interjections

A **conjunction** is a word used to connect words, phrases, or clauses in a sentence. Conjunctions are usually small words that pack a lot of power. They make sentences sound better and help to vary sentence structure.

Coordinating conjunctions join words or groups of words that are similar. The coordinating conjunctions are *and, but, or, nor, so,* and *yet*.

> **Don't forget the ball** *and* **glove.**

> **I like baseball,** *but* **I dislike soccer.**

Correlative conjunctions are used in pairs to connect words or groups of words that have equal importance in a sentence.

> *Neither* **my sister** *nor* **my brother finished the dishes.**

Conjunctive adverbs are used to connect independent clauses and are always preceded by a semicolon and followed by a comma.

> **The dinner was delicious**; *however,* **someone has to do the dishes.**

A **subordinate conjunction** joins an independent clause and a dependent clause and indicates the relationship between the two clauses.

> *Before* **I go to bed, I brush my teeth.**

An **interjection** is a word or phrase that expresses a strong or sudden emotion.

> *Hooray!*   *Yikes!*   *Wow!*   *Ugh!*

An interjection is usually set off by an exclamation point, but it can also be part of a sentence where it is generally set off by a comma.

> *Bravo!* **That was an excellent performance.**

> *Oh,* **we almost won the game!**

> ❝Only in grammar
> can you be more than perfect.❞
>
> —William Safire

COMMON ERRORS

Confusing Conjunctions

Some conjunctions, such as *without* and *unless*, and *like*, *as if*, and *as*, are frequently misused or confused.

ERROR: I cannot take the dog for a walk without I put on his leash.
CORRECT: I cannot take the dog for a walk unless I put on his leash.

ERROR: My coach acted like the win was not a big deal.
CORRECT: My coach acted as if the win was not a big deal.

Make sure students understand that *without* and *like* are prepositions that introduce prepositional phrases and that *unless* and *as if* are subordinate conjunctions.

SENTENCE DIAGRAMMING

You may wish to teach conjunctions and interjections in the context of diagramming. Review these examples. Then refer to the Diagramming section or look for Diagram It! features in the Conjunctions and Interjections section.

I ran fast, but I was late.

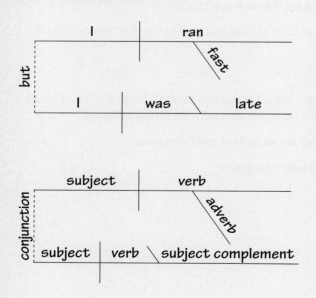

ASK AN EXPERT

Real Situations, Real Solutions

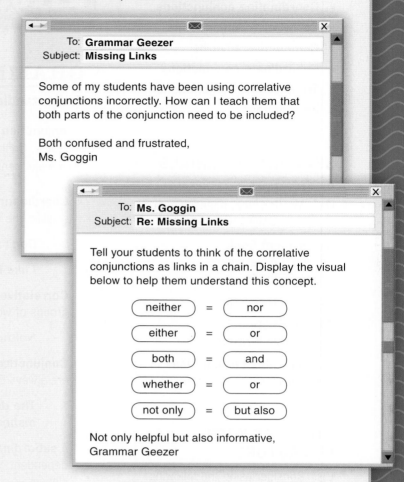

To: **Grammar Geezer**
Subject: **Missing Links**

Some of my students have been using correlative conjunctions incorrectly. How can I teach them that both parts of the conjunction need to be included?

Both confused and frustrated,
Ms. Goggin

To: **Ms. Goggin**
Subject: **Re: Missing Links**

Tell your students to think of the correlative conjunctions as links in a chain. Display the visual below to help them understand this concept.

neither	=	nor
either	=	or
both	=	and
whether	=	or
not only	=	but also

Not only helpful but also informative,
Grammar Geezer

Yikes! I almost forgot one.

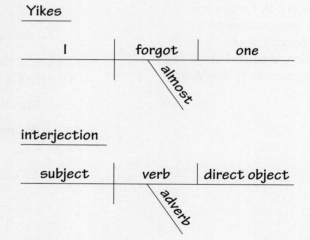

Conjunctions and Interjections

9.1 Coordinating Conjunctions

OBJECTIVES

- To identify and use coordinating conjunctions
- To identify the words, phrases, and clauses joined by coordinating conjunctions

 **Maintenance**

Assign **Practice Book** page 107, Section 9.1. After students finish,
1. Give immediate feedback.
2. Review concepts as needed.
3. Model the correct answer.

Pages 4–5 of the **Answer Key** contain tips for Daily Maintenance.

WARM-UP

Write on the board a chart with the following column headings: *Place, +, −*. Brainstorm a list of places and positive and negative adjectives that describe each place *(beach/fun/hot, movie theater/entertaining/crowded)*. Then distribute note cards on which you have written *and, but, or, so,* and *yet*. Write on the board the following sentence formulas:

What's _____ (place) like?

_____ (place) is _____ (+ −),
_____ (note card word) it is also _____ (+ −).

Have students fill in the blanks, using the note cards and information from the chart.

📖 Read from a piece of writing that the class is currently reading. Emphasize the coordinating conjunctions.

TEACH

Invite several volunteers to write on the board their Warm-Up sentences. Help students analyze the sentences. Lead them to confirm that the words on the note cards join words, phrases, or clauses that are similar. Tell students these words are called coordinating conjunctions.

Invite volunteers to read aloud about coordinating conjunctions. Have the volunteers pause after each example sentence. Ask students to identify the words, phrases, and clauses that the conjunctions join.

PRACTICE

EXERCISE 1
Review that words, phrases, and clauses can be connected by coordinating conjunctions. Have students complete this exercise independently. Instruct students to exchange papers with partners and to compare answers. Tell students to discuss any discrepancies. Review the sentences with the class.

EXERCISE 2
Remind students that coordinating conjunctions connect words, phrases, and clauses that are parallel in construction. Have students complete this activity independently. Then assign each completed sentence to three students. Ask them to write their sentences on the board. Have students compare the different sentence completions for each item.

9.1 Coordinating Conjunctions

A **conjunction** is a word used to connect words or groups of words. The four types of connectors are coordinating conjunctions, correlative conjunctions, conjunctive adverbs, and subordinate conjunctions.

A **coordinating conjunction** joins words or groups of words that are similar. The coordinating conjunctions are *and, but, or, nor, so,* and *yet.* Coordinating conjunctions connect words and phrases.

> Adventurers sought gold *or* glory. (words)
> They searched in northern South America *and* along the Amazon River for the legendary city of El Dorado. (prepositional phrases)
> They wanted to find the city *and* to gain its wealth. (infinitive phrases)

Coordinating conjunctions can also connect independent clauses to form compound sentences.

> No one found that city, *yet* the search continued.
> Francisco Coronado searched for the fabled Seven Cities, *and* Ponce de Leon searched for the Fountain of Youth.

Can you identify what is connected in these examples?

> The Seven Cities were supposedly rich in gold and in jewels.
> Coronado searched for the cities in what is present-day New Mexico, but he never found great riches.

In the first example, the conjunction connects prepositional phrases. In the second example, the conjunction connects clauses.

EXERCISE 1 Identify the coordinating conjunction in each sentence. Tell the words, phrases, or clauses that the conjunction connects.

1. Explorers and adventurers searched for the golden city of El Dorado.
2. People of many nations heard and believed tales of this rich city.
3. The dream of a city of gold was intriguing, and the search for it was undertaken by many.
4. Explorers searched long but fruitlessly for El Dorado.
5. *El Dorado* means "the gilded one," and it supposedly referred to the king of this gold-rich city.
6. Every year in a special ceremony, the king supposedly appeared, covered with ointments and sprinkled with gold dust.
7. He then bathed and washed off the gold in a lake.

Exercise 1

Conjunctions are underlined twice. The words, phrases, or clauses the conjunctions connect are underlined once.

APPLY IT NOW
Suggest that students write each coordinating conjunction on the left side of a sheet of paper, leaving space after each word in which to write sentences. After students have written a sentence for each conjunction, encourage them to tell whether words, phrases, or clauses are joined by the conjunctions. Students should demonstrate an understanding of coordinating conjunctions.

Note which students had difficulty identifying and using coordinating conjunctions. Assign **Practice Book** page 109 for further practice.

WRITING CONNECTION
Use pages 450–451 of the Writing portion of the book. Be sure to point out conjunctions and interjections in the literature excerpt and the student model.

Reteach
Have students find an article in a magazine, newspaper, nonfiction book, or novel that uses coordinating conjunctions. Tell students to underline the sentences that have coordinating conjunctions and to circle the coordinating conjunctions. Have students tally the various conjunctions and compare numbers with the other students. Then invite volunteers to write their sentences on the board.

English-Language Learners
Write on the board one sentence for each coordinating conjunction. Ask students to circle the conjunctions and locate the words, phrases, or clauses that are joined by the conjunctions. Ask students to repeat the words or word groups with the conjunction (*apples and oranges; on the field or on the court; I see you, and you see me*). Make sure students can recognize not only the conjunction but also the ideas that each conjunction connects.

Meeting Individual Needs
Auditory Give each student six note cards. Instruct students to write each conjunction on a separate card. Tell them to listen closely for one class period and to hold up the card for a conjunction each time they hear it used in everyday speech. Review the usage of conjunctions and ask students to draw conclusions about how often conjunctions are used in everyday speech.

---

8. From a boat he threw gold and jade objects into the lake as offerings to the gods.

9. El Dorado now refers to a place of fabulous wealth or to the land of one's dreams.

10. This fabulous quest for El Dorado went on primarily during the 16th and 17th centuries.

11. Some scholars believe a city like El Dorado probably existed but it didn't have the great wealth of the legends.

12. Great works of literature like *Paradise Lost* by John Milton and *Candide* by Voltaire reference El Dorado.

13. The name of El Dorado has been given to many cities in Latin America and to one county in the state of California.

14. One explorer who tried to search for the great city was Sir Walter Raleigh, yet he was unsuccessful in his task.

15. Other great mythical cities besides El Dorado were said to have existed, but they were never found by the explorers who looked for them.

16. Many explorers were unsuccessful in their quest to find El Dorado, but they helped discover many parts of the Americas we now know today.

Sir Walter Raleigh
(1552–1618)

Exercise 2
Possible answers:
1. and the play began
2. or on the dock
3. and difficult
4. or near the door
5. and I watched the ripples it made
6. and steadily
7. and the money was found
8. and I bought a book by my favorite author
9. or would you rather eat pizza
10. and slowly

EXERCISE 2 Complete each sentence with a coordinating conjunction and an appropriate word, phrase, or clause as indicated.

1. The curtain rose, _____. (clause)

2. Will you meet me in the park _____? (phrase)

3. Learning the new game was slow _____. (word)

4. Should I sit near the window _____? (phrase)

5. I tossed the stone into the water, _____. (clause)

6. We looked for the missing contact lens slowly _____. (word)

7. We searched meticulously, _____. (clause)

8. I walked into the bookstore, _____. (clause)

9. Would you rather eat Chinese food for dinner, _____? (phrase)

10. Mother stirred the beef stew on the stove carefully _____. (word)

APPLY IT NOW
Choose a topic you enjoy, such as sports, movies, or TV. Write a sentence using each coordinating conjunction. Include examples of words, phrases, and clauses connected by the conjunctions.

Conjunctions • 167

9.2 Correlative Conjunctions

OBJECTIVES
- **To identify and use correlative conjunctions**
- **To identify the words, phrases, and clauses joined by correlative conjunctions**

 **Maintenance**

Assign **Practice Book** page 107, Section 9.2. After students finish,
1. Give immediate feedback.
2. Review concepts as needed.
3. Model the correct answer.

Pages 4–5 of the **Answer Key** contain tips for Daily Maintenance.

WARM-UP

Write the following words on the board: *both, either, neither.* Tell students to write one sentence that begins with each word.

📖 Read from a piece of writing that the class is currently reading. Emphasize the correlative conjunctions.

TEACH

Invite volunteers to write their sentences on the board and to underline the conjunctions. Be sure students underline *and, or,* and *nor.* Discuss the relationship between the words connected by the conjunctions. Ask students if there are any other words in the sentences that emphasize the relationship between these words. Lead students to identify *both, either,* and *neither.* Underline these words in the sentences on the board.

Have a volunteer read aloud the first paragraph and first pair of example sentences. Ask a volunteer to explain the difference between the sentences. Direct another student to continue reading the text aloud. Challenge students to suggest a sentence for each pair of correlative conjunctions.

PRACTICE

EXERCISE 1
Review the correlative conjunctions. Remind students that correlative conjunctions are used in pairs, so in this exercise they must look for pairs of conjunctions. Have students exchange papers with partners to compare responses.

EXERCISE 2
Advise students that some sentences have coordinating conjunctions instead of correlative conjunctions. Encourage students to explain the difference between the two. *(Coordinating conjunctions are single words. Correlative conjunctions are used in pairs.)* Have students work with partners to identify the correlative conjunctions.

EXERCISE 3
Ask students to suggest strategies for supplying the missing conjunctions. Challenge students to complete the exercise independently. After students have finished, invite them to provide an appropriate conjunction for each sentence. Ask students to tell why they chose specific conjunctions.

9.2 Correlative Conjunctions

Correlative conjunctions are conjunctions that are used in pairs to connect words or groups of words that have equal importance in a sentence. The parts of the sentence that are connected should have parallel structure. Correlative conjunctions emphasize the relationship between the connected words.

> Lemonade *or* juice is a good drink for a picnic.
> *Either* lemonade *or* juice is a good drink for a picnic.

In the first sentence, the coordinating conjunction *or* joins two nouns, *lemonade* and *juice.* In the second sentence, the pair of conjunctions *either* and *or* also connects *lemonade* and *juice* but gives greater emphasis to the relationship.

These are the most commonly used correlative conjunctions:

both . . . and	not only . . . but also
either . . . or	whether . . . or
neither . . . nor	

Correlative conjunctions generally appear immediately in front of the words or phrases that are connected.

> *Neither* Sue *nor* Linda is on the picnic committee.
> *Whether* young *or* old, all students are welcome.
> Alexa is bringing *not only* fruit *but also* veggies.
> You can leave the food *either* on the table *or* in the refrigerator.

EXERCISE 1 Identify the correlative conjunctions in each sentence.

1. <u>Both</u> Lisa <u>and</u> I are on the class picnic committee.
2. We are planning <u>not only</u> the food <u>but also</u> the games.
3. <u>Both</u> my father <u>and</u> my mother have volunteered to help us.
4. <u>Whether</u> rain <u>or</u> shine, the picnic will be held.
5. In case of rain, we can use <u>either</u> the school basement <u>or</u> the gym.
6. <u>Neither</u> the principal <u>nor</u> the assistant principal can attend.
7. <u>Both</u> Mr. Alvarez <u>and</u> Mrs. Marini are helping the committee.
8. The picnic will be held on a school day— <u>either</u> on a Thursday <u>or</u> on a Friday.
9. <u>Whether</u> we play dodgeball <u>or</u> have relay races, we will have a good time.

Exercise 1
Correlative conjunctions are underlined.

APPLY

APPLY IT NOW

Suggest that students first list the correlative conjunctions at the top of their papers. Encourage students to use each set of correlative conjunctions at least once in their writing. Have students point out both parts of each set and the words, phrases, or clauses that are connected. Students should demonstrate an understanding of correlative conjunctions.

TechTip Point out that spreadsheets are an excellent tool with many benefits. You may wish to prepare a short tip sheet for students who are not familiar with spreadsheet software.

ASSESS

Note which students had difficulty using correlative conjunctions. Assign **Practice Book** page 110 for further practice.

WRITING CONNECTION

Use pages 452–453 of the Writing portion of the book.

Exercise 2

1. either . . . or
2. both . . . and
3. No correlative conjunctions
4. No correlative conjunctions
5. either . . . or
6. Neither . . . nor
7. both . . . and
8. not only. . . . but also
9. Either . . . or
10. No correlative conjunctions
11. both . . . and

EXERCISE 2 Identify the correlative conjunctions in these sentences. Not every sentence contains correlative conjunctions.

1. We asked for volunteers to bring either ice or charcoal.
2. Jason has signed up to bring both hot dogs and hamburgers.
3. Several parents and teachers will bring grills from home.
4. We will grill beef burgers, turkey burgers, and veggie burgers.
5. Most students are preparing either salads or desserts.
6. Neither ice cream nor milk is on the menu this year because many of our classmates are allergic to dairy products.
7. There will be both rides and races for fun.
8. We will have not only a trampoline but also a slide.
9. Either Jane's dad or my dad will be supervising the games.
10. Jessica or Luis will be in charge of obtaining prizes.
11. We are collecting money to pay for both the prizes and the drinks.

Exercise 3

Possible answers:
1. Both
2. but
3. Not only . . . but also
4. both
5. either
6. either . . . or
7. both
8. Both . . . and
9. Whether . . . or

EXERCISE 3 Add correlative or coordinating conjunctions to complete these sentences.

1. _____ food and drink will be available at our picnic.
2. Most of the food will be donated by volunteers, _____ some of the food will be purchased.
3. _____ will we have a lot of food at the picnic _____ beverages.
4. We need separate committees for _____ collecting money and cleaning up.
5. I will be in charge of _____ the money-collection committee or the cleanup committee.
6. Jane asked Mr. Alvarez if _____ kickball _____ potato sack races could be played at the picnic.
7. We are all looking forward to _____ the games and races.
8. _____ Jessica _____ Lisa can guess who will win.
9. _____ outside _____ indoors, we will have a great time.

APPLY IT NOW

Plan an activity such as a party, a meal, or a field trip. Write five sentences using both correlative conjunctions and coordinating conjunctions in your writing.

 Tech Tip Plan and organize your activity on a spreadsheet.

Conjunctions • 169

OBJECTIVES

- To identify and use conjunctive adverbs
- To recognize the proper use of punctuation with conjunctive adverbs

 **DAILY Maintenance**

Assign **Practice Book** page 107, Section 9.3. After students finish,
1. Give immediate feedback.
2. Review concepts as needed.
3. Model the correct answer.

Pages 4–5 of the **Answer Key** contain tips for Daily Maintenance.

WARM-UP

Write the following sentences on the board:

Ron and Doug went to the game, while their mom stayed home.

Ron and Doug went to the game; however, their mom stayed home.

Ask students to discuss the differences between the two sentences. Elicit that the sentences use different punctuation. Encourage students to identify any connecting words in the sentences.

📖 Read from a piece of writing that the class is currently reading. Emphasize the conjunctive adverbs.

TEACH

Write the word *however* on the board and ask a volunteer to write a sentence that uses the word. Point out that *however* joins two independent clauses. Ask a volunteer to underline the independent clauses. Call attention to the punctuation as you insert a semicolon before and a comma after *however*.

Explain that *however* is a type of connector called a conjunctive

adverb because it functions as both a conjunction and an adverb. Have volunteers read aloud about conjunctive adverbs.

Encourage students to provide additional sentences, one for each conjunctive adverb. Write a few sentences on the board, leaving out the punctuation. Invite students to put the semicolon and the comma in the correct places.

Ask a volunteer to read aloud the information on parenthetical expressions. Point out that a parenthetical expression can also be used to join an independent and dependent clause. Tell students that in these instances, the parenthetical expression is

surrounded by commas. Ask students to write on the board sentences with these expressions, using correct punctuation.

PRACTICE

EXERCISE 1

Encourage students to use the list in the lesson to identify the conjunctive adverbs. Have students copy the sentences, underline the conjunctive adverbs, and circle the semicolons and commas that set off the conjunctive adverbs. Ask partners to exchange papers to check each other's answers.

9.3 Conjunctive Adverbs

A **conjunctive adverb** connects independent clauses. It helps make clear the relationship between the clauses. When a conjunctive adverb connects clauses, a semicolon is used before it and a comma after it.

> **Cities offer many attractions;** *nevertheless,* **some people prefer to live in the country.**

Common conjunctive adverbs include the following:

also	hence	later	otherwise
besides	however	likewise	still
consequently	in fact	moreover	subsequently
finally	indeed	nevertheless	therefore
furthermore	instead	nonetheless	thus

Parenthetical expressions, also called explanatory expressions, are used in the same way as conjunctive adverbs. Among these are *for example, namely, on the contrary, in fact, that is,* and *on the other hand.* When a parenthetical expression joins independent clauses, it must be preceded by a semicolon and followed by a comma.

> **Missy often illustrates her compositions;** *in fact,* **she would rather draw than write.**

EXERCISE 1 Identify the conjunctive adverb in each sentence.

1. Rome was founded in 753 BC; <u>thus</u>, it is one of Europe's oldest cities.
2. The city has many old buildings; <u>however</u>, it has many modern ones.
3. In the past, residents used stones from old buildings to build new ones; <u>nevertheless</u>, many old buildings still stand.
4. The Circus Maximus, a huge oval area for races, no longer stands; <u>indeed</u>, its site is now preserved only as an open space.
5. Cars buzz around the city at all hours; <u>also</u>, riders on small motorcycles add to the congestion and noise level.
6. Rome is one of the world's richest cities in art and history; <u>therefore</u>, it is a magnet for tourists.
7. The Colosseum, a freestanding amphitheater, was begun between AD 70 and AD 80; <u>moreover</u>, it could seat 50,000 spectators.
8. The Trevi Fountain is one of the most beautiful fountains in Rome; <u>consequently</u>, many tourists come to see it and marvel at its many statues.

Exercise 1
Conjunctive adverbs are underlined.

170 • Section 9.3

Trevi Fountain in Rome, Italy

EXERCISE 2

Explain that parenthetical expressions are used in the same way as conjunctive adverbs and are punctuated the same. Have volunteers write their sentences on the board.

APPLY

APPLY IT NOW

Encourage students to write about places in their own community or state as if they are writing a postcard to a friend or relative who lives far away. Students should demonstrate an understanding of conjunctive adverbs.

> **Grammar in Action.** Students should identify the conjunctive adverb *however*. Point out the semicolon before and the comma after *however*.

ASSESS

Note which students had difficulty using conjunctive adverbs. Assign **Practice Book** pages 111–112 for further practice.

WRITING CONNECTION

Use pages 454–455 of the Writing portion of the book.

Use pages 454–455 of the Writing portion of the book.

Exercise 2

Each conjunctive adverb is preceded by a semicolon and followed by a comma.

EXERCISE 2 Rewrite these sentences, choosing the correct conjunctive adverb or parenthetical expression. Add semicolons and commas where needed.

1. Manhattan is only 13 miles long and 2 miles wide (<u>consequently</u> otherwise) land space is scarce.
2. One solution to the lack of space is to construct buildings high into the air (therefore <u>nevertheless</u>) land is still scarce.
3. Tall buildings were originally places to work (still <u>later</u>) they became places to live.
4. The Chrysler Building is no longer the tallest building in Manhattan (<u>however</u> moreover) it is still one of the most beautiful.
5. Some space was left for green areas (<u>in fact</u> nevertheless) there are more than a hundred parks in New York City.
6. Central Park is right in the middle of busy Manhattan (<u>however</u> moreover) it has many quiet and peaceful areas.
7. The human traffic in Central Park includes a never-ending flow of panting joggers (<u>moreover</u> however) there are many inline skaters on the park's roads and paths.
8. Many other cities in the United States have gained recognition; (<u>namely</u> instead) Los Angeles, Chicago, and Houston.
9. Because of its warm climate, Los Angeles attracts many residents (otherwise <u>also</u>) the work opportunities in many industries bring new residents.
10. Bright outdoor light was needed to film early motion pictures (<u>therefore</u> however) Los Angeles's sunny climate was perfect for the movie industry.
11. At one time land near Los Angeles was almost desert (<u>in fact</u> nevertheless) only snakes, lizards, and a few rabbits lived there.
12. Now irrigation pipes divert water to support the large city population (<u>furthermore</u> however) reservoirs save rainwater for use by residents.

APPLY IT NOW

Write six sentences about your town, city, or state. Use conjunctive adverbs in your sentences.

> **Grammar in Action.** Identify the conjunctive adverb in the script on p. 451.

Identify the conjunctive adverb in the script on p. 451.

Conjunctions • 171

TEACHING OPTIONS

Reteach

Write sentences with conjunctive adverbs on pairs of sentence strips— one independent clause per strip. Arrange the sentence strips on the board ledge, paired up correctly but without conjunctive adverbs. Discuss each pair of independent clauses, eliciting which conjunctive adverb best completes each sentence. Encourage students to explain the reasons for their choices, which should result in a discussion of the meaning of each conjunctive adverb. Challenge students to copy the sentences and to use the correct punctuation before and after each conjunctive adverb.

Meeting Individual Needs

Extra Support Students may have difficulty choosing the correct conjunctive adverbs because students are not sure what the words mean. Have students write the conjunctive adverbs on page 170. Ask students to look up each word in a dictionary and to write its meaning. Discuss the words to see if students fully understand the meanings. Encourage students to write sentences that show the meaning and usage of each conjunctive adverb.

Curriculum Connection

Encourage each student to research a city and to create an information poster or travel brochure about the city. Challenge students to use several conjunctive adverbs. Review students' work, encouraging students to locate the conjunctive adverbs used.

9.4 Subordinate Conjunctions

OBJECTIVES
- **To identify and use subordinate conjunctions**
- **To identify the dependent and independent clauses joined by a subordinate conjunction**

DAILY **Maintenance**

Assign **Practice Book** page 107, Section 9.4. After students finish,
1. Give immediate feedback.
2. Review concepts as needed.
3. Model the correct answer.

Pages 4–5 of the **Answer Key** contain tips for Daily Maintenance.

WARM-UP

Pass out note cards on which you have written one of the following subordinate conjunctions: *after, as if, before, how, once, than,* and *unless.* Set a timer for two minutes. Challenge students to write a sentence using the subordinate conjunction on their card.

📖 Read from a piece of writing that the class is currently reading. Emphasize the subordinate conjunctions.

TEACH

Have volunteer write on the board their Warm-Up sentences. Read the sentences aloud and ask students to listen for the words that connect the clauses. Then read the sentences a second time, transposing the two parts of each sentence, to help students hear the conjunctions more clearly.
   Explain that the words *after, as if, before, how, once, than,* and *unless* serve as subordinate

conjunctions and that they join an independent clause with a subordinate, or dependent, clause. Encourage volunteers to read aloud about subordinate conjunctions. Suggest that students write the list of subordinate conjunctions on a separate sheet of paper to help remember them.

PRACTICE

EXERCISE 1
Suggest that students start a chart with the column headings *Subordinate Conjunction, Dependent Clause,* and *Independent Clause.* Create a similar chart on the board. Invite volunteers to fill in the chart on the board with the words and clauses from students' own charts. Discuss why some clauses are dependent and others are independent.

EXERCISE 2
Have students recall the various types of connectors. Allow students to review previous sections as necessary. Have students complete the exercise independently. Ask small groups to compare and discuss their answers.

9.4 Subordinate Conjunctions

A **subordinate conjunction** is used to join an independent clause and a dependent clause and to indicate their relationship. Subordinate conjunctions typically introduce adverb clauses. These clauses describe verbs, adjectives, or adverbs in the independent clause. They tell *how, why, to what extent,* and *under what condition.* The subordinate conjunctions *where* and *when* may introduce adjective clauses, and noun clauses may be introduced by subordinate conjunctions such as *how, when,* and *whether.*

Cave painting in Lascaux, France

When we studied about prehistoric humans, we learned about their cave paintings.
I am fascinated by this time period *when written language was in its earliest form.*

In the first sentence, the subordinate conjunction *When* introduces the dependent clause *When we studied about prehistoric humans.* The dependent clause is an adverb clause, and it modifies *learned.* In the second sentence, *when* introduces an adjective clause that modifies *period* in the independent clause.

Common subordinate conjunctions include the following:

after	in order that	till
although, as though	once	unless
as, as long as	provided (that)	until
as if, as far as	since	when, whenever
as soon as	so long as	where, wherever
because	so (that)	whether
before	than	while
how	that	why
if, even if	though, even though	

EXERCISE 1 Identify the subordinate conjunction in each sentence. Then identify the dependent clause and the independent clause.

1. Experts studied the paintings in the caves at Lascaux, France, so that they could determine the early painters' techniques.
2. After those first artists had ground up charcoal and colored rocks, they mixed the resulting powders with saliva.
3. Once they had made the colors they wanted, they blew the colored liquid onto the cave walls and ceilings.

Exercise 1
Independent clauses are underlined once. Dependent clauses are underlined twice.
1. so that
2. After
3. Once
4. so that
5. Though
6. While
7. As soon as
8. Because
9. If
10. since

172 • Section 9.4

APPLY

APPLY IT NOW

Suggest that students write their paragraphs as a journal entry in the first person, conveying interesting impressions and emotions. Challenge students to use at least five subordinate conjunctions in their writing. Have students circle the conjunctions and label the clauses as dependent or independent. Students should demonstrate an understanding of subordinate conjunctions.

TechTip Have students read and assess one another's paragraphs. Encourage students to post feedback on the class blog.

ASSESS

Note which students had difficulty identifying and using subordinate conjunctions. Assign **Practice Book** page 113 for further practice.

WRITING CONNECTION

Use pages 456–457 of the Writing portion of the book.

Reteach

Have students brainstorm a list of nouns related to extracurricular activities. Write the nouns in two columns on the board. Ask a volunteer to choose one noun from each column and to compose a sentence with the two nouns in clauses connected by a subordinate conjunction. Offer the following example for the nouns *skateboarder* and *helmet*:

> **Even though** you are a good skateboarder, you should always wear a helmet.

Write students' sentences on the board and help volunteers analyze the sentences. Have volunteers circle the conjunctions and label the dependent and independent clauses.

Meeting Individual Needs

Intrapersonal Ask students to compose slogans for bumper stickers. Explain that the slogans must include subordinate conjunctions. For example:

> It doesn't matter **whom** you vote for **as long as** you vote.

> **Before** you get really angry, stop and count to 10.

Suggest that each student write several slogans and copy them onto poster board. Display the slogans on a bulletin board in the classroom.

---

4. Bumps in the limestone walls were utilized by the artists so that some of the creatures seem almost three-dimensional.

5. Though most of the figures in the caves represent animals, there are some stylized human figures.

6. While most creatures are painted in lifelike detail, one figure has the head of a buffalo and the legs of a human.

7. As soon as the caves' discovery became widely known, many visitors arrived.

8. Because the carbon dioxide in human breath caused the walls of the caves to deteriorate, there was a need for action.

9. If immediate action had not been taken, the artwork might have disappeared completely.

10. The public has not been able to view the paintings firsthand since the caves were closed to visitors in 1963.

Cave painting in Lascaux, France

Exercise 2
1. subordinate conjunction
2. conjunctive adverb
3. correlative conjunction
4. coordinating conjunction
5. conjunctive adverb
6. subordinate conjunction
7. correlative conjunction
8. subordinate conjunction

EXERCISE 2 Identify the connectors in these sentences and tell whether each is a coordinating conjunction, a correlative conjunction, a conjunctive adverb, or a subordinate conjunction.

1. Although the paintings are the first thing to attract attention, Lascaux also contains an altarlike stone.

2. There were no signs that people had actually lived in the caves; still, fires had been built in them.

3. Either worship or some other form of ritual took place there.

4. All these things are interesting, yet the major source of wonder remains the paintings.

5. The colors are still brilliant; moreover, the lifelike creatures have been captured in motion.

6. While the cave paintings are mostly positioned on walls and ceilings, experts think that scaffoldings were used to reach the higher portions of the cave.

7. Not only are there close to 600 painted animals and symbols but also nearly 1,500 engravings.

8. Because the caves were closed to the public, there was a partial replica that opened in 1983 called Lascaux II.

APPLY IT NOW

Write a brief paragraph about an amazing or a surprising experience. Use and identify subordinate conjunctions.

 TechTip Post your paragraph on the class blog.

Conjunctions • 173

OBJECTIVE

- **To recognize troublesome conjunctions and prepositions and to understand how to use them**

 **DAILY** **Maintenance**

Assign **Practice Book** page 108, Section 9.5. After students finish,
1. Give immediate feedback.
2. Review concepts as needed.
3. Model the correct answer.

Pages 4–5 of the **Answer Key** contain tips for Daily Maintenance.

WARM-UP

Put a line of tape on the floor to divide the room into halves. Identify one side as prepositions and the other as conjunctions. Read aloud a sentence containing a troublesome conjunction or preposition. Say the troublesome word and ask students to stand on the side of the room that matches how they think the word functions in the sentence. Have those who guessed incorrectly return to their seats. Repeat as time allows.

📖 Read from a piece of writing that the class is currently reading. Emphasize the troublesome conjunctions.

TEACH

Write on the board several Warm-Up sentences and underline the conjunctions. Have volunteers read aloud about troublesome conjunctions and prepositions. After each example sentence, ask students to provide additional sentences containing prepositional phrases or dependent clauses.

Explain that being able to distinguish between a phrase and a clause helps in choosing the correct word—a preposition or a conjunction. Encourage students to suggest sentences for the words *without, unless, like, as,* and *as if.* Write their sentences on the board. Discuss whether the words have been used correctly.

PRACTICE

EXERCISE 1
Tell students to analyze each sentence to determine whether the word is being used in a phrase or a clause and whether it is being used correctly. Have students exchange papers with partners to check their answers.

EXERCISE 2
Encourage students to copy each sentence, imagining that they are writing the sentences for a report about earthquakes. Suggest that students try each word in the sentence to see if it is being used correctly. Have volunteers write the sentences on the board. Ask the class to compare their sentences. Discuss the sentences and word choices as needed.

9.5 Troublesome Conjunctions

Some conjunctions are frequently misused or confused.

Unless* and *Without The word *without* is a preposition and introduces a prepositional phrase.

> **No family should be *without* an emergency kit.**

Without introduces the prepositional phrase *without an emergency kit.*

The word *unless* is a subordinate conjunction, and it introduces a dependent adverb clause.

> **No family is prepared for a disaster *unless* it has an emergency kit.**

Which word correctly completes the following?

> **Don't leave (without unless) I accompany you.**

The correct answer is the subordinate conjunction *unless,* used to introduce an adverb clause.

Like, As If,* and *As The word *like* is a preposition, and it introduces a prepositional phrase.

> **Julio looks *like* his brother.**

As if is a subordinate conjunction, and it introduces a clause.

> **Sam looks *as if* he is worried.**

As can function as a conjunction or as a preposition.

> **I crawled under a table *as* the earth shook.** (conjunction introducing a clause)
> **We studied emergency procedures *as* part of our health class.**
> (preposition in a phrase)

EXERCISE 1 Choose the correct item to complete each sentence.

1. (Without <u>Unless</u>) you have felt the ground under you heave and roll, it is hard to imagine an earthquake.
2. You feel (<u>as if</u> like) the ground under you is not solid.
3. In fact, the ground moves (as if <u>like</u>) a carpet of wavelike jelly.
4. You may not realize how scary earthquakes can be (<u>unless</u> without) you have lived through one.
5. It may seem to be the end of the world (<u>as</u> like) whole buildings wobble wildly or collapse entirely.

Exercise 1
The correct conjunction is underlined.

174 • Section 9.5

APPLY

APPLY IT NOW

Suggest that students determine whether a phrase or a clause is needed to complete each sentence. Ask volunteers to write their sentences on the board. Discuss whether the correct choice of phrase or clause has been made in each sentence. Students should demonstrate an understanding of troublesome conjunctions.

ASSESS

Note which students had difficulty recognizing troublesome conjunctions. Assign **Practice Book** pages 114–115 for further practice.

WRITING CONNECTION

Use pages 458–459 of the Writing portion of the book.

TEACHING OPTIONS

Reteach

Write the following sentences on the board:

1. It was **as if** a nightmare!

2. I left the house **as** my science homework.

3. **Like** I turned it in on time, I was going to get a bad grade.

4. It wasn't **without** I had done it on purpose.

5. **Unless** a part of my grade, it had to be turned in on time.

Instruct students to copy the sentences, replacing the underlined incorrect terms with correct ones. Invite volunteers to write on the board the corrected sentences. Have students check their rewritten sentences against those on the board, which should now contain these corrections: 1. *like*, 2. *without*, 3. *Unless*, 4. *as if*, 5. *As*.

English-Language Learners

Provide additional practice in using troublesome conjunctions and prepositions by writing sentences that include the words. Give the sentences to a student who is proficient in English and have the student work with the English-language learner, reading the sentences aloud together. In this way English-language learners can hear the correct usage of the words. After students have read the sentences together, encourage the proficient student to explain why each sentence is correct—helping the English-language learner recognize prepositional phrases and dependent clauses.

6. Objects fall (as if like) they are being thrown down.

7. Scientists (as if like) Charles F. Richter have devised various scales for measuring the size of earthquakes.

8. (Without Unless) you understand the scale, you may not realize that an earthquake measuring 7 is 10 times greater than one measuring 6.

9. (Without Unless) such measures, there would be no way to compare the magnitude of earthquakes.

10. The destructive force of earthquakes is clear (as like) you look at photos of their aftermath.

Exercise 2
1. without
2. like
3. Unless
4. as if
5. Unless
6. as
7. without
8. as if
9. as
10. as if
11. without

EXERCISE 2 Use one of the following terms to complete each sentence: *as, as if, like, unless, without*.

1. In the aftermath of an earthquake, people find themselves _____ services such as power, gas, water, and cable.

2. People debate how much preparation for disasters _____ earthquakes is useful or even possible.

3. _____ older buildings are retrofitted, they remain dangerous.

4. We must always behave _____ the next earthquake is near.

5. _____ a supply of drinking water, nonperishable food, and warm clothing is kept on hand, people are not ready for an earthquake.

6. It is important we keep the hallway of homes clear _____ this is one of the safest places to be during an earthquake.

7. One of the worst earthquakes in California took place in 1906, leaving many people _____ homes, food, or jobs.

8. The earthquake reduced San Francisco to rubble and made it appear _____ the city was crushed.

9. The earthquake occurred at 5:13 in the morning _____ many people were just starting their day or were still sleeping.

10. Buildings began to sway _____ they were dancing.

11. Other towns did not go _____ damage; San Jose, Salinas, and Santa Rosa all felt the earthquake's impact.

APPLY IT NOW

Complete these sentences to show you can use the troublesome conjunctions and prepositions correctly.

I won't go unless _____.
I won't go without _____.
You look like _____.
You look as if _____.

Conjunctions • 175

9.6 Interjections

OBJECTIVE
- To identify and use interjections in sentences

DAILY Maintenance

Assign **Practice Book** page 108, Section 9.6. After students finish,
1. Give immediate feedback.
2. Review concepts as needed.
3. Model the correct answer.

Pages 4–5 of the **Answer Key** contain tips for Daily Maintenance.

WARM-UP

Draw on the board a large exclamation point. Print out several pictures from clip art, magazines, or comics that depict funny, painful, surprising, or exciting situations. Hold up the pictures, one at a time, and ask students to call out one-word responses that would end in an exclamation point.

📖 Read from a piece of writing that the class is currently reading. Emphasize the interjections.

TEACH

Suggest the following scenarios and invite students to share the first words that come to mind. Explain that you are not looking for complete sentences but rather words that express emotions. Ask students what they might say when

they realize they've forgotten their homework.

they miss the school bus.

their favorite team wins.

they get stung by a bee.

they hear some terrific news.

List on the board the interjections that students suggest. Continue to suggest scenarios and encourage students to provide words to express how they feel.

Write the word *interjection* above your class-generated list. Explain that interjections are words that express strong emotions. Invite students to read aloud about interjections. Stress that an interjection or the sentence in which an interjection appears is always followed by an exclamation point.

PRACTICE

EXERCISE 1
Ask students how they can identify interjections. Confirm that interjections are usually followed by exclamation points and that they are usually short words conveying strong feelings. Have students work in groups to read the sentences aloud. Encourage students to express emotion as they read the interjections.

EXERCISE 2
Have students complete this exercise independently. Explain that there are no right or wrong answers and that students should answer with interjections that fit the moods or feelings of the sentences. Invite students to read aloud their completed sentences, expressing a particular feeling

---

9.6 Interjections

An **interjection** is a word or phrase that expresses a strong or sudden emotion. Interjections can be used to convey happiness, delight, anger, disgust, surprise (of a good or an unpleasant sort), impatience, pain, wonder, and so on. They can also be used to get or hold attention.

Hey! You dropped your ticket.

What do you think is expressed by the above interjection? It might be used to get attention.

Interjections may be set off from the rest of a sentence by an exclamation point.

No! I can't find my ticket.
Ouch! I just stubbed my toe.

An interjection may also be part of an exclamatory sentence. If the sentence is exclamatory, the interjection is followed by a comma, and the exclamation point is put at the end of the sentence.

Oh, how exciting the game is!
Yes, I will marry you!

These are some common interjections:

Ah!	Hey!	Oh!	Yes!
Alas!	Hooray!	Oh, dear!	Yikes!
Beware!	Hush!	Oops!	Yippie!
Bravo!	Indeed!	Ouch!	Yum!
Dear me!	Never!	Rats!	Well!
Enough!	No!	Sh!	What!
Good grief!	No way!	Stop!	Whew!
Hello!	Nonsense!	Ugh!	Wow!

EXERCISE 1 Identify the interjection in each sentence. Indicate the emotion that you think is expressed in each.

1. <u>Great</u>! We have really good seats for the game.
2. <u>Oh, dear</u>! Someone tall is sitting in front of us.
3. <u>Oh, well</u>! I can still see well enough.
4. <u>Wow</u>! That was a great shot.
5. <u>Hooray</u>! We are leading the game.
6. <u>No</u>! I can't believe the referee's call.

Exercise 1
Interjections are underlined. Answers will vary for what emotion is expressed.

while saying each interjection. Encourage students who have chosen different interjections for a sentence to read aloud their sentences.

APPLY

APPLY IT NOW

Review exclamatory and interrogative sentences. When students have finished, invite volunteers to share their e-mails with the class. Students should demonstrate an understanding of interjections.

Grammar in Action. The interjection on page 451 is *Cool!* Ask volunteers to suggest other interjections that fit the mood of the passage.

ASSESS

Note which students had difficulty identifying and using interjections. Assign **Practice Book** page 116 for further practice.

WRITING CONNECTION

Use pages 460–461 of the Writing portion of the book.

TEACHING OPTIONS

Reteach

Display an interesting image from a magazine, a book, or a poster. Invite students to use interjections to describe what they see. For example:

Wow! Look at all those people.

Oops! That person dropped his ice-cream cone.

Oh, no! That child is crying.

Beware! I see dark clouds in the sky.

Indeed! It looks as if it could rain.

Ouch! That person is stepping on someone's foot.

Encourage students to express their ideas freely. Write their responses on the board but leave out the punctuation. Invite students to supply the exclamation points. Then ask volunteers to read aloud the sentences, infusing their voices with the appropriate emotion. Challenge students to explain what emotion the interjection in each sentence conveys.

Meeting Individual Needs

Auditory Instruct students to pay attention for one day to the interjections they use in their own speech and those they hear in the speech of others. Encourage students to jot down these interjections. Invite students to share their interjections, noting particularly those that are used most frequently. Summarize the activity by discussing how interjections contribute to everyday language. *(They convey emotion; they have an immediate impact; they make language exciting.)*

---

7. <u>Bravo!</u> Joan just made a great shot for our team.
8. <u>Ah,</u> that's another foul on our team!
9. <u>Goodness!</u> It's a close game.
10. <u>Great!</u> Edwards is coming into the game.
11. <u>No!</u> Our best player looks as if she might be injured.
12. <u>Wonderful!</u> She's back in the game.
13. <u>Hey!</u> Sit down in front.
14. <u>Oh,</u> there are only two seconds left!
15. <u>Yes,</u> we've won the game!
16. <u>Yippee!</u> We have such a good team.
17. <u>Indeed,</u> the coach is the best we've ever had!
18. <u>No way!</u> Joan received the Most Valuable Player Award.
19. <u>Fantastic!</u> She deserves the award for her hard work today.
20. <u>Ah,</u> I hope we win the game next week!

Exercise 2
Answers will vary.
Possible answers:
1. Hurry! Hey!
2. Yay! Hooray!
3. Sh! Wow!
4. Look! Great! Yes!
5. Oh, no!
6. Wow! Look!
7. Hey!
8. Ugh! Ah!
9. Oh, no! Oops!
10. Wow! Hey!

EXERCISE 2 Write an interjection to go with each sentence. Use an exclamation point at the end of each interjection.

1. _____ We got places in the front row.
2. _____ We can really hear the band.
3. _____ The parade is starting.
4. _____ I took a picture of the cheerleaders.
5. _____ I don't have the right film in my camera.
6. _____ I would like to take a picture of that float.
7. _____ Those people riding on it are waving.
8. _____ It's getting hot.
9. _____ I drank all the water.
10. _____ It's the end already.

APPLY IT NOW

Imagine that you have just won a great prize. Draft an e-mail telling your friends the good news. Use interjections and exclamatory and interrogative sentences to show the different emotions associated with each.

Grammar in Action. Identify one interjection in the p. 451 script.

Interjections • 177

Conjunction and Interjection Review

ASSESS

Use the Conjunction and Interjection Review as homework, as a practice test, or as an informal assessment. Following are some examples for use.

Homework

You may wish to assign one group the odd items and another group the even items. When you next meet, review the correct answers as a group. Be sure to model how to arrive at the correct answer.

Practice Test

Use the Conjunction and Interjection Review as a diagnostic tool. Assign the entire review or only specific sections. After students have finished, identify which concepts require more attention. Reteach concepts as necessary.

Conjunction and Interjection Review

9.1
The coordinating conjunction is underlined twice. The words, phrases, or clauses it connects are underlined once.

9.1 Identify the coordinating conjunction in each sentence. Tell whether it connects words, phrases, or clauses.

1. The sun was shining, yet the forecast called for rain.
2. Tanya wanted to dig beds and to plant flowers.
3. She planted petunias in the beds and in containers.
4. She knew purple or white petunias would look best.
5. Tanya tried to finish and to clean up before the storm.
6. The clouds rolled in, and the wind picked up.
7. It rained heavily, so the flowers didn't need to be watered.
8. Tanya stored her gardening tools and gloves in the shed.
9. It rained all afternoon and into the next day.
10. Tanya was tired from her hard work, yet she looked forward to watching her garden grow.

9.2 Identify the correlative conjunctions in each sentence.

11. Either math or science is Pablo's favorite subject.
12. Neither the beaker nor the slide was cleaned after the experiment.
13. Whether you finish or not, please leave your worksheets on the desk.
14. Tom was not only studying for the exam but also practicing for the big race.
15. Both his mom and his dad help him with homework.

16. Tom wants to ace both the exam and the race.
17. Whether Pablo is my study partner or not, I will make flash cards.
18. Not only did Tom review his science homework, but also he reread the chapter.

9.3 Rewrite these sentences, choosing the correct conjunctive adverb. Add commas and semicolons where needed.

19. Stonehenge was built thousands of years ago (also nevertheless) it still stands.
20. Stonehenge may mark solar and lunar alignments (otherwise consequently) it may have been used as a calendar.
21. Stonehenge was carefully constructed (therefore still) it must have been important.
22. No one knows for sure what purpose it served (later still) many people visit Stonehenge.
23. The stones used to build the structure were large (moreover however) they were heavy.
24. Stonehenge is close to London (therefore besides) many tourists come for a day trip.
25. It is important to experience ancient history up close (thus indeed) a trip to Stonehenge would be ideal.
26. Stonehenge is an ancient relic (however finally) London is also filled with historic landmarks.

9.3
19. Stonehenge was built thousands of years ago; nevertheless, it still stands.
20. Stonehenge may mark solar and lunar alignments; consequently, it may have been used as a calendar.
21. Stonehenge was carefully constructed; therefore, it must have been important.
22. No one knows for sure what purpose it served; still, many people visit Stonehenge.
23. The stones used to build the structure were large; moreover, they were heavy.
24. Stonehenge is close to London; therefore, many tourists come for a day trip.
25. It is important to experience ancient history up close; thus, a trip to Stonehenge would be ideal.
26. Stonehenge is an ancient relic; however, London is also filled with historic landmarks.

Informal Assessment

Use the review as preparation for the formal assessment. Count the review as a portion of the grade. Have students work to find the correct answers and use their corrected review as a study guide for the formal assessment.

WRITING CONNECTION

Use pages 462–463 of the Writing portion of the book.

9.4
Subordinate conjunctions are underlined twice. Dependent clauses are underlined once

9.6

46. Hey! We can't find our tickets. Hey, we can't find our tickets!

47. Oh, dear! We will miss the start of the play. Oh, dear, we will miss the start of the play!

48. Hooray! The tickets were in my coat pocket. Hooray, the tickets were in my coat pocket!

49. Hush! I can't hear the actors. Hush, I can't hear the actors!

50. Bravo! You were very good as the lead. Bravo, you were very good as the lead!

51. Hush! Talking is not permitted in the theater. Hush, talking is not permitted in the theater!

52. Rats! I forgot my ticket at home. Rats, I forgot my ticket at home!

53. Indeed! The director is very talented. Indeed, the director is very talented!

54. Wow! What a great finale. Wow, what a great finale!

9.4 **Identify the subordinate conjunction and the dependent clause in each sentence.**

27. As if one cat weren't enough, now there are three more on the deck.

28. As long as we feed the stray cats, they will continue to come to the back door.

29. Because it was so skinny, Jeff fed the kitten.

30. Although stray cats are usually afraid of people, the kitten walked right up to Jeff.

31. Jeff took the kitten to the veterinarian before he adopted it.

32. If we can catch the adult cats, we will take them to the veterinarian as well.

33. There will be more kittens soon, unless the cats are spayed.

34. Jeff has always loved cats, while his sister prefers dogs.

35. Provided that you can care for a pet, local shelters are a good place to look for a cat to adopt.

36. A shelter will help find a new home for a stray cat, once it receives proper vaccinations.

9.5 **Choose the correct item to complete each sentence.**

37. No one should be caught (unless without) an umbrella on a rainy day.

38. Jane's feet will become wet (unless without) she wears boots.

39. Don't leave (unless without) checking the forecast.

40. Meteorologists (as like) John's dad are busy when it storms.

41. The sky looks (as if like) it might open at any minute.

42. Juan waited under an awning (as if as) the raindrops fell.

43. Molly says it looks (as if like) our game will be canceled.

44. Coach won't allow us to play the game (without unless) we get an all-clear from the referee.

45. The sky looks (as if like) it will stop soon.

9.6 **Identify the two ways to correctly punctuate each sentence.**

46. Hey we can't find our tickets

47. Oh dear we will miss the start of the play

48. Hooray the tickets were in my coat pocket

49. Hush I can't hear the actors

50. Bravo you were very good as the lead

51. Hush talking is not permitted in the theater

52. Rats I forgot my ticket at home

53. Indeed the director is very talented

54. Wow what a great finale

Tech Tip Go to www.voyagesinenglish.com for more activities.

Conjunctions and Interjections • 179

Conjunction and Interjection Challenge

ASSESS

Encourage students to read the paragraph twice before answering the questions. If students have difficulty with any question, suggest that they refer to the section that teaches the skill.

This activity can be completed by individuals, by small groups, or by the class working as a whole.

After you have reviewed conjunctions and interjections, administer the Section 9

Assessment on pages 25–26 in the **Assessment Book,** or create a customized test with the optional **Test Generator CD.**

Conjunction and Interjection Challenge

Read the selection and then answer the questions.

1. What could be more typically ethnic than Italian tomato sauce or Swiss chocolate? 2. When we think of tomatoes and chocolate, we think of Italy and Switzerland. 3. These ideas seem natural; however, both tomatoes and chocolate originated in the Americas.

4. Yes! Tomatoes are, in fact, native to Mexico and Central America, and the Aztecs grew them by AD 700. 5. Chocolate was made into a sacred drink by the Aztecs; moreover, the emperor Montezuma is said to have drunk some 50 cups of it a day. 6. Because chocolate was so precious, the cocoa bean was used even as currency. 7. The Spaniards found these products in the Americas, and they introduced them to Europeans in the 1500s.

8. Although chocolate become popular as a drink in Europe, it was only made into solid-bar form in the 1800s in the Netherlands. 9. Shortly thereafter the Swiss entered the picture. 10. It was a Swiss confectioner who made the first milk chocolate. 11. By that time the Italians had long discovered the tomato and were using it both as a fruit and as the main ingredient in savory sauces.

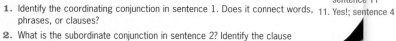

1. Identify the coordinating conjunction in sentence 1. Does it connect words, phrases, or clauses?

2. What is the subordinate conjunction in sentence 2? Identify the clause it introduces. What kind of clause is it?

3. What is the conjunctive adverb in sentence 3?

4. Identify the correlative conjunctions in sentence 3.

5. Identify the two coordinating conjunctions in sentence 4. What does each connect—words, phrases, or clauses?

6. Identify the connector in sentence 5. What type is it?

7. Identify the conjunction in sentence 6. What type is it?

8. Identify the conjunction in sentence 7. What type is it?

9. Identify the subordinate conjunction in the last paragraph. What sentence is it in?

10. Identify the correlative conjunctions in the last paragraph. What sentence is it in?

11. Find the interjection in the selection. What sentence is it in?

Conjunction and Interjection Challenge

1. or; words
2. When; When we think of tomatoes and chocolate; adverb clause
3. however
4. both . . . and
5. and, words; and, clauses
6. moreover; conjunctive adverb
7. Because; subordinate conjunction
8. and; coordinating conjunction
9. Although; sentence 8
10. both . . . and; sentence 11
11. Yes!; sentence 4

Punctuation and Capitalization

SUPPORT MATERIALS

Practice Book
Daily Maintenance, pages 117–118
Grammar, pages 119–123

Assessment Book
Section 10 Assessment,
    pages 27–28

Test Generator CD

Writing Chapter 7,
    Creative Writing

Customizable Lesson Plans
www.voyagesinenglish.com

CONNECT WITH LITERATURE

📖 Consider using the following titles throughout the section to illustrate the grammar concept:

Heartbeat by Sharon Creech
Punctuation Takes a Vacation
    by Robin Pulver
*Twenty-Odd Ducks: Why, Every
    Punctuation Mark Counts!* by
    Lynne Truss

GRAMMAR FOR GROWN-UPS

Understanding Punctuation and Capitalization

Punctuation and capitalization act as our tour guide through the maze of a sentence. They guide us to see when a sentences starts and how it ends and also where to pause or stop within a sentence. Without punctuation and capitalization, sentences would make little sense.

A **period**, a **question mark**, and an **exclamation point** are all end marks used to signal the end of a sentence.

Commas are used in a variety of ways to separate words.

> *Barack Obama, as you no doubt know, was elected president in 2008.*

Semicolons signal a partial stop in a sentence and are commonly used with conjunctive adverbs.

> *I will go to the store; however, I need to go to the bank first.*

Colons signal a full stop in a sentence and often precede a list.

> *Pat packed the following in his suitcase: clothes, toiletries, books, and CDs.*

Quotation marks are used before and after a direct quotation and for titles of shorter pieces of work.

> *"Give me liberty or give me death," said Patrick Henry.*
> *"The Raven"*

Apostrophes show possession and the omission of letters or numbers.

> *John's pencil*   *can't*   *class of '09*

In addition to being used in the first word of a sentence, **capital letters** are also used for proper nouns, titles that precede a person's name, directions when they refer to sections of the country, and certain abbreviations.

> ❝Grammar is the logic for speech,
> even as logic is the grammar of reason.❞
>
> —Richard C. Trench

COMMON ERRORS

Using Dashes Correctly

Dashes are used to indicate a change in thought. Students might use commas instead.

ERROR: Her mom, she drives an SUV, will take us to the movie.
CORRECT: Her mom—she drives an SUV—will take us to the movie.

ERROR: I quickly ran, which surprised me, out of the room.
CORRECT: I quickly ran—which surprised me—out of the room.

When students check their writing, have them read each sentence carefully for abrupt changes in thought. Make sure students are correctly punctuating these changes in thought with dashes.

SENTENCE DIAGRAMMING

You may wish to teach punctuation and capitalization in the context of diagramming. Review these examples. Then refer to the Diagramming section or look for Diagram It! features in the Punctuation and Capitalization section.

The winner was surprised; he was ecstatic.

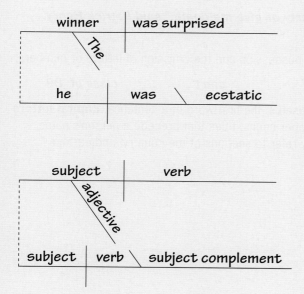

ASK AN EXPERT

Real Situations, Real Solutions

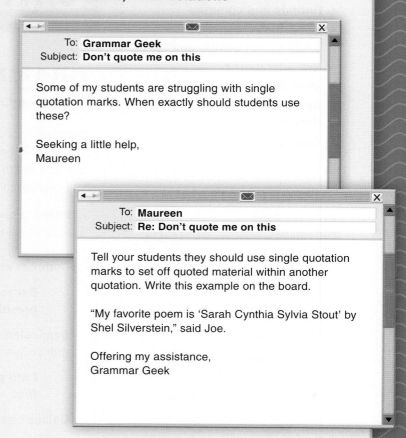

To: Grammar Geek
Subject: **Don't quote me on this**

Some of my students are struggling with single quotation marks. When exactly should students use these?

Seeking a little help,
Maureen

To: **Maureen**
Subject: **Re: Don't quote me on this**

Tell your students they should use single quotation marks to set off quoted material within another quotation. Write this example on the board.

"My favorite poem is 'Sarah Cynthia Sylvia Stout' by Shel Silverstein," said Joe.

Offering my assistance,
Grammar Geek

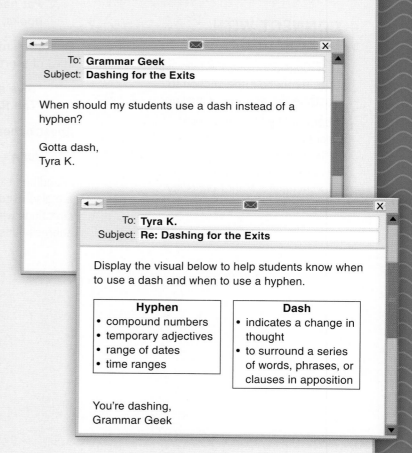

To: Grammar Geek
Subject: **Dashing for the Exits**

When should my students use a dash instead of a hyphen?

Gotta dash,
Tyra K.

To: **Tyra K.**
Subject: **Re: Dashing for the Exits**

Display the visual below to help students know when to use a dash and when to use a hyphen.

Hyphen	Dash
• compound numbers • temporary adjectives • range of dates • time ranges	• indicates a change in thought • to surround a series of words, phrases, or clauses in apposition

You're dashing,
Grammar Geek

Punctuation and Capitalization

OBJECTIVES
- To identify the uses of periods and commas in sentences
- To use periods and commas correctly

DAILY Maintenance

Assign **Practice Book** page 117, Section 10.1. After students finish,
1. Give immediate feedback.
2. Review concepts as needed.
3. Model the correct answer.

Pages 4–5 of the **Answer Key** contain tips for Daily Maintenance.

WARM-UP

Arrange the class into two teams. Read aloud from a magazine or newspaper. As you read, have a student from each team walk back and forth across the front of the classroom. Instruct students to stop when you come to a period in the reading and to change direction when you come to a comma. If a student continues walking, he or she sits down and is replaced by a teammate. Continue this activity as time permits.

📖 Read from a piece of writing that the class is currently reading. Emphasize the periods and commas.

TEACH

Copy a paragraph from the newspaper or magazine article you used in the Warm-Up, but remove all the periods and commas. Read the paragraph aloud and discuss your reading of the paragraph. Elicit from students that you did not pause as you read it. Ask students what might have prompted this type of reading. When a student suggests that perhaps the paragraph did not have any punctuation, display the paragraph. Confirm that

the paragraph does not contain punctuation. Ask students how the lack of punctuation affected their understanding of the piece. List their answers on the board.

Invite volunteers to read aloud about periods and commas. Then challenge students to insert periods and commas into the paragraph from the article.

PRACTICE

EXERCISE 1

Have students recall the rules for inserting commas and periods. Ask students to complete the exercise independently. Encourage students to use the lesson to

find answers to any punctuation questions students may have. Have students compare answers.

EXERCISE 2

Ask volunteers to name instances when a comma is required. Then have partners complete this activity. Combine sets of partners and encourage students to discuss their answers. Invite volunteers to write on the board their corrected sentences. Discuss the reason for each period and comma.

10.1 Periods and Commas

A **period** is used at the end of a declarative or an imperative sentence, after an abbreviation, and after the initials in a name.

> The poem is about a shipwreck. Recite the poem.
> Mrs. Eleanor Roosevelt
> R. A. Anaya

Commas are used for the following:

- to separate words in a series of three or more and to separate adjectives of equal importance

> Inez, Patricia, and Roberto wrote about sea disasters.
> My favorite trees are tall, leafy, green elms.

- to set off the parts of addresses, place names, and dates

> The big flood in Johnstown, Pennsylvania, occurred on May 31, 1889, and lasted no more than 10 minutes.

- to set off words of direct address and parenthetical expressions

> Lizzie, the *Titanic* disaster took place in 1912.
> The *Titanic* was called unsinkable; on the contrary, it struck an iceberg and sank in 2 hours.

- to set off nonrestrictive phrases and clauses

> Johnstown, a town in southwestern Pennsylvania, was the site of a major flood. (nonrestrictive appositive)
> The flood, which occurred because of a burst dam, left many people dead and homeless. (nonrestrictive clause)

- to set off a direct quotation or parts of a divided quotation

> "I remember a big flood," my grandmother said.
> "We evacuated our home," she continued, "in a boat!"

The *Titanic* striking an iceberg in thick fog off Newfoundland

- before coordinating conjunctions when they are used to connect clauses in a sentence and after conjunctive adverbs in compound sentences

> The South Fork dam broke, and the city of Johnstown was flooded.
> People living below the dam felt secure; consequently, they ignored the alarm.

- after the salutation in a friendly letter and after the closing in all letters

> Dear Miriam,   Yours truly,

Exercise 1
1. "Our history contains songs, poems, and stories about ships and tragedy," said Mrs. Nelson, our history teacher.
2. "Some of these," she continued, "we'll examine, class."
3. Henry W. Longfellow, a famous American poet of the 1800s, wrote a poem about a ship that sank during a storm.
4. Name some other works by Longfellow.
5. The poem, which was based on an actual event, is called "The Wreck of the *Hesperus*," and it is one of Longfellow's best-known poems.
6. The characters are a ship captain, his daughter, and an old sailor.
7. "The Sinking of the *Reuben James*," a song by Woody Guthrie, tells of another tragedy at sea.
8. The song tells of a U.S. ship torpedoed by a German submarine on October 31, 1941, near Iceland.
9. The song focuses on individuals involved in the tragedy, and originally its verses named the crew members.

APPLY

APPLY IT NOW

Remind students that a letter should include a salutation and a closing. Ask a volunteer if you can make copies of his or her letter. Distribute these copies. Discuss the punctuation of the letter, making any corrections that are needed. Students should demonstrate an understanding of using periods and commas.

ASSESS

Note which students had difficulty using periods and commas correctly. Assign **Practice Book** page 119 for further practice.

WRITING CONNECTION

Use pages 464–465 of the Writing portion of the book.

TEACHING OPTIONS

Reteach

Have students read aloud sentences from books or magazines. Write the sentences on the board, omitting the punctuation. Challenge students to suggest where commas and periods should be inserted. Have students confirm the punctuation against the original text. Encourage students to explain the rules for applying the periods and commas.

Cooperative Learning

Have small groups write on the note cards the rules for using periods and commas, one rule per card. Instruct group members to shuffle the cards and place them facedown. Have students take turns picking a card, reading the rule aloud, and composing a sentence for that rule. Instruct each group member to write the sentence on a sheet of paper, inserting the commas and periods where necessary. Tell students to review the sentence as a group. Have students continue the activity until all the cards have been read.

Meeting Individual Needs

Auditory Ask students to listen closely to the daily announcements, trying to determine whether pauses in the announcements represent periods or commas. Tell students to write sentences from the announcements, inserting punctuation as necessary. If possible, record the announcements to play during class. Write selected sentences on the board. Have students insert the commas and periods, some of which students may have written down earlier. Discuss how each sentence should be punctuated.

---

10. The *Reuben James* was the first U.S. Navy ship lost during World War II, and only 44 members of the crew survived.

Exercise 2

1. On November 10, 1975, the *Edmund Fitzgerald*, a large freighter, sank in a sudden powerful storm on Lake Superior.

2. The storm damaged the ship's communication system, and no one knows how the ship sank.

3. Yes, the ship's sinking remains a mystery.

4. The *Arthur Anderson*, the *William Clay Ford*, and the *Hilda Marjanne* all helped search for the missing boat and its crew.

5. Great Lakes Engineering Works, the company commissioned to build the great ship, had over 1,000 men working on the job.

6. Gordon Lightfoot, a Canadian folksinger, did not personally know any of the 29 dead, but he wrote a tribute to them nonetheless.

7. Lightfoot's song, which was written not long after the tragedy, is still one of his most-requested works.

EXERCISE 1 Rewrite these sentences. Add periods and commas where needed.

1. "Our history contains songs poems and stories about ships and tragedy" said Mrs Nelson our history teacher

2. "Some of these" she continued "we'll examine class"

3. Henry W Longfellow a famous American poet of the 1800s wrote a poem about a ship that sank during a storm

4. Name some other works by Longfellow

5. The poem which was based on an actual event is called "The Wreck of the *Hesperus*" and it is one of Longfellow's best-known poems

6. The characters are a ship captain his daughter and an old sailor

7. "The Sinking of the *Reuben James*" a song by Woody Guthrie tells of another tragedy at sea

8. The song tells of a US ship torpedoed by a German submarine on October 31 1941 near Iceland

9. The song focuses on individuals involved in the tragedy and originally its verses named the crew members

10. The *Reuben James* was the first US Navy ship lost during World War II and only 44 members of the crew survived

EXERCISE 2 Rewrite the following sentences to correct any errors in punctuation.

1. On November 10 1975 the *Edmund Fitzgerald* a large freighter sank in a sudden powerful storm on Lake Superior

2. The storm damaged the ship's communication system and no one knows how the ship sank

3. Yes the ship's sinking remains a mystery.

4. The *Arthur Anderson* the *William Clay Ford* and the *Hilda Marjanne* all helped search for the missing boat and its crew

5. Great Lakes Engineering Works the company commissioned to build the great ship had over 1,000 men working on the job

6. Gordon Lightfoot a Canadian folksinger did not personally know any of the 29 dead but he wrote a tribute to them nonetheless.

7. Lightfoot's song which was written not long after the tragedy is still one of his most-requested works

Out of the 2,228 people onboard the *Titanic*, only 705 survived. The ship sank on April 14, 1912.

APPLY IT NOW

Write a letter to a friend. Include lists and information about your favorite musical performers. Punctuate your letter correctly.

Punctuation • 183

10.2 Exclamation Points, Question Marks, Semicolons, and Colons

OBJECTIVE
- **To use exclamation points, question marks, semicolons, and colons correctly**

Maintenance

Assign **Practice Book** page 117, Section 10.2. After students finish,
1. Give immediate feedback.
2. Review concepts as needed.
3. Model the correct answer.

Pages 4–5 of the **Answer Key** contain tips for Daily Maintenance.

WARM-UP

Write on the board six sentences, omitting all punctuation. Leave space where a punctuation mark should appear. Before class, make large periods, commas, question marks, exclamation points, semicolons, and colons. Ask volunteers to tape the correct punctuation marks in the spaces.

📖 Read from a piece of writing that the class is currently reading. Emphasize the exclamation points, question marks, semicolons, and colons.

TEACH

Point to each punctuation mark in the Warm-Up sentences and ask students to identify each one. When pointing to exclamation points, question marks, semicolons, and colons, ask volunteers to share what they know about each punctuation mark.

Invite volunteers to read aloud about exclamation points, question marks, semicolons, and colons. Have the student pause after each rule. Discuss each rule and ask students for additional examples. Write sentences on the board for those rules that may pose the greatest challenge.

Have volunteers place the correct punctuation.

Ask students to look through books in the classroom to find examples of each punctuation mark. Write on the board the punctuation mark and the corresponding sentences from these sources. Discuss which rules apply to the punctuation used in the sentences.

PRACTICE

EXERCISE 1
Tell students that they need to consider all the parts of a sentence to help determine the proper punctuation. Instruct students to complete this activity independently. Then have a volunteer write one sentence on the board, with the punctuation in place. Ask students to check their answers against that sentence. Continue with all the sentences, discussing the use of each punctuation mark.

EXERCISE 2
Have partners complete this exercise. Suggest that they read the sentences aloud to each other. Ask students to listen for natural pauses, as well as the tone of each sentence. Have students work together to add the correct punctuation to each sentence.

10.2 Exclamation Points, Question Marks, Semicolons, and Colons

Exclamation points are used after most interjections and to end exclamatory sentences.

> Hooray! We are going to visit California.
> No, I can't find my suitcase!

Question marks are used to end interrogative sentences.

> Who put my suitcase in the basement?

A **semicolon** is used for the following:

- to separate clauses in a compound sentence when they are not joined by a conjunction

  > We left early in the morning; the roads were empty.

- to separate clauses in a compound sentence that are connected by conjunctive adverbs

  > Truckers carried freight along Route 66; furthermore, families used the highway for vacation trips.

- to separate phrases or clauses of the same type that include internal punctuation

  > Several significant dates in World War II are December 7, 1941; May 5, 1945; and August 14, 1945.

- before parenthetical expressions such as *for example* and *namely* when they are used to introduce examples

  > We traveled through several states; namely, Texas, New Mexico, Arizona, and Nevada.

A **colon** is used for the following:

- before a list when terms such as *the following* or *as follows* are used

  > The following are places I'd like to visit: Grand Canyon, Yellowstone National Park, and Hawaii.

- after the salutation of a business letter

  > Dear Professor Rosenfeld:

Exercise 1
1. Route 66 was a highway; however, it was far more than that.
2. It represented many things; namely, the romance of the open road, a chance for adventure, and a new life in the West.
3. It was one of the first highways across the United States; it was commissioned in 1926.
4. Where did the highway start and end?
5. It started near Lake Michigan in Chicago, Illinois; it ended near the Pacific Ocean in Santa Monica, California.
6. The cities that Route 66 went through included the following: Tulsa, Amarillo, Albuquerque, and Flagstaff.
7. What a great road it was!

Exercise 2
1. Other names for Route 66 are these: the Main Street of America, the Mother Road, and the Will Rogers Highway.

Invite volunteers to share their answers with the class. Discuss sentences that are difficult for some students.

TechTip Have students suggest possible search terms and list these on the board. Remind students to use a credible search engine.

APPLY

APPLY IT NOW

Discuss some well-known streets in the community and what visitors might see along them. Tell students to circle the punctuation marks in the sentences. Students should demonstrate an understanding of exclamation points, question marks, semicolons, and colons.

ASSESS

Note which students had difficulty using exclamation points, question marks, semicolons, and colons correctly. Assign **Practice Book** page 120 for further practice.

WRITING CONNECTION

Use pages 466–467 of the Writing portion of the book.

TEACHING OPTIONS

Reteach

Write each of the four punctuation marks on individual note cards. On the board write sentences that need one of the four punctuation marks, omitting the punctuation. Place the cards along the board ledge. Invite a volunteer to read aloud the first sentence. Ask students to identify the correct punctuation mark. Then have a volunteer hold the card at the point in the sentence where the punctuation mark belongs.

Meeting Individual Needs

Extra Support Encourage students to look through nonfiction texts for one example of each of the following punctuation marks: exclamation point, question mark, semicolon, and colon. Have students copy their sentences onto four separate sheets of paper, one for each mark. Direct students to write below each sentence the punctuation rule from page 184 that applies to the example.

Curriculum Connection

Have students study a road map of the United States to come up with other ideas about well-known roads besides Route 66. You might suggest the Pacific Coast Highway in the West, Route 95 in the East, and Broadway and Fifth Avenue in New York City. Ask students to choose one road and to write about the scenery they would expect to see along that road. Explain that some research may be needed before students can begin writing. Remind them to include exclamation points, question marks, semicolons, and colons in their writing. Suggest that students take "snapshots" along their roads, drawing pictures of things to see. Have students present their snapshots and writing to the class.

2. There have been songs written, such as "Will Rogers Highway" by Woody Guthrie and "Route 66" by Bobby Troup, which helped immortalize this historic highway.

3. Hotels, restaurants, and gas stations opened along the highway which catered to truck drivers and travelers alike.

4. John Steinbeck wrote *The Grapes of Wrath*; the characters in this book travel along Route 66.

5. A writer has said the following about Route 66: "It's a station wagon filled with kids wanting to know how far it is to Disneyland, a wailing ambulance fleeing a wreck on some lonely curve. It's yesterday, today, and tomorrow. Truly a road of phantoms and dreams, 66 is the romance of traveling the open highway."

6. Route 66 was officially ended in 1985; new interstate highways replaced it.

7. The old highway exists in many places; however, various sections have been renumbered.

EXERCISE 1 Rewrite the following sentences. Add exclamation points, question marks, semicolons, and colons where needed.

1. Route 66 was a highway however, it was far more than that.
2. It represented many things namely, the romance of the open road, a chance for adventure, and a new life in the West.
3. It was one of the first highways across the United States it was commissioned in 1926.
4. Where did the highway start and end
5. It started near Lake Michigan in Chicago, Illinois it ended near the Pacific Ocean in Santa Monica, California.
6. The cities that Route 66 went through included the following Tulsa, Amarillo, Albuquerque, and Flagstaff.
7. What a great road it was

EXERCISE 2 Rewrite these sentences, using the correct punctuation.

1. Other names for Route 66 are these the Main Street of America the Mother Road and the Will Rogers Highway
2. There have been songs written such as "Will Rogers Highway" by Woody Guthrie and "Route 66" by Bobby Troup which helped immortalize this historic highway
3. Hotels restaurants and gas stations opened along the highway which catered to truck drivers and travelers alike
4. John Steinbeck wrote *The Grapes of Wrath* the characters in this book travel along Route 66
5. A writer has said the following about Route 66: "It's a station wagon filled with kids wanting to know how far it is to Disneyland a wailing ambulance fleeing a wreck on some lonely curve It's yesterday today and tomorrow Truly a road of phantoms and dreams, 66 is the romance of traveling the open highway"
6. Route 66 was officially ended in 1985 new interstate highways replaced it
7. The old highway exists in many places however various sections have been renumbered

APPLY IT NOW

Choose a well-known or scenic street in your community. Write five sentences using each of these punctuation marks: exclamation point, question mark, semicolon, and colon.

Tech Tip With an adult, find a map of the original Route 66 online.

Punctuation • 185

OBJECTIVES

- **To use quotation marks, italics, and underlining correctly**
- **To distinguish which items should appear in quotation marks and which should be italicized (or underlined)**

 **DAILY Maintenance**

Assign **Practice Book** page 117, Section 10.3. After students finish,
1. Give immediate feedback.
2. Review concepts as needed.
3. Model the correct answer.

Pages 4–5 of the **Answer Key** contain tips for Daily Maintenance.

WARM-UP

Distribute copies of comic strips that do not contain dialogue. Ask students to glue the comic strips to poster board. Then have students write their own dialogue for each comic strip.

Read from a piece of writing that the class is currently reading. Emphasize the quotation marks and italics.

TEACH

Read aloud the first sentence, the first bulleted item, and the example. Point out the use of commas in divided quotations. Have students make corrections to their Warm-Up dialogues.

Ask a volunteer to read aloud the second bulleted item and the examples. Read aloud about single quotation marks and indirect quotations. Discuss the difference between direct and indirect quotations.

Have students name a few TV shows. Write suggestions on the board. Explain that each episode of a weekly TV show has a title separate from that of the series, just as a chapter in a book may have a separate title. Tell students that the series title should be in italics and the episode title should be within quotation marks. Have a volunteer read aloud the information about italics. Point out the use of underlining when handwriting.

PRACTICE

EXERCISE 1

Remind students that divided quotations need commas in addition to quotation marks. Have students complete this exercise independently. Then invite volunteers to share their answers with the class.

EXERCISE 2

Have students create a two-column chart with the headings *Quotation Marks* and *Italics*. Tell students to complete the chart to help remember which titles receive which treatment. Encourage students to refer to the chart as they complete the exercise.

EXERCISES 3

Briefly review sections 10.1 and 10.2. Have students complete this exercise independently. Then have students write their sentences on the board, with the punctuation in place. Have students discuss the sentences.

10.3 Quotation Marks and Italics

Quotation marks are used for the following:

- before and after direct quotations and around the parts of divided quotations

   "This," Mr. Small cried, "is just the sweater I've been looking for."

- to set off the titles of stories, poems, songs, magazine and newspaper articles, episodes of TV series, and radio programs

   We learned the spiritual "Deep River."
   They read Edgar Allan Poe's poem "The Bells."
   "Thanksgiving Disaster" would be a good title for my story.

Single quotation marks are used to set off quoted material within a quotation.

   "Have you read the story 'To Build a Fire'?" Mary Margaret asked.
   Mick said, "Explain the proverb 'A penny saved is a penny earned.'"

Indirect quotations do not use quotation marks.

   Mark said that his favorite literature was science fiction.

Edgar Allan Poe

Italics are used for the titles of books, magazines, newspapers, movies, TV series, ships, and works of art.

   We prayed for those aboard the aircraft carrier *Hornet*.
   Today's *Washington Post* has a photograph of Michelangelo's *Pietà*.

If you are handwriting, use underlining for italics.

   You should read the article "Sitting Pretty" in <u>Hearth and Home</u>.

EXERCISE 1 Rewrite these sentences. Add punctuation marks where needed.

1. Bottlenose dolphins the scientist explained are fascinating.
2. She continued They are known for their intelligence.
3. Do they live in families? asked a student.
4. Not exactly, but they travel in groups ranging from a dozen to several hundred individuals explained the scientist.
5. You may see these dolphins playing at the oceanarium said the scientist because they are very social creatures.

Exercise 1
1. "Bottlenose dolphins," the scientist explained, "are fascinating."
2. She continued, "They are known for their intelligence."
3. "Do they live in families?" asked a student.
4. "Not exactly, but they travel in groups ranging from a dozen to several hundred individuals," explained the scientist.

5. "You may see these dolphins playing at the oceanarium," said the scientist, "because they are very social creatures."

Exercise 2
1. In the book *Tales and Stories for Black Folks* I especially enjoyed the story "Raymond's Run" by Toni Cade Bambara.
2. George's favorite poem is "The Willow and the Gingko."
3. Nat Hentoff's novel *The Day They Came to Arrest the Book* is about the book *The Adventures of Huckleberry Finn* and a group of censors.
4. Several films tell the story of the sinking of the *Titanic*.
5. The Walt Disney movie *Sleeping Beauty* featured music by Tchaikovsky.
6. The movie *Minority Report* was based on the short story "The Minority Report," which appeared in *The Variation Man*.
7. No one knows who is portrayed in Leonardo da Vinci's famous painting *Mona Lisa*.

186 • Section 10.3

APPLY

APPLY IT NOW

After students have completed their lists, create a master list on the board. Discuss the correct punctuation. Students should demonstrate an understanding of using quotation marks and italics.

Grammar in Action Remind students to use commas with divided quotations and single quotation marks with quoted material within a quotation.

ASSESS

Note which students had difficulty using quotation marks and italics correctly. Assign **Practice Book** page 121 for further practice.

WRITING CONNECTION

Use pages 468–469 of the Writing portion of the book.

---

8. When U.S. and Canadian teams play each other, fans sing both "The Star-Spangled Banner" and "O Canada."

Exercise 3

1. The author of *Harry Potter and the Order of the Phoenix* was on the *Today Show* yesterday.

2. The article "The Magic of Potter" appeared in *Time* magazine.

3. "Do you know," asked Carol, "how Harry got to Hogwarts School?"

4. Brendan remarked, "My cousin said that *Harry Potter and the Goblet of Fire* is his favorite Harry Potter novel."

5. Carla said, "We wrote a song called 'Help Me, Hedwig.'"

6. "My favorite book is *James and the Giant Peach*," exclaimed Theresa.

7. "The book by Roald Dahl," explained Mike, "was written for his children in 1961. "

8. "The main character and hero of this book," said the teacher, "is named James Henry Trotter."

9. There are many other characters in the book; for example, some talking bugs, Aunt Sponge, and Aunt Spiker.

EXERCISE 2 Rewrite these sentences. Add quotation marks and italics where needed. You can use underlining to indicate italics.

1. In the book Tales and Stories for Black Folks I especially enjoyed the story Raymond's Run by Toni Cade Bambara.

2. George's favorite poem is The Willow and the Gingko.

3. Nat Hentoff's novel The Day They Came to Arrest the Book is about the book The Adventures of Huckleberry Finn and a group of censors.

4. Several films tell the story of the sinking of the Titanic.

5. The Walt Disney movie Sleeping Beauty featured music by Tchaikovsky.

6. The movie Minority Report was based on the short story The Minority Report, which appeared in The Variation Man.

7. No one knows who is portrayed in Leonardo da Vinci's famous painting Mona Lisa.

8. When U.S. and Canadian teams play each other, fans sing both The Star-Spangled Banner and O Canada.

EXERCISE 3 Rewrite each sentence, using correct punctuation.

1. The author of Harry Potter and the Order of the Phoenix was on the Today Show yesterday

2. The article The Magic of Potter appeared in Time magazine

3. Do you know asked Carol how Harry got to Hogwarts School

4. Brendan remarked My cousin said that Harry Potter and the Goblet of Fire is his favorite Harry Potter novel

5. Carla said We wrote a song called Help Me, Hedwig

6. My favorite book is James and the Giant Peach said Theresa

7. The book by Roald Dahl explained Mike was written for his children in 1961

8. The main character and hero of this book said the teacher is named James Henry Trotter

9. There are many other characters in the book for example some talking bugs Aunt Sponge and Aunt Spiker.

APPLY IT NOW

Make a list of all your favorite books, songs, movies, plays, works of art, and magazines. Check the punctuation of all the titles.

Grammar in Action Rewrite two lines from the play on p. 451, using quotation marks correctly.

OBJECTIVE

- To recognize when to use apostrophes, hyphens, and dashes

 **DAILY Maintenance**

Assign **Practice Book** page 117, Section 10.4. After students finish,
1. Give immediate feedback.
2. Review concepts as needed.
3. Model the correct answer.

Pages 4–5 of the **Answer Key** contain tips for Daily Maintenance.

WARM-UP

Write on the board several newspaper headlines that are punctuated incorrectly. (Include missing or misused apostrophes, hyphens, and dashes.) Arrange the class into four teams. Instruct students to add the missing punctuation or to delete incorrect punctuation. Tell students that the first team to edit the headlines correctly wins.

📖 Read from a piece of writing that the class is currently reading. Emphasize the apostrophes, hyphens, and dashes.

TEACH

Write the following on the board: *don't, we'll, Tory's book, dog's bone, sister-in-law, two-year-old.* Focus students' attention on the use of apostrophes and hyphens in these words. Ask whether students find any similarity between some of the terms *(contractions, possessives, compound nouns).*

Invite volunteers to read aloud about apostrophes and hyphens. Point out that apostrophes are used to make contractions. Explain the formation of temporary adjectives, which contain hyphens to show the relationship between the two parts. Write on the board these examples:

person with a strong will
balloon filled with hot air

strong-willed person
hot-air balloon

Have students read silently about dashes. Encourage students to suggest sentences with dashes. Write the sentences on the board and invite the students who provided the examples to put the dashes in the correct places.

PRACTICE

EXERCISE 1

Tell students to consider how words in the sentences are being used before determining the correct punctuation. Have partners complete this exercise. Discuss any discrepancies with the class.

EXERCISE 2

Explain that this exercise requires students to add quotation marks and italics (or underlining) in addition to apostrophes, hyphens, and dashes. Have partners complete this exercise. When students have finished, discuss each sentence.

EXERCISE 3

Review the use of apostrophes, hyphens, and dashes. Have

10.4 Apostrophes, Hyphens, and Dashes

An **apostrophe** is used for the following:

- to show possession

     Grady's toy soldiers   my cousins' cat

- to show the omission of letters or numbers

     can't   I'll   class of '08

- to show the plural of lowercase letters but not of capital letters unless the plural could be mistaken for a word

     a's   u's   Ps   Ns   (Exceptions: *U's* and *I's*)

A **hyphen** is used for the following:

- to divide a word between syllables at the end of a line

     My grandfather, who lives in California, will be visiting in July.

- in compound numbers from twenty-one to ninety-nine and to separate parts of some compound words

     sixty-three   mother-in-law

- to form some temporary adjectives

     The project will take *four years.*
     A *four-year* project is a big undertaking. (adjective)

A **dash** is used for the following:

- to indicate a change in thought or an interruption

     I turned suddenly—I'm still surprised I did—and left the room.

- to surround a series of words, phrases, or clauses in apposition

     Children's pets—cats, dogs, birds, and fish—are first in popularity.

EXERCISE 1 Rewrite these sentences. Add apostrophes, hyphens, and dashes where needed.

1. My father in law gave a terrific party.
2. There was a merry go round in the yard, and each child got a five minute ride.

Exercise 1
1. My father-in-law gave a terrific party.
2. There was a merry-go-round in the yard, and each child got a five-minute ride.
3. My mother-in-law hung a star-shaped piñata from a tree.
4. At first the children couldn't break it—a surprise to us all.
5. Finally it broke, and different-colored candies fell out.
6. I counted eighty-nine candy wrappers on the ground under the piñata after the children left the party.
7. My brother-in-law's band played songs—a real treat for all.
8. We'll remember the peppermint-flavored ice cream.
9. The children went home at six o'clock.
10. They'll never forget this great birthday party.

students complete this exercise independently.

 Grammar in Action. Explain that the dash is used to show an interruption.

APPLY

APPLY IT NOW

The following is the corrected sentence:

> My seventy-two-year-old grandfather—if you can believe it—walks northbound on Main Street for two miles every day.

Students should demonstrate an understanding of hyphens and dashes.

ASSESS

Note which students had difficulty using apostrophes, hyphens, and dashes. Assign **Practice Book** page 122 for further practice.

WRITING CONNECTION

Use pages 470–471 of the Writing portion of the book.

TEACHING OPTIONS

Reteach

Display an interesting picture and invite students to write three sentences about it: one sentence with an apostrophe, one with a hyphen, and one with a dash. Ask students to read their sentences aloud or to write their sentences on the board. Review the use of apostrophes, hyphens, and dashes, encouraging students to explain the rules that apply to each. Write the following sentences on the board and ask students to state the rule that applies to each:

> **The sailor's face is all scrunched up.** *(an apostrophe to show possession)*

> **The sailor has trouble with the wind-whipped sail.** *(a hyphen to form a temporary adjective)*

> **The water looks rough—I'm surprised the boat hasn't flipped yet.** *(a dash to indicate a change in thought)*

Meeting Individual Needs

Extra Challenge Have each student write a complete paragraph, using no punctuation. Explain that the paragraph can be about a topic from another class, a recent experience, or an admired person. Have students exchange their papers with partners and insert correct punctuation marks. Tell students to return the papers to the original writers. Encourage partners to discuss any punctuation marks that may have been added incorrectly or that have been missed. Monitor students' progress, helping students resolve any misunderstandings.

Exercise 2

1. Members of Mrs. Carter's eighth-grade class chose their favorite works of art.
2. Carla's favorite movie is *The Wizard of Oz.*
3. Several nominated the book *A Wrinkle in Time.*
4. Ana has seen Rodin's famous statue *The Thinker*—a wonderful experience.
5. Keshawn remarked, "My dad's favorite piece of music is the Beatles' 'Good Day Sunshine.'"
6. Carol and Christine both selected Robert Frost's poem "Stopping by Woods on a Snowy Evening."
7. Mrs. Carter reported, "My brother-in-law loves Jack London's short story 'To Light a Fire.'"
8. The novel *Great Expectations* by Charles Dickens received a number of votes—a surprise to Mrs. Carter.
9. The song "America the Beautiful" was more popular than "The Star-Spangled Banner."
10. The *Newtown Gazette* reported the results of the poll.

Exercise 3
Answers will vary.

3. My mother in law hung a star shaped piñata from a tree.
4. At first the children couldnt break it a surprise to us all.
5. Finally it broke, and different colored candies fell out.
6. I counted eighty nine candy wrappers on the ground under the piñata after the children left the party.
7. My brother in laws band played songs a real treat for all.
8. Well remember the peppermint flavored ice cream.
9. The children went home at six oclock.
10. Theyll never forget this great birthday party.

EXERCISE 2 Rewrite the following sentences, adding the correct punctuation.

1. Members of Mrs. Carters eighth grade class chose their favorite works of art.
2. Carlas favorite movie is The Wizard of Oz.
3. Several nominated the book A Wrinkle in Time.
4. Ana has seen Rodins famous statue The Thinker a wonderful experience.
5. Keshawn remarked My dads favorite piece of music is the Beatles Good Day Sunshine.
6. Carol and Christine both selected Robert Frosts poem Stopping by Woods on a Snowy Evening.
7. Mrs. Carter reported My brother in law loves Jack Londons short story To Light a Fire.
8. The novel Great Expectations by Charles Dickens received a number of votes a surprise to Mrs. Carter.
9. The song America the Beautiful was more popular than The Star Spangled Banner.
10. The Newtown Gazette reported the results of the poll.

EXERCISE 3 Write sentences using the following prompts.

1. A sentence that uses a temporary adjective
2. A sentence that uses a dash
3. A sentence to show possession
4. A sentence that uses a hyphen

APPLY IT NOW

Rewrite the following sentence using correct hyphens and dashes:

My seventy two year old grand-father if you can believe it walks northbound on Main Street for two miles every day.

Punctuation • 189

 Grammar in Action. Identify how the dash is used in the script on p. 460.

10.5 Capitalization

OBJECTIVE

• **To use capital letters correctly**

 **Maintenance**

Assign **Practice Book** page 118, Section 10.5. After students finish,
1. Give immediate feedback.
2. Review concepts as needed.
3. Model the correct answer.

Pages 4–5 of the **Answer Key** contain tips for Daily Maintenance.

WARM-UP

Write on the board the following paragraph, omitting all the *s*'s that appear at the beginning of a word:

> In September Sarah moved to Syracuse. She was sad about moving, but liked her new school. In one class she got to read her favorite story, "Stone Soup." She struggled in Spanish class, but did better in science.

Have students correct the paragraph.

📖 Read from a piece of writing that the class is currently reading. Emphasize the capital letters.

TEACH

Invite a volunteer to fill in the blank spaces in the paragraph on the board. Have the volunteer underline every word to which he or she added an *s*. Then ask volunteers to read aloud the rules for using capital letters in this lesson.

Discuss the example paragraph on the board. Make any corrections that are needed. Point out that students should have correctly capitalized words that start a sentence, proper nouns such as names and months, the title of a story, and the name of a subject derived from a proper noun. If students do not fully understand one of the rules for using capital letters, provide additional examples.

PRACTICE

EXERCISE 1

Have students turn the information in the lesson into a two-column chart with the headings *Rule* and *Example*. Encourage students to use this chart to complete this exercise. After students have finished, discuss each sentence. Prompt students to express any confusion or disagreement they have and help them understand the correction.

10.5 Capitalization

A **capital letter** is used for the following:

• the first word in a sentence, the first word in a direct quotation, and the first word of most lines of poetry and songs

> **My** favorite sport is baseball. The coach yelled, "*Slide*!"

> **And** somewhere men are laughing and somewhere children shout;
> **But** there is no joy in Mudville—mighty Casey has struck out.
> —Ernest Lawrence Thayer

• proper nouns and proper adjectives, including names of people, groups, specific buildings, particular places, months, and holidays

> *Mary's* **bat**   *American* **sports**
> *Seattle*, *Washington*   *Flatbush Avenue*
> **the** *Baseball Hall* **of** *Fame*   *Japanese* **food**

• a title when it precedes a person's name

> *Senator* **Hamilton** (*but* The senator said . . .)

• the directions north, south, east, and west, when they refer to sections of the country

> **My sister went to the college in the** *South*. (*but* Go east on Oak Street.)

• the names of deities and sacred books

> *Holy Spirit*   *Bible*   *Koran*   *Old Testament*

• the principal words in titles of works (but not the articles *a*, *and*, and *the*; coordinating conjunctions; or prepositions unless they are the first or last word)

> *To Kill a Mockingbird*   *Lord of the Flies*

• abbreviations of words that are capitalized

> *U.S.A.*   *Dr.*   *Ave.*   *Jan.*

Do not capitalize the names of subjects unless they come from proper names.

> *science*   *math*   *Spanish*

Exercise 1

1. Watching baseball ranks high among leisure-time activities in the United States.
2. When we are not watching baseball, we may be reading stories about it, such as Gary Soto's "Baseball in April" or Judith Viorst's "The Southpaw."
3. Songs like "Take Me Out to the Ball Game" are classics.
4. Take me out to the ball game. /Take me out with the crowd. /Buy me some peanuts and Cracker Jack. /I don't care if I never get back.
5. Sadly, many historic ballparks such as Ebbets Field in Brooklyn, Forbes Field in Pittsburgh, and Crosby Field in Cincinnati no longer exist.
6. In some cases the original teams moved to the West, and their old parks in the East fell to the wrecking ball.
7. It is a tradition to go to ballparks on such holidays as Memorial Day, the Fourth of July, and Labor Day.

190 • Section 10.5

APPLY

APPLY IT NOW

Suggest that students try to find passages that include a variety of capital letters, such as proper nouns and sentences within quotation marks. Have partners exchange papers again to check each other's work against the printed material. Students should demonstrate an understanding of capital letters.

💡 **TechTip** Encourage students to bring in their pictures of capital letters. Scan and post them to a class blog and challenge students to identify the capitalization rules that apply for each picture.

ASSESS

Note which students had difficulty understanding when to use capital letters. Assign **Practice Book** page 123 for further practice.

WRITING CONNECTION

Use pages 472–473 of the Writing portion of the book.

8. Baseball is played in many places, including Japan, Puerto Rico, and Mexico.
9. Some people say that baseball evolved from an English sport called rounders, but others say that Abner Doubleday invented it in Cooperstown, New York, in the 1800s.
10. Roberto Clemente, a famous Hispanic baseball player, died in a plane crash while carrying supplies to earthquake victims in Nicaragua in Central America.
11. The National Baseball Hall of Fame and Museum, located in Cooperstown, New York, displays old bats, balls, and baseball jerseys of famous players like Greg Maddux.
12. Joe DiMaggio was a famous player and was part of the New York Yankees, but he is also known for marrying film starlet Marylin Monroe.
13. Many famous movies like *Field of Dreams* and *A League of Their Own* celebrate baseball and are very popular with fans of the game.
14. *A League of Their Own* is about women who played in the All-American Girls Professional Baseball League.

EXERCISE 1 Rewrite the following sentences, adding capital letters where needed.

1. watching baseball ranks high among leisure-time activities in the united states.

2. when we are not watching baseball, we may be reading stories about it, such as gary soto's "baseball in april" or judith viorst's "the southpaw."

3. songs like "take me out to the ball game" are classics.

4. take me out to the ball game.
   take me out with the crowd.
   buy me some peanuts and cracker jack.
   i don't care if i never get back.

5. sadly, many historic ballparks such as ebbets field in brooklyn, forbes field in pittsburgh, and crosby field in cincinnati no longer exist.

6. in some cases the original teams moved to the west, and their old parks in the east fell to the wrecking ball.

7. it is a tradition to go to ballparks on such holidays as memorial day, the fourth of july, and labor day.

8. baseball is played in many places, including japan, puerto rico, and mexico.

9. some people say that baseball evolved from an english sport called rounders, but others say that abner doubleday invented it in cooperstown, new york, in the 1800s.

10. roberto clemente, a famous hispanic baseball player, died in a plane crash while carrying supplies to earthquake victims in nicaragua in central america.

11. the national baseball hall of fame and museum, located in cooperstown, new york, displays old bats, balls, and baseball jerseys of famous players like greg maddux.

12. joe dimaggio was a famous player and was part of the new york yankees, but he is also known for marrying film starlet marylin monroe.

13. many famous movies like *field of dreams* and *a league of their own* celebrate baseball and are popular with fans of the game.

14. *a league of their own* is about women who played in the all-american girls professional baseball league.

APPLY IT NOW

Copy a passage from a book, magazine, or newspaper, without the capital letters. Trade papers with a partner. See whether your classmate can correct your passage while you correct your classmate's passage.

Tech Tip Use a camera to photograph capital letters in street signs.

Capitalization • 191

TEACHING OPTIONS

Reteach

On the board create a chart with column headings for the major categories that require capitalization (*First Words, Proper Nouns, Book Titles,* and *Abbreviations*). Have students explain each rule in their own words as you enter it below the appropriate heading. Invite students to supply examples for each rule. Encourage students to write their own examples in the chart. Leave the chart on the board and tell students to refer to it when they have questions about capitalization. You might also have students use their words or phrases from the chart in sentences. Ask students to share their sentences with the class.

English-Language Learners

Capitalization rules for the English language may differ from the rules of the primary languages spoken by some students. Pair English-language learners with students proficient in the understanding of capitalization. Have the proficient student review the rules with the English-language learner. Suggest that the English-language learner write the rules and examples in his or her journal for reference. Together, have students look for examples of the capitalization rules in books, newspapers, and magazines.

Meeting Individual Needs

Intrapersonal Encourage students to read entries in their journals for possible errors in capitalization. Instruct students to look for words that have been capitalized that should not be. Tell students to circle the incorrect words and to write the correct capitalization (or missing capitalization) on a separate sheet of paper.

Punctuation and Capitalization Review

ASSESS

Use the Punctuation and Capitalization Review as homework, as a practice test, or as an informal assessment. Following are some options for use.

Homework

You may wish to assign one group the odd items and another group the even items. When you next meet, review the correct answers as a group. Be sure to model how to arrive at the correct answer.

Practice Test

Use the Punctuation and Capitalization Review as a diagnostic tool. Assign the entire review or just specific sections. After students have finished, identify which concepts require more attention. Reteach concepts as necessary.

Punctuation and Capitalization Review

10.1 Rewrite each sentence. Add periods and commas where needed.

1. W.B. Yeats was a famous Irish poet.
2. Yeats was born in Dublin, Ireland, on June 13, 1865.
3. The poet, as you may guess, wrote mainly about Irish topics.
4. Maxwell, please read one of his poems aloud.
5. "I would like to read this one," he said.
6. Maxwell finished reading "Easter 1916," and the class showered him with applause.
7. "Your reading," the teacher commented, "was magnificent."
8. My other favorite Irish writers are Oscar Wilde, James Joyce, and Patrick Kavanagh.
9. Dear Mary,
   Here is a poem I wrote for you and your family.
10. "Poetry," explained the teacher, "is another way to tell a story."

10.2 Rewrite each sentence. Add exclamation points, question marks, semicolons, and colons where needed.

11. What do we need to make pound cake for the bake sale?
12. These are the main ingredients: butter, eggs, sugar, and flour.
13. Look! Half the eggs are broken.

14. The eggs were fine at the store; they must have broken on the way home.
15. We don't have enough eggs; therefore, I must buy more.
16. Please mix all the wet ingredients; namely, butter and eggs.
17. How did the pound cake turn out?
18. Oh my, this pound cake is delicious!
19. We sold a slice of cake to Steve from Carson City, Nevada.
20. Other treats at the bake sale included cookies, tarts, pies, and brownies.
21. The last bake sale was April 14, 2009, and the next one is on September 7.
22. Ugh, I'm so full from snacking too much!

10.3 Rewrite each sentence. Add quotation marks and underlining to show italics where needed.

23. "How many students read the newspaper every day?" asked Mrs. Filippo.
24. Most students read The Daily Herald or the Morning Star each morning.
25. A few students listened to Morning Edition on the radio.
26. Mrs. Filippo brought several issues of Newsweek to the classroom.

10.4

34. My sister-in-law went to Charlie's school.
35. She graduated in '99.
36. It was the fifty-fifth class to graduate from the school.
37. There were ninety-seven students in her class.
38. Several students graduated with straight A's.
39. Many students—my brother is one—went to the same high school
40. They have known each other since they were in a high-level math class together.
41. They had their 10-year reunion last week—can you believe it?
42. My friend's sisters were both star athletes in high school.
43. His sisters—who are twins—played basketball and soccer.
44. "I graduated college in '09," she said, "with a major in prelaw."

Informal Assessment

Use the review as preparation for the formal assessment. Count the review as a portion of the grade. Have students work to find the correct answers and use their corrected review as a study guide for the formal assessment.

WRITING CONNECTION

Use pages 474–475 of the Writing portion of the book.

TEACHING OPTIONS

Putting It All Together

To review punctuation and capitalization, have students complete the following exercises:

- Write a paragraph without any punctuation or capitalization. Trade papers with a partner and correct the paragraph. Check your partner's work.

- Write 10 sentences about your favorite activity (such as cooking, swimming, or reading), using periods and commas correctly.

- Conduct online research about a current event. Write sentences about this event. Use exclamation points, question marks, semicolons, and colons.

- Develop a game that will help your classmates better understand the use of apostrophes, hyphens, and dashes. Play the game in small groups.

10.5

45. The U.S. team trained for the Summer Olympics that were held in Athens, Greece, in 2004.

46. Several training facilities are located in the West.

47. I think some swimmers train in Boulder, Colorado.

48. Is it near the University of Colorado?

49. Athletes received a good-luck message from Senator Glenn Thompson.

50. Coach Philips wants us to train at the Mountain View Aquatic Center in Loveland, Colorado.

51. Andre and Wendy swim on a team called the Boulder Poseidons.

52. If you take Pearl Street south, you can reach the base of the Flatirons foothills.

27. She asked the class to read the article "Ruffled Feathers in Birding" for homework.

28. Yesterday's _Daily Times_ featured a photograph of Michelangelo's sculpture _David_.

29. Tommy and Hunter write for the school paper, _The Janesville High Gazette_.

30. "May I interview you, Principal Markham?" asked Keisha.

31. I like to read the comics and the column "Money Sense."

32. There was a large photograph of Rodin's _The Thinker_ to accompany the article.

33. "I read the _Los Angeles Times_ and _Time_ magazine whenever I can," says Mrs. Filippo.

10.4 Rewrite each sentence. Add apostrophes, hyphens, and dashes where needed.

34. My sister in law went to Charlie's school.

35. She graduated in 99.

36. It was the fifty fifth class to graduate from the school.

37. There were ninety seven students in her class.

38. Several students graduated with straight As.

39. Many students my brother is one went to the same high school.

40. They have known each other since they were in a high level math class together.

41. They had their 10 year reunion last week can you believe it?

42. My friends sisters were both star athletes in high school.

43. His sisters who are twins played basketball and soccer.

44. "I graduated college in 09," she said, "with a major in prelaw"

10.5 Rewrite each sentence. Add capital letters where needed.

45. the u.s. team trained for the summer olympics that were held in athens, greece, in 2004.

46. several training facilities are located in the west.

47. i think some swimmers train in boulder, colorado.

48. is it near the university of colorado?

49. athletes received a good-luck message from senator glenn thompson.

50. coach philips wants us to train at the mountain view aquatic center in loveland, colorado.

51. andre and wendy swim on a team called the boulder poseidons.

52. If you take pearl street south, you can reach the base of the flatirons foothills.

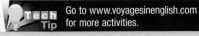

Go to www.voyagesinenglish.com for more activities.

Tech Tip Encourage students to further review punctuation and capitalization, using the additional practice and games at www.voyagesinenglish.com.

ASSESS

Encourage students to read the paragraphs twice before they start adding the punctuation. Use the Challenge as an indication of students' progress and understanding, not as a formal test. If students have difficulty with any part of the passage, remind them that they should refer to the section that teaches the skill. This activity can be completed by individuals, by small groups, or by the class working as a whole.

After you have reviewed punctuation and capitalization, administer the Section 10 Assessment on pages 27–28 in the **Assessment Book,** or create a customized test with the optional **Test Generator CD.**

You may also wish to administer the Sections 9–10 Summative Assessment on pages 41–42 of the **Assessment Book.** This test is also available on the optional **Test Generator CD.**

WRITING CONNECTION

Students can complete a formal Play script using the Writer's Workshop on pages 476–487.

Punctuation and Capitalization Challenge

Copy these paragraphs, adding whatever punctuation and capital letters are needed for clarity and correctness.

weak and thin and pallid, he awoke at last from what seemed to have been a long and troubled dream feebly raising himself in the bed with his head resting on his trembling arm he looked anxiously around

what room is this where have I been brought to said Oliver this is not the place I went to sleep in

he uttered these words in a feeble voice being very faint and weak but they were overheard at once the curtain at the bed's head was hastily drawn back and a motherly old lady, very neatly and precisely dressed, rose as she undrew it, from an arm-chair close by in which she had been sitting at needlework

—oliver twist by charles dickens

Punctuation and Capitalization Challenge

Punctuation may vary.

Weak, and thin, and pallid, he awoke at last from what seemed to have been a long and troubled dream. Feebly raising himself in the bed, with his head resting on his trembling arm, he looked anxiously around.

"What room is this? Where have I been brought to?" said Oliver. "This is not the place I went to sleep in."

He uttered these words in a feeble voice, being very faint and weak; but they were overheard at once. The curtain at the bed's head was hastily drawn back, and a motherly old lady, very neatly and precisely dressed, rose as she undrew it, from an arm-chair close by, in which she had been sitting at needle-work.

—Oliver Twist by Charles Dickens

194 • Punctuation and Capitalization Challenge

Oliver Twist asks for a second helping of porridge in this illustration by J. Mahoney.

SECTION FOCUS

- Simple sentences
- Appositives
- Compound sentences
- Compound sentence elements
- Participles
- Gerunds
- Infinitives
- Adjective clauses
- Adverb clauses
- Noun clauses

SUPPORT MATERIALS

Practice Book
Daily Maintenance, pages 124–126
Grammar, pages 127–137

Assessment Book
Section 11 Assessment,
    pages 29–32

Test Generator CD

Writing Chapter 8, Research Reports

Customizable Lesson Plans
www.voyagesinenglish.com

CONNECT WITH LITERATURE

Consider using the following titles throughout the section to illustrate the grammar concept:

A Corner of the Universe
    by Ann M. Martin
Full Tilt by Neal Shusterman
Squids Will Be Squids
    by Jon Scieszka

"No iron can pierce the heart with such force as a period put just at the right place."

—Isaac Babel

Diagramming

GRAMMAR FOR GROWN-UPS

Understanding Diagramming

A sentence diagram is a visual representation of the structure of a sentence, and it shows the reasoning behind the structure. This form of grammar instruction and practice can be especially beneficial for visual learners and English-language learners.

Diagrams demonstrate that the subject and the predicate are the most important parts of every sentences and that the remainder of a sentence is built upon these two required structural parts. In a diagram the subject and the predicate belong on one horizontal line divided by a vertical line.

Edith plays.

Edith	plays

Most sentences have direct objects or subject complements. These words are diagrammed on the main line along with the subject and predicate.

Edith plays guitar.

Edith	plays	guitar

In a sentence diagram, adjectives and adverbs are physically connected to they words they modify with a diagonal line.

Edith loudly plays her silver guitar.

Compound sentence elements are given equal treatment within a sentence, and this is reflected in a diagram. The coordinating conjunction that joins compound sentence elements is shown on a vertical dashed line in a diagram.

Edith plays the guitar and sings the lyrics.

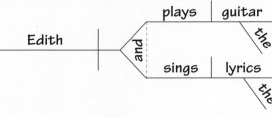

COMMON ERRORS

Singular Subjects, Plural Objects

Agreement of subject and verb can be a challenge when a singular subject is followed by a prepositional phrase with a plural object of the preposition. Diagramming can help students identify whether the verb agrees with the subject.

ERROR: A set of markers are sitting on the table.

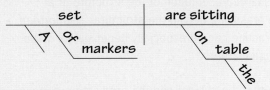

CORRECT: A set of markers is sitting on the table.

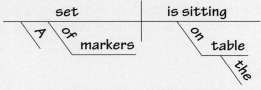

Students can mentally erase the prepositional phrase and look at the main line of the diagram.

SENTENCE DIAGRAMMING

Below is a diagramming example of a compound sentence structure. Compound sentence structures have a vertical dashed line that joins them, and the coordinating conjunction appears on this line.

Haley and Hannah made the team.

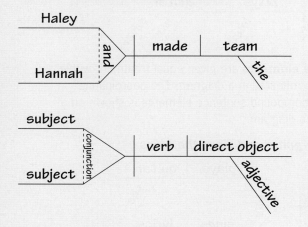

ASK AN EXPERT

Real Situations, Real Solutions

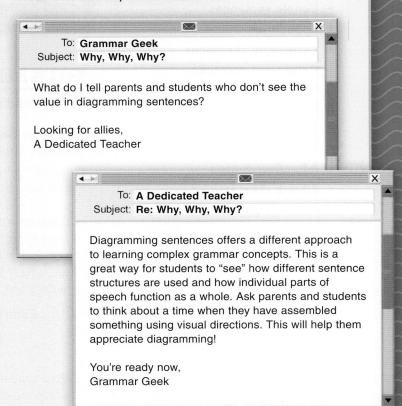

To: **Grammar Geek**
Subject: **Why, Why, Why?**

What do I tell parents and students who don't see the value in diagramming sentences?

Looking for allies,
A Dedicated Teacher

To: **A Dedicated Teacher**
Subject: **Re: Why, Why, Why?**

Diagramming sentences offers a different approach to learning complex grammar concepts. This is a great way for students to "see" how different sentence structures are used and how individual parts of speech function as a whole. Ask parents and students to think about a time when they have assembled something using visual directions. This will help them appreciate diagramming!

You're ready now,
Grammar Geek

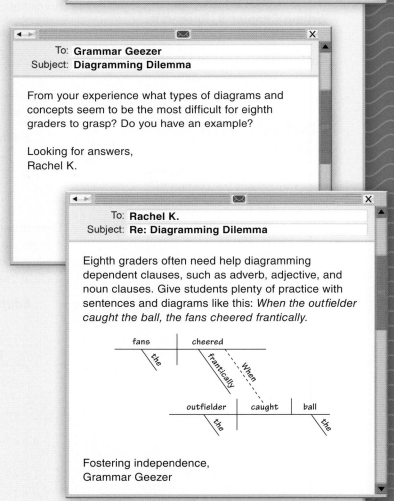

To: **Grammar Geezer**
Subject: **Diagramming Dilemma**

From your experience what types of diagrams and concepts seem to be the most difficult for eighth graders to grasp? Do you have an example?

Looking for answers,
Rachel K.

To: **Rachel K.**
Subject: **Re: Diagramming Dilemma**

Eighth graders often need help diagramming dependent clauses, such as adverb, adjective, and noun clauses. Give students plenty of practice with sentences and diagrams like this: *When the outfielder caught the ball, the fans cheered frantically.*

Fostering independence,
Grammar Geezer

Diagramming

11.1 Simple Sentences

OBJECTIVES
- **To understand the purpose for diagramming sentences**
- **To diagram a simple sentence**

 **DAILY Maintenance**

Assign **Practice Book** page 124, Section 11.1. After students finish,
1. Give immediate feedback.
2. Review concepts as needed.
3. Model the correct answer.

Pages 4–5 of the **Answer Key** contain tips for Daily Maintenance.

WARM-UP

Display various charts, diagrams, maps, and time lines. Discuss how they can provide a visual explanation and can help students learn a concept. Have partners create a chart, diagram, or time line for something they are studying in another subject. Invite volunteers to share and discuss their visuals.

TEACH

Discuss the purpose of a diagram and confirm that a diagram is a way to present information visually. Point out that the ideas expressed in sentences and paragraphs can often be presented in graphic representations.

Ask students to offer suggestions of how diagramming a sentence might be useful. Then ask students to cover all the text on the page except for the first two paragraphs. Read these paragraphs aloud. Have students uncover the example diagrams. Invite volunteers to reread aloud the two paragraphs. Point out that the information becomes much clearer as the visual representations are studied. Elicit from students how helpful the diagrams are in representing the ideas explained in the text.

PRACTICE

EXERCISE 1
Have volunteers read aloud each sentence and identify the subject and the predicate. Challenge volunteers to diagram each sentence on the board.

APPLY

APPLY IT NOW
Instruct students to begin by first writing an object complement, a prepositional phrase used as an adjective, and a prepositional phrase used as an adverb. Then have students include these in their sentences. Students should

demonstrate the ability to diagram simple sentences.

ASSESS

Note which students had difficulty diagramming simple sentences. Assign **Practice Book** page 127 for further practice.

WRITING CONNECTION
Use pages 488–489 of the Writing portion. Choose a sentence from the literature excerpt or the student model to diagram on the board. Explain the diagram.

11.1 Simple Sentences

A **diagram** is a visual outline of a sentence. It shows in a graphic manner the relationships among the various words or groups of words in a sentence. Diagramming serves two purposes. First, it helps you understand how a sentence is put together. Second, it identifies errors in a sentence and makes clear why they are errors.

In a diagram the subject, the verb, the direct object, and the subject or the object complement go on the main horizontal line. The subject is separated from the verb by a vertical line that cuts through the horizontal line. The line to separate a verb from a direct object is also vertical but does not cut through the line.

SENTENCE **Galaxies contain stars.**

| Galaxies | contain | stars |

The line to separate a subject complement from a verb slants left.

SENTENCE **The Milky Way is a galaxy.**

An object complement is placed on the horizontal line after a line slanting right.

SENTENCE **The astronomy club elected Jaime president.**

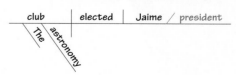

An indirect object is placed on a horizontal line under the verb.

SENTENCE **The astronomer gave the class a talk.**

196 • Section 11.1

EXERCISE 1 (Answers)

1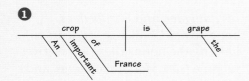

2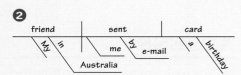

3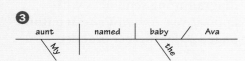

4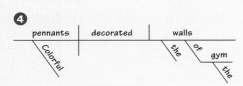

5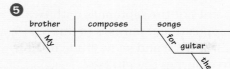

6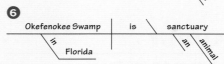

7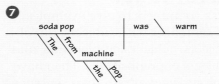

8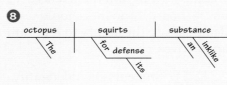

9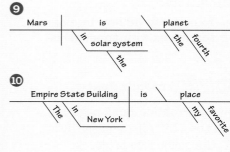

10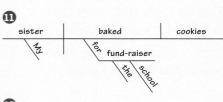

11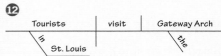

12

Adjectives, adverbs, and articles are placed under the words that they describe. In this sentence the adjective *large* describes *radish*. The adverb *slowly* describes the phrasal verb *pulled up*. The adverb *very* describes *large*.

SENTENCE **He slowly pulled up a very large radish.**

Prepositional phrases can act as adjectives or adverbs. In this sentence *in San Francisco* is an adjective phrase describing *commuters*. *On cable cars* is an adverb phrase describing *ride*.

SENTENCE **Commuters in San Francisco ride on cable cars.**

EXERCISE 1 Diagram the sentences.

1. An important crop of France is the grape.
2. My friend in Australia sent me a birthday card by e-mail.
3. My aunt named the baby Ava.
4. Colorful pennants decorated the walls of the gym.
5. My brother composes songs for the guitar.
6. Okefenokee Swamp in Florida is an animal sanctuary.
7. The soda pop from the pop machine was warm.
8. The octopus squirts an inklike substance for its defense.
9. Mars is the fourth planet in the solar system.
10. The Empire State Building in New York is my favorite place.
11. My sister baked cookies for the school fund-raiser.
12. Tourists in St. Louis visit the very impressive Gateway Arch.

APPLY IT NOW

Write and diagram five simple sentences. Include at least one object complement, one prepositional phrase used as an adjective, and one prepositional phrase used as an adverb.

Diagramming • 197

11.2 Appositives

OBJECTIVE
- **To understand how to diagram sentences with appositives**

 **DAILY Maintenance**

Assign **Practice Book** page 124, Section 11.2. After students finish,
1. Give immediate feedback.
2. Review concepts as needed.
3. Model the correct answer.

Pages 4–5 of the **Answer Key** contain tips for Daily Maintenance.

WARM-UP

Distribute to small groups note cards on which you have written two short, closely related sentences. *(Julie watched as the crowd applauded. Julie just sang the national anthem.)* Ask groups to combine the sentences by using an appositive.

TEACH

Read aloud the definition of an appositive. Then have students read aloud their Warm-Up sentences, identifying the appositive in each sentence. Invite a volunteer to read aloud the second paragraph. Discuss the example sentences, pointing out the placement of the appositives in each diagram. Be sure to point out that adjectives in an appositive phrase are diagrammed below the appositive, as shown in the first and third examples.

Have students suggest sentences that contain appositives. Then challenge students to diagram these sentences on the board.

PRACTICE

EXERCISE 1
Suggest that students first identify each appositive. After students have finished, tell partners to compare their diagrams. Also

point out the sentences with two prepositional phrases (items 5, 6, 9, 13, and 15) and show students how to diagram the phrases.

APPLY
APPLY IT NOW
Ask volunteers to give examples of sentences with subjects, direct objects, subject complements, and objects of prepositions. Then have volunteers diagram their sentences on the board. Students should demonstrate the ability to diagram appositives.

 Students should identify *Thomas L. Jennings Jr.,*

his daughter, and *Elizabeth* as appositives. Challenge students to identify the nouns these appositives rename *(son, Matilda Jennings,* and *sister).*

ASSESS

Note which students had difficulty diagramming sentences with appositives. Assign **Practice Book** page 128 for further practice.

> **WRITING CONNECTION**
> Use pages 490–491 of the Writing portion of the book.

11.2 Appositives

An **appositive** is a word or a group of words that follows a noun or a pronoun and further identifies it or adds information. An appositive names the same person, place, thing, or idea as the word it explains.

In a diagram an appositive is placed in parentheses to the right of the word it identifies. Words that describe the appositive go under it. In this sentence the appositive renames the proper noun *Shel Silverstein,* which is the subject.

SENTENCE Shel Silverstein, a humorous poet, wrote *A Light in the Attic.*

An appositive can appear in all the places in a sentence where nouns occur. In this sentence the appositive, the proper noun *Walk Two Moons,* explains the word *novel,* which is a direct object.

SENTENCE We read the novel *Walk Two Moons* for class.

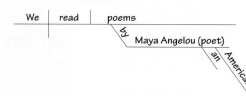

What word does the appositive in this sentence rename? How does that word function?

SENTENCE We read poems by Maya Angelou, an American poet.

The appositive, *poet,* explains the proper noun, *Maya Angelou,* which is the object of a preposition.

EXERCISE 1 (Answers)

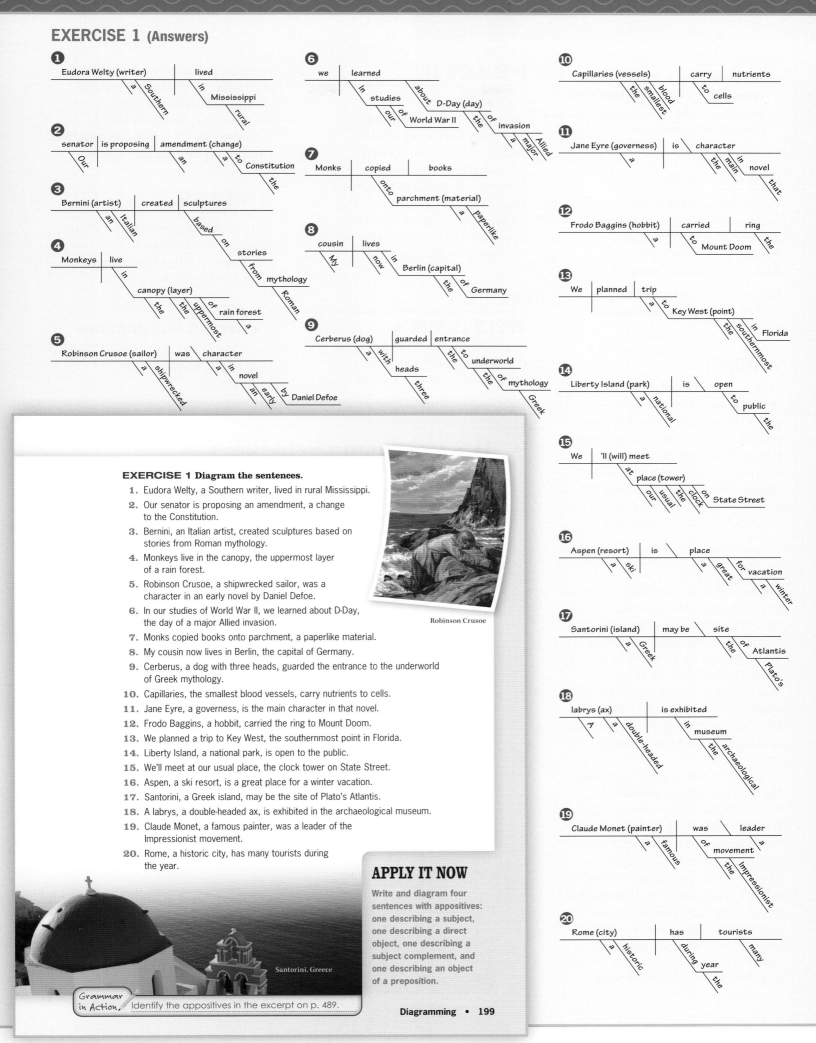

EXERCISE 1 Diagram the sentences.

1. Eudora Welty, a Southern writer, lived in rural Mississippi.
2. Our senator is proposing an amendment, a change to the Constitution.
3. Bernini, an Italian artist, created sculptures based on stories from Roman mythology.
4. Monkeys live in the canopy, the uppermost layer of a rain forest.
5. Robinson Crusoe, a shipwrecked sailor, was a character in an early novel by Daniel Defoe.
6. In our studies of World War II, we learned about D-Day, the day of a major Allied invasion.
7. Monks copied books onto parchment, a paperlike material.
8. My cousin now lives in Berlin, the capital of Germany.
9. Cerberus, a dog with three heads, guarded the entrance to the underworld of Greek mythology.
10. Capillaries, the smallest blood vessels, carry nutrients to cells.
11. Jane Eyre, a governess, is the main character in that novel.
12. Frodo Baggins, a hobbit, carried the ring to Mount Doom.
13. We planned a trip to Key West, the southernmost point in Florida.
14. Liberty Island, a national park, is open to the public.
15. We'll meet at our usual place, the clock tower on State Street.
16. Aspen, a ski resort, is a great place for a winter vacation.
17. Santorini, a Greek island, may be the site of Plato's Atlantis.
18. A labrys, a double-headed ax, is exhibited in the archaeological museum.
19. Claude Monet, a famous painter, was a leader of the Impressionist movement.
20. Rome, a historic city, has many tourists during the year.

Robinson Crusoe

Santorini, Greece

Grammar in Action. Identify the appositives in the excerpt on p. 489.

APPLY IT NOW

Write and diagram four sentences with appositives: one describing a subject, one describing a direct object, one describing a subject complement, and one describing an object of a preposition.

Diagramming • 199

11.3 Compound Sentences

OBJECTIVES

- **To identify each independent clause in a compound sentence**
- **To understand how to diagram compound sentences**

 **Maintenance**

Assign **Practice Book** page 124, Section 11.3. After students finish,
1. Give immediate feedback.
2. Review concepts as needed.
3. Model the correct answer.

Pages 4–5 of the **Answer Key** contain tips for Daily Maintenance.

WARM-UP

Write on the board *and, but,* and *or.* Have each student write a sentence on a strip of paper and place the strips into a bag. Then have a volunteer choose two strips from the bag and read the sentences aloud, combining the sentences by using a coordinating conjunction from the board.

TEACH

Explain that an independent clause is actually a sentence. Remind students that sometimes a sentence is made up of two independent clauses. Have students recall that this type of sentence is a compound sentence. Have students suggest compound sentences. Write their suggestions on the board.

Invite volunteers to read aloud the first paragraph. Review the coordinating conjunctions. Then remind students that compound sentences can also be formed by combining independent clauses using a semicolon and a conjunctive adverb. Read aloud the information about diagramming compound sentences. Discuss the example diagrams. Have students notice where the coordinating conjunction or conjunctive adverb is placed.

PRACTICE

EXERCISE 1

Diagram sentence number 5 as a class and point out the date in the diagram. Then have students complete the activity independently. Suggest that students first identify the independent clauses and the coordinating conjunctions or conjunctive adverbs.

APPLY

APPLY IT NOW

Suggest that students write compound sentences about a book or short story that the class is reading. Direct students to list coordinating conjunctions and conjunctive adverbs beforehand for reference. Students should demonstrate the ability to diagram compound sentences.

ASSESS

Note which students had difficulty diagramming compound sentences. Assign **Practice Book** page 129 for further practice.

WRITING CONNECTION

Use pages 492–493 of the Writing portion of the book.

11.3 Compound Sentences

A **compound sentence** contains two or more independent clauses. An independent clause has a subject and a predicate and can stand on its own as a sentence. Clauses in a compound sentence are usually connected by a coordinating conjunction.

In a diagram each independent clause has its own horizontal line with its subject and verb as well as any objects and complements.

- The coordinating conjunction is placed on a vertical dashed line at the left edge of the diagram.
- The line connects the main horizontal lines of the two clauses.

In the first clause of this sentence, *tourists* is the subject, *visited* is the verb, and *Philadelphia* is the direct object. In the second clause, *they* is the subject, *saw* is the verb, and *Liberty Bell* is the direct object.

SENTENCE **The tourists visited Philadelphia, and they saw the Liberty Bell.**

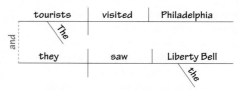

Independent clauses connected by a conjunctive adverb and a semicolon are also compound sentences. A conjunctive adverb is diagrammed in the same way as a coordinating conjunction.

SENTENCE **Our team was winning; however, it lost in the ninth inning.**

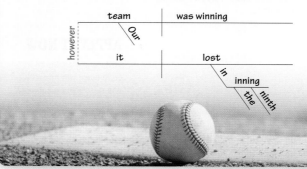

200 • Section 11.3

EXERCISE 1 (Answers)

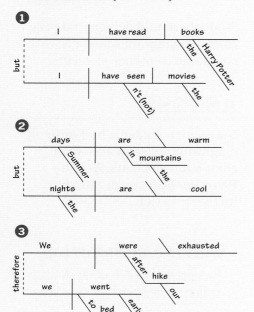
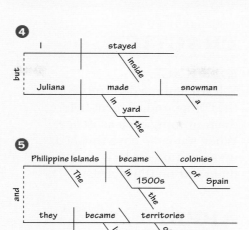
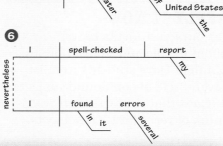
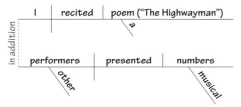

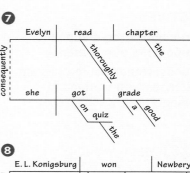
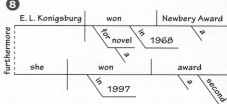
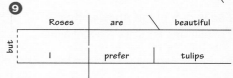
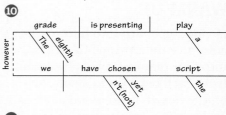
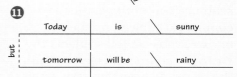

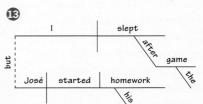

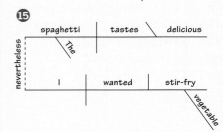

SENTENCE **I recited a poem, "The Highwayman"; in addition, other performers presented musical numbers.**

EXERCISE 1 Diagram the sentences.

1. I have read the Harry Potter books, but I haven't seen the movies.
2. Summer days are warm in the mountains, but the nights are cool.
3. We were exhausted after our hike; therefore, we went to bed early.
4. I stayed inside, but Juliana made a snowman in the yard.
5. The Philippine Islands became colonies of Spain in the 1500s, and they later became territories of the United States.
6. I spell-checked my report; nevertheless, I found several errors in it.
7. Evelyn read the chapter thoroughly; consequently, she got a good grade on the quiz.
8. E. L. Konigsburg won a Newbery Award for a novel in 1968; furthermore, she won a second award in 1997.
9. Roses are beautiful, but I prefer tulips.
10. The eighth grade is presenting a play; however, we haven't chosen the script yet.
11. Today is sunny, but tomorrow will be rainy.
12. Jana will bring some ribbon, and Corina will buy the glitter.
13. I slept after the game, but José started his homework.
14. They sky looks cloudy; however, it will not rain.
15. The spaghetti tastes delicious; nevertheless, I wanted vegetable stir-fry.

APPLY IT NOW

Write and diagram six compound sentences. Use coordinating conjunctions in three sentences and conjunctive adverbs in the other three.

Diagramming • 201

OBJECTIVES
- **To recognize the compound components of a sentence**
- **To understand how to diagram sentences with compound elements**

Assign **Practice Book** page 124, Section 11.4. After students finish,
1. Give immediate feedback.
2. Review concepts as needed.
3. Model the correct answer.

Pages 4–5 of the **Answer Key** contain tips for Daily Maintenance.

WARM-UP

Divide the board into four columns and arrange the class into four teams. Have one student from each team go to a column on the board. Read aloud a sentence containing either a compound subject, predicate, or direct object. Tell students to write the compound element on the board. Repeat this activity as time allows.

TEACH

Discuss the sentences you read in the Warm-Up. Ask students to offer sentences that contain a compound element and write three of these on the board. Tell students that other parts of a sentence, such as objects of prepositions, indirect objects, adjectives, and adverbs, can also be compound.

Have volunteers read aloud about diagramming compound subjects and compound predicates. Encourage volunteers to diagram the example sentences on the board, using the diagrams in this lesson as models.

PRACTICE

EXERCISE 1
Tell students to determine the compound element before diagramming each sentence. When students have finished, invite volunteers to write their diagrams on the board.

APPLY

APPLY IT NOW
Encourage students to write about people and things that are familiar. Have students first list several sets of compound subjects. Suggest that students then think of verbs for their subjects.

Students should demonstrate the ability to diagram sentences with compound sentence elements.

ASSESS

Note which students had difficulty diagramming sentences with compound elements. Assign **Practice Book** page 130 for further practice.

WRITING CONNECTION
Use pages 494–495 of the Writing portion of the book.

11.4 Compound Sentence Elements

The subject and the predicate in a sentence may be compound. They may consist of two or more words connected by a coordinating conjunction. Remember that a sentence with a compound subject or a compound predicate is still a simple sentence.

In a diagram the compound parts are placed on two separate lines joined to the main line. The conjunction is placed on a vertical dashed line between them. In the first sentence, the subject is compound. In the second sentence, the verb is compound.

SENTENCE **Phil and Paul are forwards on the soccer team.**

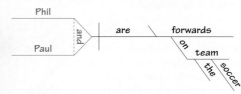

SENTENCE **The chef washed and cut vegetables for the stew.**

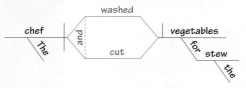

Both the subject and the verb may be compound, and each verb may have its own object.

SENTENCE **My sister and I bought groceries and prepared supper.**

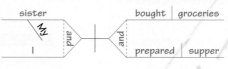

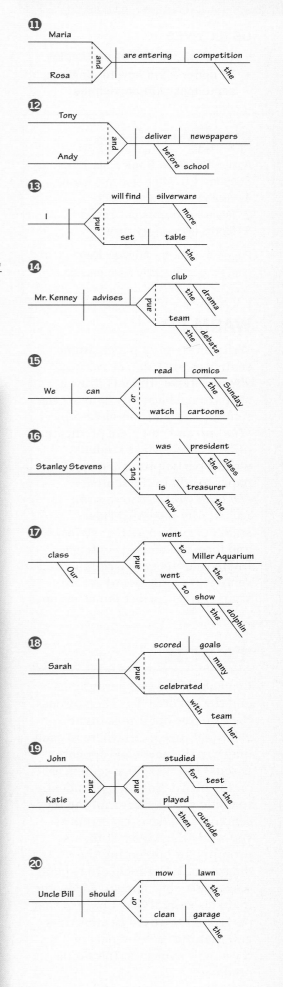

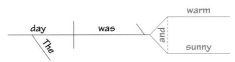

Words other than subjects and verbs may also be compound, and they are diagrammed in a similar way. In this sentence compound adjectives function as subject complements.

SENTENCE **The day was warm and sunny.**

EXERCISE 1 Diagram the sentences.

1. King Richard and King John were brothers.
2. Belize and Guatemala are located in Central America.
3. Nick sat down and read.
4. Is Sacramento or Los Angeles the capital of California?
5. Copper and zinc together form brass.
6. A telescope gathers and focuses light into a tiny point.
7. I can play the violin and the trumpet.
8. Norita ate slowly but finished the plate of linguine.
9. Kevin and Elaine are good dart players.
10. The butler cleaned and polished the silver.
11. Maria and Rosa are entering the competition.
12. Tony and Andy deliver newspapers before school.
13. I will find more silverware and set the table.
14. Mr. Kenney advises the drama club and the debate team.
15. We can read the Sunday comics or watch cartoons.
16. Stanley Stevens was the class president but is now the treasurer.
17. Our class went to the Miller Aquarium and went to the dolphin show.
18. Sarah scored many goals and celebrated with her team.
19. John and Katie studied for the test and then played outside.
20. Uncle Bill should mow the lawn or clean the garage.

APPLY IT NOW

Write and diagram four sentences: two with compound subjects and two with compound predicates.

OBJECTIVES

- To recall the use of participles
- To understand how to diagram sentences with participles

 Maintenance

Assign **Practice Book** page 125, Section 11.5. After students finish,
1. Give immediate feedback.
2. Review concepts as needed.
3. Model the correct answer.

Pages 4–5 of the **Answer Key** contain tips for Daily Maintenance.

WARM-UP

Write on strips of paper simple sentences, such as *The cat was sleeping*. Have students draw a strip from a bag and cut apart the sentence into its complete subject *(The cat)* and complete predicate *(was sleeping)*. Have students write a participle on a strip of paper to add to the sentence. *(The cat, stretched across the couch, was sleeping.)* Have students exchange their strips and form the correct sentences. Invite volunteers to write their sentences on the board. Be sure students use correct punctuation.

TEACH

Read aloud the two paragraphs and the bulleted list. Then discuss the example diagrams. Invite a volunteer to explain where in each diagram the participle appears. Discuss the Warm-Up sentences on the board. Encourage students to guide you in diagramming these sentences. Make a few errors as you work. Elicit from students prompts for correcting the diagrams. Ask students to explain why a participle appears below the main horizontal line. Confirm that participles are used as adjectives and that they are not part of the simple subject or the simple predicate.

PRACTICE

EXERCISE 1

Suggest that students rewrite each sentence without the participle and diagram these simple sentences first. Then challenge students to expand each diagram to include the participle. Point out the phrasal verb in item 10 and be sure students know how to diagram this.

APPLY

APPLY IT NOW

Suggest that students write about a favorite hobby. Encourage them to write simple sentences first

and then to insert participles. Students should demonstrate an ability to diagram sentences with participles.

ASSESS

Note which students had difficulty diagramming sentences with participles. Assign **Practice Book** page 131 for further practice.

WRITING CONNECTION

Use pages 496–497 of the Writing portion of the book.

11.5 Participles

A **participle** is a verbal that is used as an adjective. A participial phrase is made up of the participle and its objects, complements, and any modifiers. The entire phrase acts as an adjective.

In a diagram a participial phrase goes under the noun or pronoun it describes on a slanted line connecting to a horizontal line.

- The participle starts on the slanted line and extends onto the horizontal line.
- A direct object or a complement is placed after the participle.
- Any word that describes the participle or its object or complement goes on a slanted line under the correct word.

SENTENCE **Lying in the hammock, I watched the clouds in the sky.**

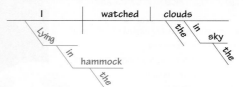

SENTENCE **The cat, stretched across the cushion, was sleeping.**

SENTENCE **The students, having removed litter from the grounds, next cleaned litter from the park.**

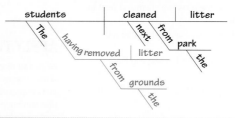

EXERCISE 1 (Answers)

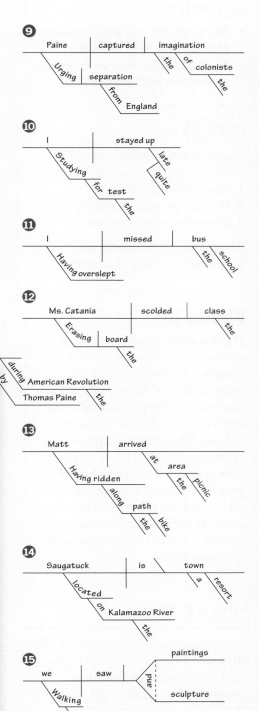

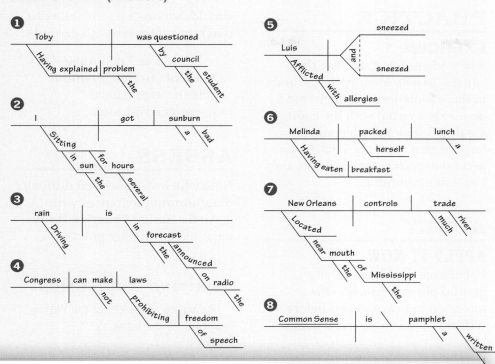

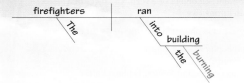

Participial adjectives, which often precede the nouns they describe, are placed just as other adjectives are.

SENTENCE **The firefighters ran into the burning building.**

EXERCISE 1 Diagram the sentences.

1. Toby, having explained the problem, was questioned by the student council.
2. Sitting in the sun for several hours, I got a bad sunburn.
3. Driving rain is in the forecast announced on the radio.
4. Congress cannot make laws prohibiting freedom of speech.
5. Afflicted with allergies, Luis sneezed and sneezed.
6. Having eaten breakfast, Melinda packed herself a lunch.
7. New Orleans, located near the mouth of the Mississippi, controls much river trade.
8. *Common Sense* is a pamphlet written by Thomas Paine during the American Revolution.
9. Urging separation from England, Paine captured the imagination of the colonists.
10. Studying for the test, I stayed up quite late.
11. Having overslept, I missed the school bus.
12. Erasing the board, Ms. Catania scolded the class.
13. Having ridden along the bike path, Matt arrived at the picnic area.
14. Saugatuck, located on the Kalamazoo River, is a resort town.
15. Walking through the art museum, we saw paintings and sculpture.
16. Playing baseball, Keith hurt his ankle.

APPLY IT NOW

Write and diagram four sentences with participial phrases.

Diagramming • 205

DAILY ⬡ Maintenance

Assign **Practice Book** page 125, Section 11.6. After students finish,
1. Give immediate feedback.
2. Review concepts as needed.
3. Model the correct answer.

Pages 4–5 of the **Answer Key** contain tips for Daily Maintenance.

WARM-UP

Place a strip of tape across the center of the classroom. Tell students that one side of the room is the participle side and the other is the gerund side. Tell students to stand on the strip of tape. Then read a sentence containing an *ing* form of a verb that is either a participle or a gerund. Tell students to stand on the side of the room that corresponds to the function of the *ing* form of the verb. Repeat as time allows.

TEACH

Challenge students to explain the difference between a participle and a gerund. Confirm that participles are adjectives and that gerunds are nouns. Discuss where a gerund might appear in a sentence diagram.

  Read aloud the first paragraph. Then have volunteers read aloud the bulleted points and the example diagrams. Point out that the gerund appears above the main horizontal line in the first two example diagrams and below the line in the last example diagram. Ask volunteers to explain the difference.

PRACTICE

EXERCISE 1

Ask students what strategy they can use to help identify the gerunds in these sentences. Confirm that a gerund is a verbal with the ending *ing* that functions as a noun. Suggest that students identify the gerund in each sentence before they begin diagramming.

APPLY

APPLY IT NOW

Encourage students to write gerund phrases *(going to the movies, practicing soccer)* before writing their sentences. Students should demonstrate an ability to diagram sentences with gerunds.

💡**TechTip** Encourage students to find an online article through a local newspaper's Web site.

ASSESS

Note which students had difficulty diagramming sentences with gerunds. Assign **Practice Book** page 132 for further practice.

WRITING CONNECTION

Use pages 498–499 of the Writing portion of the book.

11.6 Gerunds

A **gerund is a verb form ending in *ing* that is used as a noun.** A gerund can be used in a sentence as a subject, a subject complement, an object of a verb, an object of a preposition, or an appositive.

In a diagram a gerund is placed according to its function.

- The gerund is placed on a stepped line that extends onto a horizontal line.
- A direct object or a complement is placed after the gerund.
- Words that describe the gerund or its object or complement go on slanted lines.

A gerund that functions as a subject, a direct object, or a subject complement is placed on a stepped line above the main horizontal line in the appropriate position. The gerund in this sentence is used as the subject.

SENTENCE **Playing the trumpet is my favorite hobby.**

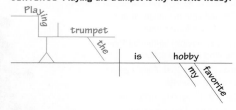

The gerund in this sentence is used as the direct object. A gerund used as a subject complement would go in a similar position, but the line before it would be slanted left. A gerund used as an appositive goes next to the word it describes in parentheses, as other appositives do.

SENTENCE **I remember writing the e-mail.**

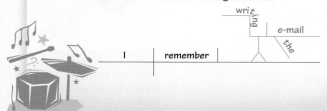

EXERCISE 1 (Answers)

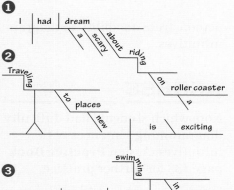
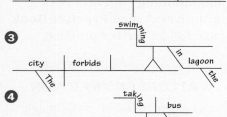
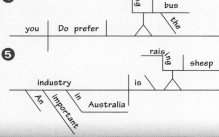

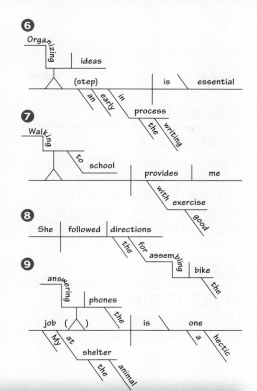

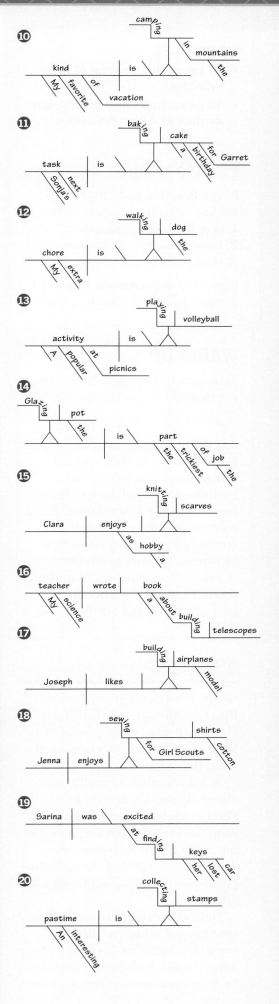

A gerund used as the object of a preposition is part of the prepositional phrase, which goes under the word it describes. A stepped line is still used, but it is not raised.

SENTENCE **Windmills are used for pumping water.**

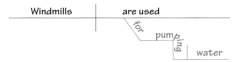

EXERCISE 1 Diagram the sentences.

1. I had a scary dream about riding on a roller coaster.
2. Traveling to new places is exciting.
3. The city forbids swimming in the lagoon.
4. Do you prefer taking the bus?
5. An important industry in Australia is raising sheep.
6. Organizing ideas, an early step in the writing process, is essential.
7. Walking to school provides me with good exercise.
8. She followed the directions for assembling the bike.
9. My job at the animal shelter, answering the phones, is a hectic one.
10. My favorite kind of vacation is camping in the mountains.
11. Sonja's next task is baking a birthday cake for Garret.
12. My extra chore is walking the dog.
13. A popular activity at picnics is playing volleyball.
14. Glazing the pot is the trickiest part of the job.
15. Clara enjoys knitting scarves as a hobby.
16. My science teacher wrote a book about building telescopes.
17. Joseph likes building model airplanes.
18. Jenna enjoys sewing cotton shirts for Girl Scouts.
19. Sarina was excited at finding her lost car keys.
20. An interesting pastime is collecting stamps.

APPLY IT NOW

Write and diagram eight sentences with gerunds. Have at least one gerund for each of these functions: subject, direct object, object of a preposition, and appositive.

Tech Tip Identify three gerunds in an online newspaper article.

Diagramming • 207

11.7 Infinitives

 **Maintenance**

Assign **Practice Book** page 125, Section 11.7. After students finish,
1. Give immediate feedback.
2. Review concepts as needed.
3. Model the correct answer.

Pages 4–5 of the **Answer Key** contain tips for Daily Maintenance.

WARM-UP

Write the following sentence on the board:

> We went to visit my grandparents.

Ask a volunteer to identify the infinitive *(to visit)* and the infinitive phrase *(to visit my grandparents)*. Tell each of four teams to write five sentences that contain infinitives. Then have students use the sentences in a rap song. Encourage students to revise the sentences to make them rhyme. Have students perform their raps for the class.

TEACH

Invite a volunteer to read aloud the definition of an infinitive. Have students read sentences from their raps and identify how each infinitive is used.

Ask a volunteer to read aloud about diagramming infinitives. Discuss each example diagram. Emphasize that the infinitive phrase in the first sentence is a direct object and that the infinitive phrase in the second sentence is an appositive.

Have students write on the board examples of infinitives used in ways other than as direct objects or appositives. Challenge volunteers to diagram these sentences. Have students use these diagrams as models.

PRACTICE

EXERCISE 1
Suggest students identify the infinitive in each sentence and how the infinitive is used. Encourage students to use the diagrams on the board as models.

APPLY

APPLY IT NOW
Have students label each noun function. Students should demonstrate an ability to diagram infinitives.

ASSESS

Note which students had difficulty diagramming sentences with infinitives. Assign **Practice Book** page 133 for further practice.

WRITING CONNECTION
Use pages 500–501 of the Writing portion of the book.

11.7 Infinitives

An **infinitive** is a verb form, usually preceded by *to*, that is used as a noun, an adjective, or an adverb.

In a diagram an infinitive is placed according to its function in the sentence.

- An infinitive itself is diagrammed like a prepositional phrase. The *to* goes on a slanted line, and the verb goes on a horizontal line.
- A direct object or a complement is placed after the verb on the horizontal line.
- A word that describes the infinitive or part of the infinitive phrase goes under the horizontal line.

An infinitive used as a subject, a direct object, a subject complement, or an appositive is placed on a stepped line above the main horizontal line in the appropriate position. In the first sentence, the infinitive is a direct object, and in the second sentence, the infinitive is an appositive.

SENTENCE **I planned to leave early.**

SENTENCE **My plan, to start a babysitting service, requires organization.**

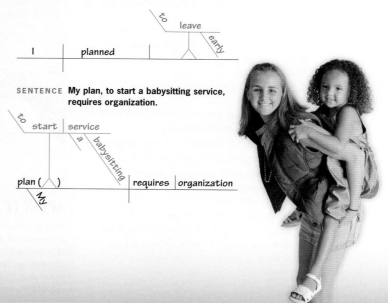

EXERCISE 1 (Answers)

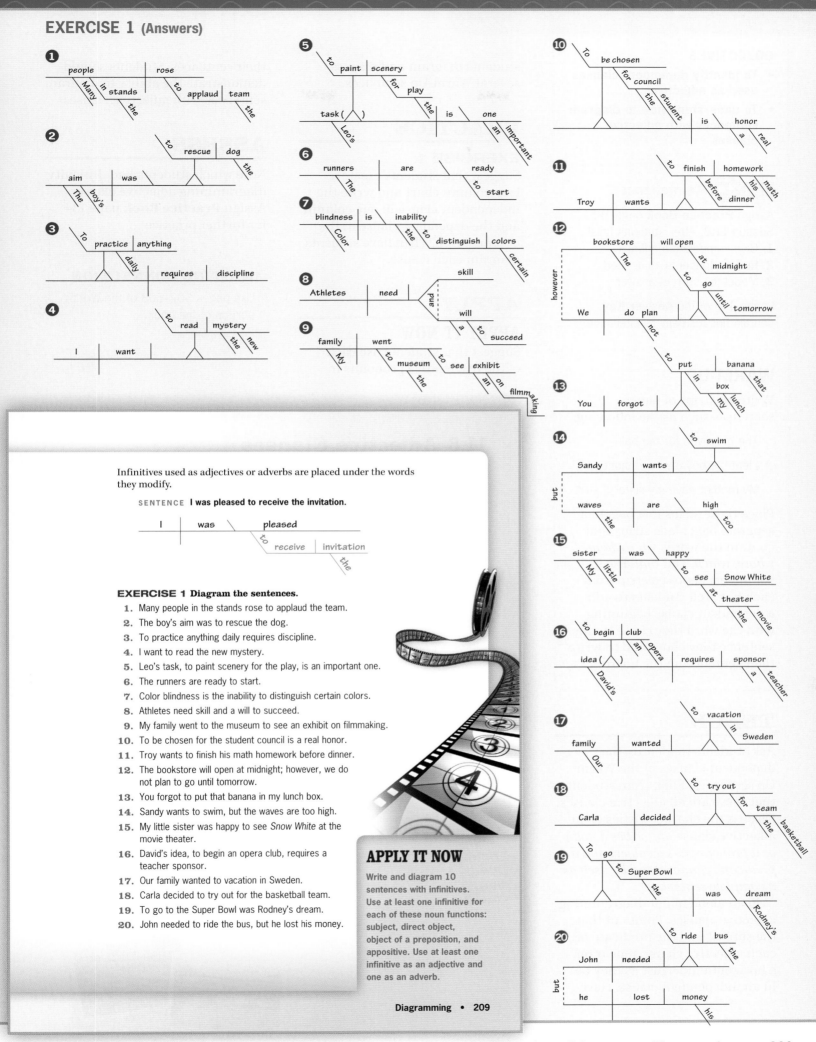

Infinitives used as adjectives or adverbs are placed under the words they modify.

SENTENCE **I was pleased to receive the invitation.**

EXERCISE 1 Diagram the sentences.

1. Many people in the stands rose to applaud the team.
2. The boy's aim was to rescue the dog.
3. To practice anything daily requires discipline.
4. I want to read the new mystery.
5. Leo's task, to paint scenery for the play, is an important one.
6. The runners are ready to start.
7. Color blindness is the inability to distinguish certain colors.
8. Athletes need skill and a will to succeed.
9. My family went to the museum to see an exhibit on filmmaking.
10. To be chosen for the student council is a real honor.
11. Troy wants to finish his math homework before dinner.
12. The bookstore will open at midnight; however, we do not plan to go until tomorrow.
13. You forgot to put that banana in my lunch box.
14. Sandy wants to swim, but the waves are too high.
15. My little sister was happy to see *Snow White* at the movie theater.
16. David's idea, to begin an opera club, requires a teacher sponsor.
17. Our family wanted to vacation in Sweden.
18. Carla decided to try out for the basketball team.
19. To go to the Super Bowl was Rodney's dream.
20. John needed to ride the bus, but he lost his money.

APPLY IT NOW

Write and diagram 10 sentences with infinitives. Use at least one infinitive for each of these noun functions: subject, direct object, object of a preposition, and appositive. Use at least one infinitive as an adjective and one as an adverb.

Diagramming • 209

OBJECTIVES

- **To identify dependent clauses used as adjectives**
- **To understand how to diagram sentences with adjective clauses**

DAILY Maintenance

Assign **Practice Book** page 125, Section 11.8. After students finish,
1. Give immediate feedback.
2. Review concepts as needed.
3. Model the correct answer.

Pages 4–5 of the **Answer Key** contain tips for Daily Maintenance.

WARM-UP

Write on strips of paper sentences such as the following:

The girl dived for the ball.

I lent the boy my headphones.

My mother gave my sister a shirt.

Place these strips in a bag. In a separate bag, place strips that contain the words *who, whom, whose, which,* and *that.* Have volunteers choose a strip from each bag. Tell students to add a dependent clause beginning with the word they chose to the sentence they chose and to write their sentence on the board.

TEACH

Ask students to identify the dependent clauses in the Warm-Up sentences. Elicit from students that these are all adjective clauses. Discuss the characteristics of an adjective clause *(describes a noun or a pronoun, has a subject and a predicate, cannot stand by itself as a complete sentence).*

Read aloud about diagramming adjective clauses. Point out that the subject and the predicate of each adjective clause appear on a horizontal line, just as they do in an independent clause. Have

students diagram and discuss several Warm-Up sentences.

PRACTICE

EXERCISE 1
Suggest that students create a two-column chart and write the independent clause in one column and the dependent clause in the other column. Then have students diagram each clause.

APPLY

APPLY IT NOW
Suggest that students use each of the five relative pronouns in

their sentences. Students should demonstrate the ability to diagram sentences with adjective clauses.

ASSESS

Note which students had difficulty diagramming adjective clauses. Assign **Practice Book** page 134 for further practice.

WRITING CONNECTION
Use pages 502–503 of the Writing portion of the book.

11.8 Adjective Clauses

An **adjective clause** is a dependent clause that describes or limits a noun or a pronoun. An adjective clause usually begins with one of the relative pronouns *(who, whom, whose, which,* or *that)* or with a subordinate conjunction *(when, where,* or *why).*

In a diagram the adjective clause and the independent clause are on separate lines, with the dependent clause beneath the independent clause.

- A dashed line connects the relative pronoun or the subordinate conjunction in the dependent clause to the word in the independent clause that is modified by the adjective clause.
- A relative pronoun is placed in the diagram according to its function in the adjective clause.

In the first sentence, *Lake Erie* is the antecedent of *which. Which* acts as the subject in the adjective clause. In the second sentence, *pictures* is the antecedent of *that. That* acts as the direct object of the verb *took* in the adjective clause.

SENTENCE **Lake Erie, which was once fairly polluted, is now much cleaner.**

Lake Erie	is	cleaner
	now	*much*
which	was	polluted
	once	*fairly*

SENTENCE **Molly showed me the pictures that she took in Italy.**

Molly	showed	pictures
	me	*the*
she	took	that
	in Italy	

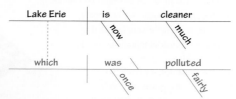

210 • Section 11.8

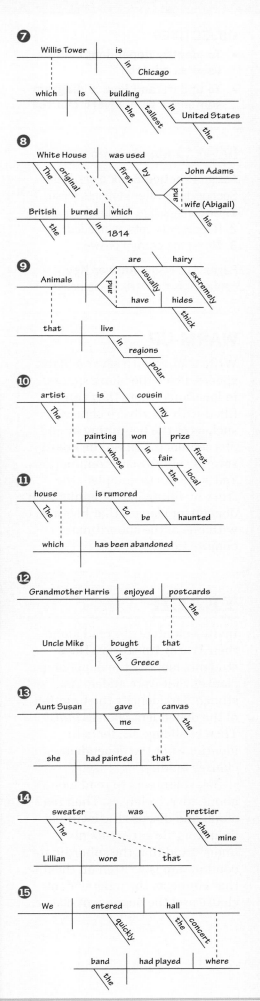

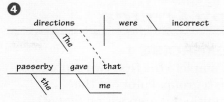

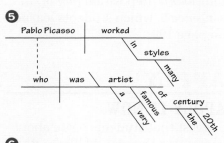

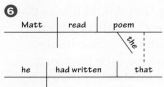

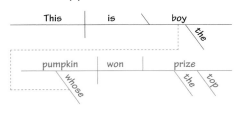

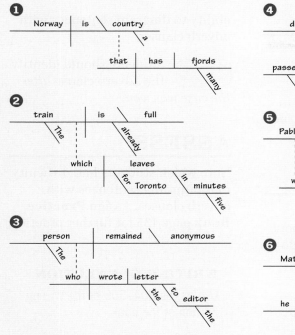

The relative pronoun *whose*, like other possessives, goes under the noun it is associated with.

SENTENCE **This is the boy whose pumpkin won the top prize.**

EXERCISE 1 Diagram the sentences.

1. Norway is a country that has many fjords.
2. The train, which leaves for Toronto in five minutes, is already full.
3. The person who wrote the letter to the editor remained anonymous.
4. The directions that the passerby gave me were incorrect.
5. Pablo Picasso, who was a very famous artist of the 20th century, worked in many styles.
6. Matt read the poem that he had written.
7. Willis Tower, which is the tallest building in the United States, is in Chicago.
8. The original White House, which the British burned in 1814, was first used by John Adams and his wife, Abigail.
9. Animals that live in polar regions are usually extremely hairy and have thick hides.
10. The artist whose painting won first prize in the local fair is my cousin.
11. The house, which has been abandoned, is rumored to be haunted.
12. Grandmother Harris enjoyed the postcards that Uncle Mike bought in Greece.
13. Aunt Susan gave me the canvas that she had painted.
14. The sweater that Lillian wore was prettier than mine.
15. We quickly entered the concert hall where the band had played.

APPLY IT NOW

Write and diagram eight sentences with adjective clauses. Use *whose* in at least one of them.

Diagramming • 211

OBJECTIVES

- **To identify dependent clauses used as adverbs**
- **To understand how to diagram sentences with adverb clauses**

 **DAILY Maintenance**

Assign **Practice Book** page 126, Section 11.9. After students finish,
1. Give immediate feedback.
2. Review concepts as needed.
3. Model the correct answer.

Pages 4–5 of the **Answer Key** contain tips for Daily Maintenance.

WARM-UP

Write a story with several blank spaces. Place the blank spaces in locations where they can be filled with an adverb clause, such as at the beginning or end of a sentence. List on the board several subordinate conjunctions. Tell students to complete the story by filling in the blanks with dependent clauses that begin with one of the subordinate conjunctions.

TEACH

Invite volunteers to read aloud their Warm-Up stories. Have students identify the dependent clauses that were added. Ask students to identify the function of the dependent clauses *(adverb)*. Then challenge students to identify what the dependent clauses modify.

Ask volunteers to read aloud about adverb clauses. Then read aloud and discuss the example diagrams. Be sure students understand that the subordinate conjunction is written on the line that connects the independent clause and the dependent clause.

PRACTICE

EXERCISE 1
Complete the first two sentences as a group. Point out the multiword preposition *(out of)* in sentence 9, which students learned on page 194.

APPLY

APPLY IT NOW
Suggest that students write about something they would like to do on a weekend. Challenge them to use a different subordinate conjunction for each sentence. Students should demonstrate an ability to diagram sentences with adverb clauses.

Grammar in Action. Students should identify the adverb clause *after the case was won.*

ASSESS

Note which students had difficulty diagramming sentences with adverb clauses. Assign **Practice Book** page 135 for further practice.

WRITING CONNECTION
Use pages 504–505 of the Writing portion of the book.

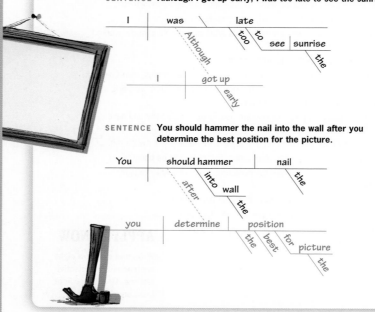

11.9 Adverb Clauses

An **adverb clause** is a dependent clause that acts as an adverb; it describes a verb, an adjective, or another adverb. Adverb clauses begin with subordinate conjunctions, such as *after, although, as, because, before, if, since, so that, unless, until, when, whenever, wherever,* and *while*.

In a diagram an adverb clause goes on its own horizontal line under the independent clause.

- The subordinate conjunction is placed on a slanted dashed line that connects the two clauses.
- The line goes from the verb in the adverb clause to the word in the independent clause that the adverb clause describes, which is usually the verb.

In the first sentence, the subordinate conjunction is *Although*. The dependent clause modifies *was*. In the second sentence, the subordinate conjunction is *after*. The independent clause modifies *should hammer*.

SENTENCE **Although I got up early, I was too late to see the sunrise.**

SENTENCE **You should hammer the nail into the wall after you determine the best position for the picture.**

212 • Section 11.9

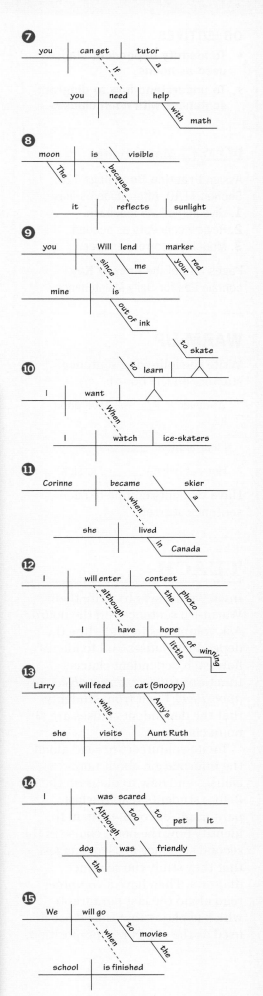

SENTENCE **I want to see the movie because *The Hobbit* is my favorite book.**

EXERCISE 1 Diagram the sentences.

1. Dylan bent the frame of his bike when he crashed into the fire hydrant.
2. Before individual cakes of soap were manufactured, grocers would cut pieces of soap from a huge block.
3. Margie played the same polka on her accordion until she memorized it.
4. When ancient Egyptian kings died, their bodies were mummified.
5. The Great Wall was built so that China would have protection from invaders.
6. The graduates tossed their caps into the air after they had received their diplomas.
7. If you need help with math, you can get a tutor.
8. The moon is visible because it reflects sunlight.
9. Will you lend me your red marker since mine is out of ink?
10. When I watch ice-skaters, I want to learn to skate.
11. Corinne became a skier when she lived in Canada.
12. I will enter the photo contest although I have little hope of winning.
13. Larry will feed Amy's cat, Snoopy, while she visits Aunt Ruth.
14. Although the dog was friendly, I was too scared to pet it.
15. We will go to the movies when school is finished.

APPLY IT NOW

Write five sentences with adverb clauses and diagram the sentences.

Diagramming • 213

Grammar in Action. Identify the adverb clause in the last sentence in the fourth paragraph of the model on p. 489.

11.10 Noun Clauses

OBJECTIVES
- **To identify dependent clauses used as nouns**
- **To understand how to diagram sentences with noun clauses**

DAILY Maintenance

Assign **Practice Book** page 126, Section 11.10. After students finish,
1. Give immediate feedback.
2. Review concepts as needed.
3. Model the correct answer.

Pages 4–5 of the **Answer Key** contain tips for Daily Maintenance.

WARM-UP

Write the following sentence starters on the board:

Whoever _____ will have good luck.

I learned that _____.

Her cat, which _____, is sick.

Have students complete each sentence starter.

TEACH

Invite volunteers to write their Warm-Up sentences on the board. Ask volunteers to underline the dependent clauses and to identify how each dependent clause functions *(subject, direct object, or appositive)*. Elicit from students that the dependent clauses are all noun clauses.

Invite volunteers to read aloud the information about noun clauses and how to diagram them. Before students read the last paragraph, encourage them to identify how the noun clause in the second sentence is used. Suggest that they study the sentence diagram. Then have a volunteer read aloud the last paragraph, which explains that the clause is used as the object of a preposition.

PRACTICE

EXERCISE 1
Tell students to first identify the noun clause in each sentence and how it is used. Make sure students are able to distinguish between a dependent noun clause and an independent clause.

APPLY

APPLY IT NOW
Suggest that students write about a research project they recently completed in science or social studies class. Encourage them to write about using the library or the Internet. Students should demonstrate an ability to diagram sentences with noun clauses.

TechTip Have students present their PowerPoint diagrams to the class.

ASSESS

Note which students had difficulty diagramming sentences with noun clauses. Assign **Practice Book** page 136 for further practice.

WRITING CONNECTION
Use pages 506–507 of the Writing portion of the book.

11.10 Noun Clauses

Dependent clauses can be used as nouns. **Noun clauses** work in sentences in the same way that nouns do. Among the words that commonly introduce noun clauses are *that, whoever, whomever, how, whether, what, whatever, when, where, which, who, whom, whose,* and *why.*

In a diagram the noun clause is placed according to its function in the sentence.

- The clause has its own horizontal line that rests on a stem connecting it to the independent clause. Except for clauses used as objects of prepositions, noun clauses are placed above the independent clause.
- If the word that introduces a noun clause has no function in the clause, it is placed on the vertical line connecting the noun clause to the independent clause. If the word that introduces the noun clause has a specific function, it is placed in the diagram according to that function.

In this sentence the noun clause is the subject. Noun clauses used as complements or direct objects are diagrammed in a similar way. Noun clauses used as appositives go in parentheses next to the nouns they describe.

SENTENCE **That the school needs a new computer lab is evident from the crowding in the old lab.**

EXERCISE 1 (Answers)

❶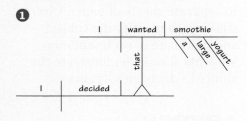

❷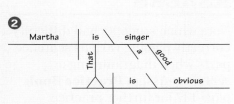

❸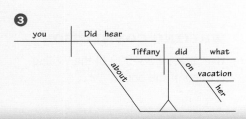

❹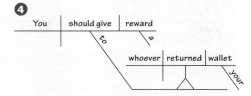

❺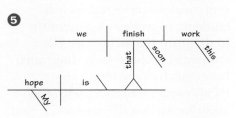

❻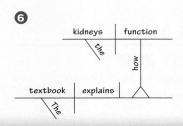

❼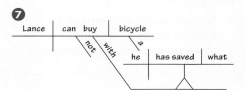

❽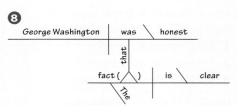

❾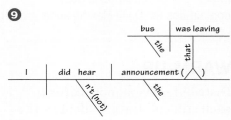

❿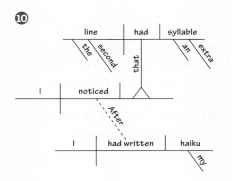

⓫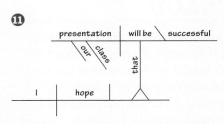

⓬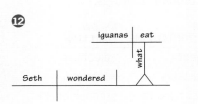

In this sentence the noun clause is the object of the preposition *to*. The word *whoever*, which introduces the noun clause, acts as its subject.

SENTENCE **The principal gave a special certificate to whoever had perfect attendance.**

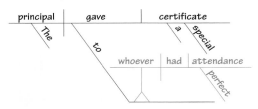

EXERCISE 1 Diagram the sentences.

1. I decided that I wanted a large yogurt smoothie.
2. That Martha is a good singer is obvious.
3. Did you hear about what Tiffany did on her vacation?
4. You should give a reward to whoever returned your wallet.
5. My hope is that we finish this work soon.
6. The textbook explains how the kidneys function.
7. Lance cannot buy a bicycle with what he has saved.
8. The fact that George Washington was honest is clear.
9. I didn't hear the announcement that the bus was leaving.
10. After I had written my haiku, I noticed that the second line had an extra syllable.
11. I hope that our class presentation will be successful.
12. Seth wondered what iguanas eat.

Iguanas eat mainly fruits and leaves, and enjoy an occasional treat such as the hibiscus.

APPLY IT NOW

Write six sentences with noun clauses and diagram the sentences. Use at least three different words to introduce the clauses.

Tech Tip Diagram a noun clause, using a PowerPoint presentation.

11.11 Diagramming Practice

OBJECTIVE

- To review the placement of various parts of a sentence when diagramming a sentence

 **Maintenance**

Assign **Practice Book** page 126, Section 11.11. After students finish,
1. Give immediate feedback.
2. Review concepts as needed.
3. Model the correct answer.

Pages 4–5 of the **Answer Key** contain tips for Daily Maintenance.

WARM-UP

Distribute several note cards to each student. Have students write on each card a sentence about their favorite activity. Encourage students to write a variety of sentences, using different types of dependent clauses. Then have students place their cards in a bag. Invite volunteers to draw a card from the bag and to diagram the sentence on the board.

TEACH

Have a volunteer read aloud the first paragraph. Begin a chart on the board to show where the parts of a sentence go in a diagram. Name a sentence part and have students explain in which column of the chart it belongs.

MAIN HORIZONTAL LINE	BELOW MAIN LINE
subjects	adjectives
predicates	adverbs
direct objects	prepositional phrases
subject complements	participles
object complements	some infinitives
	indirect objects

PRACTICE

EXERCISE 1

Have students work with partners. Suggest that they first determine the function of each word in the sentences. After doing so, ask students to work independently to diagram the sentences. Have students compare their diagrams. Invite partners to share any troublesome sentences with the class for further discussion.

APPLY

APPLY IT NOW

Tell students to copy the 10 sentences they have chosen onto 10 separate sheets of paper. Direct students to identify the subject and predicate of each sentence. Students should demonstrate the ability to diagram sentences.

ASSESS

Note which students had difficulty correctly placing various sentence parts when diagramming a sentence. Assign **Practice Book** page 137 for further practice.

> **WRITING CONNECTION**
> Use pages 508–509 of the Writing portion of the book.

11.11 Diagramming Practice

Let's review some of the basics of diagramming. Subjects, verbs, direct objects, subject complements, and object complements go on the main horizontal line. Adjectives, adverbs, prepositional phrases, participles, and some infinitives go under the words or phrases they modify.

Gerunds and infinitives used as subjects, objects, or complements go above the main horizontal line of a diagram. Gerunds used as objects of prepositions and infinitives used as adverbs and adjectives go on lines below the horizontal main line. Can you identify a gerund and an infinitive in this sentence? How are they used?

SENTENCE **To study for the test is our reason for meeting at noon.**

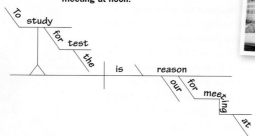

Diagrams of compound sentences and of sentences with adjective clauses, adverb clauses, and noun clauses have two horizontal lines. Review the various ways the two lines are connected. What kinds of clauses are in this sentence?

SENTENCE **Students can take lessons in French or Spanish before regular classes begin.**

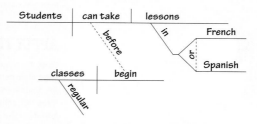

EXERCISE 1

1. Some people boil and eat acorns.

2. The temperature, rising throughout the day, set a record.

3. I can climb up the tree and climb down again before you get to the top.

4. I found an old key, but I could not find the door that it opened.

5. Schuyler plans to go to Texas in June to visit her cousins.

6. I forgot that New York was the first capital of the country.

7. Traveling to the West in a covered wagon was a difficult journey.

8. *Bronco,* which is a cowboy's term for an untamed horse, means "wild" in Spanish.

9. Jugglers need good coordination because they must keep several objects in the air at the same time.

EXERCISE 1 Write out the sentences.

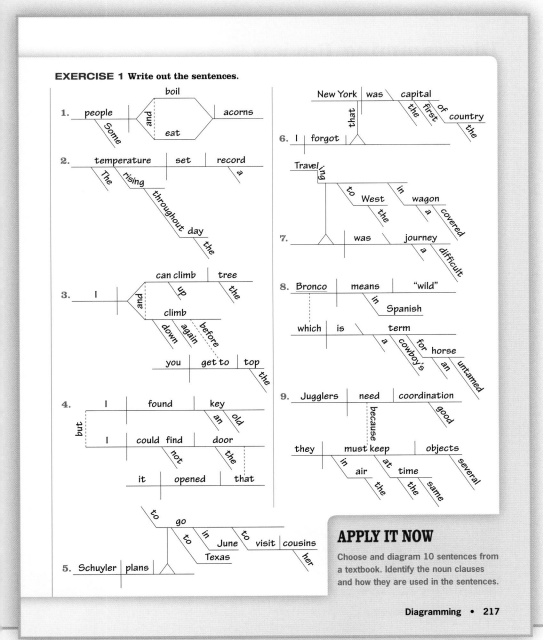

APPLY IT NOW

Choose and diagram 10 sentences from a textbook. Identify the noun clauses and how they are used in the sentences.

Diagramming • 217

Diagramming Review

ASSESS

Use the Diagramming Review as homework, as a practice test, or as an informal assessment. Following are some options for use.

Homework

When you next meet, review the diagrams as a group. Be sure to model how to arrive at the correct diagram.

Practice Test

Use the Diagramming Review as a diagnostic tool. After students have finished, identify which diagram structures require more attention. Reteach concepts as necessary.

Informal Assessment

Use the review as preparation for the formal assessment. Count the review as a portion of the grade. Have students work to diagram the sentences and use their corrected diagrams as a study guide for the formal assessment.

> **WRITING CONNECTION**
>
> Use pages 510–511 of the Writing portion of the book.

Answers

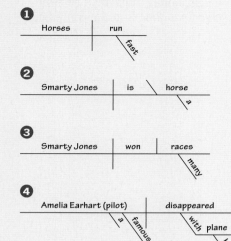
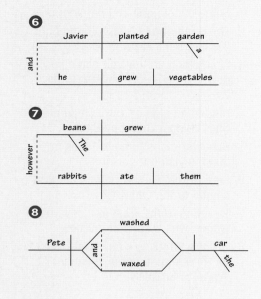

Diagramming Review

Diagram the sentences.

11.1
1. Horses run fast.
2. Smarty Jones is a horse.
3. Smarty Jones won many races.

11.2
4. Amelia Earhart, a famous pilot, disappeared with her plane.
5. We read the book *Amelia Earhart: A Biography* at school.

11.3
6. Javier planted a garden, and he grew vegetables.
7. The beans grew; however, rabbits ate them.

11.4
8. Pete washed and waxed the car.
9. Jenny and I cleaned the garage.

11.5
10. Sitting on the dock, we watched boats on the lake.
11. Tony, showing his skill, steered the boat with ease.
12. Enjoying the sand, Samantha stayed on the shore.

11.6
13. Tapping my foot is an easy dance move.
14. Lessons are useful for teaching dances.

11.7
15. Shauna wanted to make some bread.
16. The next step, to knead the dough, seemed difficult.

9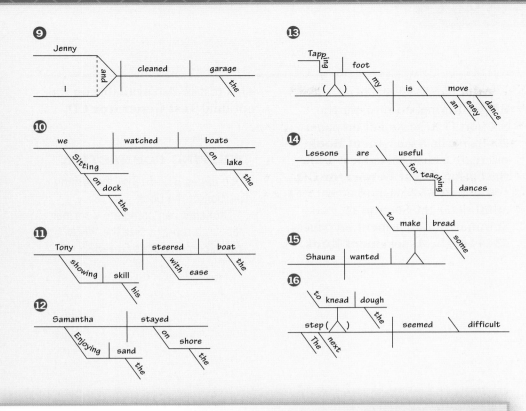

Jenny / I — and — cleaned | garage \ the

10

we | watched | boats \ on \ lake \ the
Sitting \ on \ dock \ the

11

Tony | steered | boat \ the
showing \ skill \ his | with \ ease

12

Samantha | stayed \ on \ shore \ the
Enjoying \ sand \ the

13

Tapping | foot \ my
( ) | is \ move \ an \ easy \ dance

14

Lessons | are \ useful
for teaching | dances

15

to make | bread \ some
Shauna | wanted

16

to knead | dough \ the
step ( ) | seemed \ difficult
The \ next

17

England | is connected \ by \ tunnel \ a
now
which | was separated \ from \ France
once

18

explanation | was \ fascinating
The
Mr. Johnson | gave | that

19

she | packed | toothbrush \ a
Since
Tate | was staying
overnight

20

She | arrived
for \ party \ the
after \ slumber
family | had eaten | dinner
the

21

they | fell
Although \ asleep \ early
girls | wanted | to watch | show \ the \ late
the

22

Tom | was \ artist \ a
That | good
| was \ obvious

23

artist | gave | guidance
The \ resident | to
whoever | asked
for \ help

11.8

17. England, which was once separated from France, is now connected by a tunnel.
18. The explanation that Mr. Johnson gave was fascinating.

11.9

19. Since Tate was staying overnight, she packed a toothbrush.
20. She arrived for the slumber party after the family had eaten dinner.
21. Although the girls wanted to watch the late show, they fell asleep early.

11.10

22. That Tom was a good artist was obvious.
23. The resident artist gave guidance to whoever asked for help.

11.11 Write out the sentences.

24.

I | lost | goggles \ my
therefore
I | could see \ in \ water \ the
n't (not)

25.

To rest
for \ minute \ a
| is | reason \ the
for \ floating
on \ back \ my

24

I lost my goggles; therefore, I couldn't see in the water

25

To rest for a minute is the reason for floating on my back.

Go to www.voyagesinenglish.com for more activities.

TechTip Encourage students to further review diagramming, using the additional practice and games at www.voyagesinenglish.com.

Diagramming Challenge

ASSESS

Encourage students to study the diagram closely before answering the questions independently. If students have difficulty with any questions, suggest that they refer to the section that teaches the skill. This activity can be completed by individuals, by small groups, or by the class working as a whole.

After you have reviewed diagramming, administer the Section 11 Assessment on pages 29–32 in the **Assessment Book,** or create a customized test with the optional **Test Generator CD.**

You may also wish to administer the Section 11 Summative Assessment on pages 43–44 of the **Assessment Book.**

This test is also available on the optional **Test Generator CD.**

WRITING CONNECTION

Use pages 512–513 of the Writing portion of the book.

Students can complete a formal research report using the Writer's Workshop on pages 514–525.

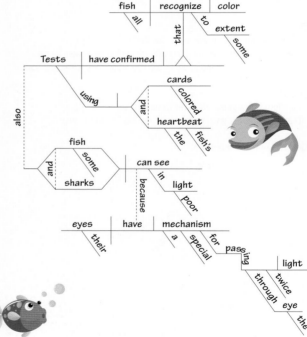

Study the diagram and then answer the questions.

1. How many clauses are in the sentence?
2. Look at the coordinating conjunctions. Identify what they connect—words, phrases, clauses, or sentences.
3. Identify the adverb clause.
4. Identify the noun clause.
5. How is *using* used in the sentence?
6. Name the gerund phrase in the sentence. How is it used?
7. Write out the sentence.

Diagramming Challenge

1. four; two independent clauses and two dependent clauses
2. *and*—connects words (*cards* and *heartbeat*) *and*—connects words (*fish* and *sharks*)
3. because their eyes have a special mechanism for passing light through the eye twice
4. that all fish recognize color to some extent
5. as a participle in the participial phrase modifying *Tests*
6. passing light through the eye twice; object of the preposition *for*
7. Tests using colored cards and the fish's heartbeat have confirmed that all fish recognize color to some extent; also, some fish and sharks can see in poor light because their eyes have a special mechanism for passing light through the eye twice.

WRITTEN AND ORAL COMMUNICATION

Chapters

CHAPTER FOCUS

LESSON 1: What Makes a Good Personal Narrative?

LESSON 2: Introduction, Body, and Conclusion

- **GRAMMAR:** Nouns and Adjectives
- **STUDY SKILLS:** Time Lines
- **WRITING SKILLS:** Varied Sentences
- **WORD STUDY:** Exact Words
- **SPEAKING AND LISTENING SKILLS:** Oral Personal Narratives
- **WRITER'S WORKSHOP:** Personal Narratives

SUPPORT MATERIALS

Practice Book
Writing, pages 138–142

Assessment Book
Chapter 1 Writing Skills, pages 45–46
Personal Narrative Writing Prompt, pages 47–48

Rubrics
Student, page 259y
Teacher, page 259z

Test Generator CD

Grammar
Sections 1 and 2, pages 1–30

Customizable Lesson Plans
www.voyagesinenglish.com

Personal Narratives

WHAT IS A PERSONAL NARRATIVE?

Personal narratives are written to share significant events in writers' lives. They are personal to the core, and at their best they are revealing and relevant to others. The writer of a good personal narrative knows how to let his or her personality shine through with the use of humor, phrasing, dialogue, or a combination of these things. Good personal narratives always have an honest voice—one that is authentic and true.

A good personal narrative includes the following:

- ☐ A topic relating to a significant experience from the writer's life
- ☐ A first-person point of view
- ☐ A structure that includes an engaging introduction, a cohesive body, and a conclusion that offers a sense of resolution
- ☐ A coherent organization that uses chronological order, flows logically, and excludes unnecessary details
- ☐ A voice that shows the writer's personality, is authentic, and uses a tone appropriate for the intended audience
- ☐ Exact words that avoid redundancy
- ☐ Natural language
- ☐ Transition words
- ☐ Varied sentence structures that avoid run-on and rambling sentences

LiNK Use the following titles to offer your students examples of well-crafted personal narratives:

In My Hands: Memories of a Holocaust Rescuer by Irene Gut Opdyke

The Land I Lost: Adventures of a Boy in Vietnam by Huynh Quang Nhuong

The Story of My Life by Helen Keller

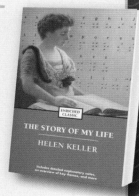

THE STORY OF MY LIFE
HELEN KELLER

"The pen that writes your life story must be held in your own hand."

—Irene C. Kassorla

WRITER'S WORKSHOP TIPS

Follow these ideas and tips to help you and your class get the most out of the Writer's Workshop:

- Review the traits of good writing. Use the chart on the inside back cover of the student and teacher editions.
- Encourage students to keep a journal to record important or interesting personal experiences.
- Fill your classroom library with autobiographies.
- Invite local businesspeople to come to class to tell how they chose their careers, how they got started, and how they overcame any difficulties.
- Invite students to bring in photo albums, scrapbooks, or other memorabilia to share information about their lives.
- As homework, have students view home movies, photo albums, or scrapbooks. Ask students to make a list of 10 life-affirming or life-altering events.

CONNECT WITH GRAMMAR

Throughout the Writer's Workshop, look for opportunities to integrate nouns and adjectives with writing personal narratives.

- ☐ Discuss how precise nouns can make writing more engaging.
- ☐ Have students add appositives to their writing to vary sentence structure.
- ☐ Have students create a list of alternative adjectives for commonly used words. Encourage students to use a thesaurus if needed.
- ☐ Talk about the differences between adjective phrases and clauses. Have students combine short sentences by using adjective phrases and clauses to vary sentence structure.

SCORING RUBRIC

Personal Narrative

0 = not evident
1 = minimal evidence of mastery
2 = evidence of development toward mastery
3 = strong evidence of mastery
4 = outstanding evidence of mastery

Ideas	POINTS
an apparent theme or purpose	
a clear focus on experience's importance	
Organization	
an engaging introduction	
a cohesive body	
a conclusion that offers a sense of resolution	
chronological order	
Voice	
identifiable writer's personality	
a sense of authenticity	
appropriate tone for intended audience	
Word Choice	
exact words	
natural language	
Sentence Fluency	
transition words	
varied sentence types	
no run-on and rambling sentences	
Conventions	
correct grammar and usage	
correct spelling, punctuation, and capitalization	
Presentation	
consistent spacing and margins	
neatness	
Additional Items	
Total	

Full-sized, reproducible rubrics can be found at the end of this chapter.

CHAPTER 1
Personal Narratives

INTRODUCING THE GENRE

Ask volunteers to share what they think constitutes a personal narrative. Use their responses to start a discussion about the genre. Make sure students understand that a personal narrative is a writer's description of something he or she experienced firsthand. Elaborate on the following characteristics in the personal narrative:

- The first-person description of events composes the body of the narrative.
- The events are related in vivid sensory language. Chronological order helps the reader become involved in the story.
- There is a sense of closure in the conclusion of the narrative. Often the conclusion restates a theme or central idea.

Point out that a personal narrative can cover a very brief period of time or a number of days, as long as it focuses on a single incident.

Reading the Literature Excerpt

Have volunteers read aloud the excerpt from *The Story of My Life*. Ask students to find examples that point to the writer describing an event that happened in her life. Have students determine other characteristics that make this a good example of a personal narrative. Then have students name books or articles they have read that share these characteristics.

LiNK The Story of My Life

The excerpts in Chapter 1 introduce students to relevant, real, published examples of personal narratives. *The Story of My Life* is a strong example of a personal narrative because it does the following:

- Tells a true story that happened to the writer
- Moves in chronological order
- Is written in the first-person point of view

As students encounter the different examples throughout the chapter, be sure to point out the characteristics they share. Also take this opportunity to point out grammar skills that students have been learning, such as rules for using nouns and adjectives.

Personal Narratives

LiNK The Story of My Life
by Helen Keller

I had now the key to all language, and I was eager to learn to use it. Children who hear acquire language without any particular effort; the words that fall from others' lips they catch on the wing, as it were, delightedly, while the little deaf child must trap them by a slow and often painful process....

At first, when my teacher told me about a new thing I asked very few questions. My ideas were vague, and my vocabulary was inadequate; but as my knowledge of things grew, and I learned more and more words, my field of inquiry broadened, and I would return again and again to the same subject, eager for further information. Sometimes a new word revived an image that some earlier experience had engraved on my brain.

I remember the morning that I first asked the meaning of the word, "love." This was before I knew many words. I had found a few early violets in the garden and brought them to my teacher ... Miss Sullivan put her arm gently around me and spelled in my hand, "I love Helen."

> This excerpt by Helen Keller, who lost her sight and hearing as a young child, is a good example of a personal narrative.

222

Reading the Student Model

Tell students they are going to read an actual personal narrative written by a student. Instruct them to read this narrative silently. When everyone has finished, ask volunteers to summarize the events in the narrative.

Point out that these events actually happened to the writer. Tell students that the pronouns *I* and *me* confirm the first-person point of view. Explain that the writer's experience had a beginning *(when the air became strangely still)* and an ending *(when the writer found his dog safe in a hole)*.

Ask students to describe the likely audience of this personal narrative, based on the tone and choice of words *(an audience similar in age and interests to the writer)*. Discuss how the language and tone might change if the audience were older, younger, or of another background.

Scavenger Hunt

Have students look through reading materials in the classroom to find examples of personal narratives. Explain that doing so will help students understand what to look for in their own narrative writing. Ask students what clues suggest that the piece is a personal narrative. Have students compare their findings to other writing genres such as a report, a letter, or a how-to article.

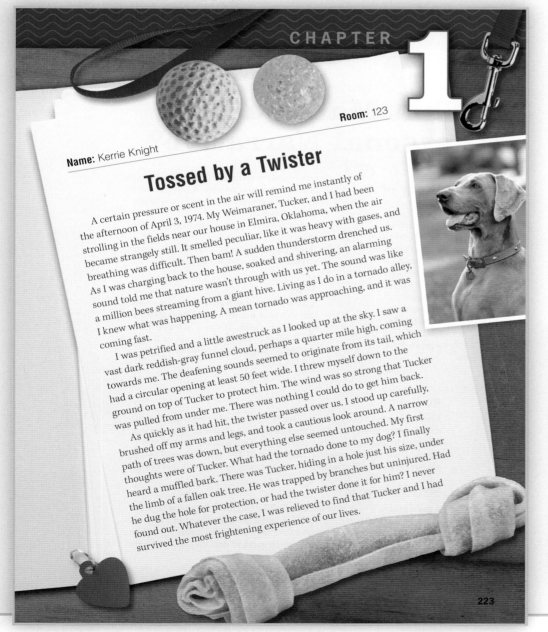

CHAPTER 1

Room: 123

Name: Kerrie Knight

Tossed by a Twister

A certain pressure or scent in the air will remind me instantly of the afternoon of April 3, 1974. My Weimaraner, Tucker, and I had been strolling in the fields near our house in Elmira, Oklahoma, when the air became strangely still. It smelled peculiar, like it was heavy with gases, and breathing was difficult. Then bam! A sudden thunderstorm drenched us. As I was charging back to the house, soaked and shivering, an alarming sound told me that nature wasn't through with us yet. The sound was like a million bees streaming from a giant hive. Living as I do in a tornado alley, I knew what was happening. A mean tornado was approaching, and it was coming fast.

I was petrified and a little awestruck as I looked up at the sky. I saw a vast dark reddish-gray funnel cloud, perhaps a quarter mile high, coming towards me. The deafening sounds seemed to originate from its tail, which had a circular opening at least 50 feet wide. I threw myself down to the ground on top of Tucker to protect him. The wind was so strong that Tucker was pulled from under me. There was nothing I could do to get him back.

As quickly as it had hit, the twister passed over us. I stood up carefully, brushed off my arms and legs, and took a cautious look around. A narrow path of trees was down, but everything else seemed untouched. My first thoughts were of Tucker. What had the tornado done to my dog? I finally heard a muffled bark. There was Tucker, hiding in a hole just his size, under the limb of a fallen oak tree. He was trapped by branches but uninjured. Had he dug the hole for protection, or had the twister done it for him? I never found out. Whatever the case, I was relieved to find that Tucker and I had survived the most frightening experience of our lives.

For Tomorrow

Have students look through magazines or newspapers at home or in the library to find two personal narratives that are written for different audiences. Students should be ready to discuss their choices and describe the intended audiences for each. Bring a personal narrative of your own to share with students.

223

OBJECTIVES

- **To examine the characteristics of a personal narrative**
- **To identify appropriate topics and titles of personal narratives**

WARM-UP

Read, Listen, Speak

Read a passage from the personal narrative you brought in as part of yesterday's For Tomorrow homework. Point out language that helps identify the target audience. Then have small groups discuss the target audience of each narrative they found, citing evidence from each piece. Have students save these narratives for a future assignment.

GRAMMAR CONNECTION

Take this opportunity to talk about singular and plural nouns. You may wish to have students point out singular and plural nouns in their Read, Listen, Speak examples.

TEACH

Ask a volunteer to read aloud the first two paragraphs at the top of the page. Choose other students to read aloud the five sections that follow. Refer to the model, "Tossed by a Twister," and ask students to identify how the writer used the five points of a personal narrative *(topic, audience, structure, coherence,* and *title).*

LiNK Discuss who the intended audience of this narrative might be. Point out language from the excerpt that aids the author in relating the events to her audience. Ask what words or sentences help the audience understand something that is unfamiliar to them.

PRACTICE

ACTIVITY A

Review the Topic section. Have students keep in mind the characteristics of a good topic when completing this activity. Give students time to work independently. When students have finished, discuss their answers. Challenge students to provide concrete support for their answers.

LESSON PERSONAL NARRATIVES

What Makes a Good Personal Narrative?

LiNK

The Story of My Life

"What is love?" I asked. She drew me closer to her and said, "It is here," pointing to my heart, whose beats I was conscious of for the first time. Her words puzzled me very much because I did not then understand anything unless I touched it.

I smelt the violets in her hand and asked . . .

"Is love the sweetness of flowers?"

Helen Keller

A personal narrative is a first-person account of an event in a writer's life. It invites readers to share the writer's experiences and his or her reactions to them.

Following are some points to keep in mind when you write a personal narrative. How closely did the writer of the personal narrative on page 223 follow these suggestions?

Topic

A good personal narrative relates an event that was unusual, memorable, or significant to the author's life. The best narratives use the incident to illustrate an idea, or theme, that many people could relate to.

Audience

Know the audience of your narrative. Is it your teacher and classmates, a close friend, or the readers of a favorite magazine? How do you want your audience to react: with smiles, tears, nods of recognition, or all three? How will you relate the events that occurred? The tone, or overall feeling, of your personal narrative depends on your answers to these questions.

Structure

A good personal narrative has a definite structure. It begins with an introduction that lures the reader in and hints at the story to come. The body, or main section, of the narrative tells what happened step-by-step. The conclusion tells the outcome of the incident and may show why the incident was significant.

APPLY

WRITER'S CORNER

Remind students that when they are brainstorming ideas, they should write quickly—using phrases to capture thoughts rather than using complete sentences. Ask students to save these ideas to use for the next Writer's Corner activity. Students should demonstrate an ability to identify appropriate topics for a personal narrative.

💡 **TechTip** You may wish to print graphic organizers from a computer program. Distribute them to partners and have them work together to fill in the graphic organizers. Have one student brainstorm ideas and the other can write them.

ASSESS

Note which students had difficulty with the characteristics of a good personal narrative. Use the Reteach option with those students who need additional reinforcement.

TEACHING OPTIONS

Reteach

Have students consider these questions:

- Was there ever a time when you lost something important? Try to remember how you felt.
- Think about a favorite time with a friend or family member. What happened? Was it unexpected?

Invite students to brainstorm ideas that these questions bring to mind. Help students identify similar experiences that might become personal narratives.

English-Language Learners

Use published writing in the English-language learners' primary languages to familiarize those students with personal narratives. Obtain lists of appropriate titles from online sources that feature writing in students' primary languages. Invite students to share examples with the class. Encourage students to identify the characteristics of a personal narrative.

Coherence

A personal narrative should maintain coherence, which means that each part of the narrative builds on what came before it. The story should be told in a logical way, usually in chronological order. Any details that aren't important to the story being told should be left out.

Title

Don't underestimate the power of a title. A title is like a snapshot of your personal narrative—it creates a first impression. If the title is short, creative, and focused on the subject or theme, the first impression will be positive.

ACTIVITY A Explain why each topic below could or could not be used for a personal narrative.

1. my favorite year in school
2. the pets I've had growing up
3. my worst basketball practice
4. the family vacation that wasn't
5. five reasons to study American history
6. the day I met my best friend
7. how my parents met
8. surviving my aunt's visit
9. all the times my mom supported me
10. my first piano lesson
11. the difference between alligators and crocodiles

WRITER'S CORNER

Use a web like the one shown to brainstorm possible topics for a personal narrative. A travel adventure or a weird dream can generate many further ideas. Write your starting topic in the center of the web. Link related thoughts to your topic, expanding your web outward.

Web diagram:
- MY SUMMER VACATION (center)
  - Summer camp
  - Trips to the beach
  - Cookout with my family
  - Growing an inch taller
  - Visiting Uncle Bart in the city
  - The fireworks show on July 4

Tech Tip Use a computer program to map out your ideas.

For Tomorrow

Have students write a list of 10 things that happen between the time they leave school and the time they sit down to do their homework. Explain that any 10 events may be used. Tell students to list the events in chronological order. Model by composing your own list of such events.

WARM-UP

Read, Listen, Speak

Share your list of events from yesterday's For Tomorrow homework. Have small groups share their lists. Point out that the lists will contain some similar items. When an unusual event is mentioned, ask students to discuss whether this event might make a good topic for a personal narrative.

GRAMMAR CONNECTION

Take this opportunity to talk about nouns used as subjects and subject complements. You may wish to have students point out nouns used as subjects and subject complements in their Read, Listen, Speak examples.

TEACH

Ask volunteers to list on the board the parts of a good personal narrative discussed yesterday *(topic, audience, structure, coherence,* and *title)*. Then lead a brief discussion reviewing specific characteristics about each of the five parts of a personal narrative *(topic relating an event in the writer's life, first-person point of view, natural authentic tone, definite structure, engaging introduction, chronological order, exact words and sensory language, and a conclusion that gives a sense of closure)*.

LiNK Point out words or phrases in the excerpt that help set the tone *(But Miss Sullivan shook her head . . .)*. Have students discuss what tone is being conveyed.

PRACTICE

ACTIVITY B

Have volunteers read aloud the personal narrative, "My Favorite Disaster." Answer the questions as a class.

ACTIVITY C

Review what makes an effective title. Discuss the first title together. Let students finish the activity independently. Encourage volunteers to explain their answers. *(The least effective titles are numbers 2, 4, and 7 because they reveal nothing about the main idea or theme of the personal narrative.)*

ACTIVITY D

Review the main points of coherence and logical flow in a personal narrative *(each part building on what came before it, chronological order, only relevant details)*. Ask a volunteer to read aloud the first paragraph in the activity. Discuss possible edits to the paragraph that would make it more coherent. Let students work independently on the second paragraph. After they have finished, invite students to discuss their answers in small groups.

ACTIVITY B Read this personal narrative. Then answer the questions that follow.

My Favorite Disaster

It took a force of nature to bring your grandpa and me together. Ray had been delivering groceries to my house for months, and I'm certain he noticed me. I surely noticed him, with his turquoise eyes and curly blond hair. But we two pitifully shy people had never muttered more than a few words to each other.

One stormy autumn evening, more than 40 years ago now, Ray delivered the groceries as usual. The wind was howling like a lonely wolf. As he put the last cardboard box of groceries on the kitchen table, we heard a sharp crack. The lights went out, and the room went dark. As I looked up, heavy drops of rain fell onto my face.

An oak had gouged a huge hole in the roof. During the time it took to find and light candles, assess the damage, and figure out what to do, Ray and I overcame our shyness. That was the beginning of our romance—a day, I sometimes say, when an ill wind brought some good.

1. What does the title tell you about this narrative?
2. Who is the intended audience?
3. How would you describe the tone?
4. Does the first sentence entice readers to continue reading? Why or why not?
5. In what way does the first sentence hint at what's to come?
6. What sensory details does the writer include?
7. Does the narrative maintain coherence? Explain how.
8. Which sentence gives the theme?
9. Identify two chronological steps that the narrator describes in the main body.
10. How is the personal narrative concluded?

ACTIVITY C Read each title for a personal narrative. Tell why you think it is or isn't effective.

1. My First and Only Scuba Dive
2. June 3, 1954
3. Why I Ran Away
4. A Rather Dull Afternoon
5. The Day My Dream Became a Nightmare
6. My Brother Is Born!
7. What Happened to Me One Day

226

APPLY

WRITER'S CORNER

Make sure students understand that they should list more than one title for each topic. When they have finished, ask volunteers to read aloud their titles. Challenge the rest of the class to guess what each topic might be. Students should demonstrate an understanding of how to create an engaging title for their personal narratives.

ASSESS

Note which students had difficulty with the characteristics of a good personal narrative. Use the Reteach option with those students who need additional reinforcement.

Practice Book page 138 provides additional practice with the characteristics of an effective personal narrative.

TEACHING OPTIONS

Reteach

Provide students with the personal narrative "A Thing Shared" by M. F. K. Fisher (or another short published piece of your choosing). Give students time to read it, and then have small groups discuss the following questions: *How well does the introduction grab the reader's attention? How well does the title hint at the topic and theme? Is the progress of the narrative coherent? What is the overall tone? What sensory details does the writer include?* Circulate around the room and offer support for each group's discussion.

Learning the Difference

Make sure students understand the difference between fictional short stories written in the first person and personal narratives. Have students look through reading materials in the classroom to find examples of each. Have students create a Venn diagram to compare and contrast the two genres. Encourage students to write a sentence summarizing the main differences between the genres.

For Tomorrow

Have students look in books or magazines at home to find examples of strong introductions and conclusions. Explain that students will discuss which introductions drew them into the piece and which conclusions ended the piece satisfactorily. Bring an example that you found or one from your own writing to share and discuss.

ACTIVITY D Read the following paragraphs for coherence. Do the events flow logically? Are only relevant details included? Edit each paragraph to make it more coherent.

1. Because I live in Hawaii, I'd seen snow in movies and on TV, but I'd never seen it firsthand. I live right near the beach, which is wonderful. Nevertheless, two months ago, armed with parka and boots, I flew from Waikiki to Minneapolis. We had to switch planes in Chicago. Three feet of snow was on the ground in Minneapolis, and more was on the way. My heart was racing. I didn't know how snow felt, tasted, or even smelled. But I was going to find out.

2. My three-year-old son Danny was screaming. People in the crowd were looking either sympathetic, annoyed, or amused—and I was sweating. How was I going to get Danny's blankie back from that innocent-looking but criminal baby elephant? Eventually, we did get it back. Dangling a bag of peanuts over the fence at the animal had accomplished nothing. So I dug our lunch out of my backpack, unwrapped a sandwich of corned beef on rye, and waved it back and forth. I still had a piece of fruit and a drink saved for later. The elephant exchanged the blanket for the sandwich, and my friend May pulled the blanket through the fence with a stick. Teamwork and ingenuity saved the day.

LiNK

The Story of My Life

Again I thought. The warm sun was shining on us. "Is this not love?" I asked, pointing in the direction from which the heat came. "Is this not love?" It seemed to me there could be nothing more beautiful than the sun, whose warmth makes all things grow. But Miss Sullivan shook her head . . .

Helen Keller

WRITER'S CORNER

Choose at least three favorite topics from the web of subjects you brainstormed on page 225. Think of some catchy titles for each possible topic.

Personal Narratives • 227

OBJECTIVES

- **To identify and write effective introductions for personal narratives**
- **To recognize effective body paragraphs of personal narratives**
- **To create concluding sentences for personal narratives**

WARM-UP

Read, Listen, Speak

Read one example you found as part of yesterday's For Tomorrow homework and discuss why it is an effective introduction or conclusion. Model the language you want students to use when they discuss their examples. Have small groups read the examples of introductions and conclusions. Instruct students to discuss whether these examples grab the reader's attention or provide a sense of closure.

GRAMMAR CONNECTION

Take this opportunity to talk about nouns used as objects and object complements. You may wish to have students point out nouns used as objects and object complements in their Read, Listen, Speak examples.

TEACH

Have volunteers read aloud the three sections on the page. Allow time for discussion. During this discussion, record the information on the board in two columns. In the column on the left write *Introduction, Body,* and *Conclusion,* with space between each. In the column on the right, list important information for each entry in the column on the left. Make sure students record this information in a notebook.

LiNK Point out the language that sets the reader's expectations and draws the reader in *(puzzled and disappointed, beautiful truth)*. Ask students what this personal narrative might be about.

PRACTICE

ACTIVITY A

Read aloud the directions and the first topic. As a class, write an effective introduction for the first topic. While writing, review the characteristics of a good introduction. Then have students complete the remainder of the activity independently. After

students have finished, have them read their introductions aloud. Let the class discuss which introductions are most effective and why.

ACTIVITY B

Have volunteers read aloud the two introductions. Discuss each one after it is read. Challenge students to use what they know about introductions to comment on each.

Point out that the second introduction wanders from the topic. Have students rewrite the second introduction independently.

LESSON **2** PERSONAL NARRATIVES

Introduction, Body, and Conclusion

Introduction

The introduction of a personal narrative sets the reader's expectations. If the introduction is bland or tedious, readers have no incentive to continue reading. The introduction may include just one sentence, or it may consist of several sentences or even paragraphs. The introduction should help the reader understand the topic of the narrative and lead the reader into the body of the narrative.

Body

The body is the core of a personal narrative, and it is generally the longest part. It uses sensory details that let the reader see, smell, hear, feel, and taste what the writer experienced. Depending on the topic and

tone, the body may include dialogue, flashbacks, and other literary devices as ways to tell an effective story. Though in many ways it is similar to a fictional story, a personal narrative describes something that actually happened to the writer. Every sentence in the body should advance the narrative. Irrelevant details are like dead weight on a sinking ship. Good writers throw them overboard!

Conclusion

The conclusion of a personal narrative is the writer's last chance to leave an impression. The conclusion can summarize the event, or it can tie the narrative together. The writer can also use the conclusion to comment or reflect upon the event, and share what he or she may have learned.

APPLY

WRITER'S CORNER

Ask volunteers to read aloud the introductions they wrote. Review the characteristics of an effective introduction. Have students save these introductions for the next Writer's Corner activity. Students should demonstrate an understanding of what is needed for a compelling introduction.

TechTip You may wish to have students use the class blog to offer constructive suggestions for revising introductions or for writing future parts of the personal narrative.

ASSESS

Note which students had difficulty with the introductions, body paragraphs, and conclusions of personal narratives. Use the Reteach option with those students who need additional reinforcement.

TEACHING OPTIONS

Reteach

Obtain a copy of E. B. White's personal narrative "Once More to the Lake" or another with a strong introduction. Ask pairs to read only the first paragraph, the introduction. Allow students time to discuss how effective it is and what details make it so effective. Have students write a critique of the introduction. Invite pairs to share their opinions with the rest of the class.

Meeting Individual Needs

Auditory Many song lyrics are written as personal narratives. Model this by playing the song "It's My Life" by Bon Jovi or another song that fits the personal narrative structure. Discuss which characteristics of a personal narrative are present in the song's lyrics. Then have students listen to the radio or look through their music collection for such songs. Ask students to analyze the song's lyrics as a personal narrative and to write a paragraph describing what characteristics of a personal narrative are found in the lyrics. Encourage students to find concrete examples and to include these in their paragraphs.

For Tomorrow

Write the following sentence on the board: *Tomorrow I have a math test.* Have students use this sentence in two paragraphs—one that has an excited tone and one that has a nervous or fearful tone. Ask students to include sensory details in each paragraph to help illustrate the tone. Write your own paragraphs to share with the class.

ACTIVITY A Imagine that you are writing a personal narrative. Choose two of the following incidents and write a short introduction in paragraph form for each.

1. helping to cook a meal for your family
2. overhearing a classmate saying something mean and untrue about you
3. going on a long road trip
4. playing in a championship game
5. moving because your mother got a new job
6. finding or losing something
7. meeting someone new

ACTIVITY B Below are two introductions for personal narratives. Choose the less effective paragraph and rewrite it to make it stronger.

1. I woke up to the sounds of a scratchy weather report on the radio and my mom insisting I get up and get dressed. The winds outside were slapping gusts of rain against our house, and my dad was packing the car with food and blankets. You'd think I'd be used to participating in an abrupt exodus alongside my fellow Dade County residents during a hurricane. But the last serious one that hit our section of Florida happened when I was too young to remember. Even with all of my family's preparations for this one, I was still in for quite a ride.

2. Ever since I learned to read, I've studied snakes, especially my favorite, the king cobra. When I was given the opportunity last year to go to India with a group from school, I hoped finally to see one up close. It was a long, tiring trip. The airplane food was bad, and I sat next to someone who talked during the whole flight. I never want to take such a long flight again.

LiNK

The Story of My Life

Someone was drawing water and my teacher placed my hand under the spout. As the cool stream gushed over one hand she spelled into the other the word water, first slowly, then rapidly. I stood still, my whole attention fixed upon the motions of her fingers. Suddenly I felt a misty consciousness as of something forgotten—a thrill of returning thought; and somehow the mystery of language was revealed to me. I knew then that "w-a-t-e-r" meant the wonderful cool something that was flowing over my hand . . .

Helen Keller

WRITER'S CORNER

Choose a topic and title from the list of possibilities you created on page 227. Write two introductions to begin your personal narrative. Be sure the first sentence of each entices your audience to continue reading. Later you can select your favorite introduction and revise it to make it even more effective.

 Tech Tip Post your introductions on the class blog for peer review.

Personal Narratives • 229

WARM-UP

Read, Listen, Speak

Share your paragraphs about a time when you had a test from yesterday's For Tomorrow activity. Model for students by discussing the tone of each paragraph and the language you used to create this tone.

Have small groups take turns reading the paragraphs they composed. Invite the rest of the group to guess which paragraph conveys an excited tone and which conveys a nervous tone. Have students provide details to support their answers.

GRAMMAR CONNECTION

Take this opportunity to talk about appositives. You may wish to have students point out appositives in their Read, Listen, Speak examples.

TEACH

Write on the board the word *body* and circle it. Ask volunteers to write on the board what they know about body paragraphs in personal narratives in a word web *(sensory details, dialogue, flashbacks, literary devices)*. As students add important pieces of information, discuss each one. Make sure students record the information in a notebook.

Repeat this procedure for conclusions, but have students lead the discussion this time. You may wish to introduce a new graphic organizer such as a concept map or a sequence organizer.

PRACTICE

ACTIVITY C

Ask a student to read the directions. Then have a volunteer read the first paragraph in the activity. Talk about the topic of the narrative and ask what sensory language the writer used to bring the audience into the scene. Have students complete the second paragraph independently.

ACTIVITY D

Ask a volunteer to read the directions and the first paragraph. Encourage students to imagine the drama of the situation as the paragraph is read. Then have students work independently to write a concluding sentence for the narrative. Ask volunteers to read their sentences aloud. Discuss any that are especially effective. Offer suggestions for others. Repeat the procedure for the remaining paragraphs.

ACTIVITY C These are paragraphs from personal narratives. Identify the topic of each, as well as the sensory details (words or phrases) used to enliven the descriptions of events.

1. Lisa and I had spoken in our made-up language many times but never in a crowd. So at the homecoming football game last week (where the most fascinating dialogue we heard was "Woo, go team!"), we decided to try some made-up French. We walked to the opposing team's side and tried hard not to crack up as we spouted vaguely French-sounding gibberish. Besides attracting a bit of attention, our goal was to converse in our invented language so convincingly that people who heard our slurred speech thought we were foreign exchange students. Lisa and I turned up our noses and pretended to insult the other team, all while masking our giggles. Then suddenly we felt a tap on our shoulders. It was a real Frenchman, with the biggest smirk on his face I had ever seen.

2. After the department store disaster, Mom, Javi, and I raced breathlessly back to the car. Actually, we raced back to the space where the car had been. Mom checked the parking receipt on which she had jotted C-7. Yes, we were standing (bug-eyed) in front of parking space C-7, but it was empty. The car was missing. Mom's forehead wrinkled like she was ready for steam to start pouring out of her ears. We huddled together miserably and discussed what to do next.

ACTIVITY D These are conclusions to personal narratives. Write a satisfying ending to complete each conclusion.

1. We'd hiked to the summit and eaten our picnic, and now we were taking a well-deserved nap in the sun before thinking about our descent. Have you ever felt as though someone was watching you when you were sleeping? That feeling was making the hairs on the back of my neck stand up. I opened my eyes cautiously and looked straight into the golden eyes of a bobcat, which was standing no more than 15 feet away from me. We looked at each other for what felt like an eternity but surely was less than a minute. I whispered, "What do you want?" Then the big cat turned and ambled off, looking over its shoulder once before disappearing into the underbrush.

APPLY

WRITER'S CORNER

Allow students time to make changes to their introductions. Encourage students to add sensory details. Then have students work with a partner to revise their introductions. Students should demonstrate an understanding of sensory details.

Grammar in Action. The objects of prepositions are *her, heart, time,* and *hand.* You may wish to ask students to identify the preposition in each phrase to help them locate the object of the preposition.

ASSESS

Note which students had difficulty with introductions, body paragraphs, and conclusions of personal narratives. Use the Reteach option with those students who need additional reinforcement.

Practice Book page 139 provides additional practice with introductions, body paragraphs, and conclusions.

TEACHING OPTIONS

Reteach

Write the following historical events on the board. Encourage students to imagine that they were present at any two of the events. Have students write an introduction and a conclusion for personal narratives about these experiences.

- **wintering at Valley Forge with General Washington**
- **surviving the sinking of the Titanic**
- **working on the intercontinental railroad**
- **watching Wilbur and Orville Wright make their first successful flight**

Meeting Individual Needs

Kinesthetic Have students in small groups act out a possible topic for a personal narrative. Ask students to determine if each topic can be turned into a successful and engaging narrative. Be sure that students provide positive feedback and suggestions to improve each actor's topic.

2. When we finally filed onstage, heads up and smiling, I completely forgot the months of practice, the fund-raising, and the social life I'd given up. Our small chorus from a small town in a small state was at Carnegie Hall, and we were about to perform for a sold-out crowd. I felt both ecstatic and a bit melancholy as I wondered whether life would ever again present me with an occasion as great as this.

3. I still have no idea what made me suspicious of the paper bag that sailed out the window of the pickup truck or why I pulled over to find out what it was. The greater mystery is how the tiny black puppy inside the bag survived the fall. He had only minor injuries and trusted me enough to lie quietly in my lap as we sped to the animal hospital. If I hadn't been busy going to school and working part-time, I would have put myself first on the list to adopt Chance (so named because my lucky discovery gave him a second chance at life).

4. After months of mowing lawns, weeding flower beds, and cleaning out old toolsheds, my day finally came. I went around to each of the houses that I had done work for and collected my wages. Mrs. Lewis offered me a "Congratulations" as she handed me an envelope. Mr. Ediza looked surly as usual, but he handed me the money without complaint. As my bag grew heavier, a feeling of pride swept over me, knowing that I had reached my goal.

5. When I got home, I slumped on the couch and told Mom that all the barbershops were closed on Monday. My hair was going to look awful for family photos that night. My mother smiled. She told me my grandmother had cut hair when she was younger. I was nervous when Grandma grabbed the scissors, but I sure looked great that night.

WRITER'S CORNER

Pick your or your classmates' favorite introduction from the ones you wrote for the previous Writer's Corner. Think of the directions your narrative might take and the themes you might want to express. Add sensory details to enhance it. Reread "Tossed by a Twister" on page 223 as a model for ideas.

Grammar in Action. Identify the objects of prepositions in the excerpt on p. 224.

Personal Narratives • 231

For Tomorrow

Have student reread the personal narrative from page 223's For Tomorrow homework. Then have them write the title and the first and last sentences on a sheet of paper. Challenge students to find evidence that the title, introduction, and conclusion communicate the theme. You may wish to do the same for your narrative.

OBJECTIVES

- To organize events into time lines
- To compose an effective sequence of events for a personal narrative using transition words

WARM-UP

Read, Listen, Speak

Read the title, introductory sentence, and concluding sentence from your narrative from the previous day's For Tomorrow activity. Ask students what they think the theme might be. Then point out some evidence from your narrative that helps identify the theme.

Have students work in small groups to share the sentences from the narratives they found. Have students discuss whether the introductory and concluding sentences communicate the themes of the personal narratives. Discuss several examples as a class.

GRAMMAR CONNECTION

Take this opportunity to talk about possessive nouns. You may wish to have students point out possessive nouns in their Read, Listen, Speak examples.

TEACH

Ask a volunteer to read aloud the first paragraph. Invite students to comment about their experiences using time lines. Give students a few moments to silently read the time line on the page. Then ask volunteers to read aloud the section Reviewing Your Time Line. Point out the revisions Keisha made to her time line. Discuss the value of constructing a time line before beginning a personal narrative. (*Since a personal experience is so familiar to a writer, he or she might forget to include pertinent details that the reader needs to know.*)

PRACTICE

ACTIVITY A

Ask students to complete the activity independently. Ask volunteers to write their completed time lines on the board. Challenge students to list which clues helped them place the events in chronological order. Tell students to save their time lines for use in Activity D.

Time Lines

For almost any project you set out to do, the right tools can help you. Just as maps and compasses help hikers chart their course, time lines help writers chart their narrative course by arranging events. Time lines are constructed by numbering events in chronological order on a vertical, a horizontal, or a diagonal line. In the example below, Keisha has created a time line to organize her personal narrative into a coherent structure. In this time line, she has recorded her memories of a scary experience she had while sailing on Lake Michigan.

Reviewing Your Time Line

When Keisha reviewed her original time line, she found some details missing. She added steps to show how the storm got worse.

When you create a time line, go over it again to jog your memory. Are any steps or details missing? Don't be afraid to add more details.

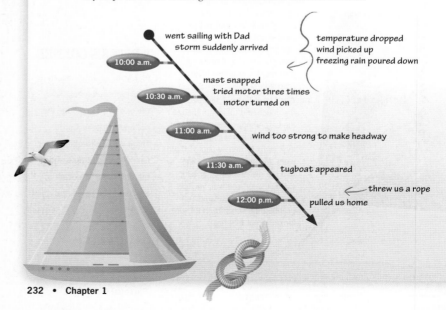

went sailing with Dad
storm suddenly arrived

10:00 a.m.

temperature dropped
wind picked up
freezing rain poured down

10:30 a.m.

mast snapped
tried motor three times
motor turned on

11:00 a.m.

wind too strong to make headway

11:30 a.m.

tugboat appeared

12:00 p.m.

threw us a rope
pulled us home

APPLY

WRITER'S CORNER

Allow time for students to make their own time lines. Encourage students to add more details after reading the time lines a second and third time. Ask students whether their time lines have enough material from which to write a personal narrative. Have students save their time lines for later work. Students should demonstrate an understanding of how time lines aid the writing process.

ASSESS

Note which students had difficulty with time lines. Use the Reteach option with those students who need additional reinforcement.

TEACHING OPTIONS

Reteach

Initiate a discussion about students' favorite TV shows and movies. Ask students to choose a favorite TV episode or movie and construct a time line of its events. Encourage students to include the characters' actions, thoughts, and feelings. Have students give the time line a title (other than the title of the show or movie) that illustrates the theme of the story. Ask volunteers to share their time lines with the class. Encourage other students to guess what show or movie the student is describing.

Meeting Individual Needs

Extra Support If some students are struggling with time lines, they might benefit from constructing a time line in another manner. Distribute note cards. Ask students to record their memories about an event, one memory per note card. Have students provide several occurrences and details. Then have students arrange the cards as on a time line.

For Tomorrow

Instruct students to make a time line of events for any day in the past week. Remind students to include sensory details, thoughts, and emotions in the time lines. Ask students to note whether they perceive a recurring theme as more details surface. Complete a similar time line of your own to share with the class.

Activity A
The Big Game
Correct sentence order: 6, 2, 4, 5, 7, 8, 1, 3

A Very Bad Day
Correct sentence order: 2, 7, 4, 3, 5, 6, 1

ACTIVITY A The events from the personal narratives below were listed out of order. Rearrange each set of events in the order in which they would have occurred. Construct a time line for each set.

The Big Game

1. I slid safely into second base just as the winning run was scored.
2. I stepped to the plate and took a deep breath.
3. Cheering wildly, my teammates rushed onto the field.
4. The opposing pitcher stared at me menacingly.
5. He blew the first two pitches right by me, and the other team cheered.
6. When the coach called my name with the game tied, I knew this could be my chance.
7. I popped the ball up behind third base and started to run.
8. The third baseman tripped, and the ball dropped to the ground.

A Very Bad Day

1. By the end of the day, I was thinking I should have just stayed in bed.
2. My mother shook me awake long after I should have woken up.
3. I had to run to catch the bus.
4. We were out of my favorite cereal, so I had to eat oatmeal instead.
5. When I got to class, I realized I had forgotten my homework.
6. At lunch I found I had forgotten my lunch money too.
7. I raced to get dressed so quickly that I slammed the closet door on my finger.

WRITER'S CORNER

Create a time line listing the events for the personal narrative you picked in the previous Writer's Corner.

Personal Narratives • 233

WARM-UP

Read, Listen, Speak

Share the time line you created as part of the For Tomorrow homework. Point out sensory language and the inclusion of emotions and thoughts. Then have small groups discuss one another's time lines and how they could be improved. Have students comment on whether any time line shows a recurring theme that might make an interesting personal narrative.

GRAMMAR CONNECTION

Take this opportunity to review nouns. You may wish to have students point out nouns in their Read, Listen, Speak examples.

TEACH

Point out that students have options when organizing information for a personal narrative. Explain that writers often use time lines to help organize events in chronological order. Review the time line on page 232.

Make a copy of Keisha's narrative in the Transition Words section. Delete the transition words from this copy. Ask a volunteer to read the paragraph about Transition Words. Have students close their books. Read the narrative in which you deleted the transition words. Then read Keisha's narrative as it appears on this page. Have students discuss the difference between the narratives. Be sure that students grasp the importance of transition words.

PRACTICE

ACTIVITY B

Conduct a group discussion about "Caught in the Storm" and elicit answers to the questions. Have students refer to Keisha's time line on page 232.

ACTIVITY C

Have students work independently to rewrite the paragraphs. Ask students to point out the benefits of using transition words *(helps connect sentences and construct events in a flowing, logical order)*. Encourage volunteers to share their finished paragraphs.

ACTIVITY D

Read the directions aloud and refer students to Activity A on page 233. Instruct students to work independently to compose their narrative paragraphs. Then have students compare paragraphs with a partner. Instruct partners to read each other's paragraphs and offer constructive feedback, paying close attention to the transition words and phrases. Allow volunteers to share their work with the class.

Transition Words

When a writer turns a series of events into a narrative, transition words help each event flow into the next. Some of these words are *first, then, later, before, during, while, next, finally, suddenly, after,* and *when.* You can also use phrases such as *at once, at last,* or *in the end* to create transitions.

Keisha used transition words to turn her time line into a narrative paragraph. Notice that she sometimes combined several events into the same sentences and added a few details.

Caught in the Storm

I was out sailing with my Dad when a storm suddenly arrived. The temperature dropped, the wind started howling, and a freezing rain pelted against our little sailboat. Suddenly, we heard a sharp crack. The mast had snapped! We knew we had to get out of there. First, we tried the motor. After three attempts, it finally caught, but we couldn't make any headway. Then out of nowhere a tugboat miraculously appeared. The captain threw us a rope, and I hitched it to our boat. Finally, we were headed home, trailing along behind the tugboat that had saved the day.

ACTIVITY B Answer the following questions about the personal narrative "Caught in the Storm."

1. What transition words were used in the paragraph?
2. What details were added that were not in the time line?
3. Which events from the time line were combined into the same sentence?

Activity B
1. Suddenly, First, After, Then, Finally
2. Answers will vary.
3. motor turned on but couldn't make headway

APPLY

WRITER'S CORNER

Allow students time to write personal narrative paragraphs, using the time lines from the previous Writer's Corner. Write on the board a list of common transition words from which students may choose when writing. Students should demonstrate an understanding of transition words and phrases.

ASSESS

Note which students had difficulty with time lines. Use the Reteach option with those students who need additional reinforcement.

Practice Book page 140 provides additional practice with time lines.

ACTIVITY C Rewrite the following paragraphs, using transition words and combining sentences so that they flow logically.

1. I had never been to a haunted house before. I told my friends that I wouldn't be scared. We waited in line. Spooky music played. I started to feel nervous. We went into the haunted house. A giant spider fell from the ceiling. I screamed. A scary clown reached out from behind a metal bar. My heart pounded. I raced through the rest of the house as fast as I could. I decided that was enough haunted houses for one year.

2. I was talking to my friend Marcy on the playground. The wind picked up. My fancy new hat blew off. I went running after it. It skipped across the playground. It rolled across the street. It landed in a puddle. I caught up to it and shook off the water. I decided not to wear it for the rest of the day.

3. The Saint Patrick's Day parade was downtown. We got there early. We set up our lawn chairs in front of a bank. The high school band marched past playing the school fight song. A pickup truck with hay and cowboys in back rumbled by. My little brother said he wanted to see the leprechauns. A clown passed us selling balloons. A man dressed like a fish came by selling bottled water. Several men rode by on mopeds, waving to the crowd. I spotted several men dressed as leprechauns near the end of the line. I held my little brother up over my head so he could see.

ACTIVITY D Choose one of the time lines from Activity A and turn it into a narrative paragraph. Use transition words and phrases to make the events flow together logically.

WRITER'S CORNER

Write two or three paragraphs of your narrative, using the time line you created in the previous Writer's Corner. Use transition words to make your paragraph flow logically. Reread the narratives at the beginning of this chapter for ideas.

Personal Narratives • 235

OBJECTIVES
- To construct compound and complex sentences
- To practice using varied sentence structures in personal narratives

WARM-UP
Read, Listen, Speak
Share your time line from yesterday's For Tomorrow homework. Discuss which events you pulled from your article to place on your time line. Tell students why you placed each event on your time line. Ask students to work with partners and share the time lines they created for homework. Encourage students to collaborate to improve their work.

GRAMMAR CONNECTION
Take this opportunity to talk about descriptive adjectives. You may wish to have students point out descriptive adjectives in their Read, Listen, Speak examples.

TEACH
Invite a volunteer to read aloud the first paragraph. Discuss the examples of simple and compound sentences. Ask another volunteer to read aloud the rest of the section, pausing for the class to discuss the example complex sentences. Have volunteers identify the structure of each example sentence (*A. compound, B. complex, C. complex, D. simple*).

LiNK Point out examples of transitional phrases, compound sentences, and complex sentences in the excerpt from "The Story of My Life."

PRACTICE

ACTIVITY A
Write on the board the two sentences for item one. As a class, create several possible answers. Discuss which is the best and why. Then have students complete the remainder of the activity independently. Ask volunteers to write their compound sentences on the board. Discuss these sentences as a class.

ACTIVITY B
Ask students to complete the activity in pairs. Then have each pair exchange papers with another pair to assess whether the complex sentences were constructed correctly. Encourage students to explore whether they might find more than one correct version. Have several volunteers share their sentences and discuss these as a class.

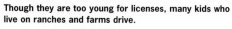

LESSON **4**   WRITING SKILLS

Varied Sentences

Most readers prefer variety in their sentences. Too many simple sentences in a row can be boring to read, but so can too many compound sentences. Too many short sentences can be choppy. Turn them all into longer sentences, however, and you may find your reader drifting to sleep. The key is to punctuate long, compound and complex sentences with shorter, simpler ones. The reader will appreciate the break.

A simple sentence has one subject and one predicate.

Students at the private school wear uniforms.

A compound sentence has two or more independent clauses joined together with a coordinating conjunction (*and, but, or, nor,* and *yet*).

Paul loves snowstorms, but Keegan detests them.

Complex sentences are formed by joining dependent and independent clauses (groups of words with subjects and predicates). They are joined with a subordinate conjunction (*after, although, as, because, for, if, so, than, which, while, unless,* and *until*) that can appear at the beginning or middle of the sentence. When the conjunction comes at the beginning of the complex sentence, a comma is usually added between the two phrases.

Though they are too young for licenses, many kids who live on ranches and farms drive.

In the sentence, *Though they are too young for licenses* is the dependent clause. It does not make sense on its own. *Many kids who live on ranches and farms drive* is the independent clause. It makes sense by itself.

See if you can identify the structure of each sentence below. Identify conjunctions and changes in punctuation.

A   **I could paint the living room, or I could use wallpaper.**

B   **Since we can't see every snowflake, how do scientists know that no two are alike?**

C   **Thomas and Juwan, who look like twins, aren't.**

D   **Hurricanes, tornadoes, and earthquakes cause billions of dollars in damages every year.**

236 • Chapter 1

APPLY

WRITER'S CORNER

Allow students time to revise their paragraphs. Encourage students to self-assess the paragraphs with these questions in mind: *Did I use compound sentences? Did I use complex sentences? Did I use a variety of sentences to add interest?* Tell students to include examples as part of a brief written self-assessment of this task. Students should demonstrate an understanding of compound and complex sentences.

ASSESS

Note which students had difficulty with varied sentences. Use the Reteach option with those students who need additional reinforcement.

TEACHING OPTIONS

Reteach

Review compound sentences. Have each student write five nouns on note cards, one noun per card. Instruct partners to use two noun cards to create a compound sentence. Explain that a noun should serve as the subject in each simple sentence within the compound sentence. Have partners continue until all 10 cards are used. Invite volunteers to read aloud the sentences they composed.

English-Language Learners

Remind students that a clause contains both a subject and a predicate. Ask students to use their answers to Activities A and B to identify the subjects and predicates in the clauses.

For Tomorrow

Provide students with a selection from a newspaper editorial column. Instruct students to circle or highlight the compound and complex sentences on the page and to consider how the writer used them. Ask students to be prepared to discuss this usage during the next class and how the sentences contributed to the writer's work. Choose another editorial column and complete the activity yourself.

Activity A

Answers will vary.
Possible answer: What are earthquakes, and what causes them?

Activity B

Answers will vary.
Possible answer: My distant relative Ferdinand Foch, who was a French military leader, was a famous WWI general.

ACTIVITY A Rewrite each pair of sentences as a compound sentence. Delete and add words as needed.

1. What are earthquakes? What causes earthquakes?

2. One type of earthquake is tectonic. Another type is volcanic.

3. I think intensity is the most significant measure of an earthquake. Magnitude is also important.

4. Seismographs record the waves from earthquakes. They help people determine how powerful an earthquake is.

5. The focus of an earthquake is the place where the first movement happens. The epicenter is the point on the surface above the focus.

6. The type of earthquake depends on where it happens. It depends on the geology of that place as well.

7. Earthquakes that occur beneath the sea are often harmless. Some cause giant destructive waves called tsunamis.

ACTIVITY B Rewrite each pair of sentences as a complex sentence. Delete and add words as needed.

1. My distant relative Ferdinand Foch was a famous WWI general. Foch was a French military leader.

2. I couldn't see the flounder's flat body. Its body blended with its surroundings.

3. We saw the Parthenon while on vacation. The Parthenon overlooks Athens.

4. My family visited the Sears Tower. The Sears Tower is located in Chicago, Illinois.

5. I learned that Ponce de León gave Florida its name. *Florida* means "full of flowers" in Spanish.

6. Our West Highland terrier is very energetic when she plays. She is also very gentle.

7. I rejoined the drama club. I had taken a year off to play basketball.

LiNK

The Story of My Life

... I was greatly puzzled and disappointed. I thought it strange that my teacher could not show me love ... "Without love you would not be happy or want to play," she said.

The beautiful truth burst upon my mind—I felt that there were invisible lines stretched between my spirit and the spirits of others.

Helen Keller

WRITER'S CORNER

Review the narrative paragraphs you wrote for the Writer's Corner on page 235. Revise them to include compound and complex sentences. Reread the personal narratives at the beginning of this chapter for ideas.

Personal Narratives • 237

Read, Listen, Speak

Read your For Tomorrow article with the class. Point out compound and complex sentences and discuss how these affect the article. Have small groups discuss the selection from the newspaper editorial. Instruct students to discuss the structure of the sentences and what effect this construction had on the flow of the article. Then ask volunteers to write on the board compound and complex sentences from the reading. Invite other volunteers to identify the phrases, independent clauses, and dependent clauses. Tell students to save this article for a future activity.

GRAMMAR CONNECTION

Take this opportunity to talk about demonstrative, interrogative, and indefinite adjectives. You may wish to have students point out demonstrative, interrogative, and indefinite adjectives in their Read, Listen, Speak examples.

TEACH

Reviews the idea that varied sentence structures can make narrative writing more interesting to read. Have students use the model narrative on page 222 or another of your choosing to point out examples of compound and complex sentences.

PRACTICE

ACTIVITY C

Have students work in pairs to rewrite the paragraphs. Ask each student to rewrite both paragraphs. Then ask the pairs to take turns reading aloud the new paragraphs, explaining the changes they made, and discussing how the changes add interest. Ask volunteers to share their paragraphs with the class.

ACTIVITY D

Give students time to complete the activity independently. Ask several volunteers to write their sentences for the first item on the board. Encourage the class to discuss the choices students made in structuring their sentences. Repeat for the remaining items.

ACTIVITY E

Have students write down several ideas to include in body paragraphs for both time lines. Assign small groups one of the time lines. Encourage students to work together to write the body paragraphs for this time line. Then have groups read their narratives aloud. Instruct other groups that worked on the same time line to offer constructive feedback.

ACTIVITY C Rewrite the paragraphs to make them more interesting by varying the structure and length of the sentences. Add or delete words, and combine or rearrange sentences as necessary.

1. We went hiking through the woods in the state park. We went hiking this weekend. The sun was shining. The air was cool. It felt good. The leaves were already changing. Green was changing to red. Green was changing to yellow and brown too. Many leaves had fallen. They smelled wonderful. We tramped through them. We saw squirrels foraging for nuts. We also saw chipmunks foraging for nuts. A flock of geese flew over. The geese were headed south. Fall was here. The signs were everywhere. Winter was approaching fast.

2. A storm was heading our way. I could see lightning in the distance. The wind was howling. The waves were choppy. Dad and I decided to stay a while longer. Dad got a bite at last. He tugged furiously. The boat rocked. Dad almost fell overboard. I held the net. My brother stood by. My uncle stood by. They waited to see if they should bring in the fish. Or should they cut the line? I looked over the side of the boat. I began to laugh. Dad pulled in the line. He had hooked the boat's anchor.

ACTIVITY D The sentences below begin personal narratives. Write two sentences of varying lengths to follow each first sentence. Your sentence types should include simple, compound, and complex sentences.

1. Who would have suspected that a family reunion could turn into such a disaster?
2. Getting a part-time job was the best and worst decision I made last year.
3. I remember the day I learned the difference between teasing and tormenting.
4. We had traveled hundreds of miles to ski, and now we were stuck.
5. Here's how an uninvited guest ruined my birthday party and my whole year.
6. An evening scuba dive seemed exciting, but also a bit scary.
7. How hard can babysitting one small boy be?
8. I arrived at the party, but I never imagined that I'd see him there dressed like a scuba diver.

APPLY

WRITER'S CORNER

Provide students with time to reread their narratives. Encourage students to thoughtfully add details to their narrative that will enhance the reader's enjoyment. Students should demonstrate an understanding of their audience and the needs of their audience.

ASSESS

Note which students had difficulty with varied sentences. Use the Reteach option with those students who need additional reinforcement.

Practice Book page 141 provides additional practice with varied sentences.

Reteach

Write on the board compound and complex sentences such as the following. Invite students to identify independent clauses and dependent clauses and to identify each sentence as compound or complex.

> He felt alone, and he had no one to talk to.

> Though the earthquake was short, it caused severe damage.

> We called Tom, who was at home sick with a cold.

Cooperative Learning

Have small groups choose three "extreme" pages from a textbook. Explain that extreme pages hold mostly text and have a variety of simple, compound, and complex sentences. Have groups discuss how these structures serve the purpose of the textbook. Encourage the class to nominate other books for "extreme reads."

ACTIVITY E Write a body paragraph based on each time line below. Use a variety of long and short sentences.

- planned picnic for a week
- 1:00 p.m.
- laid out picnic blanket and food felt a few raindrops
- 1:30 p.m.
- devoured sandwiches and salad
- 2:00 p.m.
- nervous about concert everyone lined up backstage
- 2:30 p.m. — saw a flash of lightning raced back to car
- 6:30 p.m.
- couldn't find clarinet looked in closet
- 3:00 p.m.
- 6:40 p.m.
- looked in other rooms
- 6:50 p.m.
- asked teacher
- 7:00 p.m.
- saw friend Billy playing my clarinet
- 7:10 p.m.

WRITER'S CORNER

Your personal narrative should include details that are important for the reader's understanding of what is going on. Reread your narrative. Does it include details such as setting and descriptions of the characters involved?

Personal Narratives • 239

For Tomorrow

Have students compare the newspaper editorial from yesterday's For Tomorrow homework to a page in a novel or short story. Instruct them to observe the sentence structures in each selection. Ask students to record these differences in a notebook and to bring these observations to class. Create some notes of your own to discuss with the class.

OBJECTIVES

- **To distinguish between general and specific nouns, verbs, adjectives, and adverbs**
- **To enliven personal narratives by adding vivid sensory details**

WARM-UP

Read, Listen, Speak

Discuss your examples from yesterday's For Tomorrow activity, modeling the exact language students should be using. Ask small groups to compare their examples. Have students discuss how the sentence structures fit the intended purpose. *(Newspaper articles use short, simple sentences for quicker, clearer communication. Fiction varies sentence structures for interest.)*

GRAMMAR CONNECTION

Take this opportunity to talk about comparative and superlative adjectives. You may wish to have students point out comparative and superlative adjectives in their Read, Listen, Speak examples.

TEACH

Write on the board a common adjective such as *tall, young,* or *red.* Challenge students to think of other adjectives with a similar meaning. Record these on the board. Then read the first paragraph and have a volunteer compare the sentences. Discuss the differences between these sentences. Then have a student read the second paragraph. Invite the class to name other adjectives that describe a smile and other verbs that place the man on the sofa.

Ask volunteers to read aloud the sections Nouns and Verbs. Then write the following sentence on the board:

The boy is going to be late for dinner.

Have students create a more detailed sentence by changing the nouns and verbs. Make sure students grasp that forms of the verb *be* are overused and are less interesting than more exact action verbs.

PRACTICE

ACTIVITY A

Write the eight nouns on the board. Ask students to add five specific alternatives for each noun. Have students comment on the specificity and possible uses of the replacements.

ACTIVITY B

Have students work independently to rewrite the paragraph. Appoint a students to read the original paragraph, one sentence at a time. Ask a volunteer to read the revised version of that sentence. Then ask volunteers to read their completed paragraphs.

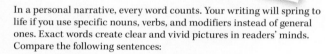

LESSON **5** WORD STUDY

Exact Words

In a personal narrative, every word counts. Your writing will spring to life if you use specific nouns, verbs, and modifiers instead of general ones. Exact words create clear and vivid pictures in readers' minds. Compare the following sentences:

The person sitting on the sofa has a nice smile.
The man perched on the sofa has a dazzling smile.

Replacing the general noun *person* with the more specific noun *man* gives readers a picture of whom the sentence is about. The verb *perch* is more distinct than *sit*. It tells readers how the man is sitting and even gives a clue about what sort of person he might be. What is a *nice* smile? The adjective *nice* is so vague that it calls to mind no particular image. *Dazzling* is exact. Readers can picture the man's stunning, bright smile.

Nouns

The more exact the noun, the more information it gives. For example:

Kendra thinks wearing a hat makes her look sophisticated.
Kendra thinks wearing a beret makes her look sophisticated.

What sort of picture does the noun *hat* call to mind? None. Unless you picture a specific kind of hat, you can't create a picture at all. A beret, on the other hand, is a certain kind of hat. It is a flat, round hat often worn to one side.

Verbs

Specific verbs tend to be action-packed and colorful. The verbs *raced, fled, dashed,* and *jogged* are livelier than *ran*. Using forms of the verb *be* (such as *is, am, are,* or *were*) will make a sentence passive and dull. Try to use an active verb instead. Which sentence below is livelier?

When the cookie was snatched by John, he was scolded by his mother.
When John snatched the cookie, his mother scolded him.

ACTIVITY C

Ask students to complete the activity independently. Encourage them to use a thesaurus to find more specific verbs.

APPLY

WRITER'S CORNER

Give students time to replace the weak or inexact words in their narrative. Ask pairs to trade papers to discuss whether the partner's narrative uses vivid verbs effectively. Students should demonstrate an understanding of exact words.

Grammar in Action. The comparative adjective in the excerpt is *more beautiful*. Remind students that comparative adjectives are used to compare two things and that superlative adjectives are used to compare more than two things.

ASSESS

Note which students had difficulty with exact words. Use the Reteach option with those students who need additional reinforcement.

TEACHING OPTIONS

⭘ Reteach

Have students review past writing to identify a sentence that lacks specific nouns and colorful verbs. Instruct students to make a list of words or phrases that would improve the sentence. Then have students write on a note card the original sentence and the revised sentence. When they have completed a few note card revisions, discuss their choices. Encourage students to make a habit of thoughtful and specific word substitutions whenever students read over their work.

⭘ Teaching Tip

Advise students against using obscure words or long lists of flowery adjectives when they make word substitutions. At the same time, encourage students to experiment with new words that enliven their sentences. Assist students by initiating writing conferences to direct students use of word substitutions.

For Tomorrow

Have students look through a textbook chapter to find a short paragraph that summarizes facts about an event or a place. Challenge students to vary sentence structure and use word substitution to enhance the paragraph. You may wish to share examples of your own summaries with the class.

ACTIVITY A Replace each general noun below with a more specific one. Think creatively. Use a thesaurus if you need ideas.

1. sport
2. animal
3. shoe
4. food
5. color
6. vehicle
7. relative
8. furniture

ACTIVITY B The following paragraph, which is the body of a personal narrative, lacks specific sensory details. Change and add sentences to insert livelier verbs.

I was very nervous at lunch last Tuesday. I knew I needed to build some energy for the debate coming up. What could I have been thinking when I ordered beef stew? I know cafeteria stew is bad. Just looking at it made me feel sick, but I was so hungry that I ate it anyway.

ACTIVITY C Replace the italicized verb in each sentence below with a more exact verb.

1. When we noticed the sky, we *came* inside instantly.
2. "Watch out for the undertow!" I *said*.
3. Andi *looked* at the presents hidden in the closet.
4. The rock climber *went* up a formidable cliff.
5. For nearly a week, rain *came* down without stopping.
6. The toddler was so shy he *talked* into his mother's ear.
7. The baby goats *ran* in the field for hours.
8. Lightning *hit* the old barn last week.
9. Lila *worked* for a month on her science fair project.
10. The goldfish *came* to the top of the bowl as I approached.

WRITER'S CORNER

Go over your narrative and circle words you feel are weak or inexact. Use a thesaurus or synonym finder to replace them. Then have a partner read your narrative and circle any words he or she feels could be replaced with more vivid or exact words. Use a thesaurus or other reference book to replace any of these as well.

Grammar in Action. Identify the comparative adjective in the excerpt on p. 237.

Personal Narratives • 241

WARM-UP

Read, Listen, Speak

Read your unedited summary from yesterday's For Tomorrow activity. Then read your revised summary to the class. Point out where you combined sentences and changed words to improve the quality of the paragraph.

Then have small groups review the paragraphs they wrote. Ask students to determine whether the edits used specific nouns and vivid verbs. Have each group share a paragraph with the class.

GRAMMAR CONNECTION

Take this opportunity to talk about concrete and abstract nouns. You may wish to have students point out concrete and abstract nouns in their Read, Listen, Speak examples.

TEACH

Ask a volunteer to read aloud the Adjectives section. Invite students to name other adjectives they often read that are overused or commonplace. Write these on the board and have students list these in a notebook. Have the class suggest alternatives to these overused adjectives.

Ask a student to read aloud the Adverbs section. Encourage volunteers to offer other adverbs or verbs that could be used in the example sentences. Keep a running list on the board of overused adjectives, adverbs, and verbs to remind students to use alternatives when writing.

PRACTICE

ACTIVITY D

Have students complete the activity independently. Instruct students to compare answers with a partner. Have volunteers share their answers with the class. Encourage students to list their specific adjectives in their notebook.

ACTIVITIES E & F

Allow students time to complete these activities independently. Ask volunteers to read aloud their sentence from Activity E and their revised sentence from Activity F. Encourage students to comment on the verb choices.

ACTIVITY G

Instruct students to revise the paragraph independently. Have a thesaurus available so that students can replace overused words. Then have students trade papers with a partner. Ask partners to identify sentences that could be improved. Discuss possible revisions as a class.

Adjectives

Specific adjectives strengthen descriptions of the nouns they precede. Describing your brother as your *little* brother gives readers important information, but describing him as your *sniveling little* brother really sharpens the image. Some adjectives are so commonplace that writers should avoid them. Adjectives such as *pretty, good, cute, great,* and *bad* are often overused. They do not really contribute to a reader's "mental picture" of the noun either. What are some other weak or overused adjectives?

Adverbs

Adverbs also help to enliven a piece of descriptive narrative, but like all modifiers, they should be used in moderation. Remember that one well-chosen, particular verb can usually accomplish more in a sentence than one or more adverbs modifying a commonplace verb.

Use adverbs sparingly to strengthen the verbs they follow.

Dana laughed at my joke.
Dana laughed *uproariously* **at my joke.**

Avoid using an adverb when a more exact verb would accomplish the job.

Koi smiled slightly at my joke.
Koi *grinned* **at my joke.**

ACTIVITY D Write an adjective that adds a specific detail to the italicized noun in each sentence.

1. A *cloud* hovered over our heads.
2. Justin is practicing jumps on his *skateboard*.
3. My *puppy* loves to doze in front of the fire on cold winter nights.
4. Have you seen the *film* about Mars exploration?
5. I got a *wet suit* and flippers for my birthday.
6. Do you think this *sweater* and shirt match?
7. We vacationed at a *ranch* in Montana.
8. One of the *fish* in the class aquarium ate another fish.
9. It's amazing that *butterflies* migrate from Canada to Mexico.
10. I hope it rains today so I can wear my *slicker*.
11. My new laptop has a *screen saver* from our climb up Mount Everest.

APPLY

WRITER'S CORNER

Give students time to complete the activity. Ask volunteers to write their sentences on the board. Elicit comments about the appropriateness of the adjectives used. Students should demonstrate an understanding of adjectives and how to replace overused adjectives.

Grammar in Action. Students should identify *love, truth, mind, spirit,* and *spirits* as abstract nouns.

ASSESS

Note which students had difficulty with exact words. Use the Reteach option with those students who need additional reinforcement.

Practice Book page 142 provides additional practice with exact words.

TEACHING OPTIONS

Reteach

Write a highly descriptive narrative paragraph incorporating trite, overused adjectives and adverbs. Have students revise the paragraph and then compare their version with the original version. Ask volunteers to describe in what ways their revised paragraphs communicate more clearly and vividly than the original.

English-Language Learners

Some words in this lesson may be especially unfamiliar to English-language learners. Work with these students to pronounce the words and discuss the nuances in meaning. If appropriate, have students pantomime the words to help them grasp the meaning.

ACTIVITY E Add an adverb that strengthens the italicized verb in each sentence.

1. My two-year-old sister *talks*, but she's not easy to understand.
2. Our dog *runs* to the door when the doorbell rings.
3. "Buy me some ice cream," Gabriel's sister *said*.
4. Marta *sang*, and she didn't need a microphone.
5. Dwayne *followed* behind me on the narrow trail.
6. The audience *clapped* after Marcus finished his speech.
7. Emotional people *cry* at sad movies.
8. The cat jumped from the bookcase just as it *fell* to the ground.
9. Justin *threw* his broken MP3 player onto the ground.
10. The pollution pouring out of the old factory *smelled*.

ACTIVITY F Select five sentences you revised in Activity E. Replace the verb and adverb with a single specific verb. Make sure the new word does not contradict or lose the meaning of the original sentence.

ACTIVITY G Below is a paragraph from a personal narrative. Rewrite it, replacing vague and overused words with specific and more interesting choices. Add detail by using adjectives and adverbs.

I was just starting to eat lunch when the Daly City earthquake happened. I heard a noise that got louder and louder. Then the shaking began. Mom got me and we went to the doorway. We lay down on the floor, and she put her body over mine. I heard lots of noises. I looked under Mom's arm. Kitchen supplies were moving, and the kitchen windows were opening and shutting. Then there was silence. The earthquake was over. When Mom opened the kitchen cabinets, broken glass and china came out. We laughed, happy to be safe.

Grammar in Action. Identify the abstract nouns in the excerpt on p. 237.

WRITER'S CORNER

Choose three sentences from Activity D. Rewrite them, using different adjectives that change the meaning of the sentences. Then review your personal narrative. Add detail with adjectives and adverbs.

Personal Narratives • 243

For Tomorrow

Challenge students to study the writing they encounter in other subject areas, magazines, newspapers, advertisements, and so on. Instruct students to record specific words they especially like or commonplace words they think should be replaced. Remind students to think of the intended audience as they make these assessments. Create your own lists of overused words and words you like.

OBJECTIVES

- **To identify characteristics of an oral personal narrative**
- **To correctly transform written narratives into oral narratives**
- **To practice valuable speaking and listening skills**

WARM-UP

Read, Listen, Speak

Discuss your lists from the previous day's For Tomorrow activity. Record these words on the board. Make sure your list uses a variety of words so that students are exposed to new vocabulary. Ask small groups to discuss the kinds of writing they encounter and the specific words they recorded as good or as too commonplace. Have groups share some of these words and create a list on the board. Encourage students to record these words and to keep a running list in their notebooks.

GRAMMAR CONNECTION

Take this opportunity to talk about adjective phrases and clauses. You may wish to have students point out adjective phrases and clauses in their Read, Listen, Speak examples.

TEACH

Have students think of someone they know who is a good storyteller, either a friend or a relative. Ask what makes this person a good storyteller. Record these characteristics on the board.

Then read aloud the first paragraph. Elicit from students more examples of personal narratives. Ask volunteers to read aloud the Purpose, Structure, and Audience sections. Then have students recall some of the personal narrative topics they brainstormed in earlier lessons. Encourage volunteers to describe the intended purpose and audience of these topics. Reiterate that naming the purpose and audience makes the preparation of an oral personal narrative easier and smoother.

PRACTICE

ACTIVITY A

Have students write the introductions independently. Then ask volunteers to read their introductions aloud. Remind students to vary their tone and word choice for the intended audience.

ACTIVITY B

Review exact and overused words. Have students work with a partner to complete the activity. Ask volunteers to share their sentences with the class. Discuss possible revisions for each sentence.

Oral Personal Narratives

You tell stories from your life, or personal narratives, every day. When you describe to your friend what happened at a party, when you tell your parents about your day at school, when you explain to your teacher why you were late for school, you are delivering a personal narrative. To tell your story well, you must remember what happened, describe it to your audience in an understandable way, and answer their questions. It takes planning and practice to guarantee success.

Purpose

Having a clear purpose will help you deliver a focused and an effective personal narrative. The purpose of your narrative can guide your word choices, imagery, and organization. The purpose of your narrative may be to relate a story about an event. It may be to share with your audience what an event has taught you. Try to have a clear purpose in mind as you begin your narrative.

Structure

An oral personal narrative is structurally organized like a written one, though the language may differ slightly. Lure your listeners with an engaging introduction. Introduce your topic and tell the story logically, using interesting details. Conclude by describing what you learned or by offering an overall message.

Audience

Who is your audience? How will your words affect them? Sometimes speaking requires a more careful choice of words than does writing. Identify your audience so that your tone and word choice will be appropriate. Some of your favorite words on paper may sound stiff or awkward when you read them aloud. Make changes to your narrative so that sentences flow and words do not sound awkward.

APPLY

SPEAKER'S CORNER

As students listen to their partner's introduction, suggest they ask themselves these questions: *Is the purpose clear? Who is the intended audience? Do the structure and word choice support the purpose and tone for the intended audience?* Encourage students to offer constructive feedback to strengthen their partners' introductions. Students should demonstrate an understanding of purpose, structure, and audience for an oral personal narrative.

TechTip You may wish to have students search an online thesaurus and print pages that provide options for common and overused words.

ASSESS

Note which students had difficulty with oral personal narratives. Use the Reteach option with those students who need additional reinforcement.

ACTIVITY A Below are titles of personal narratives to be presented to a large audience. Write a short introduction for each title. Have each introduction appeal to one of the following audiences: classmates, judges at a storytelling contest, or a community group.

1. I Was an Archaeologist for a Day
2. How I Learned to Live with My Little Brother
3. That Snap Was My Leg!
4. Two Long Weeks as a Camp Counselor
5. My Garden and How It Grew
6. A Day When Everything Went Wrong

ACTIVITY B Read aloud these sentences from personal narratives. Rewrite them so that they sound smoother and more natural when read aloud.

1. As I climbed hand over hand up the side of the cliff wall, my hand came in contact with something bumpy and warm, which turned out to be an iguana.
2. Folding laundry in my family is a complicated process and one that should not be engaged in without training because every single family member likes his or her clothes folded in a different way.
3. I was too frightened to take notice of the beauty of the spectacular branch of lightning that illuminated the sky.
4. That's the manner in which I learned that the first and most important rule to follow when cooking from a recipe is to read through all the steps slowly and with deliberation.
5. "Write the way you speak" is a phrase I have heard on many occasions from my teacher Mr. Whittaker, but he fails to understand that the advice does not always work due to the fact that my jumbled speech never sounds good when written down.

SPEAKER'S CORNER

Read your introductory paragraphs aloud several times to a partner. Ask your partner what kind of tone he or she identifies from the introduction, and what words or sentences help capture his or her interest. Replace words or sentences your partner finds boring or awkward. Reread the narratives at the beginning of this chapter for further practice.

Tech Tip With an adult, go online for synonyms of boring words.

WARM-UP

Read, Listen, Speak

Share your list of interesting events from yesterday's For Tomorrow homework. Discuss each topic and have students determine if it would make an interesting oral personal narrative.

Then have small groups share their lists of oral personal narrative topics. Instruct students to discuss the following questions: *What is the purpose of the topic—to inform or entertain? Who is the intended audience of the oral personal narrative? How would the audience and purpose shape the structure of the oral presentation?* Ask students to help one another determine and develop the strongest topics.

TEACH

Explain that some oral personal narratives are delivered extemporaneously, but others require advance preparation. As a class, think of examples of each and list these on the board. Ask why an extemporaneous oral personal narrative might make a story better. Then have a volunteer read the Prepare section. Invite another volunteer to read aloud the Present section.

Suggest that practicing listening skills is as important as practicing speaking skills. Point out that good listening skills are a sign of maturity in the listener and that active listening shows respect for the speaker. Have a volunteer read the section Listening Tips. Then ask the class to summarize the main points of the lesson.

PRACTICE

ACTIVITY C

Have students work in pairs to complete this activity. Encourage students to give each other feedback about the emotions expressed and the gestures used to communicate more clearly.

ACTIVITY D

Have pairs deliver their extemporaneous talks to each other. Challenge students to limit their talks to one minute.

APPLY

SPEAKER'S CORNER

Provide time for students to plan their oral personal narratives. Tell students that each talk should last two or three minutes. Then have small groups present their narratives. Remind students to practice listening skills as well as speaking skills. Suggest that students write a positive comment and a question about each talk to share with the speaker after each presentation. Students should demonstrate an understanding of good listening skills.

Prepare

Don't read your narrative directly from your paper. It will sound monotonous and dull. Instead, write key phrases for each idea on a sheet of paper or on note cards. You may wish to bring a visual, such as a photograph or a small object related to your story. Plan how you will use your visual beforehand.

Present

Present your personal narrative to a partner or small group. Ask your audience to critique both the content of your story and your presentation. Keep these speaking tips in mind:

- Establish eye contact with your audience. Scan across everyone in the group instead of locking eyes with one person.
- Speak clearly and slowly so that everyone can follow your narrative. Avoid saying *um, ah, well,* or *you know.*
- Vary your pitch and pace for emphasis. For example, you might slow down at a quiet moment in your story or speak with more urgency during a climactic part. Use facial expressions, gestures, and movements to reinforce your intended meaning.

Listening Tips

Just as you can become a better speaker, with practice you can become a better listener. Here are some suggestions for improving your listening skills.

- Look at the speaker. Give him or her the same attention you would want if you were speaking. Show that you are listening by smiling, nodding, or responding in some other nonverbal way at appropriate times.
- Pay close attention. Try to picture what the speaker is describing and listen for key words that signal important ideas. Figure out where the story is heading and identify the main ideas or theme of the speech.
- Don't interrupt the speaker. If you have a question or want to critique a point, write a quick note to yourself.
- At the end of the talk, ask questions or give feedback if you are invited to do so. Mention a few things you liked about the presentation and include suggestions for improvement.

TechTip You may wish to consult an online or print source that can help you set up a class podcast. Try searching under "classroom podcasts" for sites that can show you how to use this resource.

ASSESS

Note which students had difficulty with oral personal narratives. Use the Reteach option with those students who need additional reinforcement.

After you have reviewed Lessons 3–5, administer the Writing Skills Assessment on pages 45–46 in the **Assessment Book.** This test is also available on the optional **Text Generator CD.**

TEACHING OPTIONS

Reteach

Instruct small groups to devise an evaluation checklist with which to evaluate classmates' oral personal narratives. Encourage students to include items such as these: *Is the beginning sentence interesting? Does the topic hold the audience's attention? Can I hear the speaker? Does the speaker maintain eye contact?* Then have group members each present an extemporaneous personal narrative to the others. When the speaker has finished, the listeners should fill out the checklist and give it to the speaker to review.

English-Language Learners

Before students deliver their oral personal narratives, have English-language learners practice with a more fluent English speaker. The helper can provide extra support for vocabulary, pronunciation, or grammar difficulties. Remind helpers to be courteous and constructive in their comments.

Meeting Individual Needs

Extra Support Have students work in small groups. Invite one student from each group to leave the classroom while the other group members hide preselected objects somewhere in the classroom. When the student returns, have the group members take turns explaining how to find the object. Challenge students to give directions one step at a time without including the names of any classroom objects.

ACTIVITY C Read aloud each of the following sentences twice, expressing a different emotion each time you read. Vary the pacing, volume, and emphasis, as well as expressions, gestures, and movements. Ask a classmate to identify the emotions you are expressing.

1. Will a puppy that tiny survive?
2. I can see the finish line and the cheering crowd up ahead.
3. Is that really a cheesecake?
4. My eyes widened as I saw all the fish around me.
5. The grapes those people are stamping with their bare feet will become wine.

ACTIVITY D Present an extemporaneous, or unplanned, talk (about one minute long) to a partner. Keep in mind what you have learned about being a good listener when your partner is speaking. Choose from the following topics for your talk:

1. why I was late for school
2. an adventure I'll never forget
3. my first day at a new school
4. the funniest person I've ever met
5. clothes shopping with a parent
6. a great triumph playing a sport
7. something about me that people would never guess
8. the weirdest food I ever ate
9. a time when my best friend and I had a fight
10. the strangest day of my life

SPEAKER'S CORNER

Present the personal narrative idea you completed and revised in the Writer's Corner on page 237. Write your introductory sentence and some key phrases on a sheet of paper or note cards. Then present your personal narrative aloud to a small group. Reread the narratives at the beginning of this chapter for extra practice.

TechTip Record a podcast of your personal narrative.

Personal Narratives • 247

OBJECTIVE

- **To select a topic, freewrite, and organize ideas for a personal narrative**

PREWRITING AND DRAFTING

Comment on what students have learned about personal narratives.

- how to generate ideas for topics
- how to write engaging titles, introductions, and conclusions
- how to compose body paragraphs that include sensory details, exact words, and the proper tone for an intended purpose and audience

Review the steps of the writing process. Ask volunteers to write the steps on the board *(prewriting, drafting, content editing, revising, proofreading, and publishing)*. Explain that in the Writer's Workshop, students will progress through the writing process to compose a personal narrative.

Have students turn to the inside back cover of their books. Review the traits of good writing. Refer to this chart as needed. The chart is also printed on the inside back cover of your edition.

Read the opening paragraph aloud. Discuss the range of ideas students have had for personal narratives and the topics they chose to write and present orally.

Prewriting

Ask a student to read aloud this section. Remind students that the purpose of prewriting is to choose a suitable topic, to establish what supporting facts to include, and to organize ideas. Ask why prewriting is especially important when drafting a personal narrative. *(Writers rely heavily on their memories of an event to write a personal narrative.)*

👀 Explain that ideas are the foundation of writing. Point out that strong ideas supported by interesting details help make personal narratives come alive and capture the interest of the audience.

Writer's Tip Point out that brainstorming is the time for students to let their imaginations fly and to list every possible topic that comes to mind. Explain that freewriting entails taking the best idea and writing all the details about that topic.

Brainstorming

Ask a volunteer to read aloud this section. Give students time to read the brainstorming web. Invite students to comment and ask questions. Challenge students to explore several topics when brainstorming. You may wish to introduce new graphic organizers such as tree charts and idea rakes or to review those the class has already used.

Freewriting

Invite a student to read aloud the first paragraph. Encourage students to comment on freewriting techniques they have used in the past, including graphic organizers. Remind students to use a format *(phrases, words, sentences)* with which they feel

---

Prewriting and Drafting

In this chapter you have considered the characteristics of personal narratives, ways to organize your thoughts, and writing skills that will help you make your writing colorful and concise. Now you will use everything that you have learned so far to draft, revise, and publish a personal narrative.

Prewriting

Prewriting is a time to brainstorm, choose a writing topic, and freewrite to explore ideas. It is also a time to develop a plan for how you will organize and structure your writing. 👀 **Ideas** There are several prewriting techniques that you can use: lists or charts, doodles or drawings, graphic organizers, or simply jotting down ideas on paper.

Writer's Tip Brainstorming is quickly generating many ideas, recording anything that comes to mind.
Freewriting is generating more information about your brainstormed ideas.

Brainstorming

Brainstorming can assist you in choosing a topic. When you brainstorm, quickly jot all possible ideas for your topic. The following steps can assist you in brainstorming:

- Start writing ideas. Write anything that comes to mind. Use a graphic organizer such as a

clustering web to help you pursue ideas and develop themes.
- When you have run out of ideas, carefully read what you have written. Do you notice any themes or incidents that keep cropping up?

Jacob, an eighth grader, needs to think of a topic for a personal narrative. His brainstorming web is shown here. What topics for a personal narrative do they suggest to you?

Getting over fear of horses

Visiting Madison at the farm

Horses

Airplanes

Too much homework

Afraid of heights

THINGS THAT SCARE ME

Falling

Waking up late for school

Being sent to principal's office

comfortable to write freely and quickly.

Let students read Jacob's time line. Ask students to explain how Jacob transformed his brainstorming web into a time line.

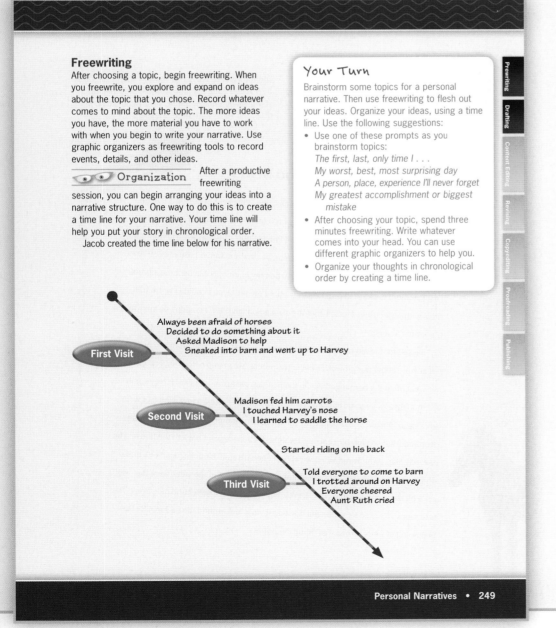 Explain that organization helps writers piece ideas together to create a captivating story. Remind students that in a personal narrative, the ideas are written in chronological order. Tell students that transferring information from freewriting to a time line is a process of organization.

Your Turn

Read this section aloud. Explain that students may use the prompts given as they brainstorm or may follow another train of thought. Allow students five to eight minutes to brainstorm topics. Encourage students to use a graphic organizer previously discussed. Then give them three minutes to freewrite. Ask students to construct a time line, writing any details that do not fit off to the side. Then have students trade papers with a partner. Instruct partners to decide if each other's time lines follow chronological order. Have students save their work.

TEACHING OPTIONS

Meeting Individual Needs

Extra Support Some students may benefit from rereading the model personal narrative on page 223 and reviewing the characteristics of a personal narrative on pages 224–225. Suggest that students use their classmates as their intended audience to focus their thoughts.

Looking Ahead

Introduce or reinforce outlining skills during the drafting phase for the personal narrative. Tell students that solid outlines can streamline prewriting, and outlining is a skill upon which students can increasingly rely. Remind students of outline styles and show them how to begin plugging in items from the prewriting and brainstorming activities into their outlines.

Freewriting

After choosing a topic, begin freewriting. When you freewrite, you explore and expand on ideas about the topic that you chose. Record whatever comes to mind about the topic. The more ideas you have, the more material you have to work with when you begin to write your narrative. Use graphic organizers as freewriting tools to record events, details, and other ideas.

Organization

After a productive freewriting session, you can begin arranging your ideas into a narrative structure. One way to do this is to create a time line for your narrative. Your time line will help you put your story in chronological order.

Jacob created the time line below for his narrative.

Your Turn

Brainstorm some topics for a personal narrative. Then use freewriting to flesh out your ideas. Organize your ideas, using a time line. Use the following suggestions:

- Use one of these prompts as you brainstorm topics:
  The first, last, only time I . . .
  My worst, best, most surprising day
  A person, place, experience I'll never forget
  My greatest accomplishment or biggest mistake
- After choosing your topic, spend three minutes freewriting. Write whatever comes into your head. You can use different graphic organizers to help you.
- Organize your thoughts in chronological order by creating a time line.

Prewriting · Drafting · Content Editing · Revising · Copyediting · Proofreading · Publishing

First Visit
Always been afraid of horses
Decided to do something about it
Asked Madison to help
Sneaked into barn and went up to Harvey

Second Visit
Madison fed him carrots
I touched Harvey's nose
I learned to saddle the horse

Started riding on his back

Third Visit
Told everyone to come to barn
I trotted around on Harvey
Everyone cheered
Aunt Ruth cried

Personal Narratives • 249

OBJECTIVE
- **To write the first draft of a personal narrative**

Drafting

Ask students to define the term *draft* as it pertains to the writing process. After a brief discussion, have a volunteer read aloud the paragraph about Jacob preparing his first draft. Give students time to read Jacob's draft, and encourage them to write questions and comments in a notebook. Then discuss Jacob's personal narrative. Elicit responses about what is effective in the piece and how it could be improved. Ask questions such as the following:

- Is the title appropriate?
- Is the introduction engaging and the conclusion satisfactory for a personal narrative?
- Does the body include relevant details in a logical order?
- Would more information or less information make the story easier to follow?

Explain that first drafts roughly establish how the narrative will flow and that students should concentrate on forming a foundation for their narrative on paper. Instruct them to focus on what personal narratives require: first-person point of view, title, introduction, body, conclusion, and a logical order.

Explain that writers gives their message life through the voice they use in their writing. Point out that this also allows the reader to hear the personality of the writer. Tell students that voice is created through word choice and tone. Explain that if students' writing is choppy or flat, the voice will not be clear. Advise students to vary sentence structure and to use exact words to create their distinctive voice.

Drafting

A draft is your first chance to develop and organize your prewriting notes into a coherent narrative. Jacob had brainstormed a topic, used freewriting to think of details, and created a time line to organize his narrative. How did these steps help Jacob write his first draft below? When do you think he decided on his title? Read Jacob's draft and reflect on these questions.

Not Too Scary

I have no idea where my fear of horses came from. Fear of horses is called equinophobia. Maybe a horse thought I was a bucket of oats when I was a baby! Just kidding. Since I live in the suburbs of Philadelphia, this fear wasn't really a big problem, at least not during the school year, but in the summer I usually visit Aunt Ruth and Uncle Henry's farm, and that's when my equinophobia became a problem. Last summer I decided to do something about my problem. I couldn't go on trail rides with my cousins. Heck, I couldn't even go on hayrides. I couldn't go anywhere on or near a horse.

I asked for the aid of my cousin Madison. Madison is 16. She promised not to tell anyone about our project. For over two weeks, we got up before anyone else. We went off to the barn together. On the first day, we just went near Harvey's stall. We thought a 15-year-old shetland pony would be the easiest to get used to. I went as close to him as I could before my mouth got dry and my heart started beating overtime. Madison fed him carrots. I watched. Then we went back to the house. The next day Harvey nickered when we approached his stall. I touched Harvey's nose, which was nice, while Madison fed him carrots. The rest of the week went that way. I got a bit more comfortable with Harvey. Harvey really is a sweet and nice pony. The next week I learned to saddle the horse and walk him around the paddok. By the beginning of week three I was riding the horse.

Writer's Tip Point out that some students may find it easier to work backward when writing their personal narratives. Explain that this means writing the body paragraphs first and saving the introduction and conclusion for last. Students may generate new ways to introduce their personal narratives or new ideas on how to bring closure to their narratives after working through the details of their body paragraphs.

Your Turn

Ask students to read aloud this section. Guide students to review the writing from their brainstorming and prewriting notes. Instruct students to use their time lines as they write. You might ask students to mark on the time lines which events to include in the introduction, in the body, and in the conclusion before beginning to write.

Review the writing skills learned in this chapter, but remind students that this is a first draft. Explain that if students don't like a word or phrase, they can cross it out and continue writing. Ask students to save their drafts for later.

At the end of that week, Madison and me called everyone down to the barn. They couldn't believe it when I put the saddle and bridle on Harvey, led him into the paddok, and got on. We trotted! I know we'll be cantering soon. My cousins were surprised. They jumped up and down. They cheered. Aunt Ruth even teared up a little, just because she was so proud of me, she said. I was proud of me! And if you break down something you're afraid of into tiny steps and do it little by little, you'll soon be proud of yourself too.

Everyone has a distinctive way of speaking that is unique. Similarly, every writer uses a distinctive voice. This voice **Voice** is based on word choice, descriptions, tone, pace, punctuation, and other stylistic devices. It is the "personality" of the narrator. If your writing sounds flat or unnatural, it does not reflect voice.

Writer's Tip Many writers find writing introductions and conclusions difficult. If that's true of you, write the body first and tackle the other parts later.

Your Turn

Look back at your freewriting and your time line as you plan to write a draft of your personal narrative. Before you begin writing your draft, recall the following characteristics of effective personal narratives:

- first-person point of view
- tone appropriate for audience
- apparent theme or purpose
- sensory details
- specific word choices

Now begin to write. If you are using a pen and paper, leave extra space between lines so you have room to edit later. If you are typing, use double-spacing. Write quickly and clearly to get all your good ideas recorded.

Personal Narratives • 251

Prewriting Pairs

You might notice that some students are uncertain about which portions of their prewriting belong in the introduction, body, and conclusion of their narratives. Encourage partners to have peer conferences to help each other organize their prewriting.

English-Language Learners

Invite students to write their drafts in their primary language. Pair students with the same primary language together and encourage them to translate their drafts into English. Have students use bilingual dictionaries or other resources if needed.

Meeting Individual Needs

Auditory Have students choose a section from their favorite book that contains an example of a unique or distinctive voice. Ask students to practice reading their sections aloud. Invite students to record their sections and to play them for the class. Encourage students to discuss the voice of the various pieces. Challenge students to analyze word choice, sentence structure and variety, and the overall tone. Encourage them to discuss their ideas.

CONTENT EDITING

Have a volunteer read aloud the first paragraph. Remind the class that a first draft is not meant to be perfect. Discuss any problems students encountered when writing their drafts. Encourage students to devise multiple solutions for these problems to avoid these issues in future assignments.

Have a volunteer read aloud the Content Editor's Checklist. Ask students what the items in the checklist are based on *(the characteristics of a personal narrative, the lessons in the chapter)*. Encourage students to suggest additions to the checklist.

Have volunteers read aloud the next two paragraphs. Discuss why a writer would ask someone to read the first draft. *(Another person can give feedback from the reader's point of view.)*

Writer's Tip Quickly review the Exact Words lesson on page 240. Remind students that the more precise their word choice is, the more engaged the reader will be.

Have a volunteer read aloud the first paragraph on page 253. Ask students to finish reading silently, stopping after Cody's comments. Allow students to refer to Jacob's draft and to discuss which of Cody's comments seem most useful for improving the content. Point out that content editing involves the following:

Editor's Workshop   Personal Narratives

Content Editing

When you content edit, you edit ideas for logic, order, and clarity. A content editor notices how well the ideas of a piece are expressed and checks to make certain that all of the necessary information is included. To help you make corrections and improvements to a personal narrative, use the checklist below as you revise your draft.

Jacob was pleased with the draft of his personal narrative. However he knew he could improve it. Armed with a red pen, the draft, and the Content Editor's Checklist, Jacob began content editing. First, he read his draft aloud and made marks beside parts of the draft that he felt needed to be deleted, replaced, or rearranged. Then he reread his draft and fine-tuned it some more. Based on the Content Editor's Checklist and your reading of his draft, what changes do you feel he needed to make?

Next, Jacob traded drafts with his classmate Cody. He knew Cody could help him by pointing out the confusing, repetitive, and awkward parts in the draft.

Writer's Tip Exact, descriptive words will make your ideas more clear and complete.

Content Editor's Checklist

☐ Does the introduction make the reader want to read more?

☐ Does the body of the narrative tell the events clearly?

☐ Is the order of events logical?

☐ Are additional details needed for clarity?

☐ Are there unnecessary details that keep the narrative from flowing?

☐ Are the ideas clearly conveyed through the choice of words?

☐ Are transition words used to help the reader follow the events?

☐ Is there a coherent balance of simple, compound, and complex sentences?

☐ Does the conclusion leave the audience with something to remember?

252

- edits to the information included in the introduction, body, and conclusion
- the overall sense and tone—the logic, order, and clarity of the writing

Point out that content editing concentrates on the clarity of the message. Ask students if there are other changes Jacob should make to his draft, based on the points in the Content Editor's Checklist. *(There are some unnecessary details in the piece. "Harvey really is a sweet and nice pony.")*

Your Turn

Ask a student to read aloud this section. Give students time to edit independently. Then have pairs trade drafts. Instruct student editors to write their comments on a separate sheet of paper or very neatly on the original draft. Allow time for the partners to confer about each other's editing. Ask students to save these comments for the next class.

TEACHING OPTIONS

Content Editor's Checklist

Encourage students to copy the Content Editor's Checklist so they can refer to it easily when they edit their own and other students' writing. Point out that a checklist such as this might change when editing other kinds of writing. You might also write the checklist on the board or have the class help you write it on a large poster board for all to see.

Meeting Individual Needs

Visual Post an example of a student-written personal narrative on a classroom blog. Have students use the Content Editor's Checklist to edit the narrative online. Encourage students to use the track changes tool if it is available. Point out that this enables students to see the edits and comments as they are added to the personal narrative. When students have finished, ask them to review their classmates' suggestions. Have students create a list of the comments that are important and revise the narrative.

Cody read a copy of Jacob's draft silently as well as aloud. Next, Cody used the Content Editor's Checklist to help him edit the draft. He made some notes on the copy and some on a separate sheet of paper.

After Cody had finished editing, he and Jacob conferred. Cody offered positive feedback first. He told Jacob that he chose a great incident to write about, one that was important to Jacob and interesting to readers. Then Cody offered the following suggestions for improving Jacob's draft:

- I like the sentence *Maybe a horse thought I was a bucket of oats as a baby!* It is funny, and it made me want to keep reading.

- Think about moving the sentence *Last summer I decided to do something about my problem.* It doesn't seem to fit. Otherwise, the way you have organized your narrative makes it easy to read.

- Can you include more description about Harvey? Some sensory words might help a reader picture what you are describing.

- Replace words like *went* and *nice* with more exact words that explain your ideas more clearly.

- I thought that your conclusion was effective. You gave some really good advice about how to do something that you were afraid to do.

Your Turn

Use the Content Editor's Checklist to guide the editing of your own draft as you follow these steps:

- Read your draft silently and aloud several times as you edit. Each time you read, you will notice something new.

- Trade drafts with a classmate. If possible, have your partner write corrections on a copy of your draft and do the same for him or her.

- Meet with your partner to discuss the drafts and make suggestions for improving them.

When you content edit your partner's draft, begin by pointing out a few things that you liked. Be honest and courteous in your comments.

Prewriting
Drafting
Content Editing
Revising
Copyediting
Proofreading
Publishing

OBJECTIVE

- **To revise the draft of a personal narrative**

REVISING

Ask students to read Jacob's draft. Discuss the revisions Jacob made based on his and his partner's edits. Point out that Jacob used double-spacing when writing his draft, and this made the revisions easier to add.

Invite volunteers to read aloud the ways Jacob improved his draft based on Cody's comments on the previous page. Ask students to explain why each improvement lies within the category of content editing. Then ask a volunteer to read aloud the paragraph after the bulleted items. Have students answer the questions.

- Jacob noticed that he could make his introduction stronger by combining some of the sentences.
- He moved the sentence to the end of the first paragraph, where it seemed more logical.
- He added the words *soft* and *velvety* to describe Harvey's nose. He also described Harvey as *gentle*.
- He replaced *went* with *sneaked*, *stood*, and *crept*.

Explain that word choice involves selecting exact words that provide a vivid picture for the reader.

Discuss that writers consider editors' feedback before incorporating it into their drafts. Point out that after considering all their partner's comments, student writers can feel free to choose those that will improve their work.

Writer's Workshop

Personal Narratives

Revising

This is Jacob's edited draft, which he revised based on his own and Cody's suggestions.

Not Too Scary

I have no idea where my fear of horses came from. ~~Fear of horses is called equinophobia.~~ , or equinophobia Maybe a horse thought I was a bucket of oats when I was a baby! ~~Just kidding.~~ Since I live in the suburbs of Philadelphia, this fear wasn't ~~really~~ a big problem, ~~at least not~~ during the school year, but in the summer I usually visit Aunt Ruth and Uncle Henry's farm, and that's when my equinophobia ~~became a problem.~~ really bothered me ~~Last summer I decided to do something about my problem.~~ I couldn't go on trail rides with my cousins, ~~Heck,~~ , and I couldn't ~~even~~ go on hayrides. In fact, I couldn't go anywhere on or near a horse. Last summer I decided to do something about it.

I asked for the aid of my cousin Madison. ~~Madison is 16.~~ 16-year-old She promised not to tell anyone about our project. For over two weeks, we got up before anyone else. We ~~went~~ off to the barn together. and sneaked On the first day, we just ~~went near~~ Harvey's stall. stood at ~~We thought a 15-year-old shetland pony would be the easiest to get used to.~~ I went as close to him as I could before my mouth got dry and my heart started beating overtime. Madison fed him carrots, crunchy as I watched. his huge teeth grind them up. Then we ~~went~~ back to the house, before anyone woke up. The crept next day Harvey nickered when we approached his stall. I touched Harvey's nose, soft and velvety which was ~~nice~~, while Madison fed him carrots. The rest of the week ~~went that~~ way. I proceeded the same ~~got~~ a bit more comfortable with Harvey. ~~Harvey really is a sweet and nice pony.~~ The became the gentle next week I learned to saddle the horse and walk him around the paddok. By the beginning of week three I was riding the horse.

Grammar in Action. Remind students that using appositives varies the length and structure of sentences within their personal narratives. (*... my fear of horses, or equinophobia, came from ...* and *... my 16-year-old cousin Madison.*)

Your Turn

Ask a volunteer to read aloud this section. Have students meet again with a classmate to discuss revisions to their drafts. If partners disagree on a revision, encourage them to consult the Content Editor's Checklist. Explain that if an edit corresponds with an item on the checklist, then it will probably improve the draft. Instruct students to keep their revised drafts for the next class.

TEACHING OPTIONS

Working on Computers

If students are working on computers, have them do their first revision on paper. Explain that once they have made all their revisions on paper, students can then enter their revisions on the computer.

Sharing the Lesson

Remind students that one way to conclude a personal narrative is to reveal a lesson learned that could help others. Have students check their conclusions carefully to make sure they are sharing the lesson effectively with the reader.

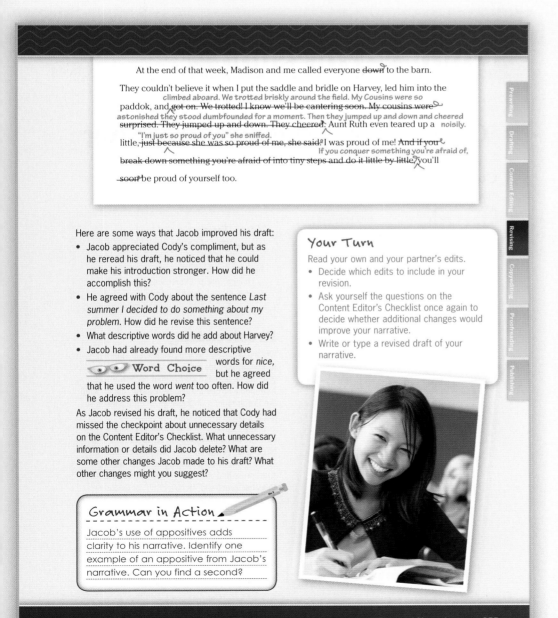

At the end of that week, Madison and me called everyone ~~down~~ to the barn.

They couldn't believe it when I put the saddle and bridle on Harvey, led him into the paddock, and ~~got on. We trotted!~~ climbed aboard. We trotted briskly around the field. My Cousins were so ~~I know we'll be cantering soon. My cousins were~~ astonished they stood dumbfounded for a moment. Then they jumped up and down and cheered ~~surprised. They jumped up and down. They cheered.~~ Aunt Ruth even teared up a noisily. "I'm just so proud of you" she sniffed. little, ~~just because she was so proud of me, she said.~~ ~~And if you~~ I was proud of me! If you conquer something you're afraid of, ~~break down something you're afraid of into tiny steps and do it little by little,~~ you'll ~~soon~~ be proud of yourself too.

Here are some ways that Jacob improved his draft:

- Jacob appreciated Cody's compliment, but as he reread his draft, he noticed that he could make his introduction stronger. How did he accomplish this?
- He agreed with Cody about the sentence *Last summer I decided to do something about my problem.* How did he revise this sentence?
- What descriptive words did he add about Harvey?
- Jacob had already found more descriptive

Word Choice — words for *nice*, but he agreed that he used the word *went* too often. How did he address this problem?

As Jacob revised his draft, he noticed that Cody had missed the checkpoint about unnecessary details on the Content Editor's Checklist. What unnecessary information or details did Jacob delete? What are some other changes Jacob made to his draft? What other changes might you suggest?

Your Turn

Read your own and your partner's edits.

- Decide which edits to include in your revision.
- Ask yourself the questions on the Content Editor's Checklist once again to decide whether additional changes would improve your narrative.
- Write or type a revised draft of your narrative.

Grammar in Action.

Jacob's use of appositives adds clarity to his narrative. Identify one example of an appositive from Jacob's narrative. Can you find a second?

OBJECTIVE

• To copyedit and proofread a personal narrative

COPYEDITING AND PROOFREADING

Copyediting

Be sure that students understand that conventions are the mechanics of a piece of writing. These include spelling, grammar, capitalization, punctuation, and formatting issues such as paragraphing.

Ask a student to read aloud the first paragraph. Invite volunteers to explain the differences between content editing and copyediting. *(A content editor looks for clarity of message, mood, tone, voice, sense, and accuracy of facts and content. A copyeditor looks for accuracy in word meaning, word choices, syntax, sentence structure, and the overall logic of the work. A content editor works with ideas; a copyeditor works with words.)*

Writer's Tip Remind students the importance of word choice in relation to tone and voice. Tell students that a clear and distinctive voice will make the personal narrative more enjoyable for the reader.

Ask a volunteer to read aloud the checklist. Encourage students to offer additions to the checklist. Lead students to the conclusion that copyeditors concentrate on the specific words and sentences of a piece, while content editors concentrate on the ideas and the overall message of a piece.

Have a student read aloud the last paragraph in the section. Explain that when students read Jacob's revised narrative, they will see the copyediting changes he made. Discuss the question in this paragraph. Lead students to point out that the revised verbs include *sneaked, crept, proceeded,* and *climbed.*

Your Turn

Read this section aloud. Allow time for students to copyedit their own drafts. Then have students trade drafts with a classmate to copyedit his or her draft. Encourage students to use the Copyeditor's Checklist.

Proofreading

Invite a volunteer to read this section aloud. Ask students if they have ever found a typographical error or a grammatical mistake in a newspaper or magazine article. Ask what they thought of this experience *(that a careless writer or editor had made the mistake).* Reinforce that during proofreading, students should check that new mistakes were not introduced through previous edits and revisions.

Copyediting and Proofreading

Copyediting

When you copyedit, you should look for accuracy in word meaning, word choice, and sentence structure, and review the overall logic of the piece. After making extensive changes to his draft, Jacob wanted to make sure that his work was logical and coherent. He used the following checklist to copyedit his draft.

Writer's Tip Unique words that suggest a feeling or tone can enhance the narrator's voice.

Copyeditor's Checklist

- [ ] Are transition words used correctly?
- [ ] Do any words seem out of place or awkward?
- [ ] Do the chosen words or phrases convey their intended meaning?
- [ ] Are there any run-on or rambling sentences?
- [ ] Do the verb tenses agree?
- [ ] Are the structures of sentences logical and grammatically correct?

What verbs did he change to more accurately convey his intended meaning?

Your Turn

Use the Copyeditor's Checklist to copyedit your draft. If possible, read the draft aloud to an editing partner. What words do you want to change? Are the sentences coherent? What does your editing partner notice?

Proofreading

Writers proofread to find mistakes in spelling, grammar, punctuation, and capitalization. They also check to make certain that no new errors have been introduced during revising. Jacob used the Proofreader's Checklist to catch mistakes in the revised draft.

A proofreader can offer a new set of eyes when editing a piece of writing. Jacob asked his friend Miles to proofread his draft. Jacob knew that because Miles had a fresh perspective, he might spot errors that Jacob and Cody had missed. After Miles had proofread Jacob's draft, Jacob used a dictionary, a thesaurus, and a language arts textbook to check the things that Miles had marked.

Have students read the Proofreader's Checklist silently. Encourage students to offer additions to the checklist. Challenge students to read Jacob's draft and to proofread for spelling and punctuation mistakes.

Common Proofreading Marks

Have students look over the proofreading marks. Ask students to add any other marks they have encountered. Encourage students to use and study the list of proofreading marks. Suggest that students use these marks every time they edit.

Your Turn

Invite a volunteer to read this section aloud. Ask students to write their own proofreader's checklist. Have students give their drafts and checklists to a partner. Allow partners time to proofread each other's drafts. Instruct students to use the proofreading marks when editing and to use a dictionary or grammar handbook to check for correctness.

TEACHING OPTIONS

Getting Advice

After the extensive editing involved in content editing and copyediting, take time to address students' questions about their revisions. Ask whether students are uncertain about some revisions. Offer advice, but also solicit answers from students.

Backward Spell-Check

Explain that one way to check students' work for misspellings is to read it backward word by word. Explain that if students read their work backward, they will look more carefully at each individual word and be less distracted by the temptation to revise the meaning of sentences.

English-Language Learners

Students whose primary language is not English may transfer the grammar and punctuation rules of their primary language to their personal narrative in English. Encourage students to work together to use conventions correctly in their personal narratives. Instruct students to consult the Grammar and Mechanics Handbook on page 527 if needed.

Proofreader's Checklist

- ☐ Are the paragraphs indented?
- ☐ Have any words been misspelled?
- ☐ Are the beginnings of sentences and proper nouns capitalized?
- ☐ Is the grammar accurate?
- ☐ Is punctuation correct?
- ☐ Were new errors introduced during editing?

Your Turn

Proofread your revised draft.

- Use the Proofreader's Checklist to help you or make one of your own that includes the kinds of errors that you make most frequently.
- If you can, proofread with a partner as Jacob and Miles did.
- Use a note card or sheet of paper so that you scan the draft one line at a time. Reading line by line will keep you from reading too quickly and missing mistakes.

Prewriting
Drafting
Content Editing
Revising
Copyediting
Proofreading
Publishing

Common Proofreading Marks

Symbol	Meaning	Example
¶	begin new paragraph	over. ¶ Begin a new
⌒	close up space	close u͜p space
∧	insert	students think (should)
ℰ	delete, omit	that the ~~the~~ book
/	lowercase letter	M̸athematics
∽	letters are reversed	letters are reve⁀rsed
≡	capitalize	w̲a̲shington
⌄ ⌄	quotation	⌄I am,⌄ I said.
⊙	period	Marta drank tea⊙

OBJECTIVE
- **To publish a personal narrative**

PUBLISHING

Have a student read aloud the information at the top of the page. Then have volunteers take turns reading aloud Jacob's finished piece. Encourage students to comment about the revisions Jacob made. Ask questions such as the following:

- How has Jacob's personal narrative improved?
- Can you identify the theme and the tone of the piece?
- Who is Jacob's audience?
- Is the sequence of events easy to follow?
- What spelling and punctuation corrections can you spot?

After discussing the changes Jacob made to his personal narrative, read the different ways that students can publish their personal narratives. Discuss the advantages and disadvantages for each publication technique.

Offer examples of publications students might contact to submit their narratives for publication.

Creative Kids
www.prufrock.com

Skipping Stones
www.skippingstones.org

Stone Soup
www.stonesoup.com

Young Voices
www.youngvoicesmagazine.com

Invite volunteers to read aloud their personal narratives. Encourage students to use the speaking and listening skills they learned in Lesson 6.

Writer's Tip Encourage students to actively research each technique discussed for publication. Tell students to investigate the submission guidelines for professional publishers.

Your Turn Tell students that presentation involves the overall appearance of a finished piece of writing. Suggest that students choose a form of presentation that enhances their personal narrative.

Ask volunteers to read this section. Then give students time to copy their finished piece. If

---

Writer's Workshop   Personal Narratives

Publishing

Publishing is the moment when you decide to share your final work. You know it is your best work and you are ready to show it to your audience. After several editing sessions, Jacob felt he had done his best. See if you can find the spelling and punctuation errors he corrected while proofreading. It was now time for the finished version. Jacob typed it on a computer and printed it out. Then he proofread it one more time to make sure there were no errors. Finally, he was ready to publish his work.

Not Too Scary

I have no idea where my fear of horses, or equinophobia, came from. Maybe a horse mistook me for a bucket of oats when I was a baby! Since I live in the suburbs of Philadelphia, this fear wasn't a big problem during the school year. But in the summer I usually visit Aunt Ruth and Uncle Henry's farm, and that's when my equinophobia really bothered me. I couldn't go on trail rides with my cousins, and I couldn't enjoy hayrides. In fact, I couldn't travel anywhere on a horse or even be anywhere near one. Last summer I decided to do something about my phobia.

I asked my 16-year-old cousin Madison for help and made her promise not to tell anyone. For over two weeks, we got up before anyone else and sneaked off to the barn together. We thought a 15-year-old Shetland pony would be the easiest horse to get used to, so that's why we chose Harvey. On the first day, we just stood at Harvey's stall. I went as close to him as I could before my mouth got dry and my heart started beating overtime. Madison fed him crunchy carrots as I watched his huge yellow teeth grind them up. Then we crept back to the house before anyone else woke up.

The next day Harvey nickered when we approached his stall. I touched Harvey's nose, which felt soft and velvety, while Madison fed him. The rest of the week proceeded the same way. Each day I became a bit more comfortable with the gentle Harvey. The next week I learned to saddle the horse and walk him around the paddock. By the beginning of the third week, I was riding.

At the end of that week, Madison and I summoned everyone to the barn. They couldn't believe it when I put the saddle and bridle on Harvey, led him into the paddock, and climbed aboard. We trotted briskly up around the field. My cousins were so astonished they stood dumbfounded for a moment. Then they jumped up and down and cheered noisily. Aunt Ruth became a little teary-eyed. "I'm just so proud of you," she sniffed. I was proud of myself! If you conquer something you're afraid of, you'll be proud of yourself too.

students are using pen and paper for their personal narratives, instruct them to write slowly and to reread each sentence as they write. Ask that they be wary of introducing errors.

Make copies of students' finished work and distribute them. Encourage students to bind the narratives with staples, string, or yarn and to add a cover if they wish. Ask students to read the narratives and to offer positive feedback to their classmates about their writing.

ASSESS

Have students assess their finished personal narratives using the reproducible Student Self-Assessment on page 259y. A separate Personal Narrative Scoring Rubric can be found on page 259z for you to use to evaluate their work.

Plan to spend tomorrow doing a formal assessment. Administer the Personal Narrative Writing Prompt on **Assessment Book** pages 47–48.

Reviewing the Process

Discuss students' experiences during the Writer's Workshop. Encourage students to share their thoughts about the steps of the writing process. Ask questions such as the following:

- How could we change the Writer's Workshops to improve them?
- Did you enjoy the writing, or editing, or both?
- In what other parts of your lives will you use the writing skills you have learned?

Portfolio Opportunity

Instruct students to begin keeping a portfolio that holds their finished pieces from the Writer's Workshops. Distribute folders or have students use their own. Ask students to decorate or label the folders as they choose. Point out that keeping a portfolio will help students track the progress they are making with their writing.

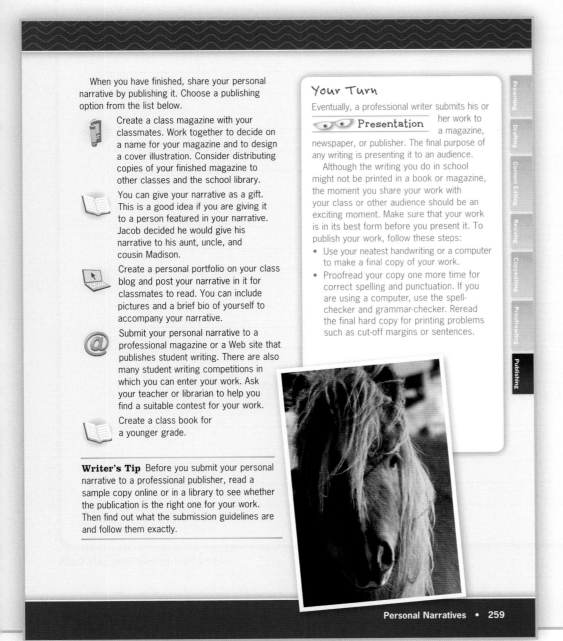

When you have finished, share your personal narrative by publishing it. Choose a publishing option from the list below.

Create a class magazine with your classmates. Work together to decide on a name for your magazine and to design a cover illustration. Consider distributing copies of your finished magazine to other classes and the school library.

You can give your narrative as a gift. This is a good idea if you are giving it to a person featured in your narrative. Jacob decided he would give his narrative to his aunt, uncle, and cousin Madison.

Create a personal portfolio on your class blog and post your narrative in it for classmates to read. You can include pictures and a brief bio of yourself to accompany your narrative.

Submit your personal narrative to a professional magazine or a Web site that publishes student writing. There are also many student writing competitions in which you can enter your work. Ask your teacher or librarian to help you find a suitable contest for your work.

Create a class book for a younger grade.

Writer's Tip Before you submit your personal narrative to a professional publisher, read a sample copy online or in a library to see whether the publication is the right one for your work. Then find out what the submission guidelines are and follow them exactly.

Your Turn

Presentation

Eventually, a professional writer submits his or her work to a magazine, newspaper, or publisher. The final purpose of any writing is presenting it to an audience.

Although the writing you do in school might not be printed in a book or magazine, the moment you share your work with your class or other audience should be an exciting moment. Make sure that your work is in its best form before you present it. To publish your work, follow these steps:

- Use your neatest handwriting or a computer to make a final copy of your work.
- Proofread your copy one more time for correct spelling and punctuation. If you are using a computer, use the spell-checker and grammar-checker. Reread the final hard copy for printing problems such as cut-off margins or sentences.

Presenting
Drafting
Content Editing
Revising
Copyediting
Proofreading
Publishing

Personal Narratives • 259

Name _____ Date _____

Personal Narrative

Ideas

	YES	NO
Does my piece show a theme or purpose?		
Do I express the experience's importance?		

Organization

Do I provide an engaging introduction?		
Do I have a cohesive body?		
Do I provide a sense of resolution in the conclusion?		
Do I use chronological order?		

Voice

Does my piece show my personality?		
Do I provide a sense of authenticity?		
Do I use a tone appropriate for my intended audience?		

Word Choice

Do I use exact words?		
Have I used natural language?		

Sentence Fluency

Do I use transition words?		
Do I use a variety of sentence types?		
Do I avoid the use of run-on and rambling sentences?		

Conventions

Do I use correct grammar?		
Do I use correct spelling, punctuation, and capitalization?		

Presentation

Are my spacing and margins consistent?		
Does my paper look neat?		

Additional Items

Name _____

Date _____ Score _____

POINT VALUES

0 = not evident
1 = minimal evidence of mastery
2 = evidence of development toward mastery
3 = strong evidence of mastery
4 = outstanding evidence of mastery

Personal Narrative

Ideas   **POINTS**

an apparent theme or purpose	
a clear focus on experience's importance	

Organization

an engaging introduction	
a cohesive body	
a conclusion that offers a sense of resolution	
chronological order	

Voice

identifiable writer's personality	
a sense of authenticity	
appropriate tone for intended audience	

Word Choice

exact words	
natural language	

Sentence Fluency

transition words	
varied sentence types	
no run-on and rambling sentences	

Conventions

correct grammar and usage	
correct spelling, punctuation, and capitalization	

Presentation

consistent spacing and margins	
neatness	

Additional Items

Total	

© LOYOLAPRESS.

CHAPTER FOCUS

LESSON 1: What Makes a Good How-to Article?

LESSON 2: Making Instructions Clear and Concise

- **GRAMMAR:** Pronouns
- **WRITING SKILLS:** Revising Sentences
- **WORD STUDY:** Roots
- **STUDY SKILLS:** Dictionary
- **SPEAKING AND LISTENING SKILLS:** How-to Talks
- **WRITER'S WORKSHOP:** How-to Articles

SUPPORT MATERIALS

Practice Book
Writing, pages 143–147

Assessment Book
Chapter 2 Writing Skills,
    pages 49–50
How-to Writing Prompt,
    pages 51–52

Rubrics
Student, page 297y
Teacher, page 297z

Test Generator CD

Grammar
Section 3, pages 32–56

Customizable Lesson Plans
www.voyagesinenglish.com

How-to Articles

WHAT IS HOW-TO WRITING?

How-to writing is a form of exposition, an avenue for providing information. It can offer guidance and direction for accomplishing a task or goal, such as giving effective presentations. How-to writing can also provide step-by-step instructions for doing or making something, such as loading software on your computer or making tamales.

A good how-to article includes the following:

- [ ] A clear focus geared toward a specific audience
- [ ] An introduction that states the purpose of the article
- [ ] Detailed, accurate step-by-step instructions in the body
- [ ] A coherent organization that expresses ideas in chronological order
- [ ] A conclusion that leaves the reader with a sense of closure
- [ ] Concise imperative sentences
- [ ] An appropriate tone for the intended audience
- [ ] Transition words to guide the reader smoothly from one step to the next
- [ ] All critical details
- [ ] No unnecessary information
- [ ] Visual aids as appropriate

LiNK Use the following titles to offer your students examples of well-crafted how-to articles:

Good Manners for Young People: How to Eat an Artichoke and Other Cool Things to Know by Louise Claude Wicks

How Rude! The Teenagers' Guide to Good Manners, Proper Behavior, and Not Grossing People Out by Alex J. Packer

How to Get Good Grades: And Still Keep Your Fabulous Reputation as a Cool Person by Kris Bearss

> "I am always doing that which I can not do, in order that I may learn how to do it."
>
> —Pablo Picasso

WRITER'S WORKSHOP TIPS

Follow these ideas and tips to help you and your class get the most out of the Writer's Workshop:

- Review the traits of good writing. Use the chart on the inside back cover of the student and teacher editions.
- Provide situations for which students can write advice columns. Make sure students understand that advice can also be a form of giving instructions.
- Have students write directions for playing a favorite game, such as soccer or checkers. Discuss which directions were most effective.
- Fill your classroom library with instruction manuals, how-to pamphlets, product brochures, and craft books.
- Explore classroom textbooks to find and compare activity directions. Discuss which are the easiest to understand and why.
- Invite students to write a favorite family recipe and bring it to class to make a class recipe book.

CONNECT WITH GRAMMAR

Throughout the Writer's Workshop, look for opportunities to integrate pronouns with writing how-to articles.

- ☐ Before drafting, discuss second-person narration and the implied "you" of the imperative mood.
- ☐ In the copyediting stage, instruct students to pay close attention to pronoun and antecedent agreement.
- ☐ Encourage students to use reflexive pronouns in their introductions and conclusions.

SCORING RUBRIC

How-to Article

0 = not evident
1 = minimal evidence of mastery
2 = evidence of development toward mastery
3 = strong evidence of mastery
4 = outstanding evidence of mastery

	POINTS
Ideas	
a clear purpose for the topic	
detailed, accurate, and complete instructions	
Organization	
an introduction that states the article's purpose	
steps presented in logical order	
a conclusion that leaves a sense of closure	
Voice	
appropriate tone	
directives in form of imperative sentences	
Word Choice	
transition words	
language specific to the topic	
Sentence Fluency	
clear, concise sentences	
logical transitions from step to step	
variety of sentence types	
Conventions	
correct grammar and usage	
correct spelling, punctuation, and capitalization	
Presentation	
consistent spacing and margins	
neatness	
visual aids as appropriate	
Additional Items	
Total	

Full-sized, reproducible rubrics can be found at the end of this chapter.

How-to Articles

INTRODUCING THE GENRE

Challenge students to discuss what they know about how-to writing, where they have seen it, and why it is important. Then ask volunteers to offer examples of how-to writing that they encounter frequently *(cooking instructions, driving directions, explanation for the completion of an assignment).*

Tell students that the characteristics of a well-written how-to article include the following:

- An introduction that clearly states the purpose
- Information that is detailed and complete
- Steps given in the order in which they should be completed
- Directions in the form of concise, imperative sentences
- A tone that is appropriate for the writer's audience

Reading the Literature Excerpt

Tell students that Benjamin Franklin conducted his kite experiment, in which he proved that lightning is a form of electricity, in 1752. Explain that when Franklin published his discovery in the *Pennsylvania Gazette*, he described the steps so thoroughly that any reader could reconstruct his entire experiment.

Have a volunteer read aloud "Electrical Kite." Have students point out reasons this is a good how-to article. Invite students to list other examples of how-to writing they have encountered.

LiNK — Electrical Kite

The excerpts in Chapter 2 introduce students to relevant, real, published examples of how-to articles. "Electrical Kite" is a strong example of a how-to article because it contains the following:

- Detailed, accurate, and complete instructions
- Steps listed in chronological order
- Imperative sentences
- Clear, error-free language

As students encounter the different examples throughout the chapter, be sure to point out the characteristics they share. Also take this opportunity to point out grammar skills that students have been learning, such as rules for using pronouns.

How-to Articles

Do not try this at home

LiNK — Electrical Kite
by Benjamin Franklin
Article from *The Pennsylvania Gazette*
October 19, 1752

Make a small cross of two light strips of cedar, the arms so long as to reach to the four corners of a large thin silk handkerchief when extended; tie the corners of the handkerchief to the extremities of the cross, so you have the body of a kite; which being properly accommodated with a tail, loop, and string, will rise in the air . . . To the top of the upright stick of the cross is to be fixed a sharp pointed wire . . . To the end of the twine, next the key may be fastened. This kite is to be raised when a thunder-gust appears to be coming on, and the person who holds the string must stand within a door or window . . . care must be taken that the twine does not touch the frame of the door. As soon as any of the thunder clouds come over the kite, the pointed wire will draw the electric fire from them, and the kite, with all the twine, will be electrified . . .

Benjamin Franklin

260

Reading the Student Model

Have volunteers read the model aloud. Ask a volunteer to point to the section in the model that explains what the how-to article will teach.

Challenge students to identify the steps for making maple syrup. Have students elaborate on the following questions:

- Are the instructions easy to follow? Why or why not?
- Are the steps complete?

- Is there any unnecessary information?
- What transition words and phrases do you notice in the piece?

Explain that this article was not written for a specific person, but for many people. Have students cite examples in the model that show the writer is trying to make sure the instructions will be understood by a large audience.

TEACHING OPTIONS

Scavenger Hunt

Have small groups find examples of how-to articles among classroom materials. Encourage students to use textbooks, magazines, catalogs, and posters. Ask students to discuss what distinguishes how-to articles from other genres.

CHAPTER 2

How to Make Your Own Maple Syrup
by Hans Whitmore

Supplies: *Drill, sugaring spouts, hammer, buckets, clothes hanger, two pans, cheesecloth, clean jars*

Every winter in Vermont, when the temperature drops to 40 or 50 degrees, I go sugaring with my grandparents. "Sugaring" is the first step for making maple syrup. The Native Americans of New England made maple syrup first, way back before Europeans arrived in America. The methods for making maple syrup have changed very little since then.

First, you need to search the woods for maple trees. There are many kinds of maple trees, but sugar maples are the best. You can identify them by their leaves, so I advise you to use a book, but black maples are OK too and are the most similar, so it's fine if you tap a black maple instead. Choose a tree that is at least 14 inches in diameter because that means it is at least 40 years old. Next, find a spot about three feet high on the sunny side of the tree and drill a two inch-deep "taphole." Make sure there are no old tapholes nearby or else you could split the tree and your spout won't fit tightly. Drill the hole at an upward angle so the sap will run nicely down your spout. Next, with a hammer, tap the sugaring spout into the hole. Be careful not to split the tree then either, or the sap will run out of the cracks and not into your bucket. After you get the spout in, simply hang your bucket under it with a wire clothes hanger so it catches the sap. It won't happen right away. The sun will warm the sap during the day, so the warmer the sun makes the tree, the more sap will thaw and run down and out of your spout. (I asked my grandpa why we can't just tap the trees in the summer for sap, and he said the trees need the cold weather to push the sap up into the trunk from the roots.) Make sure you cover your bucket everywhere except under the spout so snow and rain do not get into it.

After you have collected the sap, you need to boil it to get rid of the extra water. Do this with an adult because it needs to get very hot. You can boil it on a stove or on a fire pit, but watch it and stir it constantly because it can burn once it gets thick. Burnt syrup tastes disgusting! And skim off the scum that boils to the top because that doesn't taste very good either. Finally, pour the thickened "syrup" through cheesecloth into a new pan to cool a little, then into your syrup jars. And there you have it—homemade maple syrup to eat with your pancakes all year long!

261

For Tomorrow

Have students find two how-to articles at home or in the library. Remind students that how-to articles can be found in specialty publications such as cooking or home-improvement magazines. Bring in your own example of a how-to article.

OBJECTIVES

- **To recognize the characteristics of how-to articles**
- **To use a checklist to evaluate how-to articles**

WARM-UP
Read, Listen, Speak

Share the how-to article you brought for yesterday's For Tomorrow activity. Point out the characteristics of a how-to article in your example.

Have small groups share the how-to articles they brought for homework. Encourage students to discuss the characteristics of how-to writing in their examples.

GRAMMAR CONNECTION

Take this opportunity to talk about person, number, and gender of pronouns and subject pronouns. You may wish to have students point out person, number, and gender of pronouns and subject pronouns in their Read, Listen, Speak examples.

TEACH

Invite a volunteer to read aloud the first two paragraphs. Expand on the idea that the primary purpose of writing is to communicate information. Ask students to give examples of things they have learned to do because they read how to do them. Suggest that this learning process was the result of an effective how-to article.

Ask a volunteer to read aloud the Audience section. When the student has finished, discuss the probable audience for the model "How to Make Your Own Maple Syrup." Ask another student to read aloud the Introduction section. Have students identify and comment on the introduction for the model.

Ask volunteers to read aloud the Body and Conclusion sections. When discussing the body of a how-to article, mention that students' *Voyages in English* textbooks are similar to how-to writing because they provide instructions on how to write, and they contain many imperative sentences. Then have students discuss whether the model includes an effective body and conclusion.

LiNK Have students read the "Magic Card Trick" excerpt. Point out that the first step is numbered, and this shows chronological order. Also point out the casual language in the excerpt. Ask students who the audience might be.

PRACTICE

ACTIVITY A

Ask students to complete this activity in pairs. Remind students that their introductory sentences should state the purpose of their how-to articles and intrigue the reader. Invite volunteers to share what they wrote.

ACTIVITY B

Have students complete this activity independently. Point

What Makes a Good How-to Article?

Magic Card Trick

LiNK

What you need:
Two decks of cards. It's probably a good idea to make them full decks, too.
To Perform:
1. Give your friend the choice of either pack of cards. It doesn't matter, really. Then, ask him to shuffle his pack; you shuffle yours. Really mix them up, too. . . .

(continued on page 269)

How-to writing is a form of exposition, or informative writing, that gives directions for doing something. How-to writing can offer non-technical guidance, as in "How to Be a Good Leader," or provide step-by-step instructions, as in "How to Make Chocolate Chip Pancakes." It can be as simple as "How to Color Eggs" or as complex as "How to Build a Model of the White House." How-to writing is all around us: in the user's guides that accompany products, in magazine recipes, in craft instructions, in student handbooks. Where do you most often encounter how-to writing?

Here are a few points to keep in mind when you write a how-to article. How closely did the author of "How to Make Your Own Maple Syrup" follow these guidelines?

Audience

Before you begin, consider the audience you are writing for. This will affect both the level of detail and the tone of your writing. An audience that knows how to cook won't need to be told how to turn the oven on. An audience that has never been to your community will need more details when you give directions. If you're writing to a friend, you can use a friendly, informal tone. However, writing an instruction booklet will require a more formal tone.

Introduction

The title and the first paragraph should state clearly the purpose of the how-to article—that is, it should say what is being explained. If necessary, emphasize why the topic is significant. Why would your reader benefit from following the steps you describe? You may want to engage readers with a fascinating first sentence, which should provide background information or stress the significance of your topic.

out that thinking like the reader will help students write more effective how-to articles.

APPLY

WRITER'S CORNER

Have students work with partners to compare their lists. Challenge partners to choose the most effective topics from each list and explain why they think each topic would make an effective how-to article. Students should demonstrate an understanding of audience and topic for how-to articles.

TechTip You may wish to print graphic organizers from a computer program. Distribute them to pairs of students. Have pairs work together to fill in the graphic organizers. Have one student brainstorm ideas and the other record them.

ASSESS

Note which students had difficulty recognizing the purpose of how-to articles. Use the Reteach option with those students who need additional reinforcement.

TEACHING OPTIONS

Reteach

Bring in a board game from home and make copies of the directions. Have students work with partners to analyze the directions by discussing the following questions:

- Are the directions clear and complete?
- Were these directions written for a large audience? What evidence supports this?
- What might happen if someone missed a step?

After students have answered these questions, discuss the game's directions with the entire class.

Assorted Audiences

Have students write a how-to paragraph about how to play a common game, such as hide-and-seek or tag. Tell students that the intended audience is a group of adults. Then have students rewrite those directions for an audience of young children. Discuss how the intended audience affects the language of the paragraph.

For Tomorrow

Ask students to bring in a how-to article and to determine the audience of the piece. Challenge students to think how the writing might change based on a different audience. Bring your own example to discuss with the class.

Body

In the body of a how-to article, describe the steps required to accomplish the goal. Use imperative sentences, which are sentences written in the form of commands. Present the steps in chronological order, providing just enough detail for readers to understand clearly. Organize each step or each group of similar steps into a paragraph.

Conclusion

In the conclusion assure your audience that by following the steps as given, they will be successful, or make a prediction about the impact of their success.

ACTIVITY A Read the list of titles for how-to articles. To what audience would each appeal? Choose five titles and write engaging introductory sentences for each.

1. Recipes for Gourmet Sandwiches
2. You Can Create and Use a Blog
3. Learning to Dress Well
4. How to Run for Political Office
5. Clean the Messiest Bedroom in Less Than 15 Minutes
6. Basic Figure Skating
7. Simple Steps to a Perfect Pie Crust
8. How to Make Friends and How to Keep Them

ACTIVITY B Choose three titles from Activity A. For each title write two questions you would expect to learn the answers to if you read a how-to article on the topic.

WRITER'S CORNER

Brainstorm a list of things you know how to do. Choose a few that would make interesting and unique how-to articles.

 Use an online word web program to brainstorm ideas.

How-to Articles • 263

Read, Listen, Speak

Read your how-to article from yesterday's For Tomorrow activity. Point out specific language that helped you determine the intended audience. Explain how the language might change if the audience were different.

Have small groups discuss the intended audiences of their articles. Encourage students to point out the language that led them to this conclusion. Challenge students to discuss what aspects of their article would change with a different audience. Tell students to save their articles for future assignments

GRAMMAR CONNECTION

Take this opportunity to talk about object pronouns. You may wish to have students point out object pronouns in their Read, Listen, Speak examples.

TEACH

Invite a volunteer to read aloud the title and the first paragraph. Then ask other volunteers to read aloud the questions under the three sections of the checklist.

Have students take a few minutes to use the checklist to further assess the how-to articles they found for homework. Encourage students to use this checklist whenever they evaluate a how-to article to be sure that their evaluations are focused and precise.

Have students review the characteristics of a how-to article on pages 262–263. Then challenge students to think of other questions they can add to the checklist.

PRACTICE

ACTIVITY C

Ask students to complete the activity independently. Then have students form small groups to discuss their assessments of the writer's work.

ACTIVITY D

Invite students to use the How-to Article Checklist to evaluate the directions to the party. When students have finished, lead a group discussion to answer the questions that follow the selection.

APPLY

WRITER'S CORNER

Ask each student to trade papers with a partner and assess whether the classmate wrote a clear, engaging introduction. Have volunteers share their introductions with the class. Discuss strengths and weaknesses for each introduction. Students should demonstrate an understanding of how-to introductions.

The How-to Article Checklist

When you write a how-to article, there are many questions to keep in mind that will help make your writing clear and engaging. Use the following checklist when you evaluate your writing:

Title and Introduction

☐ Does the title clearly state the topic?

☐ Does the introduction explain the purpose of the how-to article?

☐ Does the introduction engage readers in the topic?

Body

☐ Are the steps in the right order?

☐ Are they clear?

☐ Are all the important steps included?

☐ Is there any unnecessary information?

☐ Does each step give the right level of detail?

☐ Is the tone appropriate?

Conclusion

☐ Is there a conclusion?

☐ Does it sum up the process or invite the readers to make use of or enjoy what they've learned to do?

ACTIVITY C Use the How-to Article Checklist to evaluate the following paragraph. Search for any places where the writer failed to follow the checklist. Then discuss your findings with a small group.

How to Make Hot Chocolate

Here's something you can make. Put some chocolate along with about 1/4 cup of water into a double boiler. A double boiler is two pots that fit together. You heat water in the bottom pot so that whatever you put in the top heats or melts gently. You should probably use semisweet or bittersweet chocolate. My favorite is milk chocolate, but don't use that. Oh, and chop the chocolate. Melt the chocolate. Stir it every so often. Is it smooth yet? Go ahead and stop stirring. Whisk in some hot water into the top of the double-boiler pan,

Grammar in Action. The pronouns in the excerpt are *you, it, them, it, him, you,* and *them.* Point out that *your* and *his* are not pronouns, but possessive adjectives. Then ask students to identify the pronouns that have antecedents *(him and them).* Challenge students to identify the antecedents *(friend and cards).*

ASSESS

Note which students had difficulty evaluating how-to articles. Use the Reteach option with those students who need additional reinforcement.

Practice Book page 143 provides additional work with the characteristics of an effective how-to article.

TEACHING OPTIONS

Reteach

Ask a volunteer to find simple directions for creating an origami figure. Gather materials for the activity. Make an alternative copy of the directions by deleting steps or placing them in the wrong order.

Distribute materials to small groups. Provide half the groups with the complete directions and half the groups with the edited directions. When students using the alternative directions begin to struggle, ask students to discuss what causes the problems.

Invite groups to share their experiences with the original origami directions. Ask questions such as the following:

- Did the how-to article inspire you to want to make this figure?
- What was the most difficult part? Did the writer include the necessary characteristics of a how-to article?

When students have finished the discussion, have them work together to correct the alternative directions.

---

which you have removed from the stove. If you think people will want to add sugar or whipped cream, serve those so people can add their own. Since this recipe makes 4 cups, stir 3/4 cup of milk into each mug. Be sure to use 6 ounces of chocolate. And be sure the milk in the mugs is heated so that the drink will be warm enough.

ACTIVITY D Read these directions and check them over, using the How-to Article Checklist. Then evaluate other aspects of the how-to article by answering the questions that follow.

Getting to the Party

I hope you can come to my birthday party. These are directions to help you get here the quickest and most direct way. If you need help with the directions, just give us a call at (615) 555-0309.

Since most of you will be coming from the city, I'll start from there. Take I-96 north to the Bennett Avenue exit (#87). Then proceed east (right) for about five miles. You will go through three stoplights. After a small strip mall and a gas station on the north (left), you'll see Canfield Road. Turn north (left) onto Canfield. Keep going for two or three miles until you see a sign that reads Forest Park on the east (right). That's the entrance to our subdivision. Turn into the subdivision. You'll be on Parkview Place. Follow Parkview as it curves past Meadowdale and Goldenrod Lane. Just after Goldenrod cuts in, you'll find 1001 Parkview, our big yellow house with green shutters.

Finally, you're here! We'll have a sign out front and plenty of food, music, and fun inside.

1. In which sentence is the purpose stated?
2. What is the tone of the how-to article?
3. How does the writer's audience affect the level of detail she provides?
4. What are some ways the writer clarifies the directions?
5. How well would you be able to follow these directions? Explain.
6. Can you think of ways the directions might be improved?

Grammar in Action. Name the pronouns in the p. 262 excerpt.

WRITER'S CORNER

Choose one of the how-to article ideas from the list you wrote in the Writer's Corner on page 263. Write an introduction to your article that clearly states the topic and purpose of the article, and engages the reader.

For Tomorrow

Have students write a conclusion to the how-to article idea from the Writer's Corner. Remind students to write for the same audience as they did for the introduction. Bring in a how-to article conclusion of your own to share with the class.

How-to Articles • 265

OBJECTIVE
- To write clear and concise instructions in how-to articles

WARM-UP

Read, Listen, Speak

Discuss your conclusion from yesterday's For Tomorrow homework. Point out the details that make the conclusion successful. Then have small groups discuss their conclusions. Challenge students to offer suggestions for strengthening one another's conclusions.

GRAMMAR CONNECTION

Take this opportunity to talk about pronouns after *than* or *as*. You may wish to have students point out pronouns after *than* or *as* in their Read, Listen, Speak examples.

TEACH

Write on the board the five points for writing a how-to article in paragraph form. *(Use chronological order. Divide steps into paragraphs. Use transition words and phrases. Provide enough detail. Omit unnecessary information.)* Create a column for each point. Have small groups take one of the points and read and discuss the text about that point. Then ask volunteers from each group to write important pieces of information on the board under the appropriate column. Discuss these as they are added and add to each list where appropriate. Encourage students to copy the information into their notebooks.

PRACTICE

ACTIVITY A
Ask volunteers to read their completed paragraphs aloud. Have students list on the board the transition words used in each paragraph.

ACTIVITY B
Ask students to work in pairs to complete the activity. Suggest that students follow the five points for making instructions clear and concise. Remind students to keep their intended audience in mind when rewriting the directions.

Making Instructions Clear and Concise

When writing the steps of a how-to article, the key is to make your instructions clear and concise. As you write, keep in mind the following points to make sure that the steps are logical and easy to follow.

Use Chronological Order

While writing, mentally go through the process step by step, making sure that each step is told in the order in which it should be completed. If you remember something that has been omitted, go back and add it where it belongs.

Divide Steps into Paragraphs

If your how-to article is short, you may be able to fit all the directions into a single paragraph. However, if you have long or complicated directions, put each step or group of steps in a separate paragraph.

Use Transition Words and Phrases

Using transition words such as *first, next,* and *finally,* or phrases such as *when you have finished,* helps clarify the steps in the process.

Provide Enough Detail

Don't assume that somebody will know how much water is "a little" (in a recipe) or where Main Street is (when giving directions). Be specific and use exact words when explaining a step.

Omit Unnecessary Information

Leave out any information that distracts the reader from accomplishing the task you are describing.

APPLY

WRITER'S CORNER

After students have written the rules and directions for their favorite game, encourage students to trade papers and turn the directions into paragraph form. Remind students to use transition words and to omit unnecessary information. Students should demonstrate an understanding of making instructions clear and concise.

TechTip You may wish to have students use the class blog to offer constructive suggestions for revising how-to articles.

ASSESS

Note which students had difficulty understanding the five points of writing clear and concise instructions in how-to articles. Use the Reteach option with those students who need additional reinforcement.

Activity A
Hard-boiled Eggs
Place eggs in pot.
Cover eggs with water.
Put on lid.
Turn on stove.
Bring eggs and water to a boil.
Turn off stove.
Remove pot from heat. Let eggs stand for a half hour.
Paragraphs will vary.

Chewy Nutty Popcorn Balls
Place 1 pound of caramels and 3 cups of water in a double boiler.
Melt caramels over medium heat.
Stir caramel until smooth.
Wait about 30 seconds for caramel to cool slightly.
Pour caramel over 10 cups of popcorn.
Put butter on your hands so the caramel mixture won't stick.
Form popcorn/caramel mixture into balls.
Roll popcorn balls in chopped nuts.
Store at room temperature.
Paragraphs will vary.

ACTIVITY A Arrange the steps of the following recipes in chronological order. Then write the steps in paragraph form, using transition words and phrases to help the steps flow logically. (Hint: The final step in both recipes is in the correct position.)

Hard-boiled Eggs
Turn off stove.
Bring eggs and water to a boil.
Put on lid.
Cover eggs with water.
Place eggs in pot.
Turn on stove.
Remove pot from heat. Let eggs stand for a half hour.

Chewy Nutty Popcorn Balls
Melt caramels over medium heat.
Stir caramel until smooth.
Pour caramel over 10 cups of popcorn.
Wait about 30 seconds for caramel to cool slightly.
Place 1 pound of caramels and 3 cups of water in a double boiler.
Roll popcorn balls in chopped nuts.
Put butter on your hands so the caramel mixture won't stick.
Form popcorn/caramel mixture into balls.
Store at room temperature.

ACTIVITY B Sometimes the activities that we practice daily can be the hardest to explain. Choose one of the suggested activities or come up with your own. Create a list of steps, and then write the steps in paragraph form. Be sure to make them clear and concise. Use transition words and phrases.

Tying your shoes   Making a bed   Folding a T-shirt

WRITER'S CORNER

Write the rules and directions for playing one of your favorite games or activities: baseball, basketball, a card game, a board or video game. Have a classmate familiar with the activity review it for missed or misplaced steps.

 Tech Tip Post your article on a class blog or wiki for peer review.

How-to Articles • 267

Read, Listen, Speak

Read the body of your how-to article from yesterday's For Tomorrow activity. Emphasize transition words and clarifying details. Then ask small groups to read their how-to body paragraphs to each other. Encourage students to comment on the completeness and coherence of the directions for each game and whether transitional words and phrases were used correctly.

GRAMMAR CONNECTION

Take this opportunity to talk about possessive pronouns and adjectives. You may wish to have students point out possessive pronouns and adjectives in their Read, Listen, Speak examples.

TEACH

Review the five points for writing clear and concise instructions in how-to articles. Ask volunteers to describe the effective organization of instructions. Challenge students to explain the difference between necessary detail and unnecessary information in a how-to article.

LiNK Have students read the "Magic Card Trick" excerpt. Point out the detail the writer uses in each step, and how the details make the steps clear and concise.

PRACTICE

ACTIVITY C

After students have completed this activity, invite volunteers to read aloud their how-to articles. As they read, have students say where each new paragraph begins.

ACTIVITY D

Ask students to work in pairs to finish this activity. Have volunteers read their work aloud. Ask students to point out details that were added and that are important to the how-to article. Have students list transition words and phrases that were added.

ACTIVITY E

Give students time to rewrite the instructions. Then ask partners to trade papers. Have students review each other's instructions. Direct students to the How-to Article Checklist to evaluate whether writers included the characteristics of a how-to article.

ACTIVITY C Rewrite the following how-to article. First, take the transition words and phrases below and insert them in the spaces where they belong. Then divide the how-to article into three paragraphs, putting each step or set of steps in a separate paragraph.

How to Make Perfect Coffee

Follow these steps for a delectable cup of coffee each time you brew. _____First_____, use clean equipment. Wash your coffeemaker with vinegar and water at least once a week. _____Next_____, grind the beans, which should be as fresh as possible. Make sure the grind you are using matches your brewing method: grind for 5 to 10 seconds for percolators, 10 seconds for drip and French press coffeemakers, 15 seconds for vacuum methods, and 25 to 40 seconds for espresso machines. _____Just before . . ._____, measure the ground coffee. Use 2 level tablespoons for every 6 ounces of coffee. _____Once you . . . ._____, brew the coffee with clear, pure water, following the instructions for the method you are using. _____While the . . ._____, warm the cup. Pour the coffee into the cup. _____Finally_____, enjoy your perfectly brewed cup of coffee. To enjoy the rest of the pot just as much, don't let the coffee sit on a warmer for longer than 15 or 20 minutes, and never reheat it.

Transition words and phrases

Next	Once you have measured the coffee grounds
First	While the coffee is brewing
Finally	Just before you brew the coffee

ACTIVITY D The steps presented here on how to catch a fish are out of order. First, put the steps in their proper order. Then rewrite each step as a complete sentence, using transition words or phrases in each sentence. Add detail when necessary.

1. Reel in fish.
2. Bait hook.
3. Release fish.
4. Land fish and remove hook.
5. Choose a fishing rod and reel.
6. Cast your line into the water.

APPLY

WRITER'S CORNER

Give students time to write steps for their how-to topics. When students have finished, ask them to write on the board the transition words they used. Keep a running list of transition words on chart paper as the class works to complete this chapter. Students should demonstrate an understanding of making instructions clear and concise.

💡 **TechTip** You may wish to have students post their how-to articles on a class blog. Encourage

students to review their classmates' work and to take notes on ways their classmates made their directions clear and concise.

ASSESS

Note which students had difficulty composing steps in how-to articles. Use the Reteach option with those students who need additional reinforcement.

Practice Book page 144 provides additional work with making directions clear and concise.

TEACHING OPTIONS

Reteach

Ask students to choose a familiar topic for a how-to article and to make a chart that lists the main steps and details of those steps. Remind students to list the steps in order. Write the following on the board for students to use as a model:

Getting Ready for School

Steps	Details
wake up	turn off alarm
get ready	eat breakfast, brush teeth, get dressed
pack	put lunch and homework in backpack

When students have finished, encourage volunteers to share their charts with the class. Make sure enough detail is provided for clarity.

Meeting Individual Needs

Visual Show students a video of a cooking show or home-improvement show that explains how to prepare or build something. Ask students to note the order and description of the steps. When the video has ended, challenge students to write the steps in paragraph form, using specific details and descriptions. Invite students to present what they wrote to the class.

For Tomorrow

Ask students to write a brief how-to article in paragraph form that includes both an introduction and a conclusion. Suggest that they choose a simple task such as opening a door or making a phone call. Bring in a brief how-to article of your own to share with the class.

ACTIVITY E Rewrite the instructions for using electronic voting machines to make the steps easier to understand. Use the Body portion of the How-to Article Checklist to help you.

How to Use Electronic Voting Machines

Welcome to your friendly new electronic voting machine! Follow this procedure for each office you are voting for. You'll see small square touch pads that look like buttons instead of levers as in previous elections. But really, touching a square is easier than pulling a lever. Go into the voting booth. After you touch a square, a pleasant green light will come on. Touch the square at the right of the name of each candidate you want to vote for. If you change your mind, too bad! I'm kidding. Just touch the square again, and the green light will go off. Make another selection and touch the square again.

For write-in votes, go to the Personal Choice column and touch the square marked "write in." If you make a mistake, touch the write-in square again and start over. You can spend all day making changes if you want to. Use the keypad to enter the name.

When you are satisfied with your selections, touch the large red square at the bottom of the screen to cast your vote. You will hear a click that indicates your vote has been counted. Exit the polling booth. Congratulations! You've just cast your vote.

LiNK

Magic Card Trick
(continued from page 262)

2. Switch packs, but as you do, glimpse the bottom card of your pack. Don't make a "move" out of this. Just casually tilt the deck, glimpse the card and memorize it. (If you forget this card, you're sunk!)

3. Ask your friend to fan the cards towards his face, remove any card and place it at the top of the pack. You do the same. (But don't memorize your card; keep the card in mind from Step 2)....

(continued on page 276)

WRITER'S CORNER

Write the steps for the topic you chose in the Writer's Corner on page 267. Use transition words and phrases.
Trade your work with a partner for peer review. Save your work and partner's comments to use later.

How-to Articles • 269

OBJECTIVES

- **To identify and revise run-on and rambling sentences**
- **To make every word count in the body paragraphs of how-to articles**

WARM-UP

Read, Listen, Speak

Read your how-to article from yesterday's For Tomorrow homework. Point out essential characteristics of a how-to article such as the steps being in chronological order, the use of transition words, and enough detail to avoid confusion for the reader.

Have small groups take turns reading aloud the how-to articles they wrote for homework. Have students get advice from group members on how the work might be improved. Tell students to use the How-to Article Checklist on page 264 when evaluating their classmates' how-to articles.

GRAMMAR CONNECTION

Take this opportunity to talk about intensive and reflexive pronouns. You may wish to have students point out intensive and reflexive pronouns in their Read, Listen, Speak examples.

TEACH

Have a volunteer read aloud the first paragraph. Ask students to comment on the clarity of that paragraph. *(The thoughts rambled and lost focus, making it hard to follow.)*

Ask a student to read aloud the section Run-on Sentences. Have another student read aloud the section Rambling Sentences. Invite volunteers to offer ways to rewrite the run-on sentence so that the thought is expressed more clearly. Challenge other volunteers to revise the rambling sentence so that it forms two or three shorter, more concise sentences.

PRACTICE

ACTIVITY A

Instruct pairs of students to work cooperatively to complete this activity. Then invite volunteers to write one or two revised sentences on the board. Discuss students' revisions as a group.

ACTIVITY B

Write on the board the first run-on sentence. Have volunteers write revised sentences below the original. Then give students time to complete the remaining sentences. Ask volunteers to share their answers.

LESSON **3** WRITING SKILLS

Revising Sentences

In how-to articles, as in all writing, sentences should be clear and to the point. A sentence should usually focus on one idea or event, instead of going on and on (as this one does), because if the sentence is too long, the reader will not only run out of breath (if he or she is reading aloud), but also may become confused and forget what the sentence was about in the first place.

Run-on Sentences

Run-on sentences connect more than one independent clause without using conjunctions or appropriate punctuation. A run-on sentence is grammatically incorrect.

> **Read the directions carefully before you begin to assemble the model airplane, you should have newspaper laid out on the table.**

Rambling Sentences

A rambling sentence is a sentence with many ideas that, while it may be grammatically correct, should be shortened into several sentences for clarity.

> **Gather your paints and glue on the newspaper, then open the box, take the pieces out, and lay them on the table, and begin painting the body of the airplane whatever color you want.**

Run-on and rambling sentences are undesirable in any type of writing because they confuse the reader. They cause particular problems in how-to writing because the reader needs to understand each step before moving on to the next. How would you rewrite the run-on and rambling sentences on this page?

APPLY

WRITER'S CORNER

Have volunteers write their revised sentences on the board. Discuss several different ways to revise each sentence. Students should demonstrate an understanding of revising run-on and rambling sentences.

Grammar in Action. Take this opportunity to review the difference between subject and object pronouns. Once students have identified the object pronouns, have them identify each object pronoun's antecedent *(them/maples, it/spout, it/bucket)*.

ASSESS

Note which students had difficulty revising run-on and rambling sentences. Use the Reteach option with those students who need additional reinforcement.

TEACHING OPTIONS

Reteach

Work with students to list the complete thoughts in each sentence in Activity A. Then help students identify any extra phrases or clauses. This example uses item 1.

Complete thoughts

- **You must read over the part several times.**
- **Consider the motivations of the characters.**
- **Study the lines until you have memorized them.**
- **Rehearse the role frequently with other actors.**

Meeting Individual Needs

Challenge Explain that well-known writers, especially during the Romantic and Victorian periods, used rambling sentences in their prose *(examples: Herman Melville, Charles Dickens, Emily Brontë)*. Challenge students to find selections that use rambling sentences. Ask students the following questions: *How did the rambling sentences affect your experience as the reader? What do you think was the author's purpose in using these kinds of sentences?*

For Tomorrow

Ask students to write examples of run-on and rambling sentences that might be found in how-to articles. Prepare several examples of your own to discuss with the class tomorrow.

Activity A
Sample answer
1. To learn an acting role, you must first read over the part several times. Consider the motivations of the character, then study the lines until you have memorized them. Rehearse the role frequently with other actors.

ACTIVITY A Divide these rambling sentences into several sentences.

1. To learn an acting role, you must first read over the part several times, consider the motivations of the character, then study the lines until you have memorized them and rehearse the role frequently with other actors.

2. Plan out what you will say before you go into the job interview, and bring with you a résumé and some samples of your previous work, and remember to shake the interviewer's hand and maintain frequent eye contact while you are talking.

3. To make an origami dove, take a square sheet of paper, then fold it into a rectangle and unfold it again and fold two corners into the center line.

4. I never told my brother he couldn't ever come into my room, but I asked him to knock first and wait for me to answer instead of just barging in because I need to be able to concentrate on my homework.

Activity B
Sample answer
1. Wait for the paint to dry before you glue the pieces together. Be sure you are wearing gloves.

ACTIVITY B Correct the following run-on sentences by separating them into more than one sentence.

1. Wait for the paint to dry before you glue the pieces together, be sure you are wearing gloves.

2. A bill is first introduced by a member of Congress and must be passed by both the Senate and the House of Representatives, if different versions of the bill are passed, then members of both chambers will meet in a committee to resolve any differences, it is then sent to the president to sign or veto.

3. Make sure not to park your car on the left side of the street there is a no-parking zone.

Grammar in Action. Name the object pronouns in the second paragraph of the p. 261 excerpt.

WRITER'S CORNER

Rewrite Ben Franklin's "Electrical Kite," on page 260, breaking down his run-on and rambling sentences into shorter sentences. Compare your results with a partner's results.

How-to Articles • 271

WARM-UP

Read, Listen, Speak

Write on the board your run-on sentences from yesterday's For Tomorrow homework. Discuss how these run-on sentences can be broken into clearer, concise sentences.

Have students work with a partner to compare and discuss the rambling and run-on sentences they wrote for homework. Have one student read aloud his or her original sentence. Instruct the other student to revise the sentence. Remind students that the revised sentences should state the message in a clear and concise way.

GRAMMAR CONNECTION

Take this opportunity to talk about agreement between pronouns and antecedents. You may wish to have students point out agreement between pronouns and antecedents in their Read, Listen, Speak examples.

TEACH

Ask a volunteer to read aloud the first paragraph of the section Making Every Word Count. Have another volunteer read the second paragraph and the three sets of directions for baking muffins. Encourage volunteers to explain which set of directions is clearest and to provide reasons for their answers. Then have a student read aloud the last paragraph in the section.

PRACTICE

ACTIVITY C

Give students time to complete the activity. Ask volunteers to explain the reasons for their choices. Discuss any discrepancies students may have.

ACTIVITY D

After students have completed this activity, have them trade papers with a partner to discuss the deletions each student made.

Making Every Word Count

In describing the steps in a process, every word counts. If important details are left out, readers won't be able to follow the directions. Distracting and unnecessary words can also cause confusion because readers may not be able to wade through them to figure out what to do and how to do it.

Each of the three items below describes the final steps in baking muffins. Which set of directions is the clearest and most useful?

1. Take the muffins out of the oven when they are done, and let them cool for 5 minutes. Then let them cool on a rack for a while.
2. Are your muffins ready yet? If they are, you can think about taking them out and cooling them off. It's probably a good idea to cool them for about 5 minutes in the muffin pan and then move them to a rack (if you don't have a cooling rack, you can improvise) for another 15 minutes.
3. Take the muffins out of the oven when they are golden brown, and let them cool in the muffin pan for 5 minutes. Then move them to a wire cooling rack to continue cooling for 15 minutes longer.

The first set of directions is incomplete. It leaves out critical details, such as when to take the muffins out of the oven. The next set has unnecessary information. Its first sentence is not needed, and the information in parentheses is not helpful. The last set of directions explains exactly what, when, and why. Every word counts.

ACTIVITY C Choose which set of instructions in each group is the clearest and easiest to understand. Discuss reasons for your choices.

1. a. Stir the paint, whatever color it is. Make sure you like the color you picked. Pour the paint into a roller tray, or you can use a bucket or something else. But a roller tray is best. Paint the ceiling before you paint the walls. Use tape to keep paint from getting where you don't want it to be.
   b. Whenever you paint, you should start with the ceiling. Before you begin painting, tape off the wall. Stir the paint. Then pour it into a roller tray. Use a roller as you paint the ceiling.
   c. Start with the ceiling. Use tape. If you're a really good painter, you don't have to use tape. Stir the paint, and then pour it. Paint the ceiling. Don't forget to clean the roller after you have finished using it.

APPLY

WRITER'S CORNER

Allow time for students to revise their paragraphs. Ask volunteers to read aloud their work. Challenge the class to give appropriate feedback. Students should demonstrate an understanding of revising sentences and eliminating unnecessary information

ASSESS

Note which students had difficulty writing clear and concise steps for how-to articles. Use the Reteach option with those students who need additional reinforcement.

Practice Book page 145 provides additional work with revising sentences.

2. a. Combine 4 cups of shredded Monterey jack cheese, 4 beaten eggs, and 4 ounces of canned, chopped green chilies. Spread the ingredients into an 8-inch-square baking pan. Bake at 350°F for 30 minutes.

   b. You need Monterey jack cheese. You also need 4 eggs. You need 4 ounces of green chilies. First, beat the eggs. Make sure the chilies are chopped. Combine everything and spread the mixture into an 8-inch-square baking pan. Turn the oven to 350°F. Then put in the mixture and bake it for 30 minutes.

   c. Stir together some cheese, eggs, and a bunch of chopped green chilies or another kind of chili if you like. Put the ingredients into an 8-inch-square pan. Then bake it for a while in an oven.

ACTIVITY D Identify the unnecessary sentences in the how-to article below.

Setting up an aquarium is easy, but it requires patience. Although large saltwater tanks prove to be the easiest to maintain, they are tougher to set up. You have to add salt and make sure the pH is just right, and there is other stuff to do too. So I will tell you how to set up a freshwater aquarium, which is where a novice should begin. But saltwater aquariums are very cool. First, rinse the aquarium and the gravel thoroughly because the dust will negatively affect the water quality. Never use any kind of soap, not even glass cleaner, on the outside of the aquarium. Always use gravel bought at a store because gravel from your yard can contain chemicals or bacteria that will make your fish sick. There are many medications for curing sick fish. Cover the bottom of the tank with gravel, one inch deep. Next, fill the tank with water, adding a few drops of dechlorinator or simply let the water sit for a day because chlorine evaporates from water fairly quickly. Next, rinse and add decorations. While you are waiting for the chlorine to evaporate, rinse and install the filter and heater. There are many different types of filters and heaters, so follow the directions on the box. Turn them both on, and set the heater to 78 degrees. By the way, you can choose different colors of gravel. I prefer natural colored gravel, but white is also OK. Check the water pH to make sure it is between 6.8 and 7.0. Most tap water is around this pH anyway. If not, there are chemicals you can add. Once the water has reached the proper temperature, you can purchase and add your fish. But be sure to put a hood over the top of the tank to prevent water from evaporating too quickly or fish from jumping out. And float the bags with new fish in the water for a while first so the fish can adjust gradually. I like cichlids the most. Angelfish are pretty too. An octopus is a good choice for saltwater aquariums also.

WRITER'S CORNER

Look back at the steps you wrote in the Writer's Corner on page 267. Look for any unnecessary words or phrases. Add detail for clarity. Revise your steps so that every word counts.

How-to Articles • 273

OBJECTIVE
• To understand roots of words

WARM-UP

Read, Listen, Speak

Read the steps from yesterday's For Tomorrow homework. Emphasize that there is no extra information and that every word counts in your steps.

Instruct small groups to discuss their steps. Ask students to trade papers within the group and assess whether the steps are complete, clear, easy to follow, and contain no unnecessary information.

GRAMMAR CONNECTION

Take this opportunity to talk about interrogative and demonstrative pronouns. You may wish to have students point out interrogative and demonstrative pronouns in their Read, Listen, Speak examples.

TEACH

Ask a volunteer to read aloud the first paragraph. Write on the board the word *arborvitae*. Invite volunteers to look in a dictionary definition for the origin and meanings of its roots and to write them on the board next to *arborvitae (Latin:* arbor, *tree* + vita, *life)*. Encourage students to predict the meaning of the word based solely on the meanings of its roots. Then have a student read aloud the definition of *arborvitae*. Have students name other words in the dictionary with the root *arbor*. Lead students to the conclusion that many English words and meanings are rooted in ancient words and meanings. Then ask a student to read aloud the second paragraph. Challenge students to offer words for which volunteers identify the roots.

PRACTICE

ACTIVITY A

Have partners complete this activity. Tell students to record their predictions and then to record the correct dictionary definitions. Discuss the answers as a group.

ACTIVITY B

After students have completed this activity, invite volunteers to share the additional examples for each root. If students are unfamiliar with the exact meanings of the examples given, suggest that they use a dictionary to find another word that comes from the same root as the example.

ACTIVITY C

Give students time to complete this activity. Instruct partners to use the words in oral sentences. Ask volunteers to share their answers with the class.

ACTIVITY D

Have students complete this activity independently. Invite volunteers to read aloud their words and to use each in a sentence.

LESSON **4** WORD STUDY

Roots

Knowing the meaning of a word's root and its origin can help you understand the word and use it properly in your writing. For example, knowing that the root *fort* means "strong" can help you figure out that *fortitude* means "strength" or "endurance." The meaning of *somnambulist,* "sleepwalker," is clear if you know that *somnus* means "sleep" and *ambul* means "walk."

Many roots come from Latin and Greek, and some have interesting stories behind them. In the word *companion,* for example, *com* means "with" and *pan* means "bread," so *companion* means "someone you share bread with." Knowing the roots of the word *preposterous* will show you just how preposterous the word is. The roots *pre* and *post* mean "before" and "after." The word itself is a contradiction!

ACTIVITY A Read the list of roots and example words. Write a logical definition for each root, and then check the definition in a dictionary to see how accurate you were.

	Root	Examples
1.	*migr*	migrate, immigrant
2.	*dent*	dentures, dentist
3.	*loc*	local, location
4.	*fract*	fraction, fracture
5.	*cise*	scissors, incision
6.	*son*	consonant, resonate
7.	*urb*	urban, suburb
8.	*mech*	mechanic, mechanism
9.	*ject*	inject, reject
10.	*leg*	legal, legislate
11.	*ambi*	ambivalent, ambidextrous
12.	*auto*	automatic, autograph

274 • Chapter 2

APPLY

WRITER'S CORNER
Allow time for students to search the how-to articles they have written to find an appropriate piece for this activity. Tell students to list the roots they find and to look up the meanings in a dictionary. Students should demonstrate an understanding of roots of words.

ASSESS
Note which students had difficulty understanding how to find roots and their meanings. Use the Reteach option with those students who need additional reinforcement.

TEACHING OPTIONS

Reteach
Have students make root puzzles by writing words made from roots on note cards and separating the root, using an irregular cut. Mix the puzzles together and ask students to reassemble the words. Invite students to read aloud the reassembled words and tell which part is the root. Point out that some roots might work in several words.

English-Language Learners
Instruct students to work with partners to find three words whose meanings are derived from the same root. Encourage students to also write roots with equivalent meanings from their primary language. Ask students to write on a chart the roots from both languages to display the similarities and differences among languages.

ACTIVITY B Read the list of roots, their meanings, and example words. Write a second example for each root.

	Root	Meaning	Example
1.	therm	heat	thermometer
2.	sign	mark	signature
3.	gen	born	genesis
4.	imag	likeness	image
5.	fid	faith	fidelity
6.	terra	earth	territory
7.	tox	poison	intoxicate
8.	grat	pleasing	gratuity
9.	geo	earth	geometry
10.	civ	citizen	civilian
11.	bibl	book	bibliography
12.	fin	end	final
13.	voc	call	vocal
14.	tempo	time	temporary
15.	nov	new	renovate
16.	dict	speak	predict
17.	nat	born	innate
18.	omni	all	omniscient
19.	man	hand	manual

ACTIVITY C Choose five words from the Example column of Activity B. Explain what you think each word means and then look it up in a dictionary and compare that definition with yours.

ACTIVITY D Choose five roots from Activity B. Write as many words as you can that contain each root. Check your answers in a dictionary.

WRITER'S CORNER
Examine one of the how-to articles you have written. How many words can you find with the roots from this lesson?

How-to Articles • 275

For Tomorrow
Ask students to list 10 words with roots from other languages, to identify the roots and their origins, and then to use a dictionary to write the meaning of each word. Prepare a list of your own to share with the class. In this list, choose several words that come from the same root.

WARM-UP

Read, Listen, Speak

Share your list from yesterday's For Tomorrow activity. Point out several words based on the same root. Discuss how these words are similar in meaning. Then have small groups compare their lists. Instruct groups to collaborate to list at least five words that come from the same root and are similar in meaning. Encourage students to search in textbooks or dictionaries if needed.

GRAMMAR CONNECTION

Take this opportunity to talk about relative pronouns. You may wish to have students point out relative pronouns in their Read, Listen, Speak examples.

TEACH

Review the significance of roots of words. Ask students from which languages most roots of English words are derived *(Greek and Latin)*.

LiNK Have students read the "Magic Card Trick" excerpt. Remind students that a how-to article should be in chronological order. Point out the numbered steps in the excerpt.

PRACTICE

ACTIVITY E

Give small groups time to complete this activity. Invite volunteers to write on the board the definitions of the roots. Challenge students to name the origin of each root.

ACTIVITY F

After students have completed this activity, have them trade papers with a partner to check each other's work. Invite volunteers to read aloud their additional roots.

ACTIVITY G

When students have finished the activity, ask volunteers to write their sentences on the board. Challenge other students to explain whether the words were used correctly.

ACTIVITY H

Have students work with partners to complete the chart. Encourage students to refer to a dictionary while working. Have volunteers read aloud their answers.

ACTIVITY I

After students have finished this activity, ask them to share their example words with a partner. Have students identify the roots in their partner's words.

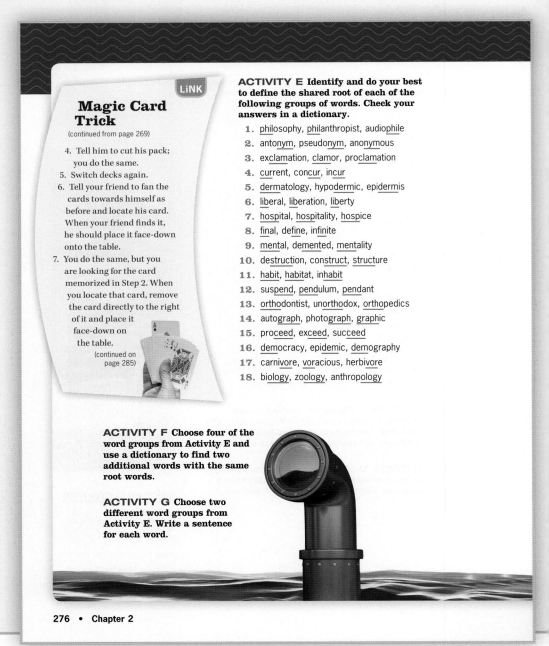

LiNK

Magic Card Trick

(continued from page 269)

4. Tell him to cut his pack; you do the same.
5. Switch decks again.
6. Tell your friend to fan the cards towards himself as before and locate his card. When your friend finds it, he should place it face-down onto the table.
7. You do the same, but you are looking for the card memorized in Step 2. When you locate that card, remove the card directly to the right of it and place it face-down on the table.

(continued on page 285)

ACTIVITY E Identify and do your best to define the shared root of each of the following groups of words. Check your answers in a dictionary.

1. philosophy, philanthropist, audiophile
2. antonym, pseudonym, anonymous
3. exclamation, clamor, proclamation
4. current, concur, incur
5. dermatology, hypodermic, epidermis
6. liberal, liberation, liberty
7. hospital, hospitality, hospice
8. final, define, infinite
9. mental, demented, mentality
10. destruction, construct, structure
11. habit, habitat, inhabit
12. suspend, pendulum, pendant
13. orthodontist, unorthodox, orthopedics
14. autograph, photograph, graphic
15. proceed, exceed, succeed
16. democracy, epidemic, demography
17. carnivore, voracious, herbivore
18. biology, zoology, anthropology

ACTIVITY F Choose four of the word groups from Activity E and use a dictionary to find two additional words with the same root words.

ACTIVITY G Choose two different word groups from Activity E. Write a sentence for each word.

APPLY

WRITER'S CORNER

Ask students to continue working with their partners to complete the Writer's Corner. Encourage students to add at least six more examples to the chart. Students should demonstrate an understanding of roots of words.

ASSESS

Note which students had difficulty identifying and defining roots. Use the Reteach option with those students who need additional reinforcement.

Practice Book page 146 provides additional work with roots.

Reteach

Ask each student to find and list four words that come from the same root. Ask students to share their words. Have volunteers find the roots.

A Roman Challenge

Remind students that the ancient Romans spoke Latin. Explain that some English words are based on Latin roots linked to the names of figures in Roman mythology. Write these words on the board with the name of the mythological figure in parentheses:

volcano (Vulcan)

cereal (Ceres)

plutonium (Pluto)

insomnia (Somnus)

martial (Mars)

Have students choose a word, define it, and research the story of the figure whose name is related to the word. Ask volunteers to share their findings with the class.

ACTIVITY H Add roots, examples, and meanings to complete the following chart. Use a dictionary if necessary.

	Root	Meaning	Example	Meaning
1.	aud	hear	audible	able to be heard
2.	ven	come	convene	assemble
3.	port	carry	transport	carry across
4.	rupt	break	erupt	break out
5.	pater	father	paternity	fatherhood
6.	multi	many	multicolored	having many colors
7.	lit, liter	letters	literature	writing
8.	hydr	water	hydrant	water faucet
9.	ann	year	anniversary	yearly recurring date
10.	mar	sea	marine	of the sea
11.	lat	side	quadrilateral	four-sided
12.	cred	believe	credible	believable
13.	bio	life	biography	story of someone's life
14.	cardi	heart	cardiology	science of the heart
15.	spec	look	spectator	observer to an event
16.	neo	new	neonate	a newborn baby
17.	mut	change	mutate	to undergo change
18.	mort	death	immortal	living forever
19.	mot	move	motivate	move someone to act
20.	pan	all	panorama	all-around view

ACTIVITY I Use a dictionary to find five roots that did not appear in Activities A–H. Define each root and think of at least two examples of words with the root.

WRITER'S CORNER

Work with a partner to expand the chart above by adding other examples of words with the same roots. Define the words you add. Keep in mind the meaning of the words and use as many as you can in your writing.

For Tomorrow

Ask students to use the model on page 261 to find words with roots in other languages. Have students write the word, its definition, and the definition of its root. Challenge students to predict the meanings before looking up each word in a dictionary. Find several words from the model to share with the class tomorrow.

OBJECTIVES

- **To examine dictionary entries and pronunciation keys**
- **To understand online dictionaries**

WARM-UP

Read, Listen, Speak

Write on the board the roots you found from yesterday's For Tomorrow activity. Discuss the definition of each word. Ask small groups to compare the lists they completed for homework. Ask students to compile a complete list of the words, their definitions, the roots within each word, and the meanings of each root. Then as a class compare group lists for accuracy.

GRAMMAR CONNECTION

Take this opportunity to talk about indefinite pronouns. You may wish to have students point out indefinite pronouns in their Read, Listen, Speak examples.

TEACH

Invite a volunteer to read aloud the first paragraph. Explain that some dictionaries have pairs of guide words (listing the first and last word on the page) and some only have one guide word (listing the first word on the page). Discuss the ways dictionaries have been useful as students work on Chapter 2.

Have another student read aloud the section Examining an Entry. Ask volunteers to identify and explain each part of the entry for *wheeze*. Allow time for students to look up *wheeze* in a dictionary. Have students answer the questions at the end of the section.

Have a volunteer read aloud the section Pronunciation. Discuss any questions students have about the pronunciation key. Ask volunteers to locate the pronunciation key in a dictionary. Encourage students to refer to the pronunciation symbols of a word and the pronunciation key at the beginning of a dictionary or at the bottom of the page whenever they have difficulty pronouncing a word.

PRACTICE

ACTIVITY A

Invite students to work in pairs to complete this activity. When they have finished, ask volunteers to share their answers. Then ask students to use each word in a sentence and to write it on the board.

Dictionary

A dictionary, whether online or in book form, is one of a writer's most valuable tools. It contains an alphabetical list of words, with information for each word, usually including meaning, pronunciation, etymology, and more. To help writers find words more quickly in paper dictionaries, letter tabs and guide words are often included. Letter tabs are located on the sides of the page. They help the writer turn directly to the first letter of the word in question. Guide words are found at the top of the page and usually are the first and last entry words on that page.

Examining an Entry

Below is a sample entry of the word *wheeze*. The key on the right identifies each part of the entry. While most dictionaries will have this information, its order sometimes varies. Some dictionaries may have other information such as synonyms or variant spellings. Find each part of the entry listed in the key below. Then look up the word in a classroom dictionary. Does it include all these parts? Can you find any others?

<table>
<tr><td>

A   B   C   D
wheeze (hwēz, wēz) *v.* **wheezed, wheez•ing.** To breathe with
                            E
difficulty, emitting a whistling sound: *The old man wheezed*
when he climbed the stairs. n. **1.** A sound of wheezing.
2. *Informal* An old joke or trite saying. [Middle English,
        G
whesen] **wheez´er** *n.* **wheez´i•ly** *adv.* **wheez´i•ness** *n.*
                              F
wheez´y *adj.*

</td><td>

A. Syllabication
B. Pronunciation
C. Part of speech
D. Word definition
E. Sample usage
F. Etymology
G. Other forms

</td></tr>
</table>

APPLY

WRITER'S CORNER

Have volunteers write their sentences on the board. Explain that it is important to try to expand their vocabulary. Tell students that learning roots and how dictionaries function will aid in expanding vocabulary. Then challenge students to use the new words in their daily writing. Students should demonstrate an understanding of dictionary entries.

TechTip You may wish to have students post their sentences from the Writer's Corner on a class blog. Have students exchange sentences using the blog, rather than paper and pencil.

ASSESS

Note which students had difficulty understanding entries in dictionaries. Use the Reteach option with those students who need additional reinforcement.

TEACHING OPTIONS

Reteach

Ask students to list on a note card the parts of a dictionary entry. Then invite students to do a library dictionary search. Give students a word and ask them to look it up in the different dictionaries in the school library. Instruct students to use their list to identify the parts of each entry. Have students also note how the entries differ among the dictionaries. If some entries are missing parts that are listed on students' cards, ask students to explain how this affects a correct understanding of the word's meaning, pronunciation, or etymology.

English-Language Learners

Invite students to name five words that they can use in everyday conversation that would "wow" their classmates. Then have students write a personal dictionary for these five words. Encourage students to create their own definitions for these words instead of using a dictionary. Have students review the parts of a dictionary entry. Encourage volunteers to share some of their words with the class.

For Tomorrow

Challenge students to create an original word and to write a dictionary entry for their word. Explain that the entry should include all the parts as in the sample in this lesson. Make up your own original word and create a dictionary entry to share with students.

Pronunciation

Pronunciations are an important part of a dictionary entry. To read the pronunciation symbols, use the pronunciation key, usually found at the beginning of a dictionary. Short keys are frequently given at the bottom of every other page as well.

a	cat	ō	go	ʉ	fur	ə	a *in* ago
ā	ape	ô	fall, for	ch	chin		e *in* agent
ä	cot, car	oo	look	sh	she		i *in* pencil
e	ten	ōō	tool	th	thin		o *in* atom
ē	me	oi	oil	*th*	then		u *in* circus
i	fit	ou	out	zh	measure		
ī	ice	u	up	ŋ	ring		

ACTIVITY A Look up the following words in a dictionary and answer these questions for each word.

splendid   cosmetic   forward   occlude   chamois

1. How is this word pronounced?
2. How many parts of speech does the word have? What are they?
3. How many definitions are there for each part of speech?
4. What are the other forms of the word if any?
5. What root does the word contain? What is the meaning of the root?
6. From what language or languages does the root word come?

WRITER'S CORNER

Turn to any three pages in a dictionary and choose an unfamiliar word from each page. Read the definition and write a sentence using each of those words. Then switch papers with a partner. Look up your partner's words in a dictionary. Then choose three different words from those pages. Write a sentence using each new word.

Tech Tip Post and switch sentences, using a class blog or wiki.

How-to Articles • 279

WARM-UP

Read, Listen, Speak

Share your original word from yesterday's For Tomorrow activity. Challenge students to guess the meaning of the word. Then discuss the dictionary entry, explaining each part.

Ask volunteers to write on the board their original words and pronunciation symbols. Challenge students to guess the meanings of the words. Then invite volunteers to use the pronunciation symbols to pronounce the words correctly.

GRAMMAR CONNECTION

Take this opportunity to talk about agreement with indefinite pronouns. You may wish to have students point out agreement with indefinite pronouns in their Read, Listen, Speak examples.

TEACH

Ask a volunteer to read aloud the section Online Dictionaries. Allow time for students to read the sample online entry. Invite volunteers to describe online dictionaries with which they are familiar. If a computer is available, conduct a search of online dictionaries as a class.

PRACTICE

ACTIVITIES B & C

Ask students to work independently to complete these activities. Invite volunteers to share their answers. Challenge volunteers to offer more words for which students can research etymologies.

ACTIVITY D

Elicit answers for this activity by leading a class discussion about the entry for *wheeze*.

ACTIVITIES E & F

Allow students time to write answers to the questions. Invite volunteers to share their answers. Discuss any discrepancies that may arise. Then ask volunteers to write on the board sentences that use *forte* and *license*.

ACTIVITY B Look up the etymologies of the following words. What is the original meaning of the word, and from what language does each word come?

theory   meander   shadow   denouement   occupy

ACTIVITY C Use each word from Activity B in a sentence that accurately illustrates one of its meanings.

Online Dictionaries

Online dictionaries don't need aids such as tabs and guide words because the computer finds the word for you. You only need to have some idea of how the word is spelled when you type it into the search window. If you misspell a word, the online dictionary site will usually provide you with possible alternatives, based on the spelling you provided.

Online dictionaries may have an audio feature that will allow you to listen to a pronunciation of the word in question. Often they provide links to other resources such as a thesaurus, an encyclopedia, or other dictionaries.

Merriam-Webster's Online Dictionary

wheeze
2 entries found.

¹ wheeze (intransitive verb)
² wheeze (noun)

Main Entry: ¹**wheeze** 🔊)
Pronunciation: \'hwēz, 'wēz\
Function: *intransitive verb*
Inflected Form(s): **wheezed; wheez·ing**
Etymology: Middle English *whesen*, probably of Scandinavian origin; akin to Old Norse *hvæsa* to hiss; akin to Old English *hwǣst* action of blowing, Sanskrit *śvasiti* he blows, snorts
Date: 15th century
1 : to breathe with difficulty usually with a whistling sound
2 : to make a sound resembling that of __wheezing__ <the bellows *wheezed*>

APPLY

WRITER'S CORNER

Allow time for students to complete this activity. Invite volunteers to write their sentences on the board. If words have multiple definitions, challenge students to write additional sentences that use other definitions. Students should demonstrate an understanding of dictionary entries.

TechTip You may wish to have students use an online dictionary to complete any activity on this page. Have students suggest online dictionaries with which they are familiar.

ASSESS

Note which students had difficulty understanding online dictionaries. Use the Reteach option with those students who need additional reinforcement.

Practice Book page 147 provides additional work with using a dictionary.

TEACHING OPTIONS

Reteach

Have students look up the words in Activity B, using an online dictionary, preferably one that provides audio pronunciations. If they are able, have students print out an entry and label the parts, using the sample dictionary entry on page 278. Reinforce the idea that online entries contain the same or similar information as paper entries, but in a slightly different format.

My Name in Symbols

Have small groups examine the pronunciation keys in classroom dictionaries. Challenge students to write their names on note cards, using symbols from a pronunciation key. Assign a student in each group to shuffle the cards and redistribute them. Have students determine which name the symbols represent and give that student his or her note card.

ACTIVITY D Answer the questions about the entry for *wheeze* and about the online dictionary page that *wheeze* is on.

1. When *wheeze* functions as a verb in a sentence, what kind of verb is it?
2. Where would you click on the page to find the definition of the noun form of *wheeze*?
3. Where would you click to hear the pronunciation of the word?
4. What is the difference between the two pronunciations of *wheeze*?
5. From what languages does *wheeze* originate? What languages have words that are akin to *wheeze*?

ACTIVITY E Use an online dictionary to answer the following questions about the word *forte*.

1. As what parts of speech can *forte* function?
2. How many pronunciations does *forte* have?
3. What is the origin of the noun form of *forte*?
4. When *forte* means "part of a sword or foil blade," how many syllables does it have?
5. What is the meaning of the adjective form of *forte*?
6. How many different definitions does *forte* have as a noun?
7. As an adjective, on which syllable is *forte* accented?

ACTIVITY F Use an online dictionary to answer the following questions about the word *license*.

1. As what parts of speech can *license* function?
2. How many variant spellings does *license* have?
3. What is the origin of the noun form of *license*?
4. Write two sentences using different forms of the word *license*.

WRITER'S CORNER

Look through an article in a newspaper or magazine. Find five words about whose meaning you are uncertain. Use a dictionary to check the words. Then write each word in a sentence.

 Tech Tip Use an online dictionary to check unfamiliar words.

How-to Articles • 281

For Tomorrow

Ask students to write a few ideas for tools that could be included in future online dictionaries to make the dictionaries more sophisticated and user-friendly. Encourage students to be creative. Write your own ideas about future online dictionaries and bring them to class to share with students.

OBJECTIVES

- To understand the characteristics of a how-to talk
- To prepare and present a how-to talk
- To practice valuable speaking and listening skills

WARM-UP

Read, Listen, Speak

Share your ideas about future online dictionaries from yesterday's homework. Determine if any of your ideas were also suggested by students.

Have a volunteer record on the board all the students' ideas for improving future online dictionaries. Encourage students to discuss the pros and cons of each idea. You may want to have students vote on the top three ideas.

GRAMMAR CONNECTION

Take this opportunity to review pronouns. You may wish to have students point out pronouns in their Read, Listen, Speak examples.

TEACH

Ask a volunteer to read aloud the first paragraph. Encourage students to share examples of how-to talks *(a cooking show, a craft or arts class)*. Invite another volunteer to read aloud the section Identify Your Audience. Ask students to identify the audiences of the examples of how-to talks discussed earlier in the lesson.

Have students silently read the sections Introduce Your Topic and Explain the Steps. Ask the class to name some visual aids for how-to talks. Read aloud the Sum Up section and discuss the ways in which how-to talks and how-to articles are similar and how they are different. As a class, create a Venn diagram to record these similarities and differences.

PRACTICE

ACTIVITY A

Have partners discuss the topics and write their ideas. When they have finished, ask each pair to present their ideas for a how-to talk to the class. Encourage students to provide feedback about the visual aids each pair chose to use for each topic.

ACTIVITY B

Allow time for students to write their steps. Then have students present and evaluate their how-to talks with their partners.

How-to Talks

In many ways telling people how to do something is easier than writing instructions, especially if you can demonstrate as you speak. It is much easier, for example, to show someone how to change a bike tire than it is to write instructions for changing a bike tire. Just as in written instructions, you have to be clear, concise, and logical. Here are some guidelines for a successful how-to talk.

Identify Your Audience

Will you have an audience of your peers? Will your audience be expert in the topic or know little about it? You must know the answers to questions like these before you can tailor your talk to your audience.

Introduce Your Topic

Identify the topic of your how-to talk for the audience immediately. Then tell them why the topic is worth their attention. How will the audience benefit?

Explain the Steps

Use visual aids to support your how-to talk. Ideally, you would demonstrate the activity, but this is not always possible. Showing how to fold napkins is easy, but showing how to discourage a bully isn't easy. If you are able to demonstrate the task, make sure everyone can see what you are doing at every step of the way.

If you can't give a demonstration, you could use a diagram, drawing, PowerPoint graphics, poster, or other visual aid. It will help your audience visualize the steps. In a PowerPoint presentation, you can use bulleted lists for any supplies needed, a series of slides to demonstrate different steps, diagrams detailing the order of steps, and clip art or photos as additional visual aids.

Be sure the steps in accomplishing the goal you set out are in chronological order.

APPLY

SPEAKER'S CORNER

Ask partners to practice their how-to talks. Remind presenters to add interesting comments to sum up their talks. Remind listeners to give constructive feedback. Invite volunteers to present their talks to the entire class. Students should demonstrate an understanding of the characteristics of a how-to talk.

 TechTip You may wish to have students incorporate a PowerPoint presentation as part of their how-to talk. Discuss how using this type of software can benefit a how-to talk.

ASSESS

Note which students had difficulty presenting a how-to talk. Use the Reteach option with those students who need additional reinforcement.

TEACHING OPTIONS

Reteach

Make a photocopy or drawing of each figure below. Give one drawing to each of three volunteers. Have the volunteers take turns giving directions for reproducing the drawing to small groups. Ask students to check their speaking and listening skills by comparing the completed drawings with the originals. If the drawings do not match the originals, discuss whether the directions were clear.

Meeting Individual Needs

Visual Have students brainstorm possible topics for a how-to talk. List these on the board. Ask students to think of possible visual aids for each topic that would not be practical to bring to class (such as a car for a topic on changing the oil). Instruct students to create a list of practical visual aids for each topic. Invite volunteers to share their lists. Discuss each visual aid, pointing out why each would work as a substitute for the impractical visual aid.

Sum Up

Avoid ending your talk with a flat statement such as "It's finished" or "That's all." Instead, remind your audience briefly of what you accomplished ("Look at the lovely basket we just made together") and how you did it ("We used bent willow branches and twine and didn't spend a cent").

ACTIVITY A Read the topics below and decide who would benefit from the following talks. What type of visual aids would you use?

1. Build a Picnic Table
2. How to Send a Text Message
3. Become a Hackey Sack Champ in Three Easy Lessons
4. How to Protect Your Computer from Viruses
5. Manage Your Time So You Have More Leisure
6. Give a Party Everyone Will Love
7. Rock Climbing
8. Steps to Keeping Computer Time Under Control
9. Quick and Easy No-Bake Recipes

ACTIVITY B Choose a title from Activity A. Choose an appropriate audience for a how-to talk on your chosen topic. Then write notes that include the steps for your talk. Present your talk to a partner, describing the visual aids you would use. Take notes on the improvements your partner suggested and save your notes for later.

SPEAKER'S CORNER

Present a talk on the how-to article you completed in the Writer's Corner on page 273. Even though your demonstration may be as simple as how to tie a shoe, make sure to break down your explanation into understandable, chronological steps. To prepare, write notes to remind yourself of your introduction and the necessary steps.

Tech Tip Make a PowerPoint presentation.

How-to Articles • 283

For Tomorrow

Ask students to watch a how-to TV program such as a cooking or home-improvement show. Have students write whether it included the characteristics of a how-to talk discussed in this lesson. Write your own critique of a how-to show based on the characteristics of a how-to talk.

WARM-UP

Read, Listen, Speak

Discuss the how-to program that you watched for yesterday's For Tomorrow homework. Point out how the program compared to the characteristics of a how-to talk.

Instruct small groups to discuss the how-to programs that students watched for homework. Ask students to share notes and to describe the characteristics of a how-to talk that were part of these shows. Make sure students point out ways the program could have been more clear for the audience.

TEACH

Ask volunteers to read aloud the sections Preparing Your Notes and Preparing Your Visual Aids. Refer to the student model on page 261. Invite students to describe what visual aids might assist in presenting a how-to talk on making maple syrup.

Have another volunteer read aloud the section Practice. Instruct students to copy the questions in this section into a notebook and to refer to them when practicing their own how-to talks.

Ask a student to read aloud the section Present. Have volunteers offer ideas for effectively presenting a talk about making maple syrup. Then have a volunteer read aloud the section Listening Tips. Encourage students to practice these tips when they listen to their classmates' how-to talks.

LiNK Have students read the "Magic Card Trick" excerpt. Bring in two decks of cards. Have two volunteers demonstrate the steps for this how-to article. Point out the detail used in each step, and how clear and concise the article is.

PRACTICE

ACTIVITY C

Have pairs of students complete this activity. Ask volunteers to share their comments about the notes and the visual aids they recommend to support the talk. Encourage students to use the notes at home to teach a parent or other adult how to make a fried peanut butter and banana sandwich.

APPLY

SPEAKER'S CORNER

Ask students to practice with small groups the how-to talks

Preparing Your Notes

Creating a set of prepared notes on note cards can help you present your how-to talk smoothly and clearly. When you prepare your notes, you might begin by listing the steps, numbering them in order from start to finish. When you have finished, review your steps, making sure you have them in the correct order.

Preparing Your Visual Aids

Presenting your visual aids clearly is just as important as speaking clearly. If you are presenting a diagram or flowchart, be sure it is large enough and placed in a position where everyone can see it. If you are demonstrating an action, make sure everyone will have a clear view. You don't want to demonstrate how to tie a shoe from the floor. If you're demonstrating how to fold a napkin, you may need to walk around the room to make sure everyone can see the napkin.

Practice

To make sure your talk goes smoothly, it will be helpful to practice it a few times. Practicing will help you be certain that you have all the materials you need and that the steps you describe will produce the goal you intend. As you practice, keep these questions in mind:

- Have I tailored my talk to my audience?
- Do I introduce my topic immediately?
- Am I speaking at a volume and pace so everyone can hear and understand me?
- Are all the steps in the right order?
- Have I eliminated all unnecessary steps?
- Do I present the visual aids clearly?
- Does my conclusion sum up what I explained?

Present

When you present your how-to talk, respond to your audience. If they are straining to hear you, speak more loudly and clearly. If they struggle to see your visual aid, raise it up or pass it around the room. If they seem bored, vary your pitch and pass quickly over steps that may be obvious. If your audience seems confused, repeat difficult steps or explain them in a different way. You can also point out common mistakes made in your activity. Stop occasionally to answer questions. In a how-to talk, understanding is the key.

they wrote for the previous Speaker's Corner. Suggest that students use items in the room for visual aids and use the questions they copied from the Practice section to improve their talks. Have volunteers present their how-to talks to the class. Students should demonstrate an understanding of the characteristics of a how-to talk.

TechTip You may wish to record students' presentations, using a webcam. Then post these on the class blog. Have students watch their own how-to talks and list ways to improve future talks.

ASSESS

Note which students had difficulty practicing and presenting a how-to talk. Use the Reteach option with those students who need additional reinforcement.

After you have reviewed Lessons 3–5, administer the Writing Skills assessment on pages 49–50 in the **Assessment Book.** This test is also available on the optional **Test Generator CD.**

TEACHING OPTIONS

Reteach

Have students work together to compile an evaluation checklist to use when practicing a how-to talk. Instruct them to get ideas from this lesson. Tell students to be sure to address all the points of a how-to talk: identifying an audience, explaining steps, summing up, using visuals, preparing notes, practicing, and presenting. You might also ask students to use the evaluation checklist to practice and give once again the how-to talk they presented for the Speaker's Corner.

Learning to Listen

Remind students that using good manners shows respect for others and helps oral presentations run smoothly. Encourage students to formulate rules for listeners to follow when classmates are presenting a how-to talk or other oral presentation. Select a student to write the rules on chart paper for display. Then ask students how they might creatively enforce the rules by using silent reminders with their classmates.

Listening Tips

In any presentation the listener's role is just as important as the speaker's role. Follow these steps when listening to a how-to talk:

- Closely watch what the speaker is doing and listen carefully. If you miss a step, you may not understand what the speaker is explaining or demonstrating.
- Do not interrupt the speaker. If you are confused by a step, raise your hand or wait for the speaker to ask for questions.
- Give the speaker the same kind of attention and feedback that you would appreciate.

ACTIVITY C Evaluate the following notes for a how-to talk. Identify any unnecessary, omitted, or out-of-order steps. Then consider a visual aid. What would you use? When would you use it?

Fried Peanut Butter and Banana Sandwich

1. Assemble ingredients/equipment
   bread, peanut butter, bananas
   frying pan

2. Make sandwich
   Spread peanut butter on two pieces of bread
   Put bananas on one piece
   Slice bananas

3. Cook sandwich
   Put sandwich in pan
   Smell the delicious scent of browning butter
   When golden brown, turn over
   When the second side is cooked, the sandwich is done

4. Eat sandwich
   Great with applesauce
   Great with a big glass of milk
   Some people prefer chocolate milk

LiNK

Magic Card Trick

(continued from page 276)

8. Now, recap—in any "You Do As I Do" trick, it's best to review what has happened: "We both shuffled our cards thoroughly. Then, we both removed a card and placed it on the top of our own deck. We then each cut our pack of cards. All the same steps, right? Next, we switched packs and looked for our chosen card and placed it face-down on the table. Since you did exactly as I did, we should have the same card, right? Let's see . . . !"

9. Ask your friend to turn over both cards and they match.

The Magnificent Montie

SPEAKER'S CORNER

Improve the how-to talk you presented for the Speaker's Corner on page 283. Use the tips you learned in this lesson. Note whether your audience's response improves.

 Tech Tip Record a podcast of your presentation.

How-to Articles • 285

PREWRITING AND DRAFTING

Comment on what students have learned about how-to articles:

• planning the introduction, body, and conclusion
• using the imperative voice
• using the How-to Article Checklist
• writing clear and concise instructions
• avoiding run-on and rambling sentences and making every word count
• using a tone appropriate for the audience

Tell students that now they will progress through the writing process to compose a how-to article to publish.

Review the steps of the writing process that students learned in the Writer's Workshop in Chapter 1. Ask volunteers to write the steps on the board (*prewriting, drafting, content editing, revising, copyediting, proofreading, publishing*). Then ask students to explain each stage of the writing process.

Ask a volunteer to read aloud the first two paragraphs.

Prewriting

Ask a volunteer to read aloud this section. Remind students that the objective of prewriting is to get all of the writer's ideas on paper. Invite students to share brainstorming techniques that work well for them.

Choosing a Topic

Have a student read aloud the section Choosing a Topic. Stress that students should choose a topic with which they are familiar for their how-to articles.

Encourage students to look through work saved from previous brainstorming and freewriting sessions.

Remind students that they should choose ideas and details that are interesting and informative. Explain that students can still write how to do an everyday task, but that the details included should shine new light on the task.

Planning the Article

Ask a volunteer to read aloud the first paragraph of this section. Discuss the steps Miguel followed to complete his sequence chart. Point out that Miguel did not use complete sentences in his chart.

Tell students that organization is the way writers put together and arrange their ideas. Remind students to use chronological order in a how-to article.

Your Turn

Allow time for students to brainstorm topics. Tell students to write every possible topic that

---

Prewriting and Drafting

Teaching someone how to do something is one of the most basic functions of writing. Often the only way to learn how to do something new is to have someone teach us how. Through writing we can teach others about games and sports, arts and crafts, and all kinds of other activities. You have practiced aspects of how-to writing throughout this chapter. Now you can use what you have learned as you share your skills and knowledge in a how-to article.

Before you prepare your how-to article, choose a topic that's just right for you and plan your article so that readers will understand the steps.

Prewriting

Prewriting is the time to choose your topic, to decide what you want to say about it, and to organize the way that you will present your ideas. For how-to articles, you brainstorm to determine what topic you know enough about to teach to someone else. Then you review the steps in the process, making certain that nothing is left out. Finally, you organize your notes to make sure the steps are in the proper sequence.

Choosing a Topic

Nearly everyone is an expert at something, whether it's constructing a model of the Taj Mahal out of sugar cubes or training a puppy to roll over. If you select a topic **Ideas** for your how-to article that you know well and genuinely care about, writing it will be fun, not a chore.

Planning the Article

Miguel, an eighth grader, has trained his dog Lobo to perform tricks. He has decided the topic of his how-to article will be how to teach a dog to wave. To help him visualize the steps in order, he used a sequence chart like this one.

Teaching Your Dog to Wave
Need: dog treats

- Tell dog to sit, then pick up dog's paw.
- Say "give paw."
- Repeat, and give treats, praise, each time.
- Second Session: Say "give paw" while putting out hand.
- When dog puts paw in hand, give praise and a treat.
- Tell dog "sit" then say "give paw wave."
- Hold out your hand higher so dog must lift his paw up higher too.
- Praise him for trying, but don't grab his paw.
- Repeat, saying just "wave."

comes to mind. Then provide students with time to choose which topic would work best for their how-to article. After students have chosen their topics, ask volunteers to share their method of choosing. Have a volunteer finish reading the Planning the Article section. Then have students read through Miguel's list of steps for teaching a dog to wave. Challenge volunteers to suggest possible revisions to improve Miguel's steps. Ask students what questions they should keep in mind when writing a list of steps. *(Are the steps in the right order? Are all the important steps included? Is there any unnecessary information?)*

Your Turn

Invite a volunteer to read aloud this section. Then have students write the steps for their topic in a sequence chart similar to Miguel's example. For topics that require many steps, tell students to consider grouping related steps to make them easier to understand. When students have finished, have them read over their lists and pretend to walk through, each step. Then have partners evaluate the order and grouping of one another's steps. Encourage partners to share comments and to provide constructive feedback. Have students save their work for the next class.

TEACHING OPTIONS

Teaching Tip

Some students may benefit from rereading the model of a how-to article on page 260. Use the model to review the characteristics of a how-to article.

Talking It Out

If students have trouble breaking their topic into steps, have them talk with a partner, explain their chosen topic, and ask for suggestions on how to proceed. Tell students to write notes while listening to their partner's suggestions. Encourage students to use these notes while drafting or revising their steps.

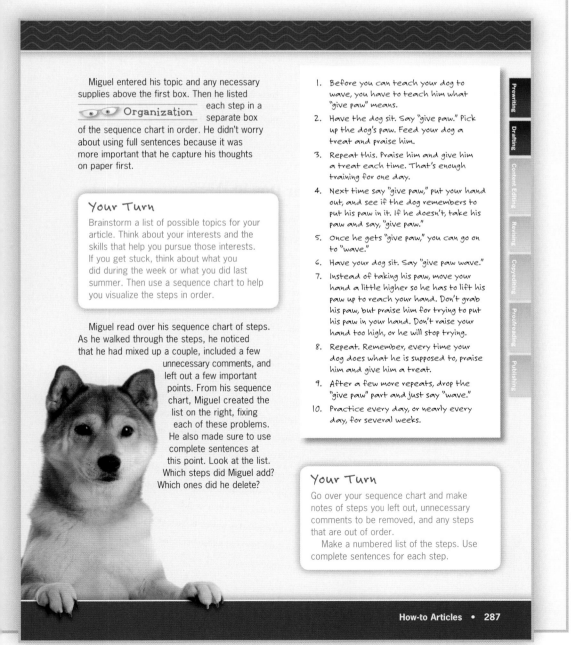

Miguel entered his topic and any necessary supplies above the first box. Then he listed

👁👁 Organization

each step in a separate box of the sequence chart in order. He didn't worry about using full sentences because it was more important that he capture his thoughts on paper first.

Your Turn

Brainstorm a list of possible topics for your article. Think about your interests and the skills that help you pursue those interests. If you get stuck, think about what you did during the week or what you did last summer. Then use a sequence chart to help you visualize the steps in order.

Miguel read over his sequence chart of steps. As he walked through the steps, he noticed that he had mixed up a couple, included a few unnecessary comments, and left out a few important points. From his sequence chart, Miguel created the list on the right, fixing each of these problems. He also made sure to use complete sentences at this point. Look at the list. Which steps did Miguel add? Which ones did he delete?

1. Before you can teach your dog to wave, you have to teach him what "give paw" means.

2. Have the dog sit. Say "give paw." Pick up the dog's paw. Feed your dog a treat and praise him.

3. Repeat this. Praise him and give him a treat each time. That's enough training for one day.

4. Next time say "give paw," put your hand out, and see if the dog remembers to put his paw in it. If he doesn't, take his paw and say, "give paw."

5. Once he gets "give paw," you can go on to "wave."

6. Have your dog sit. Say "give paw wave."

7. Instead of taking his paw, move your hand a little higher so he has to lift his paw up to reach your hand. Don't grab his paw, but praise him for trying to put his paw in your hand. Don't raise your hand too high, or he will stop trying.

8. Repeat. Remember, every time your dog does what he is supposed to, praise him and give him a treat.

9. After a few more repeats, drop the "give paw" part and just say "wave."

10. Practice every day, or nearly every day, for several weeks.

Prewriting
Drafting
Content Editing
Revising
Copyediting
Proofreading
Publishing

Your Turn

Go over your sequence chart and make notes of steps you left out, unnecessary comments to be removed, and any steps that are out of order.

Make a numbered list of the steps. Use complete sentences for each step.

How-to Articles • 287

Drafting

Read the paragraph above Miguel's article to the class. Explain that when drafting a how-to article, students should build from each step in their prewriting notes. Then have students read Miguel's how-to article silently.

After students have finished reading, encourage them to discuss Miguel's draft. First ask what Miguel did after writing the body of his article (write the introduction and conclusion). Have students refer to the How-to Article Checklist on page 264. Invite students to look back at Miguel's prewriting notes and to analyze how he transferred the notes into sentence and paragraph form. Then challenge students to point out places in the draft that Miguel expanded from his prewriting notes. Use the following questions to spark discussion:

• Is the introduction engaging?
• Are all the steps in the body necessary and in logical order?
• Is the tone appropriate for the audience?
• Did Miguel offer any extra information or troubleshooting tips throughout the article?
• Is the conclusion effective and interesting?

Discuss what Miguel did well and what ways he might improve his draft. Encourage students to write their ideas to compare with Luis's in the content editing lesson tomorrow.

Title, Introduction, and Conclusion

Have students read this section silently. Encourage volunteers to name some of their favorite titles, introductions, or conclusions from the how-to articles they have read. Ask students to explain why they liked these characteristics. Suggest that students reread their drafts to find opportunities to improve these characteristics. Then have each student trade papers with a partner to discuss whether their classmate's title, introduction, and conclusion could be more engaging.

Drafting

Miguel felt confident because he took the time to develop and organize his prewriting notes into a coherent how-to article. He revised the steps involved in teaching a dog to wave, and now he knew they worked. Read the draft of Miguel's article. After writing the body of the article first, what did Miguel add next?

Teaching Your Dog to Wave

It's not hard to teach your dog to wave, and it's a pretty nice trick. As with all dog tricks, praise your dog every time he responds correctly and give him a treat every time, or at least most of the time. Is your dog's attention starting to wander? Stop the training session. Begin again when he is rested.

Before you can teach your dog to wave you have to teach the command "Give paw." Have the dog sit. Say, "Give paw." Pick up the dog's paw. Feed your dog a treat and praise him. Repeat this, praising him and giving him a treat each time. That's enough training for one day.

Next time, say, "Give paw," put your hand out, and see whether the dog remembers to put his paw in it. If he doesnt, take his paw and say "Give paw."

Once he obeys "Give paw," you can go on to "Wave. Say, "Give paw wave." Instead of taking his paw, move your hand a little higher so he has to lift his paw up to reach your hand. Don't grab his paw, but praise him for trying to put his paw in your hand. Don't raise your hand too high, or he will stop trying. Repeat. Remember, every time your dog does what he is supposed to, praise him and give him a treat. After a few more repeats, you can drop the "Give paw" part of the command and simply say, "Wave." Practice every day, or nearly every day, for several weeks.

Doesn't your dog look nice when he waves? He's waving like a rock star to his fans, think of the other tricks you can teach him! Just remember to use only positive praise and treats during training, never punishment!

Writer's Tip Tell students that they should make each step as clear and simple as possible so that readers can easily proceed through the steps. Tell students the clearer the steps are, the more likely the reader will avoid confusion.

Your Turn

Ask a volunteer to read aloud this section. Tell students to look at the steps they wrote during the previous Your Turn. Invite students to list on the board transition words they might use in their articles. Suggest that students refer to the list while writing their drafts.

Allow time for students to compose their drafts. Move around the room to be sure that students are using transition words and including introductions and conclusions. Remind students to save their work for editing during the next class.

TEACHING OPTIONS

English-Language Learners

Have students work cooperatively when drafting their how-to articles. After students have written the first draft, ask them to circle the transition words on their drafts. Instruct students to check whether they have used each transition word correctly.

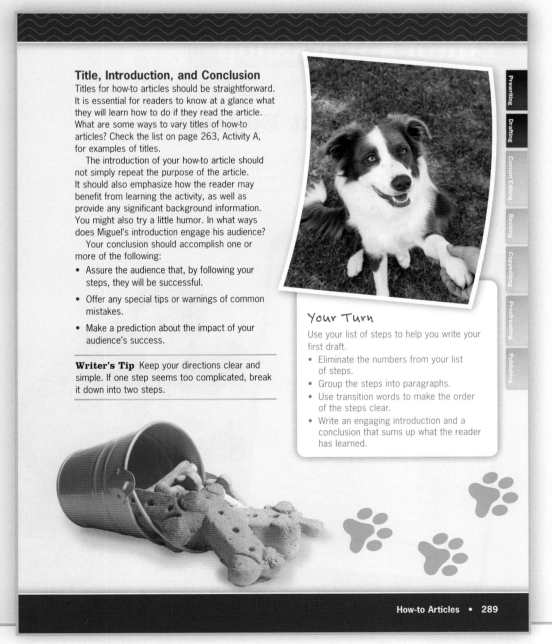

Title, Introduction, and Conclusion

Titles for how-to articles should be straightforward. It is essential for readers to know at a glance what they will learn how to do if they read the article. What are some ways to vary titles of how-to articles? Check the list on page 263, Activity A, for examples of titles.

The introduction of your how-to article should not simply repeat the purpose of the article. It should also emphasize how the reader may benefit from learning the activity, as well as provide any significant background information. You might also try a little humor. In what ways does Miguel's introduction engage his audience?

Your conclusion should accomplish one or more of the following:

- Assure the audience that, by following your steps, they will be successful.

- Offer any special tips or warnings of common mistakes.

- Make a prediction about the impact of your audience's success.

Writer's Tip Keep your directions clear and simple. If one step seems too complicated, break it down into two steps.

Your Turn

Use your list of steps to help you write your first draft.

- Eliminate the numbers from your list of steps.
- Group the steps into paragraphs.
- Use transition words to make the order of the steps clear.
- Write an engaging introduction and a conclusion that sums up what the reader has learned.

Prewriting
Drafting
Content Editing
Revising
Copyediting
Proofreading
Publishing

How-to Articles • 289

OBJECTIVE

• **To edit a first draft for content**

CONTENT EDITING

Remind students that a first draft is not meant to be perfect. Ask volunteers to share any difficulties they may have encountered when writing their drafts. Then have a volunteer read aloud the first paragraph. Discuss what a content editor's job is *(to look at logic, order, and clarity of ideas)*.

Direct students' attention to the Content Editor's Checklist. Challenge students to discuss each point on the checklist and to offer additional items to add to the checklist.

👀 Emphasize that sentence fluency, or the sound of the writing, is important. Suggest that students read their articles aloud to hear where the writing might sound awkward or choppy.

Have a student read aloud the first and second paragraphs on page 291. Then discuss why it is important to have someone else content edit a how-to article *(to learn which part of a draft might be difficult for a reader to understand)*. Have students recall how having a classmate edit their writing benefited them in the Writer's Workshop in Chapter 1.

Editor's Workshop   How-to Articles

Content Editing

The content editor reads the draft of a how-to article to see if all the steps have been included and are in the right order. The content editor also checks whether the individual steps are clear. Use the checklist below when editing a how-to article for content.

Content Editor's Checklist

☐ Does the title explain clearly what the reader will learn how to do?

☐ Does the introduction explain how the reader will benefit from reading the article?

☐ Are the steps in the process clear and easy to follow? Are they in chronological order?

☐ Is every important step included? Is every step that is included necessary?

☐ Do the steps that need explanations have them?

☐ Does the conclusion sum up the article? Does it invite readers to enjoy or use what they've learned to do? Does it offer tips or warnings?

☐ Is the tone of the article appropriate for its audience?

Ask volunteers to read aloud the third paragraph and Luis's comments on page 291. Encourage students to compare the ideas they jotted down with Luis's suggestions. Challenge volunteers to offer additional suggestions for revising Miguel's draft, referring to the Content Editor's Checklist. *(Miguel repeats the direction of giving the dog a treat too many times.)*

Your Turn

Invite a student to read aloud this section. Allow time for partners to comment on each other's drafts. Remind students to edit with care and to be clear about the revisions they suggest. Ask students to write their suggestions on a separate sheet of paper rather than writing on their partners' drafts.

Content Editor's Checklist

Encourage students to copy the checklist from page 290 so they can refer to it easily when they edit their own writing and other students'. Point out that a checklist such as this would change when editing other kinds of writing. You might also have the class help you write the checklist on chart paper for all to see.

Ask the Editor

Share with students that writers often know or suspect something is wrong with an aspect of their writing but don't know exactly how to fix it. Encourage students to create a list of possible problems in their drafts. Have students share these lists with their partners before editing.

Miguel read through his draft and used the ~~Sentence Fluency~~ Content Editor's Checklist to help him edit his draft. Then he asked his classmate Luis to read it.

Luis took his job seriously. He read the draft twice straight through. Then he used the Content Editor's Checklist as he read the draft a third time. He jotted down some suggestions, and then he and Miguel went over the draft together.

Luis told Miguel he liked his how-to article and he found it well written and easy to understand. He told Miguel that the tone was a good fit for an audience of his classmates. Luis understood how discouraging it can be to hear criticism, even if it is constructive, without hearing any praise. Then he discussed the body of Miguel's article. Here are his comments.

- The phrase *a pretty nice trick* in the introduction doesn't grab me.
- The second paragraph seems to be missing a step. What happens if the dog does the trick right the first time?
- The third paragraph is unclear. Does *next time* mean the next training session? Should the dog sit before the trainer asks him to *Give paw?*
- I think a step is missing in the third paragraph. Should the trainer repeat *Give paw* to the dog to reinforce the lesson?
- In the fourth paragraph, I didn't understand why the trainer shouldn't raise his hand too high or why the trainer should practice every day.

After their conference, Miguel began thinking about how he could use Luis's suggestions as he wrote his next draft.

Your Turn

Use the Content Editor's Checklist to help you improve your draft. What are some other ways you can improve it? Then trade how-to articles with a classmate. Again using the checklist as a guide, write comments lightly in pencil on your partner's draft. Or jot down comments on a separate sheet of paper.

When you and your partner have finished content editing each other's articles, discuss them. Be sure to start with overall reactions and positive comments. Next, clarify the written comments and corrections you made. Then you will both be ready to revise your drafts.

Prewriting / Drafting / **Content Editing** / Revising / Copyediting / Proofreading / Publishing

OBJECTIVE
- To revise the draft of a how-to article

REVISING

Have a student read aloud the sentence above Miguel's draft. Explain that revising gives the writer an opportunity to add new information, as well as to correct errors and to delete unnecessary information. Then give students time to read silently Miguel's revised draft. When they have finished, ask volunteers to compare Miguel's revisions to Luis's comments on page 291.

👀 Explain that students should use the most appropriate and specific word, but they should also define words with which readers may be unfamiliar.

Encourage volunteers to point out revisions Miguel made based on Luis's comments. Have a volunteer read the bulleted suggestions. Discuss Miguel's revisions with the class.

- He changed *pretty nice* to *show-stealing*.
- He added *Be especially enthusiastic if he begins to give you his paw.*

- Miguel clarified that *next time* means at the next training session. He also explained that the dog should sit before you give the "Give paw" command. In the last sentence in that paragraph, he added a step that he had forgotten.
- He explained why the trainer should not raise his or her hand too high and why the dog and trainer should practice every day for several weeks.
- Point out the additional detail Miguel added in the last paragraph *(like how to speak and bow)*.

Writer's Workshop
How-to Articles

Revising

After hearing Luis's comments, Miguel went to work revising his draft. Take a look at the changes he made below.

Teaching Your Dog to Wave

It's not hard to teach your dog to wave, and it's a ~~pretty nice~~ *show-stealing* trick. ~~As with all dog~~ For this and every trick you train your dog to do, praise him ~~tricks, praise your dog~~ every time he responds correctly and give him a treat ~~every time, or at least most of the time.~~ Is your dog's attention starting to wander? Stop the training session. Begin again when he is rested.

Before you can teach your dog to wave you have to teach the command "Give paw." Have the dog sit. Say "Give paw." Pick up the dog's paw. ~~Feed your dog a treat~~ several times. *Be especially enthusiastic if he begins to give you his paw on his own.* ~~and praise him.~~ Repeat this, *praising him and giving him a treat each time.* ~~That's~~ After a few repetitions, stop the training session for the day. ~~enough training for one day.~~

At the next training session, have the dog sit, ~~Next time,~~ say "Give paw," put your hand out, and see whether the dog to review. Repeat several times. remembers to put his paw in it. If he doesnt, take his paw and say "Give paw."

Once he obeys "Give paw," you can go on to "Wave. Say "Give paw wave." Instead of taking his paw, move your hand a little higher so he has to lift his paw up to reach your hand. Don't grab his paw, but praise him for trying to put his paw in your hand. become discouraged and Don't raise your hand too high, or he will stop trying. Repeat. ~~Remember: every time your dog does what he is supposed to, praise him and give him a treat.~~ After a few more repeats, you can drop the "Give paw" part of the command and simply say to make sure your dog will remember his new trick. "Wave." Practice every day, or nearly every day, for several weeks.

Doesn't your dog look nice when he waves? He's waving like a rock star to his , like how to speak and bow fans, think of ~~the~~ other tricks you can teach him! Just remember to use only positive praise and treats during training, never punishment!

Have a volunteer read aloud the final two paragraphs. Invite students to discuss what other changes they would suggest for Miguel's draft.

Your Turn

Read this section aloud. Allow time for students to consult briefly with their editing partners to clarify comments. Then have students revise their own drafts. Remind students to use the Content Editor's Checklist. Have students save their revised drafts for copyediting and proofreading during the next class.

Writer's Tip Remind students that their audience may not have any knowledge of their topic. Encourage students to provide as much detail as possible, and to be as thorough and clear as they can in each step.

Look at some of the ways Miguel revised "Teaching Your Dog to Wave."

👁👁 Word Choice

- Miguel agreed that *pretty nice* wasn't specific. With what did he replace it?
- He also agreed with Luis that the second paragraph left out what to do if the dog happened to be a quick study. What did Miguel add?
- In what ways did Miguel make the third paragraph clearer?
- What explanations did Miguel add to the fourth paragraph?
- In the last paragraph, Miguel added the name of another trick as an example because he knows that specific details create pictures in readers' minds.

When Miguel revised his draft with the help of the Content Editor's Checklist, he saw that his how-to article repeated the direction of giving the dog a treat too many times. To improve his article, he inserted *For this and every trick you train your dog to do, praise him,* in the second sentence of the first paragraph. He also deleted the repeated reminders in the second and fourth paragraphs.

What are some other changes that Miguel made to his draft? What other changes would you suggest?

Your Turn

Revise your how-to article, using your own ideas and those suggestions of your content-editing partner. After you finish revising, run through the Content Editor's Checklist again. Make sure you remembered all the corrections that you intended to make.

Writer's Tip Do not assume your reader has any prior knowledge or experience with your topic. Explain everything!

(side tabs: Prewriting, Drafting, Content Editing, Revising, Copyediting, Proofreading, Publishing)

How-to Articles • 293

OBJECTIVE
- **To copyedit and proofread a how-to article**

COPYEDITING AND PROOFREADING

Copyediting

Invite a volunteer to read aloud the first paragraph. Discuss the difference between content editing and copyediting. *(Content editing focuses on the ideas expressed. Copyediting involves checking that word choice and sentence structure are accurate.)*

Invite a student to read aloud the Copyeditor's Checklist. Encourage students to offer additions to the checklist. Then have a volunteer read aloud the revisions that Miguel made to some of his sentences. Ask students why it might help to read aloud one's draft when copyediting. *(Reading aloud makes it easier to notice awkward passages in need of revising.)*

Discuss the questions asked in the last paragraph. *(Miguel replaced* nice *with* charming.*)* Then have students list other words Miguel could have used on the board. Ask students to explain the benefit of using exact words and clear phrasing in a how-to article. *(Directions must be written clearly and concisely or the reader might become confused.)*

Your Turn

Ask a volunteer to read aloud this section. Have students work in pairs to read aloud their drafts. Suggest that as one reads, the other makes note of awkward phrases and run-on or rambling sentences. Allow time for students to correct their drafts based on these notes. Encourage students to use a dictionary and thesaurus as they work.

Proofreading

Read aloud the first paragraph. Have students name resources a proofreader can consult when proofreading a piece of writing *(dictionary, list of proofreading marks, grammar textbook).* Review the proofreading marks that students learned in Chapter 1. Challenge volunteers to write on the board any marks they know without looking in the book.

Have a volunteer read aloud the Proofreader's Checklist. Offer students a chance to add to the checklist. Suggest that it is wise for writers to personalize their checklists by adding items for mistakes the writers know they commonly make.

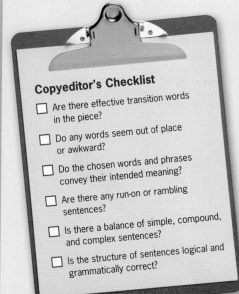

Editor's Workshop How-to Articles

Copyediting and Proofreading

Copyediting

Miguel copyedited his piece to make certain that the sentences were constructed correctly and that the piece flowed logically and coherently. He also read it to make certain that he used words and phrases that were both exact and vivid. He used the following checklist to copyedit his draft.

Miguel noticed that the last three sentences in the first paragraph were short and sounded choppy when he read them aloud. How did he improve them? See both the old and new versions below. To improve the flow, he combined them into one longer sentence.

> Is your dog's attention starting to wander? Stop the training session. Begin again when he is rested.

> If your dog's attention starts to wander, stop the training session and begin again when he is rested.

In the second paragraph, Miguel added a transition word and combined two simple sentences.

> Have the dog sit. Say "Give paw." Pick up the dog's paw.

> To begin, have the dog sit. Say "Give paw" and pick up the dog's paw.

Miguel corrected run-on sentences in the last two paragraphs, as well as a few other changes. With what word did he replace the word *nice?* Can you think of another word he could have used?

Copyeditor's Checklist

- ☐ Are there effective transition words in the piece?
- ☐ Do any words seem out of place or awkward?
- ☐ Do the chosen words and phrases convey their intended meaning?
- ☐ Are there any run-on or rambling sentences?
- ☐ Is there a balance of simple, compound, and complex sentences?
- ☐ Is the structure of sentences logical and grammatically correct?

Your Turn

Use the Copyeditor's Checklist to copyedit your draft. Pay particular attention to the rhythm of the sentences, and be on the alert for inexact and overused words. Correct run-on and rambling sentences. Have you repeated an adjective or adverb? Replace repeated adjectives and adverbs with synonyms.

Ask a volunteer to read aloud the paragraph following the Proofreader's Checklist. Have students read Miguel's how-to article silently. Discuss any additional mistakes students find.

Remind students that conventions include spelling, grammar, capitalization, and punctuation. Tell students that it is important to find and correct all conventions before writing is ready for publishing.

Your Turn

Instruct students to work in pairs to proofread their how-to articles. Make sure students are using the correct proofreading marks. Ask students to discuss each other's marks after proofreading the drafts.

Grammar in Action. Take this opportunity to review subject and object pronouns on pages 34–37. Remind students that pronouns must agree in person, number, and gender with their antecedents.

to review subject and object pronouns on pages 34–37

Proofreading Practice

Explain that some editors prefer reading aloud a piece of writing while proofreading. Suggest that reading aloud might help students find extra commas or incorrect end punctuation. Model how to indicate punctuation marks in oral reading by writing sentences on the board and demonstrating how to read them aloud (slightly pausing at commas and stopping at periods). Suggest that students use this practice when proofreading with their partners.

Meeting Individual Needs

Visual Post an example of a student's written how-to article on a class blog. Have students use the copyeditor's and proofreader's checklists to edit the article. Encourage students to use the track changes tool so that edits are clearly visible. Have students review their classmates' comments and suggestions.

Proofreading

Proofreading is the last step writers take to prepare their draft for publication. They check spelling, punctuation, capitalization, and grammar. Miguel used this Proofreader's Checklist to catch mistakes in his revised draft.

Miguel asked his classmate Ana to proofread his how-to article. Ana found several errors in **Conventions** Miguel's article. She noticed a missing apostrophe and a missing quotation mark. Can you find any other mistakes?

Proofreader's Checklist

- ☐ Are the paragraphs indented?
- ☐ Have any words been misspelled?
- ☐ Are the beginnings of sentences and proper nouns capitalized?
- ☐ Is the grammar correct?
- ☐ Is the punctuation correct?
- ☐ Were new errors introduced during editing?

Your Turn

Here are some tips to sharpen your proofreading skills.

- Use the Proofreader's Checklist to help you proofread your how-to article.
- Be sure to have a dictionary close at hand.
- Place a ruler or blank sheet of paper under each line as you read to help you pay attention to each line.
- Read very slowly and carefully.
- Proofread for one type of error at a time.
- When you have finished proofreading, trade papers with a classmate and proofread each other's work.

Grammar in Action

Make sure you use subject and object pronouns correctly, or else you will confuse your reader. Check each pronoun for agreement with its antecedent.

How-to Articles • 295

OBJECTIVE
- **To publish a how-to article**

PUBLISHING

Invite a volunteer to read aloud the first paragraph. Remind students that publishing their work means that they are ready to share their articles with an audience. Then ask volunteers to read aloud Miguel's finished how-to article. Encourage students to comment on the revisions Miguel made after copyediting and proofreading his draft. Ask questions such as the following:

- How has Miguel's how-to article improved?
- Who is Miguel's intended audience? How can you tell?
- Is the sequence of steps easy to follow? Why or why not?

Ask a volunteer to read aloud the possible ways that students can publish their how-to articles. Show the class examples of professional publications that specialize in how-to articles *(examples: craft magazines, cooking magazines, home-improvement sections of newspapers)*.

Point out the various ways students can use technology to publish their work, such as creating PowerPoint presentations, posting their articles to a classroom blog or Web site, or submitting their articles to an online magazine. Have volunteers suggest additional ideas for publication.

Writer's Workshop   How-to Articles

Publishing

After Miguel corrected the errors he and Ana found as they proofread his how-to article, he used a pen to copy the article neatly on a clean sheet of paper. Then he read it again to make sure he had copied everything correctly. This is Miguel's finished how-to article.

Teaching Your Dog to Wave

It's not hard to teach your dog to wave, and it's a show-stealing trick. For this and every trick you train your dog to do, praise him every time he responds correctly and give him a treat. If your dog's attention starts to wander, stop the training session and begin again when he is rested.

Before you can teach your dog to wave, you have to teach the command "Give paw." To begin, have the dog sit. Say, "Give paw" and pick up the dog's paw. Repeat this several times. Be especially enthusiastic if he begins to give you his paw on his own. After a few repetitions, stop the training session for the day.

At the next training session, have your dog sit, say, "Give paw," put your hand out, and see whether the dog remembers to put his paw in it. If he doesn't, take his paw and say, "Give paw" to review. Repeat several times.

Once your dog obeys "Give paw," you can go on to "Wave." Say, "Give paw wave." Instead of taking his paw, move your hand a little higher so he has to lift his paw up to reach your hand. Don't grab his paw, but praise him for trying to put his paw in your hand. Don't raise your hand too high, or he will become discouraged and stop trying. Repeat. After a few more repeats, you can drop the "Give paw" part of the command and simply say, "Wave." Practice every day, or nearly every day, for several weeks to make sure your dog will remember his new trick.

Doesn't your dog look charming when he waves like a rock star to his fans? Think of other tricks you can teach him, like how to speak and bow! Just remember to use only positive praise and treats during training, never punishment!

Your Turn

Ask a student to read this section aloud. Allow time for students to copy their how-to articles. If students are using pen and paper for their articles, point out that writing slowly and rereading each sentence as they write will keep students from introducing new errors. Encourage students to draw a graphic or picture to accompany their articles.

 Remind students that presentation deals with the appearance of their final draft. Tell students their how-to articles should be presented in a way that appeals to their audience.

ASSESS

Have students assess their finished how-to articles using the reproducible Student Self-Assessment on page 297y. A separate How-to Articles Scoring Rubric can be found on page 297z for you to use to evaluate their work.

Plan to spend tomorrow doing a formal assessment. Administer the How-to Article Writing Prompt on **Assessment Book** pages 51–52.

TEACHING OPTIONS

Portfolio Opportunity

Have students place copies of their how-to articles in their writing portfolios. Ask students to write brief summaries about skills they have learned since the previous Writer's Workshop. Have students also include goals on what they would like to improve about their writing and editing skills before the next Writer's Workshop. Tell students to date their paragraphs for reference each time they add to their portfolios.

After your teacher reviews the class's how-to articles, you can publish them for the students and adults in your school.

There are many ways you can publish your article.

 Create a class book. Work with your classmates to arrange the articles in a meaningful order, numbering the pages, and creating a table of contents that lists the titles, authors, and page numbers. Then make a cover, choosing a snappy title such as "How to Do Just About Anything." Decorate the cover and bind the book in a three-ring binder or a report cover. After everyone in class has had an opportunity to read the articles and to try out a few of them, donate the collection to the school library.

 Post it to an online how-to manual. You may also want to include images of each step. Choose images that may help depict complex steps.

 Create a class book for a younger grade. Some how-to articles such as "How to tie your shoes" may be very useful for younger students.

 Do a PowerPoint presentation. You can make the steps move on-screen in chronological order.

 Post it to your classroom's blog, wiki, or Web site. You can also include images in this medium.

Your Turn

You've worked hard to develop, express, and organize your ideas. Why not work just 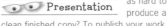 **Presentation** as hard to produce a clean finished copy? To publish your work, follow the steps below.

- Reread your how-to article to make sure you did not insert new mistakes or leave out words when you copied your draft or typed your corrections.
- If you are using a computer, run the spell-checker a final time before printing the article.
- To make the steps in the process even clearer, you may want to include an instructional graphic.

Name _____ Date _____

How-to Article

Ideas

	YES	NO
Do I have a clear purpose for the topic?		
Do I provide instruction that is detailed and complete?		

Organization

Do I clearly identify in the introduction what the article will teach?		
Do I present the steps in the order they will be completed?		
Does my conclusion leave a sense of closure?		

Voice

Do I use an appropriate tone?		
Do I use imperative sentences to state my directions?		

Word Choice

Do I use transition words?		
Do I use language specific to the topic?		

Sentence Fluency

Do I use clear, concise sentences?		
Does my piece transition logically from step to step?		
Do I use a variety of sentence types?		

Conventions

Do I use correct grammar?		
Do I use correct spelling, punctuation, and capitalization?		

Presentation

Do I use consistent spacing and margins?		
Does my paper look neat?		
Do I use visual aids when appropriate?		

Additional Items

© LOYOLAPRESS.

Name _____

Date _____ Score _____

POINT VALUES

0 = not evident
1 = minimal evidence of mastery
2 = evidence of development toward mastery
3 = strong evidence of mastery
4 = outstanding evidence of mastery

How-to Article

Ideas | POINTS

a clear purpose for the topic

detailed, accurate, and complete instructions

Organization

an introduction that states the article's purpose

steps presented in logical order

a conclusion that leaves a sense of closure

Voice

appropriate tone

directives in form of imperative sentences

Word Choice

transition words

language specific to the topic

Sentence Fluency

clear, concise sentences

logical transitions from step to step

variety of sentence types

Conventions

correct grammar and usage

correct spelling, punctuation, and capitalization

Presentation

consistent spacing and margins

neatness

visual aids as appropriate

Additional Items

_____

_____

Total

CHAPTER FOCUS

LESSON 1: What Makes a Good Business Letter?

LESSON 2: Purpose and Tone

- **GRAMMAR:** Verbs
- **WRITING SKILLS:** Adjective and Adverb Clauses
- **WORD STUDY:** Compound Words and Clipped Words
- **LITERACY SKILLS:** Writing Tools
- **SPEAKING AND LISTENING SKILLS:** Business Telephone Calls
- **WRITER'S WORKSHOP:** Business Letters

SUPPORT MATERIALS

Practice Book
Writing, pages 148–152

Assessment Book
Chapter 3 Writing Skills, pages 53–54
Business Letters Writing Prompt, pages 55–56

Rubrics
Student, page 335y
Teacher, page 335z

Test Generator CD

Grammar
Section 4, pages 57–82

Customizable Lesson Plans
www.voyagesinenglish.com

Business Letters

WHAT IS BUSINESS-LETTER WRITING?

A business letter is a formal letter written for a specific purpose. The tone of a good business letter is respectful and matches the purpose for which the letter was written. A letter of complaint, one kind of business letter, often requests compensation for a problem with a product or service. The tone of this kind of letter should be strong and persuasive.

A good business letter includes the following:

- ☐ An introduction with a clearly stated purpose
- ☐ A body with detailed information, tailored to the recipient
- ☐ A conclusion that restates the purpose and offers a sense of resolution
- ☐ A professional tone, avoiding the use of clipped words
- ☐ Adjective and adverb clauses to make sentences complete and specific
- ☐ Easy flow from one sentence to the next
- ☐ Correct business-letter format

LiNK Use the following titles to offer your students examples of well-crafted business writing:

The 7 Habits of Highly Effective Teens by Sean Covey

50 Great Businesses for Teens by Sarah Riehm

You Can Write a Business Letter by Jennifer Rozines Roy and Sherri Mabry Gordon

> ❝I think a compliment ought always to precede a complaint, where one is possible, because it softens resentment and insures for the complaint a courteous and gentle reception.❞
>
> —Mark Twain

WRITER'S WORKSHOP TIPS

Follow these ideas and tips to help you and your class get the most out of the Writer's Workshop:

- Review the traits of good writing. Use the chart on the inside back cover of the student and teacher editions.
- Fill a bulletin board in your classroom with business letters and other business communications, such as company newsletters, financial reports, and business newspapers.
- Use a graphic organizer such as a T-chart to compare and contrast characteristics of a business letter and a friendly letter.
- Encourage students to create receipts, diagrams, or other visuals for the business letters they write for the Writer's Workshop.
- Invite a local business owner to speak about effective business communication.
- To be sure that students use correct business-letter format, have them use a business-letter template and draft their letters on a computer.
- Invite a retail customer service representative to visit the class and explain characteristics of effective business letters, including what gets his or her attention and what prompts action.

CONNECT WITH GRAMMAR

Throughout the Writer's Workshop, look for opportunities to integrate verbs with writing business letters.

- ☐ Challenge students to use the perfect tenses correctly when referring to two events.
- ☐ Encourage students to use the subjunctive mood when making a request or expressing a desire.
- ☐ During revision encourage students to change sentences from the passive voice to the active voice.
- ☐ Have students check for consistency in verb tenses.
- ☐ Discuss which verb mood projects the most professional tone.

SCORING RUBRIC

Business Letter

0 = not evident
1 = minimal evidence of mastery
2 = evidence of development toward mastery
3 = strong evidence of mastery
4 = outstanding evidence of mastery

	POINTS
Ideas	
clearly stated reason for letter	
detailed information tailored to the recipient	
Organization	
an engaging introduction	
ideas presented in a logical order	
a conclusion that restates the letter's purpose	
Voice	
strong, persuasive, and respectful	
Word Choice	
business letter etiquette	
correct compound words	
professional tone	
Sentence Fluency	
problem and solutions	
adjective and adverb clauses	
logical flow from one sentence to the next	
Conventions	
correct grammar and usage	
correct spelling, punctuation, and capitalization	
Presentation	
correct business-letter format, including proper headings and addresses	
consistent spacing and margins	
neatness	
Additional Items	
Total	

Full-sized, reproducible rubrics can be found at the end of this chapter.

Business Letters

INTRODUCING THE GENRE

Ask volunteers to tell what a business letter is. Have students discuss the types of business letters people encounter, such as letters of application, letters of complaint, letters of request, and thank-you letters. Challenge students to list the parts of a business letter *(heading, inside address, salutation, body, closing, reference information).* Say that along with the correct parts, a

business letter also includes the following characteristics:

- A formal, professional tone
- A body that uses language tailored to the recipient
- A conclusion that offers a sense of resolution

Ask how a business letter differs from a friendly letter. *(The tone of a business letter is formal because the letter usually addresses someone the writer does not know and concerns a business matter.)*

Reading the Literature Excerpt

Invite volunteers to read aloud the example business letter. Encourage students to comment about the letter. Ask the following questions:

- From what point of view is the letter written?
- What is the tone of the letter, and is it appropriate?
- What writing skills (which you might have learned in previous chapters) do you notice used in the letter?

LiNK | **Business Letter**

The excerpts in Chapter 3 introduce students to real, relevant business letters. Roberta Andrews's thank-you letter is a strong example of a business letter because it has the following:

- A specific, business-related purpose
- A formal tone
- A heading, an inside address, a salutation, the body, the closing, and reference information

As students encounter the different examples of business letters throughout the chapter, be sure to point out the characteristics that the letters share. Also take this opportunity to point out grammar skills that students have been learning, such as proper verb usage.

LiNK

Business Letters

Carl Sandburg Middle School
121 E. Main St. • Greenboro, MA 01864
(617) 555-0403

November 7, 20–

Mr. Stephen H. Phillips
Managing Editor
North Fork Daily Journal
1770 Woodlawn Ave.
North Fork, MA 02171

Dear Mr. Phillips:

On behalf of my eighth-grade class, I would like to thank you for leading us on a tour of your newspaper offices. The experience fit in perfectly with our current media unit.

Some of the students were so impressed that they are already talking about joining the high school newspaper staff next year. Please accept the class photo that is enclosed as a token of our gratitude.

As a follow-up, I would like to make a request. Would anyone at your staff be available to speak to our class about life as a journalist? Perhaps you could also provide some information about potential before-school newspaper delivery jobs.

Please contact me at the phone number above to let me know if anyone would be available to speak to our students. Thanks again, and I look forward to hearing from you.

Sincerely yours,

Roberta Andrews
Roberta Andrews
Teacher

Encl: photo
cc: Martin Cohen, principal

298

- What do the abbreviations at the end of the letter below the signature mean?

Briefly discuss the importance of using a polite tone and correct format when sending business letters by e-mail. Explain that the tone of a business communication should remain the same, no matter what the medium is. Challenge volunteers to offer examples of business letters sent by e-mail. Discuss the benefits and drawbacks of these letters. *(The letter reaches the person more quickly, but some e-mail programs lack important spell-check, editing, and formatting tools that make a business letter look professional.)*

Reading the Student Model

Instruct students to read the model silently. After students have finished, ask them to point out the business-letter characteristics that they see in this letter. Then ask a volunteer to state the purpose of this letter *(to have a skateboarding park built)*. Tell students that business letters that are written to ask for something are called letters of request.

Scavenger Hunt

Have students look through reading materials in the classroom or school library for examples of business letters. Encourage students to ask other teachers, the librarian, or the office staff.

For Tomorrow

Ask students to think of two or three instances for writing a business letter. Have students write the following information for each instance: the purpose of the letter, a description of the person to whom the letter is being sent, and the tone of the letter. Bring in your own examples to share with the class.

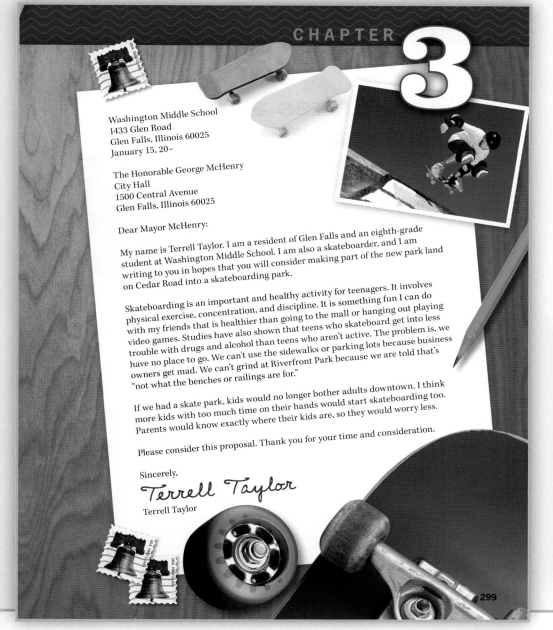

CHAPTER 3

Washington Middle School
1433 Glen Road
Glen Falls, Illinois 60025
January 15, 20–

The Honorable George McHenry
City Hall
1500 Central Avenue
Glen Falls, Illinois 60025

Dear Mayor McHenry:

My name is Terrell Taylor. I am a resident of Glen Falls and an eighth-grade student at Washington Middle School. I am also a skateboarder, and I am writing to you in hopes that you will consider making part of the new park land on Cedar Road into a skateboarding park.

Skateboarding is an important and healthy activity for teenagers. It involves physical exercise, concentration, and discipline. It is something fun I can do with my friends that is healthier than going to the mall or hanging out playing video games. Studies have also shown that teens who skateboard get into less trouble with drugs and alcohol than teens who aren't active. The problem is, we have no place to go. We can't use the sidewalks or parking lots because business owners get mad. We can't grind at Riverfront Park because we are told that's "not what the benches or railings are for."

If we had a skate park, kids would no longer bother adults downtown. I think more kids with too much time on their hands would start skateboarding too. Parents would know exactly where their kids are, so they would worry less.

Please consider this proposal. Thank you for your time and consideration.

Sincerely,

Terrell Taylor

Terrell Taylor

299

OBJECTIVES

- **To examine the characteristics and parts of business letters**
- **To follow guidelines for writing effective business letters**

WARM-UP

Read, Listen, Speak

Share your instances of writing a business letter from yesterday's For Tomorrow homework. Point out the specific details you included that are important for all business letters.

Invite small groups to share the information they collected about business letters. Encourage students to discuss the purposes, audiences, and tones of the letters. Challenge groups to discuss writing techniques that would be effective in the business letters (*short sentences, exact words, polite tone*).

GRAMMAR CONNECTION

Take this opportunity to talk about the principal parts of transitive and intransitive verbs. You may wish to have students point out principal parts of transitive and intransitive verbs in their Read, Listen, Speak examples.

TEACH

Ask a volunteer to read aloud the first paragraph. Invite students to suggest other reasons to write a business letter. Then ask volunteers to take turns reading the descriptions of the parts of a business letter. Discuss each description.

Ask the following questions: Why is it important to address the recipient of the letter with a personal title and to begin with *Dear* and close with *Sincerely yours*? (*It shows respect for the*

recipient.) How often do you think you might write business letters and when (*often—when applying for jobs, working in an office, communicating with other businesses*)?

Invite a volunteer to read aloud The Structure of a Business Letter. Discuss the first bulleted item. Reinforce the idea that the first paragraph should state the purpose of the letter. Ask students to look at the example letter and to state what the purpose of the letter is (*to thank the managing editor of a newspaper for leading a tour*). Discuss the second bulleted item and ask volunteers to point out relevant details from the example

letter. Then discuss the final bulleted item. Ask students if the writer of the example letter makes any requests. (*The writer requests a speaker to discuss careers in journalism.*)

PRACTICE

ACTIVITY A

Allow time for students to write the required information for a business letter to the publisher of their books. Then ask volunteers to share what they wrote. Encourage students to comment on whether the parts of a business letter were written correctly.

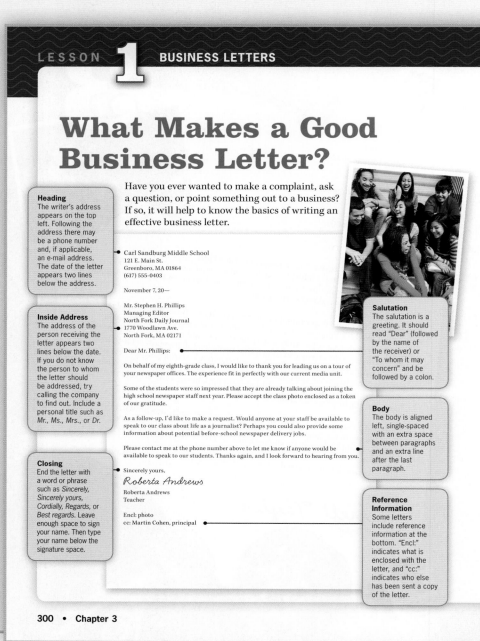

LESSON 1   BUSINESS LETTERS

What Makes a Good Business Letter?

Have you ever wanted to make a complaint, ask a question, or point something out to a business? If so, it will help to know the basics of writing an effective business letter.

Heading
The writer's address appears on the top left. Following the address there may be a phone number and, if applicable, an e-mail address. The date of the letter appears two lines below the address.

Carl Sandburg Middle School
121 E. Main St.
Greenboro, MA 01864
(617) 555-0403

November 7, 20—

Inside Address
The address of the person receiving the letter appears two lines below the date. If you do not know the person to whom the letter should be addressed, try calling the company to find out. Include a personal title such as *Mr., Ms., Mrs.,* or *Dr.*

Mr. Stephen H. Phillips
Managing Editor
North Fork Daily Journal
1770 Woodlawn Ave.
North Fork, MA 02171

Dear Mr. Phillips:

On behalf of my eighth-grade class, I would like to thank you for leading us on a tour of your newspaper offices. The experience fit in perfectly with our current media unit.

Some of the students were so impressed that they are already talking about joining the high school newspaper staff next year. Please accept the class photo enclosed as a token of our gratitude.

As a follow-up, I'd like to make a request. Would anyone at your staff be available to speak to our class about life as a journalist? Perhaps you could also provide some information about potential before-school newspaper delivery jobs.

Please contact me at the phone number above to let me know if anyone would be available to speak to our students. Thanks again, and I look forward to hearing from you.

Closing
End the letter with a word or phrase such as *Sincerely, Sincerely yours, Cordially, Regards,* or *Best regards.* Leave enough space to sign your name. Then type your name below the signature space.

Sincerely yours,

Roberta Andrews

Roberta Andrews
Teacher

Encl: photo
cc: Martin Cohen, principal

Salutation
The salutation is a greeting. It should read "Dear" (followed by the name of the receiver) or "To whom it may concern" and be followed by a colon.

Body
The body is aligned left, single-spaced with an extra space between paragraphs and an extra line after the last paragraph.

Reference Information
Some letters include reference information at the bottom. "Encl:" indicates what is enclosed with the letter, and "cc:" indicates who else has been sent a copy of the letter.

300 • Chapter 3

ACTIVITY B

Have students complete this activity independently. When students have finished, invite volunteers to read aloud their opening sentences. Ask volunteers to offer alternative opening sentences for each salutation.

APPLY

WRITER'S CORNER

Ask what kind of business letter this will be *(a letter of complaint)*. Allow time for students to write their sentences. Then have students trade papers with a partner. Ask students to read the sentences and decide whether they are an effective beginning to a business letter that makes a complaint. Students should demonstrate an understanding of the characteristics of a business letter.

ASSESS

Note which students had difficulty understanding the parts and characteristics of a business letter. Use the Reteach option with those students who need additional reinforcement.

TEACHING OPTIONS

Reteach

Give each student a copy of a business letter. (You might make photocopies of the student model on page 299.) Have students label the parts of the letter in the following ways:

- Draw a green circle around the inside address.
- Underline in blue the colon following the salutation.
- Circle in red the signature beneath the closing.
- Draw a brown circle around the reference information.
- Label each part with its name.

Business Letters Around the World

Search online for business letters written in another language, preferably in a primary language of an English-language learner. You might also ask students whose parents conduct business with other countries to bring in examples of international business letters. Discuss the various formats of the business letters, explaining that accepted formats vary from country to country. For example, people in European countries write the date as day/month/year instead of month/day/year.

For Tomorrow

Have students ask an adult family member for an old business letter. Ask students to write a paragraph that states whether the letter has the parts of a business letter that are listed on page 300. Bring in a business letter of your own and write a paragraph examining the parts of this business letter.

The Structure of a Business Letter

The best business letters are confident, polite, and concise. A good business letter can be easy to recognize, but challenging to write. Here are some guidelines for writing effective business letters.

- Begin the first paragraph with a professional and polite opening sentence that states the purpose of the letter. Get right to the point and keep it simple.
- In the next paragraph or paragraphs, offer persuasive reasoning, relevant details, statistics, or other information to support your main point. If you are enclosing something with your letter, be sure to explain what it is.
- In the closing paragraph, restate the purpose of the letter. Ask for action if appropriate. If you are making a request, thank the recipient for taking the requested action.

Read over Roberta Andrews's letter. How closely does it follow these guidelines?

ACTIVITY A Create part of a fictitious business letter that you would send from your home to the publisher of a favorite book to request an additional copy. The address can be found at the front of the book. Include the heading, inside address, salutation, closing, and reference information. Write the first paragraph of your letter stating your purpose and leave the rest of the letter blank to finish later.

ACTIVITY B When you write a formal letter to people who hold special positions, you need to use special salutations. Write an opening sentence to the following people, using the salutation given.

1. President: Dear Mr./Madam President
2. U.S. Senator: Dear Senator (surname)
3. Judge: Dear Justice (surname)
4. King/Queen: May it Please Your Majesty
5. Mayor: Sir/Madam (or) Mayor (surname)

WRITER'S CORNER

Write the first three sentences of a letter to a manufacturer or a school supply store, complaining about defective school supplies.

Business Letters • 301

WARM-UP

Read, Listen, Speak

Share your business letter from yesterday's For Tomorrow activity. As you read it to the class, point out how it compares with the example letter from yesterday's lesson. Make sure to point out any parts of the letter that are missing.

Ask small groups to share the paragraphs students wrote for homework. Encourage them to give one another feedback about their assessments of the business letters. If a student found a poorly written business letter, challenge the group members to suggest ways to improve it.

GRAMMAR CONNECTION

Take this opportunity to talk about troublesome verbs. You may wish to have students point out troublesome verbs in their Read, Listen, Speak examples.

TEACH

Review the characteristics and parts of a business letter. Ask the following questions: What greeting should you use if you don't know the name of the person to whom the letter should be addressed *("Dear Sir or Madam" or "To whom it may concern")*? What should the final paragraph accomplish *(restate the purpose and thank the recipient)*? Have a volunteer point out the parts and characteristics of a business letter in the model on page 299. Then point out the example Inside Address and Salutation on page 303.

PRACTICE

ACTIVITY C

Invite volunteers to read aloud the business letter. When they have finished, discuss as a group answers to questions 1–7. Then give students time to write their answers to question 8. Encourage students to be specific in their assessments.

ACTIVITY D

Allow time for students to rewrite the letter. Ask volunteers to read aloud their revisions and to explain why they made the changes that they did.

ACTIVITY E

After students have written their letters, ask them to trade papers with a partner. Have partners read each other's letters and assess whether the writer wrote an effective letter to the school principal.

ACTIVITY F

Have students complete this activity independently. Then invite volunteers to write their inside addresses and salutations on the board. Discuss each inside address.

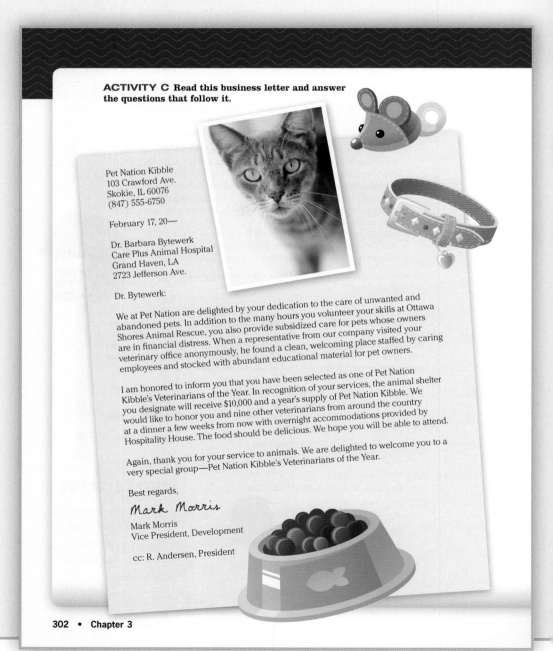

ACTIVITY C Read this business letter and answer the questions that follow it.

Pet Nation Kibble
103 Crawford Ave.
Skokie, IL 60076
(847) 555-6750

February 17, 20—

Dr. Barbara Bytewerk
Care Plus Animal Hospital
Grand Haven, LA
2723 Jefferson Ave.

Dr. Bytewerk:

We at Pet Nation are delighted by your dedication to the care of unwanted and abandoned pets. In addition to the many hours you volunteer your skills at Ottawa Shores Animal Rescue, you also provide subsidized care for pets whose owners are in financial distress. When a representative from our company visited your veterinary office anonymously, he found a clean, welcoming place staffed by caring employees and stocked with abundant educational material for pet owners.

I am honored to inform you that you have been selected as one of Pet Nation Kibble's Veterinarians of the Year. In recognition of your services, the animal shelter you designate will receive $10,000 and a year's supply of Pet Nation Kibble. We would like to honor you and nine other veterinarians from around the country at a dinner a few weeks from now with overnight accommodations provided by Hospitality House. The food should be delicious. We hope you will be able to attend.

Again, thank you for your service to animals. We are delighted to welcome you to a very special group—Pet Nation Kibble's Veterinarians of the Year.

Best regards,

Mark Morris

Mark Morris
Vice President, Development

cc: R. Andersen, President

302 • Chapter 3

APPLY

WRITER'S CORNER

As students write their reply letters, remind them to include all the necessary parts of a business letter and to use the guidelines listed on pages 300–301. Ask students to share their letters with partners. Students should demonstrate an understanding of the characteristics of a business letter.

ASSESS

Note which students had difficulty identifying the necessary parts and characteristics of a business letter. Use the Reteach option with those students who need additional reinforcement.

Practice Book page 148 provides additional practice with the parts and characteristics of an effective business letter.

TEACHING OPTIONS

Reteach

Write on the board the following information about a product:

- **the name of the product purchased**
- **the date of purchase**
- **the place of purchase**
- **a clear statement of the problem**
- **the action the writer plans to take**
- **the action the writer wants the business to take**

Discuss whether the list contains all the pertinent information to be included in a business letter of complaint. Then have students write a letter to the makers complaining about the product described. Tell them that they may make up the name and address of the company. When students have finished, ask them to trade papers with a partner. Challenge students to check each other's letters to see that they contain the information listed on the board and the characteristics students learned on pages 300–301.

Activity C

1. Heading: none; inside address: street address and city/state lines are transposed, and no zip code; salutation: no "Dear"
2. to say that Dr. Bytewerk has been named one of Pet Nation Kibble's Veterinarians of the Year.
3. second paragraph; no
4. yes; "The food should be delicious."
5. yes; date and location of awards ceremony and location of hotel.
6. Restate the letter's purpose and ask for response if needed. No, there is no request for confirming attendance at the ceremony.
7. Call or write the company.
8. No. The letter omits critical information and fails to request a needed response from the recipient. The letter buries its purpose in the second paragraph.

1. What mistakes are made in the heading, inside address, and salutation?
2. Why did Mark Morris write the letter?
3. In what paragraph does he explain his purpose? Does he make his point promptly?
4. Are any sentences irrelevant or unnecessary? If so, which ones?
5. Is any important information left out?
6. What should the last paragraph in a business letter do? Does this final paragraph do that?
7. What could Dr. Bytewerk do if she wanted to find out additional information?
8. Is this a well-written business letter? Why or why not?

Inside Address and Salutation to a Representative

The Honorable James Holt
United States House of Representatives
Washington, D.C. 20515

Dear Representative Holt:

ACTIVITY D Rewrite the letter from Activity C. Fix any mistakes in the heading, inside address, and salutation. Make any changes that would make the letter clearer and more concise, such as rearranging sentences, adding important details, or deleting unnecessary sentences.

ACTIVITY E Write a three-paragraph business letter to your principal, proposing an idea for the school to raise money for charity. State the purpose of the letter in the first paragraph. In the second paragraph, offer at least one reason to adopt the idea and restate the purpose in the third paragraph. Use your school address in the heading.

ACTIVITY F Inside addresses for people holding special positions need special titles that are often different from the title used in the salutation. Write imaginary or real inside addresses for the following people. Then match it to the proper salutation from Activity B on page 301.

1. President: The President, The White House
2. Senator/Representative: The Honorable (full name)
3. Mayor: His/Her Honor (full name)

WRITER'S CORNER

Put yourself in Dr. Bytewerk's place. Write a reply to the letter from Mark Morris of Pet Nation Kibble. Thank him for the honor, accept or decline his invitation, and ask for more information about one of the details in the letter.

For Tomorrow

Have students search online for a catalog of camping equipment. Instruct students to write a letter placing an inquiry to the catalog company, asking if the company has the necessary number and type of items students will need to plan a camping trip for 10 people. Write a letter yourself to share with the class.

Business Letters • 303

OBJECTIVES
- **To state the purpose and to set the tone of a business letter**
- **To revise a business letter**

WARM-UP

Read, Listen, Speak

Read your letter of inquiry from yesterday's For Tomorrow activity. Point out specific characteristics of a business letter.

Encourage small groups to assess whether each student's letter contains the necessary parts of a business letter. Have volunteers read their letters to the rest of the class.

GRAMMAR CONNECTION

Take this opportunity to talk about linking verbs. You may wish to have students point out linking verbs in their Read, Listen, Speak examples.

TEACH

Have a volunteer read aloud the first paragraph. Ask why an overly casual or personal tone should not be used in a business letter *(because the writer is addressing someone he or she doesn't know, and a personal tone could be offensive)*.

Ask a volunteer to read aloud the section Stating the Purpose. Reinforce that the purpose must be clear for the letter to be effective. Then allow time for students to read Taylor's letter silently. Ask a volunteer to read aloud the sentence that clearly states Taylor's purpose. *(I was surprised and disappointed to find that Crema's Lip Fix did not perform as advertised.)*

Ask a volunteer to read aloud the first paragraph of the section Setting the Tone. Challenge students to offer other words that Taylor might have used in her letter, while maintaining her polite tone *(distressed, disconcerted, astonished)*. Invite a volunteer to read aloud the second paragraph of the section. Ask students to name another detail Taylor used to persuade Crema to refund her money. *("Neither substance helped alleviate my dry lips as advertised on your TV commercial.")*

LiNK Read aloud the excerpt of the letter to General Grant. Point out that the goal or purpose of the letter is identified immediately. *(I wish to express my entire satisfaction with what you have done up to this time.)*

PRACTICE

ACTIVITY A

After students have written their paragraphs, ask volunteers to read them aloud. Discuss the tone a reply letter should have *(an apologetic tone as well as a grateful tone for the writer's input)*. Make a list of some of the words that students used to convey the appropriate tone.

LESSON **2** BUSINESS LETTERS

Purpose and Tone

People are flooded with information every day as letters, e-mails, and phone calls all fight for the recipient's attention. That's why it's important when writing a business letter to get straight to the point, explain the purpose clearly, and support it convincingly with just enough details. Writers must strive to maintain a polite, sincere tone in their letters. The tone should be neither too formal nor (even worse) overly casual and personal.

Stating the Purpose

As noted in Lesson 1, the first and most important step in writing a business letter is to identify the goal or purpose of the letter. Is it to provide information? extend an invitation? request action? Since the rest of the letter supports the purpose, it must be absolutely clear to the writer. After all, if it isn't clear to the writer, how could it possibly be clear to the reader?

Taylor was unhappy with a product she bought, so she wrote a letter to the company that manufactured it. In the first paragraph, she explained the problem. In the second paragraph, she suggested a solution.

As a longtime and loyal user of Crema products, I was surprised and disappointed to find that Crema's Lip Fix did not perform as advertised. The product separated into a gluey substance that formed a white paste on my lips and a liquid that ran off them immediately. Neither substance helped alleviate my dry lips as advertised on your TV commercials.

I feel sure that your Research and Development Department will be eager to learn of my problems with this product so that they can reformulate it if they have not already done so. I also expect your company to replace the Lip Fix with an improved reformulation if one exists or to refund the purchase price.

ACTIVITY B

Allow time for students to write a paragraph for each situation. When students have finished, ask them to trade papers with partners. Have students assess whether their partners clearly stated the purpose of each letter and used an appropriate tone. Then invite volunteers to read their paragraphs aloud.

APPLY

WRITER'S CORNER

When students have completed their letters, ask volunteers to share what they wrote. Have them read aloud the details (words or phrases) that they used to strengthen the purpose of the letters. Students should demonstrate an understanding of the purpose and tone of business letters.

ASSESS

Note which students had difficulty stating the purpose and setting the tone of a business letter. Use the Reteach option with those students who need additional reinforcement.

TEACHING OPTIONS

Reteach

Ask students to identify words or phrases that state the purpose and set the tone of the student model on page 299. Distribute photocopies of the model and instruct students to do the following:

- Underline the sentence in which the purpose is stated.
- Circle all the details that strengthen the purpose.
- Underline twice every word or phrase that helps to convey the tone of the letter (such as specific adjectives, nouns, and adverbs).

Ask students to compare their work with a partner.

Planning a Trip

Invite pairs of students to imagine they are planning a field trip for the class. Have them brainstorm a list of places of interest and kinds of information needed to plan a field trip. Then ask students to use these ideas to write a business letter requesting that the principal approve the trip. Remind students to use an appropriate tone, clearly state the purpose, and provide supporting details.

For Tomorrow

Ask students to locate the mailing address for your state tourism office by researching state tourism in the library or online. Instruct students to write a business letter to the agency, requesting information about a specific attraction within the state. Write a similar letter to share with the class.

Setting the Tone

In her letter Taylor stated the problem immediately, using clear, polite language. She used words such as *surprised* and *disappointed* and the phrase "did not perform as advertised" instead of using angrier words. She did this because she knew that business letters should always be courteous. If Taylor received no response, she could decide to write another polite but more forceful letter.

Not only did Taylor state the problem, but she also gave details and used persuasion. She explained that she is a "longtime and loyal user," a detail she hoped would help persuade the company to pay attention to her problem. Then she gave helpful details such as "The product separated into a gluey substance," which described exactly what the problem was.

ACTIVITY A Imagine that you work in the customer relations department of the Crema Company. You have just read Taylor's letter. What is your reaction to it? Write the first paragraph of a letter responding to her complaint. Pay close attention to the tone of your reply and make sure it is appropriate for the situation.

ACTIVITY B Write the first paragraph of a business letter relating to each of the following situations. Use an appropriate tone. Be sure the readers can easily figure out the purpose of each letter.

1. The clerk at a toy store was rude to your younger brother when he tried to buy a Buzzy Bee with the change in his piggy bank.
2. A student at La Mode Beauty School gave you the best haircut you ever had, and it cost only $5.
3. The photocopier has been malfunctioning, and you're not sure whether or not the new toner you ordered is the problem.

> **LiNK**
>
> **Excerpt of Letter to General Grant, Executive Mansion Washington, April 30, 1864 From President Abraham Lincoln**
>
> Not expecting to see you again before the spring campaign opens, I wish to express, in this way, my entire satisfaction with what you have done up to this time, so far as I understand it. . . . And now with a brave Army, and a just cause, may God sustain you.

WRITER'S CORNER

Complete the letter you began in Activity A. Support the purpose of the letter with relevant details. Restate the purpose of the letter in the last paragraph.

Business Letters • 305

Read, Listen, Speak

Read your letter from yesterday's For Tomorrow homework. Emphasize the purpose of the letter and the words or phrases that help create a professional tone.

Have volunteers read their letters aloud. Ask the class to identify sentences that state the purpose and words or phrases that help create the tone in each letter.

GRAMMAR CONNECTION

Take this opportunity to talk about active and passive voices. You may wish to have students point out active and passive voices in their Read, Listen, Speak examples.

TEACH

Read aloud the first paragraph in the section Revising a Business Letter. Allow time for students to read silently the business letter. Encourage them to note where the purpose is stated and the details that support the purpose. When students have finished reading, invite a volunteer to read aloud the paragraphs on the top of page 307. Ask volunteers to point out where Seth used irrelevant details. Challenge students to suggest revisions to the letter.

PRACTICE

ACTIVITY C

When students have finished rewriting the body of the letter, ask them to trade papers with a partner. Have students underline the following on their partner's paper: the sentence in which the purpose is stated and the details that strengthen the purpose. Allow time for partners to discuss their work.

ACTIVITY D & E

When students have finished these activities, have students trade papers with a partner. Tell students to circle words or phrases

that help create the writer's tone. In Activity D, remind students that although they may be annoyed that no one responded to their first letter, their tone cannot be mean or offensive.

ACTIVITY F

Have students share their letters with partners. Instruct students to look for all the parts of a business letter. Encourage students to offer one another feedback that will strengthen their letters.

ACTIVITY G

Allow time for students to complete this activity. When

Revising a Business Letter

Read and evaluate the following business letter. Can you identify the purpose easily? Is the purpose supported by relevant details?

Pearson School
17 Wright Plaza
Tucson, AZ 85705
(520) 555-0126

March 4, 20—

Mr. Donald Driver
131 Hollyhock Lane
Brunswick, MS 02138

Dear Mr. Driver:

Our class recently read your latest novel, *Platypus in Space*, and just loved it. I especially liked the beginning where the platypus stowed away on the spaceship. I wonder how it got the nerve up to do that. Anyway, the reason I am writing is because I am the president of our class, and I usually write class letters. We would like to invite you to speak at our school. It would be great if we could show you some stories that your novel inspired us to write.

We know you will be on a book tour promoting *Platypus in Space* in our area in May, so we were hoping you would be able to stop by our school to give a talk then. Any time in May would be fine for us, except Memorial Day and May 11, which is Teacher Institute Day, so we won't be having school. Our parent organization has been raising funds to pay for author talks, and most of the students would rather hear you talk than any other author. So we would be able to pay you for your talk. Please let me know how much you charge, and I will find out if we have enough in the book talk fund to pay you. We had a poll last year, and you were voted favorite author. Are you planning to write more platypus books?

Thank you for making us laugh. We hope you can speak to the students at our school in May.

Sincerely,

Seth McCall

President, Mr. Bennett's Class

cc: Mr. Bennett
    Ms. Anthony, Principal

306 • Chapter 3

students have finished, ask volunteers to share their opening paragraphs with the class. Challenge students to identify the purpose of each volunteer's paragraph.

APPLY

WRITER'S CORNER

Invite students to offer names of authors. Write the names on the board. Briefly discuss some interesting facts about each author. Then have students choose an author from the list for their letter. Encourage volunteers to share their paragraphs.

Students should demonstrate an understanding of the purpose and tone of a business letter.

ASSESS

Note which students had difficulty understanding that specific words and details help establish the tone of a business letter. Use the Reteach option with those students who need additional reinforcement.

Practice Book page 149 provides additional work with purpose and tone.

TEACHING OPTIONS

Reteach

Distribute photocopies of the letter on page 298. Invite students to identify the tone of the letter and to circle all the words that convey that tone. Then ask students to replace each word with a stronger or weaker synonym. Have students explain how their word substitutions change the tone of the letter. Lead students to the conclusion that exact wording is important in establishing the tone of a letter.

Placing an Order to the Past

Have students search in the library or online for examples of shopping catalogs from the early 20th century. Suggest that students look through a catalog to see what they might have dreamed of owning at that time. Then invite students to write a letter of request, placing an order to the catalog.

Explain that during this period in history, people often bought things from mail-order catalogs. Tell students that catalogs, like our modern online stores, provided an opportunity for people to learn about the latest fashions and inventions.

Seth's letter to Mr. Driver is well written. The tone is respectful and polite, he identifies the purpose of his letter, and he includes information Mr. Driver will need to take action. Seth's letter has some problems too.

In the first paragraph, Seth takes too long to get to the point. Does he support the purpose of the letter well? Yes and no. He does give some reasons Mr. Driver might want to visit his school. But he includes quite a few irrelevant details, which might confuse or irritate a busy author.

Remember that the writer of a successful business letter includes just enough information to make his or her point.

ACTIVITY C Rewrite the body of Seth's letter. Make sure the purpose is in the right place and strengthen the supporting details.

ACTIVITY D Rewrite the three paragraphs you wrote for Activity B. This time write the paragraphs as though no one had responded to your first letter. Modify your tone appropriately.

ACTIVITY E Write a short business letter volunteering to assist in your school library. What sort of tone is useful for this letter?

ACTIVITY F You have a great idea for a new video game and would like a local company to see your idea. Write to them requesting an interview.

ACTIVITY G Write an opening paragraph to one of the following people, using the proper inside address and salutation. (See Activity B and Activity F in Lesson 1.) Make your purpose an appropriate issue, question, or request suitable for your audience.

1. The President of the United States
2. One of your state senators
3. Your town mayor
4. Your state representative

U.S. President George Washington

WRITER'S CORNER

Choose an author to invite to visit your class. Write the first paragraph of a letter of invitation. State clearly why you want this author to visit and what would be expected of him or her.

Business Letters • 307

For Tomorrow

Ask students to finish the letter of invitation they began in the Writer's Corner. Remind them to include the necessary parts. Encourage students to use a polite tone and to include relevant supporting details. Complete a letter of invitation of your own to share with the class. Address it to your favorite author.

OBJECTIVES

- **To modify nouns and verbs by using adjective and adverb clauses**
- **To understand restrictive and nonrestrictive clauses**

WARM-UP

Read, Listen, Speak

Read aloud your letter from yesterday's For Tomorrow homework. Point out the details that help create the tone and support the purpose of the letter. Then have small groups discuss their letters of invitation. Ask students to trade papers and read aloud one another's letters, identifying the purpose of each. Have students offer suggestions for improving one another's letters.

GRAMMAR CONNECTION

Take this opportunity to talk about simple, progressive, and perfect tenses. You may wish to have students point out simple, progressive, and perfect tenses in their Read, Listen, Speak examples.

TEACH

Read the first paragraph aloud. Then ask a volunteer to define *adjective* and *adverb*. Point out that adjective and adverb clauses can provide specific details that are important to the purpose of a business letter. Read aloud the Letter of Submission example and point out the adjective clause in the second sentence *(which is titled "Angry Monkeys of the Rain Forest")*.

Invite a volunteer to read the first paragraph of the section Adjective Clauses. Read the example sentences aloud and point out that the adjective clause breaks up the sentence, avoiding a monotonous tone.

Ask a volunteer to read aloud the remainder of the Adjective Clauses section. Tell students that using clauses allows writers to share information with their reader while varying the sentence length and structure. Remind students that just as in any other type of writing, they want to create sentences that vary in structure and length, and that using adjective clauses is a way to do this.

Ask a volunteer to read aloud the section Restrictive and Nonrestrictive Clauses. Discuss the example sentences. Point out that restrictive clauses that describe things often begin with *that* and that nonrestrictive clauses that describe things often begin with *which*.

PRACTICE

ACTIVITY A

Have students complete the activity independently. Then invite volunteers to write each sentence on the board, underline the adjective clause, and circle the noun it modifies.

ACTIVITY B

After students have completed the activity, have them trade papers with a partner. Ask

---

Adjective and Adverb Clauses

Letter of Submission (Query) for Publication

Dear Agent (or Publisher):

I am requesting permission to submit my manuscript for your evaluation. My manuscript, which is titled "Angry Monkeys of the Rain Forest," is a 30–page double-spaced comedy manuscript with five illustrations. It is about a corporation that encounters hostile monkeys while trying to destroy their habitat for profit.

In business letters, as in all writing, there are many ways to make your sentences more complete or specific. One way is to modify nouns and verbs with adjectives and adverbs. Another way is to add a clause that does the same job as an adjective or an adverb. We call these clauses adjective and adverb clauses.

Adjective Clauses

Just as an adjective is a word that modifies a noun or a pronoun, an adjective clause is a clause (a group of words containing a subject and a predicate) that modifies a noun or a pronoun. An adjective clause usually begins with *whom, who, which,* or *that*. Writers use adjective clauses to shift the emphasis of a sentence, to deepen the meaning of a sentence, or to vary sentence length.

The Pueblo live in the Southwest and have a very old culture.
The Pueblo, *who live in the Southwest,* **have a very old culture.**

In the first sentence, the facts that the Pueblo live in the Southwest and have a very old culture are given equal weight. In the second sentence, emphasis shifts to the age the Pueblo's culture.

Adjective clauses can also deepen the meaning of sentences.

Odysseus was a legendary hero of the ancient Greeks.
Odysseus, *whose adventures are told in an epic poem,* **was a legendary hero of the ancient Greeks.**

The second sentence of this pair includes extra information about Odysseus. Could the same information have been communicated in a separate sentence? Certainly. However,

Statue of ancient Greek mythological hero Odysseus

students to discuss whether the meaning of each sentence changed significantly after replacing the adjective clause with a simple adjective.

APPLY

WRITER'S CORNER

After students have identified the restrictive and nonrestrictive clauses in a past piece of writing, suggest that students consider replacing simple adjectives in the same piece with adjective clauses. Students should demonstrate an understanding of adjective clauses.

ASSESS

Note which students had trouble identifying restrictive and nonrestrictive adjective clauses. Use the Reteach option with those students who need additional reinforcement.

TEACHING OPTIONS

Reteach

Write on the board the following sentences:

Mr. Smith, who lives next door, works at the city park.

Artists who create sculptures use costly raw materials.

Remind him to bring a book that he will enjoy while on vacation.

Ask students to categorize the parts of the sentences, using the chart below.

Modified Noun	Adjective Clause	Relative Pronoun
Mr. Smith	who lives next door	who

Breaking Apart Clauses

Have students break the sentences from Activity A into two separate sentences. Instruct students to do this by forming a complete sentence out of the adjective clause. Explain that this activity will show that adjective clauses help combine two separate but related ideas in one sentence.

For Tomorrow

Have students search a magazine or an online article for adjective clauses. Have students identify the clauses as restrictive or nonrestrictive. Find an article yourself and complete the same activity to share with the class tomorrow.

Activity A
1. person
2. Benjamin Franklin
3. person
4. train
5. day-care center
6. award

Activity B
1. restrictive
2. nonrestrictive
3. restrictive
4. nonrestrictive
5. nonrestrictive
6. restrictive
Sentences will vary.

using adjective clauses allows writers to select how information is communicated. The second sentence lets the writer inform the reader about the epic poem without having to use a separate sentence, which could be too distracting in an essay about famous heroes.

Restrictive and Nonrestrictive Clauses

Adjective clauses are not always optional tools for adding information about a noun. Sometimes writers need to use an adjective clause to identify the noun being modified in a sentence. This is called a restrictive clause. Nonrestrictive clauses are used to add important information that is not necessary to identify the noun in a sentence.

> **The book** *that I bought* **was too difficult.**
> **The book by Leo Tolstoy,** *which I bought*, **was too difficult.**

In the first sentence, the restrictive clause *that I bought* is necessary to identify the book. In the second sentence, the nonrestrictive clause is not necessary because *by Leo Tolstoy* identifies the book.

ACTIVITY A Identify the adjective clause in each sentence. Determine what noun each clause modifies.

1. Wise is the person who keeps silent when ignorant.
2. Benjamin Franklin, who is credited with inventing lightning rods, was a printer as well as a political leader and an inventor.
3. Pam is the person who taught us this technique.
4. That train, which leaves for New York soon, is already full.
5. Our school started a day-care center, which is very popular.
6. Congratulations on winning an award that is quite prestigious.

ACTIVITY B Look at the sentences in Activity A. Identify whether each clause is restrictive or nonrestrictive. Find three sentences that can be modified by changing an adjective clause into a simple adjective.

WRITER'S CORNER

Reread the student's letter on page 299. Identify two adjective clauses. Determine whether they are restrictive or nonrestrictive.

Business Letters • 309

WARM-UP

Read, Listen, Speak

Share your article from yesterday's For Tomorrow activity. Write the sentences that contain adjective clauses on the board. Tell whether each clause is restrictive or nonrestrictive and point out the relative pronoun for each clause.

Invite volunteers to write on the board their sentences that contain clauses. Ask students to identify the relative pronoun that starts the clause and whether each clause is restrictive or nonrestrictive.

GRAMMAR CONNECTION

Take this opportunity to talk about the indicative, imperative, and emphatic moods. You may wish to have students point out indicative, imperative, and emphatic moods in their Read, Listen, Speak examples.

TEACH

Invite a volunteer to read aloud the first two paragraphs of the section Adverb Clauses and the example sentences. Then ask volunteers to identify the verbs that the adverb clauses modify in each sentence. Invite a student to read aloud the rest of the section.

Discuss how the meaning of the first example sentence changes when the adverb *confidently* replaces the original adverb clause. Explain that this use of *confidently* provides no further detail to Colleen's thinking. Tell students that the adverb clause, *as if she were confident of the debate's outcome*, reveals to the reader why she felt confident.

PRACTICE

ACTIVITY C

Ask students to work in pairs to complete this activity. Ask volunteers to replace adverb clauses with simple adverbs. Discuss how doing so changes each sentence. Then reinforce that using adverb clauses strengthens writing and provides needed detail.

ACTIVITY D

Have students complete this activity independently. Then discuss whether the change in subordinate conjunctions altered the meanings of the sentences.

ACTIVITY E

Have students complete this activity independently. Then have volunteers write on the board their revised sentences. Discuss how the meaning of each sentence changes from the original.

ACTIVITY F

Discuss each clause with the class, determining if it is an adjective clause or an adverb clause. Then have students write their sentences independently. Ask volunteers to read aloud their sentences. Encourage students to save their most creative sentences as writing prompts for future writing.

Adverb Clauses

An adverb clause is a clause that does the same job as an adverb. An adverb clause usually modifies a verb, but can also modify an adjective or adverb in a sentence. Adverb clauses are usually introduced by subordinate conjunctions such as *although, while,* or *because.*

An adverb clause can tell when, where, why, or how something happens. It can also make a comparison or set a condition.

> **Colleen spoke** *as if she were confident of the debate's outcome.*
> *After the rain died down,* **the sun broke through the clouds.**
> **You cannot work** *if you don't have a permit.*

Like adjective clauses, adverb clauses let writers create a more vivid picture in the reader's mind or communicate a more complicated thought. A sentence such as "Colleen spoke *confidently*" would not express the same idea as the first example.

ACTIVITY C Identify the adverb clauses in the sentences below. Determine how the clause modifies the verb: by telling *when, where, why,* or *how*; by making a comparison, or by setting a condition.

1. Strike while the iron is hot.
2. Go when you are told.
3. We saw the Mounties when we were in Ottawa.
4. The rabbit ran while the turtle crawled.
5. The plant flowered because it received good care.
6. Pat devotes more time to skiing than she does to swimming.
7. I will get a loan if you need more money.
8. The computer program worked, although some of the commands were wrong.
9. The Saint Bernard played outside all day as if he didn't notice the bitter cold.
10. She saved her money so that she might attend college.

ACTIVITY D Choose five sentences from Activity C. Take out the adverb clause and add one that is introduced by a different subordinate conjunction.

Activity C

1. while the iron is hot, when
2. when you are told, when
3. when we were in Ottawa, when
4. while the turtle crawled, comparison
5. because it received good care, why
6. than she does to swimming, comparison
7. if you need more money, condition
8. although some of the commands were wrong, condition
9. as if he didn't notice the bitter cold, how
10. so that she might attend college, why

Activity D
Answers will vary.

APPLY

WRITER'S CORNER

Encourage students to be aware of how adjective and adverb clauses affect tone. Invite volunteers to share their paragraphs. Students should demonstrate an understanding of adjective and adverb clauses.

 Students should identify the following verbs with adverb clauses:

get/than teens who aren't active

can't use/because business owners get mad

can't grind/because we are told that's "not what the benches and railings are for"

Remind students that an adverb clause can also modify an adjective or an adverb.

ASSESS

Note which students had difficulty using adverb clauses. Use the Reteach option with those students who need additional reinforcement.

Practice Book page 150 provides additional work with adjective and adverb clauses.

Practice Book page 150

Activity E
Answers will vary.

ACTIVITY E Modify the verb in each sentence by inserting an adverb clause.

1. A zookeeper let us watch the lions.
2. The Native Americans decided to fight for their land.
3. Avril is studying harder than ever.
4. You can learn to play the guitar.
5. The Puritans came to America.
6. I applied for the job.
7. The students were fascinated.
8. We will terminate your account in 30 days.
9. Lila danced in the meadow.
10. James sang "The Star-Spangled Banner."
11. Keiko hit the ball.
12. Ping clapped and cheered.

Activity F
1. adverb
2. adjective
3. adjective
4. adverb
5. adjective
6. adjective
7. adverb
8. adjective
9. adverb
10. adverb

ACTIVITY F Identify whether each clause below is an adjective clause or adverb clause. Then write a sentence using each clause.

1. when the shopping bag broke
2. that we overlooked
3. which was very funny
4. if I could visit any place
5. that I'd never seen before
6. who could help me with this matter
7. as if we'd never met
8. where the weather is cold year-round
9. because he was nervous
10. until it got dark

Grammar in Action. Find verbs with adverb clauses in the p. 299 letter.

WRITER'S CORNER

You have been asked to test a new video game or toy. Write a paragraph for the body of a letter describing what you liked, disliked, or would change about the game. Use two adjective clauses and two adverb clauses.

Business Letters • 311

TEACHING OPTIONS

Reteach

Write on strips of paper sentences with adverb clauses. Cut the strips of paper, separating the adverb clause from each sentence and then separating the subordinate conjunction. Ask students to work together to reconstruct the strips to form complete sentences.

English-Language Learners

Give students extra practice working with adverbs. Provide students with a list of adverbs that end in *ly*. Cover the *ly* ending of each word and ask students to read the word they see. Have students look up the word in a dictionary and write the definition. Then challenge students to use the words from the original list of adverbs in sentences. Lead students to understand how adverbs are constructed and the role they play in a sentence.

For Tomorrow

Have students identify adjective and adverb clauses in a business letter they find at home. Ask students to write a paragraph explaining in what ways the clauses contribute to the purpose and tone of the letter. Prepare a paragraph of your own to share with the class tomorrow.

OBJECTIVES

- **To identify and to pluralize compound words**
- **To turn phrases into compounds**
- **To understand correct usage of clipped words**

WARM-UP

Read, Listen, Speak

Read aloud your business letter from yesterday's For Tomorrow activity. Point out adjective and adverb clauses and discuss how they affect the overall tone of the letter.

Have small groups discuss the business letters that they found for homework. Encourage students to use the explanations that they wrote to discuss how the use of adjective and adverb clauses affected the purpose and tone of the letters.

GRAMMAR CONNECTION

Take this opportunity to talk about the subjunctive mood. You may wish to have students point out the subjunctive mood in their Read, Listen, Speak examples.

TEACH

Invite a volunteer to read aloud the section Compound Words. Encourage students to offer additional examples of compound words. Then read aloud the section Pluralizing Compounds. Take time for students to list several examples of closed, hyphenated, and open pluralized compounds *(volleyballs, window-shoppers, maids of honor).*

Ask a volunteer to read aloud the first paragraph of the section Turning Phrases into Compounds. Discuss the example sentences

and then read aloud the paragraph that follows. Point out that when some compound words are used as nouns, they do not have a hyphen, but when the same words modify a noun, a hyphen is needed.

PRACTICE

ACTIVITY A

When students have finished, invite volunteers to write the correctly spelled compound words on the board. Ask volunteers to add two additional compound words that are not in this activity.

ACTIVITY B

After students have written the plural forms of the compound words, have students trade papers with a partner to check each other's work. Then set a timer and have partners write as many plural compound words as they can. Have the "winners" share their lists with the class.

ACTIVITY C

Have students complete this activity independently. Then as a class discuss the compound words that students wrote. Have volunteers list their words on the board.

LESSON **4** WORD STUDY

Compound Words and Clipped Words

Compound Words

Compound words, which are usually adjectives and nouns, are made up of two or more shorter words. The three kinds of compound words are

- closed compounds
  keyboard, makeup, basketball
- hyphenated compounds
  over-the-counter, twenty-five, self-respect
- open compounds
  middle school, post office, attorney general

Pluralizing Compounds

In most cases compound words should be pluralized like any other word, by adding *-s* to the end of the word. This is almost always true for closed compounds, such as *bookmarks* or *checklists*.

Some hyphenated or open compounds are pluralized differently. If the compound includes a noun followed by a word or words that modify it, pluralize the noun being modified. For example, *father-in-law* becomes *fathers-in-law* and *attorney general* becomes *attorneys general*. The words *in-law* modify *father*, while *general* describes *attorney* more specifically. If you are uncertain how to pluralize a compound, consult a dictionary.

Turning Phrases into Compounds

Sometimes it is hard to know whether two words should be written as a phrase or as a compound word. When two or more words modify the noun that follows them, they may be compounded, particularly if they might otherwise cause confusion.

We waited anxiously for our grades from the *second quarter.*
We waited anxiously for our *second-quarter* **grades.**

In the first sentence, the words *second quarter* stand alone, while in the second sentence, they modify the word *grades.*

APPLY

WRITER'S CORNER

When students have finished, invite volunteers to read aloud their sentences. Discuss differences in meaning among the sentences. Students should demonstrate an understanding of compound words.

 Students should identify two compound words. Possible answers include *skateboarder, skateboarding, skateboard, sidewalks,* and *downtown.* Remind students that compound words can be open, closed, or hyphenated.

ASSESS

Note which students had difficulty pluralizing compounds. Use the Reteach option with those students who need additional reinforcement.

Reteach

Explain that predicting whether a compound word is closed, open, or hyphenated is often difficult. Tell students that consulting a dictionary to check the spelling of a compound word can be helpful. Write these words on the board. Have students use their dictionaries to find if the words are closed, open, or hyphenated compounds. Then have students write the plural form of each.

- **great aunt**
- **keyboard**
- **school bus**
- **science fiction**
- **head set**
- **merry go round**

English-Language Learners

Provide extra practice for forming plurals of compound words. Some languages have no plural forms, and some have plural forms that are more regular than in English. Write on the board some examples of singular nouns that form plurals in a variety of ways. Work with students to form the plurals correctly.

Activity A
1. vice president
2. salesperson
3. stockbroker
4. all right
5. database
6. X-ray
7. yellow fever
8. light years or light-years
9. a lot
10. great-grandmother
11. African violet
12. blood pressure

Activity B
1. anchorwomen
2. secretaries of state
3. drive-ins
4. bills of fare
5. chiefs of staff
6. notaries public
7. wristwatches
8. also-rans
9. go-betweens
10. checkbooks
11. master sergeants
12. daughters-in-law

Activity C
Suggested answers: sandstorm, sandbar, sandman, thumbprint, handstand, handcraft, handprint, newsstand, newsprint, newsman/woman, aircraft, airman/woman, crossbar

ACTIVITY A Rewrite the incorrectly spelled compounds on the list. You may consult a dictionary for help.

1. vicepresident
2. sales person
3. stock-broker
4. alright
5. data base
6. X ray
7. yellowfever
8. lightyears
9. alot
10. greatgrandmother
11. African-violet
12. bloodpressure

ACTIVITY B Write the plural of each compound word.

1. anchorwoman
2. secretary of state
3. drive-in
4. bill of fare
5. chief of staff
6. notary public
7. wristwatch
8. also-ran
9. go-between
10. checkbook
11. master sergeant
12. daughter-in-law

ACTIVITY C Combine as many words from the first column with appropriate words from the second column to form compound words. You can use all the words more than once.

sand	storm
thumb	print
hand	stand
news	craft
air	man/woman
cross	bar

WRITER'S CORNER

Pluralize the following words and use them in sentences. Use a dictionary if you need help.

passerby

teaspoonful

six-year-old

Business Letters • 313

Grammar in Action. Find two compound words in the p. 299 letter.

For Tomorrow

Ask students to search publications for examples of adjective phrases that they can turn into compound words without losing the original meanings of the sentences. Have students replace at least three phrases with compound words. Find several examples that you can share with the class.

WARM-UP

Read, Listen, Speak

Write on the board your compound words from yesterday's For Tomorrow homework. Compare the original sentence from the letter with the revised sentence that contains the compound words. Discuss how the compound words change the tone of each sentence.

Have volunteers share their compound words with the class. Ask students how these compound words affect the overall tone of the business letters.

GRAMMAR CONNECTION

Take this opportunity to talk about modal auxiliaries. You may wish to have students point out modal auxiliaries in their Read, Listen, Speak examples.

TEACH

Ask a volunteer to read aloud the section Clipped Words. Challenge students to verbalize more examples of clipped words. For each word, have students decide whether the clipped word is so commonly used that it would be appropriate for a business letter. Remind students that casual language should be avoided in business letters.

PRACTICE

ACTIVITY D

Complete this activity as a class. Discuss each word and ask students to determine if each clipped word is appropriate for a business letter.

ACTIVITY E

After students have finished, invite volunteers to read their sentences to the class. Ask students to decide whether the clipped word would be appropriate to use in either a casual e-mail or in a business letter. Discuss how the clipped words affect the tone of each sentence.

ACTIVITY F

Have students complete this activity independently. After students have finished rewriting the letter, have them trade papers with a partner. Have students check each other's work and use proofreading marks to point out places where the letters require further revision.

Clipped Words

Many words people use every day, such as *phone* and *exam,* are clipped words, shortened versions of longer words. The word *phone* is a shortened form of *telephone,* and *exam* is short for *examination.*

Writers of business letters must be cautious when using clipped words. Many clipped words, such as *phone,* are too casual for business use. Others, such as *exam,* are so commonly used that they are acceptable in most business letters.

ACTIVITY D Write the longer word from which each clipped word comes. If you're not sure what the longer word is, look up the clipped word in a dictionary. The entry will tell you what the longer word is. Which words would be appropriate to use in a business letter?

1. bike	6. gas	11. sub	16. rep
2. fridge	7. taxi	12. limo	17. van
3. vet	8. fan	13. zoo	18. memo
4. photo	9. lunch	14. bus	19. ad
5. ref	10. math	15. flu	20. pro

ACTIVITY E Choose three clipped words in Activity D. Write three sentences that you might include in an e-mail to a friend. Include a clipped word from Activity D in each sentence. Then write three sentences that you might include in a formal business letter. In each sentence include the longer version of the clipped word. Notice how the word choice affects the tone of each sentence.

Activity D
1. bicycle
2. refrigerator
3. veteran or veterinarian
4. photograph
5. referee
6. gasoline
7. taxicab
8. fanatic
9. luncheon
10. mathematics
11. submarine or substitute
12. limousine
13. zoological garden
14. omnibus
15. influenza
16. representative
17. caravan
18. memorandum
19. advertisement
20. professional

Activity E
Accept any answers that students can justify.

APPLY

WRITER'S CORNER

When students have finished, have them share their answers with the class. Write on the board a list of technology-based clipped words and have students copy them into their notebooks. Students should demonstrate an understanding of clipped words.

ASSESS

Note which students had difficulty using clipped words. Use the Reteach option with those students who need additional reinforcement.

Practice Book page 151 provides additional work with compound words and clipped words.

Reteach

Ask students to search the model on page 298 for clipped words (photo, paper, phone). Instruct students to identify the longer word for each clipped word and to decide whether the clipped word is used appropriately. Then challenge students to offer additional clipped words that could be added to the letter.

Searching for Slang

Tell students that many slang words are clipped words. Explain that when a slang word becomes commonly used, it appears as an entry in a dictionary. Have students work with partners to search a dictionary for entries for slang words and to see if they are clipped forms of longer words. Then ask partners to collaborate on writing a formal and an informal message, one using clipped words and the other using the longer versions of the same words.

For Tomorrow

Ask students to search newspapers for examples of clipped words that are commonly used. Have students make a list of the clipped words and include the longer version of the words. Challenge students to name longer words we use now that might have common clipped versions in the future. Generate your own list to share with the class.

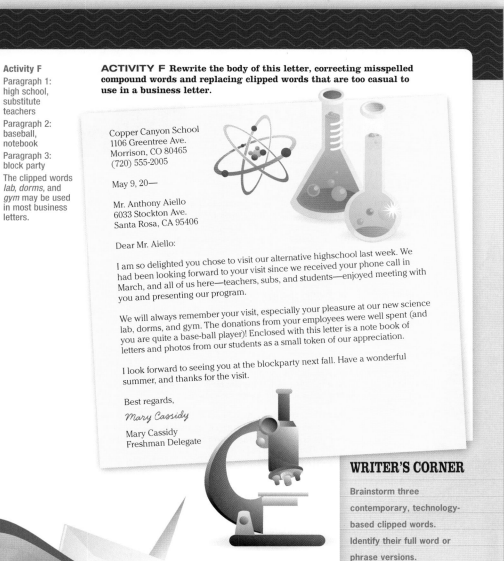

Activity F

Paragraph 1: high school, substitute teachers

Paragraph 2: baseball, notebook

Paragraph 3: block party

The clipped words *lab, dorms,* and *gym* may be used in most business letters.

ACTIVITY F Rewrite the body of this letter, correcting misspelled compound words and replacing clipped words that are too casual to use in a business letter.

Copper Canyon School
1106 Greentree Ave.
Morrison, CO 80465
(720) 555-2005

May 9, 20—

Mr. Anthony Aiello
6033 Stockton Ave.
Santa Rosa, CA 95406

Dear Mr. Aiello:

I am so delighted you chose to visit our alternative highschool last week. We had been looking forward to your visit since we received your phone call in March, and all of us here—teachers, subs, and students—enjoyed meeting with you and presenting our program.

We will always remember your visit, especially your pleasure at our new science lab, dorms, and gym. The donations from your employees were well spent (and you are quite a base-ball player)! Enclosed with this letter is a note book of letters and photos from our students as a small token of our appreciation.

I look forward to seeing you at the blockparty next fall. Have a wonderful summer, and thanks for the visit.

Best regards,

Mary Cassidy

Mary Cassidy
Freshman Delegate

WRITER'S CORNER

Brainstorm three contemporary, technology-based clipped words. Identify their full word or phrase versions.

Business Letters • 315

OBJECTIVES

- **To summarize effectively**
- **To use direct quotations correctly**
- **To paraphrase efficiently**

WARM-UP

Read, Listen, Speak

Share your list of clipped words from yesterday's For Tomorrow homework. Invite students to discuss their lists of clipped words. Write the clipped words on the board along with the longer version of the words. Then discuss some commonly used words that might have clipped versions in the future.

GRAMMAR CONNECTION

Take this opportunity to talk about agreement of subject and verb. You may wish to have students point out agreement of subject and verb in their Read, Listen, Speak examples.

TEACH

Read aloud the first paragraph and the bulleted items that follow. Reinforce that summarizing is an essential part of a business letter because business letters should be short and straight to the point.

Ask a volunteer to read aloud the next paragraph and the example sentence that follows. Point out that students will commonly use one-sentence summaries as support in their business letters.

Have students silently read the personal narrative "Tossed by a Twister" on page 223. Ask volunteers to create brief summaries of this narrative. Then read the example summary aloud. Have students compare the example summary to those offered by their classmates.

Ask a volunteer to read aloud the Direct Quotation section. Tell students that direct quotations are effective tools to support the purpose of a business letter.

PRACTICE

ACTIVITY A

Allow students time to write answers to the questions about the excerpt. Check the answers with the class, discussing each answer in detail.

Writing Tools

Summarize and Paraphrase

A summary is a condensed version of a text or other source, written in your own words. When you summarize an informational text, you restate only the main points.

- To summarize a story, you restate only important details such as the main characters, the main events, the plot, and theme.
- In a business letter, you may want to summarize only the main points. In the student's letter presented at the beginning of this chapter, the student summarizes the reasons supporting his request for a skate park.

A summary can be as long as one-third the length of the original source. It can also be as short as one sentence.

I believe that my experience as a babysitter has prepared me to take on the responsibilities of junior counselor for your camp.

Reread the personal narrative "Tossed by a Twister" in Chapter 1. A summary of "Tossed by a Twister" should read as follows:

This personal narrative is about a boy and his dog getting caught by a tornado. The boy's dog is pulled away from him by the strong winds, but the boy later finds him safely in a hole under a tree branch.

Paraphrasing is restating individual passages of a work in your own words. It is more detailed than a summary. Researchers, book reviewers, and other writers generally paraphrase a work's supporting details.

Direct Quotation

A direct quotation contains words that are identical to the original text. It must match the original text word for word. A quotation should be enclosed in quotation marks.

Whether you summarize, paraphrase, or quote, your information must be attributed to its original source. Good writers will use all three techniques in their work to avoid plagiarism and to meet the needs of their readers. Be sure to cite others' work no matter what type of medium it comes from, including Web sites, blogs, or films.

APPLY

WRITER'S CORNER

Encourage students to discuss each other's business letters, pointing out any summaries, paraphrased sentences, or direct quotations. Ask volunteers to share their business letters with the class. Students should demonstrate an understanding of summaries, direct quotations, and paraphrased sentences.

TechTip Discuss online search engines that students might use to find their sample business letters. Encourage students to suggest search engines that have been useful to them in the past.

ASSESS

Note which students had difficulty understanding how to identify summaries, direct quotations, and paraphrased sentences. Use the Reteach option with those students who need additional reinforcement.

TEACHING OPTIONS

Reteach

Give students copies of two separate articles. Provide a summary for one article. Read aloud the article and accompanying summary. Discuss which points from the article were included in the summary. Then have students make a list of main points to be included in a summary. Discuss these points, listing them on the board. Have students write their own summaries. Invite volunteers to read their summaries aloud.

Summarizing Scenes

Ask students to write a one or two paragraph summary of their favorite movie or book. Have small groups exchange papers. Encourage students to point out where summaries could be strengthened. Invite volunteers to share their summaries with the class. Challenge students to include adverb and adjective clauses in their summaries.

Activity A

1. piracy, Sir Francis Drake, the 16th century, change of character, change in loyalties, perspectives of history.

2.–5. Answers will vary.

ACTIVITY A Read the following excerpt and respond to questions.

There was another noted personage of the sixteenth century who played the part of pirate in the new world, and thereby set a most shining example to the buccaneers of those regions. This was no other than Sir Francis Drake, one of England's greatest naval commanders.

It is probable that Drake, when he started out in life, was a man of very law-abiding and orderly disposition, for he was appointed by Queen Elizabeth a naval chaplain, and, it is said, though there is some doubt about this, that he was subsequently vicar of a parish. But by nature he was a sailor, and nothing else, and after having made several voyages in which he showed himself a good fighter, as well as a good commander, he undertook, in 1572, an expedition against the Spanish settlements in the West Indies, for which he had no legal warrant whatever. . . .

Whether or not Drake's conscience had anything to do with the bungling manner in which he made this first attempt at piracy, we cannot say, but he soon gave his conscience a holiday, and undertook some very successful robbing enterprises. . . .

Whatever this gallant ex-chaplain now thought of himself, he was considered by the Spaniards as an out-and-out pirate, and in this opinion they were quite correct. During his great voyage around the world, which he began in 1577, he came down upon the Spanish-American settlements like a storm from the sea. He attacked towns, carried off treasure, captured merchant-vessels, and in fact showed himself to be a thoroughbred and accomplished pirate of the first class.

Sir Francis Drake

1. For what research topics could this excerpt be used as a resource?

2. What is the topic sentence or main idea of this excerpt? Write your answer as a one-sentence summary of this excerpt.

3. Scan the excerpt for important facts and supporting details. Use your own words and phrases to record these facts and details on note cards. You do not need to use complete sentences.

4. Paraphrase the excerpt in complete sentences, using only your note cards.

5. Which sentence would you use as a direct quotation for supporting evidence? Why?

WRITER'S CORNER

Find a business letter that includes a summary, paraphrasing, and a direct quotation. Share your letter with the class.

Tech Tip With an adult, find a sample business letter online.

Business Letters • 317

For Tomorrow

Have students find three direct quotations that they find inspiring. Tell students to write a brief paragraph describing how paraphrasing each quotation might affect the intended message. Bring in several quotations you find inspiring to discuss with the class.

WARM-UP

Read, Listen, Speak

Read your quotations from yesterday's For Tomorrow activity to the class. Ask if any students used the same quotations as you did. Have volunteers share their quotations with the class. Then discuss how the meaning of each quotation might be lost if it were paraphrased. Point out that sometimes it is better to use a direct quotation and sometimes it is better to paraphrase.

GRAMMAR CONNECTION

Take this opportunity to talk about agreement of subject and verb. You may wish to have students point out agreement of subject and verb in their Read, Listen, Speak examples.

TEACH

Have volunteers read aloud the first two paragraphs and the bulleted items that follow. Reinforce that strong writers will incorporate summaries, paraphrases, and direct quotations into their writing. Then have students write the bulleted information in their notebook. Encourage students to use these tips in all their academic subjects.

Have a volunteer read aloud the next paragraph. Allow students to silently read the news article. After students have finished reading, discuss the use of summaries, paraphrases, and direct quotations in the article.

Read aloud the tips for avoiding plagiarism. Invite students to offer other tips that would help them avoid plagiarism. Then have students write these in their notebooks.

PRACTICE

ACTIVITY B

Read aloud the directions. Write on the board a checklist containing the steps students must complete for this activity. The list should include creating a one-sentence summary, taking notes of important facts, and paraphrasing the excerpt.

Have students write their one-sentence summaries and take notes independently. Then have students compare their notes with a partner. Encourage students to discuss the important facts and supporting details with their partner. Then have students write their paraphrase of the excerpt with their partner. Remind students that when they paraphrase, they should include adverb and adjective clauses. Tell students that including adverb and adjective clauses will help avoid plagiarism and vary sentence structure.

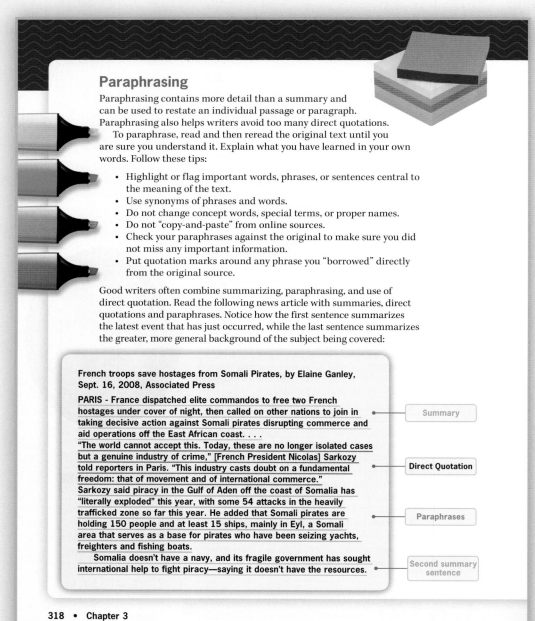

Paraphrasing

Paraphrasing contains more detail than a summary and can be used to restate an individual passage or paragraph. Paraphrasing also helps writers avoid too many direct quotations.

To paraphrase, read and then reread the original text until you are sure you understand it. Explain what you have learned in your own words. Follow these tips:

- Highlight or flag important words, phrases, or sentences central to the meaning of the text.
- Use synonyms of phrases and words.
- Do not change concept words, special terms, or proper names.
- Do not "copy-and-paste" from online sources.
- Check your paraphrases against the original to make sure you did not miss any important information.
- Put quotation marks around any phrase you "borrowed" directly from the original source.

Good writers often combine summarizing, paraphrasing, and use of direct quotation. Read the following news article with summaries, direct quotations and paraphrases. Notice how the first sentence summarizes the latest event that has just occurred, while the last sentence summarizes the greater, more general background of the subject being covered:

> French troops save hostages from Somali Pirates, by Elaine Ganley, Sept. 16, 2008, Associated Press
>
> PARIS - France dispatched elite commandos to free two French hostages under cover of night, then called on other nations to join in taking decisive action against Somali pirates disrupting commerce and aid operations off the East African coast. . . . **Summary**
>
> "The world cannot accept this. Today, these are no longer isolated cases but a genuine industry of crime," [French President Nicolas] Sarkozy told reporters in Paris. "This industry casts doubt on a fundamental freedom: that of movement and of international commerce." **Direct Quotation**
>
> Sarkozy said piracy in the Gulf of Aden off the coast of Somalia has "literally exploded" this year, with some 54 attacks in the heavily trafficked zone so far this year. He added that Somali pirates are holding 150 people and at least 15 ships, mainly in Eyl, a Somali area that serves as a base for pirates who have been seizing yachts, freighters and fishing boats. **Paraphrases**
>
> Somalia doesn't have a navy, and its fragile government has sought international help to fight piracy—saying it doesn't have the resources. **Second summary sentence**

APPLY

WRITER'S CORNER

Remind students that a summary only restates the main points. When students have finished, invite volunteers to read their summaries aloud. Encourage feedback from the class about whether summaries were done correctly. Students should demonstrate an understanding of writing summaries.

TechTip Encourage students to post their finished summaries on a class blog. Have students offer constructive responses to their classmates' summaries.

ASSESS

Note which students had difficulty summarizing, paraphrasing, and using direct quotations. Use the Reteach option with those students who need additional reinforcement.

Practice Book page 152 provides additional work with summarizing, paraphrasing, and using direct quotations.

TEACHING OPTIONS

Reteach

Have students reread the business letter on page 298. Instruct them to find three main points and to paraphrase each. Invite volunteers to write on the board the original statement along with their paraphrased statement. Discuss each example with the class.

Meeting Individual Needs

Kinesthetic Have small groups read a story and paraphrase the dialogue. Have students use the paraphrased dialogue to create a scene to perform in front of the class. Encourage students to be creative. For example, suggest that students change the setting of their scenes but keep the plot and main points the same. When students have finished, have them perform their scenes for the class.

Remember that if you use the original language from a source, it is considered plagiarism. To avoid plagiarizing, follow these steps:

- Use many different sources when conducting research on a topic.
- Set aside your research material.
- Think critically about what you have read. How was the information from different sources similar? How was it different?
- Draw your own conclusions and then start making notes. Find your own words to express your thoughts.
- Go back to your sources to make sure you have not plagiarized.

ACTIVITY B Putting several facts in one complex or compound sentence with adverb and adjective clauses is a good strategy for avoiding plagiarism when paraphrasing. Read the following excerpt. Summarize the main idea of the excerpt in one sentence. Then take notes of important facts and supporting details. Using only the information in your notes, paraphrase the excerpt in one to three compound or complex sentences with adverb and adjective clauses.

Activity B
Answers will vary.
Example of paraphrases:
Puerto Rico, which is the smallest of the Greater Antilles Islands, is a mountainous island in the West Indies whose soil is fertile and extensively cultivated with a variety of crops. This 3,550-square-mile island has beautiful weather, over twelve hundred rivers, and many springs and waterfalls.

If you will find a map of the West Indies in your atlas or geography book, you will also find Puerto Rico. It is one of the four Greater Antilles Islands, and lies east of Haiti and farthest out in the Atlantic Ocean. It is over 400 miles from the east coast of Cuba, a thousand miles from Havana, and about 1,450 miles from New York.

In size it is the smallest of the group. Its area is about 3,550 square miles. Its average length is about 95 miles; its average breadth about 35 miles. In shape it resembles the State of Connecticut, though it is only three-fourths the size of that state. . . .

The surface of Puerto Rico is mountainous. A range of hills traverses the island from east to west. The hills are low and their sides are covered with vegetation. The hills are not rocky and barren, but are cultivated to their very tops. The lower valleys are rich pasture lands or cultivated plantations. The knolls have orchards of coconuts and other trees. Coffee, protected by the shade of other trees, grows to the summits of the green hills. The ground is covered everywhere with a thick carpeting of grass.

The soil is remarkably fertile. This is due partly to the fine climate, partly to abundant moisture. The island has many fast flowing rivers. There are over 1,200 of these. In the mountains are numerous springs and waterfalls, but these are hidden by the overhanging giant ferns and plants.

WRITER'S CORNER

Write a summary of the business letter on page 298.

 Tech Tip Post your summary on the class blog.

Business Letters • 319

For Tomorrow

Have students find an article about their favorite entertainer in an encyclopedia. Tell students to write down three facts as direct quotations and to paraphrase three facts. Do the same for your favorite entertainer.

OBJECTIVES

- **To be professional and to plan what to say during a business telephone call**
- **To practice telephone listening and response skills**

WARM-UP

Read, Listen, Speak

Share with the class the direct quotations and paraphrases you wrote for yesterday's For Tomorrow homework. Ask volunteers to share their direct quotations and paraphrases. Then discuss which facts would work best as direct quotations and which would work best as paraphrases. Be sure students understand that they should incorporate both tools in their writing.

GRAMMAR CONNECTION

Take this opportunity to review verbs. You may wish to have students point out verbs in their Read, Listen, Speak examples.

TEACH

Ask students to share experiences making business telephone calls. Invite a volunteer to read aloud the first paragraph. Challenge students to explain how business telephone calls are different from personal calls. *(Business calls are made for a specific reason. Often they involve asking for something. The appropriate tone is polite and respectful. Personal calls are casual and more friendly.)*

Invite volunteers to read aloud the second paragraph and the guidelines in the section Being Professional. Then ask volunteers to paraphrase each bulleted item.

Ask volunteers to read aloud the guidelines in the section Communicating Professionally. When students have finished, explain that a variation of the golden rule can also apply to business telephone conversations. Have students explain precisely what this means. *(Speak to others the way you would like to be spoken to.)*

PRACTICE

ACTIVITY A

Allow time for students to complete the activity independently. Ask students to confer with a partner to determine if what they plan to say is appropriate. After they have practiced, ask volunteers to role-play the business conversation for the class. Discuss the positive aspects of each performed conversation.

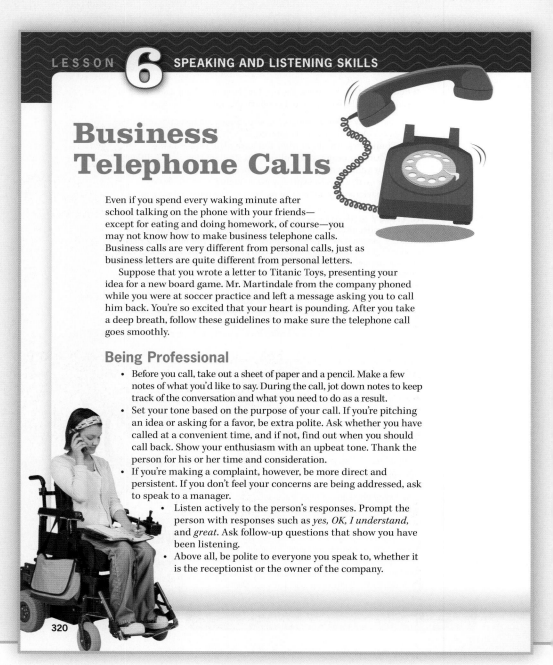

Business Telephone Calls

Even if you spend every waking minute after school talking on the phone with your friends—except for eating and doing homework, of course—you may not know how to make business telephone calls. Business calls are very different from personal calls, just as business letters are quite different from personal letters.

Suppose that you wrote a letter to Titanic Toys, presenting your idea for a new board game. Mr. Martindale from the company phoned while you were at soccer practice and left a message asking you to call him back. You're so excited that your heart is pounding. After you take a deep breath, follow these guidelines to make sure the telephone call goes smoothly.

Being Professional

- Before you call, take out a sheet of paper and a pencil. Make a few notes of what you'd like to say. During the call, jot down notes to keep track of the conversation and what you need to do as a result.
- Set your tone based on the purpose of your call. If you're pitching an idea or asking for a favor, be extra polite. Ask whether you have called at a convenient time, and if not, find out when you should call back. Show your enthusiasm with an upbeat tone. Thank the person for his or her time and consideration.
- If you're making a complaint, however, be more direct and persistent. If you don't feel your concerns are being addressed, ask to speak to a manager.
- Listen actively to the person's responses. Prompt the person with responses such as *yes, OK, I understand,* and *great.* Ask follow-up questions that show you have been listening.
- Above all, be polite to everyone you speak to, whether it is the receptionist or the owner of the company.

320

APPLY

SPEAKER'S CORNER

Have pairs of students practice aloud the messages each student would leave on Mr. Martindale's voice mail. Then invite volunteers to present their voice-mail messages to the class. Encourage feedback from students about the stated message. Challenge students to compare their classmates' messages with the business telephone call guidelines. Students should demonstrate an understanding of professional communication during business telephone calls.

TechTip You may wish to have students record their voice messages, using a recorder. Have students play their messages for the class. Encourage students to provide positive feedback for each message played.

ASSESS

Note which students had difficulty understanding communicating professionally during a business telephone call. Use the Reteach option with those students who need additional reinforcement.

TEACHING OPTIONS

Reteach

Ask students to make a business telephone call checklist. Point out that a checklist can remind students what to say if they become nervous when making the call. Have them use the following headings: *Purpose, Tone, Identify Yourself/Opening, Key Points, Polite Responses, Sum Up/Closing.*

Ask students to write notes under each heading to describe how the phone call should progress.

Business Partners

Invite students to work in pairs to role-play a business telephone call. Challenge them to write dialogue for a situation in which a complaint or a request is made. Invite pairs to present the telephone call to the class. Then ask the class to decide whether the caller followed the guidelines for making a business telephone call.

Communicating Professionally

- Immediately identify yourself and the purpose of the call. If the person you're trying to reach answers the phone, say something like "Good afternoon, this is Maris Nelson returning your call." If someone else answers, you might say "Good afternoon, this is Maris Nelson. I'm returning Mr. Martindale's call. Is he available?"
- If you're making a follow-up call, remind the person you're calling of the purpose of the call. People get busy at work, and if someone has forgotten why you're calling (or even who you are), don't take it personally.
- Sum up at the end of the conversation to make sure you both share the same understanding of what was said and what you decided to do. Thank the person for talking with you and set a time for your next conversation if one is necessary.
- If you reach someone's voice mail, leave a short message. State your name and telephone number slowly and clearly. Then briefly explain the purpose of your call. At the end of the message, state your name and phone number again so the person does not have to listen to the entire message again for this information.

ACTIVITY A Read the following scenarios. Using the guidelines, jot down notes on what you would say in a business call about each scenario.

1. A repair person fixed your washing machine last week, but it has stopped working again.
2. A famous filmmaker answered your letter. You want to invite her to speak at your school's film society.
3. You've been chosen to find out what happened to the uniforms that your team ordered. The order is now a month overdue.
4. A community foundation gives small grants to kids who have worthwhile projects. You have questions about how to apply.

SPEAKER'S CORNER

Imagine you are Maris Nelson. Practice what you would say if you reached Mr. Martindale's voice mail.

 Tech Tip Record your message and review it for improvements.

Business Letters • 321

For Tomorrow

Ask students to interview an adult about business telephone calls. Suggest that students ask the following questions: *What tone of voice did you use and why? How did you begin and end the conversation? What was the intended result of the conversation, and did you get it? What is the most important thing to keep in mind when making a business telephone call?* Conduct an interview yourself of a colleague or friend.

WARM-UP

Read, Listen, Speak

Share your interview from yesterday's For Tomorrow homework. Model what you would like students to say by pointing out the details from your interview. Then invite small groups to discuss the notes students took during their interviews. Ask students to discuss how following the guidelines for a business telephone call helped the adults' calls go more smoothly. Have students share new and pertinent information that they learned about making business telephone calls.

TEACH

Ask a volunteer to read aloud the section Listening and Response Tips. Ask why being a good listener is important during a business telephone call. (*Active listening helps both parties find solutions.*)

PRACTICE

ACTIVITY B

Allow time for students to write what they would say over the phone to launch a new product. Then invite volunteers to share their product ideas with the class.

ACTIVITY C

Have a student read aloud the questions that follow the directions. Challenge partners to practice both their listening and speaking skills. Have partners present their telephone calls to the class.

ACTIVITY D

Suggest students take notes when their partners critique the delivery of their telephone calls. Ask partners to discuss what worked and what did not work during the phone calls.

ACTIVITY E

When students have finished practicing their phone calls, lead a discussion about why it is especially important to be a good listener when someone calls you to make a complaint. (*Callers might be emotional. Solutions can come more quickly when people are calm.*)

Listening and Response Tips

Someday you may be on the receiving end of a business call. Here are some tips to help you listen and respond to the caller.

- Keep a notebook and pencil near the phone to jot down notes.
- Pay attention to the speaker's name. Refer to him or her by name.
- Listen actively. To show you are listening, offer occasional feedback or ask follow-up questions.
- If the caller explains anything complicated, repeat it back to the caller to be sure you have understood.
- Tell the caller what action you plan to take in response to the call. If you need to consult with someone else before making a decision, let the caller know.

ACTIVITY B Think of an idea for a new product that you could present over the phone to a company. For each step listed, jot down what you would say as you present your idea.

1. Greet the person.
2. Identify yourself.
3. State the purpose.
4. Describe the product.
5. Request action.
6. Thank the person.

ACTIVITY C Work with a partner to role-play the phone call you planned in Activity B. Take turns being the person making the call and the person receiving it. If you are the recipient of the call, respond as someone who is enthusiastic about the product. Use the Listening and Response Tips above. Critique each other's calls and revise your plan, taking your partner's comments into account.

As you practice your call, ask yourself the following questions:

- Did I greet the person and introduce myself politely?
- Did I concisely explain the purpose of the call?
- Did I describe the product clearly?
- Did I request action of some kind?
- Did I show that I was listening actively?
- Did I thank the person I called?

ACTIVITY F

When partners have finished practicing their telephone calls, invite volunteers to perform their calls for the class. Encourage students to provide feedback.

APPLY

SPEAKER'S CORNER

Allow time for students to present their telephone calls. When offering feedback, ask students to refer specifically to the speaking and listening guidelines on pages 320–322. Students should demonstrate an understanding of professional communication during a business telephone call.

ASSESS

Note which students had difficulty using good listening skills during a business telephone call. Use the Reteach option with those students who need additional reinforcement.

After you have reviewed Lessons 3–5, administer the Writing Skills Assessment on pages 53–54 in the **Assessment Book.** This test is also available on the optional **Test Generator CD.**

TEACHING OPTIONS

Reteach

Ask students to poll their teachers and other adults about what they consider to be good listening skills during a business telephone call. Have students compile a list of the responses and add to it the Listening and Response Tips on page 322. Encourage students to keep this list by the phone at home so they can practice these skills whenever they make a business telephone call.

Learning from Your Mistakes

Use the product idea telephone call from Activity B. Invite a volunteer to join you in presenting the telephone call to the class. As you present the call, display poor listening skills, such as continually asking your caller to repeat what he or she said, forgetting the caller's name, or using a rude tone. Then ask students to make a two-column chart about what you did wrong and how you could improve your listening skills. Ask a volunteer to role-play the same part, using good listening skills.

ACTIVITY D Practice your telephone call with a partner twice more with two different scenarios for the call's recipient. In the first scenario, the person you call is interested but not yet convinced your product will be successful. In the second scenario, the person is not interested in your product. Let your partner critique the content and delivery of your telephone call after you have finished.

ACTIVITY E Think of two more reasons you might call a business. It may be to inform the bank that your statement doesn't match the balance in your checkbook or to complain that the product you purchased doesn't work. Practice making these calls with a partner. Follow the speaking and listening tips outlined in this lesson.

ACTIVITY F Work with a partner to role-play a telephone inquiry call to a high school, magnet school, or college you wish to attend. Use the list below to develop your own set of questions to ask the recipient of your call. The recipient should jot down a list of things you have requested and repeat them back to you. Be sure to speak clearly and to the point. Make a good first impression.

1. Explain who you are and why you are calling: "I am interested in applying to your school . . ."

2. Ask any general questions that may affect your qualifications: "Do you accept applications from eighth graders who have not completed algebra?"

3. Request any information and application forms you need. Ask whether they have an informational Web site.

4. Give your full name and address, and get the full name and address of the proper person to whom you should send your application. If the application is online, make sure you ask for the e-mail address of the recipient. Even if this information is posted online, it is good to double-check to avoid confusion.

5. Ask about any special upcoming events for interested applicants. Meeting people face-to-face can give you an edge.

SPEAKER'S CORNER

Choose one of the telephone calls you practiced with a partner and present it to the class. Use cell phones as props if they are available. Concentrate your attention on the voice of your partner, who is playing the role of the receiver of the call, but turn toward the audience so they can hear you and see your face. Encourage your audience to offer feedback after you finish role-playing the call.

Business Letters • 323

OBJECTIVE

- **To prewrite, define the purpose of, and plan the paragraphs of a business letter**

PREWRITING AND DRAFTING

Review what students have learned about writing business letters:

- include the necessary parts of a business letter
- write effective openings and closings
- include a body that uses language tailored to the recipient
- establish a definite purpose and tone
- use adjective and adverb clauses
- use compound words and clipped words

Invite a volunteer to read aloud the opening paragraph. Discuss reasons students might write or receive business letters. Then discuss why business letters serve as an effective communication tool.

Prewriting

Ask a volunteer to read aloud the section Prewriting. Invite volunteers to share experiences of times they have bought something and found it to be defective. Ask what actions students took to correct what happened. Discuss how a formal letter of complaint could be beneficial in such situations.

Gathering Information

Have a volunteer read aloud this section. Tell students that the writer of a business letter might spend more time obtaining information than freewriting. Ask a volunteer to describe what information Nikki had to find *(the name of the person to whom to address her letter, the details of the things that happened).*

Defining the Purpose

Ask a student to read aloud this section. Invite a volunteer to explain why determining the purpose of the letter is accomplished during the prewriting stage. *(It is important to determine the purpose early because it shapes the content of the letter.)* Discuss the purpose of Nikki's letter and how she determined the action she wanted taken.

👓 Explain that ideas are the foundation for all types of writing. Point out the pros and cons graphic organizer and how this helped Nikki organize the ideas for her letter of complaint.

Writer's Workshop
Business Letters

Prewriting and Drafting

Telephone calls and e-mail messages are routine and effective means of business communications. But neither has the authority of business letters. Often a letter is the first contact a businessperson has with the sender, and first impressions stick. That's why learning to write effective business letters and format them properly is so important.

Prewriting

When you write a business letter, prewriting is a time for gathering information and defining your purpose.

Nikki ordered a new pair of boots this winter from Outside Adventures, a company that sells camping equipment and clothing. Boots are an important part of her wardrobe because she trudges through snow for several months every year. These boots looked perfect, tall enough so that snow wouldn't come over the top and furry inside to keep her feet warm. When they arrived, the boots fit, and she liked the way they looked. But Nikki discovered a problem after she wore them for a few hours. The left boot wouldn't stay zipped up. As Nikki got more and more annoyed by having to zip up the boot over and over, she decided to compose a letter of complaint to Outside Adventures.

Gathering Information

Nikki knew that if she sent a letter addressed *To whom it may concern*, the letter might never reach the right person. To find the person or persons to whom she should write, she called the main number for Outside Adventures. A woman in customer relations told her to address her letter to Ethan Jones, the manager of customer service. Nikki also asked for the name of the purchasing director, Barbara Smythe, just to be sure that the person who buys products knows about the defective zipper. Finally, Nikki asked for the full address of Outside Adventures.

Defining the Purpose

Nikki next considered the purpose of her letter, or what she wanted it to accomplish. She used a pros and cons graphic organizer to decide.

👓 Ideas

PURPOSE	PROS	CONS
Express Anger	Feel better	No refund on boots
Ask for new boots	I like these boots, and will have a new pair.	They may break again.
Refund	Have money to buy new boots	Have to start new search for boots I like

Your Turn

Invite a volunteer to read this section aloud. Allow students several minutes to brainstorm possible topics for their letters. Encourage students to write all possibilities. Ask volunteers to share ideas for topics. Then have students create a pros and cons graphic organizer for one topic. Instruct students to use the information in their graphic organizer to write a statement of purpose. Ask volunteers to share their statements with the class. Encourage students to comment on whether their classmates' statements of purpose are appropriate for their topics.

Freewriting

Have a volunteer read aloud this section. As students organize their ideas, tell them to write quickly so they can get all their ideas on paper. Remind students that they can add and delete items later. Tell students that if they cannot remember details such as the date of purchase or the cost, these can be researched later. Be sure students save their notes for the next class.

Freewriting

After choosing your purpose, freewrite your letter. Jot down words and phrases as quickly as they come to mind. Record details such as date of purchase, guarantees, and any costs including original purchase, shipping, or repairs.

Prewriting / Drafting / Content Editing / Revising / Copyediting / Proofreading / Publishing

Did Nikki just want to express her irritation? Did she want a refund from Outside Adventures? Did she want the boots replaced, or would a credit be better so she could choose different boots? Since Nikki liked her boots, she decided to ask for another pair and keep her fingers crossed that the zippers on the new boots would stay zipped.

Your Turn

Have you had a complaint about a product you've used recently? Maybe you've thought of a way a product might be improved. Now is your opportunity to vent—or invent. Write a letter of complaint or a letter describing an improvement. Follow these steps:

- Decide on the problem or improvement you want to communicate and the right company to receive your letter.
- Figure out the purpose of the letter, or what action you want taken. Do you want to meet with someone to present your idea? Do you want a refund? Use the pros and cons graphic organizer to help you decide.
- Write a statement of purpose, which you can use when you draft your letter.

Business Letters • 325

Drafting

Invite a student to read aloud the first paragraph. Then instruct students to read Nikki's letter silently. When they have finished, ask a volunteer to point out the parts of a business letter. (See page 300.) Ask which sentence in Nikki's letter states the purpose.

👀 Tell students that organization includes the manner in which writers put their ideas together and how certain types of writing are structured. Remind students that the organization of a business letter includes a heading, an inside address, a salutation, the body, a closing, and reference information.

Establishing a Consistent Tone

When students have finished drafting their letters, invite a volunteer to read aloud this section. Ask students to read again the questions in the section and to take some time to reread their drafts. Encourage students to pay special attention to the tone of their letters. Tell students that if they think the tone of their letter may need to be changed, make note of it on the draft so they can revise it later.

Drafting

Read over Nikki's draft. The purpose of the letter is very clear. The letter states the problem and suggests a solution. It includes polite words such as *thanks* and also includes a positive comment. But Nikki's letter does have some flaws. Can you figure out what they are?

December 12, 20—

7 Bailey Road
Clarkfield, MN 56223

Mr. Ethan Jones
Manager, Customer Service
Outside Adventures
1221 Greenview Boulevard
Racine, WI

Dear Mr. Jones:

Thanks for sending me the Outside Adventures catalog. I saw boots I wanted in it and I ordered them on November 3. They arrived promply on November 11 they looked awesome! I was so exited to get them. But they had a problem that I noticed only after I wore them for a few hours.

I was so disapointed to find out that the boots had a problem. I really needed boots and these were just the kind I wanted. I made sure that the zipper really was broken, because otherwise your boots were totally perfect tall enough so snow didn't come over the top and nice and furry to keep my feet warm. Anyway, the zipper on the left boot wouldn't stay up. How can your company make such lousy products?

I made sure the zipper was pulled up firmly. I even put a safety pin through the top of the zipper to see if that would help. It didn't, and why should I have to do this? You should send me new boots. Do you want me to send back these boots? Or do you have another suggestion? You'd better do something about this problem or you'll be sorry!

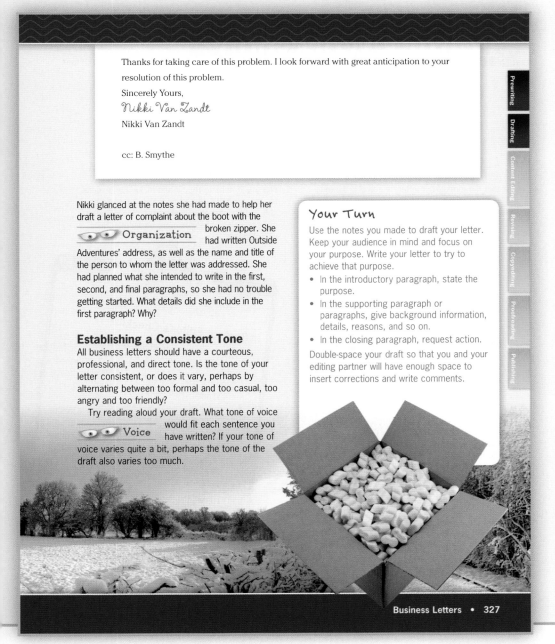

Tell students that voice is the language that helps readers hear and feel the personality of the writer. Explain that in a letter of complaint, writers should have a clear, direct purpose. Tell students they should keep a consistent, formal tone as well. Instruct students that choosing polite and professional words will help create the desired voice for a letter of complaint.

Your Turn

Have a volunteer read aloud this section. Remind students of the characteristics of a business letter's body: opening paragraph, body paragraphs that provide supporting details, and a closing paragraph. Discuss how each characteristic is important in creating an effective business letter. Then allow time for students to compose their drafts. Move around the room to make sure that students are including the necessary parts of a business letter. Suggest that students add adjective and adverb clauses where appropriate.

Thanks for taking care of this problem. I look forward with great anticipation to your resolution of this problem.

Sincerely Yours,

Nikki Van Zandt

Nikki Van Zandt

cc: B. Smythe

Nikki glanced at the notes she had made to help her draft a letter of complaint about the boot with the **Organization** broken zipper. She had written Outside Adventures' address, as well as the name and title of the person to whom the letter was addressed. She had planned what she intended to write in the first, second, and final paragraphs, so she had no trouble getting started. What details did she include in the first paragraph? Why?

Establishing a Consistent Tone

All business letters should have a courteous, professional, and direct tone. Is the tone of your letter consistent, or does it vary, perhaps by alternating between too formal and too casual, too angry and too friendly?

Try reading aloud your draft. What tone of voice **Voice** would fit each sentence you have written? If your tone of voice varies quite a bit, perhaps the tone of the draft also varies too much.

Your Turn

Use the notes you made to draft your letter. Keep your audience in mind and focus on your purpose. Write your letter to try to achieve that purpose.

- In the introductory paragraph, state the purpose.
- In the supporting paragraph or paragraphs, give background information, details, reasons, and so on.
- In the closing paragraph, request action.

Double-space your draft so that you and your editing partner will have enough space to insert corrections and write comments.

Prewriting

Drafting

Content Editing

Revising

Copyediting

Proofreading

Publishing

Business Letters • 327

OBJECTIVE
- **To edit a first draft for content**

CONTENT EDITING

Have a volunteer read aloud the first paragraph. Tell students to keep in mind the purpose of their letters and to make sure that the paragraphs support that purpose. Then ask a volunteer to read aloud the second paragraph. Point out that Nikki waited until the next day to reread her letter. Ask students what the benefits are of waiting until the next day. Discuss why it is beneficial for students to put themselves in the place of the recipient of the letter.

Tell students that sentence fluency is how sentences sound. Suggest that students read their letters aloud to hear where their writing might be unclear or awkward.

Have a volunteer read aloud the paragraph above the Content Editor's Checklist. Review the reasons writers find it helpful to have another person edit a draft for content. Then ask a volunteer to read aloud the Content Editor's Checklist. Discuss each item on the checklist and encourage students to offer additions to the checklist.

Editor's Workshop   Business Letters

Content Editing

A content editor checks ideas for logic, order, and clarity. Nikki knew how important it was that the form of her letter be correct, the tone appropriate, and the content persuasive in order for Outside Adventures to take her letter seriously.

The next day, when she was rested and could look at it with fresh eyes, Nikki turned on the computer and

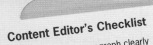
Sentence Fluency

reread the letter. She tried to put herself in the place of the person who would receive the letter, a revision strategy intended to help strengthen the content and organization. She went over the Content Editor's Checklist that the students in her class use to revise business letters and marked off each item after she checked her letter. Nikki typed questions and comments into the letter in her favorite color, bright orange. That way she could distinguish her comments from the body of the letter.

After Nikki reread the comments she made, she revised the letter. Then she asked her classmate Asha to read it and make suggestions for improvement. She knew that Asha would be able to look at it objectively and notice mistakes and confusing passages more easily than Nikki herself could.

Content Editor's Checklist

- [ ] Does the first paragraph clearly establish the purpose of the letter?
- [ ] Do the next paragraphs give reasons, examples, and details that support the purpose?
- [ ] Does the order in which the information is presented make sense, and is the information tailored to the audience?
- [ ] Do these paragraphs include only relevant information?
- [ ] Does the final paragraph restate the goal and ask for action?
- [ ] Is the tone consistent? Is it courteous and professional?

Ask a volunteer to read aloud the first paragraph on page 329. Ask students to read silently Asha's comments. Encourage students to make additional comments about Nikki's draft. *(The final sentences in the second and third paragraphs are too harsh. They need to be revised to assume a better outcome.)* Then have a volunteer read aloud the paragraph that follows Asha's comments.

Your Turn

Invite a volunteer to read aloud this section. Allow time for pairs of students to prepare and share comments on each other's drafts. If students are working on computers, encourage editing partners to make comments and revisions on printed-out versions and to type the corrections later. Remind students to offer feedback in a positive tone and to concentrate on the focus, clarity, and completeness of the letter when content editing.

TEACHING OPTIONS

Content Editor's Checklist

Encourage students to copy the checklist from page 328 so they can refer to it easily when they edit their own or other students' business letters and other writing. Ask students to place the checklist in their writing portfolios along with the checklists from previous chapters. Explain that these checklists will be helpful as students write and edit different genres.

Positive Reinforcement

Instruct students to write negative criticism about Nikki's letter. Invite volunteers to share their comments. Then challenge students to restate the negative criticism in a positive manner. Discuss how important it is to provide positive criticism when editing another student's work.

English-Language Learners

Group students who speak the same primary language. Have students trade letters within their groups. Instruct students to evaluate one another's letter, using the Content Editor's Checklist. Tell students to prepare their notes in English. When students confer, suggest that they do so in their primary language, but provide their written comments in English.

Asha read Nikki's letter several times. She consulted the Content Editor's Checklist and took a few notes. Then she and Nikki discussed the ways Asha thought the letter might be improved. Here are some of the comments Asha made to Nikki.

- Your letter states its purpose clearly and suggests a solution. I like that, but I think you should state the problem right away in the first paragraph.
- Do you really need to thank the person for sending the catalog? After all, it's routine for companies to send catalogs, hoping to sell things. Also, the person you're going to send the letter to probably didn't send the catalog.
- The tone of the last sentence in your letter is very formal. It seems quite different from the rest of the letter. I'm not sure whether it would be better to make the rest of the letter more formal or this sentence less formal, but I think you should do one or the other.

- In the last two paragraphs, you ask Mr. Jones a question, but you don't suggest whether he should write back or call you. Perhaps you could ask him to call you and add your phone number in the heading.

Asha pointed out several things that Nikki missed, such as the repetition and the inconsistent tone. After her editing conference with Asha, Nikki thought about what she would do to improve her draft.

Your Turn

Use the Content Editor's Checklist to help you revise your draft letter.

- State your purpose as clearly as you can and use details and examples to support your position. If your sentences don't bolster your argument, get rid of them.
- Trade drafts with an editing partner in your class. The two of you should read and comment on each other's letters, again using the Content Editor's Checklist as a guide.
- Begin by talking about some things you liked about the letter. Then discuss with each other your suggestions for improvement.
- Be specific and constructive in your comments. Remember that you are making suggestions. It's the writer's job to decide which comments to accept and which to reject.

Business Letters • 329

OBJECTIVE
- **To revise a business letter**

REVISING

Encourage students to discuss their experiences revising first drafts from previous chapters. Have students generate a list on the board of problems they encountered while revising. Discuss possible solutions for these issues. Then ask volunteers to share what types of changes they made to improve their work. When the discussion is complete, have students silently read Nikki's second draft.

Invite volunteers to point out the revisions Nikki made, referring to her first draft and to the comments Asha made. Ask whether Nikki maintained a consistent tone throughout the letter, and if so, to describe that tone. Challenge students to point out words or phrases that help create the tone in Nikki's letter. Have volunteers explain the improvements in the first and last paragraphs of the letter. Encourage students to comment about ways Nikki could further improve her letter. Then read aloud the paragraphs that follows Nikki's draft.

Writer's Workshop Business Letters

Revising

This is Nikki's second draft of the letter to Outside Adventures based on her own and Asha's suggestions.

December 12, 20—

7 Bailey Road
Clarkfield, MN 56223
(708) 555-1322
Mr. Ethan Jones
Manager, Customer Service
Outside Adventures
1221 Greenview Boulevard
Racine, WI

Dear Mr. Jones:

I ordered a pair of boots from an Outside Adventures catalog on November 3.
~~Thanks for sending me the Outside Adventures catalog. I saw boots I wanted in it and~~ ^P
~~I ordered them on November 3.~~ They arrived promply on November 11 ~~they looked~~ and
But I was disappointed to find that the left boot had a faulty zipper, which
~~awesome! I was so exited to get them. But they had a problem that~~ I noticed only

after I wore them for a few hours.

~~I was so disapointed to find out that the boots had a problem. I really needed boots~~ ^
~~and these were just the kind I wanted.~~ I made sure that the zipper really was broken,
                                          for our deep winter snow
because otherwise your boots were totally perfect tall enough so snow didn't come

over the top and nice and furry to keep my feet warm. ~~Anyway, the zipper on the left~~ ^
~~boot wouldn't stay up. How can your company make such lousy products?~~

Tell students that word choice is the use of everyday words in a way that supports the purpose and tone of the writing. Encourage students to use persuasive words when revising their letters of complaint.

Your Turn

Have a volunteer read aloud this section. Then allow time for students to revise their letters. When students have finished, ask them to meet again with their editing partners. Tell students to use this time to discuss the editor's suggestions and to clarify any points that may cause confusion.

TEACHING OPTIONS

Writing in Detail

As students revise their drafts, suggest that they look for opportunities to add details to their content paragraphs. Explain that these details support the purpose of the letter by giving specific reasons for the writer's complaint, praise, or request. Have students trade papers with a partner and suggest to each other where details might be added.

Business as Usual

Have small groups develop a list of questions for an interview on business letters. Suggest that the list include questions about letters that have been written and received by the subject of the interview. Then instruct students to use the list of questions to interview three adults. When students have completed their interviews, have small groups report their findings. Then discuss the findings as a class.

pulled
I made sure the zipper was pulled up firmly. I even put a safety pin through the top of the zipper to see if that would help. It didn't, and why should I have to do this? You
a pair of   If you are planning to send new boots,
should send me new boots. Do you want me to send back these boots? Or do you
have another suggestion? You'd better do something about this problem or you'll be sorry!

resolving the problem with the defective zipper. Please call me at the number
Thanks for taking care of this problem. I look forward with great anticipation to your
above to address this issue. I look forward to hearing from you as soon as possible.
resolution of this problem.

Sincerely Yours,
Nikki Van Zandt
Nikki Van Zandt

cc: B. Smythe

Preorder · Drafting · Content Editing · Revising · Copyediting · Proofreading · Publishing

Notice how Nikki improved her letter. She took out some sentences such as "How can

● ● Word Choice

your company make such lousy products?" and "You'd better do something about this problem or you'll be sorry!" How did these deletions affect the tone of her letter? In the last paragraph, she changed the tone to make it less formal. What did she add?

Compare Nikki's second draft with the first draft. In what other ways has Nikki improved her letter? In what other ways might she make her letter better?

Your Turn

- Using your own ideas and the suggestions from your editing partner, revise your letter.
- Review the Content Editor's Checklist again to make sure that you can answer yes to each question.

Business Letters • 331

OBJECTIVE
- **To copyedit and proofread a business letter**

COPYEDITING AND PROOFREADING

Copyediting

Have a volunteer read aloud the first paragraph of this section. Then have volunteers read aloud the checklist. Ask students to explain why it is important for a writer to avoid casual or inappropriate language in a business letter. Have volunteers read aloud the rest of the this section. Encourage students to point out other places in Nikki's letter where a word or phrase might be changed.

Your Turn

Invite a volunteer to read aloud this section. Allow time for editing partners to read aloud each other's drafts. Encourage students to note whether their partners correctly used compound words and clipped words.

Grammar in Action. Review active and passive voices. Tell students that passive voice may make some parts of their letter unclear and may negatively affect the overall tone of the letter.

Proofreading

Have a volunteer read aloud the first paragraph of this section. Explain that when working on a computer, it is wise to print a document to be able to proofread the paper copy. Invite volunteers to offer reasons why. *(Words, punctuation, and spaces often look different on paper than on the screen. Separating proofreading from on-screen editing helps students focus on finding mistakes.)*

Be sure students understand that conventions include spelling, grammar, punctuation, and capitalization of a piece of writing. Emphasize the importance of proofreading drafts to find and correct these types of errors.

Ask a volunteer to read aloud the rest of the section. Allow time for students to point out the mistakes that Nikki and Kay found in Nikki's letter.

Have a volunteer read aloud the Proofreader's Checklist. Review why it is helpful to have another person proofread a draft. Challenge students to add item to this checklist.

Editor's Workshop Business Letters

Copyediting and Proofreading

Copyediting

After Nikki used the Content Editor's Checklist and Asha's suggestions to help her revise her letter, she was confident that it made sense and had a clear purpose and supporting details. Because she wanted to make sure that every word was appropriate, she reviewed her letter for accuracy in word meaning, sentence structure, and logic, using the Copyeditor's Checklist.

Nikki asked Asha to read aloud the letter while Nikki listened. In that way Nikki would notice whether any words she used were too casual or whether her sentences were unclear.

Asha was uneasy with her description of the boots as *awesome*. She suspected that some people reading the letter might think that the slang word *awesome* was too casual to use in a business letter. Nikki changed *awesome* to *wonderful*. Nikki made two other word changes. She took out the word *totally* because it seemed both too casual and unnecessary. She deleted the words *nice and* from the phrase *nice and furry* for the same reason.

Nikki made sentence changes too. For example, she moved the question "Or do you have another suggestion?" and combined it with the first sentence of the paragraph.

Copyeditor's Checklist

- [ ] Are any sentences awkward or confusing?
- [ ] Is every sentence and every word in the letter needed?
- [ ] Is there a variety in sentence length?
- [ ] Is the structure of each sentence logical and grammatically correct?
- [ ] Is the letter written in the format of a business letter?
- [ ] Is the language appropriate for business communications?

Your Turn

Ask your editing partner to read aloud your revised letter or read it aloud yourself. Pay close attention to the words in each sentence. Use the Copyeditor's Checklist to help you.

Your Turn

Have a volunteer read aloud the first paragraph and the bulleted items. Allow time for students to proofread their letters. Encourage them to use proofreading marks. (See page 526.) Then ask a volunteer to read aloud the second paragraph and the bulleted items. As students work with editing partners, suggest that they read aloud each other's drafts. Point out that reading aloud will help students notice errors. When students have finished marking each other's papers, allow time for students to revise their letters accordingly.

Writer's Tip Remind students that they must be professional in the presentation of their letters as well as in the tone and content of their letters. Tell students that this means choosing a font that is professional.

TEACHING OPTIONS

Keeping Track

Explain that editors and proofreaders often use style sheets to help them remember points such as correct spelling and capitalization. Suggest that students begin a personal style sheet of words with difficult spellings or words that should be capitalized. Mention that students can refer to this style sheet whenever these words recur in this work or in other written work.

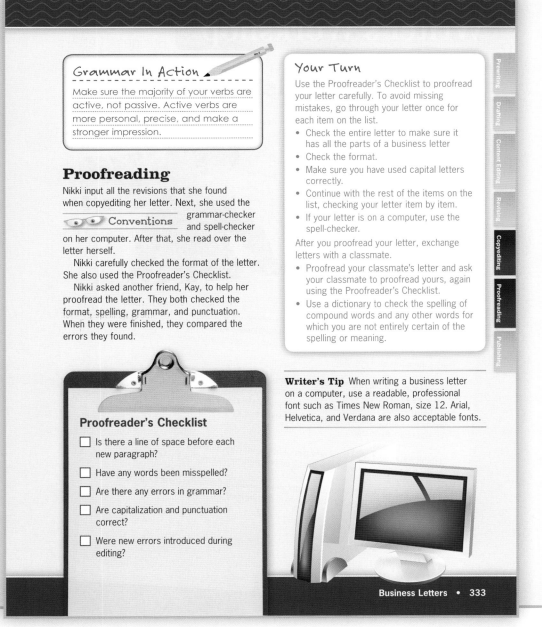

Grammar In Action

Make sure the majority of your verbs are active, not passive. Active verbs are more personal, precise, and make a stronger impression.

Proofreading

Nikki input all the revisions that she found when copyediting her letter. Next, she used the **Conventions** grammar-checker and spell-checker on her computer. After that, she read over the letter herself.

Nikki carefully checked the format of the letter. She also used the Proofreader's Checklist.

Nikki asked another friend, Kay, to help her proofread the letter. They both checked the format, spelling, grammar, and punctuation. When they were finished, they compared the errors they found.

Proofreader's Checklist

☐ Is there a line of space before each new paragraph?

☐ Have any words been misspelled?

☐ Are there any errors in grammar?

☐ Are capitalization and punctuation correct?

☐ Were new errors introduced during editing?

Your Turn

Use the Proofreader's Checklist to proofread your letter carefully. To avoid missing mistakes, go through your letter once for each item on the list.

- Check the entire letter to make sure it has all the parts of a business letter
- Check the format.
- Make sure you have used capital letters correctly.
- Continue with the rest of the items on the list, checking your letter item by item.
- If your letter is on a computer, use the spell-checker.

After you proofread your letter, exchange letters with a classmate.

- Proofread your classmate's letter and ask your classmate to proofread yours, again using the Proofreader's Checklist.
- Use a dictionary to check the spelling of compound words and any other words for which you are not entirely certain of the spelling or meaning.

Writer's Tip When writing a business letter on a computer, use a readable, professional font such as Times New Roman, size 12. Arial, Helvetica, and Verdana are also acceptable fonts.

Business Letters • 333

OBJECTIVE
• To publish a business letter

PUBLISHING

Ask volunteers to read aloud Nikki's finished letter. Encourage students to comment on it, noting the changes Nikki made after copyediting and proofreading.

As an extra challenge, discuss how Nikki might conduct a business telephone call to Mr. Jones at Outside Adventures. Ask whether Nikki might effectively use exact sentences from the letter or how she might change the wording to be more effective when speaking. Challenge pairs of students to role-play a phone call between Nikki and Mr. Jones.

After discussing the changes Nikki made to her letter, read aloud on page 335 the different ways that students can publish their business letters. Discuss the advantages and disadvantages for each publication technique.

Your Turn

Have volunteers read aloud this section. Allow time for students to copy their letters or print them from their computers. Lead students through the procedure of folding a letter. Invite students to answer the final question after students have read their classmates' letters.

Writer's Workshop
Business Letters

Publishing

This is Nikki's edited and proofread letter to Outside Adventures.

7 Bailey Road
Clarkfield, MN 56223
(708) 555-1322

December 12, 20—

Mr. Ethan Jones
Manager, Customer Service
Outside Adventures
1221 Greenview Boulevard
Racine, WI 53407

Dear Mr. Jones:

I ordered a pair of boots from an Outside Adventures catalog on November 3. They arrived promptly on November 11, and they looked wonderful! But I was disappointed to find that the left boot had a faulty zipper, which I noticed only after I wore the boots for a few hours.

I made sure that the zipper really was broken, because otherwise the boots are perfect for our deep winter snow—tall enough so snow doesn't come over the top and furry enough to keep my feet warm. I pulled the zipper up firmly. I even put a safety pin through the top of the zipper to see if that would help. It didn't, and why should I have to do this?

I think you should send me a new pair of boots, unless you have a better suggestion. If you are planning to send new boots, do you want me to send back this pair?

Thanks for resolving the problem with the defective zipper. Please call me at the number above to address this issue. I look forward to hearing from you as soon as possible.

Sincerely yours,

Nikki Van Zandt
Nikki Van Zandt

cc: B. Smythe

334

👓 Tell students that presentation deals with the final draft of their piece. Explain that students should present their letters in a way that is consistent with business communications, which is formal and professional.

ASSESS

Have students assess their finished business letters using the reproducible Student Self-Assessment on page 335y. A separate Business Letters Scoring Rubric can be found on page 335z for you to use to evaluate their work.

Plan to spend tomorrow doing formal assessment. Administer the Business Letters Writing Prompt on **Assessment Book** pages 55–56.

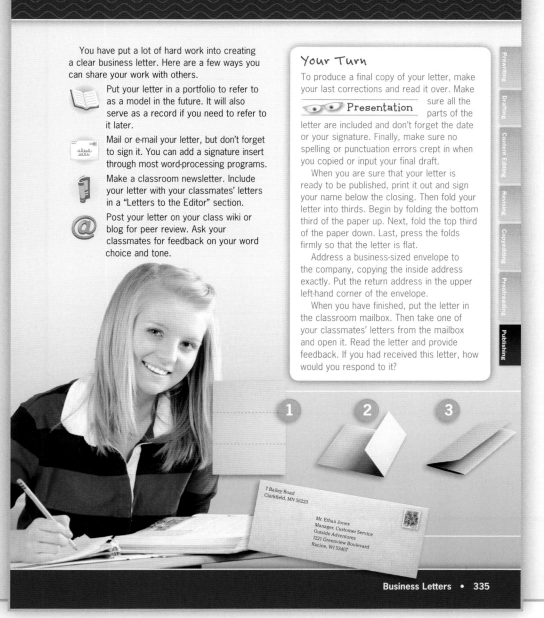

You have put a lot of hard work into creating a clear business letter. Here are a few ways you can share your work with others.

Put your letter in a portfolio to refer to as a model in the future. It will also serve as a record if you need to refer to it later.

Mail or e-mail your letter, but don't forget to sign it. You can add a signature insert through most word-processing programs.

Make a classroom newsletter. Include your letter with your classmates' letters in a "Letters to the Editor" section.

Post your letter on your class wiki or blog for peer review. Ask your classmates for feedback on your word choice and tone.

Your Turn

To produce a final copy of your letter, make your last corrections and read it over. Make

👓 **Presentation**

sure all the parts of the letter are included and don't forget the date or your signature. Finally, make sure no spelling or punctuation errors crept in when you copied or input your final draft.

When you are sure that your letter is ready to be published, print it out and sign your name below the closing. Then fold your letter into thirds. Begin by folding the bottom third of the paper up. Next, fold the top third of the paper down. Last, press the folds firmly so that the letter is flat.

Address a business-sized envelope to the company, copying the inside address exactly. Put the return address in the upper left-hand corner of the envelope.

When you have finished, put the letter in the classroom mailbox. Then take one of your classmates' letters from the mailbox and open it. Read the letter and provide feedback. If you had received this letter, how would you respond to it?

Prewriting | Drafting | Content Editing | Revising | Copyediting | Proofreading | **Publishing**

7 Bailey Road
Clarkfield, MN 56223

Mr. Ethan Jones
Manager, Customer Service
Outside Adventures
1221 Greenview Boulevard
Racine, WI 53407

Business Letters • 335

Name _____ Date _____

Business Letter

Ideas	YES	NO
Do I clearly state the reason for writing the letter?		
Do I provide detailed information that is tailored to the recipient?		

Organization		
Is my introduction engaging?		
Do I present my ideas in logical order?		
Does my conclusion restate the letter's purpose?		

Voice		
Do I use a strong, persuasive, and respectful voice?		

Word Choice		
Does my piece reflect business-letter etiquette?		
Do I use compound words correctly?		
Do I use a professional tone?		

Sentence Fluency		
Do I articulate the problem and solutions?		
Do I use adjective and adverb clauses?		
Does my piece logically flow from one sentence to the next?		

Conventions		
Do I use correct grammar?		
Do I use correct spelling, punctuation, and capitalization?		

Presentation		
Do I have the correct format for a business letter?		
Do I use consistent spacing and margins?		
Does my paper look neat?		

Additional Items

Name _____

Date _____ Score _____

POINT VALUES

0 = not evident
1 = minimal evidence of mastery
2 = evidence of development toward mastery
3 = strong evidence of mastery
4 = outstanding evidence of mastery

Business Letter

	POINTS
Ideas	
clearly stated reason for letter	
detailed information tailored to the recipient	
Organization	
an engaging introduction	
ideas presented in a logical order	
a conclusion that restates the letter's purpose	
Voice	
strong, persuasive, and respectful	
Word Choice	
business letter etiquette	
correct compound words	
professional tone	
Sentence Fluency	
problem and solutions	
adjective and adverb clauses	
logical flow from one sentence to the next	
Conventions	
correct grammar and usage	
correct spelling, punctuation, and capitalization	
Presentation	
correct business-letter format, including proper headings and addresses	
consistent spacing and margins	
neatness	
Additional Items	
Total	

©LOYOLAPRESS.

CHAPTER FOCUS

LESSON 1: What Makes a Good Description?

LESSON 2: Organization

- **GRAMMAR:** Verbals
- **WRITING SKILLS:** Graphic Organizers
- **WORD STUDY:** Figurative Language
- **STUDY SKILLS:** Thesaurus
- **SPEAKING AND LISTENING SKILLS:** Oral Descriptions
- **WRITER'S WORKSHOP:** Descriptions

SUPPORT MATERIALS

Practice Book
Writing, pages 153–157

Assessment Book
Chapter 4 Writing Skills, pages 57–58
Descriptions Writing Prompt, pages 59–60

Rubrics
Student, page 373y
Teacher, page 373z

Test Generator CD

Grammar
Section 5, pages 83–108

Customizable Lesson Plans
www.voyagesinenglish.com

Descriptions

WHAT IS DESCRIPTIVE WRITING?

A good description is like a photograph—it is an image that almost seems real. Whether as part of a larger body of work or as a complete piece, the focus on the topic is sharp and distinct, so the reader always knows what is being described. The content is illustrative, painting a picture in the reader's mind.

A good description includes the following:

- ☐ An introduction that names the two subjects
- ☐ Comparisons and contrasts of the related subjects, giving equal weight to both
- ☐ A series of paragraphs that each compare or contrast
- ☐ A conclusion that sums up the comparison, leaving readers with something to think about
- ☐ Connections are clear and logical, marked by words or phrases such as *in comparison, likewise, both, on the other hand, however,* and *instead.*
- ☐ Sentence variety
- ☐ Natural sentence transitions
- ☐ Literary techniques such as analogies, point of view, and tone
- ☐ Figurative language that evokes sensory images

LiNK Use the following titles to offer your students examples of well-crafted descriptive writing:

The King of the Golden River by John Ruskin

Machines in the Home by Rebecca Weaver

Science and Invention by Ray Spangenburg

THE KING OF THE GOLDEN RIVER

John Ruskin

> "There is . . . happiness which comes from the creative effort."
>
> —Henry Miller

WRITER'S WORKSHOP TIPS

Follow these ideas and tips to help you and your class get the most out of the Writer's Workshop:

- Review the traits of good writing. Use the chart on the inside back cover of the student and teacher editions.

- Fill your classroom library with nonfiction books that compare and contrast people, places, and ideas.

- Before they write, encourage students to draw pictures or study photographs of the subjects they will compare and contrast. Have students note similarities and differences in the visuals.

- Spend ample time on the revising stage. Organizing comparative descriptions can be difficult, and students may need extra time to revise their pieces.

- Encourage students to keep a journal to record their impressions of interesting people, places, and things.

- Create a bulletin-board display of travel posters, brochures, and pamphlets.

- Encourage students to bring in family photographs of interesting places to use as inspiration.

- Have students bring in a favorite food item and describe it, using the five senses, to the rest of the class.

CONNECT WITH GRAMMAR

Throughout the Writer's Workshop, look for opportunities to integrate verbals with descriptive writing.

- ☐ Encourage students to combine short sentences, using participle, gerund, and infinitive phrases.

- ☐ When discussing word choice, encourage students to vary their adjectives, using participles and infinitives when possible.

- ☐ During the content editing stage, have partners identify the types of verbals used as students edit one another's draft.

- ☐ Ask partners to trade their drafts and note any split infinitives or dangling participles. Have students correct any of these common errors.

SCORING RUBRIC

Description: Compare and Contrast

0 = not evident
1 = minimal evidence of mastery
2 = evidence of development toward mastery
3 = strong evidence of mastery
4 = outstanding evidence of mastery

	POINTS
Ideas	
two related subjects	
equal weight to both subjects	
Organization	
two subjects named in the introduction	
logical sentence and paragraph order	
comparison summarized in the conclusion	
Voice	
appropriate for audience	
reader's attention held	
perceivable mood	
Word Choice	
literary techniques such as figures of speech	
rich sensory details	
connecting words or phrases	
Sentence Fluency	
variety of sentences	
natural transitions between sentences	
Conventions	
correct grammar and usage	
correct spelling, punctuation, and capitalization	
Presentation	
consistent spacing and margins	
neatness	
Additional Items	
Total	

Full-sized, reproducible rubrics can be found at the end of this chapter.

CHAPTER 4
Descriptions

INTRODUCING THE GENRE

Challenge students to share what they know about descriptive writing. Ask these questions to prompt discussion:

- Where might we see descriptive writing?
- Why is descriptive writing important?
- How does descriptive writing differ from other types of writing?

Then invite students to name common literary devices used in descriptive writing *(specific adjectives and adverbs, metaphors and similes, sensory details)*. Tell students that the characteristics of descriptions include the following:

- A definite purpose and a mood that conveys the emotions expressed in the piece
- Details organized in a meaningful way
- Vivid and precise word choices that create sensory images
- Sentence variety, including figurative language

Reading the Literature Excerpt

Explain that a successful description paints a clear picture for the reader of what is being described. Then invite volunteers to read aloud *The King of the Golden River* excerpt. When students have finished, ask them what words and phrases help visualize what is being described. Challenge students to identify other characteristics of good descriptive writing within the excerpt, such as the mood or figurative language.

LiNK The King of the Golden River

The excerpts in Chapter 4 introduce students to published examples of descriptive writing. *The King of the Golden River* is an excellent example of descriptive writing because it does the following:

- Shows a sharp focus and a specific mood
- Creates vivid images through carefully selected words
- Uses a variety of adjectives to create rich, sensory details

As students encounter different examples of descriptions throughout the chapter, be sure to point out the characteristics that these descriptions share. Also take this opportunity to point out grammar skills that students have been learning, such as verbals.

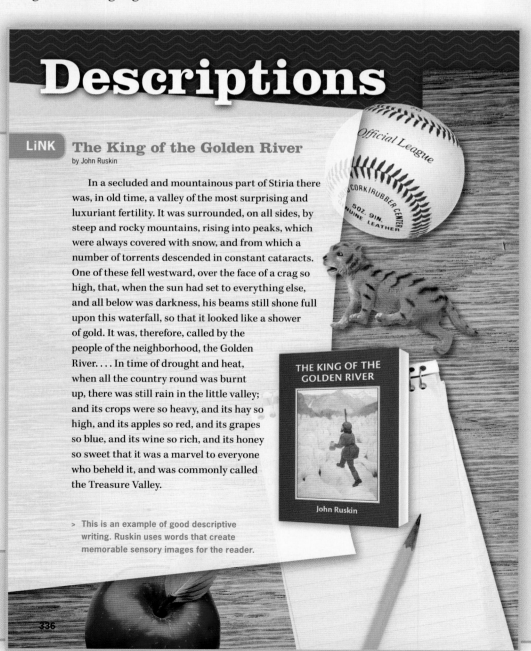

Descriptions

LiNK The King of the Golden River
by John Ruskin

In a secluded and mountainous part of Stiria there was, in old time, a valley of the most surprising and luxuriant fertility. It was surrounded, on all sides, by steep and rocky mountains, rising into peaks, which were always covered with snow, and from which a number of torrents descended in constant cataracts. One of these fell westward, over the face of a crag so high, that, when the sun had set to everything else, and all below was darkness, his beams still shone full upon this waterfall, so that it looked like a shower of gold. It was, therefore, called by the people of the neighborhood, the Golden River. . . . In time of drought and heat, when all the country round was burnt up, there was still rain in the little valley; and its crops were so heavy, and its hay so high, and its apples so red, and its grapes so blue, and its wine so rich, and its honey so sweet that it was a marvel to everyone who beheld it, and was commonly called the Treasure Valley.

> This is an example of good descriptive writing. Ruskin uses words that create memorable sensory images for the reader.

336

Reading the Student Model

Tell students they are going to read a piece of descriptive writing written by a student. Then invite volunteers to read the piece aloud.

Ask students to identify descriptive words and phrases *(cavernous, shuttle, torrent, chaotic symphony)*. Encourage students to determine whether these phrases are effective in communicating feelings or ideas.

Ask students what the mood of this piece is *(excited)* and how the writer uses descriptions to create this mood. Then ask students to point out sensory images that appeal to the senses. Then have students close their eyes. Read the piece aloud. Then ask if the writer was successful in creating a picture in their minds.

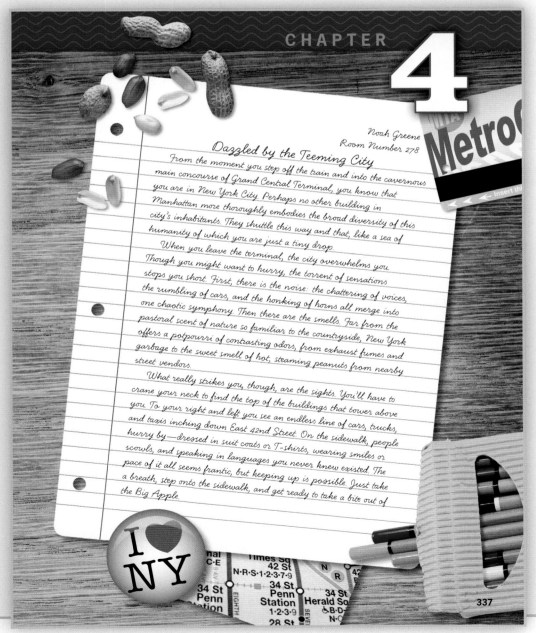

CHAPTER 4

Noah Greene
Room Number 278

Dazzled by the Teeming City

From the moment you step off the train and into the cavernous main concourse of Grand Central Terminal, you know that you are in New York City. Perhaps no other building in Manhattan more thoroughly embodies the broad diversity of this city's inhabitants. They shuttle this way and that, like a sea of humanity of which you are just a tiny drop.

When you leave the terminal, the city overwhelms you. Though you might want to hurry, the torrent of sensations stops you short. First, there is the noise: the chattering of voices, the rumbling of cars, and the honking of horns all merge into one chaotic symphony. Then there are the smells. Far from the pastoral scent of nature so familiar to the countryside, New York offers a potpourri of contrasting odors, from exhaust fumes and garbage to the sweet smell of hot, steaming peanuts from nearby street vendors.

What really strikes you, though, are the sights. You'll have to crane your neck to find the top of the buildings that tower above you. To your right and left you see an endless line of cars, trucks, and taxis inching down East 42nd Street. On the sidewalk, people hurry by—dressed in suit coats or T-shirts, wearing smiles or scowls, and speaking in languages you never knew existed. The pace of it all seems frantic, but keeping up is possible. Just take a breath, step onto the sidewalk, and get ready to take a bite out of the Big Apple.

OBJECTIVES

- **To recognize characteristics of descriptions**
- **To explore effective word choices in descriptions**
- **To establish the purpose and mood of a description**

WARM-UP

Read, Listen, Speak

Read aloud your descriptive excerpts from yesterday's For Tomorrow homework. Point out sensory details, figurative language, and descriptive details. Discuss how these contribute to the mood of each piece. Have small groups discuss their descriptions. Ask students to use the assigned questions and read aloud from the examples to support the discussion. Invite a volunteer from each group to share what their group discussed.

GRAMMAR CONNECTION

Take this opportunity to talk about participles and their placement. You may wish to have students point out participles and their placement in their Read, Listen, Speak examples.

TEACH

Invite a volunteer to read aloud the first paragraph. Encourage students to name writing genres that require descriptions. Have another volunteer read aloud the section Word Choice. Challenge students to name other vivid and precise words the author of "Dazzled by the Teeming City" might have used in his or her description.

Refer to the examples students found for the Scavenger Hunt during the previous class. Ask volunteers to use the examples again to name words and phrases that evoke the senses, including metaphors and similes.

Have a student read aloud the section Purpose and Mood. Discuss answers to the question at the end of the last paragraph. Then have students identify the purposes and moods of the Scavenger Hunt examples.

PRACTICE

ACTIVITY A

Rewrite the first sentence as a class. Then have students complete the activity independently. Challenge them to add metaphors or similes to two or three of the sentences. Ask volunteers to read aloud their sentences.

ACTIVITY B

After students have completed the activity, ask them to trade papers with a partner. Have partners comment on each other's sentences and identify the vivid words, sensory details, and figurative language in each sentence.

ACTIVITY C

Have students complete this activity in small groups. After students have finished, invite volunteers to share their rewritten phrases with the class. Tell students to write the vivid verbs in their notebook to use as a reference for their own writing.

LESSON **1** DESCRIPTIONS

What Makes a Good Description?

Descriptive writing uses vivid language to bring to life a person, a place, a thing, or an idea. Descriptions can be objective, such as describing a baby spreading cereal and bananas on her face. Descriptions also can be subjective, such as describing your feelings as you awaited your turn in the final round of the National Spelling Bee.

Word Choice

Good descriptive writing sketches its subject in words so vivid, precise, and concrete that a detailed picture forms in readers' minds. Writers choose sensory words, which evoke the senses. Metaphors, similes, and other figures of speech can create memorable word pictures.

The writer of "Dazzled by the Teeming City" chooses vivid adjectives such as *cavernous, chaotic,* and *pastoral.* He also chooses verbs that create a strong image, such as *shuttle, chattering, rumbling,* and *tower.* Finally, the writer uses similes and metaphors to create images. A symphony is a metaphor for the city sounds, the crowds are compared to a sea, and taking a bite out of an apple is a metaphor for exploring New York City.

Purpose and Mood

Mood is the overall impression or emotion expressed in a piece of writing. The careful use of vivid words is one way to set a mood for the subject of a description. The writer of "Dazzled by the Teeming City" does not describe the train he got off or the suitcase he carries. Instead, he focuses on the sights, sounds, and odors of the city because he is eager to begin his tour.

You know the writer's mood is eager anticipation when he calls the city sounds a symphony, implying that the sounds are wonderful despite the chaos. Even potentially offensive odors, such as exhaust fumes, are mingled with the mouth-watering smell of hot, steaming peanuts. How else does the writer convey mood?

APPLY

WRITER'S CORNER

After students have completed their descriptions, invite them to list the vivid and precise words on a sheet of chart paper. Post this chart in the classroom and encourage students to add words to the list as the class continues through this chapter. Students should demonstrate an understanding of word choice, purpose, and mood.

ASSESS

Note which students had difficulty understanding how effective word choice helps create sensory images in descriptions. Use the Reteach option with those students who need additional reinforcement.

TEACHING OPTIONS

Reteach

Invite volunteers to record excerpts from the variety of descriptions they have used in this lesson. Play the recording and have students list words they hear that appeal to the senses. Write headings for the five senses on the board. Invite volunteers to write the words they listed under the appropriate headings.

English-Language Learners

English-language learners may need help distinguishing between plain and vivid words. Work with small groups of students to identify examples of each. Then have students work with partners to write sentence pairs. The first sentence should use plain words, and the second sentence should replace the plain words with vivid ones.

ACTIVITY A Rewrite the sentences below to make them more interesting. Add descriptive words or substitute vivid, concrete words for vague, overused ones.

1. We went into the ballroom.
2. The happy child ran to his mother, who was waiting for him.
3. The queen placed the crown on her head and looked out at the people.
4. In the distance we saw a mountain outlined against the sky.
5. The horse ran along the track.
6. Stanley works in a small office without windows.
7. I couldn't solve a difficult puzzle like that one.
8. Seagulls flew back and forth as the waves came onto the beach.
9. My mother criticized me for staying out too late.
10. Our teacher likes to tell us about the things her dogs do.

ACTIVITY B From the topics below, choose five that interest you most. For each topic write a descriptive sentence that might appear in a paragraph describing the topic.

1. Times Square in New York City on New Year's Eve
2. the Battle of Gettysburg
3. a 100-year-old house
4. the big blizzard
5. the electricity suddenly going out
6. Wilbur in *Charlotte's Web*
7. making chocolate fudge
8. an expert juggler at work
9. the tallest building in the world
10. shopping on the day after Thanksgiving

ACTIVITY C Rewrite the following phrases. Change the nondescript verbs to vivid verbs that create more memorable word pictures and stronger moods.

1. Jesse said . . .
2. Lucy ran . . .
3. Xavier ate . . .
4. Shoshona looked . . .

WRITER'S CORNER

Choose two phrases you changed in Activity C and make them complete sentences with additional descriptive words.

For Tomorrow

Ask students to choose a special place in nature and write a description of the setting. Encourage students to use vivid words and sensory details. Remind students to establish a mood with their word choices. Write a description of one of your favorite places as well.

Descriptions • 339

WARM-UP

Read, Listen, Speak

Read aloud your description that you wrote for yesterday's homework. Tell students to raise their hands when they hear a descriptive word or phrase. Then invite volunteers to read their descriptions aloud. As students read, have students write descriptive words and phrases. After several students have read their writing, generate a list of descriptive language and add it to the class chart created in the Writer's Corner on page 339.

GRAMMAR CONNECTION

Take this opportunity to talk about gerunds used as subjects and subject complements. You may wish to have students point out gerunds used as subjects and subject complements in their Read, Listen, Speak examples.

TEACH

Review what students have learned about word choice, purpose, and mood of descriptive writing. Ask questions such as the following: What does descriptive writing attempt to do for the subject? *(create an image of it)* What is the purpose of a description? *(to create a feeling, to set a mood, to add depth and detail to a story)* What is one way to establish mood in a description? *(using words that appeal to the emotions and senses)*

PRACTICE

ACTIVITY D

Allow time for students to read the paragraphs silently. Then ask partners to write answers to the questions. When students have finished, discuss the answers as a class.

ACTIVITY E

Give students time to complete this activity independently. When students have finished, invite volunteers to read their paragraphs aloud.

ACTIVITY F

As students rewrite the sentences, encourage students to use words from the list used in the Warm-Up. When students have finished, invite volunteers to write their sentences on the board. Have several students write their revisions for each sentence. Discuss how word choice affects each sentence's mood.

ACTIVITY G

Allow time for students to rewrite the sentences. Then ask students to trade papers with a partner and discuss whether the writer used effective sensory details.

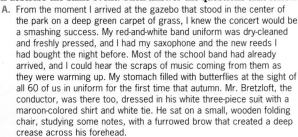

ACTIVITY D Read these paragraphs from two descriptions, both of which describe the same event. Then answer the questions that follow.

A. From the moment I arrived at the gazebo that stood in the center of the park on a deep green carpet of grass, I knew the concert would be a smashing success. My red-and-white band uniform was dry-cleaned and freshly pressed, and I had my saxophone and the new reeds I had bought the night before. Most of the school band had already arrived, and I could hear the scraps of music coming from them as they were warming up. My stomach filled with butterflies at the sight of all 60 of us in uniform for the first time that autumn. Mr. Bretzloft, the conductor, was there too, dressed in his white three-piece suit with a maroon-colored shirt and white tie. He sat on a small, wooden folding chair, studying some notes, with a furrowed brow that created a deep crease across his forehead.

B. From the moment that I arrived at the dilapidated gazebo that squatted on the park grounds like a mangy dog, a sinking sensation stole into my belly and told me the concert would not go well. The muggy, humid evening air blanketed the park and set everyone on edge. Only half of the band members had bothered to show up, and of that number, only a third were in uniform. My own red-and-white uniform still bore the mustard stain from last week's hot dog on its white tunic. Mr. Bretzloft, the conductor, was there, dressed in a gray wool suit. He was pacing back and forth, ordering the wayward players back to their assigned seats. Tired notes wheezed here and there as some members in the band warmed up.

1. What are some details that are included in both paragraphs?

2. How are the details shown differently in each paragraph?

3. Which details are sensory details? To which senses do the details appeal?

4. How would you compare the mood of the two paragraphs?

5. What are some words that helped you figure out the mood?

ACTIVITY E Choose one of the paragraphs above and write a second paragraph to the story. Use vivid words and sensory details to convey the same mood as the original paragraph.

340 • Chapter 4

APPLY

WRITER'S CORNER

When students have finished writing, ask them to reread their paragraphs for possible revisions. Suggest that students circle the adjectives and adverbs they used and then consider whether the words are vivid and provide sensory details. Students should demonstrate an understanding of word choice, purpose, and mood.

ASSESS

Note which students had difficulty understanding word choice and mood in descriptive writing. Use the Reteach option with those students who need additional reinforcement.

Practice Book page 153 provides additional work with the elements and characteristics of an effective description.

TEACHING OPTIONS

Reteach

Have small groups write a description of a photograph that you provide. Allow students time to study and to discuss the photograph. Then have students describe exactly what is pictured. Display the photographs in the classroom and have groups read their descriptions. Have students guess which photograph each description is written about.

Meeting Individual Needs

Kinesthetic Have small groups choose vivid words from the literature excerpt on page 336. Ask a volunteer from each group to act out the words in a game of charades for the entire class. Allow students who are trying to guess the words to consult the model. As each word is guessed, write it on the board. Discuss the sensory images and mood produced by these words.

For Tomorrow

Have students rewrite the student model on page 337 so that it is in a rural setting. Encourage students to consider how a city dweller might react when visiting a rural area for the first time. Have students explain how this might change the mood of the piece. Create your own rewrite of the model to share with the class.

ACTIVITY F Rewrite the sentences below, using different verbs and adjectives to set a new mood.

1. Ray straightened his starched collar and marched into the bustling office for his job interview.
2. A driving rain battered the creaky house.
3. Hanging from a nearly invisible thread, the rust-colored spider labored to spin its web.
4. Her many layers of clothing made the woman on the park bench look like an overstuffed easy chair.
5. As we crept down the rickety cellar stairs, a damp, musty smell enveloped us.
6. Alicia's joyous squeal echoed through the hall.
7. The blazing sun beat down mercilessly on the exhausted hiker.
8. As I woke up, I breathed in the smell of bacon coming from the kitchen downstairs.

ACTIVITY G Rewrite the sentences to include additional sensory details such as sights, sounds, or smells that are not mentioned in the original sentence.

1. The office building is around the corner.
2. Yolanda hung the painting on the wall.
3. Three mules stood outside the barn.
4. I can hear the concert from my apartment.
5. Isa opened the door and looked into the basement.
6. The fireworks lit up the sky.
7. We spent the summer day at the beach.
8. The mountain stood behind the valley.
9. The cat chased after the mouse.
10. Dinner simmered on the stove.

WRITER'S CORNER

Choose one of the sentences you wrote in Activity F or G and expand it into a short description.

Descriptions • 341

OBJECTIVES

• **To understand effective organization of descriptions**

• **To explore four methods of organizing descriptions**

WARM-UP

Read, Listen, Speak

Read to the class your rewritten student model from yesterday's For Tomorrow homework. When you have finished, discuss the changes you made and how those affected the model.

Invite volunteers to share their rewrites of the model. Ask students to note and respond to the writer's choice of words. Ask students to save what they wrote to use later in the lesson.

GRAMMAR CONNECTION

Take this opportunity to talk about gerunds used as objects and appositives. You may wish to have students point out gerunds used as objects and appositives in their Read, Listen, Speak examples.

TEACH

Ask a volunteer to read aloud the first paragraph. Explain that details are an important characteristic in descriptive writing. Tell students that the writer should think carefully about how best to organize those details to produce the desired mood of the piece.

Invite students to read aloud each method for organizing descriptions: Chronological Order, Spatial Order, Order of Importance, Comparison and Contrast. When students have finished, explain that a writer can incorporate aspects of more than one method of organization in a long descriptive piece. Ask how the writer organized the model on page 337 *(used chronological and spatial orders)*. Refer to the descriptions students found during the Scavenger Hunt and the ones they wrote for homework. Ask them to name or describe the method of organization used in each description.

PRACTICE

ACTIVITY A

Invite volunteers to read aloud each paragraph. Discuss the kind of organization each paragraph uses. Ask students to point out

---

Organization

Good descriptive writing never lists details at random. Writers organize the details they observe in a meaningful way to create the mood and to build important ideas or themes. Writers commonly organize descriptive writing in the following ways. Sometimes these methods are combined, and sometimes sentences depart from an overall organization for emphasis, particularly in introductions and conclusions.

Chronological Order

Descriptive writing that follows chronological order describes a scene in the order that it unfolds. This organization may be useful in describing an elaborate dance routine or telling how the sky changes colors as the sun peeks over the horizon.

Spatial Order

In spatial order, details are described in the order they appear in a given space. For example, you might describe a building from left to right, from top to bottom, or from the inside out. Can you think of any other ways that things might be described using spatial order?

Order of Importance

Another way to organize details is by order of importance, either from least to most important or from most to least important. A description of a new bike can move from the least impressive to the most impressive features, while a description of your feelings can list the strongest feelings last.

Comparison and Contrast

When writers compare and contrast, they state likenesses and differences, particularly when they describe two or more people, places, things, or ideas. Effective comparative descriptions give equal weight to the subjects being compared.

specific clues in each paragraph (such as transition words) that identify its organization.

APPLY

WRITER'S CORNER

Before students write their descriptions, suggest that they freewrite descriptive adjectives and phrases. Ask students to number the words and phrases in order of importance, and then compose their sentences. Students should demonstrate an understanding of organizing by order of importance.

TechTip Create a class blog that contains sample descriptions written by students. Then have the class review the descriptions for organization, mood, purpose, and word choice.

ASSESS

Note which students had difficulty understanding methods of organization. Use the Reteach option with those students who need additional reinforcement.

Activity A
1. spatial order
2. order of importance
3. comparison and contrast
4. chronological order

ACTIVITY A Read the descriptive paragraphs below and identify their method of organization.

1. Mies van der Rohe's Farnsworth House is an elegant example of the International Style of architecture. The house consists of two rectangular blocks, each supported by white-painted steel columns. The façade is glass, forming a transparent cube that seems to float above the ground, bracketed by the columns. From the inside, one realizes that in a glass box, the distinction between inside and outside almost disappears.

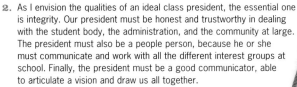

Mies van der Rohe's Farnsworth House in Plano, Illinois

2. As I envision the qualities of an ideal class president, the essential one is integrity. Our president must be honest and trustworthy in dealing with the student body, the administration, and the community at large. The president must also be a people person, because he or she must communicate and work with all the different interest groups at school. Finally, the president must be a good communicator, able to articulate a vision and draw us all together.

3. The twins' personalities couldn't be more different. Jason is shy, quiet, thoughtful, and smart. He is clueless about the music the rest of us listen to and the TV shows we watch. If I were in a jam, though, Jason would be the sibling I'd ask for help. Jenna, on the other hand, is a total social butterfly. She works just hard enough to get decent grades so she can spend the rest of her time hanging out at the mall or talking on the phone. Want to know about the supposedly private lives of pop stars? Ask Jenna.

4. To create a PowerPoint presentation, you must begin by creating your own slides from scratch or using the template given. The first slide is the title slide. Add text to this slide. Next, click on the "Next Slide" button to create a new slide. Once again start by adding the text. After this you can add movement, such as bulleted items of text that slide in from offscreen. You can also add images. When you have completed this slide, click on "Next Slide" again. If you think your slides should be placed in a different order, go to "outline" and rearrange them.

WRITER'S CORNER

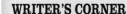

Write five sentences describing someone famous you admire. Organize the details in your writing by order of importance.

 Tech Tip Post your description on the class blog.

Descriptions • 343

Read, Listen, Speak

Read your homework from yesterday's For Tomorrow activity. Ask the class what type of organization you used. Have students identify clues that led them to their decisions. Then ask volunteers to read their rewritten models. Encourage students to identify and discuss the type of organization used in each model.

GRAMMAR CONNECTION

Take this opportunity to talk about possessives with gerunds and using *-ing* verb forms. You may wish to have students point out possessives with gerunds and using *-ing* verb forms in their Read, Listen, Speak examples.

TEACH

Read aloud the following subjects and ask students to name the method or methods of organization that would be most effective when writing a description: my two best friends *(comparison and contrast)*, the Chicago skyline *(spatial order or order of importance)*, the first day at a new school *(chronological order)*, meeting my girlfriend/boyfriend *(chronological order or order of importance)*.

LiNK Have students close their eyes. Read the excerpt aloud. Encourage students to create a visual in their minds as you read the excerpt. When finished, discuss the spatial organization and the descriptive words the author uses.

PRACTICE

ACTIVITY B

Have students complete this activity independently. Then ask volunteers to share the details they wrote and the organization they would use for each subject.

ACTIVITY C

After students have finished rewriting the paragraph, have them trade papers with a partner. Ask partners to comment on each other's papers, if necessary, offering revisions that would clarify the chronological order of events.

ACTIVITY D

Have students complete this activity in small groups. When groups are finished discussing the excerpt, conduct a class discussion about each question.

ACTIVITY E

When students have finished, invite volunteers to read aloud what they wrote. Challenge volunteers to explain how other methods of organization might be used to describe James's house.

ACTIVITY F

When students have finished, have them form small groups. Ask students to read aloud their

---

ACTIVITY B List four details you might include in writing about each of the following topics. Tell which form of organization you would use in writing a paragraph on each topic. Explain why.

1. a stray dog that wandered up to your picnic table
2. an energy-efficient home office
3. the kitchen in your home after you have made dinner
4. a perfect summer day
5. an invention that changed history
6. a fashionable shopping area of a big city
7. the most amazing person you ever met
8. the network of highways surrounding a city

ACTIVITY C Kayla wanted to describe the Independence Day fireworks celebration in chronological order. However, some events are out of sequence. Rewrite the paragraph, putting all the events Kayla described in chronological order.

An hour later, in complete darkness, the fireworks show began. After we spread out the blanket, we amused ourselves by racing out along the beach and dipping our feet in the water. The best part was the finale, a barrage of reds and yellows exploding on top of each other and lighting up the sky. Next, we dried off our feet and munched on the light snack of fruit, crackers, and cheese that we brought in our picnic basket. When the sun had finally set, but before darkness enveloped the beach, two boys nearby waved sparklers, writing their names and creating intricate patterns in the twilight air. The sun had not yet set, but had expanded into a wide, orange disk that hung close to the horizon when my mother, sister, and I arrived at the beach to wait for the show to begin. During the show, bouquets of pyrotechnics popped gracefully outward and faded just as quickly.

ACTIVITY D With a small group, read the excerpt from *The Reptile Room* on page 345 and discuss the following questions.

1. How is the excerpt organized?
2. What is the mood of the excerpt? What descriptions helped you decide the mood?
3. What sensory details does the excerpt include?

Activity C

The sun had not yet set, but had expanded into a wide, orange disk that hung close to the horizon when my mother, sister, and I arrived at the beach to wait for the show to begin. After we spread out the blanket, we amused ourselves by racing out along the beach and dipping our feet in the water. Next, we dried off our feet and munched on the light snack of fruit, crackers, and cheese that we brought in our picnic basket. When the sun had finally set, but before darkness enveloped the beach, two boys nearby waved sparklers, writing their names and creating intricate patterns in the twilight air. An hour later, in complete darkness, the fireworks show began. During the show, bouquets of pyrotechnics popped gracefully outward and faded just as quickly. The best part was the finale, a barrage of reds and yellows exploding on top of each other and lighting up the sky.

descriptions. Then have groups decide whether the organization the writer chose was effective.

APPLY

WRITER'S CORNER

When students have finished writing, lead a group discussion about the process of writing with a partner. Challenge students to discuss the collaboration. Ask students to share how they made decisions about organization. Students should demonstrate an understanding of the organization of descriptive writing.

ASSESS

Note which students had difficulty using methods of organization. Use the Reteach option with those students who need additional reinforcement.

Practice Book page 154 provides additional work with organization.

Practice Book page 154

Practice Book page 154

TEACHING OPTIONS

Reteach

Reinforce order of importance with this activity:

Order of Importance Write the following items on the board:

> **a close friend**
>
> **a deceased family member**
>
> **a parent or mentor**
>
> **a teammate, coach, or club member**

Then write the title

> **Important People in My Life**

Point out the title. Ask students to think of a person for each category and to list specific details in each person's life that make that person important. Then have students number these details in order of importance.

English-Language Learners

Encourage students to add transition words to their English vocabulary by making flash cards. Have each student look up transition words in the dictionary and record on index cards the definition of each word and its translation in the student's primary language.

Activity E
My house is easy to spot from the street because it has shrubs lining the concrete walkway to the front door. The house itself is made of red bricks and has a mahogany front door. Stepping into the tiled, rectangular entry hall from the front door bathes the visitor in warm sunlight that comes from the skylight above. A wood-paneled corridor on the left of the entry hall leads to the bedrooms. My bedroom is the first door on the left in the corridor, just past the picture of my great-grandmother. My bed is located against the far wall of my bedroom, under the window that faces the street.

ACTIVITY E James wanted to describe his house from the outside to the inside, using spatial order. But his description is confusing because the sentences are out of order. Rewrite the paragraph to describe the house from the outside to inside the writer's bedroom.

My bed is located against the far wall of my bedroom, under the window that faces the street. The house itself is made of red bricks and has a mahogany front door. A wood-paneled corridor on the left of the entry hall leads to the bedrooms. My house is easy to spot from the street because it has shrubs lining the concrete walkway to the front door. My bedroom is the first door on the left in the corridor, just past the picture of my great-grandmother. Stepping into the tiled, rectangular entry hall from the front door bathes the visitor in warm sunlight that comes from the skylight above.

ACTIVITY F Write a paragraph describing one of the following situations. Use order of importance, chronological order, comparison and contrast, or spatial order.

1. You are a sports reporter for your school newspaper and have just finished watching a game where the school record for points scored by a single player was broken. Describe the game.

2. Describe the new bike you just received. How is it different from your old bike?

3. Your birthday party must have been a success. Just look at the mess. Describe the family room and kitchen after the party.

4. You come back from Disney World just as the builders are finishing your $12 million house. You had no idea it would look like this. Describe your new mansion.

5. After years of pleading, your parents have finally agreed to let you have the pet you've always wanted. Describe the pet of your dreams.

LiNK

The Reptile Room

The room, as Violet suspected, was a dirty mess. The bed was unmade and had cracker crumbs and bits of hair all over it. Discarded newspapers and mail-order catalogs lay on the floor in untidy piles. ... The closet door was open, revealing a bunch of rusty wire coat hangers that shivered in the drafty room. The curtains over the windows were all bunched up and encrusted with something flaky ...

Lemony Snicket

WRITER'S CORNER

With a partner choose a situation from Activity F that neither of you wrote about. Write a description together. After you have finished, discuss the effectiveness of its organization.

Descriptions • 345

For Tomorrow

Have students make a list of the activities they do after school. Ask them to describe these activities two ways: using chronological order and using order of importance. Create a list of your own and organize it by chronological order and by order of importance.

OBJECTIVES
- **To use Venn diagrams when organizing ideas for a description**
- **To use word webs when organizing ideas for a description**

WARM-UP

Read, Listen, Speak

Share your list from yesterday's For Tomorrow activity. Point out the difference in the two types of organization. Then ask small groups to discuss the two lists they wrote for homework. Have students choose which method of organization worked best for them and read that description aloud. Encourage students to discuss reasons why a certain method of organization serves a subject better than another method.

GRAMMAR CONNECTION

Take this opportunity to talk about infinitives used as subjects and subject complements. You may wish to have students point out infinitives used as subjects and subject complements in their Read, Listen, Speak examples.

TEACH

Have a volunteer read aloud the first paragraph. Review why using a graphic organizer, such as a time line, is a useful writing skill. *(They are prewriting tools. They provide a visual "map" of the main points or ideas of a piece of writing. They help a writer find an effective method of organization to use when writing a draft.)*

Ask students to read aloud the section Venn Diagrams. Then allow time for students to read silently Maya's Venn diagram. Challenge volunteers to explain how the diagram organizes similarities and differences between the two libraries.

PRACTICE

ACTIVITY A

Lead a class discussion about Maya's Venn diagram. When discussing question 4, lead students to the conclusion that seeing details and ideas in a graphic organizer helps choose the mood of a piece of writing.

ACTIVITY B

Have students complete this activity independently. Then invite volunteers to write their Venn diagrams on the board. If students chose buildings familiar to the entire class, invite classmates to suggest other similarities and differences.

ACTIVITY C

As students write their sentences, remind them to use transition words that effectively connect comparisons or contrasts. Invite volunteers to read aloud their sentences. Encourage students to comment about whether they

Graphic Organizers

When you have decided how to organize a description, the right graphic organizer can help you map it out in more detail. As you learned in Chapter 1, a time line can help organize writing in chronological order. A Venn diagram is useful when comparing and contrasting two items or ideas, while a word web can help organize details in a variety of ways.

Venn Diagrams

Maya is writing about the former library in her town, which is now a Boys and Girls Club, and the new library, which was completed last year. She thinks the new library is beautiful, but she loved the comfortable, old library too. To explore her ideas and feelings about the buildings, she compares and contrasts them.

Maya begins by making a Venn diagram, which will help her sort out the differences and similarities between the two buildings. She writes the similarities between the buildings in the overlapping part of the circles and the differences in the parts of the circles that do not overlap.

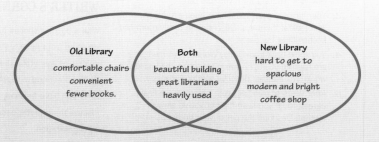

Old Library — comfortable chairs, convenient, fewer books.

Both — beautiful building, great librarians, heavily used

New Library — hard to get to, spacious, modern and bright, coffee shop

notice a particular mood emerging from the sentences.

ACTIVITY D
Have students complete this activity independently. Then have partners compare papers and discuss any differences. Invite volunteers to write their Venn diagrams on the board. Discuss each diagram as a class.

APPLY
WRITER'S CORNER
Allow time for students to complete their Venn diagrams. Invite volunteers to write their Venn diagrams on the board. If time allows, challenge students to give oral descriptions, using the information in their Venn diagrams. Students should demonstrate an understanding of Venn diagrams.

ASSESS
Note which students had difficulty constructing Venn diagrams. Use the Reteach option with those students who need additional reinforcement.

ACTIVITY A Answer the following questions about Maya's Venn diagram.

1. Which library is cozy?
2. Which library is modern?
3. Which library is more beautiful?
4. Write a summary sentence of Maya's thoughts on the libraries.

ACTIVITY B Make a Venn diagram to compare and contrast two familiar buildings. You might choose two houses in which you have lived, two schools you attended, two department stores you like, or any other buildings you know well. Write at least three differences and three similarities for each building.

ACTIVITY C Using the information from the Venn diagram on page 346, write pairs of sentences that compare and contrast the following details of the two libraries.

1. convenience
2. appearance
3. librarians
4. other features

ACTIVITY D Make a Venn diagram to compare and contrast one of the following pairs. Then write a sentence that tells the reader what the description is about.

1. spring and autumn
2. apples and oranges
3. dogs as pets and cats as pets
4. baseball and tennis

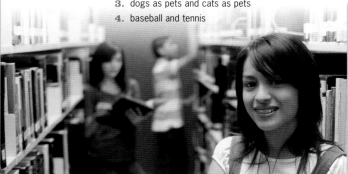

WRITER'S CORNER
Make a Venn diagram comparing two of your favorite leisure activities. How are the two activities alike? How are they different? Write your answers in a descriptive paragraph.

WARM-UP

Read, Listen, Speak

Put your Venn Diagram from yesterday's For Tomorrow activity on the board. Point out the similarities and differences and offer a summary statement for your Venn diagram. Then have students write a summary statement for their diagrams. Encourage volunteers to share their summaries with the class.

GRAMMAR CONNECTION

Take this opportunity to talk about infinitives used as direct objects. You may wish to have students point out infinitives used as direct objects in their Read, Listen, Speak examples.

TEACH

Invite a volunteer to read aloud the first four paragraphs of the section Word Webs. Have students describe their experiences working with word webs. Then allow time for students to read silently the three steps Ellen took when developing her word web. Have students study Ellen's word web. Challenge students to explain what methods of organization Ellen might use for her description, based on her word web (*spatial order because Ellen used the floor plan of the museum when recording her subtopics*).

PRACTICE

ACTIVITY E

Allow time for students to complete the activity independently. Remind them to distinguish between subtopics and details when completing their word webs. Refer students to the numbered points on page 348. Invite volunteers to write their word webs on the board.

ACTIVITY F

Have students determine their subtopics before they begin their word web. When students have finished, invite volunteers to draw their word webs on the board. Discuss the different subtopics and details that students used.

Word Webs

A word web is a graphic organizer that can help you organize your ideas in a variety of ways, such as spatial order or order of importance.

Ellen is writing a description of the city's new museum. Because the museum deals with so many aspects of the city, she used a word web to organize her thoughts about what she saw.

A word web is a useful tool for organizing a description of a place. The floor plan of a museum divides the subjects it covers into separate areas within the building. Ellen created a word web based on the separate areas of the museum.

After you finish your word web, look at it and decide if you have too much information. If so, eliminate some of the least important details from your subtopics.

This is how Ellen developed her word web for the Mayville Historical Museum.

1. Ellen started her word web with the central topic and drew a box around it. In this case the main topic is Mayville Historical Museum.
2. Next, she wrote four subtopics that are dealt with at the museum. She then drew an oval around each subtopic. The subtopics are arranged so that they stem from the main topic like spokes on a wheel.
3. Around each subtopic she wrote details relating to that particular subtopic. These are the details that will most likely fill out her description.

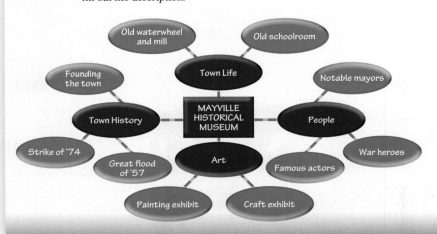

APPLY

WRITER'S CORNER

After students have finished, ask them to trade paragraphs and word webs with a partner. Have partners compare the word webs to the paragraphs. Ask partners to answer the following: *Did the writer include all relevant details from his or her word web? Did the writer effectively connect the subtopics from the word web using transition words?* Students should demonstrate an understanding of turning a word web into a descriptive paragraph.

ASSESS

Note which students had difficulty using word webs. Use the Reteach option with those students who need additional reinforcement.

Practice Book page 155 provides additional work with graphic organizers.

TEACHING OPTIONS

Reteach

Give students a selection from any genre of writing. Have them circle the sentence in which the main topic is stated. Then ask them to underline the subtopics and supporting details. Invite students to construct word webs based on the topics and details that they circled and underlined. Ask volunteers to write their word webs on the board.

Cooperative Word Webs

Challenge students to construct a class word web as a group. Ask students to choose an object or place in the school to be the subject of a description. Invite a volunteer to be the recorder and to construct a word web on the board as students suggest subtopics and details of the subject. When students have finished the word web, challenge each student to use the word web to write a description.

Study Ellen's word web on page 348. How many paragraphs do you think she will include in the body of her description? Why do you think so?

ACTIVITY E Make word webs for three of the following topics. Use a textbook, an encyclopedia, or the Internet to help you.

1. wind instruments in the orchestra
2. the parts of a flower
3. the branches of the federal government
4. types of clouds
5. Olympic Games
6. attending a ball game
7. World War II battles in Europe

ACTIVITY F With a partner make a word web for your city or town. Then write separate paragraphs in either spatial order or order of importance, using different details from the word web. Read your paragraphs to the class. Listen to your classmates' paragraphs. How similar are their paragraphs to yours? What did your classmates include that you did not?

WRITER'S CORNER

Select one of the word webs you made for Activity E. Write a paragraph using the details in your word web.

For Tomorrow

Ask students to choose a topic for a description and to construct a word web. Suggest they spend at least 5 to 10 minutes thinking about and writing subtopics and supporting details. Then challenge students to determine how best to organize the word web into paragraph form. Create a word web of your own to share with the class.

Descriptions • 349

OBJECTIVES
- **To know the purpose of a thesaurus**
- **To understand how a thesaurus is organized**
- **To understand denotation and connotation of words**

WARM-UP
Read, Listen, Speak
Draw your word web from yesterday's For Tomorrow homework on the board. Discuss what you used as subtopics and details. Then have small groups discuss the word webs they made. As groups discuss the word webs, encourage students to add subtopics or details to their word webs.

GRAMMAR CONNECTION
Take this opportunity to talk about infinitives used as appositives. You may wish to have students point out infinitives used as appositives in their Read, Listen, Speak examples.

TEACH
Invite a volunteer to read aloud the first paragraph. Encourage students to share their experiences using thesauruses. Ask why a thesaurus is especially useful when writing descriptions.

Have a volunteer read aloud the section Dictionary Thesaurus. Show students a thesaurus organized like a dictionary. Invite students to write adjectives and verbs on the board. Challenge volunteers to find synonyms for the words in the thesaurus.

Have a volunteer read aloud the section Index Thesaurus. Show students an index thesaurus.

Repeat the activity you used for a dictionary thesaurus. Discuss when students might choose to use an index thesaurus and when they might use a dictionary thesaurus.

Ask a volunteer to read aloud the section Online Thesauruses. If you have a computer available, conduct a search or have small groups of students conduct searches of online thesauruses.

PRACTICE

ACTIVITY A
Allow time for students to complete the activity independently. Then have them trade papers with a partner. Ask students to replace each synonym their partners found with another synonym for the original word. Invite volunteers to read aloud their paragraphs, incorporating the synonyms they and their partners found.

ACTIVITY B
Have students complete this activity independently. Then ask volunteers to list their synonyms on the board. Once a lengthy list has been created, encourage volunteers to share some of their sample sentences.

LESSON 4 STUDY SKILLS

Thesaurus

One of a writer's most useful tools is a thesaurus, a book of synonyms and related words. A thesaurus can help you choose precise and vivid words and avoid repeating words in your writing.

Dictionary Thesaurus
In a dictionary thesaurus, you simply look up the word that you want to replace. The book is organized alphabetically, and the writer chooses from a list of synonyms and related words that accompany each entry. The dictionary style is easy to use, but thesauruses organized this way take up more pages and are more repetitious than those that follow the index style.

Index Thesaurus
The entries of an index thesaurus are organized under classes of ideas. Under each class is a list of more specific words that make up that class. Finally, under each word is the full numbered entry that lists all the synonyms.

Using an index thesaurus takes a couple of steps. First, turn to the index at the back of the book and find the word that you want to replace. When you find that word, you will see a list of possible uses of that word, each followed by a number. Flip through the thesaurus, using the guide numbers at the top of the pages to find the number listed in the index.

Suppose you wanted to find a word to replace *prize*, which you

prize

noun: desire 100.11
award 646.2
leverage 906.1
646.2
award, reward, prize, first prize, second prize, etc;
blue ribbon; consolation prize; Nobel prize

APPLY

WRITER'S CORNER

Allow time for students to complete the Writer's Corner. Invite volunteers to write their original words and synonyms on the board. Discuss the synonyms and ask students to suggest additional synonyms. Encourage students to decide which synonyms work best. Students should demonstrate an understanding of how to use a thesaurus.

TechTip Discuss any online thesauruses that students have used. If a computer is available in the classroom, show students some reliable online thesauruses they may use.

ASSESS

Note which students had difficulty using thesauruses. Use the Reteach option with those students who need additional reinforcement.

TEACHING OPTIONS

Reteach

Have small groups turn to the section of an index thesaurus that explains how to use a thesaurus. Ask students to read this section silently. Then give students a word such as *ground*. Have them find it in the index and look through the list of synonyms. Point out that you have to know which meaning of the word you want to look up. For practice give students words to look up in the index of a thesaurus and search for synonyms.

Saying It Differently

Have groups of students choose familiar sayings. (*Practice makes perfect. You can't have your cake and eat it too.*) Challenge students to use a thesaurus to find synonyms for most of the words. Then ask groups to exchange papers and translate the created sayings back into the original sayings.

For Tomorrow

Ask students to choose a page in a book they are reading at home. Ask them to replace 10 words in the selection with synonyms. Have students use an online thesaurus to find the synonyms. Do the same with a page from your favorite book.

used too often in a description of prize-winning architecture. After *prize* in the index, you note the number 646.2, which matches the meaning of the word *prize* as it relates to *award*. Using the guide numbers at the top of the pages, you quickly locate 646.2 under *HONOR*.

You will find a list of words such as *award*, *reward*, and *blue ribbon* to choose from. Any of these words might be a good replacement for *prize*. The advantage of using an index thesaurus is that it gives you a broader range of possible word choices.

Online Thesauruses

You can also use the Internet for help with words. You can choose from dozens of online thesauruses, and most are easy to use. Usually, you type the word for which you would like to find a synonym, click on the search button, and choose a suitable word from the list of suggestions that pop up.

ACTIVITY A Read the following paragraph about writer and explorer John Wesley Powell's expedition through the American West. Use a thesaurus to replace the italicized words with more exact ones.

John Wesley Powell enjoyed naming many of the places he saw. At one point on the Colorado River, one boat was *broken* on the rocks. Powell named the site "Disaster Falls." Later he called a *part* of the river that was thick with mud "Dirty Devil." When things got very *bad* for his expedition, Powell stopped to pray for *help* by a *pretty* stream. He named the stream "Bright Angel."

Grand Canyon expedition of John Wesley Powell

ACTIVITY B Using a dictionary thesaurus, an index thesaurus, or an online thesaurus, find three synonyms to replace each word below. Then write sentences using one of the synonyms.

1. pay
2. joke
3. ruin
4. vacation
5. charm
6. manage

WRITER'S CORNER

Choose two words from the description you wrote for the Writer's Corner on page 347. Then, using a thesaurus, find two vivid synonyms for each word.

TechTip With an adult, find vivid words in an online thesaurus.

Descriptions • 351

WARM-UP

Read, Listen, Speak

Read your original selection to the class. Then read the selection with the synonyms you selected. Invite small groups of students to share their selections and the synonyms they found for homework. Suggest that students read aloud their selections, replacing the original words with the synonyms. Challenge students to discuss how well the replacements work.

GRAMMAR CONNECTION

Take this opportunity to talk about infinitives used as adjectives. You may wish to have students point out infinitives as used adjectives in their Read, Listen, Speak examples.

TEACH

Invite a volunteer to read aloud the first paragraph of the section Denotation and Connotation. Ask students to define the words *literal* and *implied*. Explain that literal meanings of words can be found in the first few definitions of a word in a dictionary. Tell students that implied meanings evolve from common usage of a word over time. Point out that sometimes these meanings and usages are also explained in the dictionary as later definitions of a word.

Have a volunteer read aloud the second paragraph of the section. Have volunteers name more examples of implied meanings of words. Reiterate the benefits of using a dictionary along with a thesaurus when writing.

LiNK Ask a volunteer to read the link aloud. Tell students that connotations associated with certain words can help establish a writer's desired tone. Discuss the connotations of some of the words in the link, such as *dreams, mortal*, and *bear*. Then point out the use of infinitives in the first line.

PRACTICE

ACTIVITY C

Have students complete this activity independently. Then ask volunteers to write the completed sentences with the replacement words on the board. Discuss the denotations and connotations of the words students chose.

ACTIVITY D

Have students complete the activity independently. Discuss the denotations and connotations of each word.

ACTIVITY E

Allow time for students to write their descriptions. Ask volunteers to read aloud their descriptions. Encourage feedback from students about the synonyms used.

ACTIVITY F

Have small groups discuss the connotations of the words. Challenge students to write a list of connotations for each group of words. Then discuss the connotations of each word as a class.

LiNK

Hamlet

To sleep, perchance to dream.
Ay, there's the rub,
For in that sleep of death what dreams may come
When we have shuffled off this mortal coil . . .
For who would bear the whips and scorns of time . . .

William Shakespeare

Denotation and Connotation

When you use a thesaurus, remember that words have both denotations, or literal meanings, and connotations, or implied meanings. Be careful when using a thesaurus to replace a word with a synonym whose meaning isn't clear to you. You may choose a word whose connotation was not what you intended. The best rule to follow is this: If you don't know the meaning of a word, look it up in a dictionary.

Here's an example of what can happen if you ignore this rule. Suppose you were describing someone with whom you liked to pass the time and whom you trusted. You might describe this person as a *friend* or *pal*, but would you want to describe that person as an *acquaintance* or a *colleague*? Obviously you would not. An acquaintance is someone you may merely nod to in the hallway, and a colleague is someone you work with.

ACTIVITY C Read each sentence and the words that follow it. Use a thesaurus and a dictionary to choose the best word to replace the italicized word in each sentence. Make sure you choose a word with the same connotation.

1. Though the building sits on marshy land, underground supports will keep the city's newest skyscraper *stable*.

   indestructible   immobile   secure   established   permanent

2. The *populace* of cities come from varied backgrounds.

   inhabitants   natives   pioneers   lodgers   occupiers

3. Some kids like wearing *hand-me-downs* from older brothers or sisters, but most don't.

   duds   tatters   clothing   rags   castoffs

4. I've never heard *yells* like the ones that erupted when our team finally won.

   cheers   screams   shouts   hooplas   hurrahs

5. Union and management hammered out an *agreement* so that the renovation of city hall could continue.

   adjustment   contract   regulation   assimilation   reconciliation

Activity C

1. immobile
2. inhabitants
3. castoffs
4. cheers
5. contract

APPLY

WRITER'S CORNER

Allow time for students to complete their paragraphs. Invite volunteers to read aloud their paragraphs. Ask students to comment on word choice and the connotations of some words the author chose. Students should demonstrate an understanding of connotations.

Grammar in Action. The two infinitives that are direct objects in the excerpt are *to hurry* and *to crane*. The other infinitive, *to find*, functions as an adverb. Follow this by asking students to identify the infinitive phrase that contains *to crane* (*to crane your neck*).

ASSESS

Note which students had difficulty understanding denotation and connotation of words. Use the Reteach option with those students who need additional reinforcement.

Practice Book page 156 provides additional work with using a thesaurus.

ACTIVITY D Use a dictionary to find the denotation of each word below. Then use a thesaurus to find three synonyms with different connotations for each word.

ACTIVITY D Use a dictionary to find the denotation of each word below. Then use a thesaurus to find three synonyms with different connotations for each word.

1. thought
2. weak
3. rare
4. shake
5. follow
6. mass

ACTIVITY E Choose two words below. Find each word in a thesaurus. Write a descriptive sentence for two synonyms of each word that you chose.

1. fake
2. eerie
3. sloppy
4. slow

ACTIVITY F Explain the differences in connotation among the words in each group. Use a dictionary if you need to check the exact meaning of any words.

1. sleepless, watchful, aware
2. gluttony, overeating, piggishness
3. solitude, loneliness, isolation
4. sociable, talkative, jolly
5. trendy, up-to-date, fashionable
6. servant, drudge, custodian
7. gab, speak up, talk
8. beast, critter, creature
9. nuke, destroy, ravage
10. camouflage, eclipse, hide

WRITER'S CORNER

Write a paragraph to follow the descriptive paragraph you wrote for the Writer's Corner on page 349. Use a thesaurus to choose words with connotations that convey the same tone as your first paragraph.

Grammar in Action. Find the two infinitives that are direct objects in the p. 337 description.

Descriptions • 353

Reteach

Ask students to write a list of 10 slang words that refer to computers, which they use in everyday conversation (*boot, crash, burn, virus, hack, spam*). Then have them write the implied meanings of those words. Challenge students to then look up the words in a dictionary and write the literal meanings of the words. Lead a discussion about the differences or similarities between the two meanings for each word.

English-Language Learners

Give students extra practice with synonyms and connotations. Have students work in pairs. Give each pair a different set of five words. Instruct students to record the words on note cards, to look up replacement words in a thesaurus, and to record the words and their connotation on separate note cards. Then ask students to shuffle the note cards and trade them with other student pairs. Challenge students to match the words with their replacement words.

For Tomorrow

Ask students to use a thesaurus to find synonyms for all the adjectives in the model on page 337. Have students list the synonyms on a separate sheet of paper so they can incorporate them into the model during the next class. Generate your own list of synonyms for the model as well.

OBJECTIVE
• To understand and use figures of speech in descriptions

WARM-UP
Read, Listen, Speak
Read the model on page 337 aloud. Then point out the adjectives used in the model. List the synonyms on the board. Then call on volunteers to share some of the synonyms they chose. Have small groups discuss the synonyms each student chose and replace the adjectives in the model. Then have a volunteer reread the model with the synonyms. Discuss how the replacement words convey the intended meaning.

GRAMMAR CONNECTION
Take this opportunity to talk about infinitives used as adverbs. You may wish to have students point out infinitives used as adverbs in their Read, Listen, Speak examples.

TEACH
Invite a volunteer to read aloud the first paragraph. Tell students that well-chosen figures of speech can create highly effective sensory images in a description. Have students read aloud the explanations of simile, clichés, metaphor, personification, and hyperbole. Ask students to give examples of each figure of speech. Then challenge volunteers to identify the figures of speech used in the model on page 337. Encourage students to discuss the images that these figures of speech create.

PRACTICE
ACTIVITY A
Discuss the example, and then allow time for students to complete the activity. Invite volunteers to share their answers. Challenge students to offer additional similes to describe the subject of each sentence.

ACTIVITY B
Have students complete the clichés independently. Then instruct pairs to collaborate on rewriting the clichés. Invite volunteers to read aloud what they have revised. Ask students to decide whether the rewrites are fresh and vivid.

Figurative Language

Like the connotations of words, figurative language goes beyond the literal meanings of words. Figures of speech such as similes, metaphors, personification, and hyperbole are examples of figurative language that can create vivid pictures in readers' minds. That's why these and other figures of speech are so useful in descriptive writing.

A **simile** uses the words *like* or *as* to compare two unrelated things.

> That high-rise looks like a glass arrow aimed at the sky.
> My pink velvet dress is as soft as a whisper.

Many similes, such as *like a ton of bricks* or *as quiet as a mouse,* are **clichés.** Clichés are similes that have become overused and worn-out. Try to avoid using clichés in your writing.

A **metaphor** is an implied comparison between two different things. It's almost like a simile except that *like* and *as* are not used.

> Max's poems are caravans of the imagination.
> Shanti's eyes are bottomless pools of feeling.

Personification is a figure of speech that allows an idea, inanimate object, or animal to take on the qualities of a person.

> Outside, the wind shrieked through the eaves of the house.
> The dog's constant barking mocked Tim's attempts to silence it.

Hyperbole is deliberate exaggeration. The exaggeration reveals the truth about something in order to emphasize an idea.

> Ana can talk until your ears fall off.
> My old dog's breath could curdle milk.

APPLY

WRITER'S CORNER

Ask which figures of speech are most often used when describing an animal *(personification, simile, metaphor)*. Allow time for students to write their sentences. Invite volunteers to read their sentences aloud. Ask students to explain the figures of speech. Have students save what they wrote to use for homework. Students should demonstrate an understanding of figurative language.

ASSESS

Note which students had difficulty understanding and constructing figures of speech. Use the Reteach option with those students who need additional reinforcement.

TEACHING OPTIONS

Reteach

Ask volunteers to write sentences containing similes, metaphors, and clichés on sentence strips. Have students use markers to draw a circle around the person, place, or thing being compared in each sentence and draw a line under the object to which it is compared. Then have students identify each example as a simile, a metaphor, or a cliché.

English-Language Learners

Point out to English-language learners the word *implied* in the explanation of a metaphor. Help students come to an understanding of how to identify the implied meaning of a phrase or sentence. Explain that to imply an idea is to express it indirectly. Ask students what ideas these sentences express indirectly.

> **Juan grabbed an apple, a package of ham, and a piece of cheese from the refrigerator** *(implied meaning—Juan is hungry)*.

> **Suzanne burst into tears when she heard that Lia couldn't come for a visit** *(implied meaning—Suzanne had looked forward to Lia's visit)*.

ACTIVITY A Identify which two things are being compared in each of the following similes. Write the quality or idea that the things share.

EXAMPLE **My brother Sam's *brain* works like a *computer*.**
A brain is compared to a computer.

1. Wind shook the branches as a mother dog shakes her pups.
2. After a demanding performance, the ballet dancer collapsed like a discarded marionette.
3. That poodle's teeth were as sharp as needles.
4. If you use the wrong ingredients for the recipe, the muffins will taste like sand.
5. That deed is as phony as a rubber chicken.
6. When he saw the scratch on the car, my father was as mad as a hornet.

Activity B
1. bee
2. log
3. clam, lark
4. envy
5. wolf
6. charm, dog
7. glove
8. horse, pig
9. baby
10. whip
11. sore thumb
12. turtle

ACTIVITY B Complete each cliché. Then work with a classmate to rewrite the clichés to make them fresh and vivid.

1. as busy as a _____
2. slept like a _____
3. as happy as a _____
4. green with _____
5. as hungry as a _____
6. works like a _____
7. fits like a _____
8. eats like a _____
9. cry like a _____
10. as smart as a _____
11. stick out like a _____
12. as slow as a _____

WRITER'S CORNER

Choose a pet or favorite animal. Use figurative language to write four sentences describing the animal.

Descriptions • 355

For Tomorrow

Ask students to add to their Writer's Corner, creating descriptive paragraphs about their favorite animal or pet. Challenge students to use personification, hyperbole, a simile, and a metaphor. Write a paragraph of your own, using figurative language.

WARM-UP

Read, Listen. Speak

Read your paragraph aloud. Point out the examples of figurative language. Discuss how the figurative language enhanced the descriptions in your paragraph. Then invite volunteers to read their paragraphs aloud. Ask students to offer feedback about the figurative language students use.

GRAMMAR CONNECTION

Take this opportunity to talk about hidden and split infinitives. You may wish to have students point out hidden and split infinitives in their Read, Listen, Speak examples.

TEACH

Review figurative language with students. Challenge volunteers to define the figures of speech discussed on page 354 and to provide an example of each one. Then ask a volunteer to tell why figurative language is useful when writing descriptions. (*It creates vivid pictures in the readers' minds.*)

Allow some time for students to search publications in the classroom for examples of figurative language.

LiNK Ask a volunteer to read the link aloud. Discuss what type of figurative language the author uses (*personification*). Encourage students to identify the examples of personification.

PRACTICE

ACTIVITY C

Discuss the example and then have students read the sentences silently. Ask volunteers to explain the metaphors. Challenge volunteers to suggest additional metaphors that would provide an accurate comparison between the two things in each sentence.

ACTIVITY D

Have students complete the activity with a partner. Instruct students to determine whether the use of hyperbole is effective.

ACTIVITY E

Have students complete this activity independently. Have students exchange papers with a partner. Tell students to determine if the similes are effective and if clichés were avoided.

ACTIVITY F

Complete this activity as a class. After students have identified the nouns and the examples of personification, ask students to determine whether the personification in each sentence evokes an appropriate image.

ACTIVITY C Explain the meaning of the metaphors in the following sentences.

EXAMPLE Those *bad grades are a stain* on my transcript.
Bad grades make a transcript look less worthy.

1. Computers are the on-ramps to the information superhighway.
2. Dan's thoughts are pebbles rattling inside a can.
3. The day before summer vacation, classrooms are three-ring circuses.
4. The governor's speech was a torpedo that sank any chance the bill had to pass the legislature.
5. Mr. Sanchez's face was stone when the workers presented their demands.

ACTIVITY D Use hyperbole to complete each sentence.

1. That bug is so ugly _____.
2. I'll be your best friend until _____.
3. It's so hot this summer _____.
4. The smell of the crowded room _____.
5. I'm hungry enough to eat _____.
6. Frank talks on the phone so long _____.
7. Uncle Hugo is such a slow driver _____.
8. Glenna has such a cheerful smile _____.
9. That cat is as old as _____.
10. The plains are so flat _____.
11. That newborn is as tiny as _____.
12. Dad bellows like _____.

ACTIVITY E Create a simile to complete each of the following sentences. Avoid using clichés.

1. The football player ran down the field _____.
2. Birds flew through the air _____.
3. The love she felt for her new baby brother _____.
4. The thunder clap sounded _____.

ACTIVITY G

Allow time for students to complete this activity independently. Ask small groups to share their sentences. Challenge students to elaborate on whether the sentences effectively describe the topics.

APPLY

WRITER'S CORNER

When students have finished their descriptions, invite volunteers to read aloud their paragraph or poem. Discuss each example with the class, determining if the figurative language creates a vivid picture in the reader's mind. Students should demonstrate an understanding of figurative language.

ASSESS

Note which students had difficulty using figures of speech when writing descriptions. Use the Reteach option with those students who need additional reinforcement.

Practice Book page 157 provides additional work with figurative language.

TEACHING OPTIONS

Reteach

Play a recording of sounds of nature. Ask students to freewrite about nature while listening to the tape. Later have students review their freewriting and challenge them to add figurative language to describe the sounds. Ask students to share what they wrote with the class.

Comparing with *Like* and *As*

Elaborate on the correct usage of *like* and *as* in a sentence. Explain that their usage is often confused, not just in sentences with similes but in many sentences. Tell students that *like* is a preposition. *As* can be a preposition or a conjunction, depending on its use. Ask volunteers to suggest sentences in which students determine whether *like* or *as* is used correctly. Say that they may use sentences from publications in the classroom or from their own writing. Write these sentences on the board as examples of correct usage.

They threw the football like all-stars (*preposition*).

We picnicked at the beach as a farewell to summer (*preposition*).

Naomi smiled as she worked (*conjunction*).

For Tomorrow

Ask students to read Ralph Waldo Emerson's poem "Concord Hymn," noting Emerson's use of hyperbole. Challenge students to find other poems that effectively use hyperbole. Find a poem that uses hyperbole on your own to share with the class.

ACTIVITY F Identify the noun that is personified in each sentence. Identify the words that give human qualities to that noun.

1. Two huge Tudor houses stand sentry at the end of the block.
2. Just when Alan recovered, a second injury robbed him of his chance to play football.
3. I'm afraid a colony of termites has gained a foothold in our basement.
4. Autumn, brightly dressed, danced through the park.
5. The shy sun peeped out from behind a cloud.
6. The clouds grew dark and cried rain upon the baseball game.
7. After a few well-placed kicks, the machine spit out our candy bars.
8. The engine is starting to cough when the car comes to a stop.
9. A tiny train crawled to the top of Mount Baldy.
10. The fields sleep under a blanket of snow.

ACTIVITY G Use personification, hyperbole, simile, or metaphor to write a descriptive sentence for each topic.

1. a pitcher who regularly throws over 90 m.p.h.
2. a bridge being demolished
3. a broken water main
4. a singer who hits high C
5. a day when 36 inches of snow falls
6. an approaching storm
7. a gymnast who performs a perfect routine on the uneven bars.

The Rubáiyát

Wake! For the Sun, who scatter'd into flight/The stars before him from the Field of Night./Drives Night along with them from Heav'n, and strikes The Sultan's Turret with a Shaft of Light.

Omar Khayyám

Nastia Liukin, 2008 Olympic gold medalist

WRITER'S CORNER

Write a paragraph or poem comparing yourself to an animal or an element of nature. Use a metaphor or a simile.

Descriptions • 357

OBJECTIVES

- To choose a topic and plan and present an oral description
- To be an effective listener

WARM-UP

Read, Listen, Speak

Read aloud the Emerson poem. Point out and discuss examples of hyperbole. Then read the poem you found for yesterday's For Tomorrow homework. Point out the uses of hyperbole. Discuss how these enhance the poem. Then have small groups discuss the poems students found that use hyperbole. Ask students to point out the examples of hyperbole. Challenge each group to choose a poem to read aloud.

GRAMMAR CONNECTION

Take this opportunity to review verbals. You may wish to have students point out verbals in their Read, Listen, Speak examples.

TEACH

Invite a volunteer to read aloud the first paragraph. Ask students to name other examples of oral descriptions. Help students understand the difference between orally describing something and explaining a process or course of action. Explain that oral descriptions consist of describing places, objects, people, and sometimes emotions. Ask a volunteer to read aloud the section Choose the Right Topic. Allow time for students to list places to talk about.

Ask volunteers to read aloud the sections Do Your Research and Let Your Words Express Mood. Discuss the importance of word choice and mood. Explain that one way oral descriptions are different from other forms of oral presentation is that each descriptive word is carefully chosen. Have a volunteer read the section Select Your Words Carefully and the paragraph that describes Wrigley Field. Have volunteers comment on whether the description provides a vivid and accurate oral presentation of the topic.

PRACTICE

ACTIVITY A

Allow time for students to choose a topic, perhaps using one that was written about earlier. Then have students record sensory details, using the chart provided. Invite volunteers to share their details. Encourage students to comment on how easy or difficult it is to recall sensory details.

Oral Description

Have you ever told friends about a favorite restaurant? What about an amusement park? You've probably described places like these to your friends many times. Presenting a talk that describes a place to an audience is not that different from describing it to your friends.

Choose the Right Topic

You are going to describe a place that genuinely made an impression on you, either positively or negatively. It might be a creepy abandoned house, an elegant hotel built in the 19th century, or a new baseball stadium with old-fashioned charm and high-tech features.

List some possible places you might talk about. Which ones interest you most? Of those places which one is clearest in your mind? Which one do you have the most to say about? Which one will intrigue your audience most? Consider these questions as you choose the topic of your talk.

Do Your Research

If you want to add factual information to bolster your description, it must be accurate. Do the necessary research in books or online to make sure you've got the facts right.

Let Your Words Express Mood

How did you feel about the place? Was it beautiful, exciting, scary, or astonishing? Make sure the emotions you associate with the place are expressed in the details you include.

Select Your Words Carefully

Make sure your description is lively and detailed. Appeal to all the senses by using vivid and specific words to explain what you saw, heard, smelled, felt, and tasted. Figures of speech will strengthen your description. Avoid clichés.

APPLY

SPEAKER'S CORNER

As students write their notes, remind them to keep in mind the intended mood of the oral description when choosing words and phrases. Tell students to think about connotations associated with certain words that can help create the intended mood. Students should demonstrate an understanding of an oral description.

Grammar in Action. The two participial phrases on page 336 are *rising into peaks* and *covered with snow.* Ask students to identify what each phrase describes *(mountains).*

ASSESS

Note which students had difficulty understanding how to choose a topic and plan an oral description. Use the Reteach option with those students who need additional reinforcement.

Read the following paragraph written by a visitor to Wrigley Field in Chicago who takes the opportunity to imagine that she witnessed Babe Ruth's famous home run. The writer will share this oral description with her drama class.

I emerged from the darkened stairwell and stepped into the brilliance of the sunlit ballpark. Standing in a sea of empty green seats, I took in the eerie silence. In the distance a lone groundskeeper pushed a wheelbarrow along the famed ivied wall that bounded the outfield. Though the stadium was empty and quiet, my mind's eye and ear took in the history that had been lived here. The roar of the crowd filled my head as I looked down at the white lines of the batter's box and imagined Babe Ruth on that fateful date when it was believed that he "called the shot." I could almost see him point toward the outfield at the place where his next home run would fly.

ACTIVITY A Choose a topic for your talk. Let the place's image flood your mind. Jot down sensory details on a list like the one below. You do not have to include all five senses on the list, but try to include as many as you can.

> My Place:
> What I see:
> What I smell:
> What I taste:
> What I hear:
> What I touch:

SPEAKER'S CORNER

Consult the chart you made in Activity A. Write notes for your talk. Include descriptive details that support the desired impression of the place.

Grammar in Action. Find the participial phrases in the p. 336 excerpt.

Descriptions • 359

TEACHING OPTIONS

Reteach

Have students choose a commercial that has made them interested in a product. Encourage students to identify the ways that the actor or announcer in the commercial described the product. Have students discuss ways that their chosen commercial was compelling *(descriptive language, figurative language, or a tone of voice that elicits an emotional response).* Have groups choose a product and write their own commercial. Challenge groups to include what was effective in their commercials.

Cooperative Learning

Have students choose a photograph or illustration from a book. Then have partners deliver impromptu oral descriptions of the photograph or illustration to each other. Instruct the students to take several minutes to create and rehearse an oral description for the same picture. Have partners deliver their prepared descriptions to each other. Encourage partners to discuss the differences between the rehearsed and the impromptu oral description.

For Tomorrow

Ask students to search a library for recordings of poetry. Challenge students to write how effectively the speaker delivered the oral presentation. Ask students to write a list of specific words that helped convey the mood of the piece. Listen to a recording of a poem and create a similar list to share.

Read, Listen, Speak

Play the recording of the poem from yesterday's For Tomorrow activity. Share your list of words that helped convey the mood of the piece. Then ask volunteers to read their poems aloud and to identify the words closely associated with the mood of the piece. Ask volunteers to identify other words that help create the mood.

TEACH

Have a volunteer read the section Organize. Ask volunteers to describe each type of organization learned in this chapter *(chronological order, spatial order, order of importance, comparison and contrast)*. Encourage students to discuss the forms of organization that would best serve the oral descriptions students began for the Speaker's Corner on page 359.

Read the Rehearse section aloud. Point out the importance of practicing your oral description in front of somebody. Tell students they may wish to practice in front of several different people to receive more feedback. Also tell students they may wish to practice in front of a mirror.

Have a volunteer read aloud the Present section. Discuss the importance of each point thoroughly. Then challenge students to add to the list of points under Present.

Read aloud the Display Visual Aids section. Discuss other options students can use as visual aids. Then have a volunteer read aloud the Be an Effective Listener section. Invite students to list additions to the bulleted list.

LiNK Invite a volunteer to read aloud the link. Point out the use of figurative and descriptive language. Ask students what the mood of the link is. Then discuss the specific words used that help create the desired mood.

PRACTICE

ACTIVITY B

Allow time for students to find a passage in an essay or a story and to practice reading it aloud. Divide the class into small groups and allow time for students to present their oral descriptions. Challenge students to follow the suggestions for being effective listeners.

Organize

Make sure that the introduction of your talk hooks the audience and that the conclusion leaves them with an idea or insight that's worth remembering.

Listeners will quickly lose interest if you present them with a disorganized mass of details. In the body of your talk, keep in mind both the overall impression and the important details you would like your audience to remember. Organize your talk by following one of the forms of organization you studied in this chapter: chronological order, spatial order, order of importance, comparison and contrast, or a combination of these.

Rehearse

Try out your talk on a classmate. He or she might notice parts that are boring or confusing. Ask your partner to make suggestions to improve the content of your talk. Ask for comments on the delivery too. Did you speak too quickly or too slowly? Could your partner understand all your words?

After you revise your talk, practice it often so that you almost know it by heart. Remember, everyone gets nervous when speaking to a group. The more you practice, the less nervous you will most likely be.

Present

Before and during your talk, remember the following points.

- Check your appearance in a mirror before you begin your talk.
- Stand up straight and breathe calmly. Avoid fidgeting or shifting from foot to foot.
- Make eye contact. Don't look only at one person or one part of the room. Glance around the entire audience.
- Be enthusiastic. Your enthusiasm will transfer to your audience.
- Use gestures for emphasis. Don't overdo it, though, or you will distract the audience from the impact of your words.
- Control your voice. Use your tone of voice to emphasize the meaning of your words. For example, prior to a dramatic moment, try slowing down and lowering your voice.

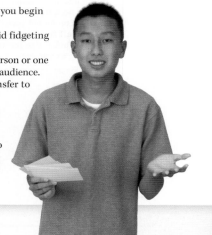

APPLY

SPEAKER'S CORNER

Ask students to present their oral descriptions to the class. Have listeners write their comments as feedback. Then have students give their notes to the speaker. Students should demonstrate an understanding of presenting an oral description.

Grammar in Action The gerund in the link is *yearning*. Ask students to identify if the gerund is a subject, subject complement, direct object, object of a preposition, or appositive *(object of a preposition)*.

ASSESS

Note which students had difficulty presenting oral descriptions. Use the Reteach option with those students who need additional reinforcement.

After you have reviewed Lessons 3–5, administer the Writing Skills Assessment on pages 57–58 in the **Assessment Book.** This test is also available on the optional **Test Generator CD.**

Display Visual Aids

If you have posters, drawings, postcards, slides, or photographs of the place, use them to illustrate your talk. Visual aids will present your audience with lots of information, leaving you free to focus on details and discuss your feelings and impressions.

Be an Effective Listener

Just as speaking before an audience is a skill that gets better with practice, listening to speakers is a skill that you can also improve. Here are some suggestions.

- Listen actively. Picture the place that the speaker is describing. Add new details to the picture in your mind as the speaker presents them. Think critically. Ask yourself if the details add up to a coherent picture.
- Listen for important ideas. Identify the mood the speaker creates for the subject.
- Do not interrupt, even if you are confused or have a question. Save questions and comments for the end of the talk.

ACTIVITY B Get used to speaking in front of an audience. Find a descriptive passage from an essay or a story. Read it aloud to a small group of classmates. Practice speaking at an appropriate pace and volume. Make sure to pronounce all the words clearly.

LiNK

The Iroquois Constitution

The thickness of your skin shall be seven spans—which is to say that you shall be proof against anger, offensive action, and criticism. Your heart shall be filled with peace and good will and your mind filled with a yearning for the welfare of the people of the confederacy.

The Iroquois Nation

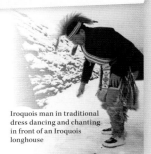

Iroquois man in traditional dress dancing and chanting in front of an Iroquois longhouse

SPEAKER'S CORNER

Present your oral description to the class. After your talk, ask for feedback from your audience. Write the helpful suggestions in a notebook or journal to review before you give another speech.

Grammar in Action. Find the gerund in the Iroquois Constitution excerpt.

Descriptions • 361

OBJECTIVE
- **To brainstorm, choose a topic, and organize ideas for a comparative description**

PREWRITING AND DRAFTING

Review what students have learned about descriptions. Encourage volunteers to name the following characteristics of a description:

- Precise and vivid word choice that accounts for the denotation and connotation of words
- A mood that conveys an emotion or overall impression
- Details that are organized in a meaningful way to create the mood
- Use of figurative language that creates vivid pictures in readers' minds

Review with students what makes an effective comparative description. Challenge students to explain how the characteristics might change in a description that compares and contrasts two things.

Ask students to explain what they have learned about using Venn diagrams, word webs, and thesauruses. Challenge volunteers to decide which of these might be used during the prewriting stage of composing a comparative description *(Venn diagrams)*. Have a volunteer write the stages of the writing process on the board. Then ask a volunteer to read aloud the first paragraph.

Prewriting

Have a student read aloud the first paragraph in this section. Discuss with students why organizing ideas is an important step in the prewriting stage of a description. *(The organization makes a description more coherent and helps set the mood.)*

👀 Explain that ideas are the foundation of writing. Tell students that strong ideas supported by strong details, sensory images, and figurative language help bring descriptions to life.

Choosing a Topic

Have a volunteer read aloud the first paragraph in this section. Invite students to finish reading the section silently. Ask volunteers to comment on Lydia's choice of topic. *(Her choice is a good topic because it focuses on specific objects and it concerns something meaningful to the writer.)* Point out that since Lydia is writing a

comparative description, she needs to freewrite for two subjects (two buildings).

Your Turn
Review with students what they have learned about choosing a topic for a description. Have a volunteer read aloud this section. Allow time for students to brainstorm topics and then to freewrite ideas. When students have finished, invite volunteers to share the topics they chose and which side of their two-part freewriting notes had more details.

Writer's Workshop
Descriptions

Prewriting and Drafting

Well-written descriptions can make people, places, and events come alive on the page. You have learned about how to organize and express descriptive details through graphic organizers and by using figurative language. Now you will use what you have learned to write a comparative description.

Prewriting

Before you write a comparative description, take
👀 **Ideas** some time to brainstorm, choose a topic, and organize your ideas. Prewriting is also the time to develop a plan for how you will structure your description. Descriptions require vivid language to be effective. Yet the details of the description need to be organized for the reader to understand them. A comparative description requires even more thought.

Choosing a Topic
The first step in writing a description that compares and contrasts is to choose two related subjects. The two subjects should have something in common, such as both being places to visit, something to do, or something to buy.

Lydia, an eighth grader, brainstormed a list of ideas that she might write about in a comparative description. Her list included ideas from restaurants to roller coasters, from buildings to baseball players.

From her list Lydia selected the topic that seemed most appealing to describe. Lydia had recently visited Chicago on a trip with her family and was fascinated by two of the city's skyscrapers—the John Hancock Center and Willis Tower.

For her freewriting exercise, Lydia drew a line down the center of a sheet of paper and wrote the name of a building on each side of the line. Under each name she wrote all the details she recalled relating to the building.

Your Turn
Use the following steps to develop your ideas:
- Write *Two Kinds of* _____ at the top of a sheet of paper and list details of your two subjects, as Lydia did.
- When you have finished, look over your paper and note which side has more details. This can serve as a guide for gathering more information.

Gathering Information
Lydia was able to remember quite a few details in her freewriting session. However, she didn't want to rely solely on the memories of her trip and felt she needed to learn more about both skyscrapers. So she gathered more information from the library and online and added it to her lists.

Gathering Information

Have a volunteer read aloud this section. Ask students to explain the benefits and drawbacks of gathering information online.

Organizing Your Ideas

Invite a student to read aloud the first paragraph in this section. Then allow time for students to read Lydia's diagram silently.

Point out that organization is the way writers put their ideas together. Review the types of organization discussed on page 342.

Have a volunteer continue reading this section aloud.

Encourage students to answer the question about Lydia's outline. Challenge students to comment on Lydia's choice of using spatial order for her comparison.

Your Turn

Ask a volunteer to read this section aloud. Review with students how to construct a Venn diagram. Allow time for students to create their Venn diagrams. Then challenge students to use a basic outline as Lydia did. Remind students to choose a method of organization that will best serve the purpose and mood of their descriptions. Invite volunteers to share their work with the class.

TEACHING OPTIONS

Working Together

After students choose a topic and freewrite, ask them to work with a partner to discuss their ideas. Ask students to assess whether their partners' free-writing notes contain equal information for both subjects. If not, have partners either help each other think of more details or help the writer choose a new topic from his or her brainstorming notes.

English-Language Learners

Encourage students to write their notes in their primary language and then to translate their notes into English. Students who struggle with vocabulary and whose primary language has a different syntax may benefit from focusing on their ideas before addressing sentence structure. Remind students that there will be time to correct structure, punctuation, and grammar later in the writing process.

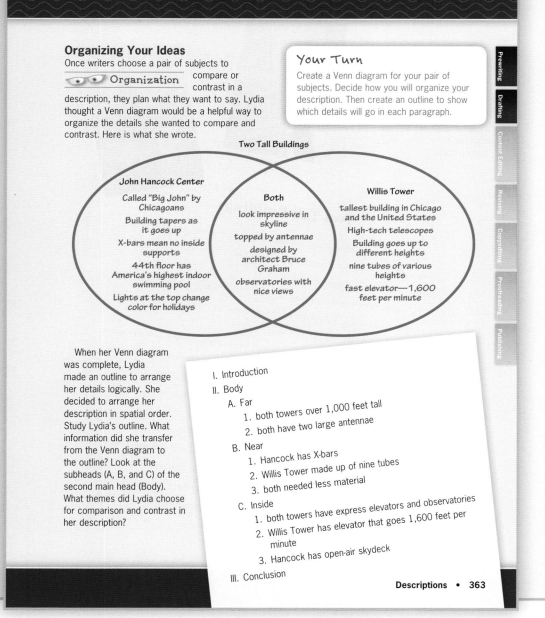

Organizing Your Ideas

Once writers choose a pair of subjects to compare or contrast in a description, they plan what they want to say. Lydia thought a Venn diagram would be a helpful way to organize the details she wanted to compare and contrast. Here is what she wrote.

Organization

Your Turn

Create a Venn diagram for your pair of subjects. Decide how you will organize your description. Then create an outline to show which details will go in each paragraph.

Prewriting
Drafting
Content Editing
Revising
Copyediting
Proofreading
Publishing

Two Tall Buildings

John Hancock Center
Called "Big John" by Chicagoans
Building tapers as it goes up
X-bars mean no inside supports
44th floor has America's highest indoor swimming pool
Lights at the top change color for holidays

Both
look impressive in skyline
topped by antennae
designed by architect Bruce Graham
observatories with nice views

Willis Tower
tallest building in Chicago and the United States
High-tech telescopes
Building goes up to different heights
nine tubes of various heights
fast elevator—1,600 feet per minute

When her Venn diagram was complete, Lydia made an outline to arrange her details logically. She decided to arrange her description in spatial order. Study Lydia's outline. What information did she transfer from the Venn diagram to the outline? Look at the subheads (A, B, and C) of the second main head (Body). What themes did Lydia choose for comparison and contrast in her description?

I. Introduction
II. Body
  A. Far
    1. both towers over 1,000 feet tall
    2. both have two large antennae
  B. Near
    1. Hancock has X-bars
    2. Willis Tower made up of nine tubes
    3. both needed less material
  C. Inside
    1. both towers have express elevators and observatories
    2. Willis Tower has elevator that goes 1,600 feet per minute
    3. Hancock has open-air skydeck
III. Conclusion

Descriptions • 363

Writer's Workshop   Descriptions

OBJECTIVE
- **To draft a comparative description**

Drafting

Invite a volunteer to read aloud the first paragraph. Tell students that when drafting a compare-and-contrast description, they should use the information they organized in their Venn diagrams. Then have volunteers take turns reading aloud Lydia's draft.

After students have finished reading, encourage them to discuss Lydia's draft. Challenge students to point out the items Lydia took from her Venn diagram and outline. Ask students if Lydia used spatial order correctly in her draft. Invite students to comment on whether spatial organization is the best fit for Lydia's comparative description.

Figurative Language

Ask a volunteer to read aloud this paragraph. Invite students to work with a partner to identify the figurative language in their first drafts. Challenge partners to determine whether figurative language was used effectively. Suggest places where adding a figure of speech would enliven the description.

Drafting

Lydia developed her Venn diagram and outline into a coherent comparative description. She had to give enough details to help readers visualize and compare and contrast the buildings. Read Lydia's draft.

Two Tall Buildings

Chicago has many tall buildings, and two of the tallest are the John Hancock Center and Willis Tower. On a recent trip to downtown Chicago with my family, I decide to visit these impressive buildings.

The similarities of the two buildings is obvious. They both go up more than 1,000 feet and architect Bruce Graham designed both buildings. On top of each, two large antennae go up into the clouds.

On closer inspection, I noticed several differences between the towers. The sides of the John Hancock Center are covered with huge X-shaped bars and they become narrower as they go up. Willis Tower has several levels of different heights, and is made up of nine tubes. Graham's designs mean less material was needed to build both buildings.

We went inside each building, we waited in similar long lines before taking an elevator that went quickly to the top. The observation areas were different. Willis Tower's elevator took us to a room with windows, while the Hancock's observatory includes an open-air skydeck that let you feel the sun and the wind blowing. While I was on the Hancock's skydeck, I learned that the building had America's highest indoor swimming pool on the 44th floor.

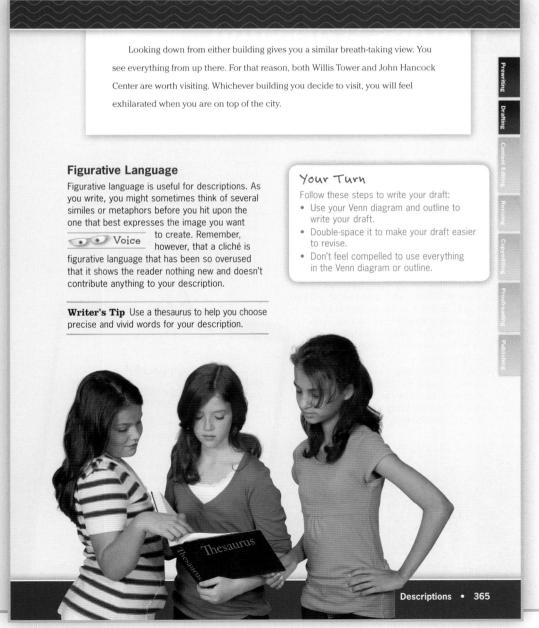

Remind students that voice is the language that helps readers hear and feel the personality of the writer. Tell students that figurative language, sensory details, and words with specific connotations will help to form their voice.

Writer's Tip Remind students to use a thesaurus to avoid using commonly repeated words. Challenge students to use synonyms that help create the desired mood of their writing.

Your Turn
Have a volunteer read this section aloud. Point out that once students start drafting their descriptions, they might not use everything in their Venn diagrams. Tell students that flow and coherent organization are particularly important when comparing two subjects.

Prewriting

Drafting

Content Editing

Revising

Copyediting

Proofreading

Publishing

Looking down from either building gives you a similar breath-taking view. You see everything from up there. For that reason, both Willis Tower and John Hancock Center are worth visiting. Whichever building you decide to visit, you will feel exhilarated when you are on top of the city.

Figurative Language

Figurative language is useful for descriptions. As you write, you might sometimes think of several similes or metaphors before you hit upon the one that best expresses the image you want to create. Remember, however, that a cliché is figurative language that has been so overused that it shows the reader nothing new and doesn't contribute anything to your description.

Voice

Writer's Tip Use a thesaurus to help you choose precise and vivid words for your description.

Your Turn
Follow these steps to write your draft:
- Use your Venn diagram and outline to write your draft.
- Double-space it to make your draft easier to revise.
- Don't feel compelled to use everything in the Venn diagram or outline.

Experimenting with Order

Have volunteers share the methods of organization they used in their drafts. Have students explain their choices. Challenge students to consider another method of organization to see how it changes the flow and mood of the description. Elicit comments about how organization affects a piece of writing. Encourage students who see the benefits of the new method of organization to use it when they next revise their drafts.

Talking It Out

Have students discuss the topic for their comparison. Explain that it is always helpful to talk about a description before writing it. Invite partners to ask questions about any details that are confusing or vague. Encourage students to describe their topics as if they were talking to family or friends who are not familiar with this topic.

Descriptions • 365

OBJECTIVE
- **To edit a first draft for content**

CONTENT EDITING

Read aloud the first paragraph. Then invite a volunteer to define content editing.

Invite a volunteer to read aloud the second and third paragraphs and the Content Editor's Checklist. Allow time for students to copy the Content Editor's Checklist into a notebook for future reference. Ask how this checklist is tailored to Lydia's task. *(It is tailored to characteristics of comparative descriptions.)* Then ask students to describe the difference between figurative language and sensory language. *(Figurative language includes figures of speech such as similes, metaphors, personification, and hyperbole. Sensory language is writing that appeals to the senses.)*

Point out Lydia's choice of an editing partner who was not familiar with her subject. Ask students why this might be useful. *(A reader not familiar with the subject would easily be able to say whether or not the details the writer included created a clear visualization in his or her head.)*

Read Lydia's draft on page 364 aloud. Have students write any ideas on how Lydia could improve her draft. Then allow time for students to read silently Sam's comments. Discuss with students any similarities between their lists and Sam's list. Ask whether students agree with Sam's comments about Lydia's draft and if they have anything else to add. *(Lydia included a few unnecessary details such as the detail about the indoor pool.)*

Editor's Workshop   Descriptions

Content Editing

Lydia knew that editing the content of a comparative description meant revising for the logic, order, and clarity of its comparisons and its contrasts. She also knew that a content editor makes sure that the things being compared and contrasted are given equal weight.

Lydia revised her draft, referring to the Content Editor's Checklist. Then she asked her friend Sam to read it. She chose Sam because he had not visited either building. In this way she might find out if he could actually visualize the details of what she had written.

Sam read through Lydia's draft carefully and then reread it, checking it against the Content Editor's Checklist. Then he had a conference with Lydia.

Sam began the conference by telling Lydia what he liked about her description. Here are Sam's comments.

- I like your topic choice. You give a pretty good sense of what these buildings look like and what they would be like to visit. You use some great words, like *breathtaking* and *exhilarated*. The description also seems to be well organized.

- You might start off with a more interesting introduction. In the opening paragraph, you should also say that you will be comparing and contrasting the two buildings.

- You seem to cover both buildings with an equal amount of detail. I don't feel as if one building is being shortchanged.

- In the second and third paragraphs, you might add more detail. I know the buildings are tall, but it's not very clear. And *Willis Tower has several levels of different heights* is kind of confusing.

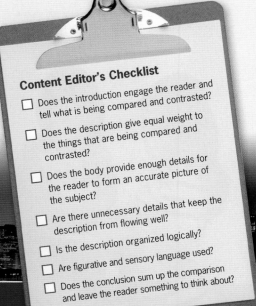

Content Editor's Checklist

☐ Does the introduction engage the reader and tell what is being compared and contrasted?

☐ Does the description give equal weight to the things that are being compared and contrasted?

☐ Does the body provide enough details for the reader to form an accurate picture of the subject?

☐ Are there unnecessary details that keep the description from flowing well?

☐ Is the description organized logically?

☐ Are figurative and sensory language used?

☐ Does the conclusion sum up the comparison and leave the reader something to think about?

366 • Chapter 4

Your Turn

Ask a volunteer to read aloud this section. Provide students with time to use the Content Editor's Checklist while they read their drafts. Then allow students time to work with editing partners to review their drafts. Encourage students to choose a partner who is unfamiliar with the subjects being compared. Remind students to word their suggestions in a constructive manner.

Grammar in Action. Remind students that participial phrases can help vary the sentence structure in their writing. Encourage students to use vivid verbs as participles to help create a clear description for their readers.

- In the third and fourth paragraphs, you identify what type of details you will be describing by using *On closer inspection* and *We went inside each building.* Can you do the same for your second paragraph?
- Instead of writing *You can see everything from up there* in the last paragraph, can you describe what you would see?

Lydia considered Sam's comments and decided to revise her draft.

Your Turn

Use the following steps to edit your draft:
- Before giving your draft to a classmate to read, review it on your own by checking it against each question in the Content Editor's Checklist.
- Trade drafts with a classmate. Refer to the Content Editor's Checklist as you read your classmate's description a few times.
- When you have finished reading your partner's draft, give your partner constructive criticism. Tell him or her the strong points of the piece before suggesting ways it might be improved. Your partner should do the same for you.

Grammar in Action

Use participial phrases to add description and sentence variety.

Descriptions • 367

Checking Facts

Tell students that content editing often involves fact-checking. Have students check the accuracy of the facts in Lydia's draft, using the library or the Internet. Then have students fact-check their editing partners' drafts or mark the facts that the writers should recheck themselves.

Intriguing Titles

Explain to students that often a reader will pick up a book because of an eye-catching title. Explain that the following are tips that students can use to help them create effective titles:

- Start with a working title. Then edit the title when the draft is done.
- Hint at something within the piece, such as an emotion, an image, or a character.
- Summarize what the piece is about.
- Think of words and phrases that have more than one meaning and that relate to your piece.

Be sure that students understand that they do not have to follow all the tips. Explain that these tips are different ways to approach writing an effective title.

OBJECTIVE

- **To revise a first draft**

REVISING

Invite volunteers to read aloud Lydia's revised draft. Challenge students to point out the revisions Lydia made based on Sam's comments. Remind students that a writer should consider all the revisions an editor suggests and then choose those that best serve the purpose, structure, tone, flow, and mood of the piece.

Remind students that sentence fluency is the sound of the writing. Suggest that students always read their writing aloud to hear where the writing might sound choppy or awkward.

Have students read aloud the paragraph on page 369. Discuss the various ways Lydia improved her draft. Have volunteers provide details on how the revisions improved Lydia's draft. Encourage students to use the characteristics of a comparative description in the discussion. Use each bullet point to discuss Lydia's revisions. Urge students to answer all the bullets.

- In the second paragraph, Lydia added the words *From a distance* to introduce the type of description in that paragraph. She decided to add a metaphor to create a stronger image about the buildings that create Chicago's skyline.

- Lydia clarified the description with a metaphor about the Sears Tower looking like a stack of building blocks. Also, she added a simile comparing the express elevator to a rocket in the fourth paragraph.

- She replaced *everything from up there* with *distant building, tiny cars, and people who look like ants*, providing specific images for the reader to visualize.

- Lydia thought the detail about the indoor pool was not needed, so she removed it.

Writer's Workshop

Revising

This is how Lydia revised her description based on her and Sam's suggestions.

Two Tall Buildings

Chicago's skyline boasts many majestic buildings, but two skyscrapers loom larger than the rest: ~~Chicago has many tall buildings, and two of the tallest are~~ the John Hancock

Center and Willis Tower. On a recent trip to downtown Chicago with my family, I
structures. I hoped to see what similarities and differences I could find.
decide to visit these impressive ~~buildings~~.

From a distance   rise confidently into the sky
The similarities of the two buildings is obvious. They ~~both go up~~ more than 1,000
, and both stand over the city's other buildings like parents watching their children.
feet ~~and~~ architect Bruce Graham designed both buildings. On top of each, two large
    dart
antennae ~~go up~~ into the clouds.

Up close
~~On closer inspection,~~ I noticed several differences between the towers. The sides
, which are covered with huge X-shaped braces, taper
of the John Hancock Center ~~are covered with huge X-shaped bars~~ and they become
, on the other hand,   that make the tower look like a stack
narrower as they go up. Willis Tower has several levels of different heights, ~~and is~~
of building blocks. The building is made up of nine support tubes of various heights.
~~made up of nine tubes.~~ Graham's designs mean less material was needed to build

both buildings.
When
We went inside each building, we waited in similar long lines before taking an
blasted to the top like a rocket   , however,
elevator that ~~went quickly to the top.~~ The observation areas were different. Willis

Tower's elevator took us to a room with windows, while the Hancock's observatory

includes an open-air skywalk that let you feel the sun and the wind blowing. ~~While~~

~~I was on the Hancock's skywalk, I learned that the building had America's highest~~

~~indoor swimming pool on the 44th floor.~~

Your Turn

Ask a volunteer to read this section aloud. Tell students that if they question a revision their editor suggested, they should refer to the Content Editor's Checklist. Explain that if the edit corresponds to an item on the checklist, then perhaps they should seriously consider making the edit. Tell students another option may be to consult another reader's opinion. If the edit simply refers to a change in wording that the editor prefers, then the writer can use his or her discretion in making the revision.

Writer's Tip Encourage students to compare their outline to their revised draft. They may find that a point of comparison was not included in their revisions. Remind students that they should refer to their outline after completing each step of the writing process.

Looking down from either building gives you a similar breath-taking view. You

distant buildings, tiny cars, and people who look like ants

see everything from up there. For that reason, both Willis Tower and John Hancock

Center are worth visiting. Whichever building you decide to visit, you will feel

exhilarated when you are on top of the city.

Notice how Lydia improved her draft. She changed the introduction to make it draw the reader in with vivid words and images. She added

👁👁 Sentence Fluency a sentence at the end

of the first paragraph to state that her description would compare and contrast the buildings.

- What did Lydia add to the second paragraph, and what effect did these additions have on her description?
- Lydia agreed that the third paragraph was unclear. How did she clarify it? What did she add to the fourth paragraph to help her readers visualize more clearly?
- Lydia agreed that in the last paragraph, saying that *you see everything* doesn't say much. How did she fix this?
- Lydia noted that Sam did not find any unnecessary details. However, she disagreed. What unnecessary details did Lydia delete from her draft?

Your Turn

Use your ideas and the ideas you got from your content editor to revise your draft.

- Don't feel obliged to use every suggestion your editor makes. Choose the ideas that you agree will make your draft stronger.
- When you have finished, go over the Content Editor's Checklist again. Have you addressed all the points on the checklist?

Writer's Tip Use your outline as an additional checklist to make sure you addressed all your points of comparison.

OBJECTIVE

- **To copyedit and proofread a draft**

COPYEDITING AND PROOFREADING

Copyediting

Invite a volunteer to read aloud the first paragraph of this section. Have students read silently the Copyeditor's Checklist. Challenge a volunteer to tell how copyediting differs from content editing. *(Content editing focuses on ideas, while copyediting focuses on words and sentences.)* Then have students list on the board any additions to the checklist.

👀 Tell students that word choice is especially important in descriptive writing. Explain that their word choice will help create the vivid images in the reader's mind that are important to descriptive writing. Encourage students to avoid overused words and to use specific verbs and adjectives to bring their writing to life.

Invite a student to continue reading aloud the paragraphs that follow the checklist. Point out that a thesaurus is a powerful tool to use while copyediting. Explain that some words, especially adjectives and adverbs, become trite from overuse, just like clichéd phrases. Tell students that a thesaurus can help a copyeditor quickly find replacement words when editing.

Your Turn

Have a student read this section aloud. When students have finished copyediting their own drafts, have them trade papers with a partner. Ask partners to use the Copyeditor's Checklist to mark revisions the writer might have missed. Encourage partners to read aloud each other's drafts to identify ineffective words or awkward phrases.

Editor's Workshop   Descriptions

Copyediting and Proofreading

Copyediting

When Lydia finished revising her draft for content, her next step was to copyedit her description. At this stage Lydia focused on making sure each sentence was clear, logical, and grammatically correct. She used the Copyeditor's Checklist to edit her draft.

When she looked it over, Lydia thought some sentences and word choices still needed work.

In the second paragraph, she found that the second sentence was a run-on sentence, so she turned the second clause into a separate sentence. She also revised the first sentence of the fourth paragraph, which was also a run-on sentence.

Lydia noticed that throughout the description 👀 **Word Choice** she overused the word *tall*. With what synonym can she replace this word?

The description also needed more comparison words such as *however* and *on the other hand*. Lydia looked for places where they might be useful.

Lydia also noticed that the last sentence in the fourth paragraph referred to feeling "the sun and the wind blowing." Why doesn't this phrase make sense, and how did Lydia fix it?

Copyeditor's Checklist

- ☐ Are there any rambling or run-on sentences?
- ☐ Are the adjectives vivid?
- ☐ Are the similes and metaphors effective?
- ☐ Are there connecting words or phrases such as *in comparison, both, on the other hand, however,* and *instead*?
- ☐ Is every sentence grammatically correct?
- ☐ Do all the sentences flow logically?
- ☐ Are any sentences awkward or confusing?
- ☐ Are any words redundant, unnecessary, or misused?

Your Turn

Use the Copyeditor's Checklist to review your revised draft.

- Check that your sentences are grammatically correct. In particular look for any rambling sentences, run-on sentences, or sentence fragments.
- Make sure every sentence is clear and logical.
- Read over your draft one more time. Make sure that no words are redundant, unnecessary, or misused.

Proofreading

Ask a volunteer to read aloud the first paragraph and the Proofreader's Checklist. Challenge students to add items to the checklist that are specific errors that students commonly make.

👀 Be sure students understand that conventions are spelling, grammar, punctuation, and capitalization of a piece of writing. Emphasize the importance of proofreading drafts to find and correct these types of errors.

Have another volunteer read aloud the rest of the section. Discuss the errors that Jennifer found in Lydia's draft. Then invite volunteers to find additional errors in Lydia's draft. Discuss these as a class.

Your Turn

Have a volunteer read this section aloud. Allow time for students to proofread drafts with a partner. Encourage students to choose partners who have not previously read their drafts.

Proofreading

Before writing the finished copy of a description, **Conventions** a good writer proofreads the draft to check for spelling, punctuation, capitalization, and grammar. A checklist like this one helps a writer proofread.

Proofreader's Checklist

- ☐ Are the paragraphs indented?
- ☐ Have any words been misspelled?
- ☐ Are capitalization and punctuation correct?
- ☐ Is the grammar accurate?
- ☐ Were new errors introduced during the editing step?

Good writers ask a proofreader to check their work for errors in grammar, mechanics, and punctuation. A proofreader will often catch errors that the writer missed.

Lydia asked Jennifer, a classmate, to proofread her report. Jennifer looked it over, using the Proofreader's Checklist, and made proofreading marks on Lydia's draft. Because Lydia did a thorough job of copyediting, Jennifer found only a few errors. She noticed that the verb *is* in the second paragraph should be changed to *are,* and in the fourth paragraph, *let* should be changed to *lets* to agree with the subject of the clause. What other errors can you find?

Your Turn

- Use the Proofreader's Checklist as you read your description.
- Read it once for each item on the list. When you have gone through the list, trade papers with a partner.
- Review your partner's draft in the same way. Be sure to use a dictionary if you are unsure of a spelling.

Descriptions • 371

PUBLISHING

Ask a volunteer to read aloud the first paragraph. Point out that Lydia reread her draft before she completed her final draft. Encourage students to do the same with their own writing. Then allow time for students to read silently Lydia's finished draft. Challenge students to point out the changes Lydia made after copyediting and proofreading. Ask a volunteer to explain why the title "Chicago's Steel Giants" is stronger than "Two Tall Buildings." Invite volunteers to share their working titles with the class. Encourage students to offer constructive feedback for these titles. Remind students that the title can help draw in the reader's attention.

Have students read aloud and discuss the many ways they might publish their descriptive essays. Have volunteers suggest additional modes of publication. Challenge students to publish their writing in a new way. Tell students that if they have already posted work to a classroom blog or on a bulletin board, they should consider creating a classroom book. Then encourage students to share their final description orally with family and friends.

Your Turn

Invite a student to read aloud the first paragraph of this section and the three bulleted points that follow. Then allow time for students to read their drafts one more time for errors and to copy it by hand or print it on a computer.

Have a volunteer read aloud the rest of the section. If you have the software available, show students how to place their descriptions in newspaper format on a computer. Allow time for students to illustrate their descriptions on the computer or on a sheet of paper.

When students have finished, divide the class into small groups

Writer's Workshop   Descriptions

Publishing

Lydia read her description again to see if it was error-free. Then she carefully typed it and added her own byline. While she read the finished draft, she realized that the title might be more interesting, so she revised it.

Chicago's Steel Giants

by Lydia Romero

Chicago's skyline boasts many majestic buildings, but two skyscrapers loom larger than the rest: the John Hancock Center and Willis Tower. On a recent trip to downtown Chicago with my family, I decided to visit these impressive structures. I hoped to see what similarities and differences I could find.

From a distance the similarities of the two buildings are obvious. They rise confidently into the sky more than 1,000 feet, and both stand over the city's other buildings like parents watching their children. Architect Bruce Graham designed both buildings. On top of each, two large antennae dart up into the clouds.

Up close, I noticed several differences between the towers. The sides of the John Hancock Center, which are covered with huge X-shaped braces, taper as they go up. Willis Tower, on the other hand, has several levels of different heights that make the tower look like a stack of building blocks. The building is made up of nine support tubes of various heights. Graham's designs mean less material was needed to build both buildings.

When we went inside each building, we waited in similar long lines before taking an elevator that blasted to the top like a rocket. The observation areas were different, however. Willis Tower's elevator took us to a room with windows, while the Hancock's observatory includes an open-air skywalk that lets you feel the sun shining and the wind blowing.

Looking down from either building, gives you a similar breathtaking view. You see distant buildings, tiny cars, and people who look like ants. For that reason, both Willis Tower and John Hancock Center are worth visiting. Whichever building you decide to visit, you will feel exhilarated when you are on top of the city.

and allow them to share their descriptions and illustrations. Encourage students to be courteous and constructive in their feedback.

👓 Tell students that presentation has to do with the overall appearance of their final draft. Encourage students to use a final format that enhances the overall impression of the piece. If using paper and pencil, encourage students to double-space and to avoid sloppy writing.

ASSESS

Have students assess their finished descriptions using the reproducible Student Self-Assessment on page 373y. A separate Descriptions Scoring Rubric can be found on page 373z for you to use to evaluate their work.

Plan to spend tomorrow doing a formal assessment. Administer the Descriptions Writing Prompt on **Assessment Book** pages 59–60.

TEACHING OPTIONS

Portfolio Opportunity

Have students place copies of their descriptions in their writing portfolios. Ask students to read the list of writing and editing skills in which they hoped to improve and to assess whether they have improved in these skills. Ask them to write and date comments about these improvements.

There are many ways to share your comparative description with your class, your friends and family, and even the public.

Create a classroom book. Your classmates may have photographs, illustrations, or other souvenirs of their experience. These are interesting items to attach to the descriptions.

Post it to a Web site that publishes student writing. Work with an adult to find one for which your description is appropriate. Lydia posted hers on a student travel Web site.

Post it on a bulletin board or on your classroom wiki. Since Lydia's description is informational, she linked it to other student entries on the class wiki about architecture and Chicago.

Make a pop-up book. Lydia's pop-up book was educational and very popular with her younger brother's class.

Whenever you publish your work, your goal is to share your thoughts and experiences with other people.

Your Turn

Once your draft has been proofread, it should be ready to publish. Before you publish your finished description, it's always a good idea to check it over one more time. Follow these steps:

• Check the content of your description to make sure you have not left out anything important or left in anything unnecessary.

• Proofread for correct spelling, grammar, capitalization, and punctuation. If your computer has a spell-checker, it can alert you to misspelled words. Make sure that when you made your corrections, you did not make any new mistakes.

• Make sure any proper names or titles are spelled correctly. People don't like seeing their names misspelled in print.

The way your description looks is important too. Be sure to use a font that is easy to read or use your best handwriting. Consider

👓 **Presentation**

adding an image to your description. You can insert an image from clipart or from a free online Web site. You might even create a small caption to place below the image.

After your description has been published, be willing to receive feedback from your peers. They will want to receive your feedback on their descriptions as well.

Prewriting
Drafting
Content Editing
Revising
Copyediting
Proofreading
Publishing

Descriptions • 373

Name _____ Date _____

Description
Compare and Contrast

Ideas	YES	NO
Do I compare and contrast two related subjects?		
Do I give equal weight to both subjects?		

Organization		
Do I name the two subjects in the introduction?		
Do I use logical sentence and paragraph order?		
Do I summarize the comparison in the conclusion?		

Voice		
Do I write appropriately for my audience?		
Does my piece grab and hold the reader's attention?		

Word Choice		
Do I use literary techniques such as simile, metaphor, and personification?		
Do I provide rich sensory details?		
Do I employ connecting words or phrases?		

Sentence Fluency		
Do I use a variety of sentence types, including those with noun clauses?		
Does my piece show natural transitions between sentences?		

Conventions		
Do I use correct grammar?		
Do I use correct spelling, punctuation, and capitalization?		

Presentation		
Do I use consistent spacing and margins?		
Does my paper look neat?		

Additional Items		

© LOYOLAPRESS.

Name _____

Date _____ Score _____

POINT VALUES

0 = not evident
1 = minimal evidence of mastery
2 = evidence of development toward mastery
3 = strong evidence of mastery
4 = outstanding evidence of mastery

Description
Compare and Contrast

	POINTS
Ideas	
two related subjects	
equal weight to both subjects	
Organization	
two subjects named in the introduction	
logical sentence and paragraph order	
comparison summarized in the conclusion	
Voice	
appropriate for audience	
reader's attention held	
perceivable mood	
Word Choice	
literary techniques such as figures of speech	
rich sensory details	
connecting words or phrases	
Sentence Fluency	
variety of sentences	
natural transitions between sentences	
Conventions	
correct grammar and usage	
correct spelling, punctuation, and capitalization	
Presentation	
consistent spacing and margins	
neatness	
Additional Items	
Total	

© LOYOLA PRESS.

SUPPORT MATERIALS

Practice Book
Writing, pages 158–162

Assessment Book
Chapter 5 Writing Skills,
     pages 61–62
Expository Writing Prompt,
     pages 63–64

Rubrics
Student, page 411y
Teacher, page 411z

Test Generator CD

Grammar
Sections 6, pages 109–122
Section 7, pages 123–138

Customizable Lesson Plans
www.voyagesinenglish.com

Expository Writing

WHAT IS EXPOSITORY WRITING?

Expository writing informs and explains, going beyond presenting surface-level knowledge of a topic to give readers a new depth of understanding. Good writers of expository essays always have in mind the purpose of informing. To present facts accurately, good expository writers work to keep their essays free of opinion.

Good expository writing includes the following:

- ☐ A clear focus on one topic
- ☐ Factual information supported by research or personal experience
- ☐ An engaging introduction that includes a topic sentence
- ☐ A logically ordered body of paragraphs that includes important main ideas supported by relevant details
- ☐ A summarizing conclusion that includes thought-provoking insights
- ☐ A neutral tone
- ☐ A confident voice
- ☐ Natural language
- ☐ Concise sentences that are free of unnecessary or redundant details
- ☐ Varied ways of providing information, such as quotations, statistics, examples, or explanations

LiNK Use the following titles to offer your students examples of well-crafted expository writing:

Gladiator by Richard Watkins

Joan of Arc: The Lily Maid by Margaret Hodges

The Story of the Greeks by H. A. Guerber

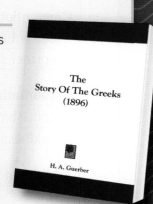

The Story Of The Greeks (1896)

H. A. Guerber

> "Words, once they are printed, have a life of their own."
>
> —Carol Burnett

WRITER'S WORKSHOP TIPS

Follow these ideas and tips to help you and your class get the most out of the Writer's Workshop:

- Review the traits of good writing. Use the chart on the inside back cover of the student and teacher editions.
- Fill your classroom library with interesting nonfiction books and magazines.
- Create a bulletin-board display of high-interest expository essays, magazine articles, and newspaper articles.
- Focus on the difference between fact and opinion and the ways students can verify the reliability of sources.
- Review how to check the reliability of a Web site.
- Reinforce the importance of using a variety of ways to incorporate information, including quotations, statistics, and examples.
- Consider creating a step-by-step completion schedule that guides students to complete each step of the process by a certain date, beginning with gathering facts about their topic.

CONNECT WITH GRAMMAR

Throughout the Writer's Workshop, look for opportunities to integrate adverbs and prepositions with expository writing.

- ☐ Suggest that students pay particular attention to adverbs of time, place, and manner when addressing the five *W*'s.
- ☐ Encourage students to avoid exaggerating adverbs. Tell students that these often are signal words for opinions and should be avoided.
- ☐ Challenge students to identify prepositional phrases during the copyediting stage of the writing process. Have students classify each prepositional phrase as an adjective or an adverb.

SCORING RUBRIC

Expository Writing

0 = not evident
1 = minimal evidence of mastery
2 = evidence of development toward mastery
3 = strong evidence of mastery
4 = outstanding evidence of mastery

	POINTS
Ideas	
a clear focus on one topic	
factual information supported by research or personal experience	
Organization	
an engaging introduction with a topic sentence	
a logically ordered body of main ideas and details	
a conclusion with summarizing insights	
Voice	
confident	
Word Choice	
natural language	
neutral tone	
Sentence Fluency	
concise sentences	
varied ways of providing information	
Conventions	
correct grammar and usage	
correct spelling, punctuation, and capitalization	
Presentation	
consistent spacing and margins	
neatness	
Additional Items	
Total	

Full-sized, reproducible rubrics can be found at the end of this chapter.

Expository Writing

INTRODUCING THE GENRE

Ask students to discuss what they know about expository writing. Encourage students to state the purpose of expository writing *(to give information about real people, places, things, or events)*. Then have students name the types of expository writing they have read, such as magazine and newspaper articles, nonfiction books, textbooks, and encyclopedia entries.

Have students discuss the characteristics of expository writing. Mention the following characteristics during the discussion:

- Includes a clear focus and informs the reader on one topic
- Includes relevant information that answers the questions *who, what, where, when, why,* and *how*
- Uses a neutral tone
- Incorporates factual information and few opinions

Reading the Literature Excerpt

Ask volunteers to read aloud the excerpt. Challenge students to answer the following questions about the model:

- How and where is the purpose of the essay stated?
- How well do the facts support the main idea?
- Are there opinions given, and, if so, are they credible or irrelevant?

Expository Writing

LiNK The Story of the Greeks

The excerpts in Chapter 5 introduce students to published examples of expository writing. *The Story of the Greeks* is a strong example of expository writing because it has the following:

- An introduction that clearly states the subject
- A main idea supported by facts, explanations, and examples
- Information that answers the questions *who, what, when, where, why,* and *how*

As students encounter different examples of expository writing throughout the chapter, be sure to discuss the characteristics that these expository pieces share. Also take this opportunity to point out grammar skills that students have been learning, such as adverbs and prepositions.

LiNK The Story of the Greeks
by H.A. Guerber

Although Greece (or Hel´las) is only half as large as the State of New York, it holds a very important place in the history of the world. It is situated in the southern part of Europe, cut off from the rest of the continent by a chain of high mountains which form a great wall on the north. It is surrounded on nearly all sides by the blue waters of the Med-it-er-ra´ne-an Sea, which stretch so far inland that it is said no part of the country is forty miles from the sea, or ten miles from the hills. Thus shut in by sea and mountains, it forms a little territory by itself, and it was the home of a noted people.

The
Story Of The Greeks
(1896)

H. A. Guerber

> This is a good example of an expository essay. The topic is stated in the first sentence, and supporting information is organized according to order of importance.

374

- Is more information required to understand the topic fully?
- How well does the tone serve the purpose of the piece?

Reading the Student Model

Encourage students to explain the differences between how-to articles and expository writing—two genres that might be easily confused. *(How-to articles explain how to perform a specific step-by-step action, encouraging the reader to perform the action. Expository writing informs the reader about a person, a place, an event, or an idea.)* Challenge students to comment on the purposes, audiences, and tones of each genre and how these characteristics differ.

Read the article aloud and discuss why this article might be of interest and who might be interested in reading it. Ask students to identify characteristics of expository writing in the model. Then have students list what other information they would like to learn about this topic.

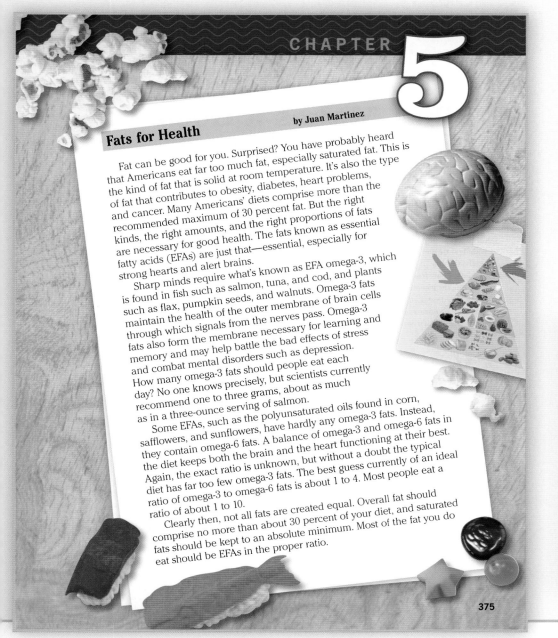

CHAPTER 5

Fats for Health

by Juan Martinez

Fat can be good for you. Surprised? You have probably heard that Americans eat far too much fat, especially saturated fat. This is the kind of fat that is solid at room temperature. It's also the type of fat that contributes to obesity, diabetes, heart problems, and cancer. Many Americans' diets comprise more than the recommended maximum of 30 percent fat. But the right kinds, the right amounts, and the right proportions of fats are necessary for good health. The fats known as essential fatty acids (EFAs) are just that—essential, especially for strong hearts and alert brains.

Sharp minds require what's known as EFA omega-3, which is found in fish such as salmon, tuna, and cod, and plants such as flax, pumpkin seeds, and walnuts. Omega-3 fats maintain the health of the outer membrane of brain cells through which signals from the nerves pass. Omega-3 fats also form the membrane necessary for learning and memory and may help battle the bad effects of stress and combat mental disorders such as depression. How many omega-3 fats should people eat each day? No one knows precisely, but scientists currently recommend one to three grams, about as much as in a three-ounce serving of salmon.

Some EFAs, such as the polyunsaturated oils found in corn, safflowers, and sunflowers, have hardly any omega-3 fats. Instead, they contain omega-6 fats. A balance of omega-3 and omega-6 fats in the diet keeps both the brain and the heart functioning at their best. Again, the exact ratio is unknown, but without a doubt the typical diet has far too few omega-3 fats. The best guess currently of an ideal diet has far too few omega-3 fats. The best guess currently of an ideal ratio of omega-3 to omega-6 fats is about 1 to 4. Most people eat a ratio of about 1 to 10.

Clearly then, not all fats are created equal. Overall fat should comprise no more than about 30 percent of your diet, and saturated fats should be kept to an absolute minimum. Most of the fat you do eat should be EFAs in the proper ratio.

375

OBJECTIVES
- To understand characteristics of expository essays
- To organize expository essays effectively

WARM-UP

Read, Listen, Speak

Read aloud the example expository essays from yesterday's For Tomorrow homework. Discuss the topic and audience of each essay. Point out language that helps create the tone of each piece. Have small groups discuss the expository essays they found. Ask students to compare the information recorded about the essays. Then challenge students to identify the tone of the essays and language that helps establish the tone.

GRAMMAR CONNECTION

Take this opportunity to talk about types of adverbs, interrogative adverbs, and adverbial nouns. You may wish to have students point out types of adverbs, interrogative adverbs, and adverbial nouns in their Read, Listen, Speak examples.

TEACH

Read aloud the first paragraph. Ask students to define neutral tone *(a tone that does not display any particular feeling or attitude toward the subject)*. Have a volunteer read aloud the section Topic and Organization. Ask students to identify the topic sentence in the model on page 375.

Review methods of organization that students already know *(chronological order, spatial order, order of importance, comparison and contrast)*. Remind students that the purpose of an expository essay is to inform. Tell them that

expository essays should make the information easy to comprehend, just like a how-to article. Explain that the information should be told in a logical way that follows a linear train of thought. Have volunteers read aloud the model on page 375. Challenge students to analyze and discuss the model's organization.

Have a volunteer read aloud the sections Supporting Paragraphs and Conclusion. Ask volunteers to identify the types of supporting details used in the model *(facts and statistics)*. Point out how the conclusion effectively summarizes the main idea of the essay.

LiNK Have a student read aloud the excerpt. Point out the neutral tone of the writing. Then ask students where and when Blackbeard ruled the seas. *(He ruled the Caribbean Sea and Atlantic Coast from 1716 to 1718.)*

PRACTICE

ACTIVITY A

Allow time for students to read silently the expository essay. Discuss the answer to each question. Challenge students to suggest ways in which the essay could be improved. List these suggestions on the board. If time permits, have students add these

---

What Makes a Good Expository Essay?

LiNK

Yo Ho! Treasure

No one knew how to drill terror into sailors' hearts like the dreaded pirate Blackbeard, who ruled the Caribbean Sea and the Atlantic Coast from 1716 to 1718. Among the legends of his cruelty: he fired randomly at his crew, and he once forced a captive to eat his own ears.

TimeforKids.com

The purpose of expository writing is to inform. Good expository writers provide relevant information about a specific topic, often answering these six questions: *who?, what?, where?, when?, why?,* and *how?* Expository writing is written in a neutral tone and takes many forms, including reports, articles, and essays. Expository essays often appear in magazines and academic journals.

Topic and Organization

The topic of an expository essay is clearly stated in a topic sentence, which appears in the introduction. The main idea, or what the writer wants to say about the topic, is often included in the topic sentence or elsewhere in the introduction.

Effective essays are well organized. Some ways of organization that can be applied to expository writing include order of importance, chronological order, and comparison and contrast. Another way to organize expository writing is to explain cause-and-effect relationships. An expository essay organized by cause and effect explains *why* something happens.

Supporting Paragraphs

Supporting paragraphs provide information that supports the main idea stated in the introduction. Each paragraph focuses on a different aspect of the topic, and all the sentences in the paragraph relate to that aspect. The support might include factual examples, statistics, or quotations.

suggestions to the essay. Then invite a volunteer to read aloud the revised essay. Discuss how the changes improved the essay.

APPLY

WRITER'S CORNER

Brainstorm possible topics with the class. Challenge students to write topic sentences for several different topics. After students have written their sentences, have partners trade papers and decide whether the topic sentences effectively introduce a main idea for an essay. Students should demonstrate an understanding of topic sentences.

TechTip Remind students that they should use only reliable Web sites when conducting research. Tell students that Web sites ending in .edu and .gov are usually reliable sources.

ASSESS

Note which students had difficulty understanding the characteristics of expository writing. Use the Reteach option with those students who need additional reinforcement.

TEACHING OPTIONS

Reteach

Have students find expository essays in textbooks or magazines. Ask students to copy the introduction, omitting the topic sentence. Have partners trade introductions. Discuss how the absence of a topic sentence affects the essay. Then have partners write topic sentences for the essays. Invite volunteers to read their introductions without topic sentences and then with topic sentences.

Curriculum Connection

Explain that social studies textbooks often combine expository and narrative writing. Point out that expository writing is used to define concepts, to give background information about a historical event, and to explain cause and effect. Mention that narrative writing is often found in sidebars or features. Challenge students to look through social studies textbooks for examples of both types of writing. Have students write assessments of how these genres serve the same or different purposes.

For Tomorrow

Have students expand their thoughts on their topic sentence from the Writer's Corner. Ask students to create an outline showing the organization and supporting details for an expository essay. Create an outline and topic sentence of your own for a similar subject to share with the class.

Conclusion

The conclusion summarizes the main idea of the essay. It leaves the reader with food for thought—a new way of looking at or thinking about the topic. This effect can be accomplished in many ways, such as through a unique insight or a thought-provoking statement.

Activity A

1. pasta
2. Since its origins thousands of years ago, pasta of many shapes and sizes has appeared in all kinds of dishes worldwide.
3. Variety of Italian pastas; pasta as a part of people's diets
4. Answers will vary.
5. When you eat your next bowl of spaghetti, think of the long and varied history of pasta.

ACTIVITY A Read the expository essay and answer the questions.

Pasta Through Time and Space

Since its origin thousands of years ago, pasta of many shapes and sizes has appeared in all kinds of dishes worldwide. *Pasta*, the Italian word for dough, is most closely identified with Italy. But pasta was discovered by the Chinese as long ago as 5000 BC.

No other country has such an astonishing variety of pasta as Italy, and the names of the different kinds describe their shapes or their uses. The pasta Americans know best is spaghetti, which means "strings" in Italian. Some other kinds include flat, wide strands of fettuccine, or "little ribbons"; lasagna, long, ripple-edged strips, whose name means "cooking pot"; narrow and flat linguine, "little tongues"; and mostaccioli, diagonally cut tubes whose name means "little mustaches." Other kinds of descriptively named pasta are radiatore, or "radiators"; vermicelli, "worms"; lumache, "snails"; and farfalle, "butterflies."

Pasta, which is made up mostly of carbohydrates, can form an important part of people's diets. Ingredients besides flour and water vary slightly, but flat strands of Italian pasta are usually made with eggs, and tube-shaped pasta is not. Many different kinds of pasta are available in grocery stores. Some are colored red or green. Some are flavored with basil or made from whole wheat. When you eat your next bowl of spaghetti, think of the long and varied history of pasta.

1. What is the topic of this essay?
2. What is the main idea?
3. What important idea is introduced in the second paragraph? the third?
4. What are some details in the second and third paragraphs?
5. Which concluding sentence sums up the main idea?

WRITER'S CORNER

Choose an original topic related to diet, health, or exercise. Write a topic sentence to introduce the idea.

Tech Tip With an adult, search online news for topics.

Expository Writing • 377

Read, Listen, Speak

Give students a copy of your outline and topic sentence from yesterday's For Tomorrow homework. Discuss the type of organization you used and point out specific supporting details in your outline. Then have small groups compare their outlines. Encourage students to discuss the organization and supporting details in their outlines. Challenge students to decide whether or not the outlines are suited for the topic sentence.

GRAMMAR CONNECTION

Take this opportunity to talk about comparative and superlative adverbs. You may wish to have students point out comparative and superlative adverbs in their Read, Listen, Speak examples.

TEACH

Review the characteristics of expository writing. Discuss the following questions:

- What tone is best for expository essays? *(a neutral tone)*
- What methods of organization work well in expository writing? *(order of importance, chronological order, comparison and contrast, and cause and effect)*
- What kinds of details can supporting paragraphs include? *(facts, statistics, and quotations)*
- What does the conclusion accomplish? *(It provides food for thought or a new way of looking at the topic.)*

LiNK Read aloud the excerpt. Ask students what the excerpt is about. Then point out that the topic is identified in the first sentence.

PRACTICE

ACTIVITY B

Have students complete the activity independently. After students have finished, invite volunteers to read their sentences aloud. If a volunteer's sentence is persuasive or entertaining, have the class offer revisions to make it informative.

ACTIVITY C

Remind students that a good conclusion summarizes the main idea and leaves the reader with a new way of looking at the topic. Have students complete the activity independently. Then have students trade papers with a partner. Challenge students to determine whether the sentences leave the reader with a lasting image or compelling thought about the topic.

ACTIVITY D

Tell students that supporting details usually appear in the form of facts, statistics, or quotations. As a class choose a topic, write a topic sentence, and write three supporting sentences. Then have students complete the activity independently. Invite volunteers to share their answers with the class.

ACTIVITY B Write a separate topic sentence for each main idea. Be sure the sentences are informational, not persuasive or entertaining.

1. team sports
2. backpacking
3. computer games
4. allowances
5. gymnastics
6. restaurants
7. museums
8. amusement parks
9. pets
10. vacations

ACTIVITY C Write a thought-provoking statement that might be included in the conclusion of an expository essay that begins with each topic sentence.

1. Smoking is bad for your health.
2. Experts agree that Jupiter is the oldest planet in the solar system.
3. A good baseball player must be able to get on base consistently.
4. Skipping breakfast is never a good idea for anyone, especially children and teenagers.
5. An essential companion to eating right is getting enough exercise.
6. Even small changes in eating habits can eventually produce big results.
7. Portion sizes at restaurants are much larger than they used to be.
8. Increasingly, Americans are exchanging their fuel-oil furnaces for gas-fired ones.
9. Discount retail stores are an enormous and growing market for value-priced consumer goods.
10. Learning to play a musical instrument can help children sharpen their math skills.

ACTIVITY D Write a topic sentence and three supporting sentences on a topic of your choice. How would you organize the information?

ACTIVITY E

Complete the first sentence as a class. Then have small groups complete this activity. When students have finished choosing methods of organization, ask volunteers to offer reasons for their answers.

APPLY

WRITER'S CORNER

Tell students to think about sources other than the library or the Internet. Suggest that students interview a family member or watch a documentary. Have students share what type of organization they would use.

Students should demonstrate an understanding of the characteristics of an expository essay.

Grammar in Action. The adverbs in the excerpt are *most, not* (twice), *always,* and *no.*

ASSESS

Note which students had difficulty organizing expository essays. Use the Reteach option with those students who need additional reinforcement.

Practice Book page 158 provides additional work with expository writing.

ACTIVITY E Read the topic sentences. Identify which way of organizing an expository essay would work best for each topic: chronological order, order of importance, comparison and contrast, or cause and effect. Explain your answers.

1. A popular type of house for pioneers living in the Great Plains was a sod house, or "soddie."

2. A base on the moon offers many advantages for space exploration.

3. Let's examine the features of the Tracker and the Forager SUVs side by side.

4. If you ask whether there is a simple way to get the proper nutrition, I respond with an emphatic yes.

5. Photosynthesis turns sunlight energy into chemical energy for plants.

6. A comparison of the typical American diet with the traditional Japanese diet reveals stark differences.

7. On casual examination a knockoff, or copy, looks much like the designer original that inspired it, but if you look closer, you'll find many differences.

8. The American Revolution and the French Revolution, while inspired by similar ideas, were very different.

9. Teaching adults to read is both different from and similar to teaching reading to children.

10. The Black Eagles of the 99th Pursuit Squadron fought Germans as well as discrimination within the U.S. Army during World War II.

11. Astronomers use the Hubble Telescope to estimate the age of the universe.

12. The type of soil in a garden determines what plants will thrive there.

Grammar in Action. Identify the adverbs in the excerpt above.

LiNK

A Weighty Issue

"What's the right weight for my height?" is one of the most common questions girls and guys have. It seems like a simple question. But, for teens, it's not always an easy one to answer. Why not? People have different body types, so there's no single number that's the right weight for everyone.

KidsHealth.org

WRITER'S CORNER

Make a list of places you might find information for the topic you chose for the Writer's Corner on page 377. Then determine the type of organization you would use for an essay on your topic.

Expository Writing • 379

LESSON 2 Fact and Opinion

OBJECTIVES

- **To use relevant, supporting facts in expository writing**
- **To use credible opinions in expository writing**

WARM-UP

Read, Listen, Speak

Read your conclusion from yesterday's For Tomorrow homework. Point out any thought-provoking statements and how the conclusion summarizes the main idea. Invite volunteers to read aloud their conclusions. Challenge students to identify any statements that are thought-provoking.

GRAMMAR CONNECTION

Take this opportunity to talk about comparisons using *as . . . as, so . . . as,* and *equally.* You may wish to have students point out comparisons using *as . . . as, so . . . as,* and *equally* in their Read, Listen, Speak examples.

TEACH

Invite a volunteer to read aloud the first paragraph. Have students read silently the examples of facts and opinions and the paragraph that follows. Challenge volunteers to explain why it is necessary for an expository essay to have more facts than opinions. *(The purpose of expository writing is to provide credible, objective information. Unsubstantiated opinions damage the credibility of the writing.)*

Ask a volunteer to read aloud the last two paragraphs. Then have students name people who might provide a credible opinion for the model on page 375 *(a doctor or nutritionist).* Explain that experts in a given subject matter can provide credible opinions for an expository essay. Point out that the writer of an expository essay

should always research sources of opinions for credibility and reliability.

Invite a volunteer to read aloud the section Use Relevant Facts. Challenge students to explain how irrelevant facts might weaken expository writing. *(They distract the reader from the pertinent details that actually inform him or her.)*

LiNK Have a volunteer read aloud the excerpt. Point out the facts in the excerpt *(In 1978 a California school district started Women's History Week, In 1981 Congress made Women's History Week a national celebration).*

PRACTICE

ACTIVITY A

Have students complete this activity independently. Discuss each sentence and invite volunteers to share their answers. Encourage students to defend their answers, using what they learned about fact and opinion.

ACTIVITY B

Tell students to identify each sentence as fact or opinion first. Then have partners trade papers and decide whether each rewritten sentence reflects an opinion or states a fact.

LESSON **2** EXPOSITORY WRITING

Fact and Opinion

LiNK

Women's History Week

In 1978, a California school district started Women's History Week to promote the teaching of women's history. It was so popular that in 1981, Congress passed a resolution making the week a celebration for the entire country!

TimeforKids.com

Facts are statements that can be verified or proved true by objective means such as checking public records or reading reference sources. Opinions are statements of judgment. Their credibility depends on the qualifications of the speaker. Most expository pieces are free of opinion or include very few opinions.

Fact: Membership at the Petoskey YMCA went up in 2009.

Opinion: The Petoskey YMCA has the best gym in the city.

The first statement is a fact because someone could check the records of the Petoskey YMCA to verify whether membership increased in 2009. The second statement is an opinion because there is no way to check it objectively. One person might think that the Petoskey YMCA is the best gym; someone else might disagree.

Some opinions are more credible than others, and good writers use credible opinions. What if a world-famous bodybuilder visited the Petoskey YMCA, as well as other gyms in the city, and said it was the best gym? The bodybuilder's opinion would be more credible than an average individual's opinion because of the bodybuilder's extensive knowledge of gyms. Keep in mind, however, that the bodybuilder's opinion would still be just an opinion, most likely not appropriate to include in an expository piece of writing. The "best" gym for an Olympic swimmer may be one with a longer pool.

A statement of fact may be proved untrue. If the person checking the Petoskey YMCA records discovered that membership in 2008 was higher than 2009, the factual statement would have been proved to be incorrect.

Use Relevant Facts

The world is full of facts. Anytime you research a topic, you are bombarded with them. When researching for an expository essay, it is important to use only the facts that are relevant to the topic. An essay describing how

APPLY

WRITER'S CORNER

After partners have discussed their sentences, invite volunteers to share what they wrote and how they identified each statement as fact or opinion. Have students save their notes for the For Tomorrow homework. Students should demonstrate an understanding of using facts and opinions in expository writing.

ASSESS

Note which students had difficulty differentiating between fact and opinion in expository writing. Use the Reteach option with those students who need additional reinforcement.

TEACHING OPTIONS

Reteach

Using a copy of the model on page 375, have students underline the facts and circle the opinions. Encourage students to explain how they decided between the two. Then have students discuss why the essay benefits from having more facts and fewer opinions.

Think It Through

Invite partners to choose a topic and to brainstorm two lists for their topic, one list for sources of factual information and one list for sources of credible opinions. When students have finished brainstorming, ask them to decide which sources would be best for an expository essay about their topic. Invite students to share their lists and explain their reasoning.

---

the Civil War began, for example, does not need to mention the fact that President Lincoln once ran a general store in New Salem, Illinois. Your job as a writer is to sort through facts and use the ones that directly support your topic's main idea.

Activity A
1. fact
2. opinion
3. opinion
4. fact
5. opinion
6. fact
7. fact
8. opinion
9. opinion
10. opinion

ACTIVITY A Identify the sentences as facts or opinions. Explain why you think each sentence is either a fact or an opinion.

1. Neil Armstrong was the first human to set foot on the moon.
2. Global warming is the most important problem we face.
3. The prettiest color for bridesmaids' dresses this year is lavender.
4. The USDA recommendations for healthful eating have changed.
5. Without a doubt, math classes are the ones that students complain about loudest and most frequently.
6. Wearing seat belts and lowering speed limits to 55 m.p.h. decreases traffic fatalities.
7. That serving of granola cereal contains five grams of sugar.
8. Aerobic exercise is more important for optimum health than anaerobic exercise.
9. The golden retriever is the best dog for people with large families.
10. This year's football team is sure to uphold our winning tradition.

Neil Armstrong

Activity B
Answers will vary.

ACTIVITY B Change the facts to opinions. Change the opinions to facts.

1. Eleanor Roosevelt traveled the world in support of social causes.
2. Nancy Reagan probably loved Ronald more than any other president's wife loved her husband.
3. Jackie Kennedy Onassis promoted American fashion designers through her choice of clothing.
4. Hillary Clinton was the first president's wife to seek an independent political career of her own.
5. Mary Todd Lincoln had the most tragic life of all the presidential wives.
6. Abigail Adams wrote, "No man ever prospered in the world without the consent and cooperation of his wife."

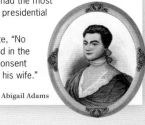
Abigail Adams

WRITER'S CORNER

In random order write five facts and five positive opinions about your school. Meet with a partner and trade papers. Identify each of your partner's sentences as a fact or an opinion. Tell why you identified each statement as you did.

For Tomorrow

Ask students to take home what they wrote for the Writer's Corner. Tell them to write an expository paragraph about the school, paying careful attention to the use of opinions. Write your own expository paragraph about the school to share with the class.

Expository Writing • 381

WARM-UP
Read, Listen, Speak

Read aloud your paragraph from yesterday's For Tomorrow homework. Model for students the use of facts as supporting details. Point out the limited use of opinions. Challenge students to identify the facts while you read your paragraph. Then have small groups share their expository paragraphs. Tell students to write the facts and opinions they hear while the students in their group read their paragraphs. Ask volunteers to share facts and opinions.

GRAMMAR CONNECTION

Take this opportunity to talk about adverb phrases and clauses. You may wish to have students point out adverb phrases and clauses in their Read, Listen, Speak examples.

TEACH

Invite a volunteer to read aloud the section Opinion Signal Words. Challenge students to name additional opinion signal words. Then ask volunteers to identify opinion signal words in expository essays they have read or written for previous activities in this chapter. Encourage students to discuss the tone these signal words communicate. Then have students compare the biased tone of opinions to the neutral tone of the excerpt on page 374. Emphasize how individual words can affect the tone of a piece.

LiNK Ask a volunteer to read aloud the excerpt. Challenge students to identify the signal words in the excerpt *(forever, immediate)*.

PRACTICE

ACTIVITY C

Have students complete this activity independently. Then have small groups discuss their answers. Invite volunteers to share their answers with the class.

ACTIVITY D

Have students complete this activity independently. Ask volunteers to read aloud their answers. Discuss each answer with the class. Then challenge students to determine what method of organization would be most effective for an expository essay on each topic.

ACTIVITY E

Remind students that their revisions should include facts and reduce the number of opinions. After students have rewritten the essay, have them trade papers with a partner. Ask students to decide whether the topic sentence and conclusion are appropriate, and whether each partner's essay has a neutral tone.

ACTIVITY F

Have students work with partners to answer the questions about their essays. If students have trouble answering any questions, encourage students to help each other improve their essays.

LiNK

The Scoop on Cereal

In 1894, one of the foods they prepared was a wheatmeal. What emerged on the other end of the rollers was to change the world forever. Instead of a unified flat sheet, the wheat came out as flakes, one for each wheat berry. They roasted the flakes and served them to their patients. They had an immediate success on their hands.

Mr.Breakfast.com

Opinion Signal Words

Clue words or phrases such as *probably, perhaps, usually, often, sometimes, I believe, I think, it's evident, obviously, everyone knows,* and *certainly* might help you identify opinions at a glance. Value words such as *pretty, creative, wonderful, good, ugly, boring, horrible, dangerous, mean,* and *unattractive* can also signal opinions.

ACTIVITY C Read the excerpt from *The Scoop on Cereal*. Identify two facts, one opinion, and one signal word or phrase.

ACTIVITY D Read each topic sentence and the set of facts that accompanies it. Determine which fact is irrelevant to the main idea of the topic and explain why.

1. Building the Panama Canal was a long and difficult engineering project.
   a. The Canal took seven years to build.
   b. Panama was once a province of Colombia.
   c. More than 232 million cubic yards of earth were moved to build the Canal.
   d. Nearly 6,000 workers died during the Canal's construction.

2. The Roman Empire grew by conquering many different lands.
   a. Rome faced the Carthaginian general Hannibal in the Second Punic War.
   b. Greece fell to Rome in 147 BC.
   c. The Roman poet Horace lived in the Augustan age.
   d. The Battle of Actium brought Egypt under Roman control.

3. Simón Bolívar helped liberate parts of South America from Spanish rule.
   a. Simón Bolívar was born in Caracas, Venezuela, on July 24, 1783.
   b. He was called the "George Washington of South America."
   c. Simón Bolívar was the first president of Colombia.
   d. Bananas are a major product of Venezuela.

Simón Bolívar

APPLY

WRITER'S CORNER

Suggest students use the library or the Internet to find an expository article. Then have students discuss their findings with a partner. Encourage students to discuss how well the writer used facts for support and if the opinions were credible. Students should demonstrate an understanding of using facts and opinions in expository writing.

TechTip Have students find their articles, using an appropriate Web site. Once students have posted their articles, have students pick several articles and identify the characteristics of good expository writing in each article.

ASSESS

Note which students had difficulty understanding how to use facts and opinions effectively in an expository essay. Use the Reteach option with those students who need additional reinforcement.

Practice Book page 159 provides additional work with facts and opinions.

TEACHING OPTIONS

Reteach

Ask students to choose a topic and to brainstorm ideas for an expository essay. Then ask them to separate their brainstorming notes into two columns: *Facts* and *Opinions*. Suggest that students refer to pages 380–381 when determining which ideas are facts and which are opinions. When students have finished, have them note whether their *Opinions* column is longer than their *Facts* column. If so, suggest that students find more facts.

Think About Your Audience

Invite students to consider the role of the audience when composing an expository essay. Explain that when students freewrite for a topic, they should think about what their readers might already know as well as what they might find new and interesting about the topic. Challenge students to reread expository essays they wrote for previous activities. Then ask students to revise the essays for a new audience.

For Tomorrow

Tell students to write a short expository essay using cause-and-effect organization. Encourage them to choose a topic that works well with cause and effect. Remind them to consider audience and tone when writing. Write your own expository essay using cause-and-effect organization.

ACTIVITY E Rewrite the persuasive essay to make it an expository essay. Take out or revise opinions so that the purpose of the essay is to inform. Include only relevant facts. Be sure to include a topic sentence and summarize the topic in the conclusion.

Breakfast in England

If you think that English breakfasts are just like American breakfasts, you couldn't be more wrong. Imagine that you are sitting down to an American breakfast on a leisurely weekend. Perhaps you will have eggs, pancakes or waffles, bacon or sausage, and, of course, orange juice. Yum! But breakfasts in England are tastier and much more interesting.

In its full traditional glory, the English breakfast has at least three courses. The first is generally eggs and bacon or ham, along with grilled tomato. You might see deviled kidneys (yech!) or mixed grill, which is a lamb chop, sausage, liver, and half a tomato. Second is a course of fruit or cereal. Third comes the fish course. It may be kippers, which are salted, dried, smoked herring, or kedgeree, an Indian dish of curried rice and lentils that may have fish, hard-boiled eggs, and cream sauce. There may be a final cold course too. Oh, and crumpets, oat cakes, and toast are on the table throughout the meal.

Now don't you think this breakfast is better than the one you usually eat? We're not sure about an American breakfast, but if you eat the English breakfast described above, you are sure to push yourself away from the table stuffed to the max.

ACTIVITY F Read the expository essay that you wrote for Activity E. Answer the following questions about your writing.

1. What is your topic?
2. What is your topic sentence?
3. What organizational pattern did you use?
4. What is one example of an opinion that you changed into a fact?
5. How did you sum up the topic in your conclusion?

WRITER'S CORNER

Read an expository news article. Record at least five facts from the article. Record any opinions you find.

 Tech Tip Share an expository news article on the class blog.

Expository Writing • 383

OBJECTIVES

- To conduct research online and determine Web site credibility
- To document Internet sources

WARM-UP

Read, Listen, Speak

Read your cause-and-effect expository essay from yesterday's For Tomorrow homework. Discuss why this type of organization is the best fit for this topic. Then discuss the audience for your writing and point out any language that helps create a neutral tone. Have small groups discuss their essays. Encourage students to discuss whether cause-and-effect organization worked well with each topic and how students created a neutral tone.

GRAMMAR CONNECTION

Take this opportunity to review adverbs. You may wish to have students point out adverbs in their Read, Listen, Speak examples.

TEACH

Ask a volunteer to read aloud the first paragraph. Invite students to discuss types of Web sites that might not be reliable and to explain why *(chat rooms, blogs, and personal Web pages because they often consist of opinions and unsubstantiated information)*.

Have a volunteer read aloud the first two paragraphs of the section Determining Web Site Credibility. Allow time for students to read silently the checklist. Then discuss each item. Encourage students to think of questions they can add to the list. Write these on the board as students suggest them and have students list the questions in their notebooks.

Ask a volunteer to finish reading the section. Point out the importance of practicing online safety. Have volunteers explain why it is important to monitor the personal information that they provide online. *(Once information is posted on the Internet, it remains available to others and cannot be totally deleted. Someone could use the information for illegal purposes.)*

Have a volunteer read aloud the section Conducting Research. Tell students that a site created and monitored by a governmental or professional organization is more reliable than a site run by individual people. Ask volunteers to give examples of sites with the extensions listed.

Invite a volunteer to read aloud the section Recording Internet Research. Have volunteers describe Internet sources that they have used for research. Remind students to make sure a site has been updated recently before using it as a source.

LiNK Tell students that UNICEF is the acronym for United Nations International Children's Emergency Fund (which is now called the United Nations Children's Fund). Have a volunteer read aloud the excerpt. Ask students if they think this would be a reliable Web site. Tell students they will get the chance

---

Evaluating Web Sites

The Internet is full of information, but only some of it is reliable enough to use in an expository piece. An important part of your work as a researcher is to determine if information from the Internet is credible and accurate. Following are some ideas for conducting good Internet research.

Determining Web Site Credibility

One main challenge in conducting research on the Internet is that almost anyone can develop a professional-looking Web site. Therefore, many Web sites contain wrong or biased information. Relying solely on the "look" of a Web site can lead a researcher to inaccurate information. Useful and reliable online Web sites include online libraries, periodicals, reputable university sites, almanacs, and encyclopedias. Fortunately, search engines often place credible sites at the top of their listings.

Once you link to a Web site, navigate it to find information. The more information you read from the Web site, the better able you will be to determine if the information is reliable. Here is a checklist of some questions to ask when evaluating Web sites.

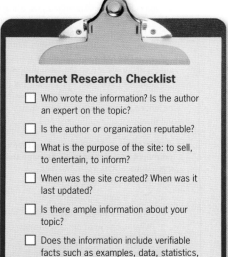

Internet Research Checklist

- [ ] Who wrote the information? Is the author an expert on the topic?
- [ ] Is the author or organization reputable?
- [ ] What is the purpose of the site: to sell, to entertain, to inform?
- [ ] When was the site created? When was it last updated?
- [ ] Is there ample information about your topic?
- [ ] Does the information include verifiable facts such as examples, data, statistics, or quotations?
- [ ] Does the information agree with what you've found in other reliable sources?

to examine this Web site in a future activity.

PRACTICE

ACTIVITY A
Allow time for small groups to write their guidelines. Invite volunteers to share their opinions. Write on the board a final list, combining suggestions from the entire class.

APPLY

WRITER'S CORNER
Discuss search engines that students have used. List these on the board. Encourage students to share what they know about search engines and to compare the success they have had with each. After students have used search engines, discuss the results. Students should demonstrate an understanding of determining reliable Web sites.

ASSESS

Note which students had difficulty understanding how to evaluate Web sites. Use the Reteach option with those students who need additional reinforcement.

TEACHING OPTIONS

Reteach
Ask partners to search sites that list Internet safety guidelines for children, such as the following:

http://yahooligans.yahoo.com

www.safeteens.com/safeteens.htm

www.safekids.com

Have students evaluate these sites to determine if they are reliable by using the Internet Research Checklist.

Surfing the Net
Have students work in groups to search the Internet for information about windsurfing. Encourage students to develop criteria to evaluate the Web sites they find, incorporating points from the Internet Research Checklist. Have students create a form that they can use to evaluate and grade each Web site about windsurfing. Suggest that they determine a number rating for each site.

Practicing online safety is important when searching Web sites, especially if you are not sure of a site's credibility. Never reveal personal information over the Internet, either through a Web site or a chat room, without first asking a parent or guardian.

Conducting Research

When doing research on the Internet, begin with a keyword search on a favorite search engine. Use words from your topic as keywords. Carefully study the Web site addresses and descriptions that come up. Link only to sites that seem professional. The three-letter extension at the end of a Web site address can help you quickly determine the site's origin. The following are some common extensions:

.com	commercial sites
.edu	sites developed by schools, from elementary schools to universities
.gov	government sites
.mil	military sites
.org	sites developed by organizations

Recording Internet Research

There are several ways to record Internet research, such as printing the Web page and highlighting the information you will use, copying and pasting the information into a word-processing file and printing it, or taking notes as you read the information on the screen. Whichever way you choose, be sure to document your sources and include the date on which you visited the site because it may be altered in the future.

ACTIVITY A Work in small groups to develop a list of guidelines to follow for online safety. Consider your safety and the safety of others.

LiNK

Fighting Chronic Malnutrition

According to UNICEF data from 2007, Guatemala has the highest percentage of chronically malnourished girls and boys in Latin America, and the fourth highest in the world.

Unicef.org

WRITER'S CORNER

Use a search engine to find five credible Web sites with information about the topic you chose in the Writer's Corner on page 377.

For Tomorrow

Ask students to research online a topic for an expository essay. Encourage students to use more than one search engine. Have students determine the credibility of the sites by using the Internet Research Checklist. Ask students to record their findings. Conduct your own online research and record your findings.

Read, Listen, Speak

Share your research from yesterday's For Tomorrow homework. Discuss what search engines you used and how you determined the reliability of each Web site. Encourage volunteers to share their research with the class. Discuss how the Internet Research Checklist helped determine if a Web site was reliable.

GRAMMAR CONNECTION

Take this opportunity to review adverbs before administering the formal assessment. You may wish to have students point out adverbs in their Read, Listen, Speak examples.

TEACH

Review the criteria for evaluating Web sites. Invite volunteers to name three-letter extensions that are reliable and to name specific Web sites with those extensions. Ask volunteers to suggest ways to record research found online and to explain why it is important to document these sources. *(It is important because students might need to refer to the sites again or cite them in a bibliography.)*

PRACTICE

ACTIVITY B

Have students examine the UNICEF Web site independently. Encourage students to refer to the checklist on page 384 while they are answering the questions. When students have finished, discuss each question and whether the site is reliable or not.

ACTIVITY C

Ask students to complete this activity independently. Discuss the reliability of each site. Then have students name sites they might check in place of those they determined to be unreliable.

ACTIVITY D

Review the search engines discussed as part of the Writer's Corner on page 385. Have students conduct their research independently. Ask volunteers to share their information with the class. Then challenge students to search other sites to find support for facts they found.

ACTIVITY E

Remind students to use the Internet Research Checklist on page 384. Invite volunteers to share what they discovered. Have students explain why the Web site they used was reliable. Discuss any sites that were not reliable.

ACTIVITY F

Review the methods for recording Internet research. Then have students complete this activity independently. Have students collaborate on writing an introduction to an expository essay, using one of the topics.

ACTIVITY B Find the UNICEF Web site and answer the following questions.

1. Does the Web site seem credible to you? Explain why or why not.
2. What is the purpose of the Web site?
3. What audience does the Web site address?
4. What information does the Web site offer?
5. In what format is the information presented to the visitor? Does the Web site use examples, statistics, surveys, expert opinions, or a combination of formats?
6. What multimedia formats (such as video, audio, or interactive documents) are offered to the visitor?
7. Does the information seem to be up-to-date? Explain why.

ACTIVITY C Suppose you were writing about international projects to immunize children against childhood diseases such as measles. Which of the following Web sites would probably have the most reliable information? Which would probably have the least reliable information? Explain your answers.

1. A pbs.org site with information about a public television show on a UNICEF immunization project
2. An .edu site publishing a report written by a fifth grader at Morningside Elementary School
3. The .com site of a large pharmaceutical company that makes vaccines
4. An .edu site on communicable diseases sponsored by a university science department
5. The .com site of a health magazine that publishes a monthly column on children's health
6. The .com site titled "Plague!" whose sponsor is not identified
7. A .gov site sponsored by the U.S. Department of Health and Human Services
8. The .org site of Citizens Against Immunizations

APPLY

WRITER'S CORNER

Tell students to use the Internet Research Checklist to determine if the Web site is reliable. Invite students to share what they found and why they believe the sites are reliable. Challenge students to make an outline on the topic. Student should demonstrate an understanding of how to identify reliable Web sites.

ASSESS

Note which students had difficulty understanding what makes a credible Web site. Use the Reteach option with those students who need additional reinforcement.

Practice Book page 160 provides additional work with evaluating Web sites.

TEACHING OPTIONS

Reteach

Have small groups describe a Web site they might develop on any topic they wish. Tell students to write a list of items that the site should include to be considered a reliable source. Encourage students to be specific and creative in determining the information they would include in the site and how they would gather reliable and original data. Have students sketch designs for their Web sites and display the sketches on a bulletin board.

Knowledge at Your Fingertips

Ask students to explore a library's electronic resources, such as access to the Internet or research databases. Have students work with partners to conduct research on topics of their choice. Encourage students to use research databases to determine how helpful these resources are to the user. Have students write an evaluation comparing Web sites, research databases, and any other sources used for research.

ACTIVITY D Type the following topics into a search engine of your choice. Link to a Web site for each topic. Evaluate the site based on the questions in Activity B on page 386. How credible is the site? How credible is the information on the site? Record one credible fact from each Web site. Compare your results with those of your classmates.

1. global warming
2. the Peace Corps
3. extreme sports
4. cartoons

ACTIVITY E Imagine that you will write an expository essay about the Boston Massacre. Find a reliable Web site about the topic. Document your source, using the Internet Research Checklist on page 384.

ACTIVITY F Do Internet research for three of the following topics. Record three facts for each topic from a reliable Web site. Document each Web site source.

1. the importance of rain forests
2. the effects of sunbathing
3. nurses in the Civil War
4. most popular dog breeds in the United States
5. biographical information about the author of the Lemony Snicket book series
6. everyday lives of pioneer women
7. the education system in Japan
8. the volcanic disaster in ancient Pompeii
9. the life cycle of a monarch butterfly
10. the best kind of dog for a person with allergies

The Boston Massacre by Paul Revere

WRITER'S CORNER

Choose one reliable Web site that you found in the Writer's Corner on page 385. Do research, using the Web site. Record at least 10 facts about your chosen topic. Document your source.

For Tomorrow

Ask students to continue their research from the Writer's Corner on page 385. Have students research more sites to gather information on their chosen topics, being sure to document their sources. Continue your research as well.

Expository Writing • 387

OBJECTIVES
- **To understand how to use noun clauses**
- **To vary sentences with noun clauses**

WARM-UP

Read, Listen, Speak

Share your research from yesterday's For Tomorrow homework. Point out reliable Web sites and discuss some Web sites that were not reliable. Invite small groups to discuss their research and how they determined which sites were reliable. Encourage students to comment on how thoroughly the sources were documented.

GRAMMAR CONNECTION

Take this opportunity to talk about single and multiword prepositions. You may wish to have students point out single and multiword prepositions in their Read, Listen, Speak examples.

TEACH

Have a volunteer read aloud the first two paragraphs. Remind students that a dependent clause is a group of words that has a subject and a predicate but does not express a complete thought. Read aloud and discuss the example sentences. Challenge students to provide additional example sentences that contain noun clauses.

Invite a student to read aloud the first paragraph and the sample sentences in the section Using Noun Clauses. Point out that the second sentence places emphasis on the subject and provides variation in sentence structure. Remind students that varying sentence structure is important in increasing the interest level of their writing. Read aloud the paragraph on the top of page 389.

Clarify any questions about noun clauses that may arise.

Ask volunteers to read aloud the rest of this section. Explain that the word *that* can link objects, people, and ideas to a subject. Challenge students to create their own sentences containing noun clauses that show a relationship between ideas.

LiNK Read aloud the excerpt. Challenge students to identify the noun clause in the excerpt and to say how the noun clause functions *(that Alcibiades had been his pupil, appositive)*.

PRACTICE

ACTIVITY A

Complete this activity as a class. Invite volunteers to rewrite each sentence so that the sentences use simple nouns instead of noun clauses. Encourage students to explain the differences in meaning between the original and the rewritten sentences.

Noun Clauses

LiNK

The Death of Socrates

This led to [Socrates'] prosecution on the double charge of blasphemy and of corrupting the Athenian youth. The fact that Alcibiades had been his pupil was used to prove the demoralizing tendency of his teachings. He was condemned to drink the fatal hemlock. The night before his death he spent with his disciples, discoursing on the immortality of the soul.

P. V. N. Myers

Socrates on trial

Noun clauses can make your writing more interesting by allowing you to communicate relationships concisely, to describe something poetically, or to place the emphasis of a sentence more precisely.

A noun clause is a dependent clause used as a noun. Noun clauses are usually introduced by introductory words such as *how, whether, what, why,* and *that.* Here are some ways that a noun clause can be used in a sentence.

As a subject

   That the polio vaccine benefits many people **has been proved.**

As a direct object

   We know *that the polio vaccine benefits many people.*

As the object of a preposition

   He spoke of *how the polio vaccine benefits many people.*

As a subject complement

   The fact is *that the polio vaccine benefits many people.*

As an appositive

   The fact *that the polio vaccine benefits many people* **cannot be denied.**

Using Noun Clauses

A writer might use a noun clause in a sentence to show relationships between ideas, to give emphasis to an idea, or to achieve sentence variety. Read these two sentences, paying close attention to each subject.

   Bryan's *defeat* **was unfortunate.** (noun)
   That Bryan was defeated **was unfortunate.** (noun clause)

APPLY

WRITER'S CORNER

Allow time for students to complete the Writer's Corner. Then have students trade papers with a partner and check whether the noun clauses were correct and labeled appropriately. Invite volunteers to read aloud their sentences. Students should demonstrate an understanding of noun clauses.

ASSESS

Note which students had difficulty identifying and using noun clauses. Use the Reteach option with those students who need additional reinforcement.

TEACHING OPTIONS

Reteach

Write the following introductory words on the board: *that, how, why, what, whether.* Have students write on strips of paper noun clauses that use these introductory words. Place the strips in a container. Tell students to select a strip and to write a sentence using the noun clause. Have students read aloud their sentences and identify the function of each clause. Have students write another sentence using the same clause with a different function.

Meeting Individual Needs

Extra Support Begin a chart with the column headings shown below. Write in the first column an introductory word for a noun clause. Have a volunteer use that word to write in the second column a noun clause. Ask the volunteer to write in the third column a complete sentence with the noun clause. Encourage students to suggest additional entries for the chart.

Introductory Word	Noun Clause	Sentence
that	that dogs are good companions	That dogs are good companions is well known.

In the first sentence, Bryan's defeat is described as an unfortunate event. In the second sentence, the emphasis shifts away from the event itself to the effect of the event. It was not the defeat that was unfortunate; it was the idea of the defeat that was unfortunate.

A noun clause reveals the relationship between things. Read the following sentences:

Henry did not know the answer to the question.
Henry did not know Sasha's response.
Henry did not know that Sasha's response answered the question.

The first sentence tells that Henry did not know the answer to the question. The second sentence tells that Henry did not know Sasha's response. The third sentence, however, links all three things to Henry: the question, the answer, and Sasha's response.

ACTIVITY A Identify the noun clause in each sentence. Tell whether it is used as a subject, a direct object, an object of a preposition, a subject complement, or an appositive.

1. What we should do next was the question.
2. Howard insisted that Andy eat the peas.
3. Whether they would pay attention to the magician was uncertain.
4. The man addressed the crowd from where he stood.
5. Why she did not call to explain her lateness disturbed us.
6. The textbook explains how the kidneys purify the blood.
7. Janet told the truth, that she had not accepted a bribe.
8. My hope is that we finish this work soon.
9. That our guests are enjoying the performance is obvious.
10. The truth is that the person who made the decision did not have all the facts.

Activity A
Noun clauses are underlined.
1. subject
2. direct object
3. subject
4. object of a preposition
5. subject
6. direct object
7. appositive
8. subject complement
9. subject
10. subject complement

WRITER'S CORNER

Use the following noun clauses in five sentences. Tell how each clause is used.

1. that she was creative
2. how the team played the game
3. what he prized most
4. that the tourists arrived
5. that the flights were canceled

For Tomorrow

Have students write an expository paragraph using their research from the previous For Tomorrow homework. Tell students to include at least three noun clauses in their writing. Write your own expository paragraph. Make sure it includes three noun clauses.

Expository Writing • 389

Read, Listen, Speak

Read aloud your expository paragraph from yesterday's For Tomorrow homework. Ask students to identify the noun clauses you included. Then challenge students to name how each clause functions in the sentence. Invite volunteers to read aloud their paragraphs. Have students identify noun clauses and their functions.

GRAMMAR CONNECTION

Take this opportunity to talk about troublesome prepositions. You may wish to have students point out troublesome prepositions in their Read, Listen, Speak examples.

TEACH

Ask a volunteer to read aloud the first two paragraphs of the section Varying Sentences with Noun Clauses. Discuss the sentence from the Gettysburg Address. Encourage students to consider the purpose of this speech and to remember that it was presented orally. Lead students to the conclusion that the way the sentence is structured adds dramatic effect by alluding to, but not specifically stating, the sacrifice that the soldiers made at Gettysburg.

Have a volunteer read aloud the rest of the section. Explain that variety in sentence structure can make any message more interesting to read, which will increase the message's effectiveness.

PRACTICE

ACTIVITY B

Complete the first two sentences as a class. Then have students finish this activity independently. Tell students to trade papers with a partner and to check each other's answers. Invite volunteers to read their sentences aloud. Challenge students to identify the function of the noun clause in each sentence.

ACTIVITY C

Have students complete this activity independently. Ask several volunteers to read their sentences for each item. Point out how each item can be rewritten in a variety of ways. Discuss how the revised sentences with noun clauses are more appealing than the original sentences. Challenge students to create a second revised sentence that is different from their first revision.

ACTIVITY D

Read aloud the five example noun clause sentences on page 388. Have volunteers write their sentences on the board. Challenge students to identify the noun clause and its function in each sentence.

Varying Sentences with Noun Clauses

Effective writers vary the lengths of their sentences. Noun clauses can be useful tools to accomplish this. A well-placed noun clause can energize writing by breaking up monotonous sentences.

In the following example from the Gettysburg Address, Abraham Lincoln uses two parallel noun clauses to draw attention to the sacrifices made by the soldiers who fought in the Battle of Gettysburg. The noun clauses are italicized.

> The world will little note, nor long remember *what we say here*, but it can never forget *what they did here*.

A writer may also shorten a sentence with a well-placed noun clause. The second sentence is less wordy and communicates the same idea as the first.

> This skateboard belongs to someone, and I think you know to whom it belongs.
> I think you know who owns this skateboard.

A noun clause will not always improve a sentence. Sometimes noun clauses just add clutter. In the example below, eliminating the noun clause improves the sentence.

> A metronome is what pianists often use to mark time.
> Pianists often use metronomes to mark time.

ACTIVITY B Complete each sentence with an appropriate noun clause.

1. _____ was long remembered.
2. The greatest attribute of the team is _____.
3. _____ was soon discovered.
4. Have you heard the news _____?
5. It was Colette's hope _____.
6. Do you believe the report _____?
7. Dan's dream, _____, seemed a possible reality.
8. What Candice wondered was _____.
9. _____ has always interested me.
10. Earl did _____.
11. Julie said _____.
12. I do not know _____.

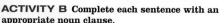

WRITER'S CORNER

Challenge students to make a cohesive paragraph out of the sentences, making sure to add a topic sentence. Invite volunteers to share their paragraphs. Point out good examples. As a class, revise examples that do not correctly use noun clauses. Students should demonstrate an understanding of noun clauses.

Note which students had difficulty understanding noun clauses. Use the Reteach option with those students who need additional reinforcement.

Practice Book page 161 provides additional work with noun clauses.

Reteach

Write a variety of noun clauses on note cards, one per card (*that the bus is leaving, how we can solve the problem, whether we win or lose*). Have a volunteer choose a card and read aloud the clause. Tell the student to the volunteer's left to make up a sentence using the clause as a subject. Encourage the next student to use the clause as an appositive, the next as a direct object, the next as the object of a preposition, and the last as a subject complement. Have students repeat the process until all the cards have been used.

Cooperative Learning

Have small groups create a list of sentence starters about their school. (*The best thing about our school is _____.*) Then have students exchange papers and complete the sentences by adding noun clauses used as subject complements. Invite a volunteer from each group to read aloud the completed sentences.

13. Her favorite saying is _____.
14. _____ is an important piece of information.
15. It cannot be denied _____.
16. The teacher's suggestion was _____.

ACTIVITY C Use noun clauses to combine each pair of sentences into one sentence. The new sentence can reveal a relationship between things or emphasize something.

1. Kyle's fear seemed unreasonable. The air conditioner could fall out the window.
2. How might such a thing happen? It was not clear to us.
3. The air conditioner had not been securely installed. That is a fact.
4. The air conditioner shook loose and fell on the car. We were stunned.
5. The screws were in the wrong places. Kyle showed us.
6. The accident had occurred. The car owner was angry.
7. The man was not hurt. He did not change his complaint.
8. He spoke to the police. People should be careful about how they install air conditioners.
9. We would not have to pay for the repair. The driver decided.
10. The insurance will pay for the repair. He hoped.
11. He had another question. How we will pay for a new air conditioner?
12. Kyle insisted. He will install it this time.
13. The police officer made a suggestion. We should use window fans instead.
14. The insurance would cover all damages. We were delighted.

ACTIVITY D Write five sentences that demonstrate the five ways noun clauses can be used: as a subject, a direct object, an object of a preposition, a subject complement, and an appositive.

WRITER'S CORNER

Using your research from the Writer's Corner on page 387, write three supporting sentences for your topic. Include a noun clause in each sentence.

For Tomorrow

Have students look through paragraphs they discovered while conducting research. Instruct students to find at least three examples of noun clauses. Challenge students to identify the function of each noun clause. Find noun clauses of your own that you can share with the class.

OBJECTIVES
- **To identify prefixes of words**
- **To understand the meanings of prefixes**

WARM-UP

Read, Listen, Speak

Write on the board the sentences containing noun clauses from yesterday's For Tomorrow homework. Have volunteers underline the noun clauses and say how each functions. Then invite volunteers to write on the board sentences they found. Challenge students to identify the noun clauses and their functions.

GRAMMAR CONNECTION

Take this opportunity to talk about words used as adverbs and prepositions. You may wish to have students point out adverbs and prepositions in their Read, Listen, Speak examples.

TEACH

Invite a volunteer to read aloud the first paragraph. Point out that, just like the word roots students studied in an earlier lesson, most prefixes are derived from Latin and Greek. Remind students that a word's antonym means the opposite of the word. Discuss the Common Prefixes chart. Challenge volunteers to name additional examples for each prefix.

Explain the difference between prefixes and roots. *(A root is a word part that carries the basic meaning of the word. A prefix is a word part added to the front of a word to change its meaning. When a prefix is removed, a complete word remains.)*

Ask volunteers to list on the board some words with prefixes. Challenge students to use a dictionary to identify the root words and prefixes of the words.

PRACTICE

ACTIVITY A

Suggest that students use a dictionary if needed. Allow time for students to work independently. Challenge students to write sentences on the board, using their example words.

ACTIVITY B

Have students complete this activity independently. Provide dictionaries for students to look up definitions if needed. Ask volunteers to write their words on the board. Discuss the definitions of the words.

ACTIVITY C

Ask students to complete this activity with partners. Discuss how the prefixes help students understand the words' definitions. Challenge students to name the origin of each prefix and to use each word in a sentence.

Prefixes

A prefix is a syllable or syllables placed at the beginning of a word to change its meaning or to make another word. Most prefixes come from other languages, such as Latin or Greek. Some prefixes change the meaning of words to make antonyms. For example, adding the prefix *il-* to the root word *legal* makes the word *illegal*, which means "not legal." This chart shows some common prefixes, their meanings, and example words. Learning the meaning of prefixes can help you figure out the meaning of the words in which you find them. Learning prefixes is a great way to increase your spoken and written vocabulary.

COMMON PREFIXES

PREFIX	MEANING	EXAMPLES
anti-	against	antiestablishment, antisocial, antiwar
dis-	not, opposite of	disagree, disarm, discontinue
il-, in-, ir-	not	illegible, inactive, irregular
inter-	between, among	interaction, interstellar, international
mis-	bad, wrong	misconduct, misfortune, misprint
mono-	one	monoculture, monorail, monotone
multi-	many, much	multipurpose, multiword, multipart
out-	surpassing	outbid, outdo, outnumber
pre-	earlier, before	prewar, preview, prehistoric
re-	again, back	recall, reappear, rewrite
under-	below, less than	underground, underpass, underage
poly-	many, more than one	polygon, polymer, polyglot

ACTIVITY D

Have students recall reliable online dictionaries discussed in previous lessons. When students have finished, invite volunteers to write on the board the words and to underline the prefixes. Then have other volunteers write the definitions.

APPLY

WRITER'S CORNER

Review the characteristics of good expository writing. Then allow time for students to write their expository pieces. Invite volunteers to read aloud their expository pieces. Challenge listeners to identify in each piece the words with prefixes. Students should demonstrate an understanding of prefixes.

ASSESS

Note which students had difficulty identifying prefixes. Use the Reteach option with those students who need additional reinforcement.

TEACHING OPTIONS

Reteach

Have students write prefixes on note cards, one per card. Tell students to write the corresponding definitions on separate note cards. Instruct students to exchange cards with a partner. Then have students match each prefix with its meaning. Tell students that they may keep a card if they are able to name and define a word that begins with the prefix on that card. The student who has the most cards at the end wins the game.

English-Language Learners

To give students practice identifying prefixes and learning their meanings, invite students to make prefix flash cards. Have students use the prefixes chart to make their flash cards. Ask students to use a dictionary to include meanings of the prefixes and example words. Encourage students whose primary languages are derived from Latin (such as Spanish, French, Italian, and Portuguese) to use their knowledge of prefixes in these languages to recognize those of similar meaning in English. Allow time for students to quiz each other, using the flash cards.

For Tomorrow

Have students look through reading material for five words with different prefixes. Tell students to record the prefixes and to predict the meanings of the words. Create a list of five words yourself.

Activity C

1. *para-*; beside, near; person who assists medical professionals
2. *super-*; above, over; a woman who succeeds in combining several roles with apparent ease
3. *circum-*; around, about; to go around
4. *hyper-*; above, beyond; highly or excessively active
5. *en-*; to put into or onto; to make into or as if into a slave
6. *post-*; after, later; a message added to a letter after the writer's signature
7. *un-*; not, opposite of; against one's country
8. *mal-*; bad, poor, wrongful; lack of proper nutrition
9. *re-*; again, anew; to write again
10. *inter-*; between, among; between states
11. *ambi-*; both; able to use both hands with equal facility
12. *intra-*; within; existing or carried on within an institution
13. *im-*; not; not fully grown or developed
14. *poly-*; many; consisting of people of many ethnic backgrounds

ACTIVITY A Choose five prefixes from the chart on page 392. Provide another example word for each prefix.

ACTIVITY B Add a prefix from the chart on page 392 to each word below. Give the meaning of each new word and write a narrative using four the words.

1. gram
2. pass
3. task
4. climax
5. game
6. election
7. change
8. democratic

ACTIVITY C Look up the following words in a dictionary. Identify each prefix and give its meaning. Then define the word. How does the meaning of the prefix help you understand the meaning of the word?

1. paramedic
2. superwoman
3. circumnavigate
4. hyperactive
5. enslave
6. postscript
7. unpatriotic
8. malnutrition
9. reword
10. interstate
11. ambidextrous
12. intramural
13. immature
14. polyethnic

ACTIVITY D Reread the excerpt on page 375. In the second and third paragraphs, there are several words that begin with prefixes. Identify the words and their prefixes. Use a dictionary to find the definition of each word. If you use an online dictionary, be sure to use a reliable site.
depression, polyunsaturated, disorder, unknown

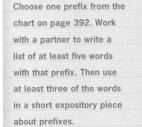

WRITER'S CORNER

Choose one prefix from the chart on page 392. Work with a partner to write a list of at least five words with that prefix. Then use at least three of the words in a short expository piece about prefixes.

Expository Writing • 393

WARM-UP
Read, Listen, Speak
Write on the board the five words containing prefixes from yesterday's For Tomorrow homework. Identify the prefixes and tell students what each prefix means. Ask students to predict what they think each word means. Have a volunteer use a dictionary to find the definition of each word. Then have students exchange lists. Tell students to use a dictionary to look up the definition of each word on the list and to check if their partner's predictions were correct.

GRAMMAR CONNECTION
Take this opportunity to talk about prepositional phrases used as adjectives. You may wish to have students point out prepositional phrases used as adjectives in their Read, Listen, Speak examples.

TEACH

Review what students learned about prefixes. Ask a volunteer to define *prefix*.

Have small groups of students search the model on page 375 for prefixes, using a dictionary to check their work. Instruct students to write on the board a list of the words containing prefixes. Discuss the meaning of each prefix and the definition of each word.

PRACTICE

ACTIVITY E
Have students work with partners to complete this activity. Invite volunteers to read aloud the dictionary definitions. Have other volunteers name additional words that have the same prefix as each word given.

ACTIVITY F
Ask students to complete this activity independently. Discuss each sentence, especially those that may have multiple answers. Then have students identify the origin of each prefix. Point out that most dictionaries include etymological information for each word and word part.

ACTIVITY G
After students have finished the activity, have volunteers re-create the chart with their answers. Encourage students to suggest additional example words for each prefix and to describe the change in meaning caused by adding each prefix.

ACTIVITY H
Have students complete this activity independently. Challenge students to write sentences that contain noun clauses. Invite volunteers to share their sentences with the class.

ACTIVITY I
Review Lesson 3 in this chapter so that students can effectively evaluate a Web site's reliability. Have students complete the research and prefix identification independently. Then have partners write topic sentences together.

ACTIVITY E Using what you know about prefixes, make an educated guess about the meaning of the following words. Consult the chart on page 392 as you work and record your ideas. Check your answers in a dictionary.

1. multilateral
2. outwit
3. monofilament
4. preorbital
5. overblown
6. misconduct
7. illogical
8. antislavery
9. aerodynamics
10. recharge

Activity F
1. syllables
2. approve
3. coastal
4. national
5. colored
6. colon
7. finals
8. graph
9. polite
10. annual

ACTIVITY F Think of the word that would best complete each sentence. The prefix of the word is given for you.

1. When Paul first wakes up, he speaks in mono_____.
2. Sara doesn't go to parties on school nights because her parents would dis_____.
3. The Intra_____ Waterways are great for boating and fishing.
4. The United Nations was established to help solve inter_____ problems.
5. The multi_____ banner attracted plenty of attention.
6. Sometimes a semi_____ divides a compound sentence.
7. The basketball team made it to the semi_____.
8. A poly_____ is commonly called a lie detector.
9. Chewing gum loudly or wearing your hat at the dinner table is considered to be im_____.
10. The school talent show is not happening this year but next year because it is a bi_____ event.

Have volunteers share their topic sentences with the class. Discuss the strengths and weaknesses of each topic sentence.

APPLY

WRITER'S CORNER

Provide dictionaries for those students who need help finding new words. Invite volunteers to share their expository paragraphs with the class. Challenge students to identify the words containing prefixes. Discuss the meaning of these words. Students should demonstrate an understanding of prefixes.

ASSESS

Note which students had difficulty understanding words with prefixes. Use the Reteach option with those students who need additional reinforcement.

Practice Book page 162 provides additional work with prefixes.

Practice Book page 162

Reteach

Have students gather examples of their writing. Tell students to trade one example with a partner and to search each other's writing for 10 words with prefixes. Have students predict the meaning of each word based on the meaning of the prefix. Then have partners return each other's papers. Ask students to determine whether each meaning is accurate. Encourage students to use dictionaries if needed.

Building Vocabulary

Write on the board the words below. Ask students to discover the root word and the prefix of each by using a dictionary and then to write each word in a sentence.

uniform

undignified

misspell

biotech

disingenuous

malapropos

ACTIVITY G Fill in the blanks on the chart below. Use a dictionary to check your answers.

PREFIX	LANGUAGE OF ORIGIN	MEANING	EXAMPLE
deca-	Greek	ten	decameter
fore-	Old English	before, earlier	**forefather**
sub-	Latin	under	submarine
aero-	Greek	air	aerospace
mega-	Greek	large	megavitamin
extra-	Latin	beyond	**extraordinary**
hyper-	Greek	excessive	hypersensitive
im-	Latin	not	impure
non-	Latin	not	nonperson
super-	Latin	above, over	**supersonic**
tele-	Greek	distant	teleconference
trans-	Latin	across, beyond	transact
nano-	Greek	one-billionth	**nanosecond**

ACTIVITY H Use each example word from the chart above in a sentence.

ACTIVITY I In the library or online, find an article, Web site, or informational text about a topic below. Identify three words with prefixes in your source. Using a dictionary, define the prefixes and the words. Then write the topic sentence for an expository essay on the topic.

1. oceanography
2. forms of government
3. prehistoric invertebrates
4. volcanoes

Jacques Cousteau, an oceanographer

A trilobite, a prehistoric invertebrate

WRITER'S CORNER

Write another example word for three prefixes in the chart above. Using the new words, write an expository paragraph about a topic of your choice.

For Tomorrow

Have students add another example word for each prefix in the chart for Activity G. Tell students they can consult a dictionary if needed. Find your own example words for each prefix to share with the class.

Expository Writing • 395

OBJECTIVES

- **To select a topic for a self-help presentation and to determine one's audience**
- **To research and organize a self-help presentation**

WARM-UP

Read, Listen, Speak

List on the board your example words from yesterday's For Tomorrow homework. Underline the prefixes. Then ask a volunteer to find each word's definition in a dictionary. Invite volunteers to write some of their example words on the board. Challenge students to identify the prefixes and predict the word's meaning.

GRAMMAR CONNECTION

Take this opportunity to talk about prepositional phrases used as adverbs. You may wish to have students point out prepositional phrases used as adverbs in their Read, Listen, Speak examples.

TEACH

Ask a volunteer to read aloud the first paragraph. Challenge students to give examples of self-help presentations *(talk shows on television, exercise classes, career seminars)*.

Have volunteers read aloud the section Selecting a Topic. Challenge students to explain the differences between how-to talks and self-help presentations. *(Self-help presentations empower listeners to solve a problem. How-to talks provide a detailed process for accomplishing a task.)*

Suggest that students recall the specific topics they chose for their how-to talks. Explain that when choosing a self-help presentation, students should narrow their topic.

Have a volunteer read aloud the section Audience. Ask a volunteer to name a topic for a self-help presentation. Challenge students to use this topic to provide answers to the three questions about the audience. Explain that developing a profile of one's audience helps a presenter choose the appropriate words and manner of speaking. Remind students that the intended audience will also affect what ideas are used and how the ideas are organized in their self-help presentations.

PRACTICE

ACTIVITY A

Have students work with a partner to complete this activity. When they have finished, ask students to share their answers. Choose a few topics and invite students to develop an audience profile for each, using the three questions in the Audience section.

Self-Help Presentations

An excellent way to share information about a topic that interests you is to tell people about it. An expository presentation might share the history of an everyday object, the scope of new technology, or the culture of a distant land. One popular type of expository talk is a self-help presentation—one in which the speaker explains how the audience might live better, more healthfully, or with fewer problems. Here are some guidelines to help you prepare and deliver an effective self-help presentation.

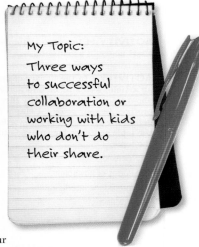

My Topic:
Three ways
to successful
collaboration or
working with kids
who don't do
their share.

Selecting a Topic

Self-help information offers new ways to solve old problems or to improve common situations. Unlike a how-to article, a self-help presentation offers approaches toward fixing something, rather than a step-by-step plan. You might start by thinking about things that you have fixed or wish you could fix.

Choose a problem, a situation, or a pet peeve you have already fixed or one that many people, including you, wish they could fix. If it is a problem you have solved, consider whether your solution would work for other people. If it is a problem that needs a solution, consider how and where you might find strategies that will serve both you and your audience. Either way, choose a topic of interest to you and your audience. Remember to narrow your topic to allow yourself time to offer examples of simple, safe, and effective self-help solutions.

396 • Chapter 5

APPLY

SPEAKER'S CORNER

Allow time for students to write their topics and to discuss them with a partner. After this discussion, ask students to consider revising their topics based on their partners' comments. Point out that this activity will help students create an audience profile. Students should demonstrate an understanding of selecting a topic for a self-help presentation.

Grammar in Action. The prepositional phrases that function as adverbs are *to an absolute minimum* and *of the fat.* Challenge students to identify which words these phrases describe (*should be kept* and *most*).

ASSESS

Note which students had difficulty understanding how to select a topic for a self-help presentation. Use the Reteach option with those students who need additional reinforcement.

TEACHING OPTIONS

Reteach

Have partners choose one of these topics: doing better in school, saving money, making friends. Instruct students to narrow their topic for a self-help presentation. Write on the board the following questions to help students narrow each topic:

- **What problems might arise in the general topic area?**
- **What problem is most common and will interest more people?**
- **Are there simple steps to finding a solution to the problem?**

Self-Help Health

Invite small group to revise the healthful eating expository model on page 375 into a self-help presentation. Instruct them to narrow the topic, to develop an audience profile, and to emphasize specific points from the written piece that the audience might put to use immediately. Have students present their ideas to the class.

Audience

Know your audience and tailor your talk to their needs. A self-help presentation is meant to offer information your listeners can use on their own to solve a problem. Ask yourself these questions:

- What does the audience already know?
- What do they wish they knew?
- What strategies will help them most help themselves?

For example, imagine how your approach to getting students to work together successfully might differ if you were talking to a group of teachers, a group of teenagers, or a group of attendance officers. Think about the way your audience looks at the topic and match your ideas, organization, and language to their needs.

ACTIVITY A Read each expository topic below. Write a narrower version of the same topic that would make an effective self-help presentation.

1. nutrition for people of all ages
2. traveling safely
3. studying
4. career education
5. repairing cars
6. running or jogging
7. lifting weights
8. potatoes and you
9. music
10. Internet safety

SPEAKER'S CORNER

Make a list of five topics for a self-help talk. Trade lists with a partner and write the problem you think each topic would address and what you would hope to learn. Discuss your responses with your partner.

Grammar in Action. Identify the prepositional phrases that function as adverbs in the last paragraph on the p. 375 model.

Expository Writing • 397

For Tomorrow

Ask students to watch a self-help presentation on television or online. Tell students to take notes about the presentation. Ask students to turn the notes into a checklist to follow when planning a self-help presentation. Watch a self-help presentation yourself. Take notes that could be used in a self-help presentation checklist.

Read, Listen, Speak

Discuss the self-help presentation you watched from yesterday's For Tomorrow homework. Write on the board the details you thought would be good additions to a self-help presentation checklist. Ask students if they had similar details in their notes. Then invite volunteers to write additional details on the board. Have students copy the finished list in their notebooks.

TEACH

Have a volunteer read aloud the first paragraph of the section Research and Organization. Discuss topics for self-help presentations that students used for previous activities. Challenge students to name print and online sources they might use to gather information. Point out that interviews are an excellent source of information and that they can offer a human connection to the topic.

Have a volunteer read aloud the rest of the section. Use the model on page 375 and lead the class through the steps of organizing a self-help presentation. Have students identify the main ideas in the introduction, body, and conclusion. Encourage volunteers to give anecdotes to open the presentation. Ask for several ideas from students for information to include in the body. Write their responses on the board. Then ask students to suggest ideas for a closing summary.

Have a volunteer read aloud the section Actively Listening. Point out the significance of asking a speaker pertinent questions after his or her presentation. Explain that asking thoughtful questions is an opportunity for listeners to learn more about the topic and to understand the speaker's

presentation more completely. Encourage students to ask questions about points that need clarification in a presentation.

PRACTICE

ACTIVITY B

After students have discussed resources with a partner, have students write their outlines. Then ask volunteers to share their outlines. Encourage feedback from the class about the information that was included in the outlines.

APPLY

SPEAKER'S CORNER

Tell students to practice their talk several times. Encourage students to experiment with different words to create their desired tone. Tell listeners to provide constructive feedback and to ask questions. Students should demonstrate an understanding of conducting self-help presentations.

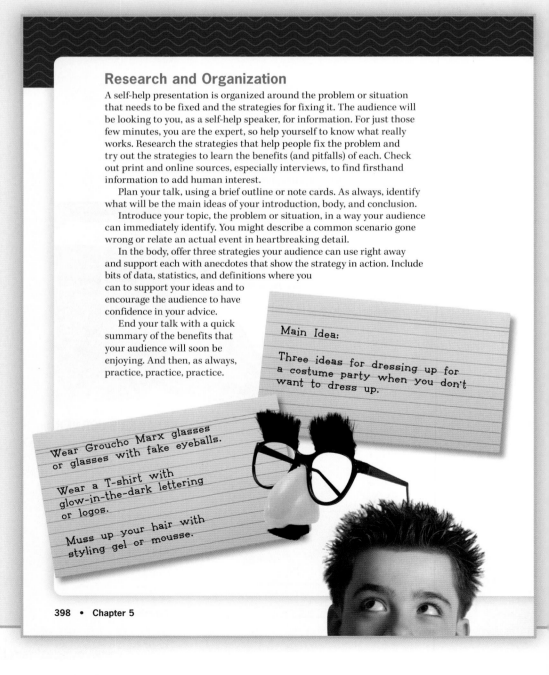

Research and Organization

A self-help presentation is organized around the problem or situation that needs to be fixed and the strategies for fixing it. The audience will be looking to you, as a self-help speaker, for information. For just those few minutes, you are the expert, so help yourself to know what really works. Research the strategies that help people fix the problem and try out the strategies to learn the benefits (and pitfalls) of each. Check out print and online sources, especially interviews, to find firsthand information to add human interest.

Plan your talk, using a brief outline or note cards. As always, identify what will be the main ideas of your introduction, body, and conclusion.

Introduce your topic, the problem or situation, in a way your audience can immediately identify. You might describe a common scenario gone wrong or relate an actual event in heartbreaking detail.

In the body, offer three strategies your audience can use right away and support each with anecdotes that show the strategy in action. Include bits of data, statistics, and definitions where you can to support your ideas and to encourage the audience to have confidence in your advice.

End your talk with a quick summary of the benefits that your audience will soon be enjoying. And then, as always, practice, practice, practice.

Main Idea:

Three ideas for dressing up for a costume party when you don't want to dress up.

Wear Groucho Marx glasses or glasses with fake eyeballs.

Wear a T-shirt with glow-in-the-dark lettering or logos.

Muss up your hair with styling gel or mousse.

TechTip You may wish to have students view their podcasts in small groups. Encourage students to provide constructive feedback to their group members. Then discuss some tips for self-help presentations.

ASSESS

Note which students had difficulty organizing self-help presentations. Use the Reteach option with those students who need additional reinforcement.

After you have reviewed Lessons 3–5, administer the Writing Skills Assessment on pages 61–62 in the **Assessment Book.** This test is also available on the optional **Test Generator CD.**

Actively Listening

When listening to a self-help presentation, follow these guidelines.

- Identify the organizational structure of the talk to increase your understanding and to help you predict what might come next.
- Try to form a picture in your mind of what the speaker is saying. Ask yourself questions such as *Does this make sense?* and *Would that strategy work for me?*
- Pay attention to any visual aids. They often allow you to see what the speaker is saying in a new way.
- At the end, limit your questions to strategies and advice you want to understand more clearly.

ACTIVITY B Discuss with a partner what resources you would use to research each topic below. Then, on your own, choose one self-help topic and write a brief outline telling what kind of information you would offer in the introduction, the body, and the conclusion of a presentation.

1. six ideas for letting go of stress
2. strategies for running a faster marathon
3. grooming a poodle at home for a fraction of the cost
4. eating in public without embarrassing yourself
5. raising your personal television viewing standards
6. a star sumo wrestler's best advice on competition
7. the benefits of learning to play a musical instrument
8. using what you know about dogs to meet people
9. finding meaning in life through nursery rhymes
10. three win-win conflict resolution techniques

SPEAKER'S CORNER

Practice your talk with a partner, varying your tone of voice and emphasizing important words. When you are the listener, describe your reaction to the speech.

 Tech Tip Record a podcast of your talk for review.

Expository Writing • 399

OBJECTIVE

- **To prewrite and plan an expository essay**

PREWRITING AND DRAFTING

Invite a volunteer to read aloud the first paragraph. Encourage students to suggest interesting topics. Be sure students understand that an expository essay can be about almost any topic a writer can research. Review what students have learned in this chapter. Mention that expository writing does the following:

- Informs the reader about a specific topic
- Includes relevant information that answers the questions *who, what, when, where, why,* and *how*
- Uses a neutral tone
- Incorporates factual information and few opinions

Prewriting

Have a student read aloud the first paragraph. Invite a volunteer to remind the class what the purpose of prewriting is *(to brainstorm ideas and plan the organization of a piece of writing)*. Encourage students to name prewriting techniques they have used in the past.

Choosing a Topic

Ask a volunteer to read aloud the first paragraph. Allow time for students to read silently the statements Denver used. Ask a volunteer to explain why using statements such as these are helpful when choosing a topic. *(They allow the writer to explore different ways of looking at the subject matter.)*

Read aloud the last paragraph in this section. Point out that Denver's topic is easy to research and that it is not too broad. Review some topics students suggested at the beginning of the lesson.

Discuss which topics might not work because they are too broad or for which research might be too difficult.

Your Turn

Have a student read aloud this section. Encourage students to use a list like Denver's while brainstorming topics. Invite volunteers to share the topics they chose. Discuss the interest level of each topic.

Gathering Ideas

Invite a volunteer to read aloud this section. Allow time for students to read silently the KWL chart that Denver wrote. Explain that this kind of organization makes it easier for a writer to see exactly what information is missing and needs to be more thoroughly researched. Mention that making this kind of chart also helps writers see that they might not know as much about a topic as they thought. Explain that gathering ideas for one topic sometimes encourages a writer to go back and brainstorm other topics.

👓 Remind students that ideas are the foundation of writing. Encourage students to choose topics that they are curious about and that will be of interest to their audience.

Writer's Workshop   Expository Writing

Prewriting and Drafting

Everyone is curious or knowledgeable about something, from Civil War battles to current tennis players. What topic do you know a lot about? What topic do you want to know more about? Any of these ideas might be an excellent topic for an expository essay. Now you will write an expository essay, using what you have discussed in this chapter.

Prewriting

The prewriting stage for writing an expository essay includes choosing a topic, gathering ideas from research, and planning the piece. Of course before you research, you need to find out what you already know.

Choosing a Topic

Denver, an eighth grader, is writing an essay for health class. He brainstormed a list of health-related topics that interested him, using a list of ideas.

I was amazed to learn _____ about health.
One healthy habit is _____.
One unhealthy habit is _____.
It's important to teach children about _____
I'd rather _____ than do any other exercise.
I just love to eat _____.
My favorite sport is _____.
I can't believe that the human body can _____

After reviewing his list, Denver chose to write about the DARE (Drug Abuse Resistance Education) program at his old school. Denver knew he could find additional information about it through research. The topic was narrow enough to maintain a clear focus in an essay.

Your Turn

Brainstorm ideas for an expository essay. Choose a topic that interests you, that you already know something about, that you can find additional information about, and that is narrow enough to maintain a clear focus. Use Denver's list if you need help.

Gathering Ideas

Denver knew that before he could make a plan for writing, he should explore his topic and do research to find important information. Denver decided to use a KWL chart to explore his topic 👓 **Ideas** and to record research. Denver filled in the Know and Want to Know columns before doing his research. Then he did some Internet research to fill in the Learned column. He checked his completed chart to be sure it answered the questions *who, what, where, when, why,* and *how.*

Writer's Tip The prewriting process includes choosing a topic, gathering ideas from research, and planning the piece.

Writer's Tip Remind students that when they plan their piece, they should think about the audience and the organization of their writing.

Planning an Expository Essay

Have a volunteer read aloud this section. Ask students why identifying the purpose and the audience of a piece is important to do before drafting. *(Knowing the purpose and the audience helps a writer maintain his or her focus and tone while writing.)*

Your Turn

Have a student read aloud this section. Allow time for students to complete KWL charts and organizational plans for their essays. When students have finished, invite volunteers to share their topics, audiences, and methods of organization.

👀 Remind students that there are many ways to organize an expository article, including order of importance, chronological order, and comparison and contrast. Suggest that students who are explaining why something happens use a cause-and-effect style of organization.

Online Time

Allow extra class time for students to conduct online research during prewriting. Review Lesson 3 on page 384. Suggest students make charts with which to rate the Web sites they discover. Make sure students document their research so that they can refer to the sites they found.

What to Write About?

If students are having difficulty choosing a topic, have them list their favorite books, movies, and television programs. Ask students to choose their three favorites and note what each is about and what they enjoy about each one. Invite students to use the subject matter or themes of these choices to help generate topic ideas. For example, if a student's favorite book is *April Morning* by Howard Fast, that student may want to research some aspect of the Revolutionary War.

What I KNOW	What I WANT to Know	What I LEARNED
• team effort by police, teachers, and parents	• What does DARE stand for?	• stands for Drug Abuse Resistance Education
• teaches kids ways to keep from drinking and taking drugs	• Which grades participate?	• There is a DARE program for every grade.
• first few lessons teach about harm	• What do expert adults think of DARE?	• Ms. Giovanni, my former principal, says, "I've seen the effects of DARE. This is one program that really works."
• next lessons teach about resisting drugs	• What else can you learn?	
• at the end kids pledge to be drug-free		• how to find role models, and the influence of media
• is in schools across America		

Prewriting · Drafting · Content Editing · Revising · Copyediting · Proofreading · Publishing

Planning an Expository Essay

Denver studied the information on his KWL chart and started to think about how he might use the information in an expository essay. He knew that he had to consider his audience, his purpose, and the organizational structure. Here is Denver's plan.

Topic: the DARE program at my old school
Audience: my health teacher
Organization Structure:

Introduction: Define program and its goals

Body: Explain program in chronological order

Conclusion: Summarize the program and its goals

Your Turn

Make a KWL chart about your topic and do your research to complete the chart. Then make an organizational plan for your expository essay.

👀 **Organization**

Record your topic, your audience, and an organizational structure, including what you will most likely place in the introduction, the body, and the conclusion.

D.A.R.E.

Expository Writing • 401

OBJECTIVE
• To draft an expository essay

Drafting

Invite a student to read aloud the first paragraph. Then allow time for students to read silently Denver's draft.

After students finish reading, discuss Denver's draft. Challenge students to point out what Denver did well and what he might improve. Suggest that students refer to the characteristics of good expository writing that they learned in Lessons 1 and 2. Use the following questions to spark discussion:

• Who is Denver's audience?
• What is the purpose of the essay?
• Is the tone appropriate for the audience?

• What words or phrases help create the tone?
• Do the supporting details offer enough support for the purpose?
• Is the topic sentence appropriate?
• Does the conclusion summarize or offer a thought-provoking statement?

After discussing these questions, challenge students to point out specific places where Denver used information from his KWL chart and the research he collected.

Drafting

Denver was ready to follow his writing plan and incorporate his KWL notes to create a draft of an expository essay. He kept in mind that he did not have to use all the information from his KWL chart. He also knew that he could add information not on the chart. Denver wrote a double-spaced draft so he would have room for revisions.

Take a DARE!

DARE is a program people have heard about but not everyone knows what it is exactly and I think they should because I participated in DARE in my last school, so I can explain it to you. Drug and alcohol abuse can cause kids problems all their lives so DARE tries to help them stay off drugs. DARE stands for Drug Abuse Resistance Education. The program is a team effort by the police department, teachers, and parents to have an educational program that teaches kids ways to keep from drinking and taking drugs.

The oficial DARE program has 17 lessons. DARE at all grades. They are about an hour long but in my old school sometimes we were having such good discussions that my teacher let us keep talking a lot longer. The first few lessons are about drugs and alcohol and the harm that they can do. Then come lessons that teach kids how to resist drugs those lessons can be fun, especially if you like to act because you do a lot of role-playing. You learn better ways to build self-esteme and manage stress than taking drugs. You also learn about the influence of the media and how to find better role models, and form a support system. At the end of the program students take a pledge to be drug-free. The last lesson is graduation, with a party and certificites.

Cause and Effect

Invite a student to read aloud this section. Ask partners to read each other's drafts. If cause-and-effect organization was used, ask students to offer suggestions for improving the flow and coherence of the piece so the cause and effect is apparent. If cause-and-effect organization was not used, challenge students to decide whether it might be incorporated.

Your Turn

Have a volunteer read aloud this section. Allow time for students to draft their essays. Remind students to focus on the purpose and audience they determined during prewriting. When they have finished, invite students to reread their drafts, paying attention to the tone. Ask if students maintained a neutral tone throughout the piece. If not, encourage students to make changes that affect the tone during content editing.

DARE is not a perfect program but overall the students I talked to like it because it gives them a chance to get to know officers and get information and ask questions they might have been afraid to ask and another good thing about the program is it teaches teachers and principals and parents too. DARE is one way to help keep kids from ruining their lives. As Ms. Eileen Giovanni, principal of Disney Middle School, says "I've seen the effects of DARE. This is one program that really works."

Cause and Effect

Cause explains why something happens. Effect explains what happens as a result. Some expository essays use cause-and-effect relationships as their organizational structure. For example, an introduction might define an effect, such as global warming. Then the body of the essay might explain several causes of the effect, such as pollution, aerosol use, and deforestation. The conclusion might then sum up the significance of the cause-and-effect relationships. Writers use words such as the following when writing an expository essay organized using cause-and-effect relationships: *as a result of, because, consequently, due to,* and *so.* Before you begin writing, determine if your expository essay topic lends itself to being structured around cause-and-effect relationships. If so, you might want to use this organizational structure for your essay.

Your Turn

Use your KWL chart and writing plan as you draft an expository essay. Feel free to change your plan if you think of information you want to add or delete.

Concentrate on getting down the important points, using the organizational structure you selected. Remember to leave extra space between the lines to leave room for revisions.

Prewriting / Drafting / Content Editing / Revising / Copyediting / Proofreading / Publishing

Expository Writing • 403

OBJECTIVE
- **To edit a first draft for content**

CONTENT EDITING

Invite a volunteer to read aloud the first and second paragraphs of this section. Discuss the advantages of having someone knowledgeable about a topic edit an expository piece for content. *(Content editing involves editing for ideas and clarity. Someone knowledgeable about a topic can offer valuable insight about whether the message or main point is clear and correctly stated.)*

Ask a volunteer to read aloud the third paragraph and the Content Editor's Checklist. Have volunteers suggest additions to the checklist based on the characteristics of expository writing students have learned in this chapter.

Have volunteers read aloud the two paragraphs at the top of page 405 and Chandra's suggestions for improvement. Pause after each suggestion is read and have students locate the area in Denver's draft that is affected. Encourage students to match Chandra's comments to the items in the Content Editor's Checklist.

Invite students to discuss whether they agree with each suggestion and how they would change the draft. Then have a volunteer read aloud the last paragraph of the section.

Ask students to comment on how Chandra worded her comments. Discuss whether she worded them constructively and included positive feedback as well as suggestions for improvement. Challenge volunteers to comment on other changes Denver could make to his draft. *(The conclusion is vague. The main idea could be summarized more clearly.)*

Content Editing

When Denver finished his draft, he thought he had written a good expository essay. But he also knew that the points the essay raised about DARE would need to be edited for logic, order, and clarity.

Denver gave his essay to Chandra, a classmate who had participated in the DARE program. He thought that her knowledge of the program would make her an ideal content editor and that she would best notice how well his ideas were expressed. He also thought she would know what information would be necessary and what would not be necessary.

Chandra used the following Content Editor's Checklist to edit Denver's draft. Chandra read Denver's draft twice, first to understand its overall purpose and to notice major problems and the second time to focus on details.

Content Editor's Checklist

- ☐ Does the essay have an identifiable topic sentence?
- ☐ Is the essay well organized? Is the organization of the essay logical?
- ☐ Are there opinions presented as facts?
- ☐ Are all the facts presented relevant to the main idea?
- ☐ Do the paragraphs in the body contain facts that support the essay's main idea?
- ☐ Are all the ideas easy to understand?
- ☐ Is all the information stated as concisely as possible?
- ☐ Does the conclusion sum up the main idea and provide additional insights?

404 • Chapter 5

Your Turn

Have a student read aloud this section. Give students time to review their own drafts. Then have students meet with a partner and comment on each other's drafts. Remind students to offer constructive and positive feedback. Tell students to consider each other's comments carefully and to use the Content Editor's Checklist as a guide when offering suggestions for improvement. Be sure students discuss each suggestion to avoid any misunderstanding.

Remind students that voice shows the writer's personality in the writing. Tell students that although expository writing is factual and has a neutral tone, they can still show their own unique voice.

Writer's Tip Tell students that they can create a confident voice by using facts and explanations that support their topic.

Chandra complimented Denver on his draft and said she understood clearly the points he made. Chandra told Denver she thought most people would understand his essay and find it interesting, especially if they had heard of the DARE program but didn't know much about it.

As with all first drafts, Chandra knew Denver would revise it. Here are her suggestions.

- The topic sentence is unclear to me. I think you should explain right away in the first paragraph what DARE stands for and what the program does.

- The essay seems to be well organized by order of importance. You begin with what DARE is, proceed to how it's organized, and end with why it's a good program.

- Although no facts are presented as opinions, the first paragraph has too much opinion for an expository essay. It's not necessary to tell the readers that you think they should participate in the program.

- Most of the facts seem to be relevant, but the fact that you participated in the program is not relevant. I would delete that part.

- The paragraphs in the essay contain sufficient information to support your main idea.

- The ideas you present are easy to understand.

- Generally, I think you should tighten up your writing. You can cut quite a bit without losing any important information. In the second paragraph, is it important to tell readers that discussions often lasted longer than required?

Denver considered Chandra's suggestions carefully. He respected her opinion and agreed with many of her suggestions. He took out unnecessary information and tightened up his writing until he was satisfied that he had improved his draft.

Your Turn

Revise your first draft, using the Content Editor's Checklist as a guide. Have you

Voice presented the important points as concisely and clearly as you possibly can?

Next, trade drafts with a partner. You and your partner should read each other's drafts and suggest improvements, if necessary, in each area on the checklist. Finally, talk over the suggestions and accept the ones that seem sensible to you.

Writer's Tip Since the purpose of an expository essay is to inform readers about a topic, the writer's voice should be confident.

Prewriting · Drafting · Content Editing · Revising · Copyediting · Proofreading · Publishing

Expository Writing • 405

OBJECTIVE
- **To revise an expository essay**

REVISING

Have students discuss their experience with revisions on previous writing projects. Ask students what types of changes they made to improve their work. Remind students that their writing will not be perfect with the first draft and that it will go through many revisions.

Have students silently read Denver's revised draft. Challenge students to discuss with partners the changes Denver made to his draft and how he incorporated Chandra's suggestions. Encourage volunteers to suggest additional changes for Denver's essay.

Read aloud the revisions Denver made that are listed on page 407. Discuss the following revisions:

- He moved the last two sentences of the introduction to the beginning of his essay.
- He deleted the fact that he had participated in the program.
- He eliminated the information about his previous teacher talking for longer than an hour.
- He decided to revise the first and second sentences to clarify the main idea.

Writer's Workshop
Expository Writing

Revising

This is Denver's draft, which shows the revisions he plans to make.

Take a DARE!

~~DARE is a program people have heard about but not everyone knows what it is exactly and I think they should because I participated in DARE in my last school, so I can explain it to you.~~ Drug and alcohol abuse can cause kids problems all their lives so, ~~DARE tries to help them stay off drugs.~~ *that's why DARE was organized.* DARE stands for Drug Abuse Resistance Education. The program is a team effort by the police department, teachers, and parents to have an educational program that teaches kids ways to keep from drinking and taking drugs.

The oficial DARE program has 17 lessons. *, which is taught at all the grades,* ~~DARE at all grades.~~ They are about an hour long ~~but in my old school sometimes we were having such good discussions that my teacher let us keep talking a lot longer.~~ The first few lessons are about drugs and alcohol and the harm that they can do. Then come lessons that teach kids how to resist drugs those lessons can be fun, especially if you like to act because you do a lot of role-playing. You learn better ways to build self-esteme and manage stress than taking drugs. You also learn about the influence of the media and how to find better role models, and form a support system. At the end of the program students take a pledge to be drug-free. The last lesson is graduation, with a party and certificites.

Remind students to read their draft aloud to check for sentence fluency. Tell students to listen for varied sentence length and style and for repetition of words.

Grammar in Action. Point out that using noun clauses can improve their writing by adding variety to their sentence structure.

Your Turn

Invite a volunteer to read aloud this section. Then allow time for students to revise their drafts. Remind students to write neatly when marking revisions. If students are revising on computers, review the editing functions in the word-processing program. Encourage volunteers to share the revisions they made. Suggest students meet again with their editing partners to discuss whether their revisions benefit the purpose and flow of each piece.

Transitions Practice

Ask students to pay special attention to the organization of their pieces while revising, especially when deleting sentences or moving them to another location in the piece. Ask why this is important (*because extensive changes might affect the logical flow and organization of a piece*). Have students work with partners to add or delete transition words in their drafts to signal the logical progression of each sentence.

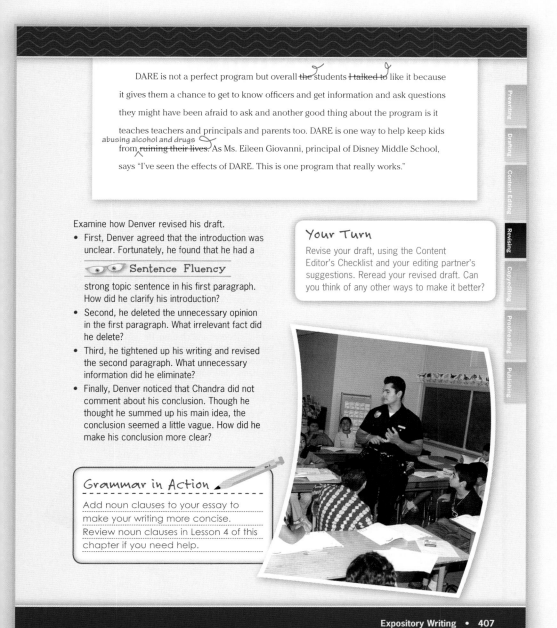

DARE is not a perfect program but overall the students I talked to like it because it gives them a chance to get to know officers and get information and ask questions they might have been afraid to ask and another good thing about the program is it teaches teachers and principals and parents too. DARE is one way to help keep kids from ~~ruining their lives~~ abusing alcohol and drugs. As Ms. Eileen Giovanni, principal of Disney Middle School, says "I've seen the effects of DARE. This is one program that really works."

Examine how Denver revised his draft.

- First, Denver agreed that the introduction was unclear. Fortunately, he found that he had a

Sentence Fluency

strong topic sentence in his first paragraph. How did he clarify his introduction?
- Second, he deleted the unnecessary opinion in the first paragraph. What irrelevant fact did he delete?
- Third, he tightened up his writing and revised the second paragraph. What unnecessary information did he eliminate?
- Finally, Denver noticed that Chandra did not comment about his conclusion. Though he thought he summed up his main idea, the conclusion seemed a little vague. How did he make his conclusion more clear?

Your Turn

Revise your draft, using the Content Editor's Checklist and your editing partner's suggestions. Reread your revised draft. Can you think of any other ways to make it better?

Grammar in Action

Add noun clauses to your essay to make your writing more concise. Review noun clauses in Lesson 4 of this chapter if you need help.

(side tabs: Prewriting, Drafting, Content Editing, Revising, Copyediting, Proofreading, Publishing)

Expository Writing • 407

OBJECTIVE
- **To copyedit and proofread an expository essay**

COPYEDITING AND PROOFREADING

Copyediting

Invite a volunteer to read aloud the first paragraph. Remind students of the difference between content editing and copyediting. *(Content editing involves looking at ideas, structure, and flow, while copyediting involves looking at individual sentences and words.)*

Tell students to choose the most precise, descriptive words, not necessarily the most unusual or exceptional. Remind students that word choice will help to establish their voice.

Ask a volunteer to read aloud the second paragraph and the Copyeditor's Checklist. Challenge students to add items to the checklist. Suggest that students refer to specific points in Lessons 1 and 2. *(Are there words that give the piece a biased tone instead of a neutral one?)*

Have a volunteer read aloud the last three paragraphs. Then ask students to match the changes

Denver made to the items on the Copyeditor's Checklist. Review run-on and rambling sentences on page 270. Ask volunteers to define them and offer examples of each. Challenge students to explain why it is important to revise run-on and rambling sentences. *(Run-on and rambling sentences lack focus and make a piece of writing difficult to follow.)*

Your Turn

Invite a student to read aloud this section. Allow time for students to read aloud their drafts and note the sound and meaning of words and sentences. Encourage students to check for one item on the checklist at a time. Suggest that students work with a partner to copyedit each other's drafts.

Proofreading

Invite a volunteer to explain why proofreading a draft is critical to the writing process *(because errors in spelling, grammar, and format can adversely affect the writing's credibility)*. Ask a volunteer to read aloud the first paragraph. Ask students why it is beneficial to have someone who has not yet seen their writing proofread it. *(It is beneficial because he or she might spot errors that the writer and the content editor missed.)*

Editor's Workshop   Expository Writing

Copyediting and Proofreading

Copyediting

Denver revised his essay, using his own and Chandra's suggestions. When he was confident that the ideas of his essay were clear and logical, he read his essay again. This time he read it for **Word Choice** word meaning, word choice, sentence structure, and the overall logic of his expository essay.

Denver used the following Copyeditor's Checklist for this task.

Copyeditor's Checklist

- ☐ Do the sentences flow smoothly?
- ☐ Are any sentences awkward or confusing?
- ☐ Are words with prefixes used correctly?
- ☐ Are any words repeated too often?
- ☐ Do transition words support the pattern of organization?
- ☐ Does the structure of the sentences vary?
- ☐ Are noun clauses used correctly?
- ☐ Is the structure of each sentence logical and grammatically correct?

Denver read his essay aloud so that he could hear how it sounded. He knew that the parts he stumbled over when he read it might trip up readers too. He took out extra words to fix those sentences.

He also corrected two run-on sentences and a rambling sentence he found in the last two paragraphs. In correcting these sentences, Denver added small details such as clearly stating the goal of the DARE strategies and describing the kind of certificates the participants receive.

Denver decided that the word *kids* was too informal to use in his essay, so he changed *kids* to *students* and *children*. He also revised the sentences that started with *you* because he wanted to keep the tone of his essay objective. He made a few other language changes.

Your Turn

Reread your revised draft, concentrating on the sound and meaning of each sentence and each word. Read the draft aloud at least once to hear how the words sound and how the sentences flow. Use the Copyeditor's Checklist to help you improve your draft.

408 • Chapter 5

Emphasize that students should remember that mistakes in spelling, grammar, and punctuation can distract readers from the topic, no matter how well the article is worded.

Have a volunteer read aloud the paragraph before the Proofreader's Checklist. Challenge students to find the mistakes in Denver's draft.

Have students read silently the Proofreader's Checklist. Ask how new errors could have been introduced during the writing process. *(Revised words and sentences could have been written or typed incorrectly, or new errors might have been introduced while correcting others.)*

Your Turn

Invite a volunteer to read aloud this section. Encourage students to work with different partners during this proofreading stage. Ask why using different partners is beneficial. *(A new pair of eyes reading a piece might notice more mistakes than someone familiar with the piece.)* Allow time for partners to proofread each other's drafts. Ask what proofreading techniques work best for students.

TEACHING OPTIONS

English-Language Learners

Be aware that students may transfer the grammar, punctuation, and capitalization rules from their primary languages to written English. For example, in Spanish a comma is not used to separate the last two items in a series joined by a conjunction: *blanco, negro y rojo (white, black and red).* Questions written in Spanish begin with an inverted question mark and end with a regular question mark. Allow extra time for students to check for errors in punctuation and capitalization, perhaps writing a modified Proofreader's Checklist of their own.

Proofreading Practice

Review proofreading marks on page 257. Have students look for errors in newspapers, magazines, or their own pieces of writing. Ask students to correct the errors with proofreading marks and then give the piece of writing to another student. Have the other student rewrite the piece, inserting the corrections indicated.

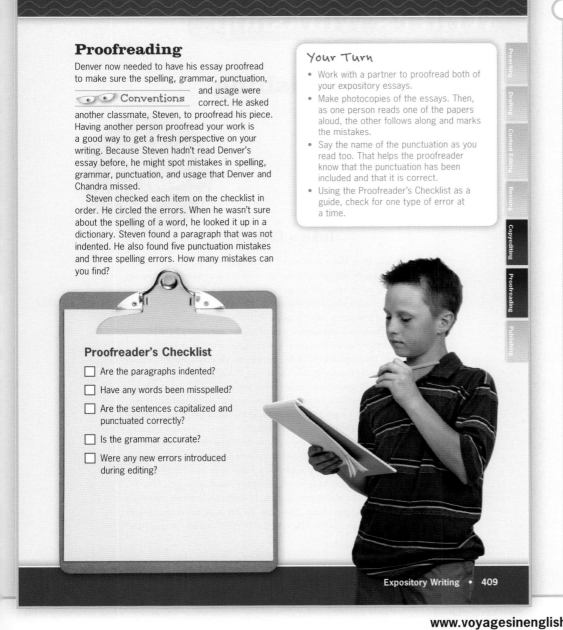

Proofreading

Denver now needed to have his essay proofread to make sure the spelling, grammar, punctuation, and usage were correct. He asked another classmate, Steven, to proofread his piece. Having another person proofread your work is a good way to get a fresh perspective on your writing. Because Steven hadn't read Denver's essay before, he might spot mistakes in spelling, grammar, punctuation, and usage that Denver and Chandra missed.

Steven checked each item on the checklist in order. He circled the errors. When he wasn't sure about the spelling of a word, he looked it up in a dictionary. Steven found a paragraph that was not indented. He also found five punctuation mistakes and three spelling errors. How many mistakes can you find?

Conventions

Your Turn

- Work with a partner to proofread both of your expository essays.
- Make photocopies of the essays. Then, as one person reads one of the papers aloud, the other follows along and marks the mistakes.
- Say the name of the punctuation as you read too. That helps the proofreader know that the punctuation has been included and that it is correct.
- Using the Proofreader's Checklist as a guide, check for one type of error at a time.

Proofreader's Checklist

☐ Are the paragraphs indented?

☐ Have any words been misspelled?

☐ Are the sentences capitalized and punctuated correctly?

☐ Is the grammar accurate?

☐ Were any new errors introduced during editing?

Expository Writing • 409

OBJECTIVE
- **To publish an expository essay**

PUBLISHING

Ask a volunteer to read aloud the first paragraph. Invite volunteers to read aloud Denver's finished piece. Challenge students to identify the changes Denver made to the piece after copyediting and proofreading. Have students compare Denver's finished version to the first draft he wrote on pages 402–403. Encourage students to comment on the tone, purpose, and organization of the essay.

Read aloud the different ways students can publish their expository essays. Then have students work together to decide on and develop a way to publish their work. Encourage students to suggest a variety of ways and to discuss the benefits and drawbacks of each. For example, students might suggest a class newspaper or magazine. If students choose this option, have them discuss the following questions:

- What should the title of the publication be?
- What are the benefits of this publication style? What are the drawbacks?

- Should any graphics be included?
- How many copies should be made?
- How can we distribute copies to other students? to parents?

Your Turn

Have a volunteer read aloud this section. Allow time for students to copy their final versions and to check their essays one more time for errors. Ask volunteers to read aloud their essays. Encourage students to offer ideas for illustrations to accompany their essays. Have students

---

Writer's Workshop   Expository Writing

Publishing

Denver edited and revised his draft several times until he felt it was good enough to publish. He made a finished version to submit to his health teacher. When he finished, he knew it was his best work, so he felt ready to share it.

Take a DARE!

DARE stands for Drug Abuse Resistance Education. The program is a team effort by the police department, teachers, and parents to teach students strategies to avoid drinking and taking drugs. Drug and alcohol abuse are serious issues that can cause lifelong problems, so that's why DARE was developed.

The official DARE program, which is taught at all the grades, has 17 lessons. Each lesson is about an hour long. The first few lessons teach about drugs and alcohol and the harm that they can do. Then come lessons that teach children strategies for resisting drugs. These lessons can be fun for students, especially students who enjoy acting because the lessons involve role-playing. The goal is to teach children better ways to build self-esteem and manage stress than taking drugs and drinking. Subsequent lessons teach about the influence of the media, ways to find good role models, and how to form a support system. At the end of the program, students take a pledge to be drug-free. The last lesson is a graduation and celebration at which certificates of completion are awarded to students who completed the program.

DARE is not a perfect program, but overall, students like the program because it gives them a chance to get to know police officers, get information, and ask questions they might have been afraid to ask previously. Another strength of the program is that it involves teachers, principals, and parents. DARE is one way to help keep children from abusing alcohol and drugs. As Ms. Eileen Giovanni, principal of Disney Middle School, says, "I've seen the effects of DARE. This is one program that really works."

design illustrations and include them with the finished pieces. Encourage students to read one another's essays during the next week and to record positive feedback.

👓 Tell students that their articles should look neat and professional. Emphasize that students' presentation should be appropriate for their chosen way to publish.

ASSESS

Have students assess their finished expository writing using the reproducible Student Self-Assessment on page 411y. A separate Expository Writing Scoring Rubric can be found on page 411z for you to use to evaluate their work.

Plan to spend tomorrow doing a formal assessment. Administer the Expository Writing Prompt on **Assessment Book** pages 63–64.

TEACHING OPTIONS

Portfolio Opportunity

Ask students to make copies of their essays for their writing portfolios. Have students reread any notes they made during the previous Writer's Workshops. Discuss whether students think they have improved their writing and editing skills.

Publishing Online

Publish students' essays on a class blog. Ask volunteers to organize those who wish to publish their essays. Encourage students to decide in what order and format to place the essays. Suggest that students also publish portions of their prewriting and drafting so that readers can see how students progressed through the writing process.

Publishing is a way for you to share your thoughts and experiences with other people. Here are a few ways to publish your expository writing.

@ Post it on your class Web site. You may want to add photographs, diagrams, or clipart. These are interesting items to attach to an expository essay. You might include a feedback questionnaire for reader comments.

📖 Create a classroom book. Ask your school librarian if your class's book could be a checkout book for a limited time.

📓 Make a classroom newsletter. Your expository essay will be a valuable resource for other students in your school who share the same interest in your topic.

📹 Read your essay aloud for Parents' Night. You might wish to record it with a video recorder.

Whenever you publish, make sure the message is clear and neatly presented.

Your Turn

Before you publish your expository essay, carefully make any needed revisions from the proofreading stage. 👓 **Presentation** If you write your essay by hand, use your best handwriting and copy your corrections accurately. If you type your essay on a computer, don't forget to do a thorough spell-check and grammar-check before printing your essay. Proofread your essay one last time, just to be sure you didn't add new mistakes or leave out any parts.

After you do a final check of your essay, you might want to add a diagram or an illustration to explain a key idea visually. You might attach this visual to the front of a folder that acts as a cover for your published piece.

Prewriting | Drafting | Content Editing | Revising | Copyediting | Proofreading | **Publishing**

Name _____ Date _____

Expository Writing

Ideas	YES	NO
Do I have a clear focus on one topic?		
Do I provide factual information supported by research or personal experience?		

Organization		
Do I include an interesting introduction with a topic sentence?		
Do I provide a logically ordered body of main ideas and details?		
Do I include a summarizing conclusion with insights?		

Voice		
Does the essay have a confident voice?		

Word Choice		
Do I use natural language?		
Do I use a neutral tone?		

Sentence Fluency		
Do I use concise sentences?		
Do I provide information in varied ways?		

Conventions		
Do I use correct grammar?		
Do I use correct spelling, punctuation, and capitalization?		

Presentation		
Do I use consistent spacing and margins?		
Is my paper neat?		

Additional Items

© Loyola Press.

Name _____

Date _____ Score _____

POINT VALUES

0 = not evident
1 = minimal evidence of mastery
2 = evidence of development toward mastery
3 = strong evidence of mastery
4 = outstanding evidence of mastery

Expository Writing

	POINTS
Ideas	
a clear focus on one topic	
factual information supported by research or personal experience	
Organization	
an engaging introduction with a topic sentence	
a logically ordered body of main ideas and details	
a summarizing conclusion with insights	
Voice	
confident	
Word Choice	
natural language	
neutral tone	
Sentence Fluency	
concise sentences	
varied ways of providing information	
Conventions	
correct grammar and usage	
correct spelling, punctuation, and capitalization	
Presentation	
consistent spacing and margins	
neatness	
Additional Items	
Total	

© Loyola Press.

CHAPTER **6** PLANNER

CHAPTER FOCUS

LESSON 1: What Makes Good Persuasive Writing?

LESSON 2: Voice and Audience

- **GRAMMAR:** Sentences
- **LITERACY SKILLS:** Advertisements
- **WRITING SKILLS:** Transition Words
- **WORD STUDY:** Suffixes
- **SPEAKING AND LISTENING SKILLS:** Persuasive Speeches
- **WRITER'S WORKSHOP:** Persuasive Writing

SUPPORT MATERIALS

Practice Book
Writing, pages 163–167

Assessment Book
Chapter 6 Writing Skills, pages 65–66
Persuasive Writing Prompt, pages 67–68

Scoring Rubric
Student, page 449y
Teacher, page 449z

Test Generator CD

Grammar
Section 8, pages 139–164

Customizable Lesson Plans
www.voyagesinenglish.com

Persuasive Writing

WHAT IS PERSUASIVE WRITING?

What power does good persuasive writing have? First, it has the power to convey a writer's values, concerns, or needs. Good persuasive writing can convince a reader to believe as the writer believes. Good persuasive writing has the power to change minds, hearts, and actions.

Good persuasive writing includes the following:

- [ ] A focus on one viewpoint regarding a specific topic
- [ ] An attempt to convince the reader to share the viewpoint
- [ ] An introduction that includes a position statement
- [ ] A body with supporting details and credible facts and opinions
- [ ] Each reason and supporting explanations in its own paragraph
- [ ] A conclusion that includes a rephrasing of the position statement
- [ ] A confident persuasive voice tailored for a specific audience
- [ ] Specific word choice to establish mood
- [ ] Transition words to connect and show relationships between ideas
- [ ] Emotional and logical appeals

LiNK Use the following titles to offer your students examples of well-crafted persuasive writing:

The American Forests by John Muir

I Have a Dream: Writing and Speeches that Changed the World by Martin Luther King Jr.

Made You Look: How Advertising Works and Why You Should Know by Shari Graydon

> " To be persuasive we must be believable; to be believable we must be credible; to be credible we must be truthful. "
>
> —Edward R. Murrow

WRITER'S WORKSHOP TIPS

Follow these ideas and tips to help you and your class get the most out of the Writer's Workshop:

- Review the traits of good writing. Use the chart on the inside back cover of the student and teacher editions.
- Make a bulletin-board display with advertisements that use propaganda. Remind students to keep their writing free of these persuasive devices.
- Fill the classroom library with political cartoons and persuasive articles from magazines and newspapers.
- Choose a popular Writer's Workshop topic and have a class debate. Discuss how the most persuasive oral arguments can translate into students' writing.
- Meet with small groups of students as they work on their persuasive essays. Discuss general concerns that apply to all students' writing.

CONNECT WITH GRAMMAR

Throughout the Writer's Workshop, look for opportunities to integrate sentences with persuasive writing.

- ☐ Point out how varying the kinds of sentences in a persuasive piece makes the writing more lively and engaging.
- ☐ Have students rewrite a simple sentence from their original persuasive draft and add either an adverb or adjective clause.
- ☐ Discuss the differences between a phrase and a clause and how both help make sentences more engaging and persuasive.

SCORING RUBRIC

Persuasive Writing

0 = not evident
1 = minimal evidence of mastery
2 = evidence of development toward mastery
3 = strong evidence of mastery
4 = outstanding evidence of mastery

	POINTS
Ideas	
one viewpoint about a specific topic	
an attempt to convince the reader to share the viewpoint	
Organization	
an introduction with a position statement	
a body with supporting details and credible facts and opinions	
a conclusion that rephrases the position statement	
Voice	
persuasive	
confident and credible	
Word Choice	
specific word choice to establish mood	
language tailored for a specific audience	
transitions words	
emotional and logical appeals	
Sentence Fluency	
rhythm and flow	
Conventions	
correct grammar and usage	
correct spelling, punctuation, and capitalization	
Presentation	
consistent spacing and margins	
neatness	
Additional Items	
Total	

Full-sized, reproducible rubrics can be found at the end of this chapter.

CHAPTER 6
Persuasive Writing

INTRODUCING THE GENRE

Ask students to discuss what they know about persuasive writing. Tell students that the purpose of persuasive writing is to convince an audience to reach a specific conclusion or decision about a topic. Have students provide examples of the genre *(opinion pieces, op-ed articles, letters to the editor, advertisements).* Discuss these characteristics of persuasive writing:

- Includes a position statement that states where the writer stands on the issue
- Includes a body with a balance of fact and opinion
- Ends with a conclusion that summarizes the position statement and leaves an impression on the reader
- Uses a tone that creates a specific mood
- Addresses a particular audience through mood and tone

Reading the Literature Excerpt

Invite volunteers to read aloud the excerpt. Ask why the topic is appropriate for a persuasive piece. *(Environmental stewardship and deforestation is a topic on which supporters and detractors have opposing points of view.)* Ask students if the writer is successful in convincing the audience to agree with his point of view.

LiNK **The American Forests**

The excerpts in Chapter 6 introduce students to relevant examples of persuasive writing. "The American Forests" is a strong example of persuasive writing because

- The speaker's point of view is clearly stated
- The speaker is trying to sway the audience to his point of view
- Arguments supporting the speaker's position are backed with facts
- The conclusion sums up the speaker's evidence and includes a call to action

As students encounter different examples of persuasive writing, be sure to point out the characteristics these examples share. You may wish to take the opportunity to point out grammar skills that students have been learning, such as different kinds of sentences.

Persuasive Writing

LiNK **The American Forests**
by John Muir

All sorts of local laws and regulations have been tried and found wanting, and the costly lessons of our own experience, as well as that of every civilized nation, show conclusively that the fate of the remnant of our forests is in the hands of the federal government, and that if the remnant is to be saved at all, it must be saved quickly. . . .

Any fool can destroy trees. They cannot run away; and if they could, they would still be destroyed—chased and hunted down as long as fun or a dollar could be got out of their bark hides, branching horns, or magnificent bole backbones. Few that fell trees plant them; nor would planting avail much towards getting back anything like the noble primeval forests. . . .

> Persuasive essays, like this one by naturalist John Muir, appeal to the public's logic and emotions to support the main topic. Muir's essay also works to convince others to share his viewpoint about preserving nature.

412

Challenge students to identify some characteristics that set persuasive writing apart from other genres.

Reading the Student Model
Ask students to describe the likely audience of the model. Discuss the tone of voice and mood the writer develops. *(The writer uses statistics that might shock an audience that knows little about deforestation. This "shock value"* sets the mood of the piece. It also has a tone of inclusiveness—that everyone can work together to be stewards of the environment.)* Invite students to comment about the piece and make suggestions for improvement.

TEACHING OPTIONS

Scavenger Hunt
Challenge students to search through reading materials in the classroom and in the library for examples of persuasive writing. Explain that doing so will help students know what to include in their own persuasive pieces. Discuss the examples students found. Ask them to identify clues that suggest the piece is persuasive. Have students compare the persuasive pieces to examples of writing in other genres and list the similarities and differences.

For Tomorrow
Ask students to search books or magazines at home for more examples of persuasive writing. Have students write the topic, the position statement, and the audience for each persuasive piece. Bring in your own example of persuasive writing and record the same information to share with the class.

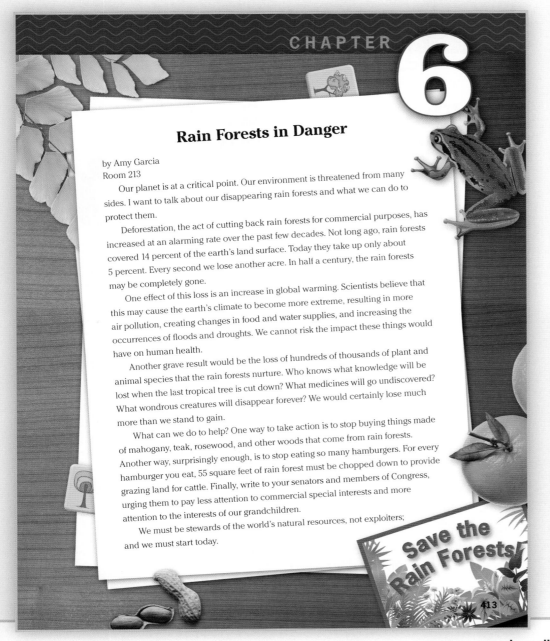

CHAPTER 6

Rain Forests in Danger

by Amy Garcia
Room 213

Our planet is at a critical point. Our environment is threatened from many sides. I want to talk about our disappearing rain forests and what we can do to protect them.

Deforestation, the act of cutting back rain forests for commercial purposes, has increased at an alarming rate over the past few decades. Not long ago, rain forests covered 14 percent of the earth's land surface. Today they take up only about 5 percent. Every second we lose another acre. In half a century, the rain forests may be completely gone.

One effect of this loss is an increase in global warming. Scientists believe that this may cause the earth's climate to become more extreme, resulting in more air pollution, creating changes in food and water supplies, and increasing the occurrences of floods and droughts. We cannot risk the impact these things would have on human health.

Another grave result would be the loss of hundreds of thousands of plant and animal species that the rain forests nurture. Who knows what knowledge will be lost when the last tropical tree is cut down? What medicines will go undiscovered? What wondrous creatures will disappear forever? We would certainly lose much more than we stand to gain.

What can we do to help? One way to take action is to stop buying things made of mahogany, teak, rosewood, and other woods that come from rain forests. Another way, surprisingly enough, is to stop eating so many hamburgers. For every hamburger you eat, 55 square feet of rain forest must be chopped down to provide grazing land for cattle. Finally, write to your senators and members of Congress, urging them to pay less attention to commercial special interests and more attention to the interests of our grandchildren.

We must be stewards of the world's natural resources, not exploiters; and we must start today.

Save the Rain Forests

413

OBJECTIVE

- To include a position statement, a body that supports the position statement, and a summarizing conclusion in a persuasive piece

WARM-UP

Read, Listen, Speak

Read aloud your persuasive writing example from yesterday's For Tomorrow homework. Point out the position statement and the audience for the writing example. Discuss the language in the piece that shows who the audience is. Then invite volunteers to share their persuasive writing examples. Discuss the position statements, the audience, and any language that helps establish who the audience is.

GRAMMAR CONNECTION

Take this opportunity to talk about kinds of sentences and adjective and adverb phrases. You may wish to have students point out kinds of sentences and adjective and adverb phrases in their Read, Listen, Speak examples.

TEACH

Ask a volunteer to read aloud the opening paragraphs. Have students name more examples of persuasive writing. Have a volunteer read aloud the section Position Statement and identify the position statement in the student model on page 413.

Have a volunteer read aloud the first paragraph of the section Supporting the Position. Allow students to read silently the statements below the first paragraph and the paragraph that follows. Ask volunteers to identify the details in the student model on page 413. Then have students

decide whether the supporting details appeal to logic or to emotion.

Invite a volunteer to read aloud the section Conclusion. Ask students how well the conclusion in the student model summarizes the position statement. Have students determine whether the conclusion is appropriate for the audience and leaves a lasting impression about the topic.

PRACTICE

ACTIVITY A

Ask a volunteer to read aloud the letter to the editor. Discuss the letter and have students answer the questions. Challenge students to offer a position statement for a letter of opposition to this letter.

What Makes Good Persuasive Writing?

Good persuasive writing focuses on one topic that can be viewed in different or opposing ways. The writer of a good persuasive essay clearly takes a position on the topic and states it. All the ideas in good persuasive writing appeal to either logic or emotion and work toward convincing readers to share the writer's viewpoint.

Persuasive writing can take many forms, including advertisements, letters to the editor, book and movie reviews, and campaign speeches. These are some of the things you should keep in mind when you write a persuasive essay.

Position Statement

A persuasive essay should begin with a position statement. This statement appears in the introduction and should tell exactly where the writer stands on the issue in question.

Supporting the Position

The body of a persuasive essay often provides readers with logical reasons to agree with the position statement. These reasons are then supported by examples or explanations, which are often opinions and statements of fact. For example, consider the model on page 413.

> **Position Statement: We must combat deforestation of the rain forests.**
> **Reason: If we don't, there will be an increase in global warming.**
> **Example (fact): Global warming causes an increase in air pollution.**
> **Explanation (opinion): We cannot risk the impact on human health.**

Writers might organize the body of a persuasive essay by developing a paragraph for each reason to agree with the position statement. The topic sentence of each supporting paragraph states the reason. The sentences that follow provide relevant examples and explanations that appeal to either logic or emotion.

APPLY

WRITER'S CORNER

Allow time for students to write their lists of ideas. Encourage students to consider ideas that have one or more opposing points of view. Have volunteers share their topics. Discuss several topics and possible points of view for these topics. Invite volunteers to read aloud their position statements. Students should demonstrate an understanding of writing position statements.

ASSESS

Note which students had difficulty understanding the characteristics of persuasive writing. Use the Reteach option with those students who need additional reinforcement.

Reteach

Locate three letters to editors that are about the same topic. Provide copies for students and invite them to underline the position statement in each. Then ask students to circle the details that support the position statements. Have students identify each detail as fact or opinion. Ask if the letters have a good balance of facts and opinions. Have students determine which letter is the most persuasive.

Fact and Opinion

Review the differences between fact and opinion by having volunteers write on the board examples of each. Point out that a fact can be verified through research. Tell students that using inaccurate facts will weaken arguments in persuasive writing. Ask volunteers to point out the statements of fact and statements of opinion in the model. Tell students that well-written persuasive pieces include a good balance of facts and credible opinions.

Conclusion

A good persuasive essay ends with a conclusion that summarizes the position statement and leaves an impact on the readers. The conclusion should not add any new reasons, but should restate the position in a convincing manner. A good persuasive conclusion might also summarize the strongest evidence supporting the position or even call on readers to take action. Any way that it is expressed, a good persuasive conclusion leaves readers thinking about the topic, even after they have finished reading the piece.

Activity A

1. Everyone eligible to vote in the United States should cast a ballot on Election Day.
2. concerned
3. The second and third sentences are facts.
4. All sentences except for the first two sentences are opinions.
5. As long as they don't vote, the truth is they are powerless. They are invisible.
6. If we want to be governed fairly, we have to make ourselves visible by voting—every one of us.

ACTIVITY A Read the body of this letter to the editor. Then answer the questions.

Everyone eligible to vote in the United States should cast a ballot on Election Day. As it stands now, when the turnout for a national election is over 50 percent, news reports comment on the high percentage of participation. That's only about half the registered voters. Many people have been discouraged from voting and encouraged to believe they are powerless. As long as they don't vote, the truth is they are powerless. They are invisible. If we want to be governed fairly, we have to make ourselves visible by voting—every one of us.

1. What is the position statement?
2. What is the general tone of the letter's body? Is the author angry, sad, concerned, or hopeful? Why do you think so?
3. What sections of the letter's body try to convince the reader through factual explanations?
4. What sections of the letter's body give opinions?
5. What are the reasons that support the position statement?
6. What is the conclusion of this essay? Does it leave an impact on the readers? Why or why not?

WRITER'S CORNER

Make a list of changes you'd like to see at home or at school, in your city or state, in our country, or in the world. Circle five ideas that are of particular interest to you and write a position statement for each.

For Tomorrow

Ask students to write a persuasive reply to the letter in Activity A. Encourage students to craft a letter that takes an opposing point of view to the one in the letter. Remind students to include a position statement. Write your own persuasive response to share with the class.

Persuasive Writing • 415

WARM-UP

Read, Listen, Speak

Read aloud your letter from yesterday's For Tomorrow homework. Discuss your position statement and point out specific details you used to support your side of the topic. Then have small groups discuss the letters they wrote for homework. Encourage students to offer feedback about whether each letter effectively persuades the reader. Invite volunteers to read aloud their letters.

GRAMMAR CONNECTION

Take this opportunity to talk about adjective clauses. You may wish to have students point out adjective clauses in their Read, Listen, Speak examples.

TEACH

Review the characteristics of persuasive writing. Discuss position statements, supporting details, and conclusions. Remind students that good persuasive writing addresses the concerns of readers who hold the opposing point of view. Ask students to name appropriate topics for persuasive pieces. Choose one topic and develop an outline for both sides of the argument.

PRACTICE

ACTIVITY B

Allow time for students to work independently to write their paragraphs. Ask students to trade papers with partners and suggest improvements to one another's paragraphs, adding details or replacing words to make the paragraphs more persuasive. You may wish to offer an added challenge and have students write a position statement for this paragraph.

ACTIVITY C

Invite students to work with partners to write two columns for each topic. Ask students to work cooperatively to write position statements for each topic. Encourage students to state their positions clearly and concisely.

ACTIVITY D

Read aloud the conclusion from the student model on page 413. Then have students complete this activity independently. Encourage volunteers to read aloud their replacements to the conclusions.

Ask students to offer feedback about whether the concluding sentences were effectively persuasive.

ACTIVITY E

Have students work in small groups to write the radio commercials. When students have finished, invite them to perform the commercial for the class. Ask volunteers whether they were persuaded to buy what was advertised and if so, why.

ACTIVITY F

Discuss examples of logical and emotional appeals. Provide supplies for students to create a

---

ACTIVITY B Read this paragraph from a newspaper editorial about the need for a community recreation center. Write another paragraph that features a different reason for its construction. Include explanations or examples to support your reason.

One reason that our community must build a recreation center is so teenagers will have something to do rather than get in trouble. Statistics show that teenagers are most likely to exhibit dangerous behaviors in the hours just after school. Teenagers of working parents will no longer have to go home to an empty house or to friends' houses that might also have no adults present. Teenagers will have a safe, fun place to go.

ACTIVITY C Read the following topics about which people have different opinions. Make a two-column chart for each topic. List all the reasons you can think of for and against the topic. Do you have more reasons for the topic or against the topic? Where do you stand on the topic? Write a position statement for each topic based on the conclusions you drew from your chart.

1. nuclear power
2. U.S. involvement in the politics of developing countries
3. professional athletes' salaries
4. eating meat
5. hunting

TOPIC:

For	Against

visual to accompany their speech. Encourage students to offer feedback after each presentation.

APPLY

WRITER'S CORNER

Encourage students to search materials in the classroom and the library for advertisements. When students have finished enhancing the advertisements, ask volunteers to share their work with the class. Ask students whether each advertisement appeals to logic or to emotion. Students should demonstrate an understanding of emotional and logical appeals.

ASSESS

Note which students had difficulty writing the parts of a persuasive piece. Use the Reteach option with those students who need additional reinforcement.

Practice Book page 163 provides additional work with the characteristics of an effective persuasive piece.

Practice Book page 163

Reteach

Choose a topic of interest to your school. Write three columns on the board with the following headings: *Position Statement, Facts,* and *Opinions.* Lead a discussion about the topic and ask students to write the points they mention under the appropriate headings. If students mention opposing position statements, then have the class choose one point of view. As a class write an introduction and body paragraph for the chosen point of view, using the information on the board.

Meeting Individual Needs

Visual Explain that advertisements are a common form of persuasion. Give small groups print advertisements that use persuasive language and images. Have students identify how the advertisement makes an emotional appeal and whether there are facts that support the position. Discuss whether the advertisements are effective and if so, why. Invite volunteers to share their advertisements with the class.

ACTIVITY D Read the following paragraphs from the conclusions of persuasive essays. Replace each of the italicized sentences with one or more powerful statements or questions that you think will lead the reader to agree with the writer.

1. Developing energy alternatives to those derived from fossil fuel makes sense financially, environmentally, and globally. *It's not too late to make a change.*

2. Lengthening the school day will disrupt extracurricular activities and increase the dangers facing students returning home at the end of each day. *These concerns are too great to ignore.*

ACTIVITY E Write two radio commercials to sell two of the items listed below. Remember to appeal to both the consumers' logic and emotions.

1. tickets to your band's rock concert
2. sandwiches for a team's fund-raising campaign
3. tickets for a school's neighborhood car wash
4. greeting cards made by your park district's photo club
5. your dog's six puppies
6. fruits and vegetables at your local farmer's market

ACTIVITY F Work with a partner. Choose a popular commercial that you have seen on television. Prepare a short speech to present to the class. Include the following:

- What product the commercial advertises
- How the commercial is presented
- How the commercial appeals to the logic of the viewer
- How the commercial appeals to the emotions of the viewer

WRITER'S CORNER

Work with a partner. Find two newspaper or magazine advertisements that appeal to both logic and emotion. Write two imperative sentences that would enhance the advertisements.

For Tomorrow

Ask students to create a list of topics about which they feel strongly. Point out that items on this list might make good topics for persuasive pieces. Also have students create a list of topics they would like to learn more about. Create similar lists of your own to share with the class.

Persuasive Writing • 417

OBJECTIVES
- **To use a tone that creates a specific mood in persuasive writing**
- **To tailor a specific voice or mood to the audience of a persuasive piece**

WARM-UP

Read, Listen, Speak

Create two columns on the board, one for topics that you feel strongly about and one for topics you would like to learn more about. Share your lists from yesterday's For Tomorrow homework. Briefly discuss each item you add to the list. Encourage students to share their lists. Discuss different points of view for each topic. Have students write in their notebooks the information on the board.

GRAMMAR CONNECTION

Take this opportunity to talk about restrictive and nonrestrictive clauses. You may wish to have students point out restrictive and nonrestrictive clauses in their Read, Listen, Speak examples.

TEACH

Invite a volunteer to read aloud the first two paragraphs and the list of moods in the Voice section. Read aloud the literature excerpt on page 412 and the student model on page 413. Discuss the mood of each piece.

Have a volunteer read aloud the paragraph that follows the list of moods. Ask volunteers to point out words in the literature excerpt and the student model that convey a particular mood.

Allow time for students to read silently the fourth paragraph and the paragraph about the Boys and Girls Club. Invite students to name words in the paragraph that help convey an enthusiastic mood (*exciting, enthusiastic, brimming, happy, possibilities, endless*).

PRACTICE

ACTIVITY A

Ask students to read the paragraph silently. Have students answer the questions in small groups. Explain that along with word choice, sentence style and punctuation can affect the mood of a piece of persuasive writing.

ACTIVITY B

Discuss words or phrases that create an angry mood. Then have students work independently to rewrite the paragraph. When they have finished, have them trade papers with partners. Ask students to decide whether the proper mood is effectively conveyed.

ACTIVITY C

Remind students that word choice is important when creating mood. Have students brainstorm words that portray a hopeful mood. List these on the board. Then have students complete the activity independently. Invite volunteers to read aloud their paragraphs.

Voice and Audience

Voice

The tone of voice in a persuasive essay sets the mood. The mood that is created can work to the writer's advantage and effectively convey a message to readers. If a writer isn't careful, however, the mood can annoy readers and perhaps even anger them.

Persuasive writers often use tone of voice to set one or more of the following moods in a piece:

uplifting	hopeful	enthusiastic
tense	concerned	warning
frank	confident	caring

To use a specific kind of voice to create a mood, writers carefully choose verbs, adjectives, and adverbs. These verbs, adjectives, and adverbs are vivid, have punch, and help bring out emotion in the reader.

The writer of this paragraph about the potential opening of a Boys and Girls Club used an upbeat and enthusiastic tone to encourage people to approve the club.

The prospect of opening a Boys and Girls Club in Riverglen is exciting for another reason. Kids get to develop important skills that they may not experience at school. Imagine a gym filled with enthusiastic volleyball players, gymnasts, and wrestlers; activity rooms brimming with happy, young people dancing, singing, building, and sewing; and a play yard alive with the sounds of jump ropes and bouncing basketballs. The possibilities for a child's personal growth are endless.

APPLY

WRITER'S CORNER

Allow students to search newspapers for a letter to the editor. Have students identify the mood and share the letter with a partner. Invite volunteers to read aloud their letters and identify the words that convey the mood. Students should demonstrate an understanding of mood in persuasive writing.

TechTip Discuss several popular magazines and newspapers. Encourage students to use these sites to find letters to the editor.

ASSESS

Note which students had difficulty understanding tone of voice and mood in persuasive writing. Use the Reteach option with those students who need additional reinforcement.

Activity A

Answers will vary. Possible answer: The mood is anger. The writer uses words such as "shameful crime" and "left out in the cold." The writer uses a rhetorical question to make an impression. The writer uses exclamation points.

ACTIVITY A A second writer wrote this paragraph about the opening of the Boys and Girls Club. How is the mood different from that of the first paragraph? What words, phrases, sentence style, and punctuation did each writer use to set the mood?

To deny the youth of Riverglen a Boys and Girls Club is a shameful crime! Where are kids supposed to go to develop important skills that they don't experience at school? Because so many schools have cut fine arts, applied arts, and athletics, many young people are left out in the cold. The boys and girls of Riverglen cannot and will not develop to their full potential unless something is done now!

ACTIVITY B Rewrite the following paragraph. Change the mood from angry to warning.

Anyone who does not think we should spend the money that our class has raised to go on a class trip to the art museum is just foolish and not thinking right. A trip to the art museum will make everybody happy and more familiar with art, which is certainly more important and valuable than the other ideas.

ACTIVITY C Rewrite the following paragraph. Change its mood from angry to hopeful.

One reason that I can't believe my parents won't let me have a sleepover is because I always do all my chores. Responsible kids should be rewarded. My parents are so unfair! Even when my brother ignores our chore chart, I still do what I'm supposed to. I take out the stinky trash, wash the filthy dog, and set the dinner table. This worker deserves a reward!

WRITER'S CORNER

Read a letter to the editor in your local newspaper. Identify the mood that is set, using the list on the preceding page. Write the words or phrases the writer uses to create the mood.

 With an adult, find letters to the editor responses online.

Read, Listen, Speak

Read your original letter from yesterday's For Tomorrow homework. Then read your rewritten letter with a new mood. Challenge students to identify the words or phrases that were added to convey the new mood. Then invite volunteers to share their letters. Encourage students to discuss whether the choice of words in each letter is appropriate for the mood the writer chose to convey.

GRAMMAR CONNECTION

Take this opportunity to talk about adverb clauses. You may wish to have students point out adverb clauses in their Read, Listen, Speak examples.

TEACH

Ask volunteers to read aloud the section Audience. Have students answer the questions. Ask a volunteer to explain why writing for a particular audience is so important when writing a persuasive piece. *(The purpose of the piece is to sway the reader toward the writer's opinion, so the tone and mood need to reach the reader and keep him or her interested.)*

Have students discuss how the tone of voice and mood might be different in two persuasive pieces about the dangers of heart disease if written for an audience of smokers and an audience of nonsmokers.

LiNK Read the excerpt aloud. Point out how the writer uses a caring mood based on the audience (the writer's mother). Discuss how the mood would

change if the audience was not as well-known to the writer. Challenge students to identify specific words that would be changed and to offer replacement words.

PRACTICE

ACTIVITY D

Ask students to work with partners to rewrite the paragraph. Invite volunteers to read aloud their paragraph. Encourage students to describe a particular audience they had in mind when rewriting the paragraph. Discuss what words or phrases were changed to convey a concerned mood.

ACTIVITY E

Have students complete this activity independently. Encourage them to write for a specific audience and to write a sentence that leaves a lasting impression with the reader. Ask volunteers to share their work.

ACTIVITY F

After students have written their introductions, ask them to trade papers with partners. Have partners determine whether each introduction includes an effective position statement and uses an appropriate tone of voice for the intended audience.

LiNK

I Wanna Iguana

Dear Mom,
I know you don't think I should have Mikey Gulligan's baby iguana when he moves, but here's why I should. If I don't take it, he goes to Stinky and Stinky's dog, Lurch, will eat it.
    You don't want that to happen, do you?
Signed,
    Your sensitive son, Alex

Karen Kaufman Orloff

Audience

A writer often chooses a particular voice or mood for a piece of writing depending on the audience. For example, a person who is trying to persuade the city council to provide money for a new park would probably use a different voice or tone from a person who is trying to persuade a group of neighbors to have a block party. Students who are trying to persuade their teachers to assign less homework would use a different tone from students who are trying to persuade their classmates to come to a pep rally.

To whom do you think the paragraphs about the Boys and Girls Club on pages 418 and 419 were addressed? Which tone do you think would work best with that particular audience?

What effect do you think the paragraph about the sleepover on page 419 had on its intended audience?

ACTIVITY D Rewrite the following paragraph. Change its mood from uplifting to concerned.

A recycling program at our school is needed for another reason. It would bring the students closer together and give us a sense of community. I just know that we can work for a common cause that bridges the gaps between all student groups at school, while at the same time reduces the amount of waste we create. Recycling is the perfect way to build a better environment, both in and out of school.

ACTIVITY E Read each position statement. Write one sentence that an active listener might argue if he or she disagreed with the statement.

1. Recycling is a waste of time and energy.
2. All students should attend college.
3. Eating three meals a day is important to your health.
4. Screaming will damage your vocal cords.
5. Drinking milk gives you strong bones.
6. Students should be required to attend physical education classes daily.

APPLY

WRITER'S CORNER

Encourage students to maintain a mood that is consistent with the position statement they wrote earlier by using similar adjectives, adverbs, and phrasing. Discuss possible moods and words that would help convey that mood. Tell students to choose an audience for their writing first. Students should demonstrate an understanding of mood and audience in persuasive writing.

Grammar in Action Students should identify the adverb clause *when the last tropical tree is cut down.* Challenge students to identify what this clause describes *(will be lost).*

ASSESS

Note which students had difficulty addressing an audience in persuasive writing. Use the Reteach option with those students who need additional reinforcement.

Practice Book page 164 provides additional work with voice and audience.

TEACHING OPTIONS

Reteach

Have students choose a topic for a persuasive piece and write a *Pro* column and a *Con* column for the topic. Tell students to write points from opposing opinions on the topic. When students have finished, ask them to note powerfully charged words and phrases in each column. Explain that these words and the emotions they evoke will provide language that students might use to persuade an audience.

Respecting Others

Discuss disrespectful techniques in persuasive writing such as name calling, personally attacking those who hold an opposite opinion, and using powerfully charged terms. Remind students that the most effective persuasive technique is a reasoned argument that shows respect for an audience and for opposing points of view. Invite students to reread the persuasive pieces they wrote and revise language that might be considered disrespectful.

ACTIVITY F Choose one of these topics and audiences. Select a voice or tone that you think would convince that audience. Then write an introduction to a persuasive essay. Use your selected topic, audience, and voice.

A. You are applying for a part-time job as a babysitter. Write the introduction of a persuasive letter of application. Give your qualifications and tell why you would be good for the job.

B. You are the editor of the school newspaper. Write the introduction for a persuasive editorial addressed to the school board. Give reasons why summer vacation should be eliminated.

C. You are a citizen who strongly believes that your community should have a recycling plan. Write the introduction for a letter to the mayor, explaining your position.

D. Your class is planning its eighth-grade party. Some students want to go horseback riding. Others want to go bowling. You don't like either activity. Write the introduction for a persuasive essay that explains why the class should choose your favorite activity.

E. Your class has been asked to help build the set and gather props for the third-grade play. Many of your classmates do not want to give up their time to help the third graders. Others feel that the third graders do not need any help. Write the introduction of a persuasive speech to be presented to your class. Give reasons why your classmates should be willing to help.

F. Your parents have given you a curfew a half hour earlier than your friends. They agreed to discuss the matter tomorrow night. Prepare by writing three reasons you believe your curfew should be extended. What voice would you use to persuade your parents?

G. You are running for class treasurer in the upcoming election. Your persuasive essay will be printed in the school paper with the other candidates' essays. Your classmates will vote based on the persuasive essays. Write your essay to convince your classmates that you are best candidate for the job.

WRITER'S CORNER

You are going to write a piece based on one of the position statements you wrote for Activity C on page 416. What mood will your piece convey? List some adjectives or adjective phrases that you will use to set the mood.

Grammar in Action Identify the adverb clause in the fourth paragraph in the student model on p. 413.

Persuasive Writing • 421

For Tomorrow

Have students study a topic for which they wrote a position statement for the Writer's Corner on page 415. Ask them to write one body paragraph for the topic. Remind students that their details should support the position statement and that they should maintain a consistent voice. Write a body paragraph of your own to share.

OBJECTIVES

- **To analyze advertisements**
- **To write different types of advertisements**

WARM-UP

Read, Listen, Speak

Read aloud your body paragraph from yesterday's For Tomorrow homework. Point out the details you included and discuss how they support the position statement. Discuss the language you used to keep a consistent tone and to establish a specific mood. Then have small groups share their paragraphs. Encourage students to offer one another feedback about the details and explain whether they support the position statement of each piece. Ask students to discuss each writer's use of facts and opinions in the supporting details.

GRAMMAR CONNECTION

Take this opportunity to talk about noun clauses used as subjects. You may wish to have students point out noun clauses used as subjects in their Read, Listen, Speak examples.

TEACH

Invite students to discuss their favorite advertisements and why the advertisements are appealing. Challenge students to explain how advertisements are a form of persuasive writing. *(They use facts, opinions, and persuasive language to convince an audience to do or to buy something.)* Ask a volunteer to read aloud the first two paragraphs. Discuss subtle advertising, such as product placement and naming rights for places and events *(U.S. Cellular Field in Chicago and the Tostitos Fiesta Bowl in Tempe, Arizona).*

Ask a volunteer to read aloud the first paragraph of the section Propaganda. Guide students to define what propaganda means *(words or devices used to urge people to act or think a certain way).* Have volunteers read aloud the descriptions of propaganda devices. After each device, ask students to discuss why each might be effective. Encourage students to name examples of each propaganda device they have encountered in advertisements.

Have volunteers read aloud the Analyzing Advertisements section and the checklist. Point out that using a checklist like this will help students think about and analyze advertisements. Encourage students to suggest additions to the checklist.

LiNK Read aloud the excerpt. Ask students what the advertisement is doing *(asking people to save food).* Challenge students to identify the propaganda device being used to persuade readers *(testimonial).*

Advertisements

The purpose of an advertisement is to persuade you to buy or do something. Drawing conclusions from and making decisions about advertisements is an important part of independent thinking.

Advertisements can be found almost everywhere. Sometimes advertisements can be obvious. Other times they can be subtle, such as placing a product in a movie or having the hero drive a certain car.

LiNK

LINCOLN said
"With malice toward none; with charity for all;...... let us strive on to finish the work we are in;---to bind up the nation's wounds;---- to do all which may achieve and cherish a just and lasting peace."

Save food
for world relief
UNITED STATES FOOD ADMINISTRATION

Propaganda

Following are specific propaganda devices that advertisers use to persuade their audience. Knowing about these devices can help consumers make wise decisions about advertisements.

Bandwagon—This device tells you to do something or buy something because many other people do it or buy it.

> **Everyone eats at Schemale's Pizza Parlor.**

Loaded words—This device uses words that will provoke an emotional response.

> **Governor Stanton's new fees are a burden on small businesses.**

Here the writer uses *burden* to describe the fees; however, the bill may be a small fee that small businesses could afford but do not want to pay.

Testimonial—This device uses the opinion of a well-known expert or celebrity. Many ads for sporting goods use testimonials.

> **Famous figure skater Shoshana Peebles says, "Mercury skates help me fly across the rink!"**

PRACTICE

ACTIVITY A

Review the different devices used in propaganda. Have students work with partners to complete this activity. When students have finished, ask them to present their answers and explain their reasoning to the class.

APPLY

WRITER'S CORNER

Have students work independently on this activity. Invite volunteers to display their advertisements and read their descriptions of the persuasive devices. Students should demonstrate an understanding of different types of advertisements.

ASSESS

Note which students had difficulty understanding how to analyze an advertisement. Use the Reteach option with those students who need additional reinforcement.

TEACHING OPTIONS

Reteach

Provide students with newspapers and magazines. Have students find an appealing advertisement. Ask them to present their ads to the rest of the class and explain why students like the advertisements. Have students use the checklist to analyze each advertisement. Lead students to discover that the analysis reinforces the reasons why the advertisement was appealing to the student who chose it.

Propaganda for Good Causes

Explain that *propaganda* is a word that has some negative connotations, but that propaganda can be used for positive reasons. Ask small groups to think of a good cause, such as a fund-raiser for a children's hospital. Challenge students to write dialogue for a television commercial advertising their cause. Tell students to use two of the four propaganda devices discussed in this lesson. Allow students to present their dialogue to the class.

Vague or sweeping generality—This device uses absolute words to describe a product or service in terms so broad that they can't possibly be proven wrong.

> **Herrmann's serves the best Polish sausage in the city!**

Analyzing Advertisements

Advertising is designed to appeal to the desires of its audience. For example, many older people want to be young or appear youthful. Pick up your favorite magazine and examine the ads inside. Pay close attention to the ads that try to create a youthful identity. They might create a perception of action or fun, or use mascots, slang, bright colors, or misleading visuals.

Use the Advertising Analysis Checklist to analyze ads.

Advertising Analysis Checklist

- ☐ Is the purpose of the writing to persuade or give information?
- ☐ What is the claim? Is the claim provable?
- ☐ What evidence is given, if any, to support the claim?
- ☐ Does just one person make the claim?
- ☐ Why is the claim being made?
- ☐ Who is making this statement? What are the qualifications of this person? Is he or she worthy of my attention?

Activity A

1. vague generality
2. vague generality
3. bandwagon and vague generality
4. loaded words
5. bandwagon
6. testimonial
7. loaded words
8. testimonial

ACTIVITY A Read each statement and identify the propaganda device or devices used.

1. Blast-O-Pod bubble gum is the best!
2. The Boomer baseball bat will help you hit the ball out of the park every time.
3. Nine out of ten dentists agree that Whitex toothpaste is effective in removing plaque from your teeth.
4. Senator Rose Dearborne is soft on crime!
5. Have a NutriBar, the snack loved by millions!
6. Where does stock car driver Miles Neff put his trust in motor oil? Under the hood of his car.
7. The Forest Bill will provide much-needed relief for our state's parks.
8. Pitcher Miguel Estrada says he never takes the mound without his Blanchard glove.

WRITER'S CORNER

Find an ad in a favorite magazine and analyze it, using the checklist. Write five sentences describing the persuasive devices used in the ad.

Persuasive Writing • 423

For Tomorrow

Ask students to find examples of each propaganda device in advertisements at home. Have students label each advertisement with the type of device used. Bring in examples of each propaganda device to share with the class.

WARM-UP

Read, Listen, Speak

Display your advertisements from yesterday's For Tomorrow homework. Discus how each is an example of a certain propaganda device. Invite volunteers to share their advertisements with the class. Have students identify the propaganda devices used in each advertisement. Discuss whether the advertisement is effective or not.

GRAMMAR CONNECTION

Take this opportunity to talk about noun clauses used as subject complements. You may wish to have students point out noun clauses used as subject complements in their Read, Listen, Speak examples.

TEACH

Invite a volunteer to read aloud the section Writing Advertisements. Ask students to name examples of advertising they have written.

Have volunteers read aloud the sections Sales Ads and Lost-and-Found Ads. Ask students where they might find or place these types of ads *(classified sections of newspapers or magazines, a flyer on a bulletin board, online auctions or message boards)*.

Ask a volunteer to read aloud the section Campaign Posters. Invite students to discuss where they have previously seen campaign posters or advertisements and whether the posters effectively represented the candidate running for office.

PRACTICE

ACTIVITY B

Have students work independently to complete this activity. Ask volunteers to answer each question from the checklist and discuss their responses.

ACTIVITY C

Review the checklist with the class. Discuss any additions to the checklist before students begin. Encourage students to choose one propaganda device for the activity. Have students complete this activity independently. Suggest that students use an object they actually own. Challenge students to write full descriptions of the item for sale and to be honest about any flaws in the item. Invite volunteers to read their ads to the class.

ACTIVITY D

Have students work with partners to complete this activity. Ask volunteers to share their lost-and-found ads with the class. Encourage students to name several places they might post their ads.

ACTIVITY E

Have students brainstorm designs and slogans for their campaign posters. When students have finished, ask volunteers to present their campaign posters to the class. Challenge students to name which propaganda device is used in each poster.

Writing Advertisements

Advertisements are a form of persuasive writing. For that reason knowing how to write an advertisement is just as important as knowing how to read one. It's also a useful skill to have if you want to place an ad on a bulletin board, in a newspaper, or online.

Any time you write a short statement trying to persuade someone to do something, you are probably writing an advertisement. For example, you might write notices for lost pets or other items, or campaign posters for student elections. Consider these suggestions when writing advertisements.

Sales Ads

Print and online sales ads need to have a clever, concise title; contain a clear description of the item; and use a persuasive tone of voice. Because online ads don't require any paper, you will probably have more space to describe your item than in a print ad. Take this opportunity to include a vivid description of the item, using what you discussed in Chapter 4. For online ads, you will probably want to provide a digital image of the item you want to sell.

Lost-and-Found Ads

Lost-and-found ads, like sales ads, need a concise and vivid description. If you can afford it, consider offering a reward for the lost item or pet. Few words can be more persuasive than *reward offered.*

Campaign Posters

Campaign posters need an eye-catching visual, such as the slogan of the candidate or graphics that bring the candidate to life on the poster. Use your imagination to think of clever slogans that help people remember the candidate's name. It's not necessary to provide details for why people should vote for your candidate. The candidate should do that in speeches and debates. The posters are there to generate positive associations with the candidate's name. If possible, the candidate's photo should appear on larger posters.

ACTIVITY F

Review the different propaganda techniques. Then have partners complete the activity. Invite volunteers to share their advertisements with the class. Have students suggest improvements for the advertisements.

APPLY

WRITER'S CORNER

Allow partners time to discuss their advertisements. Invite each pair to pick one advertisement to present to the class. Have the author of the advertisement present what he or she wrote and have the other student discuss his or her analysis of the advertisement. Students should demonstrate an understanding of different types of advertisements.

ASSESS

Note which students had difficulty writing an advertisement. Use the Reteach option with those students who need additional reinforcement.

Practice Book page 165 provides additional work with advertisements.

ACTIVITY B Use the checklist on page 423 to analyze the following ad. Examine the claims made by the ad and tell if they are credible.

Hey, kids! Come on over to the hip place to be—the Green Zone Game Palace. We've got all the hot video games, like Quester, Maw, Firelight, and the award-winning Yonk! Our prizes are the best in town! And that's not all! When you get hungry, just stop at our mouth-watering pizza bar and grab a slice that's loaded with all your favorite toppings! Everybody's in the Green Zone, so why aren't you?

ACTIVITY C Write an online sales ad. The object should be something that someone would want to own after you've owned it, such as a bike, a tennis racket, or a violin.

ACTIVITY D Write a lost-and-found ad for a lost pet. Be sure to include a vivid description and the name of the pet. If possible, design a handbill for your ad and include a picture of the pet.

ACTIVITY E Design a campaign poster for yourself for student body president. The poster should include some version of your name and a slogan by which you want your candidacy to be remembered.

ACTIVITY F Work with a partner. Write an advertisement of your choice, using some of the propaganda techniques described on pages 422–423: bandwagon, loaded words, testimonial, and vague or sweeping generality. Read aloud your advertisement and challenge your classmates to identify each technique you used.

WRITER'S CORNER

Work with a partner and analyze the ad you wrote in Activity C. Use the checklist on page 423 to guide your discussion.

Persuasive Writing • 425

OBJECTIVE
- **To use transition words and phrases to connect ideas and increase reading comprehension**

WARM-UP
Read, Listen, Speak
Read aloud your lost-and-found advertisement from yesterday's For Tomorrow homework. Point out persuasive language that you included in your advertisement. Then have small groups share their lost-and-found ads. Have students discuss why an ad was effective or how an ad could be improved to be more effective.

GRAMMAR CONNECTION
Take this opportunity to talk about noun clauses used as appositives. You may wish to have students point out noun clauses used as appositives in their Read, Listen, Speak examples.

TEACH

Invite volunteers to read aloud the first paragraph and the example transition words and phrases that follow. Point out the relationship each transition word or phrase establishes. Invite volunteers to suggest example sentences using the transition words and phrases from the lists.

Review the plot of any fairy tale. Help students write a brief summary of the fairy tale without using any transition words or phrases. Read aloud the summary. Then challenge students to add transition words or phrases. Discuss how the transition words and phrases help writing flow and make the writing easier to understand.

PRACTICE

ACTIVITY A
Allow time for students to write their lists and to share them with a partner. Invite volunteers to write on the board one word or phrase from their lists. Tell students to add to their own lists any words or phrases from the board.

ACTIVITY B
Provide an example sentence for each relationship group. Then have students complete the activity independently. Ask volunteers to read aloud their sentences. Ask other volunteers to identify the transition word or phrase in each sentence.

ACTIVITY C
Tell students to determine the relationship between the two ideas in each sentence before choosing a transition word or phrase. Then have students complete the activity independently. After students have finished, ask them to compare their answers with partners and decide whether the correct answer was chosen.

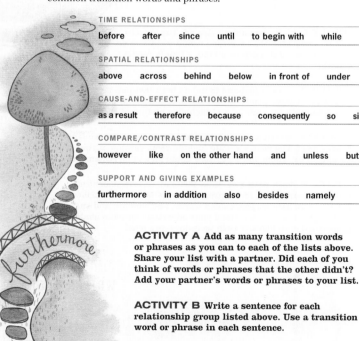

LESSON **4**   WRITING SKILLS

Transition Words

Effective writers use transition words or phrases to connect one idea to the next. These connections help writing flow and make it easier to understand. They show relationships between ideas. Here are some common transition words and phrases.

TIME RELATIONSHIPS

before	after	since	until	to begin with	while

SPATIAL RELATIONSHIPS

above	across	behind	below	in front of	under

CAUSE-AND-EFFECT RELATIONSHIPS

as a result	therefore	because	consequently	so	since

COMPARE/CONTRAST RELATIONSHIPS

however	like	on the other hand	and	unless	but

SUPPORT AND GIVING EXAMPLES

furthermore	in addition	also	besides	namely

ACTIVITY A Add as many transition words or phrases as you can to each of the lists above. Share your list with a partner. Did each of you think of words or phrases that the other didn't? Add your partner's words or phrases to your list.

ACTIVITY B Write a sentence for each relationship group listed above. Use a transition word or phrase in each sentence.

426 • Chapter 6

ACTIVITY D

Encourage students to use the lists on page 426 to determine what type of relationship each sentence should have. Ask students to complete this activity independently. Have volunteers share their sentences with the class. Discuss whether each sentence flows coherently.

APPLY

WRITER'S CORNER

Remind students to use not only the words and phrases from the lists on page 426, but also any words or phrases students added to the lists when completing Activity A. When students have finished their paragraphs, invite volunteers to read their work aloud. Discuss whether or not transition words are used correctly. Students should demonstrate an understanding of transition words.

ASSESS

Note which students had difficulty identifying transition words or phrases. Use the Reteach option with those students who need additional reinforcement.

TEACHING OPTIONS

Reteach

Secretly assign each of five groups one of the transition-word categories on page 426. Invite each group to write a story by having each student write one sentence, building on the sentence before it. Tell students that each sentence must have at least one of the words or phrases from the group's assigned word list. When students have finished, ask a volunteer from each group to read aloud the entire story. After students have shared their stories, ask volunteers to decide which transition-word category was used.

Healthy Cartoons

Discuss healthy habits such as daily exercise or eating plenty of fruits and vegetables. Invite students to use transition words and phrases as they compose cartoon panels that promote a healthy habit. Encourage students to explain their finished cartoons. Ask volunteers to name the transition words and phrases used in the cartoons.

ACTIVITY C Choose the correct transition word or phrase in parentheses to complete each sentence.

1. Our nation's energy grids used to be sufficient. With today's needs, (<u>however</u> unlike), they are not.

2. All students should respect their teachers, (since <u>yet</u>) many do not.

3. Families spend less money when children wear school uniforms. (<u>Furthermore</u> Unlike), children are less likely to compare themselves to others based on looks.

4. (While <u>Therefore</u>), our town council should allow local businesses to host live entertainment on weekends.

5. Our students deserve an all-school dance (<u>because</u> as a result) we have shown respect and maturity throughout the year.

ACTIVITY D Complete each sentence so that the ending fits the italicized transition word.

1. Treating local sewers helps control the mosquito population, *so* _____.

2. *Although* our lakes and rivers are not polluted, _____.

3. We did not go to the movie *until* _____.

4. Auto accidents among teens will rise *unless* _____.

5. Flooding is nearly out of control *across* _____.

6. *In addition* to needing the money, I have to get a summer job _____.

7. I want a new computer *so* _____.

8. *Furthermore*, I want to practice at the batting cages _____.

9. Books about pollution are easily available, *therefore* _____.

10. Going to the theater can be fun *since* _____.

11. Famous leaders of our nation are quoted *as a result* _____.

12. On the plains of Africa, elephants roam freely *but* _____.

WRITER'S CORNER

Work with a partner. Choose a relationship group from the chart on page 426. Write a persuasive paragraph, using three of the words from your chosen group.

Persuasive Writing • 427

For Tomorrow

Ask students to write a one-page letter about a real or an imaginary visit to an amusement park and to circle all the transition words or phrases in their letters. Write a letter of your own and circle all the transition words or phrases.

WARM-UP

Read, Listen, Speak

Read aloud your letter from yesterday's For Tomorrow homework. Ask students to raise their hands every time they hear a transition word or phrase. Then have small groups share their letters. Encourage volunteers to identify the transition words and phrases students used and to say whether revisions are necessary to improve the clarity of the letters. Ask each group to choose a letter to read aloud.

GRAMMAR CONNECTION

Take this opportunity to talk about noun clauses used as direct objects. You may wish to have students point out noun clauses used as direct objects in their Read, Listen, Speak examples.

TEACH

Review the transition words and phrases on page 426. Ask how the use of transition words or phrases changes a piece of writing *(improves the flow and coherence of a piece).*

Discuss correct punctuation when using transition words and phrases. Point out that commas should set off transition words that signal a distinct break in thought in a sentence but can be omitted if there is no real break. Write these examples on the board:

My sister, unlike me, likes playing sports and always wants to win.

Their research has consequently been challenged by other doctors.

Explain that some transition words, such as *however, therefore,* and *accordingly,* should be preceded by a semicolon when used between clauses of a compound sentence. Invite a volunteer to define a compound sentence. Write on the board the following example:

Zaiga says she hopes to go to Europe this summer; however, she has made no definite plans.

Ask volunteers to write other examples on the board.

PRACTICE

ACTIVITY E

Complete the first paragraph with the class. Then have students revise the remaining paragraphs independently. Encourage students to pay special attention to their use of punctuation. When they have finished, ask students to trade papers with a partner and provide feedback about whether the transition words or phrases were used effectively and with the correct punctuation.

ACTIVITY F

Review propaganda devices that appeal to emotions. Have students complete this activity independently. Invite volunteers to read their sentences aloud. Challenge students to identify the relationship between the ideas in their sentences.

ACTIVITY E Revise the following paragraphs. Use transition words or phrases to connect the ideas and make the paragraphs flow.

1. Students need more time to exercise or visit with friends. They need to relax and refresh their minds and bodies. They will go back to class relaxed and ready to work. They will be better prepared to think and learn. Recess should be extended from 15 to 20 minutes.

2. It's not difficult to set up an aquarium. Place the aquarium on a sturdy stand. Put the underwater filter on the bottom. Cover the filter with 2 or 3 inches of gravel. Make the gravel slope from the back of the aquarium to the front. Install the heater. Add some rocks to cover the heater and make the aquarium look natural. Carefully pour in the water. Plant some plants to provide hiding places. Add your fish. Enjoy many entertaining hours watching them.

3. Swimming and hiking are both good forms of exercise. Swimming benefits your whole body. Hiking mainly exercises your legs. A body of water is necessary for swimming. Hiking requires a pair of good shoes or boots. Hiking can be done in any weather. Swimming outdoors is possible only when the weather is nice. Both swimming and hiking can be done alone. Both sports are more fun when enjoyed with friends.

Austrian commemorative stamp of Franz Ferdinand

4. Driving a car with an automatic transmission is not that difficult. Look around the car for any obstructions. Step into the car. Adjust the seat and mirrors to see clearly around you. Insert the key into the ignition. Start the car. Release the emergency brake. Put the car into Drive or Reverse. Depress the accelerator lightly. Always look in the direction the car is moving. Be aware of your surroundings at all times.

5. World War I had many causes. The Great Powers of Europe formed alliances to protect one another. Archduke Franz Ferdinand was assassinated on June 28, 1914, in Sarajevo, Bosnia. Austria-Hungary blamed Serbia for the assassination and declared war on Serbia. Russia helped Serbia. Germany declared war on Russia and France. German troops invaded France through Belgium. Great Britain declared war on Germany.

Front page of a newspaper showing the assassination of Archduke Franz Ferdinand

ACTIVITY G

Remind students that they should determine the relationship between the two ideas before writing the preceding sentence. Have students complete this activity independently. When students have finished, tell them to exchange papers with partners and to check their work for correct punctuation. Encourage volunteers to read aloud their sentences.

APPLY

WRITER'S CORNER

Have students read their revision to a partner. Ask partners to assess the use of transition words and phrases. Students should demonstrate an understanding of using transition words in persuasive writing.

ASSESS

Note which students had difficulty using transition words and phrases with correct punctuation. Use the Reteach option with those students who need additional reinforcement.

Practice Book page 166 provides additional work with transition words.

Reteach

Remove the transition words and phrases from a piece of persuasive writing. Give students a copy of the piece with the transition words and phrases removed. Help students fill in the missing transition words and phrases. Encourage students to use the context of the sentences to choose appropriate transition words and phrases.

English-Language Learners

Have students begin a reference chart with transition words and phrases for persuasive writing in both English and in students' primary languages. Help students develop mnemonic devices for remembering transition words and phrases. For example, in Spanish, one way to say something is similar to something else is with the words *igual que.* Point out that *igual* is nearly identical to the English word *equal,* which is a synonym for *like.* Encourage students to note other mnemonic devices that will help them remember the meanings of transition words and phrases in English.

ACTIVITY F Write a persuasive sentence about each topic, using emotional appeal. Use the transition word or phrase in parentheses.

1. filling potholes on local streets (before)
2. allowing a class field trip to a museum (after)
3. eliminating soft drinks in school vending machines (unless)
4. hiring a full-time art teacher for school (to begin with)
5. ending poaching of animals in Africa (consequently)
6. convincing parents to raise your allowance (so)
7. convincing a teacher to raise a grade (unlike)
8. reducing water usage in the home (on the other hand)
9. recycling (as a result)
10. reinstating a school's music program (because)

ACTIVITY G The following sentences each contain a transition word or phrase. Write a sentence that you think could have come before each one.

1. While the milk was warming up, I chopped the chocolate.
2. As a result, I had to remove my muddy shoes.
3. We could not wash until the plumber was finished.
4. Furthermore, I think big cars are hard to park.
5. On the other hand, I like to ski in the winter.
6. Behind the counter, a clerk was refolding shirts.
7. In addition, the soldier was honored at the assembly.
8. Because we were excited, we decided to celebrate early.
9. Since the temperature was too high, the ice was not frozen.
10. While the dog was barking, the owner asked me to call the police.
11. However, she was still able to drive confidently.
12. Therefore, the campers were able to fall asleep.

WRITER'S CORNER

Reread a persuasive piece that you've written. Consider each paragraph. Are there any sentences that need to be connected with transition words or phrases? Revise your writing by adding them.

Persuasive Writing • 429

For Tomorrow

Have students write a persuasive paragraph using a comparison/contrast relationship. Write your own persuasive paragraph with the same relationship.

OBJECTIVES

- To understand how suffixes are added to words to make new words
- To build vocabulary by learning new words with suffixes

WARM-UP

Read, Listen, Speak

Read aloud your persuasive paragraph from yesterday's For Tomorrow homework. Point out the comparison/contrast transition words and phrases. Discuss how these words and phrases create a relationship between things. Then have small groups share their persuasive paragraphs. Have students read aloud their paragraphs without the transition words and phrases. Ask students to discuss how transition words and phrases help relate ideas more clearly.

GRAMMAR CONNECTION

Take this opportunity to talk about noun clauses used as objects of prepositions. You may wish to have students point out noun clauses used as object of prepositions in their Read, Listen, Speak examples.

TEACH

Remind students of the lessons about roots and prefixes. (See pages 274 and 392.) Review the definitions of each and ask students to provide examples of roots and prefixes. Tell students that they will learn about another important part of many words. Have a volunteer read aloud the first two paragraphs. Point out that, like a prefix, a suffix is a syllable or syllables added to a base word.

Invite students to read silently the third paragraph and the charts Verb Suffixes and Noun Suffixes. Challenge volunteers

to use example words from the charts in sentences and to write them on the board. Ask students to read silently the charts Adjective Suffixes and Adverb Suffix. Have volunteers write on the board sentences that use some of the example words in those charts. Then offer additional base words and challenge students to add suffixes to the words to make new words. Answer any questions about how to form new words by using suffixes.

LiNK Read the excerpt aloud. Point out the suffix *-ly* in the word *nobly*. Tell students this suffix changes an adjective, *noble*, into an adverb.

PRACTICE

ACTIVITY A

After students have finished this activity, challenge them to form yet another word by adding a different suffix to the example words in each sentence. Invite students to share the new words.

ACTIVITY B

Have students complete this activity independently. Instruct students to write what they think is the definition of the underlined word before using a dictionary to find the actual definition. When students have finished, ask

---

LESSON **5** WORD STUDY

Suffixes

LiNK

Gettysburg Address

The world will little note nor long remember what we say here, but it can never forget what they did here. It is for us the living rather to be dedicated here to the unfinished work which they who fought here have thus far so nobly advanced.

Abraham Lincoln

A suffix is a syllable or syllables added to the end of a word to change its meaning or to make another word. The word to which the suffix is added is called the base word.

Suffixes can be added to base words to change their parts of speech. When you write, be sure to use the correct suffix for each base word. Remember that the suffix can change the meaning of a word and that the wrong suffix can send the wrong message.

Study the suffix charts. Notice how a suffix can change a word's part of speech. Look for base words that change their spelling when a suffix is added.

VERB SUFFIXES

Suffix	Base Word	Example
-ize	legal	legalize
-ate	necessity	necessitate
-ify	identity	identify
-en	deep	deepen

NOUN SUFFIXES

Suffix	Base Word	Example
-or	act	actor
-er	teach	teacher
-ity	responsible	responsibility
-ment	agree	agreement
-ance	appear	appearance
-ness	happy	happiness

430 • Chapter 6

volunteers to identify the words with suffixes and their meanings.

ACTIVITY C
Have students complete this activity with partners. Invite volunteers to write these words on the board. Discuss any unfamiliar words.

APPLY

WRITER'S CORNER
Allow time for students to write their sentences. Challenge students to include words with suffixes in their sentences. Invite

volunteers to read aloud their sentences. Ask students to identify the words with suffixes and the infinitive phrases. Students should demonstrate an understanding of suffixes and infinitive phrases.

ASSESS

Note which students had difficulty identifying suffixes and using them to form new words. Use the Reteach option with those students who need additional reinforcement.

TEACHING OPTIONS

Reteach
Write on note cards the suffixes in the charts on pages 430 and 431, one suffix per card. Distribute the cards to partners. Have them look through books or magazines to find five nouns, verbs, adjectives, or adverbs that have the suffix shown on their note card. Ask one student from each pair to write on the board the five words. Discuss the meanings of the words, as well as the meanings of the base words to which the suffixes were added.

English-Language Learners
Have partners use a dictionary to see how the example words in the charts on pages 430 and 431 are divided into syllables. Have students take turns pronouncing each word syllable by syllable and then saying the whole word. Remind students that recognizing suffixes can help their vocabulary.

ADJECTIVE SUFFIXES

Suffix	Base Word	Example
-ful	care	careful
-less	help	helpless
-y	thirst	thirsty
-able	enjoy	enjoyable

ADVERB SUFFIX

Suffix	Base Word	Example
-ly	quick	quickly

ACTIVITY A Use an example from each chart in a separate sentence. Underline the suffixes. Trade your paper with a partner. Tell the meaning of each word with an underlined suffix.

ACTIVITY B Identify the words that contain suffixes in the following paragraph. Then give a definition for each word.

One reason that my math teacher deserves the Teacher of the Year Award is because she takes her job seriously and she treats us very kindly. She is helpful when explaining new concepts and selfless in giving her time. My math teacher makes algebra more than tolerable—she makes it interesting and fun.

ACTIVITY C Brainstorm additional base words and examples for each suffix in the suffix charts. Then choose one suffix and make a list of as many example words as you can with that suffix. Discuss the meaning of each word on your list with a partner.

WRITER'S CORNER
Write five sentences that use words with suffixes. Include at least two infinitive phrases. Underline the words with suffixes.

Persuasive Writing • 431

For Tomorrow
Ask students to search a favorite book or magazine for at least 10 words with suffixes. Ask students to write the suffixes and words on a sheet of paper and then write another word that uses each suffix they found. Create a list of your own to share with the class.

WARM-UP
Read, Listen, Speak
Write on the board your list of words containing suffixes from yesterday's For Tomorrow homework. Point out the suffix in each word and discuss how the suffix affects the meaning of the word. Then have students share their lists in small groups. Encourage students to discuss the meaning of each word and how the suffix changes it.

GRAMMAR CONNECTION
Take this opportunity to talk about simple, compound, and complex sentences. You may wish to have students point out simple, compound, and complex sentences in their Read, Listen, Speak examples.

TEACH
Review the information about suffixes on pages 430 and 431. Invite students to search the student model on page 413 for words with suffixes. Ask students to identify the base word of each. Challenge volunteers to choose a base word and to make two new words from it by adding different suffixes *(happy, happily, happier)*.

PRACTICE
ACTIVITY D
Have a volunteer read aloud the first entry of the chart. Then have partners complete the remainder of the chart. Encourage students to include more than two example words for each suffix. Write on the board the incomplete chart. When students have finished, invite volunteers to write their answers in the chart on the board. Discuss each answer with the class.

ACTIVITY E
Have students complete this activity independently. Invite volunteers to read aloud their completed sentences. Discuss each answer and any discrepancies students may have.

ACTIVITY F
Review the different types of suffixes. Complete the first word by modeling different suffixes that can be added *(socialize, socially)*. Have students complete this activity independently. Then invite volunteers to write their sentences on the board. Ask students to identify the word containing a suffix and to determine whether the word was used correctly.

ACTIVITY G
Tell students to determine if the word in each sentence should be a noun, a verb, an adjective, or an adverb. Point out that once they have done this, students should then use the charts on pages 430 and 431 to find the appropriate suffix. Have students complete this activity independently. When they have finished, discuss students' answers.

ACTIVITY D Complete a chart like the one below by writing the word, its meaning, and other words that end with the same suffix. Use the example to get started. Use a dictionary if you need help with spelling.

SUFFIX	BASE WORD	NEW WORD	MEANING	OTHER WORDS
-ize	real	realize	to come to understand	dramatize emphasize
-er	bake			
-ful	neglect			
-ly	quiet			
-ate	motive			
-hood	neighbor			
-less	friend			
-able	comfort			
-y	hand			
-ance	attend			

ACTIVITY E Complete each sentence with a word from the chart in Activity D.

1. That teacher is able to _____ her students to do well.
2. It's important to wear _____ shoes while jogging.
3. My uncle is so _____ that he can fix anything.
4. If you weren't so _____, you wouldn't lose things.
5. Please walk _____ so you won't wake the baby.
6. We are organizing a block party in my _____ for the Fourth of July.
7. Most people do not _____ how physically challenging dance class really is.
8. The teacher took _____ to determine who was missing from our class.
9. The _____ vigorously kneaded the dough.
10. He cared for the child who was alone and _____.

Activity E
1. motivate
2. comfortable
3. handy
4. neglectful
5. quietly
6. neighborhood
7. realize
8. attendance
9. baker
10. friendless

APPLY

WRITER'S CORNER

Read aloud a paragraph from a selection the class is currently reading. Point out any words that contain suffixes. Then have students do the same with a page from a novel of their choosing. Invite volunteers to write on the board the words they found that contain suffixes. Discuss the meaning and part of speech of each word. Challenge students to change the suffix to create a word that has a different function. Students should demonstrate an understanding of suffixes and noun clauses.

ASSESS

Note which students had difficulty forming new words with suffixes. Use the Reteach option with those students who need additional reinforcement.

Practice Book page 167 provides additional work with suffixes.

Practice Book page 167

Reteach

Have students make a word web for one or more of the suffixes in the lesson. Tell students to write the suffix in the center of the web. Then have them write in small ovals radiating from the center examples of words that end with that suffix. Invite students to display their word webs on a bulletin board and to continue adding new words to their maps.

Tic-Tac-Toe with Suffixes

Have students choose a partner and play tick-tack-toe with suffixes. Draw a game grid on the board and write one suffix in each box. Before students can write an *X* or an *O* in a box, they must provide three words that end with the suffix shown in the box.

ACTIVITY F Add an appropriate suffix to each word. Then give the meaning of the new word and use it in a sentence.

1. social
2. father
3. sad
4. drive
5. rely
6. profess
7. greed
8. time
9. wonder
10. enlighten
11. slow
12. grace

Activity G
1. coldness
2. enjoyment
3. motherly
4. whiten
5. harmless
6. sincerity
7. careful
8. cloudy
9. falsity or falsehood
10. bendable
11. helpful
12. kindly
13. messy
14. useful
15. slowly
16. treatment
17. doubtful
18. brightens

ACTIVITY G Add the correct suffix to the word in parentheses to complete each sentence.

1. The (cold) of the lake makes swimming unpleasant.
2. We all felt the winner's (enjoy).
3. The boy's older sister acted very (mother) toward him.
4. Will that toothpaste (white) your teeth?
5. That (harm) old dog won't hurt you.
6. The (sincere) of the speaker helped convince everyone.
7. Please be (care) when you take the bread out of the oven.
8. I hope it's not (cloud) on the day of our picnic.
9. The fact that she told a (false) shocked us all.
10. You need some (bend) wire to form the ornaments.
11. It is (help) to label each file.
12. The woman (kind) helped my mother.
13. That room is (mess) and disorganized.
14. You will not find the review session (use) unless you study.
15. We approached the car (slow).
16. He went to the hospital to receive (treat).
17. It is (doubt) that she will be on time.
18. When the sun comes out, it always (bright) my day.

WRITER'S CORNER

Choose a page in a novel. Find all the suffixes on the page and write them. Also, find two noun clauses and write them.

For Tomorrow

Ask students to write a brief review of a favorite book, persuading others to read it. Encourage students to use at least 10 words with suffixes in their review. Write your own book review using suffixes to share with the class.

Persuasive Writing • 433

OBJECTIVES

- **To understand how to compose a persuasive speech**
- **To evaluate a persuasive speech**

WARM-UP

Read, Listen, Speak

Read aloud your book review from yesterday's For Tomorrow homework. Have students identify words that contain suffixes. Then challenge students to identify the persuasive techniques used in your writing. Have small groups share their reviews. Ask students to identify the words in one another's reviews that have suffixes. Encourage students to discuss whether the reviews persuade an audience to read the books and how the reviews could be more persuasive.

GRAMMAR CONNECTION

Take this opportunity to review kinds of sentences. You may wish to have students point out kinds of sentences in their Read, Listen, Speak examples.

TEACH

Ask a volunteer to read aloud the first two paragraphs. Emphasize that listeners are more easily persuaded if the content of a speech is factual. Ask students to name examples of logical and emotional appeals that could be used in an argument.

Have volunteers read aloud the section Taking a Position on a Topic. Invite students to suggest problems in their community that could be addressed. Challenge volunteers to offer position statements for each topic.

Ask volunteers to read aloud the Audience section. Guide students to answer the questions. Point out that the audience determines how formal or informal the tone is and the best logic and facts to use.

Have volunteers read aloud the section Introduction, Body, and Conclusion. Explain that one effective emotional appeal is to use a moving story that illustrates the problem. Emphasize the importance of stating the position right away and supporting the position with reasons and research. Ask a volunteer to read aloud the section Visuals and Gestures. Explain

that gestures can be used like visual punctuation. Ask students to suggest photos that might be useful in a speech about pets on leashes.

PRACTICE

ACTIVITY A

Allow students to write their note cards individually and to present their speeches to partners. Then have partners compare the note cards they wrote from the essay. Encourage students to discuss what they did and did not choose to write on the note cards and why.

Persuasive Speeches

One of the most important reasons that speeches are made is to persuade an audience. In fact, it's no exaggeration to say that persuasive speeches have sometimes changed the course of history. Think of the impact of Martin Luther King Jr.'s "I Have a Dream" speech or Franklin Roosevelt's fireside chats.

What these speeches have in common is that they persuaded people to change the way something had been done in the past. They pointed out a problem and persuaded their audience to adopt the speaker's solution. These speeches made appeals to logic and emotion, and they supported their positions with factual evidence. Here are some guidelines to help you prepare a speech that advocates change.

Taking a Position on a Topic

To plan a speech that advocates change, first identify a problem and create a position statement that proposes a possible solution.

> **Problem: Some public school students cannot play sports because they cannot afford the extra fees.**
>
> **Position Statement (Solution): Extra fees to play sports should be eliminated for public school students.**

To choose a topic, brainstorm problems that you have encountered and select one problem from the list. Form a position statement by proposing a solution.

Like the self-help talk you gave in Chapter 5, a persuasive speech needs facts to support the position. Whether you use the Internet or other sources, it is important to research the position you take.

Audience

Keep your audience in mind when you plan your speech and use a tone that will appeal to it. Speeches that propose change need to discuss the problem in terms that are familiar to the audience.

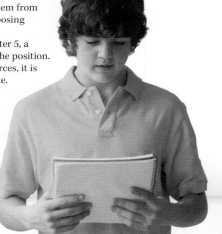

APPLY

SPEAKER'S CORNER

After students have finished, encourage them to discuss their position statements with partners. Challenge students to suggest new ideas and approaches for their partners' position statement. Students should demonstrate an understanding of topics and position statements for persuasive speeches.

TechTip Have students review classmates' position statements on the class blog. Tell students to offer feedback for each

statement. Then allow time for students to revise their position statements based on classmates' suggestions.

ASSESS

Note which students had difficulty developing a topic or position statement for a persuasive speech. Use the Reteach option with those students who need additional reinforcement.

TEACHING OPTIONS

Reteach

Ask students to name something they would like to receive as a birthday present. Challenge students to write a position statement and a short paragraph using logic, emotion, and facts to convince someone to purchase that specific gift. Explain that for a persuasive speech, the problem and the audience may vary, but the planning procedure is the same.

Flip Side

Challenge students to take the position statement they wrote for the Speaker's Corner and write a position statement for the other side of the argument with supporting reasons and explanations. After students have finished, have them discuss how seeing the other side of an argument might help them write a better persuasive speech.

For Tomorrow

Have students interview a family member about an important persuasive speech the family member remembers hearing or giving. Ask students to take notes. Encourage students to ask questions about the speaker's gestures and memorable lines. Interview a family member or colleague, asking similar questions.

Think about these questions when you plan your speech:

- What do my listeners know about this problem?
- What do they wish they knew?
- How can they become involved in the solution?

Imagine you are proposing that all pets should be leashed. Consider what parents might think about the problem. How might such a speech differ if you were speaking to your fellow students? How might it differ if you were speaking to people who don't own pets?

Introduction, Body, and Conclusion

The introduction of a persuasive speech should include a position statement that tells exactly where you stand on the issue.

The body of your speech should include both practical and persuasive reasons to agree with your position. As you offer explanations of your reasons, use strong opinion words that appeal to logic and emotion. Arrange your ideas in a logical order that creates a strong impression on the audience.

End your speech by rephrasing your position statement and giving your listeners a sense of closure. Ask your listeners to think about or act upon what you've said.

Visuals and Gestures

Think about sharing a visual, such as a thought-provoking photograph or a graphic that includes relevant statistics. Make eye contact with your audience. Consider using gestures such as nodding or shaking your head, or moving your hands to make important points.

ACTIVITY A Reread the essay on page 413 and turn it into a persuasive speech. Make note cards for your position statement, reasons and explanations, and conclusion. Ask a classmate to listen to you present your speech.

SPEAKER'S CORNER

Choose a topic for a persuasive speech to present to your class. Write a position statement and make notes that give supporting reasons and explanations.

 Tech Tip Post your statement on your class blog for peer review.

Persuasive Writing • 435

WARM-UP

Read, Listen, Speak

Share some of the important information from your interview from yesterday's For Tomorrow homework. List this information on the board. Then invite volunteers to write on the board important details they discovered through their interviews. Discuss these details. Point out how important and moving good persuasive speeches can be when emotion plays a prominent role.

TEACH

Invite a volunteer to read aloud the Practice section. Point out that a persuasive speech is a personal appeal to an audience and that it is important to take the opportunity to practice eye contact and to experiment with different gestures and inflections.

Ask a volunteer to read aloud the Listening Tips section. Discuss why it is important to recognize the difference between fact and opinion when listening to a persuasive speech. *(It allows the listener to evaluate the evidence and reasons given in the speech. It prevents the listener from being overly influenced by emotional opinion statements.)* Emphasize that students can disagree with the speaker's position but still recognize it as an effective argument and the speech as well-delivered.

PRACTICE

ACTIVITY B

Have students work in small groups to complete this activity. Invite each group to give a position statement for a few of the topics. Encourage students to explain the specific problems that were identified. Challenge students to write position statements for two opposing arguments.

ACTIVITY C

Ask students to work in the same small groups as in Activity B to develop reasons for their position statements. Have students share some of their reasons with the class. Challenge volunteers to name some counterarguments.

ACTIVITY D

Complete a similar chart on the board as a class. Then have students complete the activity independently. Ask volunteers to present their position statement along with the arguments for both sides.

Practice

The more you prepare and practice, the more comfortable you'll feel on the day of your speech. Have your note cards ready. Obtain or prepare any visuals you plan to use. When everything is ready, practice in front of a mirror or a friend or family member. As you practice, ask yourself the following questions:

- Does my introduction clearly state my position on the topic?
- Do I present both practical and emotional reasons?
- Are my reasons supported by relevant facts?
- Does my visual support my position, helping bring out favorable feelings or thoughts from the audience?
- Do I speak with emotion or emphasis so listeners believe me?
- Do I end so the audience will agree and feel a need to act?

Listening Tips

Follow these guidelines when listening to a persuasive speech:

- Listen carefully to the speaker's reasons for his or her position. Ask yourself: *Do I agree with this?*
- Listen for persuasive language. Are the speaker's emotional appeals effective? Use your own knowledge and common sense when deciding whether or not to agree with the speaker.
- Save your questions for after the speech.
- Evaluate the persuasiveness of the speech no matter your opinion. Limit your feedback to the appeals that the speaker used to persuade the audience.

ACTIVITY B Read each broad topic and determine a specific problem that relates to it. Write each problem as a complete sentence. Then develop and write a position statement that offers a solution for each problem.

1. airport security
2. the cost of auto insurance
3. genetically engineered food
4. oil drilling
5. being healthy
6. taxes
7. seatbelt laws
8. illiteracy
9. speed limits
10. women in "men's" sports
11. the space program
12. global warming

APPLY

SPEAKER'S CORNER
Encourage students to use the Listening Tips when listening to their classmates' speeches. Ask students to evaluate the speeches, using the questions at the top of page 436. Students should demonstrate an understanding of how to evaluate persuasive speeches.

ASSESS

Note which students had difficulty delivering a persuasive speech. Use the Reteach option with those students who need additional reinforcement.

After you have reviewed Lessons 3–5, administer the Writing Skills Assessment on pages 65–66 in the **Assessment Book.** This test is also available on the optional **Test Generator CD.**

TEACHING OPTIONS

Reteach
Have students take one of the position statements they have written in this lesson and develop three different ways to deliver the same words and ideas. Suggest students think about different ways to emphasize the words in the position statement. Encourage students to add different gestures to each delivery. Explain that students should make notes on the statement, underlining words they want to emphasize and noting where to use gestures. Allow students time to practice their three forms of delivery with partners. Ask students to explain which delivery they like best and why.

Talking Editorials
Provide students with editorial sections from newspapers. Have students work in groups to turn a letter to the editor into a persuasive speech, even if they disagree with the position of the letter. Tell students to develop a position statement and three reasons to use in their speech, adding reasons if the letter does not provide three. Have students make note cards. Then ask a volunteer from each group to deliver the speech to the class.

ACTIVITY C Select four position statements you wrote for Activity B. For each position statement, write three reasons to agree with it. For each reason write an explanation. Record each set of ideas on note cards.

ACTIVITY D On a sheet of paper, copy the following chart, filling in a position statement that you wrote in Activity B (but not Activity C) and three reasons that support it. Under the column *Disagree*, write three reasons that an active listener might think of to disagree with the position statement.

POSITION STATEMENT:

_____

Agree	Disagree
1. _____	1. _____
2. _____	2. _____
3. _____	3. _____

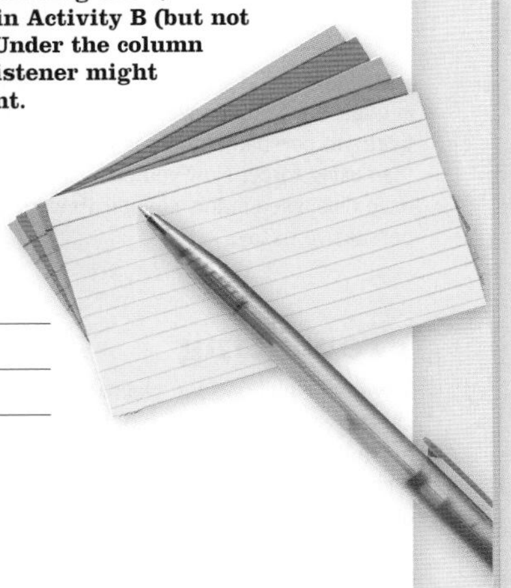

I disagree because . . .

SPEAKER'S CORNER
Present your persuasive speech, following the guidelines in this lesson. Remember that you want to convince your listeners to agree with you, so make sure your reasons and explanations are clear.

Persuasive Writing • 437

OBJECTIVE
- **To prewrite and plan a persuasive essay**

PREWRITING AND DRAFTING

Read aloud the opening paragraph. Encourage students to name the characteristics of persuasive writing and to provide specific examples of those characteristics from the writing they have done in this chapter. During the discussion, be sure to mention the following characteristics and writing skills:

- A position statement in the introduction
- A body that has an effective balance of facts and credible opinions
- Language, word choice, and tone of voice that address a specific audience
- Propaganda techniques that appeal to logic and emotion
- Transition words and phrases that help the writing flow

Prewriting

Have a volunteer read aloud this section. Ask why it is important to determine the audience and the appropriate tone of voice during prewriting. *(It provides a focus during the prewriting and drafting stages so the writer knows what facts and opinions to use.)*

Choosing a Topic

Invite a volunteer to read aloud this section. Remind students that emotional appeals in a persuasive piece can be very effective and that this is why a writer should feel strongly about the topic he or she chooses. Point out that if an emotional appeal is used incorrectly, it could make the writer's position less effective.

Explain that ideas are the foundation of all types of writing. Tell students that ideas supported with strong facts and credible opinions will help persuade their audience.

Writing for an Audience

Discuss Maya's persuasion rake. Then have a volunteer read aloud the first paragraph of this section. Discuss what tone of voice would be best suited for this topic. Then read aloud the second paragraph. Ask students why a reasonable and fair tone of voice would be effective for Maya's essay. *(Being reasonable and fair is one way for Maya to establish credibility and gain the respect of her adult audience.)*

Explain that voice creates the mood of a persuasive essay. Remind students that mood can help convey a message or could turn readers away from a message.

Your Turn

Ask a volunteer to read aloud this section. Allow time for students to brainstorm topics. When

---

Writer's Workshop   Persuasive Writing

Prewriting and Drafting

Have you ever heard the expression "The pen is mightier than the sword"? It means that using words to persuade others is more effective than using force. Now you can use what you have discussed in this chapter to write a persuasive essay.

Prewriting

Maya, an eighth grader, wants to enter an essay contest sponsored by her local city council. The prewriting stage for her persuasive essay was a time for brainstorming, choosing a topic, and planning the piece. She also thought about the audience for her essay and the right tone that would appeal to it.

Choosing a Topic

Maya brainstormed a list of possible topic ideas for her persuasive essay. When choosing a topic,

Ideas Maya wanted to identify an issue about which she felt strongly. She knew that the more passionately she feels about an issue, the better and more persuasive her writing will be.

After brainstorming a list of possible topics, she settled on persuading the Grandview city council to build a new community center. After deciding her position, she wrote her position statement at the top of a graphic organizer called a persuasion rake. Then she put her persuasive reasons on the rake as shown.

Writing for an Audience

Voice The position statement of a persuasive essay should be written with the audience in mind. What tone of voice is most likely to convince the Grandview city council to adopt Maya's position on the community center? Should the piece encourage or warn? Should the tone be upbeat or pessimistic?

Maya decided that a reasonable and fair tone of voice would be most effective for her essay.

Your Turn

Brainstorm a list of at least five issues about which you have strong feelings one way or another. Choose one topic and identify the audience you would address about that topic. Use a persuasion rake to map your reasons. Write a strong position statement that clearly shows which side of the issue you are on and sets the tone of voice you will use in a persuasive essay.

students have finished, ask them to share their topics with partners and discuss whether each topic is appropriate. Have students identify the audience and tone of voice for their pieces and then write their position statements. Invite volunteers to share their work. Encourage students to provide feedback.

Planning a Persuasive Essay

Ask a volunteer to read aloud this section. Allow time for students to read silently Maya's plan. Ask if Maya's reasons clearly support her position statement and if her reasons and explanations are likely to persuade her audience.

Tell students that organization is how a persuasive piece is structured. Tell them to follow Maya's plan when prewriting.

Your Turn

Have a volunteer read aloud this section. Allow time for students to plan their essays. Remind students to provide an explanation with every reason. Invite students to share their work with the class.

TEACHING OPTIONS

A Little Research Never Hurts

Tell students that persuasive writing sometimes requires background research. Explain that convincing factual evidence can always help prove a writer's point of view. Allow time for students to conduct research in the library or online. Review Internet safety tips. (See page 385.) Remind students to use books that have been published recently or Web sites that are reliable and have been updated recently. Explain that sometimes a writer's research can harm rather than help his or her writing if the information later proves to be false or outdated.

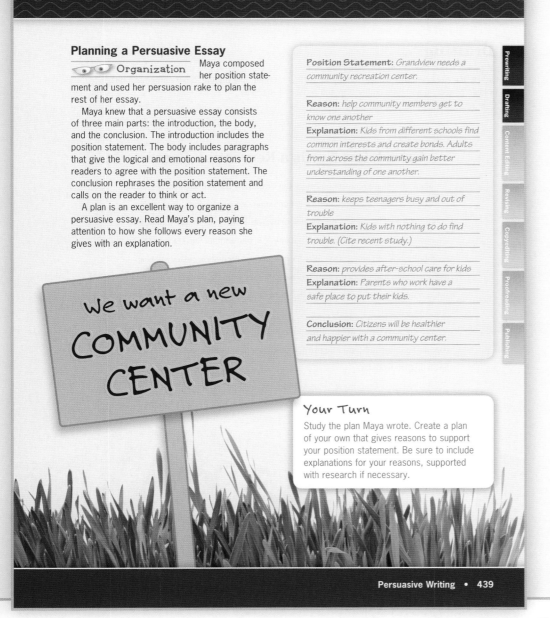

Planning a Persuasive Essay

Organization Maya composed her position statement and used her persuasion rake to plan the rest of her essay.

Maya knew that a persuasive essay consists of three main parts: the introduction, the body, and the conclusion. The introduction includes the position statement. The body includes paragraphs that give the logical and emotional reasons for readers to agree with the position statement. The conclusion rephrases the position statement and calls on the reader to think or act.

A plan is an excellent way to organize a persuasive essay. Read Maya's plan, paying attention to how she follows every reason she gives with an explanation.

We want a new COMMUNITY CENTER

Position Statement: *Grandview needs a community recreation center.*

Reason: *help community members get to know one another*
Explanation: *Kids from different schools find common interests and create bonds. Adults from across the community gain better understanding of one another.*

Reason: *keeps teenagers busy and out of trouble*
Explanation: *Kids with nothing to do find trouble. (Cite recent study.)*

Reason: *provides after-school care for kids*
Explanation: *Parents who work have a safe place to put their kids.*

Conclusion: *Citizens will be healthier and happier with a community center.*

Prewriting · Drafting · Content Editing · Revising · Copyediting · Proofreading · Publishing

Your Turn

Study the plan Maya wrote. Create a plan of your own that gives reasons to support your position statement. Be sure to include explanations for your reasons, supported with research if necessary.

Persuasive Writing • 439

Writer's Workshop   Persuasive Writing

Drafting

Invite a volunteer to read aloud the opening paragraph. Tell students that having a well-organized plan before drafting will make the drafting stage move more quickly and easily. Allow time for students to read silently Maya's draft. Ask them how Maya organized the reasons from her plan and whether they flow smoothly.

Supporting Opinions with Reasons

Ask a volunteer to read aloud the first paragraph. Discuss the opinion and reasons given and which reason is the least convincing. *("Swimming cools you off on hot days" is the least convincing reason because many things cool a person off on hot days, and this reason is not as important as the other reasons.)*

Invite a volunteer to read aloud the second and third paragraphs. Emphasize that students should use emotional and logical appeals in their writing. Remind students that they should also close their papers by rephrasing their position statements.

Ask students to work with a partner to read each other's plans, concentrating on the reasons each student gave for his or her opinion. If students think their reasons could be improved, allow time for students to add reasons or revise the original reasons.

Your Turn

Have a volunteer read aloud this section. Allow time for students to write their drafts, using pencil and paper or a computer. Encourage students to revise their plans if necessary and to use language tailored to their audiences.

Drafting

Maya knew that she had to give valid reasons for asking the city council to allocate money for such a huge project. Maya reviewed her plan and wrote a first draft, adding information and details as she went. She organized her paragraphs based on her plan.

Grandview Needs a Recreation Center

Many cities have recreation centers, but Grandview doesn't. Maybe it needs one.

Children from different schools will find common interests and create lasting bonds. As a result, there will be less school rivalrie. in addition, adults from across the community will gain a better understanding of one another and see how their neighborhoods and families are alike. Furthermore, a recreation center will keep teenagers busy and out of trouble. Recent studies show that most dangerous and riskful teenage behavior occurs between the time school is out and when parents get home from work.

A recreation center would provide after-school care for children of working parents. Parents will have a safe place to send their first through sixth graders as they finish up their workday.

As I've stated, Grandview needs a community recreation center. Citizens will be healthier and happier and Grandview will be an even better place for both adults and children.

Tell students that word choice is especially important in persuasive writing. Explain that students' word choice will help create a mood that can either enhance or distract from their position. Remind students to choose every word in their essay carefully.

Writer's Tip Tell students they need to keep their readers' interest to persuade their readers successfully. Remind students that this can be achieved by using simple, compound, and complex sentences.

Consulting Work

Encourage students to consult published persuasive pieces on their topics. Ask students to note the opinions and reasons the writer used and how he or she addressed the audience. Suggest that students also note reasons or opinions they had not thought of and whether they can address these reasons in their own drafts. Explain that students cannot copy exact text from a published piece because that is plagiarism. Tell students that they can use the information to think of additional opinions and reasons of their own.

Meeting Individual Needs

Extra Support Explain that one of the most important aspects of writing a persuasive essay is having a confident and knowledgeable writing voice. Discuss why this is important. *(Writing with confidence and knowledge is more likely to persuade an audience.)* Remind students that thoroughly researching their topic, considering opposing points of view, and being prepared to disprove rebuttals are several ways to show confidence and knowledge.

Supporting Opinions with Reasons

Opinions by themselves are not very convincing. To persuade others, writers must give solid reasons to back up their opinions. Read the following opinion and reasons. Which reason is the least convincing to you? Why?

Opinion: Everyone who is able should know how to swim.
Reason: Swimming is good exercise.
Reason: Swimming cools you off on hot days.
Reason: Swimming could save your life.

As you write your draft, be sure that you give your readers good reasons for agreeing with you. One way to do this is to list all the reasons that support your opinion and then choose the ones that will be most convincing to your audience.

Look at Maya's first draft. It starts with her position statement. The body gives reasons for wanting a recreation center, which appeal to both logic and emotion. Maya closes her speech by rephrasing her position statement.

Prewriting · **Drafting** · **Content Editing** · **Revising** · **Copyediting** · **Proofreading** · **Publishing**

Your Turn
Follow your plan as you write your draft. Keep in mind that you will probably rewrite your paper several times. Double-space between lines to make room for revisions.

Word Choice Keep your audience in mind as you write. Be sure your writing uses strong opinion words.

Writer's Tip Be sure to vary sentence length and style so that your writing remains interesting to your reader.

Persuasive Writing • 441

OBJECTIVE
- **To edit a first draft for content**

CONTENT EDITING

Ask students to recall what a content editor does *(edits a draft for overall sense and tone—the logic, order, and clarity of the writing)*. Invite a volunteer to read aloud the first paragraph. Ask why Ty was a good choice for an editing partner. *(Ty is a member of Maya's audience because he lives in Grandview. If her essay appeals to him, then it might appeal to other people in the community.)*

Ask students to read silently the second paragraph and the Content Editor's Checklist. Challenge students to discuss the following:

- How does this list differ from the Content Editor's Checklists in other chapters?
- Why are the checklists different?
- What might you add to this checklist?

Read aloud the last two paragraphs. Then have a volunteer read aloud Ty's comments on page 443. Point out that Ty gave positive, constructive feedback. Ask volunteers to match Ty's comments with points on the Content Editor's Checklist. Have volunteers offer additional suggestions for improving Maya's draft. *(Her position statement could be stronger.)* Ask a volunteer to read aloud the paragraph after Ty's comments.

Editor's Workshop
Persuasive Writing

Content Editing

Maya read over her first draft. She thought it was a good persuasive essay, but she knew that its ideas could be improved. She asked Ty, a fellow eighth grader who also lived in Grandview, to edit her draft. She wanted him to edit the essay to make sure her appeals to logic and emotion were reasonable, her essay was organized in logical order, and her ideas were clearly expressed.

Ty used the following Content Editor's checklist to edit Maya's draft.

Ty read Maya's draft a few times and checked it against the Content Editor's checklist. Then he and Maya had a conference.

First, Ty told Maya about the things that he liked. Ty thought the writing was very convincing, especially because her reasons appealed to both logic and emotion.

Content Editor's Checklist

- ☐ Does the introduction tell the position statement?
- ☐ Does each paragraph of the body give a reason for agreeing with the position statement?
- ☐ Are the reasons supported by clear and convincing explanations?
- ☐ Does the conclusion rephrase the position statement?
- ☐ Does the conclusion ask the reader to think or act?
- ☐ Does the essay use a confident, persuasive voice?
- ☐ Is the tone of the essay appropriate for the audience?

442

Your Turn

Ask a volunteer to read aloud this section. Allow time for students to read their partners' drafts and to provide feedback. Encourage students to comment on each item in the Content Editor's Checklist and to be specific in their suggestions for improvement. Remind students that their feedback should be positive and constructive.

However, there were some things in her piece that could be improved. Here are Ty's comments.

- The second paragraph doesn't tell how a recreation center relates to the recent studies. I think you should end the paragraph by linking its two main ideas.
- Some cities are thinking about having their recreation centers open all night to keep teenagers off the streets. Maybe you could mention this idea.
- Your conclusion restates your position statement but doesn't challenge the reader to think or act. Consider adding something to your conclusion.
- The essay is very confident and persuasive. You strongly believe Grandview should have a community center.
- The tone was reasonable and fair. A city council would take this essay seriously.

Maya thought that Ty's ideas were good ones, so she made most of the changes he suggested. She decided not to add his idea about the all-night center because she thought it was too controversial. She saw that Ty missed the first item of the checklist that asked about the position statement. She added a stronger position statement in the introduction.

Your Turn

Look for ways to improve your first draft by asking yourself these questions:

- Does the introduction clearly state your position?
- Does the body give good reasons that are supported by convincing explanations?
- Does the conclusion both restate your position and challenge the reader to think or act?

Trade drafts with a classmate. Read your classmate's draft several times and go over the Content Editor's Checklist. Give your honest opinion of how you think the piece could be improved and comment on the strong points too.

(Vertical tab labels: Prewriting, Drafting, Content Editing, Revising, Copyediting, Proofreading, Publishing)

Audience Editors

Have students ask a member of their potential audience to offer suggestions for revisions to students' drafts. Remind students that if they want their pieces to persuade their audience, then they should know if any parts are unclear, confusing, or potentially offensive. Invite volunteers to identify people to ask to read students' drafts. Have students write a checklist to give to that person. Suggest that students copy the checklist from page 442 and add points that are specific to their topics.

Avoiding Plagiarism

Explain that when students content edit their drafts, they should be on the alert for plagiarism. Remind students that plagiarism is quoting from a person or source without giving credit to the person or source. Tell students that facts or information that quote or closely paraphrase another's work or use another's original ideas must be credited. Tell students that one way to avoid plagiarism is to use quotation marks when writing facts from any source and to include the title of the source in the quotation.

OBJECTIVE

- **To revise the draft of a persuasive essay**

REVISING

Have students discuss their experience with revisions on previous writing projects. Ask students to describe the changes that they made to improve their work.

Read aloud the opening paragraph. Then have students silently read Maya's revised draft. Have students comment on the revisions Maya made. Point out that Maya used double-spacing

when writing her draft and clearly marked her revisions between the lines. Remind students to write neatly when marking revisions.

Ask a volunteer to read aloud the questions on page 445. Discuss the following revisions:

- Maya strengthened her position statement by clarifying the importance of the recreation center to the city.
- She linked the two ideas in the third paragraph by adding a sentence.
- Maya strengthened the conclusion by adding two sentences and directly asking the city council to act.

Remind students that a writer does not have to accept all the edits suggested by a content editor, but should at least consider them. Encourage students to read aloud their drafts while inserting revisions. Explain that sometimes revisions affect the tone of voice and organization of a piece and that the writer might not immediately recognize this.

Have a volunteer read aloud the last paragraph. Then read aloud the list of transition words and phrases. Encourage students to write these in their notebooks.

Writer's Workshop
Persuasive Writing

Revising

Revising is the time for Maya to choose which edits she wants to put in her essay. This includes the changes Ty suggested as well as those that she wants to make.

Grandview Needs a Recreation Center

Let me explain why I believe Grandview needs a recreation center. *Grandview is now a good place to live. A recreation center would make it a great place to live.* ~~Many cities have recreation centers, but Grandview doesn't. Maybe it needs one.~~ To begin with, a recreation center will help community members get to know one another. Children from different schools will find common interests and create lasting

bonds. As a result, there will be less school rivalrie. in addition, adults from across

the community will gain a better understanding of one another and see how their

neighborhoods and families are alike. Furthermore, a recreation center will keep

teenagers busy and out of trouble. Recent studies show that most dangerous and

riskful teenage behavior occurs between the time school is out and when parents get

home from work. *A recreation center would fill that void and give teenagers a healthy place to spend time.*

A recreation center would provide after-school care for children of working

parents. Parents will have a safe place to send their first through sixth graders as they

finish up their workday.

As I've stated, Grandview needs a community recreation center. Citizens will

be healthier and happier and Grandview will be an even better place for both

adults and children. *Please vote for it, plan for it, and build it. You'll be glad you did.*

Grammar in Action. Remind students that important details are essential to strong persuasive writing. Tell students to incorporate adjective and adverb phrases into their writing. Point out that doing so will also vary sentence structure and add interest to their writing.

Your Turn

Have a volunteer read aloud this section. Allow time for students to revise their drafts. Encourage students to meet again with their editing partners to review the revisions each student made. Suggest that partners clarify suggestions that were made if necessary.

Revision Practice

If students have difficulty revising their writing, you might hold individual writing conferences. Focus on one or two skills for the student to practice. Discuss suggestions to improve the student's draft. Have students work at a computer if possible. Make a copy of any piece of writing. Demonstrate how to cut and paste text and strike through words. Stress the experimental nature of revising and encourage students to try different words and sentence arrangements.

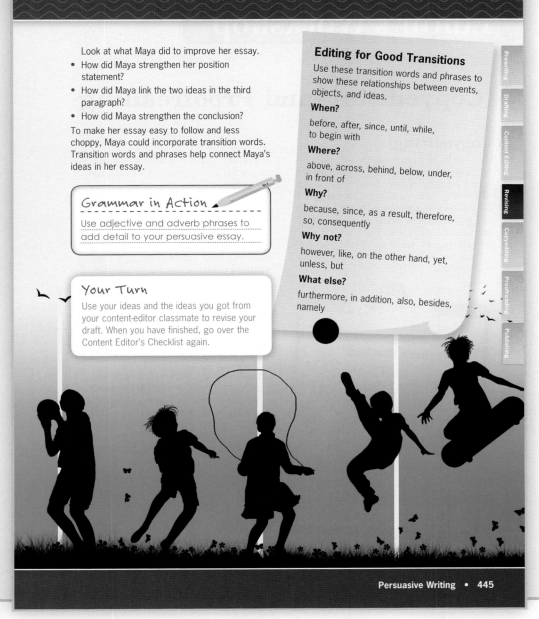

Look at what Maya did to improve her essay.
- How did Maya strengthen her position statement?
- How did Maya link the two ideas in the third paragraph?
- How did Maya strengthen the conclusion?

To make her essay easy to follow and less choppy, Maya could incorporate transition words. Transition words and phrases help connect Maya's ideas in her essay.

Grammar in Action

Use adjective and adverb phrases to add detail to your persuasive essay.

Your Turn

Use your ideas and the ideas you got from your content-editor classmate to revise your draft. When you have finished, go over the Content Editor's Checklist again.

Editing for Good Transitions

Use these transition words and phrases to show these relationships between events, objects, and ideas.

When?
before, after, since, until, while, to begin with

Where?
above, across, behind, below, under, in front of

Why?
because, since, as a result, therefore, so, consequently

Why not?
however, like, on the other hand, yet, unless, but

What else?
furthermore, in addition, also, besides, namely

Prewriting / Drafting / Content Editing / Revising / Copyediting / Proofreading / Publishing

Persuasive Writing • 445

OBJECTIVE
- To copyedit and proofread the draft of a persuasive essay

COPYEDITING AND PROOFREADING

Copyediting

Have volunteers read aloud the first paragraph. Explain that students should be especially careful when copyediting a persuasive piece. Tell students that word choice affects the tone of voice that a writer incorporates to persuade his or her audience. Ask students to discuss the differences between copyediting and content editing. *(Content editing focuses on ideas, logic, and clarity.*

Copyediting is concerned with sentence structure, word choice, and grammar.)

Have students silently read the Copyeditor's Checklist. Remind them about the lessons on suffixes and on transition words and phrases. Ask students to pay special attention to words with suffixes and to transition words and phrases when copyediting.

Ask a volunteer to read aloud the last three paragraphs. Encourage students to point out in Maya's draft where she made revisions while copyediting. Invite students to copyedit Maya's draft themselves and to suggest additional revisions.

Remind students that sentence fluency is the sound of their writing. Suggest that students always read their writing aloud to hear where the writing might sound choppy or awkward.

Your Turn

Have a volunteer read aloud this section. Ask students to copyedit their drafts and to ask themselves the questions on the checklist. When students have finished, invite volunteers to share the changes they made and how they improved the logic, word choice, and sentence structure of their drafts. Encourage partners to trade drafts and to use the

---

Copyediting and Proofreading

Copyediting

Maya revised her essay, using her own and Ty's suggestions. When she felt certain that her reasons and explanations were logical and clear, she was ready to begin copyediting her persuasive essay. Maya wanted to edit her essay for overall logic, word choice, and sentence structure. She also read her essay to make sure she used transition words and phrases properly.

Maya used the following Copyeditor's Checklist to edit her draft.

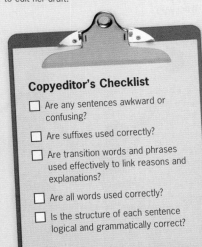

Copyeditor's Checklist

☐ Are any sentences awkward or confusing?

☐ Are suffixes used correctly?

☐ Are transition words and phrases used effectively to link reasons and explanations?

☐ Are all words used correctly?

☐ Is the structure of each sentence logical and grammatically correct?

Maya knew that she would submit her essay to members of the city council for the essay contest. She wanted her essay to be as good as she could make it.

When Maya read her essay aloud, she noticed that she jumped into the second paragraph too quickly. She added a sentence to her second paragraph to make a smoother transition from one paragraph to another.

Sentence Fluency

Maya also saw that the fourth paragraph needed a transition. She added another sentence that made the third and fourth paragraphs less choppy.

Your Turn

Look over your revised draft. Be sure that you've used transition words and phrases to help your writing flow. One way to do this is to ask yourself the questions *when, where, why* or *why not,* and *what else,* as you get to each new idea or topic. This will help you check that the ideas are correctly connected to one another.

Proofreading

Have a volunteer read aloud the first paragraph. Remind students of the importance of having a fresh pair of eyes proofread their drafts.

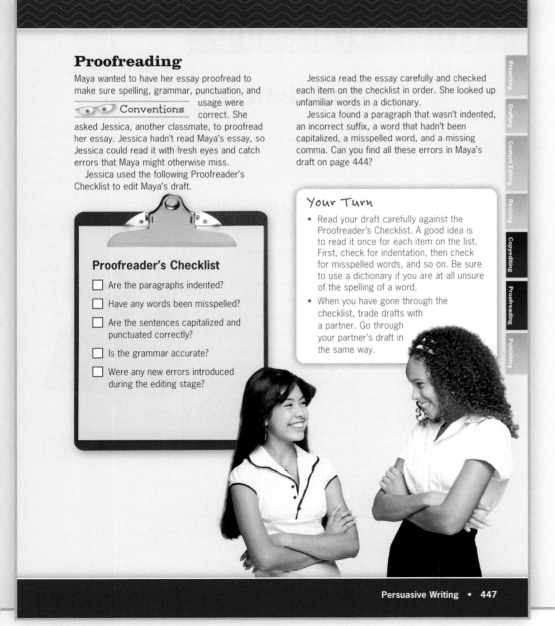 Be sure students understand that conventions include spelling, punctuation, and capitalization of a piece of writing. Emphasize the importance of proofreading drafts to find and correct these types of errors.

Invite students to read silently the second paragraph, the Proofreader's Checklist, and the two paragraphs that follow. Encourage volunteers to find where Maya corrected her draft after reviewing Jessica's corrections.

Your Turn

Ask a volunteer to read aloud this section. Allow time for students to proofread their own drafts and then to proofread a partner's draft. Have students work with a different partner when proofreading. Remind students to be sure not to introduce new errors when copyediting and proofreading their drafts.

Copyeditor's Checklist to copyedit the drafts.

TEACHING OPTIONS

Review Proofreading Marks

Have students write proofreading marks on note cards, one mark per card. (See page 526.) Then write on the board sentences with one error in each. Have students read each sentence, locate the error, and hold up the card with the mark they would use to correct the error. Choose a student who is holding up the correct card to go to the board and correct the error in the sentence.

Proofreading

Maya wanted to have her essay proofread to make sure spelling, grammar, punctuation, and **Conventions** usage were correct. She asked Jessica, another classmate, to proofread her essay. Jessica hadn't read Maya's essay, so Jessica could read it with fresh eyes and catch errors that Maya might otherwise miss.

Jessica used the following Proofreader's Checklist to edit Maya's draft.

Jessica read the essay carefully and checked each item on the checklist in order. She looked up unfamiliar words in a dictionary.

Jessica found a paragraph that wasn't indented, an incorrect suffix, a word that hadn't been capitalized, a misspelled word, and a missing comma. Can you find all these errors in Maya's draft on page 444?

Proofreader's Checklist

- ☐ Are the paragraphs indented?
- ☐ Have any words been misspelled?
- ☐ Are the sentences capitalized and punctuated correctly?
- ☐ Is the grammar accurate?
- ☐ Were any new errors introduced during the editing stage?

Your Turn

- Read your draft carefully against the Proofreader's Checklist. A good idea is to read it once for each item on the list. First, check for indentation, then check for misspelled words, and so on. Be sure to use a dictionary if you are at all unsure of the spelling of a word.

- When you have gone through the checklist, trade drafts with a partner. Go through your partner's draft in the same way.

Prewriting · Drafting · Content Editing · Revising · Copyediting · Proofreading · Publishing

Persuasive Writing • 447

OBJECTIVE
- To publish a persuasive essay

PUBLISHING

Ask students what publishing a persuasive essay might mean. *(It could mean preparing a clean final version and submitting it to an audience that students wish to persuade, presenting the article orally, or using the article as a basis for a debate.)*

Invite volunteers to read aloud the first sentence and Maya's finished draft. Encourage students to look back at Maya's drafts to see the changes she made. Encourage students to point out the changes Maya made. Discuss if these changes improved her draft. Have students suggest any other improvements for Maya's essay.

Read aloud the next two paragraphs and the ways students can publish their persuasive essays. Discuss each option and ask students to decide how they would like to publish their essays. Invite a volunteer to read aloud the final paragraph.

Your Turn

Have volunteers read aloud this section. Allow time for students to use the five points to check their drafts one more time before publishing. Then ask students to type or write their final essays.

Writer's Workshop   Persuasive Writing

Publishing

Maya corrected the errors Jessica found and printed out her finished draft.

Grandview Needs a Recreation Center

Let me explain why I believe Grandview needs a recreation center. Grandview is now a good place to live. A recreation center would make it a great place to live.

To begin with, a recreation center will help community members get to know one another. Children from different schools will find common interests and create lasting bonds. As a result, there will be less school rivalry. In addition, adults from across the community will gain a better understanding of one another and see how their neighborhoods and families are alike.

Furthermore, a recreation center will keep teenagers busy and out of trouble. Recent studies show that most dangerous and risky teenage behavior occurs between the time school is out and when parents get home from work. A recreation center would fill that void and give teenagers a healthy place to spend time.

Besides, a recreation center would provide after-school care for children with working parents. Parents will have a safe place to send their first through sixth graders as they finish up their workday.

As I've stated, Grandview needs a community recreation center. Citizens will be healthier and happier, and Grandview will be an even better place for both adults and children. Please vote for it, plan for it, and build it. You'll be glad that you did!

Explain that presentation has to do with the overall appearance of students' final drafts. Encourage students to use a final format that enhances the overall impression of the piece. If using paper and pencil, encourage students to double-space and to make sure their writing is legible.

ASSESS

Have students assess their finished persuasive essay using the reproducible Student Self-Assessment on page 449y. A separate Persuasive Writing Scoring Rubric can be found on page 449z for you to use to evaluate their work.

Plan to spend tomorrow doing a formal assessment. Administer the Persuasive Writing Prompt on **Assessment Book** pages 67–68.

Maya edited her persuasive piece again, making it even better. When she felt that her piece was ready, she printed it out. She was now ready to submit it to the contest.

There are many ways you can publish your persuasive essay.

Make a classroom newsletter. Share your ideas with others. Refine your argument by publishing your ideas for your peers to review and even disagree with. Disagreement will help you understand the opposition you hope to persuade.

Post your essay on a bulletin board or class blog for feedback. Your classmates may have additional experiences or views that will strengthen your argument.

Send your essay to the editor of your local newspaper. If your persuasive essay is something of local importance, be heard! Often it takes practice before a letter to the editor is finally published, so don't get discouraged. Read the letters of others, and keep trying.

Whenever you publish your work, your goal is to share your thoughts and experiences with other people.

Your Turn

Persuasive writing often takes the form of a letter to the editor, a magazine article, or a newspaper editorial.

Presentation

Once a piece is sent to a newspaper or magazine, it can't be taken back. If it is poorly written or full of mistakes, the editor of the magazine or newspaper will probably reject it.

You may not be sending your essay in for publication, but you will be submitting it to your teacher. Be sure that you are happy with your writing before you publish it by turning it in.

To publish, follow these steps:

1. Make sure your position statement clearly tells where you stand on the issue.
2. Make sure each reason that supports your position statement is backed up by a solid, convincing explanation.
3. Check to see that you have made appeals to both logic and emotion.
4. Use your neatest handwriting or a computer to make a finished copy of your revised draft.
5. Proofread your essay one more time for correct spelling, grammar, capitalization, and punctuation. If you can, use your computer's spell-checker.

Prewriting · Drafting · Content Editing · Revising · Copyediting · Proofreading · Publishing

Grandview Needs a Recreation Center

Persuasive Writing • 449

Name _____ Date _____

Persuasive Writing

Ideas	YES	NO
Do I focus on one viewpoint about a specific topic?		
Does the essay work to convince the reader to share my viewpoint?		

Organization		
Does the introduction include a position statement?		
Does the body include supporting details with credible facts and opinions?		
Does the conclusion rephrase the position statement?		

Voice		
Is the voice persuasive?		
Is the voice confident and credible?		

Word Choice		
Do I use specific words that establish the mood?		
Do I use language tailored to a specific audience?		
Do I use transition words?		
Do I use emotional and logical appeals?		

Sentence Fluency		
Do the sentences flow and have rhythm when put together?		

Conventions		
Do I use correct grammar?		
Do I use correct spelling, punctuation, and capitalization?		

Presentation		
Do I use consistent spacing and margins?		
Is my paper neat?		

Additional Items		

Name _____

Date _____ Score _____

POINT VALUES

0 = not evident
1 = minimal evidence of mastery
2 = evidence of development toward mastery
3 = strong evidence of mastery
4 = outstanding evidence of mastery

Persuasive Writing

Ideas

	POINTS
one viewpoint about a specific topic	
an attempt to convince the reader to share the viewpoint	

Organization

an introduction with a position statement	
a body with supporting details and credible facts and opinions	
a conclusion that rephrases the position statement	

Voice

persuasive	
confident and credible	

Word Choice

specific word choice to establish the mood	
language tailored for a specific audience	
transition words	
emotional and logical appeals	

Sentence Fluency

rhythm and flow	

Conventions

correct grammar and usage	
correct spelling, punctuation, and capitalization	

Presentation

consistent spacing and margins	
neatness	

Additional Items

Total	

© LOYOLAPRESS.

CHAPTER FOCUS

LESSON 1: What Makes Good Playwriting?

LESSON 2: Play Structure and Format

- **GRAMMAR:** Conjunctions and Interjections
- **WRITING SKILLS:** Dialogue, Monologue, and Asides
- **WORD STUDY:** Idioms, Slang, and Jargon
- **POETRY:** Free Verse
- **SPEAKING AND LISTENING SKILLS:** Reader's Theater
- **WRITER'S WORKSHOP:** Playwriting

SUPPORT MATERIALS

Practice Book
Writing, pages 168–172

Assessment Book
Chapter 7 Writing Skills,
    pages 69–70
Creative Writing: Playwriting
    Prompt, pages 71–72

Rubrics
Student, page 487y
Teacher, page 487z

Test Generator CD

Grammar
Sections 9 and 10, pages 165–194

Customizable Lesson Plans
www.voyagesinenglish.com

Creative Writing

WHAT IS PLAYWRITING?

A play is a drama designed to be performed by actors on a stage. A play script is the framework for a play—written character dialogue and stage direction.

A good play includes the following:

- ☐ Well-developed characters, including a protagonist and an antagonist
- ☐ Dialogue and stage directions
- ☐ Coherent plot structure: an organized pattern of events
- ☐ A beginning that introduces a problem, conflict, or goal
- ☐ A middle that includes rising action and a climax
- ☐ An ending that includes a resolution
- ☐ Realistic, engaging dialogue that includes idioms, slang, and jargon
- ☐ Effective use of asides, monologues, and soliloquies
- ☐ A natural voice
- ☐ Deliberate word choice, such as for humor or impact

LiNK Use the following titles to offer your students examples of well-crafted plays:

The Diary of Anne Frank by Frances Goodrich and Albert Hackett

King Midas and the Golden Touch by Charlotte Craft

A Raisin in the Sun by Lorraine Hansberry

> **"All the world's a stage."**
>
> —William Shakespeare

WRITER'S WORKSHOP TIPS

Follow these ideas and tips to help you and your class get the most out of the Writer's Workshop:

- Review the traits of good writing. Use the chart on the inside back cover of the student and teacher editions.
- Provide a creative atmosphere with a classroom library of videos of staged plays and musicals.
- Display a variety of play scripts so that students can see adaptations in play structure and format.
- Create a bulletin-board display of playbills.
- Have roundtable discussions about books that might make good play adaptations. Discuss why they would translate well to the stage.
- Encourage students to meet with you during the drafting stage to avoid writer's block or, if necessary, to eliminate it.

CONNECT WITH GRAMMAR

Throughout the Writer's Workshop, look for opportunities to integrate conjunctions, interjections, punctuation, and capitalization with writing plays.

- ☐ Have students vary sentence length by using conjunctions to combine independent clauses and words.
- ☐ Encourage students to use interjections in dialogue.
- ☐ Review the correct use of quotation marks with dialogue.
- ☐ Discuss capitalization of titles and names, including character names.

SCORING RUBRIC

Creative Writing: Playwriting

0 = not evident
1 = minimal evidence of mastery
2 = evidence of development toward mastery
3 = strong evidence of mastery
4 = outstanding evidence of mastery

Ideas	POINTS
well-developed characters, including a protagonist and an antagonist	
good plot structure	
Organization	
a beginning that introduces a problem, conflict, or goal	
a middle that includes rising action and a climax	
an ending that offers a resolution	
Voice	
natural	
Word Choice	
deliberate word choice, such as for humor or impact	
Sentence Fluency	
engaging, realistic dialogue including idioms, slang, and jargon that move the story forward	
Conventions	
correct grammar and usage	
correct spelling	
correct punctuation and capitalization	
Presentation	
standard script structure and format	
neatness	
Additional Items	
Total	

Full-sized, reproducible rubrics can be found at the end of this chapter.

Creative Writing

INTRODUCING THE GENRE

Invite students to share what they know about creative writing. Encourage students to name types of creative writing they have read, such as novels, short stories, and plays. Have volunteers discuss how being able to write creatively is important. *(Creative writing helps writers express themselves freely. Creative writing emphasizes the importance of language and helps writers better understand themselves.)*

Reading the Literature Excerpt

Explain that the excerpt is from the play *Midas the King*. Invite volunteers to share what they know about plays. Point out that the italicized words and the words in parentheses are silent directions to the actors and are not intended to be spoken aloud. Encourage students to add dramatic emphasis to the appropriate words as they read. Invite pairs of students to perform the dialogue. When one pair has finished, have other pairs perform the dialogue, encouraging them to be creative. After all volunteers have had a chance to read, invite students to comment about the dialogue. Ask students to describe what they notice about the format of the script. During the discussion introduce the following characteristics:

- Essential characteristics of a play are plot, theme, character(s), stage directions, and setting.
- Plays are usually divided into acts or scenes.
- Script format includes character and setting descriptions.

LiNK Midas the King

The excerpts in Chapter 7 introduce students to creative writing. The excerpt from *Midas the King* is a strong example of a play because it has the following:

- Stage directions
- Realistic and engaging dialogue
- Formatting so that dialogue, character's names, and stage directions are easily distinguishable

As students encounter the different examples of plays throughout the chapter, be sure to point out characteristics that the examples share. Also take this opportunity to point out grammar skills that students have been learning, such as conjunctions, interjections, punctuation, and capitalization.

Creative Writing

LiNK Midas the King
by Freddie Green, Magic Parrot Productions

Enter King Midas, then wife, daughter and fiancé strolling in the garden.

Enter four children, playing with a ball.

MIDAS: Stop right there! What are you doing in my garden?

CHILD 1: Oh, nothing, sir. We were just admiring your lovely garden!

CHILD 2: You must be very clever and wise to make a garden as good as this. Are you the gardener?

MIDAS: Gardener? I'm no gardener! I'm the King! You must be thieves, stealing my apples! I ought to have your heads chopped off right now!

DAUGHTER: Oh, father. They're not thieves! They're only children!

CHILD 4: We just wanted our ball back! That's all! It's getting late. We must be going home!

MIDAS: This is my garden! And trespassers should be executed.

WIFE: (*sternly*) Midas! If you want to please me, let them go! They are doing no harm!

> Plays, also called dramas, are performed writing pieces. King Midas is brought to life by the elements of playwriting: plot, theme, characters, setting, dialogue, and stage directions.

450

- Dialogue, character names, and stage directions are formatted so they can be easily differentiated from one another.

Encourage students to name plays they have read or performed. Ask students to describe the experience of participating in the production of a play. Have students recall the stage directions and the character and setting descriptions that were provided. Lead students to the conclusion that these characteristics are just as significant to the mood and tone of the play as is the actual dialogue.

Reading the Student Model

Ask volunteers to read "The Empty Pocket Blues." When students have finished, discuss the following questions:

- What stage directions are included?
- Does the author use setting or character descriptions?
- How do the stage directions and setting and character descriptions help create a tone and mood in the play?

CHAPTER 7

Chris Hoffm...
Room 623

The Empty Pocket Blues

CHARACTERS
CASEY   ANGELA

SETTING
A comfortable living room with a table center stage left and a couch center stage right.

SCENE 1

(CASEY *walks in with a shopping bag and sees* ANGELA *at the table with a piggy bank, counting money.*)

ANGELA: *(to herself)* One hundred and sixty-six, one hundred and sixty-seven, one hundred and sixty-eight. *(She stacks the money and updates her records.)* Only $32 to go!

CASEY: *(interested)* Cool! Let's go to the mall and buy some clothes, a new video game, and some of those trendy shoes everyone is wearing. *(He reaches over to grab the stack of money, but Angela pushes him away.)* What? You have enough to spare.

ANGELA: That's because I've been keeping track and limiting my unnecessary spending so that I can save for a new bicycle. I'm going to get the Road Rasher 3000 this summer.

CASEY: Saving isn't fun. Money is meant to be spent. I'm going to the mall.

(CASEY leaves the room. End of scene.)

SCENE 2

(ANGELA *enters wearing a bike helmet.* CASEY *is digging in the couch cushions.*)

ANGELA: I just had the best ride. The Road Rasher 3000 is the best purchase I've ever made. *(Notices CASEY)* What are you doing?

CASEY: I want to go on vacation with my friends; however, I'm broke. *(Exasperated)* Where did all my money go, anyway?

ANGELA: A penny saved is a penny earned.

451

OBJECTIVES
- To recognize the characteristics of playwriting
- To understand plot, theme, character, and setting in playwriting

WARM-UP

Read, Listen, Speak

Read aloud a portion of the one-act play from yesterday's For Tomorrow homework. Describe the plot, characters, and any other unique features of the play. Model for students the appropriate language to use when discussing plays. Then have small groups share the one-act plays they found. Encourage students to describe the characteristics and details of their play. Then have groups compile a list of characteristics of one-act plays that they believe are unique to that genre.

GRAMMAR CONNECTION

Take this opportunity to talk about coordinating conjunctions and correlative conjunctions. You may wish to have students point out coordinating conjunctions and correlative conjunctions in their Read, Listen, Speak examples.

TEACH

Ask a volunteer to read aloud the first two paragraphs. Invite students to explain what they know about the plot, theme, character, and setting of a play. Have students read silently the section Plot. Ask how the plots of plays are similar to the body of a traditionally written fiction or nonfiction story. Challenge a volunteer to explain what exposition means *(background information about the content of a play)*. Discuss the meaning of an inciting incident *(an event*

that create a problem for a main character to solve).

Suggest that students use the chart to determine the exposition, inciting incident, rising action, climax, falling action, resolution, and conclusion in the plays they found for homework. Invite students to identify these points in the pieces and to explain their choices.

Ask a volunteer to read aloud the section Theme. Challenge students to identify the theme of the model on page 451. Point out that this play's theme is stated clearly in Angela's last line of dialogue.

PRACTICE

ACTIVITY A

Allow time for partners to develop dialogue and to list their steps of rising action. Invite volunteers to perform their scenes for the class. Ask students whether the inciting incident or conflict is obvious. Encourage students to offer suggestions for each scene.

ACTIVITY B

Review the meaning of *climax, falling action,* and *resolution.* Then read aloud the model on page 451. Have students complete this activity independently. Discuss

---

What Makes Good Playwriting?

Playwriting is a unique form of writing. Unlike narrative short stories and novels, which are meant to be read, plays, also called dramas, are meant to be performed.

All plays share the same elements: plot, theme, characters, setting, dialogue, and stage directions. Here are some points to keep in mind about plays.

Plot

An effective drama is composed of a series of dramatic actions that connect the story. Plots have a beginning, a middle, and an end, no matter how many scenes the play has.

- Playwrights almost always put exposition in the beginning of a play. Through dialogue, action, and setting, exposition provides the background information about the characters and what they do. A playwright then creates an inciting incident, an event that creates a problem for a main character to solve.
- Once the problem is established, a playwright continues with action-filled events, building tension and further heightening dramatic conflict. These events are called the rising action. A playwright then leads us from the rising action to the climax, an exciting, defining moment or turning point.
- The problem is solved in the events that follow. These events, called the falling action, drive the plot to its resolution. The resolution answers remaining questions and concludes the play.

the model, inviting volunteers to explain their answers.

ACTIVITY C

Have students brainstorm play ideas for the first theme. Then have partners complete the activity. When students have finished, invite volunteers to share their ideas with the class.

APPLY

WRITER'S CORNER

Encourage students to review the information on page 452. Have volunteers share their plot summaries with the class.

Students should demonstrate an understanding of the characteristics of a play.

TechTip Take students to your school's computer lab and allow them to use PowerPoint or another type of multimedia software to create a plot diagram.

ASSESS

Note which students had difficulty understanding the characteristics of a play. Use the Reteach option with those students who need additional reinforcement.

Theme

All plays have at least one theme. A theme is the central idea, usually a generalization about human nature that the writer wants to show the audience. Effective themes can be subtle, or they can exhibit obvious lessons. Directors and designers use their interpretations of the play's theme or themes to develop their productions.

ACTIVITY A Choose one of the following inciting incidents. Act out the incident with a partner and create your own dialogue. Write a list of at least three steps that might show the rising action that follows.

A. Your best friend suddenly stops speaking to you.

B. You arrive at the music store just in time to see your friend grab the last copy of the new CD you wanted.

C. You meet someone you knew when you were younger.

D. You and a sibling break some of your parents' expensive china.

Activity B

1. Almost no information is provided. Angela seems to be responsible.

2. Casey reaches over to grab the stack of money, but Angela pushes him away. Casey goes to the mall.

3. Angela states that the Road Rasher 3000 is the best purchase she ever made.

4. Casey searches the couch cushions for extra change. He admits that he has no money.

5. "A penny saved is a penny earned."

6. Saving money is hard work; nevertheless, the rewards are great.

ACTIVITY B Look at the diagram on page 452 that shows the progress of a plot. Read the model on page 451. Then answer the questions.

1. What background information is provided about Angela?

2. Name two events that are part of the rising action.

3. What is the climax?

4. Name two events that are part of the falling action.

5. What is the resolution?

6. What is the theme of this play?

ACTIVITY C With a partner choose one of the following themes. Brainstorm ideas for a play, using your chosen theme.

1. Honesty is the best policy.

2. Slow but steady wins the race.

3. Things are not always what they seem.

4. Sticks and stones may break my bones, but names will never hurt me.

5. A stitch in time saves nine.

WRITER'S CORNER

Summarize a simple plot for a play from the scenario you acted out in Activity A. Introduce a conflict, briefly describe the rising action and climax, and finish with the falling action and resolution.

 Tech Tip Graph your plot as a PowerPoint presentation.

Creative Writing • 453

WARM-UP

Read, Listen, Speak

Display your plot summary outline from yesterday's For Tomorrow homework. Discuss the characters and theme for your play. Then invite volunteers to share their preliminary plans. Ask students to list what parts of a written piece (action, description, characters, setting) take prominence when it is made into a play.

GRAMMAR CONNECTION

Take this opportunity to talk about conjunctive adverbs. You may wish to have students point out conjunctive adverbs in their Read, Listen, Speak examples.

TEACH

Ask a student to read aloud the first paragraph of the section Character. Encourage volunteers to name the protagonists and the antagonists of some of the plays you have discussed in this chapter. Have a volunteer read aloud the second paragraph. Point out that characters are described not only through italicized directions, but also through dialogue. Explain that characters are revealed through every word spoken and every action demonstrated in a play.

Have a volunteer read aloud the tips for developing characters. Explain that if students address each of the points as they write, they will develop strong, significant characters.

Have a volunteer read aloud the section Setting. Point out that playwrights, directors, and set designers are limited to the physical space they can use to illustrate the time and place of a play. Encourage volunteers to compare play sets with those used

in film and on TV. Tell students that sometimes this limited space will inspire a playwright to be more creative when developing a setting.

Invite a volunteer to read aloud the second paragraph. Explain that sometimes a play's themes are universal and timeless. Point out that a play can be set in any location throughout the world or at any time in history and still have the same effect on the audience. Offer Shakespeare's plays as an example. Ask volunteers to name Shakespeare's plays that have been staged in modern settings.

LiNK Have students close their eyes. Then read aloud the

excerpt. Discuss how the author effectively describes the setting.

PRACTICE

ACTIVITY D

Remind students that most themes can be communicated through a variety of settings. Encourage students to be creative with their settings. Allow time for students to complete this activity independently. Invite volunteers to share their settings with the class.

ACTIVITY E

Review the terms *protagonist* and *antagonist*. Then complete the activity as a class. Challenge

Character

All plays must have at least one character, but they usually have several. In a play the central character is often called the protagonist. The character or force that opposes the main character is often called the antagonist. Opposition between the protagonist and antagonist creates the conflict of the drama, which drives the main action.

A playwright can reveal a character in a variety of ways. First, the playwright often provides a physical and social description of each main character at the beginning of a script. Then the playwright reveals what he or she wants the audience to know through the character's words and actions in the play. A playwright also reveals a character through what the other characters say about him or her.

The following tips can help you develop your characters:

- Always remember that each character must have a reason for being in the play.
- Each character must have a goal to achieve throughout the play.
- Specific physical traits can help reveal character. Brainstorm many possibilities.
- In the beginning of the play, remember to establish background information for each character.
- Each character should be interesting and believable.

Setting

Time and place in a play are just as important as the play's characters. Plays can be set in outer space, in medieval times, in fantasy worlds, or in the present—just about any place and time imaginable. Think about your daily surroundings and how they influence your everyday actions. You may act differently depending on whether you're at home, in school, or spending time with your friends. As you write a play, always have a good reason for including a specific year or location.

The same is true for the time period. Playwrights usually have a specific reason for the time and place they choose to set their story. For example, Lorraine Hansberry set her play *A Raisin in the Sun* in the South Side of Chicago during the 1950s. She wanted to show that discrimination affected African Americans who lived in Northern cities, as well as those who lived in the South.

students to explain their answers by referring to exact text in the model. Ask students if this play could take place in any time or place.

ACTIVITY F

Tell students that their character sketches should answer the questions in the activity. Invite volunteers to share their character sketches with the class.

APPLY

WRITER'S CORNER

Invite volunteers to share their paragraphs and character sketches with the class. Students should demonstrate an understanding of character and setting in a play.

ASSESS

Note which students had difficulty understanding character and setting within a play. Use the Reteach option with those students who need additional reinforcement.

Practice Book page 168 provides additional work with the characteristics of playwriting.

TEACHING OPTIONS

Reteach

Ask students to choose a specific location or person that they know very well. Have them develop an outline of a setting description or character sketch of this place or person. Explain that characters and settings of plays are most effective when the writer provides many personal details and that this is why writing about something or someone a person knows very well helps develop this skill. When students have finished, invite volunteers to share their work with the class.

Poe Production

Invite small groups to develop character sketches and setting descriptions for a play production of one of Edgar Allan Poe's short stories. Explain that the eerie mood and atmosphere of Poe's stories inspired playwrights in the past to be innovative when turning Poe's stories into plays. Have students write their descriptions in paragraph form and be as specific as they can. Encourage students to use the bulleted points on page 454 as a checklist when writing their character sketches.

ACTIVITY D Look back at the plot summary you wrote for the Writer's Corner on page 453. Choose a setting in which your plot will take place. Briefly describe the place, atmosphere, and time period. Think about interesting surroundings for your story and how the surroundings will affect your characters and their behavior.

Activity E

1. in a comfortable living room
2. Angela: counting money, piggy bank nearby, recording her earnings; Casey: tries to grab the money, wants to buy several things, rummaging in couch cushions for loose change
3. Angela
4. Casey
5. to save enough money to buy a Road Rasher 3000

ACTIVITY E Read the model on page 451. Then answer the questions about character and setting.

1. What is the setting for the play?
2. What clues in the text inform you about the goal, appearance, and personality of Angela? of Casey?
3. Who is the protagonist?
4. Who is the antagonist?
5. What is Angela's objective?

ACTIVITY F Think about the plot you developed for the Writer's Corner on page 453. Choose two characters that would likely be a part of your play. Using the questions below, write a character sketch for each character.

1. Where is your character from? How would your character speak?
2. What does your character look like? What does this say about the character?
3. What mannerisms or behaviors do your characters use?
4. How does your character relate to the other characters? to the setting?
5. What is your character doing when he or she is not talking?

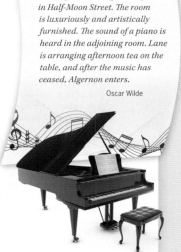

LiNK

The Importance of Being Earnest

Morning-room in Algernon's flat in Half-Moon Street. The room is luxuriously and artistically furnished. The sound of a piano is heard in the adjoining room. Lane is arranging afternoon tea on the table, and after the music has ceased, Algernon enters.

Oscar Wilde

WRITER'S CORNER

Costume is also a part of the setting and character. Think about the characters you developed for Activity F. Write a paragraph describing the clothes and props your characters would wear or use.

Creative Writing • 455

For Tomorrow

Ask students to read or view a one-person play. Ask them to write a short character sketch of the protagonist, incorporating the bulleted points on page 454. Read or view a one-person play yourself and write a character sketch to share with the class.

OBJECTIVES

- **To understand play structure and format**
- **To write character and setting descriptions**
- **To write dialogue and stage directions**

WARM-UP

Read, Listen, Speak

Provide copies of your character sketch from yesterday's For Tomorrow homework. Use the bulleted points on page 454 for the basis of a discussion about your character sketch. Then have small groups share their character sketches. Encourage students to discuss how the character in a one-person play has a unique role.

GRAMMAR CONNECTION

Take this opportunity to talk about subordinate conjunctions. You may wish to have students point out subordinate conjunctions in their Read, Listen, Speak examples.

TEACH

Invite a volunteer to read aloud the first paragraph. Review the characteristics of plot, theme, character, and setting in a play. Explain that plays are divided into acts and scenes to signal a change in setting or a significant break in the action of the play. Tell students that some plays require only one act because the play maintains a continuous momentum in the action and needs only one setting.

Ask volunteers to read aloud the section Character and Setting Description. Point out the stage location grid. Invite students who have performed in stage productions to explain the importance of recognizing stage locations and directions.

Allow time for students to read silently the example character and setting descriptions. Challenge volunteers to describe how the characters Jet and Harold might act and speak based on the descriptions. Have students note the description under Scene One. Challenge students to explain how setting descriptions help identify the mood of a play.

PRACTICE

ACTIVITY A

Explain that playwrights often write lengthy character sketches before they write the character description in the script. Allow time for students to rewrite their character sketches as character descriptions. Invite volunteers to read aloud what they wrote. Encourage feedback about the descriptions.

Play Structure and Format

Plays are usually divided into acts, each of which may contain separate scenes. Many plays have more than one act, but one-act plays are also common. A one-act play generally takes place in a shorter time than a multi-act play, and has a simpler plot and fewer characters. One-act plays share the essential elements of all plays: plot, theme, characters, setting, dialogue, and stage directions. All play scripts follow similar formats.

Character and Setting Description

Most scripts include an opening section that describes the characters and the setting. The character list provides information about each character, such as age, gender, and relationships with other characters. Characters' names are printed in all capital letters throughout the script, unless the name is used in dialogue. This is done so that actors can easily locate their lines.

Setting descriptions provide brief information for the director, actors, and designers regarding time and place.

The setting description at the opening of a scene is generally more detailed than the initial statement of time and place. Terms such as *downstage left* and *upstage center* tell where things are located and where actors move on the stage. Stage locations are always given from the perspective of the actor facing the audience.

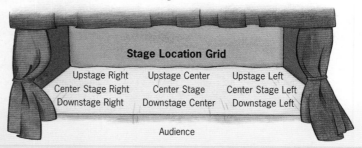

Stage Location Grid

Upstage Right	Upstage Center	Upstage Left
Center Stage Right	Center Stage	Center Stage Left
Downstage Right	Downstage Center	Downstage Left

Audience

ACTIVITY B

Have students complete this activity independently. While students are working, draw on the board a blank stage location grid. When students have finished, invite volunteers to write on the board their answers. Discuss the accuracy of each location.

APPLY

WRITER'S CORNER

When students have finished, ask them to reread the setting descriptions and identify the mood or feeling the descriptions evoke. Have volunteers share their work with the class. Students should demonstrate an understanding of how to write setting descriptions and stage directions.

ASSESS

Note which students had difficulty writing character and setting descriptions. Use the Reteach option with those students who need additional reinforcement.

TEACHING OPTIONS

Reteach

Draw on the board a three-column chart with the following headings: *Angela, Casey, Setting*. Review the play on page 451 and brainstorm words and phrases that help form the image of Angela, Casey, and the setting. Have students use these ideas to create detailed descriptions of the characters and setting as they might appear at the beginning of a script.

All in the Family

Invite each student to write character and setting descriptions for a play in which the characters are members of the student's family. Suggest students choose a scenario for the family coming together, such as a family reunion. Remind them to format their descriptions as shown on page 457. Encourage students to mention physical appearance, attitude, mannerisms, and other detailed personal traits for each character. Have students trade their finished work with a partner and determine whether the character and setting descriptions would be useful and informative to a reader's or an actor's understanding of the play.

CHARACTERS

JET: An 18-year-old female who is very ambitious and outspoken but quite naïve. She has been raised by HAROLD, her grandfather, and she will do anything to make her dreams of becoming a singer in the big city come true.

HAROLD: A stern, older man with strong values and strict views. Protective of JET.

PLACE

The action all takes place in HAROLD's New York City apartment.

TIME

A winter day sometime around 2010.

Setting is described in further detail at the beginning of each scene.

SCENE ONE

(*Lights come up on the living room of a small apartment. Upstage right, a window shows the New York City skyline. Snow is visible outside. Upstage left are a door and a coat rack. Everything is neat and in place with a warm, comfortable feel. Center stage is a large sofa with a large chair downstage right of sofa.*)

ACTIVITY A Look back at the character sketches you wrote for Activity F. Using the model above as a guide, rewrite your character sketches in the format found in the opening section of a play.

ACTIVITY B Draw a blank stage location grid. Read the Stage Location Grid on page 456 and the description of the apartment for Scene One above. Write letters in your blank grid to show where the following items would be found on the stage.

A. sofa   C. window
B. chair   D. door

WRITER'S CORNER

Use the setting description you wrote for Activity D on page 455. Rewrite it to fit the format described in this lesson. Include at least two stage locations.

For Tomorrow

Ask students to search play scripts for a setting description that conveys an eerie or a mysterious mood as well as a setting description that conveys a joyful or an optimistic mood. Find examples of each mood that you can share with the class.

Creative Writing • 457

WARM-UP
Read, Listen, Speak
Share your setting descriptions from yesterday's For Tomorrow homework. Point out the contrast in language used for each description. Invite volunteers to read aloud the descriptions they found. Tell students to pay close attention to the language used in each description. Ask students to point out specific words that add detail to the descriptions.

GRAMMAR CONNECTION
Take this opportunity to talk about troublesome conjunctions. You may wish to have students point out troublesome conjunctions in their Read, Listen, Speak examples.

TEACH
Ask a volunteer to read aloud the section Dialogue and Stage Directions. Have a volunteer point out the stage directions in the excerpt on page 450 and other plays discussed in this chapter. Point out the importance of clarity and brevity when writing stage directions.

Allow time for students to read the sample script. Ask students to read the script again, omitting the stage directions. Challenge volunteers to explain why stage directions are necessary to a play script. *(They describe the action and accentuate the spoken dialogue.)*

PRACTICE
ACTIVITY C
Remind students to review the character descriptions on page 457 before answering question 4. When students have finished, invite volunteers to share their answers with the class. Discuss each question.

ACTIVITY D
Ask students to complete this activity independently. Have them exchange papers with a partner and discuss whether each item is correct.

ACTIVITY E
Remind students to write stage directions in parentheses and to make them italicized. Also point out that stage directions should be short, clear, and necessary to the scene. Have students complete this activity independently. Discuss students' stage directions and how they differ.

ACTIVITY F
Invite students to work in small groups to complete this activity. Challenge students to write checklists for what makes effective play structures and formats. Invite volunteers to share their checklists with the class. Write the suggestions on the board and encourage students to keep a master list in their notebooks.

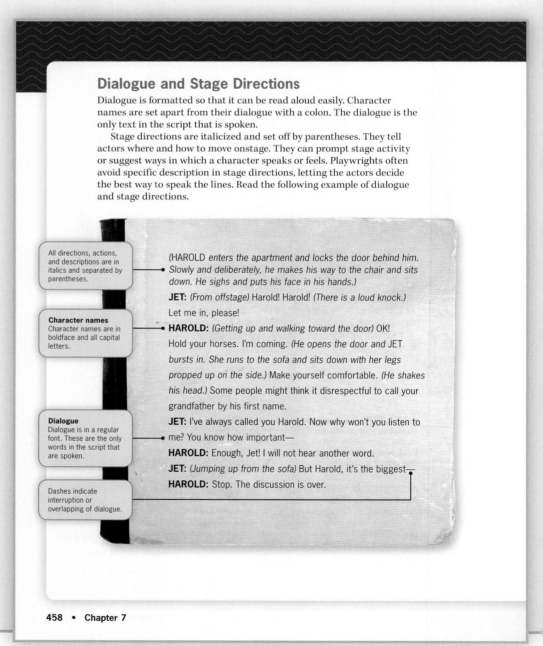

Dialogue and Stage Directions
Dialogue is formatted so that it can be read aloud easily. Character names are set apart from their dialogue with a colon. The dialogue is the only text in the script that is spoken.

Stage directions are italicized and set off by parentheses. They tell actors where and how to move onstage. They can prompt stage activity or suggest ways in which a character speaks or feels. Playwrights often avoid specific description in stage directions, letting the actors decide the best way to speak the lines. Read the following example of dialogue and stage directions.

All directions, actions, and descriptions are in italics and separated by parentheses.

Character names
Character names are in boldface and all capital letters.

Dialogue
Dialogue is in a regular font. These are the only words in the script that are spoken.

Dashes indicate interruption or overlapping of dialogue.

(HAROLD *enters the apartment and locks the door behind him. Slowly and deliberately, he makes his way to the chair and sits down. He sighs and puts his face in his hands.*)

JET: *(From offstage)* Harold! Harold! *(There is a loud knock.)* Let me in, please!

HAROLD: *(Getting up and walking toward the door)* OK! Hold your horses. I'm coming. *(He opens the door and JET bursts in. She runs to the sofa and sits down with her legs propped up on the side.)* Make yourself comfortable. *(He shakes his head.)* Some people might think it disrespectful to call your grandfather by his first name.

JET: I've always called you Harold. Now why won't you listen to me? You know how important—

HAROLD: Enough, Jet! I will not hear another word.

JET: *(Jumping up from the sofa)* But Harold, it's the biggest—

HAROLD: Stop. The discussion is over.

APPLY

WRITER'S CORNER

Allow time for students to complete their scripts independently. Then ask students to work with a partner and choose one of their scenes to perform for the class. Encourage students to point out the actions that required stage directions. Students should demonstrate an understanding of dialogue and stage directions in plays.

ASSESS

Note which students had difficulty writing dialogue and stage directions. Use the Reteach option with those students who need additional reinforcement.

Practice Book page 169 provides additional work with play structure and format.

TEACHING OPTIONS

Reteach

Tell students to choose a simple action, such as walking to their lockers with a friend and talking about their plans for the weekend. Ask students to use this action (which includes at least two people) to write a short dialogue with stage directions. Have students write a list of every physical action that happens during the scene. Tell them to use the most significant actions as stage directions. Have students write a short dialogue between the two characters, inserting the stage directions where appropriate. You might encourage students to "walk through" the scene themselves while writing their list of actions so they don't miss anything important.

Turn the Tables

Have students work with partners to write new dialogue and stage directions for the scene on page 458. Ask students to change the scene so that Jet is angry with Harold for being overprotective of her and Harold is trying to apologize. Encourage students to convey the appropriate emotions of each character in the dialogue and stage directions. Invite volunteers to perform their scenes for the class.

For Tomorrow

Ask students to choose a scene in an episode of a TV series and write stage directions that might have been in the original script for the episode. Do the same for a TV show of your choosing.

Activity C
1. Harold and Jet
2. by looking for their names in capital boldface letters
3. Jet; it is indicated in the stage directions.
4. Answers will vary.

Activity D
1. *Harold* should be in all caps and boldface.
2. *JET:* should be boldface. Dialogue should not be italicized.
3. Stage directions (except character names) should be italicized and set in parentheses.
4. Correct
5. A colon should replace the semi-colon. There should be no parentheses around the dialogue.

ACTIVITY C Read the dialogue from page 458 and answer these questions.
1. Who are the characters in this scene?
2. How can the actors quickly find their lines?
3. Which actor is supposed to knock on the door? How do you know?
4. After Harold says, "Stop. The discussion is over," what might Jet say? Write your answer in correct dialogue format.

ACTIVITY D Tell how you would retype each dialogue or stage direction correctly. Not all items have errors.
1. Harold: I am too old to worry about you.
2. JET: *You just don't realize that this is my dream!*
3. **HAROLD walks into the kitchen and begins to look very busy preparing dinner. JET slowly follows him.**
4. **JET:** Wait! Let me help you with that, Grandpa.
5. **HAROLD;** (Let's both just sit down and talk about this at dinner.)

ACTIVITY E Read the dialogue. Add four or five stage directions that you think might happen in this scenario.

JET: Will you please listen to me? I just want to talk to you.

HAROLD: There is nothing to discuss, young lady.

JET: But Harold, this is all I've ever wanted. You know I can sing. You've always said I had a pretty voice.

HAROLD: You are not going to go running around the country with a bunch of long-haired musicians!

ACTIVITY F Study a play script that you find in your classroom, in the library, or on the Internet. Compare and contrast the script to the examples in this lesson. What has the playwright done the same and differently concerning structure and format? Make a list of at least three ways that format and structure are the same and three ways that format and structure are different.

WRITER'S CORNER

Find four to six lines of dialogue from a favorite novel or story written in narrative form. Convert the lines into a short scene in script format. Use the examples in Activity E as a model. Add stage directions to show action.

Creative Writing • 459

OBJECTIVES

- To understand the use of dialogue in plays
- To understand monologues and asides in plays

WARM-UP

Read, Listen, Speak

Read aloud your scene from yesterday's For Tomorrow homework. Be sure to point out stage directions. Have small groups share their stage directions. Suggest that students discuss how stage directions illustrate the personalities of the characters. Encourage students to give one another feedback about how the stage directions could be more specific.

GRAMMAR CONNECTION

Take this opportunity to talk about interjections. You may wish to have students point out interjections in their Read, Listen, Speak examples.

TEACH

Have a volunteer read aloud the first paragraph of the section Dialogue. Emphasize that dialogue is the primary way that playwrights advance the story and present all facets of a character. Point out that how a character speaks is just as revealing of his or her personality as what the character actually says.

Ask a volunteer to read aloud the second paragraph. Have volunteers provide examples of speech from different time periods and geographical locations *(a medieval knight's formal speech, an antebellum Southern dialect, British phrasing)*. Explain that beyond the words, the sound or rhythms of a character's dialogue are very important. Point out that some of the first plays were written in lyrical verse, like poetry.

Invite volunteers to read aloud the third and fourth paragraphs and dialogue example. Ask students what a dash represents in the example *(an interruption)*. Ask students what the three dots, called an ellipsis, indicate *(a pause)*. Point out that an ellipsis would also be used if a character trailed off and did not finish a sentence.

LiNK Invite two volunteers to read aloud the excerpt. Point out the use of ellipses. Discuss what the dialogue reveals about each character.

PRACTICE

ACTIVITY A

Have partners answer and discuss the questions. Then ask students what they learned about the characters through the dialogue. Ask volunteers to explain their answers.

ACTIVITY B

Review the definitions of protagonist and antagonist. Have students complete the activity independently. Ask volunteers to justify their answers by referring to actual text in the scene.

Dialogue, Monologue, and Asides

Dialogue

Just like in other writing, dialogue in plays is the spoken words of the characters. Playwrights carefully construct dialogue to engage the audience, provide them with important information, and advance the story. In other words, dialogue reveals exposition and plot.

Dialogue is usually intended to sound like the natural speech of a specific time and place. To achieve this, many playwrights do research. Playwrights might gather writings and recordings depicting speech patterns from a specific era. The grammar, word use, style, and even cultural accent of a character are all clues that help tell the story.

Playwrights also read aloud and revise the dialogue in their scripts. If the dialogue is awkward or seems unnatural, the audience will not believe the world created on the stage.

In our everyday lives, we usually speak in complete sentences. But many times we also speak in fragments and unfinished sentences, or are interrupted by someone else. For natural-sounding dialogue, playwrights incorporate this type of speech.

JACKSON: I just wanted to tell you that I—
KIANA: It's very important to me that we get this house ready for the party.
JACKSON: But Kiana—
KIANA: Jackson, I don't have time to listen to you. We have a lot to get done and I just . . . I need to get to work.

Activity A
Answers will vary.

ACTIVITY A With a partner read aloud the dialogue above. Then answer the questions.

1. What do you know about Kiana from reading the dialogue?
2. What do you know about Jackson?
3. What do you think Jackson might say next?

ACTIVITY C

Remind students that the dialogue should seem natural and that one character is 14 years old and the other is five. Have partners complete this activity. Challenge students to include stage directions in their dialogue. Then invite volunteers to perform the scene for the class.

APPLY

WRITER'S CORNER

Ask volunteers to read aloud their conversation excerpts. When appropriate, point out interruptions, phrasing, and words that suggest natural conversation. Ask students to discuss the excerpts. Students should demonstrate an understanding of dialogue.

ASSESS

Note which students had difficulty understanding the uses of dialogue. Use the Reteach option with those students who need additional reinforcement.

TEACHING OPTIONS

Reteach

Ask students to copy the dialogue sample on page 460. Have students discuss what Jackson might say next. Then ask students to write the next four lines of dialogue for the scene. Encourage students to use natural-sounding language. Then have partners decide which new lines, if any, do not seem to fit in each dialogue. Have students make revisions where necessary. Invite volunteers to share their work with the class.

Character Cards

Have students use a note card to create a character sketch of a character. Ask students to write the character's name on the front of the card and a brief character sketch on the back. After students have finished creating their characters, ask them to work in pairs to write four to six lines of dialogue for a play, using their characters. Ask students to write a scene in which one of the characters has something the other character wants. Encourage students to use natural-sounding language that fits their different characters. Invite volunteers to share their scenes with the class.

Activity B

1. Greta
2. impassioned, determined
3. There is a legal conflict between the people and the company.
4. Speaker, MacMaster, the unnamed company
5. The people will follow Greta and march.
6. Answers will vary.

ACTIVITY B Read the excerpt from a play. Then answer the questions.

SCENE ONE

(Curtain comes up on a community center meeting hall, a large room with folding chairs in which an audience of 12 to 15 people sits. SPEAKER at the podium is interrupted abruptly by young woman who rises from audience.)

SPEAKER: *(getting louder)* As I was—

GRETA: Enough! We've heard enough. MacMaster is the biggest polluter in seven states. We've tried endless discussions. Now we've got to do something they won't forget! *(Crowd murmurs in agreement.)*

SPEAKER: But our committee has a meeting scheduled with MacMaster's lead attorney for next—

GRETA: How many meetings have we had? Ten? Twenty? Forget meetings! Let's march! *(Crowd cheers.)*

1. Which character is probably the protagonist?
2. What sort of person does Greta seem to be? How would you describe her mood?
3. What have you discovered about the plot?
4. Whom do you think the antagonist might be?
5. What is likely to happen next?
6. Does the dialogue seem natural? Why or why not?

LiNK

On the High Road

FEDYA: Are you from far off?

SAVVA: From Vologda. The town itself . . . . I live there.

FEDYA: And where is this Vologda?

TIHON: The other side of Moscow. . . .

FEDYA: Well, well, well. . . . You have come a long way, old man! On foot?

Anton Chekov

Anton Chekov, Russian writer and dramatist (1860–1904)

Activity C

Answers will vary.

ACTIVITY C Read the stage directions. Then write a brief dialogue between the two characters mentioned in the stage directions.

SCENE ONE

(Lights come up in the kitchen of a suburban home. A 14-year-old female is babysitting her 5-year-old brother. She has just discovered that the boy has made a mess. Flour, sugar, eggs, and milk are all over the counters, walls, floor, and the boy. Knowing her parents will be home soon, the girl is quick to react.)

WRITER'S CORNER

As accurately as you can, write interesting excerpts of conversations that you hear in public places. Be sure to include pauses, interruptions, and fragments.

For Tomorrow

Ask students to write a short scene of dialogue in which a character confronts a robot traveling through time. Write your own dialogue to share with the class.

Creative Writing • 461

WARM-UP

Read, Listen, Speak

Read aloud your dialogue from yesterday's For Tomorrow homework. Point out how you used the dialogue to develop the characters. Invite volunteers to read aloud their dialogues. Discuss each dialogue. Encourage students to point out strengths and to offer suggestions for improvement.

GRAMMAR CONNECTION

Take this opportunity to review conjunctions and interjections. You may wish to have students point out conjunctions and interjections in their Read, Listen, Speak examples.

TEACH

Invite a volunteer to read aloud the section Monologue. Explain that a monologue or a soliloquy is a way for a playwright to show a character's private or personal thoughts and feelings. Discuss the difference between a monologue and a soliloquy. Point out that a character's solo song in a musical is an example of a monologue.

Ask a volunteer to read aloud the section Asides. Point out that sometimes during an aside the other characters will freeze or all the lights on stage will go out except for a light on the speaker. Complete a Venn diagram comparing monologues, soliloquies, and asides like the one below.

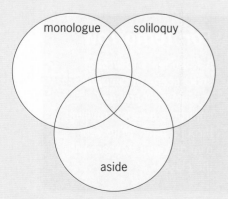

PRACTICE

ACTIVITY D

Review the definition of a monologue. Then have students complete this activity independently. Ask volunteers to read aloud their monologues. Have students discuss how the monologues suggest character traits.

ACTIVITY E

Have partners complete this activity. Invite volunteers to perform their scenes. Point out the different ways students chose to reveal the character through their asides (more dramatic, more sarcastic, more humorous).

ACTIVITY F

Review the Venn diagram from earlier in the lesson. Be sure students understand the differences between a monologue, a soliloquy, and an aside. Have students complete this activity independently. Then have partners choose one scene or combine their two scenes to perform for the class. Use the performances to point out how dialogue advances the story. Ask students to identify the aside and monologue in each performance.

Monologue

A monologue is a long speech given by one character. A monologue is always delivered within the action of the play. A monologue can be spoken to the audience or to another character. A soliloquy is similar to a monologue. It is also a long speech given by one character. In a soliloquy the speaker is always talking to himself or herself, not to others. Both monologues and soliloquies aid in character development.

Asides

An aside is dialogue in which an actor stops the play action and directly addresses the audience. During an aside it is assumed that the other characters in the play cannot hear or see it. Playwrights might use this tool to have a character seek the sympathy of the audience, to show how much smarter or more clever a character is than the others, or to give a brief commentary on what is happening on the stage. For example,

FELICIA: *(aside to audience)* I don't look that foolish, do I?

ACTIVITY D Expand the dialogue on page 460 by adding a monologue for one of the characters. Be sure the monologue consists of at least four sentences and conforms to the character's traits as you understand them.

ACTIVITY E Rewrite the following dialogue. Add two asides, one for each character. The asides can be inserted anywhere within the dialogue. Use the asides to reveal information to the audience that the other character should not know or to give some commentary about an event onstage.

JONATHA: *(turns, sees SUNHEE)* What are you doing, Sunhee?

SUNHEE: Setting the table, silly!

JONATHA: At midnight?

SUNHEE: I like to be prepared, that's all.

APPLY

WRITER'S CORNER

Invite partners to discuss asides. Have volunteers share their findings with the class. Ask volunteers what lines in the original dialogue inspired their asides and why. Students should demonstrate an understanding of asides.

ASSESS

Note which students had difficulty with monologues and asides. Use the Reteach option with those students who need additional reinforcement.

Practice Book page 170 provides additional work with dialogue, monologue, and asides.

TEACHING OPTIONS

Reteach

Have students write scenes involving two soccer players. Tell students to include a long speech in which one player is bragging to the other about how well he or she plays. Have students follow the monologue with a dialogue between the characters. Explain that at some point in the dialogue, students should insert an aside in which the nonbragging soccer player makes humorous comments about the bragging soccer player. Remind students that the bragging character will keep on talking because he or she cannot hear the aside.

Trapped in an Elevator

Have small groups write a scene for a play in which three characters are trapped in an elevator. Explain that the three characters do not know one another and are waiting for help. Encourage students to make the three characters different from one another. Tell students to pick one character who will deliver a soliloquy at the end that tells how the characters got out of the elevator. Invite volunteers to share their work with the class.

ACTIVITY F Choose two inciting incidents. Create at least six lines of dialogue for each incident. Include a monologue and an aside in each section of dialogue.

A. Gina, age 4, has just hit her whiny little brother Peter, 3, over the head with a toy truck. Their dad has witnessed the incident and is running over as quickly as he can.

B. Suddenly, odd plants that look like furry, little animals are sprouting all over town. When Carl tries to dig one up by the roots, he hears a faint noise that sounds like "Ouch!"

C. Mrs. Chen is very fond of Logan, a bright boy of 11, but his ceaseless talking constantly disrupts the class. She asks Logan to stay after class to discuss the problem.

D. Jordan's parents constantly warn him about communicating with people he doesn't know on the Internet. But he feels that he does know Paige, a friend from a chat room, so he arranges to meet her at the mall.

E. Corinne has won a scholarship to the Academy of Math and Science, a very selective boarding school. Corinne is excited, but she wonders how she will tell her best friend, Blaine, the news, especially since Blaine was not accepted.

F. Grace is forbidden to go into her sister Faith's bedroom, so of course that's where she goes every chance she gets. One day Grace is in Faith's room, trying on her sister's prom dress, when Faith, who has gotten off work early, walks in.

G. Something must have gone wrong with the science experiment Charles and Martin are conducting. They followed the steps precisely, but glowing foam has bubbled up over the beakers and is flowing all over the room.

H. Hannah wants to help, but she doesn't think it's fair that she has to take care of her brother and sister and make dinner every day that her mother works. She has a phone conversation with her father about the situation.

WRITER'S CORNER

Reread the dialogue you created for Activity E. Write a brief paragraph telling how the meaning of the play changed when you added the asides.

For Tomorrow

Ask students to read item B from Activity A on page 453. Have students write a soliloquy debating how to handle the situation. Write your own soliloquy for the same incident.

OBJECTIVE

- **To understand how and why playwrights use idioms, slang, and jargon**

WARM-UP

Read, Listen, Speak

Read aloud your soliloquy from yesterday's For Tomorrow homework. Point out the language that you used to help develop the character. Review how soliloquies differ from monologues and asides. Then invite volunteers to share their soliloquies. Encourage students to discuss how soliloquies affect a scene. Ask volunteers to point out specific language that made the soliloquies seem natural.

GRAMMAR CONNECTION

Take this opportunity to talk about periods and commas. You may wish to have students point out periods and commas in their Read, Listen, Speak examples.

TEACH

Ask a volunteer to read aloud the first paragraph. Review the terms *literal meaning* and *implied meaning*. Explain that the literal meaning of a phrase carries the exact definitions from a dictionary. Point out that a phrase acquires an implied meaning

when, over time, it is used in different written or spoken contexts that communicate a meaning for the words that is different from the literal meaning.

Have volunteers read aloud the examples of idioms listed after the first paragraph and the two paragraphs that follow. Reiterate that idioms should not be taken literally. Then ask volunteers to list on the board other examples of idioms. Discuss the meaning of each.

Have a volunteer read aloud the paragraph on page 465. Point out that idioms are a way of using natural-sounding language that makes a character realistic and

can also help develop characters. Challenge students to identify idioms in some of the playwriting they have read in this chapter.

LiNK Read aloud the excerpt. Challenge students to identify the idiom in the excerpt *(in a pickle)*. Point out that this idiom is still used today with the same meaning.

PRACTICE

ACTIVITY A

Discuss the meaning of the first idiom and ask a volunteer to use it in a sentence. Then have

---

Idioms, Slang, and Jargon

Idioms

An idiom, also called an idiomatic expression, is a phrase whose literal meaning differs from the actual meaning. Unless the implied meaning of the expression is evident, the words may not make sense. For that reason people often learn the meanings of idioms by hearing them used in proper context. The following are a few common idioms:

- *a piece of cake*
- *break the ice*
- *down in the dumps*
- *ants in her pants*

A simple task is often referred to as *a piece of cake*. *Break the ice* is an appropriate idiom for starting a conversation in awkward social settings that can seem frozen when nobody is speaking. *Down in the dumps* suggests that someone is in a rut or having a hard time. *Ants in her pants* suggests that someone is restless or jittery, as if she had ants crawling inside her pants. It is not meant to be taken literally.

Idioms enter our language from many sources. Idioms can tell us something about our history. The idiom *face the music,* which means "coming to terms with unpleasant consequences," may have come from the military. When a soldier was court-martialed, drum music was often played.

LiNK

The Tempest

TRINCULO: I have been in such a pickle since I saw you last that, I fear me, will never out of my bones: I shall not fear fly-blowing.

SEBASTIAN: Why, how now, Stephano!

William Shakespeare

students complete this activity independently. Remind students to use a dictionary if needed. After students have finished, ask volunteers to read aloud their sentences. Discuss the meaning of each idiom.

ACTIVITY B

Have partners complete this activity. When students have finished, invite volunteers to write their idioms on the board. Challenge students to use each idiom in a sentence.

APPLY

WRITER'S CORNER

Allow time for students to find examples of idioms in their writing. Discuss which idioms are more difficult to replace than others and why. Students should demonstrate an understanding of idioms.

ASSESS

Note which students had difficulty using idioms. Use the Reteach option with those students who need additional reinforcement.

TEACHING OPTIONS

Reteach

Give an example of an idiom, such as "make a mountain out of a molehill." Tell students the literal meaning of the expression as well as the implied meaning. Explain that the context in which an idiom is written or spoken reveals the implied meaning.

Ask a volunteer to give an example of an idiom and have another volunteer sketch on the board the idiom's literal meaning. Then ask a student to identify the idiom's implied meaning. Encourage students to note the difference between the visual of the idiom's literal meaning and its implied meaning.

Idiom Match

Give small groups sets of note cards with an idiom written on each card. Then give students blank note cards equal to the number of cards with idioms. Challenge students to write the implied meaning of each idiom on a blank note card. Ask groups to trade sets of cards. Have students match each idiom with its implied meaning. Challenge each group to be the first to match all the note cards.

For Tomorrow

Ask students to choose an idiom and research its origin, including how it acquired its implied meaning. Conduct research on an idiom of your choosing and share your research with the class.

Playwrights often include idioms in dialogue to create characters that seem realistic and believable. They carefully choose idioms for their characters, matching idioms to the characters' genders, ages, cultures, and personalities.

ACTIVITY A Use each of these idioms in a sentence. If you don't know a meaning, look up the most important word in a dictionary. You may be able to find the meaning of the idiom in the part of the entry that follows the definition of the word.

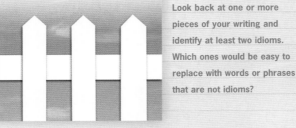

1. turn over a new leaf
2. eat your words
3. see eye to eye
4. right up my alley
5. in the same boat
6. know the ropes
7. fat chance
8. half-baked idea
9. for the birds
10. mend fences
11. all ears
12. cut corners
13. take the cake
14. see red
15. give a hand
16. lend an ear
17. keep an eye on
18. ran him ragged
19. in over your head
20. sit tight

Activity B
Possible answers:
1. make hay while the sun shines
2. give me a break
3. turn the other cheek
4. take your time
5. get a life
6. on the run
7. pull your leg
8. break a leg
9. have a ball
10. play the fool
11. go to pieces
12. throw in the towel

ACTIVITY B Some words appear in a number of idioms. Write as many idioms as you can that include each of these words.

1. make
2. give
3. turn
4. take
5. get
6. run
7. pull
8. break
9. have
10. play
11. go
12. throw

WRITER'S CORNER

Look back at one or more pieces of your writing and identify at least two idioms. Which ones would be easy to replace with words or phrases that are not idioms?

Creative Writing • 465

WARM-UP

Read, Listen, Speak

Write on the board the idiom you researched from yesterday's For Tomorrow homework. Tell students the idiom's origin and when it came into meaning. Invite volunteers to write their idioms on the board and to share their research. Challenge students to consider how a playwright might use any of the idioms to convey an emotion, such as joy or sadness.

GRAMMAR CONNECTION

Take this opportunity to talk about exclamation points, question marks, semicolons, and colons. You may wish to have students point out exclamation points, question marks, semicolons, and colons in their Read, Listen, Speak examples.

TEACH

Have a volunteer read aloud the section Slang. Discuss the last three questions with the class. Create a list on the board of slang used by students and a list of slang used by parents. Encourage students to write the lists in their notebooks for future reference. Use the lists to discuss how people of different groups use different slang words. Discuss how adding modern slang to an old play could change the audience's reaction to the play.

Ask a volunteer to read aloud the section Jargon. Invite students to give examples of jargon that they have heard. Challenge volunteers to explain how idioms, slang, and jargon differ.

PRACTICE

ACTIVITY C

Review the definition of *idiom*. When students have finished, ask whether the phrases are examples of idioms, slang, or jargon, and how students know the answer. Invite volunteers to share a definition for each item.

ACTIVITY D

Have partners complete this activity. Challenge students to search for unfamiliar examples. Then invite each pair to write two examples on the board. Ask volunteers to give the meaning and to tell whether the expression is slang or jargon.

ACTIVITY E

Brainstorm a list of idioms, slang, and jargon that might be used by a pioneer family at that time. Encourage students to brainstorm similar lists for each item. Then have partners complete this activity. After they have finished, ask students to select one item to perform for the Writer's Corner.

ACTIVITY F

Discuss the differences among idioms, slang, and jargon and be sure students understand these terms. Then have

---

Slang

Playwrights use slang carefully in their work. Slang is nonstandard, informal language. Writers must keep in mind that slang can become outdated. For example, many people in the 1950s used *swell* to describe things they liked. In the 1960s *groovy* was often used for the same meaning. Do you hear *swell* and *groovy* very often today? What adjectives do you use to describe things you like? What adjectives do your parents use?

Jargon

Another type of speech playwrights use is jargon, the special vocabulary of a particular profession or hobby. Snowboarders, computer programmers, and doctors all use jargon when they talk to others in the same profession. A playwright's task is to use enough jargon so that such characters seem real but not in a way that the audience cannot understand what the characters are saying. A playwright's goal is for all of his or her characters to speak appropriately for their age, family background, profession, and personality. All language should reflect the historical time in which a play takes place.

ACTIVITY C Write a short definition of what you think each word or phrase means. Using a dictionary or online resource, find each example and compare it to your definition.

1. best boy
2. gnarly
3. grind the rail
4. chill out
5. a four top
6. wet behind the ears
7. far out
8. cut and paste
9. with bells on
10. ASAP
11. lost his marbles
12. rain on my parade
13. LOL
14. way groovy
15. hit the hay
16. back up the hard drive

partners complete the activity independently. Discuss each sentence with the class.

APPLY

WRITER'S CORNER

Allow time for partners to discuss details about setting and characters and to read all the lines for the scene before performing. Ask students to take notes about how to improve their scenes. Allow time for revision and a second performance. After students have finished, invite them to discuss the specific suggestions or changes that improved the scenes. Students should demonstrate an understanding of idioms, slang, and jargon.

TechTip Encourage students to watch the recording of their performance and to make notes about ways to improve the performance.

ASSESS

Note which students had difficulty using idioms, slang, and jargon. Use the Reteach option with those students who need additional reinforcement.

Practice Book page 171 provides additional work with idioms, slangs, and jargon.

TEACHING OPTIONS

Reteach
Review the definitions of *slang* and *jargon*. Explain that jargon is usually used for a longer period of time than slang because jargon is associated with a profession or an interest that might have existed for many generations. Invite students to write checklists for identifying jargon and slang. Have students include points from the definitions you discussed. Name some terms that are slang or jargon and ask students to identify them by using their checklists.

Updating a Story
Review the similarities between *Romeo and Juliet* and *West Side Story*. (*They are dramas about two people who fall in love but who come from groups that do not get along.*) Provide students with excerpts from *West Side Story*. Ask students to find three examples from *West Side Story* of slang, jargon, or idioms. Ask students to write a few sentences about how slang, jargon, and idioms can update a story.

ACTIVITY D Browse through online and print newspapers and magazines to collect 20 terms of slang or jargon. For each item cite the source and provide a definition based on the context. If the definition is not clear from the source you found, research it further. (Hint: Type the word or phrase into a search engine and examine the results.)

ACTIVITY E Write a few lines of dialogue for each set of characters. Include idioms, slang, and jargon where they make sense.

1. a pioneer family heading west in a covered wagon
2. high school students at cheerleading camp
3. surgeons during an operation
4. a couple who draw cartoons for a living
5. architects and engineers at a construction site
6. two caterers getting ready for a big party
7. a boy and girl on a first date, eating at a fancy restaurant
8. a boy hopping a freight train during the Great Depression
9. twin surfers, age 13, at the beach
10. two signers of the Declaration of Independence
11. the first earthlings to land on Mars
12. two audience members watching a rodeo

Activity F
1. jargon
2. slang
3. idiom
4. slang
5. idiom
6. slang
7. jargon

ACTIVITY F Identify in each sentence whether the language used is an example of an idiom, slang, or jargon.

1. "I need a CT scan, stat!" cried the doctor on call.
2. The cowboy said, "Howdy, partner! Y'all from these parts?"
3. "Cat got your tongue?" he teased.
4. Claire's new dress is totally awesome and way cool.
5. "Well, pin a rose on your nose," Tommy grumbled.
6. "I ain't done nothin' wrong by speaking to the gentleman," cried Eliza.
7. "The suspect had a rap sheet with several priors," Officer Suarez told the chief.

WRITER'S CORNER

With a partner act out the dialogue you wrote for one item in Activity E. Does the dialogue sound realistic and believable? Explain why or why not. Revise your dialogue based on your partner's suggestions. Act it out again. Was it better the second time?

Tech Tip With your classmates, videotape your dialogue.

Creative Writing • 467

For Tomorrow

Have students write a review of the model on page 451. Tell them to write their reviews for a specific audience, such as a group of sports fans or chefs. Remind students to use the jargon, slang, and idioms of that audience. (*The Oak Street players scored a touchdown with their version of* Midas the King.) Write a review of your own for a specific audience.

OBJECTIVES

- **To identify free verse**
- **To understand the process of writing free verse**

WARM-UP

Read, Listen, Speak

Read your review from yesterday's For Tomorrow homework. Ask students to identify your intended audience. Challenge students to point out the idioms, slang, and jargon you used in your review. Have small groups share the reviews they wrote. Ask students to identify the intended audience for each review. Have each group make a list of the idioms, slang, and jargon used in each review.

GRAMMAR CONNECTION

Take this opportunity to talk about quotation marks and italics. You may wish to have students point out quotation marks and italics in their Read, Listen, Speak examples.

TEACH

Review what students know about conventional forms of poetry. Then read aloud the first paragraph, making sure students understand the definition of *free verse*. Ask students what it means to "evoke emotions and images" with words. Remind students of the definition of *figurative language*. Discuss examples of similes and metaphors.

Have volunteers read aloud the second paragraph and the poem. Ask a volunteer to use a dictionary and read aloud the definitions of *hawk* and *vermilion*. Have students give examples of how the poem evokes emotions and images *(personification of nature, nostalgic references to time past)*.

Ask a volunteer to read aloud the last paragraph. Encourage students to discuss the differences and similarities between the poet's experience and their own experiences of river roads. Invite students to suggest different ways to break the lines.

Ask a volunteer to read aloud the first paragraph of the section Free Verse Versus Prose. Allow time for students to read the prose example silently. Ask students to identify the differences they notice between the prose piece and the free verse poem. Challenge students to transform the prose piece into free verse by adding or replacing words and breaking the lines at significant points.

PRACTICE

ACTIVITY A

Allow time for students to reread the poem and to write answers to the questions. Ask students to work with partners to compare their answers. Then invite volunteers to share their answers with the class. Discuss each question and any differences in answers.

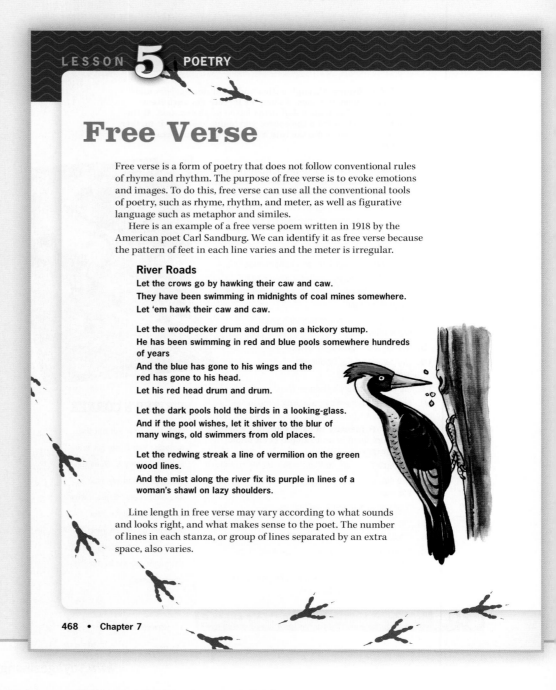

LESSON 5 POETRY

Free Verse

Free verse is a form of poetry that does not follow conventional rules of rhyme and rhythm. The purpose of free verse is to evoke emotions and images. To do this, free verse can use all the conventional tools of poetry, such as rhyme, rhythm, and meter, as well as figurative language such as metaphor and similes.

Here is an example of a free verse poem written in 1918 by the American poet Carl Sandburg. We can identify it as free verse because the pattern of feet in each line varies and the meter is irregular.

River Roads
Let the crows go by hawking their caw and caw.
They have been swimming in midnights of coal mines somewhere.
Let 'em hawk their caw and caw.

Let the woodpecker drum and drum on a hickory stump.
He has been swimming in red and blue pools somewhere hundreds of years
And the blue has gone to his wings and the red has gone to his head.
Let his red head drum and drum.

Let the dark pools hold the birds in a looking-glass.
And if the pool wishes, let it shiver to the blur of many wings, old swimmers from old places.

Let the redwing streak a line of vermilion on the green wood lines.
And the mist along the river fix its purple in lines of a woman's shawl on lazy shoulders.

Line length in free verse may vary according to what sounds and looks right, and what makes sense to the poet. The number of lines in each stanza, or group of lines separated by an extra space, also varies.

468 • Chapter 7

APPLY

WRITER'S CORNER

Tell students that the topic should be something that is important to them or part of a memory. After students have finished writing, begin a list on the board of images and emotions. Invite volunteers to name ideas associated with each image or emotion listed. Students should demonstrate an understanding of sensory images in writing.

ASSESS

Note which students had difficulty understanding free verse. Use the Reteach option with those students who need additional reinforcement.

TEACHING OPTIONS

Reteach

Have students work in small groups to create a chart that compares and contrasts free verse, conventional poetry, and prose. Tell each group to complete the chart, using ideas from the sections Free Verse and Free Verse Versus Prose.

Everyday Free Verse

Display a copy of "This Is Just to Say" by William Carlos Williams. Ask a volunteer to read aloud the poem. Encourage students to discuss the poem and how everyday events can be portrayed in poetry. Tell students that Williams's poem has been imitated in humorous ways.

Display the following free verse poem or some of your own:

> **Muddy puddle supervillain pants were no match.**
>
> **Detergent and iron powerless before you.**

Ask students to think of a commonplace event and to write a humorous free verse poem about it.

Free Verse Versus Prose

Free verse may sometimes sound like prose, or ordinary, unadorned writing, but it is not. In some ways free verse can be more difficult to write than rhymed poetry. To demonstrate the difference between free verse and prose, read the following passage:

> Crows belong to the family Corvidae, along with jays, nutcrackers, and magpies. Although crows are classified as songbirds, their usual call is a harsh caw.
>
> An adult crow is 15–18 inches long and weighs about 20 ounces. Its wingspan can be up to three feet. The beak is large, about 2½ inches long, and quite sturdy. Both males and females are entirely black.
>
> Crows flock in groups ranging from family units to several hundred—or even several thousand—birds. They fly at speeds of 25–30 miles an hour and range for food as far as 30 miles a day. Crows are omnivorous; they eat insects, grain, fruit, eggs, organic garbage, and just about anything else they can find or kill.

ACTIVITY A Reread "River Roads" and the prose passage above. Then answer the questions.

1. How does Sandburg tell the reader what sounds crows make? How does he describe their color?

2. How does the prose passage give this information? How is this different from the poem?

3. Which passage sounds like a person speaking? Why?

4. Which passage seems to be informative, and which seems to be imaginary? Why? Give examples.

5. What pictures come into your mind when you read the poem and the passage? Which are more vivid? Why?

6. What do you think is Sandburg's purpose in writing this poem?

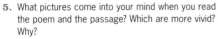

WRITER'S CORNER

Choose a topic. Freewrite 10 ideas that evoke strong sensory images and emotions for you.

Creative Writing • 469

For Tomorrow

Ask students to imagine the job they hope to have in 10 years and to write a free verse poem about one day on that job. Write a free verse poem of your own about being a teacher.

WARM-UP

Read, Listen, Speak

Read aloud the poem you wrote for yesterday's For Tomorrow homework. Discuss what characteristics make it free verse. Invite volunteers to read aloud their free verse poems. Ask students to name senses that the poems call on and images and emotions the poems evoke.

GRAMMAR CONNECTION

Take this opportunity to talk about apostrophes, hyphens, and dashes. You may wish to have students point out apostrophes, hyphens, and dashes in their Read, Listen, Speak examples.

TEACH

Invite a volunteer to read aloud the sentence under The Poetic Process and the first two paragraphs of the section Sensory Language. Allow time for students to read the poem silently. When they have finished, ask them what senses the poem engages. Have students discuss each line of the poem, mentioning any imagery or unfamiliar words.

Ask a volunteer to read aloud the first two paragraphs of the section Rhythm, Rhyme, and Repetition. Then read aloud the

example, putting extra emphasis on the stressed syllables. Read the example again and have students clap for each stressed syllable.

Read aloud the rest of the section. Point out that meter is important in poetry but is not common in free verse. Discuss how the use of assonance and alliteration can help create rhythm in free verse.

Ask a student to read aloud the section Figurative Language. Invite students to identify other examples of figurative language in the poem. Remind them that personification is a type of figurative language.

PRACTICE

ACTIVITY B

Complete one or two items with the class. Then have students complete the activity independently. Have volunteers share a few words and associated images with the class. Encourage students to offer other images for each word.

ACTIVITY C

Review assonance and alliteration. Encourage students to use one of these to help create rhythm in their poem. Have students complete this activity

The Poetic Process

The following are some tools that poets can use to write free verse.

Sensory Language

Free verse uses sensory language to create vivid pictures of its subject.

Read this passage from Robert Penn Warren's "Mediterranean Beach, Day After Storm." Warren uses sensory words to let the reader see and hear the waves crashing against the shore. Words such as *whang*, *clang*, and *fling* sound like what they mean. This is called onomatopoeia.

> How instant joy, how clang
> And whang the sun, how
> Whoop the sea, and oh,
> Sun, sing, as whiter than
> Rage of snow, let sea the spume
> Fling.

Rhythm, Rhyme, and Repetition

The mood, or attitude, of a poem can be determined by the rhythm of its language. A light, quick-moving rhythm usually conveys a whimsical thought and creates a joyous mood. Slower rhythm generally suggests a more thoughtful or sad mood.

The rhythm of a poem can often be determined by reading it aloud. Your voice will automatically stress the accented syllables. In many types of poetry, the stress falls on a regular beat. Listen for the accented syllables as you read aloud these lines from one of Shakespeare's sonnets:

> So are you to my thoughts as food to life,
> Or as sweet-seasoned showers are to the ground;

When lines of poetry have a repeated rhythm as the lines above do, they are said to have regular meter. Meter is how the words are arranged in poetry to achieve its rhythm.

Free verse does not usually follow regular meter; however, rhymes do sometimes appear in free verse poetry. Read this line of "River Roads" aloud: *And the blue has gone to his wings and the red has gone to his head.* Note the rhyme *red* and *head*. Sandburg uses a singsong rhythm to describe the woodpecker.

independently. Invite volunteers to share their poems with the class.

APPLY

WRITER'S CORNER
Remind students of the different techniques they can use to create rhythm in their poetry. After students have finished, invite them to share their poems with a partner and discuss how and why they changed the verses. Students should demonstrate an understanding of how to write free verse.

ASSESS

Note which students had difficulty understanding free verse. Use the Reteach option with those students who need additional reinforcement.

Practice Book page 172 provides additional work with free verse.

Practice Book page 172

TEACHING OPTIONS

Reteach
Write *Sensory Language* on the board above the headings *Sight, Smell, Sound, Touch,* and *Taste*. Ask students to name words that they associate with each of the senses and to write them on the board. After each heading has a short list of words, create an impromptu sensory poem by saying "I see . . ." or "I smell . . ." and so on, inviting a volunteer to complete your sentence by repeating a word from the list.

Encourage students to discuss the mood created by each sound and the length of each sound. Have students reread "River Roads" and discuss in small groups whether the poem is serious or joyful, based on its rhythm and repetition.

Meant to Be Read
Explain that reading aloud poetry that employs onomatopoeia can add to the enjoyment of the poem. Assign small groups a different part of the poem on page 470, either up to a punctuation mark or to the end of a line. Have groups practice reciting the entire poem aloud. Then ask groups to recite their different parts for the class, creating a group reading of the poem.

"River Roads" achieves its rhythm by varying its meter and repeating *Let* and the phrases *caw and caw* and *drum and drum*. Sandburg also selected words that have similar vowel sounds, such as *hawk, hawking,* and *caw*. This is called assonance. Alliteration, using words that start with the same consonant sound, is another way to build a poem's rhythm. "Mediterranean Beach" uses alliteration when it repeats the *"s"* sound in *sun, sea, snow,* and *spume*. The *"wh"* sound is repeated in *whang* and *whoop*.

Figurative Language
Free verse poetry relies heavily on metaphors, similes, and hyperbole to paint vivid images in the reader's mind. By using figurative language in poetry, two ideas that seem to make no sense can be put together. Read this line of "River Roads": *They have been swimming in midnights of coal mines somewhere*. Though it seems absurd to think of swimming in midnights, the metaphor communicates the essential blackness of the crow's feathers.

ACTIVITY B Read each abstract word. Then write several images that the word suggests to you. Use the first image that comes to mind, even if it does not make sense. Choose words that paint a picture in the reader's mind.

EXAMPLE: boredom—a drippy, wet sponge

1. sadness
2. freedom
3. honesty
4. pain
5. trust
6. bravery
7. dreams
8. justice
9. relaxation
10. beauty

ACTIVITY C Choose an image that you wrote in Activity B and write a short poem that uses that image. Use the techniques discussed in this lesson—such as rhythm, rhyme, and repetition—to write your poem. Use a rhyming dictionary or online source to help you find similar-sounding words.

WRITER'S CORNER

Write a free verse poem, using the ideas you wrote for the Writer's Corner on page 469. Add to, pare down, and alter your lines until they sound and look like poetry to you.

For Tomorrow
Ask students to write at least six lines of free verse that include onomatopoeia. Create your own free verse poem using onomatopoeia.

Creative Writing • 471

OBJECTIVES

- **To adapt a story into a script for a reader's theater performance**
- **To use a minimal setting for a reader's theater script**
- **To enhance speaking skills by rehearsing and performing a reader's theater script**

WARM-UP

Read, Listen, Speak

Read aloud your poem from yesterday's For Tomorrow homework. As you read, put extra emphasis on the examples of onomatopoeia. Then invite volunteers to read aloud their poems. Ask students to offer feedback on the use of onomatopoeia. Suggest that students also identify rhyme, if any, in each poem and clap the rhythms.

GRAMMAR CONNECTION

Take this opportunity to talk about capitalization. You may wish to have students point out capitalization in their Read, Listen, Speak examples.

TEACH

Tell students that they are going to write a script for reader's theater, a type of oral reading. Invite a volunteer to read aloud the first paragraph. Encourage students to share their experiences performing reader's theater.

Have a volunteer read aloud the section Choose a Story. Ask students to name other qualities that would be important to consider when selecting a story *(length, complexity of the plot, dialogue)*. Point out that a story with more descriptive prose than dialogue might not make engaging reader's theater, and that the writer of reader's theater needs to develop original dialogue.

Invite volunteers to read aloud the section Create a Script. Encourage students to identify additional strategies for adapting a story into a script. *(Make the most engaging prose sections of the story the most engaging sections of the script. Carry the tone and mood of the story into the script.)* Reminds students that they can use monologues, asides, idioms, slang, and jargon to develop their characters.

Ask volunteers to read aloud the section Setting the Stage. Ask students to explain why only a minimal setting is required for reader's theater.

PRACTICE

ACTIVITY A

Assign small groups one of the short stories. Allow time for groups to read or skim the stories. Then challenge students to compile a list of reasons why the stories are or are not good candidates for reader's theater. Have groups present their findings to the class.

ACTIVITY B

Review the information about character descriptions on page 456. Have students complete this activity with the same groups as in Activity A.

Reader's Theater

Reader's theater is a convenient and enjoyable way to present favorite stories in dramatic form. The scripts for reader's theater performances are generally adaptations of stories. The stories are rewritten with parts for narrators and characters so the stories can be performed for an audience. Reader's theater is a blend of reading aloud and putting on a play.

Choose a Story

Pick a story that you think performers will like and one that is suitable for the intended audience. Consider the number of parts to be read and the number of readers. Sometimes it might be necessary to combine or divide a few parts to match the number of readers. If necessary, brainstorm ideas to revise the original story to make it livelier or easier to understand or perform in script form. After you have chosen a story and revised it, you can write the script.

Create a Script

The script for reader's theater is taken from the story on which it is based. When you write the dialogue, be sure it reveals everything the audience should know about the characters and the setting. Most importantly, write dialogue to reveal the plot, including the rising action, the climax, and the resolution. Spoken dialogue in the story is assigned to characters, while descriptive and narrative prose is assigned to the narrator.

When the script is done, assign parts, and have each reader use a colored marker on a photocopied script to highlight the lines that he or she will read. Generally, if the narrator's part is the longest, consider dividing the narrator's role into smaller parts, each to be read by a different reader.

APPLY

SPEAKER'S CORNER

Have students in small groups select a section of dialogue from a short story. Have each student read aloud the group's dialogue, using different emotions and emphases than the other students. Invite students to offer feedback about which emphases and speaking techniques are the most effective. Students should demonstrate an understanding of reading dialogue in plays.

ASSESS

Note which students had difficulty reading aloud short-story dialogues for reader's theater. Use the Reteach option with those students who need additional reinforcement.

TEACHING OPTIONS

Reteach

Have a recording device available for students. Provide short monologues and have students record themselves reading the monologues aloud. Encourage students to listen to their recordings, note areas that could be improved, and rerecord the monologues, using different emphases and emotions.

Audio Books

Bring a few audio books to class and play random selections for students. Encourage them to note how the dialogue, prose, and sound effects work to make the story come alive. Have students work with partners to guess the plot of the stories based on the selections.

Setting the Stage

Setting a stage for reader's theater is simple. Because the audience relies on the narrator to paint a mental picture of the setting, there is very little need for physical props or sets. Often, the setting for reader's theater is made up of stools or chairs for the readers to sit on while another actor is speaking. You can use cardboard boxes, blocks, chairs, and other simple props to stand for just about anything the script calls for. If you like, experiment with simple lighting, sound effects, and music.

In reader's theater, the readers don't exit the performance area, but they might do simple actions such as step back or turn away from the audience to indicate that they are "offstage." Readers who move around should hold their scripts in one hand rather than resting them on a stand.

ACTIVITY A Find and read one or two of the following short stories. Determine if they would be good choices for reader's theater. Explain why or why not.

1. "Why I Live at the P.O."—Eudora Welty
2. "The Monkey's Paw"—W. W. Jacobs
3. "Dreamworld"—Isaac Asimov
4. "The Lottery"—Shirley Jackson
5. "Masque of the Red Death"—Edgar Allen Poe
6. "The Ransom of Red Chief"—O. Henry

ACTIVITY B Write character descriptions for the characters you read about in one of the short stories from Activity A. Include information about the characters' personalities that you think the actors needs to know in order to play each part. Then write a brief dialogue between two of these characters based on an event that happens in the short story.

SPEAKER'S CORNER

Choose a few lines of dialogue from a short story. Read the dialogue several different ways, in different tones of voice and emphasizing different words. Express different emotions as you read.

For Tomorrow

Ask students to select favorite short stories that are appropriate for adapting into a reader's theater performance. Have students write brief plot summaries and character lists as part of a script. Write a plot summary and character list for one of your favorite short stories to share with the class.

Creative Writing • 473

WARM-UP

Read, Listen, Speak

Share your plot summary and character list from yesterday's For Tomorrow homework. Then have small groups discuss the stories they selected. Ask students to share their plot summaries and character lists. Encourage each group to agree on the story that would work best for reader's theater. Have volunteers share which story they chose, pointing out specific reasons why it would work for reader's theater.

TEACH

Invite a volunteer to read aloud the section Rehearse. Ask students to identify additional reasons for rehearsing the performance *(to become familiar with the dialogue)*. Have a volunteer read aloud the first two paragraphs of the Perform section. Ask another student to read aloud the list of tips. Invite volunteers to suggest additions to the list.

Read aloud the Audience Tips section. Pause after each bulleted item and discuss it with the class. Be sure students understand that reader's theater is a fun way to present a story.

PRACTICE

ACTIVITY C

Review the Setting the Stage section on page 473. Then complete this activity as a class, writing on the board a list of props.

ACTIVITY D

Have students complete this activity independently. Ask volunteers to share their stage layouts with the class. Have the class vote on which is the best.

ACTIVITY E

Review idioms, slang, and jargon. Encourage students to use these as they read each line. Then allow students time to create their performance for each of the six characters. Invite volunteers to read aloud each line. Remind students to applaud when a volunteer is finished.

ACTIVITY F

Have students brainstorm a list of several short stories. Instruct students to choose the story

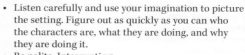

Rehearse

After choosing a story and developing the script, rehearse the performance. Practice several times, having the readers experiment with different voices and gestures. Consider switching roles among readers to experiment with dialogue styles and to keep the rehearsals interesting.

Perform

Though the scripts do not need to be memorized, the more familiar the readers are with the script, the more smoothly and expressively they will be able to read the dialogue.

Readers may want to read over the scripts both silently and aloud, making notations to remind themselves of how they want to read. They might, for example, underline words they want to emphasize or mark places where they need to make a movement.

Readers should keep these tips in mind:

- Stand or sit up straight.
- Project your voice. Speak louder, more clearly, and slower than seems natural.
- Do not let the script block your face.
- Read with feeling. Let your face show a lot of expression.
- Face the audience as much as possible, even when miming an action.
- When not reading, stay still.

Audience Tips

As the audience of reader's theater, try to imagine the world that the narrator creates in reciting the words of the script.

- Listen carefully and use your imagination to picture the setting. Figure out as quickly as you can who the characters are, what they are doing, and why they are doing it.
- Be polite. Interrupting the readers can cause them to lose their place and disrupt the performance.
- Enjoy yourself and let the readers know that you enjoyed their performance.

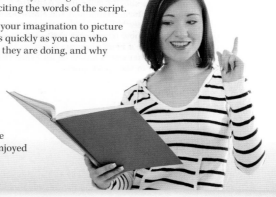

that would work best for reader's theater. When students have finished, invite volunteers to read their plot summaries aloud.

ACTIVITY G
Review Lesson 2 and 3 from this chapter. Have partners complete this activity. Tell students to decide which partner's stories would work better for reader's theater.

APPLY
SPEAKER'S CORNER
Give students time to rehearse their scripts and to perform them for the class. Encourage the

audience to follow the audience tips on page 474. Students should demonstrate an understanding of how to write and perform a reader's theater script.

ASSESS
Note which students had difficulty performing reader's theater. Use the Reteach option with those students who need additional reinforcement.

After you have reviewed Lessons 3–5, administer the Writing Skills Assessment on pages 69–70 in the **Assessment Book.** This test is also available on the optional **Test Generator CD.**

TEACHING OPTIONS

Reteach
Compile a few CDs or DVDs of modern presidential speeches, such as FDR's first inaugural address or JFK's inaugural address. Provide students with transcripts of the speeches. Have students deliver excerpts from the speeches in front of the class. Encourage students to speak authoritatively, emphasizing the appropriate words and phrases. After each speech, play the CD or DVD of the speech and compare students' speeches with the actual speeches.

News Reports
Have small groups write fictional news reports that include local news, weather, sports, and traffic. When students have finished writing, have groups present their news reports to the class. After each report, have volunteers summarize one segment of the report.

Activity C
Necessary props include: chair and table for homework, telephone or telephone ring, toys, lamp, side table for lamp, backpack, headphones

ACTIVITY C Read the following paragraph and determine what props are necessary for the scene.

Michael returns from school and sits down to start his homework. The phone rings. As he gets up to answer it, he trips over his little brother's toys and stubs his toe. Michael jumps out in pain and knocks into his mother's favorite lamp. Michael reaches out to grab the lamp before it falls and luckily makes the catch. He sets the lamp back on the side table and wipes his brow in relief. As he returns to his homework, the phone rings. Michael pulls headphones out of his backpack, puts them on, and goes back to work.

ACTIVITY D Using the example on page 456 as a template, create a picture of what the stage would look like with props for the paragraph in Activity C.

ACTIVITY E Read the line below, using the following characters. You can improvise the words to reflect the voice and gestures the character would use.

"Hello, how are you doing today? I'm feeling well."

1. a cowboy or cowgirl in the South
2. a British professor to his students
3. a hippie or flower child in the '70s
4. a mad scientist after making a breakthrough
5. an elderly woman to her grandchildren
6. a six-year-old boy playing with his toys

ACTIVITY F Select a favorite short story or novel that has more than one character and plenty of dialogue. Record the various roles that appear in the story. Then write a plot summary in paragraph form.

ACTIVITY G Write a reader's theater script based on the passage you selected in Activity F. Use the conventions of playwriting discussed in Lessons 1, 2, and 3 for writing your script.

SPEAKER'S CORNER

Work with classmates to perform the script from Activity G. Follow the suggestions in this lesson to make your performance a success.

Creative Writing • 475

PREWRITING AND DRAFTING

Review what students have learned about creative writing and playwriting. Encourage students to address the following characteristics of playwriting:

- Essential characteristics of a play are plot, theme, character(s), and setting.
- Plays are usually divided into acts or scenes.
- Script format includes character and setting descriptions that provide a context for the story.
- Dialogue, character names, and stage directions are formatted so they can be easily differentiated from one another and are useful to a reader.
- Dialogues, monologues, and asides are dramatic characteristics used in a play to communicate significant points and themes.
- Idioms, slang, and jargon are used to further develop characters.

Point out that creative writing allows a writer to explore a number of writing techniques, but still requires discipline. Explain that format and structure are necessary in a creative piece. Remind students of the specific purposes play structure and format serve *(to make a play script easy to follow, to provide background information and descriptions)*. Invite a volunteer to read aloud the first two paragraphs.

Prewriting

Ask a student to read aloud this paragraph. Explain that prewriting for a play demands more of a writer than prewriting for other genres. Point out that the writer should consider conflicts, actions, and character studies that are interesting when read silently and also when performed for an audience.

Brainstorming

Invite a volunteer to read aloud this section. Remind students of the characteristics of playwriting that include exposition, conflict, climax, and resolution. Point out that these are good points to remember when brainstorming.

Remind students that ideas are the foundation of all writing, especially creative writing. Tell students that strong ideas supported by interesting characters and dialogue help make strong creative writing.

Freewriting

Read aloud this section. Ask what the questions address *(the characteristics of playwriting)*. Explain that if a theme is not apparent after freewriting, a writer should consider freewriting on another topic.

Prewriting and Drafting

Playwriting can be a fun way to share a story. Through a script of dialogue and stage direction, you can craft a work that brings a story to life. Now you will use what you have discussed in this chapter to write a one-act play.

Jamal, an eighth grader, looked forward to writing a play. He liked listening to people talk, and the idea of writing the way people speak sounded exciting.

Prewriting

Before you sit down to write your play, take time to think about what you want to write. The prewriting stage for playwriting involves brainstorming and freewriting to develop characters and themes. It's also a time for developing the play's plot.

Brainstorming

Some playwrights begin to think of ideas for plays by brainstorming different characters and the conflicts that can be sparked between them. Characters might consist of people that playwrights know, have read or heard about, or have made up in their imaginations. Playwrights may brainstorm various themes they want to write about.

Jamal brainstormed some incidents that involved conflict from his life and his friends' lives. When he was finished, Jamal chose a conflict between himself and his mother, one in which his mother made him babysit his sister during the day for a week.

Freewriting

When Jamal decided on a conflict, he used freewriting to explore and expand his idea. To help guide his freewriting session, he asked himself the following questions:

1. Who is the protagonist? Micah
2. Who or what is the antagonist? What is the relationship to the protagonist? Mrs. Johnson. They are son and mother.
3. What is the main conflict of the play? Mrs. Johnson wants Micah to take care of the baby every afternoon while she is at work. Micah wants to hang out with his friends and look cool and thinks the baby will ruin everything.
4. What is the inciting incident? Micah and his mother get into a shouting match. Mrs. Johnson threatens to take away Micah's cell phone for a month. Micah angrily gives in.
5. How is the conflict resolved? Micah discovers that the baby attracts girls' attention. Suddenly, he is very popular, so he is pleased with his babysitting job.
6. What is the theme of the play? Good things can come from unpromising beginnings.

Your Turn

Allow time for students to brainstorm and freewrite ideas for plays. Encourage students to ask themselves the same questions Jamal asked when freewriting.

Planning the Play

Ask a volunteer to read aloud this section. Ask why plays are divided into acts and scenes *(to signal a break in the action of the play or a change in the setting)*.

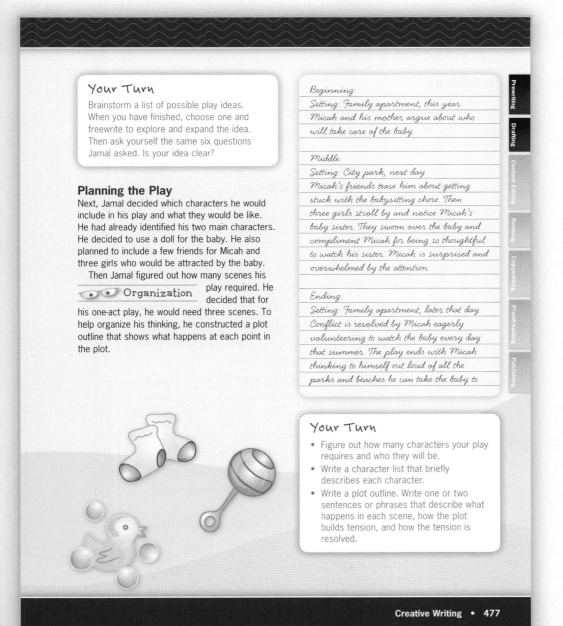 Point out that organization is the way writers put their ideas together. Explain that in creative writing, stories and plays have a plot with a beginning, a middle, and an ending.

Have students read silently Jamal's plot outline. Point out that Jamal wrote the setting for each scene and made it clear which action *(conflict, rising action, resolution)* to include in each scene. Invite students to determine if the action in the outline makes sense.

Your Turn

Ask a volunteer to read aloud this section. Remind students that they are writing one-act plays. Have students share their work and explain how the action progresses and how conflicts are resolved.

TEACHING OPTIONS

Writing Character Sketches

Have students write in paragraph form detailed sketches of their characters. Explain that the more physical and personal traits students assign to each character now, the easier it will be to draft the shorter character descriptions and dialogue later. Encourage students to identify which characters are the protagonist and the antagonist. Suggest that students turn to page 454 and use the list of tips for developing characters while writing their sketches.

Your Turn

Brainstorm a list of possible play ideas. When you have finished, choose one and freewrite to explore and expand the idea. Then ask yourself the same six questions Jamal asked. Is your idea clear?

Planning the Play

Next, Jamal decided which characters he would include in his play and what they would be like. He had already identified his two main characters. He decided to use a doll for the baby. He also planned to include a few friends for Micah and three girls who would be attracted by the baby.

Then Jamal figured out how many scenes his play required. He decided that for his one-act play, he would need three scenes. To help organize his thinking, he constructed a plot outline that shows what happens at each point in the plot.

Organization

Beginning:
Setting: Family apartment, this year
Micah and his mother argue about who will take care of the baby.

Middle:
Setting: City park, next day
Micah's friends tease him about getting stuck with the babysitting chore. Then three girls stroll by and notice Micah's baby sister. They swoon over the baby and compliment Micah for being so thoughtful to watch his sister. Micah is surprised and overwhelmed by the attention.

Ending:
Setting: Family apartment, later that day
Conflict is resolved by Micah eagerly volunteering to watch the baby every day that summer. The play ends with Micah thinking to himself out loud of all the parks and beaches he can take the baby to.

(side tabs: Prewriting, Drafting, Content Editing, Revising, Copyediting, Proofreading, Publishing)

Your Turn

- Figure out how many characters your play requires and who they will be.
- Write a character list that briefly describes each character.
- Write a plot outline. Write one or two sentences or phrases that describe what happens in each scene, how the plot builds tension, and how the tension is resolved.

Creative Writing • 477

OBJECTIVE
- To draft a script for a one-act play

Drafting

Read aloud the paragraph at the top of the page. Point out that Jamal's outline has three scenes but that this is a draft of just the first scene. Invite three volunteers to read aloud Jamal's draft—one to read the setting description, one to read Mrs. Johnson's part, and one to read Micah's part. Encourage the students to follow the stage directions in reading their parts.

Ask students whether Jamal included effective setting descriptions and stage directions. Discuss whether the characters' dialogue seems believable and if character descriptions are needed for this scene.

Writing Natural-Sounding Dialogue

Invite a volunteer to read aloud the first paragraph of this section. Ask students to point out natural-sounding language in Jamal's draft. *(Micah uses the slang word* dweeb. *Mrs. Johnson uses the idiomatic expression "What is the big deal?")* Have a volunteer read aloud the second paragraph and the example sentences. Encourage the student to use a different emphasis with each sentence to reflect the differences in tone of voice and delivery. Ask how contractions slightly change the meaning and tone of a sentence.

Have a volunteer read aloud the last two paragraphs. Ask students to reread their drafts and to note whether they used natural-sounding language. Encourage students to refer to the character sketches to determine how each character's manner of speaking could be rewritten to sound more natural. Suggest students use slang, idioms, and jargon.

Drafting

Jamal reviewed his planning notes, plot outline, and character list. Then he wrote a first draft. Here is the first scene in his script.

Baby Blues

SCENE 1

(Inside of apartment. Mrs. Johnson jigles baby who is fussing and paces as she argues with son. TV in background)

MRS. JOHNSON: *(calmly)* It will be just be for a few months until school is out. And you know you love Naomi. Besides I don't have anyone else I trust.

MICAH: *(yells)* Mom, no, I can't! Please don't make me. You just don't understand!

MRS. JOHNSON: You can, Micah and you will. I just don't have anyone else I trust. What is the big deal? It will be just for a few hours you'll have plenty of time to do homework after I get home.

MICAH: Homework I am not worried about homework! I'll look like a dweeb even stupider than I do now. Nobody else has to drag a baby around. No boys, anyway. I'll just have to stay inside and suffocate.

MRS. JOHNSON: Please do not say anything else. Do you want me to take away the cell phone? You are my hansome son so you will not look like a dweeb and I absolutely forbid you to stay inside. You need fresh air and so does Naomi. *(glares at Micah in a way that ends the argument) I am going to the kitchen to start dinner. (walks away)*

MICAH: *(to her back)* OK, fine, You win. I hope you're happy you're ruining my life! *(micah exits.)*

Tell students that voice is the writer speaking through the words on the page. Explain that the language that helps readers hear and feel the personality of the writer creates the voice. Remind students that all writers have a unique voice and that they must choose words carefully to create their own voice.

Grammar in Action. Students should identify the conjunctive adverb *Besides* in Jamal's first draft.

Your Turn
Ask a volunteer to read aloud this section. Suggest that students place the beginning, middle, and end in separate scenes. Remind students to include character and setting descriptions in the opening as well as stage directions throughout the dialogue.

TEACHING OPTIONS

Stage for One
Ask students to consider including monologues, soliloquies, and asides in their play scripts. Review the information on page 462. Invite volunteers to explain the purposes of monologues, soliloquies, and asides (*to have a character reveal personal or secret information to another character or to the audience, to provide background information*). Challenge students to add at least one monologue, soliloquy, or aside to their drafts. Ask volunteers to read aloud what they wrote and to explain its purpose in the plot of the play.

Writing Natural-Sounding Dialogue
Listen carefully to the way people speak. Notice the frequent sentence fragments, interjections, and interruptions. Use such natural-sounding speech patterns in the dialogue you write.

Read aloud the following dialogue to help you figure out where contractions would naturally appear. Choosing to use or not to use contractions can help you place the emphasis where you want it to be.

Compare the following sentences:
- You'll do what I tell you, no matter what, Missy said.
- You will do what I tell you, no matter what, Missy said.

Interruptions make for natural-sounding speech. Use dashes to indicate interrupted sentences.

Remember, though, that dialogue must sound natural to the character speaking. Think of a character type who usually speaks clearly and enunciates words fully, such as a butler who

Voice takes pride in being a perfectionist. Would slang or contractions sound natural coming from that character? Probably not.

Grammar in Action

Identify the conjunctive adverb in Jamal's first draft on p. 478.

Your Turn
Gather your planning notes, plot outline, and character list and prepare to write your first draft. Unlike Jamal's excerpt, your play draft will need to include a beginning, a middle, and an end.

What sounds natural?

Prewriting | Drafting | Content Editing | Revising | Copyediting | Proofreading | Publishing

Creative Writing • 479

OBJECTIVE

• **To edit a first draft for content**

CONTENT EDITING

Invite a student to read aloud the first paragraph. Explain that setting descriptions and dialogue are important in a play script because they signal the progression of the action. Explain that since the story is intended to be performed and not just read, students should consider reading aloud the dialogue in their drafts several times to note whether the sequence of events makes sense.

Tell students that sentence fluency is the sound of the writing. Suggest that students read their writing aloud to hear where the writing might sound choppy or awkward. Remind students that they can use assonance and alliteration to add rhythm to the sound of their sentences.

Have a volunteer read aloud the Content Editor's Checklist. Ask what the points on the checklist address *(the characteristics of playwriting)*. Point out that it is necessary for a play to include all these points.

Have students read silently the paragraph after the checklist and Evan's comments about Jamal's draft. Challenge students to identify the points on the Content Editor's Checklist that Evan specifically addressed with his comments. Point out Evan's last comment and the necessity of making the conflict, rising action, climax, and resolution clear to the audience. Challenge students to suggest other revisions to Jamal's draft. *(The draft lacks stage directions that describe what the characters are doing while they are speaking.)*

Editor's Workshop   Playwriting

Content Editing

Jamal read his first draft and thought it was a good scene. He also knew that his play would have to be edited for content. Like expository and persuasive essays, the ideas behind creative writing need to be edited for logic and clarity. Events within a play must follow a logical order that the audience can understand. He asked Evan, a classmate, to read *Baby Blues* and edit the play.

Sentence Fluency

Evan used the following Content Editor's Checklist to edit Jamal's draft.

Content Editor's Checklist

☐ Does the play have a protagonist and an antagonist?

☐ Are the characters well developed?

☐ Is the inciting incident for the main conflict included?

☐ Does the conflict make sense?

☐ Is enough exposition provided so that the audience can figure out what is going on?

☐ Do the characters have something to do onstage?

☐ Are the stage directions a good blueprint for someone to direct the play?

☐ Can a theme be inferred from the play?

☐ Does the play have a plot that has a rising action and a climax?

☐ Does the ending resolve the conflict?

Your Turn

Have a volunteer read aloud this section. Allow time for students to meet with an editing partner and offer each other suggestions. Encourage students to refer to the Content Editor's Checklist and read each other's drafts. Remind partners to offer positive as well as constructive feedback.

Writer's Tip Tell students that reading aloud all types of writing is beneficial during the writing process. Point out that this is especially useful when playwriting because the words are meant to be performed.

TEACHING OPTIONS

Thematic Editing

Invite students to discuss the themes of their plays. Suggest that they identify the points in each play where the theme evolves. Explain that sometimes a play's theme is made obvious only at the end, but that it is most effective to address the theme throughout the play. Encourage students to suggest additions or deletions to their drafts that specifically address the themes. Invite volunteers to share their themes with the class.

Evan read Jamal's draft and jotted down some questions and suggestions. Then he and Jamal got together for an editing conference. Here is what Evan had to say about Jamal's draft.

- I like your script a lot. The characters seem like real people. Mrs. Johnson and Micah both had understandable motivations that didn't feel forced.
- The conflict was very realistic. I can imagine how it would feel having to babysit every day. That would be a real problem that most kids could relate to.
- I couldn't figure out what Micah and his mother were arguing about until nearly the end of the scene. I think you should explain the conflict sooner. The audience will want to know what's going on right away.
- You repeated Mrs. Johnson's line about not having anyone to trust. Maybe you should take out the repeated words or change them.
- We learned that people often interrupt each other when they speak. Since they appear to be arguing, should your characters do this, too?
- This is only the first scene, so I don't know whether the action rises to a climax and I don't know if the conflict is resolved. But I can't wait to see how the rest of the play turns out!

Your Turn

Trade your draft script with a partner. Review each other's scripts, using the Content Editor's Checklist as a guide. Then have an editing conference.

- What did you like about your partner's script?
- Ask questions about the parts that confused you.
- Make suggestions for improvements. Be specific!
- Refer to the script as you give reasons for your opinions.

Writer's Tip You may find that reading your partner's script aloud will help both of you notice things that you missed when you read it silently.

Creative Writing • 481

OBJECTIVE
- To revise a draft of a one-act play

REVISING

Invite volunteers to read aloud the first paragraph and Jamal's revised draft. Have one student read the setting descriptions and have others read the parts of Micah and Mrs. Johnson. As students read, ask them to identify the revisions in the draft.

Read aloud the first paragraph on page 483. Then have volunteers read each of the bulleted questions about Jamal's revisions. Discuss the following answers:

- By adding *to babysit Naomi*, the audience would immediately know why Micah and Mrs. Johnson were arguing.
- Jamal removed the first instance of this line.

Explain that word choice is the use of words in a way that supports the purpose and tone of the writing. Tell students that choosing appropriate idioms, slang, or jargon can add depth to a character.

- To make dialogue sound more realistic, Jamal cut off two lines and shortened one of Mrs. Johnson's lines to *That's it!*

Writer's Workshop
Playwriting

Revising

To revise his play, Jamal carefully read his own and Evan's suggestions and selected the ones he would put into his draft. This is how he revised his scene.

Baby Blues

SCENE 1

Lights come up on the living room of a modest (~~Inside of~~ apartment. A plays Mrs. Johnson jigles baby who is fussing and paces as she argues with son, TV in background) → A couch can be seen center stage.

MRS. JOHNSON: *(calmly)* It will be just ~~be~~ for a few months until school is out. And you know you love Naomi. Besides ~~I don't have anyone else I trust~~.

MICAH: *(yells)* Mom, no, I can't! ~~Please don't make me~~. You just don't understand! *(kicks leg of couch)*

MRS. JOHNSON: You can, Micah and you will. I just don't have anyone else I trust. to babysit Naomi What is the big deal? It will be just for a few hours you'll have plenty of time to do homework after I get home.

MICAH: Homework I am not worried about homework! I'll look like a dweeb even stupider than I do now. Nobody else has to drag a baby around. No boys, anyway. I'll just have to stay inside and ~~suffocate~~.

MRS. JOHNSON: ~~Please do not say anything else~~. That's it! Do you want me to take away the cell phone? You are my hansome son so you will not look like a dweeb and I absolutely forbid you to stay inside. You need fresh air and so does Naomi. *(glares at Micah in a way that ends the argument)* I am going to the kitchen to start dinner. *(~~walks away~~)* Mrs. Johnson turns and starts walking offstage left. retreating

MICAH: *(to her back)* OK, fine, You win. I hope you're happy you're ruining my life! *(micah exits)* center stage right. Sound of door slamming is heard.

- Jamal added more stage directions, using terms learned in Lesson 2, so the reader could understand what was going on.

Challenge students to suggest additional revisions to Jamal's draft. Encourage students to explain their revisions by referring to the points on the Content Editor's Checklist.

Your Turn

Ask a volunteer to read aloud this section. Allow time for students to revise their drafts. Encourage students to meet again with their editing partners to clarify suggested revisions and to get feedback on their changes.

TEACHING OPTIONS

Revising Through Performance

Suggest that students ask classmates, friends, or family members to read aloud their drafts, assuming the different roles. Explain that when a playwright hears others read aloud his or her script, the playwright can take the role of the audience and then later use that experience to polish the play.

If students included monologues, soliloquies, or asides, encourage students to spend extra time reading them aloud or having others read them. Explain that these parts should not be too lengthy because the audience may lose track of the action. Encourage students to consider cutting superfluous text.

Jamal could see the point of Evan's comments. He went back to his draft and made some changes, which he felt improved his script quite a bit.

- Jamal explained earlier what the argument was about. What did Jamal do so that the audience would immediately know why Micah and Mrs. Johnson were arguing?

- Jamal agreed with Evan that he needlessly repeated the line about Mrs. Johnson not having anyone to trust. How can Jamal make his script more concise?

- What did Jamal do to make the dialogue Word Choice sound more realistic? Does the use of slang, idioms, and jargon work with the way Jamal's characters speak?

- Jamal noticed that Evan didn't mention what the characters were doing while they were speaking or where they were onstage. What did Jamal add so that the reader could understand what was going on?

Your Turn

Using the Content Editor's Checklist, consider your own ideas and your editor's suggestions to revise your draft script. Then read the script aloud to make sure the characters' dialogue sounds natural.

Preventing · Drafting · Content Editing · Revising · Copyediting · Proofreading · Publishing

Creative Writing • 483

OBJECTIVE
- To copyedit and proofread a one-act play

COPYEDITING AND PROOFREADING

Copyediting

Invite a volunteer to read aloud the first two paragraphs. Point out that when copyediting a play, an editor must pay special attention to the slang and other informal language to make sure the words and phrases connote their intended meanings.

Ask a volunteer to read aloud the third paragraph and the Copyeditor's Checklist. Encourage students to add to the checklist any additional questions. Point out the third item, which mentions

stage directions. Explain that during copyediting, students should check the stage locations (downstage left, upstage center) written in the draft.

Have a volunteer read aloud the paragraph after the checklist. Challenge students to predict where in Jamal's draft he made changes during copyediting by referring to the draft on page 482.

Your Turn

Have a volunteer read aloud this section. Ask students to use the Copyeditor's Checklist to edit their drafts. Encourage students to use editing partners. Remind students that a new pair of eyes may notice

errors that were missed. Remind students to spend extra time copyediting slang, idioms, jargon, and other natural-sounding language.

Proofreading

Read aloud the first paragraph. Point out that it is important to make sure new errors were not introduced during content editing.

Remind students that conventions include spelling, grammar, punctuation, and capitalization. Emphasize the importance of proofreading drafts to find and correct errors.

Editor's Workshop
Playwriting

Copyediting and Proofreading

Copyediting

Jamal was happy with the changes he made in his script. He was confident that they would help an audience understand the conflict and the reasons for Micah's and Mrs. Johnson's behavior more clearly than they would have before he improved his script.

Now he needed to copyedit his script. Copyediting a play is similar to copyediting other types of writing. You edit your draft for accuracy in word choice and sentence structure, as well as for the overall logic of the draft.

Jamal used the following Copyeditor's Checklist to edit his draft.

Jamal was still not sure about some of the words the characters said and wondered whether they sounded right. So he read the dialogue aloud. He decided that replacing some of the words with contractions would make the characters' speech sound more natural. Other dialogue lines seemed too long, so Jamal punctuated them to make them sound more like natural speech.

Your Turn

Look over your revised draft. Use the Copyeditor's Checklist to edit your draft. Be sure the sentence structure of the stage directions is logical and grammatically correct.

Copyeditor's Checklist
- [ ] Do the characters use natural-sounding idioms and slang where appropriate?
- [ ] Are proper theater terms used, such as upstage left, and do they make sense in the play?
- [ ] Does the play follow the right format for dialogue and stage directions?
- [ ] Are the lines of dialogue clear and logical?
- [ ] Are any words redundant, repeated, or misused?
- [ ] Are the nondialogue sentences grammatically correct?

484

Ask students to read aloud the second and third paragraphs. Point out the Proofreader's Checklist Rosa used to proofread Jamal's draft. Since students have used a similar checklist in every Writer's Workshop, challenge them to close their books and list the points that the checklist includes. Then ask students to identify points that are specific to playwriting *(checking the correct style and format for stage directions and characters' names)*.

Invite a volunteer to read aloud the paragraph after the checklist. Have students answer the last question.

Your Turn
Ask a volunteer to read aloud this section. Encourage partners to use dictionaries and thesauruses when proofreading each other's drafts. When students return the drafts, encourage them to return a copy of the Proofreader's Checklist, with a mark next to every item so the writer knows all the items were checked.

Writer's Tip Tell students that an extra set of eyes on their script is always helpful. Encourage students to proofread their scripts themselves, but also to have another person proofread.

TEACHING OPTIONS

Another Perspective

Challenge each student to draw a visual of a stage and use it to check the accuracy of the stage directions and locations included in their drafts. Remind students that stage locations are always from the perspective of the actor facing the audience. Ask each student to draw a visual of a stage, writing in it the nine stage locations provided on the grid on page 456. Then have students use their visuals to make sure that they wrote the stage locations and directions that they intended in their drafts.

Proofreading

Conventions Playwrights proofread their drafts to find mistakes in spelling, capitalization, punctuation, and grammar. They also check to make certain that no new errors have been introduced during the revising stage.

Most people find it difficult to catch all the mistakes when they proofread their own work. That is because they are very familiar with it, having written and revised it several times. Their eyes tend to skip over mistakes. That's why it is a good idea to ask someone else to proofread your draft. Jamal asked Rosa, another classmate, to proofread his draft.

Rosa used the following Proofreader's Checklist to proofread Jamal's play.

Proofreader's Checklist

- [ ] Are the stage directions italicized and enclosed within parentheses?
- [ ] Does each line of dialogue spoken by a different character begin on a separate line?
- [ ] Are the characters' names at the beginning of their lines in all capital letters, boldface, and followed by a colon?
- [ ] Does a line of space precede and follow each character's lines to make the script easy to read?
- [ ] Is the grammar correct?
- [ ] Is every word spelled correctly?
- [ ] Are capitalization and punctuation correct?

Rosa proofread the draft carefully word by word, consulting a dictionary when she wasn't sure about spelling. She checked off each item on the Proofreader's Checklist. Rosa found a few mistakes in Jamal's script. She found a missing colon, three examples of missing end punctuation, three missing commas, two sentences that were not capitalized, and two misspelled words. She also found characters' names that should have been capitalized and directions that should have been in italics. How many mistakes can you find in Jamal's script?

Your Turn
Read your script carefully. Check for each item on the Proofreader's Checklist one by one. After you have proofread your script as thoroughly as you can, trade scripts with a classmate. Challenge yourself to find the errors on your partner's script that he or she missed.

Writer's Tip It is a good idea to ask someone else to proofread your draft to find mistakes in spelling, capitalization, punctuation, and grammar.

Prewriting · Drafting · Content Editing · Revising · Copyediting · Proofreading · Publishing

Creative Writing • 485

OBJECTIVE

• To publish a one-act play

PUBLISHING

Have a volunteer read aloud the first paragraph.

Ask volunteers to read aloud or perform the scene in Jamal's finished script. Before they begin, encourage students to read through the scene and note the stage directions and setting descriptions. When they have finished reading or performing, have students provide feedback about whether the actors used the speaking skills from Lesson 6 and applied the appropriate emphasis on words and phrases as the stage directions indicated.

Explain that presentation has to do with the overall appearance of students' final drafts. Encourage students to use a format that enhances the overall impression of the piece.

Read aloud the options for publishing. Discuss each option and have students offer feedback for each. As an added option, you may wish to put all students' one-act plays in a single collection that can be distributed.

Writer's Workshop   Playwriting

Publishing

Jamal corrected the mistakes he and Rosa had found in his script. He made a few final editing changes too. Then he looked at his revisions again because he wanted to avoid having any errors creep into his script at the last minute. Now that his first scene looked professional, Jamal finished the play.

Baby Blues

SCENE 1

(Lights come up on the living room of a modest apartment. A sofa can be seen center stage. MRS. JOHNSON *jiggles baby who is fussing and paces as she argues with son. TV plays in the background.)*

MRS. JOHNSON: *(calmly)* It will be just for a few months until school is out. And you know you love Naomi. Besides—

MICAH: *(yells)* Mom, no, I can't! You just don't understand! *(kicks leg of sofa)*

MRS. JOHNSON: You can, Micah, and you will. I just don't have anyone else I trust to babysit Naomi. What is the big deal? It will be just for a few hours. You'll have plenty of time to do homework after I get home.

MICAH: Homework! I'm not worried about homework! I'll look like a dweeb, even stupider than I do now. Nobody else has to drag a baby around. No boys, anyway. I'll just have to stay inside and—

MRS. JOHNSON: That's it! Do you want me to take away the cell phone? You are my handsome son, so you won't look like a dweeb. And I absolutely forbid you to stay inside. You need fresh air and so does Naomi. *(She glares at Micah in a way that ends the argument.)* I'm going to the kitchen to start dinner.

*(*MRS. JOHNSON *turns and starts walking offstage left.)*

MICAH: *(to her retreating back)* Okay, fine. You win. I hope you're happy you're ruining my life!

*(*MICAH *exits center stage right. Sound of door slamming is heard.)*

Your Turn

Plan ahead to provide materials for costumes and props and perhaps a CD player for music. Have a volunteer read aloud this section. Ask students to form small groups and choose one of the students' scripts to perform for the class. Suggest that the playwright be the director of the production. Discuss ideas for simple costumes and props. Allow time for students to create costumes and a minimal set. After some rehearsal time, invite students to perform their plays for the class. Encourage the audience to practice the listening skills learned in Lesson 6.

ASSESS

Have students assess their finished play using the reproducible Student Self-Assessment on page 487y. A separate Playwriting Scoring Rubric can be found on page 487z for you to use to evaluate their work.

Plan to spend tomorrow doing a formal assessment. Administer the Playwriting Writing Prompt on **Assessment Book** pages 71–72.

TEACHING OPTIONS

Portfolio Opportunity

Have students place copies of their playwriting in their writing portfolios. Suggest that students return to these scripts at some future date and consider adding scenes or acts that further develop the plot, themes, and characters. Point out that sometimes it is beneficial to leave a piece of writing for a while and to come back to it later with a new perspective. Explain that it can be fun to revise a piece of creative writing extensively because the writer's imagination can take the story in an entirely new direction.

Performance Makes Perfect

Encourage students to perform their plays for friends or family. Suggest they spend time creating simple costumes and sets and ask friends and family members to play the characters. Invite students to videotape the performance and bring the video to school to share with the class.

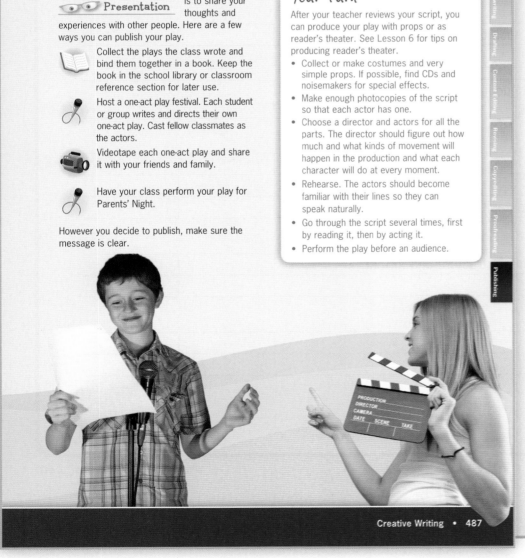

Whenever you publish your work, your goal <u>Presentation</u> is to share your thoughts and experiences with other people. Here are a few ways you can publish your play.

Collect the plays the class wrote and bind them together in a book. Keep the book in the school library or classroom reference section for later use.

Host a one-act play festival. Each student or group writes and directs their own one-act play. Cast fellow classmates as the actors.

Videotape each one-act play and share it with your friends and family.

Have your class perform your play for Parents' Night.

However you decide to publish, make sure the message is clear.

Your Turn

After your teacher reviews your script, you can produce your play with props or as reader's theater. See Lesson 6 for tips on producing reader's theater.

- Collect or make costumes and very simple props. If possible, find CDs and noisemakers for special effects.
- Make enough photocopies of the script so that each actor has one.
- Choose a director and actors for all the parts. The director should figure out how much and what kinds of movement will happen in the production and what each character will do at every moment.
- Rehearse. The actors should become familiar with their lines so they can speak naturally.
- Go through the script several times, first by reading it, then by acting it.
- Perform the play before an audience.

Creative Writing • 487

Name _____ Date _____

Creative Writing
Playwriting

Ideas

	YES	NO
Do I have well-developed characters?		
Do I have good plot structure?		

Organization

Does the beginning introduce a problem, conflict, or goal?		
Does the middle have rising action and a climax?		
Does the ending have a resolution?		

Voice

Do I use a natural voice?		

Word Choice

Do I choose words deliberately, such as for humor or impact?		

Sentence Fluency

Do I use engaging, realistic dialogue including idioms, slang, and jargon that move the story along?		

Conventions

Do I use correct grammar?		
Do I use correct spelling?		
Do I use correct punctuation and capitalization?		

Presentation

Does my play follow standard script structure and format?		
Is my final paper neat?		

Additional Items

Name _____

Date _____   Score _____

Creative Writing
Playwriting

	POINTS
Ideas	
well-developed characters, including a protagonist and an antagonist	
good plot structure	
Organization	
a beginning that introduces a problem, conflict, or goal	
a middle that includes rising action and a climax	
an ending that offers a resolution	
Voice	
natural	
Word Choice	
deliberate word choice, such as for humor or impact	
Sentence Fluency	
engaging, realistic dialogue including idioms, slang, and jargon that move the story forward	
Conventions	
correct grammar and usage	
correct spelling	
correct punctuation and capitalization	
Presentation	
standard script structure and format	
neatness	
Additional Items	
Total	

© LOYOLAPRESS.

CHAPTER FOCUS

LESSON 1: What Makes a Good Research Report?

LESSON 2: Research and Organization

- **GRAMMAR:** Diagramming
- **STUDY SKILLS:** Citing Sources
- **WRITING SKILLS:** Reference Tools
- **WORD STUDY:** Multiple-Meaning Words
- **SPEAKING AND LISTENING SKILLS:** Oral History Report
- **WRITER'S WORKSHOP:** Research Report

SUPPORT MATERIALS

Practice Book
Writing, pages 173–177

Assessment Book
Chapter 8 Writing Skills, pages 73–74
Research Report Writing Prompt, pages 75–76

Rubrics
Student, page 525y
Teacher, page 525z

Test Generator CD

Grammar
Section 11, pages 195–220

Customizable Lesson Plans
www.voyagesinenglish.com

Research Reports

WHAT IS A RESEARCH REPORT?

A research report is an expository piece that provides information on a specific topic. The information is derived from the writer gathering information from a variety of sources and then interpreting, analyzing, and drawing conclusions from the information to develop a thesis statement and supporting ideas.

A good research report includes the following:

- [ ] A clear focus on one topic
- [ ] Factual information supported by research that was gathered as notes and placed in outline form
- [ ] An introduction that includes a thesis statement
- [ ] A body of logically ordered paragraphs that include important main ideas supported by relevant details
- [ ] A summarizing conclusion
- [ ] Parenthetical notations and a Works Cited page
- [ ] Formal language and a confident voice
- [ ] A neutral tone
- [ ] A variety of sentence styles and lengths
- [ ] Varied ways of providing information, such as quotations, statistics, examples, and explanations

LiNK Use the following titles to offer your students examples of well-crafted researched writing:

Close Encounters: Exploring the Universe with the Hubble Space Telescope by Elaine Scott

Shipwreck at the Bottom of the World by Jennifer Armstrong

Who Were the Founding Fathers? Two Hundred Years of Reinventing American History by Steven H. Jaffe

> "Research is to see what everybody else has seen, and to think what nobody else has thought."
>
> —Albert Szent-Gyorgyi

WRITER'S WORKSHOP TIPS

Follow these ideas and tips to help you and your class get the most out of the Writer's Workshop:

- Review the traits of good writing. Use the chart on the inside back cover of the student and teacher editions.

- Stock the classroom library with a variety of nonfiction works to spark topic ideas.

- Invite a guest speaker, such as a marketing executive or a scientist, to explain to the class why people in his or her profession write research reports and how they are used.

- Review both library and Internet sources and ways to use these resources successfully when researching.

- Encourage students to watch the local, national, or international news for topic ideas.

- Explore the differences between an oral research report and a written research report. Emphasize the importance of practicing an oral research report and editing and revising a written research report.

- Require students to meet with you at least once during each of the following steps of writing research reports: taking notes, creating outlines, and citing works.

CONNECT WITH GRAMMAR

Throughout the Writer's Workshop, look for opportunities to integrate diagramming with writing research reports.

- ☐ When generating topics, have students diagram their topic sentences.

- ☐ To achieve clarity of purpose, have students diagram their thesis statements.

- ☐ During the copyediting stage, have students diagram any sentences that seem confusing or incorrect to their peer editors.

- ☐ Have students diagram a direct quotation from a source.

SCORING RUBRIC

Research Report

Point Values
0 = not evident
1 = minimal evidence of mastery
2 = evidence of development toward mastery
3 = strong evidence of mastery
4 = outstanding evidence of mastery

Ideas	POINTS
a clear focus on one topic	
factual information supported by research that was gathered as notes and placed in outline form	
Organization	
an interesting introduction that includes a thesis statement	
a body of logically ordered paragraphs that include important main ideas supported by relevant details	
a summarizing conclusion	
parenthetical notations and a Works Cited page	
Voice	
confident	
Word Choice	
formal language	
neutral tone	
Sentence Fluency	
varied sentence styles and lengths	
varied ways of providing information, such as quotations, statistics, examples, explanations, or related visuals	
Conventions	
correct grammar	
correct spelling	
correct punctuation and capitalization	
Presentation	
correct format for parenthetical notations and Works Cited page	
neatness	
Additional Items	
Total	

Full-sized, reproducible rubrics can be found at the end of this chapter.

CHAPTER 8
Research Reports

INTRODUCING THE GENRE

Discuss what students know about research reports. Encourage students to name research reports they have written for other classes. Remind students that writing a research report gives writers a chance to explore topics in greater depth.

Elaborate on the following characteristics of research reports:

• A narrow, focused topic and a thesis statement

• A neutral tone that avoids informal language, personal experience, and opinion statements

• Factual information supported by research

• A variety of reliable resources

• Parenthetical notations within the text

• An introduction that clearly tells what the report is about

• A body that has several main ideas and subtopics

• A conclusion that summarizes important information

• A Works Cited page that lists all the sources cited in the report

Reading the Excerpt

Clarify that the excerpt is only a portion of a research report and that it does not include all the characteristics listed.

Ask volunteers to read the excerpt aloud and to discuss the information presented in the research. Point out the parenthetical notations and discuss why these must be included. Encourage students to

---

LiNK History of the Samurai

The excerpts in Chapter 8 introduce students to relevant examples of research reports. "History of the Samurai" is a strong example of a research report because it has the following:

• A clear focus on one topic

• Factual information supported by research, including parenthetical notations

• A confident voice with formal language

As students encounter the different excerpts throughout the chapter, be sure to point out the characteristics they share. You may wish to choose sentences from the excerpts to diagram.

Research Reports

LiNK History of the Samurai
by Stephen Phillips

Though the samurai were tightly controlled by their masters, they exerted great power over the commoners and peasants under them. During the Tokugawa era (1603–1868), the samurai held the power of life or death over peasants and merchants (Morrow). This meant the samurai could murder on the spot any peasant who showed the slightest sign of disrespect.

The code by which the samurai lived was called *bushido*, or the way of the warrior. Much of the code derived from Buddhism and Confucianism, but the central tenet of the code was service to the master above all else, including their own lives (Gore 24). Because wealth was tightly controlled within Japan, frugality was a prized virtue within the code. Other virtues of *bushido* were politeness, courage, charity, and showing no fear or pain in the face of suffering. Any violation of the code or any slight sign of disrespect to a samurai's master required the samurai to pay with his life (Reynolds 50). This was called *seppuku*, and it often restored a samurai family's honor.

> A research report, like this excerpt from "History of the Samurai," is expository writing that thoroughly develops a topic and is supported with factual information and credible source material.

488

---

point out the other characteristics of a research report that can be found in the excerpt.

Reading the Student Model

Tell students that they are going to read a real student research paper about Thomas L. Jennings, the first African American to receive a patent. Have students silently read the model. When students have finished, elaborate on the characteristics of a research report. Point out the parenthetical notations and ask students what the numbers in the parentheses represent *(the page number on which the factual information can be found in the original source)*.

Challenge students to complete on the board a Venn diagram comparing the characteristics that expository writing shares with research reports. *(Both inform a reader, use a neutral tone, incorporate facts and research, and avoid opinion statements. Research reports tend to be longer. They avoid personal experience. They include citations, which are notes about the sources used to research the report.)*

TEACHING OPTIONS

Scavenger Hunt

Have small groups search the classroom and the school library for examples of writing that include a Works Cited page. Ask students to discuss what distinguishes a research report from the genres they have learned about so far.

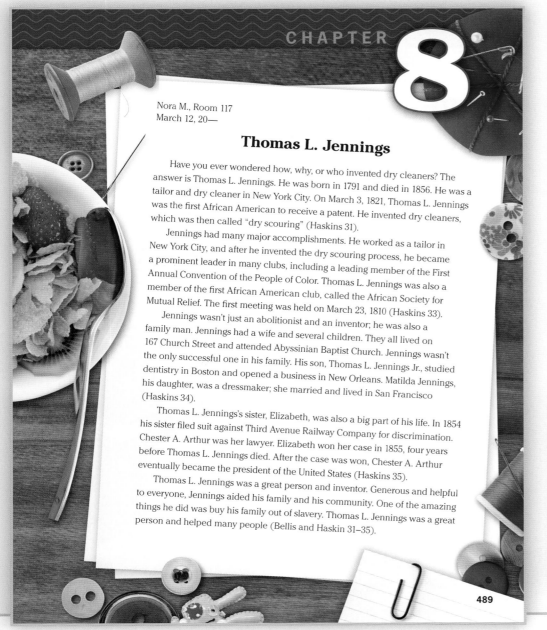

CHAPTER **8**

Nora M., Room 117
March 12, 20—

Thomas L. Jennings

Have you ever wondered how, why, or who invented dry cleaners? The answer is Thomas L. Jennings. He was born in 1791 and died in 1856. He was a tailor and dry cleaner in New York City. On March 3, 1821, Thomas L. Jennings was the first African American to receive a patent. He invented dry cleaners, which was then called "dry scouring" (Haskins 31).

Jennings had many major accomplishments. He worked as a tailor in New York City, and after he invented the dry scouring process, he became a prominent leader in many clubs, including a leading member of the First Annual Convention of the People of Color. Thomas L. Jennings was also a member of the first African American club, called the African Society for Mutual Relief. The first meeting was held on March 23, 1810 (Haskins 33).

Jennings wasn't just an abolitionist and an inventor; he was also a family man. Jennings had a wife and several children. They all lived on 167 Church Street and attended Abyssinian Baptist Church. Jennings wasn't the only successful one in his family. His son, Thomas L. Jennings Jr., studied dentistry in Boston and opened a business in New Orleans. Matilda Jennings, his daughter, was a dressmaker; she married and lived in San Francisco (Haskins 34).

Thomas L. Jennings's sister, Elizabeth, was also a big part of his life. In 1854 his sister filed suit against Third Avenue Railway Company for discrimination. Chester A. Arthur was her lawyer. Elizabeth won her case in 1855, four years before Thomas L. Jennings died. After the case was won, Chester A. Arthur eventually became the president of the United States (Haskins 35).

Thomas L. Jennings was a great person and inventor. Generous and helpful to everyone, Jennings aided his family and his community. One of the amazing things he did was buy his family out of slavery. Thomas L. Jennings was a great person and helped many people (Bellis and Haskin 31–35).

489

For Tomorrow

Ask students to find an example of a research report and bring a copy to class. Remind students to also bring a copy of the Works Cited page. Find a research report of your own to share with the class.

What Makes a Good Research Report?

OBJECTIVE

- To recognize the elements and characteristics of a research report

WARM-UP

Read, Listen, Speak

Read aloud parts of the research report from yesterday's For Tomorrow homework. Point out the characteristics of a good research report. Then have small groups compare the reports they found. Have each group create a list of characteristics and share the list with the class.

GRAMMAR CONNECTION

Take this opportunity to talk about diagramming simple sentences and appositives. You may wish to have students point out simple sentences and appositives in their Read, Listen, Speak examples.

TEACH

Ask a volunteer to read aloud the first two paragraphs. Discuss formal language. Point out that a neutral tone is an important part of formal language. Ask volunteers to define *neutral tone. (In writing, a neutral tone conveys no bias about the subject.)*

Ask a volunteer to read aloud the section Topic. Challenge students to name research topics that might fall between "crime in the United States" and "crime on my block." Ask a volunteer to name the topic of the model on page 488 *(the history of the samurai in Japanese culture).*

Have volunteers read aloud the section Thesis. Point out that a thesis statement clearly states the purpose of the report. Explain that a writer may start with one idea for a thesis statement, but change it as he or she learns more about the topic. Tell students that asking

preliminary questions about a topic will help writers prepare a preliminary thesis statement and guide them in their research.

Have a volunteer read aloud the section Organization. Point out that writers may combine different methods of organization. Ask if any students can recognize what methods of organization are used in the model on page 488.

LiNK Read the excerpt aloud. Point out that this is a good example of a thesis statement. Invite volunteers to list the questions this thesis statement answers. Then discuss possible sources for this topic.

PRACTICE

ACTIVITY A

For the first item, list on the board possible questions that might help narrow the topic. Then have small groups complete this activity. When they have finished, ask groups to share their answers. For some answers challenge volunteers to suggest ways to organize the topic.

What Makes a Good Research Report?

A research report is a comprehensive piece of expository writing that has a clear focus on one topic. This focus, expressed as the thesis statement, is supported by factual information gathered from research. Research reports are written in a confident voice that uses formal language. The conclusion to a research report summarizes the report's thesis and the important ideas raised in the body of the report.

The following are some points to keep in mind when writing your research report. How closely did the writer of the report on page 489 follow these points?

Topic

A good topic for a research report is one that interests the writer and that is neither too broad nor too narrow. Often, writers of research reports select topics that are too broad to cover adequately within a limited number of pages, such as "crime in the United States." On the other hand, a topic should not be too narrow, or a writer will not find enough information, such as "crime on my block."

The topic of a research report should also be focused and appropriate for its audience.

Thesis

A thesis statement should be clearly stated in the introduction of a research report. The rest of the paper develops the thesis.

Before settling on a thesis statement, however, many writers ask themselves preliminary questions to guide their research and maintain their focus on the topic. For example, the writer of "History of the Samurai" may have known about the samurai from watching TV or movies and was interested in discovering what role the samurai played in Japanese culture. The writer then

APPLY

WRITER'S CORNER

Provide newspapers for students. Have partners discuss the topics and offer suggestions for narrowing the topics. Encourage students to write questions they would ask about each topic. Invite volunteers to share their topics with the class. Students should demonstrate an understanding of how to narrow a topic for a research report.

TechTip Review quality search engines with the class. Also discuss how to recognize credible Internet sources. Review the Internet Research Checklist on page 384.

ASSESS

Note which students had difficulty narrowing a topic for a research report. Use the Reteach option with those students who need additional reinforcement.

TEACHING OPTIONS

Reteach

Write on the board the broad topic *musical instruments.* Invite students to list a more specific topic within that category, such as *stringed instruments,* and write their suggestions on the board. Challenge students to name increasingly specific topics. Write their answers on the board in descending order. Ask students to work with partners to select the most promising topics for a report. Then have students write five questions for each topic they choose. Have partners discuss the similarities and differences among their questions. Discuss how these questions would guide students' research.

Love Your Topic

Ask students to brainstorm a list of topics that they find interesting. Then direct students to choose two broad topics from their list and to identify three narrower topics for each (*broad topic of interest: battleships; narrowed topics: British battleships of World War II, the first ironclads, the first aircraft carriers*). Have partners review each other's narrow topics. Encourage students to suggest other narrow topics that might fit the broad topics on their partner's list.

For Tomorrow

Have students choose an appropriate topic for a research report. Ask them to write one sentence about why the topic interests them and three questions they might research about the topic. Choose a topic that interests you and do the same.

---

asked questions such as "Why did the samurai act a certain way?" or "What role did the samurai have in Japanese society?"

After exploring some library sources about the samurai, the writer learned that they were guided by a strong warrior code and that the samurai played a greater role than mere foot soldiers. By learning this new information about the samurai, the writer could better focus the report's thesis on a specific idea that is convincing and informative: the role of the samurai warrior evolved into one of the most influential features of Japanese culture.

Organization

Because research reports rely on multiple sources to support a focused thesis, good organization is especially important. Some ways of organizing research papers include cause and effect, comparison, chronological order, and order of importance.

ACTIVITY A Practice focusing topics for research reports. Suggest ways to narrow the following topics. Write the questions you would ask to focus your topic.

1. literary prizes
2. history of flight
3. energy sources
4. U.S. immigration
5. volunteer opportunities
6. the age of the dinosaurs
7. world hunger
8. women in the workforce

LiNK

Social Networking

The explosive growth in the popularity of these [social networking] sites has generated concerns among some parents, school officials, and government leaders about the potential risks posed when personal information is made available in such a public setting.

Pew Internet & American Life Project

Memorial to aviation pioneers Orville and Wilbur Wright in Kill Devil Hill, North Carolina

Tech Tip With an adult, search online to begin your topic search.

WRITER'S CORNER

Practice narrowing and broadening research topics. Look at a newspaper. How would you broaden one of the topics for a research report? How would you narrow it?

Research Reports • 491

WARM-UP

Read, Listen, Speak

Write on the board the topic you chose from yesterday's For Tomorrow homework. Tell students why this topic interests you and list the questions you would research. Point out how these questions would guide your research. Invite volunteers to write on the board their topics and to list their questions. Discuss each question and have students offer suggestions for other questions that could be researched.

GRAMMAR CONNECTION

Take this opportunity to talk about diagramming compound sentences. You may wish to have students point out compound sentences in their Read, Listen, Speak examples.

TEACH

Review the characteristics of a research report. Work with students to answer these questions:

- What are some things a writer should consider when choosing a topic?
- What is a thesis statement, and where does it appear in a research report?
- What are some ways to organize a research report?

Ask a volunteer to read aloud the Documentation section. Discuss how documentation can add credibility to a research report *(shows thorough research, allows a reader to check the reliability of a source and to check that the information from the source is used accurately)*. Then define *plagiarism* for the class and discuss why it is unethical.

PRACTICE

ACTIVITY B

After students have finished, invite volunteers to read aloud their preliminary thesis statements. Challenge volunteers to suggest an organizational method for each thesis statement.

ACTIVITY C

Discuss each method of organization and example topics for each method. Have partners complete this activity. When students have finished, ask volunteers to share and explain their choices.

ACTIVITY D

When students have filled in their charts, have them form small groups based on the topic students have chosen. Ask students to share their responses for the What I Want to Know column and to discuss sources they might use to find the information they need.

ACTIVITY E

Review how to determine if an Internet source is reliable. After students have finished, invite volunteers to share the sources they found and to describe the kinds of information in those sources.

Documentation

Research reports cite and document their sources. The bibliography that accompanies a research paper, often called the Works Cited page, lists every source the writer used in the paper. The Works Cited page is helpful to readers who want to learn more about your topic.

Documenting your sources also guards against plagiarism. Writers must avoid plagiarizing, presenting another writer's words or ideas as one's own. Plagiarizing is the theft of words and ideas and is unethical.

ACTIVITY B Choose three topics that you narrowed in Activity A. Write a preliminary thesis statement for each topic.

> EXAMPLE: **Topic:** energy sources
> **Focused topic:** alternative energy sources for electric power plants
> **Thesis:** Solar power and wind power are two alternative energy sources for our nation's power plants.

ACTIVITY C Which way would you organize a research paper about each of these topics? Would you use cause and effect, comparison, chronological order, or order of importance? Explain why that structure would be most logical.

1. elementary education in the United States and Japan
2. solving world hunger
3. gun control laws around the world
4. environmentally friendly homes
5. homeland security in an open society
6. homelessness in American cities
7. destruction of the rain forests
8. animal rights
9. history of the U.S. census
10. global climate change

Activity C
Accept any answer that students can justify.
1. comparison
2. cause and effect
3. comparison
4. cause and effect
5. cause and effect
6. comparison
7. chronological order *or* cause and effect
8. order of importance
9. chronological order
10. cause and effect

ACTIVITY F

Have partners trade papers. Challenge students to underline the thesis statement in their partner's paragraph. Ask partners to discuss ways they might organize their reports based on the thesis statements.

APPLY

WRITER'S CORNER

Ask volunteers to list on the board topics and research questions. As a class write thesis statements for each topic. Discuss sources that might be useful for these topics. Students should demonstrate an understanding of thesis statements.

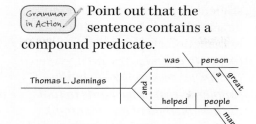

Grammar in Action. Point out that the sentence contains a compound predicate.

Thomas L. Jennings — was — person — a — great; and — helped — people — many

ASSESS

Note which students had difficulty identifying research sources. Use the Reteach option with those students who need additional reinforcement.

Practice Book page 173 provides additional work with the characteristics of a research report.

ACTIVITY D Choose one of the following topics. Then fill in a chart like the one below.

1. origin of movies
2. evolution of video games
3. high-tech kites
4. physical education in schools
5. computer viruses
6. professional women's soccer
7. exploring Mars
8. fighting wildfires
9. safe schools
10. bicycle racing
11. conquering Mount Everest
12. endangered species

TOPIC	WHAT I KNOW	WHAT I WANT TO KNOW

ACTIVITY E Briefly research the topic you chose in Activity D and find three separate sources of information about it.

ACTIVITY F Based on the information you wrote about a topic in the chart in Activity D, and the research you did in Activity E, write an introduction for a research report on the topic.

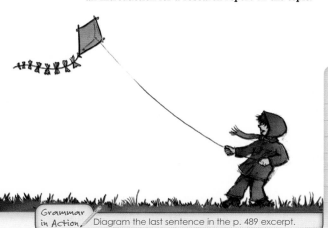

Grammar in Action. Diagram the last sentence in the p. 489 excerpt.

WRITER'S CORNER

Practice writing thesis statements or research questions for the topics you suggested in the Writer's Corner on page 491.

Research Reports • 493

OBJECTIVES
- **To record research information, using note cards**
- **To organize note cards into an outline**

WARM-UP
Read, Speak, Listen
Read aloud your article and your outline from yesterday's For Tomorrow homework. Discuss the type of organization that was used in the outline and point out specific examples of research, including parenthetical notation. Then have small groups discuss their articles and the types of organization in each. Ask groups to discuss whether the organization chosen by the writer is effective. Challenge students to name other ways to organize the same topic.

GRAMMAR CONNECTION
Take this opportunity to talk about diagramming compound sentence elements. You may wish to have students point out compound sentence elements in their Read, Listen, Speak examples.

TEACH

Ask students to discuss their experiences writing research reports in other classes. Discuss some of the challenges students faced. Ask volunteers to read aloud the opening paragraph and first two paragraphs of the section Taking Notes. Point out that writing information on note cards is a good way for a writer to become familiar with his or her topic because the writer has to absorb the information and think about how to explain it in his or her own words. Explain that when a writer uses his or her own words to take notes, the writer also avoids plagiarizing the source. Ask

students why they think it might be useful to record on note cards information about their sources *(better to organize research, easier to transfer research to an outline, simpler to rearrange cards to find the best method of organization)*.

Make sure students understand that if they wish to use a direct quotation, they should copy the words exactly on a note card and use quotation marks to remind themselves they are quoting a source directly.

Read the next two paragraphs aloud. Allow students to read silently the example note cards. Point out that the information on

a card can be written as a phrase, a sentence, or a few sentences, as long as the card has only one idea.

Ask a volunteer to read aloud the last paragraph. Challenge volunteers to summarize the points covered in the lesson.

PRACTICE

ACTIVITY A
Remind students of the benefits of using note cards to record their research. Then have students complete this activity independently. After students have finished, discuss each item.

Research and Organization

An important part of prewriting a research report is taking notes. Notes are gathered from reading the various sources that you find in the course of your research.

Taking Notes

A useful way of taking notes is to write them on note cards. This is a good way to summarize important information from your source. Summarizing will help you become familiar with what the source is saying and determine whether the information will be helpful to your research report.

When you find an important detail that relates to your topic, write it on a note card. The detail can restate a fact or an idea in your own words, or it can be a direct quotation. Then write the source's name and the page number of the source at the bottom of the card. If you quote a source, include quotation marks to remind you that you are using the source's words and not your own.

Be sure always to write just one fact on each note card. This will make it easier to rearrange your facts when you organize your notes.

Here are two note cards used by the author of the report on page 488.

Write the reference information for each source on a separate set of note cards. Be sure to list all the required information that will appear on your Works Cited page, which is discussed in Lesson 3.

> Samurai pay kept low
>
> The daimyo paid the samurai only in cash or rice.
>
> Bresson p. 89

> Samurai family wealth
>
> Samurai family pay was set at a fixed rate. If a samurai had more children, there was less money to divide.
>
> Travers p. 243

Encourage volunteers to share their answers. Record these on the board and have students compare their answers.

APPLY

WRITER'S CORNER

After students have finished, have them trade cards with a partner. Ask them to check that their partner included only one idea per card and that each card contains information about the source. Students should demonstrate an understanding of using note cards to record research information.

ASSESS

Note which students had difficulty recording research information on note cards. Use the Reteach option with those students who need additional reinforcement.

TEACHING OPTIONS

Reteach

Choose an entry in an encyclopedia that can be narrowed into subtopics. Have students decide on a subtopic of the entry that would be appropriate for a research report. Write that topic on the board. Have students write information on note cards while you read the entry aloud. Remind students to write only the information that relates to the subtopic on the board. Invite students to share their notes and to explain why they recorded that information. Check that students recorded only one idea on each card.

Note-Card News

Provide students with newspaper or online articles. Challenge students to read an article and to write information on note cards, detailing the topic of the article. Tell students to write one idea on each card. Remind them that they may use phrases but to be sure to record all the essential information. When students have finished, challenge them to retell their news articles to a partner, using only the note cards.

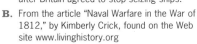

ACTIVITY A Read these sources and follow the directions.

A. From page 234 of the book *The Forgotten War* by Thomas Sommes

Tensions between the United States and two European powers, Great Britain and France, led to embargoes against all foreign trade and precipitated the War of 1812. Some Americans wanted war with France, some with Britain. However, seizures of men and ships on the high seas by Britain were too humiliating for the Americans to let stand. Negotiations to prevent war failed when Congress declared war on Britain two days after Britain agreed to stop seizing ships.

B. From the article "Naval Warfare in the War of 1812," by Kimberly Crick, found on the Web site www.livinghistory.org

The War of 1812 was fought in a series of almost isolated sea and land battles. Naval battles were fought off the coast of Africa, as well as on the Great Lakes. A victory by the Americans in the Battle of Lake Erie on September 10, 1813, allowed the Americans to move west. However, the British blockade off the Eastern seaboard kept many ships in their harbors.

C. From the article "The Myth of Unity" by Nelson Rooker in the magazine *Politics Today*, Summer 2005, page 45

Throughout the War of 1812, there were political divisions between the New England states and the Southern and Western states. New England shipbuilders hated the war because they wanted trade with Great Britain and France, and the embargoes prevented that. On the other hand, Southerners, known as War-hawks, believed British Canada could be easily conquered.

1. Write two note cards for a report about ships and shipping in the War of 1812.
2. Write five note cards, including one from each source, for a report on the War of 1812.
3. Write three note cards for a report for this thesis statement: "The War of 1812 was caused by trade embargoes."
4. Write one note card about the role of the Great Lakes in the War of 1812.

The U.S.S. *Constitution* defeats the H.M.S. *Guerriere* in a naval battle on August 19, 1812.

WRITER'S CORNER

Choose a topic that interests you and find four sources on the topic. Write three note cards from each source.

For Tomorrow

Have students use note cards to record information from a nonprint source, such as a television documentary, movie, or CD. Bring to class your own note cards from a nonprint source.

Research Reports • 495

Read, Listen, Speak

Share with the class your note cards from yesterday's For Tomorrow homework. Model for students by discussing the note-taking procedure and how it was changed by using a nonprint source. Have small groups share their note cards and describe the sources of their notes. Encourage students to discuss any challenges in the note-taking procedure.

GRAMMAR CONNECTION

Take this opportunity to talk about diagramming participles. You may wish to have students point out participles in their Read, Listen, Speak examples.

TEACH

Challenge students to predict how they might use note cards to organize their ideas. Point out that note cards make it easy to try out preliminary outlines by allowing writers to rearrange their notes physically until finding an organization that supports their thesis statement.

Invite volunteers to read aloud the first paragraph of the section Organizing Your Notes and the bulleted items that follow. Emphasize that if students identify cards that do not fit their thesis statement, they can set the cards aside for later. Point out that once students are satisfied with the arrangement of their notes, they can copy the arrangement to write their outline.

Ask a volunteer to read aloud the two paragraphs of the Outlines section. Allow students to read the example outline silently. Ask students to name the three main ideas of the outline. Challenge students to write a thesis statement based on the example outline. Then discuss how a thesis statement determines the main ideas used in the outline.

PRACTICE

ACTIVITY B

Tell students to copy each note onto a note card. Have students organize the notes independently. Then ask partners to compare and discuss their organization of the notes. Write on the board the three subtopics, creating a column under each. Invite volunteers to tape their note cards under the appropriate column. Discuss each item as it is taped to the board. Ask students to explain why certain notes were not used. Point out that some notes might be used in different parts of a report. (For example, the first note about Ghana's actual name could be used in an introduction.)

ACTIVITY C

Have students work with the same partners from Activity B to write an outline. Ask students to develop a thesis statement that would be supported by their outlines.

Organizing Your Notes

When you have completed your research and notes, gather your notes together and organize them into a preliminary outline. Follow these steps as you organize your notes:

- Separate your cards into groups of main ideas that support your thesis statement.
- Read each note card in each group. Do the notes support your thesis statement? If not, consider altering the thesis statement or taking more notes.
- Once you have decided on a thesis statement, remove any note cards that do not fit your thesis.
- Arrange the groups of note cards into a preliminary outline that best supports your thesis.
- Review your preliminary outline to see if it is in logical order according to the note cards you have organized. If not, rearrange your stacks into a more logical order.
- To help visualize your report, create a revised detailed outline from your note cards. Give a heading to each subtopic and list the related details under each subtopic.

Outlines

Using an outline lets you take all the information and sort it into smaller pieces of data that can be more easily handled. An outline can also give direction to your writing.

An outline follows a specific format. Main ideas are divided into subtopics, which are supported with details. Study this outline of a research report about how plants, animals, and humans survive in the desert.

I. Introduction
II. Plant life
   A. Roots
   B. Stems
   C. Flowers
III. Animal life
   A. Carnivores
   B. Herbivores
IV. Human life
   A. Oases
      1. Springs
      2. Wells
   B. Pipelines
V. Conclusion

ACTIVITY D

After students reread the student model, discuss possible subtopics. Have students write each item on a note card and use the cards to organize the information. Have students complete this activity independently. Then invite a volunteer to write his or her outline on the board.

APPLY

WRITER'S CORNER

Allow time for students to create outlines independently. Have students trade outlines with a partner to evaluate their partner's outline for missing information or unanswered questions. Challenge students to decide whether the organizational method suits the thesis statement. Students should demonstrate an understanding of how to organize information in an outline.

ASSESS

Note which students had difficulty creating outlines. Use the Reteach option with those students who need additional reinforcement.

Practice Book page 174 provides additional work with research and organization.

TEACHING OPTIONS

Reteach

Give students a set of note cards with the main ideas and subtopics from the example outline on page 496. Have students work as a group to arrange the cards into an outline without using their books. Then have students write an outline from the note cards they organized. Ask students to discuss how the organization of the main ideas supports the thesis statement.

Filling Out the Bones

Ask students to choose a country they are interested in learning more about. Then have students choose an organizational method and use it to make an outline based on questions. Encourage students to write three questions about the country as the main ideas in the outline. Have students trade outlines with a partner and use encyclopedias or other resources to answer the questions in outline format, listing subtopics under the main ideas. Have students return their outlines and discuss the answers.

ACTIVITY B Organize the following notes about the Ghanaian civilization of West Africa into the following three subtopics: government, trade, agriculture. Eliminate any notes that do not fit into subtopics. Then think of a thesis statement that fits the subtopics.

Eliminate note.	• Ghana's actual name was Wagadugu
subtopic government	• earliest known West African kingdom
subtopic trade	• Ghanaian kingdom was founded on gold and salt mining
subtopic agriculture	• Ghana grew crops of kola nuts
subtopic government	• Ghanaian king assisted by a council
Eliminate note.	• Ghana made advances in iron-working
subtopic trade	• trade caravans could have up to 12,000 camels
Eliminate note.	• Muslims to the north of Ghana were called Almoravids
subtopic agriculture	• the Niger River Valley provided agricultural support to Ghana
subtopic agriculture	• droughts in the area rivers helped bring about Ghana's decline
subtopic trade	• traded copper, salt, and gold with other kingdoms
subtopic government	• Ghanaian kings created a way to tax gold

Women carrying goods to market near Elmina west of Accra in Ghana

ACTIVITY C Create an outline from the subtopics and details in Activity B. The outline should identify subtopics, and the details should be listed under each subtopic.

Activity D

I. Introduction
II. Thomas L. Jennings's accomplishments
   A. Tailor
   B. Inventor
III. Family
   A. Children (Thomas, Matilda)
   B. (Sister) Elizabeth
IV. Conclusion

ACTIVITY D Reread the student model on page 489. Put the items below into an outline. Remember to add an introduction and conclusion.

1. Thomas L. Jennings's accomplishments
2. Inventor
3. Sister (Elizabeth)
4. Tailor
5. Family
6. Children (Thomas, Matilda)

WRITER'S CORNER

Sort into subtopics the notes you made on note cards from the previous Writer's Corner. Then create an outline from the groups of note cards.

For Tomorrow

Ask students to create an outline on a topic they know well, such as skateboarding or gymnastics. Encourage students to use Roman numerals for main ideas, capital letters for subtopics, and Arabic numerals for details. Create an outline of your own to share with the class.

OBJECTIVES
- **To write a Works Cited page**
- **To use parenthetical notations**

WARM-UP

Read, Listen, Speak

Write on the board the Roman numerals of your outline from yesterday's For Tomorrow homework. Discuss possible subtopics with the class. Encourage students to offer suggestions. Then fill in your complete outline. Have small groups compare outlines and discuss the way students chose to organize their outlines into main ideas and subtopics. Ask students to offer suggestions for improving each outline.

GRAMMAR CONNECTION

Take this opportunity to talk about diagramming gerunds. You may wish to have students point out gerunds in their Read, Listen, Speak examples.

TEACH

Discuss why keeping track of sources in a research report is important. Invite a volunteer to read the first paragraph aloud. Have students discuss how a reader might use a Works Cited page *(to check the credibility of sources, to find further information on the topic)*.

Ask volunteers to read aloud the first two paragraphs of the section Works Cited Page. Use the examples in the box to the right to point out the "hanging indent" and the use of an author's last name first. Explain that when the author is not known, students should alphabetize the entry by the first word of the title.

Have a volunteer read aloud the Books section. Refer students to the examples in the box and

point out in the second example that after the first author's name is listed, additional names are not reversed. Remind students that although they use italics for book titles within their writing, students should underline book titles in Works Cited entries. Have students turn to the copyright page in their books. Ask students to use the copyright page to answer the following questions about the book:

- Who is the publisher?
- Where is the publisher located?
- What year was the book most recently published?

Have volunteers read aloud the Periodicals section and the examples. Ask students to distinguish between the titles of the articles and the titles of the publications cited in both examples. Point out that in all the examples, there is a logical structure to the entries: first the author, then the title, and then the publisher information.

Provide small groups with several research sources, including books and periodicals. Have groups create a Works Cited entry for each source. Discuss these with the class.

Citing Sources

Whenever you use a source in a research report, you must tell the reader where you got your information at the point in the report where the source is used. This is called citing sources.

Works Cited Page

The Works Cited page lists every source used in the research report alphabetically according to the author's last name, when available. Use a "hanging indent" format when listing all sources so that the author's name stands away from the text of the notation. This lets the reader find the source easily. Sources that you disregarded when taking notes are not listed.

This page goes at the end of your report on a separate sheet of paper. Type the words *Works Cited* at the top of the page, centered, then begin listing the sources. Notations are written differently for different sources, but all of them follow a similar and logical pattern: first, the author's name; second, the title of the work itself; and, finally, the publisher's information. Pay close attention to the formats that follow and be sure to reproduce them in your research report.

Books

Book titles normally appear in italics but in Works Cited pages, book titles are underlined. Following the title are the city and state where the publisher is located, a colon, then the name of the publisher and the year of publication. Most of this information can usually be found on the title page of the book.

If a book has more than one author, it is alphabetized by the last name of the first author listed on the title page. If a book has more than three authors, list the first author, last name first, and then add *et al* (Latin for "and others") after the name.

> **Works Cited**
>
> Grimaldi, Helen. <u>Global Climate Change</u>. New York, NY: Wordsmith, 2001.
>
> Sperling, Arthur, and Jenny Anderson. <u>Eat Your Way to Health</u>. Emmaus, PA: Green Acres Press, 2004.

PRACTICE

ACTIVITY A

Have students complete this activity independently. When students have finished, invite volunteers to share their answers with the class. Discuss each answer, clarifying any discrepancies students may have.

APPLY

WRITER'S CORNER

If time allows, take the class to the library to complete this activity. Have volunteers write their citations on the board and discuss them. Students should demonstrate an understanding of how to write a Works Cited entry.

TechTip If possible, take students to your school's computer lab to type their Works Cited page. Discuss the proper format for a Works Cited page, using a word-processing program.

ASSESS

Note which students had difficulty writing entries for a Works Cited page. Use the Reteach option with those students who need additional reinforcement.

TEACHING OPTIONS

Reteach

Ask students to copy the examples of Works Cited entries from this lesson, each on a separate note card. Have students label their note cards by the type of entry—book or periodical. Guide students to label each part of each entry. Have them circle the punctuation marks. Then have students arrange their cards as they would appear on a Works Cited page. Suggest that students keep their cards to help write a Works Cited page.

Cooperative Learning

Provide small groups with a variety of source materials. Have students work cooperatively to create a Works Cited page listing all the sources. Have each group pass its page to another group. Challenge students to read the pages and to look for any errors in punctuation or format.

For Tomorrow

Ask students to write a Works Cited entry for their favorite book and for an entry for a magazine or newspaper article. Write Works Cited entries for your favorite book and for a magazine or newspaper article to share with the class.

Periodicals

Magazines, newspapers, and journals are called periodicals because they appear at regular intervals, or periods of time.

The titles of magazine and newspaper articles are enclosed within quotation marks. The full date of publication is included after the italics or underlined title of the publication. The pages on which the article appears follow a colon after the date. If an article begins on one page and ends on a nonsequential page, simply place a plus (+) sign after the first page on which the article appears.

> Furtado, Nellie. "Your Place in the World." *Wild Life Magazine* 15 Nov. 2005: 20–22.
>
> Groark, Virginia. "Speed Limit Cut Near Toll Plazas." *Chicago Tribune* 4 Aug. 2004, Metro, 1+.

ACTIVITY A Answer the questions that follow this Works Cited page.

> Barker, Mary, and Alan Marshall. *Genetic Modification: The Triumph of Science.* Hagerstown, MD: Scientific Press, 2002.
>
> Herbert, Kinasha. *What You See Is What You Get.* New York: Cooper Village Publishing, 2000.
>
> Walker, Stanley, and Allison Walker. *Three Easy Steps to Growing Perfect Vegetables.* Boston: Nature's Way Publishing, 2000.
>
> Brennan, Susan. "Take Two Zucchinis and Call Me Tomorrow." *Newsworthy* 18 Feb. 2001: 66–68.

1. What is the difference between titles that are italicized and titles that are enclosed within quotation marks?
2. Why are some names listed last name first and others in the reverse order?
3. What information is included for each item?
4. What might be the topic of the research report?
5. In what order should the entries above be listed?

WRITER'S CORNER

Go to your school or local library and find five books and five articles from magazines about your topic. Write a citation for each source.

 Type your Works Cited in a word processing program.

WARM-UP

Read, Listen, Speak

Distribute your Works Cited entries from yesterday's For Tomorrow homework. Point out the details that are specific to magazine or newspaper entries. Then have small groups discuss their Works Cited entries. Encourage students to check their entries for correct format and punctuation.

GRAMMAR CONNECTION

Take this opportunity to talk about diagramming infinitives. You may wish to have students point out infinitives in their Read, Listen, Speak examples.

TEACH

Ask students to name the pattern of a Works Cited entry. Invite volunteers to read aloud the section Citing Other Sources and the format for the five sources of information. Emphasize that all sources follow the same logical pattern of the author first, then the title, and then the publisher. Challenge students to identify the publisher name and type for each entry. Ask students why it is important to include in an entry the date a Web site was visited. *(Web sites can change frequently.)* Point out that many Web sites do not list authors, so writers should place the title of the article first.

Invite a volunteer to read aloud the first paragraph of the section Parenthetical Notations. Ask students to look at the excerpt on page 488 and to identify each of the parenthetical notations. Challenge a volunteer to explain why the entry for "(Morrow)" might not have a page number. *(The source could be one that does not use page numbers.)* Point out the

relationship between the example note card notes on page 494 and the parenthetical notation in the model for those notes.

Have a volunteer read aloud the paragraph and examples for the section Paraphrasing. Ask students to explain why the first paraphrase is incomplete. *(It is missing too many details.)* Tell students that paraphrasing is not copying the information with different words. Explain that writers should read the information, absorb it, and then write it in their own words.

LiNK Read the excerpt aloud and point out the parenthetical notation. Explain that the notation has the year of

publication instead of the page number. Tell students that parenthetical notations can be formatted differently in various sources.

PRACTICE

ACTIVITY B

Have students complete this activity independently. Encourage them to make note cards for their sources. Then have partners compare paragraphs. Ask students to check that their partners correctly used parenthetical notations. Encourage students to discuss what they changed when they paraphrased sources.

Citing Other Sources

Books, newspapers, and magazines are not the only sources of information available to you for a research report. The following are other sources of information and how they should be presented on your Works Cited page.

Radio and Television Programs

"Teenagers at Risk." PBS. WGVU, Grand Rapids, Michigan. 3 October 2005.

Sound Recordings

Like other citations, begin with the name of the artist, the title of the song, the title of the album, the publisher, and the date of release.

The Beatles. "Help!" *Love.* Capitol Records, 2006.

Interviews

If you speak with an expert on your research topic, make sure that you record the date of the interview. If you want to use a tape recorder, be sure to ask permission from your subject first.

Diener, Teri. Personal interview. 17 January 2005.

Online Documents

Review Chapter 5, Lesson 3, Evaluating Web Sites, before conducting research on the Internet. The notation format for online publications is similar to books and periodicals: author's name, title of the document or article, the date you accessed the Web site, and the Web site's address within angle brackets. If the Web site address is too long or cumbersome, provide the address to the Web site's home page.

Green, Robert Lane. "Abroad Appeal" *New Republic Online* 4 August 2004, <www.tnr.com>.

Encyclopedia Articles

Encyclopedia articles are often unsigned. In this case begin the notation with the title of the article. Since encyclopedias are often organized alphabetically, page or volume numbers are not necessary.

"Digestion." *World Book.* 2005 ed.

LiNK

The Reef Aquarium

In fact, in Indonesia, coral collection is done in areas already severely damaged by human industry and pollution (Wilkens, 1990).

J. Charles Delbeek and Julian Sprung

Indonesian coral garden

APPLY

WRITER'S CORNER

Remind students that paraphrasing is much more than changing a few words. Tell students they must put the information in their own words. Invite several volunteers to read aloud their paraphrases and the original source material. Discuss whether the paraphrase includes all the important details. Students should demonstrate an understanding of paraphrasing.

ASSESS

Note which students had difficulty using parenthetical notation. Use the Reteach option with those students who need additional reinforcement.

Practice Book page 175 provides additional work with citing sources.

TEACHING OPTIONS

Reteach

Ask students to create sentences that might have appeared in the sources from Activity A on page 499. Tell students to use parenthetical notation for each sentence, referring the reader to the correct source. When students have finished, have them trade papers with a partner to check for proper formatting.

Notation Rotation

Have students research a topic, using at least three sources. Tell students to use the information from the sources to write a paragraph. Ask students to write their parenthetical notations on a separate sheet of paper instead of at the end of the appropriate sentences. Invite students to trade papers and sources with a partner and use the sources to rewrite the paragraphs, inserting the parenthetical notations Ωin the correct locations.

Parenthetical Notations

One way to credit a source is to use parenthetical notations. To note a source parenthetically, paraphrase or directly quote from the source in your report. Place the author's last name and the page number of the source you used within parentheses at the end of the sentence, before the period. See the report on page 488 for examples of parenthetical notations.

Paraphrasing

When you rewrite someone else's ideas, using your own words, you are paraphrasing. Paraphrasing lets you use your own words to inform the reader what you have learned. However, because you learned your information from another source, you must note your source, just as you do for direct quotations. Effective paraphrasing requires excellent knowledge of your source material.

Study the following examples:

Original Text
Einstein often hid his fierce intellect in a bumbling, self-effacing shell. The mussed-up mop of white hair, the not-too-clean cardigan, the absent-minded-professor demeanor: all were masks.

Incomplete Paraphrase
Einstein hid his intellect behind a modest, absent-minded shell to which his hairstyle and clothing contributed.

Good Paraphrase
Einstein's messy hair and clothes, as well as his awkwardness and forgetfulness, were ways he invented to conceal his genius.

ACTIVITY B Write an expository paragraph on a topic of your choice. Consult at least two sources and use one or more quotations in your paragraph. Use parenthetical notations.

WRITER'S CORNER

Practice paraphrasing. Choose a few sentences from a nonfiction book and then write a paraphrase of them. Include a parenthetical notation. Trade papers with a classmate. Compare the paraphrase to the original. Does the original meaning remain?

For Tomorrow

Have students use the note cards they wrote for the Writer's Corner on page 495 to write paraphrased sentences with parenthetical notations. Tell students to write one sentence per source. Write several paraphrased sentences from a variety of sources that include parenthetical notations.

Research Reports • 501

OBJECTIVE

- To use almanacs, atlases, biographical references, and the *Reader's Guide to Periodic Literature*

WARM-UP

Read, Listen, Speak

Write on the board your paraphrased sentences from yesterday's For Tomorrow homework, including the parenthetical notations. Read the original material and model for students how you went about paraphrasing it. Then point out your parenthetical notations and how these may differ among sources, such as a book and a Web site. Ask volunteers to share their parenthetical notations and sentences and discuss each example.

GRAMMAR CONNECTION

Take this opportunity to talk about diagramming adjective clauses. You may wish to have students point out adjective clauses in their Read, Listen, Speak examples.

TEACH

Ask students to tell about their experiences using reference tools. List on the board examples of reference tools that students have used. Then invite volunteers to read aloud the opening paragraph and the chart.

Read aloud the Almanacs section. Show students an almanac and discuss any almanacs that students have read or used before. Have students describe the information they found in those almanacs. Point out that almanacs typically collect information that changes frequently, such as farming predictions, sports records, and population statistics.

Ask a volunteer to read aloud the Atlases section. Discuss the variety of information provided in atlases, such as topography, average temperature, population density, political borders, and roadways. Ask students to describe other kinds of information they have found in atlases.

Have a volunteer read aloud the section Biographical References. Ask students what information they expect to find in biographical references *(birth and death dates, family relationships, major accomplishments)*. Point out that biographical reference entries are usually brief and inadequate for a research report, but they can be an effective place to get basic facts.

PRACTICE

ACTIVITY A

Have small groups complete this activity. Remind students to use indexes, tabs, or tables of contents to navigate the books. Invite volunteers to share their answers and to describe how they found the information.

ACTIVITY B

Review the differences among almanacs, atlases, and biographical references. Then have students complete the activity independently. Invite volunteers to compare their answers with partners.

LESSON 4 WRITING SKILLS

Reference Tools

You can learn just about anything from reference books. Encyclopedias, almanacs, atlases, and the *Reader's Guide to Periodical Literature* are some of the most useful reference books.

REFERENCE	TYPE OF INFORMATION
almanac	annual facts, statistics, year's events
atlas	maps and other geographic information
biographical reference	information on famous people
encyclopedia	articles on specific topics
periodicals	periodic publications such as magazines
Reader's Guide to Periodical Literature	index of magazine articles

Almanacs

Almanacs are published every year, and they can cover almost any subject. Farmers were the traditional readers of almanacs. Farmers used the books to plan their crops for the coming year. Almanacs contained information about yearly weather patterns, as well as "commonsense" advice. Today there are specialized almanacs for a wide variety of topics, everything from sports to religion. General-information almanacs cover population statistics, significant events of the year, and much more. These almanacs include *The World Almanac and Book of Facts*, *TIME Almanac*, and *Farmers' Almanac*.

Atlases

An atlas is a book of maps, but it is also much more. The maps in an atlas cover political boundaries, regional climates, highways and train lines, and rivers and lakes. Atlases can also provide demographic and economic information, such as where most people in a given country live and what goods that country produces.

APPLY

WRITER'S CORNER

Tell students to create note cards for their information and to use parenthetical notations in their paragraphs. Students should demonstrate an understanding of how to use reference tools.

Grammar in Action. Ask students how independent clauses are combined within a sentence *(by a coordinating conjunction and a comma, by a semicolon, or by a conjunctive adverb and a semicolon).* Then have students identify what type of sentence this is *(compound).* Point out that the

word *samurai* functions as an adverb, modifying the adjective *family's*.

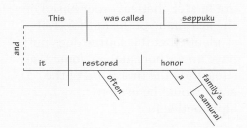

ASSESS

Note which students had difficulty identifying library reference tools. Use the Reteach option with those students who need additional reinforcement.

Biographical References

A biographical reference is a book or set of books that gives short biographies of notable people. Some popular biographical reference books include *American Men and Women of Science, Contemporary Authors, Current Biography Yearbook,* and *Who's Who in America.*

1992 Nobel Peace Prize winner

ACTIVITY A Use a current general-information almanac to answer these questions.

1. What were two top news stories of last year?
2. What was the population of the United States in 2000?
3. Who won the Nobel Peace Prize in 1992?
4. What is the origin of the name of the state of Colorado?
5. What are the highest and lowest places in the world?
6. Where were the Summer Olympic Games held in 1932?
7. Who was the National Basketball Association's Rookie of the Year in 1985?
8. What will be a good night to search the sky for meteor showers next summer?
9. What is the population of the Federated States of Micronesia?

Activity A
1. Answers will vary.
2. 281,421,906
3. Rigoberta Menchú Tum
4. from the Spanish "red" or "ruddy"
5. Mount Everest, Dead Sea
6. Los Angeles
7. Patrick Ewing
8. Answers will vary.
9. Answers will vary.

ACTIVITY B Identify which reference tool you could use to find out the information below.

1. The political boundaries of Bolivia
2. The average rainfall of your area
3. The year Thomas Edison was born
4. The winning teams of the Super Bowl for the last 10 years
5. The birthplace of Oscar Wilde
6. Urban population growth of Atlanta
7. The temperature in Australia in July

Activity B
1. atlas
2. almanac
3. biographical reference
4. (sports) almanac
5. biographical reference
6. atlas
7. almanac

WRITER'S CORNER

Look up these people in a biographical reference book. Explain in paragraph form why each one is famous.

1. Steven Spielberg
2. Mahatma Gandhi
3. Louise Nevelson
4. Kofi Annan

Grammar in Action. Diagram the last sentence in the model on p. 488.

WARM-UP

Read, Listen, Speak

Share with the class the information you researched from yesterday's For Tomorrow homework. Invite volunteers to share their information. Discuss the importance of using reference tools when writing research reports.

GRAMMAR CONNECTION

Take this opportunity to talk about diagramming adverb clauses. You may wish to have students point out adverb clauses in their Read, Listen, Speak examples.

TEACH

Have a volunteer read aloud the first paragraph of the Information Sources section. Ask students for names of search engines they have used. List these on the board and discuss the effectiveness of each. Tell students to write this information in their notebooks and to use it when conducting research. Ask a volunteer to read aloud the second paragraph. Remind students that articles are a good source of information when writing a research report.

Ask a volunteer to read aloud the last paragraph of the Information Sources section aloud. Encourage students who have used microfiche or microfilm to describe their experience. If possible, name some periodicals in your school library. Explain that some periodicals not found in the library may have searchable archives online. Emphasize that some online periodicals charge a fee to read or print older articles.

Read aloud the Plagiarism section and discuss what students can do to avoid plagiarizing. Emphasize that plagiarism is stealing.

LiNK Have students read silently the Works Cited excerpt. Point out that the entries are in alphabetical order based on the last name of the author. Tell students that if a source does not have an author, such as some Web sites, then the first word of the entry would be used to alphabetize it.

PRACTICE

ACTIVITY C

Provide small groups with atlases to complete this activity. Ask volunteers to answer the questions. Invite groups to show the class the maps they used to answer each question. Have volunteers name other kinds of information provided by those maps.

ACTIVITY D

Read aloud the list of magazine titles. Discuss the kinds of information that can be found in each magazine. If possible, have copies of the magazines so that students can look through any that are unfamiliar. Have students complete this activity independently. When students have finished, invite volunteers to share their answers with the class.

Information Sources

No search tool is totally comprehensive, so it is important to use and cite a variety of sources. A good place to begin your research may be an online search engine. There are general search engines that require a simple keyword to begin the search. Many search engines exist to help narrow the broad range of information and limit the results to guidelines you set. Visit your local or school library for a variety of search-engine options. A librarian can assist you in using specific search engines and help you find the most pertinent, helpful research for your topic.

The library will also have several reference guides that gather information and make it available to you for easy use. For your research report, you might be interested in only recent articles regarding your topic. The *Reader's Guide to Periodical Literature* is an index of articles found in popular magazines, such as *Time, Newsweek, Ebony,* and *Popular Mechanics.* This subject-and-author guide to articles from popular magazines is published twice every month, so it is a good source of up-to-date information.

When you find the article titles that you are looking for, a librarian can help you find the magazines. You might find back issues either online or in print. Often, back issues will be stored on microfilm or microfiche, an electronic machine for reading archived printed materials. If you are unfamiliar with how to use the equipment, ask a librarian to help you. Some microfilm and microfiche readers are equipped with a photocopier to make copies of the pages you need.

LiNK

Works Cited

Arendt, Hannah. 2010. *The Human Condition.* Chicago, IL: University of Chicago Press.

Aries, Philippe. 2009. *Centuries of Childhood: A Social History of Family Life.* New York: Random House.

Danah Boyd

Plagiarism

Failure to cite the source of information or ideas gathered through research is called plagiarism. Plagiarism is stealing another person's ideas or information and pretending that it is your own. Always use and cite credible sources, both online and in printed materials, and paraphrase the text in your own words and thoughts. Online search engines will help get you started, but it is your own research and diligence that will help make your research report accurate and engaging.

ACTIVITY E

Have small groups complete this activity. Invite volunteers to share their answers with the class. Discuss the possible tools for each item and whether or not those tools would be effective.

APPLY

WRITER'S CORNER

Allow time for students to locate articles in the library. Invite small groups to discuss whether their topics are suitable for a research report. Have students explain their reasoning. Students should demonstrate an understanding of how to use reference tools.

ASSESS

Note which students had difficulty using reference tools to conduct research. Use the Reteach option with those students who need additional reinforcement.

Practice Book page 176 provides additional work with reference tools.

TEACHING OPTIONS

Reteach

Ask students to select an article from a magazine in the library. Have them list the article's title and author, the name of the magazine, and the subject of the article. Then ask students to find at least one related article in the *Reader's Guide* and one related article online. Have them share the titles of the articles and explain how they might be related.

English-Language Learners

Point out some abbreviations used in the *Reader's Guide*. Write the abbreviations on the board, along with the words they represent, such as *il* for *illustration*, *p* for *page*, and *Aug* for *August*. Ask students to note any unfamiliar words. Discuss the meanings of these words.

Activity C
1. Wyoming
2. White Mountain
3. eight
4. Kentucky, Tennessee, Georgia
5. farming

ACTIVITY C Consult an atlas to answer these questions.

1. In which state is most of Yellowstone National Park?
2. What mountain range is in New Hampshire?
3. How many countries border Germany?
4. Through which states would you travel to get from Illinois to Florida the most direct way?
5. What is the principal use of the land around Dubuque, Iowa?

Activity D
1. *Architecture Digest*
2. *Newsweek*
3. *National Geographic*
4. *Rolling Stone*
5. *Consumer Reports*

ACTIVITY D Which of these magazines would you use to find information on the topics that follow?

Consumer Reports   National Geographic   Rolling Stone
Architecture Digest   Newsweek

1. building design in New Orleans, Louisiana
2. latest political and cultural news
3. the aboriginal tribes of Australia
4. profile of a popular musical group
5. comparisons of new digital cameras on the market

Aboriginal vases depicting Australian animals

Activity E
1. atlas
2. almanac
3. biographical reference
4. *Reader's Guide to Periodical Literature*
5. online search
6. *Reader's Guide to Periodical Literature*; microfiche
7. atlas, encyclopedia, online search

ACTIVITY E After an initial online search, identify which reference tools you could use to find the following information. Review and apply only the tools learned in this lesson. Some items may have more than one answer.

1. the topography of Italy
2. last year's weather in the Midwest region
3. major accomplishments of Charles Lindbergh
4. latest trends in corporations "going green"
5. the number of Web sites devoted to the TV series *Star Trek*
6. a photo of the front page of the local newspaper from 50 years ago
7. the volcanoes of the Pacific Islands

WRITER'S CORNER

Use the *Reader's Guide to Periodical Literature* to look for articles on a possible research report topic. Then read at least two of the articles. Do you still think this topic would be suitable for a four- or five-page report?

Research Reports • 505

For Tomorrow

Have students find a magazine article and an online article detailing the same country they researched for yesterday's For Tomorrow homework. Tell students to create a Works Cited entry for each article. Find a magazine article and an online article yourself and create Works Cited entries for each.

OBJECTIVES
- **To understand multiple-meaning words**
- **To understand homographs**

WARM-UP
Read, Listen, Speak
Write on the board your Works Cited entries for the articles from yesterday's For Tomorrow homework. Model for students by discussing the differences between the magazine article and the online article entries. Have small groups share the entries they wrote for their articles. Ask students to make sure their classmates have correctly written their entries.

GRAMMAR CONNECTION
Take this opportunity to talk about diagramming noun clauses. You may wish to have students point out noun clauses in their Read, Listen, Speak examples.

TEACH

Write the words *clear, groom,* and *iron* on the board. Challenge students to name at least two definitions for each of these multiple-meaning words *(clear*—free of clouds, plain or evident, to rid of objects; *groom*—someone who cares for horses, a bridegroom, to make neat; *iron*—a type of metal, a golf club, an appliance used for smoothing cloth). Ask volunteers how they know which meaning is intended when they read one of these words in a piece of writing *(by the context)*.

Invite volunteers to read aloud the first two paragraphs. Have students check their dictionaries to see how many definitions there are for such common words as *get, line, make,* and *run.* Challenge students to write a sentence for each meaning of one of these words.

PRACTICE

ACTIVITY A
Invite students to complete this activity with partners. Ask volunteers to share their answers with the class and to explain the context clues that helped determine the meaning of each word.

ACTIVITY B
Have students complete this exercise independently. Then have small groups compare their sentences. Encourage students to use a dictionary to check the correct use of the multiple-meaning words.

Multiple-Meaning Words

As you know, a word can have both literal and implied meanings. In addition, some words have more than one literal meaning. Think of the word *bridge.* One meaning of *bridge* is a structure that spans a river or other body of water. Other meanings include the area of a ship that houses the controls, a part of a musical instrument, and a part of a person's nose. Words like *bridge* are called multiple-meaning words.

Readers usually know which meaning of a word is correct by the context in which it is used. When you hear someone say "The captain has left the bridge," you assume that the captain has walked out of the ship's control room, not off a river-spanning structure.

ACTIVITY A Choose the correct meaning of the italicized word in each sentence.

1. The Reptile's second *number* was a blues tune called "Come into My Kitchen."
   a. one of a set of positive integers
   b. one of the separate offerings in a musical program
   c. a numeral used for identification

2. They played an *arrangement* for guitar and flute.
   a. an adaptation of a composition for other instruments
   b. an agreement
   c. the process of arranging

3. To gain weight, drink a *shake* instead of a glass of milk.
   a. to cause to move with jerky movements
   b. a foamy drink of milk and ice cream
   c. to disturb or agitate

4. Mike has *radical* political views.
   a. the root of a quantity
   b. advocating basic changes in current practices
   c. favoring extreme changes

APPLY

WRITER'S CORNER

Have students work independently to find multiple-meaning words in their past papers and to write the meanings. Then have partners trade papers and add any other meanings. Invite volunteers to share words that had definitions they did not previously know. Ask volunteers to name the words they found and their definitions. Students should demonstrate an understanding of multiple-meaning words.

ASSESS

Note which students had difficulty understanding multiple-meaning words. Use the Reteach option with those students who need additional reinforcement.

TEACHING OPTIONS

Reteach

Have students work in groups to write sentences for the meanings of each word not used in Activity A. Then ask students to share the sentences they wrote and to explain the context clues in their sentences that help readers distinguish each word's meaning.

English-Language Learners

Write the word *spoon* on the board. Ask students to find the word in a dictionary and name two people who might use a spoon (*a cook and a fisher*). Continue asking students to name three things that have beaks, three people involved with chips, two kinds of fingers, three things that flap or have flaps, and three types of notes. Have students write these and other multiple-meaning words in their notebooks.

5. Watching Westerns, you would assume everyone in the Old West *packed* a pistol.
   - **a.** had available for action
   - **b.** filled up with items
   - **c.** crowded to capacity

6. The new library is in an *ideal* location.
   - **a.** a goal
   - **b.** an honorable principle
   - **c.** excellent

7. Don't *gather* mushrooms unless you are positive they are edible.
   - **a.** to cause to come together
   - **b.** to pick up and enfold
   - **c.** to harvest or pick

8. Unchecked gossip can certainly *smear* someone's name.
   - **a.** to spread with a sticky substance
   - **b.** to stain the reputation of
   - **c.** to apply by spreading

ACTIVITY B The italicized words in the sentences below have more than one meaning. Write a new sentence for each word that reflects another meaning of that word.

1. Every time Emma's brother doesn't get his way, he throws a *fit*.
2. How far did stocks *fall* this week compared to last?
3. A sudden *jar* in their sleep first warned most people of the earthquake.
4. Who can *break* a dollar so Arnetta can put money in the meter?
5. The teacher described the behavior of her class as a *disgrace*.
6. After Katia sent in the *grant* application, all she could do was wait.
7. I need more *quarters* if I want to continue playing the video game.
8. The raccoons made such a *racket* last night that I couldn't sleep.

Amanita muscaria, commonly known as the fly agaric, is a poisonous fungus.

WRITER'S CORNER

Work with a partner to explore words with multiple meanings. Choose a few words from one of your papers. Think of as many meanings of the words as you can. Check a dictionary to see whether you thought of all the definitions.

For Tomorrow

Ask students to find three multiple-meaning words from today's lesson in magazines or online articles and to note which meaning is used for each. Have students write a sentence using a different meaning of each word. Find examples yourself of three words from this lesson. Write a sentence for each word, using a different meaning.

Research Reports • 507

WARM-UP

Read, Listen, Speak

Write on the board your sentences from yesterday's For Tomorrow homework. Ask volunteers to read aloud the sentences and to identify the context clues that helped determine the meaning of the word. Then invite volunteers to write their sentences on the board. Have students identify each multiple-meaning word and the clues that helped determine its meaning.

GRAMMAR CONNECTION

Take this opportunity to practice the different diagramming structures that students have learned. You may wish to have students point out different kinds of sentences to diagram in their Read, Listen, Speak examples.

TEACH

Invite a volunteer to read aloud the first paragraph. Allow time for students to look up *bridge* in a dictionary and note the two separate entries and the superscript numbers.

Have a volunteer read aloud the second paragraph and the example sentences. Ask students to name the part of speech of each homograph (*first example: verb, noun, noun; second example: verb, noun*). Invite students to suggest sentences with the homographs *bridge* and *bridge, lean* and *lean*, and *firm* and *firm*. Ask volunteers to write these sentences on the board. Challenge students to identify the part of speech of the word in each sentence.

Ask a volunteer to read aloud the rest of the text. Point out that one-syllable homographs may also have different pronunciations, such as the bird *dove* and the action *dove*.

PRACTICE

ACTIVITY C

Encourage students to use their imaginations while writing the sentences. Have partners complete this activity. Invite volunteers to share their sentences with the class.

ACTIVITY D

Discuss several examples of homographs that place the stress on different syllables. Be sure students understand what it means for a syllable to be stressed. Provide dictionaries to small groups to complete this activity. Invite groups to share their answers with the class.

ACTIVITY E

Have students complete this activity independently. Ask students to trade papers with a partner to compare sentences. Invite volunteers to share their sentences with the class.

Homographs

The word *bridge* meaning a card game has a separate entry in a dictionary from the word *bridge* referred to on page 506 because it has a different word origin. *Bridge* and *bridge* are homographs—words that are spelled the same but have different etymologies and meanings. In a dictionary a homograph is followed by a superscript number to show that it is a separate entry.

Many homographs are pronounced the same. One word *bat*, for example, means "a small, flying mammal." A second word *bat* means "a stick used to hit a ball." As a verb, this word also means "to swat or hit." You can have fun with homographs by using more than one in the same sentence.

> Pedro will *bat* at the *bat* with a *bat*.
> Can the platform *bear* the weight of the *bear*?

Some homographs that are used as different parts of speech have distinct pronunciations. This is because they are derived from separate word origins.

> Teresa waited a *minute* before she stepped onto the stage.
> Oscar found *minute* flaws in the antique vase.

In the first sentence, the noun meaning "60 seconds of time" has the stress on the first syllable. In the second sentence, the adjective meaning "tiny" has the stress on the second syllable.

ACTIVITY C Each of these words is a homograph of at least one other word. For each item, write a sentence that uses at least two of the homographs of the word. Look up the words in a dictionary if you need help. Be creative!

EXAMPLE   **A sow cannot sow corn.**

1.	ear	6.	stall	11.	lime
2.	fine	7.	long	12.	pad
3.	nag	8.	peaked	13.	lumber
4.	converse	9.	sewer	14.	boil
5.	can	10.	baste	15.	impress

APPLY

WRITER'S CORNER

Allow students to complete this activity with partners. Remind students that homographs in a dictionary are listed with superscript numbers. Encourage students to find familiar words with unfamiliar meanings. Invite students to share their homographs and sentences with the class. Students should demonstrate an understanding of homographs.

ASSESS

Note which students had difficulty understanding homographs. Use the Reteach option with those students who need additional reinforcement.

Practice Book page 177 provides additional work with multiple-meaning words.

TEACHING OPTIONS

Reteach

Write on note cards the following words that have homographs:

bow	bass
close	refuse
sow	tear
wind	would

Give partners one card and ask them to keep the word a secret. Have partners look up their word in a dictionary and find a homograph for it. Then have the students in each pair act out the two homographs simultaneously. Ask the rest of the class to name the homographs, using the correct pronunciations.

Homograph Challenge

Have small groups brainstorm a list of at least five words that have homographs. Allow groups to use a dictionary for help. Remind them that homographs have separate entries in the dictionary. After students have finished their lists, have them trade lists with another group. Challenge groups to write a sentence for each homograph on the list they receive. Invite students to share their sentences with the class.

For Tomorrow

Have students make a pair of homograph meanings similar to those in Activity D, using a pair of homographs that were not used in that activity. Find a pair of homographs yourself and write the separate meanings.

Activity D
1. a. story
   b. story
2. a. incense
   b. incense
3. a. punch
   b. punch
4. a. bore
   b. bore
5. a. entrance
   b. entrance
6. a. compact
   b. compact
7. a. mount
   b. Mount
8. a. miss
   b. miss
9. a. fritter
   b. fritter
10. a. sage
    b. sage
11. a. nail
    b. nail
12. a. kind
    b. kind
13. a. bit
    b. bit
14. a. console
    b. console

ACTIVITY D The words defined by each pair of meanings are homographs. Write the homograph for each pair. If the homographs are pronounced differently, underline the stressed syllable in each.

1. a. a tale
   b. a building floor
2. a. to make angry
   b. a fragrant substance to burn
3. a. a piercing tool
   b. to hit
4. a. to drill a hole
   b. a dull person
5. a. place of entry
   b. to delight
6. a. an agreement
   b. to crush
7. a. to climb on a horse
   b. _____ St. Helens

8. a. to avoid
   b. to feel the loss of
9. a. to waste
   b. a small cake
10. a. a wise person
    b. an herb
11. a. item used with a hammer
    b. part of a finger or toe
12. a. helpful or friendly
    b. a type of something
13. a. a part of a drill
    b. a small piece
14. a. a control panel
    b. to comfort

ACTIVITY E Each of these words is the homograph of at least one other word. Look up the words in a dictionary. Write a sentence that shows the meaning of each homograph.

1. school
2. bowl
3. lap
4. pod
5. bank
6. wake
7. light
8. case
9. elder
10. hatch
11. bail
12. mint

WRITER'S CORNER

Use a dictionary to find five other homographs that have not been discussed in this lesson. Write a sentence for each homograph that shows one of its meanings.

Research Reports • 509

OBJECTIVES

- To select, research, and organize a topic for an oral history report
- To incorporate audio and visual aids in an oral history report
- To review presentation practice and listening skills

WARM-UP

Read, Listen, Speak

Write on the board the meanings of the homographs you found for yesterday's For Tomorrow homework. Have students guess the homographs. Then ask small groups to share their homograph pairs. Tell students to guess their group members' homographs based on the meanings.

GRAMMAR CONNECTION

Take this opportunity to review diagramming. You may wish to have students point out different kinds of sentences to diagram in their Read, Listen, Speak examples.

TEACH

Ask students to brainstorm historical events or historical figures that interest them. Create a list on the the board. Then invite volunteers to read aloud the first two paragraphs and the section Choosing a Topic. Point out that sometimes the sources of inspiration are not good sources for research.

Have volunteers read aloud the section Research the Topic. Challenge volunteers to suggest tips for taking notes on note

cards. Review pages 494 and 496 if needed. Point out that while speakers do not use parenthetical notation or a Works Cited page, many credit their sources by mentioning them in the speech, especially if they use a direct quotation *(In* Common Enemies *Arthur Turling says . . .).*

Have volunteers read aloud the section Organizing Your Report. Be sure that students understand the value of writing a new set of note cards for their presentation rather than using the note cards they wrote during research.

Ask a volunteer to read aloud the section Audience. Point out that students should understand

what their audience knows about the topic. Tell students that if they are using a technical term or introducing a new concept, they should provide a brief explanation for their audience.

PRACTICE

ACTIVITY A

Have students discuss the topics in this activity with a partner. Encourage students to use encyclopedias to read about unfamiliar topics. Ask students to share topics that interest them and to explain the topics they looked up.

Oral History Report

An oral history report is a researched talk about something that occurred in the past. This can include a historical person, a significant invention, or a historical event or era. Like the research report, an oral history report must be researched, logically organized, and appropriate to its audience.

Keep these points in mind as you prepare your oral history report.

Choosing a Topic

To find a topic for your oral history report, think about historical topics that you would like to know more about. History is full of strange and fascinating stories that would appeal to you and almost any audience. Use the following tips to find a topic for your report:

- Recall ideas from your social studies or history classes that interested you. Take a few minutes to jot them down on a sheet of paper.
- Use a search engine on the Internet to look up historical people and events. Reading what others have written on a general historical topic, such as the Great Depression, can give you ideas of what you want to talk about.
- View movies that are based on historical events or time periods, such as *Apollo 13, Gone With the Wind*, or *Glory*. Consider focusing your report on the background of these events and why they became significant.
- Browse through historical almanacs. These books summarize historical events that happened on certain days of the year.

It is important to narrow your topic choices to the item you believe to have enough sources from which to draw. Remember the topic should be broad enough to cover a range of points but narrow enough to have sufficient source material.

APPLY

SPEAKER'S CORNER

Encourage students to use their notes to create an outline. Have students exchange outlines with a partner. Tell partners to look at each another's outlines for clarity and organization. Then have partners discuss the audience for the report and how to make their presentation interesting and clear. Students should demonstrate an understanding of how to choose a topic and how to organize an oral history report.

ASSESS

Note which students had difficulty selecting a topic for an oral history report. Use the Reteach option with those students who need additional reinforcement.

TEACHING OPTIONS

Reteach

Ask students to begin a chart with the headings *Movies*, *Books*, and *People*. Have students brainstorm a list of topics for each column. Discuss which topics among those listed sound like they would make the most interesting reports. Tell students to narrow the topics that are too broad for an oral history report.

History in Hollywood

Name for students a movie with a historical basis that they might have seen, such as *Titanic*. Encourage students to discuss which events in the movie are true and which are fictional. Challenge students to brainstorm a list of history topics suggested by the movie that would be appropriate for an oral history report *(history of luxury passenger ships, the building of the* Titanic, *a biography of the ship's builder or captain, a history of major nautical disasters)*.

Research the Topic

Recall what you discussed in Lesson 2 for tips on researching your report. Begin your research by locating sources from the library or the Internet.

Once you have your sources, take notes on what you read and create a set of note cards. On each card be sure to document the source, using the styles discussed in Lesson 3.

Organizing Your Report

First, think of subtopics that your notes can easily fall into. Next, organize your note cards, creating a separate pile for each subtopic. Discard any note cards that don't fall into any subtopic.

When you have organized your report, think of a thesis statement that fits your notes. Ideally, your thesis statement should summarize your topic in one sentence, such as "The American civil rights movement captured the nation's attention in the early 1960s."

Audience

Since your audience will be your classmates, make sure that everyone will be able to understand your historical report. If you learned some new terms or ideas that are critical to understanding your topic, be sure to define them for your audience.

ACTIVITY A Listed in pairs are some topics that could be assigned for an oral history report. Choose one topic from each pair and explain why that topic interests you more than the other.

1. the Great Depression or the New Deal
2. submarines in World War I or submarines in World War II
3. the Emancipation Proclamation or women's suffrage
4. the United Nations or the League of Nations
5. the Lewis and Clark expedition or the Zebulon Pike expedition
6. Anne Hutchinson's trial or the Salem trials
7. César Chávez or Mother Jones
8. The Underground Railroad or the Great Migration
9. building the Great Pyramids or building the Golden Gate Bridge
10. the cotton gin or the printing press

SPEAKER'S CORNER

Choose a topic for an oral history report to present to your class. Write a thesis statement and take notes that give supporting details and explanations.

For Tomorrow

Have students talk to a family member about an important historical event that happened during that family member's lifetime. Ask students to write a description of the event that includes the family member's recollections and impressions. Interview one of your family members and gather the same information to share with the class.

Research Reports • 511

WARM-UP

Read, Listen, Speak

Share the information you gathered from yesterday's For Tomorrow homework. Point out the specific details that made the event interesting. Retell your family member's story in a way that models how students should share their stories. Then have small groups share the historical events they discussed with their family members. Encourage students to discuss whether the events would make good oral history reports.

TEACH

Have volunteers read aloud the first two paragraphs of the section Engaging with Media. Challenge students to suggest visual and audio aids for the topics listed in Activity A on page 511. Ask volunteers to read aloud the Video or Film Clips and Audio Clips paragraphs. Ask students to name examples of video or audio clips that would be distracting or inappropriate in an oral history report. *(Using a clip of 1920s music for a report on Al Capone would be unnecessary and distracting.)* Encourage students to think of oral history reports that could use some of those same examples of video and

audio clips appropriately. *(Using a clip of 1920s music for a report on popular dance styles of the 1920s would be appropriate.)*

Invite a volunteer to read aloud the first paragraph and first bulleted list of the section Practice and Present Your Report. Remind students to practice with their visual or audio aids before making their presentations. Ask volunteers to read aloud the rest of the section. Explain that speakers are usually prepared to recommend the names of their sources in case listeners ask questions afterward that the speakers cannot answer.

Ask volunteers to read aloud the section Listening Tips. Suggest

that if students listen for a thesis statement and try to identify the organizational method used in an oral report, the report may be easier to follow.

PRACTICE

ACTIVITY B

Allow students time to prepare their oral history reports. Have students practice their reports with a partner. Encourage students to use the bulleted lists in this lesson to give feedback on their partner's reports.

Engaging with Media

Using visual and audio aids can bring your oral history report alive by letting the audience see or hear the people who made history. An oral report on the history of jazz in America, for example, could include bits of music from different jazz eras and styles. A painting of the British Army's surrender at Yorktown can help your audience imagine the event for themselves.

While you research your report, look through your sources for ideas that could be illustrated through audio or visual materials. The audio or visual aids you choose should not take away from the integrity of your report. The focus of the report should be on your presentation and what you say. Avoid using lengthy audio and video clips. Use the following suggestions to help you,

Video or Film Clips

If your topic is an event from recent history, there might be useful video or film clips that can illustrate the event. Most libraries have a broad selection of documentaries and newsreel clips.

Audio Clips

Sometimes an audience wants to hear what you're talking about. Historical events that include famous speeches are good opportunities to use audio clips in your report. If your report is on the panic caused by Orson Welles's "War of the Worlds" radio broadcast, it would probably need to include a short excerpt of the program.

Jazz sheet music approximately 1918

Practice and Present Your Report

After you finish writing your oral history report, practice presenting it. Read it aloud to a classmate. Ask yourself these questions:

- Have I used my own words?
- Is the report clear and understandable?
- Is my tone of voice calm and objective?

APPLY

SPEAKER'S CORNER

Have small groups deliver their oral history reports. Ask students to introduce their talks by discussing why they chose their topics and what sources were used for research. Encourage students to take notes and to ask questions when the speaker has finished. Students should demonstrate an understanding of how to present an oral history report.

ASSESS

Note which students had difficulty understanding how to practice and present an oral history report. Use the Reteach option with those students who need additional reinforcement.

After you have reviewed Lessons 3–5, administer the Writing Skills Assessment on pages 73–74 in the **Assessment Book.** This test is also available on the optional **Test Generator CD.**

TEACHING OPTIONS

Reteach

Ask students to divide the report they have been working on into sections for each main idea. Have students practice presenting these smaller units with a partner. Tell students to give feedback to their partners based on the bulleted lists in this lesson. Encourage students to use the feedback to make adjustments to their presentation before practicing the next part with a different partner. Allow students to present their entire report in this manner.

Listening and Looking for Topics

Take students on a tour of the multimedia resources available at your school library. Ask students to browse the materials for CDs, DVDs, videos, MP3s, and other sources that could inspire a topic for an oral history report. Have small groups discuss the visual and audio aids they chose and the topics those aids inspired. Encourage students to discuss how the audio or visual aid could be used in a presentation.

Ask your classmate to critique your presentation. He or she should comment on the following:

- The main idea
- The supporting ideas
- The appropriateness of the vocabulary
- The ease of your delivery
- Your posture, gestures, the volume of your voice, and eye contact

Based on the comments from your classmate, rewrite any parts of your report that are confusing and take out any parts that are repetitive. When you have finished revising your report, write key phrases from it on a series of note cards. That way you can maintain eye contact with your audience, and your presentation will be much more interesting.

Present your report to a group of classmates or to the entire class. Remember to stand up straight, make eye contact with the audience, and speak at an appropriate volume and pace. After you finish, ask your audience whether they have any questions.

Listening Tips

- Have a mental conversation with the speaker to stay engaged in what he or she is saying. Ask yourself questions such as *Does this report make sense?* and *Is it informative?*
- Identify the key idea or ideas in the report.
- Do not interrupt the speaker. Ask questions or make comments after the speaker has finished the presentation.
- Make at least one positive comment before offering constructive criticism about the content or presentation of the report. Ask questions about things that genuinely interest you.

ACTIVITY B Prepare your oral history report, following the guidelines in this lesson. Remember that you want to inform your listeners, so make sure your research and ideas are solid.

SPEAKER'S CORNER

Practice and present your oral history report. Remember to speak clearly, particularly when you are explaining complicated concepts. At the end of your report, invite your audience to ask questions. Answer them if you can.

OBJECTIVE
- **To prewrite and plan a research report**

PREWRITING AND DRAFTING

Tell students that in this Writer's Workshop, they will have the opportunity to plan, draft, revise, and publish their own research reports. Read aloud the first paragraph. Encourage students to name the characteristics of well-written, reliable research reports. Make sure the following points are discussed about the planning and writing of a research report:

- The report focuses on one narrow topic.
- It includes a thesis statement that is supported by factual information.
- The voice is confident, neutral, and incorporates formal language.
- Research is recorded in detail on note cards.
- An outline for the report follows a specific format and provides the writer with direction.
- Organization is focused and coherent.
- Sources are fully documented on a Works Cited page.

Prewriting

Have students silently read this section. Remind students that the prewriting stage is the time for them to explore possible topics and to look at what they already know about a number of topics.

Choosing a Topic

Invite volunteers to read aloud this section. Remind students that their topic should be narrow enough to cover comprehensively. Discuss how professional writers might go about choosing a topic for a research report. Encourage

students to explain ways they can find topics for their reports.

Explain that ideas are the foundation of writing. Tell students that their topic should be clear and of interest to their audience. Encourage students to try to find a fresh angle on their topic to add interest.

Your Turn

Ask a volunteer to read this section aloud. Allow time for students to brainstorm topics and to consult research tools. When students have finished, ask them to share their topics with the class. Invite volunteers to share the sources they used and how they chose their topics.

Researching

Have a volunteer read this section aloud. Point out Dillon's note card. Remind students that conducting research, organizing notes, and citing sources are important when writing research reports. Ask volunteers to explain why. (*The purpose of a research report is to support a thesis statement, so the factual information that supports the thesis must be thoroughly researched. Citations help form the Works Cited page and help the writer avoid plagiarism.*)

Writer's Workshop   Research Reports

Prewriting and Drafting

Throughout this chapter you have discussed what makes a good research report. You have also discussed ways to take notes and document sources. It's now time to use what you have learned in this chapter to develop, organize, and write a research report.

Prewriting

Prewriting is the time to brainstorm, choose a topic, take notes, and do research. It is also the time to explore what you already know about a topic, because your knowledge will help guide your research. Once you decide on your topic and research it, you will have an opportunity to organize and plan your research report.

Choosing a Topic

Dillon, an eighth grader, is writing a research report for science class. She brainstormed a list of possible topics that interested her. To help get herself started, she browsed the encyclopedia in her school's library and researched possible **Ideas** science topics on the Internet. After she finished browsing, she summarized her thoughts and listed them on a sheet of paper.

After reviewing her list of science-related topics, she chose to write about global warming. Dillon remembered watching a documentary film on the topic. From the film she learned that some scientists believe global warming does not exist. She disagreed with that view, so she decided the thesis of her report would be that global warming is harmful and that governments and businesses should do something about it.

Your Turn

Brainstorm a list of research topics. If you need help thinking of possible research topics, browse an encyclopedia or the Internet. Recall Activity A on page 491 and use your work to help narrow possible research topics.

Researching

Dillon knew that before she could make a plan for writing, she needed to research her topic to find important information. To help guide her research, she made a KWL chart to explore her topic. Next, she took her questions with her when she went to the library to do her research. As she gathered her sources, she jotted down her notes on cards.

Planning a Research Report

Invite a volunteer to read aloud the first paragraph. Allow time for students to read silently Dillon's outline. Challenge volunteers to explain how Dillon's outline is organized.

👓 Tell students that their method of organization will depend on their topic. Review several methods of organization, such as cause and effect, compare and contrast, and chronological order.

Your Turn

Have a volunteer read aloud this section. Allow time for students to gather information, write note cards, and compose outlines. When students have finished, invite them to share their outlines with a partner. Encourage students to offer feedback about whether the information provided in the outline is credible and whether the organization makes sense.

Is global warming real?

Polar ice caps are melting at an increased rate. Greater than 20% of polar ice caps have melted since 1979.

Bowles Global Climate Change
New York: University Press, 1999, p. 64

Planning a Research Report

Dillon studied her note cards to decide how to plan her research report. She sorted her cards into separate piles that she thought would be good subtopics for her report. When she finished, she 👓 **Organization** had a good idea about how her report should be organized. Then Dillon wrote the following outline.

Global Warming

I. Introduction: What is global warming?
   A. Definition of global warming
   B. Relation to greenhouse effect
   C. Relation to ozone layer
II. What causes global warming?
   A. Natural variation in temperatures
   B. Emissions
      1. Fossil fuels
         a. Gasoline
         b. Coal
         c. Oil and natural gas
         d. Chlorofluorocarbons
      2. Deforestation

Your Turn

Make a KWL chart about your topic and then research your topic. Use the library's resources, such as the *Reader's Guide to Periodical Literature* and other reference materials, to gather information. Write facts and information on note cards and then organize the cards into main ideas and subtopics. Write your outline on a sheet of paper.

Here are some points to keep in mind when you take notes.

- Take notes on the aspects of your topic that you will be writing about.
- Take notes on interesting ideas, strong opinions, and unique points of view. (Remember to give the author credit in your report.)
- When you find words and sentences that you want to quote directly, be sure to write them exactly as they appear in the source and enclose them within quotation marks.
- Use separate note cards for information from different sources.

STOP GLOBAL WARMING

Prewriting / Drafting / Content Editing / Revising / Copyediting / Proofreading / Publishing

Research Reports • 515

OBJECTIVE
• **To draft a research report**

Drafting

Ask a volunteer to read aloud the first and second paragraphs. Then point out that students are about to read an excerpt of Dillon's draft and that her report is actually much longer and more complete. Read aloud the first paragraph. Discuss the introduction and elicit that the opening sentence introduces Dillon's topic *(global warming)*. Ask students to identify the thesis statement. Emphasize that the topic sentence is more general, while the thesis statement narrows the topic into a specific idea that will be explained in the report.

Have students silently read the rest of Dillon's draft. After students have finished reading, review what makes up a research report *(introduction, body, conclusion, researched facts, quotations, parenthetical notations)*. Ask students to identify each of these parts in Dillon's research report. Challenge students to identify ways in which Dillon uses research to support her thesis statement.

Have students compare Dillon's draft with her outline from the previous day. Discuss what information she adapted from the outline. Then ask volunteers to suggest ways Dillon might improve her draft.

Explain that a first draft of a research report also includes a Works Cited page, which is not included in Dillon's draft. Review the information from Lesson 3 about citing sources. Remind students of the importance of consistency in citing sources and in using formal language when writing a research report. Point out that creating a Works Cited page should be fairly easy if a writer recorded the source information on his or her research note cards.

Drafting

Drafting is Dillon's first chance to develop and organize her notes and outline into a written research report.

Using her prewriting notes, Dillon followed her outline to write the first draft of her report. The following are the first page and the conclusion of Dillon's research report.

The Threat of Global Warming

This report will examine the strengths of the arguments for and against the existence of global warming and the seriousness of the threat it will also examine who is making the arguments (and who they work for and which organizations they belong to) and examine the issue of preponderance of evidence versus absolute proof. If you live in a cold climat global warming might not seem like such a bad idea. Global warming is no joke. It is a real threat to our environment and it has already begun! What is global warming? It is an increase in the average temperature of the Earth's surface, caused mostly by an increase in greenhouse gases.

Experts agree that global warming is mostly caused by burning fossil fuels, such as gasoline, coal, fuel oil and natural gas (Teeter 47). Burning hydro-carbons makes two compounds, water and carbon dioxide or CO_2 and carbon dioxide is a real heat-trapping gas. If it did not trap heat, said Dan Yarlow, "life could not exist on earth because the sun's heat would bounce off the planet" (45). Yikes! That's really scary! This process is called the "green house effect" because carbon dioxide acts like a glass roof of green house, which traps the sun's heat inside.

In conclusion, its obvious that global warming is a growing problem. And that's too bad, because we just don't want to do anything about it. The solutions to global warming, however, will not be easy to put into place. Global warming may be a difficult problem, but the solutions are within reach.

Counterarguments

Ask a volunteer to read this section aloud. Discuss why it is important for a writer to refute arguments against his or her thesis statement. Point out that Dillon learned about some scientists who insist that global warming does not exist. Explain that by showing reasons why she thinks their position is incorrect, she can strengthen her own thesis, which states that global warming is real and dangerous.

Your Turn

Have a volunteer read this section aloud. Point out that writers follow their outlines as they write, but sometimes add details or information not mentioned in their outlines, as long as the details fit with the organization of the report and support the thesis statement.

Allow time for students to draft their reports. Make sure students include all the necessary characteristics of a research report. Remind students to organize their Works Cited entries alphabetically and to be consistent in the style they use.

After students have finished writing, encourage them to trade drafts with a partner. Challenge students to identify the thesis statement in each draft.

Counterarguments

When you research your topic, you will sometimes find that certain researchers disagree with others. The work of some research may support your thesis, while the work of others does not. Points of view that run against your thesis are called counterarguments. To make your report stronger, be sure to include counterarguments when you present your research in the body of the report. Presenting counterarguments shows a reader that you have considered all points of view. Because you have done this, it makes your thesis sound more convincing.

How can I make my report stronger?

Your Turn

Follow your outline to write a first draft of your report. Be sure to note your sources properly and include a Works Cited page with your first draft.

Prewriting · Drafting · Content Editing · Revising · Copyediting · Proofreading · Publishing

Research Reports • 517

OBJECTIVE
- **To edit a draft for content**

CONTENT EDITING

Invite a volunteer to read aloud the first two paragraphs. Point out that when content editing a research report, an editor should thoroughly check that all the necessary characteristics are included, that the ideas are clearly stated, and that the structure is solid and coherent.

Ask a volunteer to read the third paragraph aloud. Have students suggest what else should be checked since this is an extended expository piece and readers will want to know that the information is reliable *(fact check the information given in the report, check correct citation of sources on Works Cited page).*

Allow time for students to read silently the Content Editor's Checklist. Ask them to suggest additions to the checklist. Review what it means to use formal language and a neutral tone. *(Word choice and phrasing convey objectivity and assure the reader that everything the writer says is reliable.)*

Invite a volunteer to read aloud the paragraph at the top of page 519. Have students read silently Eileen's comments on Dillon's draft. Ask students to explain how Eileen's comments match the points on the Content Editor's Checklist. Challenge students to offer additional suggestions for revision. *(Not all Dillon's information is cited within the body of the report. The fourth sentence in the second paragraph needs a citation.)*

Tell students that voice is the writer speaking through the words on the page. Explain that the language that helps readers hear and feel the personality of the writer creates the voice. Remind

Editor's Workshop   Research Reports

Content Editing

Dillon was proud of the draft that she had written. By organizing her notes into an outline and planning her report, Dillon found writing a draft of the research report to be far less stressful.

Dillon gave her draft to Eileen, a classmate who had also learned how to take notes and use library reference materials. Because Eileen knew what a research report should include and leave out, Dillon thought Eileen would be able to read and edit her research report effectively.

When you content edit, you edit ideas of your draft for logic, order, and clarity. Eileen read Dillon's draft to see how well Dillon's ideas were expressed. In addition, Eileen read the report to make sure all the necessary information was included. Eileen used the Content Editor's Checklist to edit Dillon's draft.

Content Editor's Checklist

☐ Does the introduction identify the topic and main ideas? Does it include a thesis statement?

☐ Does each main idea in the body of the research report support the thesis?

☐ Is the source of each researched fact or idea documented?

☐ Does the conclusion sum up the research and restate the thesis?

☐ Does the conclusion leave readers with an interesting thought or observation?

☐ Does the report use formal language and a confident tone?

☐ Is information about each source included in the Works Cited page?

students that they should use formal language with a clear, confident voice in their research reports.

Writer's Tip Tell students that when they content edit, they are looking at bigger ideas, not conventions such as correct capitalization. Remind students to look at the way factual information is used to support the thesis statement, the strength of the introduction and conclusion, and if the factual information is clearly organized.

Your Turn
Ask a volunteer to read aloud this section. Have students work with partners to edit each other's drafts. Tell students to discuss each point on the Content Editor's Checklist and to pay special attention to parenthetical notations and the Works Cited page.

TEACHING OPTIONS

An Editor's Review
Suggest that students read their research reports to their editing partners. Ask partners to take notes as they listen to the reports. Have students use the notes to summarize the reports. Encourage editing partners to work together to identify discrepancies that arise when a listener or an editor tries to identify the main ideas.

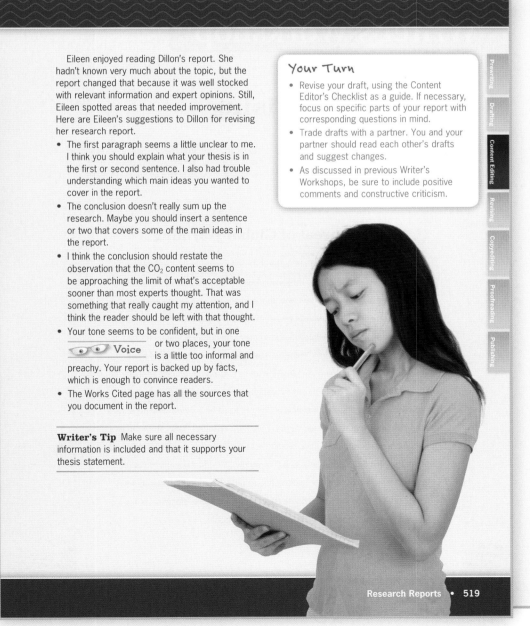

Eileen enjoyed reading Dillon's report. She hadn't known very much about the topic, but the report changed that because it was well stocked with relevant information and expert opinions. Still, Eileen spotted areas that needed improvement. Here are Eileen's suggestions to Dillon for revising her research report.

- The first paragraph seems a little unclear to me. I think you should explain what your thesis is in the first or second sentence. I also had trouble understanding which main ideas you wanted to cover in the report.
- The conclusion doesn't really sum up the research. Maybe you should insert a sentence or two that covers some of the main ideas in the report.
- I think the conclusion should restate the observation that the CO_2 content seems to be approaching the limit of what's acceptable sooner than most experts thought. That was something that really caught my attention, and I think the reader should be left with that thought.
- Your tone seems to be confident, but in one **Voice** or two places, your tone is a little too informal and preachy. Your report is backed up by facts, which is enough to convince readers.
- The Works Cited page has all the sources that you document in the report.

Writer's Tip Make sure all necessary information is included and that it supports your thesis statement.

Your Turn

- Revise your draft, using the Content Editor's Checklist as a guide. If necessary, focus on specific parts of your report with corresponding questions in mind.
- Trade drafts with a partner. You and your partner should read each other's drafts and suggest changes.
- As discussed in previous Writer's Workshops, be sure to include positive comments and constructive criticism.

Prewriting
Drafting
Content Editing
Revising
Copyediting
Proofreading
Publishing

REVISING

Ask volunteers to describe the revising stage. List on the board the types of suggestions an editor might make to help revise a research report. Then invite volunteers to read aloud the first paragraph and Dillon's revised draft, including her handwritten additions.

Have volunteers read aloud the bulleted points that detail Dillon's decisions about Eileen's comments. After each point, ask students to find the corresponding revision in the research report and to discuss the change.

- Dillon added a definition of global warming to add clarity to her introduction.
- Dillon finished the first paragraph by stating exactly what she intended to accomplish in the report.

- Dillon inserted two sentences that restated her main ideas.
- Dillon repeated the fact about the atmosphere's CO_2 content.
- Dillon deleted *Yikes! That's really scary* from the second paragraph.
- Dillon inserted a parenthetical notation in the second sentence of the second paragraph.

Writer's Workshop   Research Reports

Revising

Dillon took Eileen's suggestions seriously and worked in those that she thought were most effective. Dillon knew that revision was the time to incorporate both Eileen's suggestions and her own changes. The following is Dillon's draft, which shows the revisions that she plans to make.

The ~~Threat~~ Problem of Global Warming

This report will ~~examine the strengths of the arguments for and against the~~ argue that global warming is harmful and discuss what governments, individuals, and businesses can do to slow the affects of the problem. ~~existence of global warming and the seriousness of the threat it will also examine~~ ~~who is making the arguments (and who they work for and which organizations they~~ ~~belong to) and examine the issue of preponderance of evidence versus absolute~~ ~~proof.~~ If you live in a cold climat global warming might not seem like such a bad idea. But ~~G~~lobal warming is no joke. ~~It is a real threat to our environment and it has~~ ~~already begun! What is global warming? It~~ Global warming is an increase in the average temperature of the Earth's surface, caused mostly by an increase in greenhouse gases.

Experts agree that global warming is mostly caused by burning fossil fuels, such as gasoline, coal, fuel oil and natural gas (Teeter 47). Burning hydro-carbons makes two compounds, water and carbon dioxide or CO_2 and carbon dioxide is a real heat-trapping gas. (Laslow 345) If it did not trap heat, said Dan Yarlow, "life could not exist on earth because the sun's heat would bounce off the planet" (45). ~~Yikes! That's really scary!~~ This process is called the "green house effect" because carbon dioxide acts like a glass roof of green house, which traps the sun's heat inside.

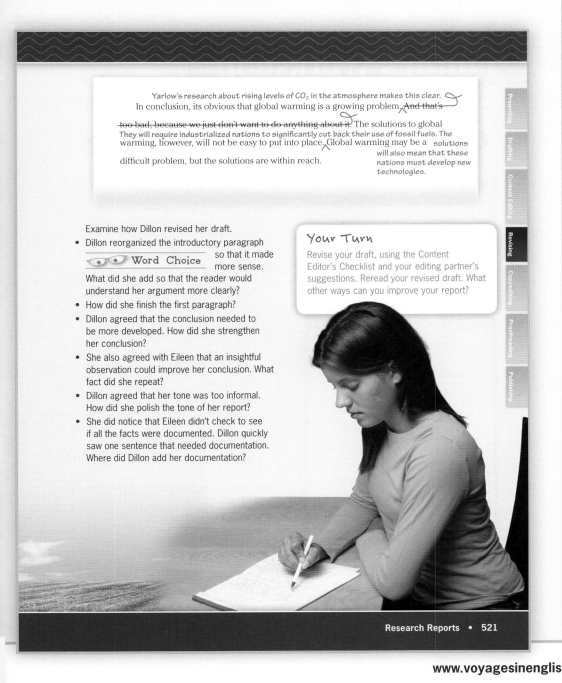

Explain that word choice is the use of words in a way that supports the purpose and tone of the writing. Remind students to keep a neutral tone when writing a research report and to define any technical terms that may be unfamiliar to their audience.

Your Turn

Have a volunteer read this section aloud. Allow time for students to revise their drafts. If students are working on computers, ask them to save their first drafts as well as their revised drafts. Explain that comparing these drafts might be useful if students decide to make further revisions at a later date.

Remind students to pay attention to the tone of their reports and to be sure it remains formal even after revising.

Piece by Piece

Suggest that students check the coherence of their research reports by reviewing main ideas individually. Tell students to check first that the main idea of each paragraph supports the thesis statement. Then tell students to examine each individual paragraph to check that the subtopics within the paragraph support the main idea of that paragraph.

Yarlow's research about rising levels of CO_2 in the atmosphere makes this clear. In conclusion, its obvious that global warming is a growing problem. And that's too bad, because we just don't want to do anything about it. The solutions to global warming, however, will not be easy to put into place. Global warming may be a difficult problem, but the solutions are within reach.

They will require industrialized nations to significantly cut back their use of fossil fuels. The solutions will also mean that these nations must develop new technologies.

Examine how Dillon revised her draft.

- Dillon reorganized the introductory paragraph

Word Choice

so that it made more sense. What did she add so that the reader would understand her argument more clearly?
- How did she finish the first paragraph?
- Dillon agreed that the conclusion needed to be more developed. How did she strengthen her conclusion?
- She also agreed with Eileen that an insightful observation could improve her conclusion. What fact did she repeat?
- Dillon agreed that her tone was too informal. How did she polish the tone of her report?
- She did notice that Eileen didn't check to see if all the facts were documented. Dillon quickly saw one sentence that needed documentation. Where did Dillon add her documentation?

Your Turn

Revise your draft, using the Content Editor's Checklist and your editing partner's suggestions. Reread your revised draft. What other ways can you improve your report?

Research Reports • 521

OBJECTIVE
- To copyedit and proofread a research report

COPYEDITING AND PROOFREADING

Copyediting

Explain that although Dillon now has a much stronger draft, she knows her report can be better. Invite a volunteer to read aloud the first two paragraphs. Remind students that revisions made after content editing might affect the overall logic of the piece because of changes to wording and sentence structure.

Ask a volunteer to read the checklist aloud. Point out the item about homographs. Invite a volunteer to define *homographs*. Encourage students to provide examples of homographs from their reports. Discuss any additions that might strengthen the checklist.

Reinforce that sentence fluency is the sound of the writing. Suggest that students always read their writing aloud to hear where it might sound choppy or awkward.

Have a volunteer read aloud the paragraphs that follow the checklist. Challenge a volunteer to explain why a thesaurus is an important tool when copyediting. *(It helps a writer find synonyms for words that are repeated too often.)* Challenge students to copyedit Dillon's draft themselves and to suggest additional changes.

Your Turn

Ask a volunteer to read this section aloud. Encourage students to trade papers with a partner after they have finished copyediting their own drafts. Suggest that students make a copy of the Copyeditor's Checklist and check each bulleted item as they copyedit their drafts.

Proofreading

Invite a volunteer to read aloud the first two paragraphs. Ask what challenges proofreading the Works Cited page poses for an editor *(must pay special attention to the use of punctuation, capitalization, and format in the citations).*

Remind students that conventions are the grammar, spelling, punctuation, and capitalization of a piece of writing. Emphasize the importance of

---

Editor's Workshop   Research Reports

Copyediting and Proofreading

Copyediting

Dillon wanted to be sure that every sentence in her report was as smooth as it could be and that it used the most accurate words to support her main ideas. When Dillon copyedited her report, she read it for accuracy in word meaning, word choice, sentence structure, and overall logic.

She used the following Copyeditor's Checklist to edit her draft.

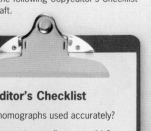

Copyeditor's Checklist
- ☐ Are homographs used accurately?
- ☐ Do the sentences flow smoothly?
- ☐ Is the sentence structure varied?
- ☐ Are any words repeated too often?
- ☐ Is the structure of each sentence logical and grammatically correct?
- ☐ Are quotations accurate and word for word?
- ☐ Are paraphrased sentences completely written in the writer's own words?

Sentence Fluency

Dillon read her essay aloud so that she could hear how it sounded.

She revised a run-on sentence in the second paragraph. Dillon also noticed that she confused *affect* with *effect*, so she corrected it.

Dillon replaced the word *real* in the second paragraph with *proven*, which was a more accurate word.

Dillon saw that she used the word *increase* too often. She read each sentence that used that word and consulted a thesaurus to see if a better word or phrase could be used. In one instance she found an alternative.

Your Turn

Reread your revised draft. Pay particular attention to the sound and meaning of each sentence and each word. Read your draft aloud at least once to make sure the sentences flow smoothly and the sentence length varies. Use the Copyeditor's Checklist to help you improve your draft.

proofreading a draft to find and correct these errors.

Read aloud the paragraph above the Proofreader's Checklist. Have volunteers read aloud the checklist and suggest additions to it based on what they will be looking for in the parenthetical citations as well as on the Works Cited page.

Have a volunteer read aloud the paragraph after the checklist. Encourage students to check Dillon's draft on pages 520–521 for errors.

Your Turn

Invite a volunteer to read this section aloud. Ask students to meet with a partner and proofread each other's drafts. Encourage students to cover their drafts with a sheet of paper and read line by line or read lines backwards to pay special attention to conventions.

Writer's Tip Tell students that reading their draft aloud will help them notice if their draft is too choppy. Remind students that doing this will help them identify where sentences should be combined or separated to create a smooth flow.

Proofreading by Genre

Ask students to read their drafts again, checking only the punctuation and capitalization in the quotations included in their drafts. Have students do an extra check of the capitalization of proper nouns. Explain that research reports often have many proper nouns and that another careful check might be required.

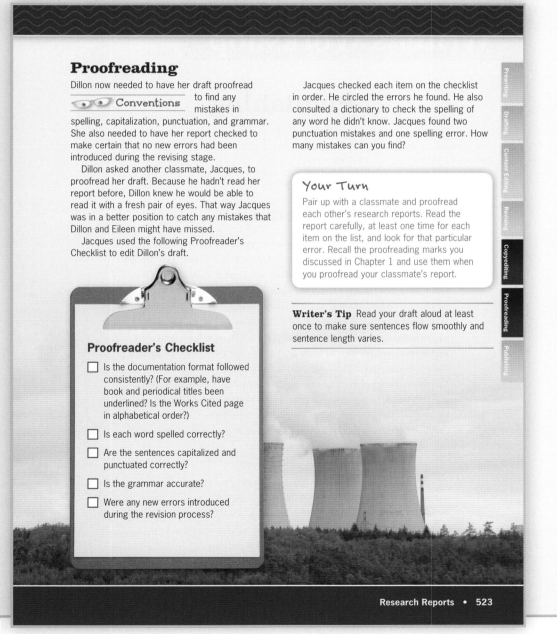

Proofreading

Dillon now needed to have her draft proofread to find any mistakes in spelling, capitalization, punctuation, and grammar. She also needed to have her report checked to make certain that no new errors had been introduced during the revising stage.

Dillon asked another classmate, Jacques, to proofread her draft. Because he hadn't read her report before, Dillon knew he would be able to read it with a fresh pair of eyes. That way Jacques was in a better position to catch any mistakes that Dillon and Eileen might have missed.

Jacques used the following Proofreader's Checklist to edit Dillon's draft.

Proofreader's Checklist

- [ ] Is the documentation format followed consistently? (For example, have book and periodical titles been underlined? Is the Works Cited page in alphabetical order?)
- [ ] Is each word spelled correctly?
- [ ] Are the sentences capitalized and punctuated correctly?
- [ ] Is the grammar accurate?
- [ ] Were any new errors introduced during the revision process?

Jacques checked each item on the checklist in order. He circled the errors he found. He also consulted a dictionary to check the spelling of any word he didn't know. Jacques found two punctuation mistakes and one spelling error. How many mistakes can you find?

Your Turn

Pair up with a classmate and proofread each other's research reports. Read the report carefully, at least one time for each item on the list, and look for that particular error. Recall the proofreading marks you discussed in Chapter 1 and use them when you proofread your classmate's report.

Writer's Tip Read your draft aloud at least once to make sure sentences flow smoothly and sentence length varies.

Prewriting
Drafting
Content Editing
Revising
Copyediting
Proofreading
Publishing

Research Reports • 523

OBJECTIVE
• **To publish a research report**

PUBLISHING

Read aloud the opening paragraph. Then ask volunteers to read aloud Dillon's research report. Remind students that this is not Dillon's entire report, but only the introduction, one body paragraph, the conclusion, and the Works Cited page.

Encourage students to identify the final copyediting and proofreading changes Dillon made. Ask students to describe the tone of the report and decide whether it flows coherently. Have them offer comparisons to the first draft on page 516.

Have volunteers read aloud the publishing options for their research reports. Discuss each method of publication. Remind students that they may use the suggestions listed or that they might consider other ways, such as presenting the report orally or creating a class magazine.

Grammar in Action. Review coordinating conjunctions, compound sentences, and the function of prepositional phrases with the class.

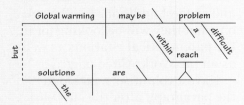

Your Turn

Ask a volunteer to read this section aloud. Have students do a final check of their drafts and then write or print out a copy for publication.

Writer's Workshop
Research Reports

Publishing

Dillon edited and revised her report several times until she was comfortable with it. She made a finished copy.

The Problem of Global Warming

If you live in a cold climate, global warming might not seem like such a bad idea. However, global warming is no joke. Global warming is a rising in the average temperature of the earth's surface caused primarily by an increase in greenhouse gases. This report will argue that global warming is harmful and will discuss what governments, individuals, and businesses can do to slow the effects of the problem.

Experts agree that global warming is mostly caused by burning fossil fuels, such as gasoline, coal, fuel oil, and natural gas (Teeter 17). These fuels are also called hydrocarbons because they are made up of carbon and hydrogen atoms. Burning these hydrocarbons makes two compounds, water and carbon dioxide, or CO_2. Carbon dioxide is a proven heat-trapping gas (Laslow 345). If it did not trap heat, said Dan Yarlow, "life could not exist on earth because the sun's heat would bounce off the planet" (45). This process is called the "greenhouse effect" because carbon dioxide acts like a glass roof of a greenhouse, which traps the sun's heat inside.

In conclusion, it is obvious that global warming is a growing problem. Yarlow's research about rising levels of CO_2 in the atmosphere makes this clear. The solutions to global warming, however, will not be easy to put into place. They will require industrialized nations to significantly cut back their use of fossil fuels. The solutions will also mean that these nations must develop new technologies. Global warming may be a difficult problem, but the solutions are within reach.

Have students follow the steps to create a classroom encyclopedia. Then challenge a committee to design a cover for the encyclopedia that they think accurately and creatively represents its content. Offer the encyclopedia to the school library to circulate.

Tell students that presentation consists of the physical appearance of their final draft. Explain that this includes neatness, consistency of margins, and the format of the Works Cited page.

ASSESS

Have students assess their finished research report using the reproducible Student Self-Assessment on page 525y. A separate Research Report Scoring Rubric can be found on page 525z for you to use to evaluate their work.

Plan to spend tomorrow doing a formal assessment. Administer the Research Report Writing Prompt on **Assessment Book** pages 75–76.

Have students choose a topic and conduct research prior to administering the Research Report Writing Prompt.

TEACHING OPTIONS

Portfolio Opportunity

Tell students to place their finished research reports in their writing portfolios. Allow time for students to review all the writing pieces in their portfolios. Discuss the eight genres of writing that students have studied in this book. Point out the differences and similarities among the genres. Encourage students to identify the characteristics of each genre and to name instances in which it would be necessary to write in one of the genres.

A Class Works Cited Page

Make photocopies of students' Works Cited pages from their research reports. Label each Works Cited page by the topic of the report. Bind the photocopies and keep them in the classroom for students to refer to whenever they want to learn more about one of the topics.

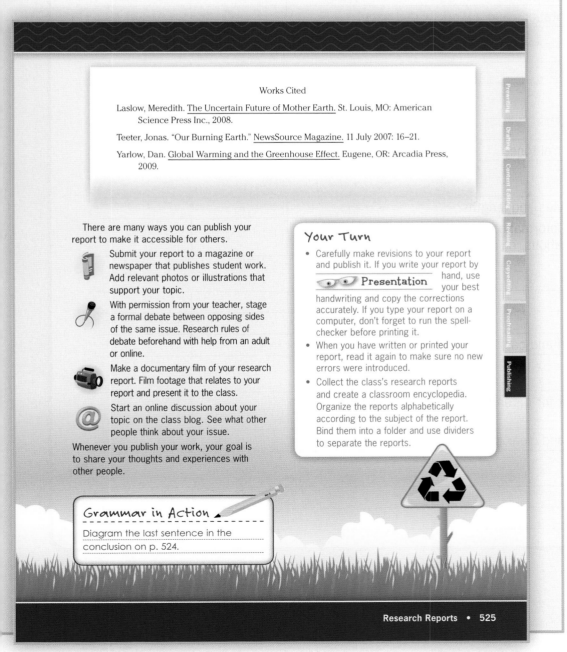

Works Cited

Laslow, Meredith. The Uncertain Future of Mother Earth. St. Louis, MO: American Science Press Inc., 2008.

Teeter, Jonas. "Our Burning Earth." NewsSource Magazine. 11 July 2007: 16–21.

Yarlow, Dan. Global Warming and the Greenhouse Effect. Eugene, OR: Arcadia Press, 2009.

There are many ways you can publish your report to make it accessible for others.

Submit your report to a magazine or newspaper that publishes student work. Add relevant photos or illustrations that support your topic.

With permission from your teacher, stage a formal debate between opposing sides of the same issue. Research rules of debate beforehand with help from an adult or online.

Make a documentary film of your research report. Film footage that relates to your report and present it to the class.

Start an online discussion about your topic on the class blog. See what other people think about your issue.

Whenever you publish your work, your goal is to share your thoughts and experiences with other people.

Your Turn

- Carefully make revisions to your report and publish it. If you write your report by hand, use your best handwriting and copy the corrections accurately. If you type your report on a computer, don't forget to run the spell-checker before printing it.
- When you have written or printed your report, read it again to make sure no new errors were introduced.
- Collect the class's research reports and create a classroom encyclopedia. Organize the reports alphabetically according to the subject of the report. Bind them into a folder and use dividers to separate the reports.

Presentation

Grammar in Action

Diagram the last sentence in the conclusion on p. 524.

Research Reports • 525

Name _____ Date _____

Research Report

Ideas

	YES	NO
Do I have a clear focus on one topic?		
Do I include factual information supported by research that was gathered as notes and placed in outline form?		

Organization

	YES	NO
Do I write an interesting introduction that includes a thesis statement?		
Do I include a body of logically ordered paragraphs that include important main ideas supported by relevant details?		
Do I write a summarizing conclusion?		
Do I include parenthetical notations and a Works Cited page?		

Voice

	YES	NO
Do I create a confident voice?		

Word Choice

	YES	NO
Do I use formal language?		
Does my writing have a neutral tone?		

Sentence Fluency

	YES	NO
Do I use varied sentence styles and lengths?		
Do I vary ways of providing information, such as quotations, statistics, examples, explanations, or related visuals?		

Conventions

	YES	NO
Do I use correct grammar?		
Do I use correct spelling?		
Do I use correct punctuation and capitalization?		

Presentation

	YES	NO
Do I have the correct format for parenthetical notations and the Works Cited page?		
Is my research report neat and clear of marks?		

Additional Items

Name _____

Date _____ Score _____

POINT VALUES

0 = not evident
1 = minimal evidence of mastery
2 = evidence of development toward mastery
3 = strong evidence of mastery
4 = outstanding evidence of mastery

Research Report

Ideas   POINTS

clear focus on one topic	
factual information supported by research that was gathered as notes and placed in outline form	

Organization

an interesting introduction that includes a thesis statement	
a body of logically ordered paragraphs that include important main ideas supported by relevant details	
a summarizing conclusion	
parenthetical notations and a Works Cited page	

Voice

confident	

Word Choice

formal language	
neutral tone	

Sentence Fluency

varied sentence styles and lengths	
varied ways of providing information, such as quotations, statistics, examples, explanations, or related visuals	

Conventions

correct grammar and usage	
correct spelling	
correct punctuation and capitalization	

Presentation

correct format for parenthetical notations and Works Cited page	
neatness	

Additional Items

Total	

Common Proofreading Marks

Use these proofreading marks to mark changes when you proofread. Remember to use a colored pencil to make your changes.

Symbol	Meaning	Example
¶	begin new paragraph	over. ¶Begin a new
⌒	close up space	close u p space
∧	insert	students∧think *should*
℗	delete, omit	that the ~~the~~ book
/	lowercase letter	/Mathematics
∿	letters are reversed	letters are reve(sr)ed
≡	capitalize	washington
∨" ∨"	quotation	∨"I am,∨" I said.
⊙	add period	Marta drank tea⊙

Not Too Scary

I have no idea where my fear of horses came from. Fear of horses is called
equinophobia, or equinaphobia. Maybe a horse thought I was a bucket of oats when I was a baby!
Just kidding. Since I live in the suburbs of Philadelphia, this fear wasn't really a big
problem, at least not during the school year, but in the summer I usually
Uncle Henry's farm, and that's when my equinophobi about my problem I couldn't go on trail anywhere

This chart from the student book is reproduced here for your convenience.

Grammar and Mechanics Handbook

Grammar

Adjectives

An adjective points out or describes a noun.

> **That** dog is **hungry**.

Adjective Clauses

An adjective clause is a dependent clause used as an adjective.
See CLAUSES.

Adjective Phrases

An infinitive phrase can be used as an adjective. See INFINITIVES.

A participial phrase can be used as an adjective. See PARTICIPLES.

A prepositional phrase can be used as an adjective. See PREPOSITIONS.

Articles

An article points out a noun. See ARTICLES.

Common Adjectives

A common adjective expresses an ordinary quality of a noun or a
pronoun: *tall* ship, *majestic* mountains.

Comparison of Adjectives

Most adjectives have three degrees of comparison: positive,
comparative, and superlative.

The positive degree of an adjective shows a quality of a noun or
a pronoun.

> My grandmother is a **tall** woman.
> The dancer is **famous**.
> LaTonya is a **careful** worker.

The comparative degree is used to compare two items or two sets of
items. This form is often followed by *than*.

> My grandfather is **taller** than my grandmother.
> The singer is **more famous** than the actor.
> James is a **less careful** worker than LaTonya.

The pages of the Grammar and Mechanics Handbook from the student book are reproduced here for your convenience.

The superlative degree is used to compare three or more items or sets of items.

> My uncle Jack is the **tallest** member of the family.
> The singer is the **most famous** person here.
> Gloria is the **least careful** worker of them all.

The adjectives *few, fewer,* and *fewest* are used to compare concrete nouns. Note that the nouns are plural in form.

> Lorna made **few** free throws.
> Gail made **fewer** free throws than Lorna.
> Mary Pat made the **fewest** free throws of all.

The adjectives *little, less,* and *least* are used to compare abstract nouns. Note that the nouns are singular in form.

> I have **little** time to practice free throws.
> My brother has **less** time to practice than I do.
> Of us all, my sister has the **least** time to practice.

Comparison with *as . . . as, so . . . as,* and *equally*

Comparisons with *as . . . as* may be made in positive or negative sentences. Comparisons with *so . . . as* may be made only in negative sentences. Never use *as* with *equally* in a comparison.

> The brown horse is **as swift as** the white horse.
> The brown horse is not **as swift as** the black horse.
> The brown horse is not **so swift as** the black horse.
> The two gray horses are **equally swift**.

Demonstrative Adjectives

A demonstrative adjective points out a definite person, place, thing, or idea. The demonstrative adjectives are *this, that, these,* and *those. This* and *that* are singular; *these* and *those* are plural. *This* and *these* refer to things or people that are near; *that* and *those* refer to things or people that are farther away.

> **This** dog is very friendly. (singular and near)
> **Those** cats are more skittish. (plural and far)

Descriptive Adjectives

A descriptive adjective gives information about a noun or pronoun. It tells about age, size, shape, color, origin, or another quality.

> I have a **sweet**, **little**, **gray**, **Persian** kitten.

The pages of the Grammar and Mechanics Handbook from the student book are reproduced here for your convenience.

Indefinite Adjectives

An indefinite adjective refers to all or any of a group of people, places, or things. Some of the most common indefinite adjectives are *all, another, any, both, each, either, every, few, many, more, most, neither, no, one, other, several,* and *some.* Note that *another, each, every, either, neither, no, one,* and *other* are always singular, and the others are plural.

> **Each** player has a glove.
> **Several** players have bats.

Interrogative Adjectives

An interrogative adjective is used in asking a question. The interrogative adjectives are *what, which,* and *whose.*

Which is usually used to ask about one or more of a specific set of people or things. *What* is used to ask about people or things but is not limited to a specific group or set. *Whose* asks about possession.

> **Which** position do you play?
> **What** time is the game?
> **Whose** equipment will you borrow?

Numerical Adjectives

A numerical adjective tells an exact number: *twenty-five children, eighth grade.*

Participial Adjectives

A participle is a verb form that is used as an adjective. A participial adjective stands alone before or after the word it modifies. See PARTICIPLES.

Position of Adjectives

Most adjectives go before the words they describe.

> **Mexican** pottery comes in many shapes.

Adjectives may also directly follow nouns.

> The vase, **ancient** and **cracked**, was found nearby.

An adjective can follow a linking verb (as a subject complement), or it can follow a direct object (as an object complement).

> The archaeologist was **excited**.
> She considered the vase **extraordinary**.

The pages of the Grammar and Mechanics Handbook from the student book are reproduced here for your convenience.

Possessive Adjectives

A possessive adjective shows possession or ownership. Possessive adjectives have antecedents. A possessive adjective must agree with its antecedent in person, number, and gender.

> John has a skateboard. **His** skateboard is silver.
> Jo and Luis have bikes. **Their** bikes are new.

Possessive adjectives change form depending on person and number. Third person singular possessive adjectives change form depending on gender.

	Singular	Plural
First Person	my	our
Second Person	your	your
Third Person	his, her, its	their

Proper Adjectives

A proper adjective is formed from a proper noun: *Brazilian* rain forest, *Chinese* emperors.

Subject Complements

An adjective may be used as a subject complement. See SUBJECT COMPLEMENTS.

Adverbs

An adverb is a word that modifies a verb, an adjective, or another adverb. Adverbs indicate *time, place, manner, degree, affirmation,* or *negation.*

> **Sometimes** my family goes to the zoo. (time)
> We like to watch the animals **there**. (place)
> We stroll **slowly** along the paths. (manner)
> Watching the animals can be **quite** entertaining. (degree)
> We'll **undoubtedly** go to the zoo next week. (affirmation)
> We **never** miss an opportunity to see the animals. (negation)

Adverb Clauses

A dependent clause can be used as an adverb. See CLAUSES.

Adverb Phrases

A prepositional phrase can be used as an adverb. See PREPOSITIONS.

The pages of the Grammar and Mechanics Handbook from the student book are reproduced here for your convenience.

Grammar

Adverbial Nouns

An adverbial noun is a noun that acts as an adverb. Adverbial nouns usually express *time, distance, measure, value,* or *direction.*

> The trip took a few **hours**. (time)
> We traveled about a hundred **miles**. (distance)
> The temperature was about 70 **degrees**. (measure)
> The bus fare was 30 **dollars**. (value)
> It was the farthest **north** I've ever been. (direction)

Comparison of Adverbs

Most adverbs have three degrees of comparison: positive, comparative, and superlative.

> Grace works **carefully**.
> Zach works **less carefully** than Grace.
> Meagen works **most carefully** of anyone in class.

> Wiley ate **rapidly**.
> David ate **less rapidly** than Wiley.
> Matt ate **least rapidly** of all.

> Carly walks **fast**.
> Maggie walks **faster** than Carly.
> Ryoko walks **fastest** of us all.

Comparison with *as . . . as, so . . . as,* and *equally*

Comparisons with *as . . . as* may be made in positive or negative sentences. Comparisons with *so . . . as* may be made only in negative sentences. Never use *as* with *equally* in a comparison.

> Isabelle sings **as well as** Lupe.
> She does not sing **as well as** Jorge.
> She does not sing **so well as** Jorge.
> Isabelle and Lupe sing **equally well**.

Conjunctive Adverbs

A conjunctive adverb connects independent clauses. A semicolon is used before a conjunctive adverb, and a comma is used after it. Common conjunctive adverbs include *also, besides, consequently, finally, furthermore, hence, however, indeed, instead, later, likewise, moreover, nevertheless, nonetheless, otherwise, still, therefore,* and *thus.*

> Ryoko walked fastest; **therefore**, he arrived first.

The pages of the Grammar and Mechanics Handbook from the student book are reproduced here for your convenience.

Interrogative Adverbs
An interrogative adverb is used to ask a question. The interrogative adverbs are *how, when, where,* and *why.*

> **When** did Ryoko arrive?

Antecedents

The noun to which a pronoun or a possessive adjective refers is its antecedent. A pronoun or a possessive adjective must agree with its antecedent in person and number. Third person singular personal, possessive, intensive, and reflexive pronouns and possessive adjectives must also agree in gender. See GENDER, NUMBER, PERSON.

Appositives

An appositive is a word (or words) that follows a noun and helps identify it or adds more information about it. An appositive names the same person, place, thing, or idea as the noun it explains. An appositive phrase is an appositive and its modifiers.

An appositive is restrictive if it is necessary to understand the sentence. It is nonrestrictive if it is not necessary. A nonrestrictive appositive is set off by commas.

> The Italian sailor **John Cabot** explored Canada.
> Magellan, **a Spanish navigator**, sailed around the world.

Articles

An article points out a noun. *The* is the definite article. It refers to a specific item or specific items in a group. *The* may be used with either singular or plural concrete nouns and with abstract nouns.

> We went to **the** park yesterday.
> **The** parks in our area are very well kept.
> **The** grass is always mowed.

A and *an* are the indefinite articles. Each is used to refer to a single member of a general group. *A* and *an* are used only with singular concrete nouns. The article *an* is used before a vowel sound. The article *a* is used before a consonant sound.

> I ate **a** sandwich and **an** apple.

The pages of the Grammar and Mechanics Handbook from the student book are reproduced here for your convenience.

Clauses

A clause is a group of words that has a subject and a predicate. An independent clause expresses a complete thought and can stand alone as a sentence. A dependent clause does not express a complete thought and cannot stand alone as a sentence.

Adjective Clauses

A dependent clause can describe a noun or a pronoun. An adjective clause usually begins with a relative pronoun *(who, whom, whose, which, that)* or a subordinate conjunction *(when, where)*. These words connect the dependent clause to the noun it modifies.

> I read a book **that was fascinating**.
> I'll never forget the place **where we met**.

A restrictive adjective clause is necessary to the meaning of the sentence. A nonrestrictive adjective clause is not necessary to the meaning. Nonrestrictive clauses are set off by commas. As a general rule, the relative pronoun *that* is used in restrictive clauses and *which* in nonrestrictive clauses.

> Chicago, **which has many tourist attractions**, is located on Lake Michigan.
> The attraction **that we liked most** was Navy Pier.

Adverb Clauses

A dependent clause can describe or give information about a verb, an adjective, or other adverb. An adverb clause can tell *where, when, why, in what way, to what extent (degree),* or *under what condition.* An adverb clause begins with a subordinate conjunction.

> We'll go **wherever you'd like**.
> We can leave **after you finish your homework**.
> **Because it's late**, we'll take a taxi.

Noun Clauses

Dependent clauses can be used as nouns. These clauses can function as subjects, complements, appositives, direct objects, indirect objects, and objects of prepositions. Most noun clauses begin with one of these introductory words: *that, who, whom, whoever, whomever, how, why, when, whether, what, where,* and *whatever.*

> **That rabbits make good pets** was a surprise to me. (subject)
> The fact is **that chinchillas make good pets too**. (subject complement)

534 • **Grammar and Mechanics Handbook**

The pages of the Grammar and Mechanics Handbook from the student book are reproduced here for your convenience.

The idea *that I could like a ferret* seems strange. (appositive)
My parents will buy me *whatever I choose*. (direct object)
I am interested in *how guinea pigs are raised*. (object of preposition)

Conjunctions

A conjunction is a word used to join two words or groups of words in a sentence.

Coordinating Conjunctions

A coordinating conjunction joins words or groups of words that are similar. The coordinating conjunctions are *and, but, nor, or, so,* and *yet.*

The boys *and* girls ran into the park. (nouns)
They played on the swings *or* in the sandbox. (prepositional phrases)
They sailed boats, *but* they didn't go swimming. (independent clauses)

Correlative Conjunctions

Correlative conjunctions are used in pairs to connect words or groups of words that have equal importance in a sentence. The most common correlative conjunctions are *both . . . and, either . . . or, neither . . . nor, not only . . . but also,* and *whether . . . or.*

Each correlative conjunction appears immediately in front of one of the words or groups of words that are connected. In sentences with *neither . . . nor,* the verb agrees with the subject closest to it.

Both my mother *and* my father like dogs.
Neither my brothers *nor* my sister likes cats.

Subordinate Conjunctions

A subordinate conjunction is used to join a dependent and an independent clause. Common subordinate conjunctions include *after, although, as, as if, as long as, because, before, even though, if, in order that, since, so that, than, though, unless, until, when, whenever, where, wherever,* and *while.*

Unless you help me, I won't finish this today.
I can't help you *until* I've completed my own project.

The pages of the Grammar and Mechanics Handbook from the student book are reproduced here for your convenience.

Direct Objects

The direct object of a sentence answers the question *whom* or *what* after the verb. A noun or an object pronoun can be used as a direct object.

Consuela made **cookies**.
The children ate **them**.

Gender

Third person singular personal, possessive, intensive, and reflexive pronouns and possessive adjectives change form depending on gender—whether the antecedent is masculine *(he, him, his, himself)*, feminine *(she, her, hers, herself)*, or neuter *(it, its, itself)*.

Gerunds

A gerund is a verb form ending in *ing* that is used as a noun. A gerund can be used in a sentence as a subject, an object, a subject complement, or an appositive.

Reading is his favorite pastime. (subject)
People from many cultures enjoy **dancing**. (direct object)
My dad likes to relax by **cooking**. (object of a preposition)
My favorite hobby is **skateboarding**. (subject complement)
Her hobby, **hiking**, requires little equipment. (appositive)

A gerund phrase consists of a gerund, its object or complement, and any descriptive words or phrases. The entire phrase acts as a noun.

Reading mysteries is a relaxing form of recreation. (subject)
Linda's hobby is **riding her bike**. (subject complement)
People around the world enjoy **watching fireworks**. (direct object)
Americans celebrate the Fourth of July by **attending firework shows**.
    (object of a preposition)
His job, **creating fireworks displays**, can be very dangerous.
    (appositive)

The pages of the Grammar and Mechanics Handbook from the student book are reproduced here for your convenience.

Indirect Objects

An indirect object tells *to whom* or *for whom*, or *to what* or *for what*, an action is done. A noun or an object pronoun can be used as an indirect object

I gave **Sven** a present.
I gave **him** a birthday card too.

Infinitives

An infinitive is a verb form, usually preceded by *to,* that is used as a noun, an adjective, or an adverb.

To study is your present job. (noun)
I have a history report **to do**. (adjective)
I went **to study** in the library. (adverb)

An infinitive phrase consists of an infinitive, its object or complement, and any descriptive words or phrases.

To finish the science report was my goal. (noun)
I made a decision **to write about bears**. (adjective)
I arrived too late **to finish it today**. (adverb)

Hidden Infinitives

A hidden infinitive is an infinitive without *to.* Hidden infinitives occur after verbs of perception such as *hear, see, know,* and *feel* and after verbs such as *let, make, dare, need,* and *help.*

I heard the birds **sing** this morning.
I'll help **build** a birdhouse.

The word *to* is also omitted after the prepositions *but* and *except* and the conjunction *than.*

I'll do anything but **mow** the lawn.
I'd rather help out than **do** nothing.

Split Infinitives

An adverb placed between *to* and the verb results in a split infinitive. Good writers try to avoid split infinitives.

The pages of the Grammar and Mechanics Handbook from the student book are reproduced here for your convenience.

Subjects of Infinitives

An infinitive used as a direct object can have a subject. The subject tells the doer of the infinitive. If the subject is a pronoun, it is always in the object form.

We wanted **her** to clean the garage.

Interjections

An interjection is a word or phrase that expresses a strong or sudden emotion, such as happiness, delight, anger, disgust, surprise, impatience, pain, or wonder.

Ouch! I stubbed my toe.
Wow, that's amazing!

Mood

Mood shows the manner in which the action or state of being of a verb is expressed.

Indicative Mood

The indicative mood is used to state a fact or ask a question. The simple tenses, the progressive tenses, and the perfect tenses are all part of the indicative mood.

I **bought** a new cell phone.
Have you ever **sent** pictures with a cell phone?
The pictures **are** amazing!

Imperative Mood

The imperative mood is used to express a command or a request. The imperative mood uses the base form of a verb. The subject of an imperative sentence is usually understood to be the second person pronoun, *you*.

Follow the directions carefully.
Watch out!

A command can be given in the first person by using *let's* before the base form of a verb.

Let's go.

The pages of the Grammar and Mechanics Handbook from the student book are reproduced here for your convenience.

Emphatic Mood

The emphatic mood gives special force to a simple present or past tense verb. To make an emphatic mood, use *do, does,* or *did* before the base form of the verb.

I **do like** to use cell phones.
I **did use** my cell phone last night.

Subjunctive Mood

The subjunctive mood is used to express a wish or a desire; to express a command, a recommendation, or a necessity after *that;* or to express something that is contrary to fact.

The past tense of a verb is used to state present wishes or desires or contrary-to-fact conditions. *Were* is used instead of *was,* and *would* is used instead of *will.*

I wish you **were** here. (a wish or desire)
If we **had** enough money, we **would** go to the movies.
   (a contrary-to-fact condition)

The base form of a verb is used in a clause after *that.*

The coach insisted that Laura **be** on time. (command after *that*)
It's imperative that she **call** him tonight. (necessity after *that*)

Nouns

A noun is a name word. A singular noun names one person, place, thing, or idea: *girl, park, ball, memory.* A plural noun names more than one person, place, thing, or idea: *girls, parks, balls, memories.*

Abstract Nouns

An abstract noun names something that cannot be seen or touched. It expresses a quality or a condition: *morality, sadness, idea, duration.*

Appositives

An appositive is a word (or words) that follows a noun and helps identify it or adds more information about it. See APPOSITIVES.

Collective Nouns

A collective noun names a group of people, animals, or things considered as one: *team, herd, bunch.*

The pages of the Grammar and Mechanics Handbook from the student book are reproduced here for your convenience.

Common Nouns

A common noun names any one of a class of people, places, or things: *reader, province, star.*

Concrete Nouns

A concrete noun names something that can be seen or touched: *table, hammer, artist, Ohio River.*

Gerunds

A gerund is a verb form ending in *ing* that is used as a noun. A gerund or a gerund phrase can be a subject, an object, a subject complement, or an appositive. See GERUNDS.

Infinitives Used as Nouns

An infinitive is a verb form, usually preceded by *to.* An infinitive or infinitive phrase used as a noun can be a subject, a subject complement, an object, or an appositive. See INFINITIVES.

Noun Clauses

A dependent clause can be used as a noun. See CLAUSES.

Noun Phrases

A gerund phrase can be used as a noun. See GERUNDS.

A prepositional phrase can be used as a noun. See PREPOSITIONS.

Possessive Nouns

A possessive noun expresses possession or ownership.

To form the singular possessive, add -'s to the singular form of the noun.

student	student**'s**	Heather	Heather**'s**

To form the possessive of a plural noun ending in *s,* add the apostrophe only. If the plural form of a noun does not end in *s,* add -'s.

cowboys	cowboys**'**	children	children**'s**

The singular possessive of a proper name ending in *s* is usually formed by adding -'s.

James	James**'s**	Mrs. Williams	Mrs. Williams**'s**

The pages of the Grammar and Mechanics Handbook from the student book are reproduced here for your convenience.

The plural possessive of a proper name is formed by adding an apostrophe to the plural of the name.

> Mr. and Mrs. Adams   the Adamses' children

The possessive of compound nouns is formed by adding -'s to the end of the term.

> commander in chief   commander in chief**'s**
> brothers-in-law   brothers-in-law**'s**

Separate possession occurs when two or more people own things independently of one another. To show separate possession, use -'s after each noun.

> Diane**'s** and Peter**'s** murals are colorful.

Joint possession occurs when two or more people own something together. To show joint possession, use -'s after the last noun only.

> Marta and Ryan**'s** mural is colorful.

Proper Nouns

A proper noun names a particular person, place, or thing: *Meryl Streep, Hollywood, Academy Award.*

Number

The number of a noun or pronoun indicates whether it refers to one person, place, thing, or idea (singular) or more than one person, place, thing, or idea (plural).

Object Complements

An object complement follows the direct object of a sentence. A noun used as an object complement follows the direct object and renames it. An adjective used as an object complement follows the direct object and describes it.

> We elected Yoko **president**.
> We found her leadership **inspiring**.

Participles

A participle is a verb form that is used as an adjective. A present participle always ends in *ing*. A past participle generally ends in *ed*.

Participial Adjectives

A participial adjective stands alone before or after the word it modifies.

> The **sobbing** child clung to her mother.
> The child, **sobbing**, clung to her mother.

A participle has voice and tense. The present participle shows a relationship between the time of the action of the participle and of the main verb. Past and perfect forms show action that was completed at some time before the action indicated by the main verb.

> The project **being started** now is supposed to end today.
>   (present passive)
> The project **started** yesterday is important. (past passive)
> Their group, **having started** late, rushed to finish.
>   (present perfect active)
> **Having been delayed** twice, the project is behind schedule.
>   (present perfect passive)

A participle that is essential to the meaning of a sentence is restrictive and is not set off by commas. A participle that is not essential to the meaning of the sentence is nonrestrictive and is set off by commas.

> The project **started on Monday** ran into terrible snags.
> The other project, **started a day later**, finished first.

Dangling Participles

A dangling participle is a participial phrase that does not modify a noun or pronoun. Dangling participles should be corrected.

> **Working hard**, the doghouse was soon finished. (incorrect)
> **Working hard**, the girls soon finished the doghouse. (correct)

Participial Phrases

A participial phrase consists of the participle and an object or a complement and any descriptive words or phrases. A participial phrase can come before or after the word it modifies.

> **Kissing the child gently**, the mother tried to soothe him.
> The child, **sobbing loudly**, refused to quiet down.

The pages of the Grammar and Mechanics Handbook from the student book are reproduced here for your convenience.

Person

Personal, possessive, intensive, and reflexive pronouns and possessive adjectives change form according to person—whether the antecedent is the person speaking (first person), being spoken to (second person), or being spoken about (third person).

Phrases

A phrase is a group of words that is used as a single part of speech.

Gerund Phrases

A gerund phrase consists of a gerund, its object or complement, and any descriptive words or phrases. See GERUNDS.

Infinitive Phrases

An infinitive phrase consists of an infinitive, its object or complement, and any descriptive words or phrases. See INFINITIVES.

Participial Phrases

A participial phrase consists of the participle, its object or complement, and any descriptive words or phrases. See PARTICIPLES.

Prepositional Phrases

A prepositional phrase is made up of a preposition, the object of the preposition, and any modifiers of the object. See PREPOSITIONS.

Verb Phrases

A verb phrase is two or more verbs that work together as a unit. A verb phrase may have one or more auxiliary verbs and a main verb.

> The boy **is studying**.
> He **has been studying** for an hour.

Predicates

The predicate of a sentence names an action or a state of being.

> The horses **jumped**.
> They **were** beautiful.

The pages of the Grammar and Mechanics Handbook from the student book are reproduced here for your convenience

Complete Predicates

The complete predicate is the verb with all its modifiers and objects or complements.

The horses **jumped all the hurdles well**.

Compound Predicates

A compound predicate contains more than one verb joined by a coordinating conjunction.

The horses **ran swiftly and jumped** over the fence.

Simple Predicates

The simple predicate is the verb or verb phrase.

The horses **have been running** for a long time.

Prepositions

A preposition is a word that shows the relationship between a noun or pronoun (the object of the preposition) and some other word in a sentence.

Prepositional Phrases

A prepositional phrase is made up of a preposition, the object of the preposition, and any modifiers of the object. A prepositional phrase may be used as an adjective, an adverb, or a noun.

She was the winner **of the game**. (adjective)
She threw her hat **into the air**. (adverb)
On the podium is where she stood. (noun)

Pronouns

A pronoun is a word used in place of a noun. The noun to which a pronoun refers is its antecedent. A pronoun must agree with its antecedent in person and number. Third person personal, possessive, intensive, and reflexive pronouns must also agree in gender. See GENDER, NUMBER, PERSON.

Demonstrative Pronouns

A demonstrative pronoun points out a particular person, place, or thing. The demonstrative pronouns are *this, that, these,* and *those. This* and *that* are singular; *these* and *those* are plural. *This* and *these* point out things that are near; *that* and *those* point out things that are farther away.

> **This** is my bike. (singular and near)
> **Those** are my skates. (plural and far)

Indefinite Pronouns

An indefinite pronoun refers to any or all of a group of people, places, or things. Indefinite pronouns can be used as subjects or objects.

> **Many** had heard about the strange old house.
> The loud noises were heard by **everyone**.

Most indefinite pronouns are singular, but some are plural. Singular indefinite pronouns include *another, anybody, anyone, anything, each, either, everybody, everyone, everything, much, neither, nobody, no one, nothing, one, other, somebody, someone,* and *something.* Plural indefinite pronouns include *both, few, many, others,* and *several.*

> **Everyone** is busy.
> **Nobody** wants to make a mistake.
> **Several** are drawing posters.
> **Others** want to use the computer.

The indefinite pronouns *all, any, more, most, none,* and *some* can be singular or plural, depending on how each is used in a sentence. These pronouns are singular and take a singular verb when they are followed by a phrase with a singular noun or an abstract noun. They are plural and take a plural verb when they are followed by a phrase with a plural noun.

> **Most** of the work was completed.
> **Most** of the projects were completed.

The indefinite pronouns *no one, nobody, none,* and *nothing* are negative words. They should never be used in sentences with other negative words such as *no, not,* or *never.*

The pages of the Grammar and Mechanics Handbook from the student book are reproduced here for your convenience.

Intensive Pronouns

Intensive pronouns end in *self* or *selves*. An intensive pronoun emphasizes a preceding noun or pronoun. It must agree with its antecedent in person, number, and gender.

My sister paid for the car **herself**.
I **myself** can't afford to buy a car.

Intensive pronouns change form depending on person and number. Third person singular intensive pronouns change form depending on gender.

	Singular	**Plural**
First Person	myself	ourselves
Second Person	yourself	yourselves
Third Person	himself	themselves
	herself	
	itself	

Interrogative Pronouns

An interrogative pronoun is used to ask a question. The interrogative pronouns are *who, whom, whose, which,* and *what.*

Who refers to people. It is often the subject of a question. *Whom* also refers to people. It is the object of a verb or a preposition.

Who is the captain of the hockey team?
Whom did he meet at the rink?
To **whom** will they sell their old skates?

Whose is used to ask about possession. *Which* is used when asking about a group or class. *What* is used for asking about things or seeking information.

Whose are those skates?
Which of the teams will be the toughest opponent?
What did you buy at the refreshment counter?
What is the date of the first game?

Object Pronouns

An object pronoun can be used as a direct or an indirect object of a verb or as the object of a preposition. The object pronouns are *me, you, him, her, it, us,* and *them.*

Tom met **her** at the video store. (direct object)
Gina wrote **him** an e-mail. (indirect object)
Martha received messages from **them**. (object of a preposition)

The pages of the Grammar and Mechanics Handbook from the student book are reproduced here for your convenience.

Personal Pronouns

Personal pronouns change form depending on person and number. Third person singular pronouns change form to reflect gender.

	Singular	Plural
First Person	I, me	we, us
Second Person	you	you
Third Person	he, she, it, him, her	they, them

Personal pronouns also change form depending on whether they are used as subjects *(I, you, he, she, it, we, they)* or objects *(me, you, him, her, it, us, them).*

Possessive Pronouns

A possessive pronoun shows possession or ownership. It takes the place of a possessive noun. Possessive pronouns must agree with their antecedents in person, number, and gender.

> The green bike is **mine**.
> Jill left **hers** near the fence.
> Joe, where is **yours**?

Possessive pronouns change form depending on person and number. Third person singular possessive pronouns change form to reflect gender.

	Singular	Plural
First Person	mine	ours
Second Person	yours	yours
Third Person	his, hers, its	theirs

Reflexive Pronouns

Reflexive pronouns end in *self* or *selves*. A reflexive pronoun can be the direct or indirect object of a verb or the object of a preposition. A reflexive pronoun generally refers to the subject of the sentence. Reflexive pronouns must agree with their antecedents in person, number, and gender.

> I consider **myself** lucky to have won. (direct object)
> He gave **himself** a pat on the back. (indirect object)
> They did it by **themselves**. (object of a preposition)

The pages of the Grammar and Mechanics Handbook from the student book are reproduced here for your convenience.

Reflexive pronouns change form depending on person and number. Third person singular reflexive pronouns change form depending on gender.

	Singular	Plural
First Person	myself	ourselves
Second Person	yourself	yourselves
Third Person	himself	themselves
	herself	
	itself	

Relative Pronouns

A relative pronoun connects an adjective clause to the noun it modifies. The relative pronouns are *who, whom, whose, which,* and *that.*

Who and *whom* refer to people. *Who* is used as the subject of an adjective clause. *Whom* is used as the object of an adjective clause.

George Washington, **who** was a famous general, was the first president of the United States.
George Washington, **whom** we call the father of our country, started out as a surveyor.

Which refers to animals, places, or things, *That* refers to people, animals, places, or things. *Whose* often refers to people but can also refer to animals, places, or things.

Mount Vernon, **which** was Washington's home, is in Virginia.
It's a place **that** many tourists visit.
They learn about Washington, **whose** possessions are displayed in the house.

Subject Pronouns

A subject pronoun can be used as the subject or the subject complement in a sentence. The subject pronouns are *I, you, he, she, it, we,* and *they.*

We went to the mall on Saturday. (subject)
The clerk we talked to was **she**. (subject complement)

The pages of the Grammar and Mechanics Handbook from the student book are reproduced here for your convenience.

Sentences

A sentence is a group of words that expresses a complete thought.

Complex Sentences

A complex sentence has one independent clause and at least one dependent clause, which may function as a noun, an adjective, or an adverb.

> He claimed that he was the fastest runner.
> The race that would decide the championship began at noon.
> Because he tripped and fell, he lost the race.

Compound Sentences

A compound sentence contains two or more independent clauses.

> The boys ran a race, and Hassan won.
> Chris was leading at the halfway mark, but he tripped and fell.
> Will they run the race again, or will Hassan get the prize?

Declarative Sentences

A declarative sentence makes a statement. It ends with a period.

> I have a new cell phone.

Exclamatory Sentences

An exclamatory sentence expresses a strong emotion. It ends with an exclamation point.

> It's so cool!

Imperative Sentences

An imperative sentence gives a command. It usually ends with a period but may end with an exclamation point. In imperative sentences the subject *you* is understood.

> Call me tomorrow.

Interrogative Sentences

An interrogative sentence asks a question. It ends with a question mark.

> Will you take my picture?

Inverted Order in Sentences

A sentence is in inverted order when the main verb or an auxiliary verb comes before the subject.

Around the chimney curled the wispy smoke.
When did you light the fireplace?
There were many birds atop the chimney.

Natural Order in Sentences

A sentence is in natural order when the verb follows the subject.

The wispy smoke curled around the chimney.

Simple Sentences

A simple sentence is one independent clause. It has a subject and a predicate, either or both of which may be compound.

Milwaukee is the largest city in Wisconsin.
Milwaukee and Green Bay have professional sports teams.
Many people in Wisconsin fish and boat in the summer.

Subject Complements

A subject complement follows a linking verb such as the forms of *be*. A noun or pronoun used as a subject complement renames the subject of the sentence; it refers to the same person, place, thing, or idea. An adjective used as a subject complement describes the subject of the sentence.

My uncle is a **police officer**.
The officer who won the medal was **he**.
His job can be **dangerous**.

Subjects

The subject names the person, place, or thing a sentence is about.

Complete Subjects

The complete subject is the simple subject plus all the words that describe it.

The tiny lamb with the black face trotted across the field.

550 • **Grammar and Mechanics Handbook**

The pages of the Grammar and Mechanics Handbook from the student book are reproduced here for your convenience.

550 • **Grammar and Mechanics Handbook**

Compound Subjects

A compound subject contains more than one noun or pronoun joined by a coordinating conjunction.

The **lamb** and its **mother** trotted across the field.

Simple Subjects

The simple subject is the noun or pronoun that a sentence is about.

The **lamb** trotted across the field.

Tenses

The tense of a verb expresses the time of the action or state of being.

Perfect Tenses

Perfect tenses consist of a form of the auxiliary verb *have* and the past participle of the main verb. The present perfect tense tells about an action that took place at an indefinite time in the past or that started in the past and continued into the present. The past perfect tense tells about an action that was completed before another action was begun or completed. The future perfect tense tells about an action that will be completed before a specific time in the future.

Present Perfect Active	He **has finished** his homework.
Past Perfect Active	He **had finished** it before dinner.
Future Perfect Active	He **will have finished** dinner by six o'clock.

The passive voice of perfect tenses is formed by inserting *been* between the auxiliary of a form of *have* and the main verb.

Present Perfect Passive	The car **has been washed**.
Past Perfect Passive	The car **had been washed** before it started to rain.
Future Perfect Passive	**The car will have been washed** by the time Dad gets home.

Progressive Tenses

Progressive tense consist of a form of the auxiliary verb *be* and the present participle of the main verb. These tenses show ongoing action.

Present Progressive	I **am reading** my math book now.
Past Progressive	I **was reading** my math book when the phone rang.
Future Progressive	I **will be reading** my math book until dinner time.

The pages of the Grammar and Mechanics Handbook from the student book are reproduced here for your convenience.

Simple Tenses

The simple present tense indicates an action that is repeated or always true. The simple past and future tenses indicate action in the past or in the future.

Simple Present	I *eat* a lot of fruit.
Simple Past	I *ate* some melon for lunch today.
Simple Future	I *am going to eat* some cherries as a snack.
	I *will eat* them after school.

Verbals

Verbals are words made from verbs. There are three kinds of verbals: participles, gerunds, and infinitives.

A participle is a verb form that is used as an adjective. A gerund is a verb form ending in *ing* that is used as a noun. An infinitive is a verb phrase, usually preceded by *to*, that is used as a noun, an adjective, or an adverb. See GERUNDS, INFINITIVES, PARTICIPLES.

The **frightened** cat ran and hid under the porch. (participle)
Getting the dog into the house was my priority. (gerund)
My hope is **to establish** a level of tolerance between Coco and Buster. (infinitive)

Verbs

A verb shows action or state of being. See MOOD, TENSES, VOICE.

Lupe **opened** her mailbox. (action)
She **was** excited to find an e-mail from Carla. (state of being)

Auxiliary Verbs

An auxiliary verb is a verb that combines with a main verb to form a verb phrase. Auxiliary verbs help show voice, mood, and tense. Some common auxiliary verbs are the forms of *be, have,* and *did.* Other auxiliary verbs are *can, could, may, might, should,* and *will.*

The pages of the Grammar and Mechanics Handbook from the student book are reproduced here for your convenience.

Intransitive Verbs

An intransitive verb does not have a receiver of its action. It does not have a direct object.

Danny **relaxed** under the big oak tree.

Some verbs can be transitive or intransitive, depending on their use in the sentence.

Danny **plays** baseball in the summer. (transitive)
He usually **plays** in Gresham Park. (intransitive)

Irregular Verbs

The past and past participle of irregular verbs are not formed by adding -d or -ed.

Present	Past	Past Participle
sing	sang	sung
write	wrote	written
put	put	put

Linking Verbs

A linking verb joins a subject with a subject complement (a noun, a pronoun, or an adjective). The subject complement renames or describes the subject.

Ms. Roberts **became** a newspaper reporter.
She **feels** proud of her work.
The author of that article **is** she.

Common linking verbs are *be, appear, become, feel, grow, look, remain, seem, smell, sound, stay, taste,* and *turn*. Some of these verbs can be transitive, intransitive, or linking verbs.

He **felt** the heat of the sun on his back. (transitive verb)
She **felt** strongly about winning the game. (intransitive)
Danny **felt** tired after the game. (linking verb)

The pages of the Grammar and Mechanics Handbook from the student book are reproduced here for your convenience.

Modal Auxiliaries

Modal auxiliaries are used to express permission, possibility, ability, necessity, obligation, and intention. They are followed by main verbs that are in the base form. The common modal auxiliaries are *may, might, can, could, must, should, will,* and *would.*

> Any amateur chef **may join** the committee. (permission)
> We **might assign** dishes at the meeting. (possibility)
> Blanca **can bake** delicious cakes. (ability)
> Everyone **must agree** on the menu. (necessity)
> Cooks **should prepare** enough food for everyone. (obligation)
> Marco **will act** as the contact person. (intention)

Phrasal Verbs

Some transitive and intransitive verbs are phrasal verbs. A phrasal verb is a combination of a main verb and a preposition or an adverb. The noun or pronoun that follows a phrasal verb is the direct object.

> He **looks after** his little brother on weekends.
> Yesterday he **set up** the croquet set.
> He **wakes up** with a smile each morning.

Principal Parts

The four basic parts of all verbs are the present, or base form; the past; the past participle; and the present participle. The past and past participles of regular verbs are formed by adding *-d* or *-ed* to the base form. The present participle is formed by adding *-ing.*

Base	Past	Past Participle	Present Participle
sail	sailed	sailed	sailing

Regular Verbs

The past and the past participles of a regular verb are formed by adding *-d* or *-ed* to the base form.

Base	Past	Past Participle
walk	walked	walked
smile	smiled	smiled
try	tried	tried
hop	hopped	hopped

The pages of the Grammar and Mechanics Handbook from the student book are reproduced here for your convenience.

Transitive Verbs

A transitive verb expresses an action that passes from a doer to a receiver. Every transitive verb has a receiver of the action. That receiver is the direct object.

Sheila *kicked* the ball into the net.

Voice

Voice shows whether the subject of a transitive verb is the doer or the receiver of the action.

Active Voice

When a transitive verb is in the active voice, the subject is the doer of the action.

Sheila *kicked* the winning goal.

Passive Voice

When a transitive verb is in the passive voice, the subject is the receiver of the action. A verb in the passive voice is formed by combining some form of *be* with the past participle of the main verb.

The winning goal *was kicked* by Sheila.

The pages of the Grammar and Mechanics Handbook from the student book are reproduced here for your convenience.

Mechanics

Capitalization and Punctuation

Apostrophes
An apostrophe is used to show possession.

    the man's coat   the boys' jackets

An apostrophe is used to show the omission of letters or numbers.

    can't   we'll   the flood of '98

An apostrophe is used to show the plural of lowercase letters but not of capital letters unless the plural could be mistaken for a word

    a's   *u*'s   *Ps*   *U*'s   *A*'s

Capital Letters
A capital letter is used for the first word in a sentence, the first word in a direct quotation, and the first word of most lines of poetry and songs.

    My dad asked, "**W**ould you like to take a trip?"

    My country, 'tis of thee,
    Sweet land of liberty.

A capital letter is used for proper nouns and proper adjectives.

    Abraham **L**incoln   the **G**ettysburg **A**ddress
    the **L**incoln **M**emorial   **W**ashington, **D.C.**
    American hero   **K**entucky rail-splitter

A capital letter is used for a title when it precedes a person's name.

    President Lincoln

A capital letter is used for the directions *North, South, East,* and *West* when they refer to sections of the country.

    We left the **S**outh and drove north toward home.

A capital letter is used for the names of deities and sacred books.

    Holy **S**pirit   **B**ible   **K**oran   **O**ld **T**estament

The pages of the Grammar and Mechanics Handbook from the student book are reproduced here for your convenience.

A capital letter is used for the principal words in titles (but not the articles *a, an,* or *the;* coordinating conjunctions; or prepositions unless they are the first or last words).

To **K**ill a **M**ockingbird   "**T**he **W**illow and the **G**ingko"

Capital letters are used for abbreviations of words that are capitalized.

Mrs.   **D**r.   **J**an.   **A**ve.

Colons

A colon is used before a list when terms such as *the following* or *as follows* are used.

I'd like to visit the following cities: New Orleans, San Francisco, and Chicago.

A colon is used after the salutation of a business letter.

Dear Senator Smith:

Commas

Commas are used to separate words in a series of three or more.

My family has two dogs, a cat, and some fish.

Commas are used to separate adjectives of equal importance before a noun.

It's a little, white, fluffy kitten.

Commas are used to set off the parts of addresses, place names, and dates.

Abraham Lincoln was born on February 12, 1809, in Hardin County, Kentucky.

Commas are used to set off words in direct address and parenthetical expressions.

Did you know, Eleanor, that the ship really sank?
Titanic was, as you may know, a popular movie.

Commas are used to set off nonrestrictive phrases and clauses.

The *Titanic*, a famous ocean liner, hit an iceberg.
The ship, which everyone had thought was unsinkable, disappeared under the icy waters.

Mechanics

Commas are used to set off a direct quotation or the parts of a divided quotation.

"I hope," said Mrs. Litwac, "you have all finished your work."

A comma is used before a coordinating conjunction that is used to connect clauses in a sentence.

I read the directions, but Joey built the model.

A comma is used after a conjunctive adverb in a compound sentence.

I missed a step in the directions; consequently, the model fell down.

Dashes

A dash is used to indicate a sudden change of thought.

My uncle cooked the whole dinner—a surprise to us all.

A dash (or dashes) is used to set off a series of words, phrases, or clauses in apposition.

The dinner—chicken, greens, and mashed potatoes—was delicious.

Exclamation Points

An exclamation point is used after most interjections and to end an exclamatory sentence.

Help! The rope is breaking!
Wow, that was close!

Hyphens

A hyphen is used to divide words between syllables at the end of a line.

The scientists studied the bone of the Tyranno-
saurus rex.

A hyphen is used in numbers from twenty-one to ninety-nine and to separate parts of some compound words.

drive-in   mother-in-law

A hyphen is used to form some temporary adjectives.

He completed the three-year project.

The pages of the Grammar and Mechanics Handbook from the student book are reproduced here for your convenience.

Italics

Italics are used to set off the titles of books, magazines, newspapers, movies, television series, ships, and works of art. If you are handwriting, use underlining for italics.

> I saw a picture of the *Titanic* in the *Atlantic Monthly*.

Periods

A period is used to end a declarative or an imperative sentence.

> The dog is hungry. Please feed it.

A period is used after an abbreviation and after the initials in a name.

> Co.　　Mrs.　　mi.　　R. L. Stevenson

Question Marks

A question mark is used to end an interrogative sentence.

> What do you feed your dog?

Quotation Marks

Quotation marks are used before and after direct quotations and around the parts of a divided quotation.

> "Why," asked my brother, "didn't you play the game?"

Quotation marks are used to set off the titles of stories, poems, songs, magazine and newspaper articles, television shows, and radio programs.

> They sang "Deep River" and "Amazing Grace."

Single quotation marks are used to set off quoted material within a quotation.

> "Did they sing 'America the Beautiful'?" Salma asked.

Semicolons

A semicolon is used to separate clauses in a compound sentence when they are not joined by a conjunction.

> It rained all afternoon; the game was cancelled.

A semicolon is used to separate clauses in a compound sentence that are connected by a conjunctive adverb.

> The water washed out the flowerbeds; furthermore, it flooded the basement.

Mechanics

Semicolons are used to separate phrases or clauses of the same type that include internal punctuation.

> There were also floods on July 8, 2001; October 22, 2003; and August 15, 2005.

A semicolon is used before expressions such as *for example* and *namely* when they are used to introduce examples.

> Many streets were under water; namely, Morris, Elm, Cornelia, and State.

The pages of the Grammar and Mechanics Handbook from the student book are reproduced here for your convenience.

Index

A

Abbreviations, capitalization of, 190, 557
Abstract nouns, 24–25, 539
Active listening. *See* **Listening tips**
Active voice, 66–67, 555
Addresses. *See also* **Business letters;**
    Salutations
    commas in, 182, 557
Adjective clauses, 144–145, 308–309, 528
    definition of, 26–27, 210, 534
    diagramming, 210–211
    noun clauses and, 154
    restrictive and nonrestrictive, 26–27,
        146–147
    subordinate conjunctions and, 144
Adjective phrases, 26–27, 130–131, 142–143, 528
    diagramming, 197
Adjectives
    common, 528
    comparative, 22–23, 116–117, 528–529
    definition of, 18, 528
    demonstrative, 20–21, 529
    dependent clauses as (*see* **Adjective clauses**)
    descriptive, 18, 529
    diagramming, 197
    hyphens in, 188
    indefinite, 20–21, 530
    infinitives as, 100–101, 209, 537
    interrogative, 20–21, 530
    numerical, 24
    as object complements, 18
    participial, 86, 205, 530, 542
    participial phrases as, 204
    position of, 530
    positive degree of, 22–23
    possessive, 40–41, 531
    prepositional phrases as, 26, 130–131
    proper, 190, 531
    specific, 242
    as subject complements, 18
    suffixes of, 431
    superlative, 22–23
Adverb clauses, 148–149, 310–311, 531
    definition of, 118–119, 212, 534
    diagramming, 212–213
    subordinate conjunctions and, 148
Adverbial nouns, 112–113, 532
Adverb phrases, 142–143, 531
    definition of, 118–119, 132
    diagramming, 197
Adverbs
    comparative, 114–115, 116–117, 532
    conjunctive (*see* **Conjunctive adverbs**)
    definition of, 110, 531
    dependent clauses as (*see* **Adverb clauses**)
    diagramming, 197
    infinitives as, 102–103, 209, 537
    interrogative, 112–113, 533
    nouns as, 112–113, 532
    positive degree, 114–115
    prepositional phrases as, 132–133
    and prepositions, words used as, 128–129
    specific, 242
    suffixes of, 431
    superlative, 114–115
    types of, 110–111
Advertisements, 422–425
    analyzing, 423
    campaign posters, 424
    lost-and-found ads, 424
    propaganda, 422–423
    sales ads, 424
    writing, 424

Affirmation, adverbs of, 110
Agreement
    with indefinite pronouns, 52
    of pronouns and antecedents, 44–45
    of subject and verb, 76–79
Alliteration, 471
Almanacs, 502
"American Forests, The," (Muir) 412
Among/between, 126
Angry with/angry at, 126
Antagonist, 454
Antecedents, 32, 44–45, 144, 533
Apostrophes, 188–189, 556
Appositive phrases, 10
Appositives
    dashes with, 188
    definition of, 10, 98, 198, 533, 539
    diagramming, 198–199
    gerunds as, 90–91, 206
    infinitives as, 98–99
    noun clauses as, 154–155, 214
Articles
    definite and indefinite, 533
    definition of, 533
    diagramming, 197
As/as, **comparisons with,** 116, 529, 532
Asides, in plays, 462, 463
As if/as/like, 174
As if/as though/like, 126
As/so, **comparisons with,** 116, 529, 532
Assonance, 471
As/than, **pronouns after,** 38–39
Atlases, 502
Audience
    how-to articles, 262
    how-to talks, 282
    oral history reports, 511
    oral personal narratives, 244
    personal narratives, 224
    persuasive essays, 420–421
    persuasive speeches, 434–435
    reader's theater, 474
    self-help presentations, 397
Audio clips, 513
Auxiliary verbs, 58, 552
    modal auxiliaries, 74–75, 554

B

Bandwagon device, 422
Base form (present tense), 58, 68, 554. *See*
    also **Prefixes; Suffixes; Verbs**
Be
    as auxiliary verb, 58, 74
    as linking verb, 64
Beside/besides, 126
Between/among, 126
Biographical references, 503
Body
    of business letters, 300
    how-to articles, 263
    personal narratives, 228
    persuasive speeches, 435
    of self-help presentation, 398
Books
    capitalization of sacred, 190, 556
    citations for, 498
Borrow/lend, 62
Brainstorming, 248, 287, 400, 476
Bring/take, 62
Business letters, 298–299. *See also* **Salutations**
    basics, 300–303
    closing, 300
    colons in, 184

    content editing, 328–329
    copyediting, 332
    drafting, 326–327
    freewriting, 325
    heading, 300
    inside address, 300
    prewriting, 324–325
    proofreading, 333
    publishing, 334–335
    purposes of, 304, 324–325
    references, 300
    revising, 306–307, 330–331
    salutations, 300
    structure of, 300–301
    tone, 305
    Writer's Workshop, 324–327, 330–331,
        334–335
Business telephone calls, 320–323

C

Campaign posters, 424
Capitalization, 190–191, 556–557
Cause and effect, 403
Character(s), in plays, 454, 456–457
Checklists
    advertising analysis, 423
    for content editors, 252, 290, 328, 366, 404,
        442, 480, 518
    for copyeditors, 256, 294, 332, 370, 408,
        446, 522
    for how-to articles, 264
    for Internet research, 384
    for proofreaders, 257, 295, 333, 371, 409,
        447, 523
Chronological order, 266, 282, 342
Citing, of sources, 498–500
Clauses. *See also* **Adjective clauses;**
    Adverb clauses; Dependent clauses;
    Nonrestrictive clauses and phrases;
    Noun clauses
    in compound sentences, 200
    definition of, 26, 534
    dependent, 144
    independent, 144, 148, 160, 172, 200, 210
    infinitive, 96
    semicolons with, 184, 559
    subordinate conjunctions and, 236
Clichés, 354, 355
Clipped words, 314–315
Closing, of business letters, 300
Clustering web, 248
Coherence, personal narratives, 225
Collective nouns, 78, 539
Colons, 184–185, 557
Commas, 182–183, 557–558
Common adjectives, 528
Common nouns, 540, 541
Comparative degree
    adjectives, 22, 24, 528
    adverbs, 114, 532
Comparisons. *See also* **Comparative degree**
    with *as/so,* 116, 532
    with *as/so/equally,* 116–117, 532
    and contrast, 342
    than and *as* in, 38–39
Complements, subject. *See* **Subject**
    complements
Complete predicates, 140, 544
Complete subjects, 140, 550
Complex sentences, 160–161, 236, 549
Complimentary close in letters, commas
    after, 182

The pages of the Index from the student book are reproduced here for your convenience.

Gerund phrases, 88, 90–91, 540, 543
Gerunds
  as appositives, 90–91
  definition of, 536
  diagramming, 206–207
  as direct objects, 88
  as nouns, 540
  as objects, 90–91
  possession with, 92–93
  as subject complements, 88–89
  as subjects, 88–89
Grammar and Mechanics Handbook, 527-560
Graphic organizers
  KWL charts, 400–401
  sequence chart, 286
  Venn diagrams, 346, 363
  word webs, 225, 248, 348–349

H

Have, as auxiliary verb, 58, 74
Heading, of business letters, 300
Hidden infinitives, 104–105, 537
History reports, oral, 510–513
Homographs, 508
How-to articles
  audience, 262
  body, 263
  checklist for, 264
  conclusions, 263, 289
  content editing, 290–291
  copyediting, 294
  details in, 266, 272
  drafting, 288–289
  instructions in, 266–267
  introductions, 262, 289
  organization, 287
  prewriting, 286
  proofreading, 295
  publishing, 296–297
  revising, 292–293
  titles, 289
  Writer's Workshop, 286–289, 292–293, 296–297
How-to talks, 282–286
  audience, 282
  listening tips, 285
  practicing, 284
  presentation of, 284
  topics, 282
  visual aids, 284
Hyperbole, 354, 356, 357
Hyphens, 188–189, 558

I

Idioms, 464–465
Imperative mood, 70–71, 538
Imperative sentences, 140, 549
In/into, 126
Indefinite adjectives, 20–21, 530
Indefinite articles, 533
Indefinite pronouns, 50–51, 545
  agreement with, 52–53
Independent clauses, 144, 148, 160, 172, 200, 210
Index thesaurus, 350–351
Indicative mood, 70–71, 538
Indirect objects
  definition of, 8, 537
  diagramming, 196
  nouns as, 8–9

Infinitive clauses, 96
Infinitive phrases, 94–95, 100, 102–103, 142, 208, 543
Infinitives
  as adjectives, 100–101, 209
  as adverbs, 102–103, 209
  as appositives, 98–99
  definition of, 537
  diagramming, 208–209
  hidden, 104–105, 537
  nouns and, 537, 540
  as objects, 96–97
  pronouns with, 100
  split, 104–105, 537
  as subject complements, 94–95
  subjects and, 94–95, 538
-ing
  in gerunds, 88, 92–93
  in present participle, 58, 84, 92
Inside address, of business letters, 300
Instructions, how-to-articles, 266–269
Intensive pronouns, 42–43, 546
Interjections, 176–177
  definition of, 538
  exclamation points with, 176–177, 558
Internet research, 384–387
Interrogative adjectives, 20–21, 530
Interrogative adverbs, 112–113, 533
Interrogative pronouns, 46–47, 546
Interrogative sentences, 140, 549
  question marks with, 184
Interviews, citations for, 500
Intransitive verbs, 60–61, 553
Introductions
  how-to articles, 262, 289
  how-to talks, 282
  personal narratives, 228
  persuasive speeches, 435
  self-help presentations, 398
Inverted order, in sentences, 550
Irregular verbs, 553
Italics, 186–187, 559

J

Jargon, 466
Joint possession, of nouns, 12

K

"King of the Golden River, The," (Ruskin) 336
KWL charts, 401

L

Language
  figurative, 354–357, 365, 471
  sensory, 470
Lay/lie, 62
Learn/teach, 62
Lend/borrow, 62
Less/fewer, 24
Less/little/least, 529
Letters. *See also* **Business letters**
  commas in, 182
Lie/lay, 62
Like/as if/as, 174
Like/as if/as though, 126
Linking verbs, 64–65, 553
Listening tips
  how-to talks, 285
  oral descriptions, 361
  oral history reports, 513

  oral personal narratives, 246
  persuasive speeches, 436
  reader's theater, 474
  self-help presentations, 399
  telephone calls, 322
Lists of items, colons with, 184
Little/less/least, 24, 529
Loaded words, 422
Lost-and-found ads, 424

M

Main verb, 58
Manner, adverbs of, 110
Media, with oral history reports, 512–513
Metaphors, 354, 356, 357, 471
Meter, in poetry, 470, 471
"Midas the King," 450
Misplaced participles, 86
Modal auxiliaries, 74–75, 554
Monologue, 462–463
Mood
  in description, 338–341
  emphatic, 70–71, 539
  imperative, 70–71, 538
  indicative, 70–71, 538
  oral descriptions, 358
  subjunctive, 70, 72–73, 539
  of verbs, 70–71
Multiple-meaning words, 506–509
Multiword prepositions, 124–125

N

Narratives, personal. *See* **Personal narratives**
Natural order, in sentences, 550
Negation, adverbs of, 110
Nonrestrictive clauses and phrases
  adjective clauses and, 146, 309, 534
  adjectives as, 26–27
  appositives as, 10–11
  commas with, 182, 557
  definition of, 10
  participles as, 84
  punctuation of, 182
Note taking, 284
  organizing, 496
  for research reports, 494–495
Noun clauses
  as appositives, 154–155
  definition of, 214, 534–535
  diagramming, 214–215
  as direct objects, 156–157
  as objects of prepositions, 158–159
  sentence variation with, 390–391
  as subject complements, 152–153
  as subjects, 150–151
  uses of, 388–389
Noun phrases, 540
Nouns
  abstract, 24–25, 539
  adverbial, 112–113, 532
  collective, 78, 539
  common, 540
  compound, 4, 12
  concrete, 24–25, 540
  definition of, 2, 539
  dependent clauses as (*see* **Noun clauses**)
  gerunds as, 540
  infinitives as, 96, 540
  number of, 541
  as object complements, 8–9, 541
  as objects, 8–9

The pages of the Index from the student book are reproduced here for your convenience.

The pages of the Index from the student book are reproduced here for your convenience.

Possessive pronouns, 40–41, 536, 547
Practicing
    how-to talks, 284
    oral descriptions, 360
    oral history reports, 512–513
    persuasive speeches, 436
Predicates, 140, 202, 543, 544
Prefixes, 392–395
Prepositional phrases
    as adjectives, 26, 130–131
    as adverbs, 132–133
    definition of, 26, 124, 142, 544
    diagramming, 197, 207
    as nouns, 134–135, 540
Prepositions. *See also* Objects of prepositions
    and adverbs, words used as, 128–129
    definition of, 124, 544
    multiword, 124
    troublesome, 126–127
Presentation
    of business letters, 335
    of descriptions, 373
    of expository essays, 411
    of how-to articles, 297
    of how-to talk, 284
    of oral description, 360
    of oral history report, 512–513
    of oral personal narrative, 246
    of personal narrative, 259
    of persuasive essays, 449
    of plays, 486
    research reports, 525
    self-help, 396–399
Present participle, 58, 554
Present perfect tense, 68
Present tense (base form), 58, 68, 554
Prewriting
    business letters, 324–325
    descriptions, 362–363
    expository essays, 400–401
    how-to articles, 286
    personal narratives, 248–249
    persuasive essays, 438–439
    playwriting, 476–477
    research reports, 514–515
Progressive tenses, 68–69, 551–552
Pronouns
    antecedents and, 44–45
    definition of, 544
    demonstrative, 46–47, 545
    gender of, 536
    indefinite, 50–51, 52–53, 545
    with infinitives, 100
    intensive, 42–43, 546
    interrogative, 46–47, 546
    number of, 541
    object, 36–37, 546
    personal, 32, 547
    possessive, 40–41, 547
    reflexive, 42–43, 547–548
    relative, 48–49, 548
    subject, 34–35, 548
    as subject complements, 6
    after *than* or *as*, 38–39
Pronunciation, in dictionaries, 279
Proofreading
    business letters, 333
    checklists, 257, 295, 333, 371, 409, 447, 485, 523
    descriptions, 371
    expository essays, 409
    how-to articles, 295
    personal narratives, 256–257
    persuasive essays, 447

playwriting, 485
    research reports, 522
Proofreading marks, 257, 526
Propaganda, 422–423
Proper adjectives, 531
    capitalization of, 190
Proper names, possessives of, 540–541
Proper nouns
    capitalization of, 190, 556
    defined, 541
    possessives of, 12
Prose, 469
Protagonist, 454
Publishing
    business letters, 334–335
    descriptions, 372–373
    expository essays, 410–411
    how-to articles, 296–297
    personal narratives, 258–259
    persuasive essays, 448–449
    playwriting, 486–487
    research reports, 524–525
Punctuation. *See* specific marks

Q

Question marks, 184–185, 559
Quotation marks, 186–187, 559
Quotations. *See also* Paraphrasing
    commas with, 182, 558
    direct, 316
    within quotations, 186, 559

R

Radio programs, citations for, 500
Rambling sentences, 270
Reader's Guide to Periodical Literature, 504–505
Reader's theater, 472–475
References
    of business letters, 300
    on note cards, 494
Reference tools
    almanacs, 502
    atlases, 502
    biographical references, 503
    dictionaries, 278–281
    Reader's Guide to Periodical Literature, 504–505
    thesaurus, 350–353
Reflexive adjectives, gender of, 536
Reflexive pronouns, 42–43, 547–548
Regular verbs, 58
Rehearsal
    oral descriptions, 360
    reader's theater, 474
Relative pronouns, 48, 144, 210, 211, 534, 548
Repetition, 470, 471
Reports. *See* Oral history reports; Research reports
Research
    conducting, 385
    oral descriptions, 358
    recording from Internet, 385
    self-help presentations, 398
Research reports, 488–489
    citing sources for, 498–501
    content editing, 518–519
    copyediting, 522
    documentation of, 492
    drafting, 516–517
    note taking for, 494–495

oral history, 510–511
    organizing, 491
    prewriting, 514–515
    proofreading, 523
    publishing, 524–525
    revising, 520–521
    thesis statements for, 490–491
    topics, 490, 514
    Writer's Workshop, 514–517, 520–521, 524–525
Restrictive clauses and phrases
    adjectives as, 26–27, 146–147, 309, 534
    appositives as, 10–11, 533
    definition of, 10
    participles as, 84
Revising
    business letters, 306–307, 330–331
    descriptions, 368–369
    expository essays, 406–407
    how-to articles, 292–293
    personal narratives, 254–255
    persuasive essays, 444–445
    playwriting, 482–483
    research reports, 520–521
    sentences, 270–271
Rhyme, 470
Rhythm, 470–471
Roots, 274–277
Run-on sentences, 270

S

Sacred books, capitalization of, 190
Sales ads, 424
Salutations
    of business letters, 300
    colons with, 184, 557
    commas after, 182
Scripts, for reader's theater, 472
Self-help presentations, 396–399
    audience, 397
    organizing, 398
    research, 398
    topics, 396
Semicolons, 184–185, 200, 559–560
Sensory language, 470
Sentences
    complex, 160–161, 236, 549
    compound (*see* Compound sentences)
    declarative, 140, 549
    definition of, 140, 549
    diagramming, 196–197
    exclamatory, 140, 549
    imperative, 140, 549
    interrogative, 140, 184, 549
    kinds of, 140–141
    natural and inverted order of, 550
    rambling, 270
    revision of, 270–271
    run-on, 270
    simple, 160–161, 550
    variation of, 236–237, 390–391
Separate possession, of nouns, 12
Sequence charts, how-to articles, 286
Series
    commas with, 182, 557
    dashes with, 558
Set/sit, 62
Setting, in plays, 454, 456–457, 473
Similes, 354, 355, 356, 357, 471
Simple predicates, 544
Simple sentences, 160–161, 236, 550
    diagramming, 196–197
Simple subjects, 551

The pages of the Index from the student book are reproduced here for your convenience.

Simple tenses, 68–69, 552
Singular nouns, 2–3, 4–5, 78
Sit/set, 62
Slang, 466
So/as, comparisons with, 529, 532
Soliloquy, 462
Sound recordings, citations for, 500
Sources, citing of, 498–501
Spatial order, 342
Speeches
    descriptions, 358–361
    history reports, 510–513
    how-to talks, 282–285
    personal narratives, 244–247
    persuasive, 434–437
    self-help, 396–399
Split infinitives, 104–105, 537
Stage directions, 458–459, 473
Stories, for reader's theater, 472
"Story of My Life, The," (Keller) 222, 224, 229
"Story of the Greeks, The," (Guerber) 374
Subject complements
    adjectives as, 18, 531
    compound adjectives as, 203
    definition of, 550
    diagramming, 196, 208
    gerunds as, 88–89, 206
    infinitives as, 94–95
    linking verbs and, 64
    noun clauses as, 152–153
    nouns as, 6
    prepositional phrases as, 134
    pronouns as, 6
Subject pronouns, 34–35, 548
Subjects
    agreement of, with verbs, 76–79
    complete, 550
    compound, 78, 202–203, 551
    definition of, 6, 140, 550
    diagramming, 196
    gerunds as, 88–89, 206
    indefinite pronouns as, 50, 52
    infinitives and, 94–95, 538
    noun clauses as, 150–151
    nouns as, 6–7
    simple, 551
    verbs and, 76
Subjunctive mood, 70, 72–73, 539
Subordinate conjunctions, 236
    adjective clauses and, 144
    adverb clauses and, 148, 212, 310
    definition of, 172, 535
    diagramming, 212
Suffixes, 430–433
Summary, 316–317
Superlative degree
    adjectives, 22, 529
    adverbs, 114
Sweeping generalities, 423
Synonyms, 350

T

Take/bring, 62
Teach/learn, 62
Telephone calls, 320–323
Television programs, citations for, 500
Tenses, verb, 58–59
    definition of, 551
    perfect, 68–69, 551
    progressive, 68–69, 551
    simple, 68–69, 552
Testimonials, 422

Than/as, pronouns after, 38–39
Theme, in plays, 453
There is/there are, 76
Thesaurus, 350–353
Thesis statements, for research reports, 490–491
Time, adverbs of, 110
Timelines, 232–235, 239
Titles
    capitalization of, 190, 556, 557
    how-to articles, 289
    italics with, 186
    personal narratives, 225
    quotation marks with, 186, 559
Tone, business letters, 305
Topics
    descriptions, 362
    expository essays, 376, 400
    how-to articles, 286–287
    how-to talks, 282
    oral descriptions, 358
    oral history reports, 510–511
    personal narratives, 224
    persuasive writing, 434, 438
    research reports, 490, 514
    self-help presentations, 396
Transition words, 234–235, 266, 426–427
    editing for, 445
Transitive verbs, 60–61, 553, 555
Troublesome conjunctions, 174–175
Troublesome prepositions, 126–127
Troublesome verbs, 62

U

Underlining, for italics, 186
Unless/without, 174

V

Vague generalities, 423
Venn diagrams, 346, 363
Verbals. *See also* Gerunds; Infinitives;
    Participles
    definition of, 84, 552
    participles as, 204
Verb phrases, 543
Verbs
    agreement of, 76–79
    auxiliary, 58, 552
    compound, 202–203
    definition of, 58, 552
    diagramming, 196
    infinitives as, 94–95
    intransitive, 60–61, 553
    irregular, 553
    linking, 64–65, 553
    main, 58
    modal auxiliaries, 74–75
    moods of, 70–73
    with object complements, 8
    objects of, 206
    phrasal, 60, 554
    plural, 78
    principal parts, 554
    regular, 58
    specific, 240
    subjects and, 76
    suffixes of, 430
    tenses of, 58–59
    transitive, 60–61, 553, 555
    troublesome, 62
    voices of, 66–67

Verse. *See* Poetry
Video clips, 512
Visual aids
    how-to talks, 284
    oral descriptions, 361
    oral history reports, 512
    persuasive speeches, 435
Voice
    active and passive, 66–67, 555
    in business letters, 327
    in expository writing, 405
    in personal narratives, 251
    in persuasive essays, 418–419
    in playwriting, 479
    of verbs, 66–67

W

Web sites, 384–387
Who/whom, 546, 548
Whose/which/what, 546, 548
Without/unless, 174
Word choice
    business letters, 331
    descriptions, 338, 370
    expository essays, 408
    how-to articles, 293
    oral descriptions, 358–359
    personal narratives, 255
    persuasive essays, 441
    playwriting, 483
    research reports, 521
Words. *See also* Details
    clipped, 314–315
    compound, 312–313, 315
    dividing with hyphens, 188
    exact, 240–243
    multiple-meaning, 506–509
    opinion signaled by, 382
    prefixes, 392–395
    roots, 274–277
    suffixes, 430–433
    transition, 234–235, 266, 426–427
    used as adverbs and prepositions, 128–129
Word webs, 225, 248, 348–349
Works Cited page, 498
Writer's Workshop
    business letters, 324–327, 330–331, 334–335
    descriptions, 362–365, 368–369, 372–373
    expository writing, 400–403, 406–407, 410–411
    how-to articles, 286–289, 292–293, 296–297
    personal narratives, 248–251, 254–255, 258–259
    persuasive essays, 438–441, 444–445, 448–449
    playwriting, 476–479, 482–483, 486–487
    research reports, 514–517, 520–521, 524–525
Writing Traits, inside back cover

Y

You, as subject, 76

The pages of the Index from the student book are reproduced here for your convenience.

Acknowledgments

Art and Photography

When there is more than one picture on a page, credits are supplied in sequence, left to right, top to bottom. Page positions are abbreviated as follows: **(t)** top, **(c)** center, **(b)** bottom, **(l)** left, **(r)** right.

Photos and illustrations not acknowledged are either owned by Loyola Press or from royalty-free sources including but not limited to Alamy, Art Resource, Big Stock, Bridgeman, Corbis/ Veer, Dreamstime, Fotosearch, Getty Images, North Wind Images, Photoedit, Smithsonian, Wikipedia. Loyola Press has made every effort to locate the copyright holders for the cited works used in this publication and to make full acknowledgment for their use. In the case of any omissions, the Publisher will be pleased to make suitable acknowledgments in future editions.

iStockphoto, Frontmatter: iii, iv, v, vi, vii, viii **Section 1:** 2, 3, 5, 6, 7, 8, 9, 11, 16 **Section 2:** 18, 20, 22, 23, 25, 26 **Section 3:** 32, 34, 37, 38, 39, 40, 42, 43, 45, 46, 47, 48, 51, 53, 56 **Section 4:** 58, 59, 60, 61, 62, 63, 64, 66, 68, 69, 70, 71, 72, 73, 74, 77, 78, 79, 82 **Section 5:** 84, 85, 87, 88, 89, 92, 93, 94, 95, 96, 99, 102, 103, 104, 105, 108 **Section 6:** 110, 111, 112, 113, 114, 115, 116, 117, 118, 119 **Section 7:** 124, 125, 126, 127, 128, 129, 130, 131, 138 **Section 8:** 140, 141, 142, 144, 145, 146, 148, 150, 151, 152, 154, 158, 160, 161, 164 **Section 9:** 167, 168, 170, 171, 172, 173, 175, 176 **Section 10:** 183, 185, 187, 189, 191 **Section 11:** 198, 200, 204, 205, 206, 208, 215 **Chapter 1:** 222, 223, 226, 227, 228, 231, 232, 233, 234, 235, 236, 237, 238, 239, 240, 241, 242, 243, 245, 247, 250, 251, 259 **Chapter 2:** 260, 261, 263, 264, 265, 267, 268, 271, 272, 273, 274, 275, 276, 277, 278, 281, 282, 283, 285, 287, 288, 289, 296, 297 **Chapter 3:** 298, 299, 301, 302, 303, 304, 306, 308, 310, 311, 312, 313, 314, 315, 316, 317, 318, 319, 320, 321, 322, 324, 325, 326, 327, 329, 330, 331, 333, 335 **Chapter 4:** 336, 337, 339, 340, 341, 342, 343, 344, 346, 347, 349, 350, 352, 353, 354, 355, 356, 357, 358, 359, 364, 366, 367, 369, 371, 373 **Chapter 5:** 374, 375, 376, 377, 378, 379, 380, 381, 382, 384, 386, 387, 389, 390, 391, 393, 394, 395, 396, 397, 398, 400, 401, 403, 404, 406 **Chapter 6:** 412, 413, 416, 420, 421, 424, 425, 429, 435, 437, 441 **Chapter 7:** 450, 451, 462, 463, 464, 465, 471, 472 **Chapter 8:** 488, 497, 500, 505, 506, 511 **Chapter 9:** 166, 168, 169, 174, 177, 180 **Chapter 10:** 182, 183, 186, 188, 189, 190, 194 **Chapter 11:** 196, 197, 199, 200, 201, 202, 203, 205, 207, 209, 210, 213, 214, 215, 220, 204–205, 218–219

Jupiterimages Unlimited, Frontmatter: v, viii **Section 2:** 19 **Section 4:** 67, 79 **Section 5:** 87, 94, 95 **Section 7:** 135 **Section 8:** 145, 155, 156, 157 **Section 9:** 166, 168, 169, 174, 177, 180 **Section 10:** 182, 183, 186, 188, 189, 190, 194 **Section 11:** 196, 197, 199, 200, 201, 202, 203, 205, 207, 209, 210, 213, 214, 215, 220, 204–205, 218–219 **Chapter 2:** 260 **Chapter 3:** 307, 308, 328 **Chapter 4:** 341, 364 **Chapter 5:** 388, 389 **Chapter 6:** 412, 414, 415, 416, 417, 418, 420, 425, 427, 429, 431, 432, 433, 435, 436, 437, 440, 442, 443, 444, 447, 448, 449 **Chapter 7:** 450, 450–451, 451, 453, 454, 454–455, 455, 457–458, 457, 459, 465, 466, 467, 468–469, 468, 469, 470, 472–473, 473, 474, 475, 477, 478, 479, 480, 481, 483, 484, 485, 487 **Chapter 8:** 488, 489, 490, 491, 492, 492–493, 496, 499, 502, 505, 506, 507, 508, 509, 515, 516, 518, 520, 522–523, 524–525

Frontmatter: iii Clockwise from upper left (a) Stock. **(b)** iStockphoto. **(c)** iStockphoto. **(d)** iStockphoto. **(e)** iStockphoto. **(f)** iStockphoto. **(g)** Hulton Archive/Getty. **vii Clockwise from upper left (a)** iStockphoto. **(b)** iStockphoto. **(c)** Kathryn Seckman Kirsch. **(d)** iStockphoto. **(e)** Leland Bobbe/ Getty. **(f)** iStockphoto.

Section 1: 10(tl) Stinger/Getty Images. **11(t)** Antar Dayal/ Getty Images.

Section 2: 30 Bruce Laurance/Getty Images.

Section 3: 33(t) Hulton Archive/Getty Images. **35** Michael Ochs Archives/2007 Getty Images. **36** HultonArchive/2003 Getty Images. **39(b)** Girl Ray/Getty Images. **41** Michael Dwyer/Alamy. **44** Antar Dayal/Getty Images. **50** William Manning/Alamy. **51(t)** Pictorial Press Ltd/Alamy.

Section 4: 64(b) Time & Life Pictures/Getty Images. **65** Pictorial Press Ltd/Alamy. **76** PanoramicImages/Getty Images. **77(b)** Tim Wright/Corbis.

Section 5: 91(t) Kathryn Seckman Kirsch. **91(b)** Trinity Mirror/ Mirrorpix/Alamy. **96(t)** AFP/2007 Getty Images. **97** Dinodia Images/Alamy. **98(t)** North Wind Picture Archives/Alamy. **100** North Wind Picture Archives/Alamy. **101(t)** Colby McLemore/ Alamy. **101(b)** Time & Life Pictures/Carl Iwasaki/Getty Images. **102(bl)** Panoramic Images/Getty Images.

Section 6: 122 Hulton Archive/Getty Images.

Section 7: 125(c) Danita Delimont/Alamy. **131(t)** Renaud Visage. **132** North Wind Picture Archives/Alamy. **135(t)** The Print Collector/Alamy. **143(t)** North Wind Picture Archives/Alamy. **143(b)** Classic Image/Alamy. **147** North Wind Picture Archives/ Alamy. **149** Ellen Rooney/Getty Images. **153(t)** Peter Horree/ Alamy. **153(b)** North Wind Picture Archives/Alamy. **159(t)** Karen Kasmauski/Science Faction/Corbis. **159(b)** 3D4Medical.com. **172(t)** Robert Harding Picture Library Ltd/Alamy. **173(tr)** Cynthia Baldauf.

Chapter 1: 222(b) Neil Fletcher/Getty Images.

Chapter 2: 260(tl) Kathryn Seckman Kirsch. **263(t)** Susan Estelle Kwas. **269(b)** PhotoStockFile/Alamy. **273(b)** Kathryn Seckman Kirsch.

Chapter 3: 289(br) Kathryn Seckman Kirsch. **293(r)** Phil Martin Photography. **295** Phil Martin Photography. **298(bl)** Phil Martin Photography. **299(cr)** Phil Martin Photography. **301(b)** Mango Productions/Corbis. **309** Blasius Erlinger/Zefa Photography/ Corbis. **334** Motofish Images/Flirt/Veer. **335** Phil Martin Photography.

Chapter 4: 337(c) Kathryn Seckman Kirsch. **337(tr)** Kathryn Seckman Kirsch. **337(bl)** Kathryn Seckman Kirsch. **338** Susan Estelle Kwas. **349(bl)** Phil Martin Photography. **351** North Wind Picture Archives/Alamy. **353(t)** Leland Bobbe/Getty Images. **357(t)** Clive Brunskill/Getty Images. **360** Phil Martin Photography. **361(t)** Nathan Benn/Alamy. **365** Phil Martin Photography. **369(bl)** Phil Martin Photography.

Chapter 5: 381(t) Corbis. **381(b)** North Wind Picture Archives/Alamy. **382(br)** Christie's Images/Corbis. **383** Images Etc Ltd/Alamy. **385** Stephen Stickler/Getty Images. **386(tl)** KASH GTorsello/Alamy. **392** Anni Betts. **395(t)** Bettmann/Corbis. **399(t)** Emely/Corbis. **399(b)** Mode Images Limited/Alamy. **401(bl)** Phil Martin Photography. **402** Phil Martin Photography. **404(bl)** Tom Carter/PhotoEdit. D.A.R.E. (logo on car). **405** Phil Martin Photography. **407** Michael Newman /PhotoEdit. **409** Phil Martin Photography.

Chapter 6: 428(t) Ivan Vdovin/Alamy. **428(b)** akg-images/Alamy.

Chapter 7: 461 Pictorial Press Ltd/Alamy.

Chapter 8: 488(cl) Asian Art & Archaeology, Inc./Corbis. **495** Smithsonian Institution/Corbis. **503** Sami Sarkis/Getty Images. **512** Brown University Library. **521(br)** Phil Martin Photography.

Literature

Excerpt from *The Reef Aquarium: Volume One* by Charles Delbeek and Julian Sprung. Copyright ©1994 Ricordea Publishing. All rights reserved.

Excerpt from "The Early Days of Breakfast Cereal." Copyright © 2009 Mr. Breakfast Enterprises. All rights reserved. Used by permission. www.mrbreakfast.com

Excerpt from "French troops save hostages from Somali pirates" by Elaine Ganley. 16 September 2008. Copyright © 2008 The Associated Press. All rights reserved. Used by permission.

Cover from *The Story of My Life* by Helen Keller. Copyright © 2005 Simon & Schuster Inc. Used by permission.

Merriam-Webster Online copyright © 2008 by Merriam-Webster, Inc. Used by permission. www.merriam-webster.com

Excerpt from "Midas the King." Copyright © 2005 Magic Parrot Productions, UK. All rights reserved. www.magicparrot.com

Cover from *Nature Writings* by John Muir. Copyright © 1992 The Library of America. Used by permission.

Excerpt from "Fighting chronic malnutrition among impoverished children in Guatemala" by Thomas Nybo. Copyright © UNICEF. All rights reserved.

Excerpt from *I Wanna Iguana* by Karen Kaufman Orloff. Text copyright © 2004 by Karen Kaufman Orloff. Published by G.P. Putnam's Sons, a division of Penguin Young Reader's Group. All rights reserved.

Cover from *The King of the Golden River* by John Ruskin. Copyright © 2007 Yesterday's Classics. Used by permission.

"River Roads" from *Cornhuskers* by Carl Sandburg, copyright © 1918 by Holt, Rinehart and Winston and renewed 1946 by Carl Sandburg. Reprinted by permission of Harcourt, Inc.

Excerpt from *The Reptile Room* by Lemony Snicket. Text copyright © 1999 by Lemony Snicket. Illustrations copyright © 1999 by Brett Helquist. Published by HarperCollins Publishers.

Excerpt from "Mediterranean Beach, Day After Storm" in *Selected Poems 1923–1975* by Robert Penn Warren. Copyright © 1966 by the author. Published by Random House, Inc.

Excerpt from "What's the Right Weight for My Height?" KidsHealth.org. Copyright © 1995–2009 The Nemours Foundation. All rights reserved. Used by permission.

Excerpt from "Why Women's History Month?" Time for Kids. Copyright © Time Inc. All rights reserved. Used by permission. www.timeforkids.com

Excerpt from "Yo Ho! Treasure." *Time for Kids.* Copyright © Time Inc. All rights reserved. Used by permission. www.timeforkids.com

All other excerpts come from public-domain sources, including Project Gutenberg.

Loyola Press has made every effort to locate the copyright holders for the cited works used in this publication and to make full acknowledgment for their use. In the case of any omissions, the publisher will be pleased to make suitable acknowledgments in future editions.

The pages of the Acknowledgments from the student book are reproduced here for your convenience.

FOR TEACHERS

Photocopy and use the following pages to help your students prepare to take tests. Whether you are preparing your students for local, state, or national tests, the purpose of these pages is to help students not only with mastery of skills and test-taking strategies, but also with building confidence and reducing the anxiety associated with testing.

Test Preparation

STRATEGIES

Three test-taking strategies that can be integrated into everyday classroom activities are following directions, budgeting time, and checking work. Reinforcing these strategies will help students develop good habits and become sophisticated test takers.

Following Directions

Encourage students to read and follow directions closely. Be sure students understand the vocabulary and concepts used in directions. Make sure students understand what they are being asked to do, and give them time to ask questions about directions. Incorporate listening and reading activities during class time to give practice in following directions. To interest them in reading directions closely, give students directions with a "twist," such as ending the directions with *disregard directions and turn in your test immediately.*

Budgeting Time

Place a time limit on select classroom activities to get students accustomed to timed activities, planning, and pacing. Estimate how much time to spend on each question or classroom activity. Encourage students to be aware of the clock as they complete time-limited classroom activities, tests, and assessments on a schedule. Invite students to figure out how much of their allotted time they can spend on each activity.

Checking Work

Help students develop a habit of checking all work—homework, in-class work, or tests. Be sure that when planning timed activities, students budget time for checking their answers. Encourage students to change answers that are incorrect. Point out that many errors can be avoided by checking work. Make checking work a requirement for every assignment.

INFORMATION

- Take some of the mystery out of standardized tests by explaining the purpose of testing, how the results will be used, and what the results mean.

- Make sure you let students know well in advance when tests are scheduled.

- Encourage students to regard tests as an opportunity to show what they've learned and how well they think, as something that they participate in rather than something out of their control that they are subjected to.

ANSWERS FOR T-570–T-577

T-572: 1. A   3. A
       2. D   4. B

T-573: C

T-574: 1. pre<u>view</u>, d   6. <u>juve</u>nile, i
       2. de<u>hydrated</u>, g   7. <u>memor</u>ize, e
       3. mani<u>cure</u>, f   8. <u>nat</u>ive, a
       4. contra<u>dict</u>ed, h   9. re<u>nov</u>ate, c
       5. auto<u>graph</u>, b   10. <u>omni</u>vores, j

T-575: Answers will vary.
T-576: Answers will vary.
T-577: Answers will vary.

> " You hit home runs not by chance but by preparation. "
>
> —Roger Maris

Name _____ Date _____

Before a Test

Preparing for tests can help your performance. There are many things you can do to prepare yourself for a test. To be as prepared as possible, be sure to

- attend class regularly
- take good notes
- do all your homework
- review your notes after each class and on a weekly basis

When you learn a test is scheduled, you should

- ask questions about the test such as the following: *What will it look like? Will it be timed? Will I be penalized for unanswered questions?*
- take practice tests and test yourself on the material you have
- check out some standardized test-preparation booklets from the library
- organize your notes, texts, and assignments according to what will be on the test
- pay attention during class test-preparation sessions

The night before a test, be sure to

- review your notes and materials instead of trying to cram new information
- prepare the materials you need to bring with you such as pencils and erasers
- eat a nutritious dinner
- get a good night's sleep

On the day of the test, be sure to

- eat a nutritious breakfast
- get to class on time
- bring the materials to class that your teacher may have requested such as several sharp pencils or a calculator

Name _____ Date _____

Taking Tests

Studying is an important part of preparing for tests, but there are also many things you can do while taking a test to improve your chances of choosing or writing correct answers.

Consider these suggestions for reading directions:

- Listen to your teacher's verbal directions before reading the written ones.
- Read all directions for a specific part of a test before beginning that portion.
- Raise your hand to ask questions about confusing directions.
- Underline key words in the directions so that you can go back and refer to them if you need a reminder.

During a test, try these tips:

- Manage your time. See how many questions there are. Divide your time so that you finish half the test before the time is half over.
- Do the easiest parts of the test first. Then go back to the harder parts.
- If your teacher advises, answer all the questions even if you have to guess.
- Read all possible choices before determining your answer.
- For open-ended questions or writing prompts, include notes, sketches, or outlines with your completed answers.
- If you make a mistake, erase it completely.
- Check all your answers before turning in your work.

Answer Sheets

When you take a standardized test, you are often given a separate answer sheet on which to record your answers. When using a separate answer sheet, do the following:

- Use only a #2 pencil to mark your answers. Do not use a pen or marker.
- Completely fill in each answer bubble.
- Do not cross out any mistakes. Erase them carefully and completely.
- Do not fold or crease the answer sheet.
- From time to time, quickly review your answer sheet to be sure that you are on the correct item number and that you didn't skip a row or section.
- Write only on your answer sheet. Do not write in your test booklet.

Apply these test-taking strategies and your scores and grades will correctly reflect your achievement.

© LOYOLAPRESS.

Name _____

Date _____

Multiple-Choice Tests

Multiple-choice items are commonly found on standardized tests. These items are written so that there is only one correct, or best, answer for each question. Each item will list several possible answers from which to choose. Some possible answers may seem to be "almost correct," so you must be careful when choosing the best answer.

To perform your best on multiple-choice tests, follow these tips:

- Before the test, check with your teacher to see if it is best to always mark an answer, even if you are not sure which one is correct. Ask your teacher if you are graded only on the items you actually answer.
- Read all the directions before you begin the test.
- Read each question carefully.
- Read all answer choices before marking any answer.
- If you find a choice that states *all of the above*, consider it only if you are sure that two or more answers are correct.
- If you find a choice that states *none of the above*, consider it only if you are sure that two or more answers are incorrect.
- First, eliminate any answers that you know are incorrect. Then take your time to think logically about the remaining choices. Go back and reread the question if you need to.
- If you are unsure of an answer, place a mark next to that item number on your answer sheet and move on to the next question. Come back to that question if there is time after finishing the rest of the test. Make an educated guess if your teacher recommended marking all the answers.

Multiple-Choice Practice

Answer the following multiple-choice questions by circling the correct answer.

1. **On a multiple-choice test, you should only consider *all of the above* as a possible answer if**

   A. you are sure that at least two answers are correct.

   B. you see it because it's always the correct answer.

   C. the subject matter is so complicated that there must be many answers.

   D. you don't know the answer.

2. **Before taking a multiple-choice test, you should**

   A. check with your teacher to see if it is best to always mark an answer.

   B. read all the directions.

   C. read each question carefully.

   D. all of the above

3. **One good strategy for taking a multiple-choice test is to**

   A. read all the choices before marking an answer.

   B. fill in the bubbles at random.

   C. look at your classmate's answer sheet.

   D. fill in the bubbles lightly if you don't know the answer.

4. **You should always**

   A. cross out mistakes on your answer sheet.

   B. completely erase a mistake on your answer sheet and then fill in the correct answer.

   C. fill in at least two bubbles, hoping that one answer will be correct.

   D. wear your lucky color.

Name _____ Date _____

Language Arts Tests: Sentence Structure

When a sentence is complete and each word in the sentence is used correctly in relation to other words, the sentence has correct sentence structure. Some language arts tests might measure your ability to determine if a sentence has correct sentence structure.

A test item might look like this:

There are several errors in the paragraph below. Choose the answer that correctly lists the number of errors and what they are.

(1) The calendar most Americans will use is called the Gregorian calendar. (2) In an ordinary year, this calendar have 365 days. (3) In the Northern Hemisphere, the year is divided into four seasons summer and winter begin at a solstice, and spring and autumn begin at an equinox.

A. No errors. Each sentence is correct.

B. Three errors. 1) "will use" should be "use" in Sentence 1; 2) "an" should be "a" in Sentence 2; and 3) Sentence 3 is a run-on sentence.

C. Three errors. 1) "will use" should be "use" in Sentence 1; 2) "have" should be "has" in Sentence 2; and 3) Sentence 3 is a run-on sentence.

D. One error. 1) "Americans" should be "American" in Sentence 1.

As you read each answer choice, think of how each sentence should read. Ask yourself the following questions:

- Is the proper verb tense used in the sentence?
- Is each sentence written clearly, completely expressing an idea?
- Do any words sound incorrect to my ear?

You would then choose the answer that best determines the errors in the paragraph.

In the example you would choose answer C because
- it clearly identifies the three errors.
- it is the best of the four answers.

Name _____   Date _____

Language Arts Tests: Roots

The root of a word gives it its basic meaning. Some words have more than one root. Some test items measure your ability to identify the root or roots in a word. The test item might look like this:

What is the root of the underlined word in the sentence?

As you read each answer choice, determine which definition matches the context of the sentences and best describes the word. Ask yourself:

- What prefixes or suffixes should I ignore?
- Which word part gives the word its basic meaning?
- Which word part gives basic meaning to other words as well?

Please don't <u>disrupt</u> your brother's nap.

A. upt   **C.** is

B. dis   **D.** rupt

You would then choose the root. In the example you would choose answer D because

- *dis* is a prefix
- *rupt* comes from the Latin word *ruptus,* meaning "to break or fracture"
- *rupt* is also the root of *rupture* and *erupt*

Underline the root in each italicized word. Write the letter of the matching root meaning.

1. We saw a *preview* of a movie based on my favorite book.   _____   **a.** born

2. There are drink stations so the runners don't get *dehydrated.*   _____   **b.** write

3. My aunt gets a *manicure* every Saturday.   _____   **c.** new

4. An eyewitness *contradicted* the burglar's story.   _____   **d.** sight

5. My cousin Jenny had the whole team *autograph* her soccer ball.   _____   **e.** remember

6. My favorite novels are in the *juvenile* fiction section of the library.   _____   **f.** care

7. It's easier to *memorize* facts when you give them a tune.   _____   **g.** water

8. Many of the rain forest's *native* plants are medicinal.   _____   **h.** say

9. Next year, the school is planning to *renovate* the auditorium.   _____   **i.** young

10. Very few known dinosaurs were *omnivores.*   _____   **j.** all

Name _____ Date _____

Writing Tests: Personal Narrative

Test items are often given in the form of a prompt, a short paragraph that tells you what to write. Follow these suggestions when writing for a prompt:

- Carefully read the prompt.
- Circle the key words that signal the genre, in this case, a personal narrative, and the key words that signal audience or purpose.
- Plan your writing. You might use a word web, a time line, notes, or a short outline.
- Write a draft based on your plan.
- Read and revise your draft.
- Copyedit and proofread your draft.

Write for the following prompt. Plan your writing on this page. Write your personal narrative on a separate sheet of paper.

> **Prompt:** The old saying "practice makes perfect" can apply to many things in life. Write about one experience in your life when "practice made perfect." Write this for a younger brother or sister.

Consider the following questions as you plan your draft:

- What have I had to practice to do well?
- Why did I want to do it?
- When, where, why, and how did I practice?
- When did I see improvement?
- What was the reward?

© LOYOLA PRESS.

Voyages in English Grade 8

Name _____   Date _____

Writing Tests: Expository Essay

Test items are often given in the form of a prompt, a short paragraph that tells you what to write. Follow these suggestions when writing for a prompt:

- Carefully read the prompt.
- Circle the key words that signal the genre, in this case, an expository essay, and the key words that signal audience or purpose.
- Plan your writing. You might use a word web, a time line, notes, or a short outline.
- Write a draft based on your plan.
- Read and revise your draft.
- Copyedit and proofread your draft.

Write for the following prompt. Plan your writing on this page. Write your expository essay on a separate sheet of paper.

> **Prompt:** There are 168 hours in every week. You go to school about 40 hours every week and sleep about 63 hours a week. That leaves about 65 hours a week of free time. Write an essay telling what activity you most enjoy doing, and give at least three reasons you would like to spend your precious 65 free hours a week on this activity.

Use the answers to the "five *w*'s" to plan your draft.

- **What** is the activity?
- **Whom** do you collaborate with when doing this activity?
- **When, where,** and **how** do you do this activity?
- **Why** do you enjoy this activity?

© LOYOLA PRESS.

Name _____ Date _____

Writing Tests: Persuasive Essay

Test items are often given in the form of a prompt, a short paragraph that tells you what to write. Follow these suggestions when writing for a prompt:

- Carefully read the prompt.
- Circle the key words that signal the genre, in this case, a persuasive essay, and the key words that signal audience or purpose.
- Plan your writing. You might use a word web, a time line, notes, or a short outline.
- Write a draft based on your plan.
- Read and revise your draft.
- Copyedit and proofread your draft.

Write for the following prompt. Plan your writing on this page. Write your persuasive essay on a separate sheet of paper.

Prompt: Conventional wisdom is that everyone is good at something. It could be a sport or an instrument, the ability to resolve conflict, or even a knack for creating problems. Think of someone you know and his or her particular talent. Describe how you discovered that talent. Invent an award for that talent and explain why this person deserves the award. You are writing to students in your class.

Person: _____ **Award:** _____

Reason #1: _____

Details: _____

_____

Reason #2: _____

Details: _____

_____

Reason #3: _____

Details: _____

_____

Brief restatement of topic and best evidence: _____

_____

_____

Scope and Sequence

E=Explored   I=Introduced   T=Taught   M=Mastered   R=Reviewed

Grammar — Grade Level	1	2	3	4	5	6	7	8
NOUNS								
common/proper	E	I	T	M	R	R	R	R
singular/plural	E	I	T	M	R	R	R	R
irregular plural			T	M	R	R	R	R
possessive			E	I	T	M	R	R
collective		E	I	T	M	R	R	R
as subjects			E	I	T	M	R	R
used in direct address			E	I	T	M		
words used as nouns and verbs			E	I	T	M	R	R
words used as nouns and adjectives			E	I	T	M		
as direct objects				E	I	T	M	R
as subject complements				E	I	T	M	R
as indirect objects					E	I	T	M
as objects of prepositions				E	I	T	M	R
concrete and abstract				E	I, T	T	M	R
showing separate and joint possession					E	I	T	M
as appositives						I	T	M
as antecedents						I	T	M
noun clauses							I, T	M
as prepositional phrases							I, T	M
as object complements							I, T	M
appositive phrases, restrictive and nonrestrictive					E	I	T	M
PRONOUNS								
singular/plural	E	I	T	M	R	R	R	R
subject	E	I	T	M	R	R	R	R
object	E	I	T	M	R	R	R	R
possessive			E	I	T	M	R	R
as compound subjects			E	I	T	M	R	R
agreement with antecedent			E	I	T	M	R	R
as direct objects				E	I	T	M	R
first/second/third person				E	I	T	M	R
in contractions				I	T	M		
as indirect objects						I	T	M	R
as objects of prepositions						I	T	M	R
as subject complements						I	T	M	R
intensive						I	T	M	R
reflexive						I	T	M	R
demonstrative						I	T	M	R
interrogative						I	T	M	R
indefinite							I	T	M
masculine/feminine/neuter						I	T	M	R
who and *whom*							I	T	M
relative							I, T	M
after *than* and *as*							I, T	M

Grammar	Grade Level	1	2	3	4	5	6	7	8
ADJECTIVES									
descriptive		E	I	T	M	R	R	R	R
comparative/superlative/positive		E	I	T	M	R	R	R	R
articles				I	T	M	R		
demonstrative		.		E	I	T	M	R	R
that tell how many		E	I	T	T	M	R	R	R
common/proper				I	T	M			
as subject complements				E	I	T	M	R	R
position of				I	T	M	R	R	R
words used as nouns or adjectives				E	I	T	M		
little, less, least					E, I	T	T	M	R
few, fewer, fewest				E	I	T	T	M	R
definite/indefinite articles					I	T	M		
repetition of articles					I, T	M			
interrogative adjectives						E	I	T	M
adjective phrases						E	I	T	M
indefinite adjectives							I	T	M
adjective clauses								I, T	M
as object complements								I, T	M
participles as adjectives								I, T	M
comparisons with *as . . . as* and *so . . . as*								I, T	M
possessive							I	T	M
numerical							I, T, M		
ADVERBS									
manner			E	I	T	M	R	R	R
time				E	I	T	M	R	R
place				E	I	T	M	R	R
negation				E	I	T	M	R	R
-er/-est					E	I	T	M	R
double negatives					E	I	T	M	R
there is/there are					I	T	M		
more/most, less/least					E	I	T	M	R
adverbial phrases						E	I	T	M
adverbial clauses						E	I	T	M
affirmation							I	T	M
degree							I	T	M
words used as adverbs and adjectives							I, T	M	R
words used as adverbs and prepositions							I	T	M
interrogative								I, T	M
adverbial nouns								I, T	M
conjunctive								I, T	M
comparisons with *as . . . as* and *so . . . so*								I, T	M
comparative							I	T	M
superlative							I	T	M

Scope and Sequence

Grammar — Grade Level	1	2	3	4	5	6	7	8
VERBS								
subject/verb agreement	E	I	T	M	R	R	R	R
action	E	I	T	M	R	R	R	R
being/linking	E	I	T	M	R	R	R	R
words used as nouns/verbs			E	I	T	M	R	R
regular/irregular	E	I	T	T	M	R	R	R
simple present	E	I	T	T	M	R	R	R
simple past	E	I	T	T	M	R	R	R
future with *will*				E	I	T	M	R
future with *going to*				E	I	T	M	R
helping (auxiliary verb)		E	I	T	M	R	R	R
principle parts			E	I	T	M	R	R
present progressive		E	I	T	M	R	R	R
past progressive		E	I	T	M	R	R	R
future progressive			E	I	T	M	R	R
verb phrases				E	I	T	M	R
present participle				E	I	T	M	R
past participle				E	I	T	M	R
present perfect				E	I	T	M	R
past perfect				E	I	T	M	R
future perfect				E	I	T	M	R
transitive/intransitive						I	T	M
active and passive voice						I	T	M
indicative mood						I	T	M
emphatic form						I	T	M
imperative mood						I	T	M
subjunctive mood						I	T	M
modal auxiliaries						I	T	M
gerunds							I, T	M
infinitives							I, T	M
phrasal verbs							I, T	M
troublesome							I	T	M
PREPOSITIONS								
phrases used as adjectives					E	I	T	M
phrases used as adverbs					E	I	T	M
objects of					E	I	T	M
words used as adverbs or prepositions						I	T	M
phrases used as nouns							I, T	M
single and multi-word							I, T	M
CONJUNCTIONS								
coordinate			E	I	T	M	R	R
correlative							I, T	M
subordinate						I	T	M	R
conjunctive adverbs							I, T	M

Grammar — Grade Level	1	2	3	4	5	6	7	8
INTERJECTIONS								
common exclamations					E	I	T	M
SENTENCES								
declarative	E	I	T	T	M	R	R	R
interrogative	E	I	T	T	M	R	R	R
exclamatory	E	I	T	T	M	R	R	R
imperative	E	I	T	T	M	R	R	R
simple	E	I	T	T	M	R	R	R
compound (conjunctions)			E	I	T	M	R	R
natural/inverted word order					I	T	M	
compound (semicolon)					E	I	T	M
complex					E	I	T	M
compound-complex							I, T	M
PARTS OF SENTENCES								
subject and predicate		E	I	T	M	R	R	R
simple subject		E	I	T	M	R	R	R
simple predicate		E	I	T	M	R	R	R
compound sentence elements			E	I	T	M	R	R
subject complement			E	I	T	M	R	R
direct object				E	I	T	M	R
complete subject				E	I	T	M	R
complete predicate				E	I	T	M	R
indirect object					E	I	T	M
object complement							I, T	M
PHRASES								
verb				E	I	T	M	R
prepositional					E	I	T	M
adverb					E	I	T	M
adjective					E	I	T	M
infinitive							I, T	M
noun							I, T	M
participle							I, T	M
gerund							I, T	M
CLAUSES								
adverb					E	I	T	M
adjective							I, T	M
independent							I, T	M
dependent							I, T	M
restrictive							I, T	M
nonrestrictive							I, T	M
noun							I, T	M
as subjects							I, T	M
as direct objects							I, T	M
as objects of prepositions							I, T	M
as complements							I, T	M
as appositives							I, T	M

Scope and Sequence

Grammar — Grade Level	1	2	3	4	5	6	7	8
PUNCTUATION/CAPITAL LETTERS								
end punctuation	E	I	T	M	R	R	R	R
capital letters	E	I	T	M	R	R	R	R
periods/capital letters in abbreviations		E	I	T	M	R	R	R
periods/capital letters in titles and initials			E	I	T	M	R	R
titles of books, stories, etc.			E	I	T	M	R	R
commas in series			E	I	T	M	R	R
commas in compound sentences			E	I	T	M	R	R
apostrophes	E	I	T	M	R	R	R	R
writing addresses			T	M	R	R	R	R
writing direct quotes			I	T	M	R	R	R
commas in direct address			I	T	M	R	R	R
commas after initial phrase			I	T	M	R	R	R
semicolons in compound sentences						I	T	M	R
colons							I	T	M
hyphens							I	T	M
italics							I	T	M
underlining	E	I	T	M	R	R	R	R
dashes							I, T	M
exclamation points	E	I	T	M	R	R	R	R
question marks	E	I	T	M	R	R	R	R
quotation marks							T	M	R
DIAGRAMMING								
subjects			E	I	T	M	R	R
predicates			E	I	T	M	R	R
possessives			E	I	T	M	R	R
adjectives			E	I	T	M	R	R
adverbs			E	I	T	M	R	R
adjective complements			E	I	T	M	R	R
compound sentence elements			E	I	T	M	R	R
compound sentences			E	I	T	M	R	R
direct objects				E	I	T	M	R
noun complements				E	I	T	M	R
indirect objects					E	I	T	M
prepositional phrases					E	I	T	M
adverb clauses					E	I	T	M
appositives							I	T	M
intensive pronouns							I	T	M
participles							I, T	M
gerunds							I, T	M
infinitives							I, T	M
noun clauses							I, T	M
adjective clauses							I, T	M
nouns in direct address							I, T	M
interjections						I	T	M

Writing

Grade Level	1	2	3	4	5	6	7	8
GENRES								
Personal Narratives	✔	✔	✔	✔	✔	✔	✔	✔
Descriptions	✔	✔	✔	✔	✔	✔	✔	✔
Comparative Description						•	•	•
Description in Paragraph Form		•	•	•	•	•	•	•
Expository Writing	✔	✔	✔	✔	✔	✔	✔	✔
Book Report/Review	•	•	•		•		•	
How-to Articles	✔	✔	✔	✔	✔	✔	✔	✔
Business, Formal, and Friendly Letters	✔	✔	✔	✔	✔	✔	✔	✔
Business or Formal Letter				•	•	•	•	•
Friendly Letter	•	•	•					
Creative Writing			✔	✔	✔	✔	✔	✔
Prose								
Fable				•				
Fantasy							•	
Folk Tale						•		
Play/Script								•
Realistic Fiction			•					
Tall Tale					•			
Trickster Tale						•		
Poetry								
Free Verse								•
Haiku				•				
Limerick							•	
Nonsense Verse					•			
Rhyming Couplets			•					
Rhyming Stanzas						•		
Persuasive Writing		✔	✔	✔	✔	✔	✔	✔
Advertisement				•		•		•
Book Review		•					•	
Persuasive Article/Essay				•	•	•	•	
Research Reports	✔	✔	✔	✔	✔	✔	✔	✔
GENRE SKILLS								
Plot Development			✔	✔	✔	✔	✔	✔
Organization	✔	✔	✔	✔	✔	✔	✔	✔
Ideas and Outlines	•	•	•	•	•	•	•	•
Spatial Order			•	•	•	•	•	•
Chronological Order	•	•	•	•	•	•	•	•
Comparing and Contrasting					•	•	•	•
Title	✔	✔	✔	✔	✔	✔	✔	✔
Topic	✔	✔	✔	✔	✔	✔	✔	✔
Introduction	✔	✔	✔	✔	✔	✔	✔	✔
Body	✔	✔	✔	✔	✔	✔	✔	✔
Conclusion	✔	✔	✔	✔	✔	✔	✔	✔
Audience	✔	✔	✔	✔	✔	✔	✔	✔

Scope and Sequence

✔ = Skill Taught   • = Subskill Taught

Writing — Grade Level	1	2	3	4	5	6	7	8
Purpose	✔	✔	✔	✔	✔	✔	✔	✔
Voice/Tone/Word Choice	✔	✔	✔	✔	✔	✔	✔	✔
Sentence Fluency	✔	✔	✔	✔	✔	✔	✔	✔
WRITING PROCESS								
Prewriting	✔	✔	✔	✔	✔	✔	✔	✔
Brainstorming	•	•	•	•	•	•	•	•
Free Writing	•	•	•	•	•	•	•	•
Organizing Ideas	•	•	•	•	•	•	•	•
Choosing a Topic	•	•	•	•	•	•	•	•
Drafting	✔	✔	✔	✔	✔	✔	✔	✔
Content Editing	✔	✔	✔	✔	✔	✔	✔	✔
Copyediting			✔	✔	✔	✔	✔	✔
Proofreading	✔	✔	✔	✔	✔	✔	✔	✔
Revising	✔	✔	✔	✔	✔	✔	✔	✔
Publishing	✔	✔	✔	✔	✔	✔	✔	✔
WRITING SKILLS								
Expanded Sentences			✔	✔	✔	✔	✔	✔
Varied Sentences			✔	✔	✔	✔	✔	✔
Revising Sentences			✔	✔	✔	✔	✔	✔
Rambling Sentences			•	•	•	•	•	•
Run-on Sentences			•	•	•	•	•	•
Redundant Words					•		•	•
Adjectives	✔	✔	✔	✔	✔	✔	✔	✔
Adjective Clauses							✔	✔
Adverb Clauses					✔	✔	✔	✔
Graphic Organizers	✔	✔	✔	✔	✔	✔	✔	✔
Five Senses Chart	•	•	•	•		•		
Venn Diagrams						•	•	•
Word Maps/Word Webs/Idea Webs			•	•	•	•	•	
Time Lines			•	•	•		•	•
Expanding Sentences			✔	✔	✔	✔	✔	
Compound Subjects and Predicates			•	•	•	•	•	
Compound Direct Objects					•	•		
Compound Objects of a Preposition						•	•	
Combining Sentences			✔	✔	✔	✔	✔	✔
Verbs			✔	✔	✔	✔	✔	✔
Using Quotations						✔	✔	✔
Dialogue, Monologue, and Asides			✔	✔	✔	✔	✔	✔
Noun Clauses							✔	✔
Sentence Types	✔	✔	✔	✔	✔	✔	✔	✔
Simple Sentences	•	•	•	•	•	•	•	•
Compound Sentences			•	•	•	•	•	•
Complex Sentences				•	•	•	•	•
Transition Words		✔	✔	✔	✔	✔	✔	✔